SWINBURNE'S POEMS

THE WORKS

OF

ALGERNON CHARLES SWINBURNE

POEMS

PHILADELPHIA

DAVID McKAY, PUBLISHER

604-8 SO. WASHINGTON SQUARE

PUBLISHERS' PREFACE

THE issuing of this edition of Swinburne in two volumes, one "Poems" and the other "Tragedies," we feel is really needed. To get the author's works before this time meant either buying the American edition in eleven volumes or collecting the English edition, in more numerous volumes, at even greater expense. The works of all the other standard poets may be had in some compact form for library use, and Swinburne surely should not be neglected. This edition, with the exception of "Rosamund," "Balen," and a few minor poems, is complete.

CONTENTS.

POEMS AND BALLADS.

....

A BALLAD OF LIFE.

I FOUND in dreams a place of wind and
    flowers,
  Full of sweet trees and color of glad
    grass,
    In midst whereof there was
A lady clothed like summer with sweet
    hours,
Her beauty, fervent as a fiery moon
  Made my blood burn and swoon
    Like a flame rained upon.
Sorrow had filled her shaken eyelids' blue,
And her mouth's sad red heavy rose all
    through
    Seemed sad with glad things gone.

She held a little cithern by the strings,
  Shaped heartwise, strung with subtle-
    colored hair
    Of some dead lute player
That in dead years had done delicious
    things.
The seven strings were named accordingly;
    The first string charity,
    The second tenderness,
The rest were pleasure, sorrow, sleep, and
    sin,
And loving kindness, that is pity's kin
    And is most pitiless.

There were three men with her, each gar-
    mented
  With gold and shod with gold upon the
    feet;
    And with plucked ears of wheat.

The first man's hair was wound upon his
    head:
His face was red, and his mouth curled and
    sad;
    All his gold garment had
    Pale stains of dust and rust.
A riven hood was pulled across his eyes;
The token of him being upon this wise
    Made for a sign of Lust.

The next was Shame, with hollow heavy
    face
  Colored like green wood when flame
    kindles it.
    He hath such feeble feet
They may not well endure in any place.
His face was full of grey old miseries,
  And all his blood's increase
    Was even increase of pain.
The last was Fear, that is akin to Death;
He is Shame's friend, and always as Shame
    saith
    Fear answers him again.

My soul said in me; This is marvellous,
  Seeing the air's face is not so delicate
    Nor the sun's grace so great,
If sin and she be kin or amorous.
And seeing where maidens served her on
    their knees,
  I bade one crave of these
    To know the cause thereof.
Then Fear said: I am Pity that was dead.
And Shame said: I am Sorrow comforted.
    And Lust said: I am Love.

3

Thereat her hands began a lute-playing
    And her sweet mouth a song in a strange
        tongue ;
    And all the while she sung
There was no sound but long tears follow-
        ing
Long tears upon men's faces, waxen white
    With extreme sad delight.
        But those three following men
Became as men raised up among the dead ;
Great glad mouths open, and fair cheeks
        made red
    With child's blood come again.

Then I said : Now assuredly I see
    My lady is perfect, and transfigureth
        All sin and sorrow and death,
Making them fair as her own eyelids be,
Or lips wherein my whole soul's life abides ;
    Or as her sweet white sides
        And bosom carved to kiss.
Now therefore, if her pity further me.

Doubtless for her sake all my days shall be
    As righteous as she is.

Forth, ballad, and take roses in both arms,
    Even till the top rose touch thee in the
        throat
Where the least thornprick harms ;
    And girdled in thy golden singing-coat,
Come thou before my lady and say this ;
    Borgia, thy gold hair's color burns in
        me,
    Thy mouth makes beat my blood in
        feverish rhymes ;
Therefore so many as these roses be,
Then it may be, seeing how sweet she is,
    That she will stoop herself none other-
        wise
    Than a blown vine-branch doth,
And kiss thee with soft laughter on thine
        eyes,
    Ballad, and on thy mouth.

A BALLAD OF DEATH.

KNEEL down, fair Love, and fill thyself
        with tears,
Girdle thyself with sighing for a girth
Upon the sides of mirth,
Cover thy lips and eyelids, let thine ears
Be filled with rumor of people sorrowing ;
Make thee soft raiment out of woven sighs
Upon the flesh to cleave,
Set pains therein and many a grievous thing,
And many sorrows after each his wise
For armlet and for gorget and for sleeve.

O Love's lute heard about the lands of death,
Left hanged upon the trees that were
        therein ;
O Love and Time and Sin,
Three singing mouths that mourn now
        under breath,
Three lovers, each one evil spoken of ;
O smitten lips where through this voice of
        mine
Came softer with her praise ;
Abide a little for our lady's love.
The kisses of her mouth were more than
    wine,

And more than peace the passage of her
        days.
O Love, thou knowest if she were good to
        see.
O Time, thou shalt not find in any land
Till, cast out of thine hand,
The sunlight and the moonlight fail from
        thee,
Another woman fashioned like as this.
O Sin, thou knowest that all thy shame in
        her
Was made a goodly thing ;
Yea, she caught Shame and shamed him
        with her kiss,
With her fair kiss, and lips much lovelier
Than lips of amarous roses in late spring.

By night there stood over against my bed
Queen Venus with a hood striped gold and
        black,
Both sides drawn fully back
From brows wherein the sad blood failed
        of red,
And temples drained of purple and full of
        death.

Her curled hair had the wave of sea-water
And the sea's gold in it.
Her eyes were as a dove's that sickeneth.
Strewn dust of gold she had shed over her,
And pearl and purple and amber on her
    feet.

Upon her raiment of dyed sendaline
Were painted all the secret ways of love
And covered things thereof,
That hold delight as grape-flowers hold
    their wine ;
Red mouths of maidens and red feet of
    doves,
And brides that kept within the bride-
    chamber
Their garment of soft shame,
And weeping faces of the wearied loves
That swoon in sleep and awake wearier,
With heat of lips and hair shed out like
flame.

The tears that through her eyelids fell on
    me
Made my own bitter where they ran be-
    tween
As blood had fallen therein,
She saying ; Arise, lift up thine eyes and
    see
If any glad thing be or any good
Now the best thing is taken forth of us ;
Even she to whom all praise
Was as one flower in a great multitude,
One glorious flower of many and glorious,
One day found gracious among many days :

Even she whose handmaiden was Love—
    to whom
At kissing times across her stateliest bed
Kings bowed themselves and shed
Pale wine, and honey with the honeycomb,
And spikenard bruised for a burnt-offering ;
Even she between whose lips the kiss be-
    came
As fire and frankincense ;
Whose hair was as gold raiment on a king,
Whose eyes were as the morning purged
    with flame,
Whose eyelids as sweet savor issuing
    thence.
Then I beheld, and lo on the other side
My lady's likeness crowned and robed and
    dead.
Sweet still, but now not red,
Was the shut mouth whereby men lived and
    died.

And sweet, but emptied of the blood's blue
    shade,
The great curled eyelids that withheld her
    eyes.
And sweet, but like spoilt gold,
The weight of color in her tresses weighed.
And sweet, but as a vesture with new dyes,
The body that was clothed with love of old.

Ah ! that my tears filled all her woven hair
And all the hollow bosom of her gown—
Ah ! that my tears ran down
Even to the place where many kisses were,
Even where her parted breast-flowers have
    place,
Even where they are cloven apart—who
    knows not this ?
Ah ! the flowers cleave apart
And their sweet fills the tender interspace ;
Ah ! the leaves grown thereof were things
    to kiss
Ere their fine gold was tarnished at the
    heart.

Ah ! in the days when God did good to
    me,
Each part about her was a righteous thing ;
Her mouth an almsgiving,
The glory of her garments charity,
The beauty of her bosom a good deed,
In the good days when God kept sight of
    us ;
Love lay upon her eyes,
And on that hair whereof the world takes
    heed :
And all her body was more virtuous
Than souls of women fashioned otherwise.

Now, ballad, gather poppies in thine hands
And sheaves of briar and many rusted
    sheaves
Rain-rotten in rank lands,
Waste marigold and late unhappy leaves
And grass that fades ere any of it be mown ;
And when thy bosom is filled full thereof
Seek out Death's face ere the light altereth,
And say "My master that was thrall to
    Love
Is become thrall to Death."
Bow down before him, ballad, sigh and
    groan,
But make no sojourn in thy outgoing ;
For haply it may be
That when thy feet return at evening
Death shall come in with thee.

LAUS VENERIS.

ASLEEP or waking is it? for her neck,
Kissed over close, wears yet a purple speck,
   Wherein the pained blood falters and
     goes out;
Soft, and stung softly—fairer for a fleck.

But though my lips shut sucking on the
    place,
There is no vein at work upon her face;
   Her eyelids are so peaceable, no doubt
Deep sleep has warmed her blood through
    all its ways.

Lo, this is she that was the world's delight;
The old grey years were parcels of her
    might;
   The strewings of the ways wherein she
     trod
Were the twain seasons of the day and
    night.

Lo, she was thus when her clear limbs en-
    ticed
All lips that now grow sad with kissing
    Christ,
   Stained with blood fallen from the feet
     of God,
The feet and hands whereat our souls were
    priced.

Alas, Lord, surely thou art great and fair.
But lo her wonderfully woven hair!
   And thou didst heal us with thy piteous
    kiss;
But see now, Lord; her mouth is lovelier.

She is right fair; what hath she done to
    thee?
Nay, fair Lord Christ, lift up thine eyes
    and see;
   Had now thy mother such a lip—like
    this?
Thou knowest how sweet a thing it is to me.

Inside the Horsel here the air is hot;
Right little peace one hath for it, God wot;

The scented dusty daylight burns the
    air,
And my heart chokes me till I hear it not.

Behold, my Venus, my soul's body, lies
With my love laid upon her garment-wise,
   Feeling my love in all her limbs and
    hair
And shed between her eyelids through her
    eyes.

She holds my heart in her sweet open
    hands
Hanging asleep; hard by her head there
    stands,
   Crowned with gilt thorns and clothed
    with flesh like fire,
Love, wan as foam blown up the salt burnt
    sands—

Hot as the brackish waifs of yellow spume
That shift and steam—loose clots of arid
    fume
   From the sea's panting mouth of dry
    desire;
There stands he, like one laboring at a
    loom.

The warp holds fast across; and every
    thread
That makes the woof up has dry specks of
    red;
   Always the shuttle cleaves clean through,
    and he
Weaves with the hair of many a ruined
    head.

Love is not glad nor sorry, as I deem;
Laboring he dreams, and labors in the
    dream,
   Till when the spool is finished, lo I see
His web, reeled off, curls and goes out like
    steam.

Night falls like fire; the heavy lights run
    low,
And as they drop, my blood and body so

Shake as the flame shakes, full of days
  and hours
That sleep not neither weep they as they
  go.

Ah yet would God this flesh of mine might
  be
Where air might wash and long leaves
  cover me,
  Where tides of grass break into foam of
    flowers,
Or where the wind's feet shine along the
  sea.

Ah yet would God that stems and roots
  were bred
Out of my weary body and my head,
  That sleep were sealed upon me with a
    seal,
And I were as the least of all his dead.

Would God my blood were dew to feed
  the grass,
Mine ears made deaf and mine eyes blind
  as glass,
  My body broken as a turning wheel,
And my mouth stricken ere it saith Alas!

Ah God, that love were as a flower or flame,
That life were as the naming of a name,
  That death were not more pitiful than
    desire,
That these things were not one thing and
  the same!

Behold now, surely somewhere there is
  death:
For each man hath some space of years, he
  saith.
  A little space of time ere time expire,
A little day, a little way of breath.

And lo, between the sundawn and the sun,
His day's work and his night's work are
  undone;
  And lo, between the nightfall and the
    light,
He is not, and none knoweth of such an
  one.

Ah God, that I were as all souls that be,
As any herb or leaf of any tree,
  As men that toil through hours of labor-
    ing night,
As bones of men under the deep sharp sea.

Outside it must be winter among men;
For at the gold bars of the gates again
  I heard all night and all the hours of it,
The wind's wet wings and fingers drip with
  rain.

Knights gather, riding sharp for cold; I
  know
The ways and woods are strangled with the
  snow;
  And with short song the maidens spin
    and sit
Until Christ's birthnight, lily-like, arow.

The scent and shadow shed about me make
The very soul in all my senses ache;
  The hot hard night is fed upon my breath,
And sleep beholds me from afar awake.

Alas, but surely where the hills grow deep,
Or where the wild ways of the sea are steep,
  Or in strange places somewhere there is
    death,
And on death's face the scattered hair of
  sleep.

There lover-like with lips and limbs that
  meet
They lie, they pluck sweet fruit of life and
  eat;
  But me the hot and hungry days devour,
And in my mouth no fruit of theirs is sweet.

No fruit of theirs, but fruit of my desire,
For her love's sake whose lips through
  mine respire;
  Her eyelids on her eyes like flower on
    flower,
Mine eyelids on mine eyes like fire on fire.

So lie we, not as sleep that lies by death,
With heavy kisses and with happy breath;
  Not as man lies by woman, when the
    bride
Laughs low for love's sake and the words
  he saith.

For she lies, laughing low with love; she
  lies
And turns his kisses on her lips to sighs,
  To sighing sound of lips unsatisfied,
And the sweet tears are tender with her
  eyes.

Ah, not as they, but as the souls that were

Slain in the old time, having found her fair;
　Who, sleeping with　her　lips upon their
　　eyes,
Heard sudden serpents hiss across her hair.

Their　blood　runs　round　the　roots　of time
　like rain:
She　casts　them　forth　and　gathers　them
　again;
　With　nerve　and　bone　she　weaves　and
　　multiplies
Exceeding pleasure out of extreme pain.

Her　little　chambers　drip　with　flower-like
　red,
Her girdles, and the chaplets of　her head,
　Her　armlets　and　her　anklets;　with her
　　feet,
She tramples all that winepress of the dead.

Her gateways smoke with　fume of flowers
　and fires,
With　loves　burnt　out　and　unassuaged de-
　sires;
　Between　her　lips　the　steam　of　them is
　　sweet,
The langor in her ears of many lyres.

Her beds are full of perfume and sad sound,
Her doors are made with music and barred
　round
With　sighing　and　with　laughter　and with
　tears,
With　tears　whereby strong souls of men are
　bound.

There is the knight Adonis that was　slain,
With flesh and blood she chains him for a
　chain;
　The body and the spirit in her ears
Cry, for her lips divide him vein by vein.

Yea, all she slayeth; yea, every man save
　me;
Me,　love,　thy　lover　that　must　cleave to
　thee
　Till　the　ending　of　the　days　and ways of
　　earth,
The shaking of the sources of the sea.

Me,　most forsaken of all souls that fell;
Me, satiated with things insatiable;
　Me,　for　whose　sake　the　extreme　hell
　　makes mirth,
Yea, laughter kindles at the heart of hell.

Alas thy　beauty！for　thy　mouth's sweet
　sake
My soul is bitter to me, my limbs　quake
　As water　as the flesh of men that weep,
　As their heart's vein whose heart goes nigh
　　to break.

Ah God, that sleep with flower-sweet finger-
　tips
Would　crush　the　fruit　of　death　upon my
　lips;
　Ah,　God,　that　death　would　tread the
　　grapes of sleep
And wring their juice upon me as it drips.

There is no change of cheer for many days,
But　change　of　chimes　high　up　in the air,
　that sways
　Rung　by the　running fingers of the wind;
And singing sorrows heard on hidden ways.

Day smiteth day in twain, night sundereth
　night,
And on mine eyes the dark sits as the light;
　Yea,　Lord,　thou　knowest　I　know not,
　　having sinned,
If heaven be clean or unclean in thy sight.

Yea, as if earth were sprinkled over me,
Such chafed harsh　earth as chokes a sandy
　sea,
　Each　pore　doth　yearn,　and　the dried
　　blood thereof
Gasps by sick fits, my heart swims heavily

There is a feverish famine in my veins;
Below her bosom, where a crushed grape
　stains
　The white and blue, there my lips caught
　　and clove
An hour since, and what mark of me re-
　mains？

I dare not always touch her, lest the kiss
Leave my lips charred.　Yea, Lord, a lit-
　tle bliss,
　Brief bitter bliss, one hath for a great sin;
Nathless thou knowest how sweet a thing
　it is.

Sin, is it sin whereby men's souls are thrust
Into the pit？yet had I a good trust
　To save my soul before it slipped therein,
Trod under by the fire-shod feet of lust.

For if mine eyes fail and my soul takes
  breath,
I look between the iron sides of death
  Into sad hell where all sweet love hath
    end,
All but the pain that never finisheth.

There are the naked faces of great kings,
The singing folk with all their lute-playings;
  There when one cometh he shall have to
    friend
The grave that covets and the worm that
  clings.

There sit the knights that were so great of
  hand,
The ladies that were queens of fair green
  land,
  Grown grey and black now, brought
    unto the dust,
Soiled, without raiment, clad about with
  sand.

There is one end for all of them; they sit
Naked and sad, they drink the dregs of it,
  Trodden as grapes in the wine-press of
    lust,
Trampled and trodden by the fiery feet.

I see the marvellous mouth whereby there
  fell
Cities and people whom the gods loved
  well,
  Yet for her sake on them the fire gat hold,
And for their sakes on her the fire of hell.

And softer than the Egyptian lote-leaf is,
The queen whose face was worth the world
  to kiss,
  Wearing at breast a suckling snake of
    gold;
And large pale lips of strong Semiramis.

Curled like a tiger's that curl back to feed;
Red only where the last kiss made them
  bleed;
  Her hair most thick with many a carven
    gem,
Deep in the mane, great-chested, like a
  steed.

Yea, with red sin the faces of them shine;
But in all these there was no sin like mine;
  No, not in all the strange great sins of
    them

That made the wine-press froth and foam
  with wine.

For I was of Christ's choosing, I God's
  knight,
No blinkard heathen stumbling for scant
  . light;
  I can well see, for all the dusty days
Gone past, the clean great time of goodly
  fight.

I smell the breathing battle sharp with
  blows,
With shriek of shafts and snapping short
  of bows;
  The fair pure sword smites out in subtle
    ways,
Sounds and long lights are shed between
  the rows

Of beautiful mailed men ; the edged light
  slips,
Most like a snake that takes short breath
  and dips
  Sharp from the beautifully bending head,
With all its gracious body lithe as lips

That curl in touching you; right in this
  wise
My sword doth, seeming fire in mine own
  eyes,
  Leaving all colors in them brown and red
And flecked with death; then the keen
  breaths like sighs,

The caught-up choked dry laughters follow-
  ing them,
When all the fighting face is grown a flame
  For pleasure, and the pulse that stuns
    the ears,
And the heart's gladness of the goodly
  game.

Let me think yet a little ; I do know
These things were sweet, but sweet such
  years ago,
  Their savor is all turned now into tears;
Yea, ten years since, where the blue rip-
  ples blow,

The blue curled eddies of the blowing
  Rhine,
I felt the sharp wind shaking grass and
  vine

Touch my blood, too, and sting me with
    delight
Through all this waste and weary body of
    mine

That never feels clear air; right gladly then
I rode alone, a great way off my men,
    And heard the chiming bridle smite and
    smite.
And gave each rhyme thereof some rhyme
    again,

Till my song shifted to that iron one;
Seeing there rode up between me and the
    sun
    Some certain of my foe's men, for his
    three
White wolves across their painted coats did
    run.

The first red-bearded, with square cheeks—
    alack,
I made my knave's blood turn his beard to
    black;
    The slaying of him was a joy to see:
Perchance too, when at night he came not
    back,

Some woman fell a-weeping, whom this
    thief
Would beat when he had drunken; yet
    small grief
    Hath any for the ridding of such knaves;
Yea, if one wept, I doubt her teen was
    brief.

This bitter love is sorrow in all lands,
Draining of eyelids, wringing of drenched
    hands,
    Sighing of hearts and filling up of graves;
A sign across the head of the world he
    stands,

As one that hath a plague-mark on his
    brows;
Dust and spilt blood do track him to his
    house
Down under earth; sweet smells of lip and
    cheek,
Like a sweet snake's breath made more
    poisonous

With chewing of some perfumed deadly
    grass,
Are shed all round his passage if he pass,

And their quenched savor leaves the
    whole soul weak,
Sick with keen guessing whence the per-
    fume was.

As one who hidden in deep sedge and reeds
Smells the rare scent made where a panther
    feeds,
    And tracking ever slotwise the warm
    smell
Is snapped upon by the sweet mouth and
    bleeds,

His head far down the hot sweet throat of
    her—
So one tracks love, whose breath is deadlier,
    And lo, one springé and you are fast in
    hell,
Fast as the gin's grip of a wayfarer.

I think now, as the heavy hours decease
One after one, and bitter thoughts increase
    One upon one, of all sweet finished things;
The breaking of the battle; the long peace

Wherein we sat clothed softly, each man's
    hair
Crowned with green leaves beneath white
    hoods of vair;
    The sounds of sharp spears at great
    tourneyings,
And noise of singing in the late sweet air.

I sang of love too, knowing nought thereof;
"Sweeter," I said, "the little laugh of
    love
Than tears out of the eyes of Magdalen,
Or any fallen feather of the Dove.

"The broken little laugh that spoils a kiss,
The ache of purple pulses, and the bliss
    Of blinded eyelids that expand again—
Love draws them open with those lips of
    his,

"Lips that cling hard till the kissed face
    has grown
Of one same fire and color with their own;
    Then ere one sleep, appeased with
    sacrifice,
Where his lips wounded, there his lips
    atone."

I sang these things long since and knew
    them not;

"Lo, here is love, or there is love, God
        wot,
    This man and that finds favor in his
        eyes,"   •
I said, "but I, what guerdon have I got?

"The dust of praise that is blown every-
        where
    In all men's faces with the common air;
    The bay-leaf that wants chafing to be
        sweet
Before they wind it in a singer's hair."

So that one dawn I rode forth sorrowing;
I had no hope but of some evil thing,
    And so rode slowly past the windy wheat,
And past the vineyard and the water-spring,

Up to the Horsel.   A great elder-tree
Held back its heaps of flowers to let me
        see
    The ripe tall grass, and one that walked
        therein,
Naked, with hair shed over to the knee.

She walked between the blossom and the
        grass;
I knew the beauty of her, what she was,
    The beauty of her body and her sin,
And in my flesh the sin of hers, alas!

Alas! for sorrow is all the end of this.
O sad kissed mouth, how sorrowful it is!
    O breast whereat some suckling sorrow
        clings,
Red with the bitter blossom of a kiss!

Ah, with blind lips I felt for you, and
        found
About my neck your hands and hair en-
        wound,
    The hands that stifle and the hair that
        stings,
I felt them fasten sharply without sound.

Yea, for my sin I had great store of bliss
Rise up, make answer for me, let thy kiss
    Seal my lips hard from speaking of my
        sin,
Lest one go mad to hear how sweet it is.

Yet I waxed faint with fume of barren
        bowers,
    2

And murmuring of the heavy-headed hours;
    And let the dove's beak fret and peck
        within
My lips in vain, and Love shed fruitless
    flowers.

So that God looked upon me when your
        hands
Were hot about me; yea, God brake my
        hands
    To save my soul alive, and I came forth
Like a man blind and naked in strange
        lands

That hears men laugh and weep, and
        knows not whence
Nor wherefore, but is broken in his sense;
    Howbeit I met folk riding from the north
Towards Rome, to purge them of their
        souls' offence.

And rode with them, and spake to none ;
        the day
Stunned me like lights upon some wizard
        way,
    And ate like fire mine eyes and mine
        eyesight ;
So rode I, hearing all these chant and pray,

And marvelled; till before us rose and fell
White cursed hills, like outer skirts of hell
    Seen where men's eyes look through the
        day to night,
Like a jagged shell's lips, harsh, untunable,

Blown in between by devils' wrangling
        breath;
Nathless we won well past that hell and
        death,
    Down to the sweet land where all airs
        are good,
Even unto Rome where God's grace tarrieth.

Then came each man and worshipped at his
        knees
Who in the Lord God's likeness bears the
        keys
    To bind or loose, and called on Christ's
        shed blood,
And so the sweet-souled father gave him
    ease.

But when I came I fell down at his feet,
Saying, "Father, though the Lord's blood
        be right sweet,

The spot it takes not off the panther's
    skin,
Nor shall an Ethiop's stain be bleached with
    it.

"Lo, I have sinned and have spat out at
    God,
Wherefore his hand is heavier and his rod
    More sharp because of mine exceeding
    sin,
And all his raiment redder than bright
    blood

" Before mine eyes ; yea, for my sake I wot
The heat of hell is waxen seven times hot
    Through my great sin." Then spake he
    some sweet word,
Giving me cheer ; which thing availed me
    not ;

Yea, scarce I wist if such indeed were said ;
For when I ceased—lo, as one newly dead
    Who hears a great cry out of hell, I heard
The crying of his voice across my head.

"Until this dry shred staff, that hath no
    whit
Of leaf nor bark, bear blossom and smell
    sweet,
Seek thou not any mercy in God's sight
For so long shalt thou be cast out from it."

Yea, what if dried-up stems wax red and
    green,
Shall that thing be which is not nor has
    been ?
    Yea, what if sapless bark was green and
    white,
Shall any good fruit grow upon my sin ?

Nay, though sweet fruit were plucked of a
    dry tree,
And though men drew sweet waters of the
    sea,
    There should not grow sweet leaves on
    this dead stem,
This waste wan body and shaken soul of
    me.

Yea, though God search it warily enough,
There is not one sound thing in all thereof ;
    Though he search all my veins through,
    searching them
He shall find nothing whole therein but
    love.

For I came home right heavy, with small
    cheer,
And lo my love, mine own soul's heart,
    more dear
    Than mine own soul, more beautiful
    than God,
Who hath my being between the hands of
    her—

Fair still, but fair for no man saving me,
As when she came out of the naked sea
    Making the foam as fire whereon she
    trod,
And as the inner flower of fire was she.

Yea, she laid nold upon me, and her mouth
Clove unto mine as soul to body doth,
    And, laughing, made her lips luxurious ;
Her hair had smells of all the sunburnt
    south,

Strange spice and flower, strange savor of
    crushed fruit
And perfume the swart kings tread under.
    foot
    For pleasure when their minds wax
    amorous,
Charred frankincense and grated sandal.
    root.

And I forgot fear and all weary things,
All ended prayers and perished thanks-
    givings,
    Feeling her face with all her eager hair
Cleave to me, clinging as a fire that clings

To the body and to the raiment, burning
    them ;
As after death I know that such-like flame
    Shall cleave to me for ever ; yea, what
    care,
Albeit I burn then, having felt the same ?

Ah love, there is no better life than this ;
To have known love, how bitter a thing it is,
    And afterward be cast out of God's sight ;
Yea, these that know not, shall they have
    such bliss

High up in barren heaven before his face
As we twain in the heavy-hearted place,
    Remembering love and all the dead de-
    light,
And all that time was sweet with for a
    space ?

For till the thunder in the trumpet be,
Soul may divide from body, but not we
 One from another; I hold thee with my
  hand,
I let mine eyes have all their will of thee,

I seal myself upon thee with my might,
Abiding alway out of all men's sight
 Until God loosen over sea and land
The thunder of the trumpets of the night,
  EXPLICIT LAUS VENERIS.

PHÆDRA.

HIPPOLYTUS; PHÆDRA : CHORUS OF TRŒZENIAN WOMEN.

HIPPOLYTUS.

Lay not thine hand upon me; let me go;
Take off thine eyes that put the gods to
  shame;
What, wilt thou turn my loathing to thy
  death?

PHÆDRA.

Nay, I will never loosen hold nor breathe
Till thou have slain me; godlike for great
  brows
Thou art, and thewed as gods are, with
  clear hair:
Draw now thy sword and smite me as thou
  art god,
For verily I am smitten of other gods,
Why not of thee?

CHORUS.

       O queen, take heed of words;
Why wilt thou eat the husk of evil speech?
Wear wisdom for that veil about thy head
And goodness for the binding of thy brows.

PHÆDRA.

Nay, but this god hath cause enow to smite;
If he will slay me, baring breast and
  throat,
I lean toward the stroke with silent mouth
And a great heart. Come, take thy sword
  and slay;
Let me not starve between desire and death,
But send me on my way with glad wet lips;
For in the vein-drawn ashen-colored palm
Death's hollow hand holds water of sweet
  draught

To dip and slake dried mouths at, as a deer
Specked red from thorns laps deep and
  loses pain.
Yea, if my mine own blood ran upon my
  mouth,
I would drink that. Nay, but be swift
  with me;
Set thy sword here between the girdle and
  breast
For I shall grow a poison if I live.
Are not my cheeks as grass, my body pale,
And my breath like a dying poisoned man's?
O whatsoever of godlike names thou be,
By thy chief name I charge thee, thou
  strong god,
And bid thee slay me. Strike, up to the
  gold,
Up to the hand-grip of the hilt; strike
  here;
For I am Cretan of my birth; strike now;
For I am Theseus' wife; stab up to the rims,
I am born daughter to Pasiphae.
See thou spare not for greatness of my
  blood,
Nor for the shining letters of my name:
Make thy sword sure inside thine hand and
  smite,
For the bright writing of my name is black,
And I am sick with hating the sweet sun.

HIPPOLYTUS

Let not this woman wail and cleave to me,
That am no part of the god's wrath with
  her;
Loose ye her hands from me lest she take
  hurt,

CHORUS.

Lady, this speech and majesty are twain;
Pure shame is of one counsel with the gods.

HIPPOLYTUS.

Man is as beast when shame stands off
　　from him.

PHÆDRA.

Man, what have I to do with shame or
　　thee ?
I am not of one counsel with the gods.
I am their kin, I have strange blood in me,
I am not of their likeness nor of thine:
My veins are mixed, and therefore am I
　　mad,
Yea therefore chafe and turn on mine own
　　flesh,
Half a woman made with half a god.
But thou wast hewn out of an iron womb
And fed with molten mother-snow for
　　milk.
A sword was nurse of thine; Hippolyta,
That had the spear to father, and the axe
To bridesman, and wet blood of sword-
　　slain men
For wedding-water out of a noble well,
Even she did bear thee, thinking of a sword,
And thou wast made a man mistakingly.
Nay, for I love thee, I will have thy hands,
Nay, for I will not loose thee, thou art
　　sweet,
Thou art my son, I am thy father's wife,
I ache toward thee with a bridal blood,
The pulse is heavy in all my married veins,
My whole face beats, I will feed full of
　　thee,
My body is empty of ease, I will be fed,
I am burnt to the bone with love, thou
　　shalt not go,
I am heartsick, and mine eyelids prick
　　mine eyes,
Thou shalt not sleep nor eat nor say a
　　word
Till thou hast slain me.　I am not good to
　　live.

CHORUS.

This is an evil born with all its teeth,
When love is cast out of the bound of love.

HIPPOLYTUS.

There is no hate that is so hateworthy.

PHÆDRA.

I pray thee turn that hate of thine my way,
I hate not it nor anything of thine.
Lo, maidens, how he burns about the brow,
And draws the chafing sword-strap down
　　his hand.
What wilt thou do? wilt thou be worse
　　than death ?
Be but as sweet as is the bitterest,
The most dispiteous out of all the gods,
I am well pleased.　Lo, do I crave so
　　much ?
I do but bid thee be unmerciful,
Even the one thing thou art.　Pity me not:
Thou wert not quick to pity.　Think of me
As of a thing thy hounds are keen upon
In the wet woods between the windy ways,
And slay me for a spoil.　This body of
　　mine
Is worth a wild beasts fell or hide of hair,
And spotted deeper than a panther's grain.
I were but dead if thou wert pure indeed;
I pray thee by thy cold green holy crown
And by the fillet-leaves of Artemis.
Nay, but thou wilt not.　Death is not like
　　thee,
Albeit men hold him worst of all the gods.
For of all gods Death only loves not gifts,
Nor with burnt-offering nor blood-sacrifice
Shalt thou do aught to get thee grace of
　　him;
He will have nought of altar and altar-song,
And from him only of all the lords in
　　heaven
Persuasion turns a sweet averted mouth.
But thou art worse: from thee with baffled
　　breath
Back on my lips my prayer falls like a blow,
And beats upon them, dumb.　What shall
　　I say?
There is no word I can compel thee with
To do me good and slay me.　But take
　　heed;
I say, be wary; look between thy feet,
Lest a snare take them though the ground
　　be good.

HIPPOLYTUS.

Shame may do most where fear is found
　　most weak:

* Æsch. Fr. Niobe :—

　μόνος θεῶν γὰρ θάνατος οὐ δώρων ἐρᾷ, κ.
τ. λ.

That which for shame's sake yet I have not
        done,
Shall it be done for fears?   Take thine own
        way;
Better the foot slip than the whole soul
        swerve.

PHÆDRA.

The man is choice and exquisite of mouth;
Yet in the end a curse shall curdle it.

CHORUS.

He goes with cloak upgathered to the lip,
Holding his eye as with some ill in sight.

PHÆDRA.

A bitter ill he hath i' the way thereof,
And it shall burn the sight out as with fire.

CHORUS.

Speak no such word whereto mischance is
        kin.

PHÆDRA.

Out of my heart and by fate's leave I speak.

CHORUS.

Set not thy heart to follow after fate.

PHÆDRA.

O women, O sweet people of this land,
O goodly city and pleasant ways thereof,
And woods with pasturing grass and great
        well-heads,
And hills with light and night between
        your leaves,
And winds with sound and silence in your
        lips,
And earth and water and all immortal
        things,
I take you to my witness what I am.
There is a god about me like as fire,
Sprung whence, who knoweth, or who
        hath heart to say?
A god more strong than whom slain beasts
        can soothe,
Or honey, or any spilth of blood-like wine,
Nor shall one please him with a whitened
        brow
Nor wheat nor wool nor aught of plaited
        leaf.

For like my mother am I stung and slain,
And round my cheeks have such red
        malady
And on my lips such fire and foam as hers.
This is that Atè out of Amathus
That breeds up death and gives it one for
        love.
She hath slain mercy, and for dead mercy's
        sake
(Being frighted with this sister that was
        slain)
Flees from before her fearful-footed shame,
And will not bear the bending of her brows
And long soft arrows flown from under
        them
As from bows bent.   Desire flows out of
        her
As out of lips doth speech: and over her
Shines fire, and round her and beneath her
        fire.
She hath sown pain and plague in all our
        house,
Love loathed of love, and mates unmatch-
        able,
Wild wedlock, and the lusts that bleat or
        low,
And marriage-fodder snuffed about of kine.
Lo how the heifer runs with leaping flank
Sleek under shaggy and speckled lies of
        hair,
And chews a horrible lip, and with harsh
        tongue
Laps alien froth and licks a loathlier mouth.
Alas, a foul first steam of trodden tares,
And fouler of these late grapes underfoot.
A bitter way of waves and clean-cut foam
Over the sad road of sonorous sea
The high gods gave king Theseus for no
        love,
Nay, but for love, yet to no loving end.
Alas the long thwarts and the fervent oars,
And blown hard sails that straightened the
        scant rope !
There were no strong pools in the hollow
        sea
To drag at them and suck down side and
        beak,
No wind to catch them in the teeth and
        hair,
No shoal, no shallow among the roaring
        reefs,
No gulf whereout the straining tides throw
        spars,
No surf where white bones twist like
        whirled white fire.

But like to death he came with death, and
    sought
And slew and spoiled and gat him that he
    would.
For death, for marriage, and for child-
    getting,
I set my curse against him as a sword;
Yea, and the severed half thereof I leave
Pittheus, because he slew not (when that
    face
Was tender, and the life still soft in it)

The small swathed child, but bred him
    for my fate.
I would I had been the first that took her
    death
Out from between wet hoofs and reddened
    teeth,
Splashed horns, fierce fetlocks of the
    brother bull !
For now shall I take death a deadlier way;
Gathering it up between the feet of love
Or off the knees of murder reaching it.

THE TRIUMPH OF TIME.

BEFORE our lives divide for ever,
    While time is with us and hands are
    free,
(Time, swift to fasten and swift to sever
Hand from hand, as we stand by the sea)
I will say no word that a man might say
Whose whole life's love goes down in a
    day;
For this could never have been; and never,
    Though the gods and the years relent,
    shall be.

Is it worth a tear, is it worth an hour,
    To think of things that are well outworn?
Of fruitless husk and fugitive flower,
    The dream foregone and the deed for-
    borne?
Though joy be done with and grief be vain,
Time shall not sever us wholly in twain;
Earth is not spoilt for a single shower;
    But the rain has ruined the ungrown corn.

It will grow not again, this fruit of my heart,
    Smitten with sunbeams, ruined with rain.
The singing seasons divide and depart
    Winter and summer depart in twain.
It will grow not again, it is ruined at root,
The bloodlike blossom, the dull red fruit;
Though the heart yet sickens, the lips yet
    smart,
    With sullen savor of poisonous pain.

I have given no man of my fruit to eat;
    I trod the grapes, I have drunken the
    wine.
Had you eaten and drunken and found it
    sweet,
    This wild new growth of the corn and
    vine,
This wine and bread without lees or leaven.
We had grown as gods, as the gods in
    heaven,
Souls fair to look upon, goodly to greet,
    One splendid spirit, your soul and mine.

In the change of years, in the coil of things,
    In the clamor and rumor of life to be
We, drinking love as the furthest springs,
Covered with love at a covering tree,
We had grown as gods, as the gods above,
Filled from the heart to the lips with love,
Held fast in his hands, clothed warm with
    his wings,
    O love, my love had you loved but me !

We had stood as the sure stars stand, and
    moved
    As the moon moves, loving the world;
    and seen
Grief collapse as a thing disproved,
    Death consume as a thing unclean,
Twain halves of a perfect heart, made fast,
Soul to soul while the years fell past;

Had you loved me once, as you have not
loved;
Had the chance been with us that has
not been.

I have put my days and dreams out of mind,
Days that are over, dreams that are done.
Though we seek life through, we shall
surely find
There is none of them clear to us now,
not one.
But clear are these things; the grass and
the sand,
Where, sure as the eyes reach, ever at hand,
With lips wide open and face burnt blind,
The strong sea-daisies feast on the sun.

The low downs lean to the sea; the stream,
One loose thin pulseless tremulous vein,
Rapid and vivid and dumb as a dream,
Works downward, sick of the sun and
the rain;
No wind is rough with the rank rare
flowers;
The sweet sea, mother of loves and hours,
Shudders and shines as the grey winds
gleam,
Turning her smile to a fugitive pain.

Mother of loves that are swift to fade,
Mother of mutable winds and hours.
A barren mother, a mother-maid,
Cold and clean as her faint salt flowers.
I would we twain were even as she,
Lost in the night and the light of the sea,
Where faint sounds falter and wan beams
wade,
Break, and are broken, and shed into
showers.

The loves and hours of the life of a man,
They are swift and sad, being born of
the sea.
Hours that rejoice and regret for a span,
Born with a man's breath, mortal as he;
Loves that are lost ere they come to birth,
Weeds of the wave, without fruit upon
earth.
I lose what I long for, save what I can,
My love, my love, and no love for me!

It is not much that a man can save
On the sands of life, in the straits of time,
Who swims in sight of the great third
wave

That never a swimmer shall cross or
climb.
Some waif washed up with the strays and
spars
That ebb-tide shows to the shore and the
stars;
Weed from the water, grass from a grave.
A broken blossom, a ruined rhyme,

There will no man do for your sake, I
think,
What I would have done for the least
word said.
I had wrung life dry for your lips to drink,
Broken it up for your daily bread :
Body for body and blood for blood,
As the flow of the full sea risen to flood
That yearns and trembles before it sink,
I had given, and lain down for you, glad
and dead.

Yea, hope at highest and all her fruit,
And time at fullest and all his dower,
I had given you surely, and life to boot,
Were we once made one for a single
hour.
But now, you are twain, you are cloven
apart,
Flesh of his flesh, but heart of my heart;
And deep in one is the bitter root,
And sweet for one is the lifelong flower.

To have died if you cared I should die for
you, clung
To my life if you bade me, played my
part
As it pleased you—these were the thoughts
that stung,
The dreams that smote with a keener
dart
Than shafts of love or arrows of death;
These were but as fire is, dust or breath,
Or poisonous foam on the tender tongue
Of the little snakes that eat my heart.

I wish we were dead together to-day,
Lost sight of, hidden away out of sight,
Clasped and clothed in the cloven clay,
Out of the world's way, out of the light,
Out of the ages of worldly weather,
Forgotten of all men altogether,
As the world's first dead, taken wholly
away.
Made one with death, filled full of the
night.

How we should slumber, how we should
    sleep,
    Far in the dark with the dreams and the
        dews !
And dreaming, grow to each other, and
    weep,
    Laugh low, live softly, murmur and muse;
Yea, and it may be, struck through by the
    dream,
Feel the dust quicken and quiver, and seem
Alive as of old to the lips, and leap
    Spirit to spirit as lovers use.

Sick dreams and sad of a dull delight;
    For what shall it profit when men are
        dead
To have dreamed, to have loved with the
    whole soul's might,
    To have looked for day when the day
        was fled ?
Let come what will, there is one thing
    worth,
To have had fair love in the life upon
    earth:
To have held love safe till the day grew
    night,
While skies had color and lips were red.

Would I lose you now? would I take you
    then,
    If I lose you now that my heart has
        need ?
And come what may after death to men,
    What thing worth this will the dead
        years breed ?
Lose life, lose all; but at least I know,
O sweet life's love, having loved you so,
Had I reached you on earth, I should lose
    not again,
    In death nor life, nor in dream or deed.

Yea, I know this well: were you once
    sealed mine,
    Mine in the blood's beat, mine in the
        breath,
Mixed into me as honey in wine,
    Not time that sayeth and gainsayeth,
Nor all strong things had severed us then;
Not wrath of gods, nor wisdom of men,
Nor all things earthly, nor all divine,
    Nor joy nor sorrow, nor life nor death.

I had grown pure as the dawn and the dew,
    You had grown strong as the sun or the
        sea.

But none shall triumph a whole life through:
    For death is one, and the fates are three.
At the door of life, by the gate of breath,
    There are worse things waiting for men than
        death;
Death could not sever my soul and you,
    As these have severed your soul from me.

You have chosen and clung to the chance
    they sent you,
    Life sweet as perfume and pure as prayer.
But will it not one day in heaven repent
    you ?
    Will they solace you wholly, the days
        that were ?
Will you lift up your eyes between sadness
    and bliss,
Meet mine, and see where the great love is,
And tremble and turn and be changed ?
    Content you;
    The gate is strait; I shall not be there.

But you, had you chosen, had you stretched
    hand,
    Had you seen good such a thing were
        done,
I too might have stood with the souls that
    stand
    In the sun's sight, clothed with the light
        of the sun;
But who now on earth need care how I
    live ?
Have the high gods anything left to give,
Save dust and laurels and gold and sand ?
    Which gifts are goodly; but I will none.

O all fair lovers about the world,
    There is none of you, none, that shall
        comfort me.
My thoughts are as dead things, wrecked
    and whirled
    Round and round in a gulf of the sea;
And still, through the sound and the strain-
    ing stream,
Through the coil and chafe, they gleam in
    a dream,
The bright fine lips so cruelly curled,
    And strange swift eyes where the soul sits
        free.

Free, without pity, withheld from woe,
    Ignorant; fair as the eyes are fair.
Would I have you change now, change at a
    blow,
    Startled and stricken, awake and aware?

Yea, if I could, would I have you see
My very love of you filling me,
And know my soul to the quick, as I know
    The likeness and look of your throat and
      hair ?

I shall not change you. Nay, though I
      might,
    Would I change my sweet one love with
      a word ?
I had rather your hair should change in a
      night,
    Clear now as the plume of a black bright
      bird;
Your face fail suddenly, cease, turn grey,
Die as a leaf that dies in a day.
I will keep my soul in a place out of sight,
    Far off, where the pulse of it is not heard.

Far off it walks, in a bleak blown space,
    Full of the sound of the sorrow of years.
I have woven a veil for the weeping face,
    Whose lips have drunken the wine of
      tears;
I have found a way for the failing feet,
A place for slumber and sorrow to meet;
There is no rumor about the place,
    Nor light, nor any that sees or hears.

I have hidden my soul out of sight, and
      said
    " Let none take pity upon thee, none
Comfort thy crying: for lo, thou art dead,
    Lie still now, safe out of sight of the sun.
Have I not built thee a grave, and wrought
Thy grave-clothes on thee of grievous
      thought,
With soft spun verses and tears unshed,
    And sweet light visions of things undone?

" I have given thee garments and balm
      and myrrh,
    And gold, and beautiful burial things.
But thou, be at peace now, make no stir;
    Is not thy grave as a royal king s ?
Fret not thyself though the end were sore;
Sleep, be patient, vex me no more.
Sleep; what hast thou to do with her ?
    The eyes that weep, with the mouth that
      sings ? "

Where the dead red leaves of the years lie
      rotten,
    The cold old crimes and the deeds thrown
      by,

The misconceived and the misbegotten,
    I would find a sin to do ere I die,
Sure to dissolve and destroy me all through,
That would set you higher in heaven, serve
      you
And leave you happy, when clean forgot-
      ten,
    As a dead man out of mind, am I.

Your lithe hands draw me, your face burns
      through me,
    I am swift to follow you, keen to see;
But love lacks might to redeem or undo me,
    As I have been, I know I shall surely be;
"What should such fellows as I do ? "
      Nay,
My part were worse if I chose to play;
For the worst is this after all; if they knew
      me,
    Not a soul upon earth would pity me.

And I play not for pity of these; but you,
    If you saw with your soul what man
      am I,
You would praise me at least that my soul
      all through
Clove to you, loathing the lives that lie;
The souls and lips that are bought and sold,
The smiles of silver and kisses of gold,
The lapdog loves that whine as they chew,
    The little lovers that curse and cry.

There are fairer women, I hear; that may
      be.
But I, that I love you and find you fair,
Who are more than fair in my eyes if they
      be,
    Do the high gods know or the great
      gods care ?
Though the swords in my heart for one
      were seven,
Would the iron hollow of doubtful heaven,
That knows not itself whether night-time
      or day be,
Reverberate words and a foolish prayer ?

I will go back to the great sweet mother,
    Mother and lover of men, the sea.
I will go down to her, I and none other,
    Close with her, kiss her and mix her
      with me;
Cling to her, strive with her, hold her fast;
O fair white mother, in days long past
Born without sister, born without brother,
    Set free my soul as thy soul is free.

O fair green-girdled mother of mine,
  Sea, that art clothed with the sun and
    the rain,
Thy sweet hard kisses are strong like wine,
  Thy large embraces are keen like pain.
Save me and hide me with all thy waves,
Find me one grave of thy thousand graves,
Those pure cold populous graves of thine,
  Wrought without hand in a world with-
    out stain.

I shall sleep, and move with the moving
  ships,
  Change as the winds change, veer in the
    tide;
My lips will feast on the foam of thy lips,
  I shall rise with thy rising, with thee
    subside;
Sleep, and not know if she be, if she were,
Filled full with life to the eyes and hair,
As a rose is fulfilled to the roseleaf tips
  With splendid summer and perfume and
    pride.

This woven raiment of nights and days,
  Were it once cast off and unwound from
    me,
Naked and glad would I walk in thy ways,
  Alive and aware of thy ways and thee;
Clear of the whole world, hidden at home,
Clothed with the green and crowned with
  the foam,
A pulse of the life of thy straits and bays,
  A vein in the heart of the streams of the
    sea.

Fair mother, fed with the lives of men,
  Thou art subtle and cruel of heart, men
    say
Thou hast taken, and shalt not render
  again;
  Thou art full of thy dead, and cold as
    they.
But death is the worst that comes of thee;
Thou art fed with our dead, O mother, O
  sea,
But when hast thou fed on our hearts? or
  when,
  Having given us love, hast thou taken
    away?

O tender-hearted, O perfect lover,
  Thy lips are bitter, and sweet thine heart.
The hopes that hurt and the dreams that
  hover,

Shall they not vanish away and apart?
But thou, thou art sure, thou art older than
  earth;
Thou art strong for death and fruitful of
  birth;
Thy depths conceal and thy gulfs discover;
  From the first thou wert; in the end thou
    art.

And grief shall endure not for ever, I know.
  As things that are not shall these things
    be;
We shall live through seasons of sun and
  of snow,
  And none be grievous as this to me.
We shall hear, as one in a trance that
  hears,
The sound of time, the rhyme of the years;
Wrecked hope and passionate pain will
  grow
  As tender things of a spring-tide sea

Sea-fruit that swings in the waves that hiss,
  Drowned gold and purple and royal
    rings.
And all time past, was it all for this?
  Times unforgotten, and treasures of
    things?
Swift years of liking, and sweet long laugh-
  ter,
That wist not well of the years thereafter
Till love woke, smitten at heart by a kiss,
  With lips that trembled and trailing
    wings?

There lived a singer in France of old,
  By the tideless dolorous midland sea.
In a land of sand and ruin and gold
  There shone one woman, and none but
    she.
And finding life for her love's sake fail,
Being fain to see her, he bade set sail,
Touched land, and saw her as life grew
  cold,
  And praised God, seeing; and so died he.

Died, praising God for his gift and grace:
  For she bowed down to him weeping,
    and said
" Live;" and her tears were shed on his
  face
  Or ever the life in his face was shed.
The sharp tears fell through her hair, and
  stung

Once, and her close lips touched him and
  clung
Once, and grew one with his lips for a
  space;
And so drew back, and the man was
  dead.

O brother, the gods were good to you.
  Sleep, and be glad while the world en-
  dures.
Be well content as the years wear through;
  Give thanks for life, and the loves and
  lures;
Give thanks for life, O brother, and death,
For the sweet last sound of her feet, her
  breath,
For gifts she gave you, gracious and few,
  Tears and kisses, that lady of yours.

Rest and be glad of the gods; but I,
  How shall I praise them, or how take
  rest ?
There is not room under all the sky
  For me that know not of worst or best,
Dream or desire of the days before,
Sweet things or bitterness, any more.
Love will not come to me now though I
  die,
  As love came close to you, breast to
  breast.

I shall never be friends again with roses;
  I shall loathe sweet tunes, where a note
  grown strong
Relents and recoils, and climbs and closes,
  As a wave of the sea turned back by
  song.

There are sounds where the soul's delight
  takes fire,
Face to face with its own desire;
A delight that rebels, a desire that reposes,
  I shall hate sweet music my whole life
  long.

The pulse of war and passion of wonder,
  The heavens that murmur, the sounds
  that shine,
The stars that sing and the loves that
  thunder,
The music burning at heart like wine,
An armed archangel whose hands raise up
All senses mixed up in the spirit's cup
Till flesh and spirit are molten in sunder—
  These things are over, and no more mine.

These were a part of the playing I heard
  Once, ere my love and my heart were at
  strife;
Love that sings and hath wings as a bird,
  Balm of the wound and heft of the knife,
Fairer than earth is the sea, and sleep
Than overwatching of eyes that weep,
Now time has done with his one sweet
  word,
  The wine and leaven of lovely life.

I shall go my ways, tread out my measure,
  Fill the days of my daily breath
With fugitive things not good to treasure,
  Do as the world doth, say as it saith;
But if we had loved each other—O sweet,
Had you felt, lying under the palms of
  your feet,
The heart of my heart, beating harder with
  pleasure
  To feel you tread it to dust and death—

Ah, had I not taken my life up and given
  All that life gives and the years let go,
The wine and honey, the balm and leaven,
  The dreams reared high and the hopes
  brought low ?
Come life, come death, not a word be said;
Should I lose you living, and vex you dead ?
I never shall tell you on earth; and in
  heaven
  If I cry to you then, will you hear or
  know ?

LES NOYADES.

WHATEVER a man of the sons of men
　　Shall say to his heart of the lords above,
They have shown man verily, once and
　　　　again,
　　Marvellous mercies and infinite love.

In the wild fifth year of the change of
　　　　things,
　　When France was glorious and blood-
　　　　red, fair
With dust of battle and deaths of kings,
　　A queen of men, with helmeted hair;

Carrier came down to the Loire and slew,
　　Till all the ways and the waves waxed
　　　　red:
Bound and drowned, slaying two by two,
　　Maidens and young men, naked and wed.

They brought on a day to his judgment-
　　　　place
　　One rough with labor and red with fight,
And a lady noble by name and face,
　　Faultless, a maiden, wonderful, white.

She knew not, being for shame's sake blind,
　　If his eyes were hot on her face hard by.
And the judge bade strip and ship them,
　　　　and bind
　　Bosom to bosom to drown and die.

The white girl winced and whitened; but
　　　　he
　　Caught fire, waxed bright as a great
　　　　bright flame
Seen with thunder far out on the sea,
　　Laughed hard as the glad blood went
　　　　and came.

Twice his lips quailed with delight, then
　　　　said,
　　" I have but a word to you all, one word
Bear with me; surely I am but dead:"
　　And all they laughed and mocked him
　　　　and heard.

" Judge, when they open the judgment-
　　　　roll,
　　I will stand upright before God and pray:
' Lord God, have mercy on one man's soul,
　　For his mercy was great upon earth, I
　　　　say.

" ' Lord, if I loved thee—Lord, if I
　　　　served—
　　If these who darkened thy Son's fair face
I fought with, sparing not one, nor swerved
　　A hand's-breadth, Lord, in the perilous
　　　　place—

" ' I pray thee say to this man, O Lord,
　　Sit thou for him at my feet on a throne.
I will face thy wrath, though it bite as a
　　　　sword,
　　And my soul shall burn for his soul and
　　　　atone.

" ' For Lord, thou knowest, O God most
　　　　wise,
　　How gracious on earth were his deeds
　　　　toward me.
Shall this be a small thing in thine eyes,
　　That is greater in mine than the whole
　　　　great sea ?'

" I have loved this woman my whole life
　　　　long,
　　And even for love's sake when have I
　　　　said
' I love you?' when have I done you
　　　　wrong,
　　Living ? but now I shall have you dead.

" Yea, now, do I bid you love me, love ?
　　Love me or loathe, we are one not twain.
But God be praised in his heaven above
　　For this my pleasure and that my pain !

" For never a man, being mean like me,
　　Shall die like me till the whole world
　　　　dies.

I shall drown with her, laughing for love ;
and she
  Mix with me, touching me, lips and
  eyes.

"Shall she not know me and see me all
  through,
  Me, on whose heart as a worm she trod ?
You have given me, God requite it you,
  What man yet never was given of God."

O sweet one love, O my life's delight,
  Dear, though the days have divided us,
Lost beyond hope, taken far out of sight,
  Not twice in the world shall the gods do
  thus.

Had it been so hard for my love? but I,
  Though the gods gave all that a god can
  give,
I had chosen rather the gift to die,
  Cease, and be glad above all that live.

For the Loire would have driven us down
  to the sea,
And the sea would have pitched us from
  shoal to shoal;
And I should have held you, and you held
  me,
  As flesh holds flesh, and the soul the
  soul.

Could I change you, help you to love
  me, sweet,
Could I give you the love that would
  sweeten death,
We should yield, go down, locked hands
  and feet,
  Die, drown together, and breath catch
  breath;

But you would have felt my soul in a kiss,
  And known that once if I loved you well;
And I would have given my soul for this
  To burn for ever in burning hell.

A LEAVE-TAKING.

LET us go hence, my songs; she will not
  hear.
Let us go hence together without fear;
Keep silence now, for singing-time is over
And over all old things and all things dear.
She loves not you nor me as all we love her.
Yea, though we sang as angels in her ear,
  She would not hear.

Let us rise up and part; she will not know.
Let us go seaward as the great winds go,
Full of blown sand and foam; what help is
  there ?
There is no help, for all these things are so,
And all the world is bitter as a tear.
And how these things are, though ye strove
to show,
  She would not know.

Let us go home and hence; she will not
  weep,
We gave love many dreams and days to
  keep,
Flowers without scent, and fruits that would
  not grow,
Saying, 'If thou wilt, thrust in thy sickle
  and reap.'
All is reaped now; no grass is left to mow;
And we that sowed, though all we fell on
  sleep,
  She would not weep.

Let us go hence and rest; she will not love.
She shall not hear us if we sing hereof,
Nor see love's ways, how sore they are and
  steep.
Come hence, let be, lie still; it is enough.

Love is a barren sea, bitter and deep;
And though she saw all heaven in flower
    above,
        She would not love.

Let us give up, go down; she will not care.
Though all the stars made gold of all the air,
And the sea moving saw before it move
One moon-flower making all the foam-
    flowers fair;
Though all those waves went over us, and
    drove
Deep down the stifling lips and drowning
    hair
        She would not care.

Let us go hence, go hence; she will not
    see.
Sing all once more together: surely she,
She too, remembering days and words that
    were,
Will turn a little toward us, sighing; but
    we,
We are hence, we are gone, as though we
    had not been there.
Nay, and though all men seeing had pity
    on me,
        She would not see.

ITYLUS.

SWALLOW, my sister, O sister swallow,
    How can thine heart be full of the spring?
    A thousand summers are over and
        dead.
What hast thou found in the spring to follow?
    What hast thou found in thine heart to
        sing?
    What wilt thou do when the summer is
        shed?

O swallow, sister, O fair swift swallow,
    Why wilt thou fly after spring to the
        south,
    The soft south whither thine heart is
        set?
Shall not the grief of the old time follow?
    Shall not the song thereof cleave to thy
        mouth?
    Hast thou forgotten ere I forget?

Sister, my sister, O fleet sweet swallow,
    Thy way is long to the sun and the south;
    But I, fulfilled of my heart's desire,
Shedding my song upon height, upon
    hollow,

From tawny body and sweet small mouth
    Feed the heart of the night with fire.

I the nightingale all spring through,
    O swallow, sister, O changing swallow,
All spring through till the spring be done,
Clothed with the light of the night on the
    dew,
    Sing, while the hours and the wild birds
        follow,
    Take flight and follow and find the
        sun.

Sister, my sister, O soft light swallow,
    Though all things feast in the spring's
        guest-chamber,
    How hast thou heart to be glad there
        of yet?
For where thou fliest I shall not follow,
    Till life forget and death remember,
    Till thou remember and I forget.

Swallow, my sister, O singing swallow,
    I know not how thou hast heart to sing.
    Hast thou the heart? is it all past over?

Thy lord the summer is good to follow,
  And fair the feet of thy lover the spring:
    But what wilt thou say to the spring
      thy lover?

O swallow, sister, O fleeting swallow,
  My heart in me is a molten ember
    And over my head the waves have met.
But thou wouldst tarry or I would follow,
  Could I forget or thou remember,
    Couldst thou remember and I forget.

O sweet stray sister, O shifting swallow
  The heart's division divideth us.
    Thy heart is light as a leaf of a tree;
But mine goes forth among sea-gulfs hollow
  To the place of the slaying of Itylus,
    The feast of Daulis, the Thracian sea.

O swallow, sister, O rapid swallow,
  I pray thee sing not a little space.
    Are not the roofs and the lintels wet?
The woven web that was plain to follow,
  The small slain body, the flower-like
    face,
      Can I remember if thou forget?

O sister, sister, thy first-begotten!
  The hands that cling and the feet that
    follow,
      The voice of the child's blood crying
        yet
*Who hath remembered me? who hath for-
    gotten?*
  Thou hast forgotten, O summer swallow,
    But the world shall end when I forget.

ANACTORIA.

τίνοςαὖ τὺ πειθοῖ
μάψ σαγηνεύσας φιλότατα;

SAPPHO.

MY life is bitter with thy love; thine eyes
Blind me, thy tresses burn me, thy sharp
    sighs
Divide my flesh and spirit with soft sound,
And my blood strengthens, and my veins
    abound.
I pray thee sigh not, speak not, draw not
    breath;
Let life burn down, and dream it is not
    death.
I would the sea had hidden us, the fire
(Wilt thou fear that, and fear not my de-
    sire?)
Severed the bones that bleach, the flesh
    that cleaves,
And let our sifted ashes drop like leaves.

I feel thy blood against my blood: my pain
Pains thee, and lips bruise lips, and vein
    stings vein.
Let fruit be crushed on fruit, let flower on
    flower,
Breast kindle breast, and either burn one
    hour.
Why wilt thou follow lesser loves? are
    thine
Too weak to bear these hands and lips of
    mine?
I charge thee for my life's sake, O too sweet
To crush love with thy cruel faultless feet,
I charge thee keep thy lips from hers or his,
Sweetest, till theirs be sweeter than my
    kiss.

Lest I too lure, a swallow for a dove,
Erotion or Erinna to my love.
I would my love could kill thee; I am
    satiated
With seeing thee live, and fain would have
    thee dead.
I would earth had thy body as fruit to eat,
And no mouth but some serpent's found
    thee sweet.
I would find grievous ways to have thee
    slain,
Intense device, and superflux of pain;
Vex thee with amorous agonies, and shake
Life at thy lips, and leave it there to ache;
Strain out thy soul with pangs too soft to
    kill,
Intolerable interludes, and infinite ill;
Relapse and reluctation of the breath,
Dumb tunes and shuddering semitones of
    death.
I am weary of all thy words and soft
    strange ways,
Of all love's fiery nights and all his days,
And all the broken kisses salt as brine
That shuddering lips make moist with
    waterish wine,
And eyes the bluer for all those hidden
    hours
That pleasure fills with tears and feeds
    from flowers,
Fierce at the heart with fire that half comes
    through,
But all the flower-like white-stained round
    with blue;
The fervent underlid, and that above
Lifted with laughter or abashed with love;
Thine amorous girdle, full of thee and fair,
And leavings of the lilies in thine hair.
Yea, all sweet words of thine and all thy
    ways,
And all the fruit of nights and flower of
    days,
And stinging lips wherein the hot sweet
    brine
That love was born of burns and foams
    like wine,
And eyes insatiable of amorous hours,
Fervent as fire and delicate as flowers,
Colored like night at heart, but cloven
    through
Like night with flame, dyed round like
    night with blue,
Clothed with deep eyelids under and
    above—
Yea, all thy beauty sickens me with love;

Thy girdle empty of thee and now not fair,
And ruinous lilies in thy languid hair.
Ah, take no thought for Love's sake; shall
    this be,
And she who loves thy lover not love thee?
Sweet soul, sweet mouth of all that laughs
    and lives,
Mine is she, very mine; and she forgives.
For I beheld in sleep the light that is
In her high place in Paphos, heard the kiss
Of body and soul that mix with eager tears
And laughter stinging through the eyes and
    ears;
Saw Love, as burning flame from crown to
    feet,
Imperishable, upon her storied seat;
Clear eyelids lifted toward the north and
    south,
A mind of many colors and a mouth
Of many tunes and kisses; and she bowed,
With all her subtle face laughing aloud,
Bowed down upon me, saying, "Who
    doth the wrong,
Sappho?" but thou—thy body is the song,
Thy mouth the music; thou art more than I,
Though my voice die not till the whole
    world die;
Though men that hear it madden; though
    love weep,
Though nature change, though shame be
    charmed to sleep.
Ah, wilt thou slay me lest I kiss thee dead?
Yet the queen laughed from her sweet heart
    and said:
"Even she that flies shall follow for thy
    sake,
And she shall give thee gifts that would not
    take,
Shall kiss that would not kiss thee" (yea,
    kiss me)
"When thou wouldst not"—when I would
    not kiss thee!
Ah, more to me than all men as thou art,
Shall not my songs assuage her at the
    heart?
Ah, sweet to me as life seems sweet to
    death,
Why should her wrath fill thee with fear-
    ful breath?
Nay, sweet, for is she God alone? hath she
Made earth and all the centuries of the sea,
Taught the sun ways to travel, woven most
    fine
The moonbeams, shed the starbeams forth
    as wine,

Bound with her myrtles, beaten with her
rods,
The young men and the maidens and the
gods?
Have we not lips to love with, eyes for
tears,
And summer and flower of women and of
years?
Stars for the foot of morning, and for noon
Sunlight, and exaltation of the moon;
Waters that answer waters, fields that wear
Lilies, and languor of the Lesbian air?
Beyond those flying feet of fluttered doves,
Are there not other gods for other loves?
Yea, though she scourge thee, sweetest,
for my sake,
Blossom not thorns, and flowers not blood
should break.
Ah that my lips were tuneless lips, but
pressed
To the bruised blossom of thy scourged
white breast!
Ah that my mouth for Muses' milk were
fed
On the sweet blood thy sweet small wounds
had bled!
That with my tongue I felt them, and could
taste
The faint flakes from thy bosom to the
waist!
That I could drink thy veins as wine, and
eat
Thy breasts like honey! that from face to
feet
Thy body were abolished and consumed,
And in my flesh thy very flesh entombed!
Ah, ah, thy beauty! like a beast it bites,
Stings like an adder, like an arrow smites.
Ah sweet, and sweet again, and seven times
sweet,
The paces and the pauses of thy feet!
Ah sweeter than all sleep or summer air
The fallen fillets fragrant from thine hair!
Yea, though their alien kisses do me wrong,
Sweeter thy lips than mine with all their
song;
Thy shoulders whiter than a fleece of white,
And flower-sweet fingers good to bruise or
bite
As honeycomb of the inmost honey-cells,
With almond-shaped and rose-leaf colored
shells,
And blood like purple blossom at the tips
Quivering; and pain made perfect in thy
lips

For my sake when I hurt thee; O that I
Durst crush thee out of life with love, and
die,
Die of thy pain and my delight, and be
Mixed with thy blood and molten into thee!
Would I not plague thee dying overmuch?
Would I not hurt thee perfectly? not touch
Thy pores of sense with torture, and make
bright
Thine eyes with bloodlike tears and grievous
light?
Strike pang from pang as note is struck
from note,
Catch the sob's middle music in thy throat,
Take thy limbs living, and new-mould with
these
A lyre of many faultless agonies?
Feed thee with fever and famine and fine
drouth,
With perfect pangs convulse thy perfect
mouth,
Make thy life shudder in thee and burn
afresh,
And wring thy very spirit through the
flesh?
Cruel? but love makes all that love him
well
As wise as heaven and crueller than hell.
Me hath love made more bitter toward
thee
Than death toward man; but were I made
as he
Who hath made all things to break them
one by one,
If my feet trod upon the stars and sun
And souls of men as his have alway trod,
God knows I might be crueller than God.
For who shall change with prayers or
thanksgivings
The mystery of the cruelty of things?
Or say what God above all gods and years,
With offering and blood-sacrifice of tears,
With lamentation from strange lands, from
graves
Where the snake pastures, from scarred
mouths of slaves,
From prison, and from plunging prows of
ships
Through flame like foam of the sea's closing
lips—
With thwartings of strange signs, and
wind-blown hair
Of comets, desolating the dim air,
When darkness is made fast with seals and
bars,

3

And fierce reluctance of disastrous stars,
Eclipse, and sound of shaken hills, and
wings
Darkening, and blind inexpiable things—
With sorrow of laboring moons, and alter-
ing light
And travail of the planets of the night,
And weeping of the weary Pleiads seven,
Feeds the mute melancholy lust of heaven?
Is not this incense bitterness, his meat
Murder? his hidden face and iron feet
Hath not man known, and felt them on
their way
Threaten and trample all things and every
day?
Hath he not sent us hunger? who hath
cursed
Spirit and flesh with longing? filled with
thirst
Their lips who cried unto him? who bade
exceed
The fervid will, fall short the feeble deed,
Bade sink the spirit and the flesh aspire,
Pain animate the dust of dead desire,
And life yield up her flower to violent fate?
Him would I reach, him smite, him dese-
crate,
Pierce the cold lips of God with human
breath,
And mix his immortality with death.
Why hath he made us? what had all we
done
That we should live and loathe the sterile
sun,
And with the moon wax paler as she wanes,
And pulse by pulse feel time grow through
our veins?
Thee too the years shall cover; thou shalt
be
As the rose born of one same blood with
thee,
As a song sung, as a word said, and fall
Flower-wise, and be not any more at all,
Nor any memory of thee anywhere;
For never Muse has bound above thine hair
The high Pierian flower whose graft out-
grows
All summer kinship of the mortal rose
And colour of deciduous days, nor shed
Reflex and flush of heaven about thine
head,
Nor reddened brows made pale by floral
grief
With splendid shadow from that lordlier
leaf.

Yea, thou shalt be forgotten like spilt wine,
Except these kisses of my lips on thine
Brand them with immortality; but me—
Men shall not see bright fire nor hear the
sea,
Nor mix their hearts with music, nor be-
hold
Cast forth of heaven with feet of awful
gold
And plumeless wings that make the bright
air blind,
Lightning with thunder for a hound behind
Hunting through fields unfurrowed and un-
sown—
But in the light and laughter, in the moan
And music, and in grasp of lip and hand
And shudder of water that makes felt on
land
The immeasurable tremor of all the sea,
Memories shall mix and metaphors of me.
Like me shall be the shuddering calm of
night,
When all the winds of the world for pure
delight
Close lips that quiver and fold up wings
that ache;
When nightingales are louder for love's
sake,
And leaves tremble like lute-strings or like
fire;
Like me the one star swooning with desire
Even at the cold lips of the sleepless moon,
As I at thine; like me the waste white
noon,
Burnt through with barren sunlight; and
like me
The land-stream and the tide-stream in the
sea.
I am sick with time as these with ebb and
flow,
And by the yearning in my veins I know
The yearning sound of waters; and mine
eyes
Burn as that beamless fire which fills the
skies
With troubled stars and travailing things of
flame;
And in my heart the grief consuming them
Labors, and in my veins the thirst of these,
And all the summer travail of the trees
And all the winter sickness; and the earth
Filled full with deadly works of death and
birth,
Sore spent with hungry lusts of birth and
death,

Has pain like mine in her divided breath ;
Her spring of leaves is barren, and her
    fruit
Ashes ; her boughs are burdened, and her
    root
Fibrous and gnarled with poison; under-
    neath
Serpents have gnawn it through with tortu-
    ous teeth
Made sharp upon the bones of all the dead,
And wild birds rend her branches over-
    head.
These, woven as raiment for his word and
    thought,
These hath God made, and me as these,
    and wrought
Song. and hath lit it at my lips; and me
Earth shall not gather though she feed on
    thee.
As a shed tear shalt thou be shed; but I—
Lo, earth may labor, men live long and
    die,
Years change and stars, and the high God
    devise
New things, and old things wane before his
    eyes
Who wields and wrecks them, being more
    strong than they—
But, having made me, me he shall not slay.
Nor slay nor satiate, like those herds of his
Who laugh and live a little, and their kiss
Content, them, and their loves are swift
    and sweet,
And sure death grasps and gains them with
    slow feet,
Love they or hate they, strive or bow their
    knees—
And all these end; he hath his will of these.
Yea, but albeit he slay me, hating me—
Albeit he hide me in the deep dear sea
And cover me with cool wan foam, and
    ease
This soul of mine as any soul of these,
And give me water and great sweet waves,
    and make
The very sea's name lordlier for my sake,
The whole sea sweeter—albeit I die indeed
And hide myself and sleep and no man
    heed,
Of me the high God hath not all his will.
Blossom of branches, and on each high hill
Clear air and wind, and under in clamorous
    vales
Fierce noises of the fiery nightingales,
Buds burning in the sudden spring like fire,

The wan washed sand and the waves' vain
    desire,
Sails seen like blown white flowers at sea,
    and words
That bring tears swiftest, and long notes of
    birds
Violently singing till the whole world
    sings—
I Sappho shall be one with all these things,
With all high things for ever; and my face
Seen once, my songs once heard in a strange
    place,
Cleave to men's lives, and waste the days
    thereof
With gladness and much sadness and long
    love.
Yea, they shall say, earth's womb has borne
    in vain
New things, and never this best thing again;
Borne days and men, borne fruits and wars
    and wine,
Seasons and songs, but no song more like
    mine.
And they shall know me as ye who have
    known me here,
Last year when I loved Atthis, and this
    year
When I love thee; and they shall praise
    me, and say
"She hath all time as all we have our day,
Shall she not live and have her will "—
    even I?
Yea, though thou diest, I say I shall not
    die.
For these shall give me of their souls, shall
    give
Life, and the days and loves wherewith I
    live,
Shall quicken me with loving, fill with
    breath,
Save me and serve me, strive for me with
    death.
Alas, that neither moon nor snow nor
    dew
Nor all cold things can purge me wholly
    through,
Assuage me nor allay me nor appease,
Till supreme sleep shall bring me bloodless
    ease;
Till time wax faint in all his periods;
Till fate undo the bondage of the gods,
And lay, to slake and satiate me all through,
Lotus and Lethe on my lips like dew,
And shed around and over and under me
Thick darkness and the insuperable sea.

HYMN TO PROSERPINE.

(AFTER THE PROCLAMATION IN ROME OF THE CHRISTIAN FAITH.)

Vicisti, Galilæe.

I HAVE lived long enough, having seen one
    thing, that love hath an end ;
Goddess and maiden and queen, be near
    me now and befriend.
Thou art more than the day or the morrow,
    the seasons that laugh or that weep ;
For these give joy and sorrow ; but thou,
    Proserpina, sleep.
Sweet is the treading of wine, and sweet
    the feet of the dove ;
But a goodlier gift is thine than foam of the
    grapes or love.
Yea, is not even Apollo, with hair and
    harpstring of gold,
A bitter God to follow, a beautiful God to
    behold ?
I am sick of singing ; the bays burn deep
    and chafe : I am fain
To rest a little from praise and grievous
    pleasure and pain.
For the Gods we know not of, who give us
    our daily breath,
We know they are cruel as love or life, and
    lovely as death.
O Gods dethroned and deceased, cast forth,
    wiped out in a day !
From your wrath is the world released, re-
    deemed from your chains, men say.
New Gods are crowned in the city, their
    flowers have broken your rods ;
They are merciful, clothed with pity, the
    young compassionate Gods.
But for me their new device is barren, the
    days are bare ;
Things long past over suffice, and men for-
    gotten that were.
Time and the Gods are at strife: ye dwell
    in the midst thereof,
Draining a little life from the barren breasts
    of love.
I say to you, cease, take rest ; yea, I say
    to you all, be at peace,

Till the bitter milk of her breast and the
    barren bosom shall cease.
Wilt thou yet take all, Galilean ? but these
    thou shalt not take,
The laurel, the palms and the pæan, the
    breast of the nymphs in the brake ;
Breasts more soft than a dove's, that tremble
    with tenderer breath;
And all the wings of the Loves, and all the
    joy before death;
All the feet of the hours that sound as a
    single lyre,
Dropped and deep in the flowers, with
    strings that flicker like fire.
More than these wilt thou give, things fairer
    than all these things ?
Nay, for a little we live, and life hath
    mutable wings.
A little while and we die; shall life not
    thrive as it may ?
For no man under the sky lives twice, out-
    living his day.
And grief is a grievous thing, and a man
    hath enough of his tears:
Why should he labour, and bring fresh
    grief to blacken his years?
Thou hast conquered, O pale Galilean; the
    world has grown grey from thy breath;
We have drunken of things Lethean, and
    fed on the fulness of death.
Laurel is green for a season, and love is
    sweet for a day;
But love grows bitter with treason, and
    laurel outlives not May.
Sleep, shall we sleep after all? for the world
    is not sweet in the end;
For the old faiths loosen and fall, the new
    years ruin and rend.
Fate is a sea without shore, and the soul is
    a rock that abides;
But her ears are vexed with the roar and
    her face with the foam of the tides.

O lips that the live blood faints in, the
  leavings of racks and rods !
O ghastly glories of saints, dead limbs of
  gibbeted Gods !
Though all men abase them before you in
  spirit, and all knees bend,
I kneel not neither adore you, but standing, look to the end.
All delicate days and pleasant, all spirits
  and sorrows are cast
Far out with the foam of the present that
  sweeps to the surf of the past:
Where beyond the extreme sea-wall, and
  between the remote sea-gates,
Waste water washes, and tall ships founder,
  and deep death waits:
Where, mighty with deepening sides, clad
  about with the seas as with wings,
And impelled of invisible tides, and fulfilled of unspeakable things,
White-eyed and poisonous finned, shark-
  toothed and serpentine-curled,
Rolls, under the whitening wind of the
  future, the wave of the world.
The depths stand naked in sunder behind
  it, the storms flee away;
In the hollow before it the thunder is taken
  and snared as a prey;
In its sides is the north-wind bound; and
  its salt is of all men's tears;
With light of ruin, and sound of changes,
  and pulse of years:
With travail of day after day, and with
  trouble of hour upon hour;
And bitter as blood is the spray; and the
  crests are as fangs that devour:
And its vapor and storm of its steam as the
  sighing of spirits to be;
And its noise as the noise in a dream; and
  its depth as the roots of the sea:
And the height of its heads as the height of
  the utmost stars of the air:
And the ends of the earth at the might
  thereof tremble, and time is made bare.
Will ye bridle the deep sea with reins, will
  ye chasten the high sea with rods?
Will ye take her to chain her with chains,
  who is older than all ye Gods?
All ye as a wind shall go by, as a fire shall
  ye pass and be past;
Ye are Gods, and behold ye shall die, and
  the waves be upon you at last.
In the darkness of time, in the deeps of the
  years, in the changes of things,
Ye shall sleep as a slain man sleeps, and
  the world shall forget you for kings.

Though the feet of thine high priests tread
  where thy lords and our forefathers trod,
Though these that were Gods are dead, and
  thou being dead art a God,
Though before thee the throned Cytherian
  be fallen, and hidden her head,
Yet thy kingdom shall pass, Galilean, thy
  dead shall go down to thee dead.
Of the maiden thy mother, men sing as a
  goddess with grace clad around;
Thou art throned where another was king;
  where another was queen she is crowned.
Yea, once we had sight of another: but now
  she is queen, say these.
Not as thine, not as thine was our mother,
  a blossom of flowering seas,
Clothed round with the world's desire as
  with raiment, and fair as the foam,
And fleeter than kindled fire, and a goddess,
  and mother of Rome.
For thine came pale and a maiden, and
  sister to sorrow; but ours,
Her deep hair heavily laden with odour and
  color of flowers,
White rose of the rose-white water, a silver
  splendor, a flame,
Bent down unto us that besought her, and
  earth grew sweet with her name.
For thine came weeping, a slave among
  slaves, and rejected; but she
Came flushed from the full-flushed wave,
  and imperial, her foot on the sea,
And the wonderful waters knew her, the
  winds and the viewless ways,
And the roses grew rosier, and bluer the
  sea-blue stream of the bays.
Ye are fallen, our lords by what token? we
  wist that ye should not fall.
Ye were all so fair that are broken; and
  one more fair than ye all.
But I turn to her still, having seen she
  shall surely abide in the end;
Goddess and maiden and queen, be near
  me now and befriend.
O daughter of earth, of my mother, her
  crown and blossom of birth,
I am also, I also, thy brother; I go as I
  came unto earth.
In the night where thine eyes are as moons
  are in heaven, the night where thou art,
Where the silence is more than all tunes,
  where sleep overflows from the heart,
Where the poppies are sweet as the rose in
  our world, and the red rose is white,
And the wind falls faint as it blows with
  the fume of the flowers of the night,

And the murmur of spirits that sleep in the
    shadow of Gods from afar
Grows dim in thine ears and deep as the
    deep dim soul of a star,
In the sweet low light of thy face, under
    heavens untrod by the sun,
Let my soul with their souls find place, and
    forget what is done and undone.
Thou art more than the Gods who number
    the days of our temporal breath;
For these give labor and slumber; but thou,
    Proserpina, death.

Therefore now at thy feet I abide for a
    season in silence.   I know
I shall die as my fathers died, and sleep as
    they sleep; even so.
For the glass of the years is brittle wherein
    we gaze for a span ;
A little soul for a little bears up this corpse
    which is man.*
So long I endure, no longer; and laugh not
    again, neither weep.
For there is no God found stronger than
    death ; and death is a sleep.

ILICET.

THERE is an end of joy and sorrow ;
Peace all day long, all night, all morrow,
    But never a time to laugh or weep.
The end is come of pleasant places,
The end of tender words and faces,
    The end of all, the poppied sleep.

No place for sound within their hearing,
No room to hope, no time for fearing,
    No lips to laugh, no lids for tears.
The old years have run out all their measure;
No chance of pain, no chance of pleasure,
    No fragment of the broken years.

Outside of all the worlds and ages,
There where the fool is as the sage is,
    There where the slayer is clean of blood,
No end, no passage, no beginning,
There where the sinner leaves off sinning,
    There where the good man is not good.

There is not one thing with another,
But Evil saith to Good: My brother,
    My brother, I am one with thee :
They shall not strive nor cry forever :
No man shall chose between them : never
    Shall this thing end and that thing be.

Wind wherein seas and stars are shaken
Shall shake them, and they shall not waken;

None that has lain down shall arise ;
The stones are sealed across their places ;
    One shadow is shed on all their faces,
    One blindness cast on all their eyes.

Sleep, is it sleep perchance that covers
Each face, as each face were his lover's ?
    Farewell; as men that sleep fare well.
The grave's mouth laughs unto derision
Desire and dread and dream and vision,
    Delight of heaven and sorrow of hell.

No soul shall tell nor lip shall number
The names and tribes of you that slumber ;
    No memory, no memorial.
" Thou knowest "—who shall say thou
    knowest ?
    There is none highest and none lowest :
    An end, an end, an end of all.

Good night, good sleep, good rest from
    sorrow,
To these that shall not have good morrow;
    The gods be gentle to all these.
Nay, if death be not, how shall they be ?
Nay, is there help in heaven ? it may be
    All things and lords of things shall cease.

---

*ψυχάριον εἶ βαστάζον νεκρόν.
                        EPICTETUS.

The stooped urn, filling, dips and flashes;
The bronzed brims are deep in ashes;
　The pale old lips of death are fed.
Shall this dust gather flesh hereafter?
Shall one shed tears or fall to laughter,
　At sight of all these poor old dead?

Nay, as thou wilt; these know not of it;
Thine eyes' strong weeping shall not profit,
　Thy laughter shall not give thee ease;
Cry aloud, spare not, cease not crying,
Sigh, till thou cleave thy sides with sighing,
　Thou shalt not raise up one of these.

Burnt spices flash, and burnt wine hisses,
The breathing flame's mouth curls and
　　kisses
　The small dried rows of frankincense;
All round the sad red blossoms smoulder,
Flowers colored like the fire, but colder,
　In sign of sweet things taken hence;

Yea, for their sake and in death's favor
Things of sweet shape and of sweet savor
　We yield them, spice and flower and wine;
Yea, costlier things than wine or spices,
Whereof none knoweth how great the price
　　is,
　And fruit that comes not of the vine.

From boy's pierced throat and girl's pierced
　　bosom
Drips, reddening round the blood-red
　　blossoms,
.　The slow delicious bright soft blood,
Bathing the spices and the pyre,
Bathing the flowers and fallen fire,
　Bathing the blossom by the bud.

Roses whose lips the flame had deadened
Drink till the lapping leaves are reddened
　And warm wet inner petals weep ;
The flower whereof sick sleep gets leisure,
Barren of balm and purple pleasure,
　Fumes with no native steam of sleep.

Why will ye weep ? what do ye weeping ?
For walking folk and people sleeping,
　And sands that fill and sands that fall,
The days rose-red, the poppied hours,
Blood, wine, and spice and fire and flowers,
.　There is one end of one and all.

Shall such an one lend love or borrow ?
Shall these be sorry　for thy sorrow ?

Shall these give thanks for words or
　　breath ?
Their hate is as their loving-kindness;
The frontlet of their brows is blindness,
　The armlet of their arms is death.

Lo, for no noise or light of thunder
Shall these grave-clothes be rent in sunder,
　He that hath taken, shall he give?
He hath rent them: shall he bind to-
　　gether ?
He hath bound them: shall he break the
　　tether ?
He hath slain them: shall he bid them live ?

A little sorrow, a little pleasure,
Fate metes us from the dusty measure
　That holds the date of all of us;
We are born with travail and strong crying,
And from the birth-day to the dying
　The likeness of our life is thus.

One girds himself to serve another,
Whose father was the dust, whose mother
　The little dead red worm therein;
They find no fruit of things they cherish;
The goodness of a man shall perish,
　It shall be one thing with his sin.

In deep wet ways by grey old gardens
Fed with sharp spring the sweet fruit har-
　　dens;
　They know not what fruits wane or grow;
Red summer burns to the utmost ember;
They know not, neither can remember,
　The old years and flowers they used to
　　know.

Ah, for their sakes, so trapped and taken,
For theirs, forgotten and forsaken,
Watch, sleep not, gird thyself with prayer.
Nay, where the heart of wrath is broken,
Where long love ends as a thing spoken,
　How shall thy crying enter there?

Though the iron sides of the old world falter
The likeness of them shall not alter
　For all the rumor of periods,
The stars and seasons that come after
The tears of latter men, the laughter
　Of the old unalterable gods.

Far up above the years and nations,
The high gods, clothed and crowned with
　　patience,

Endure through days of death-like date;
They bear the witness of things hidden;
Before their eyes all life stands chidden,
    As they before the eyes of Fate.

Not for their love shall Fate retire,
Nor they relent for our desire,

Nor the graves open for their call.
The end is more than joy and anguish,
Than lives that laugh and lives that lan-
    guish,
    The poppied sleep, the end of all!

HERMAPHRODITUS.

I.

LIFT up thy lips, turn round, look back for
    love,
    Blind love that comes by night and casts
        out rest;
    Ot all things tired thy lips look weariest,
Save the long smile that they are wearied
    of.
Ah sweet, albeit no love be sweet enough,
    Choose of two loves and cleave unto the
        best;
    Two loves at either blossom of thy breast
Strive until one be under and one above.
Their breath is fire upon the amorous air,
Fire in thine eyes and where thy lips sus-
    pire:
And whosoever hath seen thee, being so
    fair,
    Two things turn all his life and blood to
        fire;
A strong desire begot on great despair,
    A great despair cast out by strong desire.

II.

Where between sleep and life some brief
        space is,
    With love like gold bound round about
        the head,
    Sex to sweet sex with lips and limbs is
        wed,
Turning the fruitful feud of hers and his

To the waste wedlock of a sterile kiss;
    Yet from them something like as fire is
        shed
    That shall not be assuaged till death be
        dead,
Though neither life nor sleep can find out
        this.
Love made himself of flesh that perisheth
    A pleasure-house for all the loves his kin;
But on the one side sat a man like death,
    And on the other a woman sat like sin.
So with veiled eyes and sobs between his
        breath
    Love turned himself and would not enter
        in.

III.

Love, is it love or sleep or shadow or light
    That lies between thine eyelids and thine
        eyes?
    Like a flower laid upon a flower it lies,
Or like the night's dew laid upon the night.
Love stands upon thy left hand and thy
        right,
    Yet by no sunset and by no moonrise
    Shall make thee man and ease a woman's
        sighs,
Or make thee woman for a man's delight.
To what strange end hath some strange
        god made fair
    The double blossom of two fruitless
        flowers?
Hid love in all the folds of all thy hair,

Fed thee on summers, watered thee with
   showers,
Given all the gold that all the seasons wear
   To thee that art a thing of barren hours?

IV.

Yea, love, I see; it is not love but fear.
   Nay, sweet, it is not fear but love, I
      know;
   Or wherefore should thy body's blossom
      blow
So sweetly, or thine eyelids leave so clear
Thy gracious eyes that never made a tear—
   Though for their love our tears like blood
      should flow,

Though love and life and death should
   come and go,
So dreadful, so desirable, so dear?
Yea, sweet, I know; I saw in what swift
   wise
   Beneath the woman's and the water's
      kiss
Thy moist limbs melted into Salmacis,
And the large light turned tender in thine
   eyes,
And all thy boy's breath softened into
   sighs;
   But Love being blind, how should he
      know of this?

Au Musée du Louvre, Mars 1863.

FRAGOLETTA.

O Love! what shall be said of thee?
The son of grief begot by joy?
Being sightless, wilt thou see?
Being sexless, wilt thou be
Maiden or boy?

I dreamed of strange lips yesterday
And cheeks wherein the ambiguous blood
Was like a rose's—yea
A rose's when it lay
Within the bud.

What fields have bred thee, or what groves
Concealed thee, O mysterious flower,
O double rose of Love's,
With leaves that lure the doves
From bud to bower?

I dare not kiss it, lest my lip
Press harder than an indrawn breath,
And all the sweet life slip
Forth, and the sweet leaves drip,
Bloodlike, in death.

O sole desire of my delight!
O sole delight of my desire!
Mine eyelids and eyesight
Feed on thee day and night
Like lips of fire.

Lean back thy throat of carven pearl,
Let thy mouth murmur like the dove's;
Say, Venus hath no girl,
No front of female curl,
Among her Loves.

Thy sweet low bosom, thy close hair,
Thy strait soft flanks and slenderer feet,
Thy virginal strange air,
Are these not over fair
For Love to greet?

How should he greet thee? what new name,
Fit to move all men's hearts, could move
Thee, deaf to love or shame,
Love's sister, by the same
Mother as Love?

Ah, sweet, the maiden's mouth is cold,
Her breast-blossoms are simply red,
Her hair mere brown or gold,
Fold over simple fold
Binding her head.

Thy mouth is made of fire and wine,
Thy barren bosom takes my kiss
And turns my soul to thine
And turns thy lip to mine,
And mine it is.

Thou hast a serpent in thine hair,
In all the curls that close and cling;
And ah, thy breast-flower!
Ah love, thy mouth too fair
To kiss and sting.

Cleave to me, love me, kiss mine eyes
Satiate thy lips with loving me;
Nay, for thou shalt not rise;
Lie still as Love that dies
For love of thee.

Mine arms are close about thine head,
My lips are fervent on thy face,
And where my kiss hath fed
Thy flower-like blood leaps red
To the kissed place.

O bitterness of things too sweet
O broken singing of the dove!
Love's wings are over fleet,
And like the panther's feet
The feet of Love.

RONDEL.

THESE many years since we began to
      be,
What have the gods done with us? what
      with me,
What with my love? they have shown me
      fates and fears,
Harsh springs, and fountains bitterer than
      the sea,
Grief a fixed star, and joy a vane that
      veers,
      These many years.

With her, my love, with her have they
      done well?
But who shall answer for her? who shall
      tell

Sweet things or sad, such things as no man
      hears?
May no tears fall, if no tears ever fell,
From eyes more dear to me than starriest
      spheres
      These many years!

But if tears ever touched, for any grief,
Those eyelids folded like a white-rose leaf,
Deep double shells where through the eye-
      flower peers,
Let them weep once more only, sweet and
      brief,
Brief tears and bright, for one who gave
      her tears
      These many years.

SATIA TE SANGUINE.

IF you loved me ever so little,
    I could bear the bonds that gall,
  I could dream the bonds were brittle;
    You do not love me at all.

O beautiful lips, O bosom
    More white than the moon's and warm,
A sterile, a ruinous blossom
    Is blown your way in a storm.

As the lost white feverish limbs
Of the Lesbian Sappho, adrift
In foam where the sea-weed swims,
Swam loose for the streams to lift.

My heart swims blind in a sea
That stuns me ; swims to and fro,
And gathers to windward and lee
Lamentation, and mourning, and woe.

A broken, an emptied boat,
Sea saps it, winds blow apart,
Sick and adrift and afloat,
The barren waif of a heart.

Where, when the gods would be cruel,
Do they go for a torture ? where
Plant thorns, set pain like a jewel?
Ah, not in the flesh, not there :

The racks of earth and the rods
Are weak as foam on the sands ;
In the heart is the prey for gods,
Who crucify hearts, not hands.

Mere pangs corrode and consume,
Dead when life dies in the brain ;
In the infinite spirit is room
For the pulse of an infinite pain.

I wish you were dead, my dear ;
I would give you, had I to give,
Some death too bitter to fear ;
It is better to die than live.

I wish you were stricken of thunder
And burnt with a bright flame through,
Consumed and cloven in sunder,
I dead at your feet like you.

If I could but know after all,
I might cease to hunger and ache,
Though your heart were ever so small
If it were not a stone or a snake.

You are crueller, you that we love,
Than hatred, hunger, or death;
You have eyes and breasts like a dove
And you kill men's hearts with a breath.

As plague in a poisonous city
Insults and exults on her dead,
So you, when pallid for pity
Comes love, and fawns to be fed.

As a tame beast writhes and wheedles,
He fawns to be fed with wiles;
You carve him a cross of needles,
And whet them sharp as your smiles.

He is patient of thorn and whip,
He is dumb under axe or dart;
You suck with a sleepy red lip
The wet red wounds in his heart.

You thrill as his pulses dwindle,
You brighten and warm as he bleeds,
With insatiable eyes that kindle
And insatiable mouth that feeds.

Your hands nailed love to the tree,
You stript him, scourged him with rods,
And drowned him deep in the sea
That hides the dead and their gods.

And for all this, die will he not;
There is no man sees him but I;
You came and went and forgot;
I hope he will some day die.

A LITANY.

ἐν οὐρανῷ φαεννὰς
κρύψω παρ᾽ ὑμὶν αὐγὰς,
μιας πρὸ νυκτὸς ἑπτὰ νύκτας ἕξετε, κ.τ.λ.
                                        Anth. Sac.

FIRST ANTIPHONE.

ALL the bright lights of heaven
I will make dark over thee :

One night shall be as seven
That its skirts may cover thee;
I will send on thy strong men a sword

On thy remnant a rod;
Ye shall know that I am the Lord.
Saith the Lord God.

SECOND ANTIPHONE.

All the bright lights of heaven
 Thou hast made dark over us;
One night has been as seven
 That its skirts might cover us;
Thou has sent on our strong men a sword,
 On our remnant a rod;
We know that thou art the Lord,
 O Lord our God.

THIRD ANTIPHONE.

As the treeses and wings of the wind
 Are scattered and shaken,
I will scatter all them that have sinned,
 There shall none be taken;
As a sower that scattered seed,
 So will I scatter them;
As one breaketh and shattereth a reed,
 I will break and shatter them.

FOURTH ANTIPHONE.

As the wings and the locks of the wind
 Are scattered and shaken,
Thou hast scattered all them that have
 sinned,
 There was no man taken.
As a sower that scattereth seed,
 So hast thou scattered us;
As one breaketh and shattereth a reed,
 Thou hast broken and shattered us.

FIFTH ANTIPHONE.

From all thy lovers that love thee
 I God will sunder thee;
I will make darkness above thee,
 And thick darkness under thee;
Before me goeth a light,
 Behind me a sword;
Shall a remnant find grace in my sight?
 I am the Lord.

SIXTH ANTIPHONE.

From all our lovers that love us
 Thou god didst sunder us;
Thou madest darkness above us,
 And thick darkness under us;
Thou hast kindled thy wrath for a light,
 And made ready thy sword;

Let a remnant find grace in thy sight,
 We beseech thee, O Lord.

SEVENTH ANTIPHONE.

Wilt thou bring fine gold for a payment
 For sins on this wise?
For the glittering of raiment
 And the shining of eyes,
For the painting of faces
 And the sundering of trust,
For the sins of thine high places
 And delight of thy lust?

For your high things ye shall have lowly,
 Lamentations for song ;
For, behold, I God am holy,
 I the Lord am strong ;
Ye shall seek me and shall not reach me
 Till the wine-press be trod;
In that hour ye shall turn and beseech me
 Saith the Lord God.

EIGHTH ANTIPHONE.

Not with fine gold for a payment,
 But with coin of sighs
But with rending of raiment
 And with weeping of eyes,
But with shame of stricken faces
 And with strewing of dust
For the sin of stately places
 And lordship of lust;

With voices of men made lowly
 Made empty of song,
O Lord God most holy,
 O God most strong,
We reach out hands to reach thee
 Ere the wine-press be trod;
We beseech thee, O Lord, we beseech thee
 O Lord our God.

NINTH ANTIPHONE.

In that hour thou shalt say to the night,
 Come down and cover us;
To the cloud on thy left and thy right,
 Be thou spread over us;
A snare shall be as thy mother,
 And a curse thy bride;
Thou shalt put her away, and another
 Shall lie by thy side.

Thou shalt neither rise up by day
Nor lie down by night.

Would God it were dark ! thou shalt say;
  Would God it were light !
And the sight of thine eyes shall be made
  As the burning of fire ;
And thy soul shall be sorely afraid
  For thy soul's desire.

Ye whom your lords loved well,
  Putting silver and gold on you,
The inevitable hell
  Shall surely take hold on you ;
Your gold shall be for a token,
  Your staff for a rod ;
With the breaking of bands ye are broken,
  Saith the Lord God.

TENTH ANTIPHONE.

In our sorrow we said to the night,
  Fall down and cover us ;
To the darkness at left and at right,
  Be thou shed over us ;
We had breaking of spirit to mother

And cursing to bride;
And one was slain, and another
  Stood up at our side.

We could not arise by day,
  Nor lie down by night;
Thy sword was sharp in our way,
  Thy word in our sight;
The delight of our eyelids was made
  As the burning of fire,
And our souls became sorely afraid
  For our soul's desire.

We whom the world loved well,
  Laying silver and gold on us,
The kingdom of death and of hell
  Riseth up to take hold on us;
Our gold is turned to a token,
  Our staff to a rod;
Yet shalt thou bind them up that were
  broken
O Lord our God.

A LAMENTATION.

1.

WHO hath known the ways of time
  Or trodden behind his feet ?
    There is no such man among men.
For chance overcomes him, or crime
  Changes; for all things sweet
    In time wax bitter again.
Who shall give sorrow enough,
  Or who the abundance of tears?
Mine eyes are heavy with love
  And a sword gone through mine ears,
    A sound like a sword and fire,
    For pity, for great desire;
Who shall ensure me thereof,
  Lest I die, being full of my fears ?

Who hath known the ways and the wrath
  The sleepless spirit, the root
    And blossom of evil will,

The divine device of a god ?
Who shall behold it or hath ?
  The twice-tongued prophets are mute,
  The many speakers are still;
    No foot has travelled or trod,
No hand has meted, his path.
  Man's fate is a blood-red fruit,
    And the mighty gods have their fill
    And relax not the rein, or the rod.

Ye were mighty in heart from of old,
  Ye slew with the spear, and are slain.
Keen after heat is the cold,
  Sore after summer is rain,
And melteth man to the bone.
    As water he weareth away,
    As a flower, as an hour in a day
Fallen from laughter to moan.
But my spirit is shaken with fear
  Lest an evil thing begin.

New-born, a spear for a spear,
  And one for another sin,
Or ever our tears began,
  It was known from of old and said;
One law for a living man,
  And another law for the dead.
For these are fearful and sad,
  Vain, and things without breath;
    While he lives let a man be glad,
      For none hath joy of his death.

II.

Who hath known the pain, the old pain of
    earth,
  Or all the travail of the sea,
The many ways and waves, the birth
Fruitless, the labor nothing worth ?
  Who hath known, who knoweth, O gods ?
    not we.

There is none shall say he hath seen,
  There is none he hath known.
Though he saith, Lo, a lord have I been,
  I have reaped and sown;
I have seen the desire of mine eyes,
  The beginning of love,
The season of kisses and sighs
  And the end thereof
I have known the ways of the sea,
  All the perilous ways;
Strange winds have spoken with me,
  And the tongues of strange days.
I have hewn the pine or ships;
  Where steeds run arow,
I have seen from their bridled lips
  Foam blown as the snow,
With snapping of chariot-poles
  And with straining of oars
I have grazed in the race the goals,
  In the storm the shores;
As a greave is cleft with an arrow
  At the joint of the knee,
I have cleft through the sea-straits narrow
  To the heart of the sea.
When air was smitten in sunder
  I have watched on high
The ways of the stars and the thunder
  In the night of the sky;
Where the dark brings forth light as a
    flower,
  As from lips that dissever ;
One abideth the space of an hour,
  One endureth for ever.
Lo, what hath he seen or known

Of the way and the wave
Unbeholden, unsailed-on, unsown,
  From the breast to the grave?

Or ever the stars were made, or skies,
  Grief was born, and the kinless night,
  Mother of gods without form or name.
And light is born out of heaven and dies,
  And one day knows not another's light,
    But night is one, and her shape the
      same.
But dumb the goddesses underground
  Wait, and we hear not on earth if their
    feet
    Rise, and the night wax loud with
      their wings;
Dumb, without word or shadow of sound;
  And sift in scales and winnow as wheat
    Men's souls, and sorrow of manifold
      things.

III.

Nor less of grief than ours
  The gods wrought long ago
    To bruise men one by one ;
But with the incessant hours
  Fresh grief and greener woe
    Spring, as the sudden sun
Year after year makes flowers;
  And these die down and grow,
    And the next year lacks none.

As these men sleep, have slept
  The old heroes in time fled,
    No dream-divided sleep;
And holier eyes have wept
  Than ours when on her dead
    Gods have seen Thetis weep,
With heavenly hair far-swept
    Back, heavenly hands outspread
      Round what she could not keep.

Could not one day withhold,
  One night ; and like as these
    White ashes of no weight,
Held not his urn the cold
  Ashes of Heracles !
    For all things born one gate
Opens, no gate of gold ;
  Opens; and no man sees
    Beyond the gods and fate.

ANIMA ANCEPS

Till death have broken
Sweet life's love-token,
Till all be spoken
    That shall be said,
What dost thou praying,
O soul, and playing
With song and saying,
    Things flown and fled
For this we know not—
That fresh springs flow not
And fresh grief grows not
    When men are dead;
When strange years cover
Lover and lover,
And joys are over
    And tears are shed.

If one day's sorrow
Mar the day's morrow—
If man's life borrow
    And man's death pay—
If souls once taken,
If lives once shaken,
Arise, awaken,
    By night, by day—

Why with strong crying
And years of sighing,
Living and dying,
    Fast ye and pray?
For all your weeping,
Waking and sleeping;
Death comes to reaping
    And takes away.
Though time rend after
Roof-tree from rafter,
A little laughter
    Is much more worth
Than thus to measure
The hour, the treasure,
The pain, the pleasure,
    The death, the birth;
Grief, when days alter,
Like joy shall falter;
Song-book and psalter,
    Mourning and mirth.
Live like the swallow;
Seek not to follow
Where earth is hollow
    Under the earth.

IN THE ORCHARD.

(PROVENÇAL BURDEN.)

Leave go my hands, let me catch breath and see ;
Let the dew-fall drench either side of me ;
    Clear apple-leaves are soft upon that moon
Seen sidelong like a blossom in the tree ;
    Ah God, ah God, that day should be so soon.

The grass is thick and cool, it lets us lie.
Kissed upon either cheek and either eye,
    I turn to thee as some green afternoon
Turns toward sunset, and is loth to die;
    Ah God, ah God, that day should be so soon.

Lie closer, lean your face upon my side,
Feel where the dew fell that has hardly
    dried,
  Hear how the blood beats that went nigh
    to swoon;
The pleasure lives there when the sense
    has died;
  Ah God, ah God, that day should be so
    soon.

O my fair lord, I charge you leave me this:
Is it not sweeter than a foolish kiss ?
  Nay take it then, my flower, my first in
    June,
My rose, so like a tender mouth it is :
  Ah God, ah God, that day should be so
    soon.

Love, till dawn sunder night from day
    with fire,
Dividing my delight and my desire,
  The crescent life and love the plenilune,
Love me though dusk begin and dark re-
    tire;
  Ah God, ah God, that day should be so
    soon.

Ah, my heart fails my blood draws back ;
    I know,
When life runs over, life is near to go ;
  And with the slain of love love's ways
    are strewn,
And with their blood, if love will have it
    so ;
  Ah God, ah God, that day should be so
    soon.

Ah, do thy will now ; slay me if thou wilt;
There is no building now the walls are
    built,
  No quarrying now the corner-stone is
    hewn,
No drinking now the vine's whole blood is
    spilt ;
  Ah God, ah God, that day should be so
    soon.

Nay, slay me now ; nay, for I will be slain;
Pluck thy red pleasure from the teeth of
    pain,
  Break down thy vine ere yet grape-
    gatherers prune,
Slay me ere day can slay desire again ;
  Ah God, ah God, that day should be so
    soon.

Yea, with thy sweet lips, with thy sweet
    sword; yea,
Take life and all, for I will die, I say;
  Love, I gave love, is life a better boon ?
For sweet night's sake I will not live till
    day;
  Ah God, ah God, that day should be so
    soon.

Nay, I will sleep then only; nay, but go.
Ah sweet, too sweet to me, my sweet, I
    know
  Love, sleep, and death go to the sweet
    same tune;
Hold my hair fast, and kiss me through
    it so.
  Ah God, ah God, that day should be so
    soon.

A MATCH.

If love were what the rose is,
  And I were like the leaf,
Our lives would grow together
In sad or singing weather,
Blown fields or flowerful closes,
  Green pleasure or grey grief;
If love were what the rose is,
  And I were like the leaf.

If I were what the words are,
  And love were like the tune,
With double sound and single
Delight our lips would mingle,
With kisses glad as birds are
  That get sweet rain at noon;
If I were what the words are
  And love were like the tune.

If you were life, my darling,
  And I your love were death,
We'd shine and snow together
Ere March made sweet the weather
With daffodil and starling
  And hours of fruitful breath;
If you were life, my darling,
  And I your love were death.

If you were thrall to sorrow,
  And I were page to joy,
We'd play for lives and seasons
With loving looks and treasons
And tears of night and morrow
  And laughs of maid and boy;
If you were thrall to sorrow,
  And I were page to joy.

If you were April's lady,
  And I were lord in May,
We'd throw with leaves for hours
And draw for days with flowers,
Till day like night were shady
  And night were bright like day;
If you were April's lady,
  And I were lord in May.

If you were queen of pleasure,
  And I were king of pain,
We'd hunt down love together,
Pluck out his flying-feather,
And teach his feet a measure,
  And find his mouth a rein;
If you were queen of pleasure,
  And I were king of pain.

FAUSTINE.

Ave Faustina Imperatrix, morituri te salutant.

Lean back, and get some minutes' peace;
  Let your head lean
Back to the shoulder with its fleece
  Of locks, Faustine.

The shapely silver shoulder stoops,
  Weighed over clean
With state of splendid hair that droops
  Each side, Faustine.

Let me go over your good gifts
  That crown you queen;
A queen whose kingdom ebbs and shifts
  Each week, Faustine.

Bright heavy brow well gathered up:
  White gloss and sheen;
Carved lips that make my lips a cup
  To drink, Faustine.

Wine and rank poison, milk and blood,
  Being mixed therein

Since first the devil threw dice with God
  For you, Faustine.

Your naked new-born soul, their stake,
  Stood blind between;
God said "let him that wins her take
  And keep Faustine."

But this time Satan throve, no doubt;
  Long since, I ween,
God's part in you was battered out;
  Long since, Faustine.

The die rang sideways as it fell,
  Rang cracked and thin,
Like a man's laughter heard in hell
  Far down, Faustine.

A shadow of laughter like a sigh,
  Dead sorrow's kin;
So rang, thrown down, the devil's die
  That won Faustine.

4

A suckling of his breed you were,
 One hard to wean;
But God, who lost you, left you fair,
 We see, Faustine.

You have the face that suits a woman
 For her soul's screen—
The sort of beauty that's called human
 In hell, Faustine.

You could do all things but be good
 Or chaste of mien;
And that you would not if you could,
 We know, Faustine.

Even he who cast seven devils out
 Of Magdalene
Could hardly do as much, I doubt,
 For you, Faustine.

Did Satan make you to spite God?
 Or did God mean
To scourge with scorpions for a rod
 Our sins, Faustine?

I know what queen at first you were,
 As though I had seen
Red gold and black imperious hair
 Twice crown Faustine.

As if your fed sarcophagus
 Spared flesh and skin,
You come back face to face with us,
 The same Faustine.

She loved the games men played with death,
 Where death must win;
As though the slain man's blood and breath
 Revived Faustine.

Nets caught the pike, pikes tore the net;
 Lithe limbs and lean
From drained-out pores dripped thick red
  sweat
 To soothe Faustine.

She drank the steaming drift and dust
 Blown off the scene;
Blood could not ease the bitter lust
 That galled Faustine.

All round the foul fat furrows reeked,
 Where blood sank in;
The circus splashed and seethed and shrieked
 All round Faustine.

But these are gone now: years entomb
 The dust and din;
Yea, even the bath's fierce reek and fume
 That slew Faustine.

Was life worth living then? and now
 Is life worth sin?
Where are the imperial years? and how
 Are you, Faustine?

Your soul forgot her joys, forgot
 Her times of teen;
Yea, this life likewise will you not
 Forget, Faustine?

For in the time we know not of
 Did fate begin
Weaving the web of days that wove
 Your doom, Faustine.

The threads were wet with wine, and all
 Were smooth to spin;
They wove you like a Bacchanal,
 The first Faustine.

And Bacchus cast your mates and you
 Wild grapes to glean;
Your flower-like lips dashed with dew
 From his, Faustine.

Your drenched loose hands were stretched
  to hold
 The vine's wet green,
Long ere they coined in Roman gold
 Your face, Faustine.

Then after change of soaring feather
 And winnowing fin,
You woke in weeks of feverish weather,
 A new Faustine.

A star upon your birthday burned,
 Whose fierce serene
Red pulseless planet never yearned
 In heaven, Faustine.

Stray breaths of Sapphic song that blew
 Through Mitylene
Shook the fierce quivering blood in you
 By night, Faustine.

The shameless nameless loves that makes
 Hell's iron gin
Shut on you like a trap that breaks
 The soul, Faustine.

And when your veins were void and dead,
  What ghosts unclean
Swarmed round the straitened barren bed
  That hid Faustine?

What sterile growths of sexless root
  Or epicene?
What flower of kisses without fruit
  Of love, Faustine?

What adders came to shed their coats?
  What coiled obscene
Small serpents with soft stretching throats
  Caressed Faustine?

But the time came of famished hours,
  Maimed loves and mean,
This ghastly thin-faced time of ours,
  To spoil Faustine.

You seem a thing that hinges hold,
  A love-machine
With clockwork joints of supple gold—
  No more, Faustine.

Not godless, for you serve one God,
  The Lampsacene,
Who metes the gardens with his rod;
  Your lord, Faustine.

If one should love you with real love
  (Such things have been,
Things your fair face knows nothing of
  It seems, Faustine);

That clear hair heavily bound back,
  The lights wherein
Shift from dead blue to burnt-up black
  Your throat, Faustine,

Strong, heavy, throwing out the face
  And hard bright chin
And shameful scornful lips that grace
  Their shame, Faustine,

Curled lips, long since half kissed away,
  Still sweet and keen;
You'd give him—poison shall we say?
  Or what, Faustine?

A CAMEO.

THERE was a graven image of Desire
  Painted with red blood on a ground
    of gold
  Passing between the young men and
    the old,
And by him Pain, whose body shone like
    fire,
And Pleasure with gaunt hands that grasp-
    ed their hire.
  Of his left wrist, with fingers clenched
    and cold,
  The insatiable Satiety kept hold,
Walking with feet unshod that pashed the
    mire,
The senses and the sorrows and the sins,
  And the strange loves that suck the
    breasts of Hate
Till lips and teeth bite in their sharp
    indenture,
Followed like beasts with flap of wings
    and fins. [grate,
  Death stood aloof behind a gaping
  Upon whose lock was written *Perad-
    venture.*

SONG BEFORE DEATH.

(FROM THE FRENCH.)

1795

SWEET mother, in a minute's span
  Death parts thee and my love of thee
Sweet love, that yet art living man,

Come back, true love, to comfort me.
Back, ah, come back! ah wellaway!
But my love comes not any day.

As roses, when the warm West blows,
  Break to full flower and sweeten spring,
My soul would break to a glorious rose
  In such wise at his whispering
In vain I listen ; wellaway !
My love says nothing any day.

You that will weep for pity of love
  On the low place where I am lain,
I pray you, having wept enough,
  Tell him for whom I bore such pain
That he was yet, ah ! wellaway !
My true love to my dying day.

ROCOCO.

Take hand and part with laughter;
  Touch lips and part with tears;
Once more and no more after,
  Whatever comes with years.
We twain shall not remeasure
  The ways that left us twain;
Nor crush the lees of pleasure
  From sanguine grapes of pain.

We twain once well in sunder,
  What will the mad gods do
For hate with me, I wonder,
  Or what for love with you ?
Forget them till November,
  And dream there's April yet,
Forget that I remember,
  And dream that I forget.

Time found our tired love sleeping,
  And kissed away his breath;
But what should we do weeping,
  Though light love sleep to death ?
We have drained his lips at leasure,
  Till there's not left to drain
A single sob of pleasure,
  A single pulse of pain.

Dream that the lips once breathless
  Might quicken if they would;
Say that the soul is deathless;
  Dream that the gods are good;
Say march may wed September,
  And time divorce regret;
But not that you remember,
  And not that I forget.

We have heard from hidden places
  What love scarce lives and hears:
We have seen on fervent faces
  The pallor of strange tears:
We have trod the wine-vats treasure,
  Whence, ripe to steam and stain,
Foams round the feet of pleasure
  The blood-red must of pain.

Remembrance may recover
  And time bring back to time
The name of your first lover,
  The ring of my first rhyme;
But rose-leaves of December
  The frosts of June shall fret,
The day that you remember,
  The day that I forget.

The snake that hides and hisses
  In heaven we twain have known;
The grief of cruel kisses,
  The joy whose mouth makes moan;
The pulses pause and measure,
  Where in one furtive vein
Throbs through the heart of pleasure
  The purpler blood of pain.

We have done with tears and treasons
  And love for treason's sake;
Room for the swift new seasons,
  The years that burn and break,
Dismantle and dismember
  Men's days and dreams, Juliette;
For love may not remember,
  But time will not forget.

Life treads down love in flying,
  Time withers him at root;
Bring all dead things and dying,
  Reaped sheaf and ruined fruit,
Where, crushed by three days' pressure
  Our three days' love lies slain;
And earlier leaf of pleasure,
  And latter flower of pain.

Breathe close upon the ashes,
  It may be flame will leap;
Unclose the soft close lashes,
  Lift up the lids and weep.
Light love's extinguised ember,
  Let one tear leave it wet
For one that you remember
  And ten that you forget.

STAGE LOVE.

WHEN the game began between them for a jest,
He played king and she played queen to match the best ;
Laughter soft as tears, and tears that turned to laughter,
These were things she sought for years and sorrowed after.

Pleasure with dry lips, and pain that walks by night ;
All the sting and all the stain of long delight ;
These were things she knew not of, that knew not of her,
When she played at half a love with half a lover.

Time was chorus, gave them cues to laugh or cry ;
They would kill, befool, amuse him, let him die ;
Set him webs to weave to-day and break to-morrow,
Till he died for good in play, and rose in sorrow.

What the years mean ; how times dies and is not slain ;
How love grows and laughs and cries and wanes again ;
These were things she came to know, and take their measure,
When the play was played out so for one man's pleasure.

THE LEPER.

NOTHING is better, I well think,
  Than love; the hidden well-water
Is not so delicate to drink:
  This was well seen of me and her.

I served her in a royal house;
  I served her wine and curious meat
For will to kiss between her brows
  I had no heart to sleep or eat.

Mere scorn God knows she had of me;
   A poor scribe, nowise great or fair,
Who plucked his clerk's hood back to see
   Her curled up lips and amorous hair.

I vex my head with thinking this.
   Yea, though God always hated me,
And hates me now that I can kiss
   Her eyes, plait up her hair to see

How she then wore it on the brows,
   Yet am I glad to have her dead
Here in this wretched wattled house
   Where I can kiss her eyes and head.

Nothing is better, I well know,
   Than love; no amber in cold sea
Or gathered berries under snow:
   That is well seen of her and me.

Three thoughts I make my pleasure of:
   First I take heart and think of this:
That knight's gold hair she chose to love,
   His mouth she had such will to kiss.

Then I remember that sundawn
   I brought him by a privy way
Out at her lattice, and thereon
   What gracious words she found to say.

(Cold rushes for such little feet—
   Both feet could lie into my hand.
A marvel was it of my sweet
   Her upright body could so stand.)

"Sweet friend, God give you thank and
     grace
   Now am I clean and whole of shame,
Nor shall men burn me in the face
   For my sweet fault that scandals them."

I tell you over word by word.
   She, sitting edgewise on her bed,
Holding her feet, said thus.   The third,
   A sweeter thing than these, I said.

God, that makes time and ruins it,
   And alters not abiding God,
Changed with disease her body sweet,
   The body of love wherein she abode.

Love is more sweet and comlier
   Than a dove's throat strained out to sing.
All they spat out and cursed at her
   And cast her forth for a base thing.

They cursed her, seeing how God had
     wrought
   This curse to plague her, a curse of his.
Fools were they surely, seeing not
   How sweeter than all sweet she is.

He that had held her by the hair,
   With kissing lips blinding her eyes,
Felt her bright bosom, strained and bare,
   Sigh under him, with short mad cries

Out of her throat and sobbing mouth
   And body broken up with love,
With sweet hot tears his lips were loth
   Her own should taste the savor of,

Yea, he inside whose grasp all night
   Her fervent body leapt or lay,
Stained with sharp kisses red and white,
   Found her a plague to spurn away.

I hid her in this wattled house,
   I served her water and poor bread,
For joy to kiss between her brows
   Time upon time I was nigh dead.

Bread failed; we got but well-water
   And gathered grass with dropping seed.
I had such joy of kissing her,
   I had small care to sleep or feed.

Sometimes when service made me glad
   The sharp tears leapt between my lids,
Falling on her, such joy I had
   To do the service God forbids.

"I pray you let me be at peace,
   Get hence, make room for me to die."
She said that: her poor lip would cease,
   Put up to mine, and turn to cry.

I said, "Bethink yourself how love
   Fared in us twain, what either did;
Shall I unclothe my soul thereof?
   That I should do this, God forbid."

Yea, though God hateth us, he knows
   That hardly in a little thing
Love faileth of the work it does
   Till it grow ripe for gathering.

Six months, and now my sweet is dead
   A trouble takes me; I know not
If all were done well, all well said,
   No word or tender deed forgot.

Too sweet, for the least part in her,
  To have shed life out by fragments; yet,
Could the close mouth catch breath and
    stir,
I might see something I forget.

Six months, and I sit still and hold
  In two cold palms her cold two feet.
Her hair, half grey half ruined gold,
  Thrills me and burns me in kissing it.

Love bites and stings me through, to see
  Her keen face made of sunken bones.
Her worn-off eyelids madden me,
  That were shot through with purple once.

She said, " Be good with me; I grow
  So tired for shame's sake, I shall die
If you say nothing:" even so.
  And she is dead now and shame put by.

Yea, and the scorn she had of me
  In the old time, doubtless vexed her
    then.
I never should have kissed her. See
  What fools God's anger makes of men !

She might have loved me a little too,
  Had I been humbler for her sake.

But that new shame could make love new
  She saw not—yet her shame did make.

I took too much upon my love,
  Having for such mean service done
Her beauty and all the ways thereof,
  Her face and all the sweet thereon.

Yea, all this while I tended her,
  I know the old love held fast his part :
I know the old scorn waxed heavier,
  Mixed with sad wonder, in her heart.

It may be all my love went wrong—
  A scribe's work writ awry and blurred,
Scrawled after the blind evensong—
  Spoilt music with no perfect word.

But surely I would fain have done
  All things the best I could. Perchance
Because I failed, came short of one,
  She kept at heart that other man's.

I am grown blind with all these things :
  It may be now she hath in sight
Some better knowledge ; still there clings
  The old question. Will not God do
    right ?

En ce temps-là estoyt dans ce pays grand nombre de ladres et de meseaulx, ce dont le roy eut grand desplaisir, ven que Dieu dust en estre moult griefvement courroucé. Ores il advint qu'une noble damoyselle appelée Yolande de Sallières estant atteincte et touste guastée de ce vilain mal, tous ses amys et ses parens ayant devant leurs yeux la paour de Dieu la firent issir fors de leurs maisons et oncques ne voulurent recepvoir ni reconforter chose mauldicte de Dieu et à tous les hommes puante et abhominable. Ceste dame avoyt esté moult belle et gracieuse de formes, et de son corps elle estoyt large et de vie lascive. Pourtant nul des amans qui l avoyent souventesfois accollée et basiée moult tendrement ne voulust plus héberger si laide femme et si détestable pescheresse. Ung seul clerc qui feut premiérement son lacquays et son entremetteur en matière d amour la recut chez luy et la récéla dans une petite cabane. Là mourut la meschinette de grande misère et de male mort : et après elle décéda ledist clerc qui pour grand amour l avcyt six mois durant soignée, làvée, habillée et deshabillée tous les jours de ses mains propres. Mesme dist-on que ce meschant homme et mauldict clerc remémourant de la grande beauté passée et guastée de ceste femme se délectoyt maintesfois à la baiser sur sa bouche orde et lépreuse et l accoller doulcement de ses mains amoureuses. Aussy est-il mort de ceste mesme maladie abhominable. Cecy advint prés Fontainebellant en Gastinois. Et quand ouyt le roy Philippe ceste adventure moult en estoyt esmerveillé.

        Grandes Chroniques de France, 1505.

A BALLAD OF BURDENS.

THE burden of fair women. Vain delight,
  And love self-slain in some sweet shame-
    ful way,
And sorrowful old age that comes by night
  As a thief comes that has no heart by
    day,
    And change that finds fair cheeks and
      leaves them grey,
And weariness that keeps awake for hire,
  And grief that says what pleasure used
    to say;
This is the end of every man's desire.

The burden of bought kisses. This is sore,
  A burden without fruit in childbearing;
Between the nightfall and the dawn three-
    score,
  Threescore between the dawn and even-
    ing.
  The shuddering in thy lips, the shudder-
    ing
In thy sad eyelids tremulous like fire,
  Makes love seem shameful and a
    wretched thing.
This is the end of every man's desire.

The burden of sweet speeches. Nay, kneel
    down,
  Cover thy head, and weep; for verily
These market-men that buy thy white and
    brown
  In the last days shall take no thought
    for thee.
  In the last days like earth thy face shall
    be,
Yea, like sea-marsh made thick with brine
    and mire,
  Sad with sick leavings of the sterile sea.
This is the end of every man's desire.

The burden of long living. Thou shalt
    fear
  Waking, and sleeping mourn upon thy
    bed;
And say at night " Would God the day
    were here,"
  And say at dawn " Would God the day
    were dead."

With weary days thou shalt be clothed
    and fed,
And wear remorse of heart for thine attire,
  Pain for thy girdle and sorrow upon thine
    head;
This is the end of every man's desire.

The burden of bright colors. Thou shalt
    see
  Gold tarnished, and the grey above the
    green;
And as the thing thou seest thy face shall be,
  And no more as the thing beforetime
    seen.
  And thou shalt say of mercy " It hath
    been,"
And living, watch the old lips and loves
    expire,
  And talking, tears shall take thy breath
    between.
This is the end of every man's desire.

The burden of sad sayings. In that day
  Thou shalt tell all thy days and hours,
    and tell
Thy times and ways and words of love, and
    say
How one was dear and one desirable,
  And sweet was life to hear and sweet to
    smell,
But now with lights reverse the old hours
    retire
  And the last hour is shod with fire from
    hell.
This is the end of every man's desire.

The burden of four seasons. Rain in
    spring,
  White rain and wind among the tender
    trees;
A summer of green sorrows gathering,
  Rank autumn in a mist of miseries,
  With sad face set towards the year, that
    sees
The charred ash drop out of the dropping
    pyre,
  And winter wan with many maladies;
This is the end of every man's desire.

The burden of dead faces. Out of sight
  And out of love, beyond the reach of
    hands,
Changed in the changing of the dark and
    light,
  They walk and weep about the barren
    lands
  Where no seed is nor any garner stands,
Where in short breaths the doubtful days
    respire,
  And time's turned glass lets through the
    sighing sands;
  This is the end of every man's desire.

The burden of much gladness. Life and
    lust
  Forsake thee, and the face of thy delight;
And underfoot the heavy hour strews dust;

And overhead strange weathers burn and
    bite:
  And where the red was, lo the bloodless
    white,
And where truth was, the likeness of a
    liar,
  And where day was, the likeness of the
    night;
This is the end of every man's desire.

L'ENVOY.

Princes, and ye whom pleasure quickeneth,
  Heed well this rhyme before your plea-
    sure tire;
For life is sweet, but after life is death.
  This is the end of every man's desire.

RONDEL.

KISSING her hair I sat against her feet,
  Wove and unwove it, wound and found it
    sweet
Made fast therewith her hands, drew down
    her eyes,
Deep as deep flowers and dreamy like dim
    skies;
With her own tresses bound and found ner
    fair,
    Kissing her hair.

Sleep were no sweeter than her face to me,
Sleep of cold sea-bloom under the cold sea;
What pain could get between my face and
    hers?
What new sweet thing would love not relish
    worse?
Unless, perhaps, white death had kissed
    me there,
    Kissing her hair?

BEFORE THE MIRROR.

(VERSES WRITTEN UNDER A PICTURE.)

INSCRIBED TO J. A. WHISTLER.

WHITE rose in red rose-garden
  Is not so white;
Snowdrops that plead for pardon

  And pine for fright
Because the hard East blows
Over their maiden rows
  Grow not as this face grows from pale to
    bright.

Behind the veil, forbidden
  Shut up from sight,
Love, is there sorrow hidden,
  Is there delight ?
Is joy thy dower of grief,
White rose of weary leaf,
  Late rose whose life is brief, whose loves
    are light ?

Soft snows that hard winds harden
  Till each flake bite
Fill all the flowerless garden
  Whose flowers took flight
Long since when summer ceased,
And men rose up from feast.
  And warm west wind grew east, and
    warm day night.

II.

" Come snow. come wind or thunder
  High up in air,
I watch my face, and wonder
  At my bright hair;
Nought else exalts or grieves
The rose at heart, that heaves
  With love of her own leaves and lips that
    pair.

" She knows not loves that kissed her
  She knows not where,
Art thou the ghost, my sister,
  White sister there,
Am I the ghost, who knows ?
My hand, a fallen rose,
  Lies snow-white on white snows, and
    takes no care.

" I cannot see what pleasures
  Or what pains were;
What pale new loves and treasures
  New years will bear;
What beam will fall, what shower,
What grief or joy for dower;
  But one thing knows the flower; the
    flower is fair."

III.

Glad, but not flushed with gladness,
  Since joys go by;
Sad, but not bent with sadness,
  Since sorrows die;
Deep in the gleaming glass
She sees all past things pass,
  And all sweet life that was lie down and
    lie.

There glowing ghosts of flowers
  Draw down, draw nigh;
And wings of swift spent hours
  Take flight and fly;
She sees by formless gleams,
She hears across cold streams,
  Dead mouths of many dreams that sing
    and sigh.

Face fallen and white throat lifted,
  With sleepless eye
She sees old loves that drifted,
  She knew not why,
Old loves and faded fears
Float down a stream that hears
  The flowing of all men's tears beneath
    the sky.

EROTION.

Sweet for a little even to fear, and sweet,
O love, to lay down fear at love's fair feet;
Shall not some fiery memory of his breath
Lie sweet on lips that touch the lips of
    death ?
Yet leave me not; yet, if thou wilt, be free;
Love me no more, but love my love of thee.
Love where thou wilt, and live thy life;
    and I,
One thing I can, and one love cannot—die.

Pass from me; yet thine arms, thine eyes,
    thine hair,
Feed my desire and deaden my despair.
Yet once more ere time change us, ere my
    cheek
Whiten, ere hope be dumb or sorrow speak,
Yet once more ere thou hate me, one full
    kiss;
Keep other hours for others, save me this.
Yea, and I will not (if it please thee) weep.

Lest thou be sad; I will but sigh, and sleep.
Sweet, does death hurt? thou canst not do
   me wrong:
I shall not lack thee, as I loved thee, long.
Hast thou not given me above all that live
Joy, and a little sorrow shalt not give?
What even though fairer fingers of strange
   girls
Pass nestling through thy beautiful boy's
   curls
As mine did, or those curled lithe lips of
   thine
Meet theirs as these, all theirs come after
   mine;
And though I were not, though I be not,
   best,
I have loved and love thee more than all
   the rest.
O love, O lover, loose or hold me fast,
I had thee first, whoever have thee last;

Fairer or not, what need I know, what care?
To thy fair bud my blossom once seemed
   fair.
Why am I fair at all before thee, why
At all desired? seeing thou art fair, not I.
I shall be glad of thee, O fairest head,
Alive, alone, without thee, with thee, dead;
I shall remember while the light lives yet.
And in the night-time I shall not forget.
Though (as thou wilt) thou leave me ere
   life leave,
I will not, for thy love I will not, grieve;
Not as they use who love not more than I,
Who love not as I love thee though I die;
And though thy lips, once mine, be oftener
   prest
To many another brow and balmier breast,
And sweeter arms, or sweeter to thy mind,
Lull thee or lure, more fond thou wilt not
   find.

IN MEMORY OF WALTER SAVAGE LANDOR.

BACK to the flower-town, side by side,
   The bright months bring,
New-born, the bridegroom and the bride,
   Freedom and spring.

The sweet land laughs from sea to sea,
   Filled full of sun;
All things come back to her, being free;
   All things but one.

In many a tender wheaten plot
   Flowers that were dead
Live, and old suns revive; but not
   That holier head.

By this white wandering waste of sea,
   Far north, I hear
One face shall never turn to me
   As once this year:

Shall never smile and turn and rest
   On mine as there,
Nor one most sacred hand be prest
   Upon my hair.

I came as one whose thoughts half linger,
   Half run before;
The youngest to the oldest singer
   That England bore.

I found him whom I shall not find
   Till all grief end,
In holiest age our mightiest mind,
   Father and friend.

But thou, if anything endure,
   If hope there be,
O spirit that man's life left pure,
   Man's death set free,

Not with disdain of days that were
        Look earthward now;
Let dreams revive the reverend hair,
        The imperial brow;

Come back in sleep, for in the life
        Where thou art not
We find none like thee.   Time and strife
        And the world's lot.

Move thee no more; but love at least
        And reverent heart

May move thee, royal and released,
        Soul, as thou art.

And thou, his Florence, to thy trust
        Receive and keep,
Keep safe his dedicated dust,
        His sacred sleep.

So shall thy lovers, come from far,
        Mix with thy name
As morning-star with evening-star
        His faultless fame.

A SONG IN TIME OF ORDER.   1852.

PUSH hard across the sand,
        For the salt wind gathers breath;
Shoulder and wrist and hand,
        Push hard as the push of death.

The wind is as iron that rings,
        The foam-heads loosen and flee;
It swells and welters and swings,
        The pulse of the tide of the sea.

And up on the yellow cliff
        The long corn flickers and shakes;
Push, for the wind holds stiff,
        And the gunwale dips and rakes.

Good hap to the fresh fierce weather,
        The quiver and beat of the sea !
While three men hold together,
        The kingdoms are less by three.

Out to the sea with her there,
        Out with her over the sand,
Let the kings keep the earth for their share !
        We have done with the sharers of land.

They have tied the world in a tether,
        They have bought over God with a fee;
While three men hold together,
        The kingdoms are less by three.

We have done with the kisses that sting,
        The thief's mouth red from the feast,
The blood on the hands of the king,
        And the lie at the lips of the priest.

Will they tie the winds in a tether,
        Put a bit in the jaws of the sea ?
While three men hold together,
        The kingdoms are less by three.

Let our flag run out straight in the wind !
        The old red shall be floated again
When the rank that are thin shall be
        thinned,
        When the names that were twenty are
        ten;

When the devil's riddle is mastered
        And the galley-bench creaks with a
        Pope,
We shall see Buonaparte the bastard
        Kick heels with his throat in a rope.

While the shepherd sets wolves on his
        sheep
        And the emperor halters his Kine,
While Shame is a watchman asleep
        And Faith is a keeper of swine.

Let the wind shake our flag like a feather,
  Like the plumes of the foam of the sea!
While three men hold together,
  The kingdoms are less by three.

All the world has its burdens to bear,
  From Cayenne to the Austrian whips;

Forth, with the rain in our hair
  And the salt sweet foam in our lips;

In the teeth of the hard glad weather,
  In the blown wet face of the sea;
While three men hold together,
  The kingdoms are less by three.

A SONG IN TIME OF REVOLUTION. 1860.

THE heart of the rulers is sick, and the
  high-priest covers his head:
For this is the song of the quick that is
  heard in the ears of the dead.

The poor and the halt and the blind are
  keen and mighty and fleet:
Like the noise of the blowing of wind is
  the sound of the noise of their feet.

The wind has the sound of a laugh in the
  clamor of days and of deed :
The priests are scattered like chaff, and
  the rulers broken like reeds.

The high-priest sick from qualms, with his
  raiment bloodily dashed;
The thief with branded palms, and the liar
  with cheeks abashed.

They are smitten, they tremble greatly, they
  are pained for their pleasant things :
For the house of the priests made stately,
  and the might in the mouth of the
  kings.

They are grieved and greatly afraid ; they
  are taken, they shall not flee:
For the heart of the nations is made as the
  strength of the springs of the sea.

They were fair in the grace of gold, they
  walked with delicate feet :
They were clothed with the cunning of old,
  and the smell of their garments was
  sweet.

For the breaking of gold in their hair they
  halt as a man made lame:
They are utterly naked and bare; their
  mouths are bitter with shame.

Wilt thou judge thy people now, O king
  that wast found most wise ?
Wilt thou lie any more, O thou whose
  mouth is emptied of lies ?

Shall God make a pact with thee, till his
  hook be found in thy sides ?
Wilt thou put back the time of the sea, or
  the place of the season of tides ?

Set a word in thy lips, to stand before God
  with a word in thy mouth :
That " the rain shall return in the land,
  and the tender dew after drouth."

But the arm of the elders is broken, their
  strength is unbound and undone:
They wait for a sign of a token; they cry,
  and there cometh none.

Their moan is in every place, the cry of
  them filleth the land:
There is shame in the sight of their face,
  there is fear in the thews of their hand.

They are girdled about the reins with a
  curse for the girdle thereon:
For the noise of the rending of chains the
  face of their color is gone.

For the sound of the shouting of men they
    are grievously stricken at heart:
They are smitten asunder with pain, their
    bones are smitten apart.

There is none of them all that is whole;
    their lips gape open for breath:
They are clothed with sickness of soul,
    and the shape of the shadow of death.

The wind is thwart in their feet; it is full
    of the shouting of mirth;
As one shaketh the sides of a sheet so it
    shaketh the ends of the earth.

The sword, the sword is made keen; the
    iron has opened its mouth;
The corn is red that was green; it is bound
    for the sheaves of the south.

The sound of a word was shed, the sound
    of the wind as a breath

In the ears of the souls that were dead, in
    the dust of the deepness of death;

Where the face of the moon is taken, the
    ways of the stars undone,
The light of the whole sky shaken, the
    light of the face of the sun:

Where the waters are emptied and broken,
    the waves of the waters are stayed;
Where God has bound for a token the
    darkness that maketh afraid;

Where the sword was covered and hidden,
    and dust had grown in its side,
A word came forth which was bidden, the
    crying of one that cried:

The sides of the two-edged sword shall be
    bare, and its mouth shall be red,
For the breath of the face of the Lord that
    is felt in the bones of the dead,

TO VICTOR HUGO

IN the fair days when God
    By man as godlike trod,
And each alike was Greek, alike was free,
    God's lightning spared, they said,
    Alone the happier head
Whose laurels screened it; fruitless grace
    for thee,
    To whom the high gods gave of right
Their thunders and their laurels and their
    light.

Sunbeams and bays before
    Our master's servants wore,
For these Appollo left in all men's lands
    But far from these ere now
    And watched with jealous brow
Lay the blind lightnings shut between
    God's hands,
    And only loosed on slaves and kings
The terror of the tempest of their wings.

Born in those younger years
    That shone with storms of spears
And shook in the wind blown from a dead
    world's pyre,
    When by her back-blown hair
    Napoleon caught the fair
And fierce Republic with her feet of fire,
    And stayed with iron words and hands
Her flight, and freedom in a thousand lands

Thou sawest the tides of things
    Close over heads of kings,
And thine hand felt the thunder and to
    thee
    Laurels and lightnings were
    As sunbeams and soft air
Mixed each in other, or as mist with sea
    Mixed, or as memory with desire,
Or the lute's pulses with the louder lyre.

For thee man's spirit stood
Disrobed of flesh and blood,
And bear the heart of the most secret hours;
And to thine hand more tame
Than birds in winter came
High hopes and unknown flying forms of
  . powers,
And from thy table fed, and sang
Till with the tune men's ears took fire and
  rang.

Even all men's eyes and ears
With fiery sound and tears
Waxed hot, and cheeks caught flame and
  eyelids light,
  . At those high songs of thine
  That stung the sense like wine,
Or fell more soft than dew or snow by
  night,
  Or wailed as in some flooded cave
Sobs the strong broken spirit of a wave.

But we, our master, we
Whose hearts, uplift to thee,
Ache with the pulse of thy remembered
  song,
  We ask not nor await
  From the clenched hands of fate,
As thou, remission of the world's old
  wrong;
  Respite we ask not, nor release;
Freedom a man may have, he shall not
  peace.

Though thy most fiery hope
Storm heaven, to set wide ope
The all-sought-for gate whence God or
  Chance debars
  All feet of men, all eyes—
  The old night resumes her skies,
Her hollow hiding-place of clouds and
  stars,
  Where nought save these is sure in
  sight
And, paven with death, our days are
  roofed with night.

One thing we can; to be
Awhile, as men may, free;
But not by hope or pleasure the most stern
  Goddess, most awful-eyed,
  Sits, but on either side
Sits sorrow and the wrath of hearts that
  burn,
  Sad faith, that cannot hope or fear,

And memory grey with many a flowerless
  year.

Not that in stranger's wise
I lift not loving eyes
To the fair foster-mother France, that gave
  Beyond the pale fleet foam
  Help to my sires and home,
Whose great sweet breast could shelter
  those and save
  Whom from her nursing breasts and
  hands
Their land cast forth of old on gentler
  lands.

Not without thoughts that ache
For theirs and for thy sake,
I, born of exiles, hail thy banished head
  I whose young song took flight
  Toward the great heat and light
On me a child from thy far splendor shed,
  From thine high place of soul and
  song,
Which, fallen on eyes yet feeble, made
  them strong.

Ah, not with lessening love,
For memories born hereof,
I look to that sweet mother-land, and see
  The old fields and fair full streams,
  And skies, but fled like dreams
The feet of freedom and the thought of
  thee;
  And all between the skies and graves
The mirth of mockers and the shame of
  slaves.

She, killed with noisome air,
Even she! and still so fair,
Who said "Let there be freedom," and
  there was
  Freedom; and as a lance
  The fiery eyes of France
Touched the world's sleep and as a sleep
  made pass
  Forth of men's heavier ears and eyes
Smitten with fire and thunder from new
  skies.

Are they men's friends indeed
Who watch them weep and bleed?
Because thou hast loved us, shall the gods
  love thee?
  Thou first of men and friend,
  Seest thou, even thou, the end?

Thou knowest what hath been, knowest
　　　thou what shall be ?
Evils may pass and hopes endure;
But fade is dim, and all the gods obscure.

　　O nursed in airs apart,
　　O poet highest of heart,
Hast thou seen time, who hast seen so
　　　many things ?
　　Are not the years more wise,
　　More sad than keenest eyes,
The years with soundless feet and sounding
　　　wings ?
　　Passing we hear them not, but past
The clamor of them thrills us, and their
　　blast.

　　Thou art chief of us, and lord;
　　Thy song is as a sword
Keen-edged and scented in the blade from
　　flowers;
　　Thou art lord and king but we
　　Lift younger eyes; and see
Less of high hope, less light on wandering
　　hours ;
　　Hours that have borne men down so
　　long,
Seen the right fail, and watched uplift the
　　wrong.

　　But thine imperial soul
　　As years and ruins roll
To the same end, and all things and all
　　dreams
　　With the same wreck and roar
　　Drift on the dim same shore,
Still in the bitter foam and brackish
　　streams
　　Tracks the fresh water-spring to be
And sudden sweeter fountains in the sea.

　　As once the high God bound
　　With many a rivet round
Man's saviour, and with iron nailed him
　　through,
　　At the wild end of things,
　　Where even his own bird's wings
Flagged whence the sea shone like a drop
　　of dew,
　　From Caucasus beheld below
Past fathoms of unfathonable snow;

　　So the strong God, the chance
　　Central of circumstance,
Still shows him exile who will not be slave;

　　All thy great fame and thee
　　Girt by the dim strait sea
With multitudinous walls of wandering
　　wave;
　　Shows us our greatest from his throne
Fate-stricken, and rejected of his own.

　　Yea, he is strong, thou say'st,
　　A mystery many-faced,
The wild beasts know him and the wild
　　birds flee;
　　The blind night sees him, death
　　Shrinks beaten at his breath,
And his right hand is heavy on the sea:
　　We know he hath made us, and is
　　king;
We know not if he care for anything.

　　Thus much, no more, we know;
　　He bade what is be so,
Bade light be and bade night be, one by
　　one;
　　Bade hope and fear, bade ill
　　And good redeem and kill,
Till all men be aweary of the sun
　　And this world burn in its own flame
And bear no witness longer of his name.

　　Yet though all this be thus,
　　Be those men praised of us
Who have loved and wrought and sorrowed
　　and not sinned
　　For fame or fear or gold,
　　Nor waxed for winter cold,
Nor changed for changes of the worldly
　　wind;
　　Praised above men of men be these.
Till this one world and work we know
　　shall cease.

　　Yea, one thing more than this,
　　We know that one thing is,
The splendor of a spirit without blame
　　That not the laboring years
　　Blind-born, nor any fears,
Nor men nor any gods can tire or tame;
　　But purer power with fiery breath
Fills, and exalts above the gulfs of death.

　　Praised above men be thou,
　　Whose laurel-laden brow,
Made for the morning, droops not in the
　　night;
　　Praised and beloved, that none
　　Of all thy great things done

Flies higher than thy most equal spirits flight;
    Praised, that nor doubt nor hope could
        bend

Earth's loftiest head, found upright to the
    end.

BEFORE DAWN.

SWEET life, if life were stronger,
Earth clear of years that wrong he,
Then two things might live longer,
    Two sweeter things than they;
Delight, the rootless flower,
And love, the bloomless bower;
Delight that lives an hour,
    And love that lives a day.

From evensong to daytime,
When April melts in Maytime,
Love lengthens out his playtime,
    Love lessens breath by breath,
And kiss by kiss grows older
On listless throat or shoulder
Turned sidewise now, turned colder
    Than life that dreams of death.

This one thing once worth giving
Life gave, and seemed worth living;
Sin sweet beyond forgiving
    And brief beyond regret:
To laugh and love together
And weave with foam and feather
And wind and words the tether
    Our memories play with yet.

Ah, one thing worth beginning,
One thread in life worth spinning,
Ah sweet, one sin worth sinning
    With all the whole soul's will;
To lull you till one stilled you,
To kiss you till one killed you,
To feed you till one filled you,
    Sweet lips, if love could fill;

To hunt sweet Love and lose him
Between white arms and bosom,
Between the bud and blossom,
    Between your throat and chin;
5

To say of shame—what is it?
Of virtue—we can miss it,
Of sin—we can but kiss it,
    And it's no longer sin:

To feel the strong soul, stricken
Through fleshly pulses, quicken
Beneath swift sighs that thicken,
    Soft hands and lips that smite;
Lips that no love can tire,
With hands that sting like fire,
Weaving the web Desire
    To snare the bird Delight.

But love so lightly plighted,
Our love with torch unlighted,
Paused near us unaffrighted,
    Who found and left him free;
None, seeing us cloven in sunder,
Will weep or laugh or wonder;
Light love stands clear of thunder,
    And safe from winds at sea.

As, when late larks give warning,
Of dying lights and dawning,
Night murmurs to the morning,
    "Lie still, O love, lie still;"
And half her dark limbs cover
The white limbs of her lover,
With amorous plumes that hover
    And fervent lips that chill;

As scornful day represses
Night's void and vain caresses,
And from her cloudier tresses
    Unwinds the gold of his,
With limbs from limbs dividing
And breath by breath subsiding;
For love has no abiding,
    But dies before the kiss.

So hath it been, so be it;
    For who shall live and flee it ?
But look that no man see it
    Or hear it unaware;

Lest all who love and choose him
See Love, and so refuse him;
For all who find him lose him,
    But all have found him fair.

DOLORES.

(NOTRE-DAME DES SEPT DOULEURS.)

COLD eyelids that hide like a jewel
    Hard eyes that grow soft for an hour ;
The heavy white limbs, and the cruel
    Red mouth like a venomous flower ;
When these are gone by with their glories,
    What shall rest of thee then, what re-
        main,
O mystic and sombre Dolores
    Our Lady of Pain ?

Seven sorrows the priests give their Virgin;
    But thy sins, which are seventy times
        seven,
Seven ages would fail thee to purge in,
    And then they would haunt thee in
        heaven:
Fierce midnights and famishing morrows,
    And the loves that complete and control
All the joys of the flesh, all the sorrows
    That wear out the soul.

O garment not golden but gilded,
    O garden where all men may dwell,
O tower not of ivory, but builded
    By hands that reach heaven from hell;
O mystical rose of the mire,
    O house not of gold but of gain,
O house of unquenchable fire,
    Our Lady of Pain !

O lips full of lust and of laughter,
    Curled snakes that are fed from my breast
Bite hard, lest remembrance come after
    And press with new lips where you
        pressed.
For my heart too springs up at the pressure,

Mine eyelids too moisten and burn ;
Ah, feed me and fill me with pleasure,
    Ere pain come in turn.

In yesterday's reach and to-morrow's,
    Out of sight though they lie of to-day,
There have been and there yet shall be sor
    rows,
    That smite not and bite not in play.
The life and the love thou despisest,
    These hurt us indeed, and in vain,
O wise among women, and wisest,
    Our Lady of Pain.

Who gave thee thy wisdom ? what stories
    That stung thee, what visions that smote?
Wert thou pure and a maiden, Dolores,
    When desire took thee first by the throat?
What bud was the shell of a blossom
    That all men may smell to and pluck ?
What milk fed thee first at what bosom ?
    What sins gave thee suck ?

We shift and bedeck and bedrape us,
    Thou art noble and nude and antique;
Libitina thy mother, Priapus
    Thy father, a Tuscan and Greek.
We play with light loves in the portal,
    And wince and relent and refrain;
Loves die, and we know thee immortal,
    Our Lady of Pain.

Fruits fail and love dies and time ranges;
    Thou art fed with perpetual breath,
And alive after infinite changes,

And fresh from the kisses of death ;
Of languors rekindled and rallied,
  Of barren delights and unclean,
Things monstrous and fruitless, a pallid
  And poisonous queen.

Could you hurt me, sweet lips, though I
      hurt you ?
  Men touch them, and change in a trice
The lilies and languors of virtue
  For the raptures and roses of vice;
Those lie where thy foot on the floor is,
  These crown and caress thee and chain,
O splendid and sterile Dolores,
  Our Lady of Pain.

There are sins it may be to discover,
  There are deeds it may be to delight.
What new work wilt thou find for thy lover?
  What new passions for daytime or night ?
What spells that they know not a word of
  Whose lives are as leaves overblown ?
What tortures undreampt of, unheard of,
  Unwritten, unknown ?

Ah beautiful passionate body
  That never has ached with a heart !
On thy mouth though the kisses are bloody,
  Though they sting till it shudder and
      smart,
More kind than the love we adore is,
  They hurt not the heart or the brain,
O bitter and tender Dolores,
  Our Lady of Pain.

As our kisses relax and redouble,
  From the lips and the foam and the fangs
Shall no new sin be born for men's trouble,
  No dream of impossible pangs ?
With the sweet of the sins of old ages
  Wilt thou satiate thy soul as of yore ?
Too sweet is the rind, say the sages,
  Too bitter the core.

Hast thou told all thy secrets the last time,
  And bared all thy beauties to one ?
Ah, where shall we go then for pastime,
  If the worst that can be has been done ?
But sweet as the rind was the core is;
  We are fain of thee still, we are fain,
O sanguine and subtle Dolores,
  Our Lady of Pain.

By the hunger of change and emotion,
  By the thirst of unbearable things,
By despair, the twin-born of devotion,

  By the pleasure that winces and stings,
The delight that consumes the desire,
  The desire that outruns the delight,
By the cruelty deaf as a fire
  And blind as the night,

By the ravenous teeth that have smitten
  Through the kisses that blossom and bud,
By the lips intertwisted and bitten
  Till the foam has a savor of blood,
By the pulse as it rises and falters,
  By the hands as they slacken and strain,
I adjure thee, respond from thine altars,
  Our Lady of Pain.

Wilt thou smile as a woman disdaining
  The light fire in the veins of a boy ?
But he comes to thee sad, without feigning,
  Who has wearied of sorrow and joy;
Less careful of labor and glory
  Than the elders whose hair has uncurled;
And young, but with fancies as hoary
  And grey as the world.

I have passed from the outermost portal
  To the shrine where a sin is a prayer;
What care though the service be mortal ?
  O our lady of Torture, what care ?
All thine the last wine that I pour is,
  The last in the chalice we drain,
O fierce and luxurious Dolores,
  Our Lady of Pain.

All thine the new wine of desire,
  The fruit of four lips as they clung
Till the hair and the eyelids took fire,
  The foam of a serpentine tongue,
The froth of the serpents of pleasure,
  More salt than the foam of the sea,
Now felt as a flame, now at leisure
  As wine shed for me.

Ah thy people, thy children, thy chosen,
  Marked cross from the womb and per-
      verse !
They have found out the secret to cozen
  The gods that constrain us and curse;
They alone, they are wise, and none other;
  Give me place, even me, in their train,
O my sister, my spouse, and my mother,
  Our Lady of Pain.

For the crown of our life as it closes
  Is darkness, the fruit thereof dust;
No thorns go as deep as a rose's,

And love is more cruel than lust.
Time turns the old days to derision,
  Our loves into corpses or wives;
And marriage and death and division
  Make barren our lives.

And pale from the past we draw nigh thee
  And satiate with comfortless hours;
And we know thee, how all men belie thee,
  And we gather the fruit of thy flowers;
The passion that slays and recovers,
  The pangs and the kisses that rain
On the lips and the limbs of thy lovers,
  Our Lady of Pain.

The desire of thy furious embraces
  Is more than the wisdom of years,
On the blossom though blood lie in traces,
  Though the foliage be sodden with tears.
For the lords in whose keeping the door is
  That opens on all who draw breath
Gave the cypress to love, my Dolores,
  The myrtle to death.

And they laughed, changing hands in the
    measure,
  And they mixed and made peace after
    . strife;
Pain melted in tears, and was pleasure;
  Death tingled with blood, and was life.
Like lovers they melted and tingled,
  In the dusk of thine innermost fame;
In the darkness they murmured and min-
    gled,
  Our Lady of Pain.

In a twilight where virtues are vices,
  In thy chapels, unknown of the sun,
To a tune that enthralls and entices,
  They were wed, and the train were as
    one.
For the tune from thine altar hath sounded
  Since God bade the world's work begin,
And the fume of thine incense abounded,
  To sweeten the sin.

Love listens, and paler than ashes,
  Through his curls as the crown on them
    slips,
Lifts languid wet eyelids and lashes,
  And laughs with insatiable lips.
Thou shalt hush him with heavy caresses,
  With music that scares the profane;
Thou shalt darken his eyes with thy tresses,
  Our Lady of Pain.

Thou shalt blind his bright eyes though he
    wrestle,
  Thou shalt chain his light limbs though
    he strive;
In his lips all thy serpents shall nestle,
  In his hands all thy cruelties thrive.
In the daytime thy voice shall go through
    him,
  In his dreams he shall feel thee and ache;
Thou shalt kindle by night and subdue him
  Asleep and awake.

Thou shalt touch and make redder his roses
  With juice not of fruit nor of bud;
When the sense in the spirit reposes,
  Thou shalt quicken the soul through the
    blood.
Thine, thine the one grace we implore is,
  Who would live and not languish or feign,
O sleepless and deadly Dolores,
  Our Lady of Pain.

Dost thou dream, in a respite of slumber,
  In a lull of the fires of thy life,
Of the days without name, without number,
  When thy will stung the world into strife,
When, a goddess, the pulse of thy passion
  Smote kings as they revelled in Rome;
And they hailed thee re-risen, O Thalassian,
  Foam-white, from the foam ?

When thy lips had such lovers to flatter,
  When the city lay red from thy rods,
And thine hands were as arrows to scatter
  The children of change and their gods ;
When the blood of thy foemen made fervent
  A sand never moist from the main,
As one smote them, their lord and thy
    servant,
  Our Lady of Pain.

On sands by the storm never shaken,
  Nor wet from the washing of tides;
Nor by foam of the waves overtaken,
  Nor winds that the thunder bestrides;
But red from the print of thy paces,
  Made smooth for the world and its lords,
Ringed round with a flame of fair faces,
  And splendid with swords.

There the gladiator, pale for thy pleasure,
  Drew bitter and perilous breath;
There torments laid hold on the treasure
  Of limbs too delicious for death ;
When thy gardens were lit with live torches;

When the world was a steed for thy rein;
When the nations lay prone in thy porches,
  Our Lady of Pain.

When, with flame all around him aspirant,
  Stood flushed, as a harp-player stands,
The implacable beautiful tyrant,
  Rose-crowned, having death in his hands;
And a sound as the sound of loud water
  Smote far through the flight of the fires,
And mixed with the lightning of slaughter
  A thunder of lyres.

Dost thou dream of what was and no more
    is,
  The old kingdoms of earth and the
    kings?
Dost thou hunger for these things, Dolores,
  For these, in a world of new things?
But thy bosom no fasts could emaciate,
  No hunger compel to complain
Those lips that no bloodshed could satiate,
  Our Lady of Pain.

As of old when the world's heart was
    lighter,
  Through thy garments the grace of thee
    glows,
The white wealth of thy body made whiter
  By the blushes of amorous blows,
And seamed with sharp lips and fierce fin-
    gers,
  And branded by kisses that bruise;
When all shall be gone that now lingers,
  Ah, what shall we lose?

Thou wert fair in the fearless old fashion,
  And thy limbs are as melodies yet,
And move to the music of passion
  With lithe and lascivious regret,
What ailed us, O gods, to desert you
  For creeds that refuse and restrain?
Come down and redeem us from virtue,
  Our Lady of Pain.

All shrines that were Vestal are flameless;
  But the flame has not fallen from this,
Though obscure be the god, and though
    nameless
  The eyes and the hair that we kiss;
Low fires that love sits by and forges
  Fresh heads for his arrows and thine;
Hair loosened and soiled in mid orgies
  With kisses and wine.

Thy skin changes country and color,
  And shrivels or swells to a snake's.
Let it brighten and bloat and grow duller,
  We know it, the flames and the flakes,
Red brands on it smit.en and bitten,
  Round skies where a star is a stain,
And the leaves with thy litanies written,
  Our Lady of Pain.

On thy bosom though many a kiss be,
  There are none such as knew it of old.
Was it Alciphron once or Arisbe,
  Male ringlets or feminine gold
That thy lips met with under the statue,
  Whence a look shot out sharp after
    thieves
From the eyes of the garden god at you
  Across the fig-leaves?

Then still, through dry seasons, and mois-
    ter,
  One god had a wreath to his shrine;
The love was the pearl of his oyster,*
  And Venus rose red out of wine.
We have all done amiss, choosing rather
  Such loves as the wise gods disdain;
Intercede for us thou with thy father,
  Our Lady of Pain.

In spring he had crowns of his garden,
  Red corn in the heat of the year,
Then hoary green olives that harden
  When the grape-blossom freezes with fear;
And milk-budded myrtles with Venus
  And vine-leaves with Bacchus he trod;
And ye said, "We have seen, he hath seen
    us,
  A visible God."

What broke off the garlands that girt you?
  What sundered you spirit and clay?
Weak sins yet alive are as virtue
  To the strength of the sins of that day.
For dried is the blood of thy lover,
  Ipsithilla, contracted the vein;
Cry aloud, "Will he rise and recover,
  Our Lady of Pain?"

Cry aloud; for the old world is broken:
  Cry out; for the Phrygian is priest,
And rears not the bountiful token
  And spreads not the fatherly feast.

---

* " Nam te præcipuè in suis urbibus colit ora
Hellespontia, cæteris ostreosior oris."
                    CATULL. *Carm* xviii

From the midmost of Ida, from shady
  Recesses that murmur at morn,
They have brought and baptized her, Our
    Lady,
  A goddess new-born.

And the chaplets of old are above us,
  And the oyster-bed teems out of reach;
Old poets outsing and outlove us,
  And Catullus makes mouths at our speech.
Who shall kiss, in thy father's own city,
  With such lips as he sang with, again ?
Intercede for us all of thy pity,
  Our Lady of Pain.

Out of Dindymus heavily laden
  Her lions draw bound and unfed
A mother, a mortal, a maiden,
  A queen over death and the dead.
She is cold, and her habit is lowly,
  Her temple of branches and sods;
Most fruitful and virginal, holy,
  A mother of gods.

She hath wasted with fire thine high places,
  She hath hidden and marred and made
    sad
The fair limbs of the Loves, the fair faces
  Of gods that were goodly and glad.
She slays, and her hands are not bloody;
  She moves as a moon in the wane,
White-robed, and thy raiment is ruddy,
  Our Lady of Pain.

They shall pass and their places be taken,
  The gods and the priests that are pure.
They shall pass, and shalt thou not be
    shaken ?
  They shall perish, and shalt thou endure ?
Death laughs, breathing close and relentless
  In the nostrils and eyelids of lust,
With a pinch in his fingers of scentless
  And delicate dust.

But the worm shall revive thee with kisses,
  Thou shalt change and transmute as a
    god,
As the rod to a serpent that hisses,
  As the serpent again to a rod.
Thy life shall not cease though thou doff it;
  Thou shalt live until evil be slain,
And good shall die first, said thy prophet,
  Our Lady of Pain.

Did he lie ? did he laugh ? does he know it,
  Now he lies out of reach, out of breath,
Thy prophet, thy preacher, thy poet,
  Sin's child by incestuous Death ?
Did he find out in fire at his waking,
  Or discern as his eyelids lost light,
When the bands of the body were breaking
  And all came in sight?

Who has known all the evil before us,
  Or the tyrannous secrets of time ?
Though we match not the dead men that
    bore us
  At a song, at a kiss, at a crime—
Though the heathen outface and outlive us,
  And our lives and our longings are twain—
Ah, forgive us our virtues, forgive us,
  Our Lady of Pain.

Who are we that embalm and embrace thee
  With spices and savors of song ?
What is time, that his children should face
    thee;
  What am I, that my lips do thee wrong ?
I could hurt thee—but pain would delight
    thee ;
  Or caress thee—but love would repel;
And the lovers whose lips would excite thee
  Are serpents in hell.

Who now shall content thee as they did,
  Thy lovers, when temples were built
And the hair of the sacrifice braided
  And the blood of the sacrifice spilt,
In Lampsacus fervent with faces,
  In Aphaca red from thy reign,
Who embraced thee with awful embraces,
  Our Lady of Pain ?

Where are they, Cotytto or Venus,
  Astarte or Ashtaroth, where ?
Do their hands as we touch come between
    us ?
  Is the breath of them hot in thy hair ?
From their lips have thy lips taken fever,
  With the blood of their bodies grown red ?
Hast thou left upon earth a believer
  If these men are dead ?

They were purple of raiment and golden,
  Filled full of thee, fiery with wine,
Thy lovers, in haunts unbeholden,
  In marvellous chambers of thine.
They are fled, and their footprints escape
    us,

Who appraise thee, adore, and abstain,
O daughter of Death and Priapus,
  Our Lady of Pain.

What ails us to fear overmeasure,
  To praise thee with timorous breath,
O mistress and mother of pleasure,
  The one thing as certain as death?
We shall change as the things that we
      cherish,
  Shall fade as they faded before,

As foam upon water shall perish
  As sand upon shore

We shall know what the darkness discovers,
  If the grave-pit be shallow or deep;
And our fathers of old, and our lovers,
  We shall know if they sleep not or sleep
We shall see whether hell be not heaven,
  Find out whether tares be not grain,
And the joys of thee seventy times seven,
  Our Lady of Pain.

THE GARDEN OF PROSERPINE.

HERE, where the world is quiet,
  Here, where all trouble seems
Dead winds' and spent waves' riot
  In doubtful dreams of dreams;
I watch the green field growing
For reaping folk and sowing,
For harvest time and mowing,
  A sleepy world of streams.

I am tired of tears and laughter,
  And men that laugh and weep
Of what may come hereafter
  For men that sow to reap:
I am weary of days and hours,
Blown buds of barren flowers,
Desires and dreams and powers
  And everything but sleep.

Here life has death for neighbor,
  And far from eye or ear
Wan waves and wet winds labor,
  Weak ships and spirits steer;
They drive adrift, and whither
They wot not who make thither;
But no such winds blow hither,
  And no such things grow here.

No growth of moor or coppice,
  No heather-flower or vine,

But bloomless buds of poppies,
  Green grapes of Proserpine,
Pale beds of blowing rushes
Where no leaf blooms or blushes,
Save this whereout she crushes
  For dead men deadly wine.

Pale, without name or number,
  In fruitless fields of corn,
They bow themselves and slumber
  All night till light is born;
And like a soul belated,
In hell and heaven unmated,
By cloud and mist abated
  Comes out of darkness morn.

Though one were strong as seven,
  He too with death shall dwell,
Nor wake with wings in heaven,
  Nor weep for pains in hell;
Though one were fair as roses,
His beauty clouds and closes;
And well though love reposes,
  In the end it is not well.

Pale, beyond porch and portal,
  Crowned with calm leaves, she stands
Who gathers all things mortal
  With cold immortal hands:

Her languid lips are sweeter
Than love's who fears to greet her
To men that mix and meet her
　　From many times and lands.

She waits for each and other,
　　She waits for all men born;
Forgets the earth her mother,
　　The life of fruits and corn;
And spring and seed and swallow
Take wing for her and follow
Where summer song rings hollow
　　And flowers are put to scorn.

There go the loves that wither,
　　The old loves with wearier wings;
And all dead years draw thither,
　　And all disastrous things;
Dead dreams of days forsaken
Blind buds that snows have shaken,
Wild leaves that winds have taken,
　　Red strays of ruined springs.

We are not sure of sorrow,
　　And joy was never sure;

To-day will die to-morrow;
　　Time stoops to no man's lure;
And love, grown faint and fretful
With lips but half regretful
Sighs, and with eyes forgetful
　　Weeps that no loves endure.

From too much love of living,
　　From hope and fear set free,
We thank with brief thanksgiving
　　Whatever gods may be
That no life lives for ever;
That dead men rise up never;
That even the weariest river
　　Winds somewhere safe to sea.

Then star nor sun shall waken,
　　Nor any change of light:
Nor sound of waters shaken,
　　Nor any sound or sight:
Nor wintry leaves nor vernal,
Nor days nor things diurnal;
Only the sleep eternal
　　In an eternal night.

HESPERIA.

OUT of the golden remote wild west where
　　the sea without shore is,
　　Full of the sunset, and sad, if at all, with
　　the fulness of joy,
As a wind sets in with the autumn that
　　blows from the region of stories,
　　Blows with a perfume of songs and of
　　memories beloved from a boy,
Blows from the capes of the past oversea to
　　the bays of the present,
　　Filled as with shadow of sound with the
　　pulse of invisible feet,
Far out to the shallows and straits of the
　　future, by rough ways or pleasant,

Is it thither the wind's wings beat? is it
　　hither to me, O my sweet?
For thee, in the stream of the deep tide-
　　wind blowing in with the water,
　　Thee I behold as a bird borne in with the
　　wind from the west,
Straight from the sunset, across white waves
　　whence rose as a daughter
　　Venus thy mother, in years when the
　　world was a water at rest.
Out of the distance of dreams, as a dream
　　that abides after slumber,
　　Strayed from the fugitive flock of the
　　night, when the moon overhead

Wanes in the wan waste heights of the
heaven, and stars without number
Die without sound, and are spent like
lamps that are burnt by the dead,
Comes back to me, stays by me, lulls me
with touch of forgotten caresses,
One warm dream clad about with a fire
as of life that endures;
The delight of thy face, and the sound of
thy feet, and the wind of thy tresses,
And all of a man that regrets, and all of
a maid that allures.

But thy bosom is warm for my face and
profound as a manifold flower,
Thy silence as music, thy voice as an
odor that fades in a flame;
Not a dream, not a dream is the kiss of thy
mouth, and the bountiful hour
That makes me forget what was sin, and
would make me forget were it shame.
Thine eyes that are quiet, thine hands that
are tender, thy lips that are loving,
Comfort and cool me as dew in the dawn
of a moon like a dream;
And my heart yearns baffled and blind,
moved vainly toward thee, and moving
As the refluent seaweed moves in the
languid exuberant stream,
Fair as a rose is on earth, as a rose under
water in prison,
That stretches and swings to the slow
passionate pulse of the sea,
Closed up from the air and the sun, but
alive, as a ghost re-arisen,
Pale as the love that revives as a ghost
re-arisen in me.
From the bountiful infinite west, from the
happy memorial places
Full of the stately repose and the lordly
delight of the dead,
Where the fortunate islands are lit with the
light of ineffable faces,
And the sound of a sea without wind is
about them, and sunset is red,
Come back to redeem and release me from
love that recalls and represses,
That cleaves to my flesh as a flame, till
the serpent has eaten his fill;
From the bitter delights of the dark, and
the feverish, the furtive caresses
That murder the youth in a man or ever
his heart have its will.

Thy lips cannot laugh and thine eyes cannot weep; thou art pale as a rose is,
Paler and sweeter than leaves that cover
the blush of the bud;
And the heart of the flower is compassion,
and pity the core it encloses,
Pity, not love, that is born of the breath
and decays with the blood.
As the cross that a wild nun clasps till the
edge of it bruises her bosom,
So love wounds as we grasp it, and
blackens and burns as a flame;
I have loved overmuch in my life: when the
live bud bursts with the blossom,
Bitter as ashes or tears is the fruit, and
the wine thereof shame.
As a heart that its anguish divides is the
green bud cloven asunder;
As the blood of a man self-slain is the
flush of the leaves that allure;
And the perfume as poison and wine to
the brain, a delight and a wonder;
And the thorns are too sharp for a boy,
too slight for a man, to endure.
Too soon did I love it, and lost love's rose;
and I cared not for glory's:
Only the blossoms of sleep and of plea-
sure were mixed in my hair.
Was it myrtle or poppy thy garland was
woven with, O my Dolores?
Was it pallor or slumber, or blush as of
blood, that I found in thee fair?
For desire is a respite from love, and the
flesh not the heart is her fuel;
She was sweet to me once, who am fled
and escaped from the rage of her
reign;
Who behold as of old time at hand as I
turn, with her mouth growing cruel,
And flushed as with wine with the blood
of her lovers,
Our Lady of Pain.
Low down where the thicket is thicker with
thorns than with leaves in the summer,
In the brake is a gleaming of eyes and a
hissing of tongues that I knew;
And the lithe long throats of her snakes
reach round her, their mouths overcome her,
And her lips grow cool with their foam,
made moist as a desert with dew.
With the thirst and the hunger of lust
though her beautiful lips be so bitter

With the cold foul foam of the snakes
    they soften and redden and smile;
And her fierce mouth sweetens, her eyes
    wax wide and her eyelashes glitter,
  And she laughs with a savor of blood in
    her face, and a savor of guile.
She laughs, and her hands reach hither, her
    hair blows hither and hisses,
As a low-lit flame in a wind, back-blown
    till it shudder and leap;
Let her lips not again lay hold on my soul,
    nor her poisonous kisses,
  To consume it alive and divide from thy
    bosom, Our Lady of Sleep.
Ah daughter of sunset and slumber, if now
    it return into prison,
  Who shall redeem it anew ? but we, if
    thou wilt, let us fly;
Let us take to us, now that the white skies
    thrill with a moon unarisen,
Swift horses of fear or of love, take flight
    and depart and not die.
They are swifter than dreams, they are
    stronger than death; there is none
    that hath ridden,
None that shall ride in the dim strange
    ways of his life as we ride:

By the meadows of memory, the highlands
    of hope, and the shore that is hidden,
Where life breaks loud and unseen, a
    sonorous invisible tide;
By the sands where sorrow has trodden,
    the salt pools bitter and sterile,
  By the thundering reef and the low sea-
    wall and the channel of years,
Our wild steeds press on the night, strain
    hard through pleasure and peril,
  Labor and listen and pant not or pause
    for the peril that nears;
And the sound of them trampling the way
    cleaves night as an arrow asunder,
  And slow by the sand-hill and swift by
    the down with its glimpses of grass
Sudden and steady the music, as eight hoofs
    trample and thunder,
  Rings in the ear of the low blind wind of
    the night as we pass;
Shrill shrieks in our faces the blind bland
    air that was mute as a maiden,
  Stung into storm by the speed of our
    passage, and deaf where we past;
And our spirits too burn as we bound, thine
    holy but mine heavy-laden,
As we burn with the fire of our flight ; ah,
    love, shall we win at the last ?

LOVE AT SEA.

WE are in love's land to-day;
    Where shall we go ?
Love, shall we start or stay,
    Or sail or row ?
There's many a wind and way,
And never a May but May;
We are in love's hand to-day;
    Where shall we go ?

Our landwind is the breath
Of sorrows kissed to death
    And joys that were;

Our ballast is a rose;
Our way lies where God knows
    And love knows where.
        We are in love's hand to-day—

Our seamen are fledged Loves,
Our masts are bills of doves,
    Our decks fine gold;
Our ropes are dead maids' hair,
Our stores are love-shafts fair
    And manifold.
        We are in love's land to-day—

Where shall we land you, sweet?
On fields of strange men's feet,
   Or fields near home?
Or where the fire-flowers blow,
Or where the flowers of snow
   Or flowers of foam?
      We are in love's hand to-day—

Land me, she says, where love
Shows but one shaft, one dove,
   One heart, one hand.
—A shore like that, my dear,
Lies where no man will steer,
   No maiden land.
      Imitated from Theophile Gautier.

APRIL

FROM THE FRENCH OF THE VIDAME DE CHARTRES.

12—?

WHEN the fields catch flower
   And the underwood is green,
And from bower unto bower
   The songs of the birds begin,
   I sing with sighing between.
When I laugh and sing,
   I am heavy at heart for my sin;
I am sad in the spring
   For my love that I shall not win,
For a foolish thing.

This profit I have of my woe,
   That I know, as I sing,
I know he will needs have it so
   Who is master and king,
   Who is lord of the spirit of spring.
I will serve her and will not spare
   Till her pity awake
Who is good, who is pure, who is fair,
   Even her for whose sake
Love hath ta'en me and slain unaware.

O my Lord, O Love,
   I have laid my life at thy feet;
Have thy will thereof,
   Do as it please thee with it,
   For what shall please thee is sweet.
I am come unto thee
   To do thee service, O Love;

Yet cannot I see
   Thou wilt take any pity thereof,
Any mercy on me.

But the grace I have long time sought
   Comes never in sight,
If in her it abideth not,
   Through thy mercy and might,
   Whose heart is the world's delight.
Thou hast sworn without fail I shall die,
   For my heart is set
On what hurts me, I wot not why,
   But cannot forget
What I love, what I sing for and sigh.

She is worthy of praise,
   For this grief of her giving is worth
All the joy of my days
   That lie between death's day and birth
   All the lordship of things upon earth.
Nay, what have I said?
   I would not be glad if I could;
My dream and my dread
   Are of her, and for her sake I would
That my life were fled.

Lo, sweet, if I durst not pray to you,
   Then were I dead;
If I sang not a little to say to you,
   (Could it be said)
   O my love, how my heart would be fed;

Ah sweet who hast hold of my heart
　For thy love's sake I live,
Do but tell me, ere either depart,
　What a lover may give

For a woman so fair as thou art.
The lovers that disbelieve,
　False rumors shall grieve
And evil-speaking shall part.

BEFORE PARTING.

A MONTH or twain to live on honeycomb
Is pleasant; but one tires of scented time,
Cold sweet recurrence of accepted rhyme,
And that strong purple under juice and
　foam
Where the wine's heart has burst;
Nor feel the latter kisses like the first.

Once yet, this poor one time; I will not
　pray
Even to change the bitterness of it,
The bitter taste ensuing on the sweet,
To make your tears fall where your soft hair
　lay
All blurred and heavy in some perfumed
　wise
Over my face and eyes.

And yet who knows what end the scythed
　wheat
Makes of its foolish poppies' mouths of
　red ?
These were not sown, these are not har-
　vested,
They grow a month and are cast under feet
And none has care thereof,
As none has care of a divided love.

I know each shadow of your lips by rote,
Each change of love in eyelids and eye-
　brows;
The fashion of fair temples tremulous
With tender blood, and color of your throat;
I know not how love is gone out of this,
Seeing that all was his.

Love's likeness there endures upon all
　these:
But out of these one shall not gather love.
Day hath not strength nor the night shade
　enough
To make love whole and fill his lips with
　ease,
As some bee-builded cell
Feels at filled lips the heavy honey swell.

I know not how this last month leaves your
　hair
Less full of purple color and hid spice,
And that luxurious trouble of closed eyes
Is mixed with meaner shadow and waste
　care;
And love, kissed out by pleasure, seems not
　yet
Worth patience to regret.

THE SUNDEW.

A LITTLE marsh-plant, yellow green,
And pricked at lip with tender red.
Tread close, and either way you tread
Some faint black water jets between
Lest you should bruise the curious head.

A live thing may be; who shall know?
The summer knows and suffers it;
For the cool moss is thick and sweet
Each side, and saves the blossom so
That it lives out the long June heat.

The deep scent of the heather burns
About it; breathless though it be,
Bow down and worship; more than we,
Is the least flower whose life returns,
Least weed renascent in the sea.

We are vexed and cumbered in earth's sight
With wants, with many memories;
These see their mother what she is,
Glad-growing, till August leave more bright
The apple-colored cranberries.

Wind blows and bleaches the strong grass,
Blown all one way to shelter it
From trample of strayed kine, with feet

Felt heavier than the moorhen was,
Strayed up past patches of wild wheat

You call it sundew: how it grows,
If with its color it have breath,
If life taste sweet to it, if death
Pain its soft petal, no man knows:
Man has no sight or sense that saith.

My sundew, grown of gentle days,
In these green miles the spring begun
Thy growth ere April had half done
With the soft secret of her ways
Or June made ready for the sun.

O red-lipped mouth of marsh-flower,
I have a secret halved with thee.
The name that is love's name to me
Thou knowest, and the face of her
Who is my festival to see.

The hard sun, as thy petals knew,
Colored the heavy moss-water:
Thou wert not worth green midsummer
Nor fit to live to August blue,
O sundew, not remembering her.

FÉLISE.

Mais où sont les neiges d'antan.

WHAT shall be said between us here,
  Among the downs, between the trees,
In fields that knew our feet last year,
  In sight of quiet sands and seas,
  This year, Félisé?

Who knows what word were best to say?
  For last year's leaves lie dead and red
On this sweet day, in this green May,

E

And barren corn makes bitter bread.
What shall be said?

Here as last year the fields begin,
  A fire of flowers and glowing grass;
The old fields we laughed and lingered in,
  Seeing each our souls in last year's glass,
  Félisé, alas!

Shall we not laugh, shall we not weep,
  Not we, though this be as it is?
For love awake or love asleep
  Ends in a laugh, a dream, a kiss,
  A song like this.

I that have slept awake, and you
  Sleep, who last year were well awake.
Though love do all that love can do,
  My heart will never ache or break
  For your heart's sake.

The great sea, faultless as a flower,
  Throbs, trembling under beam and
    breeze,
And laughs with love of the amorous hour.
  I found you fairer once, Félise,
  Than flowers or seas.

We played at bondsman and at queen;
  But as the days change men change too;
I find the grey sea's notes of green,
  The green sea's fervent flakes of blue,
  More fair than you.

Your beauty is not over fair
  Now in mine eyes, who am grown up
    wise.
The smell of flowers in all your hair
  Allures not now; no sigh replies
  If your heart sighs.

But you sigh seldom, you sleep sound,
  You find love's new name good enough.
Less sweet I find it than I found
  The sweetest name that ever love
  Grew weary of.

My snake with bright bland eyes, my snake
  Grown tame and glad to be caressed.
With lips athirst for mine to slake
  Their tender fever! who had guessed
  You loved me best?

I had died for this last year, to know
  You loved me.   Who shall turn on fate?
I care not if love come or go
  Now, though your love seek mine for
    mate.
  It is too late.

The dust of many strange desires
  Lies deep between us; in our eyes
Dead smoke of perishable fires
  Flickers, a fume in air and skies,
  A steam of sighs.

You loved me and you loved me not;
  A little, much, and overmuch.
Will you forget as I forgot?
  Let all dead things lie dead; none such
  Are soft to touch.

I love you and I do not love,
  Too much, a little, not at all;
Too much, and never yet enough.
  Birds quick to fledge and fly at call
  Are quick to fall.

And these love longer now than men,
  And larger loves than ours are these.
No diver brings up love again
  Dropped once, my beautiful Félise,
  In such cold seas.

Gone deeper than all plummets sound,
  Where in the dim green dayless day
The life of such dead thing lies bound
  As the sea feeds on, wreck and stray
  And castaway.

Can I forget? yea, that can I,
  And that can all men; so will you,
Alive, or later, when you die,
  Ah, but the love you plead was true?
  Was mine not too?

I loved you for that name of yours
  Long ere we met, and long enough.
Now that one thing of all endures—
  The sweetest name that ever love
  Waxed weary of.

Like colors in the sea, like flowers,
  Like a cat's splendid circled eyes
That wax and wane with love for hours,
  Green as green flame, blue-grey like skies,
  And soft like sighs—

And all these only like your name,
  And your name full of all of these.
I say it, and it sounds the same—
  Save that I say it now at ease,
  Your name, Félise.

I said " she must be swift and white
  And subtly warm, and half perverse
And sweet like sharp soft fruit to bite,
  And like a snake's love lithe and fierce."
  Men have guessed worse.

What was the song I made of you
  Here where the grass forgets our feet
As afternoon forgets the dew ?
Ah that such sweet things should be fleet,
  Such fleet things sweet !

As afternoon forgets the dew,
  As time in time forgets all men,
As our old place forgets us two,
  Who might have turned to one thing
     then,
  But not again.

O lips that mine have grown into
  Like April's kissing May,
O fervent eyelids letting through
Those eyes the greenest of things blue,
  The bluest of things grey,

If you were I and I were you,
  How could I love you, say ?
How could the roseleaf love the rue,
The day love nightfall and her dew,
  Though night may love the day ?

You loved it may be more than I;
  We know not; love is hard to seize,
And all things are not good to try;
  And lifelong loves the worst of these
  For us, Félise.

Ah, take the season and have done,
  Love well the hour and let it go:
Two souls may sleep and wake up one,
  Or dream they wake and find it so,
  And then—you know.

Kiss me once hard as though a flame
  Lay on my lips and made them fire;
The same lips now, and not the same;
  What breath shall fill and re-inspire
  A dead desire ?

The old song sounds hollower in mine ear
  Than thin keen sounds of dead men's
     speech—
A noise one hears and would not hear;
  Too strong to die, too weak to reach
  From wave to beach.

We stand on either side the sea,
  Stretch hands, blow kisses, laugh and
     lean
I toward you, you toward me;
  But what hears either save the keen
  Grey sea between ?

A year divides us, love from love,
  Though you loved now, though **I** loved
    then.
The gulf is strait, but deep enough ;
  Who shall recross, who among men
  Shall cross again ?

Love was a jest last year, you said,
  And what lives surely, surely dies.
Even so ; but now that love is dead,
  Shall love rekindle from wet eyes,
  From subtle sighs ?

For many loves are good to see;
  Mutable loves, and loves perverse;
But there is nothing, nor shall be,
  So sweet, so wicked, but my verse
  Can dream of worse.

For we that sing and you that love
  Know that which man may, only we.
The rest live under us; above,
  Live the great gods in heaven, and see
  What things shall be.

So this thing is and must be so;
  For man dies, and love also dies.
Though yet love's ghost moves to and fro
  The sea-green mirrors of your eyes,
  And laughs, and lies.

Eyes colored like a water-flower,
  And deeper than the green sea's glass;
Eyes that remember one sweet hour—
  In vain we swore it should not pass;
  In vain, alas !

Ah my Félise, if love or sin,
  If shame or fear could hold it fast,
Should we not hold it ? Love wears thin,
  And they laugh well who laugh the last.
  Is it not past ?

The gods, the gods are stronger; time
  Falls down before them, all men's knees
Bow, all men's prayers and sorrows climb
  Like incense towards them; yea, for
    these
  Are gods, Félise.

Immortal are they, clothed with powers,
  Not to be comforted at all;
Lords over all the fruitless hours;
  Too great to appease, too high to appal,
  Too far to call.

For none shall move the most high gods,
  Who are most sad, being cruel; none
Shall break or take away the rods
  Wherewith they scourge us, not as one
    That smites a son.

By many a name of many a creed
  We have called upon them, since the
    sands
Fell through time's hour-glass first, a seed
  Of life; and out of many lands
    Have we stretched hands.

When have they heard us? who hath
    known
  Their faces, climbed unto their feet,
Felt them and found them? Laugh or
    groan,
  Doth heaven remurmur and repeat
    Sad sounds or sweet?

Do the stars answer? in the night
  Have ye found comfort? or by day
Have ye seen gods? What hope, what light,
  Falls from the farthest starriest way
    On you that pray?

Are the skies wet because we weep,
  Or fair because of any mirth?
Cry out; they are gods; perchance they
    sleep;
  Cry; thou shalt know what prayers are
    worth,
    Thou dust and earth.

O earth, thou art fair; O dust, thou art
    great
  O laughing lips and lips that mourn,
Pray, till ye feel the exceeding weight
  Of God's intolerable scorn,
    Not to be borne.

Behold, there is no grief like this;
  The barren blossom of thy prayer,
Thou shalt find out how sweet it is.
  O fools and blind, what seek ye there,
    High up in the air?

Ye must have gods, the friends of men,
  Merciful gods, compassionate,
And these shall answer you again.
  Will ye beat always at the gate,
    Ye fools of fate?

Ye fools and blind; for this is sure,
  That all ye shall not live, but die.
Lo, what thing have ye found endure?
  Or what thing have have ye found on
    high
    Past the blind sky?

The ghosts of words and dusty dreams,
  Old memories, faiths infirm and dead.
Ye fools; for which among you deems
  His prayer can alter green to red
    Or stones to bread?

Why should ye bear with hopes and fears
  Till all these things be drawn in one,
The sound of iron-footed years,
  And all the oppression that is done
    Under the sun?

Ye might end surely, surely pass
  Out of the multitude of things,
Under the dust, beneath the grass,
  Deep in dim death, where no thought
    stings,
    No record clings.

No memory more of love or hate,
  No trouble, nothing that aspires,
No sleeplesss labor thwarting fate,
  And thwarted; where no travail tires,
    Where no faith fires.

All passes, nought that has been is,
  Things good and evil have one end.
Can anything be otherwise
  Though all men swear all things would
    mend
    With God to friend?

Can ye beat off one wave with prayer,
  Can ye move mountains? bid the flower
Take flight and turn to a bird in the air?
  Can ye hold fast for shine or shower
    One wingless hour?

Ah sweet, and we too, can we bring
  One sigh back, bid one smile revive?
Can God restore one ruined thing,
  Or he who slays our souls alive
    Make dead things thrive?

Two gifts perforce he has given us yet,
  Though sad things stay and glad things
    fly;
Two gifts he has given us, to forget
  All glad and sad things that go by,
  And then to die.

We know not whether death be good,
  But life at least it will not be :
Men will stand saddening as we stood,
  Watch the same fields and skies as we
  And the same sea.

Let this be said between us here,
  One love grows green when one turns
    grey;
This year knows nothing of last year;
  To-morrow has no more to say
  To yesterday.

Live and let live, as I will do,
  Love and let love, and so will I.
But, sweet, for me no more with you :
  Not while I live, not though I die.
  Good-night, good-bye.

AN INTERLUDE.

In the greenest growth of the Maytime,
  I rode where the woods were wet,
Between the dawn and the daytime;
  The spring was glad that we met.

There was something the season wanted,
  Though the ways and the woods smelt
    sweet;
The breath at your lips that panted,
  The pulse of the grass at your feet.

You came, and the sun came after,
  And the green grew golden above;
And the flag-flowers lightened with laugh-
    ter,
  And the meadow sweet shook with love.

Your feet in the full-grown grasses
  Moved soft as a weak wind blows;
You passed me as April passes,
  With face made out of a rose.

By the stream where the stems were slender,
  Your bright foot paused at the sedge;
It might be to watch the tender
  Light leaves in the springtime hedge.

On boughs that the sweet month blanches,
  With flowery frost of May :
It might be a bird in the branches,
  It might be a thorn in the way.

I waited to watch you linger
  With foot drawn back from the dew,
Till a sunbeam straight like a finger
  Struck sharp through the leaves at you

And a bird overhead sang *Follow*,
  And a bird to the right sang *Here*;
And the arch of the leaves was hollow,
  And the meaning of May was clear.

I saw where the sun's hand pointed,
  I knew what the bird's note said;
By the dawn and the dewfall anointed,
You were queen by the gold on your head.

As the glimpse of a burnt-out ember
  Recalls a regret of the sun,
I remember, forget, and remember
  What Love saw done and undone.

I remember the way we parted,
  The day and the way we met;
You hoped we were both broken-hearted,
  And knew we should both forget.

And May with her world in flower
  Seemed still to murmur and smile
As you murmured and smiled for an hour;
  I saw you turn at the stile.

6

A hand like a white wood-blossom
  You lifted, and waved, and passed,
With head hung down to the bosom,
And pale, as it seemed, at last.

And the best and the worst of this is
  That neither is most to blame
If you've forgotten my kisses
  And I've forgotten your name.

HENDECASYLLABICS.

In the month of the long decline of roses
I, beholding the summer dead before me,
Set my face to the sea and journeyed silent,
Gazing eagerly where above the sea-mark
Flame as fierce as the fervid eyes of lions
Half divided the eyelids of the sunset;
Till I heard as it were a noise of waters
Moving tremulous under feet of angels
Multitudinous, out of all the heavens;
Knew the fluttering wind, the fluttered
  foliage,
Shaken fitfully, full of sound and shadow;
And saw, trodden upon by noiseless angels,
Long mysterious reaches fed with moon-
  light,
Sweet sad straits in a soft subsiding
  channel,
Blown about by the lips of winds I knew
  not,
Winds not born in the north nor any
  quarter,
Winds not warm with the south nor any
  sunshine;
Heard between them a voice of exultation,
" Lo, the summer is dead, the sun is faded,
Even like as a leaf the year is withered,

All the fruits of the day from all her
  branches
Gathered, neither is any left to gather.
All the flowers are dead, the tender blos-
  soms,
All are taken away ; the season wasted,
Like an ember among the fallen ashes.
Now with light of the winter days, with
  moonlight,
Light of snow, and the bitter light of hoar-
  frost,
We bring flowers that fade not after autumn,
Pale white chaplets and crowns of latter
  seasons,
Fair false leaves (but the summer leaves
  were falser,)
Woven under the eyes of stars and planets
When low light was upon the windy reaches
Where the flower of foam was blown, a lily
Dropt among the sonorous fruitless furrows
And green fields of the sea that make no
  pasture:
Since the winter begins, the weeping winter,
All whose flowers are tears, and round his
  temples
Iron blossom of frost is bound for ever."

SAPPHICS.

All the night sleep came not upon my eyelids,
Shed not dew, nor shook nor unclosed a
  feather,
Yet with lips shut close and with eyes of
  iron
    Stood and beheld me.

Then to me so lying awake a vision
Came without sleep over the seas and
  touched me,
Softly touched mine eyelids and lips; and I
  too,
    Full of the vision,

Saw the white implacable Aphrodite,
Saw the hair unbound, and the feet un-
        sandalled
Shine as fire of sunset on western waters;
    Saw the reluctant

Feet, the straining plumes of the doves
        that drew her,
Looking always, looking with necks re-
        verted,
Back to Lesbos, back to the hills where-
        under
    Shone Mitylene;

Heard the flying feet of the Loves behind
        her
Make a sudden thunder upon the waters,
As the thunder flung from the strong un-
        closing
    Wings of a great wind.

So the goddess fled from her place, with
        awful
Sound of feet and thunder of wings around
        her;
While behind a clamour of singing women
    Severed the twilight.

Ah the singing, ah the delight, the passion!
All the Loves wept, listening; sick with
        anguish,
Stood the crowned nine Muses about Apollo;
    Fear was upon them,

While the tenth sang wonderful things they
        knew not.
Ah the tenth, the Lesbian ! the nine were
        silent,
None endured the sound of her song for
        weeping;
    Laurel by laurel,

Faded all their crowns; but about her fore-
        head,
Round her woven tresses and ashen temples
White as dead snow, paler than grass in
        summer,
    Ravaged with kisses,

Shone a light of fire as a crown for ever.
Yea, almost the implacable Aphrodite
Paused, and almost wept; such a song was
        that song,
    Yea, by her name too

Called her, saying, "Turn to me, O my
        Sappho;"
Yet she turned her face from the Loves, she
        saw not
Tears or laughter darken immortal eyelids,
    Heard not about her

Fearful fitful wings of the doves departing,
Saw not how the bosom of Aphrodite
Shook with weeping, saw not her shaken
        raiment,
    Saw not her hands wrung;

Saw the Lesbians kissing across their
        smitten
Lutes with lips more sweet than the sound
        of lute-strings,
Mouth to mouth and hand upon hand, her
        chosen,
    Fairer than all men;

Only saw the beautiful lips and fingers,
Full of songs and kisses and little whispers,
Full of music; only beheld among them
    Soar, as a bird soars

Newly fledged, her visible song, a marvel,
Made of perfect sound and exceeding
        passion,
Sweetly shapen, terrible, full of thunders,
    Clothed with the wind's wings.

Then rejoiced she, laughing with love, and
        scattered
Roses, awful roses of holy blossom;
Then the Loves thronged sadly with hidden
        faces
    Round Aphrodite,

Then the Muses, stricken at heart, were
        silent;
Yea, the gods waxed pale; such a song
        was that song.
All reluctant, all with a fresh repulsion,
    Fled from before her.

All withdrew long since, and the land was
        barren,
Full of fruitless women and music only.
Now perchance, when winds are assuaged
        at sunset,
    Lulled at the dewfall,

the grey sea-side, unassuaged, unheard of,
Unbeloved, unseen in the ebb of twilight,
Ghosts of outcast women return lamenting,
Purged not in Lethe,

Clothed about with flame and with tears, and singing
Songs that move the heart of the shaken heaven,
Songs that break the heart of the earth with pity,
Hearing, to hear them.

AT ELEUSIS.

MEN of Eleusis, ye that with long staves
Sit in the market-houses, and speak words
Made sweet with wisdom as the rare wine is
Thickened with honey; and ye sons of these
Who in the glad thick streets go up and down
For pastime or grave traffic or mere chance;
And all fair women having rings of gold
On hands or hair; and chiefest over these
I name you, daughters of this man the king,
Who dipping deep smooth pitchers of pure brass
Under the bubbled wells, till each round lip
Stooped with loose gurgle of waters incoming,
Found me an old sick woman, lamed and lean,
Beside a growth of builded olive boughs
Whence multiplied thick song of thick-plumed throats—
Also wet tears filled up my hollow hands
By reason of my crying into them—
And pitied me ; for as cold water ran
And washed the pitchers full frcm lip to lip,
So washed both eyes full the strong salt of tears.
And ye put water to my mouth, made sweet
With brown hill-berries; so in time I spoke
And gathered my loose knees from under me.
Moreover in the broad fair halls this month
Have I found space and bountiful abode
To please me.   I Demeter speak of this,
Who am the mother and the mate of things:
For as ill men by drugs or singing words

Shut the doors inward of the narrowed womb
Like a lock bolted with round iron through,
Thus I shut up the body and sweet mouth
Of all soft pasture and the tender land,
So that no seed can enter in by it
Though one sow thickly, nor some grain get out
Past the hard clods men cleave and bite with steel
To widen the sealed lips of them for use.
None of you is there in the peopled street
But knows how all the dry-drawn furrows ache
With no green spot made count of in the black:
How the wind finds no comfortable grass
Nor is assuaged with bud nor breath of herbs;
And in hot autumn when ye house the stacks,
All fields are helpless in the sun, all trees
Stand as a man stripped out of all but skin.
Nevertheless ye sick have help to get
By means and stablished ordinance of God;
For God is wiser than a good man is.
But never shall new grass be sweet in earth
Till I get righted of my wound and wrong
By changing counsel of ill-minded Zeus.
For of all other gods is none save me
Clothed with like power to build and break the year.
I make the lesser green begin, when spring
Touches not earth but with one fearful foot;
And as a careful gilder with grave art
Soberly colors and completes the face,

Mouth, chin and all, of some sweet work
    in stone,
I carve the shapes of grass and tender corn
And color the ripe edges and long spikes
With the red increase and the grace of gold.
No tradesman in soft wools is cunninger
To kill the secret of the fat white fleece
With stains of blue and purple wrought in it.
Three moons were made and three moons
    burnt away
While I held journey hither out of Crete
Comfortless, tended by grave Hecate
Whom my wound stung with double iron
    point;
For all my face was like a cloth wrung out
With close and weeping wrinkles, and both
    lids
Sodden with salt continuance of tears.
For Hades and the sidelong will of Zeus
And that lame wisdom that has writhen
    feet,
Cunning, begotten in the bed of Shame,
These three took evil will at me, and made
Such counsel that when time got wing to fly
This Hades out of summer and low fields
Forced the bright body of Persephone:
Out of pure grass, where she lying down,
    red flowers
Made their sharp little shadows on her
    sides,
Pale heat, pale color on pale maiden flesh—
And chill water slid over her reddening
    feet,
Killing the throbs in their soft blood; and
    birds,
Perched next her elbow and pecking at
    her hair,
Stretched their necks more to see her than
    even to sing.
A sharp thing is it I have need to say;
For Hades holding both white wrists of
    hers
Unloosed the girdle and with knot by knot
Bound her between his wheels upon the
    seat,
Bound her pure body, holiest yet and dear
To me and God as always, clothed about
With blossoms loosened as her knees went
    down,
Let fall as she let go of this and this
By tens and twenties, tumbled to her feet,
White waifs or purple of the pasturage.
Therefore with only going up and down
My feet were wasted, and the gracious air,
To me discomfortable and dun, became

As weak smoke blowing in the under world.
And finding in the process of ill days
What part had Zeus herein and how as
    mate
He coped with Hades, yokefellow in sin,
I set my lips against the meat of gods
And drank not, neither ate nor slept in
    heaven.
Nor in the golden greeting of their mouths
Did ear take note of me, nor eye at all
Track my feet going in the ways of them.
Like a great fire on some strait slip of land
Between two washing inlets of wet sea
That burns the grass up to each lip of
    beach
And strengthens, waxing in the growth of
    wind
So burnt my soul in me at heaven and
    earth,
Each way a ruin and a hungry plague,
Visible evil; nor could any night
Put cool between mine eyelids, nor the sun
With competence of gold fill out my want.
Yea so my flame burnt up the grass and
    stones,
Shone to the salt-white edges of thin sea,
Distempered all the gracious work, and
    made
Sick change, unseasonable increase of days
And scant avail of seasons; for by this
The fair gods faint in hollow heaven: there
    comes
No taste of burnings of the twofold fat
To leave their palates smooth, nor in their
    lips
Soft rings of smoke and weak scent wander-
    ing;
All cattle waste and rot, and their ill smell
Grows alway from the lank unsavory flesh,
That no man slays for offering; the sea
And waters moved beneath the heath and
    corn
Preserve the people of fin-twinkling fish,
And river-flies feed thick upon the smooth;
But all earth over is no man or bird
(Except the sweet race of the kingfisher)
That lacks not and is wearied with much
    loss.
Meantime the purple inward of the house
Was softened with all grace of scent and
    sound
In ear and nostril perfecting my praise;
Faint grape-flowers and cloven honey-cake
And the just grain with dues of the shed
    salt

Made me content: yet my hand loosened not
Its gripe upon your harvest all year long.
While I, thus woman-muffled in wan flesh
And waste externals of a perished face,
Preserved the levels of my wrath and love
Patiently ruled; and with soft offices
Cooled the sharp noons and busied the
    warm nights
In care of this my choice, this child my
    choice,
Triptolemus, the king's selected son:
That this fair yearlong body, which hath
    grown
Strong with strange milk upon the mortal
    lip
And nerved with half a god, might so in-
    crease
Outside the bulk and the bare scope of
    man:
And waxen over large to hold within
Base breath of yours and this impoverished
    air,
I might exalt him past the flame of stars,
The limit and walled reach of the great
    world.
Therefore my breast made common to his
    mouth
Immortal savors, and the taste whereat
Twice their hard life strains out the colored
    veins
And twice its brain confirms the narrow
    shell.
Also at night, unwinding cloth from cloth
As who unhusks an almond to the white
And pastures curiously the purer taste,
I bared the gracious limbs and the soft feet,
Unswaddled the weak hands, and in mid
    ash
Laid the sweet flesh of either feeble side,
More tender for impressure of some touch
Than wax to any pen; and lit around
Fire, and made crawl the white worm-
    shapen flame,
And leap in little angers spark by spark
At head at once and feet; and the faint hair
Hissed with rare sprinkles in the closer
    curl,
And like scaled oarage of a keen thin fish
In sea-water, so in pure fire his feet
Struck out, and the flame bit not in his
    flesh
But like a kiss it curled his lip, and heat
Fluttered his eyelids; so each night I blew
The hot ash red to purge him to full god.
Ill is it when fear hungers in the soul

For painful food, and chokes thereon, being
    fed;
And ill slant eyes interpret the straight sun,
But in their scope its white is wried to
    black:
By the queen Metaneira mean I this;
For with sick wrath upon her lips and
    heart,
Narrowing with fear the spleenful passages,
She thought to thread this webs's fine ravel
    out,
Nor leave her shuttle split in combing it;
Therefore she stole on us, and with hard
    sight
Peered, and stooped close; then with pale
    open mouth
As the fire smote her in the eyes between
Cried, and the child's laugh sharply short-
    ening
As fire doth under rain, fell off; the flame
Writhed once all through and died, and in
    thick dark
Tears fell from mine on the child's weep-
    ing eyes,
Eyes dispossessed of strong inheritance
And mortal fallen anew. Who not the less
From bud of beard to pale-grey flower of
    hair
Shall wax vinewise to a lordly vine, whose
    grapes
Bleed the red heavy blood of swoln soft
    wine,
Subtle with sharp leaves' intricacy, until
Full of white years and blossom of hoary
    days
I take him perfected; for whose one sake
I am thus gracious to the least who stands
Filleted with white wool and girt upon
As he whose prayer endures upon the lip
And falls not waste: wherefore let sacrifice
Burn and run red in all the wider ways;
Seeing I have sworn by the pale temples'
    band
And poppied hair of gold Persephone
Sad-tressed and pleached low down about
    her brows,
And by the sorrow in her lips and death
Her dumb and mournful-mouthéd minister,
My word for you is eased of its harsh weight
And doubled with soft promise; and your
    king
Triptolemus, this Celeus dead and swathed
Purple and pale for golden burial,
Shall be your helper in my services,
Dividing earth and reaping fruits thereof

In fields where wait, well girt, well-
wreathen, all
The heavy-handed seasons all year through;
Saving the choice of warm spear-headed
grain,

And stooping sharp to the slant-sided share
All beasts that furrow the remeasured
land
With their bowed necks of burden equable.

AUGUST

THERE were four apples on the bough,
Half gold half red, that one might know
The blood was ripe inside the core;
The color of the leaves was more
Like stems of yellow corn that grow
Through all the gold June meadow's floor.

The warm smell of the fruit was good
To feed on, and the split green wood,
With all its bearded lips and stains
Of mosses in the cloven veins,
Most pleasant, if one lay or stood
In sunshine or in happy rains.

There were four apples on the tree,
Red stained through gold, that all might
see
The sun went warm from core to rind;
The green leaves made the summer blind
In that soft place they kept for me
With golden apples shut behind.

The leaves caught gold across the sun
And where the bluest air begun,
Thirsted for song to help the heat;
As I to feel my lady's feet
Draw close before the day were done;
Both lips grew dry with dreams of it.

In the mute August afternoon
They trembled to some undertune
Of music in the silver air;
Great pleasure was it to be there
Till green turned duskier and the moon
Colored the corn-sheaves like gold hair.

That August time it was delight
To watch the red moons wane to white
'Twixt grey seamed stems of apple-trees;
A sense of heavy harmonies
Grew on the growth of patient night,
More sweet than shapen music is.

But some three hours before the moon
The air, still eager from the noon,
Flagged after heat, not wholly dead;
Against the stem I leant my head;
The color soothed me like a tune,
Green leaves all round the gold and red.

I lay there till the warm smell grew
More sharp, when flecks of yellow dew
Between the round ripe leaves had blurred
The rind with stain and wet; I heard
A wind that blew and breathed and blew,
Too weak to alter its one word.

The wet leaves next the gentle fruit
Felt smoother, and the brown tree-root
Felt the mould warmer: I too felt
(As water feels the slow gold melt
Right throught it when the day burns mute)
The peace of time wherein love dwelt.

There were four apples on the tree,
Gold stained on red that all might see
The sweet blood filled them to the core:
The color of her hair is more
Like stems of fair faint gold, that be
Mown from the harvest's middle-floor.

A CHRISTMAS CAROL.*

THREE damsels in the queen's chamber,
    The queen's mouth was most fair;
She spake a word of God's mother
    As the combs went in her hair.
      Mary that is of might,
      Bring us to thy Son's sight.

They held the gold combs out from her,
    A span's length off her head;
She sang this song of God's mother
    And of her bearing-bed.
      Mary most full of grace,
      Bring us to thy Son's face.

When she sat at Joseph's hand,
    She looked against her side;
And either way from the short silk band
    Her girdle was all wried.
      Mary that all good may,
      Bring us to thy Son's way.

Mary had three women for her bed,
    The twain were maiden's clean;
Tne first of them had white and red,
    The third had riven green.
      Mary that is so sweet,
      Bring us to thy Son's feet.

She had three women for her hair,
    Two were gloved soft and shod;
The third had feet and fingers bare,
    She was the likest God.
      Mary that wieldeth land,
      Bring us to thy Son's hand.

She had three woman for her ease,
    The twain were good women:
The first two were the two Maries,
    The third was Magdalen.
      Mary that perfect is,
      Bring us to thy Son's kiss.

Joseph had three workmen in his stall,
    To serve him well upon;
The first of them were Peter and Paul,
      The third of them was John.
      Mary, God's handmaiden,
      Bring us to thy Son's ken.

"If your child be none other man's,
    But if it be very mine,
The bedstead shall be gold two spans,
    The bedfoot silver fine."
      Mary that made God mirth,
      Bring us to thy Son's birth.

"If the child be some other man's,
    And if it be none of mine,
The manger shall bestraw two spans,
    Betwixen kine and kine."
      Mary that made sin cease,
      Bring us to thy Son's peace.

Christ was born upon this wise,
    It fell on such a night,
Neither with sounds of psalteries,
    Nor with fire for light.
      Mary that is God's spouse,
      Bring us to thy Son's house.

The star came out upon the east
    With a great sound and sweet·
Kings gave gold to make him feast
    And myrrh for him to eat.
      Mary, of thy sweet mood,
      Bring us to thy Son's good.

He had two handmaids at his head,
    One handmaid at his feet;
The twain of them were fair and red
    The third one was right sweet.
      Mary that is most wise,
      Bring us to thy Son's eyes. Amen.

---

* Suggested by a drawing of Mr. D. G. Rossetti's.

THE MASQUE OF QUEEN BERSABE.

A MIRACLE-PLAY

KING DAVID.

KNIGHTS mine, all that be in hall,
I have a council to you all,
Because of this thing God lets fall
    Among us for a sign.
For some days hence as I did eat
From kingly dishes my good meat,
There flew a bird between my feet
    As red as any wine.
This bird had a long bill of red
And a gold ring above his head;
Long time he sat and nothing said,
Put softly down his neck and fed
    From the gilt patens fine:
And as I marvelled at the last
He shut his two keen eyën fast
And suddenly woxe big and brast
    Ere one should tell to nine.

PRIMUS MILES.

Sir, note this that I will say;
That Lord who maketh corn with hay
And morrows each of yesterday,
    He hath you in his hand.

SECUNDUS MILES (*Paganus quidam*).

By Satan I hold no such thing;
For if wine swell within a king
Whose ears for drink are hot and ring,
The same shall dream of wine-bibbing
    Whilst he can lie or stand.

QUEEN BERSABE.

Peace now, lords, for God is head.
Ye chirk as starlings that be fed
And gape as fishes newly dead;
The devil put your bones to bed,
    Lo, this is all to say.

SECUNDUS MILES.

By Mahound, lords, I have good will
This devil's bird to wring and spill;
For now meseems our game goes ill,
    Ye have scant hearts to play.

TERTIUS MILES.

Lo, sirs, this word is there said,
That Urias the knight is dead
Through some ill craft; by Poulis head,
I doubt his blood hath made so red
This bird that flew from the queen's bed
    Whereof ye have such fear.

KING DAVID.

Yea, my good knave, and is it said
That I can raise men from the dead?
By God I think to have his head
Who saith words of my lady's bed
    For any thief to hear.
    Et percutiat eum in capite.

QUEEN BERSABE.

I wis men shall spit at me,
And say it were but right for thee
That one should hang thee on a tree;
Ho! it were a fair thing to see
The big stones bruise her false body;
    Fie! who shall see her dead?

KING DAVID.

I rede you have no fear of this.
For as ye wot, the first good kiss
I had must be the last of his;
Now are ye queen of mine, I wis,
And lady of a house that is
    Full rich of meat and bread.

PRIMUS MILES.

I bid you make good cheer to be
So fair a queen as all men see.
And hold us for your lieges free;
By Peter's soul that hath the key,
　　Ye have good hap of it.

SECUNDUS MILES.

I would that he were hanged and dead
Who hath no joy to see your head
With gold about it, barred on red;
I hold him as a sow of lead
　　That is so scant of wit.

Tunc dicat NATHAN *propheta.*

O king, I have a word to thee;
The child that is in Bersabe
Shall wither without light to see ;
This word is come of God by me
　　For sin that ye have done.
Because herein ye did not right,
To take the fair one lamb to smite
That was of Urias the knight;
　　Ye wist he had but one.
Full many sheep I wot ye had,
And many women, when ye bade
To do your will and keep you glad;
And a good crown about your head
　　With gold to show thereon.
This Urias had one poor house
With low-barred latoun shot-windows
And scant of corn to fill a mouse ;
And rusty basnets for his brows,
　　To wear them to the bone.
Yea the roofs also, as men sain,
Were thin to hold against the rain;
Therefore what rushes were there lain
Grew wet withouten foot of men;
The stancheons were all gone in twain
　　As sick man's flesh is gone.
Nathless he had great joy to see
The long hair of this Bersabe
Fall round her lap and round her knee
Even to her small soft feet, that be
Shod now with crimson royally
　　And covered with clean gold.
Likewise great joy he had to kiss
Her throat, where now the scarlet is
Against her little chin, I wis,
　　That then was but cold.
No scarlet then her kirtle had
And little gold about it sprad;

But her red mouth was always glad
To kiss, albeit the eyes were sad
　　With love they had to hold.

SECUNDUS MILES.

How ! old thief, thy wits are lame;
To clip such it is no shame;
I rede you in the devil's name,
Ye come not here to make men game;
By Termagaunt that maketh grame,
　　I shall to-bete thine head.
　　Hic Diabolus capiat eum.
This knave hath sharp fingers, perfay;
Mahound you thank and keep alway,
And give you good knees to pray;
What man hath no lust to play,
The devil wring his ears, I say ;
There is no more but wellaway,
　　For now am I dead.

KING DAVID.

Certes his mouth is wried and black,
Full little pence be in his sack;
This devil hath him by the back,
　　It is no boot to lie.

NATHAN.

Sitteth now still and learn of me
A little while and ye shall see
The face of God's strength presently.
All queens made as this Bersabe,
All that were fair and foul ye be,
　　Come hither; it am I.
　　Et hic omnes cantabunt.

HERODIAS.

I am the queen Herodias.
This headband of my temples was
　　King Herod's gold band woven me,
This broken dry staff in my hand
Was the queen's staff of a great land
　　Betwixen Perse and Samarie.
For that one dancing of my feet,
The fire is come in my green wheat
　　From one sea to the other sea.

AHOLIBAH.

I am the queen Aholibah.
My lips kissed dumb the word of *Ah*
　　Sighed on strange lips grown sick
　　　　thereby
God wrought to me my royal bed:

The inner work thereof was red,
  The outer work was ivory,
My mouth's heat was the heat of flame
For lust towards the kings that came
  With horsemen riding royally.

CLEOPATRA.

I am the queen of E'hiope.
Love bade my kissing eyelids ope
  That men beholding might praise love.
My hair was wonderful and c rled;
My lips held fast the mouth the world
  To spoil the strength and speech there-
    of.
The latter triumph in my breath
Bowed down the beaten brows of death,
  Ashamed they had not wrath enough.

ABIHAIL.

I am the queen of Tyrians.
My hair was glorious for twelve spans,
  That dried to loose dust afterward.
My stature was a strong man's length:
My neck was like a place of strength
  Built with white walls, even and hard.
Like the first noise of rain leaves catch
One from another, snatch by snatch,
  Is my praise, hissed against and marred.

AZUBAH.

I am the queen of Amorites.
My face was like a place of lights
  With multitudes at festival.
The glory of my gracious brows
Was like God's house made glorious
  With colors upon either wall.
Between my brows and hair there was
A white space like a space of glass
  With golden candles over all.

AHOLAH.

I am the queen of Amalek.
There was no tender touch or fleck
  To spoil my body or bared feet.
My words were soft like dulcimers,
And the first sweet of grape-flowers
  Made each side of my bosom sweet.
My raiment was as tender fruit
Whose rind smells sweet of spice-tree root,
  Bruised balm-blossom and budded
    wheat.

AHINOAM.

I am the queen Ahinoam
Like he throat of a soft slain lamb
  Was my throat, softer veined than his:
My lips were as two grapes the sun
Lays his whole weight of heat upon
  Like a mouth heavy with a kiss:
My hair's pure purple a wrought fleece,
My temples therein as a piece
  Of a pomegranate's cleaving is.

ATARAH.

I am the queen Sidonian.
My face made faint the face of man,
  And strength was bound between my
    brows.
Spikenard was hidden in my ships,
Honey and wheat and myrrh in strips,
  White wools that shine as color does
Soft linen dyed upon the fold,
Split spice and cores of scented gold
  Cedar and broken calamus.

SEMIRAMIS.

I am the queen Semiramis.
The whole world and the sea that is
  In fashion like a chrysopras,
The noise of all men laboring,
The priest's mouth tired through thanks-
    giving,
  The sound of love in the blood's pause,
The strength of love in the blood's beat,
All these were cast beneath my feet
  And all found lesser than I was.

HESIONE.

I am the queen Hesione.
The seasons that increased in me
  Made my face fairer than all men's.
I had the summer in my hair;
And all the pale gold autumn air
  Was as the habit of my sense.
My body was as fire that shone;
God's beauty that makes all things one
  Was one among my handmaidens.

CHRYSOTHEMIS.

I am the queen of Samothrace.
God, making roses, made my face
  As a rose filled up full with red.
My prows made sharp the straitened seas
From Pontus to that Chersonese

Whereon the ebbed Asian stream is
    shed.
My hair was as sweet scent that drips;
Love's breath begun about my lips
    Kindled the lips of people dead.

THOMYEIS.

I am the queen of Scythians.
My strength was like no strength of man's,
    My face like day, my breast like
        spring.
My fame was felt in the extreme land
That hath sunshine on the one hand
    And on the other star-shining.
Yea, and the wine there fails of breath;
Yea, and their life is waste like death;
    Yea, and there death is a glad thing.

HARHAS.

I am the queen of Anakim.
In the spent years whose speech is dim,
    Whose raiment is the dust and death,
My stately body without stain
Shone as the shining race of rain
    Whose hair a great wind scattereth,
Now hath God turned my lips to sighs,
Plucked off mine eyelids from mine eyes,
And sealed with seals my way of breath.

MYRRHA.

I am the queen Arabian.
The tears wherewith mine eyelids ran
    Smelt like my perfumed eyelids' smell.
A harsh thirst made my soft mouth hard,
That ached with kisses afterward;
    My brain rang like a beaten bell.
As tears on eyes, as fire on wood,
Sin fed upon my breath and blood,
    Sin made my breasts subside and swell.

PASIPHAE.

I am the queen Pasiphae.
Not all the pure clean-colored sea
    Could cleanse or cool my yearning
        veins;
Nor any root nor herb that grew,
Flag-leaves that let green water through,
    Nor washing of the dews and rains.
From shame's pressed core I wrung the
        sweet
Fruit's savour that was death to eat,
    Whereof no seed but death remains.

SAPPHO.

I am the queen of Lesbians.
My love, that had no part in man's,
    Was sweeter than all shape of sweet.
The intolerable infinite desire
Made my face pale like faded fire
    When the ashen pyre falls through with
        heat.
My blood was hot wan wine of love,
And my song's sound the sound thereof,
    The sound of the delight of it.

MESSALINA.

I am the queen of Italy.
These were the signs God set on me;
    A barren beauty subtle and sleek,
Curled carven hair, and cheeks worn wan
With fierce false lips of many a man,
    Large temples where the blood ran
        weak,
A mouth athirst and amorous
And hungering as the grave's mouth does
    That, being an-hungered, cannot speak.

AMESTRIS.

I am the queen of Persians.
My breasts were lordlier than bright swans,
    My body as amber fair and thin.
Strange flesh was given my lips for bread,
With poisonous hours my days were fed,
    And my feet shod with adder-skin.
In Shushan toward Ecbatane
I wrought my joys with tears and pain,
    My loves with blood and bitter sin.

EPHRATH.

I am the queen of Rephaim.
God, that some while refraineth him,
    Made in the end a spoil of me.
My rumor was upon the world
As strong sound of swoln water hurled
    Through porches of the straining sea.
My hair was like the flag-flower,
And my breasts carven goodlier
    Than beryl with chalcedony.

PASITHEA.

I am the queen of Cypriotes.
Mine oarsmen, laboring with brown throats,
    Sang of me many a tender thing.
My maidens, girdled loose and braced
With gold from bosom to white waist.

Praised me between their wool-comb-
    ing.
All that praise Venus all night long
With lips like speech and lids like song
    Praised me till song lost heart to sing.

ALACIEL.

I am the queen Alaciel.
My mouth was like that moist gold cell
    Whereout the thickest honey drips
Mine eyes were as a grey-green sea;
The amorous blood that smote on me
    Smote to my feet and finger-tips.
My throat was whiter than the dove.
Mine eyelids as the seals of love,
    And as the doors of love my lips.

ERIGONE.

I am the queen Erigone
The wild wine shed as blood on me
    Made my face brighter than a bride's.
My large lips had the old thirst of earth,
Mine arms the might of the old sea's girth
    Bound round the whole world's iron
        sides.
Within mine eyes and in mine ears
Were music and the wine of tears,
    And light, and thunder of the tides.
Et hic exeant, et dicat Bersabe regina;

Alas, God, for thy great pity
And for the might that is in thee,
Behold, I woful Bersabe
Cry out with stoopings of my knee
And thy wrath laid and bound on me
    Till I may see thy love.
Behold, Lord, this child is grown
Within me between bone and bone
To make me mother of a son,
Made of my body with strong moan;
There shall not be another one
    That shall be made hereof.

KING DAVID.

Lord God, alas, what shall I sain ?
Lo, thou art as an hundred men
Both to break and build again:
The wild ways thou makest plain,
Thine hands hold the hail and rain,
And thy fingers both grape and grain;
Of their largess we be all well fain,
    And of their great pity;
The sun thou madest of good gold,

Of clean silver the moon cold,
All the great stars thou hast told
As thy cattle in thy fold
Every one by his name of old;
Wind and water thou hast in hold,
    Both the land and the long sea;
Both the green sea and the land,
Lord God, thou hast in hand,
Both white water and grey sand;
Upon thy right or thy left hand
There is no man that may stand;
    Lord, thou rue on me.
O wise Lord, if thou be keen
To note things amiss that been,
I am not worth a shell of bean
More than an old mare meagre and lean
For all my wrong-doing with my queen,
    But it began of her body.
For it fell in the hot May
I stood within a paven way
Built of fair bright stone, perfay,
That is as fire of night and day
    And lighteth all my house.
Therein be neither stones nor sticks,
Neither red nor white bricks,
But for cubits five or six
There is most goodly sardonyx
    And amber laid in rows.
It goes round about my roofs,
(If ye list ye shall have proofs)
There is good space for horse and hoofs,
    Plain and nothing perilous.
For the fair green weather's heat,
And for the smell of leaves sweet,
It is no marvel, well ye weet,
    A man to waxen amorous.
This I say now by my case
That spied forth of that royal place;
There I saw in no great space
Mine own sweet, both body and face,
    Under the fresh boughs.
In a water that was there
She wesshe her goodly body bare
And dried it with her owen hair:
Both her arms and her knees fair,
    Both bosom and brows;
Both shoulders and eke thighs
Tho she wesshe upon this wise;
Ever she sighed with little sighs,
    And ever she gave God thank.
Yea, God wot I can well see yet
Both her breast and her sides all wet
And her long hair withouten let
Spread sideways like a drawing net;
Full dear bought and full far fet

Was that sweet thing there y-set:
It were a hard thing to forget
How both lips and eyen met,
    Breast and breath sank.
So goodly a sight as there she was,
Lying looking on her glass
By wan water in green grass,
    Yet saw never man.
So soft and great she was and bright
With all her body waxen white,
I woxe nigh blind to see the light
Shed out of it to left and right;
This bitter sin from that sweet sight
    Between us twain began.

NATHAN.

Now, sir, be merry anon,
For ye shall have a full wise son,
Goodly and great of flesh and bone;
There shall no king be such an one
    I swear by Godis rood.
Therefore, lord, be merry here,
And go to meat withouten fear,
And hear a mass with goodly cheer;
For to all folk ye shall be dear,
    And all folk of your blood.

    Et tunc dicant Laudamus.

ST. DOROTHY.

It hath been seen and yet it shall be seen
That out of tender mouths God's praise
    hath been
Made perfect, and with wood and simple
    string
He that played music sweet as shawm-
    playing
To please himself with softness of all sound;
And no small thing but hath been some-
    time found
Full sweet of use, and no such humbleness
But God hath bruised withal the sentences
And evidence of wise men witnessing;
No leaf that is so soft a hidden thing
It never shall get sight of the great sun;
The strength of ten has been the strength
    of one,
And lowliness has waxed imperious.
    There was in Rome a man Theophilus
Of right great blood and gracious ways,
    that had
All noble fashions to make people glad
And a soft life of pleasurable days;
He was a goodly man for one to praise,
Flawless and whole upward from foot to
    head;
His arms were a red hawk that alway fed
On a small bird with feathers gnawed upon,

Beaten and plucked about the bosom-bone
Whereby a small round fleck like fire there
    was:
They called it in their tongue lampadias;
This was the banner of the lordly man.
In many straits of sea and reaches wan
Full of quick wind, and many a shaken
    firth,
It had seen fighting days of either earth,
Westward or east of waters Gaditane
(This was the place of sea-rocks under Spain
Called after the great praise of Hercules)
And north beyond the washing Pontic seas,
Far windy Russian places fabulous,
And salt fierce tides of storm-swoln Bos-
    phorus.
    Now as this lord came straying in Rome
    town
He saw a little lattice open down
And after it a press of maidens' heads
That sat upon their cold small quiet beds
Talking, and played upon short-stringed
    lutes;
And other some ground perfume out of roots
Gathered by marvellous moons in Asia
Saffron and aloes and wild cassia,
Colored all through and smelling of the
    sun:

And over all these was a certain one
Clothed softly, with sweet herbs about her
  hair
And bosom flowerful; her face more fair
Than sudden-singing April in soft lands;
Eyed like a gracious bird, and in both
  hands
She held a psalter painted green and red.
  This Theophile laughed at the heart, and
  said;
Now God so help me hither and St. Paul,
As by the new time of their festival
I have good will to take this maid to wife.
And herewith fell to fancies of her life
And soft half-thoughts that ended suddenly.
This is man's guise to please himself, when
  he
Shall not see one thing of his pleasant
  things,
Nor with outwatch of many travailings
Come to be eased of the least pain he hath
For all his love and all his foolish wrath
And all the heavy manner of his mind.
Thus is he like a fisher fallen blind
That casts his nets across the boat awry
To strike the sea, but lo, he striketh dry
And plucks them back all broken for his
  pain
And bites his beard and casts across again
And reaching wrong slips over in the sea.
So hath this man a strangled neck for fee,
For all his cost he chuckles in his throat.
This Theophile that little hereof wote
Laid wait to hear of her what she might be:
Men told him she had name of Dorothy,
And was a lady of a worthy house.
Thereat this knight grew inly glorious
That he should have a love so fair of place.
She was a maiden of most quiet face,
Tender of speech and had no hardihood
But was nigh feeble of her fearful blood;
Her mercy in her was so marvellous
From her least years, that seeing her school-
  fellows
That read beside her stricken with a rod,
She would cry sore and say some word to
  God
That he would ease her fellow of his pain.
There is no touch of sun or fallen rain
That ever fell on a more gracious thing.
  In middle Rome there was in stone-
  working
The church of Venus painted royally.
The chapels of it were some two or three,
In each of them her tabernacle was

And a wide window of six feet in glass
Colored with all her works in red and gold.
The altars had bright cloths and cups t₁
  hold
The wine of Venus for the services,
Made out of honey and crushed wood-
  berries
That shed sweet yellow through the thick
  wet red,
That on high days was borne upon the head
Of Venus' priest for any man to drink;
So that in drinking he should fall to think
On some fair face, and in the thought
  thereof
Worship, and such should triumph in his
  love.
For this soft wine that did such grace and
  good
Was new trans-shaped and mixed with love's
  own blood,
That in the fighting Trojan time was bled;
For which came such a woe to Diomed
That he was stifled after in hard sea.
And some said that this wine-shedding
  should be
Made of the falling of Adonis' blood,
That curled upon the thorns and broken
  wood
And round the gold silk shoes on Venus'
  feet;
The taste thereof was as hot honey sweet
And in the mouth ran soft and riotous.
This was the holiness of Venus' house.
  It was their worship that in August days
Twelve maidens should go through their
  Roman ways
Naked, and having gold across their brows
And their hair twisted in short golden rows.
To minister to Venus in this wise :
And twelve men chosen in their companies
To match these maidens by the altar-stair,
All in one habit, crowned upon the hair
Among these men was chosen Theophile.
  This knight went out and prayed a little
  while,
Holding queen Venus by her hands and
  knees;
I will give thee twelve royal images
Cut in glad gold, with marvels of wrought
  stone
For thy sweet priest to lean and pray upon,
Jasper and hyacinth and chrysopras,
And the strange Asian thalamite that was
Hidden twelve ages under heavy sea
Among the little sleepy pearls, to be

A shrine lit over with soft candle-flame
Burning all night red as hot brows of shame,
So thou wilt be my lady without sin.
Goddess that art all gold outside and in,
Help me to serve thee in thy holy way.
Thou knowest, Love, that in my bearing day
There shone a laughter in the singing stars
Round the gold ceiléd bride-bed wherein
    Mars
Touched thee and had thee in your kissing
    wise.
Now, therefore, sweet kiss thou my maiden's
    eyes
That they may open graciously towards me;
And this new fashion of thy shrine shall be
As soft with gold as thine own happy head.
The goddess, that was painted with face
    red
Between two long green tumbled sides of
    sea,
Stooped her neck sideways, and spake
    pleasantly:
Thou shalt have grace as thou art thrall of
    mine.
And with this came a savor of shed wine
And plucked-out petals from a rose's head:
And softly with slow laughs of lip she said,
Thou shalt have favor all thy days of me.
    Then came Theophilus to Dorothy,
Saying: O sweet, if one should strive or
    speak
Against God's ways, he gets a beaten cheek
For all his wage and shame above all men.
Therefore I have no will to turn again
When God saith "go," lest a worse thing
    fall out.
Then she, misdoubting lest he went about
To catch her wits, made answer somewhat
    thus:
I have no will, my lord Theophilus,
To speak against this worthy word of yours;
Knowing how God's will in all speech en-
    dures,
That save by grace there may no thing be
    said.
Then Theophile waxed light from foot to
    head,
And softly fell upon this answering.
It is well seen you are a chosen thing
To do God service in his gracious way.
I will that you make haste and holiday
To go next year upon the Venus stair,
Covered none else, but crowned upon your
    hair,
And do the service that a maiden doth.

She said: but I that am Christ's maid were
    loth
To do this thing that hath such bitter name.
Thereat his brows were beaten with sore
    shame
And he came off and said no other word.
Then his eyes chanced upon his banner-
    bird,
And he fell fingering at the staff of it
And laughed for wrath and stared between
    his feet.
And out of a chafed heart he spake as thus:
Lo how she japes at me Theophilus,
Feigning herself a fool and hard to love;
Yet in good time for all she boasteth of
She shall be like a little beaten bird.
And while his mouth was open in that word
He came upon the house Janiculum,
Where some went busily, and other some
Talked in the gate called the gate glorious.
The emperor, which was one Gabalus,
Sat over all and drank chill wine alone.
To whom is come Theophilus anon,
And said as thus: *Beau sire, Dieu vous aide.*
And afterward sat under him, and said
All this thing through as ye have wholly
    heard.
    This Gabalus laughed thickly in his
    beard.
Yea, this is righteousness and maiden rule.
Truly, he said, a maid is but a fool.
And japed at them as one full villainous,
In a lewd wise, this heathen Gabalus,
And sent his men to bind her as he bade.
Thus have they taken Dorothy the maid,
And haled her forth as men hale pick-
    purses:
A little need God knows they had of this,
To hale her by her maiden gentle hair.
Thus went she lowly, making a soft prayer,
As one who stays the sweet wine in his
    mouth,
Murmuring with eased lips and is most
    loth
To have done wholly with the sweet of it.
    Christ king, fair Christ, that knowest all
    men's wit
And all the feeble fashion of my ways,
O perfect God, that from all yesterdays
Abidest whole with morrows perfected,
I pray thee by thy mother's holy head
Thou help me to do right, that I not slip:
I have no speech nor strength upon my lip,
Except thou help me who art wise and
    sweet.

Do this too for those nails that clove thy feet,
Let me die maiden after many pains.
Though I be least among thy handmaidens,
Doubtless I shall take death more sweetly thus.
　Now have they brought her to King Gabalus,
Who laughed in all his throat some breathing-whiles.
By God, he said, if one should leap two miles,
He were not pained about the sides so much.
This were a soft thing for a man to touch.
Shall one so chafe that hath such little bones?
And shook his throat with thick and chuckled moans
For laughter that she had such holiness.
What aileth thee, wilt though do services
It were good fare to fare as Venus doth.
　Then said this lady with her maiden mouth,
Shamefaced, and something paler in the cheek:
Now, sir, albeit my wit and will to speak
Give me no grace in sight of worthy men,
For all my shame yet know I this again,
I may not speak, nor after downlying
Rise up to take delight in lute-playing,
Nor sing nor sleep, nor sit and fold my hands,
But my soul in some measure understands
God's grace laid like a garment over me.
For this fair God that out of strong sharp sea
Lifted the shapely and green-colored land,
And hath the weight of heaven in his hand
As one might hold a bird, and under him
The heavy golden planets beam by beam
Building the feasting-chambers of his house,
And the large world he holdeth with his brows,
And with the light of them astonisheth
All place and time and face of life and death
And motion of the north wind and the south,
And is the sound within his angel's mouth
Of singing words and words of thanksgiving,
And is the color of the latter spring
And heat upon the summer and the sun,
And is beginning of all things begun
And gathers in him all things to their end,
7

And with the fingers of his hand doth bend
The stretched-out sides of heaven like a sail,
And with his breath he maketh the red pale
And fills with blood faint faces of men dead,
And with the sound between his lips are fed
Iron and fire and the white body of snow,
And blossom of all trees in places low,
And small bright herbs about the little hills,
And fruit pricked softly with birds' tender bills,
And flight of foam about green fields of sea,
And fourfold strength of the great winds that be
Moved always outward from beneath his feet,
And growth of grass and growth of sheaved wheat
And all green flower of goodly-growing lands;
And all these things he gathers with his hands
And covers all their beauty with his wings;
The same, even God that governs all these things,
Hath set my feet to be upon his ways.
Now therefore for no painfulness of days
I shall put off this service bound on me.
Also, fair sir, ye know this certainly,
How God was in his flesh full chaste and meek
And gave his face to shame, and either cheek
Gave up to smiting of men tyrannous.
　And here with a great voice this Galabus
Cried out and said: By God's blood and his bones,
This were good game betwixen night and nones
For one to sit and hearken to such saws:
I were as lief fall in some big beast's jaws
As hear these women's jaw-teeth chattering;
By God a woman is the harder thing,
One may not put a hook into her mouth.
Now by St. Luke I am so sore adrouth
For all these saws I must needs drink again
But I pray God deliver all us men
From all such noise of women and their heat.
That is a noble scripture, well I weet,
That likens women to an empty can;
When God said that he was a full wise man.
I trow no man may blame him as for that.
　And herewithal he drank a draught, and spat

And said: Now shall I make an end hereof.
Come near all men and hearken for God's
love,
And ye shall hear a jest or twain, God wot.
And spake as thus with mouth full thick and
hot;
But thou do this thou shalt be shortly slain.
Lo, sir, she said, this death and all this
pain
I take in penance of my bitter sins.
Yea, now, quoth Gabalus, this game begins.
Lo, without sin one shall not live a span.
Lo, this is she that would not look on man
Between her fingers folded in thwart wise.
See how shame hath smitten in her eyes
That was so clean she had not heard of
shame.
Certes, he said, by Gabalus my name,
This two years back I was not so well
pleased.
This were good mirth for sick men to be
eased
And rise up whole and laugh at hearing of.
I pray thee show us something of thy love,
Since thou wast maid thy gown is waxen
wide.
Yea, maid I am, she said, and somewhat
sighed,
As one who thought upon the low fair
house
Where she sat working, with soft bended
brows
Watching her threads, among the school-
maidens.
And she thought well now God hath brought
her thence
She should not come to sew her gold again.
Then cried King Gabalus upon his men
To have her forth and draw her with steel
gins.
And as a man hag-ridden beats and grins
And bends his body sidelong in his bed,
So wagged ne with his body and knave's
head,
Gaping at her, and blowing with his breath.
And in good time he gat an evil death
Out of his lewdness with his cursed wives:
His bones were hewn asunder as with
knives
For his misliving, certes it is said.
But all the evil wrought upon this maid,
It were full hard for one to handle it.
For her soft blood was shed upon her feet,
And all her body's color bruised and faint.
But she, as one abiding God's great saint,

Spake not nor wept for all this travail hard.
Wherefore the king commanded afterward
To slay her presently in all men's sight.
And it was now an hour upon the night
And winter-time, and a few stars began.
The weather was yet feeble and all wan
For beating of a weighty wind and snow.
And she came walking in soft wise and
slow,
And many men with faces piteous.
Then came this heavy cursing Gabalus,
That swore full hard into his drunken beard;
And faintly after without any word
Came Theophile some paces off the king.
And in the middle of this wayfaring
Full tenderly beholding her he said:
    There is no word of comfort with men
dead
Nor any face and color of things sweet;
But always with lean cheeks and lifted feet
These dead men lie all aching to the blood
With bitter cold, their brows withouten
hood
Beating for chill, their bodies swathed full
thin:
Alas, what hire shall any have herein
To give his life and get such bitterness?
Also the soul going forth bodiless
Is hurt with naked cold, and no man saith
If there be house or covering for death
To hide the soul that is discomforted.
    Then she beholding him a little said:
Alas, fair lord, ye have no wit of this;
For on one side death is full poor of bliss
And as ye say full sharp of bone and lean:
But on the other side is good and green
And hath soft flower of tender-colored hair
Grown on his head, and a red mouth as
fair
As may be kissed with lips: thereto his
face
Is as God's face, and in a perfect place
Full of all sun and color of straight boughs
And waterheads about a painted house
That hath a mile of flowers either way
Outward from it, and blossom-grass of May
Thickening on many a side for length of
heat,
Hath God set death upon a noble seat
Covered with green and flowered in the
fold,
In likeness of a great king grown full old
And gentle with new temperance of blood;
And on his brows a purfled purple hood,
They may not carry any golden thing;

And plays some tune with subtle fingering
On a small cithern, full of tears and sleep
And heavy pleasure that is quick to weep
And sorrow with the honey in her mouth;
And for this might of music that he doth
Are all souls drawn toward him with great
    love
And weep for sweetness of the noise thereof
And bow to him with worship of their
    knees;
And all the field is thick with companies
Of fair-clothed men that play on shawms
    and lutes
And gather honey of the yellow fruits
Between the branches waxen soft and wide;
And all this peace endures in either side
Of the green land, and God beholdeth all.
And this is girdled with a round fair wall
Made of red stone and cool with heavy
    leaves
Grown out against it, and green blossom
    cleaves
To the green chinks, and lesser wall-weed
    sweet,
Kissing the crannies that are split with
    heat,
And branches where the summer draws to
    head.
    And Theophile burnt in the cheek, and
    said:
Yea, could one see it, this were marvellous.
I pray you, at your coming to this house,
Give me some leaf of all those tree-branches;
Seeing how so sharp and white our weather
    is,
There is no green nor gracious red to see.
    Yea, sir, she said, that shall I certainly.
And from her long sweet throat without a
    fleck
Undid the gold, and through her stretched
    out neck
The cold axe clove, and smote away her
    head:
Out of her throat the tender blood full red
Fell suddenly through all her long soft hair.
And with good speed for hardness of the air
Each man departed to his house again.
    Lo, as fair color in the face of men
At seed-time of their blood, or in such wise
As a thing seen increaseth in men's eyes,
Caught first far off by sickly fits of sight—
So a word said, if one shall hear aright,
Abides against the season of its growth.
This Theophile went slowly, as one doth
That is not sure for sickness of his feet;

And counting the white stonework of the
    street,
Tears fell out of his eyes for wrath and love,
Making him weep more for the shame
    thereof
Than for true pain: so went he half a mile.
And women mocked him, saying: Theo-
    phile,
Lo, she is dead; what shall a women have
That loveth such an one? so Christ me save,
I were as lief to love a man new-hung.
Surely this man has bitten on his tongue,
This makes him sad and writhled in his fac
    And when they came upon the paven
    place
That was called sometime the place amor-
    ous,
There came a child before Theophilus,
Bearing a basket, and said suddenly:
Fair sir, this is my mistress Dorothy
That sends you gifts; and with this he was
    gone.
In all this earth there is not such an one
For color and straight stature made so fair.
The tender growing gold of his pure hair
Was as wheat growing, and his mouth as
    flame.
God called him Holy after his own name;
With gold cloth like fire burning he was
    clad.
But for the fair green basket that he had,
It was filled up with heavy white and red:
Great roses stained still where the first rose
    bled,
Burning at heart for shame their heart with-
    holds:
And the sad color of strong marigolds
That have the sun to kiss their lips for
    love;
The flower that Venus' hair is woven of,
The color of fair apples in the sun,
Late peaches gathered when the heat was
    done
And the slain air got breath; and after these
The fair faint-headed poppies drunk with
    ease,
And heaviness of hollow lilies red.
    Then cried they all that saw these things,
    and said
It was God's doing, and was marvellous.
And in brief while this knight Theophilus
Is waxen full of faith, and witnesseth
Before the king of God and love and death,
For which the king bade hang him pre-
    sently.

A gallows of a goodly piece of tree
This Gabalus hath made to hang him on.
Forth of this world lo Theophile is gone
With a wried neck, God give us better
    fare
Than his that hath a twisted throat to wear;
But truly for his love God hath him brought
There where his heavy body grieves him
    nought
Nor all the people plucking at his feet:

But in his face his lady's face is sweet,
And through his lips her kissing lips are
    gone:
God send him peace, and joy of such an one,
    This is the story of St. Dorothy.
I will you of your mercy pray for me
Because I wrote these sayings for your
    grace,
That I may one day see her in the face.

THE TWO DREAMS.

(FROM BOCCACCIO.)

I WILL that if I say a heavy thing
Your tongues forgive me; seeing ye know
    that spring
Has flecks and fits of pain to keep her
    sweet,
And walks somewhile with winter-bitten
    feet.
Moreover it sounds often well to let
One string, when ye play music, keep at
    fret
The whole song through; one petal that is
    dead
Confirms the roses, be they white or red;
Dead sorrow is not sorrowful to hear
As the thick noise that breaks mid weeping
    were;
The sick sound aching in a lifted throat
Turns to sharp silver of a perfect note;
And though the rain falls often, and with
    rain
Late autumn falls on the old red leaves like
    pain,
I deem that God is not disquieted.
Also while men are fed with wine and
    bread,
They shall be fed with sorrow at his hand.
    There grew a rose-garden in Florence
    land

More fair than many; all red summers
    through
The leaves smelt sweet and sharp of rain,
    and blew
Sideways with tender wind; and therein fell
Sweet sound wherewith the green waxed
    audible,
As a bird's will to sing disturbed his throat
And set the sharp wings forward like a boat
Pushed through soft water, moving his
    brown side
Smooth-shapen as a maid's, and shook with
    pride
His deep warm bosom, till the heavy sun's
Set face of heat stopped all the songs at
    once.
The ways were clean to walk and delicate;
And when the windy white of March grew
    late,
Before the trees took heart to face the sun
With ravelled raiment of lean winter on,
The roots were thick and hot with hollow
    grass.
    Some roods away a lordly house there
    was,
Cool with broad courts and latticed passage
    wet
From rush-flowers and lilies ripe to set,

Sown close among the strewings of the
　floor;
And either wall of the slow corridor
Was dim with deep device of gracious
　things;
Some angel's steady mouth and weight of
　wings
Shut to the side; or Peter with straight stole
And beard cut black against the aureole
That spanned his head from nape to crown;
　there
Mary's gold hair, thick to the girdle-tie
Wherein was bound a child with tender
　feet;
Or the broad cross with blood nigh brown
　on it.
　　Within this house a righteous lord abode,
Ser Averardo; patient of his mood,
And just of judgment; and to child he had
A maid so sweet that her mere sight made
　glad
Men sorrowing, and unbound the brows of
　hate;
And where she came, the lips that pain
　made strait
Waxed warm and wide, and from untender
　grew
Tender as those that sleep brings patience to.
Such long locks had she, that with knee
　to chin
She might have wrapped and warmed her
　feet therein.
Right seldom fell her face on weeping wise;
Gold hair she had, and golden-colored
　eyes,
Filled with clear light and fire and large
　repose
Like a fair hound's; no man there is but
　knows
Her face was white, and thereto she was
　tall;
In no wise lacked there any praise at all
To her most perfect and pure maidenhood;
No sin I think there was in all her blood.
　　She, where a gold grate shut the roses in,
Dwelt daily through deep summer weeks,
　through green
Flushed hours of rain upon the leaves ;
　and there
Love made him room and space to worship
　her
With tender worship of bowed knees, and
　wrought
Such pleasure as the pained sense palates
　not

For weariness, but at one taste undoes
The heart of its strong sweet, is ravenous
Of all the hidden honey, words and sense
Fail through the tune's imperious preval-
　ence.
　　In a poor house this lover kept apart,
Long communing with patience next his
　heart
If love of his might move that face at all,
Tuned evenwise with colors musical;
Then after length of days he said thus:—
　　" Love,
For love's own sake and for the love there-
　of
Let no harsh words untune your gracious
　mood;
For good it were, if anything be good
To comfort me in this pain's plague of
　mine;
Seeing thus, how neither sleep nor bread
　nor wine
Seems pleasant to me; yea, no thing that is
Seems pleasant to me; only I know this,
Love's ways are sharp for palms of piteous
　feet
To travel, but the end of such is sweet:
Now do with me as seemeth you the best."
She mused a little, as one holds his guest
By the hand musing, with her face borne
　down:
Then said: " Yea, though such bitter seed
　be sown,
Have no more care of all that you have
　said;
Since if there is no sleep will bind your
　head,
Lo, I am fain to help you certainly;
Christ knoweth, sir, if I would have you
　die;
There is no pleasure when a man is dead. "
Thereat he kissed her hands and yellow
　head
And clipped her fair long body many times;
I have no wit to shape in written rhymes
A scanted tithe of this great joy they had
　　They were too near love's secret to be
　　glad
As whoso deems the core will surely melt
From the warm fruit his lips caress, hath
　felt
Some bitter kernel where the teeth shut
　hard:
Or as sweet music sharpens afterward,
Being half disrelished both for sharp and
　sweet;
As sea-water, having killed over-heat

In a man's body, chills it with faint ache;
So their sense, burdened only for love's
    sake,
Failed for pure love; yet so time served
    their wit,
They saved each day some gold reserves of
    it,
Being wiser in love's riddle than such be
Whom fragments feed with his chance
    charity.
All things felt sweet were felt sweet over-
    much;
The rose-thorn's prickle dangerous to
    touch,
And flecks of fire in the thin leaf-shadows;
Too keen the breathèd honey of the rose,
Its red too harsh a weight on feasted eyes;
They were so far gone in love's histories,
Beyond all shape and color and mere breath
Where pleasure has for kinsfolk sleep and
    death,
And strength of soul and body waxen blind
For weariness, and flesh entoiled with
    mind,
When the keen edge of sense foretasteth
    sin.
    Even this green place the summer caught
    them in
Seemed half deflowered and sick with
    beaten leaves
In their strayed eyes; these gold flower-
    fumed eyes
Burnt out to make the sun's love offering,
The midnoon's prayer, the rose's thanks-
    giving,
The tree's weight burdening the strength-
    less air,
The shape of her stilled eyes, her colored
    hair,
Her body's balance from the moving feet—
All this, found fair, lacked yet one grain of
    sweet
It had some warm weeks back: so perisheth
On May's new lip the tender April breath:
So those same walks the wind sowed lilies
    in
All April through, and all their latter kin
Of languid leaves whereon the Autumn
    blows—
The dead red raiment of the last year's
    rose—
The last year's laurel, and the last year's
    love,
Fade, and grow things that death grows
    weary of.

What man will gather in red summer-time
The fruit of some obscure and hoary rhyme
Heard last midwinter, taste the heart in it,
Mould the smooth semitones afresh, refit
The fair limbs ruined, flush the dead blood
    through
With color, make all broken beauties new
For love's new lesson—shall not such find
    pain
When the marred music laboring in his
    brain
Frets him with sweet sharp fragments, and
    lets slip
One word that might have satisfied his
    lip—
One touch that might put fire in all the
    chords?
This was her pain: to miss from all sweet
    words
Some taste of sound, diverse and delicate—
Some speech the old love found out to
    compensate
For seasons of shut lips and drowsiness—
Some grace, some word the old love found
    out to bless
Passionless months and undelighted weeks.
The flowers had lost their summer-scented
    cheeks
Their lips were no more sweet than daily
    breath:
The year was plagued with instances of
    death.
    So fell it, these were sitting in cool grass
With leaves about, and many a bird there
    was
Where the green shadow thickliest im-
    pleached
Soft fruit and writhen spray and blossom
    bleached
Dry in the sun or washed with rains to
    white:
Her girdle was pure silk, the bosom bright
With purple as purple water and gold
    wrought in.
One branch had touched with dusk her lips
    and chin,
Made violet of the throat, abashed with
    shade
The breast's bright plaited work: but
    nothing frayed
The sun's large kiss on the luxurious hair.
Her beauty was new color to the air
And music to the silent many birds.
Love was an-hungered for some perfect
    words

To praise her with; but only her low name
"Andrevuola" came thrice, and thrice put
   shame
In her clear cheek, so fruitful with new red
That for pure love straightway shame's self
   was dead.
    Then with lids gathered as who late had
     wept
She began saying: ' I have so little slept
My lids drowse now against the very sun;
Yea, the brain aching with a dream begun
Beats like a fitful blood; kiss but both
   brows,
And you shall pluck my thoughts grown
   dangerous
Almost away." He said thus, kissing them:
  "O sole sweet thing that God is glad to
   name,
My one gold gift, if dreams be sharp and
   sore
Shall not the waking time increase much
   more
With taste and sound, sweet eyesight or
   sweet scent ?
Has any heat too hard and insolent
Burnt bare the tender married leaves, un-
   done
The maiden grass shut under from the sun ?
Where in this world is room enough for
   pain ?"
    The feverish finger of love had touched
    again
Her lips with happier blood; the pain lay
   meek
In her fair face, nor altered lip nor cheek
With pallor or with pulse; but in her mouth
Love thirsted as a man wayfaring doth,
Making it humble as weak hunger is.
She lay close to him, bade do this and this,
Say that, sing thus: then almost weeping-
   ripe
Crouched, then laughed low. As one that
   fain would wipe
The old record out of old things done and
   dead,
She rose, she heaved her hands up, and
   waxed red
For wilful heart and blameless fear of
   blame;
Saying "Though my wits be weak, this is
   no shame
For a poor maid whom love so punisheth
With heats of hesitation and stopped breath
That with my dreams I live yet heavily
For pure sad heart and faith's humility.

Now be not wroth and I will shew you
   this.
   " Methought our lips upon their second
   kiss
Met in this place, and a fair day we had
And fair soft leaves that waxed and were
   not sad
With shaken rain or bitten through with
   drouth;
When I, beholding ever how your mouth
Waited for mine, the throat being fallen
   back,
Saw crawl thereout a live thing flaked with
   black
Specks of brute slime and leper-colored
   scale,
A devil's hide with foul flame-writhen grail
Fashioned where hell's heat festers loath-
   somest;
And that brief speech may ease me of the
   rest,
Thus were you slain and eaten of the thing.
My waked eyes felt the new day shuddering
On their low lids, felt the whole east so
   beat,
Pant with close pulse of such a plague-
   struck heat,
As if the palpitating dawn drew breath
For horror, breathing between life and
   death,
Till the sun sprang blood-bright and vio-
   lent."
So finishing, her soft strength wholly spent,
She gazed each way, lest some brute-hoovèd
   thing,
The timeless travail of hell's childbearing,
Should threat upon the sudden: whereat he,
For relish of her tasted misery
And tender little thornprick of her pain,
Laughed with mere love. What lover
   among men
But hath his sense fed sovereignly 'twixt
   whiles
With tears and covered eyelids and sick
   smiles
And soft disaster of a painèd face ?
What pain, established in so sweet a place,
But the plucked leaf of it smells fragrantly ?
What color burning man's wide-open eye
But may be pleasurably seen ? what sense
Keeps in its hot sharp extreme violence
No savor of sweet things ? The bereaved
   blood
And emptied flesh in their most broken
   mood

Fail not so wholly, famish not when thus
Past honey keeps the starved lip covetous.
Therefore this speech from a glad mouth
　　began,
Breathed in her tender hair and temples
　　wan
Like one prolonged kiss while the lips had
　　breath:
"Sleep, that abides in vassalage of death
And in death's service wears out half his
　　age,
Hath his dreams full of deadly vassalage,
Shadow and sound of things ungracious;
Fair shallow faces, hooded bloodless brows,
And mouths past kissing; yea, myself have
　　had
As harsh a dream as holds your eyelids sad.
　　"This dream I tell you came three nights
　　ago;
In full mid sleep I took a whim to know
How sweet things might be; so I turned
　　and thought;
But save my dream all sweet availed me
　　not.
First came a smell of pounded spice and
　　scent
Such as God ripens in some continent
Of utmost amber in the Syrian sea;
And breaths as though some costly rose
　　could be
Spoiled slowly, wasted by some bitter fire
To burn the sweet out leaf by leaf, and tire
The flower's poor heart with heat and
　　waste, to make
Strong magic for some perfumed woman's
　　sake.
Then a cool naked sense beneath my feet
Of bud and blossom; and sound of veins
　　that beat
As if a lute should play of its own heart
And fearfully, not smitten of either part;
And all my blood it filled with sharp and
　　sweet
As gold swoln grain fills out the huskèd
　　wheat;
So I rose naked from the bed, and stood
Counting the mobile measure in my blood
Some pleasant while, and through each
　　limb there came
Swift little pleasures pungent as a flame.
Felt in the thrilling flesh and veins as
　　much
As the outer curls that feel the comb's first
　　touch
Thrill to the roots and shiver as from fire;

And blind between my dream and my de-
　　sire
I seemed to stand and held my spirit still
Lest this should cease. A child whose
　　fingers spill
Honey from cells forgotten of the bee
Is less afraid to stir the hive and see
Some wasp's bright back inside, than I to
　　feel
Some finger-touch disturb the flesh like
　　steel.
I prayed thus; Let me catch a secret here
So sweet, it sharpens the sweet taste of
　　fear
And takes the mouth with edge of wine; I
　　would
Have here some color and smooth shape as
　　good
As those in heaven whom the chief garden
　　hides
With low grape-blossom veiling their white
　　sides
And lesser tendrils that so bind and blind
Their eyes and feet, that if one come
　　behind
To touch their hair they see not, neither
　　fly;
This would I see in heaven and not die.
So praying; I had nigh cried out and knelt,
So wholly my prayer filled me: till I felt
In the dumb night's warm weight of glow-
　　ing gloom
Somewhat that altered all my sleeping-
　　room,
And made it like a green low place wherein
Maids mix to bathe : one sets her small
　　warm chin
Against a ripple that the angry pearl
May flow like flame about her: the next
　　curl
Dips in some eddy colored of the sun
To wash the dust well out; another one
Holds a straight ankle in her hand and
　　swings
With lavish body sidelong, so that rings
Of fierce sweet water, swollen and splendid,
　　fail
All round her fine and floated body pale,
Swayed flower fashion, and her balanced
　　side
Swerved edgeways lets the weight of water
　　slide,
As taken in some underflow of sea
Swerves the banked gold of sea-flowers;
　　but she

Pulls down some branch to keep her per-
  fect head
Clear of the river: even from wall to bed,
I tell you, was my room transfigured so.
Sweet, green and warm it was, nor could
  one know
If there were walls or leaves, or if there was
No bed's green curtain, but mere gentle
  grass.
There were set also hard against the feet
Gold plates with honey and green grapes
  to eat,
With the cool water's noise to hear in
  rhymes:
And a wind warmed me full of furze and
  limes
And all hot sweets the heavy summer fills
To the round brim of smooth cup-shapen
  hills.
Next the grave walking of a woman's feet
Made my veins hesitate, and gracious heat
Made thick the lids and leaden on mine
  eyes:
And I thought ever, surely it were wise
Not yet to see her: this may last (who
  knows ?)
Five minutes; the poor rose is twice a rose
Because it turns a face to her, the wind
Sings that way; hath this woman ever
  sinned,
I wonder ? as a boy with apple-rind,
I played with pleasures, made them to my
  mind,
Changed each ere tasting. When she came
  indeed,
First her hair touched me, then I grew to
  feed
On the sense of her hand; her mouth at
  last
Touched me between the cheek and lip
  and past
Over my face with kisses here and there
Sown in and out across the eyes and hair.
Still I said nothing; till she set her face
More close and harder on the kissing-place,
And her mouth caught like a snake's mouth,
  and stung
So faint and tenderly, the fang scarce
  clung
More than a bird's foot: yet a wound it
  grew,
A great one, let this red mark witness you
Under the left breast; and the stroke there-
  of
So clove my sense that I woke out of love

And knew not what this dream was nor
  had wit;
But now God knows if I have skill of it."
  Hereat she laid one palm against her
  lips
To stop their trembling; as when water
  slips
Out of a beak-mouthed vessel with faint
  noise
And chuckles in the narrow throat and
  cloys
The carven rims with murmuring, so came
Words in her lips with no word right of
  them,
A beaten speech thick and disconsolate,
Till his smile ceasing waxed compassionate
Of her sore fear that grew from anything—
The sound of the strong summer thickening
In heated leaves of the smooth apple-trees:
The day's breath felt about the ash-branches
And noises of the noon whose weight still
  grew
On the hot heavy-headed flowers, and
  drew
Their red mouths open till the rose-heart
  ached;
For eastward all the crowding rose was
  slaked
And soothed with shade: but westward all
  its growth
Seemed to breathe hard with heat as a man
  doth
Who feels his temples newly feverous.
And even with such motion in her brows
As that man hath in whom sick days begin,
She turned her throat and spake, her voice
  being thin
As a sick man's, sudden and tremulous;
" Sweet, if this end be come indeed on us,
Let us love more;" and held his mouth
  with hers.
As the first sound of flooded hill-waters
Is heard by people of the meadow-grass,
Or ever a wandering waif of ruin pass
With whirling stones and foam of the brown
  stream
Flaked with fierce yellow: so beholding
  him
She felt before tears came her eyelids wet,
Saw the face deadly thin where life was
  yet,
Heard his throat's harsh last moan before
  it clomb:
And he, with close mouth passionate and
  dumb

Burned at her lips: so lay they without
   speech,
Each grasping other, and the eyes of each
Fed in the other's face: till suddenly
He cried out with a little broken cry
This word "O help me, sweet, I am but
   dead."
And even so saying, the color of fair red
Was gone out of his face, and his blood's
   beat
Fell, and stark death made sharp his up-
   ward feet
And pointed hands: and without moan he
   died.
Pain smote her sudden in the brows and
   side,
Strained her lips open and made burn her
   eyes:
For the pure sharpness of her miseries
She had no heart's pain, but mere body's
   wrack;
But at the last her beaten blood drew back
Slowly upon her face, and her stunned
   brows
Suddenly grown aware and piteous
Gathered themselves, her eyes shone, her
   hard breath
Came as though one nigh dead came back
   from death;
Her lips throbbed, and life trembled through
   her hair.
   And in brief while she thought to bury
   there
The dead man that her love might lie with
   him
In a sweet bed under the rose-roots dim
And soft earth round the branched apple-
   trees,

Full of hushed heat and heavy with great
   ease,
And no man entering divide him thence.
Wherefore she bade one of her hand-
   maidens
To be her help to do upon this wise.
And saying so the tears out of her eyes
Fell without noise and comforted her heart:
Yea, her great pain eased of the sorest part
Began to soften in her sense of it.
There under all the little branches sweet
The place was shapen of his burial;
They shed thereon no thing funereal,
But colored leaves of latter rose-blossom,
Stems of soft grass, some withered red and
   some
Fair and flesh-blooded; and spoil splendider
Of marigold and great spent sunflower.
   And afterward she came back without
   word
To her own house; two days went, and the
   third
Went, and she showed her father of this
   thing.
And for great grief of her soul's travailing
He gave consent she should endure in
   peace
Till her life's end; yea, till her time should
   cease,
She should abide in fellowship of pain.
And having lived a holy year or twain
She died of pure waste heart and weariness.
And for love's honor in her love's distress
This word was written over her tomb's
   head;
"Here dead she lieth, for whose sake Love
   is dead."

AHOLIBAH.

In the beginning God made thee
   A woman well to look upon,
Thy tender body as a tree
   Whereon cool wind hath always blown
   Till the clean branches be well grown.

There was none like thee in the land;
   The girls that were thy bondwomen
Did bind thee with a purple band;
   Upon thy forehead, that all men,
   Should know thee for God's hand-
   maiden.

Strange raiment clad thee like a bride,
　With silk to wear on hands and feet
And plates of gold on either side:
　Wine made thee glad, and thou didst
　　　eat
　Honey, and choice of pleasant meat.

And fishers in the middle sea
　Did get thee sea-fish and sea-weeds
In color like the robes on thee;
　And curious work of plaited reeds,
　And wools wherein live purple bleeds.

And round the edges of thy cup
　Men wrought thee marvels out of gold,
Strong snakes with lean throats lifted up,
　Large eyes whereon the brows had
　　　hold,
　And scaly things their slime kept cold.

For thee they blew soft wind in flutes
　And ground sweet roots for cunning
　　　scent;
Made slow because of many lutes,
　The wind among thy chambers went
　Wherein no light was violent.

God called thy name Aholibah,
　His tabernacle being in thee,
A witness through waste Asia;
　Thou wert a tent sewn cunningly
　With gold and colors of the sea.

God gave thee gracious ministers
　And all their work who plait and
　　　weave:
The cunning of embroiderers
　That sew the pillow to the sleeve,
　And likeness of all things that live.

Thy garments upon thee were fair
　With scarlet and with yellow thread;
Also the weaving of thine hair
　Was as fine gold upon thy head,
　And thy silk shoes were sewn with red.

All sweet things he bade sift, and ground
　As a man grindeth wheat in mills
With strong wheels alway going round;
　He gave thee corn, and grass that fills
　The cattle on a thousand hills.

The wine of many seasons fed
　Thy mouth, and made it fair and clean;
Sweet oil was poured out on thy head
　And ran down like cool rain between
　The strait close locks it melted in.

The strong men and the captains knew
　Thy chambers wrought and fashioned
With gold and covering of blue,
　And the blue raiment of thine head
　Who satest on a stately bed.

All these had on their garments wrought
　The shape of beasts and creeping
　　　things,
The body that availeth not,
　Flat backs of worms and veinèd wings,
　And the lewd bulk that sleeps and
　　　stings.

Also the chosen of the years,
　The multitude being at ease,
With sackbuts and with dulcimers
　And noise of shawms and psalteries
　Made mirth within the ears of these.

But as a common woman doth,
Thou didst think evil and devise;
The sweet smell of thy breast and mouth
　Thou madest as the harlot's wise,
　And there was painting on thine eyes.

Yea, in the woven guest-chamber
　And by the painted passages
Where the strange gracious paintings were,
　State upon state of companies,
　There came on thee the lust of these.

Because of shapes on either wall
　Sea-colored from some rare blue shell
At many a Tyrian interval,
　Horsemen on horses, girdled well,
　Delicate and desirable,

Thou saidest: I am sick of love:
Stay me with flagons, comfort me
With apples for my pain thereof
　Till my hands gather in his tree
　That fruit wherein my lips would be.

Yea, saidest thou, I will go up
　When there is no more shade than one
May cover with a hollow cup,
　And make my bed against the sun
　Till my blood's violence be done.

Thy mouth was leant upon the wall
　Against the painted mouth, thy chin
Touched the hair's painted curve and fall;
　Thy deep throat, fallen lax and thin,
　Worked as the blood's beat worked
　　　therein.

Therefore, O thou Aholibah,
   God is not glad because of thee;
And thy fine gold shall pass away
   Like those fair coins of ore that be
   Washed over by the middle sea.

Then will one make thy body bare
   To strip it of all gracious things,
And pluck the cover from thine hair,
   And break the gift of many kings,
   Thy wrist-rings and thine ankle-rings.

Likewise the man whose body joins
   To thy smooth body, as was said,
Who hath a girdle on his loins
   And dyed attire upon his head—
   The same who, seeing, worshipped,

Because thy face was like the face
   Of a clean maiden that smells sweet,
Because thy gait was as the pace
   Of one that opens not her feet
   And is not heard within the street—

Even he, O thou Aholibah,
   Made separate from thy desire,
Shall cut thy nose and ears away
   And bruise thee for thy body's hire
   And burn the residue with fire.

Then shall the heathen people say
   The multitude being at ease,
Lo, this is that Aholibah
   Whose name was blown among strange
      seas,
   Grown old with soft adulteries.

Also her bed was made of green,
   Her windows beautiful for glass
That she had made her bed between:
   Yea, for pure lust her body was
   Made like white summer-colored grass

Her raiment was a strong man's spoil;
   Upon a table by a bed
She set mine incense and mine oil
   To be the beauty of her head
   In chambers walled about with red.

Also between the walls she had
   Fair faces of strong men portrayed;
All girded round the loins, and clad
   With several cloths of woven braid
   And garments marvellously made.

Therefore the wrath of God shall be
   Set as a watch upon her way;
And whoso findeth by the sea
   Blown dust of bones will hardly say
   If his were that Aholibah.

LOVE AND SLEEP.

Lying asleep between the strokes of night
   I saw my love lean over my sad bed,
   Pale as the duskiest lily's leaf or head,
Smooth-skinned and dark, with bare throat
     made to bite,
Too wan for blushing and too warm for
     white,
   But perfect-colored without white or red.
   And her lips opened amorously, and
     said—
I wist not what, saving one word—De-
   light.

And all her face was honey to my mouth,
   And all her body pasture to mine eyes;
     The long lithe arms and hotter hands
      than fire,
The quivering flanks, hair smelling of the
     south,
     The bright light feet, the splendid supple
      thighs
      And glittering eyelids of my soul's
       desire.

MADONNA MIA.

UNDER green apple boughs
That never a storm will rouse,
My lady hath her house
  Between two bowers;
In either of the twain
Red roses full of rain;
She hath for bondwomen
  All kind of flowers.

She hath no handmaid fair
To draw her curled gold hair
Through rings of gold that bear
  Her whole hair's weight;
She hath no maids to stand
Gold-clothed on either hand;
In all the great green land
  None is so great.

She hath no more to wear
But one white hood of vair
Drawn over eyes and hair,
  Wrought with strange gold,
Made for some great queen's head,
Some fair great queen since dead;
And one strait gown of red
  Against the cold.

Beneath her eyelids deep
Love lying seems asleep,
Love, swift to wake, to weep,
  To laugh to gaze;
Her breasts are like white birds,
And all her gracious words
As water-grass to herds
  In the June-days.

To her all dews that fall
And rains are musical;
Her flowers are fed from all,
  Her joys from these;
In the deep-feathered firs
Their gift of joy is hers,
In the least breath that stirs
  Across the trees.

She grows with greenest leaves,
Ripens with reddest sheaves,
Forgets, remembers, grieves,
  And is not sad;
The quiet lands and skies
Leave light upon her eyes;
None knows her, weak or wise,
  Or tired or glad.

None knows, none understands,
What flowers are like her hands;
Though you should search all lands
  Wherein time grows,
What snows are like her feet,
Though his eyes burn with heat
Through gazing on my sweet,
  Yet no man knows.

Only this thing is said;
That white and gold and red,
God's three chief words, man's bread
  And oil and wine,
Were given her for dowers,
And kingdom of all hours,
And grace of goodly flowers
  And various vine.

This is my lady's praise:
God after many days
Wrought her in unknown ways,
  In sunset lands;
This was my lady's birth;
God gave her might and mirth
And laid his whole sweet earth
  Between her hands.

Under deep apple-boughs
My lady hath her house;
She wears upon her brows
  The flower thereof;
All saying but what God saith
To her is as vain breath;
She is more strong than death,
  Being strong as love.

THE KING'S DAUGHTER.

WE were ten maidens in the green corn,
　　Small red leaves in the mill-water:
Fairer maidens never were born,
　　Apples of gold for the king's daughter.

We were ten maidens by a well-head,
　　Small white birds in the mill-water:
Sweeter maidens never were wed,
　　Rings of red for the king's daughter.

The first to spin, the second to sing,
　　Seeds of wheat in the mill-water;
The third may was a goodly thing,
　　White bread and brown for the king's
　　　　daughter.

The fourth to sew and the fifth to play,
　　Fair green weed in the mill-water;
The sixth may was a goodly may,
　　White wine and red for the king's
　　　　daughter.

The seventh to woo, the eighth to wed,
　　Fair thin reeds in the mill-water;
The ninth had gold work on her head,
　　Honey in the comb for the king's daughter.

The ninth had gold work round her hair,
　　Fallen flowers in the mill-water;
The tenth may was goodly and fair,
　　Golden gloves for the king's daughter.

We were ten maidens in a field green,
　　Fallen fruit in the mill-water;
Fairer maidens never have been,
　　Golden sleeves for the king's daughter.

By there comes the king's young son,
　　A little wind in the mill-water;
"Out of ten maidens ye'll grant me one,'
　　A crown of red for the king's daughter.

"Out of ten mays ye'll give me the
　　　　best,"
　　A little rain in the mill-water;
A bed of yellow straw for all the rest,
　　A bed of gold for the king's daughter.

He's ta'en out the goodliest,
　　Rain that rains in the mill-water;
A comb of yellow shell for all the rest,
　　A comb of gold for the king's daughter.

He's made her bed to the goodliest,
　　Wind and hail in the mill-water;
A grass girdle for all the rest,
　　A girdle of arms for the king's daughter.

He's set his heart to the goodliest,
　　Snow that snows in the mill-water;
Nine little kisses for all the rest,
　　An hundredfold for the king's daughter.

He's ta'en his leave at the goodliest,
　　Broken boats in the mill-water;
Golden gifts for all the rest,
　　Sorrow of heart for the king's daughter.

"Ye'll make a grave for my fair body,"
　　Running rain in the mill-water;
"And ye'll streek my brother at the side of
　　　　me,"
　　The pains of hell for the king's daughter.

AFTER DEATH.

THE four boards of the coffin lid
Heard all the dead men did.

The first curse was in his mouth,
Made of grave's mould and deadly drouth.

The next curse was in his head,
Made of God's work discomfited.

The next curse was in his hands,
Made out of two grave-bands.

The next curse was in his feet,
Made out of a grave-sheet.

" I had fair coins red and white,
And my name was as great light;

I had fair clothes green and red,
And strong gold bound round my head.

But no meat comes in my mouth,
Now I fare as the worm doth;

And no gold binds in my hair,
Now I fare as the blind fare.

My live thews were of great strength,
Now I am waxen a span's length;

My live sides were full of lust,
Now are they dried with dust."

The first board spake and said:
" Is it best eating flesh or bread ?"

The second answered it:
" Is wine or honey the more sweet ?"

The third board spake and said:
" Is red gold worth a girl's gold head ?"

The fourth made answer thus:
" All these things are as one with us."

The dead man asked of them:
" Is the green land stained brown with
    flame ?

Have they hewn my son for beasts to eat,
And my wife's body for beasts' meat ?

Have they boiled my maid in a brass pan,
And built a gallows to hang my man ?"

The boards said to him:
" This is a lewd thing that ye deem.

Your wife has gotten a golden bed,
All the sheets are sewn with red.

Your son has gotten a coat of silk,
The sleeves are soft as curded milk.

Your maid has gotten a kirtle new,
All the skirt has braids of blue.

Your man has gotten both ring and glove,
Wrought well for eyes to love."

The dead man answered thus:
" What good gift shall God give us ?"

The boards answered him anon:
"'Flesh to feed hell's worm upon."

MAY JANET.

(BRETON.)

" STAND up, stand up, thou May Janet,
  And go to the wars with me."
He's drawn her by both hands
  With her face against the sea.

" He that strews red shall gather white,
  He that sows white reap red.
Before your face and my daughter's
  Meet in a marriage bed.

"Gold coin shall grow in the yellow field,
  Green corn in the green sea-water,
And red fruit grow of the rose's red,
  Ere your fruit grow in her."

"But I shall have her by land, ' he said,
  "Or I shall have her by sea,
Or I shall have her by strong treason
  And no grace go with me."

Her father's drawn her by both hands,
  He's rent her gown from her,
He's ta'en the smock round her body,
  Cast in the sea-water.

The captain's drawn her by both sides
  Out of the fair green sea;
  "Stand up, stand up, thou May Janet,
And come to the war with me."

The first town they came to
  There was a blue bride-chamber;
He clothed her on with silk
  And belted her with amber.

The second town they came to
  The bridesmen feasted knee to knee;
He clothed her on with silver,
  A stately thing to see.

The third town they came to
  The bridesmaids all had gowns of gold;
He clothed her on with purple,
  A rich thing to behold.

The last town they came to
  He clothed her white and red,
With a green flag either side of her
  And a gold flag overhead.

THE BLOODY SON.

(FINNISH.)

"O WHERE have ye been the morn sae late,
  My merry son, come tell me hither?
O where have ye been the morn sae late?
  And I wot I hae but anither."
"By the water-gate, by the water-gate
  O dear mither."

"And whattin kin' o' wark had ye there to
    make,
  My merry son, come tell me hither?
And whatten kin' o' wark had ye there to
    make?
  And I wot I hae but anither."
"I watered my steeds with water frae the
    lake,
  O dear mither."

"Why is your coat sae fouled the day
  My merry son, come tell me hither?
Why is your coat sae fouled the day?

And I wot I hae but anither."
"The steeds wer stamping sair by the
    weary banks of clay,
  O dear mither."

"And where gat ye thae sleeves of red,
  My merry son, come tell me hither?
And where gat ye thae sleeves of red?
  And I wot I hae but anither."
"I have slain my ae brither by the weary
    water-head,
  O dear mither."

"And where will ye gang to mak your
    mend?
  My merry son, come tell me hither?
And where will ye gang to mak your mend?
  And I wot I hae not anither."
"The warldis way, to the warldis end,
  O dear mither."

And what will ye leave your father dear,
  My merry son, come tell me hither ?
And what will ye leave your father dear ?
  And I wot I hae not anither ”
“ The wood to fell and the logs to bear,
For he'll never see my body mair,
  O dear mither.”

“ And what will ye leave your mither dear,
  My merry son, come tell me hither ?
And what will ye leave your mither dear ?
  And I wot I hae not anither ”
“ The wool to card and the wool to wear,
For ye'll never see my body mair,
  O dear mither.”

“ And what will ye leave for your wife to take,
  My merry son, come tell me hither ?
And what will ye leave for your wife to take ?
  And I wot I hae not anither.”
“ A goodly gown and a fair new make,
For she'll do nae mair for my body's sake,
  O dear mither.”

“ And what will ye leave your young son fair,
  My merry son, come tell me hither ?
And what will ye leave your young son fair ?
  And I wot ye hae not anither.”
“ A twiggen school-rod for his body to bear,
Though it garred him greet he'll get nae mair,
  O dear mither.”

“ And what will ye leave your little daughter sweet ?
  My merry son, come tell me hither ?

And what will ye leave your little daughter sweet ?
  And I wot ye hae not anither.”
“ Wild mulberries for her mouth to eat,
She'll get nae mair though it garred her greet,
  O dear mither.”

“And when will ye come back frae roamin',
  My merry son, come tell me hither ?
And when will ye come back frae roamin' ?
  And I wot I hae not anither.”
“ When the sunrise out of the north is comen,
  O dear mither.”

“ When shall the sunrise on the north side be,
  My merry son, come tell me hither ?
When shall the sunrise on the north side be ?
  And I wot I hae not anither.”
“ When chuckie-stanes shall swim in the sea,
  O dear mither,”

“ When shall stanes in the sea swim,
  My merry son, come tell me hither ?
When shall stanes in the sea swim ?
  And I wot I hae not anither.”
“ When birdies' feathers are as lead therein,
  O dear mither.”

“ When shall feathers be as lead,
  My merry son, come tell me hither ?
When shall feathers be as lead ?
  And I wot I hae not anither.”
“ When God shall judge between the quick and dead,
  O dear mither.”

THE SEA-SWALLOWS.

This fell when Christmas lights were done,
  Red rose leaves will never make wine;
But before the Easter lights begun;
  The ways are sair fra' the Till to the Tyne.

Two lovers sat where the rowan blows
  And all the grass is heavy and fine,
By the gathering place of the sea-swallows
  When the wind brings them over Tyne.

8

Blossom of broom will never make bread,
　Red rose leaves will never make wine:
Between her brows she is grown red,
　That was full white in the fields by Tyne.

"O what is this thing ye have on,
　Show me now, sweet daughter of mine?"
"O father, this is my little son
　That I found hid in the sides of Tyne."

"O what will ye give my son to eat,
　Red rose leaves will never make wine?"
"Fen-water and adder's meat,
　The ways are sair fra' the Till to the
　　Tyne."

"Or what will ye get my son to wear,
　Red rose leaves will never make wine?"
"A weed and a web of nettle's hair,
　The ways are sair fra' the Till to the
　　Tyne."

"Or what will ye take to line his bed,
　Red rose leaves will never make wine?"
"Two black stones at the kirkwall's head,
　The ways are sair fra' the Till to the
　　Tyne."

"Or what will ye give my son for land,
　Red rose leaves will never make wine?"
"Three girl's paces of red sand,
　The ways are sair fra' the Till to the
　　Tyne.

"Or what will ye give me for my son,
　Red rose leaves will never make wine?"
"Six times to kiss his young mouth on,
　The ways are sair fra' the Till to the
　　Tyne."

"But what have ye done with the bearing-
　　bread,
　And what have ye made with the wash-
　　ing-wine?
Or where have ye made your bearing-bed,
　To bear a son in the sides of Tyne?"

"The bearing-bred is soft and new,
　There is no soil in the straining wine;
The bed was made between green and blue,
　It stands full soft by the sides of Tyne.

"The fair grass was my bearing-bread,
　The well-water my washing-wine;
The low leaves were my bearing-bed,
　And that was best in the sides of Tyne."

"O daughter, if ye have done this thing,
　I wot the greater grief is mine;
This was a bitter child-bearing,
　When ye were got by the sides of Tyne."

"About the time of sea-swallows
　That fly full thick by six and nine,
Ye'll have my body out of the house,
　To bury me by the sides of Tyne.

"Set nine stones by the wall for twain,
　Red rose leaves will never make wine;
For the bed I take will measure ten,
　The ways are sair fra' the Till to the
　　Tyne.

"Tread twelve girl's paces out for three,
　Red rose leaves will never make wine;
For the pit I made has taken me,
　The ways are sair fra' the Till to the
　　Tyne."

THE YEAR OF LOVE.

There were four loves that one by one,
Following the seasons and the sun,
Passed over without tears, and fell
Away without farewell.

The first was made of gold and tears,
The next of aspen-leaves and fears,
The third of rose-boughs and rose-roots,
The last love of strange fruits.

These were the four loves faded. Hold
Some minutes fast the time of gold
When our lips each way clung and clove
To a face full of love.

The tears inside our eyelids met,
Wrung forth with kissing, and wept wet
The faces cleaving each to each
Where the blood served for speech.

The second, with low patient brows
Bound under aspen-colored boughs
And eyes made strong and grave with sleep
And yet too weak to weep—

The third, with eager mouth at ease
Fed from late autumn honey, lees
Of scarce gold left in latter cells
With scattered flower-smells—

Hair sprinkled over with spoilt sweet
Of ruined roses, wrists and feet

Slight-swathed, as grassy girdled sheaves
Hold in stray poppy-leaves—

The fourth, with lips whereon has bled
Some great pale fruit's slow color, shed
From the rank bitter husk whence drips
Faint blood between her lips—

Made of the heat of whole great Junes
Burning the blue dark round their moons
(Each like a mown red marigold)
So hard the flame keeps hold—

These are burnt thoroughly away.
Only the first holds out a day
Beyond these latter loves that were
Made of mere heat and air.

And now the time is winterly
The first loves fades too: none will see,
When April warms the world anew,
The place wherein love grew.

DEDICATION.

1865.

THE sea gives her shells to the shingle,
    The earth gives her streams to the sea;
They are many, but my gift is single,
    My verses, the first fruits of me.
Let the wind take the green and the grey
        leaf,
    Cast forth without fruit upon air;
Take rose-leaf and vine-leaf and bay-leaf
    Blown loose from the hair.

The night shakes them round me in legions
    Dawn drives them before her like dreams;
Time sheds them like snows on strange
        regions,
    Swept shoreward on infinite streams;

Leaves pallid and sombre and ruddy,
    Dead fruits of the fugitive years;
Some stained as with wine and made
        bloody,
    And some as with tears.

Some scattered in seven years' traces,
    As they fell from the boy that was then;
Long left among idle green places,
    Or gathered but now among men;
On seas full of wonder and peril,
    Blown white round the capes of the
        north;
Or in islands where myrtles are sterile
    And loves bring not forth.

O daughters of dreams and of stories
  That life is not wearied of yet,
Faustine, Fragoletta, Dolores,
  Félise and Yolande and Juliette,
Shall I find you not still, shall I miss you,
  When sleep, that is true or that seems,
Comes back to me hopeless to kiss you,
  O daughters of dreams.

They are past as a slumber that passes,
  As the dew of a dawn of old time;
More frail than the shadows on glasses,
  More fleet than a wave or a rhyme.
As the waves after ebb drawing seaward,
  When their hollows are full of the night,
So the birds that flew singing to me-ward
  Recede out of sight.

The songs of dead seasons, that wander
  On wings of articulate words;
Lost leaves that the shore-wind may squan-
    der,
  Light flocks of untameable birds;
Some sang to me dreaming in class time
  And truant in hand as in tongue;
For the youngest were born of boy's pas-
    time,
  The eldest are young.

Is there shelter while life in them lingers,
  Is there hearing for songs that recede,
Tunes touched from a harp with men's
    fingers
  Or blown with boy's mouth in a reed?
Is there place in the land of your labor,
  Is there room in your world of delight,
Where change has not sorrow for neighbor
  And day has not night?

In their wings though the sea-wind yet
    quivers,
  Will you spare not a space for them there
Made green with the running of rivers
  And gracious with temperate air;
In the fields and the turreted cities,
  That cover from sunshine and rain
Fair passions and bountiful pities
  And loves without stain?

In a land of clear colors and stories,
  In a region of shadowless hours,
Where earth has a garment of glories
  And a murmur of musical flowers;
In woods where the spring half uncovers
  The flush of her amorous face,
By the waters that listen for lovers,
  For these is there place?

For the song-birds of sorrow, that muffle
  Their music as clouds do their fire:
For the storm-birds of passion, that ruffle
  Wild wings in a wind of desire;
In the stream of the storm as it settles
  Blown seaward, borne far from the sun,
Shaken loose on the darkness like petals
  Dropt one after one?

Though the world of your hands be more
    gracious
  And lovelier in lordship of things
Clothed round by sweet art with the
    spacious
  Warm heaven of her imminent wings,
Let them enter, unfledged and nigh fainting,
  For the love of old loves and lost times;
And receive in your palace of painting
  This revel of rhymes.

Though the seasons of man full of losses
  Make empty the years full of youth,
If but one thing be constant in crosses,
  Change lays not her hand upon truth;
Hopes die, and their tombs are for token
  That the grief as the joy of them ends
Ere time that breaks all men has broken
  The faith between friends.

Though the many lights dwindle to one
    light,
  There is help if the heaven has one;
Though the skies be discrowned of the
    sunlight
  And the earth dispossessed of the sun,
They have moonlight and sleep for repay-
    ment,
  When, refreshed as a bride and set free
With stars and sea-winds in her raiment,
  Night sinks on the sea.

SONGS OF TWO NATIONS.

I. A SONG OF ITALY.

II. ODE ON THE PROCLAMATION OF THE
FRENCH REPUBLIC.

III. DIRÆ.

I saw the double-featured statue stand
Of Memnon or of Janus, half with night
ᵕ eiled, and fast bound with iron; half with light
Crowned, holding all men's future in his hand.

And all the old westward face of time grown grey
Was writ with cursing and inscribed for death
But on the fac. that met the morning's breath
Fear died of hope as darkness dies of day.

INSCRIBED

WITH ALL DEVOTION AND REVERENCE

TO

JOSEPH MAZZINI.

1867.

A SONG OF ITALY.

UPON a windy night of stars that fell
　　At the wind's spoken spell,
Swept with sharp strokes of agonizing
　　light
　　From the clear gulf of night,
Between the fixed and fallen glories one
　　Against my vision shone,
More fair and fearful and divine than they
　　That measure night and day,
And worthier worship; and within mine
　　eyes
　　The formless folded skies
Took shape and were unfolded like as
　　flowers.
　　And I beheld the hours
As maidens, and the days as laboring men,
　　And the soft nights again
As wearied women to their own souls wed,
　　And ages as the dead.
And over these living, and them that died,
　　From one to the other side
A lordlier light than comes of earth or air
　　Made the world's future fair.
A woman like to love in face, but not
　　A thing of transient lot—
And like to hope, but having hold on
　　truth—
　　And like to joy or youth,
Save that upon the rock her feet were
　　set—
　　And like what men forget,
Faith, innocence, high thought, laborious
　　peace—
　　And yet like none of these,
Being not as these are mortal, but with
　　eyes
　　That sounded the deep skies
And clove like wings or arrows their clear
　　way
　　Through night and dawn and day—
So fair a presence over star and sun
　　Stood, making these as one.
For in the shadow of her shape were all
　　Darkened and held in thrall,
So mightier rose she past them; and I felt
　　Whose form, whose likeness knelt
With covered hair and face and clasped
　　her knees;

And knew the first of these
Was Freedom, and the second Italy.
　　And what sad words said she
For mine own grief I knew not, nor had
　　heart
　　Therewith to bear my part
And set my songs to sorrow; nor to hear
　　How tear by sacred tear
Fell from her eyes as flowers or notes that
　　fall
　　In some slain feaster's hall
Where in mid music and melodious breath
　　Men singing have seen death.
So fair, so lost, so sweet she knelt; or so
　　In our lost eyes below
Seemed to us sorrowing; and her speech
　　being said,
　　Fell, as one who falls dead.
And for a little she too wept, who stood
　　Above the dust and blood
And thrones and troubles of the world;
　　then spake,
　　As who bids dead men wake.

' Because the years were heavy on thy
　　head;
　　Because dead things are dead;
Because thy chosen on hill-side, city and
　　plain
　　Are shed as drops of rain;
Because all earth was black, all heaven
　　was blind,
　　And we cast out of mind;
Because men wept, saying *Freedom*, know-
　　ing of thee,
　　Child, that thou wast not free:
Because wherever blood was not shame was
　　Where thy pure foot did pass;
Because on Promethean rocks distent
　　Thee fouler eagles rent;
Because a serpent stains with slime and
　　foam
　　This that is not thy Rome;
Child of my womb, whose limbs were made
　　in me,
　　Have I forgotten thee?
In all thy dreams through all these years
　　on wing,

Hast thou dreamed such a thing?
The mortal mother-bird outsoars her nest,
  The child outgrows the breast;
But suns as stars shall fall from heaven and
    cease,
  Ere we twain be as these;
Yea, utmost skies forget their utmost sun,
  Ere we twain be not one.
My lesser jewels sewn on skirt and hem,
  I have no heed of them
Obscured and flawed by sloth or craft or
    power;
  But thou, that wast my flower,
The blossom bound between my brows and
    worn
  In sight of even and morn
From the last ember of the flameless west
  To the dawn's baring breast—
I were not Freedom if thou wert not free,
  Nor thou wert Italy.
O mystic rose ingrained with blood, im-
    pearled
  With tears of all the world!
The torpor of their blind brute-ridden
    trance
  Kills England and chills France;
And Spain sobs hard through strangling
    blood; and snows
  Hide the huge eastern woes.
But thou, twin-born with morning, nursed
    of noon,
  And blessed of star and moon!
What shall avail to assail thee any more,
  From sacred shore to shore?
Have Time and Love not knelt down at
    thy feet,
  Thy sore, thy soiled, thy sweet,
Fresh from the flints and mire of murderous
    ways
  And dust of travelling days?
Hath Time not kissed them, Love not
    washed them fair,
  And wiped with tears and hair?
Though God forget thee, I will not forget;
  Though heaven and earth be set
Against thee, O unconquerable child,
  Abused, abased, reviled,
Lift thou not less from no funereal bed
  Thine undishonored head;

Love thou not less, by lips of thine once
    prest,
  This my now barren breast;
Seek thou not less, being well assured
    thereof,
  O child, my latest love.

For now the barren bosom shall bear fruit,
  Songs leap from lips long mute,
And with my milk the mouths of nations
    fed
  Again be glad and red
That were worn white with hunger and
    sorrow and thirst;
  And thou, most fair and first,
Thou whose warm hands and sweet live
    lips I feel
  Upon me for a seal,
Thou whose least looks, whose smiles and
    little sighs,
  Whose passionate pure eyes,
Whose dear fair limbs that neither bonds
    could bruise
  Nor hate of men misuse,
Whose flower-like breath and bosom, O my
    child,
  O mine and undefiled,
Fill with such tears as burn like bitter
    wine
  These mother's eyes of mine,
Thrill with huge passions and primeval
    pains
  The fulness of my veins.
O sweetest head seen higher than any
    stands,
  I touch thee with mine hands,
I lay my lips upon thee, O thou most
    sweet,
  To lift thee on thy feet
And with the fire of mine to fill thine eyes;
  I say unto thee, Arise.'

She ceased, and heaven was full of flame
    and sound,
  And earth's old limbs unbound
Shone and waxed warm with fiery dew and
    seed
  Shed through her at this her need;
And highest in heaven, a mother and full
    of grace,
  With no more covered face,
With no more lifted hands and bended
    knees,
  Rose, as from sacred seas
Love, when old time was full of plenteous
    springs,
  That fairest-born of things,
The land that holds the rest in tender
    thrall
  For love's sake in them all,
That binds with words and holds with eyes
  and hands

All hearts in all men's lands.
So died the dream whence rose the live
  desire
    That here takes form and fire,
A spirit from the splendid grave of sleep
  Risen, that ye should not weep,
Should not weep more nor ever, O ye that
  hear
    And ever have held her dear,
Seeing now indeed she weeps not who
  wept sore,
    And sleeps not any more.
Hearken ye towards her, O people exalt
  your eyes;
    Is this a thing that dies?

Italia! by the passion of the pain
    That bent and rent thy chain;
Italia! by the breaking of the bands,
    The shaking of the lands;
Beloved, O men's mother, O men's queen,
    Arise, appear, be seen!
Arise, array thyself in manifold
    Queen's raiment of wrought gold;
With girdles of green freedom, and with
  red
    Roses, and white snow shed
Above the flush and frondage of the hills
    That all thy deep dawn fills
And all thy clear night veils and warms
  with wings
    Spread till the morning sings;
The rose of resurrection, and the bright
    Breast lavish of the light,
The lady lily like the snowy sky
    Ere the stars wholly die;
As red as blood, and whiter than a wave
    Flowers grown as from thy grave,
From the green fruitful grass in Maytime
  hot,
    Thy grave, where thou art not.
Gather the grass and weave, in sacred
  sign
    Of the ancient earth divine,
The holy heart of things, the seed of
  birth,
    The mystical warm earth.
O thou her flower of flowers, with treble
  braid
    Be thy sweet head arrayed,
In witness of her mighty motherhood
    Who bore thee and found thee good,
Her fairest-born of children, on whose
  head
    Her green and white and red

Are hope and light and life, inviolate
    Of any latter fate.
Fly, O our flag, through deep Italian
  air,
    Above the flags that were,
The dusty shreds of shameful battle-flags
    Trampled and rent in rags,
As withering woods in autumn's bitterest
  breath
    Yellow, and black as death;
Black as crushed worms that sicken in the
  sense,
    And yellow as pestilence.
Fly, green as summer and red as dawn and
  white
    As the live heart of light,
The blind bright womb of color unborn,
  that brings
    Forth all fair forms of things,
As freedom all fair forms of nations dyed
    In divers-colored pride.
Fly, fleet as wind on every wind that blows
    Between her seas and snows,
From Alpine white, from Tuscan green,
  and where
    Vesuvius reddens air.
Fly! and let all men see it, and all kings
  wail,
    And priests wax faint and pale,
And the cold hordes that moan in misty
  places
    And the funereal races
And the sick serfs of lands that wait and
  wane
    See thee and hate thee in vain.
In the clear laughter of all winds and
  waves,
    In the blown grass of graves,
In the long sound of fluctuant boughs of
  trees,
    In the broad breath of seas,
Bid the sound of thy flying folds be
  heard;
    And as a spoken word
Full of that fair god and that merciless
    Who rends the Pythoness,
So be the sound and so the fire that saith
    She feels her ancient breath
And the old blood move in her immortal
  veins.

Strange travail and strong pains,
Our mother, hast thou borne these many
  years
    While thy pure blood and tears

Mixed with the Tyrrhene and the Adrian
　　sea;
　　Light things were said of thee,
As of one buried deep among the dead;
　　Yea, she hath been, they said,
She was when time was younger, and is
　　not:
The very cerecloths rot
That flutter in the dusty wind of death,
　　Not moving with her breath;
Far seasons and forgotten years enfold
　　Her dead corpse old and cold
With　many　windy　winters　and　pale
　　springs:
　　She is none of this world's things.
Though her dead head like a live garland
　　wear
　　The golden-growing hair
That flows over her breast down to her
　　feet,
　　Dead queens, whose life was sweet
In sight of all men living, have been
　　found
　　So cold, so clad, so crowned,
With all things faded and with one thing
　　fair,
　　Their old immortal hair,
When flesh and bone turned dust at touch
　　of day:
　　And she is dead as they.

So men said sadly, mocking; so the slave,
　　Whose life was his soul's grave:
So, pale or red with change of fast and
　　feast,
　　The sanguine-sandalled priest
So the Austrian, when his fortune came to
　　flood,
　　And the warm wave was blood;
With wings that widened and with beak
　　that smote,
　　So shrieked through either throat
From the hot horror of its northern nest
　　That double-headed pest;
So, triple-crowned with fear and fraud and
　　shame,
　　He of whom treason came,
The herdsman of the Gadarean swine;
　　So all his ravening kine,
Made fat with poisonous pasture; so not
　　we,
　　Mother, beholding thee.
Make answer, O the crown of all our
　　slain,
　　Ye that were one, being twain,

Twain brethren, twin-born to the second
　　birth,
　　Chosen out of all our earth
To be the prophesying stars that say
　　How hard is night on day,
Stars in serene and sudden heaven rerisen
　　Before the sun break prison
And ere the moon be wasted ; fair first
　　flowers
　　In that red wreath of ours
Woven with the lives of all whose lives
　　were shed
　　To crown their mother's head
With leaves of civic cypress and thick
　　yew,
　　Till the olive bind it too,
Olive and laurel and all loftier leaves
　　That victory wears or weaves
At her fair feet for her beloved brow;
　　Hear, for she too hears now,
O Pisacane, from Calabrian sands;
　　O all heroic hands
Close on the sword-hilt, hands of all her
　　dead;
　　O many a holy head,
Bowed for her sake even to her reddening
　　dust;
　　O chosen, O pure and just,
Who counted for a small thing life's estate,
　　And died, and made it great;
Ye whose names mix with all her memo-
　　ries; ye
　　Who rather chose to see
Death, than our more intolerable things;
　　Thou whose name withers kings,
Agesilao; thou too, O chiefliest thou,
　　The slayer of splendid brow,
Laid where the lying lips of fear deride
　　The foiled tyrannicide,
Foiled, fallen, slain, scorned, and happy,
　　being in fame,
　　Felice, like thy name,
Not like thy fortune; father of the fight,
　　Having in hand our light.
Ah, happy ! for that sudden-swerving
　　hand
　　Flung light on all thy land,
Yea, lit blind France with compulsory
　　ray,
　　Driven down a righteous way;
Ah, happiest ! for from thee the wars be-
　　gan,
　　From thee the fresh springs ran;
From thee the lady land that queens the
　　earth
　　Gat as she gave new birth,

O sweet mute mouths, O all fair dead of
    ours,
  Fair in our eyes as flowers,
Fair without feature, vocal without voice,
  Strong without strength, rejoice !
Hear it with ears that hear not, and on
    eyes
  That see not let it rise,
Rise as a sundawn; be it as dew that
    drips
  On dumb and dusty lips;
Eyes have ye not, and see it; neither ears,
  And there is none but hears.
This is the same for whom ye bled and
    wept;
  She was not dead, but slept.
This is that very Italy which was
  And is and shall not pass.

But thou, though all were not well done,
    O chief,
  Must thou take shame or grief?
Because one man is not as thou or ten,
  Must thou take shame for men ?
Because the supreme sunrise is not yet,
  Is the young dew not wet ?
Wilt thou not yet abide a little while,
  Soul without fear or guile,
Mazzini,—O our prophet, O our priest,
  A little while at least ?
A little hour of doubt and of control,
  Sustain thy sacred soul;
Withhold thine heart, our father, but an
    hour;
  Is it not here, the flower,
Is it not blown and fragrant from the root,
  And shall not be the fruit ?
Thy children, even thy people thou hast
    made,
  Thine, with thy words arrayed,
Clothed with thy thoughts and girt with
    thy desires,
  Yearn up toward thee as fires.
Art thou not father, O father, of all these ?
  From thine own Genoese
To where of nights the lower extreme
    lagune
  Feels its Venetian moon,
Nor suckling's mouth nor mother's breast
    set free
  But hath that grace through thee.
The milk of life on death's unnatural brink
  Thou gavest them to drink,
The natural milk of freedom; and again
  They drank, and they were men.

The wine and honey of freedom and of
    faith
  They drank, and cast off death.
Bear with them now; thou art holier: yet
    endure,
  Till they as thou be pure.
Their swords at least that stemmed half
    Austria's tide
  Bade all its bulk divide;
Else, though fate bade them for a breath's
    space fall,
  She had not fallen at all.
Not by their hands they made time's
    promise true;
  Not by their hands, but through.
Nor on Custoza ran their blood to waste,
  Nor fell their fame defaced
Whom stormiest Adria with tumultuous
    tides
  Whirls undersea and hides.
Not his, who from the sudden-settling
    deck
  Looked over death and wreck
To where the mother's bosom shone, who
    smiled
  As he, so dying, her child;
For he smiled surely, dying, to mix his
    death
  With her memorial breath;
Smiled, being most sure of her, that in no
    wise,
  Die whoso will, she dies:
And she smiled surely, fair and far above,
  Wept not, but smiled for love.
Thou too, O splendor of the sudden
    sword
  That drove the crews abhorred
From Naples and the siren-footed strand
  Flash from thy master's hand
Shine from the middle summer of the
    seas
  To the old Æolides,
Outshine their fiery fumes of burning
    night,
  Sword, with thy midday light;
Flame as a beacon from the Tyrrhene
    foam
  To the rent heart of Rome,
From the island of her lover and thy lord,
  Her saviour and her sword,
In the fierce year of failure and of fame,
  Art thou not yet the same
That wast as lightning swifter than all
    wings
  In the blind face of kings?

When priests took counsel to devise de-
    spair,
  And princes to forswear,
She clasped thee, O her sword and flag-
    bearer
  And staff and shield to her,
O Garibaldi; need was hers and grief,
  Of thee and of the chief,
And of another girt in arms to stand
  As good of hope and hand,
As high of soul and happy, albeit indeed
  The heart should burn and bleed,
So but the spirit shake not nor the breast
  Swerve, but abide its rest.
As theirs did and as thine, though ruin
    clomb
  The highest wall of Rome,
Though treason stained and spilt her lustral
    water,
  And slaves led slaves to slaughter,
And priests, praying and slaying, watched
    them pass
  From a strange France, alas,
That was not freedom; yet when these
    were past,
  Thy sword and thou stood fast,
Till new men seeing thee where Sicilian
    waves
  Hear now no sound of slaves,
And where thy sacred blood is fragrant still
  Upon the Bitter Hill,
Seeing by that blood one country saved and
    stained,
  Less loved thee crowned than chained,
And less now only than the chief: for he,
  Father of Italy,
Upbore in holy hands the babe new-born
  Through loss and sorrow and scorn,
Of no man led, of many men reviled;
  Till lo, the new-born child
Gone from between his hands, and in its
    place,
  Lo, the fair mother's face.
Blessed is he of all men, being in one
  As father to her and son,
Blessed of all men living, that he found
  Her weak limbs bared and bound,
And in his arms and in his bosom bore,
  And as a garment wore
Her weight of want, and as a royal dress
  Put on her weariness.
As in faith's hoariest histories men read,
  The strong man bore at need
Through roaring rapids when all heaven
  was wild

  The likeness of a child
That still waxed greater and heavier as he
    trod,
  And altered, and was God.
Praise him, O winds that move the molten
    air,
  O light of days that were,
And light of days that shall be; land and
    sea,
  And heaven and Italy:
Praise him, O storm and summer, shore
    and wave,
  O skies and every grave;
O weeping hopes, O memories beyond
    tears,
  O many and murmuring years,
O sounds far off in time and visions far,
  O sorrow with thy star;
And joy with all thy beacons; ye that
    mourn,
  And ye whose light is born;
O fallen faces, and O souls arisen,
  Praise him from tomb and prison,
Praise him from heaven and sunlight; and
    ye floods,
  And windy waves of woods;
Ye valleys and wild vineyards, ye lit lakes
  And happier hillsides brakes,
Untrampled by the cursed feet that trod
  Fields golden from their god,
Fields of their god forsaken, whereof none
  Sees his face in the sun,
Hears his voice from the floweriest wilder-
    ness;
And, barren of his tresses,
Ye bays unplucked and laurels unen-
    twined,
  That no men break or bind,
And myrtles long forgetful of the sword,
  And olives unadored,
Wisdom and love, white hands that save
    and slay,
  Praise him; and ye as they,
Praise him, O gracious might of dews and
    rains
  That feed the purple plains,
O sacred sunbeams bright as bare steel
    drawn,
  O cloud and fire and dawn;
Red hills of flame, white Alps, green
    Apennines,
  Banners of blowing pines,
Standards of stormy snows, flags of light
    leaves,
  Three wherewith Freedom weaves

One ensign that once woven and once un-
　　furled
　　Makes day of all a world,
Makes blind their eyes who knew not, and
　　outbraves
　　The waste of iron waves;
Ye fields of yellow fullness, ye fresh foun-
　　tains,
　　And mists of many mountains;
Ye moons and seasons, and ye days and
　　nights;
　　Ye starry-headed heights,
And gorges melting sunward from the
　　snow,
　　And all strong streams that flow,
Tender as tears, and fair as faith, and
　　pure
　　As hearts made sad and sure
At once by many sufferings and one love;
　　O mystic deathless dove
Held to the heart of earth and in her
　　hands
　　Cherished, O lily of lands,
White rose of time, dear dream of praises
　　past—
　　For such as these thou wast,
That art as eagles setting to the sun,
　　As fawns that leap and run,
As a sword carven with keen floral gold,
　　Sword for an armed god's hold,
Flower for a crowned god's forehead—O
　　our land,
　　Reach forth thine holiest hand,
O mother of many sons and memories,
　　Stretch out thine hand to his
That raised and gave thee life to run and
　　leap
　　When thou wast full of sleep,
That touched and stung thee with young
　　blood and breath
　　When thou wast hard on death.
Praise him, O all her cities and her crowns,
　　Her towers and thrones of towns;
O noblest Brescia, scarred from foot to
　　head
　　And breast-deep in the dead,
Praise him from all the glories of the graves
　　That yellow Mela laves
With gentle and golden water, whose fair
　　flood
　　Ran wider with thy blood :
Praise him, O born of that heroic breast,
　　O nursed thereat and blest,
Verona, fairer than thy mother fair,
　　But not more brave to bear :

Praise him, O Milan, whose imperial tread
　　Bruised once the German head ;
Whose might, by northern swords left
　　desolate,
　　Set foot on fear and fate :
Praise him, O long mute mouth of melodies,
　　Mantua, with louder keys,
With mightier chords of music even than
　　rolled
　　From the large harps of old,
When thy sweet singer of golden throat and
　　tongue,
　　Praising his tyrant, sung ;
Though now thou sing not as of other days,
　　Learn late a better praise.
Not with the sick sweet lips of slaves that
　　sing,
　　Praise thou no priest or king,
No brow-bound laurel of discoloured leaf,
　　But him, the crownless chief.
Praise him, O star of sun-forgotten times,
　　Among their creeds and crimes
That wast a fire of witness in the night,
　　Padua, the wise men's light :
Praise him, O sacred Venice, and the sea
　　That now exults through thee,
Full of the mighty morning and the sun,
　　Free of things dead and done ;
Praise him from all the years of thy great
　　grief,
　　That shook thee like a leaf
With winds and snows of torment, rain that
　　fell
　　Red as the rains of hell,
Storms of black thunder and of yellow flame,
　　And all ill things but shame ;
Praise him with all thy holy heart and
　　strength ;
　　Through thy walls' breadth and length
Praise him with all thy people, that their
　　voice
　　Bid the strong soul rejoice,
The fair clear supreme spirit beyond stain,
　　Pure as the depth of pain,
High as the head of suffering, and secure
　　As all things that endure.
More than thy blind lord of an hundred
　　years
　　Whose name our memory hears,
Home-bound from harbours of the Byzantine
　　Made tributary of thine,
Praise him who gave no gifts from oversea,
　　But gave thyself to thee.
O mother Genoa, through all years that run,
　　More than that other son,

Who first beyond the seas of sunset prest
    Even to the unfooted west,
Whose black-blown flag scared from their
    sheltering seas
    The unknown Atlantides,
And as flame climbs through cloud and
    vapour clomb
Through streams of storm and foam,
Till half in sight they saw land heave and
    swim—
    More than this man praise him.
One found a world new-born from virgin
    sea ;
    And one found Italy.
O heavenliest Florence, from the mouths of
    flowers
    Fed by melodious hours,
From each sweet mouth that kisses light
    and air,
    Thou whom thy fate made fair,
As a bound vine or any flowering tree,
    Praise him who made thee free.
For no grape-gatherers trampling out the
    wine
    Tread thee, the fairest vine ;
For no man binds thee, no man bruises,
    none
    Does with thee as these have done.
From where spring hears loud through ner
    long lit vales
    Triumphant nightingales,
In many a fold of fiery foliage hidden.
    Withheld as things forbidden,
But clamorous with innumerable delight
    In May's red, green, and white,
In the far-floated standard of the spring,
    That bids men also sing,
Our flower of flags, our witness that are
    free,
    Our lamp for land and sea ;
From where Majano feels through corn and
    vine
    Spring move and melt as wine,
And Fiesole's embracing arms enclose
    The immeasurable rose ;
From hill-sides plumed with pine, and
    heights wind-worn
    That feel the refluent morn,
Or where the moon's face warm and
    passionate
    Burns, and men's hearts grow great,
And the swoln eyelids labor with sweet
    tears,
    And in their burning ears

Sound throbs like flame, and in their eyes
    new light
    Kindles the trembling night ;
From faint illumined fields and starry valleys
    Wherefrom the hill-wind sallies,
From Valombrosa, from Valdarno raise
    One Tuscan tune of praise.
O lordly city of the field of death,
    Praise him with equal breath,
From sleeping streets and gardens, and the
    stream
    That threads them as a dream
Threads without light the untravelled ways
    of sleep
    With eyes that smile or weep ;
From the sweet sombre beauty of wave and
    wall
    That fades and does not fall ;
From colored domes and cloisters fair
    with fame,
    Praise thou and thine his name.
Thou too, O little laurelled town of towers,
    Clothed with the flame of flowers,
From windy ramparts girdled with young
    gold,
    From thy sweet hill-side fold
Of wallflowers and the acacia's belted
    bloom
    And every blowing plume,
Halls that saw Dante speaking, chapels
    fair
    As the outer hills and air,
Praise him who feeds the fire that Dante
    fed,
    Our highest heroic head,
Whose eyes behold through floated cloud
    and flame
    The maiden face of fame
Like April's in Valdelsa ; fair as flowers,
    And patient as the hours ;
Sad with slow sense of time, and bright
    with faith
    That levels life and death ;
The final fame, that with a foot sublime
    Treads down reluctant time ;
The fame that waits and watches and is
    wise,
    A virgin with chaste eyes,
A goddess who takes hands with great
    men's grief ;
    Praise her, and him, our chief.
Praise him, O Siena, and thou her deep
    green spring,
    O Fonte Branda, sing :

Shout from the red clefts of thy fiery crags,
　Shake out thy flying flags
In the long wind that streams from hill to
　hill ;
　Bid thy full music fill
The desolate red waste of sunset air
　And fields the old time saw fair,
But now the hours ring void through
　ruined lands,
　Wild work of mortal hands ;
Yet through thy dead Maremma let his
　name
　Take flight and pass in flame,
And the red ruin of disastrous hours
　Shall quicken into flowers.
Praise him, O fiery child of sun and sea,
　Naples, who bade thee be ;
For till he sent the swords that scourge
　and save,
　Thou was not, but thy grave.
But more than all these praise him and
　give thanks,
　Thou, from thy Tiber's banks,
From all thine hills and from thy supreme
　dome,
　Praise him, O risen Rome.
Let all thy children cities at thy knee
　Lift up their voice with thee,
Saying 'for thy love's sake and our per-
　ished grief
　We laud thee, O our chief ;'
Saying 'for thine hand and help when
　hope was dead
　We thank thee, O our head ;'
Saying 'for thy voice and face within our
　sight
　We bless thee, O our light ;
For waters cleansing us from days defiled
　We praise thee, O our child.'

So with an hundred cities' mouths in one
　Praising thy supreme son,
Son of thy sorrow, O mother, O maid and
　mother,
　Our queen, who serve none other,
Our lady of pity and mercy, and full of grace,
　Turn otherwhere thy face,
Turn for a little and look what things are
　these
　Now fallen before thy knees ;
Turn upon them thine eyes who hated
　thee,
　Behold what things they be,
Italia: these are stubble that were steel,
　Dust, or a turning wheel ;

As leaves, as snow, as sand, that were so
　strong ;
　And howl, for all their song,
And wail, for all their wisdom ; they that
　were
　So great, they are all stript bare,
They are made empty of beauty, and all
　abhorred ;
　They are shivered, and their sword ;
They are slain who slew, they are heart-
　less who were wise ;
　Yea, turn on these thine eyes,
O thou, soliciting with soul sublime
　The obscure soul of time,
Thou, with the wounds thy holy body
　bears
　From broken swords of theirs,
Thou, with the sweet swoln eyelids that
　have bled
　Tears for thy thousands dead,
And upon these, whose swords drank up
　like dew
　The sons of thine they slew,
These, whose each gun blasted with mur-
　dering mouth
　Live flowers of thy fair south,
These, whose least evil told in alien ears
　Turned men's whole blood to tears,
These, whose least sin remembered for
　pure shame
　Turned all those tears to flame,
Even upon these, when breaks the extreme
　blow
　And all the world cries woe,
When heaven reluctant rains long-suffering
　fire
　On these and their desire,
When his wind shakes them and his waters
　whelm
　Who rent thy robe and realm,
When they that poured thy dear blood
　forth as wine
　Pour forth their own for thine,
On these, on these have mercy : not in
　hate,
　But full of sacred fate,
Strong from the shrine and splendid from
　the god,
　Smite, with no second rod.
Because they spared not, do thou rather
　spare :
　Be not one thing they were.
Let not one tongue of theirs who hate thee
　say
　That thou wast even as they.

Because their hands were bloody, be thine
 white ;
 Show light where they shed night :
Because they are foul, be thou the rather
 pure ;
 Because they are feeble, endure ;
Because they had no pity, have thou pity.

And thou, O supreme city,
O priestless Rome that shalt be, take in trust
 Their names, their deeds, their dust,
Who held life less than thou wert ; be the
 least
 To thee indeed a priest,
Priest and burnt-offering and blood-sacri-
 fice
 Given without prayer or price,
A holier immolation than men wist,
 A costlier eucharist,
A sacrament more saving ; bend thine head
 Above these many dead
Once, and salute with thine eternal eyes
 Their lowest head that lies.
Speak from thy lips of immemorial speech
 If but one word for each.
Kiss but one kiss on each thy dead son's
 mouth
 Fallen dumb or north or south.
And laying but once thine hand on brow
 and breast,
 Bless them, through whom thou art
 blest.
And saying in ears of these thy dead 'Well
 done,'
 Shall they not hear 'O son '?
And bowing thy face to theirs made pale
 for thee,
 Shall the shut eyes not see ?
Yea, through the hollow-hearted world of
 death,
 As light, as blood, as breath,
Shall there not flash and flow the fiery
 sense,
 The pulse of prescience ?
Shall not these know as in times overpast
 Thee loftiest to the last ?
For times and wars shall change, kingdoms
 and creeds,
 And dreams of men, and deeds ;
Earth shall grow grey with all her golden
 things,
 Pale peoples and hoar kings ;
But though her thrones and towers of
 nations fall,
 Death has no part in all ;

In the air, nor in the imperishable sea,
 Nor heaven, nor truth, nor thee.
Yea, let all sceptre-stricken nations lie,
 But live thou though they die ;
Let their flags fade as flowers that storm
 can mar,
 But thine be like a star ;
Let England's, if it float not for men free,
 Fall, and forget the sea ;
Let France's, if it shadow a hateful head,
 Drop as a leaf drops dead ;
Thine let what storm soever smite the rest
 Smite as it seems him best ;
Thine let the wind that can, by sea or
 land,
 Wrest from thy banner-hand.
Die they in whom dies freedom, die and
 cease,
 Though the world weep for these ;
Live thou and love and lift when these lie
 dead
 The green and white and red.

O our Republic that shalt bind in bands
 The kingdomless far lands
And link the chainless ages ; thou that
 wast
 With England ere she past
Among the faded nations, and shalt be
 Again, when sea to sea
Calls through the wind and light of morn-
 ing time,
 And throneless clime to clime
Makes antiphonal answer ; thou that art
 Where one man's perfect heart
Burns, one man's brow is brightened for
 thy sake,
 Thine, strong to make or break ;
O fair Republic hallowing with stretched
 hands
 The limitless free lands
When all men's heads for love, not fear,
 bow down
 To thy sole royal crown,
As thou to freedom ; when man's life
 smells sweet;
 And at thy bright swift feet
A bloodless and a bondless world is laid ;
 Then, when thy men are made,
Let these indeed as we in dreams behold
 One chosen of all thy fold,
One of all fair things fairest, one exalt
 Above all fear or fault,
One unforgetful of unhappier men
 And us who loved her then ;

With eyes that outlook suns and dream on
  graves ;
  With voice like quiring waves ;
With heart the holier for their memories'
  sake
Who slept that she might wake ;
With breast the sweeter for that sweet
  blood lost,
  And all the milkless cost ;
Lady of earth, whose large equality
  Bends but to her and thee ;
Equal with heaven, and infinite of years,

And splendid from quenched tears ;
Strong with old strength of great things
  fallen and fled,
  Diviner for her dead ;
Chaste of all stains and perfect from all
  scars,
  Above all storms and stars,
All winds that blow through time, all
  waves that foam,
  Our Capitolian Rome.

1867.

ODE ON PROCLAMATION OF THE FRENCH REPUBLIC.

SEPTEMBER 4TH, 1870.

À VICTOR HUGO.

αἴλινον αἴλινον εἰπὲ, τὸ δ᾿ εὖ νικάτω

STROPHE I.

With songs and crying and sound of ac-
  clamations,
  Lo, the flame risen, the fire that falls in
  showers !
Hark ; for the word is out among the na-
  tions :
  Look; for the light is up upon the hours ;
O fears, O shames, O many tribulations,
  Yours were all yesterdays, but this day
  ours.
Strong were your bonds linked fast with
  lamentations,
  With groans and tears built into walls
  and towers :
Strong were your works and wonders of
  high stations,
  Your forts blood-based, and rampires of
  your powers :
Lo now the last of divers desolations,
  The hand of time, that gathers hosts like
  flowers ;
Time, that fills up and pours out generations;
  Time, at whose breath confounded empire
  cowers.

STR. 2.

What are these moving in the dawn's
  red gloom ?
What is she waited on by dread and
  doom,
Ill ministers of morning, bondsmen born of
  night ?
If that head veiled and bowed be morning's head,
If she come walking between doom and
  dread,
Who shall rise up with song and dance
  before her sight ?

Are not the night's dead heaped about
  her feet ?
Is not death swollen, and slaughter full
  of meat ?
What, is their feast a bride-feast, where
  men sing and dance ?
A bitter, a bitter bride-song and a shrill
Should the house raise that such bride-
  followers fill,
Wherein defeat weds ruin, and takes for
  bride-bed France.

For nineteen years deep shame and sore
   desire
Fed from men's hearts with hungering
   fangs of fire,
And hope fell sick with famine for the food
   of change.
  Now is change come, but bringing funeral
   urns ;
  Now is day nigh, but the dawn blinds
   and burns ;
Now time long dumb hath language, but
   the tongue is strange.

We that have seen her not our whole
   lives long,
We to whose ears her dirge was cradle-
   song,
The dirge men sang who laid in earth her
   living head,
  Is it by such light that we live to see
  Rise, with rent hair and raiment, Liberty?
Does her grave open only to restore her
   dead ?

Ah, was it this we looked for, looked
   and prayed,
This hour that treads upon the prayers
   we made,
This ravening hour that breaks down good
   and ill alike ?
  Ah, was it thus we thought to see her
   and hear,
  The one love indivisible and dear ?
Is it her head that hands which strike down
   wrong must strike?

STR. 3.

Where is hope, and promise where, in all
   these things,
Shocks of strength with strength, and jar
   of hurtling kings ?
  Who of all men, who will show us any
   good ?
Shall these lightenings of blind battles give
   men light ?
Where is freedom ? who will bring us in
   her sight,
  That have hardly seen her footprint where
   she stood ?

STR. 4.

Who is this that rises red with wounds and
   splendid,
  All her breast and brow made beautiful
   with scars,

9

Burning bare as naked daylight, undefended,
  In her hands for spoils her splintered
   prison-bars,
In her eyes the light and fire of long pain
   ended,
  In her lips a song as of the morning
   stars ?

STR. 5.

O torn out of thy trance,
O deathless, O my France,
O many-wounded mother, O redeemed to
   reign !
  O rarely sweet and bitter
  The bright brief tears that glitter
On thine unclosing eyelids, proud of their
   own pain ;
  The beautiful brief tears
  That wash the stains of years
White as the names immortal of thy chosen
   and slain.
  O loved so much so long,
  O smitten with such wrong,
O purged at last and perfect without spot
   or stain,
  Light of the light of man,
  Reborn republican,
At last, O first Republic, hailed in heaven
   again !
  Out of the obscene eclipse
  Re-risen, with burning lips
To witness for us if we looked for thee in
   vain.

STR. 6.

Thou wast the light whereby men saw
Light, thou the trumpet of the law
  Proclaiming manhood to mankind ;
   And what if all these years were blind
And shameful ? hath the sun a flaw
Because one hour hath power to draw
  Mist round him wreathed as links to
   bind ?
And what if now keen anguish drains
The very wellspring of thy veins
  And very spirit of thy breath ?
The life outlives them and disdains ;
The sense which makes the soul remains,
  And blood of thought which travaileth
To bring forth hope with procreant pains
O thou that satest bound in chains
Between thine hills and pleasant plains
  As whom his own soul vanquisheth,
Held in the bonds of his own thought,
Whence very death can take off nought,

Nor sleep, with bitterer dreams than
　　death,—
What though thy thousands at thy knees
Lie thick as grave-worms feed on these,
Though thy green fields and joyous places
Are populous with blood-blackening faces
　　And wan limbs eaten by the sun ?
Better an end of all men's races,
　　Better the world's whole work were
　　done.
And life wiped out of all our traces,
　　And there were left to time not one,
Than such as these that fill thy graves
Should sow in slaves the seed of slaves.

ANTISTROPHE I.

Not of thy sons, O mother many-wounded,
　　Not of thy sons are slaves ingraffed and
　　grown.
Was it not thine, the fire whence light re-
　　bounded
From kingdom on rekindling kingdom
　　thrown,
From hearts confirmed on tyrannies con-
　　founded,
　　From earth on heaven, fire mightier than
　　his own ?
Not thine the breath wherewith time's
　　clarion sounded,
　　And all the terror in the trumpet blown ?
The voice whereat the thunders stood
　　astounded
As at a new sound of a God unknown ?
And all the seas and shores within them
　　bounded
Shook at the strange speech of thy lips
　　alone,
And all the hills of heaven, the storm-
　　surrounded,
　　Trembled, and all the night sent forth a
　　groan.

ANT. 2.

What hast thou done that such an hour
　　should be
More than another clothed with blood to
　　thee ?
Thou hast seen many a bloodred hour be-
　　fore this one.
What art thou that thy lovers should
　　misdoubt ?
What is this hour that it should cast hope
　　out ?
If hope turn back and fall from thee, what
　　hast thou done ?

Thou hast done ill against thine own
　　soul ; yea,
Thine own soul hast thou slain and
　　burnt away,
Dissolving it with poison into foul thin fume.
Thine own life and creation of thy fate
Thou hast set thy hand to unmake and
　　discreate ;
And now thy slain soul rises between dead
　　and doom.

Yea, this is she that comes between
　　them led ;
That veiled head is thine own soul's
　　buried head,
The head that was as morning's in the
　　whole world's sight.
These wounds are deadly on thee, but
　　deadlier
Those wounds the ravenous poison left
　　on her ;
How shall her weak hands hold thy weak
　　hands up to fight ?

Ah, but her fiery eyes, her eyes are these
That gazing, make thee shiver to the
　　knees
And the blood leap within thee, and the
　　strong joy rise.
What, doth her sight yet make thine
　　heart to dance ?
O France, O freedom, O the soul of
　　France,
Are ye then quickened, gazing in each
　　other's eyes ?

Ah, and her words, the words where-
　　with she sought thee
Sorrowing, and bare in hand the robe
　　she wrought thee
To wear when soul and body were again
　　made one,
　　And fairest among women, and a bride.
Sweet-voiced to sing the bridegroom to
　　her side,
The spirit of man, the bridegroom brighter
　　than the sun !

ANT. 3.

Who shall help me ? who shall take me by
　　the hand ?
Who shall teach mine eyes to see, my feet
　　to stand,
　　Now my foes have stripped and wound-
　　ed me by night ?

Who shall heal me ? who shall come to
take my part ?
Who shall set me as a seal upon his heart,
As a seal upon his arm made bare for
fight ?

ANT. 4.

If thou know not, O thou fairest among
women,
If thou see not where the signs of him
abide,
Lift thine eyes up to the light that stars
grow dim in,
To the morning whence he comes to
take thy side.
None but he can bear the light that love
wraps him in,
When he comes on earth to take himself
a bride.

ANT. 5.

Light of light, name of names,
Whose shadows are live flames,
The soul that moves the wings of worlds
upon their way :
Life, spirit, blood and breath
In time and change and death
Substant through strength and weakness,
ardor and decay ;
Lord of the lives of lands,
Spirit of man, whose hands
Weave the web through wherein man's
centuries fall as prey ;
That art within our will
Power to make, save, and kill,
Knowledge and choice, to take extremities
and weigh ;
In the soul's hand to smite
Strength, in the soul's eye sight ;
That to the soul art even as is the soul to
clay ;
Now to this people be
Love ; come, to set them free,
With feet that tread the night, with eyes
that sound the day.

ANT. 6.

Thou that wast on their fathers dead
As effluent God effused and shed,
Heaven to be handled, hope made flesh,
Break for them now time's iron mesh ;
Give them thyself for hand and head,
Thy breath for life, thy love for bread,
Thy thought for spirit to refresh,

Thy bitterness to pierce and sting,
Thy sweetness for a healing spring,
Be to them knowledge, strength, life,
light,
Thou to whose feet the centuries cling
And in the wide warmth of thy wing
Seek room and rest as birds by night,
O thou the kingless people's king,
To whom the lips of silence sing,
Called by thy name of thanksgiving
Freedom, and by thy name of might
Justice, and by thy secret name
Love ; the same need is on the same
Men, be the same God in their sight !
From this their hour of bloody tears
Their praise goes up into thine ears,
Their bruised lips clothe thy name with
praises,
The song of thee their crushed voice
raises,
Their grief seeks joy for psalms to bor-
row,
With tired feet seeks her through time's
mazes
Where each day's blood leaves pale the
morrow,
And from their eyes in thine there gazes
A spirit other far than sorrow—
A soul triumphal, white and whole
And single, that salutes thy soul.

EPODE.

All the lights of the sweet heaven that sing
together ;
All the years of the green earth that bare
man free ;
Rays and lightings of the fierce or tender
weather,
Heights and lowlands, wastes and head-
lands of the sea,
Dawns and sunset, hours that hold the
world in tether,
Be our witnesses and seals of things to be.
Lo the mother, the Republic universal,
Hands that hold time fast, hands feeding
men with might,
Lips that sing the song of the earth, that
make rehearsal
Of all seasons, and the sway of day with
night,
Eyes that see as from a mountain the dis-
persal,
The huge ruin of things evil, and the
flight ;

Large exulting limbs, and bosom godlike
    moulded
      Where the man-child hangs, and womb
      wherein he lay;
Very life that could it die would leave the
    soul dead,
      Face whereat all fears and forces flee
      away,
Breath that moves the world as winds a
    flower-bell folded,
      Feet that trampling the gross darkness
      beat out day.
      In the hour of pain and pity,
      Sore spent, a wounded city,
Her foster-child seeks to her, stately where
    she stands;
      In the utter hour of woes,
      Wind-shaken, blind with blows,
Paris lays hold upon her, grasps her with
    child's hands;
      Face kindles face with fire,
      Hearts take and give desire,
Strange joy breaks red as tempest on tor-
    mented lands.
      Day to day, man to man,
      Plights love republican,
And faith and memory burn with passion
    toward each other;
      Hope, with fresh heavens to track,
      Looks for a breath's space back,
Where the divine past years reach hands
    to this their brother;
      And souls of men whose death
      Was light to her and breath
Send word of love yet living to the living
    mother.
      They call her, and she hears;
      O France, thy marvellous years,
The years of the strong travail, the
    triumphant time,
      Days terrible with love,
      Red-shod with flames thereof,
Call to this hour that breaks in pieces
    crown and crime;
      The hour with feet to spurn,
      Hands to crush, fires to burn
The state whereto no latter foot of man
    shall climb.
      Yea, come what grief now may
      By ruinous night or day,
One grief there cannot, one the first and
    last grief, shame.
      Come force to break thee and bow
      Down, shame can come not now,

Nor, though hands wound thee, tongues
    make mockery of thy name:
      Come swords and scar thy brow,
      No brand there burns it now,
No spot but of thy blood marks thy white-
    fronted fame.
      Now though the mad blind morrow
      With shafts of iron sorrow
Should split thine heart, and whelm thine
    head with sanguine waves;
      Though all that draw thy breath
      Bled from all veins to death,
And thy dead body were the grave of all
    their graves,
      And thine unchilded womb
      For all their tombs a tomb,
At least within thee as on thee room were
    none for slaves.
      This power thou hast, to be,
      Come death or come not, free;
That in all tongues of time's this praise be
    chanted of thee,
      That in thy wild worst hour
      This power put in thee power,
And moved as hope around and hung as
    heaven above thee,
      And while earth sat in sadness
      In only thee put gladness,
Put strength and love, to make all hearts
    of ages love thee.
      That in death's face thy chant
      Arose up jubilant,
And thy great heart with thy great peril
    grew more great:
      And sweet for bitter tears
      Put out the fires of fears,
And love made lovely for thee loveless hell
    and hate;
      And they that house with error,
      Cold shame and burning terror,
Fled from truth risen and thee made migh-
    tier than thy fate.
      This shall all years remember;
      For this thing shall September
Have only name of honour, only sign of
    white.
      And this year's fearful name,
      France, in thine house of fame
Above all names of all thy triumphs shalt
    thou write,
      When, seeing thy freedom stand
      Even at despair's right hand,
The cry thou gavest at heart was only of
    delight.

DIRÆ.

Guai a voi, anime prave.
DANTE.
Soyez maudits, d'abord d'être ce que vous êtes,
Et puis soyez maudits d'obséder les poètes !
VICTOR HUGO.

I.—A DEAD KING.

[*Ferdinand II. entered Malebolge May 22nd, 1859.*]

Go down to hell. This end is good to see ;
  The breath is lightened and the sense at
    ease
Because thou art not ; sense nor breath
  there is
In what thy body was, whose soul shall be
Chief nerve of hell's pained heart eternally.
Thou art abolished from the midst of
  these
  That art what thou wast : Pius from his
    knees
Blows off the dust that flecked them, bowed
  for thee.
Yea, now the long-tongued slack-lipped
  litanies
  Fail, and the priest has no more prayer
    to sell—
Now the last Jesuit found about thee is
  The beast that made thy fouler flesh his
    cell—
Time lays his finger on thee, saying, 'Cease;
  Here is no room for thee ; go down to
    hell.'

II.—A YEAR AFTER.

IF blood throbs yet in this that was thy
  face,
  O thou whose soul was full of devil's
    faith,
  If in thy flesh the worm's bite slackeneth
In some acute red pause of iron days,
Arise now, gird thee, get thee on thy ways,
  Breathe off the worm that crawls and
    fears not breath ;
  King, it may be thou shalt prevail on
    death ;

King, it may be thy soul shall find out
  grace.
O spirit that hast eased the place of Cain,
  Weep now and howl, yea weep now sore;
    for this
  That was thy kingdom hath spat out its
    king.
Wilt thou plead now with God ? behold
  again,
  Thy prayer for thy son's sake is turned
    to a hiss,
  Thy mouth to a snake's whose slime out-
    lives the sting,

III.—PETER'S PENCE FROM
PERUGIA.

ISCARIOT, thou grey-grown beast of blood.
  Stand forth to plead ; stand, while red
    drops run here
  And there down fingers shaken with foul
    fear,
Down the sick shivering chin that stooped
  and sued,
Bowed to the bosom, for a little food
  At Herod's hand, who smites thee cheek
    and ear.
  Cry out, Iscariot ; haply he will hear ;
Cry, till he turn again to do thee good.
Gather thy gold up, Judas, all thy gold,
  And buy thee death ; no Christ is here to
    sell,
But the dead earth of poor men bought and
  sold,
  While year heaps year above thee safe in
    hell,
To grime thy grey dishonourable head
With dusty shame, when thou art damned
  and dead.

IV.—PAPAL ALLOCUTION.

' Popule mi, quid tibi feci?'

What hast thou done? Hark, till thine
ears wax hot,
Judas; for these and these things hast
thou done.
Thou hast made earth faint,and sickened
the sweet sun,
With fume of blood that reeks from limbs
that rot;
Thou hast washed thine hands and mouth,
saying, 'Am I not
Clean?' and thy lips were bloody, and
there was none
To speak for man against thee, no, not
one;
This hast thou done to us, Iscariot.
Therefore though thou be deaf and heaven
be dumb,
A cry shall be from under to proclaim
In the ears of all who shed men's
blood or sell
Pius the Ninth, Judas the Second, come
Where Boniface out of the filth and flame
Barks for his advent in the clefts of
hell.*

V.—THE BURDEN OF AUSTRIA.

1866.

O DAUGHTER of pride,wasted with misery,
With all the glory that thy shame put on
Stripped off thy shame, O daughter of
Babylon,
Yea, whoso be it, yea, happy shall he be
That as thou hast served us hath rewarded
thee.
Blessed, who throweth against war's
boundary stone
Thy warrior brood,and breaketh bone by
bone
Misrule thy son, thy daughter Tyranny.
That landmark shalt thou not remove for
shame,
But sitting down there in a widow's weed
Wail; for what fruit is now of thy red fame?
Have thy sons too and daughters learnt
indeed
What thing it is to weep, what thing to
bleed?
Is it not thou that now art but a name?†

*Dante, 'Inferno,' xix. 53.
† 'A geographical expression.'—Metternich of Italy.

VI.—LOCUSTA.

COME close and see her and hearken. This
is she.
Stop the ways fast against the stench that
nips
Your nostril as it nears her. Lo, the lips
That between prayer and prayer find time
to be
Poisonous, the hands holding a cup and
key,
Key of deep hell, cup whence blood reeks
and drips;
The loose lewd limbs, the reeling hinge-
less hips,
The scurf that is not skin but leprosy.
This haggard harlot grey of face and green
With the old hand's cunning mixes her
new priest
The cup she mixed her Nero, stirred and
spiced.
She lisps of Mary and Jesus Nazarene
With a tongue tuned, and head that
bends to the east,
Praying. There are who say she is bride
of Christ.

VII.—CELÆNO.

THE blind king hides his weeping eyeless
head,
Sick with the helpless hate and shame
and awe,
Till food have choked the glutted hell-
bird's craw
And the foul cropful creature lie as dead
And soil itself with sleep and too much
bread;
So the man's life serves under the beast's
law,
And things whose spirit lives in mouth
and maw
Share shrieking the soul's board and soil
her bed,
Till man's blind spirit, their sick slave re-
sign
Its kingdom to the priests whose souls
are swine,
And the scourged serf lie reddening from
their rod,
Discrowned, disrobed, dismantled, with
lost eyes
Seeking where lurks in what conjectual
skies
That triple-headed hound of hell their God.

VIII.—A CHOICE.

FAITH is the spirit that makes man's body
and blood
Sacred, to crown when life and death
have ceased
His heavenward head for high fame's
holy feast ;
But as one swordstroke swift as wizard's rod
Made Cæsar carrion and made Brutus God,
Faith false or true, born patriot or born
priest,
Smites into semblance or of man or beast
The soul that feeds on clean or unclean food.
Lo here the faith that lives on its own light,
Visible music ; and lo there, the foul
Shape without shape, the happy throat
and howl.
Sword of the spirit of man ! arise and
smite,
And sheer through throat and claw and
maw and tongue
Kill the beast faith that lives on its own
dung.

IX.—THE AUGURS.

LAY the corpse out on the altar ; bid the
elect
Slaves clear the ways of service spiritual,
Sweep clean the stalled soul's serviceable
stall,
Ere the chief priest's dismantling hands
detect
The ulcerous flesh of faith all scaled and
specked
Beneath the bandages that hid it all,
And with sharp edgetools œcumenical
The leprous carcases of creeds dissect.
As on the night ere Brutus grew divine
The sick-souled augurs found their ox or
swine
Heartless ; so now too by their after art
In the same Rome, at an uncleaner shrine,
Limb from rank limb, and putrid part
from part,
They carve the corpse—a beast without
a heart.

X.—A COUNSEL.

O STRONG Republic of the nobler years
Whose white feet shine beside time's
fairer flood
That shall flow on the clearer for our
blood

Now shed, and the less brackish for our
tears ;
When time and truth have put out hopes
and fears
With certitude, and love has burst the
bud,
If these whose powers then down the
wind shall scud
Still live to feel thee smite their eyes and
ears,
When thy foot's tread hath crushed their
crowns and creeds.
Care thou not then to crush the beast that
bleeds,
The snake whose belly cleaveth to the
sod,
Nor set thine heel on men as on their
deeds ;
But let the worm Napoleon crawl untrod,
Nor grant Mastai the gallows of his God.

1869.

XI.—THE MODERATES.

Virtutem videant intabescantque relictâ.

SHE stood before her traitors bound and
bare,
Clothed with her wounds and with her
naked shame
As with a weed of fiery tears and flame,
Their mother-land, their common weal and
care,
And they turned from her and denied, and
sware
They did not know this woman nor her
name.
And they took truce with tyrants and
grew tame,
And gathered up cast crowns and creeds to
wear,
And rags and shards regilded. Then she
took
In her bruised hands their broken pledge,
and eyed
These men so late so loud upon her side
With one inevitable and tearless look,
That they might see her face whom they
forsook ;
And they beheld what they had left, and
died.

February, 1870.

XII.—INTERCESSION.

Ave Cæsar Imperator, moriturum te saluto.

I.

O DEATH, a little more, and then the
    worm ;
    A little longer, O Death, a little yet,
    Before the grave gape and the grave-
        worm fret ;
Before the sanguine-spotted hand infirm
Be rottenness, and that foul brain, the
    germ
    Of all ill things and thoughts, be stop-
        ped and set ;
    A little while, O Death, ere he forget,
A small space more of life, a little term ;
A little longer ere he and thou be met,
    Ere in that hand that fed thee to thy
        mind
The poison-cup of life be overset ;
    A little respite of disastrous breath,
Till the soul lift up her lost eyes, and find
    Nor God nor help nor hope, but thee O
        Death.

II.

Shall a man die before his dying day,
    Death ? and for him though the utter
        day be nigh,
Not yet, not yet we give him leave to die ;
We give him grace not yet that men should
    say
He is dead, wiped out, perished and past
    away.
    Till the last bitterness of life go by,
    Thou shalt not slay him ; till those last
        dregs run dry,
O thou last lord of life ! thou shalt not slay.
Let the lips live a little while and lie,
    The hand a little, and falter, and fail of
        strength,
And the soul shudder and sicken at the sky ;
    Yea, let him live, though God nor man
        would let
Save for the curse' sake ; then at bitter
    length,
    Lord, will we yield him to thee, but not
    yet.

III.

Hath he not deeds to do and days to see
    Yet ere the day that is to see him dead ?
    Beats there no brain yet in the poisonous
    head.

Throbs there no treason ? if no such thing
    there be,
If no such thought, surely this is not he.
    Look to the hands then ; are the hands
    not red ?
    What are the shadows about this man's
    bed ?
Death, was not this the cupbearer to thee ?
Nay, let him live then, till in this life's
    stead
    Even he shall pray for that thou hast to
    give ;
Till seeing his hopes and not his memories
    fled
    Even he shall cry upon thee a bitter cry,
    That life is worse than death ; then let
        him live,
    Till death seem worse than life ; then
        let him die.

IV.

O watcher at the guardless gate of kings,
    O doorkeeper that serving at their feast
    Hast in thine hand their doomsday drink
        and seest
With eyeless sight the soul of unseen
    things ;
Thou in whose ear the dumb time coming
    sings,
    Death, priest and king that makest of
        king and priest
    A name, a dream, a less thing than the
        least,
Hover awhile above him with closed wings,
Till the coiled soul, an evil snake-shaped
    beast,
    Eat its base bodily lair of flesh away ;
If haply, or ever its cursed life have ceased,
    Or ever thy cold hands cover his head
    From sight of France and freedom and
        broad day,
    He may see these and wither and be
        dead.

PARIS, *September, 1869.*

XIII.—THE SAVIOUR OF SOCIETY.

I.

O SON of man, but of what man who
    knows ?
    That broughtest healing on thy leathern
    wings
    To priests, and under them didst gather
    kings,

And madest friends to thee of all man's
    foe's ;
Before thine incarnation, the tale goes,
    Thy virgin mother, pure of sensual
        stings.
    Communed by night with angels of
        chaste things,
And, full of grace, untimely felt the throes
Of motherhood upon her, and believed
    The obscure annunciation made when
        late
    A raven-feathered raven-throated dove
    Croaked salutation to the mother of
        love
    Whose misconception was immaculate,
And when her time was come she miscon-
    ceived.

II.

Thine incarnation was upon this wise,
    Saviour ; and out of east and west were
        led
To thy foul cradle by thy planet red
Shepherds of souls that feed their sheep
    with lies
Till the utter soul die as the body dies,
    And the wise men that ask but to be fed
    Though the hot shambles be their board
        and bed
And sleep on any dunghill shut their eyes,
So they lie warm and fatten in the mire ;
    And the high priest enthroned yet in thy
        name,
Judas, baptised thee with men's blood for
    hire ;
    And now thou hangest nailed to thine
        own shame
    In sight of all time, but while heaven
        has flame
Shalt find no resurrection from hell-fire.
December, 1869.

XIV.—MENTANA : SECOND ANNI-
VERSARY.

Est-ce qu'il n'est pas temps que la foudre se prouve,
Cieux profonds, en broyant ce chien, fils de la louve?
    La Légende des Siècles :—*Rathbert.*

I.

By the dead body of Hope, the spotless lamb
    Thou threwest into the high priest's
        slaughtering-room,
    And by the child Despair born red
        therefrom

As, thank the secret sire picked out to cram
With spurious spawn thy misconceiving
    dam,
    Thou, like a worm from a town's com-
        mon tomb,
    Didst creep from forth the kennel of her
        womb,
Born to break down with catapult and ram
Man's builded towers of promise, and with
    breath
And tongue to track and hunt his hopes to
    death ;
    O, by that sweet dead body abused and
        slain
And by that child mismothered—dog, by all
Thy curses thou hast cursed mankind
    withal,
    With what curse shall man curse thee
        back again ?

II.

By the brute soul that made man's soul its
    food ;
    By time grown poisonous with it ; by the
        hate
    And horror of all souls not miscreate ;
By the hour of power that evil hath on
    good ;
And by the incognizable fatherhood
    Which made a whorish womb the shame-
        ful gate
    That opening let out loose to fawn on
        fate
A hound half-blooded ravening for man's
    blood ;
(What prayer but this for these should any
    say,
    Thou dog of hell, but this that Shakespeare
        said ?)
By night deflowered and desecrated day,
    That fall as one curse on one cursed head,
'Cancel his bond of life, dear God, I pray,
    That I may live to say, the dog is dead !'
1869.

XV.—MENTANA : THIRD ANNI-
VERSARY.

I.

Such prayers last year were put up for thy
    sake ;
    What shall this year do that hath lived to
        see
    The piteous and unpitied end of thee ?

What moan, what cry, what clamour shall
    it make,
Seeing as a reed breaks all thine empire
    break,
    And all thy great strength as a rotten
      tree,
    Whose branches made broad night from
      sea to sea,
And the world shuddered when a leaf would
    shake ?
From the unknown deep wherein those
    prayers were heard,
From the dark height of time there sounds
    a word,
    Crying, Comfort ; though death ride on
      this red hour,
    Hope waits with eyes that make the
      morning dim,
Till liberty, reclothed with love and power,
    Shall pass and know not if she tread on
    him.

II.

The hour for which men hungered and had
    thirst,
    And dying were loth to die before it
      came,
Is it indeed upon thee ? and the lame
Late foot of vengeance on thy trace accurst
For years insepulchred and crimes in-
    hearsed,
    For days marked red or black with blood
      or shame,
    Hath it outrun thee to tread out thy
      name ?
This scourge, this hour, is this indeed the
    worst ?
O clothed and crowned with curses, canst
    thou tell ?
    Have thy dead whispered to thee what
      they see
    Whose eyes are open in the dark on thee
Ere spotted soul and body take farewell
    Or what of life beyond the worm's may
      be
Satiate the immitigable hours in hell ?
1870.

XVI.—THE DESCENT INTO HELL.

January 9th, 1873.

I.

O NIGHT and death, to whom we grudged
    him then,

When in man's sight he stood not yet un-
    done,
Your king, your priest, your saviour, and
    your son,
We grudge not now, who know that not
    again
Shall this curse come upon the sins of
    men,
Nor this face look upon the living sun
That shall behold not so abhorred an
    one
In all the days whereof his eye takes ken.
The bond is cancelled, and the prayer is
    heard
    That seemed so long but weak and wasted
      breath ;
    Take him, for he is yours, O night and
      death.
Hell yawns on him whose life was as a
    word
Uttered by death in hate of heaven and
    light,
A curse now dumb upon the lips of night.

II.

What shapes are these and shadows with-
    out end
    That fill the night full as a storm of
      rain
    With myriads of dead men and women
      slain,
Old with young, child with mother, friend
    with friend,
That on the deep mid wintering air impend,
    Pale yet with mortal wrath and human
      pain,
    Who died that this man dead now too
      might reign,
Toward whom their hands point and their
    faces bend ?
The ruining flood would redden earth and
    air
    If for each soul whose guiltless blood was
      shed
    There fell but one drop on this one man's
      head
Whose soul to-night stands bodiless and
    bare,
For whom our hearts give thanks who put
    up prayer,
    That we have lived to say, the dog is
    dead.

XVII.—APOLOGIA.

IF wrath embitter the sweet mouth of song,
  And make the sunlight fire before those
     eyes
  That would drink draughts of peace from
     the unsoiled skies,
The wrongdoing is not ours, but ours the
     wrong,
Who hear too loud on earth and see too long
  The grief that dies not with the groan
     that dies,

Til! the strong bitterness of pity cries
Within us, that our anger should be strong.
For chill is known by heat and heat by
     chill,
And the desire that hope makes love to
     still
  By the fear flying beside it or above,
  A faclon fledged to follow a fledgeling
     dove,
And by the fume and flame of hate of ill
  The exuberant light and burning bloom
     of love.

SONGS BEFORE SUNRISE.

DEDICATION.

TO

JOSEPH MAZZINI.

TAKE, since you bade it should bear,
  These, of the seed of your sowing,
    Blossom or berry or weed.
Sweet though they be not, or fair,
  That the dew of your word kept grow
    ing,
    Sweet at least was the seed.

Men bring you love-offerings of tears,
  And sorrow the kiss that assuages,
And slaves the hate-offering of wrongs,
And time the thanksgiving of years,
  And years the thanksgiving of ages ;
    I bring you my handful of songs.

If a perfume be left, if a bloom
  Let it live till Italia be risen,
    To be strewn in the dust of her car
When her voice shall awake from the tomb
  England, and France from her prison,
    Sisters, a star by a star.

I bring you the sword of a song,
  The sword of my spirit's desire,
    Feeble ; but laid at your feet,

That which was weak shall be strong,
  That which was cold shall take fire,
    That which was bitter be sweet.

It was wrought not with hands to smite
  Nor hewn after swordsmiths' fashion,
    Nor tempered on anvil of steel ;
But with visions and dreams of the night
  But with hope and the patience of passion,
    And the signet of love for a seal.

Be it witness, till one more strong,
  Till a loftier lyre, till a rarer
    Lute praise her better than I,
Be it witness before you, my song,
  That I knew her, the world's banner-
    bearer,
    Who shall cry the republican cry.

Yea, even she as at first,
  Yea, she alone and none other,
    Shall cast down, shall build up, shall
      bring home ;
Slake earth's hunger and thirst,
  Lighten, and lead as a mother ;
    First name of the world's names, Rome.

PRELUDE.

BETWEEN the green bud and the red
Youth sat and sang by Time, and shed
From eyes and tresses flowers and tears,
From heart and spirit hopes and fears,
Upon the hollow stream whose bed
Is channelled by the foamless years;
And with the white the gold-haired head
Mixed running locks, and in Time's ears
Youth's dreams hung singing, and Time's truth
Was half not harsh in the ears of Youth.

Between the bud and the blown flower
Youth talked with joy and grief an hour,
With footless joy and wingless grief
And twin-born faith and disbelief
Who share the seasons to devour;
And long ere these made up their sheaf
Felt the winds round him shake and shower
The rose-red and the blood-red leaf,
Delight whose germ grew never grain,
And passion dyed in its own pain.

Then he stood up, and trod to dust
Fear and desire, mistrust and trust,
And dreams of bitter sleep and sweet,
And bound for sandals on his feet
Knowledge and patience of what must
And what things may be, in the heat
And cold of years that rot and rust
And alter; and his spirit's meat
Was freedom, and his staff was wrought
Of strength, and his cloak woven of thought.

For what has he whose will sees clear
To do with doubt and faith and fear,
Swift hopes and slow despondencies?
His heart is equal with the sea's
And with the sea-wind's, and his ear
Is level to the speech of these,
And his soul communes and takes cheer
With the actual earth's equalities,
Air, light, and night, hills, winds, and streams,
And seeks not strength from strengthless dreams.

His soul is even with the sun
Whose spirit and whose eyes are one,
Who seeks not stars by day nor light
And heavy heat of day by night.
Him can no God cast down, whom none
Can lift in hope beyond the height
Of fate and nature and things done
By the calm rule of might and right
That bids men be and bear and do,
And die beneath blind skies or blue.

To him the lights of even and morn
Speak no vain things of love or scorn,
Fancies and passions miscreate
By man in things dispassionate.
Nor holds he fellowship forlorn
With souls that pray and hope and hate,
And doubt they had better not been born,
And fain would lure or scare off fate
And charm their doomsman from their doom
And make fear dig its own false tomb.

He builds not half of doubts and half
Of dreams his own soul's cenotaph
Whence hopes and fears with helpless eyes,
Wrapt loose in cast-off cerecloths, rise
And dance and wring their hands and laugh,
And weep thin tears and sigh light sighs,
And without living lips would quaff
The living spring in man that lies,
And drain his soul of faith and strength
It might have lived on a life's length.

He hath given himself and hath not sold
To God for heaven or man for gold,
Or grief for comfort that it gives,
Or joy for grief's restoratives,
He hath given himself to time, whose fold
Shuts in the mortal flock that lives
On its plain pasture's heat and cold
And the equal year's alternatives,
Earth, heaven, and time, death, life, and he,
Endure while they shall be to be.

" Yet between death and life are hours
To flush with love and hide in flowers;
What profit save in these?" men cry:
" Ah, see, between soft earth and sky,

What only good things here are ours !"
  They say, "what better wouldst thou try,
What sweeter sing of ? or what powers
    Serve, that will give thee ere thou die
More joy to sing and be less sad,
More heart to play and grow more glad ?"

Play then and sing ; we too have played,
We likewise, in that subtle shade.
  We too have twisted through our hair
  Such tendrils as the wild Loves wear,
And heard what mirth the Mænads made,
  Till the wind blew our garlands bare
And left their roses disarrayed,
    And smote the summer with strange air,
And disengirdled and discrowned
The limbs and locks that vine-wreaths
    bound.

We too have tracked by star-proof trees
The tempest of the Thyiades
  Scare the loud night on hills that hid
  The blood-feasts of the Bassarid,
Heard their song's iron cadences
  Fright the wolf hungering from the kid,
Outroar the lion-throated seas,
  Outchide the north-wind if it chid,
And hush the torrent-tongued ravines
With thunders of their tambourines.

But the fierce flute whose notes acclaim
Dim goddesses of fiery fame,
  Cymbal and clamorous kettledrum,
  Timbrels and tabrets, all are dumb
That turned the high chill air to flame ;
  The singing tongues of fire are numb
  That called on Cotys by her name
  Edonian, till they felt her come
And maddened, and her mystic face
Lightened along the streams of Thrace.

For Pleasure slumberless and pale,
And Passion with rejected veil,
  Pass, and the tempest-footed throng
  Of hours that follow them with song
Till their feet flag and voices fail,
  And lips that were so loud so long
Learn silence. or a wearier wail ;
  So keen is change, and time so strong,
To weave the robes of life and rend
And weave again till life have end.

But weak is change, but strengthless time,
To take the light from heaven or climb

The hills of heaven with wasting feet.
  Songs they can stop that earth found
    meet,
But the stars keep their ageless rhyme :
  Flowers they can slay that spring thought
    sweet.

But the stars keep their spring sublime ;
  Passions and pleasures can defeat,
Actions and agonies control,
And life and death, but not the soul.

Because man's soul is man's God still,
What wind soever waft his will
  Across the waves of day and night
  To port or shipwreck, left or right,
By shores and shoals of good and ill ;
  And still its flame at mainmast height
Through the rent air that foam-flakes fill
Sustains the indomitable light
Whence only man hath strength to steer
Or helm to handle without fear.

Save his own soul's light overhead,
None leads him, and none ever led,
  Across birth's hidden harbor bar,
  Past youth where shoreward shallows are,
Through age that drives on toward the red
  Vast void of sunset hailed from far,
To the equal waters of the dead ;
  Save his own soul he hath no star,
And sinks, except his own soul guide,
Helmless in middle turn of tide.

No blast of air or fire of sun
Puts out the light whereby we run
  With girdled loins our lamplit race,
  And each from each takes heart of grace
And spirit till his turn be done,
  And light of face from each man's face
In whom the light of trust is one ;
  Since only souls that keep their place
By their own light, and watch things roll,
And stand, have light for any soul.

A little time we gain from time
To set our seasons in some chime,
  For harsh or sweet or loud or low,
  With seasons played out long ago
And souls that in their time and prime
  Took part with summer or with snow,
Lived abject lives out or sublime,
  And had their chance of seed to sow
For service or disservice done
To those days dead and this their son.

A little time that we may fill
Or with such good works or such ill
As loose the bonds or make them strong
Wherein all manhood suffers wrong.
By rose-hung river and light-foot rill

There are who rest not ; who think long
Till they discern as from a hill
At the sun's hour of morning song,
Known of souls only, and those souls free,
The sacred spaces of the sea.

THE EVE OF REVOLUTION.

I.

THE trumpets of the four winds of the
    world
    From the ends of the earth blow battle ;
    the night heaves,
With breasts palpitating and wings refurled,
    With passion of couched limbs, as one
    who grieves
Sleeping, and in her sleep she sees uncurled
    Dreams serpent-shapen, such as sickness
    weaves,
Down the wild wind of vision caught and
    whirled,
    Dead leaves of sleep, thicker than autumn
    leaves,
        Shadows of storm-shaped things,
        Flights of dim tribes of kings,
    The reaping men that reap men for
    their sheaves,
        And, without grain to yield,
        Their scythe-swept harvest-field
    Thronged thick with men pursuing and
    fugitives,
    Dead foliage of the tree of sleep,
Leaves blood-colored and golden, blown
    from deep to deep.

2.

I hear the midnight on the mountains cry
    With many tongues of thunders, and I
    hear
Sound and resound the hollow shield of
    sky
    With trumpet-throated winds that charge
    and cheer,
And through the roar of the hours that
    fighting fly,
    Through flight and fight and all the
    fluctuant fear,
A sound sublimer than the heavens are
    high,
    A voice more instant than the winds are
    clear,

Say to my spirit, "Take
    Thy trumpet too, and make
A rallying music in the void night's ear,
    Till the storm lose its track,
    And all the night go back ;
Till, as through sleep false life knows
    true life near,
Thou know the morning through the
    night,
And through the thunder silence, and
    through darkness light."

3.

I set the trumpet to my lips and blow.
    The height of night is shaken, the skies
    break,
The winds and stars and waters come and
    go
    By fits of breath and light and sound,
    that wake
As out of sleep, and perish as the show
    Built up of sleep, when all her strengths
    forsake
The sense-compelling spirit ; the depths
    glow,
    The heights flash, and the roots and
    summits shake
        Of earth in all her mountains,
        And the inner foamless fountains
    And wellsprings of her fast-bound forces
    quake ;
        Yea, the whole air of life
        Is set on fire of strife,
Till change unmake things made and
    love remake ;
Reason and love, whose names are one,
Seeing reason is the sunlight shed from love
    the sun.

4.

The night is broken eastward ; is it day,
    Or but the watchfires trembling here and
    there,

Like hopes on memory's devastated way,
   In moonless wastes of planet-stricken
      air?
O many-childed mother great and grey,
   O multitudinous bosom, and breasts that
     bare
Our fathers' generations, whereat lay
   The weanling peoples and the tribes that
     were,
      Whose new-born mouths long dead
      Those ninefold nipples fed,
   Dim face with deathless eyes and wither-
     ed hair,
      Fostress of obscure lands,
      Whose multiplying hands
   Wove the world's web with divers races
     fair
      And cast it waif-wise on the stream,
The waters of the centuries, where thou
   sat'st to dream;

5.

O many-minded mother and visionary,
   Asia, that sawest their westering waters
     sweep
With all the ships and spoils of time to
   carry
   And all the fears and hopes of life to
     keep,
Thy vesture wrought of ages legendary
   Hides usward thine impenetrable sleep,
And thy veiled head, night's oldest tribu-
   tary,
   We know not if it speak or smile or weep.
      But where for us began
      The first live light of man
   And first-born fire of deeds to burn and
     leap,
      The first war fair as peace
      To shine and lighten Greece,
   And the first freedom moved upon the
     deep,
      God's breath upon the face of time
Moving, a present spirit, seen of men
   sublime;

6.

There where our east looks always to thy
   west,
   Our mornings to thine evenings, Greece
     to thee,
These lights that catch the mountains crest
   by crest,
   Are they of stars or beacons that we see?

Taygetus takes here the winds abreast,
   And there the sun resumes Thermopylæ;
The light is Athens where those remnants
   rest,
   And Salamis the sea-wall of that sea.
      The grass men tread upon
      Is very Marathon
   The leaves are of that time-unstricken
     tree
      That storm nor sun can fret
      Nor wind, since she that set
   Made it her sign to men whose shield
     was she;
      Here, as dead time his deathless
      things,
Eurotas and Cephisus keep their sleepless
   springs.

7

O hills of Crete, are these things dead? O
   waves,
   O many-mouthed streams, are these
     springs dry?
Earth, dost thou feed and hide now none
   but slaves?
Heaven, hast thou heard of men that
   would not die?
Is the land thick with only such men's
   graves
   As were ashamed to look upon the sky?
Ye dead, whose name outfaces and out-
   braves
   Death, is the seed of such as you gone by?
      Sea, have thy ports not heard
      Some Marathonian word
   Rise up to landward and to Godward fly?
      No thunder, that the skies
      Sent not upon us, rise
   With fire and earthquake and a cleaving
     cry?
      Nay, light is here, and shall be
      light,
Though all the face of the hour be over-
   borne with night.

8.

I set the trumpet to my lips and blow.
   The night is broken northward; the pale
     plains
And footless fields of sun-forgotten snow
   Feel through their creviced lips and iron
     veins
Such quick breath labor and such clean
   blood flow

As summer-stricken spring feels in her
    pains
When dying May bears June, too young to
    know
The fruit that waxes from the flower that
    wanes ;
    Strange tyrannies and vast,
    Tribes frost-bound to their past,
Lands that are loud all through their
    length with chains,
    Wastes where the wind's wings
      break,
    Displumed by daylong ache
And anguish of blind snows and rack-
    blown rains,
    And ice that seals the White Sea's
      lips,
Whose monstrous weights crush flat the
    sides of shrieking ships :

9.

Horrible sights and sounds of the unreached
    pole,
    And shrill fierce climes of inconsolable
      air,
Shining below the beamless aureole
    That hangs about the north-wind's hurt-
      ling hair,
A comet-lighted lamp, sublime and sole
    Dawn of the dayless heaven where suns
      despair :
Earth, skies, and waters, smitten into soul,
    Feel the hard veil that iron centuries wear
      Rent as with hands in sunder,
      Such hands as make the thunder
And clothe with form all substance and
    strip bare :
    Shapes, shadows, sounds and lights
    Of their dead days and nights
    Take soul of life too keen for death to
      bear ;
      Life, conscience, forethought, will,
      desire,
Flood men's inanimate eyes and dry-drawn
    hearts with fire.

10.

Light, light, and light ! to break and melt
    in sunder
    All clouds and chains that in one bond-
    age bind
Eyes, hands, and spirits, forged by fear and
    wonder

And sleek fierce fraud with hidden knife
    behind ;
There goes no fire from heaven before their
    thunder,
Nor are the links not malleable that wind
Round the snared limbs and souls that ache
    thereunder ;
The hands are mighty, were the head not
    blind.
    Priest is the staff of king,
    And chains and clouds one thing,
And fettered flesh with devastated mind.
    Open thy soul to see,
    Slave, and thy feet are free ;
Thy bonds and thy beliefs are one in kind,
    And of thy fears thine irons wrought
Hang weights upon thee fashioned out of
    thine own thought.

II.

O soul, O God, O glory of liberty,
    To night and day their lightning and
    their light !
With heat of heart thou kindlest the quick
    sea,
    And the dead earth takes spirit from thy
      sight ;
The natural body of things is warm with
    thee,
    And the world's weakness parcel of thy
      might ;
Thou seest us feeble and forceless, fit to be
    Slaves of the years that drive us left and
      right,
      Drowned under hours like waves
      Wherethrough we row like slaves ;
But if thy finger touch us, these take
    flight.
    If but one sovereign word
    Of thy live lips be heard,
What man shall stop us, and what God
    shall smite ?
    Do thou but look in our dead eyes,
They are stars that light each other till thy
    sundawn rise.

12

Thou art the eye of this blind body of man,
    The tongue of this dumb people ; shalt
    thou not
See, shalt thou speak not for them ? Time
    is wan
    And hope is weak with waiting, and swift
    thought

Hath lost the wings at heel wherewith he
　ran,
　　And on the red pit's edge sits down dis-
　　traught
To talk with death of days republican
　　And dreams and fights long since dreamt
　　　out and fought ;
　　　Of the last hope that drew
　　　To that red edge anew
　The firewhite faith of Poland without
　　spot ;
　　　Of the blind Russian might,
　　　And fire that is not light ;
　Of the green Rhineland where thy spirit
　　wrought ;
　　　But though time, hope, and memory
　　　tire,
Canst thou wax dark as they do, thou whose
　light is fire?

13.

I set the trumpet to my lips and blow.
　　The night is broken westward ; the wide
　　sea
That makes immortal motion to and fro
　　From world's end unto world's end, and
　　shall be
When nought now grafted of men's hands
　　shall grow
　　And as the weed in last year's waves are
　　we
Or spray the sea-wind shook a year ago
　From its sharp tresses down the storm
　　to lee,
　　　The moving god that hides
　　　Time in its timeless tides
　Wherein time dead seems live eternity,
　　　That breaks and makes again
　　　Much mightier things than men,
　Doth it not hear change coming, or not
　　see ?
　　　Are the deeps deaf and dead and
　　　blind,
To catch no light or sound from landward
　of mankind ?

14.

O thou, clothed round with raiment of
　white waves,
　　Thy brave brows lightening through the
　　grey wet air,
Thou, lulled with sea-sounds of a thousand
　caves,
　　And lit with sea-shine to thine inland lair,

Whose freedom clothed the naked souls of
　slaves
　　And stripped the muffled souls of tyrants
　　bare,
O, by the centuries of thy glorious graves,
By the live light of the earth that was thy
　care,
　　　Live, thou must not be dead,
　　　Live ; let thine armed head
　Lift itself up to sunward and the fair
　　　Daylight of time and man,
　　　Thine head republican,
　With the same splendor on thine helmless
　　hair
　　　That in his eyes kept up a light
Who on thy glory gazed away their sacred
　sight ;

15.

Who loved and looked their sense to death
　on thee ;
　　Who taught thy lips imperishable things,
And in thine ears outsang thy singing sea ;
　Who made thy foot firm on the necks of
　kings
And thy soul somewhile steadfast—woe are
　we
It was but for a while, and all the strings
Were broken of thy spirit ; yet had he
　Set to such tunes and clothed it with
　　such wings
　　　It seemed for his sole sake
　　　Impossible to break,
　And woundless of the worm that waits
　　and stings,
　　　The golden-headed worm
　　　Made headless for a term,
　The king-snake whose life kindles with
　　the spring's,
　　　To breathe his soul upon her bloom,
And while she marks not turn her temple
　to her tomb.

16.

By those eyes blinded and that heavenly
　head
　　And the secluded soul adorable.
O Milton's land, what ails thee to be dead ?
　Thine ears are yet sonorous with his shell
That all the songs of all thy sea-line fed
　With motive sound of spring-tides at mid
　swell,
And through thine heart his thought as
　blood is shed,

Requickening thee with wisdom to do
   well ;
   Such sons were of thy womb,
   England, for love of whom
Thy name is not yet writ with theirs that
   fell,
   But, till thou quite forget
   What were thy children, yet
On the pale lips of hope is as a spell ;
   And Shelley's heart and Landor's
     mind
Lit thee with latter watch-fires ; why wilt
   thou be blind ?

17.

Though all were else indifferent, all that
   live
   Spiritless shapes of nations ; though
     time wait
In vain on hope till these have help to give,
And faith and love crawl famished from
   the gate ;
Canst thou sit shamed and self-contempla-
   tive
With soulless eyes on thy secluded fate ?
Though time forgive them, thee shall he
   forgive
Whose choice was in thine hand to be so
   great ?
   Who cast out of thy mind
   The passion of man's kind,
And made thee and thine old name sep-
   arate ?
   Now when time looks to see
   New names and old and thee
Build up our one Republic state by state,
   England with France, and France
     with Spain,
And Spain with sovereign Italy strike
   hands and reign.

18.

O known and unknown fountain-heads that
   fill
   Our dear life-springs of England ! O
     bright race
Of streams and waters that bear witness
   still
   To the earth her sons were made of ! O
     fair face
Of England, watched of eyes death cannot
   kill,
   How should the soul that lit you for a
     space

Fall through sick weakness of a broken will
   To the dead cold damnation of disgrace ?
   Such wind of memory stirs
   On all green hills of hers,
Such breath of record from so high a
   place,
   From years whose tongue of flame
   Prophesied in her name
Her feet should keep truth's bright and
   burning trace,
   We needs must have her heart with
     us,
Whose hearts are one with man's; she must
   must be dead or thus.

19.

Who is against us ? who is on our side ?
   Whose heart of all men's hearts is one
     with man's ?
Where art thou that wast prophetess and
   bride,
   When truth and thou trod under time and
     chance ?
What latter light of what new hope shall
   guide
   Out of the snares of hell thy feet, O
     France ?
What heel shall bruise these heads that hiss
   and glide,
   What wind-blow out these fen-born fires
     that dance
   Before thee to thy death ?
   No light, no life, no breath,
From thy dead eyes and lips shall take
   the trance,
   Till on that deadliest crime
   Reddening the feet of time
Who treads through blood and passes,
   time shall glance
   Pardon, and Italy forgive,
And Rome arise up whom thou slewest, and
   bid thee live.

20.

I set the trumpet to my lips and blow.
   The night is broken southward ; the
     springs run,
The daysprings and the watersprings that
   flow
   Forth with one will from where their
     source was one,
Out of the might of morning: high and low,
   The hungering hills feed full upon the
     sun,

The thirsting valleys drink of him and glow
  As a heart burns with some divine thing
     done,
    Or as blood burns again
    In the bruised heart of Spain,
A rose renewed with red new life begun,
  Dragged down with thorns and
    briers,
  That puts forth buds like fires
Till the whole tree take flower in unison,
  And prince that clogs and priest that
    clings
Be cast as weeds upon the dunghill of dead
  things.

21.

Ah heaven, bow down, be nearer ! This is
  she,
  Italia, the world's wonder, the world's
    care,
Free in her heart ere quite her hands be free,
  And lovlier than her lovliest robe of air.
The earth hath voice, and speech is in the
  sea,
  Sounds of great joy, too beautiful to bear ;
All things are glad because of her, but we
  Most glad, who loved her when the worst
    days were.
    O sweetest, fairest, first,
    O flower, when times were worst,
  Thou hadst no stripe wherein we had no
    share,
    Have not our hearts held close,
    Kept fast the whole world's rose ?
  Have we not worn thee at heart whom
    none would wear ?
    First love and last love, light of lands
Shall we not touch thee full-blown with our
  lips and hands ?

22.

O too much loved, what shall we say of
  thee ?
  What shall we make of our heart's burn-
    ing fire,
The passion in our lives that fain would be
  Made each a brand to pile into the pyre
That shall burn up thy foemen, and set free
  The flame whence thy sun-shadowing
    wings aspire ?
Love of our life, what more than men are we,
  That this our breath for thy sake should
    expire,
    For whom to joyous death
    Glad gods might yield their breath,

  Great gods drop down from heaven to
    serve for hire ?
    We are but men, are we,
    And thou art Italy ;
  What shall we do for thee with our de-
    sire ?
    What gift shall we deserve to give ?
How shall we die to do thee service or how
  live ?

23.

The very thought in us how much we love
  thee
  Makes the throat sob with love and blinds
    the eyes,
How should love bear thee, to behold
    above thee
  His own light burning from reverberate
    skies ?
They give thee light, but the light given
    them of thee
  Makes faint the wheeling fires that fall
    and rise.
What love, what life, what death of man's
    should move thee,
  What face that lingers or what foot that
    flies ?
    It is not heaven that lights
    Thee with such days and nights,
  But thou that heaven is lit from in such
    wise.
    O thou her dearest birth,
    Turn thee to lighten earth,
  Earth too bore thee and yearns to
    thee and cries ;
    Stand up, shine, lighten, become
    flame,
Till as the sun's name through all nations
  be thy name.

24.

I take the trumpet from my lips and sing.
  O life immeasurable and imminent love,
And fear like winter leading hope like
  spring,
  Whose flower-bright brows the day-star
    sits above,
Whose hand unweariable and untiring wing
Strike music from a world that wailed and
  strove,
Each bright soul born and every glorious
  thing,
  From very freedom to man's joy thereof,
    O time, O change and death,
    Whose now not hateful breath

But gives the music swifter feet to move
  Through sharp remeasuring tones
  Of refluent antiphones
More tender-tuned than heart or throat
    of dove,
    Soul into soul, song into song,
Life changing into life, by laws that work
  not wrong ;

25.

O natural force in spirit and sense, that art
  One thing in all things, fruit of thine
    own fruit,
O thought illimitable and infinite heart
  Whose blood if life in limbs indissolute
That still keeps hurtless thine invisible part
  And inextirpable thy viewless root
Whence all sweet shafts of green and
    each thy dart
  Of sharpening leaf and bud resundering
    shoot ;
    Hills that the day-star hails,
    Heights that the first beam scales,
And heights that souls outshining suns
    salute,
    Valleys for each mouth born
    Free now of plenteous corn,
Waters and woodlands musical or mute ;
  Free winds that brighten brows as free
And thunder and laughter and lightning of
  the sovereign sea ;

26.

Rivers and springs, and storms that seek
    your prey
  With strong wings ravening through the
    skies by night
Spirits and stars that hold one choral way ;
  O light of heaven, and thou the heaven-
    lier light

Aflame above the souls of men that sway
  All generations of all years with might ;
O sunrise of the repossessing day,
  And sunrise of all-renovating right ;
    And thou, whose trackless foot
    Mocks hope's or fear's pursuit,
  Swift Revolution, changing depth with
    height ;
    And thou, whose mouth makes one
    All songs that seek the sun,
Serene Republic of a world made white ;
  Thou, Freedom, whence the soul's
    springs ran ;
Praise earth for man's sake living, and for
  earth's sake man.

27.

Make yourselves wings, O tarrying feet of
    fate,
  And hidden hour that hast our hope to
    bear,
A child-god, through the morning-colored
    gate
That lets love in upon the golden air,
Dead on whose threshold lies heart-broken
    hate.
Dead discord, dead injustice, dead despair;
  O love long looked for, wherefore wilt
    thou wait,
  And shew not yet the dawn on thy bright
    hair,
    Not yet thine hand released
    Refreshing the faint east,
Thine hand reconquering heaven, to seat
    man there ?
    Come forth, be born and live
    Thou that hast help to give
And light to make man's day of man-
    hood fair ;
  With flight outflying the spherèd sun,
Hasten thine hour and halt not, till thy
  work be done.

A WATCH IN THE NIGHT.

1.

WATCHMAN, what of the night ?—
  Storm and thunder and rain,
  Lights that waver and wane,
Leaving the watchfires unlit.
Only the balefires are bright,
  And the flash of the lamps now and then
From a palace where spoilers sit,
  Trampling the children of men.

2.

Prophet, what of the night ?—
  I stand by the verge of the sea,
  Banished, uncomforted, free,
Hearing the noise of the waves
And sudden flashes that smite
  Some man's tyrannous head,
Thundering, heard among graves
  That hide the hosts of his dead.

3.

Mourners, what of the night ?—
  All night through without sleep
  We weep, and we weep, and we weep.
Who shall give us our sons ?
Beaks of raven and kite,
  Mouths of wolf and of hound,
Give us them back whom the guns
  Shot for your dead on the ground.

4.

Dead men, what of the night ?—
  Cannon and scaffold and sword,
  Horror of gibbet and cord,
Mowed us as sheaves for the grave,
Mowed us down for the right.
  We do not grudge or repent.
Freely to freedom we gave
  Pledges, till life should be spent.

5.

Statesman, what of the night ?—
  The night will last me my time.
  The gold on a crown or a crime
Looks well enough yet by the lamps.
Have we not fingers to write,
  Lips to swear at a need ?
Then, when danger decamps,
  Bury the word with the deed.

6.

Warrior, what of the night ?—
  Whether it be not or be
  Night, is as one thing to me.
I for one, at the least,
Ask not of dews if they blight,
  Ask not of flames if they slay,
Ask not of prince or of priest
  How long ere we put them away

7.

Master, what of the night ?—
  Child, night is not at all
  Anywhere, fallen or to fall,
Save in our star-stricken eyes.
Forth of our eyes it takes flight,
  Look we but once nor before
Nor behind us, but straight on the skies
  Night is not then any more.

8.

Exile, what of the night ?—
  The tides and the hours run out,
  The seasons of death and of doubt,
The night-watches bitter and sore.
In the quicksands leftward and right
  My feet sink down under me ;
But I know the scents of the shore
  And the broad blown breaths of the sea.

9.

Captives, what of the night ?—
  It rains outside overhead
  Always, a rain that is red,
And our faces are soiled with the rain.
Here in the seasons' despite
  Day-time and night-time are one,
Till the curse of the kings and the chain
  Break, and their toils be undone.

10.

Christian, what of the night ?—
  I cannot tell ; I am blind.
  I halt and hearken behind
If haply the hours will go back
And return to the dear dead light,
  To the watchfires and stars that of old
Shone where the sky now is black,
  Glowed where the earth now is cold.

11.

High priest, what of the night ?—
  The night is horrible here
  With haggard faces and fear,
Blood, and the burning of fire.
Mine eyes are emptied of sight,
  Mine hands are full of the dust,
If the God of my faith be a liar,
  Who is it that I shall trust ?

12.

Princes, what of the night ?—
  Night with pestilent breath
  Feeds us, children of death
Clothes us close with her gloom.
Rapine and famine and fright
  Crouch at our feet and are fed.
Earth where we pass is a tomb,
  Life where we triumph is dead.

13.

Martyrs, what of the night ?—
  Nay, is it night with you yet ?
  We, for our part, we forget
What night was, if it were.
The loud red mouth of the fight
Are silent and shut where we are.
  In our eyes the tempestuous air
  Shines as the face of a star.

14.

England, what of the night ?—
  Night is for slumber and sleep,
  Warm, no season to weep.
Let me alone till the day.
Sleep would I still if I might,
  Who have slept for two hundred years.
Once I had honor, they say ;
  But slumber is sweeter than tears.

15.

France, what of the night ?—
  Night is the prostitute's noon,
  Kissed and drugged till she swoon,
Spat upon, trod upon, whored.
With bloodred rose-garlands dight,
  Round me reels in the dance
Death, my saviour, my lord,
  Crowned ; there is no more France.

16.

Italy, what of the night ?—
  Ah, child, child, it is long !
  Moonbeam and starbeam and song
Leave it dumb now and dark.

Yet I perceive on the height
  Eastward, not now very far,
A song too loud for the lark,
  A light too strong for a star.

17.

Germany, what of the night ?—
  Long has it lulled me with dreams ;
  Now at midwatch, as it seems,
Light is brought back to mine eyes,
And the mastery of old and the might
  Lives in the joints of mine hands,
Steadies my limbs as they rise,
  Strengthens my foot as it stands.

18.

Europe, what of the night ?—
  Ask of heaven, and the sea
  And my babes on the bosom of me,
Nations of mine, but ungrown.
There is one who shall surely requite
  All that endure or that err :
She can answer alone :
  Ask not of me, but of her.

19.

Liberty, what of the night ?—
  I feel not the red rains fall,
  Hear not the tempest at all,
Nor thunder in heaven any more.
All the distance is white
  With the soundless feet of the sun.
Night, with the woes that it wore,
  Night is over and done.

SUPER FLUMINA BABYLONIS.

By the waters of Babylon we sat down and
    wept,
  Remembering thee,
That for ages of agony hast endured, and
    slept,
  And wouldst not see.

By the waters of Babylon we stood up and
    sang,
  Considering thee,
That a blast of deliverance in the darkness
    rang,
  To set thee free.

And with trumpets and thunderings and
    with morning song
  Came up the light ;
And thy spirit uplifted thee to forget thy
    wrong
  As day doth night.

And thy sons were dejected not any more,
    as then
  When thou wast shamed ;
When thy lovers went heavily without
    heart, as men
  Whose life was maimed.

In tho desolate distances, with a great
    desire,
    For thy love's sake,
With our hearts going back to thee, they
    were filled with fire,
    Were nigh to break.

It was said to us : " Verily ye are great of
    heart,
    But ye shall bend ;
Ye are bondsmen and bondswomen, to be
    scourged and smart,
    To toil and tend. "

And with harrows men harrowed us, and
    subdued with spears,
    And crushed with shame ;
And the summer and winter was, and the
    length of years,
    And no change came.

By the rivers of Italy, by the sacred streams,
    By town, by tower,
There was feasting with revelling, there
    was sleep with dreams,
    Until thine hour.

And they slept and they rioted on their
    rose-hung beds,
    With mouths on flame,
And with love-locks vine-chapleted, and
    with rose-crowned heads
    And robes of shame.

And they knew not their forefathers, nor
    the hills and streams
    And words of power,
Nor the gods that were good to them, but
    with songs and dreams
    Filled up their hour.

By the rivers of Italy, by the dry streams'
    beds,
    When thy time came,
There was casting of crowns from them,
    from their young men's heads,
    The crowns of shame.

By the horn of Eridanus, by the Tiber
    mouth,
    As thy day rose,
They arose up and girded them to the
    north and south,
    By seas, by snows.

As a water in January the frost confines,
    Thy kings bound thee ;
As a water in April is, in the new-blown
    vines,
    Thy sons made free.

And thy lovers that looked for thee, and
    that mourned from far,
    For thy sake dead,
We rejoiced in the light of thee, in the
    signal star
    Above thine head.

In thy grief had we followed thee, in thy
    passion loved,
    Loved in thy loss ;
In thy shame we stood fast to thee, with
    thy pangs were moved,
    Clung to thy cross.

By the hillside of Calvary we beheld thy
    blood,
    Thy bloodred tears,
As a mother's in bitterness, an unebbing
    flood,
    Years upon years.

And the north was Gethsemane, without
    leaf or bloom,
    A garden sealed ;
And the south was Aceldama, for a sanguine
    fume
    Hid all the field.

By the stone of the sepulchre we returned
    to weep,
    From far, from prison ;
And the guards by it keeping it we beheld
    asleep,
    But thou wast risen.

And an angel's similitude by the unsealed
    grave,
    And by the stone :
And the voice was angelical, to whose
    words God gave
    Strength like his own.

" Lo, the graveclothes of Italy that are
    folded up
    In the grave's gloom !
And the guards as men wrought upon with
    charmed cup,
    By the open tomb

"And her body most beautiful, and her shining head,
    These are not here ;
For your mother, for Italy, is not surely dead :
    Have ye no fear.

"As of old time she spake to you, and you hardly heard,
    Hardly took heed,
So now also she saith to you, yet another word,
    Who is risen indeed.

"By my saying she saith to you, in your ears she saith,
    Who hear these things,
Put no trust in men's royalties, nor in great men's breath,
    Nor words of kings.

"For the life of them vanishes and is no more seen,
    Nor no more known ;
Nor shall any remember him if a crown hath been,
    Or where a throne.

"Unto each man his handiwork, unto each his crown,
    The just Fate gives ;
Whoso takes the world's life on him and his own lays down,
    He, dying so, lives.

"Whoso bears the whole heaviness of the wronged world's weight
    And puts it by,
It is well with him suffering, though he face man's fate ;
    How should he die ?

"Seeing death has no part in him any more, no power
    Upon his head ;
He has bought his eternity with a little hour,
    And is not dead.

"For an hour, if ye look for him, he is no more found,
    For one hour's space ;
Then ye lift up your eyes to him and behold him crowned,
    A deathless face.

"On the mountains of memory, by the world's well-springs,
    In all men's eyes,
Where the light of the life of him is on all past things,
    Death only dies.

"Not the light that was quenched for us, nor the deeds that were,
    Nor the ancient days,
Nor the sorrows not sorrowful, nor the face most fair
    Of perfect praise."

So the angel of Italy's resurrection said,
    So yet he saith ;
So the son of her suffering, that from breasts nigh dead
    Drew life, not death.

That the pavement of Golgotha should be white as snow,
    Not red, but white ;
That the waters of Babylon should no longer flow,
    And men see light.

THE HALT BEFORE ROME.

SEPTEMBER. 1867.

Is it so, that the sword is broken,
    Our sword, that was halfway drawn ?
Is it so, that the light was a spark,
That the bird we hailed as the lark
Sang in her sleep in the dark,
And the song we took for a token
    Bore false witness of dawn ?

Spread in the sight of the lion,
    Surely, we said, is the net
Spread but in vain, and the snare
Vain ; for the light is aware,
And the common, the chainless air,
Of his coming whom all we cry on ;
    Surely in vain is it set.

Surely the day is on our side,
   And heaven, and the sacred sun ;
Surely the stars, and the bright
Immemorial inscrutable night :
Yea, the darkness, because of our light,
Is no darkness, but blooms as a bower-side
   When the winter is over and done ;

Blooms underfoot with young grasses
   Green, and with leaves overhead,
Windflowers white, and the low
New-dropped blossoms of snow ;
And or ever the May winds blow,
And or ever the March wind passes,
   Flames with anemones red.

We are here in the world's bower-garden,
   We that have watched out the snow.
Surely the fruitfuller showers,
The splendider sunbeams are ours ;
Shall winter return on the flowers,
And the frost after April harden,
   And the fountains in May not flow ?

We have in our hands the shining
   And the fire in our hearts of a star.
Who are we that our tongues should palter,
Hearts bow down, hands falter,
Who are clothed as with flame from the
    altar,
That the kings of the earth, repining,
   Far off, watch from afar ?

Woe is ours if we doubt or dissemble,
   Woe, if our hearts not abide.
Are our chiefs not among us, we said,
Great chiefs, living and dead,
To lead us glad to be led ?
For whose sake, if a men of us tremble
   He shall not be on our side.

What matter if these lands tarry,
   That tarried (we said) not of old ?
France, made drunken by fate,
England, that bore up the weight
Once of men's freedom, a freight
Holy, but heavy to carry
   For hands overflowing with gold.

Though this be lame, and the other
   Fleet, but blind from the sun,
And the race be no more to these,
Alas ! nor the palm to seize,
Who are weary and hungry of ease,
Yet, O Freedom, we said, O our mother,
   Is there not left to thee one ?

Is there not left of thy daughters,
   Is there not one to thine hand ?
Fairer than these, and of fame
Higher from of old by her name ;
Washed in her tears, and in flame
Bathed as in baptism of waters,
   Unto all men a chosen land.

Her hope in her heart was broken,
   Fire was upon her, and clomb,
Hiding her, high as her head ;
And the world went past her and said
(We heard it say) she was dead ;
And now, behold, she hath spoken,
   She that was dead, saying, "Rome."

O mother of all men's nations,
   Thou knowest if the deaf world heard !
Heard not now to her lowest
Depths, where the strong blood slowest
Beats at her bosom, thou knowest,
In her toils, in her dim tribulations,
   Rejoiced not, hearing the word.

The sorrowful, bound unto sorrow,
   The woe-worn people, and all
That of old were discomforted,
And men that famish for bread,
And men that mourn for their dead,
She bade them be glad on the morrow,
   Who endured in the day of her thrall.

The blind, and the people in prison,
   Souls without hope, without home,
How glad were they all that heard !
When the winged white flame of the word
Passed over men's dust, and stirred
Death ; for Italia was risen,
   And risen her light upon Rome.

The light of her sword in the gateway
   Shone, an unquenchable flame,
Bloodless, a sword to release,
A light from the eyes of peace,
To bid grief utterly cease,
And the wrong of the old world straight-
    way
   Pass from the face of her fame :

Hers, whom we turn to and cry on,
   Italy, mother of men :
From the light of the face of her glory,
At the sound of the storm of her story,
That the sanguine shadows and hoary
Should flee from the foot of the lion,
   Lion-like, forth of his den.

As the answering of thunder to thunder
  Is the storm-beaten sound of her past ;
As the calling of sea unto sea
Is the noise of her years yet to be ;
For this ye knew not is she,
Whose bonds are broken in sunder ;
  This is she at the last.

So spake we aloud, high-minded,
  Full of our will ; and behold,
The speech that was halfway spoken
Breaks, as a pledge that is broken,
As a king's pledge, leaving in token
Grief only for high hopes blinded,
  New grief grafted on old.

We halt by the walls of the city,
  Within sound of the clash of her chain.
Hearing, we know that in there
The lioness chafes in her lair,
Shakes the storm of her hair,
Struggles in hands without pity,
  Roars to the lion in vain.

Whose hand is stretched forth upon her ?
  Whose curb is white with her foam ?
Clothed with the cloud of his deeds,
Swathed in the shroud of his creeds,
Who is this that has trapped her and leads,
Who turns to despair and dishonor
  Her name, her name that was Rome ?

Over fields without harvest or culture,
  Over hords without honor or love,
Over nations that groan with their kings,
As an imminent pestilence flings
Swift death from her shadowing wings,
So he, who hath claws as a vulture,
  Plumage and beak as a dove.

He saith, "I am pilot and haven,
  Light and redemption I am
Unto souls overlabored," he saith ;
And to all men the blast of his breath
Is a savour of death unto death ;
And the Dove of his worship a raven,
  And a wolf-cub the life-giving Lamb.

He calls his sheep as a shepherd,
  Calls from the wilderness home,
"Come unto me and be fed,"
To feed them with ashes for bread
And grass from the graves of the dead,
Leaps on the fold as a leopard,
  Slays, and says, "I am Rome."

Rome, having rent her in sunder,
  With the clasp of an adder he clasps ;
Swift to shed blood are his feet,
And his lips, that have man for their meat,
Smoother than oil, and more sweet
Than honey, but hidden thereunder
  Festers the poison of asps.

As swords are his tender mercies,
  His kisses as mortal stings ;
Under his hallowing hands
Life dies down in all lands
Kings pray to him, prone where he stands,
And his blessings, as other men's curses,
  Disanoint where they consecrate kings.

With an oil of unclean consecration,
  With effusion of blood and of tears,
With uplifting of cross and of keys,
Priest, though thou hallow us these,
Yet even as they cling to thy knees
Nation awakens by nation,
  King by king disappears.

How shall the spirit be loyal
  To the shell of a spiritless thing ?
Erred once, in only a word,
The sweet great song that we heard
Poured upon Tuscany, erred,
Calling a crowned man royal
  That was no more than a king.

Sea-eagle of English feather,
  A song-bird beautiful-souled,
She knew not them that she sang ;
The golden trumpet that rang
From Florence, in vain for them, sprang
As a note in the nightingales' weather
  Far over Fiesole rolled.

She saw not—happy, not seeing—
  Saw not as we with her eyes
Aspromonte ; she felt
Never the heart in her melt
As in us when the news was dealt
Melted all hope out of being,
  Dropped all dawn from the skies.

In that weary funeral season,
  In that heart-stricken grief-ridden time,
The weight of a king and the worth,
With anger and sorrowful mirth,
We weighed in the balance of earth,
And light was his word as a treason,
  And heavy his crown as a crime.

Banners of kings shall ye follow
  None, and have thrones on your side
None ; ye shall gather and grow
Silently, row upon row,
Chosen of Freedom to go
Gladly where darkness may swallow,
  Gladly where death may divide.

Have we not men with us royal,
  Men the masters of things?
In the days when our life is made new,
All souls perfect and true
Shall adore whom their forefathers slew ;
And these indeed shall be loyal,
  And those indeed shall be kings.

Yet for a space they abide with us,
  Yet for a little they stand,
Bearing the heat of the day.
When their presence is taken away,
We shall wonder and worship, and say,
" Was not a star on our side with us?
  Was not a God at our hand ? "

These, O men, shall ye honor,
  Liberty only, and these.
For thy sake and for all men's and mine,
Brother, the crowns of them shine
Lighting the way to her shrine,
That our eyes may be fastened upon her,
  That our hands may encompass her knees.

In this day is the sign of her shown to you ;
  Choose ye, to live or to die.
Now is her harvest in hand ;
Now is her light in the land ;
Choose ye, to sink or to stand,
For the might of her strength is made
    known to you
  Now, and her arm is on high.

Serve not for any man's wages,
  Pleasure nor glory nor gold ;
Not by her side are they won
Who saith unto each of you, " Son,
Silver and gold have I none ;
I give but the love of all ages,
  And the life of my people of old."

Fear not for any man's terrors ;
  Wait not for any man's word ;
Patiently, each in his place,
Gird up your loins to the race ;
Following the print of her pace,
Purged of desires and of errors,
  March to the tune ye have heard.

March to the tune of the voice of her,
  Breathing the balm of her breath,
Loving the light of her skies.
Blessed is he on whose eyes
Dawns but her light as he dies ;
Blessed are ye that make choice of her,
  Equal to life and to death.

Ye that when faith is nigh frozen,
  Ye that when hope is nigh gone,
Still, over wastes, over waves,
Still, among wrecks, among graves,
Follow the splendor that saves,
Happy, her children, her chosen,
  Loyally led of her on.

The sheep of the priests, and the cattle
  That feed in the penfolds of kings,
Sleek is their flock and well-fed ;
Hardly she giveth you bread,
Hardly a rest for the head,
Till the day of the blast of the battle
  And the storm of the wind of her wings.

Ye that have joy in your living,
  Ye that are careful to live,
You her thunders go by :
Live, let men be, let them lie,
Serve your season, and die ;
Gifts have your masters for giving,
  Gifts hath not Freedom to give ;

She, without shelter or station,
  She, beyond limit or bar,
Urges to slumberless speed
Armies that famish, that bleed,
Sowing their lives for her seed,
That their dust may rebuild her a nation,
  That their souls may relight her a star.

Happy are all they that follow her ;
  Them shall no trouble cast down ;
Though she slay them, yet shall they trust
    in her,
For unsure there is nought nor unjust in her,
Blemish is none, neither rust in her ;
Though it threaten, the night shall not
    swallow her,
  Tempest and storm shall not drown.

Hither, O strangers, that cry for her,
  Holding your lives in your hands,
Hither, for here is your light,
Where Italy is, and her might ;
Strength shall be given you to fight,
Grace shall be given you to die for her,
  For the flower, for the lady of lands ;

Turn ye, whose anguish oppressing you
　　Crushes, asleep and awake,
For the wrong which is wrought as of yore ;
That Italia may give of her store,
Having these things to give and no more ;
Only her hands on you, blessing you ;
　　Only a pang for her sake ;

Only her bosom to die on ;
　　Only her heart for a home,
And a name with her children to be
From Calabrian to Adrian sea
Famous in cities made free
That ring to the roar of the lion
　　Proclaiming republican Rome.

MENTANA: FIRST ANNIVERSARY.

At the time when the stars are grey,
　　And the gold of the molten moon
Fades, and the twilight is thinned,
And the sun leaps up, and the wind,
Alight rose, not of the day,
　　A stronger light than of noon.

As the light of a face much loved
　　Was the face of the light that clomb ·
As a mother whitened with woes
Her adorable ... . arose;
As the sound of a .... hat is moved,
　　Her voice went forth upon Rome.

At her lips it fluttered and failed
　　Twice, and sobbed ...to song,
And sank as a flame sinks under ;
Then spake, and the speech was thunder,
And the cheek as he heard it paled
　　Of the wrongdoer grown grey with the
　　wrong.

"Is it time, is it time appointed,
　　Angel of time, is it near ?
For the spent night aches into day
When the kings shall slay not or pray,
And the high-priest, accursed and anointed,
　　Sickens to deathward with fear.

"For the bones of my slain are stirred,
　　And the seed of my earth in her womb
Moves as the heart of a bud
Beating with odorous blood
To the tune of the loud first bird
　　Burns and yearns into bloom.

"I lay my hand on her bosom,
　　My hand on the heart of my earth,
And I feel as with shiver and sob
The triumphant heart in her throb,
The dead petals dilate into blossom,
　　The divine blood beat into birth.

"O my earth, are the springs in thee dry ?
　　O sweet, is thy body a tomb ?
Nay, springs out of springs derive,
And summers from summers alive,
And the living from them that die ;
　　No tomb is here, but a womb.

"O manifold womb and divine,
　　Give me fruit of my children, give !
I have given thee my dew for thy root,
Give thou me for my mouth of thy fruit ;
Thine are the dead that are mine,
　　And mine are thy sons that live.

"O goodly children, O strong
　　Italian spirits, that wear
Could time or the world misdoubt you,
My glories as garments about you,
Behold, in disproof of the wrong,
　　The field of the grave-pits there.

"And ye that fell upon sleep,
　　We have you too with us yet.
Fairer than life or than youth
Is this, to die for the truth :
No death can sink you so deep
　　As their graves whom their brethren for-
　　get.

"Were not your pains as my pains ?
　　As my name are your names not divine ?
Was not the light in your eyes
Mine, the light of my skies,
And the sweet shed blood of your veins,
　　O my beautiful martyrs, mine ?

"Of mine earth were your dear limbs
　　made,
　　Of mine air was your sweet life's breath ;
At the breasts of my love ye were fed,
O my children, my chosen, my dead,
At my breasts where again ye are laid,
　　At the old mother's bosom, in death.

"But ye that live. O their brothers,
  Be ye to me as they were ;
Give me, my children that live,
What these dead grudged not to give,
Who alive were son's of your mother's,
  Whose lips drew breath of your air.

"Till darkness by dawn be cloven,
  Let youth's self mourn and abstain ;
And love's self find not an hour,

And spring's self wear not a flower,
And Lycoris, with hair unenwoven,
  Hail back to the banquet in vain.

"So sooner and surer the glory
  That is not with us shall be,
And stronger the hands that smite
The heads of the sons of night,
And the sound throughout earth of our story
  Give all men heart to be free."

BLESSED AMONG WOMEN.

TO THE SIGNORA CAIROLI.

I.

BLESSED was she that bare,
  Hidden in flesh most fair,
For all men's sake the likeness of all love ;
  Holy that virgin's womb,
  The old record saith, on whom
The glory of God alighted as a dove ;
  Blessed, who brought to gracious
    birth
The sweet-souled Saviour of a man-tor-
    mented earth.

2.

But four times art thou blest,
  At whose most holy breast
Four times a godlike soldier-saviour hung ;
  And thence a fourfold Christ
  Given to be sacrificed
To the same cross as the same bosom clung;
  Poured the same blood, to leave the
    same
Light on the many-folded mountain-skirts
    of fame.

3.

Shall they and thou not live,
  The children thou didst give
Forth of thine hands, a godlike gift, to
    death,
  Through fire of death to pass
  For her high sake that was
Thine and their mother, that gave all you
    breath ?
  Shall ye not live till time drop dead,
O mother, and each her children's conse-
    crated head ?

4.

Many brought gifts to take
  For her love's supreme sake,
Life and life's love, pleasure and praise
    and rest,
  And went forth bare ; but thou,
  So much once richer, and now
Poorer than all these, more than these be
    blest ;
  Poorer so much, by so much given,
Than who gives earth for heaven's sake,
    not for earth's sake heaven.

5.

Somewhat could each soul save,
  What thing soever it gave,
But thine, mother, what has thy soul kept
    back ?
  None of thine all, not one,
  To serve thee and be thy son,
Feed with love all thy days, lest one day
    lack ;
  All thy whole life's love, thine
    heart's whole,
Thou hast given as who gives gladly, O
    thou the supreme soul.

6.

The heart's pure flesh and blood,
  The heaven thy motherhood,
The live lips, the live eyes, that lived on
    thee ;
  The hands that clove with sweet
  Blind clutch to thine, the feet
That felt on earth their first way to thy
    knee ;

The little laughter of mouths milk-
fed,
Now open again to feed on dust among the
dead ;

7.

The fair,   strong,   yonng men's
strength,
Light of life-days and length,
And glory of earth seen under and stars
above,
And years that bring to tame
Now the wild falcon fame,
Now, to . stroke smooth, the dove-white
breast of love ;   .
The life unlived, the unsown seeds,
Suns unbeholden, sons unsung, and undone
deeds.

8.

Therefore shall man's love be
As an own son to thee,
And the world's worship of thee for a child ;
All thine own land as one
New-born, a nursing son,
All thine own people a new birth undefiled ;
And all the unborn Italian time,
And all its glory, and all its works, thy
sèed sublime.

9.

That henceforth no man's breath,
Saying "Italy," but saith
In that Most sovereign word thine equal
name ;
Nor can one speak of thee
But he saith " Italy,"
Seeing in two sons one co-eternal flame ;
One heat, one heaven, one heart, one fire,
One light, one love, one benediction, one
desire.

10.

Blest above praise and prayer
And incense of men's air,
Thy place is higher than where such voices
rise
As in men's temples make
Music for some vain sake,
This God's or that God's, in one weary
wise ;
Thee the soul silent, the shut heart,

The locked lips of the spirit praise thee
that thou art.

I.

Yea, for man's whole life's length,
And with man s whole soul's
strength,
We praise thee, O holy, and bless thee, O
mother of lights ;
And send forth as on wings
The world s heart's thanksgiving
Song-birds to sing thy days through and
thy nights ;
And wrap thee around and arch thee
above
With the air of benediction and the heaven
of love.

12.

And toward thee our unbreathed
words
Fly speechless, winged as birds,
As the Indian flock, children of Paradise,
The winged things without feet,
Fed with God's dew for meat,
That live in the air and light of the utter
skies ;
So fleet, so flying a footless flight,
With wings for fleet love seeks thee, to
partake thy sight.

13.

Love like a clear sky spread
Bends over thy loved head,
As a new heaven bends over a new-born
earth,
When the old night's womb is great
With young stars passionate
And fair new planets fiery-fresh from birth ;
And moon-white here, there hot
like Mars,
Souls that are worlds shine on thee, spirits
that are stars.

14.

Till the whole sky burns through
With heaven's own heart-deep hue,
With psssion-colored glories of lit souls ;
And thine above all names
Writ highest with lettering flames
Lightens, and all the old starriest auroles
And all the old holiest memories
Wane.

And the old names of love's chosen, found
in thy sight vain.

15.

And crowned heads are discrowned,
And stars sink without sound,
And love's self for thy love's sake waxes
    pale ;
Seeing from his storied skies
In what new reverent wise
Thee Rome's most highest, her sovereign
    daughters, hail ;
Thee Portia, thee Veturia grey,
Thee Arria, thee Cornelia, Roman more
    than they.

16.

Even all these as all we
Subdue themselves to thee,
Bow their heads haloed, quench their fiery
    fame ;
Seen through dim years divine,
Their faint lights feminine
Sink, then spring up rekindled from thy
    flame ;
Fade, then reflower aud reillume
From thy fresh spring their wintering age
    with new-blown bloom.

17.

To thy much holier head
Even theirs, the holy and dead,
Bow themselves each one from her heaven-
    ward height ;
Each in her shining turn,
All tremble toward thee and yearn
To melt in thine their consummated light ;
Till from day's Capitolian dome
One glory of many glories lighten upon
    Rome.

18.

Hush thyself, song, and cease,
Close, lips, and hold your peace;
What help hast thou, what part have ye
    herein ?

But you, with sweet shut eyes,
Heart-hidden memories,
Dreams and dumb thoughts that keep
    what things have been
Silent, and pure of all words saiu,
Praise without song the living, without dirge
    the dead.

19.

Thou, strengthless in these things,
Song, fold thy feebler wings,
And as a pilgrim go forth girt and shod
    And where the new graves are,
    And where the sunset star,
To the pure spirit of man that men call God,
    To the high soul of things, that is
Made of men's heavenlier hopes and might-
    ier memories ;

20.

To the elements that make
For the soul's living sake
This raiment of dead things, of shadow and
    trance,
    That give us chance and time
    Wherein to aspire and climb
And set our life's work higher than time or
    chance ;
    The old sacred elements, that give
The breath of life to days that die, to deeds
    that live ;

21.

To them, veiled gods and great,
There bow thee and dedicate
The speechless spirit in these thy weak words
    hidden ;
    And mix thy reverent breath
    With holier air of death,
At the high feast of sorrow a guest unbidden,
    Till with divine triumphal tears
Thou fill men's eyes who listen with a
    heart that hears.

THE LITANY OF NATIONS.

μᾶ Γᾶ, μᾶ Γᾶ, βοὰν
φοβερὸν ἀπότρεπε.

ÆSCH. *Supp 890.*

CHORUS.

IF with voice of words or prayers thy sons
   may reach thee,
   We thy latter sons, the men thine after-
      birth,
   We the children of thy grey-grown age,
      O Earth,
O our mother everlasting, we beseech thee,
By the sealed and secret ages of thy life ;
   By the darkness wherein grew thy sacred
      forces ;
   By the songs of stars thy sisters in their
      courses ;
By thine own song hoarse and hollow and
   shrill with strife ;
By thy voice distuned and marred of modu-
   lation ;
   By thy discord of thy measures march
      with theirs ;
   By the beauties of thy bosom, and the
      cares ;
By thy glory of growth, and the splendor
   of thy station ;
By the shame of men thy children, and the
   pride ;
   By the pale-cheeked hope that sleeps and
      weeps and passes,
   As the grey dew from the morning
      mountain-grasses ;
   By the white-lipped sightless memories
      that abide ;
By the silence and the sound of many
   sorrows ;
   By the joys that leapt up living and fell
      dead ;
   By the veil that hides thy hands and
      breasts and head,
Wrought of divers colored days and nights
   and morrows ;
Isis, thou that knowest of God what worlds
   are worth,
   Thou the ghost of God, the mother un-
      created,

Soul for whom the floating forceless ages
      waited
As our forceless fancies wait on thee, O
   Earth ;
Thou the body and soul, the father-God
   and mother,
   If at all it move thee, knowing of all
      things done
   Here where evil things and good things
      are not one,
But their faces are as fire against each other;
By thy morning and thine evening, night
   and day ;
   By the first white light that stirs and
      strives and hovers
   As a bird above the brood her bosom
      covers,
By the sweet last star that takes the west-
   ward way ;
By the night whose feet are shod with snow
   or thunder,
   Fledged with plumes of storm, or sound-
      less as the dew ;
   By the vesture bound of many-folded
      blue
Round her breathless breasts, and all the
   woven wonder ;
By the golden-growing eastern stream of
   sea ;
   By the sounds of sunrise moving in the
      mountains ;
   By the forces of the floods and unsealed
      fountains ;
Thou that badest man be born, bid man be
   free.

GREECE.

I am she that made thee lovely with my
      beauty
   From north to south ;
Mine, the fairest lips, took first the fire of
      duty
   From thine own mouth

11

Mine, the fairest eyes, sought first thy laws
   and knew them
     Truths undefiled ;
Mine, the fairest hands, took freedom first
   into them,
     A weanling child.
By my light, now he lies sleeping, seen
   above him
     Where none sees other :
By my dead that loved and living men that
   love him ;
     (*Cho.*) Hear us, O mother.

ITALY.

I am she that was the light of thee enkindled
     When Greece grew dim ;
She whose life grew up with man's free life,
   and dwindled
     With wane of him
She that once by sword and once by word
   imperial
     Struck bright thy gloom ;
And a third time, casting off these years
   funeral,
     Shall burst thy tomb.
By that bond 'twixt thee and me whereat
   affrighted
     Thy tyrants fear us ;
By that hope and this remembrance re-
   united :
     (*Cho.*) O mother, hear us.

SPAIN.

I am she that set my seal upon the nameless
     West worlds of seas ;
And my sons as brides took unto them the
   tameless
     Hesperides.
Till my sins and sons through sinless lands
   dispersèd,
     With red flame shod,
Made accurst the name of man, and thrice
   accursèd
     The name of God.
Lest for those past fires the fires of my repentance
     Hell's fume yet smother,
Now my blood would buy remission of my
   sentence ;
     (*Cho.*) Hear us, O mother.

FRANCE.

I am she that was thy sign and standard-
   bearer,
     Thy voice and cry ;
She that washed thee with her blood and
   left thee fairer,
     The same was I.
Were not these the hands that raised thee
   fallen and fed thee,
     These hands defiled ?
Was not I thy tongue that spake, thine eye
   that led thee,
     Not I thy child ?
By the darkness on our dreams, and the
   dead errors
     Of dead times near us ;
By the hopes that hang around thee, and
   the terrors ;
     (*Cho.*) O mother, hear us.

RUSSIA.

I am she whose hands are strong and her
   eyes blinded
     And lips athirst
Till upon the night of nations many-minded
     One bright day burst :
Till the myriad stars be molten into one
   light,
     And that light thine ;
Till the soul of man be parcel of the sunlight,
     And thine of mine.
By the snows that blanch not him nor
   cleanse from slaughter
     Who slays his brother ;
By the stains and by the chains on me thy
   daughter ;
     (*Cho.*) Hear us, O mother

SWITZERLAND.

I am she that shews on mighty limbs and
   maiden
     Nor chain nor stain ;
For what blood can touch these hands with
   gold unladen,
     These feet what chain ?
By the surf of spears one shieldless bosom
   breasted
     And was my shield,
Till the plume-plucked Austrian vulture-
   heads twin crested
     Twice drenched the field ;

By the snows and souls untrampled and
    untroubled
    That shine to cheer us,
Light of those to these responsive and re-
    doubled ;
    (Cho.) O mother, hear us.

GERMANY.

I am she beside whose forest-hidden foun-
    tains
    Slept freedom armed,
By the magic born to music in my
    mountains
    Heart-chained and charmed.
By those days the very dream whereof
    delivers
    My soul from wrong ;
By the sounds that make of all my ringing
    rivers
    None knows what song ;
By the many tribes and names of my division
    One from another ;
By the single eye of sun-compelling vision ;
    (Cho.) Hear us, O mother.

ENGLAND.

I am she that was and was not of thy
    chosen,
    Free, and not free ;
She that fed thy springs, till now her springs
    are frozen ;
    Yet I am she.
By the sea that clothed and sun that saw
    me splendid
    And fame that crowned.
By the song-fires and the sword-fires mixed
    and blended
    That robed me round ;
By the star that Milton's soul for Shelley's
    lighted,
    Whose rays insphere us ;
By the beacon-bright Republic far-off
    sighted ;
    (Cho.) O mother, hear us.

CHORUS.

Turn away from us the cross-blown blasts
    of error,
    That drown each other ;
Turn away the fearful cry, the loud tongued
    terror,
    O Earth, O mother.

Turn away their eyes who track, their hearts
    who follow,
    The pathless past ;
Shew the soul of man, as summer shows the
    swallow,
    The way at last.
By the sloth of men that all too long endure
    men
    On man to tread ;
By the cry of men, the bitter cry of poor
    men
    That faint for bread ;
By the blood-sweat of the people in the
    garden
    Inwalled of kings ;
By his passion interceding for their pardon
    Who do these things ;
By the sightless souls and fleshless limbs
    that labor
    For not their fruit ;
By the foodless mouth with foodless heart
    for neighbor,
    That, mad, is mute ;
By the child that famine eats as worms the
    blossom
    —Ah God, the child !
By the milkless lips that strain the blood-
    less bosom
    Till woe runs wild ;
By the pastures that give grass to feed the
    lamb in,
    Where men lack meat ;
By the cities clad with gold and shame and
    famine ;
    By field and street ;
By the people, by the poor man, by the
    master
    That men call slave ;
By the cross-winds of defeat and of disaster,
    By wreck by wave ;
By the helm that keeps us still to sunwards
    driving,
    Still eastward bound,
Till, as night-watch ends, day burn on eyes
    reviving,
    And land be found :
We thy children, that arraign not nor im-
    peach thee
    Though no star steer us,
By the waves that wash the morning we
    beseech thee,
    O mother, hear us,

HERTHA.

I AM that which began ;
　　Out of me the years roll ;
　　Out of me God and man ;
　　I am equal and Whole ;
God changes, and man, and the form of
　　them bodily ; I am the soul.

Before ever land was,
　　Before ever the sea,
　　Or soft hair of the grass,
　　Or fair limbs of the tree,
Or the flesh-colored fruit of my branches,
　　I was, and thy soul was in me.

First life on my sources
　　First drifted and swam ;
　　Out of me are the forces
　　That save it or damn ;
Out of me man and woman, and wild-beast
　　and bird ; before God was, I am.

Beside or above me
　　Nought is there to go ;
　　Love or unlove me,
　　Unknow me or know,
I am that which unloves me and loves ; I
　　am stricken, and I am the blow.

I the mark that is missed
　　And the arrows that miss,
　　I the mouth that is kissed
　　And the breath in the kiss,
The search, and the sought, and the seeker,
　　the soul and the body that is.

I am that thing which blesses
　　My spirit elate ;
　　That which caresses
　　With hands uncreate
My limbs unbegotten that measure the
　　length of the measure of fate.

But what thing dost thou now,
　　Looking Godward, to cry
　　" I am I, thou art thou,
　　I am low, thou art high ?"
I am thou, whom thou seekest to find him ;
　　find thou but thyself, thou art I.

I the grain and the furrow,
　　The plough-cloven clod
　　And　the　ploughshare　drawn
　　thorough,
　　The germ and the sod,
The deed and the doer, the seed and the
　　sower, the dust which is God.

Hast thou known how I fashioned
　　thee,
　　Child, underground ?
　　Fire that impassioned thee,
　　Iron that bound,
Dim changes of water, what thing of all
　　these hast thou known of or found ?

Canst thou say in thine heart
　　Thou has seen with thine eyes
　　With what cunning of art
　　Thou wast wrought in what wise,
By what force of what stuff thou wast shap-
　　en, and shown on my breast to the skies?

Who hath given, who hath sold it
　　thee,
　　Knowledge of me ?
Hath the wilderness told it thee ?
　　Hast thou learnt of the sea ?
Hast thou communed in spirit with night ?
　　have the winds taken counsel with thee?

Have I set such a star
　　To show light on thy brow
　　That thou sawest from afar
　　What I show to thee now ?
Have ye spoken as brethren together, the
　　sun and the mountains and thou ?

What is here, dost thou know it ?
　　What was, hast thou known ?
　　Prophet nor poet
　　Nor tripod nor throne
Nor spirit nor flesh can make answer, but
　　only thy mother alone.

Mother, not maker,
　　Born, and not made ;
　　Though her children forsake her,
　　Allured or afraid,
Praying prayers to the God of their fashion,
　　she stirs not for all that have prayed.

A creed is a rod.
And a crown is of night ;
But this thing is God,
To be man with thy might,
To grow straight in the strength of thy
spirit, and live out thy life as the light.

I am in thee to save thee,
As my soul in thee saith,
Give thou as I gave thee,
Thy life-blood and breath,
Green leaves of thy labor, white flowers of
thy thought, and red fruit of thy death.

Be the ways of thy giving
As mine were to thee ;
The free life of thy living,
Be the gift of it free ;
Not as servant to lord, nor as master to
slave, shalt thou give thee to me.

O children of banishment,
Souls overcast,
Were the lights ye see vanish meant
Alway to last,
Ye would know not the sun overshining the
shadows and stars overpast.

I that saw where ye trod
The dim paths of the night
Set the shadow called God
In your skies to give light ;
But the morning of manhood is risen, and
the shadowless soul is in sight.

The tree many-rooted
That swells to the sky
With frondage red-fruited,
The life-tree am I ;
In the buds of your lives is the sap of my
leaves : ye shall live and not die.

But the Gods of your fashion
That take and that give,
In their pity and passion
That scourge and forgive,
They are worms that are bred in the bark
that falls off : they shall die and not
live.

My own blood is what stanches
The wounds in my bark :
Stars caught in my branches
Make day of the dark,
And are worshipped as suns till the sunrise
shall tread out their fires as a spark.

Where dead ages hide under
The live roots of the tree,
In my darkness the thunder
Make utterance of me ;
In the clash of my boughs with each other
ye hear the waves sound of the sea.

That noise is of Time,
As his feathers are spread
And his feet set to climb
Through the boughs overhead,
And my foliage rings round him and rustles,
and branches are bent with his tread.

The storm-winds of ages
Blow through me and cease,
The war-wind that rages,
The spring-wind of peace,
Ere the breath of them roughen my tresses,
ere one of my blossoms increase.

All sounds of all changes,
All shadows and lights
On the world's mountain-ranges
And stream-riven heights,
Whose tongue is the wind's tongue and lan-
guage of storm-clouds on earth-shaking
nights ;

All forms of all faces,
All works of all hands
In unsearchable places
Of time-stricken lands,
All death and all life, and all reigns and all
ruins, drop through me as sands.

Though sore be my burden
And more than ye know,
And my growth have no guerdon
But only to grow,
Yet I fail not of growing for lightnings
above me or deathworms below.

These too have their part in me,
As I too in these ;
Such fire is at heart in me,
Such sap is this tree's,
Which hath in it all sounds and all secrets
of infinite lands and of seas.

In the spring-colored hours
When my mind was as May's,
There brake forth of me flowers
By centuries of days,
Strong blossoms with perfume of manhood,
shot out from my spirit as rays.

And the sound of them springing
  And smell of their shoots
Were as warmth and sweet singing
  And strength to my roots ;
And the lives of my children made perfect
  with freedom of soul were my fruits.

I bid you but be ;
  I have need not of prayer ;
I have need of you free
  As your mouths of mine air ;
That my heart may be greater within me,
  beholding the fruits of me fair.

More fair than strange fruit is
  Of faiths ye espouse ;
In me only the root is
  That blooms in your boughs ;
Behold now your God that ye made you,
  to feed him with faith of your vows.

In the darkening and whitening
  Abysses adored,
With dayspring and lightning
  For lamp and for sword,
God thunders in heaven, and his angels
  are red with the wrath of the Lord.

O my sons, O too dutiful
  Toward Gods not of me,
Was not I enough beautiful ?
  Was it hard to be free ?
For behold, I am with you, am in you and
  of you ; look forth now and see.

Lo, winged with world's wonders,
  With miracles shod,
With the fires of his thunders
  For raiment and rod,
God trembles in heaven, and his angels are
  white with the terror of God.

For his twilight is come on him,
  His anguish is here ;
And his spirits gaze dumb on him,
  Grown grey from his fear ;
And his hour taketh hold on him stricken,
  the last of his infinite year.

Thought made him and breaks him,
  Truth slays and forgives ;
But to you, as time takes him,
  This new thing it gives,
Even love, the beloved Republic, that feeds
  upon freedom and lives.

For truth only is living,
  Truth only is whole,
And the love of his giving
  Man's polestar and pole ;
Man, pulse of my centre, and fruit of my
  body, and seed of my soul.

One birth of my bosom ;
  One beam of mine eye ;
One topmost blossom
  That scales the sky ;
Man, equal and one with me, man that is
  made of me, man that is I.

BEFORE A CRUCIFIX.

HERE, down between the dusty trees,
  At this lank edge of haggard wood,
Women with labor-loosened knees,
  With gaunt backs bowed by servitude,
Stop, shift their loads, and pray, and fare
Forth with souls easier for the prayer.

The suns have branded black, the rains
  Striped grey this piteous God of theirs ;
The face is full of prayers and pains,
  To which they bring their pains and
    prayers ;
Lean limbs that shew the laboring bones,
And ghastly mouth that gapes and groans.

God of this grievous people, wrought
  After the likeness of their race,
By faces like thine own besought,
  Thine own blind helpless eyeless face,
I too, that have nor tongue nor knee
For prayer, I have a word to thee.

It was for this then, that thy speech
  Was blown about the world in flame
And men's souls shot up out of reach
  Of fear or lust or thwarting shame—
That thy faith over souls should pass
As sea-winds burning the grey grass ?

It was for this, that prayers like these
  Should spend themselves about thy feet,
And with hard overlabored knees
  Kneeling, these slaves of men should
    beat
Bosoms too lean too suckle sons
And fruitless as their orisons?

It was for this, that men should make
  Thy name a fetter on men's necks,
Poor men's made poorer for thy sake,
  And women's withered out of sex?
It was for this, that slaves should be,
Thy word was passed to set men free?

The nineteenth wave of the ages rolls
  Now deathward since thy death and
    birth.
Hast thou fed full men's starved-out souls?
  Hast thou brought freedom upon earth?
Or are there less oppressions done
In this wild world under the sun?

Nay, if indeed thou be not dead,
  Before thy terrene shrine be shaken,
Look down, turn usward, bow thine head;
  O thou that wast of God forsaken,
Look on thine household here, and see
These that have not forsaken thee.

Thy faith is fire upon their lips,
  Thy kingdom golden in their hands;
They scourge us with thy words for whips,
  They brand us with thy words for
    brands;
The thrist that made thy dry throat shrink
To their moist mouths commends the drink.

The toothèd thorns that bit thy brows
  Lighten the weight of gold on theirs;
Thy nakedness enrobes thy spouse
  With the soft sanguine stuff she wears
Whose old limbs use for ointment yet
Thine agony and bloody sweat.

The blinding buffets on thine head
  On their crowned heads confirm the
    crown;
Thy scourging dyes their raiment red,
  And with thy bands they fasten down
For burial in the blood-bought field
The nations by thy stripes unhealed.

With iron for thy linen bands
  And unclean cloths for winding-sheet

They bind the people's nail-pierced hands,
  They hide the people's nail-pierced feet:
And what man or what angel known
Shall roll back the sepulchral stone?

But these have not the rich man's grave
  To sleep in when their pain is done.
These were not fit for God to save.
  As naked hell-fire is the sun
In their eyes living, and when dead
These have not where to lay their head.

They have no tomb to dig, and hide;
  Earth is not theirs, that they should
    sleep.
On all these tombless crucified
  No lovers' eyes have time to weep.
So still, for all man's tears and creeds,
The sacred body hangs and bleeds.

Through the left hand a nail is driven,
  Faith, and another through the right,
Forged in the fires of hell and heaven,
  Fear that puts out the eye of light:
And the feet soiled and scarred and pale
Are pierced with falsehood for a nail.

And priests against the mouth divine
  Push their sponge full of poison yet
And bitter blood for myrrh and wine,
  And on the same reed is it set
Wherewith before they buffeted
The people's disanointed head.

O sacred head, O desecrate,
  O labor-wounded feet and hands,
O blood poured forth in pledge to fate
  Of nameless lives in divers lands,
O slain and spent and sacrificed
People, the grey-grown speechless Christ!

Is there a gospel in the red
  Old witness of thy wide-mouthed wounds?
From thy blind stricken tongueless head
  What desolate evangel sounds
A hopeless note of hope deferred?
What word, if there be any word?

O son of man, beneath man's feet
  Cast down, O common face of man
Whereon all blows and buffets meet,
  O royal, O republican
Face of the people bruised and dumb
And longing till thy kingdom come!

The soldiers and the high priests part
  Thy vesture : all thy days are pierced,
And all the nights that eat thine heart.
  And that one seamless coat of Christ,
The freedom of the natural soul,
They cast their lots for to keep whole.

No fragment of it save the name
  They leave thee for a crown of scorns
Wherewith to mock thy naked shame
  And forehead bitten through with thorns
And, marked with sanguine sweat and tears,
The stripes of eighteen hundred years.

And we seek yet if God or man
  Can loosen thee as Lazarus,
Bid thee rise up republican
  And save thyself and all of us ;
But no disciple's tongue can say
When thou shalt take our sins away.

And mouldering now and hoar with moss
  Between us and the sunlight swings
The phantom of a Christless cross
  Shadowing the sheltered heads of kings
And making with its moving shade
The souls of harmless men afraid.

It creaks and rocks to left and right,
  Consumed of rottenness and rust,
Worm-eaten of the worms of night,
  Dead as their spirits who put trust,
Round its base muttering as they sit,
In the time-cankered name of it.

Thou, in the day that breaks thy prison,
  People, though these men take thy name,
And hail and hymn thee rearisen,
  Who made songs erewhile of thy shame,
Give thou not ear ; for these are they
Whose good day was thine evil day.

Set not thine hand unto their cross
  Give not thy soul up sacrificed.
Change not the gold of faith for dross
  Of Christian creeds that spit on Christ.
Let not thy tree of freedom be
Regrafted from that rotting tree.

This dead God here against my face
  Hath help for no man ; who hath seen
The good works of it, or such grace
  As thy grace in it, Nazarene,
As that from thy live lips which ran
For man's sake, O thou son of man ?

The tree of faith ingraffed by priests
  Puts its foul foliage out above thee,
And round it feed man-eating beasts
  Because of whom we dare not love thee ;
Though hearts reach back and memories
    ache,
We cannot praise thee for their sake.

O hidden face of man, whereover
  The years have woven a viewless veil,
If thou wast verily man's lover,
  What did thy love or blood avail ?
Thy blood the priests make poison of,
And in gold shekels coin thy love.

So when our souls looks back to thee
  They sicken, seeing against thy side,
Too foul to speak of or to see,
  The leprous likeness of a bride,
Whose kissing lips through his lips grown
Leave their God rotten to the bone.

When we would see thee man, and know
  What heart thou hadst toward men indeed,
Lo, thy blood-blackened altars ; lo,
  The lips of priests that pray and feed
While their own hell's worm curls and licks
The poison of the crucifix.

Thou bad'st let children come to thee ;
  What children now but curses come ?
What man in that God can be
  Who sees their worship, and is dumb ?
No soul that lived, loved, wrought, and
    died,
Is this their carrion crucified.

Nay, if their God and thou be one,
  If thou and this thing be the same,
Thou shouldst not look upon the sun ;
  The sun grows haggard at thy name.
Come down, be done with, cease, give o'er ;
Hide thyself, strive not, be no more.

TENEBRÆ.

At the chill high tide of the night,
  At the turn of the fluctuant hours,
When the waters of time are at height,
In a vision arose on my sight
  The kingdoms of earth and the powers.

In a dream without lightening of eyes
  I saw them, children of earth,
Nations and races arise,
Each one after his wise,
  Signed with the sign of his birth.

Sound was none of their feet,
  Light was none of their faces ;
In their lips breath was not, or heat,
But a subtle murmur and sweet
  As of water in wan waste places.

Pale as from passionate years,
  Years unassuaged of desire,
Sang they soft in mine ears,
Crowned with jewels of tears,
  Girt with girdles of fire.

A slow song beaten and broken,
  As is were from the dust and the dead,
As of spirits athirst unsloken,
As of things unspeakable spoken,
  As of tears unendurable shed.

In the manifold sound remote,
  In the molten murmur of song,
There was but a sharp sole note
Alive on the night and afloat,
  The cry of the world's heart's wrong.

As the sea in the strait sea-caves,
  The sound came straitened and strange ;
A noise of the rending of graves,
A tidal thunder of waves,
  The music of death and of change.

"We have waited so long," they say.
  "For a sound of the God, for a breath,
For a ripple of the refluence of day,
For the fresh bright wind of the fray,
  For the light of the sunrise of death.

"We have prayed not, we, to be strong,
  To fulfil the desire of our eyes ;
—Howbeit they have watched for it long,
Watched, and the night did them wrong,
  Yet they say not of day shall it rise ?

"They are fearful and feeble with years,
  Yet they doubt not of day if it be ;
Yea, blinded and beaten with tears,
Yea, sick with foresight of fears,
  Yet a little, and hardly, they see.

"We pray not, we, for the palm,
  For the fruit ingraffed of the fight,
For the blossom of peace and the balm,
And the tender triumph and calm
  Of crownless and weaponless right.

"We pray not, we, to behold
  The latter august new birth,
The young day's purple and gold,
And divine, and rerisen as of old,
  The sun-god of Freedom on earth.

"Peace. and world's honor, and fame,
  We have sought after none of these
    things :
The light of a life like flame
Passing the storm of a name
  Shaking the strongholds of kings :

"Nor, fashioned of fire and of air,
  The splendor that burns on his head
Who was chiefest in ages that were,
Whose breath blew palaces bare,
  Whose eye shone tyrannies dead ;

"All these things in your day
  Ye shall see, O our sons, and shall hold
Surely ; but we, in the grey
Twilight, for one thing we pray,
  In that day though our memories be cold:

"To feel on our brows as we wait
  An air of the morning, a breath
From the springs of the east, from the gate
Whence freedom issues. and fate,
  Sorrow and triumph, and death :

"From a land whereon time hath not trod,
  Where the spirit is bondless and bare,
And the world's rein breaks, and the rod,
And the soul of a man which is God,
  He adores without altar or prayer :

"For alone of herself and her right
  She takes, and alone gives grace :
And the colors of things lose light,
And the forms, in the limitless white
  Splendor of space without space :

" And the blossom of man from his tomb
  Yearns open, the flower that survives ;
And the shadows of changes consume
In the colorless passionate bloom
  Of the live light made of our lives :

" Seeing each life given is a leaf
  Of the manifold multiform flower,
And the least among these, and the chief.
As an ear in the red ripe sheaf
  Stored for the harvesting hour.

" O spirit of man, most holy,
  The measure of things and the root ;
In our summers and winters a lowly
Seed, putting forth of them slowly
  Thy supreme blossom and fruit ;

" In thy sacred and perfect year.
  The souls that were parcel of thee
In the labor and life of us here
Shall be rays of thy sovereign sphere,
  Springs of thy motion shall be.

" There is the fire that was man,
  The light that was love, and the breath
That was hope ere deliverance began,

And the wind that was life for a span,
  And the birth of new things which is
    death.

" There, whosoever had light,
  And, having, for men's sake gave ;
All that warred against night,
All that were found in the fight
  Swift to be slain and to save ;

"Undisbranched of the storms that disroot
    us
  Of the lures that enthrall unenticed :
The names that exalt and transmute us :
The blood-bright splendour of Brutus,
  The snow-bright splendor of Christ.

' There all chains are undone ;
  Day there seems but as night ;
Spirit and sense are as one
In the light not of star nor of sun :
  Liberty there is the light.

" She, sole mother and maker,
  Stronger than sorrow, than strife ;
Deathless, though death overtake her ;
Faithful, though faith should forsake her ;
  Spirit, and saviour, and life."

HYMN OF MAN.

(DURING THE SESSION IN ROME OF THE ŒCUMENICAL COUNCIL.)

IN the grey beginning of years, in the
    twilight of things that began,
The word of the earth in the ears of the
    world, was it God ? was it man ?
The word of the earth to the spheres her
    sisters, the note of her song,
The sound of her speech in the ears of the
    starry and sisterly throng,
Was it praise or passion or prayer, was it
    love or devotion or dread,
When the veils of the shining air first wrapt
    her jubilant head ?
When her eyes new-born of the night saw
    yet no star out of reach ;
When her maiden mouth was alight with
    the flame of musical speech ;
When her virgin feet were set on the terrible
    heavenly way.
And her virginal lids were wet with the dew
    of the birth of the day :
Eyes that had looked not on time, and ears
    that had heard not of death ;

Lips that had learnt not the rhyme of change
    and passionate breath,
The rhythmic anguish of growth, and the
    motion of mutable things,
Of love that longs and is loth, and plume-
    plucked hope without wings,
Passions and pains without number, and
    life that runs and is lame,
From slumber again to slumber, the same
    race set for the same,
Where the runners outwear each other, but
    running with lampless hands
No man takes light from his brother till
    blind at the goal he stands :
Ah, did they know, did they dream of it,
    counting the cost and the worth ?
The ways of her days, did they seem then
    good to the new-souled earth ?
Did her heart rejoice, and the might of her
    spirit in her then,
Child yet no child of the night, and mother-
    less mother of men ?

Was it Love brake forth flower-fashion, a
  bird with gold on his wings,
Lovely, her firstborn passion, and impulse
  of firstborn things?
Was Love that nestling indeed that under
  the plume of the night
Was hatched and hidden as seed in the
  furrow, and brought forth bright?
Was it Love lay shut in the shell world-
  shaped, having over him there
Black world-wide wings that impel the
  might of the night through air?
And bursting his shell as a bird, night
  shook through her sail-stretched vans,
And her heart as a water was stirred, and
  its heat was the firstborn man's
For the waste of the dead void air took
  form of a world at birth,
And the waters and firmaments were, and
  light, and the life-giving earth.
The beautiful bird unbegotten that night
  brought forth without pain
In the fathomless years forgotten whereover the dead gods reign,
Was it love, life, godhead, or fate? we say
  the spirit is one
That moved on the dark to create out of
  darkness the stars and the sun.
Before the growth was the grower, and
  the seed ere the plant was sown;
But what was seed of the sower? and the
  grain of him, whence was it grown?
Foot after foot ye go back and travail and
  make yourselves mad;
Blind feet that feel for the track where
  highway is none to be had.
Therefore the God that ye make you is
  grievous, and gives not aid,
Because it is but for your sake that the
  God of your making is made.
Thou and I and he are not gods made
  men for a span,
But God, if a God there be, is the sub-
  stance of men which is man.
Our lives are as pulses or pores of his man-
  ifold body and breath;
As waves of his sea on the shores where
  birth is the beacon of death.
We men, the multiform features of man,
  whatsoever we be,
Recreate him of whom we are creatures,
  and all we only are he.
For each man of all men is God, but God
  is the fruit of the whole;
Indivisible spirit and blood, indiscernible
  body from soul.

Not men's but man's is the glory of godhead, the kingdom of time,
The mountainous ages made hoary with
  snows for the spirit to climb.
A God with the world inwound whose
  clay to his footsole clings;
A manifold God fast-bound as with iron
  of adverse things.
A soul that labours and lives, an emotion,
  a strenuous breath,
From the flame that its own mouth gives
  reillumed and refreshed with death.
In the sea whereof centuries are waves the
  live God plunges and swims;
His bed is in all men's graves, but the
  worm hath not hold on his limbs.
Night puts out not his eyes, nor time
  sheds change on his head;
With such fire as the stars of the skies are
  the roots of his heart are fed.
Men are the thoughts passing through it,
  the veins that fulfil it with blood,
With spirit of sense to renew it as springs
  fulfilling a flood.
Men are the heartbeats of man, the plumes
  that feather his wings,
Storm-worn, since being began, with the
  wind and thunder of things.
Things are cruel and blind; their strength
  detains and deforms:
And the wearying wings of the mind still
  beat up the stream of their storms.
Still, as one swimming up stream, they
  strike out blind in the blast,
In thunders of vision and dream, and
  lightning of future and past.
We are baffled and caught in the current
  and bruised upon edges of shoals;
As weeds or as reeds in the torrent of
  things are the wind-shaken souls.
Spirit by spirit goes under, a foam-bell's
  bubble of breath,
That blows and opens in sunder and blurs
  not the mirror of death.
For a worm or a thorn in his path is a
  man's soul quenched as a flame;
For his lust of an hour or his wrath shall
  the worm and the man be the same.
O God sore stricken of things! they have
  wrought him a raiment of pain;
Can a God shut eyelids and wings at a
  touch on the nerves of the brain?
O shamed and sorrowful God, whose force
  goes out at a blow!

What world shall shake at his nod ? at his
  coming what wilderness glow ?
What help in the work of his hands ? what
  light in the track of his feet ?
His days are snowflakes or sands, with cold
  to consume him and heat.
He is servant with Change for lord, and for
  wages he hath to his hire
Folly and force, and a sword that devours,
  and a ravening fire,
From the bed of his birth to his grave he is
  driven as a wind at their will :
Lest Change bow down as his slave, and
  the storm and the sword be still ;
Lest earth spread open her wings to the
  sunward, and sing with the spheres ;
Lest man be master of things, to prevail on
  their forces and fears.
By the spirit are things overcome ; they are
  stark, and the spirit hath breath ;
It hath speech, and their forces are dumb ;
  it is living and things are of death.
But they know not the spirit for master,
  they feel not force from above,
While man makes love to disaster, and
  woos desolation with love.
Yea, himself too hath made himself chains,
  and his own hands plucked out his
  eyes ;
For his own soul only constrains him, his
  own mouth only denies.
The herds of kings and their hosts and the
  flocks of the high priests bow
To a master whose face is a ghost's ; O
  thou that wast God, is it thou ?
Thou madest man in the garden ; thou
  temptedst man, and he fell ;
Thou gavest him poison and pardon for
  blood and burnt-offering to sell.
Thou hast sealed thine elect to salvation,
  fast locked with faith for the key ;
Make now for thyself expiation, and be
  thine atonement for thee.
Ah, thou that darkenest heaven—ah, thou
  that bringest a sword—
By the crimes of thine hands unforgiven
  they beseech thee to hear them, O
  Lord.
By the balefires of ages that burn for thine
  incense, by creed and by rood,
By the famine and passion that yearn and
  that hunger to find of thee food,
By the children that asked at thy throne of
  the priests that were fat with thine hire
For bread, and thou gavest a stone ; for
  light, and thou madest them fire ;

By the kiss of thy peace like a snake's kiss,
  that leaves the soul rotten at root ;
By the savors of gibbets and stakes thou
  hast planted to bear to thee fruit ;
By torture and terror and treason, that
  make to thee weapons and wings ;
By thy power upon men for a season, made
  out of the malice of things ;
O thou that hast built thee a shrine of the
  madness of man and his shame,
And hast hung in the midst for a sign of his
  worship the lamp of thy name ;
That hast shown him for heaven in a vision
  a void world's shadow and shell,
And hast fed thy delight and derision with
  fire of belief as of hell ;
That has fleshed on the souls that believe
  thee the fang of the death-worm fear,
With anguish of dreams to deceive them
  whose faith cries out in thine ear ;
By the face of the spirit confounded before
  thee and humbled in dust,
By the dread wherewith life was astounded
  and shamed out of sense of its trust,
By the scourges of doubt and repentance
  that fell on the soul at thy nod,
Thou art judged, O judge, and the sentence
  is gone forth against thee, O God.
Thy slave that slept is awake ; thy slave
  but slept for a span ;
Yea, man thy slave shall unmake thee, who
  made thee lord over man.
For his face is set to the east, his feet on
  the past and its dead ;
The sun rearisen is his priest, and the heat
  thereof hallows his head.
His eyes take part in the morning ; his
  spirit outsounding the sea
Asks no more witness or warning from
  temple or tripod or tree.
He hath set the centuries at union ; the
  night is afraid at his name ;
Equal with life, in communion with death,
  he hath found them the same.
Past the wall unsurmounted that bars out
  our vision with iron and fire
He hath sent forth his soul for the stars to
  comply with and suns to conspire.
His thought takes flight for the centre
  wherethrough it hath part in the whole;
The abysses forbid it not enter : the stars
  make room for the soul.
Space is the soul's to inherit ; the night is
  hers as the day ;
Lo, saith man, this is my spirit ; how shall
  not the worlds make way ?

Space is thought's, and the wonders thereof, and the secret of space ;
Is thought not more than the thunders and
lightnings ? shall thought give place ?
Is the body not more than the vesture, the
life not more than the meat ?
The will than the word or the gesture, the
heart than the hands or the feet ?
Is the tongue not more than the speech is ?
the head not more than the crown ?
And if higher than is heaven be the reach
of the soul, shall not heaven bow down?
Time, father of life, and more great than
than the life it begat and began,
Earth's keeper and heaven's and their fate,
lives, thinks, and hath substance in
man.
Time's motion that throbs in his blood is
the thought that gives heart to the skies,
And the springs of the fire that is food to
the sunbeams are light to his eyes.
The minutes that beat with his heart are
the words to which worlds keep chime,
And the thought in his pulses is part of the
blood and the spirit of time.
He saith to the ages, Give ; and his soul
foregoes not her share ;
Who are ye that forbid him to live, and
would feed him with heavenlier air ?
Will ye feed him with poisonous dust, and
restore him with hemlock for drink,
Till he yield you his soul up in trust, and
have heart not to know or to think ?
He hath stirred him, and found out the
flaw in his fetters, and cast them behind ;
His soul to his soul is a law, and his mind
is a light to his mind.
The seal of his knowledge is sure, the truth
and his spirit are wed ;
Men perish, but man shall endure ; lives
die, but the life is not dead.
He hath sight of the secrets of season, the
roots of the years and the fruits ;
His soul is at one with the reason of things
that is sap to the roots.
He can hear in their changes a sound as the
conscience of consonant spheres ;
He can see through the years flowing round
him the law lying under the years.
Who are ye that would bind him with curses
and blind him with vapor of prayer?
Your might is as night that disperses when
light is alive in the air.
The bow of your godhead is broken, the arm
of your conquest is stayed ;

Though ye call down God to bear token,
for fear of you none is afraid.
Will ye turn back times, and the courses of
stars, and the season of souls ?
Shall God s breath dry up the sources that
feed time full as it rolls?
Nay, cry on him then till he show you a
sign, till he lift up a rod ;
Hath he made not the nations to know him
of old if indeed he be God ?
Is no heat of him left in the ashes of thous-
ands burnt up for his sake ?
Can prayer not rekindle the flashes that
shone in his face from the stake ?
Cry aloud ; for your God is a God and a
Saviour ; cry, make yourselves lean ;
Is he drunk or asleep, that the rod of his
wrath is unfelt and unseen ?
Is the fire of his old loving-kindness gone
out, that his pyres are acold ?
Hath he gazed on himself unto blindness,
who made men blind to behold ?
Cry out, for his kingdom is shaken ; cry
out, for the people blaspheme ;
Cry aloud till his godhead awaken ; what
doth he to sleep and to dream ?
Cry, cut yourselves, gash you with knives
and with scourges, heap on to you dust;
Is his life but as other gods' lives ? is not
this the Lord God of your trust ?
Is not this the great God of your sires, that
with souls and with bodies was fed,
And the world was on flame with his fires ?
O fools, he was God, and is dead.
He will hear not again the strong crying of
earth in his ears as before,
And the fume of his multitudes dying shall
flatter his nostrils no more.
By the spirit he ruled as his slave is he slain
who was mighty to slay,
And the stone that is sealed on his grave he
shall rise not and roll not away.
Yea, weep to him, lift up your hands ; be
your eyes as a fountain of tears ;
Where he stood there is nothing that stands;
if he call, there is no man that hears.
He hath doffed his king's raiment of lies
now the wane of his kingdom is come;
Ears hath he, and hears not ; and eyes, and
he sees not ; and mouth, and is dumb.
His red king's raiment is ripped from him
naked, his staff broken down :
And the signs of his empire are stripped from
him shuddering; and where is his crown?
And in vain by the wellsprings refrozen ye
cry for the warmth of his sun—

O God, the Lord God of thy chosen, thy
 will in thy kingdom be done.
Kingdom and will hath he none in him left
 him, nor warmth in his breath ;
Till his corpse be cast out of the sun will ye
 know not the truth of his death ?
Surely, ye say, he is strong, though the
 times be against him and men ;
Yet a little, ye say, and how long, till he
 come to show judgment again ?
Shall God then die as the beasts die ? who
 is it hath broken his rod ?
O God, Lord God of thy priests, rise up
 now and show thyself God.

They cry out, thine elect, thine aspirants
 to heavenward, whose faith is as flame;
O thou the Lord God of our tyrants, they
 call thee, their God, by thy name.
By thy name that in hell-fire was written,
 and burned at the point of thy sword,
Thou art smitten, thou God, thou art smitten ; thy death is upon thee, O Lord
And the love-song of earth as thou diest
 resounds through the wind of her
 wings—
Glory to Man in the highest ! for Man is
 master of things.

THE PILGRIMS.

WHO is your lady of love, O ye that pass
Singing ? and is it for sorrow of that which
 was
  That ye sing sadly, or dream of what
  shall be ?
   For gladly at once and sadly it seems
   ye sing.
—Our lady of love by you is unbeholden ;
For hands she hath none, nor eyes, nor lips,
 nor golden
  Treasure of hair, nor face nor form ; but
  we
   That love, we know her more fair
   than anything.

—Is she a queen, having great gifts to
 give ?
—Yea, these ; that whoso hath seen her
 shall not live
  Except he serve her sorrowing, with
  strange pain,
   Travail and bloodshedding and bitterer
   tears ;
And when she bids die he shall surely die.
And he shall leave all things under the sky
 And go forth naked under sun and rain
  And work and wait and watch out all
  his years.

—Hath she on earth no place of habitation ?
—Age to age calling, nation answering
 nation,
  Cries out, Where is she ? and there is
  none to say ;
   For if she be not in the spirit of men.

For if in the inward soul she hath no
 place,
In vain they cry unto her, seeking her face,
 In vain their mouths make much of her ;
 for they
  Cry with vain tongues, till the heart
  lives again.

—O ye that follow, and have ye no repentance ?
For on your brows is written a mortal
 sentence,
 An hieroglyph of sorrow, a fiery sign,
  That in your lives ye shall not pause
  or rest,
Nor have the sure sweet common love, nor
 keep
Friends and safe days, nor joy of life nor
 sleep.
 —These have we not, who have one
  thing, the divine
  Face and clear eyes of faith and fruitful breast.

—And ye shall die before your thrones be
 won.
—Yea, and the changed world and the
 liberal sun
 Shall move and shine without us, and
 we lie
  Dead ; but if she too move on earth
  and live,
But if the old world with all the old irons
 rent

Laugh and give thanks, shall we be not
 content ?
 Nay, we shall rather live, we shall not
 die,
 Life being so little and death so good
 to give.

And these men shall forget you—Yea,
 but we
Shall be a part of the earth and the ancient
 sea,
 And heaven high air august, and awful
 fire,
 And all things good ; and no man's
 heart shall beat
But somewhat in it of our blood once shed
Shall quiver and quicken, as now in us the
 dead
 Blood of men slain and the old same
 life's desire
 Plants in their fiery footprints our fresh
 feet.

But ye that might be clothed with all
 things pleasant,
 Ye are foolish that put off the fair soft
 present,
 That clothe yourselves with the cold
 future air ;
 When mother and father and tender
 sister and brother
And the old live love that was shall be as
 ye,
Dust, and no fruit of loving life shall be.
 —She shall be yet who is more than
 all these were,
 Than sister or wife or father unto us or
 mother.

—Is this worth life, is this, to win for
 wages ?
Lo, the dead mouths of the awful grey
 grown ages,
 The venerable, in the past that is their
 prison,
 In the outer darkness, in the unopening grave,
Laugh, knowing how many as ye now say
 have said,
How many, and all are fallen, are fallen
 and dead :

Shall ye dead rise, and these dead have not
 risen :
 —Not we but she, who is tender and
 swift to save.

—Are ye not weary and faint not by the
 way
Seeing night by night devoured of day by
 day,
 Seeing hour by hour consumed in sleepless fire ?
 Sleepless ; and ye too, when shall ye
 too sleep ?
— We are weary in heart and head, in hands
 and feet,
And surely more than all things sleep were
 sweet,
 Than all things save the inexorable desire
 Which whoso knoweth shall neither
 faint nor weep.

—Is this so sweet that one were fain to
 follow ?
Is this so sure where all men's hopes are
 hollow,
 Even this your dream, that by much
 tribulation
 Ye shall make whole flawed hearts,
 and bowed necks straight ?
—Nay though our life were blind, our
 death were fruitless,
Not therefore were the whole world's high
 hope rootless :
 But man to man, nation would turn to
 nation,
 And the old life live, and the old
 great world be great.

—Pass on then and pass by us and let us be,
For what light think ye after life to see ?
And if the world fare better will ye know ?
 And if man triumph who shall seek you
 and say ?
—Enough of light is this for one life's span,
That all men born are mortal, but not man:
 And we men bring death lives by night
 to sow,
 That man may reap and eat and live
 by day.

ARMAND BARBÈS.

I.

FIRE out of heaven, a flower of perfect
    fire,
  That where the roots of life are had its
    root
  And where the fruits of time are brought
    forth fruit ;
A faith made flesh, a visible desire
That heard the yet unbreathing years re-
    spire,
  And speech break forth of centuries that
    sit mute
  Beyond all feebler footprint of pursuit ;
That touched the highest of hope and went
    up higher ;
A heart love-wounded whereto love was
    law,
A soul reproachless without fear or flaw.
A shining spirit without shadow of shame,
A memory made of all men's love and
    awe ,
  Being disembodied, so thou be the same,
  What need, O soul, to sign thee with thy
    name ?

II.

All woes of all men sat upon thy soul
  And all their wrongs were heavy on thy
    head ;
  With all their wounds thy heart was
    pierced and bled.
And in thy spirit as in a mourning scroll
The world's huge sorrows were inscribed
    by roll,
  All theirs on earth who serve and faint
    for bread,
  All banished men's, all theirs in prison
    dead,
Thy love had heart and sword-hand for the
    whole.
" This was my day of glory," didst thou say,
  When, by the scaffold thou hadst hope to
    climb
For thy faith's sake they brought thee re-
    spite ; " Nay,
I shall not die then, I have missed my day."
  O hero, O our help, O head sublime,
  Thy day shall be commensurate with
    time.

QUIA MULTUM AMAVIT.

AM I not he that hath made thee and be-
    gotten thee,
  I, God, the spirit of man ?
Wherefore now these eighteen years hast
    thou forgotten me,
  From whom thy life began ?
Thy life-blood and thy life-breath and thy
    beauty,
  Thy might of hands and feet,
Thy soul made strong for divinity of duty
  And service which was sweet.
Through the red sea brimmed with blood
    didst thou not follow me,
  As one that walks in trance ?
Was the storm strong to break or the sea
    to swallow thee,
  When thou wast free and France ?
I am Freedom, God and man, O France,
    that plead with thee ;
  How long now shall I plead ?

Was I not with thee in travail, and in need
    with thee,
  Thy sore travail and need ?
Thou wast fairest and first of my virgin-
    vested daughters,
  Fairest and foremost thou ;
And thy breast was white, though thy hands
    were red with slaughters,
  Thy breast, a harlot's now.
O foolish virgin and fair among the fallen,
  A ruin where satyrs dance,
A garden wasted for beasts to crawl and
    brawl in,
  What hast thou done with France ?
Where is she who bared her bosom but to
    thunder,
  Her brow to storm and flame,
And before her face was the red sea cloven
    in sunder,
  And all its waves made tame ?

And the surf wherein the broad-based rocks
    were shaking
She saw far off divide,
At the blast of the breath of the battle
    blown and breaking,
    And weight of wind and tide ;
And the ravin and the ruin of thronèd
    nations
    And every royal race,
And the kingdoms and kings from the state
    of their high stations
    That fell before her face.
Yea, great was the fall of them, all that rose
    against her,
    From the earth s old-historied
      heights ;
For my hands were fire, and my wings as
    walls that fenced her,
    Mine eyes as pilot-lights.
Not as guerdons given of kings the gifts I
    brought her,
    Not strengths that pass away;
But my heart, my breath of life, O France,
    O daughter,
    I gave thee in that day,
Yea, the heart's blood of a very God I gave
    thee,
    Breathed in thy mouth his breath;
Was my word as a man's having no more
    strength to save thee
    From this worse thing than death ?
Didst thou dream of it only, the day that I
    stood nigh thee,
    Was all its light a dream?
When that iron surf roared backwards and
    went by thee
    Unscathed of storm or stream :
When thy sons rose up and thy young men
    stood together,
    One equal face of fight,
And my flag swam high as the swimming
    sea-foam s feather
    Laughing, a lamp of light ?
Ah the lordly laughter and light of it, that
    lightened
    Heaven-high, the heaven's whole
      length !
Ah the hearts of heroes pierced, the bright
    lips whitened
    Of strong men in their strength !
Ah the banner-poles, the stretch of straight-
    ening streamers
    Straining their full reach out !
Ah the men's hands making true the dreams
    of dreamers,
    The hopes brought forth in doubt !

12

Ah the noise of horse, the charge and thun-
    der of drumming,
    And swaying and sweep of swords !
Ah the light that led them through of the
    world's life coming,
    Clear of its lies and lords !
By the lightning of the lips of guns whose
    flashes
    Made plain the strayed world's way;
By the flame that left her dead old sins in
    ashes,
    Swept out of sight of day ;
By thy children whose bare feet were shod
    with thunder,
    Their bare hands mailed with fire ;
By the faith that went with them, waking
    fear and wonder,
    Heart's love and high desire ;
By the tumult of the waves of nations wak-
    ing
    Blind in the loud wide night ;
By the wind that went on the world's waste
    waters, making
    Their marble darkness white,
As the flash of the flakes of the foam flared
    lamplike, leaping
    From wave to gladdening wave,
Making wide the fast-shut eyes of thraldom
    sleeping
    The sleep of the unclean grave ;
By the fire of equality, terrible, devouring,
    Divine, that brought forth good ;
By the lands it purged and wasted and left
    flowering
    With bloom of brotherhood ;
By the lips of fraternity that for love's sake
    uttered
    Fierce words and fires of death,
But the eyes were deep as love's and the
    fierce lips fluttered
    With love's own living breath ;
By the weaponed hands, brows helmed, and
    bare feet spurning
    The bared head of a king :
By the storm of sunrise round thee risen and
    burning,
    Why hast thou done this thing ?
Thou hast mixed thy limbs with the son of
    a harlot of a stranger.
Mouth to mouth limb to limb,
Thou, bride of a God, because of the brides
    man Danger,
    To bring forth seed to him.
For thou thoughtest only the terrible bride
    groom wakes me,
    When I would sleep, to go;

The fire of his mouth consumes, and the red
   kiss shakes me,
   More bitter than a blow.
Rise up, my beloved, go forth to meet the
   stranger,
   Put forth thine arm, he saith :
Fear thou not at all though the bridesman
   should be Danger,
   The bridesmaid should be Death.
I the bridegroom, am I not with thee, O
   bridal nation
   O wedded France to strive ?
To destroy the sins of the earth with divine
   devastation,
   Till none be left alive ?
Lo her growths of sons, foliage of men and
   frondage,
   Broad boughs of the old-world tree,
With iron of shame and with pruning-hooks
   of bondage
   They are shorn from sea to sea.
Lo, I set wings to thy feet that have been
   wingless,
   Till the utter race be run ;
Till the priestless temples cry to the thrones
   made kingless,
   Are we not also undone ?
Till the immeasurable Republic arise and
   enlighten
   Above these quick and dead,
And her awful robes be changed, and her
   red robes whiten,
   Her warring-robes of red
But thou wouldst not, saying, I am weary
   and faint to follow,
   Let me lie down and rest ;
And hast sought out shame to sleep with,
   mire to wallow,

Yea, a much fouler breast :
And thine own hast made prostitute, sold
   and shamed and bared it,
   Thy bosom which was mine,
And the bread of the world I gave thee
   hast soiled, and shared it
   Among these snakes and swine.
As a harlot thou wast handled and polluted,
   Thy faith held light as foam,
That thou sentest men thy sons, thy sons
   imbruted,
   To slay thine elder Rome.
Therefore, O harlot, I gave thee to the
   accurst one,
   By night to be defiled,
To thy second shame, and a fouler than
   the first one,
   That got thee first with child.
Yet I know thee turning back now to be
   hold me,
   To bow thee and make thee bare,
Not for sin s sake but penitence, by my feet
   to hold me,
   And wipe them with thine hair.
And sweet ointment of thy grief thou hast
   brought thy master,
   And set before thy lord,
From a box of flawed and broken alabaster,
   Thy broken spirit, poured.
And love-offerings, tears and perfumes,
   hast thou given me,
   To reach my feet and touch ;
Therefore thy sins, which are many, are
   forgiven thee,
   Because thou hast loved much.

18 brumaire, an 78.

GENESIS.

In the outer world that was before this
   earth,
   That was before all shape or space was
   born,
Before the blind first hour of time had
   birth,
   Before night knew the moonlight or the
   morn ;

Yea, before any world had any light,
   Or anything called God or man drew
   breath,

Slowly the strong sides of the heaving
   night
   Moved, and brought forth the strength
   of life and death.

And the sad shapeless horror increate
   That was all things and one thing, without fruit,
Limit, or law ; where love was none, nor
   hate,
   Where no leaf came to blossom from no
   root ;

The very darkness that time knew not of,
    Nor God laid hand on, nor was man
        found there,
Ceased, and was cloven in several shapes;
        above
    Light, and night under, and fire, earth,
        water, and air.

Sunbeams and starbeams, and all colored
        things,
    All forms and all similitudes began;
And death, the shadow cast by life's wide
        wings,
    And God, the shade cast by the soul of
        man.

Then between shadow and substance, night
        and light,
    Then between birth and death, and deeds
        and days
The illimitable embrace and the amorous
        fight
    That of itself begets, bears, rears, and
        slays,

The immortal war of mortal things, that is
    Labor and life and growth and good and
        ill,
The mild antiphonies that melt and kiss,
    The violent symphonies that meet and
        kill,

All nature of all things began to be.
    But chiefliest in the spirit (beast or man,
Planet of heaven or blossom of earth or sea)
    The divine contraries of life began.

For the great labor of growth, being many,
        is one;
    One thing the white death and the ruddy
        birth;
The invisible air and the all-beholden sun,
    And barren water and many-childed earth.

And these things are made manifest in men
    From the beginning forth unto this day:

Time writes and life records them, and again
    Death seals them lest the record pass
        away.

For if death were not, then should growth
        not be,
    Change, nor the life of good nor evil things;
Nor were there night at all nor light to see,
    Nor water of sweet nor water of bitter
        springs.

For in each man and each year that is born
    Are sown the twin seeds of the strong
        twin powers;
The white seed of the fruitful helpful morn,
    The black seed of the barren hurtful
        hours.

And he that of the black seed eateth fruit,
    To him the savor as honey shall be sweet;
And he in whom the white seed hath struck
        root,
    He shall have sorrow and trouble and
        tears for meat.

And him whose lips the sweet fruit hath
        made red
    In the end men loathe and make his
        name a rod;
And him whose mouth on the unsweet fruit
        hath fed
    In the end men follow and know for very
        God.

And of these twain, the black seed and the
        white,
    All things come forth endured of men and
        done;
And still the day is great with child of night,
    And still the black night labors with the
        sun.

And each man and each year that lives on
        earth
    Turns hither or thither, and hence or
        thence is fed;
And as a man before was from his birth,
    So shall a man be after among the dead.

TO WALT WHITMAN IN AMERICA.

SEND but a song oversea for us.
　　Heart of their hearts who are free,
Heart of their singer, to be for us
　　More than our singing can be ;
Ours, in the tempest at error,
With no light but the twilight of terror ;
　　Send us a song oversea !

Sweet-smelling of pine-leaves and grasses,
　　And blown as a tree through and through
With the winds of thee keen mountain-
　　passes,
　　And tender as sun-smitten dew ;
Sharp-tongued as the winter that shakes
The wastes of your limitless lakes,
　　Wide-eyed as the sea-line's blue.

O strong-winged soul with prophetic
　　Lips hot with the bloodbeats of song
With tremor of heartstrings magnetic,
　　With thoughts as thunders in throng,
With consonant ardors of chords
That pierce men's souls as with swords
　　And hale them hearing along,

Make us too music, to be with us
　　As a word from a world's heart warm, ·
To sail the dark as a sea with us,
　　Full-sailed, outsinging the storm,
A song to put fire in our ears
Whose burning shall burn up tears,
　　Whose sign bid battle reform ;

A note in the ranks of a clarion,
　　A word in the wind of cheer,
To consume as with lightning the carrion
　　That makes time foul for us here ;
In the air that our dead things infest
A blast of the breath of the west,
　　Till east way as west way is clear.

Out of the sun beyond sunset,
　　From the evening whence morning shall
　　　be,
With the rollers in measureless onset,
　　With the van of the storming sea,
With the world-wide wind, with the breath
That breaks ships driven upon death,
　　With the passion of all things free,

With the sea-steeds footless and frantic,
　　White myriads for death to bestride
In the charge of the ruining Atlantic
　　Where deaths by regiments ride,
With clouds and clamors of waters,
With a long note shriller than slaughter's
　　On the furrowless fields world-wide,

With terror, with ardor and wonder,
　　With the soul of the season that wakes
When the weight of a whole year's thunder
　　In the tidestream of autumn breaks,
Let the flight of the wide-winged word
Come over, come in and be heard,
　　Take form and fire for our sakes.

For a continent bloodless with travail
　　Here toils and brawls as it can,
And the web of it who shall unravel
　　Of all that peer on the plan ;
Would fain grow men, but they grow not,
And fain be free, but they know not
　　One name for freedom and man ?

One name, not twain for division ;
　　One thing, not twain, from the birth ;
Spirit and substance and vision,
　　Worth more than worship is worth ;
Unbeheld, unadored, undivined,
The cause, the centre, the mind,
　　The secret and sense of the earth.

Here as a weakling in irons,
　　Here as a weanling in bands
As a prey that the stake-net environs,
　　Our life that we looked for stands ;
And the man-child naked and dear,
Democracy, turns on us here
　　Eyes trembling with tremulous hands.

It sees not what season shall bring to it
　　Sweet fruit of its bitter desire ;
Few voices it hears yet sing to it,
　　Few pulses of hearts reaspire ;
Foresees not time, nor forehears
The noises of imminent years,
　　Earthquake, and thunder, and fire :

When crowned and weaponed and curbless
  It shall walk without helm or shield
The bare burnt furrows and herbless
  Of wars last flame-stricken field,
Till godlike, equal with time,
It stand in the sun sublime,
  In the godhead of man revealed.

Round your people and over them
  Light like raiment is drawn,
Close as a garment to cover them
  Wrought not of mail nor of lawn :
Here, with hope hardly to wear,
Naked nations and bare
  Swim, sink, strike out for the dawn.

Chains are here, and a prison,
  Kings, and subjects, and shame :
If the God upon you be arisen.
  How should our songs be the same ?
How in confusion of change,
How shall we sing, in a strange
  Land songs praising his name ?

God is buried and dead to us
  Even the spirit of earth.
Freedom : so have they said to us,
  Some with mocking and mirth,
Some with heartbreak and tears :
And a God without eyes, without ears
  Who shall sing of him dead in the birth ?

The earth god Freedom, the lonely
  Face lightening, the footprint unshod.
Not as one man crucified only
  Nor scoured with but one life's rod:
The soul that is substance or nations,
Reincarnate with fresh generations ;
  The great god Man, which is God.

But in weariest of years and obscurest
  Doth it live not at heart of all things
The one God and one spirit, a purest
  Life, fed from unstanchable springs :
Within love ; within hatred it is,
And its seed in the stripe as the kiss,
  And in slaves is the germ, and in kings.

Freedom we call it, for holier
  Name of the soul's there is none ;
Surelier it labors, if slowlier,
  Than the metres of star or of sun
Slowlier than life unto breath
Surelier than time unto death,
  It moves till its labor be done.

Till the motion be done and the measure
  Circling through season and clime.
Slumber and sorrow and pleasure,
  Vision of virtue and crime ;
Till consummate with conquering eyes,
A soul disembodied, it rise
  From the body transfigured of time.

Till it rise and remain and take station
  With the stars of the world that rejoice ;
Till the voice of its heart's exultation
  Be as theirs an invariable voice
By no discord of evil estranged,
By no pause by no breach in it changed
  By no clash in the chord of its choice.

It is one with the world's generations,
  With the spirit the star and the sod :
With the kingless and king-stricken nation,
  With the cross, and the chain, and the rod
The most high, the most secret, most lonely,
The earth-soul Freedom, that only
  Lives, and that only is God

CHRISTMAS ANTIPHONES.

I.

IN CHURCH.

Thou whose birth on earth
  Angels sang to men,
While thy stars made mirth,
Saviour, at thy birth.
  This day born again :

As this night was bright
  With thy cradle ray,

Very light of light,
Turn the wild world's night
  To thy perfect day.

God whose feet made sweet
  Those wild ways they trod,
From thy fragrant feet
Staining field and street
  With the blood of God ;

God whose breast is rest
  In the time of strife,

In thy secret breast
Sheltering souls opprest
  From the heat of life ;

God whose eyes are skies
  Love-lit as with spheres
By the lights that rise,
To thy watching eyes,
  Orbèd lights of tears ;

God whose heart hath part
  In all grief that is,
Was no man's the dart
That went through thine heart,
  And the wound not his ?

Where the pale souls wail,
  Held in the bonds of death,
Where all spirits quail,
Came thy Godhead pale
  Still from human breath—

Pale from life and strife,
  Wan with manhood, came
Forth of mortal life,
Pierced as with a knife,
  Scarred as with a flame.

Thou the Word and Lord
  In all time and space
Heard, beheld, adored,
With all ages poured
  Forth before thy face,

Lord, what worth in earth
  Drew thee down to die ?
What therein was worth,
Lord, thy death and birth ?
  What beneath thy sky ?

Light above all love
  By thy love was lit,
And brought down the Dove
Feathered from above
  With the wings of it.

From the height of night,
  Was not thine the star
That led forth with might
By no wordly light
  Wise men from afar ?

Yet the wise men's eyes
  Saw thee not more clear

Than they saw thee rise
  Who in shepherd s guise
Drew as poor men near.

Yet thy poor endure,
  And are with us yet,
Be thy name a sure
Refuge for thy poor
  Whom men's eyes forget.

Thou whose ways we praise,
  Clear alike and dark,
Keep our works and ways
This and all thy days
  Safe inside thine ark.

Who shall keep thy sheep,
  Lord, and lose not one ?
Who save one shall keep,
Lest the shepherds sleep ?
  Who beside the Son ?

From the grave-deep wave,
  From the sword and flame,
Thou, even thou, shalt save
Souls of king and slave
  Only by thy Name.

Light not born with morn
  Or her fires above,
Jesus virgin-born,
Held of men in scorn,
  Turn their scorn to love.

Thou whose face gives grace
  As the sun's doth heat,
Let thy sunbright face
Lighten time and space
  Here beneath thy feet.

Bid our peace increase,
  Thou that madest morn ;
Bid oppressions cease ;
Bid the night be peace ;
  Bid the day be born.

II.

OUTSIDE CHURCH.

WE whose days and ways
  All the night makes dark,
What day shall we praise
Of these weary days
  That our life-drops mark ?

We whose mind is blind,
　Fed with hope of nought ;
Wastes of worn mankind,
Without heart or mind,
　Without meat or thought ;

We with strife of life
　Worn till all life cease,
Want, a whetted knife,
Sharpening strife on strife,
　How should we love peace ?

Ye whose meat is sweet
　And your wine-cup red,
Us beneath your feet
Hunger grinds as wheat,
　Grinds to make you bread.

Ye whose night is bright
　With soft rest and heat,
Clothed like day with light,
Us the naked night
　Slays from street to street.

Hath your God no rod,
　That ye tread so light ?
Man on us as God,
God as man hath trod,
　Trod us down with might.

We that one by one
　Bleed from either's rod,
What for us hath done
Man beneath the sun,
　What for us hath God ?

We whose blood is food
　Given your wealth to feed,
From the Christless rood
Red with no God's blood,
　But with man's indeed ;

How shall we that see
　Night-long overhead
Life, the flowerless tree,
Nailed whereon as we
　Were our fathers dead—

We whose ear can hear,
　Not whose tongue can name.
Famine, ignorance, fear.
Bleeding tear by tear
　Year by year of shame,

Till the dry life die
　Out of bloodless breast.

Out of beamless eye,
Out of mouths that cry
　Till death feed with rest—

How shall we as ye,
　Though ye bid us, pray ?
Though ye call, can we
Hear you call, or see,
　Though ye show us day ?

We whose name is shame,
　We whose souls walk bare,
Shall we call the same
God as ye by name,
　Teach our lips your prayer ?

God, forgive and give,
　For His sake who died ?
Nay, for ours who live,
How shall we forgive
　Thee, then, on our side ?

We whose right to light
　Whom the blind beams smite
Heaven's high noon denies,
That for you shine bright,
　And but burn our eyes,

With what dreams of beams
　Shall we build up day,
At what sourceless streams
Seek to drink in dreams
　Ere they pass away ?

In what street shall meet,
　At what market-place,
Your feet and our feet,
With one goal to greet,
　Having run one race ?

What one hope shall ope
　For us all as one
One some horoscope,
Where the soul sees hope
　That outburns the sun ?

At what shrine what wine,
　At what board what bread,
Salt as blood or brine,
Shall we share in sign
　How we poor were fed ?

In what hour what power
　Shall we pray for morn,
If your perfect hour,
When all day bears flower,
　Not for us is born ?

III.

BEYOND CHURCH.

YE that weep in sleep,
  Souls and bodies bound,
Ye that all night keep
Watch for change, and weep
  That no change is found ;

Ye that cry and die,
  And the world goes on
Without ear or eye,
And the days go by
  Till all days are gone ;

Man shall do for you,
  Men the sons of man,
What no God would do
That they sought unto
  While the blind years ran.

Brotherhood of good,
  Equal laws and rights,
Freedom, whose sweet food
Feeds the multitude
  All their days and nights,

With the bread full-fed
  Of her body blest
And the soul's wine shed
From her table spread
  Where the world is guest,

Mingling me and thee,
  When like light of eyes
Flashed through thee and me
Truth shall make us free,
  Liberty make wise ;

These are they whom day
  Follows and gives light
Whence they see to slay
Night, and burn away
  All the seed of night.

What of thine and mine,
  What of want and wealth,
When one faith is wine
For my heart and thine
  And one draught is health?

For no sect elect
  Is the soul's wine poured
And her table decked ;
Whom should man reject
  From man's common board ?

Gods refuse and choose ;
  Grudge and sell and spare ;
None shall man refuse,
None of all men lose,
  None leave out of care.

No man's might of sight
  Knows that hour before ;
No man's hand hath might
To put back that light
  For one hour the more.

Not though all men call,
  Kneeling with void hands,
Shall they see light fall
Till it come for all
  Tribes of men and lands.

No desire brings fire
  Down from heaven by prayer,
Though man's vain desire
Hang faith's wind struck lyre
  Out in tuneless air.

One hath breath and saith
  What the tune shall be—
Time, who puts his breath
Into life and death,
  Into earth and sea.

To and fro years flow.
  Fill their tides and ebb,
As his fingers go
Weaving to and fro
  One unfinished web.

All the range of change
  Hath its bounds therein,
All the lives that range
All the byways strange
  Named of death or sin.

Star from far to star
  Speaks, and white moons wake.
Watchful from afar
What the night's ways are
  For the morning's sake.

Many names and flames
  Pass and flash and fall,
Night-begotten names,
And the night reclaims,
  As she bare them, all.

But the sun is one,
And the sun's name Right ;
And when light is none
Saving of the sun,
All men shall have light.

All shall see and be
Parcel of the morn ;
Ay, though blind were we,
None shall choose but see
When that day is born.

A NEW YEAR'S MESSAGE.

TO JOSEPH MAZZINI.

" Send the stars light, but send not love to me."—*Shelley.*

I.

Out of the dawning heavens that hear
Young wings and feet of the new year
Move through their twilight, and shed round
Soft showers of sound,
Soothing the season with sweet rain,
If greeting come to make me fain,
What is it I can send again ?

2.

I know not if the year shall send
Tidings to usward as a friend,
And salutation, and such things
Bear on his wings
As the soul turns and thirsts unto
With hungering eyes and lips that sue
For that sweet food which makes all new.

3.

I know not if his light shall be
Darkness, or else light verily :
I know but that it will not part
Heart's faith from heart,
Truth from the trust in truth, nor hope
From sight of days unscaled that ope
Beyond one poor year's horoscope.

4.

That faith in love which love's self gives,
O master of my spirit, lives,
Having in presence unremoved
Thine head beloved,
The shadow of thee, the semitone
Of thy voice heard at heart and known,
The light of thee not set nor flown.

5.

Seas, lands, and hours, can these divide
Love from love's service, side from side,
Though no sound pass nor breath be heard
Of one good word ?
To send back words of trust to thee
Were to send wings to love, when he
With his own strong wings covers me.

6.

Who shall teach singing to the spheres,
Or motion to the flight of years ?
Let soul with soul keep hand in hand
And understand,
As in one same abiding-place
We keep one watch for one same face
To rise in some short sacred space.

7.

And all space midway is but nought
To keep true heart from faithful thought,
As under twilight stars we wait
By Time's shut gate
Till the slow soundless hinges turn,
And through the depth of years that yearn
The face of the Republic burn.

1870.

MATER DOLOROSA.

Citoyen, lui dit Enjolras, ma mère, c'est la République.—Les Miserables.

WHO is this that sits by the way, by the
  wild wayside,
In a rent stained raiment, the robe of a
  cast-off bride,
In the dust, in the rainfall sitting, with
  soiled feet bare,
With the night for a garment upon her,
  with torn wet hair ?
She is fairer of face than the daughters of
  men, and her eyes,
Worn through with her tears, are deep as
  the depth of skies.

This is she for whose sake being fallen, for
  whose abject sake,
Earth groans in the blackness of darkness,
  and men's hearts break.
This is she for whose love, having seen her
  the men that were
Poured life out as water, and shed their
  souls upon air
This is she for whose glory their years were
  counted as foam ;
Whose face was a light upon Greece, was
  a fire upon Rome

Is it now not surely a vain thing, a foolish
  and vain,
To sit down by her, mourn to her, serve
  her, partake in the pain ?
She is grey with the dust of time on his
  manifold ways,
Where her faint feet stumble and falter
  through yearlong days
Shall she help us at all, O fools, give fruit
  or give fame,
Who herself is a name despised, a rejected
  name ?

We have not served her for guerdon.   If
  any do so,
That his mouth may be sweet with such
  honey, we care not to know
We have drunk from a wine-unsweetened,
  a perilous cup,
A draught very bitter.   The kings of the
  earth stood up,

And the rulers took counsel together to
  smite her and slay;
And the blood of her wounds is given us
  to drink to-day.

Can these bones live ? or the leaves that
  are dead leaves bud ?
Or the dead blood drawn from her veins be
  in your veins blood ?
Will ye gather up water again that was
  drawn and shed ?
In the blood is the life of the veins, and her
  veins are dead
For the lives that are over are over, and
  past things past ;
She had her day, and it is not ; was first,
  and is last.

Is it nothing unto you then, all ye that pass
  by
If her breath be left in her lips if she live
  now or die ?
Behold now, O people, and say if she be
  not fair
Whom your fathers followed to find her
  with praise and prayer,
And rejoiced having found her, though roof
  they had none nor bread;
But ye care not; what is it to you if her own
  day be dead ?

It was well with our fathers; their sound
  was in all men's heads;
There was fire in their hearts, and the
  hunger of fight in their hands.
Naked and strong they went forth on her
  strength like flame,
For her loves and her name's sake of old,
  her republican name.
But their children by kings made quiet, by
  priests made wise,
Love better the heat of their hearths than
  the light of her eyes.

Are they children of these thy children indeed who have sold
O golden goddess the light of thy face for
  gold ?

Are they sons indeed the sons of thy dayspring of hope,
Whose lives are in fief of an emperor, whose
  souls of a Pope?
Hide then thine head, O beloved; thy time
  is done;
Thy kingdom is broken in heaven, and
  blind thy sun.

What sleep is upon you, to dream she indeed
  shall rise,
When the hopes are dead in her heart as
  the tears in her eyes?
If ye sing of her dead will she stir? if ye
  weep for her, weep?
Come away now, leave her; what hath she
  to do but sleep?

But ye that mourn are alive, and have years
  to be;
And life is good, and the world is wiser
  than we.

Yea, wise is the world and mighty, with
  years to give,
And years to promise; but how long now
  shall it live?
And foolish and poor is faith, and her ways
  are bare,
Till she find the way of the sun, and the
  morning air,
In that hour shall this dead face shine as
  the face of the sun,
And the soul of man and her soul and the
  world's be one.

MATER TRIUMPHALIS.

MOTHER of man's time-travelling genera-
  tions,
  Breath of his nostrils, heartblood of his
    heart,
God above all Gods worshipped of all na-
  tions,
  Light above light, law beyond law thou
    art.

Thy face is as a sword smiting in sunder
  Shadows and chains and dreams and iron
    things;
The sea is dumb before thy face, the thunder
  Silent, the skies are narrower than thy
    wings.

Angels and Gods, spirit and sense, thou
  takest
  In thy right hand as drops of dust or dew;
The temples and the towers of time thou
  breakest,
  His thoughts and words and works, to
    make them new.

All we have wandered from thy ways, nave
  hidden
  Eyes from thy glory and ears from calls
    they heard;
Called of thy trumpets vainly, called and
  chidden,
  Scourged of thy speech and wounded of
    thy word

We have known thee and have not known
  thee; stood beside thee,
  Felt thy lips breathe, set foot where thy
    feed trod,
Loved and renounced and worshipped and
  denied thee,
  As thou thou wert but as another God.

" One hour for sleep," we said, " and yet
  one other;
  All day we served her, and who shall
    serve by night?
Not knowing of thee, thy face not knowing,
  O mother,
  O light wherethrough the darkness is as
    light.

Men that forsook thee hast thou not for-
  saken,
  Races of men that knew not hast thou
    known;
Nations that slept thou hast doubted not to
  waken
  Worshippers of strange Gods to make
    thine own.

All old grey histories hiding thy clear fea-
  tures,
  O secret spirit and sovereign, all men's
    tales,
Creeds woven of men thy children and thy
  creatures,
  They have woven for vestures of thee and
    for veils.

Thine hands, without election or exemption,
  Feed all men fainting from false peace or
    strife,
O thou, the resurrection and redemption,
  The godhead and the manhood and the
    life.

The wings shadow the waters ; thine eyes
    lighten
  The horror of the hollows of the night ;
The depths of the earth and the dark places
    brighten
  Under thy feet, whiter than fire is white.

Death is subdued to thee, and hell's bands
    broken ;
  Where thou art only is heaven ; who
    hears not thee,
Time shall not hear him ; when men's
    names are spoken,
  A nameless sign of death shall his name
    be.

Deathless shall be the death, the name be
    nameless ;
  Sterile of stars his twilight time of death;
With fire of hell shall shame consume him
    shameless,
  And dying, all the night darken his death.

The years are as thy garments, the world's
    ages
  As sandals bound and loosed from thy
    swift feet ;
Time serves before thee, as one that hath
    for wages
  Praise or shame only, bitter words or
    sweet.

Thou sayest " Well done, " and all a cen-
    tury kindles ;
  Again thou sayest " Depart from sight
    of me, "
And all the light of face of all men dwindles,
  And the age is as the broken glass of
    thee.

The night is as a seal set on men's faces,
  On faces fallen of men that take no
    light
Nor give light in the deeps of the dark
    places,
  Blind things incorporate with the body of
    night.

Their souls are serpents winterbound and
    frozen,
  Their shame is as a tame beast, at their
    feet
Couched ; their cold lips deride thee and
    thy chosen,
  Their lying lips made grey with dust for
    meat.

Then when their time is full and days run
    over,
  The splendor of thy sudden brow made
    bare
Darkens the morning ; thy bared hands
    uncover
  The veils of light and night and the awful
    air.

And the world naked as a new-born maiden
  Stands virginal and splendid as at birth,
With all thine heaven of all its light un-
    laden,
  Of all its love unburdened all thine earth.

For the utter earth and the utter air of
    heaven
  And the extreme depth is thine and the
    extreme height ;
Shadows of things and veils of ages riven
  Are as men's kings unkingdomed in thy
    sight.

Through the iron years, the centuries
    brazen gated,
  By the ages barred impenetrable doors,
From the evening to the morning have we
    waited,
  Should thy foot haply sound on the awful
    floors.

The floors untrodden of the sun's feet
    glimmer,
  The star-unstricken pavements of the
    night ;
Do the lights burn inside ? the lights was
    dimmer
  On festal faces withering out of sight.

The crowned heads lose the light on them:
    it may be
  Dawn is at hand to smite the loud feast
    dumb :
To blind the torch-lit centuries till the day
    be,
  The feasting kingdoms till thy kingdom
    come.

Shall it not come? deny they or dissemble,
  Is it not even as lightning from on high
Now? and though many a soul close eyes
    and tremble,
  How should they tremble at all who love
    thee as I?

I am thine harp between thine hands, O
    mother!
  All my strong chords are strained with
    love of thee.
We grapple in love and wrestle, as each
    with other
  Wrestle the wind and the unreluctant
    sea.

I am no courtier of thee sober-suited,
  Who loves a little for a little pay.
Me not thy winds and storms nor thrones
    disrooted
  Nor molten crowns nor thine own sins
    dismay.

Sinned hast thou sometime, therefore art
    thou sinless;
  Stained hast thou been, who art there-
    fore without stain;
Even as man's soul is kin to thee, but
    kinless
  Thou, in whose womb Time sows the
    all-various grain.

I do not bid thee spare me, O dreadful
    mother!
  I pray thee that thou spare not, of thy
    grace.
How were it with me then, if ever another
  Should come to stand before thee in this
    my place?

am the trumpet at thy lips, thy clarion
  Full of thy cry, sonorous with thy breath;
The grave of souls born worms and creeds
    grown carrion
  Thy blast of judgment fills with fires of
    death.

Thou art the player whose organ-keys are
    thunders,
  And I beneath thy foot the pedal prest;
Thou art the ray whereat the rent night
    sunders,
  And I the cloudlet borne upon thy breast.

I shall burn up before thee, pass and perish,
  As haze in sunrise on the red sea-line;

But thou from dawn to sunsetting shalt
    cherish
  The thoughts that led and souls that
    lighted mine.

Reared between night and noon and truth
    and error,
  Each twilight-travelling bird that trills
    and screams
Sickens at midday, nor can face for terror
  The imperious heaven's inevitable ex-
    tremes.

I have no spirit of skill with equal fingers
  At sign to sharpen or to slacken strings;
I keep no time of song with gold-perched
    singers
  And chirp of linnets on the wrists of
    kings.

I am thy storm-thrush of the days that
    darken,
  Thy petrel in the foam that bears thy
    bark
To port through night and tempest; if
    thou hearken,
  My voice is in thy heaven before the
    lark.

My song is in the mist that hides thy
    morning,
  My cry is up before the day for thee;
I have heard thee and beheld thee and give
    warning,
  Before thy wheels divide the sky and sea.

Birds shall wake with thee voiced and
    feathered fairer,
  To see in summer what I see in spring;
I have eyes and heart to endure thee, O
    thunder-bearer,
  And they shall be who shall have tongues
    to sing.

I have love at least, and have not fear, and
    part not
  From thine unnavigable and wingless
    way;
Thou tarriest, and I have not said thou art
    not,
  Nor all thy night long have denied thy
    day.

Darkness to daylight shall lift up thy pæan,
  Hill to hill thunder, vale cry back to vale

With wind-notes as of eagles Æschylean,
 And Sappho singing in the nightingale.

Sung to by mighty sons of dawn and
 daughters,
 Of this night's songs thine ear shall keep
 but one ;
That supreme song which shook the channelled waters,

And called thee skyward as God calls
 the sun.

Come, though all heaven again be fire
 above thee ;
 Though death before thee come to clear
 thy sky ;
Let us but see in his thy face who love thee;
 Yea, though thou slay us, arise and let
 us die.

A MARCHING SONG.

WE mix from many lands,
 We march for very far ;
 In hearts and lips and hands
 Our staffs and weapons are ;
The light we walk in darkens sun and
 moon and star.

It doth not flame and wane
 With years and spheres that roll,
 Storm cannot shake nor stain
 The strength that makes it whole,
The fire that moulds and moves it of the
 sovereign soul.

We are they that have to cope
 With time till time retire ;
 We live on hopeless hope,
 We feed on tears and fire ;
Time, foot by foot, gives back before our
 sheer desire.

From the edge of harsh derision,
 From discord and defeat,
 From doubt and lame division,
 We pluck the fruit and eat ;
And the mouth finds it bitter, and the
 spirit sweet.

We strive with time at wrestling
 Till time be on our side
And hope, our plumeless nestling,
 A full-fledged eaglet ride
Down the loud length of storm its wind-
 ward wings divide.

We are girt with our belief,
 Clothed with our will and crowned;
Hope, fear, delight, and grief,
 Before our will give ground;
Their calls are in our ears as shadows of
 dead sound.

All but the heart forsakes us,
 All fails us but the will;
Keen treason tracks and takes us
 In pits for blood to fill ;
Friend falls from friend, and faith for faith
 lays wait to kill.

Out under moon and stars
 And shafts of the urgent sun
Whose face on prison bars
 And mountain-heads is one,
Our march is everlasting till time's march
 be done.

Whither we know, and whence,
 And dare not care where through.
Desires that urge the sense,
 Fears changing old with new,
Pearls and pains beset the ways we press
 into ;

Earth gives us thorns to tread,
 And all her thorns are trod ;
Through lands burnt black and red
 We pass with feet unshod ;
Whence we would be man shall not keep us,
 nor man's God.

Through the great desert beasts
 Howl at our backs by night,
And thunder-forging priests
 Blow their dead bale-fires bright,
And on their broken anvils beat out bolts
 for fight.

Inside their sacred smithies,
 Though hot the hammer rings,
Their steel links snap like withies,
 Their chains like twisted strings,
Their surest fetters are as plighted words
 of kings.

O nations undivided,
　O single people and free,
We dreamers, we derided,
　We mad blind men that see,
We bear you witness ere ye come that ye
　shall be.

Ye sitting among tombs,
　Ye standing round the gate,
Whom fire-mouthed war consumes,
　Or cold-lipped peace bids wait,
All tombs and bars shall open, every grave
　and grate.

The locks shall burst in sunder,
　The hinges shrieking spin,
When time, whose hand is thunder,
　Lays hand upon the pin,
And shoots the bolts reluctant, bidding all
　men in.

These eyeless times and earless,
　Shall these not see and hear,
And all their hearts burn fearless
　That were afrost for fear ?
Is day not hard upon us, yea, not our day
　near ?

France ? from its grey dejection
　Make manifest the red
Tempestuous resurrection
　Of thy most sacred head !
Break thou the covering cerecloths ; rise up
　from the dead.

And thou, whom sea-walls sever
　From lands unwalled with seas,
Wilt thou endure for ever,
　O Milton's England, these ?
Thou that wast his Republic, wilt thou
　clasp their knees ?

These royalties rust-eaten,
　These worm-corroded lies,
That keep thine head storm-beaten
　And sunlike strength of eyes
From the open heaven and air of intercepted
　skies ;

These princelings with gauze winglets
　That buzz in the air unfurled,
These summer-swarming kinglets
　These thin worms crowned and
　　curled,
That bask and blink and warm themselves
　about the world ;

These fanged meridian vermin,
　Shrill gnats that crowd the dusk,
Night-moths whose nestling ermine
　Smells foul of mould and musk,
Blind flesh-flies hatched by dark and ham-
　pered in their husk ;

These honors without honor,
　These ghost-like gods of gold,
This earth that wears upon her
　To keep her heart from cold
No memory more of men that brought it
　fire of old ;

These limbs, supine, unbuckled,
　In rottenness of rest,
These sleepy lips blood-suckled
　And satiate of thy breast,
These dull wide mouths that drain thee dry
　and call thee blest ;

These masters of thee mindless
　That wear thee out of mind,
These children of thee kindless
　That use thee out of kind,
Whose hands strew gold before thee and
　contempt behind ;

Who have turned thy name to laughter,
　Thy sea-like sounded name
That now none hearkens after
　For faith in its free fame,
Who have robbed thee of thy trust and given
　thee of their shame ;

These hours that mock each other,
　These years that kill and die,
Are these thy gains, our mother,
　For all thy gains thrown by ?
Is this that end whose promise made thine
　heart so high ?

With empire and with treason
　The first right hand made fast,
But in man's nobler season
　To put forth help the last,
Love turns from thee, and memory disavows
　thy past.

Lest thine own sea disclaim thee,
　Lest thine own sons despise,
Lest lips shoot out that name thee
　And seeing thee men shut eyes,
Take thought with all thy people, turn thine
　head and rise.

Turn thee, lift up thy face ;
　What ails thee to be dead ?

Ask of thyself for grace,
  Seek of thyself for bread,
And who shall starve or shame thee, blind
  or bruise thine head?

The same sun in thy sight,
  The same sea in thine ears,
That saw thine hour at height,
  That sang thy song of years,
Behold and hearken for thee, knowing thy
  hopes and fears.

O people, O perfect nation,
  O England that shall be,
How long till thou take station?
  How long till thralls live free?
How long till all thy soul be one with all
  thy sea?

Ye that from south to north,
  Ye that from east to west,
Stretch hands of longing forth
  And keep your eyes from rest,
Lo, when ye will, we bring you gifts of
  what is best.

From the awful northland pines
  That skirt their wan dim seas
To the ardent Apennines
  And sun-struck Pyrenees,
One frost on all their frondage bites the
  blossoming trees.

The leaves look up for light,
  For heat of helpful air;
The trees of oldest height
  And thin storm-shaken hair
Seek with gaunt hands up heavenward if the
  sun be there.

The woods where souls walk lonely,
  The forests girt with night,
Desire the day-star only
  And firstlings of the light
Not seen of slaves nor shining in their
  masters' sight.

We have the morning star,
  O foolish people, O kings!
With us the day-springs are,
  Even all the fresh day-springs;
For us, and with us, all the multitudes of
  things.

O sorrowing hearts of slaves,
  We heard you beat from far!
We bring the light that saves,
  We bring the morning star;

Freedom's good things we bring you,
  whence all good things are.

With us the winds and fountains
  And lightnings live in tune;
The morning-colored mountains
  That burn into the noon,
The mist's mild veil on valleys muffled from
  the moon:

The thunder-darkened highlands
  And lowlands hot with fruit,
Sea-bays and shoals and islands,
  And cliffs that foil man's foot,
And all the flower of large-limbed life and
  all the root:

The clangor of sea-eagles
  That teach the morning mirth
With baying of heaven's beagles
  That seek their prey on earth,
By sounding strait and channel, gulf and
  reach and firth.

With us the fields and rivers,
  The grass that summer thrills,
The haze where morning quivers,
  The peace at heart of hills,
The sense that kindles nature, and the
  soul that fills.

With us all natural sights,
  All notes of natural scale;
With us the starry lights;
  With us the nightingale;
With us the heart and secret of the worldly
  tale.

The strife of things and beauty,
  The fire and light adored,
Truth, and life-lightening duty,
  Love without crown or sword,
That by his might and godhead makes man
  god and lord.

These have we, these are ours,
  That no priests give nor kings;
The honey of all these flowers,
  The heart of all these springs;
Ours, for where freedom lives not, there
  live no good things.

Rise, ere the dawn be risen;
  Come, and be all souls fed;
From field and street and prison
  Come, for the feast is spread;
Live, for the truth is living; wake, for
  night is dead.

SIENA.

INSIDE this northern summer's fold
The fields are full of naked gold,
Broadcast from heaven on lands it loves ;
The green veiled air is full of doves;
Soft leaves that sift the sunbeams let
Light on the small warm grasses wet
Fall in short broken kisses sweet,
And break again like waves that beat
Round the sun's feet.

But I, for all this English mirth
Of golden-shod and dancing days,
And the old green-girt sweet-hearted earth
Desire what here no spells can raise.
Far hence, with holier heavens above,
The lovely city of my love
Bathes deep in the sun-satiate air
That flows round no fair thing more fair
Her beauty bare.

There the utter sky is holier, there
More pure the intense white height of air,
More clear men's eyes that mine would
    meet,
And the sweet springs of things more sweet.
There for this one warm note of doves
A clamor of a thousand loves
Storms the night's ear, the day's assails,
From the tempestuous nightingales,
And fills, and fails.

O gracious city well-beloved,
    Italian, and a maiden crowned,
Siena, my feet are no more moved
    Toward thy strange-shapen mountain-
        bound :
But my heart in me turns and moves
O lady loveliest of my loves,
Toward thee, to lie before thy feet
And gaze from thy fair fountain-seat
Up the sheer street ;

And the house midway hanging see
That saw Saint Catherine bodily,
Felt on its floors her sweet feet move,
And the live light of fiery love
Burn from her beautiful strange face,
As in the sanguine sacred place
Where in pure hands she took the head
Severed, and with pure lips still red
Kissed the lips dead.

13

For years through, sweetest of the saints,
    In quiet without cease she wrought,
Till cries of men and fierce complaints
    From   outward   moved   her   maiden
        thought ;
And prayers she heard and sighs toward
    France,
"God, send us back deliverance,
Send back thy servant, lest we die ! "
With an exceeding bitter cry
They smote the sky.

Then in her sacred saving hands
She took the sorrows of the lands,
With maiden palms she lifted up
The sick time's blood-embittered cup,
And in her virgin garment furled
The faint limbs of a wounded world.
Clothed with calm love and clear desire,
She went forth in her soul's attire,
A missive fire.

Across the might of men that strove
    It shone, and over heads of kings ;
And molten in red flames of love
    Were swords and many monstrous things ;
And shields were lowered, and snapt were
    spears,
And sweeter-tuned the clamorous years ;
And faith came back, and peace, that were
Fled ; for she bade, saying, " Thou, God's
    heir,
Hast thou no care

" Lo, men lay waste thine heritage
Still, and much heathen people rage
Against thee, and devise vain things.
What comfort in the face of kings,
What counsel is there ? Turn thine eyes
And thine heart from them in like wise ;
Turn thee unto thine holy place
To help us that of God for grace
Require thy face.

For who shall hear us if not thou
    In a strange land ? what doest thou there?
Thy sheep are spoiled, and the ploughers
    plough
    Upon us ; why hast thou no care
For all this, and beyond strange hills
Liest unregardful what snow chills

Thy foldless flock, or what rains beat?
Lo, in thine ears, before thy feet,
Thy lost sheep bleat.

" And strange men feed on faultless lives,
And there is blood, and men put knives,
Shepherd, unto the young lamb's throat ;
And one hath eaten, and one smote,
And one had hunger and is fed
Full of the flesh of these, and red
With blood of these as who drinks wine.
And God knoweth, who hath sent thee a
    sign,
If these were thine."

But the Pope's heart within him burned,
    So that he rose up, seeing the sign,
And came among them; but she turned
    Back to her daily way divine,
And fed her faith with silent things,
And lived her life with curbed white wings,
And mixed herself with heaven and died:
And now on the sheer city-side
Smiles like a bride.

You see her in the fresh clear gloom,
Where walls shut out the flame and bloom,
Of full-breathed summer, and the roof
Keeps the keen ardent air aloof
And sweet weight of the violent sky:
There bodily beheld on high,
She seems as one hearing in tune
Heaven within heaven, at heaven's full
    noon,
In sacred swoon:

A solemn swoon of sense that aches
    With imminent blind heat of heaven,
While all the wide-eyed spirit wakes,
    Vigilant of the supreme Seven,
Whose choral flames in God's sight move,
Made unnendurable with love,
That without wind or blast or breath
Compels all things through life and death
Whither God saith.

There on the dim side-chapel wall
Thy mighty touch memorial,
Razzi, raised up, for ages dead,
And fixed for us her heavenly head :
And, rent with plaited thorn and rod,
Bared the live likeness of her God
To men's eyes turning from strange lands,
Where, pale from thine immortal hands,
Christ wounded stands ;

And the blood blots his holy hair
    And white brows over hungering eyes
That plead against us, and the fair
    Mute lips forlorn of words or sighs
In the great torment that bends down
His bruised head with the bloomless crown,
White as the unfruitful thorn-flower,
A God beheld in dreams that were
Beheld of her.

In vain on all these sins and years
Falls the sad blood, fall the slow tears :
In vain poured forth as watersprings,
Priests, on your altars, and ye, kings,
About your seats of sanguine gold ;
Still your God, spat upon and sold,
Bleeds at your hands ; but now is gone
All his flock from him saving one ;
Judas alone.

Surely your race it was that he,
    O men signed backward with his name,
Beholding in Gethsemane
    Bled the red bitter sweat of shame,
Knowing how the word of Christian should
Mean to men evil and not good,
Seem to men shameful for your sake,
Whose lips, for all the prayers they make,
Man's blood must slake.

But blood nor tears ye love not, you
That my love leads my longing to,
Fair as the world's old faith of flowers,
O golden goddesses of ours !
From what Idalian rose-pleasance
Hath Aphrodite bidden glance
The lovlier lightnings of your feet ?
From what sweet Papian sward or seat
Led you more sweet ?

O white three sisters, three as one,
    With flowerlike arms for flowery bands
Your linked limbs glitter like the sun,
    And time lies beaten at your hands.
Time and wild years and wars and men
Pass, and ye care not whence or when ;
With calm lips over sweet for scorn,
Ye watch-night pass, O children born
Of the old world morn.

Ah, in this strange and shrineless place,
What doth a goddess, what a Grace,
Where no Greek worships her shrined limbs
With wreaths and Cytherean hymns ?
Where no lute makes luxurious
The adoring airs in Amathus,

Till the maid, knowing her mother near,
Sobs with love, aching with sweet fear?
What do ye here?

For the outer land is sad, and wears
A raiment of a flaming fire;
And the fierce fruitless mountain stairs
  Climb, yet seem wroth and loth to aspire,
Climb, and break, and are broken down,
And through their clefts and crests the town
Looks west and sees the dead sun lie,
In sanguine death that stains the sky
With angry dye.

And from the war-worn wastes without
In twilight, in the time of doubt,
One sound comes of one whisper where
  Moved with low motions of slow air
The great trees nigh the castle swing
In the sad colored evening;
" *Ricorditi di me che son
La Pia* "—that small sweet word alone
Is not yet gone.

    " *Ricorditi di me* "—the sound
Sole out of deep dumb days remote
Across the fiery and fatal ground
  Comes tender as a hurt bird's note
To where a ghost with empty hands,
A woe-worn ghost, her palace stands
In the mid city, where the strong
Bells turn the sunset air to song,
And the towers throng.

With other face, with speech the same,
A mightier maiden's likeness came
Late among mourning men that slept,
A sacred ghost that went and wept,
Whit as the passion-wounded Lamb,
Saying, ' Ah, remember me, that am
Italia." (From deep sea to sea
Earth heard, earth knew her, that this was she.)
" *Ricorditi.* "

    Love made me of all things fairest thing,
    And hate unmade me; this knows he
Who with God's sacerdotal ring
  Enringed mine hand, espousing me
Yea, in thy myriad-mooded woe,
Yea, Mother, hast thou not said so?
Have not our hearts within us stirred,
O thou most holiest, at thy word?
Have we not heard?

As this dead tragic land that she
Found deadly, such was time to thee;
Years passed thee withering in the red
Maremma, years that deemed thee dead,
Ages that sorrowed or that scorned;
And all this while though all they mourned
Thou sawest the end of things unclean,
And the unborn that should see thee a queen.
Have we not seen?

The weary poet, thy sad son,
  Upon thy soil, under thy skies,
Saw all Italian things save one—
  Italia; this thing missed his eyes;
The old mother might, the breast, the face,
That reared, that lit the Roman race;
This not Leopardi saw; but we,
What is it, Mother, that we see,
What if not thee?

Look thou from Siena southward home,
Where the priest's pall hangs rent on Rome,
And through the red rent swaddling bands
Toward thine she strains her laboring hands.
Look thou and listen, and let be
All the dead quick all the bond free;
In the blind eyes let there be sight;
In the eighteen centuries of the night
Let there be light.

Bow down the beauty of thine head,
  Sweet, and with lips of living breath
Kiss thy sons sleeping, and thy dead,
  That there be no more sleep or death.
Give us thy light, thy might, thy love,
Whom thy face seen afar above
Drew to thy feet; and when being free,
Thou hast blest thy children born to thee,
Bless also me.

Me that when others played or slept
Sat still under thy cross and wept.
Me who so early and unaware
Felt fall on bent bared brows and hair
(Thin drops of the overflowing flood!)
The bitter blessing of thy blood;
The sacred shadow of thy pain,
Thine, the true maiden-mother, slain
And raised again.

Me consecrated, if I might,
  To praise thee, or to love at least,
O mother of all men's dear delight
  Thou madest a choral-souled boy pries

Before my lips had leave to sing,
Or my hands hardly strength to cling
About the intolerable tree
Whereto they had nailed my heart and thee
And said, " Let be.

For to thee too the high Fates gave
Grace to be sacrificed and save,
That being arisen, in the equal sun,
God and the People should be one;
By those red roads thy footprints trod,
Man more divine, more human God,
Saviour; that where no light was known
But darkness, and a daytime down,
Light should be shown.

Let there be light, O Italy !
For our feet falter in the night,
O lamp of living years to be,
O light of God, let there be light !
Fill with a love keener than flame
Men sealed in spirit wtth thy name,
The cities and the Roman skies,

Where men with other than man's eyes
Saw thy sun rise.

For theirs thou wast and thine were they
Whose names outshine thy very day;
For they are thine and theirs thou art
Whose blood beats living in man's heart,
Remembering ages fled and dead
Wherein for thy sake these men bled;
They that saw Trebia, they that see
Mentana, they in years to be
That shall see thee.

For thine are all of us, and ours
Thou; till the seasons bring to birth
A perfect people, and all the powers
Be with them that bear fruit on earth;
Till the inner heart of man be one
With freedom, and the sovereign sun;
And Time, in likeness of a guide,
Lead the Republic as a bride
Up to God's side.

COR CORDIUM.

O heart of hearts, the chalice of love's
fire,
Hid round with flowers and all the
bounty of bloom.
O wonderful and perfect heart for whom
The lyrist liberty made life a lyre;
O heavenly heart at whose most dear
desire
Dead love, living and singing, cleft his
tomb,
And with him risen and regent in death's
room
All day thy choral palses rang full choir;
O heart whose beating blood was running
song,
O sole thing sweeter than thine own
songs were,
Help us for thy free love's sake to be
free.
True for thy truth's sake, for thy strength's
sake strong,
Till very liberty make clean and fair
The nursing earth as the sepulchral
sea.

IN SAN LORENZO.

Is thine hour come to wake, O slumbering
Night ?
Hath not the Dawn a message in thine
ear ?
Though thou be stone, and sleep, yet
shalt thou hear
When the word falls from heaven—Let
there be light,
Thou knowest we would not do thee despite
To wake thee while the old sorrow and
shame were near;
We spakè not loud for thy sake, and
for fear
Lest thou shouldst lose the rest that was
thy right,
The blessing given thee that was thine
alone,
The happiness to sleep and to be stone;
Nay, we kept silence of thee for thy sake
Albeit we knew thee alive, and left with
thee
The great good gift to feel not nor to see
But will not yet thine Angel bid thee
wake ?

TIRESIAS.

PART I.

It is an hour before the hour of dawn.
Set in mine hand my staff and leave me
here
Outside the hollow house that blind men
fear,
More blind than I who live on life with-
drawn
And feel on eyes that see not but foresee
The shadow of death which clothes
Antigone.

Here lay her living body that here lies
Dead, if man living know what thing is
death,
If life be all made up of blood and
breath,
And no sense be save as of ears and eyes,
But heart there is not, tongue there is
not found,
To think or sing what verge hath life or
bound.

In the beginning when the powers that
made
The young child man a little loved him,
seeing
His joy of life and fair face of his being,
And bland and laughing with the man-
child played,
As friends they saw on our divine one
day
King Cadmus take to queen Harmonia.

The strength of soul that builds up as with
hands
Walls spiritual and towers and towns of
thought
Which only fate, not force, can bring to
nought,
Took then to wife the light of all men's
lands,
War's child and love's, most sweet and
wise and strong,
Order of things and rule and guiding
song.

It was long since : yea, even the sun that
saw
Remembers hardly what was, nor how
long,

And now the wise heart of the worldly
song
Is perished, and the holy hand of law
Can set no tune on time, nor help again
The power of thought to build up life for
men.

Yea, surely are they now transformed or
dead,
And sleep below this world, where no
sun warms,
Or move about it now in formless forms
Incognizable, and all their lordship fled ;
And where they stood up singing crawl
and hiss
With fangs that kill behind their lips that
kiss.

Yet though her marriage-garment, seeming
fair
Was dyed in sin and woven of jealousy
To turn their seed to poison, time shall
see
The gods reissue from them, and repair
Their broken stamp of godhead, and
again
Thought and wise love sing words of law
to men.

I, Tiresias the prophet, seeing in Thebes
Much evil, and the misery of men's
hands
Who sow with fruitless wheat the stones
and sands,
With fruitful thorns the fallows and warm
glebes,
Bade their hands hold lest worse hap
came to pass,
But which of you had heed of Tiresias ?

I am as Times self in mine own wearied
mind,
Whom the strong heavy-footed years
have led
From night to night and dead men unto
dead,
And from the blind hope to the memory
blind ;
For each man's life is woven, as Time's
life is,
Of blind young hopes and old blind
memories.

I am a soul outside of death and birth.
  I see before me and afterward I see.
  O child, O corpse, the live dead face of
    thee,
Whose life and death are one thing upon
    earth
  Where day kills night and night again
    kills day
  And dies : but where is that Harmonia ?

O all-beholden light not seen of me,
  Air, and warm winds that under the sun's
    eye
  Stretch your strong wings at morning ;
    and thou, sky,
Whose hollow circle engirdling earth and
    sea
  All night the set stars limit, and all day
  The moving sun remeasures ; ye, I say,

Ye heights of hills, and thou Dircean
    spring
  Inviolable, and ye towers that saw cast
    down
  Seven kings keen-sighted toward your
    seven-faced town
And quenched the red seed of one sightless
    king ;
  And thou, for death less dreadful than
    for birth,
  Whose wild leaves hide the horror of the
    earth,

O mountain whereon gods made chase of
    kings,
  Cithæron, thou that sawest on Pentheus
    dead
  Fangs of a mother fasten and wax red
And satiate with a son thy swollen springs,
  And heardst her cry fright all thine eyries'
    nests
  Who gave death suck at sanguine-suck-
    ling breasts ;

Yea, and a grief more grievous, without
    name,
  A curse too grievous for the name of
    grief,
  Thou sawest, and heardst the rumor scare
    belief
Even unto death and madness, when the
    flame
  Was lit whose ashes dropped about the
    pyre

That of two brethren made one sundering
    fire ;

O bitter nurse, that on thine hard bare knees
  Rear'dst for his fate the bloody-footed
    child
  Whose hands should be more bloodily
    defiled
And the old blind feet walk wearier ways
    than these,
  Whose seed, brought forth in darkness
    unto doom,
  Should break as fire out of his mother's
    womb ;

I bear you witness as ye bear to me,
  Time, day, night, sun, stars, life, death,
    air, sea, earth,
  And ye that round the human house of
    birth
Watch with veiled heads and weaponed
    hands, and see
  Good things and evil, strengthless yet and
    dumb,
  Sit in the clouds with cloudlike hours to
    come ;

Ye forces without form and viewless powers
  That have the keys of all are years in hold,
  That prophecy too late with tongues of
    gold,
In a strange speech whose words are per-
    ished hours,
  I witness to you what good things ye give
  As ye to me what evil while I live.

What should I do to blame you, what to
    praise,
  For floral hours and hours funeral ?
  What should I do to curse or bless at all
For winter-woven or summer-colored days?
  Curse he that will and bless whoso can,
  I have no common part in you with man.

I hear a springing water, whose quick sound
  Makes softer the soft sunless patient air,
  And the wind's hand is laid on my thin
    hair
Light as a lover's, and the grasses round
  Have odors in them of green bloom and
    rain
  Sweet as the kiss wherewith sleep kisses
    pain.

I hear the low sound of the spring of time,
Still beating as the low live throb of blood
And where its waters gathered head and
flood
I hear change moving on them, and the
chime
Across them of reverberate wings of
hours
Sounding, and feel the future air of
flowers.

The wind of change is soft as snow, and
sweet
The sense thereof as roses in the sun,
The faint wind springing with the spring
that run,
The dim sweet smell of flowering hopes, and
heat
Of unbeholden sunrise ; yet how long
I know not, till the morning put forth
song.

I prophesy of life, who live with death ;
Of joy, being sad ; of sunlight, who am
blind ;
Of man, whose ways are alien from man-
kind
And his lips are not parted with man's
breath ;
I am a word out of the speechless years,
The tongue of time, that no man sleeps
who hears.

I stand a shadow across the door of doom,
Athwart the lintel of death's house, and
wait ;
Nor quick nor dead, nor flexible by fate,
Nor quite of earth nor wholly of the tomb ;
A voice, a vision, light as fire or air,
Driven between days that shall be and
that were.

I prophesy, with feet upon a grave,
Of death cast out and life devouring death
As flame doth wood and stubble with a
breath ;
Of freedom, though all manhood were one
slave ;
Of truth, though all the world were liar ; of
love,
That time nor hate can raze the witness of.

Life that was given for love's sake and his
law's
Their powers have no more power on ;
they divide

Spoils wrung from lust or wrath of man
or pride,
And keen oblivion without pity or pause
Sets them on fire and scatters them on
air
Like ashes shaken from a suppliant's hair.

But life they lay no hand on ; life once
given
No force of theirs hath competence to
take ;
Life that was given for some divine
thing's sake,
To mix the bitterness of earth with heaven,
Light with man's night, and music with
his breath,
Dies not, but makes its living food of
death.

I have seen this, who live where men are
not,
In the high starless air of fruitful night
On that serenest and obscurest height
Where dead and unborn things are one in
thought
And whence the live unconquerable
springs
Feed full of force the torrents of new
things.

I have seen this, who saw long since, being
man,
As now I know not, if indeed I be,
The fair bare body of Wisdom good to
see
And evil whence my light and night began ;
Light on the goal and darkness on the
way,
Light all through night and darkness
all through day.

Mother, that by that Pegasean spring
Didst fold round in thine arms thy
blinded son,
Weeping " O holiest, what thing hast
thou done,
What, to my child ? woe's me that see the
thing !
Is this thy love to me-ward, and hereof
Must I take sample how the gods can
love ?

"O child, thou hast seen indeed, poor
  child of mine,
  The breasts and flanks of Pallas bare in
  sight,
  But never shalt see more the dear sun's
  light,
O Helicon, how great a pay is thine
  For some poor antelopes and wild-deer
  dead,
  My child's eyes hast thou taken in their
  stead—"

Mother, thou knowest not what he had to
  give,
  Thy goddess though then angered, for
  mine eyes ;
  Fame and foreknowledge, and to be most
  most wise,
And centuries of high-thoughted life to
  live,
  And in mine hand this guiding staff to be
  As eyesight to the feet of men that see.

Perchance I shall not die at all, nor pass
  The general door and lintel of men dead,
  Yet even the very tongue of wisdom said
What grace should come with death to
  Tiersias,
  What special honor that God's hand
  accord
  Who gathers all men's nations as their
  lord.

And sometimes when the secret eye of
  thought
  Is changed with obscuration, and the
  sense
  Aches with long pain of hollow prescience,
And fieryforesight with foresuffering bought
  Seems even to infect my spirit and consume,
  Hunger and thirst come on me for the
  tomb.

I could be fain to drink my death and
  sleep,
  And no more wrapt about with bitter
  dreams
  Talk with the stars and with the winds
  and streams
And with the inevitable years, and weep;
  For how should he who communes with
  the years
  Be sometime not a living spring of tears?

O child, that guided of thine only will
  Didst set thy maiden foot against the
  gate
  To strike it oper ere thine hour of fate,
Antigone, men say not thou dist ill,
  For love's sake and the reverence of his
  awe
  Divinely dying, slain by mortal law;

For love is awful as immortal death,
  And through thee surely hast thy brother
  won
  Rest, out of sight of our world-weary sun,
And in the dead land where ye ghosts draw
  breath,
  A royal place and honor; so wast thou
  Happy, though earth have hold of thee
  too now.

So hast thou life and name inviolable
  And joy it may be, sacred and severe,
  Joy secret-souled beyond all hope or fear,
A monumental joy wherein to dwell
  Secluse and silent, a selected state,
  Serene possession of thy proper fate.

Thou art not dead as these are dead who
  live
  Full of blind years, a sorrow-shaken
  kind,
  Nor as these are am I the prophet blind;
They have not life that have nor heart to
  give
  Life, nor have eyesight who lack heart
  to see
  When to be not is better than to be

O ye whom time but bears with for a span,
  How long will ye be blind and dead, how
  long
  Make your own souls part of your own
  soul's wrong ?
Son of the word of the most high gods,
  man,
  Why wilt thou make thine hour of light
  and breath
  Emptier of all but shame than very
  death?

Fool, wilt thou live for ever? though thou
  care
  With all thine heart for life to keep it
  fast,
  Shall not thine hand forego it at the last ?
  Lo, thy sure hour shall take thee by the
  hair

Sleeping, or when thou knowest not, or
wouldst fly ;
And as men died much mightier shalt
thou die.

Yea, they are dead, men much more worth
than thou ;
The savour of heroic lives that were,
Is it not mixed into thy common air ?
The sense of them is shed about thee now :
Feel not thy brows a wind blowing from
far ?
Aches not thy forehead with a future
star ?

The light that thou may'st make out of thy
name
Is in the wind of this same hour that
drives,
Blown within reach but once of all men's
lives ;
And he that puts forth hand upon the flame
Shall have it for a garland on his head
To sign him for a king among the dead.

But these men that the lessening years be-
hold,
Who sit the most part without flame or
crown,
And brawl and sleep and wear their life-
days down
With joys and griefs ignobler than of old
And care not if the better day shall be,—
Are these or art thou dead, Antigone ?

PART II.

As when one wakes out of a waning dream
And sees with instant eyes the naked
thought
Whereof the vision as a web was wrought,
I saw beneath a heaven of cloud and gleam,
Ere yet the heart of the young sun waxed
brave,
One like a prophet standing by a grave.

In the hoar heaven was hardly beam or
breath,
And all the colored hills and fields were
grey,
And the wind wandered seeking for the
day,
And wailed as though he had found her
done to death
And this grey hour had built to bury her
The hollow twilight for a sepulchre.

But in my soul I saw as in a glass
A pale and living body full of grace
There lying, and over it the prophet's
face
Fixed ; and the face was not of Tiresias,
For such a starry fire was in his eyes
As though their light it was that made
the skies.

Such eyes should God's have been when
very love
Looked forth of them and set the sun
aflame,
And such his lips that called the light by
name
And bade the morning forth at sound
thereof ;
His face was sad and masterful as fate,
And like a star's his look compassionate.

Like a star's gazed on of sad eyes so long
It seems to yearn with pity, and all its
fire
As a man's heart to tremble with desire
And heave as though the light would bring
forth song
Yet from his face flashed lightning on
the land,
And like the thunder-bearer's was his
hand.

The steepness of strange stairs had tried his
feet,
And his lips yet seemed sick of that salt
bread
Wherewith the lips of banishment are
fed ;
But nothing was there in the world so
sweet
As the most bitter love, like God's own
grace,
Wherewith he gazed on that fair buried
face.

Grief and glad pride and passion and sharp
shame,
Wrath and remembrance, faith and hope
and hate
And pitiless pity of days degenerate,
Where in his eyes as an incorporate flame
That burned about her, and the heart
thereof
And central flower was very fire of love.

But all about her grave wherein she slept
  Were noises of the wild wind-footed
    years
  Whose footprints flying were full of blood
    and tears,
Shrieks as of Mænads on their hills that
    leapt
  And yelled as beasts of ravin, and their
    meat
  Was the rent flesh of their own sons to
    eat :

And fiery shadows passing with strange
    cries ;
  And Sphinx-like shapes about the ruined
    lands,
  And the red reek of parricidal hands
And intermixture of incestuous eyes,
  And light as of that self-divided flame
  Which made an end of the Cadmean
    name.

And I beheld again, and lo the grave,
  And the bright body laid therein as dead,
  And the same shadow across another
    head
That bowed down silent on that sleeping
    slave
  Who was the lady of empire from her
    birth
  And light of all the kingdoms of the
    earth.

Within the compass of the watcher's hand
  All strengths of other men and divers
    powers
  Were held at ease and gathered up as
    flowers ;
His heart was as the heart of his whole
    land,
  And at his feet as natural servants lay
  Twilight and dawn and night and labor-
    ing day.

He was most awful of the sons of God.
  Even now men seeing seemed at his lips
    to see
  The trumpet of the judgment that should
    be,
And in his right hand terror for a rod,
  And in the breath that made the moun-
    tains bow
  The horned fire of Moses on his brow

The strong wind of the coming of the
    Lord
  Had blown as flame upon him, and
    brought down
  On his bare head from heaven fire for a
    crown,
And fire was girt upon him as a sword
  To smite and lighten, and on what ways
    he trod
  There fell from him the shadow of a God.

Pale, with the whole world's judgment in
    his eyes,
  He stood and saw the grief and shame
    endure
  That he, though highest of angels, might
    not cure,
And the same sins done under the same
    skies,
  And the same slaves to the same tyrants
    thrown,
  And fain he would have slept, and fain
    been stone.

But with unslumbering eyes he watched the
    sleep
  That sealed her sense whose eyes were
    suns of old ;
  And the night shut and opened, and
    behold,
The same grave where those prophets came
    to weep,
  But she that lay therein had moved and
    stirred,
  And where those twain had watched her
    stood a third.

The tripled rhyme that closed in Paradise
  With Love's name sealing up its starry
    speech—
  The tripled might of hand that found in
    reach
All crowns beheld far off of all men's eyes,
  Song, color, carven wonders of live
    stone—
  These were not, but the very soul alone.

The living spirit, the good gift of grace,
  The faith which takes of its own blood
    to give
  That the dead veins of buried hope may
    live,
Came on her sleeping, face to naked face,

And from a soul more sweet than all the
    south
    Breathed love upon her sealed and
    breathless mouth.

Between her lips the breath was blown as
    fire,
    And through her flushed veins leapt the
    liquid life
And with sore passion and ambiguous
    strife
The new birth rent her and the new desire
The will to live, the competence to be,
The sense to hearken and the soul to see.

And the third prophet standing by her
    grave
    Stretched forth his hand and touched
    her, and her eyes,
    Opened as sudden suns in heaven might
    rise,
And her soul caught from his the faith to
    save ;
    Faith above creeds faith beyond records,
    born

Of the pure, naked, fruitful, awful morn.
For in he daybreak now that night was
    dead
    The light, the shadow, the delight, the
    pain,
    The purpose and the passion of those
    twain,
Seemed gathered on that third prophetic
    head,
    And all their crowns were as one crown,
    and one
    His face with her face in the living sun.

For even with that communion of their
    eyes
    His whole soul passed into her and made
    her strong ;
    And all the sounds and shows of shame
    and wrong,
The hands that slays, the lip that mocks
    and lies,
    Temples and thrones that yet men seem
    to see,—
    Are these dead or art thou dead, Italy ?

THE SONG OF THE STANDARD.

MAIDEN most beautiful, mother most boun-
    tiful, lady of lands,
Queen and republican, crowned of the
    centuries whose years are thy sands,
See for thy sake what we bring to thee,
    Italy, here in our hands.

This is the banner thy gonfalon, fair in the
    front of thy fight,
Red from the hearts that were pierced for
    thee, white as thy mountains are white,
Green as the spring of thy soul everlasting,
    whose life-blood is light.

Take to thy bosom thy banner, a fair bird
    fit for the nest,
Feathered for flight into sunrise or sunset,
    for eastward or west,
Fledged for the flight everlasting, but held
    yet warm to thy breast.

Gather it close to thee, song-bird or storm-
    bearer, eagle or dove,
Lift it to sunward, a beacon beneath to the
    beacon above,
Green as our hope in it, white as our faith
    in it, red as our love.

Thunder and splendor of lightning are hid
    in the folds of it furled ;
Who shall unroll it but thou, as thy bolt to
    be handled and hurled,
Out of whose lips is the honey, whose bosom
    the milk of the world ?

Out of thine hands hast thou fed us with
    pasture of color and song ;
Glory and beauty by birthright to thee as
    thy garments belong ;
Out of thine hands thou shalt give us as
    surely deliverance from wrong.

Out of thine eyes thou hast shed on us love
    as a lamp in our night,
Wisdom a lodestar to ships, and remem-
    brance a flame-colored light ;
Out of thine eyes thou shalt shew us as
    surely the sundawn of right.

Turn to us, speak to us, Italy, mother, but
    once and a word,
None shall not follow thee, none shall not
    serve thee, not one that has heard ;
Twice hast thou spoken a message, and time
    is athirst for the third.

Kingdom and empire of peoples thou hadst,
    and thy lordship made one
North sea and south sea and east men and
    west men that look on the sun ;
Spirit was in thee and counsel, when soul
    in the nations was none.

Banner and beacon thou wast to the cen-
    turies of stormwind and foam,
Ages that clashed in the dark with each
    other, and years without home ;
Empress and prophetess wast thou, and
    what wilt thou now be, O Rome ?

Ah, by the faith and the hope and the love
    that have need of thee now,
Shines not thy face with the forethought of
    freedom, and burns not thy brow ?
Who is against her but all men ? and who
    is beside her but thou ?

Art thou not better than all men ? and
    where shall she turn but to thee ?
Lo, not a breath, not a beam, not a beacon
    from midland to sea ;
Freedom cries out for a sign among nations,
    and none will be free.

England in doubt of her, France in despair
    of her, all without heart—
Stand on her side in the vanward of ages,
    and strike on her part !
Strike but one stroke for the love of her
    love of thee, sweet that thou art !

Take in thy right hand thy banner, a strong
    staff fit for thine hand ;
Forth at the light of it lifted shall foul things
    flock from the land ;
Faster than stars from the sun shall they
    fly, being lighter than sand.

Green thing to green in the summer makes
    answer, and rose-tree to rose ;
Lily by lily the year becomes perfect ; and
    none of us knows
What thing is fairest of all things on earth
    as it brightens and blows.

This thing is fairest in all time of all things,
    in all time is best—
Freedom, that made thee, our mother, and
    suckled hers sons at thy breast ;
Take to thy bosom the nations, and there
    shall the world come to rest.

ON THE DOWNS.

A FAINT sea without wind or sun ;
A sky like flameless vapor dun ;
    A valley like an unsealed grave
That no man cares to weep upon,
    Bare, without boon to crave,
        Or flower to save.

And on the lip's edge of the down,
Here where the bent-grass burns to brown
    In the dry sea-wind, and the heath
Crawls to the cliff-side and looks down,
    I watch, and hear beneath
        The low tide breathe.

Along the long lines of the cliff,
Down the flat sea-line without skiff
    Or sail or black-blown fume for mark,
Through wind-worn heads of heath and stiff
    Stems blossomless and stark
        With dry sprays dark,

I send mine eyes out as for news
Of comfort that all these refuse,
    Tidings of light or living air
From windward where the low clouds muse
    And the sea blind and bare
        Seems full of care.

So is it now as it was then,
And as men have been such are men,
    There as I stood I seem to stand,
Here sitting chambered, and again
    Feel spread on either hand
        Sky, sea, and land.

As a queen taken and stripped and bound
Sat earth, discolored and discrowned ;
    As a king's palace empty and dead
The sky was without light or sound ;
    And on the summer's head
        Were ashes shed,

Scarce wind enough was on the sea,
Scarce hope enough there moved in me,
 To sow with live blown flowers of white
The green plain's sad serenity,
 Or with stray thoughts of light
  Touch my soul's sight.

By footless ways and sterile went
My thought unsatisfied, and bent
 With blank unspeculative eyes
On the untracked sands of discontent
 Where, watched of helpless skies,
  Life hopeless lies.

East and west went my soul to find
Light, and the world was bare and blind
 And the soil herbless where she trod
And saw men laughing scourge mankind,
 Unsmitten by the rod
  Of any God.

Out of time's blind old eyes were shed
Tears that were mortal, and left dead
 The heart and spirit of the years,
And on man's fallen and helmless head
 Time's disanointing tears
  Fell cold as fears.

Hope flowering had but strength to bear
The fruitless fruitage of despair ;
 Grief trod the grapes of joy for wine,
Whereof love drinking unaware
 Died as one undivine

   And made no sign.
And soul and body dwelt apart ;
And weary wisdom without heart
 Stared on the dead round heaven and
  sighed,
"Is death too hollow as thou art,
 Or as man's living pride "
  And saying so died.

And my soul heard the songs and groans
That are about and under thrones,
 And felt through all time's murmur thrill
Fate's old imperious semitones
 That made of good and ill
  One same tune still.

Then "Where is God ? and where is aid ?
Or what good end of these ?" she said ;
 "Is there no God or end at all,

Nor reason with unreason weighed
Nor force to disenthral
 Weak feet that fall ?

"No light to lighten and no rod
To chasten men ? Is there no God ?"
So girt with anguish, iron-zoned,
Went my soul weeping as she trod
 Between the men enthroned
  And men that groaned.

O fool, that for brute cries of wrong
Heard not the grey glad mother's song
Ring response from the hills and waves,
But heard harsh noises all day long
 Of spirits that were slaves
  And dwelt in graves.

The wise word of the secret earth
Who knows what life and death are worth,
 And how no help and no control
Can speed or stay things come to birth
 Nor all world's wheels's that roll
  Crush one born soul.

With all her tongues of life and death,
With all her bloom and blood and breath,
 From all years dead and all things done,
In the ear of man the mother saith,
 "There is no God, O son,
  If thou be none."

So my soul sick with watching heard
That day the wonder of that word,
 And as one springs out of a dream
Sprang, and the stagnant wells were stirred
 Whence flows through gloom and gleam
  Thought's soundless stream.

Out of pale cliff and sunburnt heath,
Out of the low sea curled beneath
 In the land's bending arm embayed,
Out of all lives that thought hears breathe
  Life within life inlaid.
   Was answer made.

A multitudinous monotone
Of dust and flower and seed and stone,
 In the deep sea-rock's mid-sea sloth,
In the live waters trembling zone,
 In all men love and loathe,
  One God at growth.

One forceful nature uncreate
That feeds itself with death and fate,

Evil and good, and change and time,
That within all men lies at wait
　　Till the hour shall bid them climb
　　　And live sublime.

For all things come by fate to flower
At their unconquerable hour,
　　And time brings truth, and truth makes
　　　free,
And freedom fills time's veins with power,
　As, brooding on that sea,
　　My thought filled me.

And the sun smote the clouds and slew
And from the sun the sea's breath blew,
　　And white waves laughed and turned and
　　　fled

The long green heaving sea-field through,
　And on them overhead
　　The sky burnt red.

Like a furled flag that wind sets free,
On the swift summer-colored sea
　　Shook out the red lines of the light,
The live sun's standard, blown to lee
　　Across the live sea's white
　　　And green delight.

And with divine triumphant awe
My spirit moved within me saw,
　　With burning passion of stretched eyes,
Clear as the light's own firstborn law,
　　In windless wastes of skies
　　　Time's deep dawn rise.

MESSIDOR.

PUT in the sickles and reap ;
　For the morning of harvest is red,
　　And the long large ranks of the corn
　　　Colored and clothed as the morn
Stand thick in the fields and deep
　For them that faint to be fed.
Let all that hunger and weep
　Come hither, and who would have bread
Put in the sickles and reap.

Colored and clothed as the morn,
　The grain grows ruddier than gold,
　　And the good strong sun is alight
　　　In the mists of the day-dawn white,
And the crescent, a faint sharp horn,
　In the fear of his face turns cold
As the snakes of the night-time that creep
　From the flag of our faith unrolled.
Put in the sickles and reap.

In the mists of the day-dawn white
　That roll round the morning star,
　　The large flame lightens and grows
　　　Till the red gold harvest-rows,
Full-grown, are full of the light
　As the spirits of strong men are,
Crying, Who shall slumber or sleep ?
　Who put back morning or mar ?
Put in the sickles and reap.

Till the red-gold harvest-rows
　For miles through shudder and shine
　　In the wind's breath, fed with the sun,
　　A thousand spear-heads as one

Bowed as for battle to close
　Line in rank against line
With place and station to keep
　Till all men's hands at a sign
Put in the sickles and reap.

A thousand spear-heads as one
　Wave as with swing of the sea
　　When the mid tide sways at its height
　　For the hour is for harvest or fight
In face of the just calm sun,
　As the signal in season may be
And the lot in the helm may leap
　When chance shall shake it ; but ye,
Put in the sickles and reap.

For the hour is for harvest or fight
　To clothe with raiment of red ;
　　O men sore stricken of hours,
　　　Lo, this one, is not it ours,
To glean, to gather, to smite ?
　Let none make risk of his head
Within reach of the clean scythe-sweep,
　When the people that lay as the dead
Put in the sickles and reap.

Lo, this one, is not it ours,
　Now the ruins of dead things rattle
　　As dead men's bones in the pit,
　　　Now the kings wax lean as they sit
Girt round with memories of powers,
　With musters counted as cattle
And armies folded as sheep
　Till the red blind husbandman battle
Put in the sickles and reap.

Now the kings wax lean as they sit,
  The people grow strong to stand ;
  The men they trod on and spat,
  The dumb dread people that sat
As corpses cast in a pit,
  Rise up with God at their hand,
And thrones are hurled on a heap,
  And strong men, sons of the land,
Put in the sickles and reap.

The dumb dread people that sat
  All night without screen for the night,
  All day without food for the day,
  They shall not give their harvest away,
They shall eat of its fruit and wax fat :
  They shall see the desire of their sight,
Though the ways of the seasons be steep,
  They shall climb with face to the light,
Put in the sickles and reap.

ODE ON THE INSURRECTION IN CANDIA.

STR. 1.

I LAID my laurel-leaf
    At the white feet of grief,
Seeing how with covered face and plumeless wings,
        With unreverted head
        Veiled, as who mourns his dead,
Lay Freedom couched between the
thrones of kings,
        A wearied lion without lair,
And bleeding from base wounds, and vexed
with alien air.

STR. 2.

Who was it, who, put poison to thy mouth,
    Who lulled with craft or chant thy vigi-
lant eyes,
O light of all men, lamp to north and
south,
    Eastward and westward, under all men's
skies ?
For if thou sleep, we perish, and thy name
    Dies with the dying of our ephemeral
breath ;
And if the dust of death o'ergrows thy
flame,
    Heaven also is darkened with the dust of
death.
If thou be mortal, if thou change or cease,
If thine hand fail, or thine eyes turn from
Greece,
Thy first-born, and the first-fruits of thy
fame,
God is no God, and man is moulded out
of shame.

STR. 3.

Is there change in the secret skies,
    In the sacred places that see
        The divine beginning of things,
            The weft of the web of the world ?

Is Freedom a worm that dies,
    And God no God of the free ?
        Is heaven like as earth with her kings
            And time as a serpent curled
            Round life as a tree ?

From the steel-bound snows of the north
    From the mystic mother, the east,
        From the sands of the fiery south,
            From the low-lit clouds of the west,
A sound of a cry is gone forth ;
    Arise, stand up from the feast,
        Let wine be far from the mouth,
        Let no man sleep or take rest,
            Till the plague hath ceased.

Let none rejoice or make mirth
    Till the evil thing be stayed,
        Nor grief be lulled in the lute,
        Nor hope be loud on the lyre ;
Let none be glad upon the earth.
    O music of young man and maid,
    O songs of the bride, be mute.
        For the light of her eyes, her desire,
        Is the soul dismayed.

It is not a land new-born
    That is scourged of a stranger's hand,
    That is rent and consumed with flame,
        We have known it of old, this face,
With the cheeks and the tresses torn,
    With shame on the brow as a brand.
    We have named it of old by name,
        The land of the royallest race,
        The most holy land.

STR. 4.

Had I words of fire,
    Whose words are weak as snow
Were my heart a lyre
    Whence all its love might flow

In the mighty modulations of desire,
In the notes wherewith man's passion
worships woe ;

> Could my song release
>   The thought weak words confine,
> And my grief, O Greece,
>   Prove how it worships thine ;
It would move with pulse of war the limbs
    of peace
Till she flushed and trembled and became
    divine.

> (Once she held for true
>   This truth of sacred strain ;
> Though blood drip like dew
>   And life run down like rain,
It is better that war spare but one or two
Than that many live, and liberty be slain.)

> Then with fierce increase
>   And bitter mother's mirth,
> From the womb of peace,
>   A womb that yearns for birth,
As a man-child should deliverance come to
    Greece,
As a saviour should the child be born on
    earth.

STR. 5.

O that these my days had been
Ere white peace and shame were wed
Without torch or dancers' din
Round the unsacred marriage bed !
For of old the sweet-tongued law,
Freedom, clothed with all men's love,
Girt about with all men's awe,
With the wild war-eagle mated
The white breast of peace the dove,
And his ravenous heart abated
And his windy wings were furled
In an eyrie consecrated
Where the snakes of strife uncurled,
And her soul was soothed and sated
With the welfare of the world.

ANT. 1.

But now, close-clad with peace,
While war lays hand on Greece,
The kingdoms and their kings stand by to
    see ;
    "Aha, we are strong," they say,
    "We are sure, we are well," even they;
"And if we serve, what ails ye to be free ?
    We are warm, clothed round with peace
        and shame ;
But ye lie dead and naked, dying for a
    name."

ANT. 2.

O kings and queens and nations miserable
    O fools and blind, and full of sins and
        fears,
With these it is, with you it is not well ;
    Ye have one hour, but these the im-
        mortal years.
These for a pang, a breath, a pulse o' pain,
    Have honor, while that honor on earth
        shall be ;
Ye for a little sleep and sloth shall gain
    Scorn, while one man of all men born is
        free.
Even as the depth more deep than night or
    day,
The sovereign heaven that keeps its eldest
    way,
So without chance or change, so without
    stain,
The heaven of their high memories shall
    not wax nor wane.

ANT. 3.

As the soul on the lips of the dead
    Stands poising her wings for flight,
        A bird scarce quit of her prison,
        But fair without form or flesh,
So stands over each man's head
    A splendor of imminent light,
        A glory of fame rearisen,
        Of day rearisen afresh
            From the hells of night.

In the hundred cities of Crete
    Such glory was not of old,
        Though her name was great upon earth
        And her face was fair on the sea.
The words of her lips were sweet,
    Her days were woven with gold,
        Her fruits came timely to birth ;
        So fair she was, being free,
            Who is bought and sold.

So fair, who is fairer now
    With her children dead at her side,
        Unsceptered, unconsecrated,
            Unapparelled, unhelped, unpitied,
With blood for gold on her brow,
    Where the towery tresses divide ;
        The goodly, the golden-gated,
            Many-crowned, many-named, many
                cities,
            Made like as a bride.

And these are the bridegroom's gifts ;
Anguish that straitens the breath.
    Shame, and the weeping of mothers,
        And the suckling dead at the breast,
White breast that a long sob lifts ;
And the dumb dead mouth, which saith,
    " How long, and how long, my
        brothers ? "
        And wrath which endures not rest,
        And the pains of death.

ANT. 4.

Ah, but would that men,
    With eyelids purged by tears,
Saw, and heard again
    With consecrated ears,
All the clamor, all the splendor, all the
    slain,
All the lights and sounds of war, the fates
    and fears ;

Saw far off aspire,
    With crash of mine and gate,
From a single pyre
    The myriad flames of fate,
Soul by soul transfigured in funereal fire,
Hate made weak by love, and love made
    strong by hate ;

Children without speech,
    And many a nursing breast ;
Old men in the breach,
    Where death sat down a guest ;
With triumphant lamentation made for
    each,
Let the world salute their ruin and their
    rest.

In one iron hour
    The cresent flared and waned,
As from tower to tower,
    Fire-scathed and sanguine-stained,
Death with flame in hand, an open blood-
    red flower,
Passed, and where it bloomed no bloom
    of life remained.

ANT. 5.

Hear thou, earth, the heavy-hearted
Weary nurse of waning races :
From the dust of years departed,
From obscure funereal places,
Raise again thy sacred head ;
Lift the light up of thine eyes ;

14

Where are they of all thy dead
That did more than these men dying
In their godlike Grecian wise ?
Not with garments rent and sighing,
Neither gifts of myrth and gold,
Shall their sons lament them lying ;
Lest the fame of them wax cold ;
But with lives to lives replying,
And a worship from of old.

EPODE.

O sombre heart of earth and swoln with
    grief,
    That in thy time wast as a bird for mirth,
Dim womb of life and many a seed and
    sheaf,
    And full of changes, ancient heart of
        earth,
From grain and flower, from grass and
    every leaf,   [birth,
    Thy mysteries and thy multitudes of
From hollow and hill, from vales and all
    thy springs,
    From all shapes born and breath of all
        lips made.
From thunders, and the sound of winds
    and wings,
    From light, and from the solemn sleep
        of shade,
From the full fountains of all living things,
    Speak, that this plague be stayed.
Bear witness all the ways of death and life
If thou be with us in the world's old
    If thou be mother indeed,   [strife,
        And from these wounds that bleed
Gather in thy great breast the dews that
    fall,
    And on thy sacred knees
    Lull with mute melodies,
Mother, thy sleeping sons in death's dim
    hall.
    For these thy sons, behold,
    Sons of thy sons of old,
Bear witness if these be not as they were ;
    If that high name of Greece
    Depart, dissolve, decease
From mouths of men and memories like
    as air.
    By the last milk that drips
    Dead on the child's dead lips,
By old men's white unviolated hair,
    By sweet unburied faces
    That fill those red high places
Where death and freedom found one lion's
    lair,

By all the bloodred tears
  That fill the chaliced years,
The vessels of the sacrament of time,
  Wherewith, O thou most holy,
  O Freedom, sure and slowly
Thy ministrant white hands cleanse earth
    of crime ;
  Though we stand off afar
  Where slaves and slaveries are,
Among the chains and crowns of poisonous
    peace ;
  Though not the beams that shone
  From rent Arcadion
Can melt her mists and bid her snows de-
    crease ;

Do thou with sudden wings
  Darken the face of kings,
But turn again the beauty of thy brows on
    Greece ;
  Thy white and woundless brows,
  Whereto her great heart bows ;
Give her the glories of thine eyes to see ;
  Turn thee, O holiest head,
  Toward all thy quick and dead,
For love's sake of the souls that cry for
    thee ;
  O love, O light, O flame,
  By thine own Grecian name,
We call thee and we charge thee that all
    these be free.

Jan. 1867.

"NON DOLET."

It does not hurt. She looked along the knife
  Smiling, and watched the thick drops
    mix and run
Down the sheer blade ; not that which
    had been done
Could hurt the sweet sense of the Roman
  wife,
But that which was to do yet ere the strife
  Could end for each for ever, and the sun :
Nor was the palm yet nor was peace yet
    won
While pain had power upon her husband's
  life.

It does not hurt, Italia. Thou art more
  Than bride to bridegroom ; how shalt
    thou not take
  The gift love's blood has reddened for
    thy sake?
Was not thy lifeblood given for us be-
    fore ?
And if love's heartblood can avail thy
    need,
And thou not die, how should it hurt
    indeed ?

EURYDICE.

TO VICTOR HUGO.

Orpheus, the night is full of tears and cries,
  And hardly for the storm and ruin shed
  Can even thine eyes be certain of her head
Who never passed out of thy spirit's eyes,
But stood and shone before them in such
  wise
  As when with love her lips and hands
    were fed,
  And with mute mouth out of the dusty dead
Strove to make answer when thou bad'st
  her rise.

Yet viper-stricken must her lifeblood feel
  The fang that stung her sleeping, the
    foul germ
  Even when she wakes of hell's most
    poisonous worm,
Though now it writhe beneath her wound-
    ed heel.
  Turn yet, she will not fade nor fly from
    thee ;
  Wait, and see hell yield up Eurydice.

AN APPEAL.

I.

ART thou indeed among these,
Thou of the tyrannous crew,
The kingdoms fed upon blood,
O queen from of old of the seas,
England, art thou of them too
That drink of the poisonous flood,
That hide under poisonous trees?

II.

Nay, thy name from of old,
Mother, was pure, or we dreamed;
Purer we held thee than this,
Purer fain would we hold;
So goodly a glory it seemed,
A fame so bounteous of bliss,
So more precious than gold.

III.

A praise so sweet in our ears,
That thou in the tempest of things
As a rock for a refuge shouldst stand,
In the bloodred river of tears
Poured forth for the triumph of kings;
A safeguard, a sheltering land,
In the thunder and torrent of years.

IV.

Strangers came gladly to thee,
Exiles, chosen of men,
Safe for thy sake in thy shade,
Sat down at thy feet and were free.
So men spake of thee then;
Now shall their speaking be stayed?
Ah, so let it not be!

V.

Not for revenge or affright,
Pride, or a tyrannous lust,
Cast from thee the crown of thy praise,
Mercy was thine in thy might;
Strong when thou wert, thou wert just;
Now, in the wrong-doing days,
Cleave thou, thou at least, to the right.

VI.

How should one charge thee, how sway,
Save by the memories that were?
Not thy gold nor the strength of thy ships,
Nor the might of thine armies at bay,
Made thee, mother, most fair;
But a word from republican lips
Said in thy name in thy day.

VII.

Hast thou said it, and hast thou forgot?
Is thy praise in thine ears as a scoff?
Blood of men guiltless was shed,
Children, and souls without spot,
Shed, but in places far off;
Let slaughter no more be, said
Milton; and slaughter was not.

VIII.

Was it not said of thee too,
Now, but now, by thy foes,
By the slaves that had slain their France.
And thee would slay as they slew—
"Down with her walls that enclose
Freemen that eye us askance,
Fugitives, men that are true!"

IX.

This was thy praise or thy blame
From bondsman or freeman—to be
Pure from pollution of slaves,
Clean of their sins, and thy name
Bloodless, innocent, free;
Now if thou be not, thy waves
Wash not from off thee thy shame.

X.

Freeman he is not, but slave,
Whoso in fear for the State
Cries for surety of blood,
Help of gibbet and grave;
Neither is any land great
Whom, in her fear-stricken mood,
These things only can save.

XI.

Lo, how fair from afar,
Taintless of tyranny, stands
The mighty daughter, for years
Who trod the winepress of war ;
Shines with immaculate hands ;
Slays not a foe, neither fears ;
Stains not peace with a scar.

XII.

Be not as tyrant or slave,
England ; be not as these,
Thou that wert other than they.
Stretch out thine hand, but to save ;
Put forth thy strength, and release ;
Lest there arise, if thou slay,
Thy shame as a ghost from the grave.

November 20, 1867.

PERINDE AC CADAVER.

In a vision Liberty stood
　By the childless charm-stricken bed
Where, barren of glory and good,
Knowing nought if she would not or would,
　England slept with her dead.

Her face that the foam had whitened,
　Her hands that were strong to strive,
Her eyes whence battle had lightened,
Over all was a drawn shroud tightened
　To bind her asleep and alive.

She turned and laughed in her dream
　With grey lips arid and cold ;
She saw not the face as a beam
Burn on her, but only a gleam
　Through her sleep as of new-stamped
　　gold.

But the goddess, with terrible tears
　In the light of her down-drawn eyes,
Spake fire in the dull sealed ears ;
"Thou, sick with slumbers and fears,
　Wilt thou sleep now indeed or arise ?

" With dreams and with words and with
　　light
　Memories and empty desires
Thou hast wrapped thyself round all night;
Thou hast shut up thine heart from the
　　right,
　And warmed thee at burnt-out fires.

" Yet once if I smote at thy gate,
　Thy sons would sleep not, but heard ;
O thou that wast found so great,
Art thou smitten with folly or fate
　That thy sons have forgotten my word ?

" O Cromwell's mother, O breast
　That suckled Milton ! thy name
That was beautiful then, that was blest,
Is it wholly discrowned and deprest,
　Trodden under by sloth into shame ?

" Why wilt thou hate me and die ?
　For none can hate me and live.
What ill have I done to thee ? why
Wilt thou turn from me fighting, and fly,
　Who would follow thy feet and forgive ?

" Thou hast seen me stricken, and said,
　What is it to me ? I am strong ;
Thou hast seen me bowed down on my
　　dead
And laughed and lifted thine head,
　And washed thine hands of my wrong.

" Thou hast put out the soul of thy sight ;
　Thou hast sought to my foemen as friend,
To my traitors that kiss me and smite,
To the kingdoms and empires of night
　That begin with the darkness, and end.

" Turn thee, awaken, arise,
　With the light that is risen on the lands,
With the change of the fresh-colored skies;
Set thine eyes on mine eyes,
　Lay thy hands in my hands."

She moved and mourned as she heard,
　Sighed and shifted her place,
As the wells of her slumber were stirred
By the music and wind of the word,
　Then turned and covered her face.

" Ah," she said in her sleep,
  " Is my work not done with and done?
Is there corn for my sickle to reap?

And strange is the pathway and steep,
  And sharp overhead is the sun.

" I have done thee service enough,
  Loved thee enough in my day;
Now nor hatred nor love
Nor hardly remembrance thereof
  Lives in me to lighten my way.

" And is it not well with us here?
  Is change as good as is rest?
What hope should move me, or fear,
That eye should open or ear,
  Who have long since won what is best?

" Where among us are such things
  As turn men's hearts into hell?
Have we not queens without stings,
Scotched princes, and fangless kings?
  Yea," she said, " we are well.

" We have filed the teeth of the snake
  Monarchy, how should it bite?

Should the slippery slow thing wake,
It will not sting for my sake;
  Yea," she said, " I do right."

So spake she, drunken with dreams,
  Mad; but again in her ears
A voice as of storm-swelled streams
Spake; " No brave shame then redeems
  Thy lusts of sloth and thy fears?

" Thy poor lie slain of thine hands,
  Their starved limbs rot in thy sight;
As a shadow the ghost of thee stands
Among men living and lands,
  And stirs not leftward or right.

" Freeman he is not, but slave,
  Who stands not out on my side;
His own hand hollows his grave,
Nor strength is in me to save
  Where strength is none to abide.

" Time shall tread on his name
  That was written for honor of old,
Who hath taken in change for fame
Dust, and silver, and shame,
  Ashes, and iron, and gold."

MONOTONES.

BECAUSE there is but one truth;
  Because there is but one banner;
  Because there is but one light;
Because we have with us our youth
  Once, and one chance and one manner
  Of service, and then the night;

Because we have found not yet
  Any way for the world to follow
  Save only that ancient way;
Whosoever forsake or forget,
  Whose faith soever be hollow,
  Whose hope soever grow grey;

Because of the watchwords of kings
  That are many and strange and unwritten,
  Diverse, and our watchword is one;
Therefore, though seven be the strings,
  One string, if the harp be smitten,
  Sole sounds, till the tune be done;

Sounds without cadence or change
  In a weary monotonous burden,
  Be the keynote of mourning or mirth;

Free, but free not to range;
  Taking for crown and for guerdon
  No man's praise upon earth;

Saying one sole word evermore,
  In the ears of the charmed world saying,
  Charmed by spells to its death;
One that chanted of yore
  To a tune of the sword-sweep's playing
  In the lips of the dead blew breath;

Therefore I set not mine hand
  To the shifting of changed modulations
  To the smiting of manifold strings;
While the thrones of the throned men stand
  One song for the morning of nations,
  One for the twilight of kings.

One chord, one word, and one way,
  One hope as our law, one heaven,
  Till slain be the great one wrong;
Till the people it could not slay,
  Risen up, have for one star seven,
  For a single, a sevenfold song.

THE OBLATION.

Ask nothing more of me sweet,
  All I can give you I give
  Heart of my heart, were it more.
More would be laid at your feet :
  Love that should help you to live,
  Song that should spur you to soar.

All things were nothing to give
  Once to have sense of you more,
  Touch you and taste of you sweet,

Think you and breathe you and live,
  Swept of your wings as they soar,
  Trodden by chance of your feet.

I that have love and no more
  Give you but love of you, sweet :
  He that hath more, let him give ;
He that hath wings, let him soar ;
  Mine is the heart at your feet
  Here, that must love you to live.

A YEAR'S BURDEN.

Fire and wild light of hope and doubt and
    fear,
Wind of swift change, and clouds and hours
    that veer
As the storm shifts of the tempestuous year ;
  Cry wellaway, but well befall the right.

Hope sits yet hiding her war-wearied eyes,
Doubt sets her forehead earthward and
    denies,
But fear brought hand to hand with danger
    dies,
  Dies and is burnt up in the fire of fight.

Hearts bruised with loss and eaten through
    with shame
Turn at the time's touch to devouring
    flame ;
Grief stands as one that knows not her own
    name,
  Nor if the star she sees bring day or night.

No song breaks with it on the violent air,
But shrieks of shame, defeat, and brute de-
    spair ;
Yet something at the star's heart far up
    there
  Burns as a beacon in our shipwrecked
    sight.

O strange fierce light of presage, unknown
    star,
Whose tongues shall tell us what thy secrets
    are,
What message trembles in thee from so far?
  Cry wellaway, but well befall the right.

From shores laid waste across an iron sea
Where the waifs drift of hopes that were to
    be,
Across the red rolled foam we look for thee,
  Across the fire we look up for the light.

From days laid waste across disastrous
    years,
From hopes cut down across a world of
    fears,
We gaze with eyes too passionate for tears,
  Where faith abides though hope be put to
    flight.

Old hope is dead, the grey-haired hope
    grown blind
That talked with us of old things out of
    mind,
Dreams, deeds and men the world has left
    behind ;
  Yet, though hope die, faith lives in hope's
    despite.

Ay, with hearts fixed on death and hope-
    less hands
We stand about our banner while it stands
Above but one field of the ruined lands ;
  Cry wellaway, but well befall the right.

Though France were given for prey to bird
    and beast,
Though Rome were rent in twain of king
    and priest,
The soul of man, the soul is safe at least
  That gives death life and dead men
    hands to smite.

Are ye so strong, O kings, O strong
   men? Nay,
Waste all ye will and gather all ye may,
Yet one thing is there that ye shall not
   slay,
    Even thought, that fire nor iron can
    affright.

The woundless and invisible thought that
   goes
Free throughout time as north or south
   wind blows,
Far throughout space as east or west sea
   flows,
    And all dark things before it are made
    bright.

Thy thought, thy word, O soul republican,
O spirit of life, O God whose name is
   man:
What sea of sorrows but thy sight shall
   span?
    Cry wellaway, but well befall the right.

With all its coils crushed, all its rings uncurled,
The one most poisonous worm that soiled
   the world
Is wrenched from off the throat of man,
   and hurled
    Into deep hell from empire's helpless
    height.

Time takes no more infection of it now;
Like a dead snake divided of the plough,
The rotten thing lies cut in twain; but
   thou,
    Thy fires shall heal us of the serpent's
    bite.

Ay, with red cautery and a burning brand
Purge thou the leprous leaven of the
   land;

Take to thee fire, and iron in thine hand,
   Till blood and tears have washed the
   soiled limbs white.

We have sinned against thee in dreams
   and wicked sleep;
Smite, we will shrink not; strike, we will
   not weep:
Let the heart feel thee; let thy wound go
   deep;
    Cry wellaway, but well befall the right.

Wound us with love, pierce us with longing, make
Our souls thy sacrifices; turn and take
Our hearts for our sin-offerings lest they
   break,
    And mould them with thine hands and
    give them might.

Then, when the cup of ills is drained indeed,
Will we come to thee with our wounds
   that bleed,
With famished mouths and hearts that
   thou shalt feed,
    And see thee worshipped as the world's
    delight.

There shall be no more wars nor kingdoms won,
But in thy sight whose eyes are as the sun
All names shall be one name, all nations
   one,
    All souls of men in man's one soul unite.

O sea whereon men labor, O great sea
That heaven seems one with, shall these
   things not be?
O earth, our earth, shall time not make us
   free?
    Cry wellaway, but well befall the right.

EPILOGUE.

BETWEEN the wave-ridge and the strand
I let you forth in sight of land,
   Songs that with storm-crossed wings and
     eyes
   Strain eastward till the darkness dies ;
Let signs and beacons fall or stand,
   And stars and balefires set and rise;
Ye, till some lordlier lyric hand
 · Weave the beloved brows their crown,
At the beloved feet lie down.

And whatsoever of life or light
Love hath to give you, what of might
   Or heart or hope is yours to live,
   I charge you take in trust to give
For very love's sake, in whose sight,
   Through poise of hours alternative
And seasons plumed with light or night,
   Ye live and move and have your breath,
   To sing with on the ridge of death.

I charge you faint not all night through
For love's sake that was breathed on you
   To be to you as wings and feet
   For travel, and as blood to heat
And sense of spirit to renew
   And bloom of fragrance to keep sweet
And fire of purpose to keep true
   The life, if life in such things be,
   That I would give you forth of me.

Out where the breath of war may bear,
Out in the rank moist reddened air
   That sounds and smells of death, and
     hath
   No light but death's upon its path
Seen through the black wind's tangled hair,
   I send you past the wild time's wrath
To find his face who bade you bear
   Fruit of his seed to faith and love,
   That he may take the heart thereof.

By day or night, by sea or street,
Fly till ye find and clasp his feet
   And kiss as worshippers who bring
   Too much love on their lips to sing,
But with hushed heads accept and greet
   The presence of some heavenlier thing
In the near air ; so may ye meet
   His eyes, and droop not utterly
   For shame's sake at the light you see.

Not utterly struck spiritless
For shame's sake and unworthiness
   Of these poor forceless hands that come
   Empty, these lips that should be dumb,
This love whose seal can but impress
   These weak word-offerings wearisome
Whose blessings have not strength to bless,
   Nor lightnings fire to burn up aught
   Nor smite with thunders of their thought.

One thought they have, even love ; one
     light,
Truth, that keeps clear the sun by night ;
   One chord, of faith as of a lyre ;
   One heat, of hope as of a fire ;
One heart, one music, and one might,
   One flame, one altar, and one choir ;
And one man's living head in sight
   Who said, when all time's sea was foam,
   "Let there be Rome,"—and there was
     Rome.

As a star set in space for token
Like a live word of God's mouth spoken,
   Visible sound, light audible,
   In the great darkness thick as hell
A stanchless flame of love unsloken,
   A sign to conquer and compel,
A law to stand in heaven unbroken
   Whereby the sun shines, and where
     through
   Time's eldest empires are made new

So rose up on our generations
That light of the most ancient nations,
   Law, life, and light, on the world's way,
   The very God of very day,
The sun-god ; from their star-like stations
   Far down the night in disarray
Fled, crowned with fires of tribulations,
   The suns of sunless years, whose light
   And life and law were of the night.

The naked kingdom quenched and stark
Drave with their dead things down the dark
   Helmless ; their whole world, throne by
     throne,
   Fell, and its whole heart turned to stone.
Hopeless ; their hands that touched our ark
   Withered ; and lo, aloft, alone,
On time's white waters man's one bark,
   Where the red sundawn's open eye
   Lit the soft gulf of low green sky.

So for a season piloted
It sailed the sunlight, and struck red
  With fire of dawn reverberate
  The wan face of incumbent fate
That paused half pitying overhead
And almost had foregone the freight
Of those dark hours the next day bred
  For shame, and almost had forsworn
  Service of night for love of morn.

Then broke the whole night in one blow,
Thundering ; then all hell with one throe
  Heaved, and brought forth beneath the
    stroke
  Death ; and all dead things moved and
    woke
That the dawn's arrows had brought low,
At the great sound of night that broke
Thundering, and all the old world-wide
    woe ;
  And under night's loud-sounding dome
  Men sought her, and she was not Rome.

Still with blind hands and robes blood-wet
Night hangs on heaven, reluctant yet,
  With black blood dripping from her eyes
  On the soiled lintels of the skies,
With brows and lips that thirst and threat,
  Heart-sick with fear lest the sun rise,
And aching with her fires that set,
  And shuddering eredawn bursts her bars,
  Burns out with all her beaten stars.

In this black wind of war they fly
Now, ere that hour be in the sky
  That brings back hope, and memory back,
  And light and law to lands that lack ;
That spiritual sweet hour whereby
  The bloody-handed night and black
Shall be cast out of heaven to die ;
  Kingdom by kingdom, crown by crown,
  The fires of darkness are blown down.

Yet heavy, grievous yet the weight
Sits on us of imperfect fate.
  From wounds of other days and deeds
  Still this day's breathing body bleeds ;
Still kings for fear and slaves for hate
  Sow lives of men on earth like seeds
In the red soil they saturate ;
  And we, with faces eastward set,
  Stand sightless of the morning yet.

And many for pure sorrow's sake
Look back and stretch back hands to take

Gifts of night's giving, ease and sleep,
Flowers of night's grafting, strong to
    steep
The soul in dreams it will not break,
  Songs of soft hours that sigh and sweep
Its lifted eyelids nigh to wake
  With subtle plumes and lulling breath
  That soothe its weariness to death.

And many, called of hope and pride,
Fall ere the sunrise from our side.
  Fresh lights and rumors of fresh fames
  That shift and veer by night like flames,
Shouts and blown trumpets, ghosts that
    glide
  Calling, and hail them by dead names,
Fears, angers, memories, dreams divide
  Spirit from spirit, and wear out
  Strong hearts of men with hope and
    doubt.

Till time beget and sorrow bear
The soul-sick eyeless child despair,
  That comes among us, mad and blind,
  With counsels of a broken mind,
Tales of times dead and woes that were,
  And, prophesying against mankind,
Shakes out the horror of her hair
  To take the sunlight with its coils
  And hold the living soul in toils.

By many ways of death and moods
Souls pass into their servitudes.
  Their young wings weaken, plume by
    plume
  Drops, and their eyelids gather gloom
And close against man's frauds and feuds,
  And their tongues call they know not
    whom
To help in their vicissitudes ;
  For many slaveries are, but one
  Liberty, single as the sun.

One light, one law, that burns up strife,
And one sufficiency of life.
  Self-stablished, the sufficing soul
  Hears the loud wheels of changes roll,
Sees against man man bare the knife,
  Sees the world severed, and is whole ;
Sees force take dowerless fraud to wife,
  And fear from fraud's incestuous bed
  Crawl forth and smite his father dead :

Sees death made drunk with war, sees time
Weave many-colored crime with crime,
  State overthrown on ruining state,
  And dares not be disconsolate.

Only the soul hath feet to climb,
  Only the soul hath room to wait
Hath brows and eyes to hold sublime
  Above all evil and all good,
  All strength and all decrepitude.

She only, she since earth began,
The many-minded soul of man,
  From one incognisable root
  That bears such divers-colored fruit,
Hath ruled for blessing or for ban
  The flight of seasons and pursuit ;
She regent, she republican,
  With wide and equal eyes and wings
  Broods on things born and dying things.

Even now for love or doubt of us
The hour intense and hazardous
  Hangs high with pinions vibrating
  Whereto the light and darkness cling
Dividing the dim season thus,
  And shakes from one ambiguous wing
Shadow, and one is luminous
  And day falls from it ; so the past
  Torments the future to the last.

And we that cannot hear or see
The sounds and lights of liberty,
  The witness of the naked God
  That treads on burning hours unshod
With instant feet unwounded ; we
  That can trace only where he trod
By fire in heaven or storm at sea,
  Not know the very present whole
  And naked nature of the soul ;,

We that see wars and woes and kings,
And portents of enormous things,
  Empires, and agonies, and slaves,
  And whole flame of town-swallowing
    graves ;
That hear the harsh hours clap sharp wings
  Above the roar of ranks like waves,
From wreck to wreck as the world swings ;
  Know but that men there are who see
  And hear things other far than we,

By the light sitting on their brows,
The fire wherewith their presence glows,
  The music falling with their feet,
  The sweet sense of a spirit sweet
That with their speech or motion grows
  And breathes and burns men's hearts
    with heat ;
By these signs there is none but knows
  Men who have life and grace to give,
  Men who have seen the soul and live.

By the strength sleeping in their eyes,
The lips wheron their sorrow lies
  Smiling, the lines of tears unshed,
  The large divine look of one dead
That speaks out of the breathless skies
  In silence, when the light is shed
Upon man's soul of memories ;
  The supreme look that sets love free,
  The look of stars and of the sea ;

By the strong patient godhead seen
Implicit in their mortal mien,
  The conscience of a God held still
  And thunders ruled by their own will
And fast-bound fires that might burn clean
  This worldly air that foul things fill,
And the afterglow of what has been,
  That, passing, shows us without word
  What they have seen, what they have
    heard ;

By all these keen and burning signs
The spirit knows them and divines.
  In bonds, in banishment, in grief,
  Scoffed at and scourged with unbelief,
Foiled with false trusts and thwart designs,
  Stripped of green days and hopes in leaf,
Their mere bare body of glory shines
  Higher, and man gazing surelier sees
  What light, what comfort is of these.

So I now gazing ; till the sense
Being set on fire of confidence
  Strains itself sunward, feels out far
  Beyond the bright and morning star,
Beyond the extreme wave's refluence,
  To where the fierce first sunbeams are
Whose fire intolerant and intense
  As birthpangs whence day burns to be
Parts breathless heaven from breathing sea.

I see not, know not, and am blest,
Master, who know that thou knowest,
  Dear lord and leader, at whose hand
  The first days and the last days stand,
With scars and crowns on head and breast,
  That fought for love of the sweet land
Or shall fight in her latter quest ;
  All the days armed and girt and crowned
  Whose glories ring thy glory round.

Thou sawest, when all the world was blind,
The light that should be of mankind,
  The very day that was to be ;
  And how shalt thou not sometime se.

Thy city perfect to thy mind
· Stand face to living face with thee,
And no miscrowned man's head behind ;
   The hearth of man, the human home,
   The central flame that shall be Rome ?

As one that ere a June day rise
Makes seaward for the dawn and tries
   The water with delighted limbs
   That taste the sweet dark sea and swims
Right eastward under strengthening skies,
   And sees the gradual rippling rims
Of waves whence day breaks blossom-wise
   Take fire ere light peer well above,
   And laughs from all his heart with love ;

And softlier swimming with raised head
Feels the full flower of morning shed
   And fluent sunrise round him rolled
   That laps and laves his body bold
With fluctuant heaven in water's stead,
   And urgent through the growing gold
Strikes, and sees all the spray flash red,
   And his soul takes the sun, and yearns
   For joy wherewith the sea's heart burns ;

So the soul seeking through the dark
Heavenward, a dove without an ark,

Transcends the unnavigable sea
Of years that wear out memory ;
So calls a sunward-singing lark,
   In the ear of souls that should be free ;
So points them toward the sun for mark
   Who steer not for the stress of waves,
   And seek strange helmsmen, and are
     slaves.

For if the swimmer's eastward eye
Must see no sunrise—must put by
   The hope that lifted him and led
   Once, to have light about his head,
To see beneath the clear low sky
   The green foam-whitened wave wax red
And all the morning's banner fly—
   Then, as earth's helpless hopes go down,
   Let earth's self in the dark tides drown.

Yea, if no morning must behold
Man, other than were they now cold,
   And other deeds than past deeds done,
   Nor any near or far-off sun
Salute him risen and sunlike-souled,
   Free, boundless, fearless, perfect, one,
Let man's world die like worlds of old,
   And here in heaven's sight only be
   The sole sun of a worldless sea.

POEMS AND BALLADS.

THE LAST ORACLE.

(A. D. 361.)

εἴπατε τῷ βασιλῆϊ, χαμαὶ πέσε δαίδαλος αὐλά ·
οὐκέτι Φοῖβος ἔχει καλύβαν, οὐ μάντιδα δάφνην,
οὐ παγὰν λαλέουσαν · ἀπέσβετο καὶ λάλον ὕδωρ.

YEARS have risen and fallen in darkness or
in twilight,
　Ages waxed and waned that knew not thee
nor thine,
While the world sought light by night and
sought not thy light,
　Since the sad last pilgrim left thy dark mid
shrine.
Dark the shrine and dumb the fount of song
thence welling,
　Save for words more sad than tears of
blood, that said:
*Tell the king, on earth has fallen the glorious
dwelling,*
　*And the watersprings that spake are quenched
and dead.*
Not a cell is left the God, no roof, no cover;
　*In his hand the prophet laurel flowers no
more.*
And the great king's high sad heart, thy true
last lover,
　Felt thine answer pierce and cleave it to
the core.
　And he bowed down his hopeless head
　　In the drift of the wild world's tide,
　And dying, *Thou hast conquered,* he said,
　　Galilean ; he said it, and died.
　And the world that was thine and was
ours
　　When the Graces took hands with the
Hours
　Grew cold as a winter wave
　In the wind from a wide-mouthed grave,
　　As a gulf wide open to swallow
　　　The light that the world held dear.
　O father of all of us, Paian, Apollo,
　　Destroyer and healer, hear !

Age on age thy mouth was mute, thy face
was hidden,
　And the lips and eyes that loved thee blind
and dumb;
Song forsook their tongues that held thy
name forbidden,

Light their eyes that saw the strange God's
kingdom come.
Fire for light and hell for heaven and psalms
for pæans
　Filled the clearest eyes and lips most sweet
of song,
When for chant of Greeks the wail of Gali-
leans
　Made the whole world moan with hymns of
wrath and wrong.
Yea, not yet we see thee, father, as they saw
thee,
　They that worshipped when the world was
theirs and thine,
They whose words had power by thine own
power to draw thee
　Down from heaven till earth seemed more
than heaven divine.
　For the shades are about us that hover
　　When darkness is half withdrawn
　And the skirts of the dead night cover
　　The face of the live new dawn.
　For the past is not utterly past
　Though the word on its lips be the last,
　　And the time be gone by with its creed
　When men were as beasts that bleed,
　　As sheep or as swine that wallow,
　　In the shambles of faith and of fear.
　O father of all of us, Paian, Apollo,
　　Destroyer and healer, hear !

Yet it may be, lord and father, could we know
it,
　We that love thee for our darkness shall
have light
More than ever prophet hailed of old or poet
　Standing crowned and robed and sovereign
in thy sight.
To the likeness of one God their dreams en-
thralled thee,
　Who wast greater than all Gods that waned
and grew;
Son of God the shining son of Time they
called thee,
　Who wast older, O our father, than they
knew.
For no thought of man made Gods to love or
honor
　Ere the song within the silent soul began,
Nor might earth in dream or deed take heaven
upon her

Till the word was clothed with speech by
   lips of man.
And the word and the life wast thou,
   The spirit of man and the breath;
And before thee the Gods that bow
   Take life as thine hands and death.
For these are as ghosts that wane,
That are gone in an age or twain;
Harsh, merciful, passionate, pure,
They perish, but thou shalt endure;
Be their life as the swan's or the swallow,
   They pass as the flight of a year.
O father of all of us, Paian, Apollo,
   Destroyer and healer, hear!

Thou the word, the light, the life, the breath,
   the glory,
   Strong to help and heal, to lighten and to
     slay,
Thine is all the song of man, the world's
   whole story ;
   Not of morning and of evening is thy day.
Old and younger Gods are buried or begotten
From uprising to downsetting of thy sun,
Risen from eastward, fallen to westward and
   forgotten,
   And their springs are many, but their end
     is one.
Divers births of godheads find one death ap-
   pointed,
   As the soul whence each was born makes
     room for each;
God by God goes out, discrowned and dis-
   anointed,
   But the soul stands fast that gave them
     shape and speech.
   Is the sun yet cast out of heaven ?
   Is the song yet cast out of man ?
   Life that had song for its leaven
     To quicken the blood that ran
Through the veins of the songless years
More bitter and cold than tears,
Heaven that had thee for its one
Light, life, word, witness, O sun,
Are they soundless and sightless and
   hollow,
   Without eye, without speech, without
     ear ?
O father of all of us, Paian, Apollo,
   Destroyer and healer, hear!

Time arose and smote thee silent at his warning,
   Change and darkness fell on men that fell
     from thee:
Dark thou satest, veiled with light, behind
   the morning,

Till the soul of man should lift up eyes
   and see.
Till the blind mute soul get speech again and
   eyesight,
Man may worship not the light of life within;
In his sight the stars whose fires grow dark in
   thy sight
   Shine as sunbeams on the night of death
     and sin.
Time again is risen with mightier word of
   warning,
   Change hath blown again a blast of louder
     breath;
Clothed with clouds and stars and dreams that
   melt in morning,
   Lo, the Gods that ruled by grace of sin and
     death !
   They are conquered, they break, they
     are stricken,
     Whose might made the whole world
      pale;
   They are dust that shall rise not or
     quicken
     Though the world for their death's sake
      wail.
   As a hound on a wild beast's trace,
   So time as their godhead in chase ;
   As wolves when the hunt makes head,
   They are scattered, they fly, they are fled;
   They are fled beyond hail, beyond hollo.
     And the cry of the chase, and the cheer.
O father of all of us, Paian, Apollo,
   Destroyer and healer, hear !
Day by day thy shadow shines in heaven be-
   holden,
   Even the sun, the shining shadow of thy
     face :
King, the ways of heaven before thy feet grow
   golden ;
   God, the soul of earth is kindled with thy
     grace.
In thy lips the speech of man whence Gods
   were fashioned,
   In thy soul the thought that makes them
     and unmakes ;
By thy light and heat incarnate and impas-
   sioned,
   Soul to soul of man gives light for light and
     takes.
As they knew thy name of old time could we
   know it,
   Healer called of sickness, slayer invoked of
     wrong,
Light of eyes that saw thy light, God, king,
   priest, poet,
   Song should bring thee back to heal us with
     thy song.

For thy kingdom is past not away,
  Nor thy power from the place thereof
    hurled ;
Out of heaven they shall cast not the day,
  They shall cast not out song from the
    world.
By the song and the light they give
We know thy works that they live ;
With the gift thou hast given us of speech
We praise, we adore, we beseech,
  We arise at thy bidding and follow,
    We cry to thee, answer, appear,
O father of all of us, Paian, Apollo,
  Destroyer and healer, hear !

IN THE BAY.

I .

BEYOND the hollow sunset, ere a star
Take heart in heaven from eastward, while
  the west
Fulfilled of watery resonance and rest,
Is as a port with clouds for harbor bar
To fold the fleet in of the winds from far
That stir no plume now of the bland sea's
  breast;

II.

Above the soft sweep of the breathless bay
Southwestward, far past flight of night and
  day,
Lower than the sunken sunset sinks, and
  higher
Than dawn can freak the front of heaven with
  fire,
My thought with eyes and wings made wide
  makes way
To find the place of souls that I desire.

III.

If any place for any soul there be,
Disrobed and disentrammelled ; if the might,
The fire and force that filled with ardent light
The souls whose shadow is half the light we
  see,
Survive and be suppressed not of the night ;
This hour should show what all day hid from
  me.

IV.

Night knows not, neither is it shown to day,
By sunlight nor by starlight is it shown,
Nor to the full moon's eve nor footfall known,

Their world's untrodden and unkindled way.
Nor is the breath nor music of it blown
With sounds of winter or with winds of May.

V.

But here, where light and darkness reconciled
Hold earth between them as a weanling child
Between the balanced hands of death and
  birth,
Even as they held the new-born shape of earth
When first life trembled in her limbs and
  smiled,
Here hope might think to find what hope were
  worth.

VI.

Past Hades, past Elysium, past the long
Slow smooth strong lapse of Lethe—past the
  toil
Wherein all souls are taken as a spoil,
The Stygian web of waters—if your song
Be quenched not, O our brethren, but be strong
As ere ye too shook off our temporal coil ;

VII.

If yet these twain survive your worldly breath,
Joy trampling sorrow, life devouring death,
If perfect life possess your life all through
And like your words your souls be deathless
  too,
To-night, of all whom night encompasseth,
My soul would commune with one soul of you.

VIII.

Above the sunset might I see thine eyes
That were above the sundawn in our skies,
Son of the songs of morning,—thine that were
First lights to lighten that rekindling air
Where through men saw the front of England
  rise
And heard thine loudest of the lyre-notes
  there—

IX.

If yet thy fire have not one spark the less,
O Titan, born of her a Titaness,
Across the sunrise and the sunset's mark
Send of thy lyre one sound, thy fire one spark,
To change this face of our unworthiness,
Across this hour dividing light from dark.

X.

To change this face of our chill time, that hears
No song like thine of all that crowd its ears,
Of all its lights that lighten all day long

Sees none like thy most fleet and fiery sphere's
Outlightening Sirius—in its twilight throng
No thunder and no sunrise like thy song.

XI.

Hath not the sea-wind swept the sea-line bare
To pave with stainless fire through stainless
    air
A passage for thine heavenlier feet to tread
Ungrieved of earthly floor work? hath it spread
No covering splendid as the sun-god's hair
To veil or to reveal thy lordlier head?

XII.

Hath not the sunset shown across the sea
A way majestical enough for thee?
What hour save this should be thine hour—
    and mine,
If thou have care of any less divine
Than thine own soul ; if thou take thought of
    me,
Marlowe, as all my soul takes thought of thine?

XIII.

Before the moon's face as before the sun
The morning star and evening star are one
For all men's lands as England. O, if night
Hang hard upon us,—ere our day take flight,
Shed thou some comfort from thy day long
    done
On us pale children of the latter light !

XIV.

For surely, brother and master and lord and
    king,
Where'er thy footfall and thy face make spring
In all souls' eyes that meet thee wheresoe'er,
And have thy soul for sunshine and sweet air—
Some late love of thine old live land should
    cling,
Some living love of England, round thee there.

XV.

Here from her shore across her sunniest sea
My soul makes question of the sun for thee,
And waves and beams make answer. When
    thy feet
Made her ways flowerier and their flowers
    more sweet
With childlike passage of a god to be,
Like spray these waves cast off her foemen's
    fleet.

XVI.

Like foam they flung it from her, and like weed
Its wrecks were washed from scornful shoal to
    shoal,
From rock to rock reverberate ; and the whole
Sea laughed and lightened with a deathless
    deed
That sowed our enemies in her field for seed
And made her shores fit harborage for thy soul.

XVII.

Then in her green south fields, a poor man's
    child,
Thou hast thy short sweet fill of half-blown
    joy,
That ripens all of us for time to cloy
With full-blown pain and passion; ere the
    wild
World caught thee by the fiery heart, and
    smiled
To make so swift end of the godlike boy.

XVIII.

For thou, if ever godlike foot there trod
These fields of ours, wert surely like a god.
Who knows what splendor of strange dreams
    was shed
With sacred shadow and glimmer of gold and
    red
From hallowed windows, over stone and sod,
On thine unbowed bright insubmissive head?

XIX.

The shadow stayed not, but the splendor stays.
Our brother, till the last of English days.
No day nor night on English earth shall be
For ever, spring nor summer, Junes nor Mays,
But somewhat as a sound or gleam of thee
Shall come on us like morning from the sea.

XX.

Like sunrise never wholly risen, nor yet
Quenched; or like sunset never wholly set,
A light to lighten as from living eyes
The cold unlit close lids of one that lies
Dead, or a ray returned from death's far skies
To fire us living lest our lives forget.

XXI.

For in that heaven what light of lights may be,
What splendor of what stars, what spheres of
    flame

Sounding, that none may number nor may
    name,
We know not, even thy brethren; yea, not we
Whose eyes desire the light that lightened thee,
Whose ways and thine are one way and the
    same.

XXII.

But if the riddles that in sleep we read,
And trust them not, be flattering truth indeed,
As he that rose our mightiest called them,—he,
Much higher than thou as thou much higher
    than we—
There, might we say, all flower of all our
    seed,
All singing souls are as one sounding sea.

XXIII.

All those that here were of thy kind and kin,
Beside thee and below thee, full of love,
Full-souled for song,—and one alone above
Whose only light folds all your glories in—
With all birds' notes frum nightingale to dove
Fill the world whither we too fain would win.

XXIV.

The world that sees in heaven the sovereign
    light
Of sunlike Shakespeare, and the fiery night
Whose stars were watched of Webster; and
    beneath,
The twin-souled brethren of the single wreath,
Grown in king's gardens, plucked from
    pastoral heath,
Wrought with all flowers for all men's heart's
    delight.

XXV.

And that fixed fervor, iron-red like Mars,
In the mid moving tide of tenderer stars,
That burned on loves and deeds the darkest
    done,
Athwart the incestuous prisoner's bride-house
    bars ;
And thine, most highest of all their fires but
    one,
Our morning star, sole risen before the sun.

XXVI.

And one light risen since theirs to run such
    race
Thou has seen, O Phoshor, from thy pride of
    place.

Thou hast seen Shelley, him that was to thee
As light to fire or dawn to lightning ; me,
Me likewise, O our brother, shall thou see,
And I behold thee, face to glorious face?

XXVII.

You twain the same swift year of manhood
    swept.
Down the steep darkness, and our father
    wept.
And from the gleam of Apollonian tears
A holier aureole rounds your memories, kept
Most fervent-fresh of all the singing spheres,
And April-colored through all months and
    years.

XXVIII.

You twain fate spared not half your fiery span;
The longer date fulfils the lesser man
Ye from beyond the dark dividing date
Stand smiling, crowned as gods with foot on
    fate.
For stronger was your blessing than his ban,
And earliest whom he struck, he struck too
    late.

XXIX.

Yet love and loathing, faith and unfaith yet
Bind less to greater souls in unison,
And one desire that makes three spirits as
    one
Takes great and small as in one spiritual net
Woven out of hope toward what shall yet be
    done
Ere hate or love remember or forget.

XXX.

Woven out of faith and hope and love too
    great
To bear the bonds of life and death and fate:
Woven out of love and hope and faith too
    dear
To take the print of doubt and change and
    fear:
And interwoven with lines of wrath and hate
Blood-red with soils of many a sanguine year.

XXXI.

Who cannot hate, can love not; if he grieve,
His tears are barren as the unfruitful rain
That rears no harvest from the green sea's
    plain,

And as thorns crackling this man's laugh is
vain.
Nor can belief touch, kindle, smite, reprieve
His heart who has not heart to disbelieve.

XXXII.

But you, most perfect in your hate and love,
Our great twin-spirited brethren; you that
stand
Head by head glittering, hand made fast in
hand,
And underfoot the fang-drawn worm that
strove
To wound you living; from so far above,
Look love, not scorn, on ours that was our
land.

XXXIII.

For love we lack, and help and heat and light
To clothe us and to comfort us with might.
What help is ours to take or give? but ye—
O, more than sunrise to the blind cold sea,
That wailed aloud with all her waves all night,
Much more, being much more glorious, should
you be.

XXXIV.

As fire to frost, as ease to toil, as dew
To flowerless fields, as sleep to slackening
pain,
As hope to souls long weaned from hope
again
Returning, or as blood revived anew
To dry-drawn limbs and every pulseless vein,
Even so toward us should no man be but you.

XXXV.

One rose before the sunrise was, and one
Before the sunset, lovelier than the sun.
And now the heaven is dark and bright and
loud
With wind and starry drift and moon and
cloud,
And night's cry rings in straining sheet and
shroud,
What help is ours if hope like yours be none?

XXXVI.

O well-beloved, our brethren, if ye be,
Then are we not forsaken. This kind earth
Made fragrant once for all time with your
birth,

And bright for all men with your love, and
worth
The clasp and kiss and wedlock of the sea,
Were not your mother if not your brethren
we.

XXXVII.

Because the days were dark with gods and
kings
And in time's hand the old hours of time as
rods,
When force and fear set hope and faith at
odds,
Ye failed not nor abased your plume-plucked
wings;
And we that front not more disastrous things,
How should we fail in face of kings and gods?

XXXVIII.

For now the deep dense plumes of night are
thinned
Surely with winnowing of the glimmering wind
Whose feet are fledged with morning; and the
breath
Begins in heaven that sings the dark to death.
And all the night wherein men groaned and
sinned
Sickens at heart to hear what sundawn saith.

XXXIX.

O first-born sons of hope and fairest, ye
Whose prows first clove the thought-un-
sounded sea
Whence all the dark dead centuries rose to
bar
The spirit of man lest truth should make him
free,
The sunrise and the sunset, seeing one star,
Take heart as we to know you that ye are.

XL.

Ye rise not and ye set not; we that say
Ye rise and set like hopes that set and rise
Look yet but seaward from a land-locked bay;
But where at last the sea's line is the sky's
And truth and hope one sunlight in your eyes,
No sunrise and no sunset marks their day.

A FORSAKEN GARDEN.

In a coign of the cliff between lowland and
highland,
   At the sea-down's edge between windward
   and lee,

15

Walled round with rocks as an inland island,
 The ghost of a garden fronts the sea.
A girdle of brushwood and thorn encloses
 The steep square slope of the blossomless
  bed
Where the weeds that grew green from the
  graves of its roses
   Now lie dead.

The fields fall southward, abrupt and broken,
 To the low last edge of the long lone land.
If a step should sound or a word be spoken,
 Would a ghost not rise at the strange guest's
  hand?
So long have the gray bare walks lain guest-
  less,
 Through branches and briers if a man make
  way,
He shall find no life but the sea-wind's, restless
  Night and day.

The dense hard passage is blind and stifled
 That crawls by a track none turn to climb
To the strait waste place that the years have
  rifled
 Of all but the thorns that are touched not
  of time.
The thorns he spares when the rose is taken;
 The rocks are left when he wastes the
  plain.
The wind that wanders, the weeds wind-
  shaken,
   These remain.

Not a flower to be prest of the foot that falls
  not;
 As the heart of a dead man the seed-plots
  are dry;
From the thicket of thorns whence the night-
  ingale calls not,
 Could she call, there were never a rose to
  reply.
Over the meadows that blossom and wither
 Rings but the note of a sea-bird's song;
Only the sun and the rain come hither
  All year long.

The sun burns sere and the rain dishevels
 One gaunt bleak blossom of scentless breath.
Only the wind here hovers and revels
 In a round where life seems barren as death.
Here there was laughing of old, there was
  weeping,
Haply, of lovers none ever will know,
 Whose eyes went seaward a hundred
  sleeping
   Years ago.

Heart handfast in heart as they stood, 'Look
  thither,'
 Did he whisper? 'Look forth from the
  flowers to the sea;
For the foam-flowers endure when the rose-
  blossoms wither,
 And men that love lightly may die—but we?'
And the same wind sang and the same waves
  whitened,
 And or ever the garden's last petals were
  shed,
In the lips that had whispered, the eyes that
  had lightened,
   Love was dead.

Or they loved their life through, and then
  went whither?
 And were one to the end—but what end
  who knows?
Love deep as the sea as a rose must wither,
 As the rose-red seaweed that mocks the
  rose.
Shall the dead take thought for the dead to
  love them?
 What love was ever as deep as a grave?
They are loveless now as the grass above
  them
   Or the wave.

All are at one now, roses and lovers,
 Not known of the cliffs and the fields and
  the sea.
Not a breath of the time that has been hovers
 In the air now soft with a summer to be.
Not a breath shall there sweeten the seasons
  hereafter
 Of the flowers or the lovers that laugh now
  or weep,
When as they that are free now of weeping
  and laughter
   We shall sleep.

Here death may deal not again forever;
 Here change may come not till all change
  end.
From the graves they have made they shall
  rise up never,
 Who have left nought living to ravage and
  rend.
Earth, stones, and thorns of the wild ground
  growing,
 While the sun and the rain live, these shall
  be;
Till a last wind's breath upon all these blow-
  ing
   Roll the sea.

Till the slow sea rise and the sheer cliff
  crumble,
  Till terrace and meadow the deep gulfs
  drink,
Till the strength of the waves of the high
  tides humble
The fields that lessen, the rocks that shrink,
Here now in his triumph where all things
  falter,
  Stretched out on the spoils that his own
  hand spread,
As a god self-slain on his own strange altar,
  Death lies dead.

RELICS.

THIS flower that smells of honey and the sea,
White laurustine, seems in my hand to be
  A white star made of memory long ago
Lit in the heaven of dear times dead to me.

A star out of the skies love used to know
Here held in hand, a stray left yet to show
  What flowers my heart was full of in the
  days
That are long since gone down dead memory's
  flow.

Dead memory that revives on doubtful ways,
Half hearkening what the buried season says
  Out of the world of the unapparent dead
Where the lost Aprils are, and the lost
  Mays.

Flower, once I knew thy star-white brethren
  bred
Nigh where the last of all the land made
  head
  Against the sea, a keen-faced promontory,
Flowers on salt wind and sprinkled sea-dews
  fed.

Their hearts were glad of the free place's
  glory;
The wind that sang them all his stormy story
  Had talked all winter to the sleepless
  spray,
And as the sea's their hues were hard and
  hoary.

Like things born of the sea and the bright
  day,
They laughed out at the years that could not
  slay,
  Live sons and joyous of unquiet hours,
And stronger than all storms that range for
  prey.

And in the close indomitable flowers
A keen-edged odor of the sun and showers
  Was as the smell of the fresh honeycomb
Made sweet for mouths of none but para
  mours.

Out of the hard green wall of leaves that
  clomb
They showed like windfalls of the snow-soft
  foam,
  Or feathers from the weary south-wind's
  wing,
Fair as the spray that it came shoreward
  from.

And thou, as white, what word hast thou to
  bring?
If my heart hearken, whereof wilt thou sing?
  For some sign surely thou too hast to bear,
Some word far south was taught thee of the
  spring.

White like a white rose, not like these that
  were
Taught of the wind's mouth and the winter
  air,
  Poor tender thing of soft Italian bloom,
Where once thou grewest, what else for me
  grew there.

Born in what spring and on what city's tomb,
By whose hand wast thou reached, and
  plucked for whom?
  There hangs about thee, could the soul's
  sense tell,
An odor as of love and of love's doom.

Of days more sweet than thou wast sweet to
  smell,
Of flower-soft thoughts that came to flower
  and fell,
  Of loves that lived a lily's life and died,
Of dreams now dwelling where dead roses
  dwell.

O white birth of the golden mountain-side
That for the sun's love makes its bosom wide
  At sunrise, and with all its woods and
  flowers
Takes in the morning to its heart of pride!

Thou hast a word of that one land of ours,
And of the fair town called of the fair towers,
  A word for me of my San Gimignan,
A word of April's greenest-girdled hours.

Of the breached walls whereon the wall-
flowers ran
Called of Saint Fina, breachless now of man,
   Though time with soft feet break them
      stone by stone,
Who breaks down hour by hour his own
      reign's span.

Of the cliff overcome and overgrown
That all that flowerage clothed as flesh clothes
      bone,
   That garment of acacias made for May,
Whereof here lies one witness overblown.

The fair brave trees with all their flowers at
      play,
How king-like they stood up into the day!
   How sweet the day was with them, and the
      night!
Such words of message have dead flowers to
      say.

This that the winter and the wind made
      bright,
And this that lived upon Italian light,
   Before I throw them and these words away,
Who knows but I what memories too take
      flight?

AT A MONTH'S END.

THE night last night was strange and shaken:
   More strange the change of you and me.
Once more, for the old love's love forsaken,
   We went out once more toward the sea.

For the old love's love-sake dead and buried,
   One last time, one more and no more,
We watched the waves set in, the serried
   Spears of the tide storming the shore.

Hardly we saw the high moon hanging,
   Heard hardly through the windy night
Far waters ringing, low reefs clanging,
   Under wan skies and waste white light.

With chafe and change of surges chiming.
   The clashing channels rocked and rang
Large music, wave to wild wave timing,
   And all the choral water sang.

Faint lights fell this way, that way floated,
   Quick sparks of sea-fire keen like eyes
From the rolled surf that flashed, and noted
   Shores and faint cliffs and bays and skies.

The ghost of sea that shrank up sighing
   At the sand's edge, a short sad breath
Trembling to touch the goal, and dying
   With weak heart heaved up once in death—

The rustling sand and shingle shaken
   With light sweet touches and small sound—
These could not move us, could not waken
   Hearts to look forth, eyes to look round.

Silent we went an hour together,
   Under gray skies by waters white.
Our hearts were full of windy weather,
   Clouds and blown stars and broken light.

Full of cold clouds and moonbeams drifted
   And streaming storms and straying fires,
Our souls in us were stirred and shifted
   By doubts and dreams and foiled desires.

Across, aslant, a scudding sea-mew
   Swam, dipped, and dropped, and grazed
      the sea :
And one with me I could not dream you ;
   And one with you I could not be.

As the white wing the white wave's fringes
   Touched and slid over and flashed past—
As a pale cloud a pale flame tinges
   From the moon's lowest light and last—

As a star feels the sun and falters,
   Touched to death by diviner eyes—
As on the old gods' untended altars
   The old fire of withered worship dies—

(Once only, once the shrine relighted
   Sees the last fiery shadow shine,
Last shadow of flame and faith benighted,
   Sees falter and flutter and fail the shrine)

So once with fiery breath and flying
   Your winged heart touched mine and went,
And the swift spirits kissed, and sighing,
   Sundered and smiled and were content.

That only touch, that feeling only,
   Enough we found, we found too much;
For the unlit shrine is hardly lonely
   As one the old fire forgets to touch.

Slight as the sea's sight of the sea-mew,
   Slight as the sun's sight of the star :
Enough to show one must not deem you
   For love's sake other than you are.

Who snares and tames with fear and danger
   A bright beast of a fiery kin,

Only to mar, only to change her
  Sleek supple soul and splendid skin?

Easy with blows to mar and maim her,
  Easy with bonds to bind and bruise ;
What profit, if she yield her tamer
  The limbs to mar, the soul to lose?

Best leave or take the perfect creature,
  Take all she is or leave complete ;
Transmute you will not form or feature,
  Change feet for wings or wings for feet.

Strange eyes, new limbs, can no man give
    her ;
  Sweet is the sweet thing as it is.
No soul she hath, we see, to outlive her ;
  Hath she for that no lips to kiss?

So may one read his weird, and reason,
  And with vain drugs assuage no pain.
For each man in his loving season
  Fools and is fooled of these in vain.

Charms that allay not any longing,
  Spells that appease not any grief,
Time brings us all by handfuls, wronging
  All hurts with nothing of relief.

Ah, too soon shot, the fool's bolt misses !
  What help? the world is full of loves ;
Night after night of running kisses,
  Chirp after chirp of changing doves.

Should Love disown or disesteem you
  For loving one man more or less ?
You could not tame your light white sea-mew,
  Nor I my sleek black pantheress.

For a new soul let whoso please pray,
  We are what life made us, and shall be.
For you the jungle and me the sea-spray,
  And south for you and north for me.

But this one broken foam-white feather
  I throw you off the hither wing,
Splashed stiff with sea-scurf and salt weather,
  This song for sleep to learn and sing—

Sing in your ear when, daytime over,
  You, couched at long length on hot sand
With some sleek sun-discolored lover,
  Wince from his breath as from a brand:

Till the acrid hour aches out and ceases,
  And the sheathed eyeball sleepier swims,
The deep flank smooths its dimpling creases,
  And passion loosens all the limbs :

Till dreams of sharp gray north-sea weather
  Fall faint upon your fiery sleep,
As on strange sands a strayed bird's feather
  The wind may choose to lose or keep.

But I, who leave my queen of panthers,
  As a tired honey-heavy bee
Gilt with sweet dust from gold-grained anthers
  Leaves the rose-chalice, what for me ?

From the ardors of the chaliced centre,
  From the amorous anthers' golden grime,
That scorch and smutch all wings that enter,
  I fly forth hot from honey-time.

But as to a bee's gilt thighs and winglets
  The flower-dust with the flower-smell clings;
As a snake's mobile rampant ringlets
  Leave the sand marked with print of rings;

So to my soul in surer fashion
  Your savage stamp and savor hangs ;
The print and perfume of old passion,
  The wild-beast mark of panther's fangs.

SESTINA.

I SAW my soul at rest upon a day
  As the bird sleeping in the nest of night,
Among soft leaves that give the starlight way
  To touch its wings but not its eyes with light;
So that it knew as one in visions may,
  And knew not as men waking, of delight.

This was the measure of my soul's delight ;
  It had no power of joy to fly by day,
Nor part in the large lordship of the light ;
  But in a secret moon-beholden way
Had all its will of dreams and pleasant night,
  And all the love and life that sleepers may.

But such life's triumph as men waking may
  It might not have to feed its faint delight
Between the stars by night and sun by day,
  Shut up with green leaves and a little light;
Because its way was as a lost star's way,
  A world's not wholly known of day or night.

All loves and dreams and sounds and gleams
    of night
  Made it all music that such minstrels may,
And all they had they gave it of delight;
  But in the full face of the fire of day
What place shall be for any starry light, ·
  What part of heaven in all the wide sun's
    way ?

Yet the soul woke not, sleeping by the way,
  Watched as a nursling of the large-eyed
      night,
And sought no strength nor knowledge of the
      day,
  Nor closer touch conclusive of delight,
Nor mightier joy nor truer than dreamers may,
  Nor more of song than they, nor more of
      light.
For who sleeps once and sees the secret light
  Whereby sleep shows the soul a fairer way
Between the rise and rest of day and night,
  Shall care no more to fare as all men may,
But he is place of pain or of delight,
  There shall he dwell, beholding night as
      day.

Song, have thy day and take thy fill of light
  Before the night be fallen across thy way;
Sing while he may, man hath no long delight.

THE YEAR OF THE ROSE.

From the depths of the green garden-closes
Where the summer in darkness dozes
  Till autumn pluck from his hand
  An hour-glass that holds not a sand ;
From the maze that a flower-belt encloses
  To the stones and sea-grass on the strand
How red was the reign of the roses
  Over the rose-crowned land !

The year of the rose is brief ;
From the first blade blown to the sheaf,
  From the thin green leaf to the gold,
  It has time to be sweet and grow old,
To triumph and leave not a leaf
  For witness in winter's sight
  How lovers once in the light
Would mix their breath with its breath,
  And its spirit was quenched not of night,
As love is subdued not of death.

In the red-rose land not a mile
Of the meadows from stile to stile,
  Of the valleys from stream to stream,
  But the air was a long sweet dream
And the earth was a sweet wide smile
  Red-mouthed of a goddess, returned
  From the sea which had borne her and
      burned,
That with one swift smile of her mouth
  Looked full on the north as it yearned,
And the north was more than the south.

For the north, when winter was long,
In his heart had made him a song,
  And clothed it with wings of desire,
  And shod it with shoon as of fire,
To carry the tale of his wrong
  To the south-west wind by the sea,
  That who might bear it but he
To the ears of the goddess unknown
  Who waits till her time shall be
To take the world for a throne ?

In the earth beneath, and above
In the heaven where her name is love,
  She warms with light from her eyes
  The seasons of life as they rise,
And her eyes are as eyes of a dove,
  But the wings that lift her and bear
  As an eagle's, and all her hair
As fire by wind's breath curled,
  And her passage is song through the air,
And her presence is spring through the world.

So turned she northward and came,
And the white-thorn land was aflame
  With the fires that were shed from her feet,
  That the north, by her love made sweet,
Should be called by a rose-red name ;
  And a murmur was heard as of doves,
  And a music beginning of loves
In the light that the roses made,
  Such light as the music loves.
The music of man with maid.

But the days drop one upon one,
And a chill soft wind is begun
  In the heart of the rose-red maze
  That weeps for the roseleaf days
And the reign of the rose undone
  That ruled so long in the light,
  And by spirit, and not by sight,
Through the darkness thrilled with its breath,
  Still ruled in the viewless night,
As love might rule over death.

The time of lovers is brief ;
From the fair first joy to the grief
  That tells when love is grown old,
  From the warm wild kiss to the cold,
From the red to the white-rose leaf,
  They have but a season to seem
  As roseleaves lost on a stream
That part not and pass not apart
  As a spirit from dream to dream,
As a sorrow from heart to heart.

From the bloom and the gloom that encloses
The death-bed of Love where he dozes

Till a relic be left not of sand
To the hour-glass that breaks in his hand ;
From the change in the gray garden-closes
To the last stray grass of the strand,
A rain and ruin of roses
Over the red rose-land.

A WASTED VIGIL.

I.

COULDST thou not watch with me one hour?
Behold,
Dawn skims the sea with flying feet of gold,
With sudden feet that graze the gradual sea ;
Couldst thou not watch with me?

II.

What, not one hour? for star by star the night
Falls, and her thousands world by world take
flight;
They die, and day survives, and what of thee ?
Couldst thou not watch with me?

III.

Lo, far in heaven the web of night undone,
And on the sudden sea the gradual sun ;
Wave to wave answers, tree responds to tree ;
Couldst thou not watch with me?

IV.

Sunbeam by sunbeam creeps from line to line,
Foam by foam quickens on the brightening
brine ;
Sail by sail passes, flower by flower gets free ;
Couldst thou not watch with me?

V.

Last year, a brief while since, an age ago,
A whole year past, with bud and bloom and
snow,
O moon that wast in heaven, what friends
were we !
Couldst thou not watch with me?

VI.

Old moons, and last year's flowers, and last
year's snows
Who now saith to thee, moon ? or who saith,
rose ?
O dust and ashes, once found fair to see !
Couldst thou not watch with me?

VII.

O dust and ashes, once thought sweet to
smell !
With me it is not, is it with thee well ?
O sea-drift blown from windward back to lee !
Couldst thou not watch with me?

VIII.

The old year's dead hands are full of their
dead flowers,
The old days are full of dead old loves of ours.
Born as a rose, and briefer born than she;
Couldst thou not watch with me?

IX.

Could two days live again of that dead year,
One would say, seeking us and passing here,
Where is she? and one answering, *Where is
he?*
Couldst thou not watch with me?

X.

Nay, those two lovers are not anywhere;
If we were they, none knows us what we were,
Nor aught of all their barren grief and glee.
Couldst thou not watch with me?

XI.

Half false, half fair, all feeble, be my verse
Upon thee not for blessing nor for curse
For some must stand, and some must fall or
flee;
Couldst thou not watch with me?

XII.

As a new moon above spent stars thou wast;
But stars endure after the moon is past.
Couldst thou not watch one hour, though I
watch three ?
Couldst thou not watch with me?

XIII.

What of the night? The night is full, the
tide
Storms inland, the most ancient rocks divide;
Yet some endure, and bow nor head nor
knee;
Couldst thou not watch with me?

XIV.

Since thou art not as these are, go thy ways
Thou hast no part in all my nights and days.
Lie still, sleep on, be glad—as such things
be;
Thou couldst not watch with me.

THE COMPLAINT OF LISA.

(*Double Sestina*.)

DECAMERON, X. 7.

THERE is no woman living that draws breath
So sad as I, though all things sadden her.
There is not one upon life's weariest way
Who is weary as I am weary of all but death.
Toward whom I look as looks the sunflower
All day with all his whole soul toward the sun;
While in the sun's sight I make moan all day,
And all night on my sleepless maiden bed
Weep and call out on death, O Love, and thee,
That thou or he would take me to the dead,
And know not what thing evil I have done
That life should lay such heavy hand on me.

Alas, Love, what is this thou wouldst with me?
What honor shalt thou have to quench my breath,
Or what shall my heart broken profit thee?
O Love, O great god Love, what have I done,
That thou shouldst hunger so after my death?
My heart is harmless as my life's first day:
Seek out some false fair woman, and plague her
Till her tears even as my tears fill her bed:
I am the least flower in thy flowery way,
But till my time be come that I be dead
Let me live out my flower-time in the sun
Though my leaves shut before the sunflower.

O Love, Love, Love, the kingly sunflower!
Shall he the sun hath looked on look on me,
That live down here in shade, out of the sun,
Here living in the sorrow and shadow of death?
Shall he that feeds his heart full of the day
Care to give mine eyes light, or my lips breath?
Because she loves him shall my lord love her
Who is as a worm in my lord's kingly way?
I shall not see him or know him alive or dead;
But thou, I know thee, O Love, and pray to thee
That in brief while my brief life-days be done,
And the worm quickly make my marriage-bed.

For underground there is no sleepless bed:
But here since I beheld my sunflower
These eyes have slept not, seeing all night and day
His sunlike eyes, and face fronting the sun.
Wherefore if anywhere be any death,
I would fain find and fold him fast to me,
That I may sleep with the world's eldest dead,
With her that died seven centuries since, and her
That went last night down the night-wandering way.
For this is sleep indeed, when labor is done,
Without love, without dreams, and without breath,
And without thought, O name unnamed! of thee.

Ah, but, forgetting all things, shall I thee?
Wilt thou not be as now about my bed.
There underground as here before the sun?
Shall not thy vision vex me alive and dead,
Thy moving vision without form or breath?
I read long since the bitter tale of her
Who read the tale of Launcelot on a day,
And died, and had no quiet after death,
But was moved ever along a weary way,
Lost with her love in the underworld; ah me,
O my king, O my lordly sunflower,
Would God to me too such a thing were done!

But if such sweet and bitter things be done,
Then, flying from life, I shall not fly from thee,
For in that living world without a sun
Thy vision will lay hold upon me dead,
And meet and mock me, and mar my peace in death.
Yet if being wroth God had such pity on her,
Who was a sinner and foolish in her day,
That even in hell they twain should breathe one breath,
Why should he not in some wise pity me?
So if I sleep not in my soft strait bed
I may look up and see my sunflower
As he the sun, in some divine strange way.

O poor my heart, well knowest thou in what way
This sore sweet evil unto us was done.
For on a holy and a heavy day
I was arisen out of my still small bed
To see the knights tilt, and one said to me
'The king,' and seeing him, somewhat stopped my breath,
And if the girl spake more, I heard not her,

For only I saw what I shall see when dead,
A kingly flower of knights, a sunflower,
That shown against the sunlight like the sun,
And like a fire, O heart, consuming thee,
The fire of love that lights the pyre of death.

Howbeit I shall not die an evil death
Who have loved in such a sad and sinless
    way,
That this my love, lord, was no shame to thee.
So when mine eyes are shut against the sun,
O my soul's sun, O the world's sunflower,
Thou nor no man will quite despise me dead.
And dying I pray with all my low last breath
That thy whole life may be as was that day,
That feast-day that made troth-plight death
    and me,
Giving the world light of thy great deeds
    done ;
And that fair face brightening thy bridal bed,
That God be good as God hath been to her.

That all things goodly and glad remain with
    her,
All things that make glad life and goodly
    death ;
That as a bee sucks from a sunflower
Honey, when summer draws delighted breath,
Her soul may drink of thy soul in like way,
And love make life a fruitful marriage-bed
Where day may bring forth fruits of joy to
    day
And night to night till days and nights be
    dead.
And as she gives light of her love to thee,
Give thou to her the old glory of days long
    done ;
And either give some heat of light to me,
To warm me where I sleep without the sun.

O sunflower made drunken with the sun,
O knight whose lady's heart draws thine to
    her,
Great king, glad lover, I have a word to thee.
There is a weed lives out of the sun's way,
Hid from the heat deep in the meadow's bed,
That swoons and whitens at the wind's least
    breath,
A flower star-shaped, that all a summer day
Will gaze her soul out on the sunflower
For very love till twilight finds her dead.
But the great sunflower heeds not her poor
    death,
Knows not when all her loving life is done ;
And so much knows my lord the king of me.

Aye, all day long he has no eye for me ;
With golden eye following the golden sun

From rose-colored to purple-pillowed bed,
From birthplace to the flame-lit place of
    death,
From eastern end to western of his way.
So mine eye follows thee, my sunflower,
So the white star-flower turns and yearns to
    thee,
The sick weak weed, not well alive or dead,
Trod underfoot if any pass by her,
Pale, without color of summer or summer
    breath
In the shrunk shuddering petals, that have
    done
No work but love, and die before the day.

But thou, to-day, to-morrow, and every day,
Be glad and great, O love whose love slays
    me.
Thy fervent flower made fruitful from the sun
Shall drop its golden seed in the world's way,
That all men thereof nourished shall praise
    thee
For grain and flower and fruit of works well
    done ;
Till thy shed seed, O shining sunflower,
Bring forth such growth of the world's garden-
    bed
As like the sun shall outlive age and death.
And yet I would thine heart had heed of her
Who loves thee alive ; but not till she be
    dead.
Come, Love, then, quickly, and take her ut-
    most breath.

Song, speak for me who am dumb as are the
    dead ;
From my sad bed of tears I send forth thee,
To fly all day from sun's birth to sun's death
Down the sun's way after the flying sun,
For love of her that gave thee wings and
    breath
Ere day be done, to seek the sunflower.

FOR THE FEAST OF GIORDANO BRUNO,

PHILOSOPHER AND MARTYR.

I.

Son of the lightning and the light that glows
    Beyond the lightning's or the morning's
    light,
        Soul splendid with all-righteous love of
        right,
In whose keen fire all hopes and fears and
    woes

Were clean consumed, and from their ashes rose
  Transfigured, and intolerable to sight
  Save of purged eyes whose lids had cast off night,
In love's and wisdom's likeness when they close,
Embracing, and between them truth stands fast,
  Embraced of either ; thou whose feet were set
  On English earth while this was England yet,
Our friend that art, our Sidney's friend that wast,
Heart hardier found and higher than all men's past,
  Shall we not praise thee though thine own forget ?

II.

Lift up thy light on us and on thine own,
  O soul whose spirit on earth was as a rod
  To scourge off priests, a sword to pierce their God,
A staff for man's free thought to walk alone,
A lamp to lead him far from shrine and throne
  On ways untrodden where his fathers trod
  Ere earth's heart withered at a high priest's nod
And all men's mouths that made not prayer made moan.
From bonds and torments and the ravening flame
  Surely thy spirit of sense rose up to greet
  Lucretius, where such only spirits meet,
And walk with him apart till Shelley came
  To make the heaven of heavens more heavenly sweet
And mix with yours a third incorporate name.

AVE ATQUE VALE.

IN MEMORY OF CHARLES BAUDELAIRE.

Nous devrions pourtant lui porter quelques fleurs ;
Les morts, les pauvres morts, ont de grandes douleurs,
Et quand Octobre souffle, émondeur des vieux arbres,
Son vent mélancolique a l'entour de leurs marbres,
Certe, ils doivent trouver les vivants bien ingrats.
                Les Fleurs du Mal.

I.

SHALL I strew on thee the rose or rue or laurel,
  Brother, on this that was the veil of thee ?
Or quiet sea-flower moulded by the sea,
Or simplest growth of meadow-sweet or sorrel,
  Such as the summer-sleepy Dryads weave,
  Waked up by snow-soft sudden rains at eve ?
Or wilt thou rather, as on earth before,
  Half-faded fiery blossoms, pale with heat
  And full of bitter summer, but more sweet
To thee than gleanings of a northern shore
  Trod by no tropic feet ?

II.

For always thee the fervid languid glories
  Allured of heavier suns in mightier skies;
  Thine ears knew all the wandering watery sighs
Where the sea sobs round Lesbian promontories,
  The barren kiss of piteous wave to wave
  That knows not where is that Leucadian grave
Which hides too deep the supreme head of song.
  Ah, salt and sterile as her kisses were,
  The wild sea winds her and the green gulfs bear
Hither and thither, and vex and work her wrong,
  Blind gods that cannot spare.

III.

Thou sawest, in thine old singing season, brother,
  Secrets and sorrows unbeheld of us :
  Fierce loves, and lovely leaf-bud poisonous,
Bare to thy subtler eye, but for none other
  Blowing by night in some unbreathed-in clime;
  The hidden harvest of luxurious time,
Sin without shape, and pleasure without speech;
  And where strange dreams in a tumultuous sleep
  Make the shut eyes of stricken spirits weep;
And with each face thou sawest the shadow on each,
  Seeing as men sow men reap.

IV.

O sleepless heart and sombre soul unsleeping,
  That were athirst for sleep and no more life
  And no more love, for peace and no more strife !
Now the dim gods of death have in their keeping

Spirit and body and all the springs of
song,
Is it well now where love can do no
wrong,
Where stingless pleasure has no foam or fang
Behind the unopening closure of her lips ?
Is it not well where soul from body slips
And flesh from bone divides without a pang
As dew from flower-bell drips ?

v.

It is enough; the end and the beginning
Are one thing to thee, who art past the
end.
O hand unclasped of unbeholden friend,
For thee no fruits to pluck, no palms for
winning,
No triumph and no labor and no lust,
Only dead yew-leaves and a little dust.
O quiet eyes wherein the light saith nought,
Whereto the day is dumb, nor any night
With obscure finger silences your sight,
Nor in your speech the sudden soul speaks
thought,
Sleep, and have sleep for light.

vi.

Now all strange hours and all strange loves
are over,
Dreams and desires and sombre songs
and sweet,
Hast thou found place at the great knees
and feet
Of some pale Titan-woman like a lover,
Such as thy vision here solicited,
Under the shadow of her fair vast head,
The deep division of prodigious breasts,
The solemn slope of mighty limbs asleep,
The weight of awful tresses that still keep
The savor and shade of old-world pine-forests
Where the wet hill-winds weep ?

vii.

Hast thou found any likeness for thy vision ?
O gardener of strange flowers, what bud,
what bloom,
Hast thou found sown, what gathered in
the gloom ?
What of despair, of rapture, of derision,
What of life is there, what of ill or good ?
Are the fruits gray like dust or bright like
blood ?
Does the dim ground grow any seed of ours,
The faint fields quicken any terrene root,
In low lands where the sun and moon are
mute
And all the stars keep silence ? Are there
flowers
At all, or any fruit ?

viii.

Alas, but though my flying song flies after,
O sweet strange elder singer, thy more
fleet
Singing, and footprints of thy fleeter feet,
Some dim derision of mysterious laughter
From the blind tongueless warders of the
dead,
Some gainless glimpse of Proserpine's
veiled head,
Some little sound of unregarded tears
Wept by effaced unprofitable eyes,
And from pale mouths some cadence of
dead sighs—
These only, these the hearkening spirit hears,
Sees only such things rise.

ix.

Thou art far too far for wings of words to
follow,
Far too far off for thought or any prayer.
What ails us with thee, who art wind and
air ?
What ails us gazing where all seen is hollow ?
Yet with some fancy, yet with some
desire,
Dreams pursue death as winds a flying
fire,
Our dreams pursue our dead and do not find.
Still, and more swift than they, the thin
flames flies,
The low light fails us in elusive skies,
Still the foiled earnest ear is deaf, and blind
Are still the eluded eyes.

x.

Not thee, O never thee, in all time's changes,
Not thee, but this the sound of thy sad
soul,
The shadow of thy swift spirit, this shut
scroll
I lay my hand on, and not death estranges
My spirit from communion of thy song—
These memories and these melodies that
throng
Veiled porches of a Muse funereal—
These I salute, these touch, these clasp
and fold
As though a hand were in my hand to
hold,
Or through mine ears a mourning musical
Of many mourners rolled.

xi.

I among these, I also, in such station
As when the pyre was charred, and piled
the sods,

And offering to the dead made, and their
  gods,
The old mourners had, standing to make
  libation,
  I stand, and to the gods and to the dead
  Do reverence without prayer or praise,
    and shed
Offering to these unknown, the gods of gloom,
  And what of honey and spice my seed-
    lands bear,
  And what I may of fruits in this chilled
    air,
And lay, Orestes-like, across the tomb
  A curl of severed hair.

XII.

But by no hand nor any treason stricken,
  Not like the low-lying head of Him, the
    King,
  The flame that made of Troy a ruinous
    thing,
Thou liest and on this dust no tears could
  quicken
  There fall no tears like theirs that all
    men hear
  Fall tear by sweet imperishable tear
Down the opening leaves of holy poet's pages.
  Thee not Orestes, not Electra mourns;
  But bending us-ward with memorial urns
The most high Muses that fulfil all ages
  Weep, and our God's heart yearns.

XIII.

For, sparing of his sacred strength, not often
  Among us darkling here the lord of light
  Makes manifest his music and his might
In hearts that open and in lips that soften
  With the soft flame and heat of songs
    that shine.
  Thy lips indeed he touched with bitter
    wine,
And nourished them indeed with bitter bread;
  Yet surely from his hand thy soul's food
    came,
  The fire that scarred thy spirit at his
    flame
Was lighted, and thine hungering heart he
  fed
  Who feeds our hearts with fame.

XIV.

Therefore he too now at thy soul's sunsetting,
  God of all suns and songs, he too bends
    down

To mix his laurel with thy cypress crown
And save thy dust from blame and from for-
  getting.
  Therefore he too, seeing all thou wert
    and art,
  Compassionate, with sad and sacred
    heart,
Mourns thee of many his children the last
  dead,
  And hallows with strange tears and alien
    sighs
  Thine unmelodious mouth and sunless
    eyes,
And over thine irrevocable head
  Sheds light from the under skies.

XV.

And one weeps with him in the ways Lethean,
  And stains with tears her changing
    bosom chill;
  That obscure Venus of the hollow hill,
That thing transformed which was the
  Cytherean,
  With lips that lost their Grecian laugh
    divine
  Long since, and face no more called Ery-
    cine
A ghost, a bitter and luxurious god.
  Thee also with fair flesh and singing
    spell
  Did she, a sad and second prey, compel
Into the footless places once more trod,
  And shadows hot from hell.

XVI.

And now no sacred staff shall break in blos-
  som,
  No choral salutation lure to light
  A spirit with perfume and sweet night
And love's tired eyes and hands and barren
  bosom.
  There is no help for these things; none
    to mend,
  And none to mar; not all our songs, O
    friend,
Will make death clear or make life durable.
  Howbeit with rose and ivy and wild vine
  And with wild notes about this dust of
    thine
At least I fill the place where white dreams
  dwell
  And wreathe an unseen shrine.

XVII.

Sleep; and if life was bitter to thee, pardon,
    If sweet, give thanks; thou hast no more
        to live
    And to give thanks is good, and to for-
        give.
Out of the mystic and the mournful garden
    Where all day through thine hands in
        barren braid
    Wove the sick flowers of secrecy and
        shade,
Green buds of sorrow and sin, and remnants
    gray,
    Sweet-smelling, pale with poison, san-
        guine-hearted,
    Passions that sprang from sleep and
        thoughts that started,
Shall death not bring us all as thee one day
    Among the days departed?

XVIII.

For thee, O now a silent soul, my brother,
    Take at my hands this garland, and fare-
        well.
    Thin is the leaf, and chill the wintry
        smell,
And chill the solemn earth, a fatal mother,
    With sadder than the Niobean womb,
    And in the hollow of her breasts a tomb.
Content thee, howsoe'er, whose days are
    done:
    There lies not any troublous thing before,
    Nor sight nor sound to war against thee
        more,
For whom all winds are quiet as the sun,
    All waters as the shore.

MEMORIAL VERSES.

ON THE DEATH OF THEOPHILE GAUTIER.

Death, what hast thou to do with me? So
    saith
Love, with eyes set against the face of Death;
    What have I done, O thou strong Death,
        to thee,
That mine own lips should wither from thy
    breath?

Though thou be blind as fire or as the sea,
Why should thy waves and storms make war
    on me?
    Is it for hate thou hast to find me fair,
Or for desire to kiss, if it might be,

My very mouth of song, and kill me there?
So with keen rains vexing his crownless hair,
    With bright feet bruised from no delightful
        way,
Through darkness and the disenchanted air,

Lost Love went weeping half a winter's day.
And the armed wind that smote him seemed
    to say,
    How shall the dew live when the dawn is
        fled,
Or wherefore should the Mayflower outlast
    May?

Then Death took Love by the right hand and
    said,
Smiling: Come now and look upon thy dead.
    But Love cast down the glories of his eyes,
And bowed down like a flower his flowerless
    head.

And Death spake, saying: What ails thee in
    such wise,
Being God, to shut thy sight up from the
    skies?
    If thou canst see not, hast thou ears to
        hear?
Or is thy soul too as a leaf that dies?

Even as he spake with fleshless lips of fear,
But soft as sleep sings in a tired man's ear,
    Behold, the winter was not, and its might
Fell, and fruits broke forth of the barren
    year.

And upon earth was largess of great light,
And moving music winged for world-wide
    flight,
    And shapes and sounds of gods beheld and
        heard
And day's foot set upon the neck of night.

And with such song the hollow ways were
    stirred
As of a god's heart hidden in a bird,
    Or as the whole soul of the sun in spring
Should find full utterance in one flower-soft
    word,

And all the season should break forth and
    sing
From one flower's lips, in one rose triumph-
    ing;
    Such breath and light of song as of a flame
Made ears and spirits of them that heard it
    ring.

And Love beholding knew not for the same
The shape that led him, nor in face nor name,
    For he was bright and great of thews and
        fair,
And in Love's eyes he was not Death, but
    Fame.

Not that gray ghost whose life is empty and
    bare
And his limbs moulded out of mortal air,
    A cloud of change that shifts into a shower
And dies and leaves no light for time to wear:

But a god clothed with his own joy and power,
A god re-risen out of his mortal hour
    Immortal, king and lord of time and space,
With eyes that look on them as from a tower.

And where he stood the pale sepulchral place
Bloomed, as new life might in a bloodless
    face,
    And where men sorrowing came to seek a
        tomb
With funeral flowers and tears for grief and
    grace,

They saw with light as of a world in bloom
The portal of the House of Fame illume
    The ways of life wherein we toiling tread,
And watched the darkness as a brand con-
    sume.

And through the gates where rule the death-
    less dead
The sound of a new singer's soul was shed
    That sang among his kinsfolk, and a beam
Shot from the star on a new ruler's head.

A new star lighting the Lethean stream,
A new song mixed into the song supreme
    Made of all souls of singers and their
        might,
That makes of life and time and death a
    dream.

Thy star, thy song, O soul that in our sight
Wast as a sun that made for man's delight
    Flowers and all fruits in season, being so
        near
The sun-god's face, our god that gives us
    light.

To him of all gods that we love or fear
Thou among all men by thy name wast dear,
    Dear to the god that gives us spirit of song
To bind and burn all hearts of men that hear.

The god that makes men's words too swe
    and strong
For life or time or death to do them wrong,
    Who sealed with his thy spirit for a sign
And filled it with his breath thy whole life long.

Who made thy moist lips fiery with new wine
Pressed from the grapes of song the sovereign
    vine,
    And with all love of all things loveliest
Gave thy soul power to make them more
    divine.

That thou might'st breathe upon the breath-
    less rest
Of marble, till the brows and lips and breast
    Felt fall from off them as a cancelled curse
That speechless wherewith they lived opprest,

Who gave thee strength and heat of spirit to
    pierce
All clouds of form and color that disperse,
    And leave the spirit of beauty to remould
In types of clean chryselephantine verse.

Who gave thee words more golden than fine
    gold
To carve in shapes more glorious than of old,
    And build thy songs up in the sight of time
As statues set in godhead manifold:

In sight and scorn of temporal change and
    clime
That meet the sun re-risen with refluent rhyme
    —As god to god might answer face to face—
From lips whereon the morning strikes sublime.

Dear to the god, our god who gave thee place
Among the chosen of days, the royal race,
    The lords of light, whose eyes of old and
        ears
Saw even on earth and heard him for a space.

There are the souls of those once mortal years
That wrought with fire of joy and light of
    tears
    In words divine as deeds that grew thereof
Such music as he swoons with love who hears.

There are the lives that lighten from above
Our under lives, the spheral souls that move
    Through the ancient heaven of song-illumined
        air
Whence we that hear them singing die with
    love.

There all the crowned Hellenic heads, and
        there
The old gods who made men godlike as they
        were,
    The lyric lips wherefrom all songs take fire,
Live eyes, and light of Apollonian hair.

There, round the sovereign passion of that lyre
Which the stars hear and tremble with desire,
    The ninefold light Pierian is made one
That here we see divided, and aspire,

Seeing, after this or that crown to be won ;
But where they hear the singing of the sun,
    All form, all sound, all color, and all thought
Are as one body and soul in unison.

There the song sung shines as a picture
        wrought
The painted mouths sing that on earth say
        nought,
    The carven limbs have sense of blood and
        growth
And large-eyed life that seeks nor lacks not
        aught.

There all the music of thy living mouth
Lives, and all lovers wrought of thine hand in
        youth
    And bound about the breasts and brows
        with gold
And colored pale or dusk from north to south.

Fair living things made to thy will of old,
Born of thy lips, no births of mortal mould,
    That in the world of song about thee wait
Where thought and truth are one and mani-
        fold.

Within the graven lintels of the gate
That here divides our vision and our fate,
    The dreams we walk in and the truths of
        sleep,
All sense and spirit have life inseparate.

There what one thinks, in his to grasp and
        keep ;
There are no dreams, but very joys to reap,
    No foiled desires that die before delight,
No fears to see across our joys and weep.

There hast thou all thy will of thought and
        sight,
All hope for harvest, and all heaven for flight ;
    The sunrise of whose golden-mouthed glad
        head
To paler songless ghosts was heat and light.

Here where the sunset of our year is red
Men think of thee as of the summer dead,
    Gone forth before the snows, before thy day,
With unshod feet, with brows unchapleted.

Couldst thou not wait till age had wound, they
        say,
Round those wreathed brows his soft white
        blossoms ? Nay
    Why shouldst thou vex thy soul with this
        harsh air,
Thy bright-winged soul, once free to take its
        way ?

Nor for men's reverence hadst thou need to
        wear
The holy flower of gray time-hallowed hair ;
    Nor were it fit that aught of thee grew old,
Fair lover all thy days of all things fair.

And hear we not thy words of molten gold
Singing ? or is their light and heat acold
    Whereat men warmed their spirits ? Nay,
        for all
These yet are with us, ours to hear and hold.

The lovely laughter, the clear tears, the call
Of love to love on ways where shadows fall,
    Through doors of dim division and disguise,
And music made of doubts unmusical ;

The love that caught strange light from death's
        own eyes,*
And filled death's lips with fiery words and
        sighs,
    And half asleep let feed from veins of his
Her close red warm snake's mouth, Egyptian-
        wise :

And that great night of love more strange than
        this,†
When she that made the whole world's bale
        and bliss
    Made king of the whole world's desire a
        slave,
And killed him in mid kingdom with a kiss ;

Veiled loves that shifted shapes and shafts,
        and gave,‡
Laughing, strange gifts to hands that durst
        not crave,
    Flowers double-blossomed, fruits of scent
        and hue
Sweet as the bride-bed, stranger than the
        grave ;

*La Morte Amoureuse.
†Une Nuit de Cléopâtre.   ‡Mademoiselle de Maupin

All joys and wonders of old lives and new
That ever in love's shine or shadow grew,
    And all the grief whereof he dreams and
      grieves,
And all sweet roots fed on his light and dew;

All these through thee our spirit of sense per-
    ceives,
As threads in the unseen woof thy music
    weaves,
    Birds caught and snared that fill our ears
      with thee,
Bay-blossoms in thy wreath of brow-bound
    leaves.

Mixed with the masque of death's old comedy
Though thou too pass, have here our flowers,
    that we
    For all the flowers thou gav'st upon thee
      shed,
And pass not crownless to Persephone.

Blue lotus-blooms and white and rosy-red
We wind with poppies for thy silent head,
    And on this margin of the sundering sea
Leave thy sweet light to rise upon the dead.

SONNET.

(WITH A COPY OF "MADEMOISELLE DE MAUPIN.")

THIS is the golden book of spirit and sense,
    The holy writ of beauty; he that wrought
    Made it with dreams and faultless words
      and thought
That seeks and finds and loses in the dense
Dim air of life that beauty's excellence
    Wherewith love makes one hour of life
      distraught
And all hours after follow and find not aught.
Here is that height of all love's eminence
Where man may breathe but for a breathing-
    space
And feel his soul burn as an altar-fire
To the unknown God of unachieved desire,
And from the middle mystery of the place
    Watch lights that break, hear sounds as of
      a quire,
But see not twice unveiled the veiled God's
    face.

AGE AND SONG.

(TO BARRY CORNWALL.)

I.

IN vain men tell us time can alter
Old loves or make old memories falter,
    That with the old year the old year's life
      closes.
The old dew still falls on the old sweet flowers,
The old sun revives the new-fledged hours,
    The old summer rears the new-born roses.

II.

Much more a Muse that bears upon her
Raiment and wreath and flower of honor,
    Gathered long since and long since woven,
Fades not or falls as fall the vernal
Blossoms that bear no fruit eternal,
    By summer or winter charred or cloven.

III.

No time casts down, no time upraises,
Such loves, such memories, and such praises,
    As need no grace of sun or shower,
No saving screen from frost or thunder,
To tend and house around and under
    The imperishable and fearless flower.

IV.

Old thanks, old thoughts, old aspirations,
Outlive men's lives and lives of nations,
    Dead, but for one thing which survives—
The inalienable and unpriced treasure,
The old joy of power, the old pride of pleasure,
    That lives in light above men's lives.

IN MEMORY OF BARRY CORNWALL.

(OCTOBER 4, 1874.)

I.

IN the garden of death, where the singers
    whose names are deathless
    One with another make music unheard of
      men,
Where the dead sweet roses fade not of lips
    long breathless,
    And the fair eyes shine that shall weep not
      or change again,
Who comes now crowned with the blossom
    of snow-white years?

What music is this that the world of the dead
    men hears?

II.

Beloved of men, whose words on our lips
    were honey,
    Whose name in our ears and our fathers'
      ears was sweet,
Like summer gone forth of the land his songs
    made sunny,
    To the beautiful veiled bright world where
      the glad ghosts meet,
Child, father, bridegroom and bride, and an-
    guish and rest,
No soul shall pass of a singer than this more
    blest.

III.

Blest for the years' sweet sake that were
    filled and brightened,
    As a forest with birds, with the fruit and
      the flower of his song ;
For the souls' sake blest that heard, and their
    cares were lightened,
    For the hearts' sake blest that have fostered
      his name so long ;
By the living and dead lips blest that have
    loved his name,
And clothed with their praise and crowned
    with their love for fame.

IV.

Ah, fair and fragrant his fame as flowers
    that close not,
    That shrink not by day for heat or for cold
      by night,
As a thought in the heart shall increase when
    the heart's self knows not,
    Shall endure in our ears as a sound, in our
      eyes as a light ;
Shall wax with the years that wane and the
    seasons' chime,
As a white rose thornless that grows in the
    garden of time.

V.

The same year calls, and one goes hence with
    another,
    And men sit sad that were glad for their
      sweet songs' sake ;
The same year beckons, and elder with
    younger brother
    Takes mutely the cup from his hand that
      we all shall take.*

    * Sydney Dobell died August 22, 187.
16

They pass ere the leaves be past or the snows
    be come ;
And the birds are loud, but the lips that out-
    sang them dumb.

VI.

Time takes them home that we loved, fair
    names and famous,
    To the soft long sleep, to the broad sweet
      bosom of death ;
But the flower of their souls he shall take not
    away to shame us,
    Nor the lips lack song for ever that now
      lack breath.
For with us shall all the music and perfume
    that die not dwell,
Though the dead to our dead bid welcome,
    and we farewell.

EPICEDE.

(James Lorimer Graham died at Florence. April 30
1876.)

LIFE may give for love to death
    Little ; what are life's gifts worth
    To the dead wrapt round with earth?
Yet from lips of living breath
    Sighs or words we are fain to give,
    All that yet, while yet we live,
Life may give for love to death.

Dead so long before his day,
    Passed out of the Italian sun
    To the dark where all is done
Fallen upon the verge of May ;
    Here at life's and April's end
    How should song salute my friend
Dead so long before his day?

Not a kindlier life or sweeter
    Time, that lights and quenches men,
    Now may quench or light again,
Mingling with the mystic metre
    Woven of all men's lives with his
    Not a clearer note than this,
Not a kindlier life or sweeter.

In this heavenliest part of earth
    He that living loved the light,
    Light and song, may rest aright,
One in death, if strange in birth,

With the deathless dead that make
Life the lovelier for their sake
In this heavenliest part of earth.

Light, and song, and sleep at last—
  Struggling hands and suppliant knees
  Get no goodlier gift than these.
Song that holds remembrance fast
  Light that lightens death, attend
  Round their graves who have to friend
Light, and song, and sleep at last.

TO VICTOR HUGO.

HE had no children, who for love of men,
  Being God, endured of Gods such things
    as thou,
  Father; nor on his thunder-beaten brow
Fell such a woe as bows thine head again,
Twice bowed before, though godlike, in man's
    ken,
  And seen too high for any stroke to bow
  Save this of some strange God's that bends
    it now
The third time with such weight as bruised it
    then.
Fain would grief speak, fain utter for love's
    sake
Some word; but comfort who might bid thee
    take?
  What God in your own tongue shall talk
    with thee,
Showing how all souls that look upon the
    sun
Shall be for thee one spirit and thy son,
  And thy soul's child the soul of man to be?

January 3, 1876.

INFERIAE.

SPRING, and the light and sound of things on
    earth
Requickening, all within our green sea's
    girth;
A time of passage or a time of birth
  Fourscore years since as this year, first and
    last.

The sun is all about the world we see,
The breath and strength of very spring; and
  we

Live, love, and feed on our own hearts; but
  he
  Whose heart fed mine has passed into the
    past.

Past, all things born with sense and blood
    and breath;
The flesh hears nought that now the spirit
    saith.
If death be like as birth and birth as death,
  The first was fair—more fair should be the
    last.
Fourscore years since, and come but one
    month more
The count were perfect of his moral score
Whose sail went seaward yesterday from shore
  To cross the last of many an unsailed sea.

Light, love and labor up to life's last height,
These three were stars unsetting in his sight
Even as the sun is life and heat and light
  And sets not nor is dark when dark are we.

The life, the spirit, and the work were one
That here—ah, who shall say, that here are
    done
Nor I, that know not; father, not thy son,
  For all the darkness of the night and sea.

A BIRTH-SONG.

For Olivia Frances Madox Rossetti, born September
20, 1875.)

    OUT of the dark sweet sleep
    Where no dreams laugh or weep
      Borne through bright gates of birth
    Into the dim sweet light
    Where day still dreams of night
      While heaven takes form on earth,
White rose of spirit and flesh, and lily of love,
    What note of song have we
    Fit for the birds and thee,
Fair nestling couched beneath the mother-
    dove?

    Nay, in some more divine
    Small speechless song of thine
      Some news too good for words
    Heart-hushed and smiling, we
    Might hope to have of thee,
      The youngest of God's birds,
If thy sweet sense might mix itself with ours,
    If ours might understand
    The language of thy land,

Ere thine become the tongue of mortal
hours:
Ere thy lips learn too soon
Their soft first human tune,
Sweet, but less sweet than now,
And thy raised eyes to read
Glad and good things indeed,
But none so sweet as thou :
Ere thought lift up their flower-soft lids to see
What life and love on earth
Bring thee for gifts at birth,
But none so good as thine who hast given us
thee:

Now, ere thy sense forget
The heaven that fills it yet,
Now, sleeping or awake,
If thou couldst tell, or we
Ask and be heard of thee,
For love's undying sake,
From thy dumb lips divine and bright mute
speech
Such news might touch our ear
That then would burn to hear
Too high a message now for man's to reach.

Ere the gold hair of corn
Had withered wast thou born,
To make the good time glad ;
The time that but last year
Fell colder than a tear
On hearts and hopes turned sad.
High hopes and hearts requickening in thy
dawn,
Even theirs whose life-springs, child,
Filled thine with life and smiled,
But then wept blood for half their own with-
drawn.*

If death and birth be one,
And set with rise of sun,
And truth with dreams divine,
Some word might come with thee
From over the still sea
Deep hid in shade or shine,
Crossed by the crossing sails of death and birth,
Word of some sweet new thing
Fit for such lips to bring,
Some word of love, some afterthought of
earth.

If love be strong as death,
By what so natural breath
As thine could this be said ?
By what so lovely way

* Oliver Madox Brown died November 5, 1874, in his
twentieth year.

Could love send word to say
He lives and is not dead ?
Such word alone were fit for only thee,
If his and thine have met
Where spirits rise and set,
His whom we see not, thine whom scarce we
see :

His there new-born, as thou
New-born among us now;
His, here so fruitful-souled,
Now veiled and silent here,
Now dumb as thou last year,
A ghost of one year old:
If lights that change their sphere in changing
meet,
Some ray might his not give
To thine who wast to live,
And make thy present with his past life
sweet?

Let dreams that laugh or weep,
All glad and sad dreams, sleep;
Truth more than dreams is dear.
Let thoughts that change and fly,
Sweet thoughts and swift, go by;
More than all thought is here.
More than all hope can forge or memory
feign
The life that in our eyes,
Made out of love's life, lies,
And flower-like fed with love for sun and rain.

Twice royal in its root
The sweet small olive-shoot
Here set in sacred earth;
Twice dowered with glorious grace
From either heaven-born race
First blended in its birth;
Fair God or Genius of so fair an hour
For love of either name
Twice crowned, with love and fame,
Guard and be gracious to the fair-named
flower.

————

EX-VOTO.

WHEN their last hour shall rise
Pale on these mortal eyes,
Herself like one that dies,
And kiss me dying
The cold last kiss, and fold
Close round my limbs her cold
Soft shade as raiment rolled
And leave them lying.

If aught my soul would say
Might move to hear me pray
The birth-god of my day
  That he might hearken,
This grace my heart should crave,
To find no landward grave
That worldly springs make brave,
  World's winters darken,

Nor grow through gradual hours
The cold blind seed of flowers
Made by new beams and showers
  From limbs that moulder,
Nor take my part with earth,
But find for death's new birth
A bed of larger girth,
  More chaste and colder.

Not earth's for spring and fall,
Not earth's at heart, not all
Earth's making, though men call
  Earth only mother,
Not hers at heart she bare
Me, but thy child, O fair
Sea, and thy brother's care,
  The wind thy brother.
Yours was I born, and ye,
The sea-wind and the sea,
Made all my soul in me
  A song forever,
A harp to string and smite
For love's sake of the bright
Wind and the sea's delight,
  To fail them never:

Not while on this side death
I hear what either saith
And drink of either's breath
  With heart's thanksgiving
That in my veins like wine
Some sharp salt blood of thine,
Some springtide pulse of brine
  Yet leaps up living.

When thy salt lips wellnigh
Sucked in my mouth's last sigh,
Grudged I so much to die
  This death as others ?
Was it no ease to think
The chalice from whose brink
Fate gave me death to drink
  Was thine,—my mother's ?

Thee too, the all-fostering earth,
Fair as thy fairest birth,
More than thy worthiest worth,
  We call, we know thee,

More sweet and just and dread
Than live men highest of head
Or even thy holiest dead
  Laid low below thee.

The sunbeam on the sheaf,
The dewfall on the leaf,
All joy, all grace, all grief,
  Are thine for giving;
Of thee our loves are born,
Our lives and loves, that mourn
And triumph ; tares with corn,
  Dead seed with living:

All good and ill things done
In eyeshot of the sun
t last in thee made one
  Rest well contented ;
All words of all man's breath
And works he doth or saith,
All wholly done to death,
  None long lamented.

A slave to sons of thee,
Thou, seeming, yet art free ;
But who shall make the sea
  Serve even in seeming ?
What plough shall bid it bear
Seed to the sun and the air,
Fruit for thy strong sons' fare,
  Fresh wine's foam streaming ?

What oldworld son of thine,
Made drunk with death as wine,
Hath drunk the bright sea's brine
  With lips of laughter ?
Thy blood they drink; but he
Who hath drunken of the sea
Once deeplier than of thee
  Shall drink not after.

Of thee thy sons of men
Drink deep, and thirst again;
For wine in feasts, and then
  In fields for slaughter;
But thirst shall touch not him
Who hath felt with sense grown dim
Rise, covering lip and limb,
  The wan sea's water.

All fire of thirst that aches
The salt sea cools and slakes
More than all springs or lakes,
  Freshets or shallows;
Wells where no beam can burn
Through frondage of the fern
That hides from hart and hern
  The haunt it hallows.

Peace with all graves on earth
For death or sleep or birth
Be alway, one in worth
    One with another;¹
But when my time shall be,
O mother, O my sea,
Alive or dead, take me,
    Me too, my mother.

A BALLAD OF DREAMLAND.

I HID my heart in a nest of roses,
    Out of the sun's way, hidden apart;
In a softer bed than the soft white snow's is,
    Under the roses I hid my heart.
Why would it sleep not? why should it
    start,
When never a leaf of the rose-tree stirred?
What made sleep flutter his wings and part?
Only the song of a secret bird.

Lie still, I said, for the wind's wing closes,
    And mild leaves muffle the keen sun's dart;
Lie still, for the wind on the warm sea dozes,
    And the wind is unquieter yet than thou art.
Does a thought in thee still as a thorn's
    wound smart?
Does the fang still fret thee of hope deferred?
What bids the lids of thy sleep dispart?
Only the song of a secret bird.

The green land's name that a charm encloses,
    It never was writ in the traveller's chart,
And sweet on its trees as the fruit that grows
    is,
    It never was sold in the merchant's mart.
The swallows of dreams through its dim
    fields dart,
And sleep's are the tunes in its tree-tops
    heard;
    No hound's note wakens the wildwood hart,
Only the song of a secret bird.

ENVOI.

In the world of dreams I have chosen my part.
    To sleep for a season and hear no word
Of true love's truth or of light love's art,
    Only the song of a secret bird.

CYRIL TOURNEUR.

A SEA that heaves with horror of the night,
    As maddened by the moon that hangs
    aghast

With strain and torment of the ravening
    blast,
Haggard as hell, a bleak blind bloody light;
No shore but one red reef of rock in sight,
    Whereon the waifs of many a wreck were
    cast
    And shattered in the fierce nights over-
    past
Wherein more souls toward hell than heaven
    took flight;
And 'twixt the shark-toothed rocks and
    swallowing shoals
A cry as out of hell from all these souls
    Sent through the sheer gorge of the
    slaughtering sea,
Whose thousand throats, full-fed with life by
    death,
Fill the black air with foam and furious
    breath;
    And over all these one star—Chastity.

A BALLAD OF FRANCOIS VILLON,

PRINCE OF ALL BALLAD-MAKERS.

BIRD of the bitter bright gray golden morn
    Scarce risen upon the dusk of dolorous
    years,
First of us all and sweetest singer born
    Whose far shrill note the world of new men
    hears
    Cleave the cold shuddering shade as
    twilight clears;
When song new-born put off the old world's
    attire
And felt its tune on her changed lips expire,
    Writ foremost on the roll of them that came
Fresh girt for service of the latter lyre,
    Villon, our sad bad glad mad brother's
    name!

Alas the joy, the sorrow and the scorn,
    That clothed thy life with hopes and sins
    and fears,
And gave thee stones for bread and tares for
    corn
    And plume-plucked jail-birds for thy
    starveling peers
    Till death clipt close their flight with shame-
    ful shears;
Till shifts came short and loves were hard to
    hire,
When lilt of song nor twitch of twangling
    wire
    Could buy thee bread or kisses; when light
    fame

Spurned like a ball and haled through brake
        and briar,
    Villon, our sad bad glad mad brother's
        name !

Poor splendid wings so frayed and soiled and
        torn !
    Poor kind wild eyes so dashed with light
        quick tears !
Poor perfect voice, most blithe when most
        forlorn,
    That rings athwart the sea whence no man
        steers
    Like joy-bells crossed with death-bells in
        our ears !
What far delight has cooled the fierce desire
That like some ravenous bird was strong to
        tire
    On that frail flesh and soul consumed with
        flame,
But left more sweet than roses to respire,
    Villon, our sad bad glad mad brother's
        name ?

ENVOI.

Prince of sweet songs made out of tears and
        fire,
A harlot was thy nurse, a God thy sire ;
    Shame soiled thy song, and song assoiled
        thy shame.
But from thy feet now death has washed the
        mire,
Love reads our first at head of all our quire,
    Villon, our sad bad glad mad brother's
        name.

PASTICHE.

Now the days are all gone over
Of our singing, love by lover.
Days of summer-colored seas
Blown adrift, through beam and breeze.

Now the nights are all past over
Of our dreaming, dreams that hover
In a mist of fair false things,
Nights afloat on wide wan wings.

Now the loves with faith for mother,
Now the fears which hope for brother,
Scarce are with us as strange words,
Notes from songs of last year's birds.

Now all good that comes or goes is
As the smell of last year's roses,
As the radiance in our eyes
Shot from summer's ere he dies.

Now the morning faintlier risen
Seems no God come forth of prison,
But a bird of plume-plucked wing,
Pale with thoughts of evening.

Now hath hope, outraced in running
Given the touch up of his cunning
And the palm he thought to wear
Even to his own strong child—despair.

BEFORE SUNSET.

In the lower lands of day
    On the hither side of night,
There is nothing that will stay,
    There are all things soft to sight;
    Lighted shade and shadowy light
In the wayside and the way,
    Hours the sun has spared to smite.
Flowers the rain has left to play.

Shall these hours run down and say
    No good thing of thee and me ?
Time that made us and will slay
    Laughs at love in me and thee;
    But if here the flowers may see
One whole hour of amorous breath,
    Time shall die, and love shall be
Lord as time was over death.

SONG.

Love laid his sleepless head
On a thorny rosy bed;
And his eyes with tears were red,
And pale his lips as the dead.

And fear and sorrow and scorn
Kept watch by his head forlorn.
Till the night was overworn
And the world was merry with morn.

And Joy came up with the day
And kissed Love's lips as he lay,
And the watchers ghostly and gray
Sped from his pillow away.

And his eyes as the dawn grew bright,
And his lips waxed ruddy as light:
Sorrow may reign for a night,
But day shall bring back delight.

A VISION OF SPRING IN WINTER.

I.

O TENDER time that love thinks long to see,
  Sweet foot of spring that with her footfall
    sows
  Late snowlike flowery leavings of the
    snows,
Be not too long irresolute to be;
O mother-month, where have they hidden
  thee?
  Out of the pale time of the flowerless rose
I reach my heart out toward the springtime
  lands.
  I stretch my spirit forth to the fair hours,
    The purplest of the prime;
I lean my soul down over them, with hands
  Made wide to take the ghostly growths of
    flowers;
    I send my love back to the lovely time.

II.

Where has the greenwood hid thy gracious
  head?
  Veiled with what visions while the gray
    world grieves,
  Or muffled with what shadows of green
    leaves,
What warm intangible green shadows spread
To sweeten the sweet twilight for thy bed?
  What sleep enchants thee? what delight
    deceives?
Where the deep dreamlike dew before the
  dawn
  Feels not the fingers of the sunlight yet
    Its silver web unweave,
Thy footless ghost on some unfooted lawn
  Whose air the unrisen sunbeams fear to
    fret
    Lives a ghost's life of daylong dawn
      and eve.

III.

Sunrise it sees not, neither set of star,
  Large nightfall, nor imperial plenilune,
  Nor strong sweet shape of the full-breasted
    noon;
But where the silver-sandalled shadows are,
Too soft for arrows of the sun to mar,
  Moves with the mild gait of an ungrown
    moon:
Hard overhead the half-lit crescent swims,
  The tender-colored night draws hardly
    breath.

The light is listening;
They watch the dawn of slender-shapen limbs,
Virginal, born again of doubtful death,
    Chill foster-father of the weanling
      spring.

IV.

As sweet desire of day before the day,
  As dreams of love before the true love born
  From the outer edge of winter overworn
The ghost arisen of May before the May
Takes through dim air her unawakened way,
  The gracious ghost of morning risen ere
    morn.
With little unblown breasts and child-eyed
  looks
  Following, the very maid, the girl-child
    spring,
    Lifts windward her bright brows,
Dips her light feet in warm and moving brooks,
And kindles with her own mouth's coloring
    The fearful firstlings of the plumeless
      boughs.

V.

I seek thee sleeping, and awhile I see,
  Fair face that art not, how thy maiden
    breath
  Shall put at last the deadly days to death
And fill the fields and fire the woods with thee
And seaward hollows where my feet would be
  When heaven shall hear the word that
    April saith
To change the cold heart of the weary time,
  To stir and soften all the time to tears,
    Tears joyfuller than mirth;
As even to May's clear height the young days
  climb
  With feet not swifter than those fair first
    years
    Whose flowers revive not with thy
      flowers on earth.

VI.

I would not bid thee, though I might, give
  back
  One good thing youth has given and borne
    away;
  I crave not any comfort of the day
That is not, nor on time's retrodden track
Would turn to meet the white-robed hours
  or black
    That long since left me on their mortal way;
Nor light nor love that has been, nor the
  breath

That comes with the morning from the sun
    to be
    And sets light hope on fire ;
No fruit, no flower thought once too fair for
    death,
    No flower nor hour once fallen from life's
    green tree,
        No leaf once plucked or once fulfilled
        desire.

VII.

The morning song beneath the stars that fled
    With twilight through the moonless moun-
    tain air,
    While youth with burning lips and wreath-
    less hair
Sang toward the sun that was to crown his
    head,
Rising ; the hopes that triumphed and fell
    dead,
    The sweet swift eyes and songs of hours
    that were ;
These may'st thou not give back forever ;
    these,
    As at the sea's heart all her wrecks lie
    waste,
        Lie deeper than the sea ;
But flowers thou may'st, and winds, and
    hours of ease,
    And all its April to the world thou may'st
        Give back, and half my April back to
        me.

CHORIAMBICS.

LOVE, what ailed thee to leave life that was
    made lovely, we thought, with love?
What sweet visions of sleep lured thee away,
    down from the light above ?

What strange faces of dreams, voices that
    called, hands that were raised to wave,
Lured or led thee, alas, out of the sun, down
    to the sunless grave ?

Ah, thy luminous eyes! once was their light
    fed with the fire of day ;
Now their shadowy lids cover them close,
    hush them and hide away.

Ah, thy snow-colored hands! once were they
    chains, mighty to bind me fast;
Now no blood in them burns, mindless of
    love, senseless of passion past.

Ah, thy beautiful hair ! so was it once braided
    for me, for me ;
Now for death is it crowned, only for death,
    lover and lord of thee.

Sweet, the kisses of death set on thy lips,
    colder are they than mine ;
Colder surely than past kisses that love
    poured for thy lips as wine.

Lov'st thou death? is his face fairer than
    love's, brighter to look upon ?
Seest thou light in his eyes, light by which
    love's pales and is overshone?

Lo, the roses of death, gray as the dust, chiller
    of leaf than snow!
Why let fall from thy hand love's that were
    thine, roses that loved thee so?

Large red lilies of love, sceptral and tall,
    lovely for eyes to see;
Thornless blossom of love, full of the sun,
    fruits that were reared for thee.

Now death's poppies alone circle thy hair,
    girdle thy breasts as white;
Bloodless blossoms of death, leaves that have
    sprung never against the light.

Nay then, sleep if thou wilt ; love is content;
    what should he do to weep ?
Sweet was love to thee once; now in thine
    eyes sweeter than love is sleep.

AT PARTING.

FOR a day and a night Love sang to us,
    played with us,
    Folded us round from the dark and the
    light;
And our hearts were fulfilled of the music he
    made with us,
Made with our hearts and our lips while he
    stayed with us,
        Stayed in mid passage his pinions from
        flight
            For a day and a night.

From his foes that kept watch with his wings
    had he hidden us,
    Covered us close from the eyes that would
    smite,
From the feet that had tracked and the
    tongues that had chidden us

Sheltering in shade of the myrtles forbidden
  us
Spirit and flesh growing one with delight
    For a day and a night.

But his wings will not rest and his feet will
  not stay for us:
Morning is here in the joy of its might;
With his breath has he sweetened a night
  and a day for us;
Now let him pass, and the myrtles make way
  for us;
Love can but last in us here at his height
    For a day and a night.

———

A SONG IN SEASON.

I.

THOU whose beauty
  Knows no duty
Due to love that moves thee never;
  Thou whose mercies
  Are men's curses,
And thy smile a scourge forever;

II.

Thou that givest
  Death and livest
On the death of thy sweet giving;
  Thou that sparest
  Not nor carest
Though thy scorn leave no love living;

III.

Thou whose rootless
  Flower is fruitless
As the pride its heart encloses,
  But thine eyes are
  As May skies are,
And thy words like spoken roses;

IV.

Thou whose grace is
  In men's faces
Fierce and wayward as thy will is;
  Thou whose peerless
  Eyes are tearless,
And thy thoughts as cold sweet lilies;

V.

Thou that takest
  Hearts and makest
Wrecks of loves to strew behind thee,

Whom the swallow
  Sure should follow,
Finding summer where we find thee;

VI.

Thou that wakest
  Hearts and breakest,
And thy broken hearts forgive thee,
  That wilt make no
  Pause and take no
Gift that love for love might give thee.

VII.

Thou that bindest
  Eyes and blindest,
Serving worst who served thee longest ;
  Thou that speakest,
  And the weakest
Heart is his that was the strongest ;

VIII.

Take in season
  Thought with reason ;
Think what gifts are ours for giving ;
  Hear what beauty
  Owes of duty
To the love that keeps it living.

IX.

Dust that covers
  Long dead lovers
Song blows off with breath that brightens;
  At its flashes
  Their white ashes
Burst in bloom that lives and lightens.

X.

Had they bent not
  Head or lent not
Ear to love and amorous duties,
  Song had never
  Saved forever,
Love, the least of all their beauties.

XI.

All the golden
  Names of olden
Women yet by men's love cherished,
  All our dearest
  Thoughts hold nearest,
Had they loved not, all had perished

XII.

If no fruit is
Of thy beauties,
Tell me yet, since none may win them,
What and wherefore
Love should care for
Of all good things hidden in them?

XIII.

Pain for profit
Comes but of it,
If the lips that lure their lover's
Hold no treasure
Past the measure
Of the lightest hour that hovers.

XIV.

If they give not
Or forgive not
Gifts or thefts for grace or guerdon,
Love that misses
Fruit of kisses
Long will bear no thankless burden.

XV.

If they care not
Though love were not,
If no breath of his burn through them,
Joy must borrow
Song from sorrow,
Fear teach hope the way to woo them.

XVI.

Grief has measures
Soft as pleasure's,
Fear has moods that hope lies deep in,
Songs to sing him,
Dreams to bring him,
And a red-rose bed to sleep in.

XVII.

Hope with fearless
Looks and tearless
Lies and laughs too near the thunder;
Fear hath sweeter
Speech and meeter
For heart's love to hide him under.

XVIII.

Joy by daytime
Fills his playtime
Full of songs loud mirth takes pride in;

Night and morrow
Weave round sorrow
Thoughts as soft as sleep to hide

XIX.

Graceless faces,
Loveless graces,
Are but motes in light that quicken,
Sands that run down
Ere the sundown,
Rose-leaves dead ere autumn sicken.

XX.

Fair and fruitless
Charms are bootless
Spells to ward off age's peril;
Lips that give not
Love shall live not,
Eyes that meet not eyes are sterile.

XXI.

But the beauty
Bound in duty
Fast to love that falls off never
Love shall cherish
Lest it perish,
And its roots bears fruit forever.

TWO LEADERS.

βᾶτε δόμον, μεγάλοι φιλοτίμοι
Νυκτὸς παῖδες ἄπαιδες, ὑπ' εὐφρονι πομπᾷ.

I.

O GREAT and wise, clear-souled and high of
heart,
One the last flower of Catholic love, that
grows
Amid bare thorns their only thornless rose,
From the fierce juggling of the priests' loud
mart
Yet alien, yet unspotted and apart
From the blind hard foul rout whose shame-
less shows
Mock the sweet heaven whose secret no
man knows
With prayers and curses and the soothsayer's
art;
One like a storm-god of the northern foam
Strong, wrought of rock that breasts and
breaks the sea
And thunders back its thunder, rhyme
for rhyme
Answering, as though to outroar the tides
of time

And bid the world's wave back—what
song should be
Theirs that with praise would bring and sing
you home ?

II.

With all our hearts we praise you whom ye
hate,
High souls that hate us; for our hopes are
higher,
And higher than yours the goal of our de-
sire,
Though high your ends be as your hearts are
great.
Your world of Gods and kings, of shrine and
state,
Was of the night when hope and fear stood
nigher,
Wherein men walked by light of stars and
fire
Till man by day stood equal with his fate.
Honor not hate we give you, love not fear,
Last prophets of past kind, who fill the
dome
Of great dead Gods with wrath and wail, nor
hear
Time's word and man's: 'Go honored
hence, go home,
Night's childless children; here your hour is
done;
Pass with the stars, and leave us with the
sun.'

VICTOR HUGO IN 1877.

'Dazzle mine eyes, or do I see three suns?'

Above the spring-tide sundawn of the year,
A sunlike star, not born of day or night,
Filled the fair heaven of spring with
heavenlier light,
Made of all ages orbed in one sole sphere
Whose light was as a Titan's smile or tear ;
Then rose a ray more flowerlike, starry
white,
Like a child's eye grown lovelier with
delight,
Sweet as a child's heart-lightening laugh to
hear ;
And last a fire from heaven, a fiery rain
As of God's wrath on the unclean cities,
fell
And lit the shuddering shades of half-
seen hell
That shrank before it and were cloven in
twain;

A beacon fired by lightning, whence all
time
Sees red the bare black ruins of a crime.

CHILD'S SONG.

What is gold worth, say,
Worth for work or play,
Worth to keep or pay,
Hide or throw away,
Hope about or fear?
What is love worth, pray ?
Worth a tear ?

Golden on the mould
Lie the dead leaves rolled
Of the wet woods old,
Yellow leaves and cold,
Woods without a dove ;
Gold is worth but gold ;
Love's worth love.

TRIADS.

I.

I.

The word of the sun to the sky,
The word of the wind to the sea,
The word of the moon to the night,
What may it be ?

II.

The sense to the flower of the fly,
The sense of the bird to the tree,
The sense to the cloud of the light,
Who can tell me ?

III.

The song of the fields to the kye,
The song of the lime to the bee,
The song of the depth to the height,
Who knows all three ?

II.

I.

The message of April to May
That May sends on into June
And June give out to July
For birthday boon;

II.

The delight of the dawn in the day,
  The delight of the day in the noon,
    The delight of a song in a sigh
          That breaks the tune ;

III.

The secret of passing away,
  The cost of the change of the moon,
    None knows it with ear or with eye,
          But all will soon.

III.

I.

The live wave's love for the shore,
  The shore's for the wave as it dies,

The love of the thunder-fire
          That sears the skies,

II.

We shall know not though life wax hoar,
  Till all life, spent into sighs,
    Burn out as consumed with desire
          Of death's strange eyes :

III.

Till the secret be secret no more
  In the light of one hour as it flies,
    Be the hour as of suns that expire
          Or suns that rise.

FOUR SONGS OF FOUR SEASONS.

I. WINTER IN NORTHUMBERLAND.

I.

Outside the garden
The wet skies harden;
The gates are barred on
  The summer side:
Shut out the flower-time,
'Sunbeam and shower-time;
Make way for our time,'
  Wild winds have cried.
Green once and cheery,
The woods, worn weary,
Sigh as the dreary
  Weak sun goes home:
A great wind grapples
The wave, and dapples
The dead green floor of the sea with foam.

II.

Through fell and moorland,
And salt-sea foreland,
Our noisy norland
  Resounds and rings;
Waste waves thereunder
Are blown in sunder,
And winds make thunder
  With cloudwide wings;
Sea-drift makes dimmer
The beacon's glimmer;
Nor sail nor swimmer
  Can try the tides;
And snowdrifts thicken
Where, when leaves quicken,
Under the heather the sundew hides.

III.

Green land and red land,
Moorside and headland,
Are white as dead land,
  Are all as one;
Nor honied heather

Nor bells to gather,
Fair with fair weather
  And faithful sun:
Fierce frost has eaten
All flowers that sweeten
The fells rain-beaten;
  And winds their foes
Have made the snow's bed
Down in the rose-bed;
Deep in the snow's bed bury the rose.

IV.

Bury her deeper
Than any sleeper;
Sweet dreams will keep her
  All day, all night;
Though sleep benumb her
And time o'ercome her,
She dreams of summer,
  And takes delight,
Dreaming and sleeping
In love's good keeping,
While rain is weeping
  And no leaves cling;
Winds will come bringing her
Comfort, and singing her
Stories and songs and good news of the spring.

V.

Draw the white curtain
Close, and be certain
She takes no hurt in
  Her soft low bed;
She feels no colder,
And grows not older,
Though snows enfold her
  From foot to head;
She turns not chilly
Like weed and lily
In marsh or hilly
  High watershed,

Or green soft island
In lakes of highland ;
She sleeps awhile, and she is not dead.

VI.

For all the hours,
Come sun, come showers,
Are friends of flowers,
    And fairies all ;
When frost entrapped her,
They came and lapped her
In leaves, and wrapped her
    With shroud and pall ;
In red leaves wound her,
With dead leaves bound her
Dead brows, and round her
    A death-knell rang ;
Rang the death-bell for her,
Sang 'is it well for her,
Well, is it well with you, rose ?' they sang.

VII.

O what and where is
The rose now, fairies,
So shrill the air is,
    So wild the sky ?
Poor last of roses,
Her worst of woes is
The noise she knows is
    The winter's cry ;
His hunting hollo
Has scared the swallow ;
Fain would she follow
    And fain would fly ;
But wind unsettles
Her poor last petals ;
Had she but wings, and she would not die.

VIII.

Come, as you love her,
Come close and cover
Her white face over,
    And forth again
Ere sunset glances
On foam that dances,
Through lowering lances
    Of bright white rain ;
And make your playtime
Of winter's daytime
As if the Maytime
    Were here to sing ;
As if the snowballs
Were soft like blowballs,
Blown in a mist from the stalk in the spring.

IX.

Each reed that grows in
Our stream is frozen,
The fields it flows in
    Are hard and black ;
The water-fairy
Waits wise and wary
Till time shall vary
    And thaws come back.
'O sister, water,'
The wind besought her,
'O twin-born daughter
    Of spring with me,
Stay with me, play with me,
Take the warm way with me,
Straight for the summer and oversea.'

X.

But winds will vary,
And wise and wary
The patient fairy
    Of water waits ;
All shrunk and wizen,
In iron prison,
Till spring re-risen
    Unbar the gates ;
Till, as with clamor
Of axe and hammer,
Chained streams that stammer
    And struggle in straits
Burst bonds that shiver,
And thaws deliver
The roaring river in stormy spates.

XI.

In fierce March weather
White waves break tether,
And whirled together
    At either hand,
Like weeds uplifted,
The tree-trunks rifted
In spars are drifted,
    Like foam or sand,
Past swamp and sallow,
And reed-beds callow,
Through pool and shallow,
    To wind and lee,
Till, no more tongue-tied,
Full flood and young tide
Roar down the rapids and storm the sea.

XII.

As men's cheeks faded
On shores invaded,
When shorewards waded
    The lords of fight ;
When churl and craven
Saw hard on haven
The wide-winged raven
    At mainmast height ;
When monks affrighted
To windward sighted
The birds full-flighted
    Of swift sea-kings ;
So earth turns paler
When Storm the sailor
Steers in with a roar in the race of his wings.

XIII.

O strong sea-sailor,
Whose cheeks turn paler
For wind or hail or
    For fear of thee ?
O far sea-farer,
O thunder-bearer,
Thy songs are rarer
    Than soft songs be.
O fleet-foot stranger,
O north-sea ranger
Through days of danger
    And ways of fear,
Blow thy horn here for us,
Blow the sky clear for us,
Send us the song of the sea to hear.

XIV.

Roll the strong stream of it
Up, till the scream of it
Wake from a dream of it
    Children that sleep,
Seamen that fare for them
Forth, with a prayer for them ;
Shall not God care for them,

Angels not keep?
Spare not the surges
Thy stormy scourges ;
Spare us the dirges
    Of wives that weep.
Turn back the waves for us :
Dig no fresh graves for us,
Wind, in the manifold gulfs of the deep.

XV.

O stout north-easter,
Sea-king, land-waster,
For all thine, haste, or
    Thy stormy skill,
Yet hast thou never,
For all endeavor,
Strength to dissever
    Or strength to spill,
Save of his giving
Who gave our living,
Whose hands are weaving
    What ours fulfill ;
Whose feet tread under
The storms and thunder ;
Who made our wonder to work his will.

XVI.

His years and hours,
His world's blind powers,
His stars and flowers,
    His nights and days,
Sea-tide and river,
And waves that shiver,
Praise God, the giver
    Of tongues to praise.
Winds in their blowing,
And fruits in growing ;
Time in its going,
    While time shall be ;
In death and living,
With one thanksgiving,
Praise him whose hand is the strength of the sea

2. SPRING IN TUSCANY.

ROSE-RED lilies that bloom on the banner ;
  Rose-cheeked gardens that revel in spring ;
    Rose-mouthed acacias that laugh as they
      climb,

Like plumes for a queen's hand fashioned to
      fan her
  With wind more soft than a wild dove's wing,
What do they sing in the spring of their time ?

If this be the rose that the world hears singing,
 Soft in the soft night, loud in the day,
  Songs for the fire-flies to dance as they
    hear ;
If that be the song of the nightingale, spring-
    ing
 Forth in the form of a rose in May,
  What do they say of the way of the year ?

What of the way of the world gone Maying,
 What of the work of the buds in the bowers,
  What of the will of the wind on the wall,
Fluttering the wall-flowers, sighing and playing,
 Shrinking again as a bird that cowers,
  Thinking of hours when the flowers have
    to fall ?

Out of the throats of the loud birds shower-
    ing,
 Out of the folds where the flag-lilies leap,
  Out of the mouths of the roses stirred,
Out of the herbs on the walls reflowering,
 Out of the heights where the sheer snows
    sleep,
  Out of the deep and the steep, one word.

One from the lips of the lily-flames leaping,
 The glad red lilies that burn in our sight,
  The great live lilies for standard and
    crown ;
One from the steeps where the pines stand
    sleeping,
 One from the deep land, one from the height,
  One from the light and the might of the
    town.

The lowlands laugh with delight of the high-
    lands,
 Whence May winds feed them with balm
    and breath

From hills that beheld in the years behind
A shape as of one from the blest souls' islands,
 Made fair by a soul too fair for death,
  With eyes on the light that should smite
    them blind.

Vallombrosa remotely remembers,
 Perchance, what still to us seems so near,
  That time not darkens it, change not mars
The foot that she knew when her leaves were
    September's,
 The face lift up to the star-blind seer,
  That saw from his prison arisen his stars.

And Pisa broods on her dead, not mourning,
 For love of her loveliness given them in fee
  And Prato gleams with the glad monk's
    gift
Whose hand was there as the hand of morning
 And Siena, set in the sand's red sea,
  Lifts loftier her head than the red sand's
    drift.

And far to the fair south-westward lightens,
 Girdled and sandalled and plumed with
    flowers,
  At sunset over the love-lit lands,
The hill-side's crown where the wild hill
    brightens,
 Saint Fina's town of the Beautiful Towers,
  Hailing the sun with a hundred hands.

Land of us all that have loved thee dearliest,
 Mother of men that were lords of man,
  Whose name in the world's heart works a
    spell,
My last song's light, and the star of mine earli-
    est,
 As we turn from thee, sweet, who wast our
    for a span,
  Fare well we may not who say farewell.

3. SUMMER IN AUVERGNE.

The sundawn fills the land
Full as a feaster's hand
Fills full with bloom of bland
 Bright wine his cup ;
Flows full to flood that fills
From the arch of air it thrills
Those rust-red iron hills
 With morning up ;

Dawn, as a panther's springs,
With fierce and fire-fledged wings
Leaps on the land that rings
 From her bright feet
Thro' all its lava-black
Cones that cast answer back
And cliffs of footless track
 Where thunders meet.

The light speaks wide and loud
From deeps blown clean of cloud
As tho' days' heart were proud
　　And heaven's were glad ;
The towers brown-striped and grey
Take fire from heaven of day
As tho' the prayers they pray
　　Their answers had.

Higher in these high first hours
Wax all the keen church towers,
And higher all hearts of ours
　　Than the old hills' crown,
Higher than the pillared height
Of that strange cliff-side bright
With basalt towers whose might
　　Strong time bows down.

'Shut out the flower time
Half sun's half shower time,
Make way for our time,'

Wild winds have cried.
What is love worth ? nay,
Tell me, dear.

And the old fierce ruin there
Of the old wild princes' lair
Whose blood in mine hath share
　　Gapes gaunt and great
Toward heaven that long ago
Watched all the wan land's woe
Whereon the wind would blow
　　Of their bleak hate.

Dead are those deeds ; but yet
Their memory seems to fret
Lands that might else forget
　　That old world's brand ;
Dead all their sins and days ;
Yet in this red climes rays
Some fiery memory stays
　　That scars their land.

4. AUTUMN IN CORNWALL.

THE year lies fallen and faded
On cliffs by clouds invaded,
With tongues of storms upbraided,
　　With wrath of waves bedinned ;
And inland, wild with warning,
As in deaf ears or scorning,
The clarion even and morning
　　Rings of the south-west wind.

The wild bents wane and wither
In blasts whose breath bows hither
Their grey-grown heads and thither,
　　Unblest of rain or sun ;
The pale fierce heavens are crowded
Wite shapes like dreams beclouded,
As though the old year enshrouded
　　Lay, long ere life were done.

Full-charged with old-world wonders,
From dusk Tintagel thunders
A note that smites and sunders
　　The hard froze-fields of air ;
A trumpet stormier-sounded
Than once from lists rebounded
When strong men sense-confounded
　　Fell thick in tourney there.

From scarce a duskier dwelling
Such notes of wail rose welling
Thro' the outer darkness, telling
　　In the awful singer's ears
What souls the darkness covers,
What love-lost souls of lovers,
Whose cry still hangs and hovers
　　In each man's born that hears.

For there by Hector's brother
And yet some thousand other
He that had grief to mother
　　Passed pale from Dante's sight ;
With one fast linked as fearless,
Perchance, there only tearless ;
Iseult, and Tristram, peerless
　　And perfect queen and knight.

A shrill-winged sound comes flying
North, as of wild souls crying
The cry of things undying,
　　That know what life must be ?
Or as the old year's heart, stricken
Too sore for hope to quicken
By thoughts like thorns that thicken,
　　Broke, breaking with the sea.

17

THE WHITE CZAR.

[In an English magazine of 1877 there appeared a version of some insolent lines addressed by "A Russian Poet to the Empress of India." To these the first of the two following sonnets was designed to serve by way of counterblast. The writer will scarcely be suspected of royalism or imperialism; but it seemed to him that an insult levelled by Muscovite lips at the ruler of England might perhaps be less unfitly than unofficially resented by an Englishman who was also a republican.]

I.

GEHAZI by the hue that chills thy cheek
　And Pilate by the hue that sears thine hand
　Whence all earth's waters cannot wash the
　　brand
That signs thy soul a manslayer's though thou
　　speak
All Christ, with lips most murderous and most
　　meek—
　Thou set thy foot where England's used to
　　stand!
　Thou reach thy rod forth over Indian land!
Slave of the slaves that call thee lord, and
　　weak
As their foul tongues who praise thee! son of
　　them

Whose presence put the snows and stars to
　　shame
　In centuries dead and damned that reek be-
　　low
Curse-consecrated, crowned with crime and
　　flame,

To them that bare thee like them shalt
　　thou go
Forth of man's life—a leper white as snow.

II.

Call for clear water, wash thine hands, be
　　clean,
　Cry, *What is truth?* O Pilate; thou shalt
　　know
　Haply too soon, and gnash thy teeth for
　　woe
Ere the outer darkness take thee round unseen
That hides the red ghosts of thy race obscene,
　Bound nine times round with hell's most
　　dolorous flow
And in its pools thy crownless head lie low
By his of Spain who dared an English queen
With half a world to hearten him for fight,
Till the wind gave his warriors and their might
　To shipwreck and the corpse-encumbered
　　sea;
But thou, take heed, ere yet thy lips wax white,
　Lest as it was with Philip so it be,
O white of name and red of hand, with thee

RIZPAH.

How many sons, how many generations,
　For how long years hast thou bewept, and
　　known

Nor end of torment nor surcease of moan,
　Rachel or Rizpah, wofullest of nations,
Crowned with the crowning sign of desolation.

And couldst not even scare off with hand or
    groan
Those carrion birds devouring bone by
    bone
The children of thy thousand tribulations?
Thou wast our warrior once; thy sons long
    dead

Against a foe less foul than this made head,
    Poland, in years that sound and shine afar;
Ere the east beheld in thy bright sword-blade's
    stead
The rotten corpse-light of the Russian star
That lights towards hell his bondslaves and
    their Czar.

TO LOUIS KOSSUTH.

LIGHT of our fathers' eyes, and in our own
    Star of the unsetting sunset! for thy name,
    That on the front of noon was as a flame
In the great year nigh twenty years agone
When all the heavens of Europe shook and
    shone
    With stormy wind and lightning, keeps its
    fame
And bears its witness all day through the
    same;

Not for past days and great deeds past alone,
Kossuth, we praise thee as our Landor praised,
But that now too we know thy voice up-
    raised,
    Thy voice, the trumpet of the truth of God,
Thine hand, the thunder-bearer's, raised to
    smite
    As with heaven's lightning for a sword and
    rod
Men's heads abased before the Muscovite.

TRANSLATIONS FROM THE FRENCH OF VILLON.

THE COMPLAINT OF THE FAIR ARMOURESS.

1.

MESEEMETH I heard cry and groan
    That sweet who was the armourer's maid;
For her young years she made sore moan,
    And right upon this wise she said;
    "Ah fierce old age with foul bald head,
To spoil fair things thou art over fain;
    Who holdeth me? who? would God I were
    dead!
Would God I were well dead and slain!

2.

"Lo, thou hast broken the sweet yoke
    That my high beauty held above
All priests and clerks and merchant-folk;
    There was not one but for my love
    Would give me gold and gold enough,
Though sorrow his very heart had riven,
    To win from me such wage thereof
As now no thief would take if given.

3.

"I was right chary of the same,
　God wot it was my great folly,
For love of one sly knave of them,
　Good store of that same sweet had he ;
For all my subtle wiles, perdie,
God wot I loved him well enow ;
　Right evilly he handled me,
But he loved well my gold, I trow.

4.

"Though I gat bruises green and black,
　I loved him never the less a jot ;
Though he bound burdens on my back,
　If he said 'Kiss me,' and heed it not,'
　Right little pain I felt, God wot,
When that foul thief's mouth, found so sweet,
　Kissed me—Much good thereof I got !
I keep the sin and the shame of it.

5.

"And he died thirty year agone.
　I am old now, no sweet thing to see ;
By God, though, when I think thereon,
　And of that good glad time, woe's me,
　And stare upon my changed body
Stark naked, that has been so sweet,
　Lean, wizen, like a small dry tree,
I am nigh mad with the pain of it.

6.

"Where is my faultless forehead's white
　The lifted eyebrows, soft gold hair
Eyes wide apart and keen of sight,
　With subtle skill in the amorous air ;
　The straight nose, great nor small, but fair,
The small carved ears of shapeliest growth,
　Chin dimpling, color good to wear,
And sweet red splendid kissing mouth ?

7.

"The shapely slender shoulders small,
　Long arms, hands wrought in glorious wise,
Round little breasts, the hips withal
　High, full of flesh, not scant of size,
　Fit for all amorous masteries ;
*** ***** *****, *** *** ****** **** ***
******* ******, *** ** ******
** * ***** ****** ** **** *****?

8.

"A writhled forehead, hair gone grey,
　Fallen eyebrows, eyes gone blind and red,
Their laughs and looks all fled away,
　Yea, all that smote men's hearts are fled ;
　The bowed nose, fallen from goodlihead ;
Foul flapping ears like water-flags ;
　Peaked chin, and cheeks all waste and dead,
And lips that are two skinny rags :

9.

"Thus endeth all the beauty of us.
　The arms made short, the hands made lean,
The shoulders bowed and ruinous,
　The breasts, alack ! all fallen in ;
　The flanks too, like the breasts, grown thin
** *** *** ***** *****, *** ** ** !
*** *** **** ******, ** ****** *** ****,
**** *** **** ****** ****** ** *******-****

10.

"So we make moan for the old sweet days,
　Poor old light women, two or three
Squatting about the straw-fire's blaze,
　The bosom crushed against the knee,
　Like fagots on a heap we be,
Round fires soon lit, soon quenched and done ;
　And we were once so sweet, even we !
Thus fareth many and many an one."

A DOUBLE BALLAD OF GOOD COUNSEL.

Now take your fill of love and glee,
  And after balls and banquets hie ;
In the end ye'll get no good for fee,
  But just heads broken by and by ;
  Light loves make beasts of men that sigh ;
They changed the faith of Solomon,
  And left not Samson lights to spy ;
Good luck has he that deals with none !

Sweet Orpheus, lord of minstrelsy,
  For this with flute and pipe came nigh
The danger of the dog's heads three
  That ravening at hell's door doth lie ;
  Fain was Narcissus, fair and shy,
For love's love lightly lost and won,
  In a deep well to drown and die ;
Good luck has he that deals with none !

Sardana, flower of chivalry,
  Who conquered Crete with horn and cry,
For this was fain a maid to be
  And learn with girls the thread to ply ;
King David, wise in prophecy,
  Forgot the fear of God for one
  Seen washing either shapely thigh ;
Good luck has he that deals with none !

For this did Amnon, craftily
  Feigning to eat of cakes of rye,
Deflower his sister fair to see,
  Which was foul incest ; and hereby
  Was Herod moved, it is no lie,
To lop the head of Baptist John
  For dance and jig and psaltery ;
Good luck has he that deals with none !

Next of myself I tell, poor me,
  How thrashed like clothes at wash was I
Stark naked, I must needs agree ;
  Who made me eat so sour a pie
  But Katherine of Vaucelles ? thereby
Noé took third part of that fun ;
  Such wedding-gloves are ill to buy ;
Good luck has he that deals with none !

But for that young man fair and free
  To pass those young maids lightly by,
Nay, would you burn him quick, not he :
  Like broom-horsed witches though he fry,
  They are sweet as civet in his eye ;
But trust them, and you're fooled anon ;
  For white or brown, and low or high,
Good luck has he that deals with none !

A FRAGMENT ON DEATH.

And Paris be it or Helen dying,
  Who dies soever, dies with pain.
He that lacks breath and wind for sighing,
  His gall bursts on his heart ; and then

He sweats, God knows what sweat ! again,
  No man may ease him of his grief ;
  Child, brother, sister, none were fain
To bail him thence for his relief.

Death makes him shudder, swoon, wax pale,
  Nose bend, veins stretch, and breath sur-
    render,
Neck swell, flesh soften, joints that fail
  Crack their strained nerves and arteries
    slender.
  O woman's body found so tender,
Smooth, sweet, so precious in men's eyes,

    Must thou too bear such count to render?
Yes ; or pass quick into the skies.

   † [In the original here follows Villon's masterpiece,
the matchless *Ballad of the Ladies of Old Times*, so
incomparably rendered in the marvellous version of
Mr. Rossetti ; followed in its turn by the succeeding
poem, as inferior to its companion as is my attempt at
translation of it to his triumph in that higher and
harder field.—A. C. S.]

BALLAD OF THE LORDS OF OLD TIME.

AFTER THE FORMER ARGUMENT.

WHAT more ?   Where is the third Calixt,
  Last of that name now dead and gone,
Who held four years the Papalist ?
  Alphonso king of Aragon,
  The gracious lord, duke of Bourbon,
And Arthur, duke of old Britaine ?
  And Charles the Seventh, that worthy
    one ?
Even with the good knight Charlemain.

The Scot too, king of mount and mist,
  With half his face vermilion,
Men tell us, like an amethyst
  From brow to chin that blazed and shone ;
  The Cypriote king of old renown,
Alas ! and that good king of Spain,

Whose name I cannot think upon ?
Even with the good knight Charlemain.

No more to say of them I list ;
  'Tis all but vain, all dead and done :
For death may no man born resist,
  Nor make appeal when death comes on.
  I make yet one more question ;
Where's Lancelot, king of far Bohain ?
  Where's he whose grandson called him son ?
Even with the good knight Charlemain.

Where is Guesclin, the good Breton ?
  The lord of the eastern mountain-chain,
And the good late duke of Alençon ?
  Even with the good knight Charlemain.

BALLAD OF THE WOMEN OF PARIS.

ALBEIT the Venice girls get praise
  For their sweet speech and tender air,
And tho' the old women have wise ways
  Of chaffering for amorous ware,
  Yet at my peril dare I swear,
Search Rome, where God's grace mainly tar-
    ries,
  Florence and Savoy, everywhere,
There's no good girl's lip out of Paris.

The Naples women, as folk prattle,
  Are sweetly spoken and subtle enough :

German girls are good at tattle,
  And Prussians make their boast thereof ;
Take Egypt for the next remove,
  Or that waste land the Tartar harries,
  Spain or Greece, for the matter of love,
There's no good girl's lip out of Paris.

Breton and Swiss know nought of the matter,
  Gascony girls or girls of Toulouse ;
Two fishwomen with a half hour's chatter
  Would shut them up by threes and twos ;
  Calais, Lorraine, and all their crews.

(Names enow the mad song marries)
England and Picardy, search them and
   choose,
There's no good girl's lip out of Paris.

Prince, give praise to our French ladies
   For the sweet sound their speaking **carries ;**
'Twixt Rome and Cadiz many a maid is,
   But no good girl's lip out of Paris.

BALLAD WRITTEN FOR A BRIDEGROOM

**WHICH VILLON GAVE TO A GENTLEMAN NEWLY MARRIED TO SEND TO HIS WIFE WHOM HE HAD
WON WITH THE SWORD.**

At daybreak, when the falcon claps his wings,
No whit for grief, but noble heart and high,
With loud glad noise he stirs himself and
   springs,
And takes his meat and toward his lure draws
   nigh ;
Such good I wish you ! Yea, and heartily
I am fired with hope of true love's meed to get;
Know that Love writes it in his book ; for why,
This is the end for which we twain are met.

Mine own heart's lady with no gainsayings
You shall be always wholly till I die ;
And in my right against all bitter things
Sweet laurel with fresh rose its force shall try ;
Seeing reason wills not that I cast love by
(Nor here with reason shall I chide or fret)
Nor cease to serve, but serve more constantly ;
This is the end for which we twain are met.

And, which is more, when grief about me
   clings
Through Fortune's fit and fume of jealousy,
Your sweet kind eye beats down her threaten-
   ings
As wind doth smoke ; such power sits in your
   eye.
Thus in your field my seed of harvestry
Thrives, for the fruit is like me that I set ;
God bids me tend it with good husbandry ;
This is the end for which we twain are met.

Princess, give ear to this my summary ;
That heart of mine your heart's love should
   forget,
Shall never be ; like trust in you put I :
This is the end for which we twain are met.

BALLAD AGAINST THE ENEMIES OF FRANCE.

May he fall in with beasts that scatter fire,
   Like Jason, when he sought the fleece of
   gold,
Or change from man to beast three years entire,
   As King Nebuchadnezzar did of old ;
Or else have times as shameful and as bad
As Trojan folk for ravished Helen had ;
Or gulfed with Proserpine and Tantalus
Let hell's deep fen devour him dolorous,

   With worse to bear than Job's worst suf-
   ferance,
Bound in his prison-maze with Dædalus,
   Who could wish evil to the state of
   France !

May he four months, like bitterns in the mire,
   Howl with head downmost in the lake-
   springs cold,

Or to bear harness like strong bulls for hire
    To the Great Turk for money down be
      sold ;
Or thirty years like Magdalen live sad,
With neither wool nor web of linen clad ;
Drown like Narciss', or swing down pendulous
Like Absalom with locks luxurious,
    Or liker Judas fallen to reprobance ;
Or find such death as Simon sorcerous,
    Who could wish evil to the state of France !

May the old times come of fierce Octavian's
    ire,
    And in his belly molton coin be told ;
May he like Victor in the mill expire,
    Crushed between moving millstones on
      him rolled,
Or in deep sea drenched breathless, more
    adrad

Than in the whale's bulk Jonas, when God
    bade :
From Phœbus' light, from Juno's treasure-
    house
Driven, and from joys of Venus amorous,
    And cursed of God most high to the utter-
      ance,
As was the Syrian king Antiochus,
    Who could wish evil to the state of France !

ENVOY.

Prince, may the bright-winged brood of Æolus
To sea-king Glaucus' wild wood cavernous
    Bear him bereft of peace and hope's least
      glance,
For worthless is he to get good of us,
    Who could wish evil to the state of France !

THE DISPUTE OF THE HEART AND BODY OF FRANÇOIS VILLON.

WHO is this I hear ?—Lo, this is I, thine
    heart,
    That holds on merely now by a slender string.
Strength fails me, shape and sense are rent
    apart,
    The blood in me is turned to a bitter thing,
    Seeing thee skulk here like a dog shivering.—
Yea, and for what ?—For that thy sense found
    sweet.—
What irks it thee ?—I feel the sting of it.—
    Leave me at peace.—Why ?—Nay now, leave
    me at peace ;
I will repent when I grow ripe in wit.—
    I say no more.—I care not though thou
    cease.—
What art thou, trow ?—A man worth praise,
    perfay.—
    This is thy thirtieth year of wayfaring.—
'Tis a mule's age.—Art thou a boy still ?—
    Nay.--
    Is it hot lust that spurs thee with its sting,
    Grasping thy throat ? Know'st thou not
    anything ?—
Yea, black and white, when milk is specked
    with flies,
I can make out.—No more ?—Nay, in no wise.
    Shall I begin again the count of these ?—

Thou art undone.—I will make shift to rise.—
    I say no more.—I care not though thou
    cease.—

I have the sorrow of it, and thou the smart.
    Wert thou a poor mad fool or weak of wit,
Then might'st thou plead this pretext with
    thine heart ;
    But if thou know not good from evil a whit,
    Either thy head is hard as stone to hit,
Or shame, not honor, gives thee most content.
What canst thou answer to this argument ?—
    When I am dead I shall be well at ease.—
God ! what good luck ?—Thou art over elo-
    quent.—
    I say no more.—I care not though thou
    cease.—

Whence is this ill ?—From sorrow and not
    from sin.
    When Saturn packed my wallet up for me
I well believe he put these ills therein.—
    Fool, wilt thou make thy servant lord of
    thee ?
    Hear now the wise King's counsel ; thus
    saith he ;
All power upon the stars a wise man hath ;

There is no planet that shall do him scathe.—
  Nay, as they made me I grow and I de-
    crease.—
What say'st thou ?—Truly this is all my faith.—
  I say no more.—I care not though thou
    cease.—

Would'st thou live still ?—God help me that I
    may !—
Then thou must—What ? turn pentitent and
    pray ?—

Read always —What ?—Grave words and good
    to say ;
Leave off the ways of fools, lest they dis-
    please.—
Good ; I will do it.—Wilt thou remember ?—
    Yea.—
Abide not till there come an evil day.

  I say no more.—I care not though thou
    cease.—

EPISTLE IN FORM OF A BALLAD TO HIS FRIENDS.

Have pity, pity, friends, have pity on me,
  Thus much at least, may it please you, of
    your grace !
I lie not under hazel or hawthorn-tree
  Down in this dungeon ditch, mine exile's
    place
By leave of God and fortune's foul disgrace.
Girls, lovers, glad young folk and newly wed,
Jumpers and jugglers, tumbling heel o er head,
  Swift as a dart, and sharp as needle-ware,
Throats clear as bells that ring the kine to shed,
  Your poor old friend, what, will you leave
    him there ?

Singers that sing at pleasure, lawlessly,
  Light, laughing, gay of word and deed, that
    race
And run like folk light-witted as ye be
  And have in hand nor current coin nor base,
Ye wait too long, for now he's dying apace.
Rhymers of lays and roundels sung and read,
Ye'll brew him broth too late when he lies dead.
  Nor wind nor lightning, sunbeam nor fresh air,
May pierce the thick wall's bound where lies
    his bed ;

  Your poor old friend, what, will you leave
    him there ?

O noble folk from tithes and taxes free,
  Come and behold him in this piteous case,
Ye that nor king nor emperor holds in fee,
  But only God in heaven : behold his face
Who needs must fast, Sundays and holidays,
  Which makes his teeth like rakes ; and when
    he hath fed
With never a cake for banquet but dry bread,
  Must drench his bowels with much cold
    watery fare,
With board nor stool, but low on earth instead ;
  Your poor old friend, what, will you leave
    him there ?

Princes afore-named, old and young foresaid,
Get me the king's seal and my pardon sped,
  And hoist me in some basket up with care :
So swine will help each other ill bested,
For where one squeaks they run in heaps ahead.
  Your poor old friend, what, will you leave
    him there ?

THE EPITAPH IN FORM OF A BALLAD

WHICH VILLON MADE FOR HIMSELF AND HIS COMRADES, EXPECTING TO BE HANGED ALONG WITH THEM.

Men, brother men, that after us yet live,
Let not your hearts too hard aginst us be ;
For if some pity of us poor men ye give,
The sooner God shall take of you pity.
Here we are five or six strung up, you see,
And here the flesh that all too well we fed
Bit by bit eaten and rotten, rent and shred,

And we the bones grow dust and ash withal;
Let no man laugh at us discomforted,
But pray to God that he forgive us all.

If we call on you, brothers, to forgive,
Ye should not hold our prayer in scorn, though
    we
Were slain by law ; ye know that all alive

Have not wit alway to walk righteously ;
Make therefore intercession heartily
With him that of a virgin's womb was bred,
That his grace be not as a dry well-head
For us, nor let hell's thunder on us fall ;
We are dead, let no man harry or vex us dead,
But pray to God that he forgive us all.

The rain has washed and laundered us all five,
And the sun dried and blackened ; yea, perdie,
Ravens and pies with beaks that rend and rive
Have dug our eyes out, and plucked off for
    fee
Our beards and eyebrows ; never are we free,

Not once, to rest ; but here and there still
    speed,
Drive at its wild will by the wind's change/
    led,
More pecked of birds than fruits on garden-
    wall ;
Men, for God's love, let no gibe here be said,
But pray to God that he forgive us all.

Prince Jesus, that of all art lord and head,
Keep us, that hell be not our bitter bed ;
We have nought to do in such a master's hall.
Be not ye therefore of our fellowhead,
But pray to God that he forgive us all.

THE CHILDREN OF THE POOR.

FROM THE FRENCH OF VICTOR HUGO.

TAKE heed of this small child of earth ;
    He is great : he hath in him God most
        high.
Children before their fleshly birth
    Are lights alive in the blue sky.

In our light bitter world of wrong
    They come ; God gives us them awhile.
His speech is in their stammering tongue,
    And his forgiveness in their smile.

Their sweet light rests upon our eyes
    Alas ! their right to joy is plain.

If they are hungry, Paradise
    Weeps, and, if cold, Heaven thrills with
        pain.

The want that saps their sinless flower
    Speaks judgment on sin's ministers.
Man holds an angel in his power.
    Ah ! deep in Heaven what thunder stirs,

When God seeks out these tender things
    Whom in the shadow where we sleep
He sends us clothed about with wings,
    And find them ragged babes that weep !

NOCTURNE.

LA nuit écoute et se penche sur l'onde
Pour y cueillir rien qu'un souffle d'amour;
Pas de lueur, pas de musique au monde,
Pas de sommeil pour moi ni de séjour.
O mère, ô Nuit, de ta source profonde
Verse-nous, verse enfin l'oubli du jour.

Verse l'oubli de l'angoisse et du jour;
Chante; ton chant assoupit l'âme et l'onde:
Fais de ton sein pour mon âme un séjour,
Elle est bien lasse, ô mère, de ce monde,
Où le baiser ne veut pas dire amour,
Où l'âme aimée est moins que toi profonde.

Car toute chose aimée est moins profonde,
O Nuit, que toi, fille et mère du jour;
Toi dont l'attente est le répit du monde,
Toi dont le souffle est plein de mots d'amour,
Toi dont l'haleine enfle et réprime l'onde,
Toi dont l'ombre a tout le ciel pour séjour.

La misère humble et lasse, sans séjour,
S'abrite et dort sous ton aile profonde;
Tu fais à tous l'aumône de l'amour;
Toutes les soifs viennent boire à ton onde,
Tout ce qui pleure et se dérobe au jour,
Toutes les faims et tous les maux du monde.

Moi seul je veille et ne vois dans ce monde
Que ma douleur qui n'ait point de séjour
Où s'abriter sur ta rive profonde

Et s'endormir sous tes yeux loin du jour;
Je vais toujours cherchant au bord de l'onde
Le sang du beau pied blessé de l'amour.

La mer est sombre où tu naquis, amour,
Pleine des pleurs et des sanglots du monde;
On ne voit plus le gouffre où nait le jour
Luire et frémir sous ta leuer profonde;
Maisdans les cœurs d'homme où tu fais séjour
La douleur monte et baisse comme une onde.

ENVOI.

Fille de l'onde et mère de l'amour,
Du haut séjour plein de ta paix profonde
Sur ce bas monde épands un peu de jour.

THEOPHILE GAUTIER.

POUR mettre une couronne au front d'une
  chanson,
Il semblait qu'en passant son pied semât des
  roses,
Et que sa main cueillît comme des fleurs
  écloses
Les étoiles au fond du ciel en floraison.

Sa parole de marbre et d'or aviat le son
Desclaironsde l'été chassantles jours moroses;

Comme en Thrace Apollon banni des grands
  cieux roses,
Il regardait du cœur l'Olympe, sa maison.

Le soleil fut pour lui le soleil du vieux monde,
Et son œil recherchait dans les flots embrasés
Le sillon immortel d'où s'élança sur l'onde
Vénus, que la mer molle enivrait de baisers:
Enfin, dieu ressaisi de sa splendeur prmeière,
Il trône, et son sépulcre est bâti de lumière.

ODE.

(LE TOMBEAU DE THEOPHILE GAUTIER.)

QUELLE fleur, ô Mort, quel joyau, quel
  chant,
Quel vent, quel rayon de soleil couchant,
Sur ton front penché, sur ta main avide,
Sur l'âpre pâleur de ta l'èvre aride,
  Vibre encore et luit?
Ton sein est sans lait, ton oreille est vide,
  Ton œil plein de nuit.

Ta bouche est sans souffle et ton front sans
  ride;
Mais l'éclair voilé d'une flamme humide,
Flamme éclose au cœur d'un ciel pluvieux,
Rallume ta lèvre et remplit tes yeux
  De lueurs d'opale;
Ta bouche est vermeille et ton front joyeux,
  O toi qui fus pâle.

Comme aux jours divins la mère des
    dieux,
Reine au sein fécond, au corps radieux,
Tu surgis au bord de la tombe amère;
Tu nous apparais, ô Mort, vierge et mère,
    Effroi des humains,
Le divin laurier sur la tête altière
    Et la lyre aux mains.

Nous reconnaissons, courbés vers la terre,
Que c'est la splendeur de ta face austère
Qui dore la nuit de nos longs malheurs;
Que la vie ailée aux mille couleurs,
    Dont tu n'es que l'âme,
Refait par tes mains les prés et les fleurs,
    La rose et la femme.

Lune constante! astre ami des douleurs
Qui luis à travers la brume des pleurs!
Quelle flamme au fond de ta clarté molle

Eclate et rougit, nouvelle auréole,
    Ton doux front voilé?
Quelle étoile, ouvrant ses ailes, s'envole
    Du ciel étoilé?

Pleurant ce rayon de jour qu'on lui vole,
L'homme exècre en vain la Mort triste et folle;
Mais l'astre qui fut à nos yeux si beau,
Là-haut, loin d'ici, dans un ciel nouveau
    Plein d'autres étoiles,
Se lève, et pour lui la nuit du tombeau
    Entr'ouvre ses voiles.

L'âme est dans le corps comme un jeune
    oiseau
Dont l'aile s'agite au bord du berceau;
La mort, déliant cette aile inquiète,
Quand nous écoutons la bouche muette
    Qui nous dit adieu,
Fait de l'homme infime et sombre un poëte,
    Du poëte un dieu.

IN OBITUM THEOPHILI POETÆ.

O LUX Pieridum et laurigeri deliciæ dei,
Vox leni Zephyro lenior, ut veris amans
    novi
Tollit floridulis implicitum primitiis caput,
Ten' ergo abripuit non rediturum, ut redeunt
    novo
Flores vere novi, te quoque mors irrevoca-
    bilem?
Cur vatem neque te Musa parens, te neque
    Gratiæ,
Nec servare sibi te potuit fidum animi Venus?
Quæ nunc ipsa magis vel puero te Cinyreïo,
Te desiderium et flebilibus lumen amoribus,

Amissum queritur, sanguineis fusa comam
    genis.
Tantis tu lacrymis digne, comes dulcis Apol-
    lini,
Carum nomen eris dîs superis atque sodalibus
Nobis, quîs eadem quæ tibi vivo patuit via
Non æquis patet, at te sequimur passibus
    haud tuis,
At mæsto cinerem carmine non illacrymabi-
    lem
Tristesque exuvias floribus ac fletibus integris
Unà contegimus, nec citharâ nec sine tibiâ,
Votoque unanimæ vocis Ave dicimus et Vale.

AD CATULLUM.

CATULLE frater, ut velim comes tibi
Remota per vireta, per cavum nemus
Sacrumque Ditis haud inhospiti specus,
Pedem referre, trans aquam Stygis ducem
Secutus unum et unicum, Catulle, te,
Ut ora vatis optimi reviserem,
Tui meique vatis ora, quem scio
Venustiorem adîsse vel tuo lacum,
Benigniora semper arva vel tuis,
Ubi serenus accipit suos deus,
Tegitque myrtus implicata laureâ,

Manuque mulcet halituque consecrat
Fovetque blanda mors amabili sinu,
Et ore fama fervido colit viros
Alitque qualis unus ille par tibi
Britannus unicusque in orbe præstitit
Amicus ille noster, ille ceteris
Poeta major, omnibusque floribus
Priore Landor inclytum rosâ caput
Revinxit extulitque, quam tuâ manu
Recepit ac refovit integram suâ.

DEDICATION.

1878.

SOME nine years gone, as we dwelt together
In the sweet hushed heat of the south French
　　weather
　　Ere autumn fell on the vine-tressed hills
Or the season had shed one rose-red feather,

Friend, whose fame is a flame that fills
All eyes it lightens and hearts it thrills
　　With joy to be born of the blood which
　　bred
From a land that the grey sea girds and chills

The heart and spirit and hand and head
Whose might is as light on a dark day shed,
　　On a day now dark as a land's decline
Where all the peers of your praise are dead;

In a land and season of corn and vine
I pledged you a health from a beaker of mine
　　But half-way filled to the lip's edge yet
With hope for honey and song for wine.

Nine years have risen and eight years set
Since there by the wellspring our hands on it
　　met:
　　And the pledge of my songs that were
　　then to be,
I could wonder not, friend, though a friend
　　should forget.

For life's helm rocks to the windward and lee,
And time is as wind, and as waves are we;
　　And song is as foam that the sea-winds
　　fret,
Though the thought at its heart should be
　　deep as the sea.

POEMS AND BALLADS.

THIRD SERIES.

[To William Bell Scott, Poet and Painter, I dedicate these poems. In memory of many years.]

MARCH: AN ODE.

1887.

I.

ERE frost-flower and snow-blossom faded and
fell, and the splendour of winter had
passed out of sight,
The ways of the woodlands were fairer and
stranger than dreams that fulfil us in
sleep with delight;
The breath of the mouths of the winds had
hardened on tree-tops and branches that
glittered and swayed
Such wonders and glories of blossomlike snow
or of frost that outlightens all flowers till
it fade
That the sea was not lovelier than here was
the land, nor the night than the day, nor
the day than the night,
Nor the winter sublimer with storm than the
spring: such mirth had the madness and
might in thee made,
March, master of winds, bright minstrel and
marshal of storms that enkindle the season they smite.

II.

And now that the rage of thy rapture is satiate
with revel and ravin and spoil of the
snow,
And the branches it brightened are broken,
and shattered the tree-tops that only thy
wrath could lay low,
How should not thy lovers rejoice in thee,
leader and lord of the year that exults to
be born
So strong in thy strength and so glad in thy
gladness whose laughter puts winter and
sorrow to scorn?
Thou hast shaken the snows from thy wings,
and the frost on thy forehead is molten:
thy lips are aglow

As a lover's that kindle with kissing, and earth,
with her raiment and tresses yet wasted
and torn,
Takes breath as she smiles in the grasp of thy
passion to feel through her spirit the
sense of thee flow.

III.

Fain, fain would we see but again for an hour
what the wind and the sun have dispelled
and consumed,
Those full deep swan-soft feathers of snow
with whose luminous burden the branches
implumed
Hung heavily, curved as a half-bent bow, and
fledged not as birds are, but petalled as
flowers,
Each tree-top and branchlet a pinnacle jewelled and carved, or a fountain that shines
as it showers,
But fixed as a fountain is fixed not, and
wrought not to last till by time or by
tempest entombed,
As a pinnacle carven and gilded of men: for
the date of its doom is no more than an
hour's,
One hour of the sun's when the warm wind
wakes him to wither the snow-flowers
that froze as they bloomed.

IV.

As the sunshine quenches the snowshine; as
April subdues thee, and yields up his
kingdom to May;
So time overcomes the regret that is born of
delight as it passes in passion away,
And leaves but a dream for desire to rejoice
in or mourn for with tears or thanksgivings; but thou,
Bright god that art gone from us, maddest
and gladdest of months, to what goal
hast thou gone from us now?

For somewhere surely the storm of thy
 laughter that lightens, the beat of thy
 wings that play,
Must flame as a fire through the world, and
 the heavens that we know not rejoice in
 thee: surely thy brow
Hath lost not its radiance of empire, thy spirit
 the joy that impelled it on quest as for
 prey.

v.

Are thy feet on the ways of the limitless
 waters, thy wings on the winds of the
 waste north sea?
Are the fires of the false north dawn over
 heavens where summer is stormful and
 strong like thee
Now bright in the sight of thine eyes? are the
 bastions of icebergs assailed by the blast
 of thy breath?
Is it March with the wild north world when
 April is waning? the word that the
 changed year saith,
Is it echoed to northward with rapture of
 passion reiterate from spirits triumphant
 as we
Whose hearts were uplift at the blast of thy
 clarions as men's rearisen from a sleep
 that was death
And kindled to life that was one with the
 world's and with thine? hast thou set
 not the whole world free?

vi.

For the breath of thy lips is freedom, and
 freedom's the sense of thy spirit, the
 sound of thy song,
Glad god of the north-east wind, whose heart
 is as high as the hands of thy kingdom
 are strong,

Thy kingdom whose empire is terror and joy,
 twin-featured and fruitful of births
 divine,
Days lit with the flame of the lamps of the
 flowers, and nights that are drunken
 with dew for wine,
And sleep not for joy of the stars that deepen
 and quicken, a denser and fierier
 throng,
And the world that thy breath bade whiten
 and tremble rejoices at heart as they
 strengthen and shine,
And earth gives thanks for the glory bequeathed her, and knows of thy reign
 that it wrought not wrong.

vii.

Thy spirit is quenched not, albeit we behold
 not thy face in the crown of the steep
 sky's arch,
And the bold first buds of the whin wax
 golden, and witness arise of the thorn
 and the larch:
Wild April, enkindled to laughter and storm
 by the kiss of the wildest of winds that
 blow,
Calls loud on his brother for witness; his
 hands that were laden with blossom are
 sprinkled with snow,
And his lips breathe winter, and laugh, and
 relent; and the live woods feel not the
 frost's flame parch;
For the flame of the spring that consumes not
 but quickens is felt at the heart of the
 forest aglow,
And the sparks that enkindled and fed it were
 strewn from the hands of the gods of the
 winds of March.

THE COMMONWEAL.

1887.

i.

EIGHT hundred years and twenty-one
 Have shone and sunken since the land
 Whose name is freedom bore such brand
As marks a captive, and the sun
 Beheld her fettered hand.

ii.

But ere dark time had shed as rain
 Or sown on sterile earth as seed
 That bears no fruit save tare and
  weed
An age and half an age again,
 She rose on Runnymede.

III.

Out of the shadow, starlike still,
　She rose up radiant in her right,
　And spake, and put to fear and flight
The lawless rule of aweless will
　That pleads no right save might.

IV.

Nor since hath England ever borne
　The burden laid on subject lands,
　The rule that curbs and binds all hands
Save one, and marks for servile scorn
　The heads it bows and brands.

V.

A commonweal arrayed and crowned
　With gold and purple, girt with steel
　At need, that foes must fear or feel,
We find her, as our fathers found,
　Earth's lordliest commonweal.

VI.

And now that fifty years are flown
　Since in a maiden's hand the sign
　Of empire that no seas confine
First as a star to seaward shone,
　We see their record shine.

VII.

A troubled record, foul and fair,
　A simple record and serene,
　Inscribes for praise a blameless queen,
For praise and blame an age of care
　And change and ends unseen.

VIII.

Hope, wide of eye and wild of wing,
　Rose with the sundawn of a reign
　Whose grace should make the rough ways
　　plain,
And fill the worn old world with spring,
　And heal its heart of pain.

IX.

Peace was to be on earth; men's hope
　Was holier than their fathers had,
　Their wisdom not more wise than glad:
They saw the gates of promise ope,
　And heard what love's lips bade.

X.

Love armed with knowledge, winged and wise
　Should hush the wind of war, and see,
　They said, the sun of days to be
Bring round beneath serener skies
　A stormless jubilee.

XI.

Time, in the darkness unbeholden
　That hides him from the sight of fear
　And lets but dreaming hope draw near,
Smiled and was sad to hear such golden
　Strains hail the all-golden year.

XII.

Strange clouds have risen between, and wild
　Red stars of storm that lit the abyss
　Wherein fierce fraud and violence kiss
And mock such promise as beguiled
　The fiftieth year from this.

XIII.

War upon war, change after change,
　Hath shaken thrones and towers to dust,
　And hopes austere and faiths august
Have watched in patience stern and strange
　Men's works unjust and just.

XIV.

As from some Alpine watch-tower's portal
　Night, living yet, looks forth for dawn,
　So from time's mistier mountain lawn
The spirit of man, in trust immortal,
　Yearns toward a hope withdrawn.

XV.

The morning comes not, yet the night
　Wanes, and men's eyes win strength to
　　see
　Where twilight is, where light shall be
When conquered wrong and conquering right
　Acclaim a world set free.

XVI.

Calm as our mother-land, the mother
　Of faith and freedom, pure and wise,
　Keeps watch beneath unchangeful skies,
When hath she watch the woes of other
　Strange lands with alien eyes?

XVII.

Calm as she stands alone, what nation
  Hath lacked an alms from English hands
  What exiles from what stricken lands
Have lacked the shelter of the station
  Where higher than all she stands?

XVIII.

Though time discrown and change dismantle
  The pride of thrones and towers that frown,
  How should they bring her glories down—
The sea cast round her like a mantle,
  The sea-cloud like a crown?

XIX.

The sea, divine as heaven and deathless,
  Is hers, and none but only she
  Hath learnt the sea's word, none but we
Her children hear in heart the breathless
  Bright watchword of the sea.

XX.

Heard not of others, or misheard
  Of many a land for many a year,
  The watchword Freedom fails not here
Of hearts that witness if the word
  Find faith in England's ear.

XXI.

She, first to love the light, and daughter
  Incarnate of the northern dawn,
  She, round whose feet the wild waves fawn
When all their wrath of warring water
  Sounds like a babe's breath drawn,

XXII.

How should not she best know, love best,
  And best of all souls understand
  The very soul of freedom, scanned
Far off, sought out in darkling quest
  By men at heart unmanned?

XXIII.

They climb and fall, ensnared, enshrouded,
  By mists of words and toils they set
  To take themselves, till fierce regret
Grows mad with shame, and all their clouded
  Red skies hang sunless yet.

XXIV.

But us the sun, not wholly risen
  Nor equal now for all, illumes
  With more of light than cloud that looms;
Of light that leads forth souls from prison
  And breaks the seals of tombs.

XXV.

Did not her breasts who reared us rear
  Him who took heaven in hand, and weighed
  Bright world with world in balance laid?
What Newton's might could make not clear
  Hath Darwin's might not made?

XXVI.

The forces of the dark dissolve,
  The doorways of the dark are broken:
  The word that casts out night is spoken,
And whence the springs of things evolve
  Light born of night bears token.

XXVII.

She, loving light for light's sake only,
  And truth for only truth's, and song
  For song's sake and the sea's, how long
Hath she not borne the world her lonely
  Witness of right and wrong?

XXVIII.

From light to light her eyes imperial
  Turn, and require the further light,
  More perfect than the sun's in sight,
Till star and sun seem all funereal
  Lamps of the vaulted night.

XXIX.

She gazes till the strenuous soul
  Within the rapture of her eyes
  Creates or bids awake, arise,
The light she looks for, pure and whole
  And worshipped of the wise.

XXX.

Such sons are hers, such radiant hands
  Have borne abroad her lamp of old,
  Such mouths of honey-dropping gold
Have sent across all seas and lands
  Her fame as music rolled.

18

XXXI.

As music made of rolling thunder
    That hurls through heaven its heart
        sublime,
    Its heart of joy, in charging chime,
So ring the songs that round and under
    Her temple surge and climb.

XXXII.

A temple not by men's hands builded,
    But moulded of the spirit, and wrought
    Of passion and imperious thought;
With light beyond all sunlight gilded,
    Whereby the sun seems nought.

XXXIII.

Thy shrine, our mother, seen for fairer
    Than even thy natural face, made fair
    With kisses of thine April air
Even now, when spring thy banner-bearer
    Took up thy sign to bear;

XXXIV.

Thine annual sign from heaven's own arch
    Given of the sun's hand into thine,
    To rear and cheer each wildwood shrine
But now laid waste by wild-winged March,
    March, mad with wind like wine.

XXXV.

From all thy brightening downs whereon
    The windy seaward whin-flower shows
    Blossom whose pride strikes pale the rose
Forth is the golden watchword gone
    Whereat the world's face glows.

XXXVI.

Thy quickening woods rejoice and ring
    Till earth seems glorious as the sea:
    With yearning love too glad for glee
The world's heart quivers toward the spring
    As all our hearts toward thee.

XXXVII.

Thee, mother, thee, our queen, who givest
    Assurance to the heavens most high
    And earth whereon her bondsmen sigh
That by the sea's grace while thou livest
    Hope shall not wholly die.

XXXVIII.

That while thy free folk hold the van
    Of all men, and the sea-spray shed
    As dew more heavenly on thy head
Keeps bright thy face in sight of man,
    Man's pride shall drop not dead.

XXXIX.

A pride more pure than humblest prayer,
    More wise than wisdom born of doubt,
    Girds for thy sake men's hearts about
With thrust and triumph that despair
    And fear may cast not out.

XL.

Despair may ring men's hearts, and fear
    Bow down their heads to kiss the dust,
    Where patriot memories rot and rust,
And change makes faint a nation's cheer,
    And faith yields up her trust.

XLI.

Not here this year have true men known,
    Not here this year may true men know,
    That brand of shame-compelling woe
Which bids but brave men shrink or groan
    And lays but honour low.

XLII.

The strong spring wind blows notes of praise,
    And hallowing pride of heart, and cheer
    Unchanging, toward all true men here
Who hold the trust of ancient days
    High as of old this year.

XLIII.

The days that made thee great are dead;
    The days that now must keep thee great
    Lie not in keeping of thy fate;
In thine they lie, whose heart and head
    Sustain thy charge of state.

XLIV.

No state so proud, no pride so just,
    The sun, through clouds at sunrise curled
    Or clouds across the sunset whirled,
Hath sight of, nor has man such trust
    As thine in all the world.

XLV.

Each hour that sees the sunset's crest
  Make bright thy shores ere day decline
  Sees dawn the sun on shores of thine,
Sees west as east and east as west
  On thee their sovereign shine.

XLVI.

The sea's own heart must needs wax proud
  To have born the world a child like thee.
  What birth of earth might ever be
Thy sister? Time, a wandering cloud,
  Is sunshine on thy sea.

XLVII.

Change mars not her; and thee, our mother,
  What change that irks or moves thee mars?
  What shock that shakes? what chance that
    jars?
Time gave thee, as he gave none other,
  A station like a star's.

XLVIII.

The storm that shrieks, the wind that wages
  War with the wings of hopes that climb
  Too high toward heaven in doubt sublime,
Assail not thee, approved of ages
  The towering crown of time.

XLIX.

Toward thee this year thy children turning
  With souls uplift of changeless cheer
  Salute with love that casts out fear,
With hearts for beacons round thee burning,
  The token of this year.

L.

With just and sacred jubilation
  Let earth sound answer to the sea
  For witness, blown on winds as free,
How England, how her crowning nation,
  Acclaims this jubilee.

THE ARMADA.

1588 : 1888.

I.

I.

England, mother born of seamen, daughter
  fostered of the sea,
Mother more beloved than all who bear not
  all their children free,
Reared and nursed and crowned and cherished by the sea-wind and the sun,
Sweetest land and strongest, face most
  fair and mightiest heart in one,
Stands not higher than when the centuries
  known of earth were less by three,
When the strength that struck the whole
  world pale fell back from hers undone.

II.

At her feet were the heads of her foes bowed
  down, and the strengths of the storm of
  them stayed,
And the hearts that were touched not with
  mercy with terror were touched and
  amazed and affrayed:
Yea, hearts that had never been molten
  with pity were molten with fear as with
  flame,
And the priests of the Godhead whose temple
  is hell, and his heart is of iron and fire,
And the swordsmen that served and the seamen that sped them, whom peril could
  tame not or tire,
Were as foam on the winds of the waters
  of England which tempest can tire not
  or tame.

III.

They were girded about with thunder, and
  lightning came forth of the rage of their
  strength,
And the measure that measures the wings of
  the storm was the breadth of their force
  and their length:
And the name of their might was invincible,
  covered and clothed with the terror of
  God;
With his wrath were they winged, with his
  love were they fired, with the speed of
  his winds were they shod;
With his soul were they filled, in his trust were
  they comforted: grace was upon them
  as night,
And faith as the blackness of darkness: the
  fume of their balefires was fair in his
  sight;

The reek of them sweet as a savour of myrrh
    in his nostrils: the world that he made,
Theirs was it by gift of his servants: the wind,
    if they spake in his name, was afraid,
And the sun was a shadow before it, the stars
    were astonished with fear of it: fire
Went up to them, fed with men living, and lit
    of men's hands for a shrine or a pyre;
And the east and the west wind scattered their
    ashes abroad, that his name should be
    blest
Of the tribes of the chosen whose blessings are
    curses from uttermost east unto west.

II.

I.

Hell for Spain, and heaven for England,—
    God to God, and man to man,—
Met confronted, light with darkness, life with
    death: since time began,
    Never earth nor sea beheld so great a stake
    before them set,
    Save when Athens hurled back Asia from
    the lists wherein they met;
Never since the sands of ages through the
    glass of history ran
    Saw the sun in heaven a lordlier day than
    this that lights us yet.

II.

For the light that abides upon England, the
    glory that rests on her godlike name,
The pride that is love and the love that is
    faith, a perfume dissolved in flame,
    Took fire from the dawn of the fierce July
    when fleets were scattered as foam
And squadrons as flakes of spray; when gal-
    leon and galliass that shadowed the sea
Were swept from her waves like shadows that
    pass with the clouds they fell from, and
    she
    Laughed loud to the wind as it gave to
    her keeping the glories of Spain and
    Rome.

III.

Three hundred summers have fallen as leaves
    by the storms in their season thinned,
Since northward the war-ships of Spain came
    sheer up the way of the south-west
    wind:

Where the citadel cliffs of England are flanked
    with bastions of serpentine,
Far off to the windward loomed their hulls,
    an hundred and twenty-nine,
All filled full of war, full-fraught with battle
    and charged with bale;
Then store-ships weighted with cannon; and
    all were an hundred and fifty sail.
The measureless menace of darkness anhun-
    gered with hope to prevail upon light,
The shadow of death made substance, the
    present and visible spirit of night,
Came, shaped as a waxing or waning moon
    that rose with the fall of day,
To the channel where couches the Lion in
    guard of the gate of the lustrous bay.
Fair England, sweet as the sea that shields
    her, and pure as the sea from stain,
Smiled, hearing hardly for scorn that stirred
    her the menace of saintly Spain.

III.

I.

'They that ride over ocean wide with hempen
    bridle and horse of tree,'
How shall they in the darkening day of wrath
    and anguish and fear go free?
How shall these that have curbed the seas not
    feel his bridle who made the sea?

God shall bow them and break them now: for
    what is man in the Lord God's sight?
Fear shall shake them, and shame shall break,
    and all the noon of their pride be night:
These that sinned shall the ravening wind of
    doom bring under, and judgment smite.

England broke from her neck the yoke, and
    rent the fetter, and mocked the rod:
Shrines of old that she decked with gold she
    turned to dust, to the dust she trod:
What is she, that the wind and sea should
    fight beside her, and war with God?

Lo, the cloud of his ships that crowd her chan-
    nel's inlet with storm sublime,
Darker far than the tempests are that sweep
    the skies of her northmost clime;
Huge and dense as the walls that fence the
    secret darkness of unknown time.

Mast on mast as a tower goes past, and sail
   by sail as a cloud's wing spread;
Fleet by fleet, as the throngs whose feet keep
   time with death in his dance of dread;
Galleons dark as the helmsman's bark of old
   that ferried to hell the dead.

Squadrons proud as their lords, and loud with
   tramp of soldiers and chant of priests;
Slaves there told by the thousandfold, made
   fast in bondage as herded beasts;
Lords and slaves that the sweet free waves
   shall feed on, satiate with funeral feasts.

Nay, not so shall it be, they know; their priests
   have said it; can priesthood lie?
God shall keep them, their God shall sleep
   not: peril and evil shall pass them by:
Nay, for these are his children; seas and winds
   shall bid not his children die.

II.

So they boast them, the monstrous host whose
   menace mocks at the dawn: and here
They that wait at the wild sea's gate, and
   watch the darkness of doom draw near,
How shall they in their evil day sustain the
   strength of their hearts for fear?

Full July in the fervent sky sets forth her
   twentieth of changing morns:
Winds fall mild that of late waxed wild: no
   presage whispers or wails or warns:
Far to west on the bland sea's breast a sailing
   crescent uprears her horns.

Seven wide miles the serene sea smiles between them stretching from rim to rim:
Soft they shine, but a darker sign should bid
   not hope or belief wax dim:
God's are these men, and not the sea's: their
   trust is set not on her but him.

God's? but who is the God whereto the
   prayers and incense of these men rise?
What is he, that the wind and sea should fear
   him, quelled by his sunbright eyes?
What, that men should return again, and hail
   him Lord of the servile skies?

Hell's own flame at his heavenly name leaps
   higher and laughs, and its gulfs rejoice:

Plague and death from his baneful breath
   take life and lighten, and praise his
   choice:
Chosen are they to devour for prey the tribes
   that hear not and fear his voice.

Ay, but we that the wind and sea gird round
   with shelter of storms and waves
Know not him that ye worship, grim as
   dreams that quicken from dead men's
   graves:
God is one with the sea, the sun, the land that
   nursed us, the love that saves.

Love whose heart is in ours, and part of all
   things noble and all things fair;
Sweet and free as the circling sea, sublime
   and kind as the fostering air;
Pure of shame as is England's name, whose
   crowns to come are as crowns that were.

IV.

I.

But the Lord of darkness, the God whose
   love is a flaming fire,
The master whose mercy fulfils wide hell till
   its tortures tire,
He shall surely have heed of his servants who
   serve him for love, not hire.

They shall fetter the wing of the wind whose
   pinions are plumed with foam:
For now shall thy horn be exalted, and now
   shall thy bolt strike home;
Yea, now shall thy kingdom come, Lord God
   of the priests of Rome.

They shall cast thy curb on the waters, and
   bridle the waves of the sea:
They shall say to her, Peace, be still: and
   stillness and peace shall be:
And the winds and the storms shall hear them,
   and tremble, and worship thee.

Thy breath shall darken the morning, and
   wither the mounting sun;
And the daysprings, frozen and fettered, shall
   know thee, and cease to run;
The heart of the world shall feel thee, and die,
   and thy will be done.

The spirit of man that would sound thee, and
   search out causes of things,

Shall shrink and subside and praise thee: and
    wisdom, with plume-plucked wings,
Shall cower at thy feet and confess thee, that
    none may fathom thy springs.

The fountains of song that await but the wind
    of an April to be
To burst the bonds of the winter, and speak
    with the sound of a sea,
The blast of thy mouth shall quench them:
    and song shall be only of thee.

The days that are dead shall quicken, the
    seasons that were shall return;
And the streets and the pastures of England,
    the woods that burgeon and yearn,
Shall be whitened with ashes of women and
    children and men that burn.

For the mother shall burn with the babe
    sprung forth of her womb in fire,
And bride with bridegroom, and brother
    with sister, and son with sire;
And the noise of the flames shall be sweet in
    thine ears as the sound of a lyre.

Yea, so shall thy kingdom be stablished, and
    so shall the signs of it be:
And the world shall know, and the wind shall
    speak, and the sun shall see,
That these are the works of thy servants,
    whose works bear witness to thee.

II.

But the dusk of the day falls fruitless, whose
    light should have lit them on:
Sails flash through the gloom to shoreward,
    eclipsed as the sun that shone:
And the west wind wakes with dawn, and the
    hope that was here is gone.

Around they wheel and around, two knots to
    the Spaniard's one,
The wind-swift warriors of England, who
    shoot as with shafts of the sun,
With fourfold shots for the Spaniard's, that
    spare not till day be done.

And the wind with the sundown sharpens,
    and hurtles the ships to the lee,
And Spaniard on Spaniard smites, and shatters
    and yields; and we,

Ere battle begin, stand lords of the battle,
    acclaimed of the sea.

And the day sweeps round to the nightward;
    and heavy and hard the waves
Roll in on the herd of the hurtling galleons;
    and masters and slaves
Reel blind in the grasp of the dark strong
    wind that shall dig their graves.

For the sepulchres hollowed and shaped of
    the wind in the swerve of the seas,
The graves that gape for their pasture, and
    laugh, thrilled through by the breeze,
The sweet soft merciless waters, await and
    are fain of these.

As the hiss of a Python heaving in menace of
    doom to be
They hear through the clear night round them
    whose hours are as clouds that flee,
The whisper of tempest sleeping, the heave
    and the hiss of the sea.

But faith is theirs, and with faith are they
    girded and helmed and shod:
Invincible are they, almighty, elect for a sword
    and a rod;
Invincible even as their God is omnipotent,
    infinite, God.

In him is their strength, who have sworn that
    his glory shall wax not dim:
In his name are their war-ships hallowed as
    mightiest of all that swim:
The men that shall cope with these, and con-
    quer, shall cast out him.

In him is the trust of their hearts; the desire
    of their eyes is he;
The light of their ways, made lightning for
    men that would fain be free:
Earth's hosts are with them, and with them
    is heaven: but with us is the sea.

V.

I.

And a day and a night pass over;
    And the heart of their chief swells high;
For England, the warrior, the rover,
    Whose banners on all winds fly,
Soul-stricken, he saith, by the shadow of
    death, holds off him, and draws not nigh.

And the wind and the dawn together
   Make in from the gleaming east:
And fain of the wild glad weather
   As famine is fain of feast,
And fain of the fight, forth sweeps in its might
the host of the Lord's high priest.

And lightly before the breeze
   The ships of his foes take wing:
Are they scattered, the lords of the seas?
   Are they broken, the foes of the king?
And ever now higher as a mounting fire the
hopes of the Spaniard spring.

And a windless night comes down:
   And a breezeless morning, bright
With promise of praise to crown
   The close of the crowning fight,
Leaps up as the foe's heart leaps, and glows
with lustrous rapture of light.

And stinted of gear for battle
   The ships of the sea's folk lie,
Unwarlike, herded as cattle,
   Six miles from the foeman's eye
That fastens as flame on the sight of them
tame and offenceless, and ranged as to
die.

Surely the souls in them quail,
   They are stricken and withered at
      heart,
When in on them, sail by sail,
   Fierce marvels of monstrous art,
Tower darkening on tower till the sea-winds
cower-crowds down as to hurl them apart.

And the windless weather is kindly,
   And comforts the host in these;
And their hearts are uplift in them
      blindly,
   And blindly they boast at ease
That the next day's fight shall exalt them, and
smite with destruction the lords of the
seas.

II.

And lightly the proud hearts prattle,
   And lightly the dawn draws nigh,
The dawn of the doom of the battle
   When these shall falter and fly;
No day more great in the roll of fate filled
ever within the sky.

To fightward they go as to feastward,
   And the tempest of ships that drive
Sets eastward ever and eastward,
   Till closer they strain and strive;
And the shots that rain on the hulls of Spain
are as thunders afire and alive.

And about them the blithe sea smiles
   And flashes to windward and lee
Round capes and headlands and isles
   That heed not if war there be;
Round Sark, round Wight, green jewels of
light in the ring of the golden sea.

But the men that within them abide
   Are stout of spirit and stark
As rocks that repel the tide,
   As day that repels the dark;
And the light bequeathed from their swords
unsheathed shines lineal on Wight and
on Sark.

And eastward the storm sets ever,
   The storm of the sails that strain
And follow and close and sever
   And lose and return and gain;
And English thunder divides in sunder the
holds of the ships of Spain.

Southward to Calais, appalled
   And astonished, the vast fleet veers;
And the skies are shrouded and palled,
   But the moonless midnight hears
And sees how swift on them drive and drift
strange flames that the darkness fears.

They fly through the night from shore-
      ward,
   Heart-stricken till morning break,
And ever to scourge them forward
   Drives down on them England's Drake,
And hurls them in as they hurtle and spin and
stagger, with storm to wake.

VI.

I.

And now is their time come on them.
For eastward they drift and reel,
   With the shallows of Flanders ahead,
      with destruction and havoc at heel,
   With God for their comfort only, the
      God whom they serve; and here
Their Lord, of his great loving-kindness,
   may revel and make good cheer;

Though ever his lips wax thirstier with
drinking, and hotter the lusts in him
swell;
For he feeds the thirst that consumes him
with blood, and his winepress fumes
with the reek of hell.

II.

Fierce noon beats hard on the battle;
the galleons that loom to the lee
Bow down, heel over, uplifting their
shelterless hulls from the sea:
From scuppers aspirt with blood, from
guns dismounted and dumb,
The signs of the doom they looked for,
the loud mute witnesses come.
They press with sunset to seaward for comfort: and shall not they find it there?
O servants of God most high, shall his winds
not pass you by, and his waves not spare?

III.

The wings of the south-west wind are widened; the breath of his fervent lips,
More keen than a sword's edge, fiercer than
fire, falls full on the plunging ships.
The pilot is he of their northward flight, their
stay and their steersman he;
A helmsman clothed with the tempest, and
girdled with strength to constrain the
sea.
And the host of them trembles and quails,
caught fast in his hand as a bird in the
toils;
For the wrath and the joy that fulfil him are
mightier than man's, whom he slays and
spoils.
And vainly, with heart divided in sunder, and
labour of wavering will,
The lord of their host takes counsel with hope
if haply their star shine still,
If haply some light be left them of chance to
renew and redeem the fray;
But the will of the black south-wester is lord
of the councils of war to-day.
One only spirit it quells not, a splendour un-
darkened of chance or time;
Be the praise of his foes with Oquendo for
ever, a name as a star sublime.
But here what aid in a hero's heart, what help
in his hand may be?
For ever the dark wind whitens and blackens
the hollows and heights of the sea,

And galley by galley, divided and desolate,
founders; and none takes heed,
Nor foe nor friend, if they perish; forlorn,
cast off in their uttermost need,
They sink in the whelm of the waters, as peb-
bles by children from shoreward hurled,
In the North Sea's waters that end not, nor
know they a bourn but the bourn of the
world.
Past many a secure unavailable harbour, and
many a loud stream's mouth,
Past Humber and Tees and Tyne and Tweed,
they fly, scourged on from the south,
And torn by the scourge of the storm-wind
that smites as a harper smites on a lyre,
And consumed of the storm as the sacrifice
loved of their God is consumed with fire,
And devoured of the darkness as men that are
slain in the fires of his love are devoured,
And deflowered of their lives by the storms, as
by priests is the spirit of life deflowered.
For the wind, of its godlike mercy, relents not,
and hounds them ahead to the north,
With English hunters at heel, till now is the
herd of them past the Forth,
All huddled and hurtled seaward; and now
need none wage war upon these,
Nor huntsmen follow the quarry whose fall is
the pastime sought of the seas.
Day upon day upon day confounds them, with
measureless mists that swell,
With drift of rains everlasting and dense as
the fumes of ascending hell.
The visions of priest and of prophet beholding
his enemies bruised of his rod
Beheld but the likeness of this that is fallen on
the faithful, the friends of God.
Northward, and northward, and northward
they stagger and shudder and swerve
and flit,
Dismantled of masts and of yards, with sails
by the fangs of the storm-wind split.
But north of the headland whose name is
Wrath, by the wrath or the ruth of the
sea,
They are swept or sustained to the westward,
and drive through the rollers aloof to the
lee.
Some strive yet northward for Iceland, and
perish: but some through the storm-hewn
straits
That sunder the Shetlands and Orkneys are
borne of the breath which is God's or
fate's:

And some, by the dawn of September, at last
    give thanks as for stars that smile,
For the winds have swept them to shelter and
    sight of the cliffs of a Catholic isle.
Though many the fierce rocks feed on, and
    many the merciless heretic slays,
Yet some that have laboured to land with
    their treasure are trustful, and give God
    praise.
And the kernes of murderous Ireland, athirst
    with a greed everlasting of blood,
Unslakable ever with slaughter and spoil,
    rage down as a ravening flood,
To slay and to flay of their shining apparel
    their brethren whom shipwreck spares;
Such faith and such mercy, such love and
    such manhood, such hands and such
    hearts are theirs.
Short shrift to her foes gives England, but
    shorter doth Ireland to friends; and worse
Fare they that come with a blessing on treason
    than they that come with a curse.
Hacked, harried, and mangled of axes and
    skenes, three thousand naked and dead
Bear witness of Catholic Ireland, what sons
    of what sires at her breasts are bred.
Winds are pitiful, waves are merciful, tempest
    and storm are kind:
The waters that smite may spare, and the
    thunder is deaf, and the lightning is blind:
Of these perchance at his need may a man,
    though they know it not, yet find grace;
But grace, if another be hardened against him,
    he gets not at this man's face.
For his ear that hears and his eye that sees
    the wreck and the wail of men,
And his heart that relents not within him, but
    hungers, are like as the wolf's in his den.
Worthy are these to worship their master, the
    murderous Lord of lies,
Who hath given to the pontiff his servant the
    keys of the pit and the keys of the skies.
Wild famine and red-shod rapine are cruel,
    and bitter with blood are their feasts;
But fiercer than famine and redder than
    rapine the hands and the hearts of priests.
God, God bade these to the battle; and here,
    on a land by his servants trod,
They perish, a lordly blood-offering, subdued
    by the hands of the servants of God.
These also were fed of his priests with faith,
    with the milk of his word and the wine;
These two are fulfilled with the spirit of dark-
    ness that guided their quest divine.

And here, cast up from the ravening sea on
    the mild land's merciful breast,
This comfort they find of their fellows in
    worship; this guerdon is theirs of their
    quest.
Death was captain, and doom was pilot, and
    darkness the chart of their way;
Night and hell had in charge and in keeping
    the host of the foes of day.
Invincible, vanquished, impregnable, shat-
    tered, a sign to her foes of fear,
A sign to the world and the stars of laughter,
    the fleet of the Lord lies here.
Nay, for none may declare the place of the
    ruin wherein she lies;
Nay, for none hath beholden the grave
    whence never a ghost shall rise.
The fleet of the foemen of England hath
    found not one but a thousand graves;
And he that shall number and name them shall
    number by name and by tale the waves.

VII.

I.

Sixtus, Pope of the Church whose hope takes
    flight for heaven to dethrone the sun,
Philip, king that wouldst turn our spring to
    winter, blasted, appalled, undone,
Prince and priest, let a mourner's feast give
    thanks to God for your conquest won.

England's heel is upon you: kneel, O priest,
    O prince, in the dust, and cry,
'Lord, why thus? art thou wroth with us
    whose faith was great in thee, God most
    high?
Whence is this, that the serpent's hiss derides
    us? Lord, can thy pledged word lie?

'God of hell, are its flames that swell quenched
    now for ever, extinct and dead?
Who shall fear thee? or who shall hear the
    word thy servants who feared thee said?
Lord, art thou as the dead gods now, whose
    arm is shortened, whose rede is read?

'Yet we thought it was not for nought thy
    word was given us, to guard and guide:
Yet we deemed that they had not dreamed
    who put their trust in thee. Hast thou
    lied?
God our Lord, was the sacred sword we drew
    not drawn on thy Church's side?

'England hates thee as hell's own gates; and
  England triumphs, and Rome bows
  down:
England mocks at thee; England's rocks cast
  off thy servants to drive and drown:
England loathes thee; and fame betroths and
  plights with England her faith for crown.

'Spain clings fast to thee; Spain, aghast with
  anguish, cries to thee; where art thou?
Spain puts trust in thee; lo, the dust that soils
  and darkens her prostrate brow!
Spain is true to thy service; who shall raise up
  Spain for thy service now?

'Who shall praise thee, if none may raise thy
  servants up, nor affright thy foes?
Winter wanes, and the woods and plains forget the likeness of storms and snows:
So shall fear of thee fade even here: and what
  shall follow thee no man knows.'

Lords of night, who would breathe your blight
  on April's morning and August's noon,
God your Lord, the condemned, the abhorred,
  sinks hellward, smitten with deathlike
  swoon:
Death's own dart in his hateful heart now
  thrills, and night shall receive him soon.

God the Devil, thy reign of revel is here for
  ever eclipsed and fled:
God the Liar, everlasting fire lays hold at last
  on thee, hand and head:
God the Accurst, the consuming thirst that
  burns thee never shall here be fed.

II.

England, queen of the waves whose green
  inviolate girdle enrings thee round,
Mother fair as the morning, where is now the
  place of thy foemen found?
Still the sea that salutes us free proclaims
  them stricken, acclaims thee crowned.

Times may change, and the skies grow strange
  with signs of treason and fraud and fear:
Foes in union of strange communion may rise
  against thee from far and near:
Sloth and greed on thy strength may feed as
  cankers waxing from year to year.

Yet, though treason and fierce unreason
  should league and lie and defame and
  smite,
We that know thee, how far below thee the
  hatred burns of the sons of night,
We that love thee, behold above thee the witness written of life in light.

Life that shines from thee shows forth signs
  that none may read not but eyeless
  foes:
Hate, born blind, in his abject mind grows
  hopeful now but as madness grows:
Love, born wise, with exultant eyes adores thy
  glory, beholds and glows.

Truth is in thee, and none may win thee to lie,
  forsaking the face of truth:
Freedom lives by the grace she gives thee,
  born again from thy deathless youth:
Faith should fail, and the world turn pale,
  wert thou the prey of the serpent's
  tooth.

Greed and fraud, unabashed, unawed, may
  strive to sting thee at heel in vain:
Craft and fear and mistrust may leer and
  mourn and murmur and plead and plain:
Thou art thou: and thy sunbright brow is
  hers that blasted the strength of Spain.

Mother, mother beloved, none other could
  claim in place of thee England's
  place:
Earth bears none that beholds the sun so
  pure of record, so clothed with grace:
Dear our mother, nor son nor brother is thine,
  as strong or as fair of face.

How shalt thou be abased? or how shall fear
  take hold of thy heart? of thine,
England, maiden immortal, laden with charge
  of life and with hopes divine?
Earth shall wither, when eyes turned hither
  behold not light in her darkness shine.

England, none that is born thy son, and lives
  by grace of thy glory, free,
Lives and yearns not at heart and burns with
  hope to serve as he worships thee;
None may sing thee: the sea-wind's wing beats
  down our songs as it hails the sea.

TO A SEAMEW.

When I had wings, my brother,
  Such wings were mine as thine:
Such life my heart remembers
In all as wild Septembers
  As this when life seems other,
  ' Though sweet, than once was mine;
When I had wings, my brother,
  Such wings were mine as thine.

Such life as thrills and quickens
  The silence of thy flight,
Or fills thy note's elation
With lordlier exultation
Than man's, whose faint heart sickens
  With hopes and fears that blight
Such life as thrills and quickens
  The silence of thy flight.

Thy cry from windward clanging
  Makes all the cliffs rejoice;
Though storm clothe seas with sorrow,
Thy call salutes the morrow;
While shades of pain seem hanging
  Round earth's most rapturous voice,
Thy cry from windward clanging
  Makes all the cliffs rejoice.

We, sons and sires of seamen,
  Whose home is all the sea,
What place man may, we claim it;
But thine—whose thought may name it?
Free birds live higher than freemen,
  And gladlier ye than we—
We, sons and sires of seamen,
  Whose home is all the sea.

For you the storm sounds only
  More notes of more delight
Than earth's in sunniest weather:
When heaven and sea together
Join strengths against the lonely
  Lost bark borne down by night,
For you the storm sounds only
  More notes of more delight.

With wider wing, and louder
  Long clarion-call of joy,
Thy tribe salutes the terror
Of darkness, wild as error,
But sure as truth, and prouder
  Than waves with man for toy;
With wider wing, and louder
  Long clarion-call of joy.

The wave's wing spreads and flutters,
  The wave's heart swells and breaks;
One moment's passion thrills it,
One pulse of power fulfils it
And ends the pride it utters
  When, loud with life that quakes,
The wave's wing spreads and flutters,
  The wave's heart swells and breaks.

But thine and thou, my brother,
  Keep heart and wing more high
Than aught may scare or sunder;
The waves whose throats are thunder
Fall hurtling each on other,
  And triumph as they die;
But thine and thou, my brother,
  Keep heart and wing more high.

More high than wrath or anguish,
  More strong than pride or fear,
The sense or soul half hidden
In thee, for us forbidden,
Bids thee nor change nor languish,
  But live thy life as here,
More high than wrath or anguish,
  More strong than pride or fear.

We are fallen, even we, whose passion
  On earth is nearest thine;
Who sing, and cease from flying;
Who live, and dream of dying:
Grey time, in time's grey fashion,
  Bids wingless creatures pine:
We are fallen, even we, whose passion
  On earth is nearest thine.

The lark knows no such rapture,
  Such joy no nightingale,
As sways the songless measure
Wherein thy wings take pleasure:
Thy love may no man capture,
  Thy pride may no man quail;
The lark knows no such rapture,
  Such joy no nightingale.

And we, whom dreams embolden,
  We can but creep and sing
And watch through heaven's waste hollow
The flight no sight may follow
To the utter bourne beholden
  Of none that lack thy wing:
And we, whom dreams embolden,
  We can but creep and sing.

Our dreams have wings that falter,
　Our hearts bear hopes that die;
For thee no dream could better
A life no fears may fetter,
A pride no care can alter,
　That wots not whence or why
Our dreams have wings that falter,
　Our hearts bear hopes that die.

With joy more fierce and sweeter
　Than joys we deem divine
Their lives by time untarnished,
Are girt about and garnished,

Who match the wave's full metre
　And drink the wind's wild wine
With joy more fierce and sweeter
　Than joys we deem divine.

Ah, well were I for ever,
　Wouldst thou change lives with me,
And take my song's wild honey,
And give me back thy sunny
Wide eyes that weary never,
　And wings that search the sea;
Ah, well were I for ever,
　Wouldst thou change lives with me.

Beachy Head, September, 1886.

PAN AND THALASSIUS.

A LYRICAL IDYL.

THALASSIUS.

Pan!

PAN.

O sea-stray, seed of Apollo,
　What word wouldst thou have with me?
My ways thou wast fain to follow
　Or ever the years hailed thee
　　Man.

Now
If August brood on the valleys,
　If satyrs laugh on the lawns,
What part in the wildwood alleys
　Hast thou with the fleet-foot fauns—
　　Thou?

See!
Thy feet are a man's—not cloven
　Like these, not light as a boy's:
The tresses and tendrils inwoven
　That lure us, the lure of them cloys
　　Thee.

Us
The joy of the wild woods never
　Leaves free of the thirst it slakes:
The wild love throbs in us ever
　That burns in the dense hot brakes
　　Thus.

Life,
Eternal, passionate, awless,
　Insatiable, mutable, dear,
Makes all men's law for us lawless:
　We strive not: how should we fear
　　Strife?

We,
The birds and the bright winds know not
　Such joys as are ours in the mild
Warm woodland; joys such as grow not
　In waste green fields of the wild
　　Sea.

No;
Long since, in the world's wind veering,
　Thy heart was estranged from me:
Sweet Echo shall yield thee not hearing:
　What have we to do with thee?
　　Go.

THALASSIUS.

Ay!
Such wrath on thy nostril quivers
　As once in Sicilian heat
Bade herdsmen quail, and the rivers
　Shrank, leaving a path for thy feet
　　Dry?

Nay,
Low down in the hot soft hollow
Too snakelike hisses thy spleen:
'O sea-stray, seed of Apollo!'
What ill hast thou heard or seen?
Say.

Man
Knows well, if he hears beside him
The snarl of thy wrath at noon,
What evil may soon betide him,
Or late, if thou smite not soon,
Pan.

Me
The sound of thy flute, that flatters
The woods as they smile and sigh,
Charmed fast as it charms thy satyrs,
Can charm no faster than I
Thee.

Fast
Thy music may charm the splendid
Wide woodland silence to sleep
With sounds and dreams of thee blended
And whispers of waters that creep
Past.

Here
The spell of thee breathes and passes
And bids the heart in me pause,
Hushed soft as the leaves and the grasses
Are hushed if the storm's foot draws
Near.

Yet
The panic that strikes down strangers
Transgressing thy ways unaware
Affrights not me nor endangers
Through dread of thy secret snare
Set.

PAN.
Whence
May man find heart to deride me?
Who made his face as a star
To shine as a God's beside me?
Nay, get thee away from us, far
Hence.

THALASSIUS.
Then
Shall no man's heart, as he raises
A hymn to thy secret head,
Wax great with the godhead he praises:
Thou, God, shalt be like unto dead
Men.

PAN.
Grace
I take not of men's thanksgiving,
I crave not of lips that live;
They die, and behold, I am living,
While they and their dead Gods give
Place.

THALASSIUS.
Yea:
Too lightly the words were spoken
That mourned or mocked at thee dead:
But whose was the word, the token,
The song that answered and said
Nay?

PAN.
Whose
But mine, in the midnight hidden,
Clothed round with the strength of night
And mysteries of things forbidden
For all but the one most bright
Muse?

THALASSIUS.
Hers
Or thine, O Pan, was the token
That gave back empire to thee
When power in thy hands lay broken
As reeds that quake if a bee
Stirs?

PAN.
Whom
Have I in my wide woods need of?
Urania's limitless eyes
Behold not mine end, though they read of
A word that shall speak to the skies
Doom.

THALASSIUS.
She
Gave back to thee kingdom and glory,
And grace that was thine of yore,
And life to thy leaves, late hoary
As weeds cast up from the hoar
Sea.

Song
Can bid faith shine as the morning
Though light in the world be none:
Death shrinks if her tongue sound warning,
Night quails, and beholds the sun
Strong.

PAN.
Night
Bare rule over men for ages
  Whose worship wist not of me
And gat but sorrows for wages,
  And hardly for tears could see
    Light.

Call
No more on the starry presence
  Whose light through the long dark swam:
Hold fast to the green world's pleasance:
  For I that am lord of it am
    All.

THALASSIUS.
God,
God Pan, from the glad wood's portal
  The breaths of thy song blow sweet:
But woods may be walked in of mortal
  Man's thought, where never thy feet
    Trod.

Thine
All secrets of growth and of birth are,
  All glories of flower and of tree,
Wheresoever the wonders of earth are;
  The words of the spell of the sea
    Mine.

A BALLAD OF BATH.

LIKE a queen enchanted who may not laugh
    or weep,
  Glad at heart and guarded from change
    and care like ours,
Girt about with beauty by days and nights
    that creep
Soft as breathless ripples that softly shore-
    ward sweep,
  Lies the lovely city whose grace no grief
    deflowers.
Age and grey forgetfulness, time that shifts
    and veers,
  Touch not thee, our fairest, whose charm no
    rival nears,
  Hailed as England's Florence of one
    whose praise gives grace,
Landor, once thy lover, a name that love
    reveres:
  Dawn and noon and sunset are one before
    thy face.

Dawn whereof we know not, and noon whose
    fruit we reap,
  Garnered up in record of years that fell
    like flowers,
Sunset liker sunrise along the shining steep
Whence thy fair face lightens, and where thy
    soft springs leap,
  Crown at once and gird thee with grace of
    guardian powers.
Loved of men beloved of us, souls that fame
    inspheres,
All thine air hath music for him who dreams
    and hears;
  Voices mixed of multitudes, feet of friends
    that pace,

Witness why for ever, if heaven's face clouds
    or clears,
  Dawn and noon and sunset are one before
    thy face.

Peace hath here found harbourage mild as
    very sleep:
  Not the hills and waters, the fields and
    wildwood bowers,
Smile or speak more tenderly, clothed with
    peace more deep,
Here than memory whispers of days our mem-
    ories keep
  Fast with love and laughter and dreams of
    withered hours.
Bright were these as blossoms of old, and
    thought endears
Still the fair soft phantoms that pass with
    smiles or tears,
  Sweet as roseleaves hoarded and dried
    wherein we trace
Still the soul and spirit of sense that lives and
    cheers:
  Dawn and noon and sunset are one before
    thy face.

City lulled asleep by the chime of passing
    years,
Sweeter smiles thy rest than the radiance
    round thy peers;
  Only love and lovely remembrance here
    have place.
Time on thee lies lighter than music on men's
    ears;
  Dawn and noon and sunset are one before
    thy face.

IN A GARDEN.

BABY, see the flowers!
  —Baby sees
Fairer things than these,
Fairer though they be than dreams of
  ours.

Baby, hear the birds!
  —Baby knows
Better songs than those,
Sweeter though they sound than sweetest
  words.

Baby, see the moon!
  —Baby's eyes
Laugh to watch it rise,
Answering light with love and night with
  noon.

Baby, hear the sea!
  —Baby's face
Takes a graver grace,
Touched with wonder what the sound may be.

Baby, see the star!
  —Baby's hand
Opens, warm and bland,
Calm in claim of all things fair that are.

Baby, hear the bells!
  —Baby's head
Bows, as ripe for bed,
Now the flowers curl round and close their
  cells.

Baby, flower of light,
  Sleep, and see
Brighter dreams than we,
Till good day shall smile away good night.

A RHYME.

BABE, if rhyme be none
  For that sweet small word
Babe, the sweetest one
  Ever heard,

Right it is and meet
  Rhyme should keep not true
Time with such a sweet
  Thing as you.

Meet it is that rhyme
  Should not gain such grace;
What is April's prime
  To your face?

What to yours is May's
  Rosiest smile? what sound
Like your laughter sways
  All hearts round?

None can tell in metre
  Fit for ears on earth
What sweet star grew sweeter
  At your birth.

Wisdom doubts what may be:
  Hope, with smile sublime,
Trusts: but neither, baby,
  Knows the rhyme.

Wisdom lies down lonely;
  Hope keeps watch from far;
None but one seer only
  Sees the star.

Love alone, with yearning
  Heart for astrolabe,
Takes the star's height, burning
  O'er the babe.

BABY-BIRD.

BABY-BIRD, baby-bird,
  Ne'er a song on earth
May be heard, may be heard,
  Rich as yours in mirth.

All your flickering fingers,
  All your twinkling toes,
Play like light that lingers
  Till the clear song close.

Baby-bird, baby-bird,
　　Your grave majestic eyes
Like a bird's warbled words
　　Speak, and sorrow dies.

Sorrow dies for love's sake,
　　Love grows one with mirth,
Even for one white dove's sake,
　　Born a babe on earth.

Baby-bird, baby-bird,
　　Chirping loud and long,
Other birds hush their words,
　　Hearkening toward your song.

Sweet as spring though it ring,
　　Full of love's own lures,
Weak and wrong sounds their song,
　　Singing after yours.

Baby-bird, baby-bird,
　　The happy heart that hears
Seems to win back within
　　Heaven, and cast out fears.

Earth and sun seem as one
　　Sweet light and one sweet word
Known of none here but one,
　　Known of one sweet bird.

OLIVE.

I.

Who may praise her?
Eyes where midnight shames the sun,
Hair of night and sunshine spun,
Woven of dawn's or twilight's loom,
Radiant darkness, lustrous gloom,
Godlike childhood's flowerlike bloom,
None may praise aright, nor sing
Half the grace wherewith like spring
　　Love arrays her.

II.

Love untold
Sings in silence, speaks in light
Shed from each fair feature, bright
Still from heaven, whence toward us, now
Nine years since, she deigned to bow
Down the brightness of her brow,
Deigned to pass through mortal birth:
Reverence calls her, here on earth,
　　Nine years old.

III.

Love's deep duty,
Even when love transfigured grows
Worship, all too surely knows
How, though love may cast out fear,
Yet the debt divine and dear
Due to childhood's godhead here
May by love of man be paid
Never; never song be made
　　Worth its beauty.

IV.

Nought is all
Sung or said or dreamed or thought
Ever, set beside it; nought
All the love that man may give—
Love whose prayer should be, 'Forgive!'
Heaven, we see, on earth may live;
Earth can thank not heaven, we know,
Save with songs that ebb and flow,
　　Rise and fall.

V.

No man living,
No man dead, save haply one
Now gone homeward past the sun,
Ever found such grace as might
Tune his tongue to praise aright
Children, flowers of love and light,
Whom our praise dispraises: we
Sing, in sooth, but not as he
　　Sang thanksgiving.

VI.

Hope that smiled,
Seeing her new-born beauty, made
Out of heaven's own light and shade,
Smiled not half so sweetly: love,
Seeing the sun, afar above,
Warm the nest that rears the dove,
Sees, more bright than moon or sun,
All the heaven of heavens in one
　　Little child.

VII.

Who may sing her?
Wings of angels when they stir
Make no music worthy her:
Sweeter sound her shy soft words
Here than songs of God's own birds
Whom the fire of rapture girds
Round with light from love's face lit:
Hands of angels find no fit
 Gifts to bring her.

VIII.

Babes at birth
Wear as raiment round them cast,
Keep as witness toward their past,
Tokens left of heaven; and each,

Ere its lips learn mortal speech,
Ere sweet heaven pass on pass reach,
Bears in undiverted eyes
Proof of unforgotten skies
 Here on earth.

IX.

Quenched as embers
Quenched with flakes of rain or snow
Till the last faint flame burns low,
All those lustrous memories lie
Dead with babyhood gone by:
Yet in her they dare not die:
Others, fair as heaven is, yet,
Now they share not heaven, forget:
 She remembers.

A WORD WITH THE WIND.

LORD of days and nights that hear thy word
 of wintry warning,
 Wind, whose feet are set on ways that
 none may tread,
Change the nest wherein thy wings are fledged
 for flight by morning,
 Change the harbour whence at dawn thy
 sails are spread.
Not the dawn, ere yet the imprisoning night
 has half released her,
 More desires the sun's full face of cheer,
 than we,
Well as yet we love the strength of the iron-
 tongued north-easter,
 Yearn for wind to meet us as we front the
 sea.
All thy ways are good, O wind, and all the
 world should fester,
 Were thy fourfold godhead quenched, or
 stilled thy strife:
Yet the waves and we desire too long the
 deep south-wester,
 Whence the waters quicken shoreward,
 clothed with life.
Yet the field not made for ploughing save of
 keels nor harrowing
 Save of storm-winds lies unbrightened by
 thy breath:
Banded broad with ruddy samphire glow the
 sea-banks narrowing
 Westward, while the sea gleams chill and
 still as death.

Sharp and strange from inland sounds thy
 bitter note of battle,
 Blown between grim skies and waters sul-
 len-souled,
Till the baffled seas bear back, rocks roar and
 shingles rattle,
 Vexed and angered and anhungered and
 acold.
Change thy note, and give the waves their
 will, and all the measure,
 Full and perfect, of the music of their
 might,
Let it fill the bays with thunderous notes and
 throbs of pleasure,
 Shake the shores with passion, sound at
 once and smite.
Sweet are even the mild low notes of wind and
 sea, but sweeter
 Sounds the song whose choral wrath of
 raging rhyme
Bids the shelving shoals keep tune with
 storm's imperious metre,
 Bids the rocks and reefs respond in rapturous chime.
Sweet the lisp and lulling whisper and luxurious laughter,
 Soft as love or sleep, of waves whereon the
 sun
Dreams, and dreams not of the darkling hours
 before nor after,
 Winged with cloud whose wrath shall bid
 love's day be done.

19

Yet shall darkness bring the awakening sea
    a lordlier lover,
  Clothed with strength more amorous and
    more strenuous will,
Whence her heart of hearts shall kindle and
    her soul recover
  Sense of love too keen to lie for love's
    sake still.
Let thy strong south-western music sound,
    and bid the billows
  Brighten, proud and glad to feel thy
    scourge and kiss
Sting and soothe and sway them, bowed as
    aspens bend or willows,
  Yet resurgent still in breathless rage of
    bliss.
All to-day the slow sleek ripples hardly bear
    up shoreward,
  Charged with sighs more light than laugh-
    ter, faint and fair,
Like a woodland lake's weak wavelets lightly
    lingering forward,
  Soft and listless as the slumber-stricken
    air.
Be the sunshine bared or veiled, the sky
    superb or shrouded,
  Still the waters, lax and languid, chafed
    and foiled,
Keen and thwarted, pale and patient, clothed
    with fire or clouded,
  Vex their heart in vain, or sleep like ser-
    pents coiled.

Thee they look for, blind and baffled, wan
    with wrath and weary,
  Blown for ever back by winds that rock the
    bird:
Winds that seamews breast subdue the sea,
    and bid the dreary
  Waves be weak as hearts made sick with
    hope deferred.
Let thy clarion sound from westward, let the
    south bear token
  How the glories of thy godhead sound and
    shine:
Bid the land rejoice to see the land-wind's
    broad wings broken,
  Bid the sea take comfort, bid the world be
    thine.
Half the world abhors thee beating back the
    sea, and blackening
  Heaven with fierce and woful change of
    fluctuant form:
All the world acclaims thee shifting sail again,
    and slackening
  Cloud by cloud the close-reefed cordage of
    the storm.
Sweeter fields and brighter woods and lordlier
    hills than waken
  Here at sunrise never hailed the sun and
    thee:
Turn thee then, and give them comfort, shed
    like rain and shaken
  Far as foam that laughs and leaps along
    the sea.

NEAP-TIDE.

FAR off is the sea, and the land is afar:
  The low banks reach at the sky,
  Seen hence, and are heavenward high;
Though light for the leap of a boy they are,
  And the far sea late was nigh.

The fair wild fields and the circling downs,
  The bright sweet marshes and meads
  All glorious with flowerlike weeds,
The great grey churches, the sea-washed towns,
  Recede as a dream recedes.

The world draws back, and the world's light
    wanes,
  As a dream dies down and is dead;
  And the clouds and the gleams overhead
Change, and change; and the sea remains,
  A shadow of dreamlike dread.

Wild, and woful, and pale, and grey,
  A shadow of sleepless fear,
  A corpse with the night for bier,
The fairest thing that beholds the day
  Lies haggard and hopeless here.

And the wind's wings, broken and spent, sub-
    side;
  And the dumb waste world is hoar,
  And strange as the sea the shore;
And shadows of shapeless dreams abide
  Where life may abide no more.

A sail to seaward, a sound from shoreward
  And the spell were broken that seems
  To reign in a world of dreams
Where vainly the dreamer's feet make forward
  And vainly the low sky gleams.

The sea-forsaken forlorn deep-wrinkled
  Salt slanting stretches of sand
  That slope to the seaward hand,
Were they fain of the ripples that flashed and
    twinkled
    And laughed as they struck the strand?

As bells on the reins of the fairies ring
  The ripples that kissed them rang,
  The light from the sundawn sprang,
And the sweetest of songs that the world may
    sing
    Was theirs when the full sea sang.

Now no light is in heaven; and now
  Not a note of the sea-wind's tune
  Rings hither: the bleak sky's boon
Grants hardly sight of a grey sun's brow—
    A sun more sad than the moon.

More sad than a moon that clouds beleaguer
  And storm is a scourge to smite,
  The sick sun's shadowlike light

Grows faint as the clouds and the waves wax
    eager,
    And withers away from sight.

The day's heart cowers, and the night's heart
    quickens:
  Full fain would the day be dead
  And the stark night reign in his stead:
The sea falls dumb as the sea-fog thickens
    And the sunset dies for dread.

Outside of the range of time, whose breath
  Is keen as the manslayer's knife
  And his peace but a truce for strife,
Who knows if haply the shadow of death
    May be not the light of life?

For the storm and the rain and the darkness
    borrow
  But an hour from the suns to be,
  But a strange swift passage, that we
May rejoice, who have mourned not to-day,
    to-morrow,
    In the sun and the wind and the sea.

BY THE WAYSIDE.

SUMMER'S face was rosiest, skies and woods
    were mellow,
Earth had heaven to friend, and heaven had
    earth to fellow,
  When we met where wooded hills and
    meadows meet.
Autumn's face is pale, and all her late leaves
    yellow,
  Now that here again we greet.

Wan with years whereof this eightieth nears
    December,
  Fair and bright with love, the kind old
    face I know
Shines above the sweet small twain whose
    eyes remember
Heaven, and fill with April's light this pale
    November,
  Though the dark year's glass run low.

Like a rose whose joy of life her silence utters
When the birds are loud, and low the lulled
    wind mutters,
  Grave and silent shines the boy nigh three
    years old.
Wise and sweet his smile, that falters not nor
    flutters,
  Glows, and turns the gloom to gold.

Like the new-born sun's that strikes the dark
    and slays it,
  So that even for love of light it smiles and
    dies,
Laughs the boy's blithe face whose fair fourth
    year arrays it
All with light of life and mirth that stirs and
    sways it
  And fulfils the deep wide eyes.

Wide and warm with glowing laughter's ex-
    ultation,
Full of welcome, full of sunbright jubilation,
  Flash my taller friend's quick eyebeams,
    charged with glee;
But with softer still and sweeter salutation
  Shine my smaller friend's on me.

Little arms flung round my bending neck,
    that yoke it
  Fast in tender bondage, draw my face
    down too
Toward the flower-soft face whose dumb deep
    smiles invoke it,
Dumb, but love can read the radiant eyes
    that woke it,
  Blue as June's mid heaven is blue.

How may men find refuge, how should hearts
    be shielded,
From the weapons thus by little children
    wielded,
   When they lift such eyes as light this
    lustrous face—
Eyes that woke love sleeping unawares, and
    yielded,
   Love for love, a gift of grace,

Grace beyond man's merit, love that laughs,
    forgiving
   Even the sin of being no more a child, nor
    worth
Trust and love that lavish gifts above man's
    giving,
Touch or glance of eyes and lips the sweetest
    living,
   Fair as heaven and kind as earth?

NIGHT.

I.

FROM THE ITALIAN OF GIOVANNI STROZZI.

NIGHT, whom in shape so sweet thou here
    may'st see
   Sleeping, was by an Angel sculptured thus
   In marble, and since she sleeps hath life
    like us:
Thou doubt'st? Awake her: she will speak
    to thee.

II.

FROM THE ITALIAN OF MICHELANGELO BUO-
NARROTI.

Sleep likes me well, and better yet to know
   I am but stone. While shame and grief
    must be,
   Good hap is mine, to feel not, nor to see:
Take heed, then, lest thou wake me: ah, speak
    low.

IN TIME OF MOURNING.

'RETURN,' we dare not as we fain
   Would cry from hearts that yearn:
Love dares not bid our dead again
   Return.

   O hearts that strain and burn
As fires fast fettered burn and strain!
Bow down, lie still, and learn.

The heart that healed all hearts of pain
   No funeral rites inurn:
Its echoes, while the stars remain,
   Return.

May, 1885.

THE INTERPRETERS.

I.

DAYS dawn on us that make amends for many
   Sometimes,
When heaven and earth seem sweeter even
    than any
   Man's rhymes.

Light had not all been quenched in France,
    or quelled
   In Greece,
Had Homer sung not, or had Hugo held
   His peace.

Had Sappho's self not left her word thus
    long
   For token,
The sea round Lesbos yet in waves of song
   Had spoken.

II.

And yet these days of subtler air and finer
   Delight,
When lovelier looks the darkness, and
    diviner
   The light—

The gift they give of all these golden
hours,
Whose urn
Pours forth reverberate rays or shadowing
showers
In turn—

Clouds, beams, and winds that make the live
day's track
Seem living—
What were they did no spirit give them
back
Thanksgiving?

III.

Dead air, dead fire, dead shapes and shadows,
telling
Time nought;
Man gives them sense and soul by song, and
dwelling
In thought.

In human thought their being endures, their
power
Abides:
Else were their life a thing that each light
hour
Derides.

The years live, work, sigh, smile, and die,
with all
They cherish;
The soul endures, though dreams that fed it
fall
And perish.

IV.

In human thought have all things habitation·
Our days
Laugh, lower, and lighten past, and find no
station
That stays.

But thought and faith are mightier things
than time
Can wrong,
Made splendid once with speech, or made
sublime
By song.

Remembrance, though the tide of change that
rolls
Wax hoary,
Gives earth and heaven, for song's sake and
the soul's,
Their glory.

July 16th, 1885.

THE RECALL.

RETURN, they cry, ere yet your day
Set, and the sky grow stern:
Return, strayed souls, while yet ye may
Return.

But heavens beyond us yearn;
Yea, heights of heaven above the sway
Of stars that eyes discern.

The soul whose wings from shoreward
stray
Makes toward her viewless bourne
Though trustless faith and unfaith say,
Return.

BY TWILIGHT.

IF we dream that desire of the distance above us
Should be fettered by fear of the shadows that
seem,
If we wake, to be nought, but to hate or to
love us
If we dream.

Night sinks on the soul, and the stars as they
gleam
Speak menace or mourning, with tongues to
reprove us

That we deemed of them better than terror
may deem.

But if hope may not lure us, if fear may not
move us,
Thought lightens the darkness wherein the
supreme
Pure presence of death shall assure us, and
prove us
If we dream.

A BABY'S EPITAPH.

APRIL made me: winter laid me here away
    asleep.
Bright as Maytime was my daytime; night is
    soft and deep:
Though the morrow brings forth sorrow, well
    are ye that weep.

Ye that held me dear beheld me not a twelve-
    month long:
All the while ye saw me smile, ye knew not
    whence the song

Came that made me smile, and laid me here,
    and wrought you wrong.

Angels, calling from your brawling world one
    undefiled,
Homeward bade me, and forbade me here to
    rest beguiled:
Here I sleep not: pass, and weep not here
    upon your child.

ON THE DEATH OF SIR HENRY TAYLOR.

FOURSCORE and five times has the gradual
    year
    Risen and fulfilled its days of youth and
        eld
    Since first the child's eyes opening first
        beheld
Light, who now leaves behind to help us
    here
Light shed from song as starlight from a
    sphere
    Serene as summer; song whose charm
        compelled

The sovereign soul made flesh in Arte-
    velde
To stand august before us and austere,
Half sad with mortal knowledge, all sublime
With trust that takes no taint from change
    or time,
Trust in man's might of manhood.   Strong
    and sage,
    Clothed round with reverence of remem-
        bering hearts,
He, twin-born with our nigh departing age,
    Into the light of peace and fame departs.

IN MEMORY OF JOHN WILLIAM INCHBOLD.

FAREWELL: how should not such as thou fare
    well,
    Though we fare ill that love thee, and
        that live,
And know, whate'er the days wherein we
    dwell
    May give us, thee again they will not
        give?

Peace, rest, and sleep are all we know of death,
    And all we dream of comfort: yet for thee,
Whose breath of life was bright and strenuous
    breath,
    We think the change is other than we see.

The seal of sleep set on thine eyes to-day
    Surely can seal not up the keen swift light
That lit them once for ever.   Night can slay
    None save the children of the womb of
        night.

The fire that burns up dawn to bring forth
    noon
    Was father of thy spirit: how shouldst
        thou
Die as they die for whom the sun and
    moon
    Are silent?   Thee the darkness holds not
        now:

Them, while they looked upon the light, and
    deemed
    That life was theirs for living in the sun,
The darkness held in bondage: and they
    dreamed,
    Who knew not that such life as theirs was
        none.

To thee the sun spake, and the morning sang
    Notes deep and clear as life or heaven:
        the sea

That sounds for them but wild waste music
    rang
    Notes that were lost not when they rang
    for thee.

The mountains clothed with light and night
    and change,
    The lakes alive with wind and cloud and
    sun
Made answer, by constraint sublime and
    strange,
    To the ardent hand that bade thy will be
    done.

We may not bid the mountains mourn, the
    sea
    That lived and lightened from thine hand
    again
Moan, as of old would men that mourned as
    we
    A man beloved, a man elect of men,

A man that loved them. Vain, divine and
    vain,
    The dream that touched with thoughts or
    tears of ours
The spirit of sense that lives in sun and rain,
    Sings out in birds, and breathes and fades
    in flowers.

Not for our joy they live, and for our grief
    They die not. Though thine eye be closed,
    thine hand
Powerless as mine to paint them, not a leaf
    In English woods or glades of Switzerland

Falls earlier now, fades faster. All our love
    Moves not our mother's changeless heart,
    who gives
A little light to eyes and stars above,
    A little life to each man's heart that lives.

A little life to heaven and earth and sea,
    To stars and souls revealed of night and
    day,
And change, the one thing changeless: yet
    shall she
    Cease too, perchance, and perish. Who
    shall say?

Our mother Nature, dark and sweet as sleep,
    And strange as life and strong as death,
    holds fast,
Even as she holds our hearts alive, the deep
    Dumb secret of her first-born births and
    last.

But this, we know, shall cease not till the
    strife
    Of nights and days and fears and hopes
    find end;
This, through the brief eternities of life,
    Endures, and calls from death a living
    friend;

The love made strong with knowledge,
    whence confirmed
    The whole soul takes assurance, and the
    past
(So by time's measure, not by memory's,
    termed)
    Lives present life, and mingles first with
    last.

I, now long since thy guest of many days,
    Who found thy hearth a brother's, and
    with thee
Tracked in and out the lines of rolling
    bays
    And banks and gulfs and reaches of the
    sea—

Deep dens wherein the wrestling water sobs
    And pants with restless pain of refluent
    breath
Till all the sunless hollow sounds and throbs
    With ebb and flow of eddies dark as
    death—

I know not what more glorious world, what
    waves
    More bright with life,—if brighter aught
    may live
Than those that filled and fled their tidal
    caves—
    May now give back the love thou hast
    to give.

Tintagel, and the long Trebarwith sand,
    Lone Camelford, and Boscastle divine
With dower of southern blossom, bright and
    bland
    Above the roar of granite-baffled brine,

Shall hear no more by joyous night or day
    From downs or causeways good to rove
    and ride
Or feet of ours or horse-hoofs urge their
    way
    That sped us here and there by tower and
    tide.

The headlands and the hollows and the waves,
  For all our love, forget us: where I am
Thou art not: deeper sleeps the shadow on
      graves
    Than in the sunless gulf that once we
    swam.

Thou hast swum too soon the sea of death:
      for us
  Too soon, but if truth bless love's blind
  belief
Faith, born of hope and memory, says not
    thus:
  And joy for thee for me should mean not
  grief.

And joy for thee, if ever soul of man
  Found joy in change and life of ampler
  birth
Than here pens in the spirit for a span,
  Must be the life that doubt calls death
  on earth.

For if, beyond the shadow and the sleep,
  A place there be for souls without a stain,
Where peace is perfect, and delight more deep
  Than seas or skies that change and shine
  again,

There none of all unsullied souls that live
  May hold a surer station: none may lend
More light to hope's or memory's lamp, nor
    give
  More joy than thine to those that called
  thee friend.

Yea, joy from sorrow's barren womb is born
  When faith begets on grief the godlike child:
As midnight yearns with starry sense of morn
  In Arctic summers, though the sea wax
  wild,

So love, whose name is memory, thrills at
    heart,
  Remembering and rejoicing in thee, now
Alive where love may dream not what thou
    art
  But knows that higher than hope or love
  art thou.

'Whatever heaven, if heaven at all may be,
  Await the sacred souls of good men dead,
There, now we mourn who loved him here, is
    he.'
  So,' sweet and stern of speech, the Roman
  said,

Erect in grief, in trust erect, and gave
  His deathless dead a deathless life even
  here
Where day bears down on day as wave on
    wave
  And not man's smile fades faster than
  his tear.

Albeit this gift be given not me to give,
  Nor power be mine to break time's silent
  spell,
Not less shall love that dies not while I live
  Bid thee, beloved in life and death, fare-
  well.

NEW YEAR'S DAY.

New Year, be good to England. Bid her
    name
  Shine sunlike as of old on all the sea:
  Make strong her soul: set all her spirit free:
Bind fast her homeborn foes with links of
    shame
More strong than iron and more keen than
    flame:
  Seal up their lips for shame's sake: so
  shall she
Who was the light that lightened freedom be,
For all false tongues, in all men's eyes the
    same.

O last-born child of Time, earth's eldest
    lord,
  God undiscrowned of godhead, who for
  man
    Begets all good and evil things that
    live,
Do thou, his new-begotten son, implored
  Of hearts that hope and fear not, make
  thy span
    Bright with such light as history bids
    thee give.

                    Jan. 1, 1889.

TO SIR RICHARD F. BURTON.

(ON HIS TRANSLATION OF THE ARABIAN NIGHTS.)

WESTWARD the sun sinks, grave and glad; but far
Eastward, with laughter and tempestuous tears,
Cloud, rain, and splendour as of orient spears,
Keen as the sea's thrill toward a kindling star,
The sundawn breaks the barren twilight's bar
And fires the mist and slays it. Years on years
Vanish, but he that hearkens eastward hears
Bright music from the world where shadows are.

Where shadows are not shadows. Hand in hand
A man's word bids them rise and smile and stand
And triumph. All that glorious orient glows
Defiant of the dusk. Our twilight land
Trembles; but all the heaven is all one rose,
Whence laughing love dissolves her frosts and snows.

NELL GWYN.

SWEET heart, that no taint of the throne or the stage
Could touch with unclean transformation, or alter
To the likeness of courtiers whose consciences falter
At the smile or the frown, at the mirth or the rage,
Of a master whom chance could inflame or assuage,
Our Lady of Laughter, invoked in no psalter,
Adored of no faithful that cringe and that palter,

Praise be with thee yet from a hag-ridden age.

Our Lady of Pity thou wast: and to thee
All England, whose sons are the sons of the sea,
Gives thanks, and will hear not if history snarls
When the name of the friend of her sailors is spoken:
And thy lover she cannot but love—by the token
That thy name was the last on the lips of King Charles.

CALIBAN ON ARIEL.

'His backward voice is to utter foul speeches and to detract.'

HE tongue is loosed of that most lying slave,
Whom stripes may move, not kindness. Listen: 'Lo,
The real god of song, Lord Stephano,
That's a brave god, if ever god were brave,
And bears celestial liquor: but,' the knave
(A most ridiculous monster) howls, 'we know
From Ariel's lips what springs of poison flow,
The chicken-heart blasphemer! Hear him rave!'

Thou poisonous slave, got by the devil himself
Upon thy wicked dam, the witch whose name
Is darkness, and the sun her eyes' offence,
Though hell's hot sewerage breed no loathlier elf,
Men cry not shame upon thee, seeing thy shame
So perfect: they but bid thee—'Hag-seed, hence!'

THE WEARY WEDDING.

O DAUGHTER, why do ye laugh and weep,
  One with another?
For woe to wake and for will to sleep,
  Mother, my mother.

But weep ye winna the day ye wed,
  One with another.
For tears are dry when the springs are dead,
  Mother, my mother.

Too long have your tears run down like rain,
  One with another.
For a long love lost and a sweet love slain,
  Mother, my mother.

Too long have your tears dripped down like
    dew,
  One with another.
For a knight that my sire and my brethren
    slew,
  Mother, my mother.

Let past things perish and dead griefs lie,
  One with another.
O fain would I weep not, and fain would I die,
  Mother, my mother.

Fair gifts we give ye, to laugh and live,
  One with another.
But sair and strange are the gifts I give,
  Mother, my mother.

And what will ye give for your father's love?
  One with another.
Fruits full few and thorns enough,
  Mother, my mother.

And what will ye give for your mother's sake?
  One with another.
Tears to brew and tares to bake,
  Mother, my mother.

And what will ye give your sister Jean?
  One with another.
A bier to build and a babe to wean,
  Mother, my mother.

And what will ye give your sister Nell?
  One with another.
The end of life and beginning of hell,
  Mother, my mother.

And what will ye give your sister Kate?
  One with another.
Earth's door and hell's gate,
  Mother, my mother.

And what will ye give your brother Will?
  One with another.
Life's grief and world's ill,
  Mother, my mother.

And what will ye give your brother Hugh?
  One with another.
A bed of turf to turn into,
  Mother, my mother.

And what will ye give your brother John?
  One with another.
The dust of death to feed upon,
  Mother, my mother.

And what will ye give your bauld bridegroom?
  One with another.
A barren bed and an empty room,
  Mother, my mother.

And what will ye give your bridegroom's
    friend?
  One with another.
A weary foot to the weary end,
  Mother, my mother.

And what will ye give your blithe bridesmaid?
  One with another.
Grief to sew and sorrow to braid,
  Mother, my mother.

And what will ye drink the day ye're wed?
  One with another.
But ae drink of the wan well-head,
  Mother, my mother.

And whatten a water is that to draw?
  One with another.
We maun draw thereof a', we maun drink
    thereof a',
  Mother, my mother.

And what shall ye pu' where the well rins deep?
  One with another.
Green herb of death, fine flower of sleep,
  Mother, my mother.

Are there ony fishes that swim therein?
   One with another.
The white fish grace, and the red fish sin,
   Mother, my mother.

Are there ony birds that sing thereby?
   One with another.
O when they come thither they sing till they
     die,
   Mother, my mother.

Is there ony draw-bucket to that well-head?
   One with another.
There's a wee well-bucket hangs low by a
     thread,
   Mother, my mother.

And whatten a thread is that to spin?
   One with another.
It's green for grace, and it's black for sin,
   Mother, my mother.

And what will ye strew on your bride-cham-
     ber floor?
   One with another.
But one strewing and no more,
   Mother, my mother.

And whatten a strewing shall that one be?
   One with another.
The dust of earth and sand of the sea,
   Mother, my mother.

And what will ye take to build your bed?
   One with another.
Sighing and shame and the bones of the
     dead,
   Mother, my mother.

And what will ye wear for your wedding gown?
   One with another.
Grass for the green and dust for the brown,
   Mother, my mother.

And what will ye wear for your wedding lace?
   One with another.
A heavy heart and a hidden face,
   Mother, my mother.

And what will ye wear for a wreath to your
     head?
   One with another.
Ash for the white and blood for the red,
   Mother, my mother.

And what will ye wear for your wedding
     ring?
   One with another.
A weary thought for a weary thing,
   Mother, my mother.

And what shall the chimes and the bell-ropes
     play?
   One with another,
A weary tune on a weary day,
   Mother, my mother.

And what shall be sung for your wedding
     song?
   One with another.
A weary word of a weary wrong,
   Mother, my mother,

The world's way with me runs back,
   One with another,
Wedded in white and buried in black,
   Mother, my mother.

The world's day and the world's night,
   One with another,
Wedded in black and buried in white,
   Mother, my mother.

The world's bliss and the world's teen,
   One with another,
It's red for white and it's black for green,
   Mother, my mother.

The world's will and the world's way,
   One with another,
It's sighing for night and crying for day,
   Mother, my mother.

The world's good and the world's worth,
   One with another,
It's earth to flesh and it's flesh to earth,
   Mother, my mother.

*   *   *   *   *   *

When she came out at the kirkyard gate,
   (One with another)
The bridegroom's mother was there in wait
   (Mother, my mother.)

O mother, where is my great green bed,
   (One with another)
Silk at the foot and gold at the head,
   Mother, my mother?

Yea, it is ready, the silk and the gold,
    One with another.
But line it well that I lie not cold,
    Mother, my mother.

She laid her cheek to the velvet and vair,
    One with another;
She laid her arms up under her hair.
    (Mother, my mother.)

Her gold hair fell through her arms fu'
    low,
    One with another:
Lord God, bring me out of woe!
    (Mother, my mother.)

Her gold hair fell in the gay reeds green,
    One with another:
Lord God, bring me out of teen!
    (Mother, my mother.)

*   *   *   *   *   *

O mother, where is my lady gone?
    (One with another.)
In the bride-chamber she makes sore moan:
    (Mother, my mother.)

Her hair falls over the velvet and vair,
    (One with another)
Her great soft tears fall over her hair.
    (Mother, my mother.)

When he came into the bride's chamber,
    (One with another)
Her hands were like pale yellow amber.
    (Mother, my mother.)

Her tears made specks in the velvet and
    vair,
    (One with another)
The seeds of the reeds made specks in her
    hair.
    (Mother, my mother.)

He kissed her under the gold on her head;
    (One with another)
The lids of her eyes were like cold lead.
    (Mother, my mother.)

He kissed her under the fall of her chin;
    (One with another)
There was right little blood therein.
    (Mother, my mother.)

He kissed her under her shoulder sweet;
    (One with another)
Her throat was weak, with little heat.
    (Mother, my mother.)

He kissed her down by her breast-flowers red,
    One with another;
They were like river-flowers dead.
    (Mother, my mother.)

What ails you now o' your weeping, wife?
    (One with another.)
It ails me sair o' my very life.
    (Mother, my mother.)

What ails you now o' your weary ways?
    (One with another.)
It ails me sair o' my long life-days.
    (Mother, my mother.)

Nay, ye are young, ye are over fair.
    (One with another.)
Though I be young, what needs ye care?
    (Mother, my mother.)

Nay, ye are fair, ye are over sweet.
    (One with another.)
Though I be fair, what needs ye greet?
    (Mother, my mother.)

Nay, ye are mine while I hold my life.
    (One with another.)
O fool, will ye marry the worm for a wife?
    (Mother, my mother.)

Nay, ye are mine while I have my breath.
    (One with another.)
O fool, will ye marry the dust of death?
    (Mother, my mother.)

Yea, ye are mine, we are handfast wed,
    One with another.
Nay, I am no man's; nay, I am dead,
    Mother, my mother.

THE WINDS.

O WEARY fa' the east wind,
  And weary fa' the west:
And gin I were under the wan waves wide
  I wot weel wad I rest.

O weary fa' the north wind,
  And weary fa' the south:
The sea went ower my good lord's head
  Or ever he kissed my mouth.

Weary fa' the windward rocks,
  And weary fa' the lee:
They might hae sunken sevenscore ships,
  And let my love's gang free.

And weary fa' ye, mariners a',
  And weary fa' the sea:
It might hae taken an hundred men,
  And let my ae love be.

A LYKE-WAKE SONG.

FAIR of face, full of pride,
Sit ye down by a dead man's side.

Ye sang songs a' the day:
Sit down at night in the red worm's way.

Proud ye were a' day long:
Ye'll be but lean at evensong.

Ye had gowd kells on your hair:
Nae man kens what ye were.

Ye set scorn by the silken stuff:
Now the grave is clean enough.

Ye set scorn by the rubis ring:
Now the worm is a saft sweet thing.

Fine gold and blithe fair face,
Ye are come to a grimly place.

Gold hair and glad grey een,
Nae man kens if ye have been.

A REIVER'S NECK-VERSE.

SOME die singing, and some die swinging,
  And weel mot a' they be:
Some die playing, and some die praying,
  And I wot sae winna we, my dear,
  And I wot sae winna, we.

Some die sailing, and some die wailing,
  And some die fair and free:
Some die flyting, and some die fighting,
  But I for a fause love's fee, my dear,
  But I for a fause love's fee.

Some die laughing, and some die quaffing,
  And some die high on tree:
Some die spinning, and some die sinning,
  But faggot and fire for ye, my dear,
  Faggot and fire for ye.

Some die weeping, and some die sleeping,
  And some die under sea:
Some die ganging, and some die hanging,
  And a twine of a tow for me, my dear,
  A twine of a tow for me.

THE WITCH-MOTHER.

'O WHERE will ye gang to and where will ye
    sleep,
  Against the night begins?'
'My bed is made wi' cauld sorrows,
  My sheets are lined wi' sins.

'And a sair grief sitting at my foot,
  And a sair grief at my head;
And dule to lay me my laigh pillows,
  And teen till I be dead.

'And the rain is sair upon my face,
    And sair upon my hair;
And the wind upon my weary mouth,
    That never may man kiss mair.

'And the snow upon my heavy lips,
    That never shall drink nor eat;
And shame to cledding, and woe to wedding,
    And pain to drink and meat.

But woe be to my bairns' father,
    And ever ill fare he:
He has tane a braw bride hame to him,
    Cast out my bairns and me.'

'And what shall they have to their marriage
        meat
    This day they twain are wed?'
'Meat of strong crying, salt of sad sighing,
    And God restore the dead.'

'And what shall they have to their wedding
        wine
    This day they twain are wed?'
'Wine of weeping, and draughts of sleeping,
    And God raise up the dead.'

She's tane her to the wild woodside,
    Between the flood and fell:
She's sought a rede against her need
    Of the fiend that bides in hell.

She's tane her to the wan burnside,
    She's wrought wi' sang and spell:
She's plighted her soul for doom and dole
    To the fiend that bides in hell.

She's set her young son to her breast,
    Her auld son to her knee:
Says, 'Weel for you the night, bairnies,
    And weel the morn for me.'

She looked fu' lang in their een, sighing,
    And sair and sair grat she:
She has slain her young son at her
        breast,
    Her auld son at her knee.

She's sodden their flesh wi' saft water,
    She's mixed their blood with wine:
She's tane her to the braw bride-house,
    Where a' were boun' to dine.

She poured the red wine in his cup,
    And his een grew fain to greet:
She set the baked meats at his hand,
    And bade him drink and eat.

Says, 'Eat your fill of your flesh, my lord,
    And drink your fill of your wine,
For a' thing's yours and only yours
    That has been yours and mine.'

Says, 'Drink your fill of your wine, my
        lord,
    And eat your fill of your bread:
I would they were quick in my body again,
    Or I that bare them dead.'

He struck her head frae her fair body,
    And dead for grief he fell:
And there were twae mair sangs in heaven
    And twae mair sauls in hell.

THE BRIDE'S TRAGEDY.

THE wind wears roun', the day wears doun,
    The moon is grisly grey;
There's nae man rides by the mirk muir-
        sides,
    Nor down the dark Tyne's way.'
    In, in, out and in,
    Blaws the wind and whirls the whin.

'And winna ye watch the night wi' me,
    And winna ye wake the morn?
Foul shame it were that your ae mither
    Should brook her ae son's scorn.'
    In, in, out and in,
    Blaws the wind and whirls the whin.

'O mither, I may not sleep nor stray,
    My weird is ill to dree;
For a fause faint lord of the south seaboard
    Wad win my bride of me.'
    In, in, out and in,
    Blaws the wind and whirls the whin.

'The winds are strang, and the nights are
        lang,
    And the ways are sair to ride:
And I maun gang to wreak my wrang,
    And ye maun bide and bide.'
    In, in, out and in,
    Blaws the wind and whirls the whin.

'Gin I maun bide and bide, Willie,
  I wot my weird is sair:
Weel may ye get ye a light love yet,
  But never a mither mair.'
    In, in, out and in,
    Blaws the wind and whirls the whin.

O gin the morrow be great wi' sorrow,
  The wyte be yours of a':
But though ye slay me that haud and stay me,
  The weird ye will maun fa'.'
    In, in, out and in,
    Blaws the wind and whirls the whin.

When cocks were crawing and day was daw-
    ing,
  He's boun' him forth to ride:
And the ae first may he's met that day
  Was fause Earl Robert's bride.
    In, in, out and in,
    Blaws the wind and whirls the whin.

O blithe and braw were the bride-folk a',
  But sad and saft rade she;
And sad as doom was her fause bridegroom,
  But fair and fain was he.
    In, in, out and in,
    Blaws the wind and whirls the whin.

'And winna ye bide, sae saft ye ride,
  And winna ye speak wi' me?
For mony's the word and the kindly word
  I have spoken aft wi' thee.'
    In, in, out and in,
    Blaws the wind and whirls the whin.

'My lamp was lit yestreen, Willie,
  My window-gate was wide:
But ye camena nigh me till day came by me
  And made me not your bride.'
    In, in, out and in,
    Blaws the wind and whirls the whin.

He's set his hand to her bridle-rein,
  He's turned her horse away:
And the cry was sair, and the wrath was mair,
  And fast and fain rode they.
    In, in, out and in,
    Blaws the wind and whirls the whin.

But when they came by Chollerford,
  I wot the ways were fell;
For broad and brown the spate swang down,
  And the lift was mirk as hell.
    In, in, out and in,
    Blaws the wind and whirls the whin.

'And will ye ride yon fell water,
  Or will ye bide for fear?
Nae scathe ye'll win o' your father's kin,
  Though they should slay me here.'
    In, in, out and in,
    Blaws the wind and whirls the whin.

'I had liefer ride yon fell water,
  Though stange it be to ride,
Than I wad stand on the fair green strand
  And thou be slain beside.'
    In, in, out and in,
    Blaws the wind and whirls the whin.

'I had liefer swim yon wild water,
  Though sair it be to bide,
Than I wad stand at a strange man's hand,
  To be a strange man's bride.'
    In, in, out and in,
    Blaws the wind and whirls the whin.

'I had liefer drink yon dark water,
  Wi' the stanes to make my bed,
And the faem to hide me, and thou beside me,
  Than I wad see thee dead.'
    In, in, out and in,
    Blaws the wind and whirls the whin.

He's kissed her twice, he's kissed her thrice,
  On cheek and lip and chin:
He's wound her rein to his hand again,
  And lightly they leapt in.
    In, in, out and in,
    Blaws the wind and whirls the whin.

Their hearts were high to live or die,
  Their steeds were stark of limb:
But the stream was starker, the spate was
    darker,
  Than man might live and swim.
    In, in, out and in,
    Blaws the wind and whirls the whin.

The first ae step they strode therein,
  It smote them foot and knee:
But ere they wan to the mid water
  The spate was as the sea.
    In, in, out and in,
    Blaws the wind and whirls the whin.

But when they wan to the mid water,
  It smote them hand and head:
And nae man knows but the wave that flows
  Where they lie drowned and dead.
    In, in, out and in,
    Blaws the wind and whirls the whin.

A JACOBITE'S FAREWELL.

1716.

There's nae mair lands to tyne, my dear,
  And nae mair lives to gie:
Though a man think sair to live nae mair,
  There's but one day to die

For a' things come and a' days gane,
  What needs ye rend your hair?
But kiss me till the morn's morrow,
  Then I'll kiss ye nae mair.

O lands are lost and life's losing,
  And what were they to gie?
Fu' mony a man gives all he can,
  But nae man else gives ye.

Our king wons ower the sea's water,
  And I in prison sair:
But I'll win out the morn's morrow,
  And ye'll see me nae mair.

A JACOBITE'S EXILE.

1746.

The weary day rins down and dies,
  The weary night wears through:
And never an hour is fair wi' flower,
  And never a flower wi' dew.

I would the day were night for me,
  I would the night were day:
For then would I stand in my ain fair land,
  As now in dreams I may.

O lordly flow the Loire and Seine,
  And loud the dark Durance:
But bonnier shine the braes of Tyne
  Than a' the fields of France;
And the waves of Till that speak sae still
  Gleam goodlier where they glance.

O weel were they that fell fighting
  On dark Drumossie's day:
They keep their hame ayont the faem,
  And we die far away.

O sound they sleep, and saft, and deep,
  But night and day wake we;
And ever between the sea-banks green
  Sounds loud the sundering sea.

And ill we sleep, sae sair we weep,
  But sweet and fast sleep they;
And the mool that haps them roun' and laps
    them
  Is e'en their country's clay;
But the land we tread that are not dead
  Is strange as night by day.

Strange as night in a strange man's sight,
  Though fair as dawn it be:
For what is here that a stranger's cheer
  Should yet wax blithe to see?

The hills stand steep, the dells lie deep,
  The fields are green and gold:
The hill-streams sing, and the hill-sides ring,
  As ours at home of old.

But hills and flowers are nane of ours,
  And ours are oversea:
And the kind strange land whereon we stand,
  It wotsna what were we
Or ever we came, wi' scathe and shame,
  To try what end might be.

Scathe, and shame, and a waefu' name,
  And a weary time and strange,
Have they that seeing a weird for dreeing
  Can die, and cannot change.

Shame and scorn may we thole that mourn,
  Though sair be they to dree:
But ill may we bide the thoughts we hide,
  Mair keen than wind and sea.

Ill may we thole the night's watches,
  And ill the weary day:
And the dreams that keep the gates of sleep,
  A waefu' gift gie they;
For the sangs they sing us, the sights they
    bring us,
  The morn blaws all away.

On Aikenshaw the sun blinks braw,
  The burn rins blithe and fain:
There's nought wi' me I wadna gie
  To look thereon again.

On Keilder-side the wind blaws wide;
  There sounds nae hunting-horn
That rings sae sweet as the winds that beat
  Round banks where Tyne is born.

The Wansbeck sings with all her springs,
  The bents and braes give ear;
But the wood that rings wi' the sang she
    sings
  I may not see nor hear;
For far and far thae blithe burns are,
  And strange is a' thing near.

The light there lightens, the day there bright-
    ens,
  The loud wind there lives free:
Nae light comes nigh me or wind blaws by me
  That I wad hear or see.

But O gin I were there again,
  Afar ayont the faem,
Cauld and dead in the sweet saft bed
  That haps my sires at hame!

We'll see nae mair the sea-banks fair,
  And the sweet grey gleaming sky,
And the lordly strand of Northumberland,
  And the goodly towers thereby:
And none shall know but the winds that blow
  The graves wherein we lie.

THE TYNESIDE WIDOW.

THERE'S mony a man loves land and life,
  Loves life and land and fee;
And mony a man loves fair women,
  But never a man loves me, my love,
  But never a man loves me.

O weel and weel for a' lovers,
  I wot weel may they be;
And weel and weel for a' fair maidens,
  But aye mair woe for me, my love,
  But aye mair woe for me.

O weel be wi' you, ye sma' flowers,
  Ye flowers and every tree;
And weel be wi' you, a' birdies,
  But teen and tears wi' me, my love,
  But teen and tears wi' me.

O weel be yours, my three brethren,
  And ever weel be ye;
Wi' deeds for doing and loves for wooing,
  But never a love for me, my love,
  But never a love for me.

And weel be yours, my seven sisters,
  And good love-days to see,
And long life-days and true lovers,
  But never a day for me, my love,
  But never a day for me.

Good times wi' you, ye bauld riders,
  By the hieland and the lee;
And by the leeland and by the hieland
  It's weary times wi' me, my love,
  It's weary times wi' me.

Good days wi' you, ye good sailors,
  Sail in and out the sea;
And by the beaches and by the reaches
  It's heavy days wi' me, my love,
  It's heavy days wi' me.

I had his kiss upon my mouth,
  His bairn upon my knee;
I would my soul and body were twain,
  And the bairn and the kiss wi' me, my love,
  And the bairn and the kiss wi' me.

The bairn down in the mools, my dear,
  O saft and saft lies she;
I would the mools were ower my head,
  And the young bairn fast wi' me, my love,
  And the young bairn fast wi' me.

The father under the faem, my dear,
  O sound and sound sleeps he;
I would the faem were ower my face,
  And the father lay by me, my love,
  And the father lay by me.

I would the faem were ower my face,
  Or the mools on my ee-bree;
And waking, time with a' lovers,
  But sleeping-time wi' me, my love,
  But sleeping-time wi' me.

I would the mools were meat in my
    mouth,
  The saut faem in my ee;
And the land-worm and the water-worm
  To feed fu' sweet on me, my love,
  To feed fu' sweet on me.

My life is sealed with a seal of love,
  And locked with love for a key;

And I lie wrang and I wake lang,
  But ye tak' nae thought for me, my love,
  But ye tak' nae thought for me.

We were weel fain of love, my dear,
  O fain and fain were we;
It was weel with a' the weary world,
  But O, sae weel wi' me, my love,
  But O, sae weel wi' me.

We were nane ower mony to sleep, my dear,
  I wot we were but three;
And never a bed in the weary world
  For my bairn and my dear and me, my love,
  For my bairn and my dear and me.

DEDICATION.

THE years are many, the changes more,
Since wind and sun on the wild sweet
    shore
  Where Joyous Gard stands stark by the
    sea
With face as bright as in years of yore

Shone, swept, and sounded, and laughed for
    glee
More deep than a man's or a child's may be,
  On a day when summer was wild and glad,
And the guests of the wind and the sun were
    we.

The light that lightens from seasons clad
With darkness now, is it glad or sad?
  Not sad but glad should it shine, meseems,
On eyes yet fain of the joys they had.

For joy was there with us; joy that gleams
And murmurs yet in the world of dreams

  Where thought holds fast, as a constant
    warder,
The days when I rode by moors and streams,

Reining my rhymes into buoyant order
Through honied leagues of the northland
    border.
  Though thought or memory fade, and prove
A faithless keeper, a thriftless hoarder,

One landmark never can change remove,
One sign can the years efface not. Love,
  More strong than death or than doubt may
    be,
Treads down their strengths, and abides
    above.

Yea, change and death are his servants: we,
Whom love of the dead links fast, though free.
  May smile as they that beheld the dove
Bear home her signal across the sea.

SONGS OF THE SPRINGTIDES.

DEDICATION.

TO EDWARD JOHN TRELAWNY.

A sea-mew on a sea-king's wrist alighting,
  As the north sea-wind caught and strained and curled
The raven-figured flag that led men fighting
  From field to green field of the water-world,
Might find such brief high favour at his hand
  For wings imbrued with brine, with foam impearled,
As these my songs require at yours on land,
  That durst not save for love's free sake require,
Being lightly born between the foam and sand,
  But reared by hope and memory and desire
Of lives that were and life that is to be,
  Even such as filled his heavenlier song with fire
Whose very voice, that sang to set man free,
  Was in your ears as ever in ours his lyre,
Once, ere the flame received him from the sea.

THALASSIUS.

Upon the flowery forefront of the year,
One wandering by the grey-green April sea
Found on a reach of shingle and shallower
    sand
Inlaid with starrier glimmering jewellery
Left for the sun's love and the light wind's
    cheer
Along the foam-flowered strand
Breeze-brightened, something nearer sea than
    land
Though the last shoreward blossom-fringe was
    near,
A babe asleep with flower-soft face that gleamed
To sun and seaward as it laughed and dreamed,
Too sure of either love for either's fear,
Albeit so birdlike slight and light, it seemed
Nor man nor mortal child of man, but fair
As even its twin-born tenderer spray-flowers
    were,
That the wind scattered like an Oread's hair.

For when July strewed fire on earth and sea
The last time ere that year,
Out of the flame of morn Cymothoe
Beheld one brighter than the sun bright sphere
Move toward her from its fieriest heart, whence
    trod
The live sun's very God,
Across the foam-bright water-ways that are
As heavenlier heavens with star for answering
    star,
And on her eyes and hair and maiden mouth
Felt a kiss falling fiercer than the South
And heard above afar
A noise of songs and wind-enamoured wings
And lutes and lyres of milder and mightier
    strings,
And round the resonant radiance of his car
Where depth is one with height,
Light heard as music, music seen as light
And with that second moondawn of the spring's
That fosters the first rose,
A sun-child whiter than the sunlit snows
Was born out of the world of sunless things

That round the round earth flows and ebbs
    and flows.

But he that found the sea-flower by the
    sea
And took to foster like a graft of earth
Was born of man's most highest and heaven-
    liest birth,
Free-born as winds and stars and waves are
    free ;
A warrior grey with glories more than years,
Though more of years than change the quick
    to dead
Had rained their light and darkness on his
    head
A singer that in time's and memory's ears
Should leave such words to sing as all his
    peers
Might praise with hallowing heat of rapturous
    tears
Till all the days of human flight were fled.
And at his knees his fosterling was fed
Not with man's wine and bread
Nor mortal mother-milk of hopes and fears,
But food of deep memorial days long sped ;
For bread with wisdom and with song for wine
Clear as the full calms emerald hyaline.
And from his grave glad lips the boy would
    gather
Fine honey of song-notes goldener than gold,
More sweet than bees make of the breathing
    heather,
That he, as glad and bold,
Might drink as they, and keep his spirit from
    cold.
And the boy loved his laurel-laden hair
As his own father's risen on the eastern air,
And that less white brow-binding baylea
    bloom
More than all flowers his father's eyes relume
And those high songs he heard,
More than all notes of any landward bird,
More than all sounds less free
Than the wind's quiring to the choral sea.

High things the high song taught him ; how
  the breath
Too frail for life may be more strong than
  death ;
And this poor flash of sense in life, that gleams
As a ghost's glory in dreams,
More stabile than the world's own heart's root
  seems,
By that strong faith of lordliest love which
  gives
To death's own sightless-seeming eyes a light
Clearer, to death's bare bones a verier might,
Than shines or strikes from any man that lives.
How he that loves life overmuch shall die
The dog's death, utterly :
And he that much less loves it than he hates
All wrongdoing that is done
Anywhere always underneath the sun
Shall live a mightier life than time's or fate's.
One fairer thing he shewed him, and in might
More strong than day and night
Whose strengths build up time's towering
  period :
Yea, one thing stronger and more high than
  God,
Which if man had not, then should God not be:
And that was Liberty.
And gladly should man die to gain, he said,
Freedom ; and gladlier, having lost, lie dead.
For man's earth was not, nor the sweet sea-
  waves
His, nor his own land, nor its very graves,
Except they bred not, bore not, hid not slaves:
But all of all that is,
Were one man free in body and soul, were his.
  And the song softened, even as heaven by
  night
Softens, from sunnier down to starrier light,
And with its moonbright breath
Blessed life for death's sake, and for life's sake
  death.
Till as the moon's own beam and breath con-
  fuse
In one clear hueless haze of glimmering hues
The sea's line and the land's line and the sky's,
And light for love of darkness almost dies,
As darkness only lives for light's dear love,
Whose hands the web of night is woven of :
So in that heaven of wondrous words were life
And death brought out of strife ;
Yea, by that strong spell of serene increase
Brought out of strife to peace.

  And the song lightened, as the wind at morn
Flashes, and even with lightning of the wind

Night's thick-spun web is thinned
And all its weft unwoven and overworn
Shrinks, as might love from scorn.
And as when wind and light on water and
  land
Leap as twin gods from heavenward hand in
  hand,
And with the sound and splendor of their leap
Strike darkness dead, and daunt the spirit of
  sleep,
And burn it up with fire ;
So with the light that lightened from the lyre
Was all the bright heat in the child's heart
  stirred
And blown with blasts of music into flame
Till even his sense became
Fire, as the sense that fires the singing bird
Whose song calls night by name.
And in the soul within the sense began
The manlike passion of a godlike man,
And in the sense within the soul again
Thoughts that make men of gods and gods of
  men.

  For love the high song taught him : love
  that turns
God's heart toward man as man's to Godward ;
  love
That life and death and life are fashioned of,
From the first breath that burns
Half kindled on the flowerlike yeanling's lip,
So light and faint that life seems like to slip,
To that yet weaklier drawn
When sunset dies of night's devouring dawn
But the man dying not wholly as all men dies
If aught be left of his in live men's eyes
Out of the dawnless dark of death to rise ;
If aught of deed or word
Be seen for all time or of all time heard.
Love, that though body and soul were over-
  thrown
Should live for love's sake of itself alone,
Though spirit and flesh were one thing doom-
  ed and dead,
Not wholly annihilated.
Seeing even the hoariest ash-flake that the
  pyre
Drops, and forgets the thing was once afire
And gave its heart to feed the pile's full flame
Till its own heart its own heat overcame,
Outlives its own life, though by scarce a span
As such men dying outlive themselves in man,
Outlive themselves for ever ; if the heat
Outburn the heart that kindled it, the sweet
Outlast the flower whose soul it was, and flit

Forth of the body of it
Into some new shape of a strange perfume
More potent than its light live spirit of bloom,
How shall not something of that soul relive,
That only soul that had such gifts to give
As lighten something even of all men's doom
Even from the laboring womb
Even to the seal set on the unopening tomb?
And these the loving light of song and love
Shall wrap and lap round and impend above,
Imperishable ; and all springs born illume
Their sleep with brighter thoughts than wake
 the dove
To music, when the hillside winds resume
The marriage-song of heather-flower and
 broom
And all the joy thereof.

And hate the song too taught him : hate of all
That brings or holds in thrall
Of spirit or flesh, free-born ere God began,
The holy body and sacred soul of man.
And wheresoever a curse was or a chain,
A throne for torment or a crown for bane
Rose, moulded out of poor men's molten pain,
There, said he, should man's heaviest hate be
 set
Inexorably, to faint not or forget
Till the last warmth bled forth of the last vein
In flesh that none should call a king's again,
Seeing wolves and dogs and birds that plague-
 strike air
Leave the last bone of all the carrion bare.

And hope the high song taught him : hope
 whose eyes
Can sound the seas unsoundable, the skies
Inaccessible eyesight ; that can see
What earth beholds not, hear what wind and
 sea
Hear not, and speak what all these crying in
 one
Can speak not to the sun.
For in her sovereign eyelight all things are
Clear as the closest seen and kindlier star
That marries morn and even and winter and
 spring
With one loves golden ring.
For she can see the days of man, the birth
Of good and death of evil things on earth
Inevitable and infinite, and sure
As present pain is, or herself is pure.
Yea, she can hear and see, beyond all things
That lighten from before Time's thunderous
 wings

Through the awful circle of wheel-winged
 periods,
The tempest of the twilight of all Gods :
And higher than all the circling course the
 ran
The sundawn of the spirit that was man.

And fear the song too taught him ; fear t
 be
Worthless the dear love of the wind and sea
That bred him fearless, like a sea-mew reared
In rocks of man's foot feared,
Where nought of wingless life may sing o
 shine.
Fear to wax worthless of that heaven he had
When all the life in all his limbs was glad
And all the drops in all his veins were wine
And all the pulses music ; when his heart,
Singing, bade heaven and wind and sea bea
 part
In one live song's reiterance, and they bore :
Fear to go crownless of the flower he wore
When the winds loved him and the water
 knew,
The blithest life that clove their blithe li
 through
With living limbs exultant, or held strife
More amorous than all dalliance aye anew
With the bright breath and strength of thei
 large life,
With all strong wrath of all sheer winds tha
 blew,
All glories of all storms of the air that fell
Prone, ineluctable,
With roar from heaven of revel, and with hu
As of heaven turned hell.
For when the red blast of their breath had
 made
All heaven aflush with light more dire tha
 shade,
He felt it in his blood and eyes and hair
Burn as if all the fires of the earth and air
Had laid strong hold upon his flesh, and stun
The soul behind it as with serpent's tongue,
Forked like the loveliest lightnings : nor could
 bear
But hardly, half distraught with strong delight
The joy that like a garment wrapped hir
 round
And lapped him over and under
With raiment of great light
And rapture of great sound
At every loud leap earthward of the thunde
From heaven's most furthest bound :
So seemed all heaven in hearing and in sight

Alive and mad with glory and angry joy,
That something of its marvellous mirth and
    might
Moved even to madness, fledged as even for
    flight,
The blood and spirit of one but mortal boy.

So, clothed with love and fear that love
    makes great,
And armed with hope and hate,
He set first foot upon the spring-flowered ways
That all feet pass and praise.
And one dim dawn between the winter and
    spring,
In the sharp harsh wind harrying heaven and
    earth
To put back April that had borne his birth
From sunward on her sunniest shower-struck
    wing,
With tears and laughter for the dew-dropt
    thing,
Slight as indeed a dew-drop, by the sea
One met him lovelier than all men may be,
God-featured, with God's eyes ; and in their
    might
Somewhat that drew men's own to mar their
    sight,
Even of all eyes drawn toward him : and his
    mouth
Was as the very rose of all men's youth,
One rose of all the rose-beds in the world :
But round his brows the curls were snakes that
    curled,
And like his tongue a serpent's ; and his voice
Speaks death, and bids rejoice.
Yet then he spake no word, seeming as dumb,
A dumb thing mild and hurtless ; nor at first
From his bowed eyes seemed any light to
    come,
Nor his meek lips for blood or tears to thirst :
But as one blind and mute in mild sweet wise
Pleading for pity of piteous lips and eyes,
He strayed with faint bare lily-lovely feet
Helpless, and flowerlike sweet :
Nor might man see , not having word hereof,
That this of all gods was the great god Love.

And seeing him lovely and like a little child
That wellnigh wept for wonder that it smiled
And was so feeble and fearful, with soft speech
The youth bespake him softly ; but there fell
From the sweet lips no sweet word audible
That ear or thought might reach :
No sound to make the dim cold silence glad,

No breath to thaw the hard harsh air with
    heat ;
Only the saddest smile of all things sweet,
Only the sweetest smile of all things sad.

And so they went together one green way
Till April dying made free the world for May ;
And on his guide suddenly Love's face turned,
And in his blind eyes burned
Hard light and heat of laughter ; and like
    flame
That opens in a mountain's ravening mouth
To blear and sear the sunlight from the south,
His mute mouth opened, and his first word
    came :
' Knowest thou me now by name ? '
And all his stature waxed immeasurable,
As of one shadowing heaven and lightening
    hell ;
And statelier stood he than a tower that stands
And darkens with its darkness far-off sands
Whereon the sky leans red ;
And with a voice that stilled the winds he said:
'I am he that was thy lord before thy birth,
I am he that is thy lord till thou turn earth :
I make the night more dark, and all the morrow
Dark as the night whose darkness was my
    breath :
O fool, my name is sorrow ;
Thou fool, my name is death.'

And he that heard spake not, and looked
    right on
Again, and Love was gone.
Through many a night toward many a
    wearier day
His spirit bore his body down its way.
Through many a day toward many a wearier
    night
His soul sustained his sorrows in her sight.
And earth was bitterer, and heaven, and even
    the sea
Sorrowful even as he.
And the wind helped not, and the sun was
    dumb ;
And with too long stress of grief to be
His heart grew sere and numb.

And one bright eve ere summer in autumn
    sank
At stardawn standing on a grey sea-bank
He felt the wind fitfully shift and heave
As toward a stormier eve ;
And all the wan wide sea shuddered ; and
    earth

Shook underfoot as toward some timeless
 birth,
Intolerable and inevitable ; and all
Heaven, darkling, trembled like a stricken
 thrall.
And far out of the quivering east, and far
From past the moonrise and its guiding star,
Began a noise of tempest and a light
That was not of the lightning ; and a sound
Rang with it round and round
That was not of the thunder; and a flight
As of blown clouds by night,
That was not of them ; and with songs and
 cries
That sang and shrieked their soul out at the skies
A shapeless earthly storm of shapes began
From all ways round to move in on the man,
Clamorous against him silent ; and their feet
Were as the wind's are fleet,
And their shrill songs were as wild birds' are
 sweet.

And as when all the world of earth was
 wronged
And all the host of all men driven afoam
By the red hand of Rome,
Round some fierce amphitheatre overthronged
With fair clear faces full of bloodier lust
Than swells and stings the tiger when his
 mood
Is fieriest after blood
And drunk with trampling of the murderous
 must
That soaks and stains the tortuous close-coiled
 wood
Made monstrous with its myriad-mustering
 brood,
Face by fair face panted and gleamed and
 pressed,
And breast by passionate breast
Heaved hot with ravenous rapture, as they
 quaffed
The red ripe full fume of the deep live draught,
The sharp quick reek of keen fresh bloodshed,
 blown
Through the dense deep drift up to the emper-
 or's throne
From the under steaming sands
With clamour of all-applausive throats and
 hands,
Mingling in mirthful time
With shrill blithe mockeries of the lithe-
 limbed mime :
So from somewhence far forth of the unbe-
 holden,

Dreadfully driven from over and after and
 under,
Fierce, blown through fifes of brazen blast and
 golden,
With sound of chiming waves that drown the
 thunder
Or thunder that strikes dumb the sea's own
 chimes,
Began the bellowing of the bull-voiced mimes,
Terrible ; firs bowed down as briars or palms
Even as the breathless blast as of a breeze
Fulfilled with clamor and clangor and storms
 of psalms ;
Red hands rent up the roots of oldworld trees,
Thick flames of torches tossed as tumbling
 seas
Made mad the moonless and infuriate air
That, ravening, revelled in the riotous hair
And raiment of the furred Bassarides.

So came all those in on him ; and his heart,
As out of sleep suddenly struck astart,
Danced, and his flesh took fire of theirs, and
 grief
Was as a last year's leaf
Blown dead far down the wind's way ; and he
 set
His pale mouth to the brightest mouth it met
That laughed for love against his lips, and
 bade
Follow ; and in following all his blood grew
 glad
And as again a sea-bird's ; for the wind
Took him to bathe him deep round breast and
 brow
Not as it takes a dead leaf drained and
 thinned,
But as the brightest bay-flower blown on bough,
Set springing toward it singing : and they rode
By many a vine-leafed, many a rose-hung road,
Exalt with exultation : many a night
Set all its stars upon them as for spies
On many a moon-bewildering mountain-height
Where he rode only by the fierier light
Of his dread lady's hot sweet hungering eyes.
For the moon wandered witless of her way,
Spell-stricken by strong magic in such wise
As wizards use to set the stars astray.
And in his ears the music that makes mad
Beat always ; and what way the music bade,
That always rode he ; nor was any sleep
His, nor from height nor deep.
But heaven was as red iron, slumberless,
And had no heart to bless ;
And earth lay sere and darkling as distraught,

And help in her was nought.

Then many a midnight, many a morn and
even,
His mother, passing forth of her fair heaven,
With goodlier gifts than all save gods can give
From earth or from the heaven where sea-
things live,
With shine of sea-flowers through the bay-
leaf braid
Woven for a crown her foam-white hands had
made
To crown him with land's laurel and sea-dew,
Sought the sea-bird that was her boy : but he
Sat panther-throned beside Erigone,
Riding the red ways of the revel through
Midmost of pale-mouthed passion's crownless
crew.

Till on some winter's dawn of some dim year
He let the vine-bit on the panther's lip
Slide, and the green rein slip,
And set his eyes to seaward, nor gave ear
If sound from landward hailed him, dire or
dear ;
And passing forth of all those fair fierce ranks
Back to the grey sea-banks,
Against a sea-rock lying, aslant the steep,
Fell after many sleepless dreams on sleep.

And in his sleep the dun green light was
shed
Heavily round his head
That through the veil of sea falls fathom-deep,
Blurred like a lamp's that when the night
drops dead
Dies ; and his eyes gat grace of sleep to see
The deep divine dark dayshine of the sea,
Dense water-walls and clear dusk . water-ways,
Broad-based, or branching as a sea-flower
sprays
That side or this dividing ; and anew
The glory of all her glories that he knew.
And in sharp rapture of recovering tears
He woke on fire with yearnings of old years,
Pure as one purged of pain that passion bore,
Ill child of bitter mother ; for his own
Looked laughing toward him from her midsea
throne,
Up toward him there ashore.

Thence in his heart the great same joy be-
gan,
Of child that made him man :
And turned again from all hearts else on quest,
He communed with his own heart. and had
rest.

And like sea-winds upon loud waters ran
His days and dreams together, till the joy
Burned in him of the boy.
Till the earth's great comfort and the sweet
sea's breath
Breathed and blew life in where was heartless
death,
Death spirit-stricken of soul-sick days, where
strife
Of thought and flesh made mock of death and
life.
And grace returned upon him of his birth
Where heaven was mixed with heavenlike sea
and earth ;
And song shot forth strong wings that took the
sun
From inward, fledged with might of sorrow
and mirth
And father's fire made mortal in his son.
Nor was not spirit of strength in blast and
breeze
To exalt again the sun's child and the sea's :
For as wild mares in Thessaly grow great
With child of ravishing winds, that violate
Their leaping length of limb with manes like
fire
And eyes outburning heaven's
With fires more violent than the lightning
levin's
And breath drained out and desperate of desire
Even so the spirit in him, when winds grew
strong,
Grew great with child of song.
Nor less than when his veins first leapt for joy
To draw delight in such as burns a boy,
Now too the soul of all his senses felt
The passionate pride of deep sea-pulses dealt
Through nerve and jubilant vein
As from the love and largess of old time,
And with his heart again
The tidal throb of all the tides keep rhyme
And charm him from his own soul's separate
sense
With infinite and invasive influence
That made strength sweet in him and sweet-
ness strong,
Being now no more a singer, but a song.

Till one clear day when brighter sea-wind
blew
And louder sea-shine lightened, for the waves
Were full of godhead and the light that saves,
His father's, and their spirit had pierced him
through,
He felt strange breath and light all round him
shed

That bowed him down with rapture; and he knew
His father's hand, hallowing his humbled head,
And the old great voice of the old good time, that said :

'Child of my sunlight and the sea, from birth
A fosterling and fugitive on earth ;
Sleepless of soul as wind or wave or fire,
A manchild with an ungrown God's desire ;
Because thou hast loved nought mortal more than me,
Thy father, and thy mother-hearted sea ;
Because thou hast set thine heart to sing, and sold

Life and life's love for song, God's living gold
Because thou hast given thy flower and fire o youth
To feed men's hearts with visions, truer than truth ;
Because thou hast kept in those world-wandering eyes
The light that makes me music of the skies ;
Because thou hast heard with world-unwearied ears
The music that puts light into the spheres ;
Have therefore in thine heart and in thy mouth
The sound of song that mingles north and south,
The song of all the winds that sing of me,
And in thy soul the sense of all the sea.'

ON THE CLIFFS.

ἱμερόφωνος ἀηδών.

SAPPHO.

BETWEEN the moondawn and the sundown here
The twilight hangs half starless ; half the sea
Still quivers as for love or pain or fear
Or pleasure mightier than these all may be
A man's live heart might beat
Wherein a God's with mortal blood should meet
And fill its pulse too full to bear the strain
With fear or love or pleasure's twin-born, pain.
Fiercely the gaunt woods to the grim soil cling
That bears for all fair fruits
Wan wild sparse flowers of windy and wintry spring
Between the tortive serpent-shapen roots
Wherethrough their dim growth hardly strikes and shoots
And shews one gracious thing
Hardly, to speak for summer one sweet word
Of summer's self scarce heard.
But higher the steep green sterile fields, thick-set

With flowerless hawthorn even to the upward verge
Whence the woods gathering watch new cliff emerge
Higher than their highest of crowns that sea winds fret,
Hold fast, for all that night or wind can say,
Some pale pure colour yet,
Too dim for green and luminous for grey.
Between the climbing inland cliffs above
And these beneath that breast and break the bay,
A barren peace to soft for hate or love
Broods on an hour to dim for night or day.
O wind, O wingless wind that walk'st the sea
Weak wind, wing-broken, wearier wind than we
Who are yet not spirit-broken, maimed like thee
Who wail not in our inward night as thou
In the outer darkness now,
What word has the old sea given thee for mine ear

From thy faint lips to hear?
For some word would she send me, knowing
    not how.

Nay, what far other word
Than ever of her was spoken, or of me
Or all my winged white kinsfolk of the sea
Between fresh wave and wave was ever heard,
Cleaves the clear dark enwinding tree with
    tree
Too close for stars to separate and to see
Enmeshed in multitudinous unity?
What voice of what strong God hath stormed
    and stirred
The fortressed rock of silence, rent apart
Even to the core Night's all maternal heart?
What voice of God grown heavenlier in a bird,
Make keener of edge to smite
Than lightning,—yea, thou knowest, O moth-
    er Night,
Keen as that cry from thy strange children
    sent
Wherewith the Athenian judgment-shrine was
    rent,
For wrath that all their wrath was vainly spent,
Their wrath for wrong made right
By justice in her own divine despite
That bade pass forth unblamed
The sinless matricide and unashamed?
Yea, what new cry is this, what note more
    bright
Than their song's wing of words was dark of
    flight,
What word is this thou hast heard,
Thine and not thine or theirs, O Night, what
    word
More keen than lightning and more sweet than
    light?
As all men's hearts grew godlike in one bird
And all those hearts cried on thee, crying with
    might,
Hear us, O mother Night!

Dumb is the mouth of darkness as of death:
Light, sound and life are one
In the eyes and lips of dawn that draw the sun
To hear what first child's word with glimmer-
    ing breath
Their weak wan weanling child the twilight
    saith;
But night makes answer none.

God, if thou be god.—bird, if bird thou be,—
Do thou then answer me.
For but one word, what wind soever blow,

Is blown up usward ever from the sea.
In fruitless years of youth dead long ago
And deep beneath their own dead leaves and
    snow
Buried, I heard with bitter heart and sere
The same sea's word unchangeable, nor knew
But that mine own life-days were changeless
    too
And sharp and salt with unshed tear on tear
And cold and fierce and barren; and my
    soul,
Sickening, swam weakly with bated breath
In a deep sea like death,
And felt the wind buffet her face with brine
Hard, and harsh thought on thought in long
    bleak roll
Blown by keen gusts of memory sad as thine
Heap the weight up of pain, and break, and
    leave
Strength scarce enough to grieve
In the sick heavy spirit, unmanned with strife
Of waves that beat at the tired lips of life.

Nay, sad may be man's memory, sad may be
The dream he weaves him as for shadow of
    thee,
But scarce one breathing-space, one heartbeat
    long,
Wilt thou take shadow of sadness on thy song.
Not thou, being more than man or man's desire,
Being bird and God in one,
With throat of gold and spirit of the sun;
The sun whom all our souls and songs call sire,
Whose godhead gave thee, chosen of all our
    quire,
Thee only of all that serve, of all that sing
Before our sire and king,
Borne up some space on time's world-wander-
    ing wing,
This gift, this doom, to bear till time's wing
    tire—
Life everlasting of eternal fire.

Thee only of all; yet can no memory say
How many a night and day
My heart has been as thy heart, and my life
As thy life is, a sleepless hidden thing,
Full of the thirst and hunger of winter and
    spring,
That seeks its food not in such love or strife
As fill men's hearts with passionate hours and
    rest.
From no loved lips and on no loving breast
Have I sought ever for such gifts as bring
Comfort, to stay the secret soul with sleep.

The joys, the loves, the labors, whence men
    reap
Rathe fruit of hopes and fears,
I have made not mine ; the best of all my
    days
I have been as those fair fruitless summer strays,
Those water-waifs that but the sea-wind steers,
Flakes of glad foam or flowers on footless ways
That take the wind in season and the sun,
And when the wind wills is their season done.

For all my days as all thy days from birth
My heart as thy heart was in me as thee,
Fire ; and not all the fountains of the sea
Have waves enough to quench it, nor on earth
Is fuel enough to feed,
While day sows night and night sows day for
    seed.

We were not marked for sorrow, thou nor I,
For joy nor sorrow, sister, were we made,
To take delight and grief to live and die,
Assuaged by pleasures or by pains affrayed
That melt men's hearts and alter ; we retain
A memory mastering pleasure and all pain,
A spirit within the sense of ear and eye,
A soul behind the soul, that seeks and sings
And makes our life move only with its wings
And feed but from its lips, that in return
Feed of our hearts wherein the old fires that
    burn
Have strength not to consume
Nor glory enough to exalt us past our doom.

Ah, ah, the doom (thou knowest whence rang
    that wail)
Of the shrill nightingale !
(From whose wild lips, thou knowest, that
    wail was thrown)
For round about her have the great gods cast
A wing-borne body, and clothed her close and
    fast
With a sweet life that hath no part in moan.
But me, for me (how hadst thou heart to hear ?)
Remains a sundering with the two-edged spear.

Ah, for her doom ! so cried in presage then
The bodeful bondslave of the king of men,
And might not win her will.
Too close the entangling dragnet woven of
    crime,
The snare of ill new-born of elder ill,
The curse of new time for an elder time,
Had caught, and held her yet,
Enmeshed intolerably in the intolerant net,

Who thought with craft to mock the God most
    high,
And win by wiles his crown of prophecy
From the Sun's hand sublime,
As God were man, to spare or to forget,

But thou,—the gods have given thee and for-
    given thee
More than our master gave
That strange-eyed spirit-wounded strange-ton
    gued slave
There questing houndlike where the roofs red-
    wet
Reeked as a wet red grave.
Life everlasting has their strange grace given
    thee,
Even hers whom thou wast wont to sing and
    serve
With eyes, but not with song, too swift to
    swerve ;
Yet might not even thine eyes estranged estrange
    her,
Who seeing thee too, but inly, burn and bleed
Like that pale princess-priest of Priam's seed,
For stranger service gave thee guerdon, stranger
If this indeed be guerdon, this indeed
Her mercy, this thy meed—
That thou, being more than all we born, being
    higher
Than all heads crowned of him that only gives
The light whereby man lives,
The bay that bids man moved of God's
    desire
Lay hand on lute or lyre,
Set lip to trumpet or deflowered green reed—
If this were given thee for a grace indeed,
That thou, being first of all these, thou alone
Shouldst have the grace to die not, but to live
And loose nor change one pulse of song, one
    tone
Of all that were thy lady's and thine own,
Thy lady's whom thou criedst on to forgive,
Thou, priest and sacrifice on the altar-stone
Where none may worship not of all that live,
Love's priestess, errant on dark ways diverse ;
If this were grace indeed for Love to give,
If this indeed were blessing and no curse.

Love's priestess, mad with pain and joy of
    song,
Song's priestess, mad with joy and pain of
    love,
Name above all names that are lights above,
We have loved, praised, pitied, crowned and
    done thee wrong.

) thou past praise and pity; thou the sole
Utterly deathless, perfect only and whole
Immortal, body and soul.
For over all whom time hath overpast
The shadow of sleep inexorable is cast,
The implacable sweet shadow of perfect sleep
That gives not back what life gives death to
    keep;
Yea, all that lived and loved and sang and
    sinned
Are all borne down death's cold sweet sound-
    less wind
That blows all night and knows not whom its
    breath,
Darkling, may touch to death:
But one that wind hath touched and changed
    not,—one
Whose body and soul are parcel of the sun;
One that earth's fire could burn not, nor the
    sea
Quench; nor might human doom take hold on
    thee;
All praise, all pity, all dreams have done thee
    wrong,
All love, with eyes love-blinded from above;
Song's priestess, mad with joy and pain of love,
Love's priestess, mad with pain and joy of
    song.

Hast thou none other answer then for me
Than the air may have of thee,
Or the earth's warm woodlands girdling with
    green girth
Thy secret sleepless burning life on earth,
Or even the sea that once, being woman
    crowned
And girt with fire and glory of anguish round,
Thou wert so fain to seek to, fain to crave
If she would hear thee and save
And give thee comfort of thy great green grave?
Because I have known thee always who thou
    art,
Thou knowest, have known thee to thy heart's
    own heart,
Nor ever have given light ear to storied song
That did thy sweet name sweet unwitting
    wrong,
Nor ever have called thee nor would call for
    shame,
Thou knowest, but inly by thine only name,
Sappho—because I have known thee and lov-
    ed, hast thou
None other answer now?
As brother and sister were we, child and bird,
Since thy first Lesbian word

Flamed on me, and I knew not whence I knew
This was the song that struck my whole soul
    through,
Pierced my keen spirit of sense with edge more
    keen,
Even when I knew not,—even ere sooth was
    seen,—
When thou was but the tawny sweet winged
    thing
Whose cry was but of spring.

And yet even so thine ear should hear me—
    yea,
Hear me this nightfall by this northland bay,
Even for their sake whose loud good word I
    had,
Singing of thee in the all-beloved clime
Once, where the windy wine of spring makes
    mad
Our sisters of Majano, who kept time
Clear to my choral rhyme.
Yet was the song acclaimed of these aloud
Whose praise had made mute humbleness mis-
    proud,
The song with answering song applauded thus,
But of that Daulian dream of Itylus.
So but for love's love haply was it—nay,
How else?—that even their song took my
    song's part,
For love of love and sweetness of sweet heart,
Or god-given glorious madness of mid May
And heat of heart and hunger and thirst to
    sing,
Full of the new wine of the wind of spring.

Or if this were not, and it be not sin
To hold myself in spirit of thy sweet kin,
In heart and spirit of song;
If this my great love do thy grace no wrong.
Thy grace that gave me grace to dwell therein;
If thy gods thus be my gods, and their will
Made my song part of thy song—even such
    part
As man's hath of God's heart—
And my life like as thy life to fulfil;
What have our gods then given us? Ah, to
    thee,
Sister, much more, much happier than to me,
Much happier things they have given, and
    more of grace
Than falls to man's light race;
For lighter are we, all our love and pain
Lighter than thine, who knowest of time of
    place
Thus much, that place nor time

Can heal or hurt or lull or change again
The singing soul that makes his soul sublime
Who hears the far fall of its fire-fledged rhyme
Fill darkness as with bright and burning rain
Till all the live gloom inly glows, and light
Seems with the sound to cleave the core of
    night.

The singing soul that moves thee, and that
    moved
When thou wast woman, and their songs divine
Who mixed for Grecian mouths heaven's lyric
    wine
Fell dumb, fell down reproved
Before one sovereign Lesbian song of thine.
That soul, though love and life had fain held
    fast,
Wind-winged with fiery music, rose and past
Through the indrawn hollow of earth and
    heaven and hell,
As through some strait sea-shell
The wide sea's immemorial song,—the sea
That sings and breathes in strange men's ears
    of thee
How in her barren bride-bed, void and vast,
Even thy soul sang itself to sleep at last.

To sleep? Ah, then, what song is this, that
    here
Makes all the night one ear,
One ear fulfilled and mad with music, one
Heart kindling as the heart of heaven, to hear
A song more fiery than the awakening sun
Sings, when his song sets fire
To the air and clouds that build the dead
    night's pyre?
O thou of divers-coloured mind, O thou
Deathless, God's daughter subtle-souled—lo,
    now,
Now to the song above all songs, in flight
Higher than the day-star's height,   [night!
And sweet as sound the moving wings of
Thou of the divers-coloured seat—behold,
Her very song of old!—
O deathless, O God's daughter subtle-souled!
That same cry through this boskage overhead
Rings round reiterated,
Palpitates as the last palpitated,
The last that panted through her lips and died
Not down this grey north sea's half sapped
    cliff-side
That crumbles toward the coastline, year by
    year
More near the sands and near;
The last loud lyric fiery cry she cried, [here.
Heard once on heights Leucadian.—heard not

Not here; for this that fires our northland
This is the song that made   [night,
Love fearful, even the heart of love afraid,
With the great anguish of its great delight.
No swan-song, no far-fluttering half-drawn
    breath,
No word that love of love's sweet nature saith,
No dirge that lulls the narrowing lids of death,
No healing hymn of peace-prevented strife,—
This is her song of life.

I loved thee,—hark, one tenderer note than
    all—
Atthis, of old time, once—one low long fall,
Sighing—one long low lovely loveless call,
Dying—one pause in song so flamelike fast—
Atthis, long since in old time overpast—
One soft first pause and last.
One,—then the old rage of rapture's fieriest
    rain
Storms all the music-maddened night again.

Child of God, close craftswoman, I beseech thee
Bid not ache nor agony break nor master,
Lady, my spirit—
O thou her mistress, might her cry not reach
    thee?
Our Lady of all men's loves, could Love go
    past her,
Pass, and not hear it?

She hears not as she heard not; hears not me
O treble-natured mystery,—how should she
Hear, or give ear?—who heard and heard not
    thee;
Heard, and went past, and heard not; but all
    time
Hears all that all the ravin of his years
Hath cast not wholly out of all men's ears
And dulled to death with deep dense funeral
    chime
Of their reiterate rhyme.
And now of all songs uttering all her praise,
All hers who had thy praise and did thee
    wrong,
Abides one song yet of her lyric days,
Thine only, this thy song.

O soul triune, woman and god and bird,
Man, man at least has heard.
All ages call thee conqueror, and thy cry
The mightiest as the least beneath the sky
Whose heart was ever set to song, or stirred
With wind of mounting music blown more high
Than wildest wing may fly,
Hath heard or hears,—even Æschylus as I.
But when thy name was woman, and thy word

Human,—then haply, surely then meseems
This thy bird's note was heard on earth of
none,
Of none save only in dreams.
In all the world then surely was but one
Song ; as in heaven at highest one sceptred sun
Regent, on earth here surely without fail
One only, one imperious nightingale.
Dumb was the field, the woodland mute, the
lawn
Silent ; the hill was tongueless as the vale
Even when the last fair waif of cloud that felt
Its heart beneath the coloring moonrays melt,
At high midnoon of midnight half withdrawn,
Bared all the sudden deep divine moondawn.
Then, unsaluted by her twin-born tune,
That latter timeless morning of the moon
Rose past its hour of moonrise ; clouds gave
way
To the old reconquering ray,
But no song answering made it more than day;
No cry of song by night
Shot fire into the cloud-constraining light.
One only, one Æolian island heard
Thrill, but through no bird's throat,
In one strange manlike maiden's godlike note,
The song of all these as a single bird.
Till the sea's portal was as funeral gate
For that sole singer in all time's ageless date
Singled and signed for so triumphal fate,
All nightingales but one in all the world
All her sweet life were silent ; only then,
When her life's wing of womanhood was furled,
Their cry, this cry of thine was heard again,
As of me now, of any born of men.

Through sleepless clear spring nights filled full
of thee,
Rekindled here, thy ruling song has thrilled
The deep dark air and subtle tender sea
And breathless hearts with one bright sound
fulfilled.
Or at midnoon to me
Swimming, and birds about my happier head
Skimming, one smooth soft way by water and
air,
To these my bright born brethren and to me

Hath not the clear wind borne or seemed to
bear
A song wherein all earth and heaven and sea
Were molten in one music made of thee
To enforce us, O our sister of the shore,
Look once in heart back landward and adore ?
For songless were we sea-mews, yet had we
More joy than all things joyful of thee—more,
Haply, than all things happiest ; nay, save thee
In thy strong rapture of imperious joy
Too high for heart of sea-borne bird or boy,
What living things were happiest if not we ?
But knowing not love nor change nor wrath
nor wrong,
No more we knew of song.

Song, and the secrets of it, and their might,
What blessings curse it and what curses bless,
I know them since my spirit had first in sight,
Clear as thy song's words or the live sun's
light,
The small dark body's Lesbian loveliness
That held the fire eternal; eye and ear
Were as a god's to see, a god's to hear,
Through all his hours of daily and nightly
chime,
The sundering of the two-edged spear of time :
The spear that pierces even the sevenfold
shields
Of mightiest Memory, mother of all songs
made,
And wastes all songs as roseleaves kissed and
frayed
As here the harvest of the foam-flowered fields;
But thine the spear may waste not that he
wields
Since first the God whose soul is man's live
breath,
The sun whose face hath our sun's face for
shade,
Put all the light of life and love and death
Too strong for life, but not for love too strong,
Where pain makes peace with pleasure in thy
song,
And in thine heart, where love and song make
strife,
Fire everlasting of eternal life.

THE GARDEN OF CYMODOCE.

Sea, and bright wind, and heaven of ardent air,
More dear than all things earth-born ; O to me
Mother more dear than love's own longing, sea,
More than love's eyes are, fair,
Be with my spirit of song as wings to bear,
As fire to feel and breathe and brighten ; be
A spirit of sense more deep of deity,
A light of love, if love may be, more strong
In me than very song.
For song I have loved with second love, but thee,
Thee first, thee, mother ; ere my songs had breath,
That love of loves, whose bondage makes man free,
Was in me strong as death.
And seeing no slave may love thee, no, not one
That loves not freedom more,
And more for thy sake loves her, and for hers
Thee : or that hates not, on whate'er thy shore
Or what thy wave soever, all things done
Of man beneath the sun
In his despite and thine, to cross and curse
Your light and song that as with lamp and verse
Guide safe the strength of our sphered universe,
Thy breath it was, thou knowest, and none but thine,
That taught me love of one thing more divine.

    Ah, yet my youth was old,
    Its first years dead and cold
    As last year's autumn's gold,
And all my spirit of singing sick and sad and sere,
    Or ever I might behold
    The fairest of thy fold
    Engirt, enringed, enrolled,
In all thy flower-sweet flock of islands dear and near.

    Yet in my heart I deemed
    The fairest things, meseemed,
    Truth, dreaming, ever dreamed,

Had made mine eyes already like a god's to see :
    Of all sea-things that were
    Clothed on with water and air,
    That none could live more fair
Than thy sweet love long since had shown for love to me.

    I knew not, mother of mine,
    That one birth more divine
    Than all births else of thine
That hang like flowers or jewels on thy deep soft breast
    Was left for me to shine
    Above thy girdling line
    Of bright and breathing brine,
To take mine eyes with rapture and my sense with rest.

    That this was left for me,
    Mother, to have of thee,
    To touch, to taste, to see,
To feel as fire fulfilling all my blood and breath,
    As wine of living fire
    Keen as the heart's desire
    That makes the heart its pyre
And on its burning visions burns itself to death.

For here of all thy waters, here of all
Thy windy ways the wildest, and beset
As some beleaguered city's war-breached wall
With deaths enmeshed all round it in deep net,
Thick sown with rocks deadlier than steel, and fierce
With loud cross-countering currents, where the ship
Flags, flickering like a wind-bewildered leaf,
The densest weft of waves that prow may pierce
Coils round the sharpest warp of shoals that dip
Suddenly, scarce well under for one brief
Keen breathing space between the streams adverse,
Scarce showing the fanged edge of one hungering lip
Or one tooth lipless of the ravening reef ;
And midmost of the murderous water's web

All around it stretched and spun,
Laughs, reckless of rough tide and raging ebb
The loveliest thing that shines against the sun.

O flower of all wind-flowers and sea-flowers,
   Made lovelier by love of the sea
Than thy golden own field-flowers, or tree-
      flowers
   Like foam of the sea-facing tree !
No foot but the sea-mew's there settles
   On the spikes of thine anthers like horns,
With snow-colored spray for thy petals,
   Black rocks for thy thorns.

Was it here, in the waste of his waters,
   That the lordly north wind, when his love
On the fairest of many king's daughters
   Bore down for a spoil from above,
Chose forth of all farthest far islands,
   As a haven to harbor her head,
Of all lowlands on earth and all highlands,
   His bride-worthy bed ?

Or haply, my sea-flower, he found thee
   Made fast as with anchors to land,
And broke, that his waves might be round
      thee,
   Thy fetters like rivets of sand ?
And afar by the blast of him drifted
   Thy blossom of beauty was borne,
As a lark by the heart in her lifted
   To mix with the morn ?

By what rapture of rage, by what vision
   Of a heavenlier heaven than above,
Was he moved to devise thy divison
   From the land as a rest for his love ?
As a nest when his wings would remeasure
   The ways were of old they would be,
As a bride-bed upbuilt for his pleasure
   By sea-rock and sea ?

For in no deeps of midmost inland May
More flower-bright flowers the hawthorn, or
      more sweet
Swells the wild gold of the earth for wander-
      ing feet ;
For on no northland way
Crowds the close whin-bloom closer, set like
      thee
With thorns about for fangs of sea-rock shown
Through blithe lips of the bitter brine to lee ;
Nor blithelier landward comes the sea-wind
      blown,
Nor blithelier leaps the land-wind back to sea :

21

Nor louder springs the living song of birds
To shame our sweetest words.
And in the narrowest of thine hollowest hold
For joy thine aspens quiver as though for cold,
And many a self-lit flower-illumined tree
Outlaughs with snow-bright or with rose-bright
      glee
The laughter of the fields whose laugh is gold.
Yea, even from depth to height,
Even thine own beauty with its own delight
Fulfils thine heart in thee an hundredfold
Beyond the larger hearts of islands bright
With less intense contraction of desire
Self-satiate, centred in its own deep fire ;
Of shores not self-enchanted and entranced
By heavenly severance from all shadow of mirth
Or mourning upon earth ;
As thou, by no similitude enhanced,
By no fair foil made fairer, but alone
Fair as could be no beauty save thine own,
And wondrous as no world-beholden wonder :
Throned, with the world's most perilous sea
      for throne,
And praised from all its choral throats of
      thunder.

Yet one praise hast thou, holier
   Then praise of theirs may be,
To exalt thee, wert thou lowlier
   Than all that take the sea
With shores whence waves ebb slowlier
   Than these fall off from thee :

That One, whose name gives glory,
   One man whose life makes light,
One crowned and throned in story
   Above all empire's height,
Came, where thy straits run hoary,
   To hold thee fast in sight ;

With hallowing eyes to hold thee,
   With rapturous heart to read,
To encompass and enfold thee
   With love whence all men feed,
To brighten and behold thee,
   Who is mightiest of man's seed :
More strong than strong disaster,
   For fate and fear too strong ;
Earth's friend, whose eyes look past her,
   Whose hands would purge of wrong
Our lord, our light, our master,
   Whose word sums up all song.

Be it April or September
   That plays his perfect part,
Burn June or blow December,

Thou canst not in thine heart
But rapturously remember,
  All heavenlike as thou art,

Whose footfall made thee fairer,
  Whose passage more divine,
Whose hand, our thunder-bearer,
  Held fire that bade thee shine
With subtler glory and rarer
  Than thrills the sun's own shrine.

Who knows how then his godlike banished gaze
Turned haply from its goal of natural days
And homeward hunger for the clear French
    clime,
Toward English earth, whereunder now the
    Accursed
Rots, in the hate of all men's hearts inhearsed,
A carrion ranker to the sense of time
For that sepulchral gift of stone and lime
By royal grace laid on it, less of weight
Than the load laid by fate,
Fate, misbegotten child of his own crime,
Son of as foul a bastard-bearing birth
As even his own on earth ;
Less heavy than the load of cursing piled
By loyal grace of all souls undefiled
On one man's head, whose reeking soul made
    rotten
The loathed live corpse on earth once misbe-
    gotten ?
But when our Master's homeless feet were here,
France yet was foul with joy more foul than
    fear,
And slavery chosen, more vile by choice of
    chance
Than dull damnation of inheritance
From Russian year to year.
Alas fair mother of men, alas my France,
What ailed thee so to fall, that wert so dear
For all men's sake to all men, in such trance,
Plague-stricken ? Had the very Gods, that
    saw
Thy glory lighten on us for a law,
Thy gospel go before us for a guide,
Had these waxed envious of our love and awe
Or was it less their envy than thy pride
That bared thy breast for the obscene vulture-
    claw,
High priestess, by whose mouth Love prophe-
    sied
That fate should yet mean freedom ? Howso-
    ever,
That hour, the helper of men's hearts, we
praise,

Which blots out of man's book of after days
The name above all names abhorred for ever.
And His name shall we praise not, whom there
    flowers,
These rocks and ravening waters bound for
    girth
Round this wild starry spanlong plot of earth,
Beheld, the mightier for those heavier hours
That bowed his heart not down
Nor marred one crowning blossom of his
    crown ?
For surely, might we say,
Even from the dark deep sea-gate that makes
    way
Through channelled darkness for the darkling
    day
Hardly to let men's faltering footfall win
The sunless passage in,
Where breaks a world aflower against the sun,
A small sweet world of wave-encompassed
    wonders,
Kept from the wearier landward world asunder
With violence of wild waters, and with thunder
Of many winds as one,
To where the keen sea-current grinds and frets
The black bright sheer twin flameless Altarlets
That lack no live blood-sacrifice they crave
Of shipwreck and the shrine-subservient wave,
Having for priest the storm-wind, and for choir
Lightnings and clouds whose prayers and
    praise are fire,
All the isle acclaimed him coming ; she, the
    least
Of all things loveliest that the sea's love hides
From strange men's insult, walled about with
    tides
That bid strange guests back from her flower-
    strewn feast,
Set all her fields aflower, her flowers aflame,
To applaud him that he came.
Nor surely flashed not something of delight
Through that steep strait of rock whose twin-
    cliffed height
Links crag with crag reiterate, land with land,
By one sheer thread of narrowing precipice
Bifront, that binds and sunders
Abyss from hollower imminent abyss
And wilder isle with island, blind for bliss
Of sea that lightens and of wind that thunders ;
Nor pealed not surely back from deep to steep
Reverberate acclamation, steep to deep
Inveterately reclaiming and replying
Praise, and response applausive ; nor the sea,
For all the sea-wind's crying,
Knew not the song her sister, even as she

Thundering, or like her confluent spring-tides
  brightening,
And like her darkness lightening ;
The song that moved about him silent, now
Both soundless wings refolded and refurled
On that Promethean brow,
Then quivering as for flight that wakes the
  world.

From the roots of the rocks underlying the
  gulfs that engird it around
Was the isle not enkindled with light of him
  landing, or thrilled not with sound ?
Yea, surely the sea like a harper laid hand on
  the shore as a lyre,
As the lyre in his own for a birthright of old
  that was given of his sire,
And the hand of the child was put forth on
  the chords yet alive and aflame
From the land of the God that had wrought it
  in heaven ; and the hand was the same.
And the tongue of the child spake, singing ;
  and never a note that he sang,
But the strings made answer unstricken, as
  though for the God they rang.
And the eyes of the child shone, lightening ;
  and touched as by life at his nod,
They shuddered with music, and quickened as
  though from the glance of the God.
So trembled the heart of the hills and the
  rocks to receive him, and yearned
With desirous delight of his presence and love
  that beholding him burned.
Yea, down through the mighty twin hollows
  where never the sunlight shall be,
Deep sunk under imminent earth, and subdued
  to the stress of the sea,
That feel when the dim week changes by change
  of their tides in the dark,
As the wave sinks under within them, reluctant,
  removed from its mark,
Even there in the terror of twilight in bloom
  with its blossoms ablush,
Did a sense of him touch not the gleam of their
  flowers with a fiercer flush ?
Though the sun they behold not for ever, yet
  knew they not over them One
Whose soul was the soul of the morning, whose
  song was the song of the sun ?
But the secrets inviolate of sunlight in hollows
  untrodden of day,
Shall he dream what are these who beholds
  not ? or he that hath seen, shall he say ?
For the path is for passage of sea-mews ; and
  he that hath glided and leapt

Over sea-grass and sea-rock, alighting as one
  from a citadel crept
That his foemen beleaguer, descending by
  darkness and stealth, at the last
Peers under, and all is as hollow to hellward,
  agape and aghast.
But afloat and afar in the darkness a tremulous
  color subsides
From the crimson high crest of the purple-
  peaked roof to the soft-colored sides
That brighten as ever they widen till downward
  the level is won
Of the soundless and colorless water that
  knows not the sense of the sun :
From the crown of the culminant arch to the
  floor of the lakelet abloom,
One infinite blossom of blossoms innumerable
  aflush through the gloom.
All under the deeps of the darkness are glim-
  mering ; all over impends
An immeasurable infinite flower of the dark
  that dilates and descends,
That exults and expands in its breathless and
  blind efflorescence of heart
As it broadens and bows to the wave-ward,
  and breathes not, and hearkens apart.
As a beaker inverse at a feast on Olympus, exhausted of wine,
But inlaid as with rose from the lips of Dione
  that left it divine :
From the lips everliving of laughter and love
  everlasting, that leave
In the cleft of his heart who shall kiss them a
  snake to corrode it and cleave.
So glimmers the gloom into glory, the glory
  recoils into gloom
That the eye of the sun could not kindle, the
  lip not of Love could relume.
So darkens reverted the cup that the kiss of her
  mouth set on fire :
So blackens a brand in his eyeshot asmoulder
  awhile from the pyre.
From the beam from beneath and without it
  refrangent again from the wave
Strikes up through the portal a ghostly reverse
  on the dome of the cave,
On the depth of the dome ever darkling and
  dim to the crown of its arc :
That the sun-colored tapestry, sunless for ever,
  may soften the dark.
But within through the side-seen archway
  aglimmer again from the right
Is the seal of the sea's tide set on the mouth
  of the mystery of night.
And the seal on the seventh day breaks but a
  little, that man by its mean

May behold what the sun hath not looked on,
   the stars of the night have not seen.

Even like that hollow-bosomed rose, inverse
And infinite, the heaven of thy vast verse,
Our Master, over all our souls impends,
Imminent ; we, with heart-enkindled eyes
Upwondering, search the music-moulded skies
Sphere by sweet sphere, concordant as it blends
Light of bright sound, sound of clear light, in
   one,
As all the stars found utterance through the
   sun.
And all that heaven is like a rose in bloom,
Flower-colored, where its own sun's fires
   illume
As from one central and imperious heart
The whole sky's every part :
But lightening still and darkling downward. lo
The light and darkness of it,
The leaping of tne lamping levin afar
Between the full moon and the sunset star,

The war-song of the sounding skies aglow,
That have the herald thunder for their prophet :
From north to south the lyric lights that leap,
The tragic sundawns reddening east and west
As with bright blood from one Promethean
   breast,
The peace of noon that strikes the sea to sleep,
The wail over the world of all that weep,
The peace of night when death brings life or
   rest.
Goddess who gatherest all the herded waves
Into thy great sweet pastureless green fold,
Even for our love of old,
I pray thee by thy power that slays and saves
Take thou my song of this thy flower to keep
Who hast my heart in hold ;
And from thine high place of thy garden-steep,
Where one sheer terrace oversees thy deep
From the utmost rock-reared height
Down even to thy dear depths of night and
   light,
Take my song's salutation ; and on me
Breathe back the benediction of thy sea.

BIRTHDAY ODE

FOR THE ANNIVERSARY FESTIVAL OF

VICTOR HUGO.

FEBRUARY 26TH, 1880.

Between two seas the sea-bird's wing makes halt,
   Wind-weary ; while with lifting head he waits
   For breath to reinspire him from the gates
That open still toward sunrise on the vault
High-domed of morning, and in flight's default
   With spreading sense of spirit anticipates
   What new sea now may lure beyond the straits
His wings exulting that her winds exalt
And fill them full as sails to seaward spread,
   Fulfilled with fair speea's promise. Pass, my song,
Forth to the heaven of thy desire and dread,
   The presence of our lord, long loved and long
Far off above beholden, who to thee
Was as light kindling all a windy sea.

BIRTHDAY ODE

FOR THE ANNIVERSARY FESTIVAL OF VICTOR HUGO, FEBRUARY 26, 1880.

SPRING, born in heaven ere many a spring-
 time flown,   *strophe* I.
Dead spring that sawest on earth
A babe of deathless birth,
A flower of rosier flowerage than thine own,
A glory of goodlier godhead ; even this day,
That floods the mist of February with May,
And strikes death dead with sunlight, and the
 breath
Whereby the deadly doers are done to death,
They that in day's despite
Would crown the imperial night,
And in deep hate of insubmissive spring
Rethrone the royal winter for a king,
This day that casts the days of darkness down
Low as a broken crown,
We call thee from the gulf of deeds and days,
Deathless and dead, to hear us whom we praise.

A light of many lights about thine head,
     antistrophe I.
Lights manifold and one,
Stars molten in a sun,
A sun of divers beams incorporated,
Compact of confluent aureoles, each more fair
Than man, save only at highest of man, may
 wear,
So didst thou rise, when this our grey-grown
 age
Had trod two paces of his pilgrimage,
Two paces through the gloom
From his fierce father's tomb,
Led by cross lights of lightnings, and the
 flame
That burned in darkness round one darkling
 name ;
So didst thou rise, nor knewest thy glory, O
 thou
Re-risen upon us now,
The glory given thee for a grace to give,
And take the praise of all men's hearts that
 live.

  First in the dewy ray *epode* I.
   Ere dawn be slain of day
The fresh crowned lilies of discrowned kings'
 prime
   Sprang splendid as of old
   With moonlight-coloured gold
And rays refract from the oldworld heaven of
 time ;

Pale with proud light of stars decreased
In westward wane reluctant from the con-
 quering east.
But even between their golden olden bloom
       str. 2.
Strange flowers of wildwood glory,
 With frost and moonshine hoary,
Thrust up the new growths of their green-
 leaved gloom,
Red buds of ballad blossom, where the dew
Blushed as with bloodlike passion, and its hue
Was as the life and love of hearts on flame,
And fire from forth of each live chalice came :
Young sprays of elder song,
Stem straight and petal strong,
Bright foliage with dark frondage overlaid,
And light the lovelier for its lordlier shade ;
And morn and even made loud in woodland
 lone
With cheer of clarions blown,
And through the tournay's clash and clarion's
 cheer
Laugh to laugh echoing, tear washed off by
 tear.

Then eastward far past northland lea and
 lawn   *ant.* 2.
Beneath a heavier light
Of stormier day and night
Began the music of the heaven of dawn ;
Bright sound of battle along the Grecian
 waves,
Loud light of thunder above the Median
 graves,
New strife, new song on Æschylean seas,
Canaris risen above Themistocles ;
Old glory of warrior ghosts
Shed fresh on filial hosts,
With dewfall redder than the dews of day,
And earth-born lightnings out of bloodbright
 spray ;
Then through the flushed grey gloom on
 shadowy sheaves
Low flights of falling leaves ;
And choirs of birds transfiguring as they
 throng
All the world's twilight and the soul's to song.
  Voices more dimly deep *ep.* 2.
   Than the inmost heart of sleep,
And tenderer than the rose-mouthed morning
 lips ;

And midmost of them heard
The viewless water's word,
The sea's breath in the wind's wing and the ship's,
That bids one swell and sound and smite
And rend that other in sunder as with fangs by night.

But ah ! the glory of shadow and mingling ray,
The story of morn and even
Whose tale was writ in heaven
And had for scroll the night, for scribe the day !
For scribe the prophet of the morning, far
Exalted over twilight and her star ;
For scroll beneath his Apollonian hand
The dim twin wastes of sea and glimmering land.
Hark, on the hill-wind, clear
For all men's hearts to hear
Sound like a stream at nightfall from the steep
That all time's depths might answer, deep to deep,
With trumpet-measures of triumphal wail
From windy vale to vale,
The crying of one for love that strayed and sinned
Whose brain took madness of the mountain wind.

Between the birds of brighter and duskier wing,
What mightier-moulded forms
Girt with red clouds and storms
Mix their strong hearts with theirs that soar and sing ?
Before the storm-blast blown of death's dark horn
The marriage moonlight withers, that the morn
For two made one may find three made by death
One ruin at the blasting of its breath ;
Clothed with heart's flame renewed
And strange new maidenhood,
Faith lightens on the lips that bloomed for hire
Pure as the lightning of love's first-born fire :
Wide-eyed and patient ever, till the curse
Find where to fall and pierce,
Keen expiation whets with edge more dread
A father's wrong to smite a father's head.

Borgia, supreme from birth
As loveliest born on earth

Since earth bore ever women that were fair ;
Scarce known of her own house
If daughter or sister or spouse ;
Who holds men's hearts yet helpless with her hair ;
The direst of divine things made,
Bows down her amorous aureole half suffused with shade.

As red the fire-scathed royal northland bloom,
That left our story a name
Dyed through with blood and flame
Ere her life shrivelled from a fierier doom
Than theirs her priests bade pass from earth in fire
To slake the thirst of God their Lord's desire :
As keen the blast of love-enkindled fate
That burst the Paduan tyrant's guarded gate :
As sad the softer moan
Made one with music's own
For one whose feet made music as they fell
On ways by loveless love made hot from hell;
But higher than these and all the song thereof
The perfect heart of love,
The heart by fraud and hate once crucified,
That, dying, gave thanks, and in thanksgiving died.

Above the windy walls that rule the Rhine
A noise of eagles' wings
And wintry war-time rings,
With roar of ravage trampling corn and vine
And storm of wrathful wassail dashed with song
And under these the watch of wreakless wrong,
With fire of eyes anhungered ; and above
These, the light of the stricken eyes of love,
The faint sweet eyes that follow
The wind-outwinging swallow,
And face athirst with young wan yearning mouth
Turned after toward the unseen all-golden south,
Hopeless to see the birds back ere the wane,
Or the leaves born again ;
And still the might and music mastering fate
Of life more strong than death and love than hate.

In special strength biform
Stand the twin sons of storm
Transfigured by transmission of one hand
That gives the new-born time
Their semblance more sublime
Than once it lightened over each man's land ;

There Freedom's winged and wide-
mouthed hound,
And here our high Dictator, in his son discrowned.

What strong-limbed shapes of kindred throng
round these
Before, between, behind,
Sons born of one man's mind,
Fed at his hands and fostered round his knees ?
Fear takes the spirit in thraldom at his nod,
And pity makes it as the spirit of God,
As his own soul that from her throne above
Sheds on all souls of men her showers of love,
On all earth's evil and pain
Pours mercy forth as rain
And comfort as the dewfall on dry land ;
And feeds with pity from a faultless hand
All by their own fault stricken, all cast out
By all men's scorn or doubt,
Or with their own hands wounded, or by fate
Brought into bondage of men's fear or hate.

In violence of strange visions north and south
Confronted, east and west,
With frozen or fiery breast,
Eyes fixed or fevered, pale or bloodred mouth,
Kept watch about his dawn-enkindled dreams ;
But ere high noon a light of nearer beams
Made his young heaven of manhood more be-
nign,
And love made soft his lips with spiritual wine,
And left them fired, and fed
With sacramental bread,
And sweet with honey of tenderer words than
tears
To feed men's hopes and fortify men's fears,
And strong to silence with benignant breath
The lips that doom to death,
And swift with speech like fire in fiery lands
To melt the steel's edge in the headsman's
hands.

Higher than they rose of old,
New builded now, behold,
The live great likeness of Our Lady's
towers ;
And round them like a dove
Wounded, and sick with love,
One fair ghost moving, crowned with fateful
flowers,
Watched yet with eyes of bloodred lust
And eyes of love's heart broken and unbroken
trust.

But sadder always under shadowier skies,
More pale and sad and clear
Waxed always, drawn more near,
The face of Duty lit with Love's own eyes ;
Till the awful hands that culled in rosier
hours
From fairy-footed fields of wild old flowers
And sorcerous woods of Rhineland, green and
hoary,
Young children's chaplets of enchanted story,
The great kind hands that showed
Exile its homeward road,
And, as man's helper made his foeman God,
Of pity and mercy wrought themselves a rod,
And opened for Napoleon's wondering kin
France, and bade enter in,
And threw for all the doors of refuge wide,
Took to them lightning in the thunder-tide.

For storm on earth above had risen from under,
Out of the hollow of hell,
Such storm as never fell
From darkest deeps of heaven distract with
thunder ;
A cloud of cursing, past all shape of thought,
More foul than foulest dreams, and overfraught
With all obscene things and obscure of birth
That ever made infection of man's earth ;
Having all hell for cloak
Wrapped round it as a smoke
And in its womb such offspring so defiled
As earth bare never for her loathliest child,
Rose, brooded, reddened, broke, and with its
breath
Put France to poisonous death ;
Yea, far as heaven's red laboring eye could
glance,
France was not, save in men cast forth of
France.

Then,—while the plague-sore grew
Two darkling decades through,
And rankled in the festering flesh of time,—
Where darkness binds and frees
The wildest of wild seas
In fierce mutations of the unslumbering
clime,
There, sleepless too, o'er shuddering wrong
One hand appointed shook the reddening
scourge of song.

And through the lightnings of the apparent
word
Dividing shame's dense night
Sounds lovelier than the light

And light more sweet than　song from night's
　　own bird
Mixed　each　their　hearts　with other, till　the
　　gloom
Was glorious as with all the stars in bloom,
Sonorous as with all the spheres in chime
Heard far through flowering heaven : the sea,
　　sublime
Once only with its own
Old wind's and waters' tone,
Sad only or glad with its own glory, and crown-
　　ed
With its own light, and thrilled with its own
　　sound,
Learnt now their song, more sweet than heav-
　　en's may be,
Who pass away by sea ;
The song that takes of old love's land farewell,
With pulse of plangent water like a knell.
And louder ever and louder and yet more loud
Till night be shamed of morn
Rings the Black Huntsman's horn
Through darkening deeps beneath the covering
　　cloud,
Till all the wild beasts of the darkness hear ;
Till the Czar quake, till Austria cower for fear,
Till the king breathe not, till the priest wax pale,
Till spies and slayers on seats of judgment
　　quail,
Till mitre and cowl bow down
And crumble as a crown,
Till Cæsar driven to the lair and hounded
　　Pope
Reel breathless and drop heartless out of hope,
And one the uncleanest kinless beast of all
Lower than his fortune fall ;
The wolfish waif of casual empire, born
To turn all hate and horror cold with scorn.
　　Yea, even at night's full noon
　　Light's birth-song brake in tune,
　Spake, witnessing that with us one must be,
　God ; naming so by name
　That priests have brought to shame
The strength whose scourge sounds on the
　　smitten sea ;
　The mystery manifold of might
Which bids the wind give back to night the
　　things of night.

Even God, the unknown of all　time ; force
　　or thought,
Nature or fate or will,
Clothed round with good and ill,
Veiled　and　revealed　of　all　things　and　of
　　nought,

Hooded　and　helmed　with　mystery, girt　and
　　shod
With light and darkness, unapparent God.
Him　the　high　prophet　o'er　his　wild　work
　　bent
Found indivisible ever and immanent
At hidden heart of truth,
In forms of age and youth
Transformed and transient ever ; masked and
　　crowned,
From all bonds loosened and with all bonds
　　bound,
Diverse　and　one　with all　things ; love　and
　　hate,
Earth, and the starry state
Of heaven immeasurable, and years that flee
As clouds and winds and rays across the sea.

But　higher　than　stars　and　deeper　than　the
　　waves
Of day and night and morrow
That roll for all time, sorrow
Keeps ageless watch over perpetual graves.
From dawn to morning of the soul in flower,
Through toils and dreams and visions, to that
　　hour
When　all　the　deeps　were　opened, and　one
　　doom
Took two sweet lives to embrace them and en-
　　tomb,
The strong song plies its wing
That makes the darkness ring
And the deep light reverberate sound as deep ;
Song soft as flowers or grass more soft than
　　sleep,
Song bright as heaven above the mounting
　　bird,
Song like a god's tear heard
Falling, fulfilled of life and death and light,
And all the stars and all the shadow of night.

　　Till, when its flight hath past
　　Time's loftiest mark and last,
　The goal where good kills evil with a kiss,
　　And Darkness in God's sight
　　Grows as his brother Light,
　And heaven and hell one heart whence all
　　　the abyss
　　　Throbs with love's music ; from his
　　　trance
Love waking leads it home to her who stayed
　　in France.

But now from all the world old winds of the
　　air

One blast of record rings
As from time's hidden springs
With roar of rushing wings and fires that bear
Toward north and south sonorous, east and
west,
Forth of the dark wherein its records rest
The story told of the ages, writ nor sung
By man's hand ever nor by mortal tongue
Till, godlike with desire,
One tongue of man took fire,
One hand laid hold upon the lightning, one
Rose up to bear time witness what the sun
Had seen, and what the moon and stars of
night
Beholding lost not light:
From dawn to dusk what ways man wander-
ing trod
Even through tne twilight of the gods to God.

From dawn of man and woman twain and one,
When the earliest dews impearled
The front of all the world
Ringed with aurorean aureole of the sun,
To days that saw Christ's tears and hallowing
breath
Put life for love's sake in the lips of death,
And years as waves whose brine was fire,
whose foam
Blood, and the ravage of Neronian Rome ;
And the eastern crescent's horn
Mightier awhile than morn ;
And knights whose lives were flights of eagles'
wings,
And lives like snakes' lives of engendering
kings ;
And all the ravin of all the swords that reap
Lives cast as sheaves on heap
From all the billowing harvest-fields of fight ;
And sounds of love-songs lovelier than the
light.

The grim dim thrones of the east
Set for death's riotous feast
Round the bright board where darkling cen-
turies wait,
And servile slaughter, mute,
Feeds power with fresh red fruit,
Glitter and groan with mortal food of fate ;
And throne and cup and lamp's bright
breath
Bear witness to their lord of only night and
death.

Dead freedom by live empire lies defiled,
And murder at his feet

Plies lust with wine and meat,
With offering of an old man and a child
With holy body and blood, inexpiable
Communion in the sacrament of hell,
Till, reeking from their monstrous eucharist,
The lips wax cold that murdered where they
kissed,
And empire in mid feast
Fall as a slaughtered beast
Headless, and ease men's hungering hearts of
fear
Lest God were none in heaven, to see nor hear,
And purge his own pollution with the flood
Poured of his black base blood
So first found healing, poisonous as it poured ;
And on the clouds the archangel cleanse his
sword

As at the word unutterable that made
Of day and night division,
From vision on to vision,
From dream to dream, from darkness into
shade,
From sunshine into sunlight, moves and lives
The steersman's eye, the helming hand that
gives
Life to the wheels and wings that whirl along
The immeasurable impulse of the sphere of
song
Through all the eternal years,
Beyond all stars and spheres,
Beyond the washing of the waves of time,
Beyond all heights where no thought else may
climb,
Beyond the darkling dust of suns that were,
Past height and depth of air ;
And in the abyss whence all things move that
are
Finds only living Love, the sovereign star.

Nor less the weight and worth
Found even of love on earth
To wash all stain of tears and sins away,
On dying lips alit
That living knew not it,
In the winged shape of song with death to
play :
To warm young children with its wings,
And try with fire the heart elect for godlike
things.

For all worst wants of all most miserable
With divine hands to deal
All balms and herbs that heal,
Among all woes whereunder poor men dwell

Our Master sent his servant Love, to be
On earth his witness ; but the strange deep
    sea,
Mother of life and death inextricate,
What work should Love do there, to war
    with fate ?
Yet there must Love too keep
At heart of the eyeless deep
Watch, and wage war wide-eyed with all its
    wonders,
Lower than the lightnings of its waves, and
    thunders
Of seas less monstrous than the births they
    bred ;
Keep high there heart and head,
And conquer : then for prize of all toils past
Feel the sea close them in again at last.

A day of direr doom arisen thereafter
With cloud and fire in strife
Lightens and darkens life
Round one by man's hand masked with living
    laughter,
A man by men bemonstered, but by love
Watched with blind eyes as of a wakeful dove
And wooed by lust, that in her rosy den
As fire on flesh feeds on the souls of men,
To take the intense impure
Burnt-offering of her lure,
Divine and dark and bright and naked, strange
With ravenous thirst of life reversed and
    change,
As though the very heaven should shrivel and
    swell
With hunger after hell,
Run mad for dear damnation, and desire
To feel it light thrilled through with stings of
    fire.

Above a windier sea,
    The glory of Ninety-three
Fills heaven with blood-red and with rose-
    red beams
    That earth beholding grows
    Herself one burning rose
Flagrant and fragrant with strange deeds
    and dreams,
    Dreams dyed as love's own flower, and
        deeds
Stained as with love's own life-blood, that for
    love's sake bleeds.
And deeper than all deeps of sea and skies
Wherein the shadows are
Called sun and moon and star
That rapt conjecture meets with mounting eyes,

Loud with strange waves and lustrous with
    new spheres,
Shines, masked at once and manifest of years,
Shakespeare, a heaven of heavenly eyes be-
    holden ;
And forward years as backward years grow
    golden
With light of deeds and words
And flight of God's fleet birds,
Angels of wrath and love and truth and pity ;
And higher on exiled eyes their natural city
Dawns down the depths of vision, more sub-
    lime
Than all truths born of time ;
And eyes that wept above two dear sons dead
Grow saving stars to guard one hopeless head.
Bright round the brows of banished age had
    shone
In vision flushed with truth
The rosy glory of youth
On streets and woodlands where in days long
    gone
Sweet love sang light and loud and deep and
    dear :
And far the trumpets of the dreadful year
Had pealed and wailed in darkness : last arose
The song of children, kindling as a rose
At breath of sunrise, born
Of the red flower of morn
Whose face perfumes deep heaven with odor-
    ous light
And thrills all through the wings of souls in
    flight
Close as the press of children at His knee
Whom if the high priest see,
Dreaming, as homeless on dark earth he trod,
The lips that praise him shall not know for
    God.

O sovereign spirit, above
    All offering but man's love,
All praise and prayer and incense undefiled !
    The one thing stronger found
    Than towers with iron bound ;
The one thing lovelier than a little child,
    And deeper than the seas are deep,
And tenderer than such tears of love as angels
    weep.

Dante, the seer of all things evil and good,
Beheld two ladies, Beauty
And high life-hallowing Duty,
That strove for sway upon his mind and mood
And held him in alternating accord
Fast bound at feet of either : but our lord,

The seer and singer of righteousness and
   wrong
Who stands now master of all the keys of
   song,
Sees both as dewdrops run
Together in the sun,
For him not twain but one thing twice divine ;
Even as his speech and song are bread and
   wine
For all souls hungering and all hearts athirst
At best of days and worst,
And both one sacrament of Love's great giving
To feed the spirit and sense of all souls living.

The seventh day in the wind's month ten years
   gone
Since heaven-espousing earth
Gave the Republic birth,
The mightiest soul put mortal raiment on
That came forth singing ever in man's ears
Of all souls with us, and through all these
   years

Rings yet the lordliest, waxen yet more strong,
That on our souls hath shed itself in song,
Poured forth itself like rain
On souls like springing grain
That with its procreant beams and showers
   were fed
For living wine and sacramental bread ;
Given all itself as air gives life and light,
Utterly, as of right ;
The goodliest gift our age hath given, to be
Ours, while the sun gives glory to the sea.

Our Father and Master and Lord,
   Who hast thy song for sword,
For staff thy spirit, and our hearts for throne;
   As in past years of wrong,
   Take now my subject song,
To no crowned head made humble but thine
   own ;
   That on thy day of worldly birth
Gives thanks for all thou hast given past thanks
   of all on earth.

TRISTRAM OF LYONESSE.

PRELUDE.

TRISTRAM AND ISEULT.

LOVE, that is first and last of all things made,
The light that has the living world for shade,
The spirit that for temporal veil has on
The souls of all men woven in unison,
One fiery raiment with all lives inwrought
And lights of sunny and starry deed and
 thought,
And alway through new act and passion new
Shines the divine same body and beauty
 through,
The body spiritual of fire and light
That is to worldly noon as noon to night ;
Love, that is flesh upon the spirit of man
And spirit within the flesh whence breath be-
 gan ;
Love, that keeps all the choir of lives in
 chime ;
Love, that is blood within the veins of time ;
That wrought the whole world without stroke
 of hand,
Shaping the breadth of sea, the length of land,
And with the pulse and motion of his breath
Through the great heart of the earth strikes
 life and death,
The sweet twain chords that make the sweet
 tune live
Through day and night of things alternative,
Through silence and through sound of stress
 and strife,
And ebb and flow of dying death and life ;
Love, that sounds loud or light in all men's
 ears,
Whence all men's eyes take fire from sparks
 of tears,
That binds on all men's feet or chains or
 wings ;
Love, that is root and fruit of terrene things ;
Love, that the whole world's waters shall not
 drown,
The whole world's fiery forces not burn down ;

Love, that what time his own hands guard
 his head
The whole world's wrath and strength shall
 not strike dead ;
Love, that if once his own hands make his
 grave
The whole world's pity and sorrow shall not
 save ;
Love that for very life shall not be sold,
Nor bought nor bound with iron nor with
 gold ;
So strong that heaven, could love bid heaven
 farewell,
Would turn to fruitless and unflowering hell ;
So sweet that hell, to hell could love be given,
Would turn to splendid and sonorous heaven ;
Love that is fire within thee and light above,
And lives by grace of nothing but of love ;
Through many and lovely thoughts and much
 desire
Led these twain to the life of tears and fire ;
Through many and lovely days and much de-
 light
Led these twain to the lifeless life of night.
 Yea, but what then ? albeit all this were
 thus,
And soul smote soul and left it ruinous,
And love led love as eyeless men lead men,
Through chance by chance to deathward—
 Ah, what then ?
Hath love not likewise led them further yet,
Out through the years where memories rise
 and set,
Some large as suns, some moon-like warm
 and pale,
Some starry-sighted, some through clouds
 that sail
Seen as red flame through spectral float of
 fume,
Each with the blush of its own special bloom

332.

On the fair face of its own coloured light,
Distinguishable in all the host of night,
Divisible from all the radiant rest
And separable in splendour? Hath the best
Light of love's all, of all that burn and move,
A better heaven than heaven is? Hath not
      love
Made for all these their sweet particular air
To shine in, their own beams and names to
      bear,
Their ways to wander and their wards to
      keep,
Till story and song and glory and all things
      sleep?
Hath he not plucked from death of lovers
      dead
Their musical soft memories, and kept red
The rose of their remembrance in men's eyes,
The sunsets of their stories in his skies,
The blush of their dead blood in lips that
      speak
Of their dead lives, and in the listener's
      cheek
That trembles with the kindling pity lit
In gracious hearts for some sweet fever-fit,
A fiery pity enkindled of pure thought
By tales that make their honey out of nought,
The faithless faith that lives without belief
Its light life through, the griefless ghost of
      grief?
Yea, as warm night refashions the sere blood
In storm-struck petal or in sun-struck bud,
With tender hours and tempering dew to cure
The hunger and thirst of day's distemperature
And ravin of the dry discolouring hours,
Hath he not bid relume their flameless flow-
      ers
With summer fire and heat of lamping song,
And bid the short-lived things, long dead,
      live long,
And thought remake their wan funereal
      fames,
And the sweet shining signs of women's
      names
That mark the months out and the weeks
      anew
He moves in changeless change of seasons
      through
To fill the days up of his dateless year
Flame from Queen Helen to Queen Guene-
      vere?
For first of all the sphery signs whereby
Love severs light from darkness, and most
      high,
In the white front of January there glows

The rose-red sign of Helen like a rose :
And gold-eyed as the shore flower shelterless
Whereon the sharp-breathed sea blows bitter-
      ness,
A storm-star that the seafarers of love
Strain their wind-wearied eyes for glimpses
      of,
Shoots keen through February's grey frost
      and damp
The lamplike star of Hero for a lamp ;
The star that Marlowe sang into our skies
With mouth of gold, and mourning in his
      eyes ;
And in clear March across the rough blue sea
The signal sapphire of Alcyone
Makes bright the blown brows of the wind-
      foot year ;
And shining like a sunbeam-smitten tear
Full ere it fall, the fair next sign in sight
Burns opal-wise with April-coloured light
When air is quick with song and rain and
      flame,
My birth-month star that in love's heaven
      hath name
Iseult, a light of blossom and beam and
      shower,
My singing sign that makes the song-tree
      flower ;
Next like a pale and burning pearl beyond
The rose-white sphere of flower-named Rosa-
      mond
Signs the sweet head of Maytime ; and for
      June
Flares like an angered and storm-reddening
      moon
Her signal sphere, whose Carthaginian pyre
Shadowed her traitor's flying sail with fire ;
Next, glittering as the wine-bright jacinth-
      stone,
A star south-risen that first to music shone,
The keen girl-star of golden Juliet bears
Light northward to the month whose fore-
      head wears
Her name for flower upon it, and his trees
Mix their deep English song with Veronese ;
And like an awful sovereign chrysolite
Burning, the supreme fire that blinds the
      night,
The hot gold head of Venus kissed by Mars,
A sun-flower among small sphered flowers of
      stars,
The light of Cleopatra fills and burns
The hollow of heaven whence ardent August
      yearns ;
And fixed and shining as the sister-shed

Sweet tears for Phaethon disorbed and dead,
The pale bright autumn's amber-coloured
sphere,
That through September sees the saddening
year
As love sees change through sorrow, hath to
name
Francesca's ; and the star that watches flame
The embers of the harvest overgone
Is Thisbe's, slain of love in Babylon,
Set in the golden girdle of sweet signs
A blood-bright ruby ; last save one light
shines
An eastern wonder of sphery chrysopras,
The star that made men mad, Angelica's ;
And latest named and lordliest, with a sound
Of swords and harps in heaven that ring it
round,
Last love-light and last love-song of the
year's,
Gleams like a glorious emerald Guenevere's.
These are the signs wherethrough the year
sees move,
Full of the sun, the sun-god which is love,
A fiery body blood-red from the heart
Outward, with fire-white wings made wide
apart,
That close not and unclose not, but upright
Steered without wind by their own light and
might
Sweep through the flameless fire of air that
rings
From heaven to heaven with thunder of
wheels and wings
And antiphones of motion-moulded rhyme
Through spaces out of space and timeless
time.
So shine above dead chance and conquered
change
The sphered signs and leave without their
range
Doubt and desire, and hope with fear for
wife,
Pale pains, and pleasures long worn out of
life.
Yea, even the shadows of them spiritless,
Through the dim door of sleep that seem to
press,
Forms without form, a piteous people and
blind
Men and no men, whose lamentable kind
The shadow of death and shadow of life com-
pel
Through semblances of heaven and false-
faced hell,

Through dreams of light and dreams of dark-
ness tost
On waves innavigable, are these so lost ?
Shapes that wax pale and shift in swift strange
wise,
Void faces with unspeculative eyes,
Dim things that gaze and glare, dead mouths
that move,
Featureless heads discrowned of hate and
love,
Mockeries and masks of motion and mute
breath,
Leavings of life, the superflux of death—
If these things and no more than these things
be
Left when man ends or changes, who can see ?
Or who can say with what more subtle sense
Their subtler natures taste in air less dense
A life less thick and palpable than ours,
Warmed with faint fires and sweetened with
dead flowers
And measured by low music? how time fares
In that wan time-forgotten world of theirs,
Their pale poor world too deep for sun or star
To live in, where the eyes of Helen are,
And hers who made as God's own eyes to shine
The eyes that met them of the Florentine,
Wherein the godhead thence transfigured lit
All time for all men with the shadow of it?
Ah, and these too felt on them as God's
grace
The pity and glory of this man's breathing
face ;
For these too, these my lovers, these my
twain,
Saw Dante, saw God visible by pain,
With lips that thundered and with feet that
trod
Before men's eyes incognisable God ;
Saw love and wrath and light and night and
fire
Live with one life and at one mouth respire,
And in one golden sound their whole soul
heard
Sounding, one sweet immitigable word.
They have the night who had like us the
day ;
We, whom day binds, shall have the night as
they.
We, from the fetters of the light unbound,
Healed of our wound of living, shall sleep
sound.
All gifts but one the jealous God may keep
From our soul's longing, one he cannot—
sleep.

This, though he grudge all other grace to prayer,
This grace his closed hand cannot choose but spare.
This, though his ear be sealed to all that live,
Be it lightly given or lothly, God must give.
We, as the men whose name on earth is none,
We too shall surely pass out of the sun ;
Out of the sound and eyeless light of things,
Wide as the stretch of life's time-wandering wings,
Wide as the naked world and shadowless,
And long-lived as the world's own weariness.
Us too, when all the fires of time are cold,
The heights shall hide us and the depths shall hold.
Us too, when all the tears of time are dry,
The night shall lighten from her tearless eye.
Blind is the day and eyeless all its light,
But the large unbewildered eye of night
Hath sense and speculation ; and the sheer
Limitless length of lifeless life and clear,
The timeless space wherein the brief worlds move
Clothed with light life and fruitful with light love,
With hopes that threaten, and with fears that cease,
Past fear and hope, hath in it only peace.
    Yet of these lives inlaid with hopes and fears,
Spun fine as fire and jewelled thick with tears,

These lives made out of loves that long since were,
Lives wrought as ours of earth and burning air,
Fugitive flame and water of secret springs,
And clothed with joys and sorrows as with wings,
Some yet are good, if aught be good, to save
Some while from washing wreck and wrecking wave.
Was such not theirs, the twain I take, and give
Out of my life to let their dead life live
Some days of mine, and blow my living breath
Between dead lips forgotten even of death ?
So many and many of old have given my twain
Love and life song and honey-parted pain,
Whose root is sweetness and whose fruit is sweet,
So many and with such joy have tracked their feet,
What should I do to follow ? yet I too,
I have the heart to follow, many or few
Be the feet gone before me ; for the way,
Rose-red with remnant roses of the day
Westward, and eastward white with stars that break,
Between the green and foam is fair to take
For any sail the sea-wind steers for me
From morning into morning, sea to sea.

I.

THE SAILING OF THE SWALLOW.

ABOUT the middle music of the spring
Came from the castled shore of Ireland's king
A fair ship stoutly sailing, eastward bound
And south by Wales and all its wonders round
To the loud rocks and ringing reaches home
That take the wild wrath of the Cornish foam,
Past Lyonesse unswallowed of the tides
And high Carlion that now the steep sea hides
To the wind-hollowed heights and gusty bays
Of sheer Tintagel, fair with famous days.
Above the stem a gilded swallow shone,

Wrought with straight wings and eyes of glittering stone
As flying sunward oversea, to bear
Green summer with it through the singing air.
And on the deck between the rowers at dawn,
As the bright sail with brightening wind was drawn,
Sat with full face against the strengthening light
Iseult, more fair than foam or dawn was white.

Her gaze was glad past love's own singing of,
And her face lovely past desire of love.
Past thought and speech her maiden motions were,
And a more golden sunrise was her hair.
The very veil of her bright flesh was made
As of light woven and moonbeam-colored shade
More fine than moonbeams ; white her eyelids shone
As snow sun-stricken that endures the sun,
And through their curled and coloured clouds of deep
Luminous lashes thick as dreams in sleep
Shone as the sea's depth swallowing up the sky's
The springs of unimaginable eyes.
As the wave's subtler emerald is pierced through
With the utmost heaven's inextricable blue,
And both are woven and molten in one sleight
Of amorous color and implicated light
Under the golden guard and gaze of noon,
So glowed their aweless amorous plenilune,
Azure and gold and ardent grey, made strange
With fiery difference and deep interchange
Inexplicable of glories multiform :
Now as the sullen sapphire swells toward storm
Foamless, their bitter beauty grew acold,
And now afire with ardour of fine gold.
Her flower-soft lips were meek and passionate,
For love upon them like a shadow sate
Patient, a foreseen vision of sweet things,
A dream with eyes fast shut and plumeless wings
That knew not what man's love or life should be,
Nor had it sight nor heart to hope or see
What thing should come, but childlike satisfied
Watched out its virgin vigil in soft pride
And unkissed expectation ; and the glad
Clear cheeks and throat and tender temples had
Such maiden heat as if a rose's blood
Beat in the live heart of a lily-bud.
Between the small round breasts a white way led
Heavenward, and from slight foot to slender head
The whole fair body flower-like swayed and shone
Moving, and what her light hand leant upon

Grew blossom-scented ; her warm arms began
To round and ripen for delight of man
That they should clasp and circle : her fresh hands,
Like regent lilies of reflowering lands
Whose vassal firstlings, crown and star and plume,
Bow down to the empire of that sovereign bloom,
Shone sceptreless, and from her face there went
A silent light as of a God content ;
Save when, more swift and keen than love or shame,
Some flash of blood, light as the laugh of flame,
Broke it with sudden beam and shining speech,
As dream by dream shot through her eyes, and each
Outshone the last that lightened, and not one
Showed her such things as should be borne and done,
Though hard against her shone the sunlike face
That in all change and wreck of time and place
Should be the star of her sweet living soul.
Nor had love made it as his written scroll
For evil will and good to read in yet ;
But smooth and mighty, without scar or fret,
Fresh and high-lifted was the helmless brow
As the oak-tree flower that tops the topmost bough,
Ere it drop off before the perfect leaf ;
And nothing save his name he had of grief,
The name his mother, dying as he was born,
Made out of sorrow in very sorrow's scorn,
And set it on him smiling in her sight,
Tristram ; who now, clothed with sweet youth and might,
As a glad witness wore that bitter name,
The second symbol of the world for fame.
Famous and full of fortune was his youth
Ere the beard's bloom had left his cheek unsmooth,
And in his face a lordship of strong joy
And height of heart no chance could curb or cloy
Lightened, and all that warmed them at his eyes
Loved them as larks that kindle as they rise
Toward light they turn to music love the blue strong skies.

So like the morning through the morning
moved
Tristram, a light to look on and be loved.
Song sprang between his lips and hands, and
shone
Singing, and strengthened and sank down
thereon
As a bird settles to the second flight,
Then from beneath his harping hands with
might
Leapt, and made way and had its fill and
died,
And all whose hearts were fed upon it sighed
Silent, and in them all the fire of tears
Burned as wine drunken not with lips but
ears.
And gazing on his fervent hands that made
The might of music all their souls obeyed
With trembling strong subservience of delight,
Full many a maid that had him once in sight
Thought in the secret rapture of her heart
In how dark onset had these hands borne
part
How oft, and were so young and sweet of
skill ;
And those red lips whereon the song burned
still,
What words and cries of battle had they flung
Athwart the swing and shriek of swords, so
young ;
And eyes as glad as summer, what strange
youth
Fed them so full of happy heart and truth,
That had seen sway from side to sundering
side
The steel flow of that terrible springtide
That the moon rules not, but the fire and
light
Of men's hearts mixed in the mid mirth of
fight.
Therefore the joy and love of him they had
Made thought more amorous in them and
more glad
For his fame's 'sake remembered, and his
youth
Gave his fame flowerlike fragrance and soft
growth
As of a rose requickening, when he stood
Fair in their eye, a flower of faultless blood.
And that sad queen to whom his life was
death,
A rose plucked forth of summer in mid breath,
A star fall'n out of season in mid throe
Of that life's joy that makes the star's life
glow,

22

Made their love sadder toward him and more
strong,
And in mid change of time and fight and song
Chance cast him westward on the low sweet
strand
Where songs are sung of the old green Irish
land,
And the sky loves it, and the sea loves best,
And as a bird is taken to man's breast
The sweet-souled land where sorrow sweet
est sings
Is wrapt round with them as with hands and
wings
And taken to the sea's heart as a flower.
There in the luck and light of his good hour
Came to the king's court like a noteless man
Tristram, and while some half a season ran
Abode before him harping in his hall,
And taught sweet craft of new things musical
To the dear maiden mouth and innocent
hands
That for his sake are famous in all lands.
Yet was not love between them, for their fate
Lay wrapt in its appointed hour at wait,
And had no flower to show yet, and no sting.
But once being vexed with some past wound
the king
Bade give him comfort of sweet baths, and
then
Should Iseult watch him as his handmaiden,
For his more honour in men's sight, and ease
The hurts he had with holy remedies
Made by her mother's magic in strange hours
Out of live roots and life-compelling flowers.
And finding by the wound's shape in his
side
This was the knight by whom their strength
had died
And all their might in one man overthrown
Had left their shame in sight of all men
shown,
She would have slain him swordless with his
sword ;
Yet seemed he to her so great and fair a lord
She heaved up hand and smote not ; then said
he,
Laughing—'What comfort shall this dead
man be,
Damsel ? what hurt is for my blood to heal ї
But set your hand not near the toothèd steel
Lest the fang strike it.'—' Yea, the fang,' she
said,
' Should it not sting the very serpent dead
That stung my uncle ? for his slayer art thou,
And half my mother's heart is bloodless now

Through thee, that mad'st the veins of all her
kin
Bleed in his wounds whose veins through thee
ran thin.
Yet thought she how their hot chief's violent
heart
Had flung the fierce word forth upon their
part
Which bade to battle the best knight that
stood
On Arthur's, and so dying of his wild mood
Had set upon his conqueror's flesh the seal
Of his mishallowed and anointed steel,
Whereof the venom and enchanted might
Made the sign burn here branded in her sight.
These things she stood recasting, and her soul
Subsiding till its wound of wrath were whole
Grew smooth again, as though still softening
stole
Through all its tempered passion ; nor might
hate
Keep high the fire against him lit of late ;
But softly from his smiling sight she passed.
And peace thereafter made between them fast
Made peace between two kingdoms, when he
went
Home with hands reconciled and heart con-
tent,
To bring fair truce 'twixt Cornwall's wild
bright strand
And the long wrangling wars of that loud
land.
And when full peace was struck betwixt them
twain
Forth must he fare by those green straits
again,
And bring back Iseult for a plighted bride
And set to reign at Mark his uncle's side.
So now with feast made and all triumphs done
They sailed between the moonfall and the sun
Under the spent stars eastward; but the queen
Out of wise heart and subtle love had seen
Such things as might be, dark as in a glass,
And lest some doom of these should come to
pass
Bethought her with her secret soul alone
To work some charm for marriage and alone
And strike the heart of Iseult to her lord
With power compulsive more than stroke of
sword.
Therefore with marvellous herbs and spells
she wrought
To win the very wonder of her thought,
And brewed it with her secret hands and
blest

And drew and gave out of her secret breast
To one her chosen and Iseult's handmaiden,
Brangwain, and bade her hide from sight of
men
This marvel covered in a golden cup,
So covering in her heart the counsel up
As in the gold the wondrous wine lay close :
And when the last shout with the last cup rose
About the bride and bridegroom bound to bed.
Then should this one word of her will be said
To her new-married maiden child, that she
Should drink with Mark this draught in unity,
And no lip touch it for her sake but theirs :
For with long love and consecrating prayers
The wine was hallowed for their mouths to
pledge ;
And if a drop fell from the beaker's edge
That drop should Iseult hold as dear as
blood
Shed from her mother's heart to do her good.
And having drunk they twain should be one
heart
Who were one flesh till fleshly death should
part—
Death, who parts all.   So Brangwain swore,
and kept
The hid thing by her while she waked or
slept.
And now they sat to see the sun again
Whose light of eye had looked on no such
twain
Since Galahault in the rose-time of the year
Brought Launcelot first to sight of Guene-
vere.
    And Tristram caught her changing eyes
and said :
' As this day raises daylight from the dead
Might not this face the light of a dead man ? '
And Iseult, gazing where the sea was wan
Out of the sun's way, said : ' I pray you not
Praise me, but tell me there in Camelot,
Saving the queen, who hath most name of
fair ?
I would I were a man and dwelling there,
That I might win me better praise than
yours,
Even such as you have ; for your praise en-
dures,
That with great deeds ye wring from mouths
of men,
But ours—for shame, where is it ? Tell me
then,
Since woman may not wear a better here,
Who of this praise hath most save Guene-
vere ? '

And Tristram, lightening with a laugh
     held in—
' Surely a little praise is this to win,
A poor praise and a little ! but of these
Hapless, whom love serves only with bowed
     knees.
Of such poor women fairer face hath none
That lifts her eyes alive against the sun
Than Arthur's sister, whom the north seas
     call
Mistress of isles ; so yet majestical
Above the crowns on younger heads she
     moves,
Outlightening with her eyes our late-born
     loves.'
     ' Ah,' said Iseult, ' is she more tall than I ?
Look, I am tall ; ' and struck the mast hard
     by,
With utmost upward reach of her bright
     hand ;
' And look, fair lord, now, when I rise and
     stand,
How high with feet uplifted I can touch
Standing straight up ; could this queen do
     thus much ?
Nay, over tall she must be then, like me ;
Less fair than lesser women.   May this be,
That still she stands the second stateliest
     there,
So more than many so much younger fair,
She, born when yet the king your lord was
     not,
And has the third knight after Launcelot
And after you to serve her ? nay, sir, then
God made her for a godlike sign to men.'
     ' Ay,' Tristram answered, ' for a sign, a
     sign—
Would God it were not ! for no planets shine
With half such fearful forecast of men's fate
As a fair face so more unfortunate.'
     Then with a smile that lit not on her brows
But moved upon her red mouth tremulous
Light as a sea-bird's motion oversea,
' Yea,' quoth Iseult, ' the happier hap for me,
With no such face to bring men no such fate.
Yet her might all we women born too late
Praise for good hap, who so enskied above
Not more in age excels us than man's love.'
     There came a glooming light on Tristram's
     face
Answering : ' God keep you better in his
     grace
Than to sit down beside her in men's sight.
For if men be not blind whom God gives
     light

And lie not in whose lips he bids truth live,
Great grief shall she be given, and greater give,
For Merlin witnessed of her years ago
That she should work woe and should suffer
     woe
Beyond the race of women : and in truth
Her face, a spell that knows nor age nor
     youth,
Like youth being soft, and subtler-eyed than
     age,
With lips that mock the doom her eyes
     presage,
Hath on it such a light of cloud and fire,
With charm and change of keen or dim de-
     sire,
And over all a fearless look of fear
Hung like a veil across its changing cheer,
Made up of fierce foreknowledge and sharp
     scorn,
That it were better she had not been born.
For not love's self can help a face which
     hath
Such insubmissive anguish of wan wrath,
Blind prescience and self-contemptuous hate
Of her own soul and heavy-footed fate,
Writ broad upon its beauty : none the less
Its fire of bright and burning bitterness
Takes with as quick a flame the sense of men
As any sunbeam, nor is quenched again
With any drop of dewfall ; yea, I think
No herb of force or blood-compelling drink
Would heal a heart that ever it made hot.
Ay, and men too that greatly love her not,
Seeing the great love of her and Lamoracke,
Make no great marvel, nor look strangely
     back
When with his gaze about her she goes by
Pale as a breathless and star-quickening sky
Between moonrise and sunset, and moves out
Clothed with the passion of his eyes about
As night with all her stars, yet night is black ;
And she, clothed warm with love of Lamor-
     acke,
Girt with his worship as with girdling gold,
Seems all at heart anhungered and acold,
Seems sad at heart and loveless of the light,
As night, star-clothed or naked, is but night.'
     And with her sweet eyes sunken, and the
     mirth
Dead in their look as earth lies dead in earth
That reigned on earth and triumphed, Iseult
     said :
' Is it her shame of something done and dead
Or fear of something to be born and done
That so in her soul's eye puts out the sun ?'

And Tristram answered: 'Surely, as I think,
This gives her soul such bitterness to drink,
The sin born blind, the sightless sin unknown,
Wrought when the summer in her blood was blown,
But scarce aflower, and spring first flushed her will
With bloom of dreams no fruitage should fulfil,
When out of vision and desire was wrought
The sudden sin that from the living thought
Leaps a live deed and dies not: then there came
On that blind sin swift eyesight like a flame
Touching the dark to death, and made her mad
With helpless knowledge that too late forbade
What was before the bidding; and she knew
How sore a life dead love should lead her through
To what sure end how fearful; and though yet
Nor with her blood nor tears her way be wet
And she look bravely with set face on fate,
Yet she knows well the serpent hour at wait
Somewhere to sting and spare not; ay, and he,
Arthur'——
      'The king, quoth Iseult suddenly,
'Doth the king too live so in sight of fear?
They say sin touches not a man so near
As shame a woman; yet he too should be
Part of the penance, being more deep than she
Set in the sin.'
      'Nay,' Tristram said, ' for thus
It fell by wicked hap and hazardous,
That wittingly he sinned no more than youth
May sin and be assoiled of God and truth,
Repenting; since in his first year of reign
As he stood splendid with his foemen slain
And light of new-blown battles, flushed and hot
With hope and life, came greeting from King Lot
Out of his wind-worn islands oversea,
And homage to my king and fealty
Of those north seas wherein the strange shapes swim,
As from his man; and Arthur greeted him
As his good lord and courteously, and bade
To his high feast; who coming with him had
This Queen Morgause of Orkney, his fair wife,

In the green middle Maytime of her life,
And scarce in April was our king's as then,
And goodliest was he of all flowering men,
And of what graft as yet himself knew not;
But cold as rains in autumn was King Lot
And grey-grown out of season: so there sprang
Swift love between them, and all spring through sang
Light in their joyous hearing; for none knew
The bitter bond of blood between them two.
Twain fathers but one mother, till too late
The sacred mouth of Merlin set forth fate
And brake the secret seal on Arthur's birth,
And showed his ruin and his rule on earth
Inextricable, and light on lives to be.
For surely, though time slay us, yet shall we
Have such high name and lordship of good days
As shall sustain us living, and men's praise
Shall burn a beacon lit above us dead.
And of the king how shall not this be said
When any of us from any mouth has praise,
That such were men in only this king's days,
In Arthur's? yea, come shine or shade, no less
His name shall be one name with knightliness,
His fame one light with sunlight. Yet in sooth
His age shall bear the burdens of his youth
And bleed from his own bloodshed; for indeed
Blind to him blind his sister brought forth seed,
And of the child between them shall be born
Destruction: so shall God not suffer scorn,
Nor in men's souls and lives his law lie dead.'
      And as one moved and marvelling Iseult said:
'Great pity it is and strange it seems to me
God could not do them so much right as we,
Who slay not men for witless evil done;
And these the noblest under God's glad sun
For sin they knew not he that knew shall slay,
And smite blind men for stumbling in fair day.
What good is it to God that such should die?
Shall the sun's light grow sunnier in the sky
Because their light of spirit is clean put out?'
      And sighing, she looked from wave to cloud about,
And even with that the full-grown feet of day
Sprang upright on the quivering water-way,
And his face burned against her meeting face

Most like a lover's filled with great love's
  grace
Whose glance takes fire and gives ; the quick
  sea shone
And shivered like spread wings of angels
  blown
By the sun's breath before him ; and a low
Sweet gale shook all the foam-flowers of thin
  snow
As into rain-fall of sea-roses shed
Leaf by wild leaf on that green garden-bed
Which tempests till and sea-winds turn and
  plough :
For rosy and fiery round the running prow
Fluttered the flakes and feathers of the spray,
And bloomed like blossoms cast by God away
To waste on the ardent water ; swift the
  moon
Withered to westward as a face in swoon
Death-stricken by glad tidings : and the
  height
Throbbed and the centre quivered with de-
  light
And the depth quailed with passion as of
  love,
Till like the heart of some new-mated dove
Air, light, and wave seemed full of burning
  rest,
With motion as of one God's beating breast.
  And her heart sprang in Iseult, and she
  drew
With all her spirit and life the sunrise through,
And through her lips the keen triumphant air
Sea-scented, sweeter than land-roses were,
And through her eyes the whole rejoicing
  east
Sun-satisfied, and all the heaven at feast
Spread for the morning ; and the imperious
  mirth
Of wind and light that moved upon the earth,
Making the spring, and all the fruitful might
And strong regeneration of delight
That swells the seedling leaf and sapling man,
Since the first life in the first world began
To burn and burgeon through void limbs and
  veins,
And the first love with sharp sweet procreant
  pains
To pierce and bring forth roses ; yea, she felt
Through her own soul the sovereign morning
  melt,
And all the sacred passion of the sun ;
And as the young clouds flamed and were un-
  done
About him coming, touched and burnt away

In rosy ruin and yellow spoil of day,
The sweet veil of her body and corporal sense
Felt the dawn also cleave it, and incense
With light from inward and with effluent heat
The kindling soul through fleshly hands and
  feet.
And as the august great blossom of the dawn
Burst, and the full sun scarce from sea with-
  drawn
Seemed on the fiery water a flower afloat,
So as a fire the mighty morning smote
Throughout her, and incensed with the influ-
  ent hour
Her whole soul's great mystical red flower
Burst, and the bud of her sweet spirit broke
Rose-fashion, and the strong spring at a
  stroke
Thrilled, and was cloven, and from the full
  sheath came
The whole rose of the woman red as flame :
And all her Mayday blood as from a swoon
Flushed, and May rose up in her and was
  June.
So for a space her heart as heavenward
  burned :
Then with half summer in her eyes she
  turned,
And on her lips were April yet, and smiled,
As though the spirit and sense unreconciled
Shrank laughing back, and would not ere its
  hour
Let life put forth the irrevocable flower.
  And the soft speech between them grew
  again
With questionings and records of what men
Rose mightiest, and what names for love or
  fight
Shone starriest overhead of queen or knight.
There Tristram spake of many a noble thing,
High feast and storm of tournay round the
  king,
Strange quest by perilous lands of marsh and
  brake,
And circling woods branch-knotted like a
  snake,
And places pale with sins that they had seen
Where was no life of red fruit or of green
But all was as a dead face wan and dun ;
And bowers of evil builders whence the sun
Turns silent, and the moon holds hardly
  light
Above them through the sick and star-crossed
  night ;
And of their hands through whom such holds
  lay waste,

And all their strengths dishevelled and de-
faced
Fell ruinous, and were not from north to
south :
And of the might of Merlin's ancient mouth,
The son of no man's loins, begot by doom
In speechless sleep out of a spotless womb ;
For sleeping among graves where none had
rest
And ominous houses of dead bones unblest
Among the grey grass rough as old rent hair
And wicked herbage whitening like despair
And blown upon with blasts of dolorous
breath
From gaunt rare gaps and hollow doors of
death,
A maid unspotted, senseless of the spell,
Felt not about her breathe some thing of hell
Whose child and hers was Merlin ; and to
him
Great light from God gave sight of all things
dim
And wisdom of all wondrous things, to say
What root should bear, what fruit of night or
day,
And sovereign speech and counsel higher than
man ;
Wherefore his youth like age was wise and
wan,
And his age sorrowful and fain to sleep ;
Yet should sleep never, neither laugh nor
weep,
Till in some depth of deep sweet land or sea
The heavenly hands of holier Nimue,
That was the nurse of Launcelot, and most
sweet
Of all that move with magical soft feet
Among us, being of lovelier blood and breath,
Should shut him in with sleep as kind as
death :
For she could pass between the quick and
dead :
And of her love toward Pelleas, for whose
head
Love-wounded and world-wearied she had
won
A place beyond all pain in Avalon ;
And of the fire that wasted afterward
The loveless eyes and bosom of Ettarde,
In whose false love his faultless heart had
burned ;
And now being rapt from her, her lost heart
yearned
To seek him, and passed hungering out of
life :

And after all the thunder-hours of strife
That roared between King Claudas and King
Ban
How Nimue's mighty nursling waxed to man,
And how from his first field such grace he got
That all men's hearts bowed down to Launce-
lot,
And how the high prince Galahault held him
dear
And led him even to love of Guenevere
And to that kiss which made break forth as
fire
The laugh that was the flower of his desire,
The laugh that lightened at her lips for bliss
To win from love so great a lover's kiss :
And of the toil of Balen all his days
To reap but thorns for fruit and tears for
praise,
Whose hap was evil as his heart was good,
And all his works and ways by wold and
wood
Led through much pain to one last labouring
day
When blood for tears washed grief with life
away :
And of the kin of Arthur, and their might ;
The misborn head of Mordred, sad as night,
With cold waste cheeks and eyes as keen as
pain,
And the close angry lips of Agravaine ;
And gracious Gawain, scattering words as
flowers,
The kindliest head of worldly paramours ;
And the fair hand of Gareth, found in fight
Strong as a sea-beast's tushes and as white ;
And of the king's self, glorious yet and glad
For all the toil and doubt of doom he had,
Clothed with men's loves and full of kingly
days.
  Then Iseult said : ' Let each knight have
his praise
And each good man good witness of his
worth ;
But when men laud the second name on earth,
Whom would they praise to have no worldly
peer
Save him whose love makes glorious Guene-
vere ?'
  ' Nay,' Tristram said, ' such man as he is
none.'
  ' What,' said she, ' there is none such under
sun
Of all the large earth's living ? yet I deemed
Men spake of one—but maybe men that
dreamed,

Fools and tongue-stricken, witless, babbler's
     breed—
That for all high things was his peer indeed
Save this one highest, to be so loved and
     love.'
   And Tristram said : 'Little wit had these
     thereof ;
For there is none such in the world as this.'
   ' Ay, upon land,' quoth Iseult, ' none such is,
I doubt not, nor where fighting folk may be ;
But were there none such between sky and sea,
The world's whole worth were poorer than I
     wist.'
   And Tristram took her flower-white hand
     and kissed,
Laughing ; and through his fair face as in
     shame
The light blood lightened. ' Hear they no
     such name ? '
She said ; and he, ' If there be such a word,
I wot the queen's poor harper hath not heard.'
Then, as the fuller-feathered hours grew long,
He holp to speed their warm slow feet with
     song.

Love, is it morning risen or night deceased
That makes the mirth of this triumphant east ?
   Is it bliss given or bitterness put by
That makes most glad men's hearts at love's high
     feast ?
     Grief smiles, joy weeps, that day should live and
     die.

' Is it with soul's thirst or with body's drought
That summer yearns out sunward to the south,
   With all the flowers that when thy birth drew
     nigh
Were molten in one rose to make thy mouth ?
     O love, what care though day should live and
     die ?

Is the sun glad of all the love on earth,
The spirit and sense and work of things and worth ?
   Is the moon sad because the month must fly
And bring her death that can but bring back birth ?
     For all these things as day must live and die.

' Love, is it day that makes thee thy delight
Or thou that seest day made out of thy light ?
   Love, as the sun and sea are thou and I,
Sea without sun dark, sun without sea bright ;
     The sun is one though day should live and die.

' O which is elder, night or light, who knows ?
And life or love, which first of these twain grows ?
   For life is born of love to wail and cry,
And love is born of life to heal his woes,
     And light of night, that day should live and die.

' O sun of heaven above the worldly sea,
O very love, what light is this of thee !
   My sea of soul is deep as thou art high,
But all thy light is shed through all of me,
     As love's through love, while day shall live and
     die.

' Nay,' said Iseult, ' your song is hard to
     read.'
   ' Ay ? ' said he : ' or too light a song to
     heed,
Too slight to follow, it may be ? Who shall
     sing
Of love but as a churl before a king
If by love's worth men rate his worthiness ?
Yet as the poor churl's worth to sing is less,
Surely the more shall be the great king's grace
To show for churlish love a kindlier face.'
   ' No churl,' she said, ' but one in sooth-
     sayer's wise
Who tells but truths that help no more than
     lies.
I have heard men sing of love a simpler way
Than these wrought riddles made of night
     and day,
Like jewelled reins whereon the rhyme-bells
     hang.'
   And Tristram smiled and changed his song
     and sang.

' The breath between my lips of lips not mine,
Like spirit in sense that makes pure sense divine,
   Is as life in them from the living sky
That entering fills my heart with blood of thine
   And thee with me, while day shall live and die.

' Thy soul is shed into me with thy breath,
And in my heart each heartbeat of thee saith
   How in thy life the offsprings of me lie,
Even one life to be gathered of one death
   In me and thee, though day may live and die.

' Ah, who knows now if in my veins it be
My blood that feels life sweet, or blood of thee,
   And this thine eyesight kindled in mine eye
That shows me in thy flesh the soul of me,
     For thine made mine, while day may live and
     die ?

' Ah, who knows yet if one be twain or one,
And sunlight separable again from sun,
   And I from thee with all my lifesprings dry,
And thou from me with all thine heartbeats done,
   Dead separate souls while day shall live and die ?

' I see my soul within thine eyes, and hear
My spirit in all thy pulses thrill with fear,
   And in my lips the passion of thee sigh,
And music of me made in mine own ear ;
   Am I not thou while day shall live and die ?

' Art thou not I as I thy love am thou ?
So let all things pass from us ; we are now,
   For all that was and will be, who knows why ?
And all that is and is not, who knows how ?
     Who knows ? God knows why day should live
     and die.'

And Iseult mused and spake no word, but
     sought

Through all the hushed ways of her tongue-
  less thought
What face or covered likeness of a face
In what veiled hour or dream-determined
  place
She seeing might take for love's face, and
  believe
This was the spirit to whom all spirits cleave.
For that sweet wonder of the twain made one
And each one twain, incorporate sun with
  sun,
Star with star molten, soul imbued,
And all the soul's works, all their multitude,
Made one thought and one vision and one
  song,
Love—this thing, this, laid hand on her so
  strong
She could not choose but yearn till she should
  see.
So went she musing down her thoughts ; but
  he,
Sweet-hearted as a bird that takes the sun
With clear strong eyes, and feels the glad god
  run
Bright through his blood and wide rejoicing
  wings,
And opens all himself to heaven and sings,
Made her mind light and full of noble mirth
With words and songs the gladdest grown on
  earth,
Till she was blithe and high of heart as he.
So swam the Swallow through the springing
  sea.
    And while they sat at speech as at a feast,
Came a light wind fast hardening forth of the
  east
And blackening till its might had marred the
  skies :
And the sea thrilled as with heart-sundering
  sighs
One after one drawn, with each breath it
  drew,
And the green hardened into iron blue,
And the soft light went out of all its face.
Then Tristram girt him for an oarsman's
  place
And took his oar and smote, and toiled with
  might
In the east wind's full face and the strong
  sea's spite
Labouring ; and all the rowers rowed hard,
  but he
More mightily than any wearier three,
And Iseult watched him rowing with sinless
  eyes

That loved him but in holy girlish wise
For noble joy in his fair manliness
And trust and tender wonder ; none the less
She thought if God had given her grace to
  be
Man, and make war on danger of earth and
  sea,
Even such a man she would be ; for his stroke
Was mightiest as the mightier water broke,
And in sheer measure like strong music drave
Clean through the wet weight of the wallow-
  ing wave,
And as a tune before a great king played
For triumph was the tune their strong strokes
  made,
And speed the ship through with smooth strife
  of oars
Over the mid sea's grey foam-paven floors,
For all the loud breach of the waves at will.
So for an hour they fought the storm out
  still,
And the shorn foam spun from the blades,
  and high
The keel sprang from the wave-ridge, and
  the sky
Glared at them for a breath's space through
  the rain ;
Then the bows with a sharp shock plunged
  again
Down, and the sea clashed on them, and so
  rose
The bright stem like one panting from swift
  blows,
And as a swimmer's joyous beaten head
Rears itself laughing, so in that sharp stead
The light ship lifted her long quivering bows
As might the man his buffeted strong brows
Out of the wave-breach ; for with one stroke
  yet
Went all men's oars together, strongly set
As to loud music, and with hearts uplift
They smote their strong way through the
  drench and drift.
Till the keen hour had chafed itself to death
And the east wind fell fitfully, breath by
  breath,
Tired ; and across the thin and slackening
  rain
Sprang the face southward of the sun again.
Then all they rested and were eased at heart ;
And Iseult rose up where she sat apart,
And with her sweet soul deepening her deep
  eyes
Cast the furs from her and subtle embroid-
  eries

That wrapped her from the storming rain and
spray,
And shining like all April in one day,
Hair, face, and throat dashed with the stray-
ing showers,
She stood the first of all the whole world's
flowers,
And laughed on Tristram with her eyes, and
said,
' I too have heart then, I was not afraid.'
And answering some light courteous word of
grace
He saw her clear face lighten on his face
Unwittingly, with unenamoured eyes,
For the last time. A live man in such wise
Looks in the deadly face of his fixed hour
And laughs with lips wherein he hath no
power
To keep the life yet some five minutes' space.
So Tristram looked on Iseult face to face
And knew not, and she knew not. The last
time—
The last that should be told in any rhyme
Heard anywhere on mouths of singing men
That ever should sing praise of them again ;
The last hour of their hurtless hearts at
rest,
The last that peace should touch them breast
to breast,
The last that sorrow far from them should
sit,
This last was with them, and they knew not
it.
  For Tristram being athirst with toil now
spake,
Saying, ' Iseult, for all dear love's labour's
sake
Give me to drink, and give me for a pledge
The touch of four lips on the beaker's edge.'
And Iseult sought and would not wake Brang-
wain
Who slept as one half dead with fear and
pain,
Being tender-natured ; so with hushed light
feet
Went Iseult round her, with soft looks and
sweet
Pitying her pain ; so sweet a spirited thing
She was, and daughter of a kindly king.
And spying what strange bright secret charge
was kept
Fast in that maid's white bosom while she
slept,
She sought and drew the gold cup forth and
smiled

Marvelling, with such light wonder as a child
That hears of glad sad life in magic lands ;
And bare it back to Tristram with pure
hands
Holding the love-draught that should be for
flame
To burn out of them fear and faith and
shame,
And lighten all their life up in men's sight,
And make them sad for ever. Then the
knight
Bowed toward her and craved whence had
she this strange thing
That might be spoil of some dim Asian
king,
By starlight stolen from some waste place of
sands,
And a maid bore it here in harmless hands.
And Iseult, laughing—' Other lords that
be
Feast, and their men feast after them ; but
we,
Our men must keep the best wine back to
feast
Till they be full and we of all men least
Feed after them and fain to fare so well :
So with mine handmaid and your squire it
fell
That hid this bright thing from us in a
wile : '
And with light lips yet full of their swift
smile
And hands that wist not though they dug a
grave,
Undid the hasps of gold, and drank, and
gave,
And he drank after, a deep glad kingly
draught :
And all their life changed in them, for they
quaffed
Death ; if it be death so to drink, and fare
As men who change and are what these twain
were.
And shuddering with eyes full of fear and
fire
And heart-strung with a serpentine desire
He turned and saw the terror in her eyes
That yearned upon him shining in such
wise
As a star midway in the midnight fixed.
  Their Galahault was the cup, and she that
mixed ;
Nor other hand there needed, nor sweet
speech
To lure their lips together ; each on each

Hung with strange eyes and hovered as a bird [word ;
Wounded, and each mouth trembled for a
Their heads neared, and their hands were drawn in one,

And they saw dark, though still the unsunken sun
Far through fine rain shot fire into the south ;
And their four lips became one burning mouth.

II.

THE QUEEN'S PLEASANCE.

OUT of the night arose the second day,
And saw the ship's bows break the shoreward spray.
As the sun's boat of gold and fire began
To sail the sea of heaven unsailed of man,
And the soft waves of sacred air to break
Round the prow launched into the morning's lake,
They saw the sign of their sea-travel done.
  Ah, was not something seen of yester-sun,
When the sweet light that lightened all the skies
Saw nothing fairer than one maiden's eyes,
That whatsoever in all time's years may be
To-day's sun nor to-morrow's sun shall see ?
Not while she lives, not when she comes to die
Shall she look sunward with that sinless eye.
  Yet fairer now than song may show them stand
Tristram and Iseult, hand in amorous hand,
Soul-satisfied, their eyes made great and bright
With all the love of all the livelong night ;
With all its hours yet singing in their ears
No mortal music made of thoughts and tears,
But such a song, past conscience of man's thought,
As hearing he grows god and knows it not.
Nought else they saw nor heard but what the night
Had left for seal upon their sense and sight,
Sound of past pulses beating, fire of amorous light.
Enough, and overmuch, and never yet
Enough, though love still hungering feed and fret,
To fill the cup of night which dawn must overset.
For still their eyes were dimmer than with tears

And dizzier from diviner sounds their ears
Than though from choral thunders of the quiring spheres.
They heard not how the landward waters rang,
Nor saw where high into the morning sprang,
Riven from the shore and bastioned with the sea,
Toward summits where the north wind's nest might be,
A wave-walled palace with its eastern gate
Full of the sunrise now and wide at wait,
And on the mighty-moulded stairs that clomb
Sheer from the fierce lip of the lapping foam
The knights of Mark that stood before the wall.
So with loud joy and storm of festival
They brought the bride in up the towery way
That rose against the rising front of day,
Stair based on stair, between the rocks unhewn,
To those strange halls wherethrough the tidal tune
Rang loud or lower from soft or strengthening sea,
Tower shouldering tower, to windward and to lee,
With change of floors and stories, flight on flight,
That clomb and curled up to the crowning height
Whence men might see wide east and west in one
And on one sea waned moon and mounting sun.
And severed from the sea-rock's base, where stand
Some worn walls yet, they saw the broken strand,
The beachless cliff that in the sheer sea dips,
The sleepless shore inexorable to ships,

And the straight causeway's spare gaunt spine
  between
The sea-spanned walls and naked mainland's
  green.
  On the mid stairs, between the light and dark,
Before the main tower's portal stood King
  Mark,
Crowned : and his face was as the face of one
Long time athirst and hungering for the sun
In barren thrall of bitter bonds, who now
Thinks here to feel its blessing on his brow.
A swart lean man, but kinglike still of guise,
With black streaked beard and cold unquiet
  eyes,
Close-mouthed, gaunt-cheeked, wan as a
  morning moon,
Though hardly time on his worn hair had
  strewn
The thin first ashes from a sparing hand :
Yet little fire there burnt upon the brand,
And way-worn seemed he with life's way-
  faring.
So between shade and sunlight stood the king,
And his face changed nor yearned not toward
  his bride ;
But fixed between mild hope and patient pride,
Abode what gift of rare or lesser worth
This day might bring to all his days on earth.
But at the glory of her when she came
His heart endured not : very fear and shame
Smote him, to take her by the hand and kiss,
Till both were molten in the burning bliss,
And with a thin flame flushing his cold face
He led her silent to the bridal place.
There were they wed and hallowed of the
  priest ;
And all the loud time of the marriage feast
One thought within three hearts was as a fire,
Where craft and faith took counsel with desire.
For when the feast had made a glorious end
They gave the new queen for her maids to
  tend
At dawn of bride-night and thereafter bring
With marriage music to the bridegroom king.
Then by device of craft between them laid
To him went Brangwain delicately, and
  prayed
That this thing even for love's sake might
  not be,
But without sound or light or eye to see
She might come in to bride-bed : and he
  laughed,
As one that wist not well of wise love's craft,
And bade all bridal things be as she would
But of his gentleness he gat not good ;

For clothed and covered with the nuptial dark
Soft like a bride came Brangwain to King
  Mark,
And to the queen came Tristram ; and the
  night
Fled, and ere danger of detective light
From the king sleeping Brangwain slid away,
And where had lain her handmaid Iseult lay.
And the king waking saw beside his head
That face yet passion-coloured, amorous red
From lips not his, and all that strange hair
  shed
Across the tissued pillows, fold on fold,
Innumerable, incomparable, all gold,
To fire men's eyes with wonder, and with love
Men's hearts ; so shone its flowering crown
  above
The brows enwound with that imperial wreath,
And framed with fragrant radiance round the
  face beneath.
  And the king marvelled, seeing with sudden
    start
Her very glory, and said out of his heart ;
' What have I done of good for God to bless
That all this he should give me, tress on tress,
All this great wealth and wondrous ? Was it
  this
That in mine arms I had all night to kiss,
And mix with me this beauty? this that seems
More fair than heaven doth in some tired
  saint's dreams,
Being part of that same heaven ? yea, more,
  for he,
Though loved of God so, yet but seems to see,
But to me sinful such great grace is given
That in mine hands I hold this part of heaven
Not to mine eyes lent merely. Doth God
  make
Such things so godlike for man's mortal sake ?
Have I not sinned, that in this fleshly life
Have made of her a mere man's very wife ?'
  So the king mused and murmured ; and
    she heard
The faint sound trembling of each breathless
  word
And laughed into the covering of her hair.
  And many a day for many a month as fair
Slid over them like music ; and as bright
Burned with love's offerings many a secret
  night.
And many a dawn to many a fiery noon
Blew prelude, when the horn's heart-kindling
  tune
Lit the live woods with sovereign sound of
  mirth

Before the mightiest huntsman hailed on earth
Lord of its lordliest pleasure, where he rode
Hard by her rein whose peerless presence
    glowed
Not as that white queen's of the virgin hunt
Once, whose crown-crescent braves the night-
    wind's brunt,
But with the sun for frontlet of a queenlier
    front.
For where the flashing of her face was turned
As lightning was the fiery light that burned
From eyes and brows enkindled more with
    speed
And rapture of the rushing of her steed
Than once with only beauty ; and her mouth
Was as a rose athirst that pants for drouth
Even while it laughs for pleasure of desire,
And all her heart was as a leaping fire.
Yet once more joy they took of woodland
    ways
Than came of all those flushed and fiery days
When the loud air was mad with life and
    sound,
Through many a dense green mile, of horn
    and hound
Before the king's hunt going along the wind,
And ere the timely leaves were changed or
    thinned,
Even in mid maze of summer. For the
    knight
Forth was once ridden toward some frontier
    fight
Against the lewd folk of the Christless lands
That warred with wild and intermittent hands
Against the king's north border ; and there
    came
A knight unchristened yet of unknown name,
Swart Palamede, upon a secret quest,
To high Tintagel, and abode as guest
In likeness of a minstrel with a king.
Nor was there man could sound so sweet a
    string,
Save Tristram only, of all held best on earth.
And one loud eve, being full of wine and
    mirth,
Ere sunset left the walls and waters dark,
To that strange minstrel strongly swore King
    Mark,
By all that makes a knight's faith firm and
    strong,
That he for guerdon of his harp and song
Might crave and have his liking.   Straight
    there came
Up the swart cheek a flash of swarthier flame,
And the deep eyes fulfilled of glittering night

Laughed out in lightnings of triumphant
    light
As the grim harper spake : ' O king, I crave
No gift of man that king may give to slave,
But this thy crowned queen only, this thy
    wife,
Whom yet unseen I loved, and set my life
On this poor chance to compass, even as here,
Being fairer famed than all save Guenevere.'
Then as the noise of seaward storm that
    mocks
With roaring laughter from reverberate rocks
The cry from ships near shipwreck, harsh
    and high
Rose all the wrath and wonder in one cry
Through all the long roof's hollow depth and
    length
That hearts of strong men kindled in their
    strength
May speak in laughter lion-like, and cease,
Being wearied : only two men held their
    peace
And each glared hard on other ; but King
    Mark
Spake first of these : " Man, though thy craft
    be dark
And thy mind evil that begat this thing,
Yet stands the word once plighted of a king
Fast : and albeit less evil it were for me
To give my life up than my wife, or be
A landless man crowned only with a curse,
Yet this in God's and all men's sight were
    worse,
To live soul-shamed, a man of broken troth,
Abhorred of men as I abhor mine oath
Which yet I may forswear not.' And he
    bowed
His head and wept : and all men wept aloud,
Save one, that heard him weeping ; but the
    queen
Wept not : and statelier yet than eyes had
    seen
That ever looked upon her queenly state
She rose, and in her eyes her heart was great
And full of wrath seen manifest and scorn
More strong than anguish to go thence for-
    lorn
Of all men's comfort and her natural right.
And they went forth into the dawn of night.
Long by wild ways and clouded light they
    rode,
Silent ; and fear less keen at heart abode
With Iseult than with Palamede : for awe
Constrained him, and the might of love's
    high law,

That can make lewd men royal ; and his
    heart
Yearned on her, if perchance with amorous
    art
And soothfast skill of very love he might
For courtesy find favor in her sight
And comfort of her mercies : for he wist
More grace might come of that sweet mouth
    unkissed
Than joy for violence done it, that should
    make
His name abhorred for shame's disloyal sake.
And in the stormy starlight clouds were
    thinned
And thickened by short gusts of changing
    wind
That panted like a sick man's fitful breath :
And like a moan of lions hurt to death
Came the sea's hollow noise along the night.
But ere its gloom from aught but foam had
    light
They halted, being aweary : and the knight
As reverently forbore her where she lay
As one that watched his sister's sleep till day.
Nor durst he kiss or touch her hand or hair
For love and shamefast pity, seeing how fair
She slept, and fenceless from the fitful air.
And shame at heart stung nigh to death de-
    sire,
But grief at heart burned in him like a fire
For hers and his own sorrowing sake, that
    had
Such grace for guerdon as makes glad men
    sad,
To have their will and want it. And the day
Sprang : and afar along the wild waste way
They heard the pulse and press of hurrying
    horse-hoofs play :
And like the rushing of a ravenous flame
Whose wings make tempest of the darkness,
    came
Upon them headlong as in thunder borne
Forth of the darkness of the labouring morn
Tristram : and up forthright upon his steed
Leapt, as one blithe of battle, Palamede,
And mightily with shock of horse and man
They lashed together : and fair that fight
    began
As fair came up that sunrise : to and fro,
With knees nigh staggered and stout heads
    bent low
From each quick shock of spears on either
    side,
Reeled the strong steeds heavily, haggard-
    eyed

And heartened high with passion of their
    pride
As sheer the stout spears shocked again, and
    flew
Sharp-splintering : then, his sword as each
    knight drew,
They flashed and foined full royally, so long
That but to see so fair a strife and strong
A man might well have given out of his life
One year's void space forlorn of love or strife.
As when a bright north-easter, great of heart,
Scattering the strengths of squadrons, hurls
    apart
Ship from ship labouring violently, in such
    toil
As earns but ruin—with even so strong recoil
Back were the steeds hurled from the spear
    shock, fain
And foiled of triumph : then with tightened
    rein
And stroke of spur, inveterate, either knight
Broe in again upon his foe with might,
Heart-hungry for the hot-mouthed feast of
    fight
And all athirst of mastery : but full soon
The jarring notes of that tempestuous tune
Fell, and its mighty music made of hands
Contending, clamorous through the loud waste
    lands,
Broke at once off ; and shattered from his
    steed
Fell, as a mainmast ruining, Palamede,
Stunned : and those lovers left him where he
    lay,
And lightly through green lawns they rode
    away.
    There was a bower beyond man's eye more
    fair
Than ever summer dews and sunniest air
Fed full with rest and radiance till the boughs
Had wrought a roof as for a holier house
Than aught save love might breathe in ;
    fairer far
Than keeps the sweet light back of moon and
    star
From high kings' chambers : there might
    love and sleep
Divide for joy the darkling hours, and keep
With amorous alternation of sweet strife
The soft and secret ways of death and life
Made smooth for pleasure's feet to rest and
    run
Even from the moondawn to the kindling sun,
Made bright for passion's feet to run and
    rest

Between the midnight's and the morning's
    breast,
Where hardly though her happy head lie
    down
It may forget the hour that wove its crown ;
Where hardly though her joyous limbs he laid
That m.y forget the mirth that midnight
    made.
And thither, ere sweet night had slain sweet
    day,
Iseult and Tristram took their wandering
    way,
And rested, and refreshed their hearts with
    cheer
In hunters' fashion of the woods ; and here
More sweet it seemed, while this might be,
    to dwell
And take of all world's weariness farewell
Than reign of all world's lordship queen and
    king.
Nor here would time for three moons' changes
    bring
Sorrow nor thought of sorrow ; but sweet
    earth
Fostered them like her babes of eldest birth,
Reared warm in pathless woods and cherished
    well.
And the sun sprang above the sea and fell,
And the stars rose and sank upon the sea ;
And outlaw-like, in forest wise and free,
The rising and the setting of their lights
Found those twain dwelling all those days
    and nights.
And under the change of sun and star and
    moon
Flourished and fell the chaplets woven of
    June,
And fair through fervours of the deepening
    sky
Panted and passed the hours that lit July,
And each day blessed them out of heaven
    above,
And each night crowned them with the crown
    of love.
Nor till the might of August overhead
Weighed on the world was yet one roseleaf
    shed
Of all their joy's warm coronal, nor aught
Touched them in passing ever with a thought
That ever this might end on any day
Or any night not love them where they lay ;
But like a babbling tale of barren breath
Seemed all report and rumour held of death,
And a false bruit the legend tear-impearled
That such a thing as change was in the world.

And each bright song upon his lips that came,
Mocking the powers of change and death by
    name,
Blasphemed their bitter godhead, and defied
Time, though clothed round with ruin as
    kings with pride,
To blot the glad life out of love : and she
Drank lightly deep of his philosophy
In that warm wine of amorous words which is
Sweet with all truths of all philosophies.
For well he wist all subtle ways of song,
And in his soul the secret eye was strong
That burns in meditation, till bright words
Break flamelike forth as notes from fledgeling
    birds
That feel the soul speak through them of the
    spring.
So fared they night and day as queen and
    king
Crowned of a kingdom wide as day and night
Nor ever cloudlet swept or swam in sight
Across the darkling depths of their delight
Whose stars no skill might number, nor
    man's art
Sound the deep stories of its heavenly heart.
Till, even for wonder that such life should
    live,
Desires and dreams of what death's self
    might give
Would touch with tears and laughter and
    with speech
The lips and eyes of passion, fain to reach,
Beyond all bourne of time or trembling sense,
The verge of love's last possible eminence.
Out of the heaven that storm nor shadow
    mars,
Deep from the starry depth beyond the stars,
A yearning ardour without scope or name
Fell on them, and the bright night's breath
    of flame
Shot fire into their kisses ; and like fire
The lit dews lightened on the leaves, as
    higher
Night's heart beat on toward midnight.   Far
    and fain
Somewhiles the soft rush of rejoicing rain
Solaced the darkness, and from steep to steep
Of heaven they saw the sweet sheet lightning
    leap
And laugh its heart out in a thousand smiles,
When the clear sea for miles on glimmering
    miles
Burned as though dawn were strewn abroad
    astray,
Or, showering out of heaven all heaven's array

Had paven instead the waters : fain and far
Somewhiles the burning love of star for star
Spake words that love might wellnigh seem
    to hear
In such deep hours as turn delight to fear
Sweet as delight's self ever.   So they lay
Tranced once, nor watched along the fiery
    bay
The shrine of summer darkness palpitate and
    play.
She had nor sight nor voice ; her swooning
    eyes
Knew not if night or light were in the skies ;
Across her beauty sheer the moondawn shed
.Its light as on a thing as white and dead ;
Only with stress of soft fierce hands she prest
Between the throbbing blossoms of her breast
His ardent face, and through his hair her
    breath
Went quivering as when life is hard on death ;
And with strong trembling fingers she strained
    fast
His head into her bosom ; till at last,
Satiate with sweetness of that burning bed,
His eyes afire with tears, he raised his head
And laughed into her lips ; and all his heart
Filled hers ; then face from face fell, and
    apart
Each hung on each with panting lips, and felt
Sense into sense and spirit in spirit melt.
    ' Hast thou no sword ?   I would not live
    till day ;
O love, this night and we must pass away,
It must die soon, and let not us die late.'
    ' Take thou my sword and slay me ; nay,
    but wait
Till day be risen ; what, wouldst thou think
    to die
Before the light take hold upon the sky ? '
    ' Yea, love ; for how shall we have twice,
    being twain,
This very night of love's most rapturous
    reign ?
Live thou and have thy day, and year by year
Be great, but what shall I be ? Slay me here ;
Let me die not when love lies dead, but now
Strike through my heart : nay, sweet, what
    heart hast thou ?
Is it too much I ask thee, and spend my
    breath
In asking ? nay, thou knowest it is but death.
Hadst thou true heart to love me, thou
    wouldst give
This : but for hate's sake thou wilt let me
    live.'

Here he caught up her lips with his, and
    made
The wild prayer silent in her heart that
    prayed,
And strained her to him till all her faint
    breath sank
And her bright light limbs palpitated and
    shrank
And rose and fluctuated as flowers in rain
That bend them and they tremble and rise
    again
And heave and straighten and quiver all
    through with bliss
And turn afresh their mouths up for a kiss,
Amorous, athirst of that sweet influent love ;
So, hungering toward his hovering lips above,
Her red-rose mouth yearned silent, and her
    eyes
Closed, and flashed after, as though June's
    darkest skies
The divine heartbeats of the deep live light
Make open and shut the gates of the outer
    night.
    Long lay they still, subdued with love, nor
    knew
If cloud or light changed colour as it grew,
If star or moon beheld them ; if above
The heaven of night waxed fiery with their
    love,
Or earth beneath were moved at heart and
    root
To burn as they, to burn and bring forth fruit
Unseasonable for love's sake ; if tall trees
Bowed, and close flowers yearned open, and
    the breeze
Failed and fell silent as a flame that fails :
And all that hour unheard the nightingales
Clamoured, and all the woodland soul was
    stirred,
And depth and height were one great song
    unheard,
As though the world caught music and took
    fire
From the instant heart alone of their desire.
    So sped their night of nights between
    them : so,
For all fears past and shadows, shine and
    snow,
That one pure hour all-golded where they lay
Made their life perfect and their darkness day.
And warmer waved its harvest yet to reap,
Till in the lovely fight of love and sleep
At length had sleep the mastery ; and the dark
Was lit with soft live gleams they might not
    mark,

Fleet butterflies, each like a dead flower's ghost,
White, blue, and sere leaf-coloured ; but the most
White as the sparkle of snow-flowers in the sun
Ere with his breath they lie at noon undone
Whose kiss devours their tender beauty, and leaves
But raindrops on the grass and sere thin leaves
That were engraven with traceries of the snow
Flowerwise ere any flower of earth's would blow ;
So swift they sprang and sank, so sweet and light
They swam the deep dim breathless air of night.
Now on her rose-white amorous breast half bare,
Now on her slumberous love-dishevelled hair,
The white wings lit and vanished, and afresh
Lit soft as snow lights on her snow-soft flesh,
On hand or throat or shoulder ; and she stirred
Sleeping, and spake some tremulous bright word,
And laughed upon some dream too sweet for truth,
Yet not so sweet as very love and youth

That there had charmed her eyes to sleep at last.
Nor woke they till the perfect night was past,
And the soft sea thrilled with blind hope of light.
But ere the dusk had well the sun in sight
He turned and kissed her eyes awake and said,
Seeing earth and water neither quick nor dead
And twilight hungering toward the day to be,
' As the dawn loves the sunlight I love thee.'
And even as rays with cloudlets in the skies
Confused in brief love's bright contentious wise,
Sleep strove with sense rekindling in her eyes ;
And as the flush of birth scarce overcame
The pale pure pearl of unborn light with flame
Soft as may touch the rose's heart with shame
To break not all reluctant out of bud,
Stole up her sleeping cheek her waking blood ;
And with the lovely laugh of love that takes
The whole soul prisoner ere the whole sense wakes,
Her lips for love's sake bade love's will be done.
And all the sea lay subject to the sun.

III.

TRISTRAM IN BRITTANY.

' " As the dawn loves the sunlight I love thee ; "
As men that shall be swallowed of the sea
Love the sea's lovely beauty ; as the night
That wanes before it loves the young sweet light,
And dies of loving ; as the worn-out noon
Loves twilight, and as twilight loves the moon
That on its grave a silver seal shall set—
We have loved and slain each other, and love yet.

Slain ; for we live not surely, being in twain :
In her I lived, and in me she is slain,
Who loved me that I brought her to her doom,
Who loved her that her love might be my tomb.
As all the streams on earth and all fresh springs
And sweetest waters, every brook that sings,
Each fountain where the young year dips its wings

First, and the first-fledged branches of it
wave,
Even with one heart's love seek one bitter
grave.
From hills that first see bared the morning's
breast,
And heights the sun last yearns to from the
west,
All tend but toward the sea, all born most
high
Strive downward, passing all things joyous
by,
Seek to it and cast their lives in it and die.
So strive all lives for death which all lives
win;
So sought her soul to my soul, and therein
Was poured and perished : O my love, and
mine
Sought to thee and died of thee and died as
thine.
As the dawn loves the sunlight that must
cease
Ere dawn again may rise and pass in peace ;
Must die that she being dead may live
again,
To be by his new rising nearly slain.
So rolls the great wheel of the great world
round,
And no change in it and no fault is found,
And no true life of perdurable breath,
And surely no irrevocable death.
Day after day night comes that day may
break,
And day comes back for night's reiterate
sake.
Each into each dies, each of each is born :
Day past is night, shall night past not be
morn ?
Out of this moonless and faint-hearted night
That love yet lives in, shall there not be
light ?
Light strong as love, that love may live in
yet ?
Alas, but how shall foolish hope forget
How all these loving things that kill and die
Meet not but for a breath's space and pass
by ?
Night is kissed once of dawn and dies, and
day
But touches twilight and is rapt away.
So may my love and her love meet once
more,
And meeting be divided as of yore.
Yea, surely as the day-star loves the sun
And when he hath risen is utterly undone,

23

So is my love of her and hers of me—
And its most sweetness bitter as the sea.
Would God yet dawn might see the sun and
die !'
    Three years had looked on earth and passed
it by
Since Tristram looked on Iseult, when he
stood
So communing with dreams of evil and good,
And let all sad thoughts through his spirit
sweep
As leaves through air or tears through eyes
that weep
Or snowflakes through dark weather : and his
soul,
That had seen all those sightless seasons roll
One after one, wave over weary wave,
Was in him as a corpse is in its grave.
Yet, for his heart was mighty, and his might
Through all the world as a great sound and
light,
The mood was rare upon him ; save that here
In the low sundawn of the lightening year
With all last year's toil and its triumph done
He could not choose but yearn for that set sun
Which at this season saw the firstborn kiss
That made his lady's mouth one fire with his.
Yet his great heart being greater than his
grief
Kept all the summer of his strength in leaf
And all the rose of his sweet spirit in flower ;
Still his soul fed upon the sovereign hour
That had been or that should be ; and once
more
He looked through drifted sea and drifting
shore
That crumbled in the wave-breach, and again
Spake sad and deep within himself : ' What
pain
Should make a man's soul wholly break and
die,
Sapped as weak sand by water ?   How shall I
Be less than all less things that endure
And strive and yield when time is ?   Nay,
full sure
All these and we are parts of one same end ;
And if through fire or water we twain tend
To that sure life where both must be made one,
If one we be, what matter ?   Thou, O sun,
The face of God, if God thou be not—nay,
What but God should I think thee, what
should say,
Seeing thee rerisen, but very God ?—should
I,
I fool, rebuke thee sovereign in thy sky,

The clouds dead round thee and the air alive,
The winds that lighten and the waves that strive
Toward this shore as to that beneath thy breath,
Because in me my thoughts bear all towards death?
O sun, that when we are dead wilt rise as bright,
Air deepening up toward heaven, and nameless light,
And heaven immeasurable, and faint clouds blown
Between us and the lowest aerial zone
And each least skirt of their imperial state—
Forgive us that we held ourselves so great!
What should I do to curse you? I indeed
Am a thing meaner than this least wild seed
That my foot bruises and I know not—yet
Would not be mean enough for worms to fret
Before their time and mine was.
　　　　　　' Ah, and ye
Light washing weeds, blind waifs of dull blind sea,
Do ye so thirst and hunger and aspire,
Are ye so moved with such long strong desire
In the ebb and flow of your sad life, and strive
Still toward some end ye shall not see alive—
But at high noon ye know it by light and heat
Some half-hour, till ye feel the fresh tide beat
Up round you, and at night's most bitter noon
The ripples leave you naked to the moon?
And this dim dusty heather that I tread,
These half-born blossoms, born at once and dead,
Sere brown as funeral cloths, and purple as pall,
What if some life and grief be in them all?
　　' Ay, what of these? but, O strong sun! O sea!
I bid not you, divine things! comfort me,
I stand not up to match you in your sight—
Who hath said ye have mercy toward us, ye who have might?
And though ye had mercy, I think I would not pray
That ye should change your counsel or your way
To make our life less bitter: if such power
Be given the stars on one deciduous hour,
And such might be in planets to destroy
Grief and rebuild, and break and build up joy,
What man would stretch forth hand on them to make
Fate mutable, God foolish, for his sake?

For if in life or death be aught of trust,
And if some unseen just God or unjust
Put soul into the body of natural things
And in time's pauseless feet and worldwide wings
Some spirit of impulse and some sense of will
That steers them through the seas of good and ill
To some incognizable and actual end,
Be it just or unjust, foe to man or friend,
How should we make the stable spirit to swerve,
How teach the strong soul of the world to serve,
The imperious will in time and sense in space
That gives man life turn back to give man place—
The conscious law lose conscience of its way,
The rule and reason fail from night and day,
The streams flow back toward whence the springs began,
That less of thirst might sear the lips of man?
Let that which is be, and sure strengths stand sure,
And evil or good and death or life endure,
Not alterable and rootless, but indeed
A very stem born of a very seed
That brings forth fruit in season : how should this
Die that was sown, and that not be which is,
And the old fruit change that came of the ancient root,
And he that planted bid it not bear fruit,
And he that watered smite his vine with drouth
Because its grapes are bitter in our mouth,
And he that kindled quench the sun with night
Because its beams are fire against our sight,
And he that tuned untune the sounding spheres
Because their song is thunder in our ears :
How should the skies change and the stars, and time
Break the large concord of the years that chime,
Answering, as wave to wave beneath the moon
That draws them shoreward, mar the whole tide's tune
For the instant foam's sake on one turning wave—
For man's sake that is grass upon a grave?

How should the law that knows not soon or
   late,
For whom no time nor space is—how should
   fate,
That is not good nor evil, wise nor mad,
Nor just nor unjust, neither glad nor sad—
How should the one thing that hath being,
   the one
That moves not as the stars move or the sun
Or any shadow or shape that lives or dies
In likeness of dead earth or living skies,
But its own darkness and its proper light
Clothe it with other names than day or night,
And its own soul of strength and spirit of
   breath
Feed it with other powers than life or death—
How should it turn from its great way to give
Man that must die a clearer space to live?
Why should the waters of the sea be cleft,
The hills be molten to his right and left,
That he from deep to deep might pass dry-
   shod,
Or look between the viewless heights on
   God?
Hath he such eyes as, when the shadows flee,
The sun looks out with to salute the sea?
Is his hand bounteous as the morning's hand?
Or where the night stands hath he feet to
   stand
Will the storm cry not when he bids it cease?
Is it his voice that saith to the east wind,
   Peace!
Is his breath mightier than the west wind's
   breath?
Doth his heart know the things of life and
   death?
Can his face bring forth sunshine and give
   rain,
Or his weak will that dies and lives again
Make one thing certain or bind one thing
   fast,
That as he willed it shall be at the last?
How should the storms of heaven and kindled
   lights
And all the depths of things and topless
   heights
And air and earth and fire and water change
Their likeness, and the natural world grow
   strange,
And all the limits of their life undone
Lose count of time and conscience of the sun,
And that fall under which was fixed above,
That man might have a larger hour for love?'
  So musing with close lips and lifted eyes
That smiled with self-contempt to live so wise,

With silent heart so hungry now so long,
So late grown clear, so miserably made
   strong,
About the wolds a banished man he went,
The brown wolds bare and sad as banish-
   ment,
By wastes of fruitless flowerage, and grey
   downs
That felt the sea-wind shake their wild-flower
   crowns
As though fierce hands would pluck from
   some grey head
The spoils of majesty despised and dead,
And fill with crying and comfortless strange
   sound
Their hollow sides and heights of herbless
   ground.
Yet as he went fresh courage on him came,
Till dawn rose too within him as a flame,
The heart of the ancient hills and his were
   one;
The winds took counsel with him, and the
   sun
Spake comfort; in his ears the shout of birds
Was as the sound of clear sweet-spirited
   words,
The noise of streams as laughter from above
Of the old wild lands, and as a cry of love
Spring's trumpet-blast blown over moor and
   lea:
The skies were red as love is, and the sea
Was as the floor of heaven for love to tread.
So went he as with light about his head,
And in the joyous travail of the year
Grew April-hearted; since nor grief nor
   fear
Can master so a young man's blood so long
That it shall move not to the mounting song
Of that sweet hour when earth replumes her
   wings
And with fair face and heart set heavenward
   sings
As an awakened angel unaware
That feels his sleep fall from him, and his
   hair
By some new breath of wind and music
   stirred,
Till like the sole song of one heavenly bird
Sounds all the singing of the host of heaven,
And all the glories of the sovereign Seven
Are as one face of one incorporate light,
And as that host of singers in God's sight
Might draw toward one that slumbered, and
   arouse
The lips requickened and rekindling brows,

So seemed the earthly host of all things born
In sight of spring and eyeshot of the morn,
All births of land or waifs of wind and sea,
To draw toward him that sorrowed, and set
    free
From presage and remembrance of all pains
The life that leapt and lightened in his veins.
So with no sense abashed nor sunless look,
But with exalted eyes and heart, he took
His part of sun or storm-wind, and was glad,
For all things lost, of these good things he
    had.
  And the spring loved him surely, being
    from birth
One made out of the better part of earth,
A man born as at sunrise ; one that saw
Not without reverence and sweet sense of
    awe
But wholly without fear of fitful breath
The face of life watched by the face of death;
And living took his fill of rest and strife,
Of love and change, and fruit and seed of
    life,
And when his time to live in light was done
With unbent head would pass out of the sun:
A spirit as morning, fair and clear and strong,
Whose thought and work were as one harp
    and song
Heard through the world as in a strange
    king's hall
Some great guest's voice that sings of festival.
So seemed all things to love him, and his
    heart
In all their joy of life to take such part,
That with the live earth and the living sea
He was as one that communed mutually
With naked heart to heart of friend to friend:
And the star deepening at the sunset's end,
And the moon fallen before the gate of day
As one sore wearied with vain length of way,
And the winds wandering, and the streams
    and skies,
As faces of his fellows in his eyes.
Nor lacked there love where he was evermore
Of man and woman, friend of sea or shore,
Not measurable with weight of graven gold,
Free as the sun's gift of the world to hold
Given each day back to man's reconquering
    sight
That loses but its lordship for a night.
And now that after many a season spent
In barren ways and works of banishment,
Toil of strange fights and many a fruitless
    field,
Ventures of quest and vigils under shield,

He came back to the strait of sundering sea
That parts green Cornwall from grey Brittany,
Where dwelt the high king's daughter of the
    lands,
Iseult, named alway from her fair white hands,
She looked on him and loved him ; but being
    young
Made shamefastness a seal upon her tongue,
And on her heart, that none might hear its
    cry,
Set the sweet signet of humility.
Yet when he came a stranger in her sight,
A banished man and weary, no such knight
As when the Swallow dipped her bows in foam
Steered singing that imperial Iseult home,
This maiden with her sinless sixteen years
Full of sweet thoughts and hopes that played
    at fears
Cast her eyes on him but in courteous wise,
And lo, the man's face burned upon her eyes
As though she had turned them on the naked
    sun :
And through her limbs she felt sweet passion
    run
As fire that flowed down from her face, and
    beat
Soft through stirred veins on even to her hands
    and feet
As all her body were one heart on flame,
Athrob with love and wonder and sweet
    shame.
And when he spake there sounded in her ear
As 'twere a song out of the graves of years
Heard and again forgotten, and again
Remembered with a rapturous pulse of pain
But as the maiden mountain snow sublime
Takes the first sense of April's trembling
    time
Soft on a brow that burns not though it
    blush
To feel the sunrise hardly half aflush,
So took her soul the sense of change, no
    thought
That more than maiden love was more than
    nought.
Her eyes went hardly after him, her cheek
Grew scarce a goodlier flower to hear him
    speak,
Her bright mouth no more trembled than a
    rose
May for the least wind's breathless sake that
    blows
Too soft to sue save for a sister's kiss,
And if she sighed in sleep she knew no
    this.

Yet in her heart hovered the thoughts of
　　things
Past, that with lighter or with heavier wings
Beat round her memory, till it burned
With grief that brightened and with hope
　　yearned,
Seeing him so great and sad, nor knowing
　　what fate
Had bowed and crowned a head so sad and
　　great.
Nor might she guess but little, first or last,
Though all her heart so hung upon his past,
Of what so bowed him for what sorrow's
　　sake :
For scarce of aught at any time he spake
That from his own land oversea had sent
His lordly life to barren banishment.
Yet still or soft or keen remembrance clung
Close round her of the least word from his
　　tongue
That fell by chance of courtesy, to greet
With grace of tender thanks her pity, sweet
As running streams to men's way-wearied
　　feet.
And when between strange words her name
　　would fall
Suddenly straightway to that lure's recall
Back would his heart bound as the falconer's
　　bird
And tremble and bow down before the word.
　　Iseult '—and all the cloudlike world grew
　　flame,
And all his heart flashed lightning at her
　　name ;
　　Iseult '—and all the wan waste weary skies
Shone as his queen's own love-enkindled eyes.
And seeing the bright blood in his face leap
　　up
As red wine mantling in a royal cup
To hear the sudden sweetness of the sound
Ring, but ere well his heart had time to
　　bound
His cheek would change, and grief bow down
　　his head,
　　Haply,' the girl's heart, though she spake
　　not, said,
This name of mine was worn of one long
　　dead,
Some sister that he loved : ' and therewithal
Would pity bring her heart more deep in
　　thrall.
But once, when winds about the world made
　　mirth,
And March held revel hard on April's birth
Till air and sea were jubilant as earth,

Delight and doubt in sense and soul began,
And yearning of the maiden toward the man,
Harping on high before her : for his word
Was fire that kindled in her heart that heard,
And alway through the rhymes reverberate
　　came
The virginal soft burden of her name.
And ere the full song failed upon her ear
Joy strove within her till it cast out fear,
And all her heart was as his harp, and rang
Swift music, made of hope whose birthnote
　　sprang
Bright in the blood that kindled as he sang.

' Stars know not how we call them, nor may flowers
Know by what happy name the hovering hours
　　Baptize their new-born heads with dew and
　　　flame :
And Love, adored of all time as of ours,
　　Iseult, knew nought for ages of his name.

' With many tongues men called on him, but he
Wist not which word of all might worthiest be
　　To sound for ever in his ear the same,
Till heart of man might hear and soul might see,
　　Iseult, the radiance ringing from thy name.

' By many names men called him, as the night
By many a name calls many a starry light,
　　Her several sovereigns of dividual fame ;
But day by one name only calls aright,
　　Iseult, the sun that bids men praise his name.

' In many a name of man his name soared high
And song shone round it soaring, till the sky
　　Rang rapture, and the world's fast-founded
　　　frame
Trembled with sense of triumph, even as I,
　　Iseult, with sense of worship at thy name.

' In many a name of woman smiled his power
Incarnate, as all summer in a flower,
　　Till winter bring forgetfulness or shame :
But thine, the keystone of his topless tower,
　　Iseult, is one with Love's own lordliest name.

' Iseult my love, Iseult my queen twice crowned,
In thee my death, in thee my life lies bound :
　　Names are there yet that all men's hearts acclaim,
But Love's own heart rings answer to the sound,
　　Iseult, that bids it bow before thy name.'

There ceased his voice yearning upon the
　　word,
Struck with strong passion dumb : but she
　　that heard
Quailed to the heart, and trembled ere her
　　eyes
Durst let the loving light within them rise,
And yearn on his for answer : yet at last,
Albeit not all her fear was overpast,
Hope, kindling even the frost of fear apace

With sweet fleet bloom and breath of gradual
   grace,
Flushed in the changing roses of her face.
And ere the strife took truce of white with
   red,
Or joy for soft shame's sake durst lift up head,
Something she would and would not fain have
   said,   [be,
And wist not what the fluttering word would
But rose and reached forth to him her hand:
   and he,

Heart-stricken, bowed his head and dropped
   his knee,
And on her fragrant hand his lips were
   fire;
And their two hearts were as one trembling
   lyre
Touched by the keen wind's kiss with brief
   desire
And music shuddering at its own delight.
So dawned the moonrise of their marriage
   night.

IV.

THE MAIDEN MARRIAGE.

SPRING watched her last moon burn and fade
   with May
While the days deepened toward a bridal day.
And on her snowbright hand the ring was set
While in the maiden's ear the song's word yet
Hovered, that hailed as love's own queen by
   name
Iseult: and in her heart the word was flame;
A pulse of light, a breath of tender fire,
Too dear for doubt, too driftless for desire.
Between her father's hand and brother's led
From hall to shrine, from shrine to marriage-
   bed,
She saw not how by hap at home-coming
Fell from her new lord's hand a royal ring,
Whereon he looked, and felt the pulse astart
Speak passion in his faith-forsaken heart.
For this was given him of the hand wherein
That heart's pledge lay for ever: so the sin
That should be done if truly he should take
This maid to wife for strange love's faithless
   sake
Struck all his mounting spirit abashed, and
   fear
Fell cold for shame's sake on his changing
   cheer.
Yea, shame's own fire that burned upon his
   brow
To bear the brand there of a broken vow
Was frozen again for very fear thereof
That wrung his heart with keener pangs than
   love.

And all things rose upon him, all things past
Ere last they parted, cloven in twain at last,
Iseult from Tristram, Tristram from the
   queen;
And how men found them in the wild woods
   green
Sleeping, but sundered by the sword between,
Dividing breast from amorous breast a span,
But scarce in heart the woman from the man
As far as hope from joy or sleep from truth,
And Mark that saw them held for sacred
   sooth
These were no fleshly lovers, by that sign
That severed them, still slumbering; so di-
   vine
He deemed it: how at waking they beheld
The king's folk round the king, and uncom-
   pelled
Were fain to follow and fare among them
   home
Back to the towers washed round with rolling
   foam
And storied halls wherethrough sea-music
   rang:
And how report thereafter swelled and sprang
A full-mouthed serpent, hissing in men's ears
Word of their loves: and one of all his peers
That most he trusted, being his kinsman born
A man base-moulded for the stamp of scorn
Whose heart with hate was keen and cold
   and dark,
Gave note by midnight whisper to King Mark

Where he might take them sleeping ; how ere
  day
Had seen the grim next morning all away
Fast bound they brought him down a weary
  way
With forty knights about him, and their chief
That traitor who for trust had given him grief,
To the old hoar chapel, like a strait stone
  tomb
Sheer on the sea-rocks, there to take his
  doom :
Now, seeing he needs must die, he bade them
  yet
Bethink them if they durst for shame forget
What deeds for Cornwall had he done, and
  wrought
For all their sake what rescue, when he
  fought
Against the fierce foul Irish foe that came
To take of them for tribute in their shame
Three hundred heads of children ; whom in
  fight
His hard redeeming slew Moraunt the knight
That none durst lift his eyes against, not one
Had heart but he, who now had help of none,
To take the battle ; whence great shame it
  were
To knighthood, yea, foul shame on all men
  there,
To see him die so shamefully : nor durst
One man look up, nor one make answer first,
Save even the very traitor, who defied
And would have slain him naked in his pride,
But he, that saw the sword plucked forth to
  slay,
Looked on his hands and wrenched their
  bonds away,
Haling those twain that he went bound be-
  tween
Suddenly to him, and kindling in his mien
Shone lion-fashion forth with eyes alight,
And lion-wise leapt on that kinsman knight
And wrung forth of his felon hands with
  might
The sword that should have slain him weapon-
  less
And smote him sheer down : then came all
  the press
All raging in upon him ; but he wrought
So well for his deliverance as they fought
That ten strong knights rejoicingly he slew,
And took no wound, nor wearied : then the
  crew
Waxed greater, and their cry on him ; but he
Had won the chapel now above the sea

That chafed right under : then the heart in
  him
Sprang, seeing the low cliff clear to leap, and
  swim
Right out by the old blithe way the sea-mew
  takes
Across the bounding billow-belt that breaks
For ever, but the loud bright chain it makes
To bind the bridal bosom of the land
Time shall unlink not ever, till his hand
Fall by its own last blow dead : thence again
Might he win forth into the green great main
Far on beyond, and there yield up his breath
At least, with God's will, by no shameful
  death,
Or haply save himself, and come anew
Some long day later, ere sweet life were
  through.
And as the sea-gull hovers high, and turns
With eyes wherein the keen heart glittering
  yearns
Down toward the sweet green sea whereon
  the broad noon burns,
And suddenly, soul-stricken with delight,
Drops, and the glad wave gladdens, and the
  light
Sees wing and wave confuse their fluttering
  white,
So Tristram one brief breathing-space apart
Hung, and gazed down ; then with exulting
  heart
Flunged : and the fleet foam round a joyous
  head
Flashed, that shot under, and ere a shaft had
  sped
Rose again radiant, a rejoicing star,
And high along the water-ways afar
Triumphed : and they deemed he needs must
  die ;
But Gouvernayle his squire, that watched
  hard by,
Sought where perchance a man might win
  ashore,
Striving, with strong limbs labouring long
  and sore,
And there abode an hour : till as from fight
Crowned with hard conquest won by master.
  ing might,
Hardly, but happier for the imperious toil,
Swam the knight in forth of the close waves
  coil,
Sea-satiate, bruised with buffets of the brine,
Laughing, and flushed as one afire with wine :
All this came hard upon him in a breath ;
And how he marvelled in his heart that death

Should be no bitterer than it seemed to be
There, in the strenuous impulse of the sea
Born as to battle deathward : and at last
How all his after seasons overpast
Had brought him darkling to this dark sweet
    hour,
Where his foot faltered nigh the bridal bower,
And harder seemed the passage now to pass,
Though smoother-seeming than the still sea's
    glass,
More fit for very manhood's heart to fear,
Than all straits past of peril.   Hardly here
Might aught of all things hearten him save
    one,
Faith : and as men's eyes quail before the
    sun
So quailed his heart before the star whose
    light
Put out the torches of his bridal night,
So quailed and shrank with sense of faith's
    keen star
That burned as fire beheld by night afar
Deep in the darkness of his dreams ; for all
The bride-house now seemed hung with
    heavier pall
Than clothes the house of mourning.   Yet
    at last,
Soul-sick with trembling at the heart, he
    passed
Into the sweet light of the maiden bower
Where lay the lonely lily-featured flower
That, lying within his hand to gather, yet
Might not be gathered of it.   Fierce regret
And bitter loyalty strove hard at strife
With amorous pity toward the tender wife
That wife indeed might never be, to wear
The very crown of wedlock ; never bear
Children, to watch and worship her white hair
When time should change, with hand more
    soft than snow,
The fashion of its glory ; never know
The loveliness of laughing love that lives
On little lips of children : all that gives
Glory and grace and reverence and delight
To wedded woman by her bridal right,
All praise and pride that flowers too fair to
    fall,
Love that should give had stripped her of
    them all
And left her bare for ever.   So his thought
Consumed him, as a fire within that wrought
Visibly, ravening till its wrath were spent :
So pale he stood, so bowed and passion-rent,
Before the blithe-faced bride-folk, ere he
    went

Within the chamber, heavy-eyed : and there
Gleamed the white hands and glowed th
    glimmering hair
That might but move his memory more o
    one more fair,
More fair than all this beauty : but in sooth
So fair she too shone in her flower of youth
That scarcely might man's heart hold fast it
    truth,
Though strong, who gazed upon her : fo
    her eyes
Were emerald-soft as evening-coloured skies,
And a smile in them like the light therein
Slept, or shone out in joy that knew not sin,
Clear as a child's own laughter : and her
    mouth,
Albeit no rose full-hearted from the south
And passion-colored for the perfect kiss
That signs the soul for love and stamps it his,
Was soft and bright as any bud new-blown ;
And through her cheek the gentler lifebloom
    shone
Of mild wild roses nigh the northward sea.
So in her bride-bed lay the bride : and he
Drew nigh, and all the high sad heart in him
Yearned on her, seeing the twilight meek and
    dim
Through all the soft alcove tremblingly lit
With hovering silver, as a heart in it
Beating, that burned from one deep lamp
    above,
Fainter than fire of torches, as the love
Within him fainter than a bridegroom's fire,
No marriage-torch red with the heart's desire,
But silver-soft, a flameless light that glowed
Starlike along night's dark and starry road
Wherein his soul was traveller.   And he
    sighed,
Seeing, and with eyes set sadly toward his
    bride
Laid him down by her, and spake not ; but
    within
His heart spake, saying how sore should be
    the sin
To break toward her, that of all womankind
Was faithfullest, faith plighted, or unbind
The bond first linked between them when
    they drank
The love-draught : and his quick blood sprang
    and sank,
Remembering in the pulse of all his veins
That red swift rapture, all its fiery pains
And all its fierier pleasures : and he spake
Aloud, one burning word for love's keen
    sake—

' Iseult ; ' and full of love and lovelier fear
A virgin voice gave answer—' I am here.'
And a pang rent his heart at root : but still,
For spirit and flesh were vassals to his will,
Strong faith held mastery on them : and the breath
Felt on his face did not his will to death,
Nor glance nor lute-like voice nor flower-soft touch
Might so prevail upon it overmuch
That constancy might less prevail than they,
For all he looked and loved her as she lay
Smiling ; and soft as bird alights on bough
He kissed her maiden mouth and blameless brow,
Once, and again his heart within him sighed:
But all his young blood's yearning toward his bride,

How hard soe'er it held his life awake
For passion, and sweet nature's unforbidden sake,
And will that strove unwillingly with will it might not break,
Fell silent as a wind abashed, whose breath
Dies out of heaven, suddenly done to death,
When in between them on the dumb dusk air
Floated the bright shade of a face more fair
Than hers that hard beside him shrank and smiled
And wist of all no more than might a child.
So had she all her heart's will, all she would,
For love's sake that sufficed her, glad and good,
All night safe sleeping in her maidenhood.

V.

ISEULT AT TINTAGEL.

But that same night in Cornwall oversea
Couched at Queen Iseult's hand, against her knee,
With keen kind eyes that read her whole heart's pain
Fast at wide watch lay Tristram's hound Hodain,
The goodliest and the mightiest born on earth,
That many a forest day of fiery mirth
Had plied his craft before them ; and the queen
Cherished him, even for those dim years between,
More than of old in those bright months far flown
When ere a blast of Tristram's horn was blown
Each morning as the woods rekindled, ere
Day gat full empire of the glimmering air,
Delight of dawn would quicken him, and fire
Spring and pant in his breath with bright desire
To be among the dewy ways on quest :
But now perforce at restless-hearted rest

He chafed through days more barren than the sand,
Soothed hardly but soothed only with her hand,
Though fain to fawn thereon and follow, still
With all his heart and all his loving will
Desiring one divided from his sight,
For whose lost sake dawn was as dawn of night
And noon as night's noon in his eyes was dark.
But in the halls far under sat King Mark,
Feasting, and full of cheer, with heart uplift,
As on the night that harper gat his gift :
And music revelled on the fitful air,
And songs came floated up the festal stair,
And muffled roar of wassail, where the king
Took heart from wine-cups and the quiring string
Till all his cold thin veins rejoiced and ran
Strong as with lifeblood of a kinglier man.
But the queen shut from sound her wearied ears,
Shut her sad eyes from sense of aught save tears,

And wrung her hair with soft fierce hands,
  and prayed :
' O God, God born of woman, of a maid,
Christ, once in flesh of thine own fashion
  clad ;
O very love, so glad in heaven and sad
On earth for earth's sake alway : since thou
  art
Pure only, I only impure of spirit and heart,
Since thou for sin's sake and the bitter doom
Didst as a veil put on a virgin's womb,
I that am none, and cannot hear or see
Or shadow or likeness or a sound of thee
Far off, albeit with man's own speech and
  face
Thou shine yet and thou speak yet, showing
  forth grace—
Ah me ! grace only shed on souls that are
Lit and led forth of shadow by thy star—
Alas ! to these men only grace, to these,
Lord, whom thy love draws Godward, to thy
  knees—
I, can I draw thee me-ward, can I seek,
Who love thee not, to love me ? seeing how
  weak,
Lord, all this little love I bear thee is,
And how much is my strong love more than
  this,
My love that I love man with, that I bear
Him sinning through me sinning ? wilt thou
  care,
God, for this love, if love be any, alas,
In me to give thee, though long since there
  was,
How long, when I too, Lord, was clean, even
  I,
That now am unclean till the day I die—
Haply by burning, harlot-fashion, made
A horror in all hearts of wife and maid,
Hateful, not knowing if ever in these mine
  eyes
Shone any light of thine in any wise
Or this were love at all that I bore thee ? '
  And the night spake, and thundered on the
  sea,
Ravening aloud for ruin of lives : and all
The bastions of the main cliff's northward
  wall
Rang response out from all their deepening
  length,
As the east wind girded up his godlike
  strength
And hurled in hard against that high-towered
  hold
The fleeces of the flock that knows no fold,

The rent white shreds of shattering storm :
  but she
Heard not nor heeded wind or storming sea,
Knew not if night were mild or mad with
  wind.
  ' Yea, though deep lips and tender hair be
  thinned,
Though cheek wither, brow fade, and bosom
  wane,
Shall I change also from this heart again
To maidenhood of heart and holiness ?
Shall I more love thee, Lord, or love him
  less—
Ah miserable ! though spirit and heart be
  rent,
Shall I repent, Lord God ? shall I repent ?
Nay, though thou slay me ! for herein I am
  blest,
That as I loved him yet I love him best—
More than mine own soul or thy love or thee,
Though thy love save and my love save not
  me.
Blest am I beyond women even herein,
That beyond all born women is my sin,
And perfect my transgression : that above
All offerings of all others is my love,
Who have chosen it only, and put away for
  this
Thee, and my soul's hope, Saviour, of the kiss
Wherewith thy lips make welcome all thine
  own
When in them life and death are overthrown ;
The sinless lips that seal the death of sin,
The kiss wherewith their dumb lips touched
  begin
Singing in heaven,
  ' Where we shall never, love,
Never stand up nor sing ! for God above
Knows us, how too much more than God to
  me
Thy sweet love is, my poor love is to thee !
Dear, dost thou see now, dost thou hear to-
  night,
Sleeping, my waste wild speech, my face worn
  white,
—Speech once heard soft by thee, face once
  kissed red !—
In such a dream as when men see their dead
And know not if they know if dead these be
Ah love, are thy days my days, and to thee
Are all nights like as my nights ? does the sun
Grieve thee ? art thou soul-sick till day be
  done,
And weary till day rises ? is thine heart
Full of dead things as mine is ? Nay, thou art

Man, with man's strength and praise and
  pride of life,
No bondwoman, no queen, no loveless wife
That would be shamed albeit she had not
  sinned.'
  And swordlike was the sound of the iron
  wind,
And as a breaking battle was the sea.
  'Nay, Lord, I pray thee let him love not
  me,
Love me not any more, nor like me die,
And be no more than such a thing as I.
Turn his heart from me, lest my love too lose
Thee as I lose thee, and his fair soul refuse
For my sake thy fair heaven, and as I fell
Fall, and be mixed with my soul and with
  hell.
Let me die rather, and only ; let me be
Hated of him so he be loved of thee,
Lord : for I would not have him with me
  there
Out of thy light and love in the unlit air,
Out of thy sight in the unseen hell where I
Go gladly, going alone, so thou on high
Lift up his soul and love him—Ah, Lord,
  Lord,
Shalt thou love as I love him ? she that
  poured
From the alabaster broken at thy feet
An ointment very precious, not so sweet
As that poured likewise forth before thee then
From the rehallowed heart of Magdalen,
From a heart broken, yearning like the dove,
An ointment very precious which is love—
Couldst thou being holy and God, and sinful
  she
Love her indeed as surely she loved thee ?
Nay, but if not, then as we sinners can
Let us love still in the old sad wise of man.
For with less love than my love, having had
Mine, though God love him he shall not be
  glad.
And with such love as my love, I wot well,
He shall not lie disconsolate in hell :
Sad only as souls for utter love's sake
Here, and a little sad, perchance, for me—
Me happy, me more glad than God above,
In the utmost hell whose fires consume not
  love !
For in the waste ways emptied of the sun
He would say—" Dear, thy place is void, and
  one
Weeps among angels for thee, with his face
Veiled, saying, *O sister, how thy chosen
  place*

Stands *desolate that God made fair for thee !
Is heaven not sweeter, and we thy brethren, we
Fairer than love on earth and life in hell ?"*
And I—with me were all things then not
  well ?
Should I not answer—" O love, be well con-
  tent ;
Look on me, and behold if I repent."
This were more to me than an angel's wings.
Yea, many men pray God for many things,
But I pray that this only thing may be.'
  And as a full field charging was the sea,
And as the cry of slain men was the wind.
  'Yea, since I surely loved him, and he
  sinned
Surely, though not as my sin his be black,
God, give him to me—God, God, give him
  back !
For now how should we live in twain or die ?
I am he indeed, thou knowest, and he is I.
Not man and woman several as we were,
But one thing with one life and death to bear,
How should one love his own soul overmuch ?
And time is long since last I felt the touch,
The sweet touch of my lover, hand and
  breath,
In such delight as puts delight to death,
Burn my soul through, till spirit and soul and
  sense,
In the sharp grasp of the hour, with violence
Died, and again through pangs of violent
  birth
Lived, and laughed out with refluent might of
  mirth ;
Laughed each on other and shuddered into
  one,
As a cloud shuddering dies into the sun.
Ah, sense is that or spirit, soul or flesh,
That only love lulls or awakes afresh ?
Ah, sweet is that or bitter, evil or good,
That very love allays not as he would ?
Nay, truth is this or vanity, that gives
No love assurance when love dies or lives ?
This that my spirit is wrung withal, and yet
No surelier knows if haply thine forget,
Thou that my spirit is wrung for, nor can say
Love is not in thee dead as yesterday?
Dost thou feel, thou, this heartbeat whence
  my heart
Would send thee word what life is mine apart,
And know by keen response what life is
  thine ?
Dost thou not hear one cry of all of mine ?
O Tristram's heart, have I no part in thee ?'
  And all her soul was as the breaking sea,

And all her heart anhungered as the wind.
' Dost thou repent thee of the sin we
    sinned ?
Dost thou repent thee of the days and nights
That kindled and that quenched for us their
    lights,
The months that feasted us with all their
    hours,
The ways that breathed of us in all their
    flowers,
The dells that sang of us with all their doves ?
Dost thou repent thee of the wildwood loves ?
Is thine heart changed, and hallowed? art
    thou grown
God's and not mine ? Yet, though my heart
    make moan,
Fain would my soul give thanks for thine, if
    thou
Be saved—yea, fain praise God, and knows
    not how.
How should it know thanksgiving ? nay, or
    learn
Aught of the love wherewith thine own should
    burn,
God's, that should cast out as an evil thing
Mine ? yea, what hand of prayer have I to
    cling,
What heart to prophesy, what spirit of sight
To strain insensual eyes toward increate light,
Who look but back on life wherein I sinned ?'
    And all their past came wailing in the wind,
And all their future thundered in the sea.
' But if my soul might touch the time to be,
If hand might handle now or eye behold
My life and death ordained me from of old,
Life palpable, compact of blood and breath,
Visible, present, naked, very death,
Should I desire to know before the day
These that I know not, nor is man that may ?
For haply, seeing, my heart would break for
    fear,
And my soul timeless cast its load off here,
'Its load of life too bitter, love too sweet,
And fall down shamed and naked at thy feet,
God, who wouldst take no pity of it, nor give
One hour back, one of all its hours to live
Clothed with my mortal body, that once
    more,
Once, on this reach of barren beaten shore,
This stormy strand of life, ere sail were set,
Had haply felt love's arms about it yet—
Yea, ere death's bark put off to seaward,
    might
With many a grief have bought me one de-
    light

That then should know me never. Ah, what
    years
Would I endure not, filled up full with tears,
Bitter like blood and dark as dread of death,
To win one amorous hour of mingling breath,
One fire-eyed hour and sunnier than the
    sun,
For all these nights and days like nights but
    one ?
One hour of heaven born once, a stormless
    birth,
For all these windy weary hours of earth ?
One, but one hour from birth of joy to death,
For all these hungering hours of feverish
    breath ?
And I should lose this, having died and
    sinned.'
    And as man's anguish clamouring cried the
    wind,
And as God's anger answering rang the sea
    ' And yet what life—Lord God, what life
    for me
Has thy strong wrath made ready ? Dost
    thou think
How lips whose thirst hath only tears to
    drink
Grow grey for grief untimely ? Dost thou
    know,
O happy God, how men wax weary of woe—
Yea, for their wrong's sake that thine hand
    hath done
Come even to hate thy semblance in the sun ?
Turn back from dawn and noon and all thy
    light
To make their souls one with the soul of
    night ?
Christ, if thou hear yet or have eyes to see,
Thou that hadst pity, and hast no pity on me,
Know'st thou no more, as in this life's sharp
    span,
What pain thou hadst on earth, what pain
    hath man ?
Hast thou no care, that all we suffer yet ?
What help is ours of thee if thou forget ?
What profit have we though thy blood were
    given,
If we that sin bleed and be not forgiven ?
Not love but hate, thou bitter God and
    strange,
Whose heart as man's heart hath grown cold
    with change,
Not love but hate thou showest us that have
    sinned.'
    And like a world's cry shuddering was the
    wind,

And like a God's voice threatening was the
　　sea.
　' Nay, Lord, for thou wast gracious ; nay,
　　in thee
No change can come with time or varying
　　fate,
No tongue bid thine be less compassionate,
No sterner eye rebuke for mercy thine,
No sin put out thy pity—no, not mine.
Thou knowest us, Lord, thou knowest us, all
　　we are,
He, and the soul that hath his soul for star :
Thou knowest as I know, Lord, how much
　　more worth
Than all souls clad and clasped about with
　　earth,
But most of all, God, how much more than I,
Is this man's soul that surely shall not die.
What righteousness, what judgment, Lord
　　most high,
Were this, to bend a brow of doom as grim
As threats me, me the adulterous wife, on
　　him ?
There lies none other nightly by his side :
He hath not sought, he shall not seek a
　　bride.
Far as God sunders earth from heaven above,
So far was my love born beneath his love.
I loved him as the sea-wind loves the sea,
To rend and ruin it only and waste : but he,
As the sea loves a sea-bird loved he me,
To foster and uphold my tired life's wing,
And bounteously beneath me spread forth
　　spring,
A springtide space whereon to float or fly,
A world of happy water, whence the sky
Glowed goodlier, lightening from so glad a
　　glass,
Than with its own light only.　Now, alas !
Cloud hath come down and clothed it round
　　with storm,
And gusts and fits of eddying winds deform
The feature of its glory.　Yet be thou,
God, merciful : nay, show but justice now,
And let the sin in him that scarce was his
Stand expiated with exile : and be this
The price for him, the atonement this, that I
With all the sin upon me live, and die

With all thy wrath on me that most have
　　sinned.'
　And like man's heart relenting sighed the
　　the wind,
And as God's wrath subsiding sank the sea.
　' But if such grace be possible—if it be
Not sin more strange than all sins past, and
　　worse
Evil, that cries upon thee for a curse,
To pray such prayers from such a heart, do
　　thou
Hear, and make wide thine hearing toward
　　me now ;
Let not my soul and his for ever dwell
Sundered : though doom keep always heaven
　　and hell
Irreconcilable, infinitely apart,
Keep not in twain for ever heart and heart
That once, albeit by not thy law, were one ;
Let this be not thy will, that this be done.
Let all else, all thou wilt of evil, be,
But no doom, none, dividing him and me.'
　By this was heaven stirred eastward, and
　　there came
Up the rough ripple a labouring light like
　　flame ;
And dawn, sore trembling still and grey with
　　fear,
Looked hardly forth, a face of heavier cheer
Than one which grief or dread yet half en-
　　shrouds,
Wild-eyed and wan, across the cleaving
　　clouds.
And Iseult, worn with watch long held on
　　pain,
Turned, and her eye lit on the hound Hodain,
And all her heart went out in tears : and he
Laid his kind head along her bended knee,
Till round his neck her arms went hard, and
　　all
The night past from her as a chain might fall :
But yet the heart within her, half undone,
Wailed, and was loth to let her see the sun.
　And ere full day brought heaven and earth
　　to flower,
Far thence, a maiden in a marriage bower,
That moment, hard by Tristram, oversea,
Woke with glad eyes Iseult of Brittany.

VI.

JOYOUS GARD.

A LITTLE time, O Love, a little light,
A little hour for ease before the night.
Sweet Love, that art so bitter ; foolish Love,
Whom wise men know for wiser, and thy
　　dove
More subtle than the serpent ; for thy sake
These pray thee for a little beam to break,
A little grace to help them; lest men think
Thy servants have but hours like tears to
　　drink.
O Love, a little comfort, lest they fear
To serve as these have served thee who stand
　　here.
　For these are thine, thy servants these, that
　　stand
Here nigh the limit of the wild north land,
At margin of the grey great eastern sea,
Dense-islanded with peaks and reefs, that see
No life but of the fleet wings fair and free
Which cleave the mist and sunlight all day
　　long
With sleepless flight and cries more glad than
　　song.
Strange ways of life have led him hither,
　　here
To win fleet respite from desire and fear,
With armistice from sorrow ; strange and
　　sweet
Ways trodden by forlorn and casual feet
Till kindlier chance woke toward them kindly
　　will
In happier hearts of lovers, and their ill
Found rest, as healing surely might it not,
By gift and kingly grace of Launcelot
At gracious bidding given of Guenevere.
For in the trembling twilight of this year
Ere April sprang from hope to certitude
Two hearts of friends fast linked had fallen
　　at feud
As they rode forth on hawking, by the sign
Which gave his new bride's brother Ganhar-
　　dine
To know the truth of Tristram's dealing,
　　how
Faith kept of him against his marriage vow

Kept virginal his bride-bed night and morn ;
Whereat, as wroth his blood should suffer
　　scorn,
Came Ganhardine to Tristram, saying, ' Be-
　　hold,
We have loved thee, and for love we have
　　shown of old
Scorn hast thou shown us : wherefore is thy
　　bride
Not thine indeed, a stranger at thy side,
Contemned ? what evil hath she done, to be
Mocked with mouth-marriage and despised
　　of thee,
Shamed, set at nought, rejected ? ' But there
　　came
On Tristram's brow and eye the shadow and
　　flame
Confused of wrath and wonder, ere he spake,
Saying, ' Hath she bid thee for thy sister's
　　sake
Plead with me, who believed of her in heart
More nobly than to deem such piteous part
Should find so fair a player ? or whence hast
　　thou
Of us this knowledge ? ' ' Nay,' said he, ' but
　　now,
Riding beneath these whitethorns overhead,
There fell a flower into her girdlestead
Which laughing she shook out, and smiling
　　said—
" Lo, what large leave the wind hath given
　　this stray,
To lie more near my heart than till this day
Aught ever since my mother lulled me lay
Or even my lord came ever ; " whence I wot
We are all thy scorn, a race regarded not
Nor held as worth communion of thine
　　own,
Except in her be found some fault alone
To blemish our alliance.' Then replied
Tristram, ' Nor blame nor scorn may touch
　　my bride,
Albeit unknown of love she live, and be
Worth a man worthier than her love thought
　　me.

Faith only, faith withheld me, faith forbade
The blameless grace wherewith love's grace
  makes glad
All lives linked else in wedlock ; not that less
I loved the sweet light of her loveliness,
But that my love toward faith was more : and
  thou,
Albeit thine heart be keen against me now,
Couldst thou behold my very lady, then
No more of thee than of all other men
Should this my faith be held a faithless fault.'
And ere that day their hawking came to halt
Being sore of him entreated for a sign,
He sware to bring his brother Ganhardine
To sight of that strange Iseult : and thereon
Forth soon for Cornwall are these brethren
  gone,
Even to that royal pleasance where the hunt
Rang ever of old with Tristram's horn in front
Blithe as the queen's horse bounded at his
  side :
And first of all her dames forth pranced in
  pride
That day before them, with a ringing rein
All golden-glad, the king's false bride Brang-
  wain,
The queen's true handmaid ever : and on her
Glancing, ' Be called for all time truth-teller,
O Tristram, of all true men's tongues alive,'
Quoth Ganhardine ; ' for may my soul so
  thrive
As yet mine eye drank never sight like this.'
' Ay ?' Tristram said, ' and she thou look'st
  on is
So great in grace of goodliness, that thou
Hast less thought left of wrath against me
  now,
Seeing but my lady's handmaid ? Nay, be-
  hold ;
See'st thou no light more golden than of gold
Shine where she moves in midst of all, above
All, past all price or praise or prayer of love ?
Lo, this is she.' But as one mazed with wine
Stood, stunned in spirit and stricken, Gan-
  hardine,
And gazed out hard against them : and his
  heart
As with a sword was cloven, and rent apart
As with strong fangs of fire ; and scarce he
  spake,
Saying how his life for even a handmaid's sake
Was made a flame within him. And the
  knight
Bade him, being known of none that stood in
  sight,

Bear to Brangwain his ring, that she unseen
Might give in token privily to the queen
And send swift word where under moon or
  sun
They twain might yet be no more twain but
  one.
And that same night, under the stars that
  rolled
Over their warm deep wildwood nights of old
Whose hours for grains of sand shed sparks
  of fire,
Such way was made anew for their desire
By secret wile of sickness feigned, to keep
The king far off her vigils or her sleep,
That in the queen's pavilion midway set
By glimmering moondawn were those lovers
  met,
And Ganhardine of Brangwain gat him grace.
And in some passionate soft interspace
Between two swells of passion, when their
  lips
Breathed, and made room for such brief speech
  as slips
From tongues athirst with draughts of amor-
  ous wine
That leaves them thirstier than the salt sea's
  brine,
Was counsel taken how to fly, and where
Find covert from the wide world's ravening
  air
That hunts with storm the feet of nights and
  days
Through strange thwart lines of life and
  flowerless ways.
Then said Iseult : ' Lo, now the chance is
  here
Foreshown me late by word of Guenevere,
To give me comfort of thy rumoured wrong,
My traitor Tristram, when report was strong
Of me forsaken and thine heart estranged :
Nor should her sweet soul toward me yet be
  changed
Nor all her love lie barren, if mine hand
Crave harvest of it from the flowering land.
See therefore if this counsel please thee not,
That we take horse in haste for Camelot
And seek that friendship of her plighted troth
Which love shall be full fain to lend, nor loth
Shall my love be to take it.' So next night
The multitudinous stars laughed round their
  flight,
Fulfilling far with laughter made of light
The encircling deeps of heaven : and in brief
  space
At Camelot their long love gat them grace

Of those fair twain whose heads men's praise
impearled
As love's two lordliest lovers in the world :
And thence as guests for harbourage past they
forth
To win this noblest hold of all the north.
Far by wild ways and many days they rode,
Till clear across June's kingliest sunset
glowed
The great round girth of goodly wall that
showed
Where for one clear sweet season's length
should be
Their place of strength to rest in, fain and
free,
By the utmost margin of the loud lone sea.
  And now, O Love, what comfort? God
most high,
Whose love is as a flower's to live and die,
Whose light is everlasting : Lord, whose
breath
Speaks music through the deathless lips of
death
Whereto time's heart rings answer : Bard,
whom time
Hears, and is vanquished with a wandering
rhyme
That once thy lips made fragrant : Seer,
whose sooth
Joy knows not well, but sorrow knows for
truth,
Being priestess of thy soothsayings : Love,
what grace
Shall these twain find at last before thy face?
  This many a year they have served thee,
and deserved,
If ever man might yet of all that served,
Since the first heartbeat bade the first man's
knee
Bend, and his mouth take music, praising
thee,
Some comfort ; and some honey indeed of
thine
Thou hast mixed for these with life's most
bitter wine
Commending to their passionate lips a draught
No deadlier than thy chosen of old have
quaffed
And blessed thine hand, their cupbearer's :
for not
On all men comes the grace that seals their
lot
As holier in thy sight, for all these feuds
That rend it, than the light-souled multi-
tude's.

Nor thwarted of thine hand nor blessed ; but
these
Shall see no twilight, Love, nor fade at ease,
Grey-grown and careless of desired delight,
But lie down tired and sleep before the night.
These shall not live till time or change may
chill
Or doubt divide or shame subdue their will,
Or fear or slow repentance work them wrong,
Or love die first : these shall not live so long.
Death shall not take them drained of dear true
life
Already, sick or stagnant from the strife,
Quenched : not with dry-drawn veins and lin-
gering breath
Shall these through crumbling hours crouch
down to death.
Swift, with one strong clean leap, ere life's
pulse tire,
Most like the leap of lions or of fire,
Sheer death shall bound upon them : one pang
past,
The first keen sense of him shall be their last,
Their last shall be no sense of any fear,
More than their life had sense of anguish
here.
  Weeks and light months had fled at swal-
low's speed
Since here their first hour sowed for them the
seed
Of many sweet as rest or hope could be ;
Since on the blown beach of a glad new sea
Wherein strange rocks like fighting men stand
scarred
They saw the strength and help of Joyous
Gard.
Within the full deep glorious tower that stands
Between the wild sea and the broad wild
lands
Love led and gave them quiet : and they drew
Life like a God's life in each wind that blew,
And took their rest, and triumphed. Day by
day
The mighty moorlands and the sea-walls grey,
The brown bright waters of green fells that
sing
One song to rocks and flowers and birds on
wing,
Beheld the joy and glory that they had,
Passing, and how the whole world made them
glad,
And their great love was mixed with all things
great,
As life being lovely, and yet being strong like
fate.

For when the sun sprang on the sudden sea
Their eyes sprang eastward, and the day to be
Was lit in them untimely : such delight
They took yet of the clear cold breath and
    light
That goes before the morning, and such grace
Was deathless in them through their whole
    life's space
As dies in many with their dawn that dies
And leaves in pulseless hearts and flameless
    eyes
No light to lighten and no tear to weep
For youth's high joy that time has cast on
    sleep.
Yea, this old grace and height of joy they had,
To lose no jot all that made them glad
And filled their springs of spirit with such fire
That all delight fed in them all desire ;
And no whit less than in their first keen crime
The spring's breath blew through all their
    summer time,
And in their skies would sunlike Love con-
    fuse
Clear April colours with hot August hues,
And in their hearts one light of sun and moon
Reigned, and the morning died not of the
    noon :
Such might of life was in them, and so high
Their heart of love rose higher than fate
    could fly.
And many a large delight of hawk and hound
The great glad land that knows no bourne or
    bound,
Save the wind's own and the outer sea-bank's,
    gave
Their days for comfort ; many a long blithe
    wave
Buoyed their blithe bark between the bare
    bald rocks,
Deep, steep, and still, save for the swift free
    flocks
Unshepherded, uncompassed, unconfined,
That when blown foam keeps all the loud air
    blind
Mix with the wind's their triumph, and par-
    take
The joy of blasts that ravin, waves that break,
All round and all below their mustering
    wings,
A clanging cloud that round the cliff's edge
    clings
On each bleak bluff breaking the strenuous
    tides
That rings reverberate mirth when storm be-
    strides
24

The subject night in thunder : many a noon
They took the moorland's or the bright sea's
    boon
With all their hearts into their spirit of sense,
Rejoicing, where the sudden dells grew dense
With sharp thick flight of hillside birds, or
    where
On some strait rock's ledge in the intense
    mute air
Erect against the cliff's sheer sunlit white
Blue as the clear north heaven, clothed warm
    with light,
Stood neck to bended neck and wing to wing
With heads fast hidden under, close as cling
Flowers on one flowering almond-branch in
    spring,
Three herons deep asleep against the sun,
Each with one bright foot downward poised,
    and one
Wing-hidden hard by the bright head, and all
Still as fair shapes fixed on some wondrous
    wall
Of minster-aisle or cloister-close or hall
To take even time's eye prisoner with delight.
Or, satisfied with joy of sound and sight,
They sat and communed of things past : what
    state
King Arthur, yet unwarred upon by fate,
Held high in hall at Camelot, like one
Whose lordly life was as the mounting sun
That climbs and pauses on the point of noon,
Sovereign : how royal rang the tourney's tune
Through Tristram's three days' triumph, spear
    to spear,
When Iseult shone enthroned by Guenevere,
Rose against rose, the highest adored on earth,
Imperial : yet with subtle notes of mirth
Would she bemock her praises, and bemoan
Her glory by that splendour overthrown
Which lightened from her sister's eyes elate ;
Saying how by night a little light seems
    great,
But less than least of all things, very nought,
When dawn undoes the web that darkness
    wrought ;
How like a tower of ivory well designed
By subtlest hand subserving subtlest mind,
Ivory with flower of rose incarnadined
And kindling with some God therein revealed,
A light for grief to look on and be healed,
Stood Guenevere : and all beholding her
Were heartstruck even as earth at midsum-
    mer
With burning wonder, hardly to be borne.
So was that amorous glorious lady born,

A fiery memory for all storied years :
Nor might men call her sisters crowned her
  peers,
Her sister queens, put all by her to scorn :
She had such eyes as are not made to mourn ;
But in her own a gleaming ghost of tears
Shone, and their glance was slower than
  Guenevere's,
And fitfuller with fancies grown of grief ;
Shamed as a Mayflower shames an autumn
  leaf
Full well she wist it could not choose but be
If in that other's eyeshot standing she
Should lift her looks up ever : wherewithal
Like fires whose light fills heaven with festi-
  val
Flamed her eyes full on Tristram's ; and he
  laughed,
Answering, ' What wile of sweet child-hearted
  craft
That children forge for children, to beguile
Eyes known of them not witless of the wile
But fain to seem for sport's sake self-deceived,
Wilt thou find out now not to be believed ?
Or how shall I trust more than ouphe or elf
Thy truth to me-ward, who beliest thyself ?'
' Nor elf nor ouphe or aught of airier kind,'
Quoth she, ' though made of moonbeams
  moist and blind,
Is light if weighed with man's winged weight-
  less mind.
Though thou keep somewise troth with me,
  God wot,
When thou didst wed, I doubt, thou thought-
  est not
So charily to keep it.'   ' Nay,' said he,
' Yet am not I rebukable by thee
As Launcelot, erring, held me ere he wist
No mouth save thine of mine was ever kissed
Save as a sister's only, since we twain
Drank first the draught assigned our lips to
  drain
That Fate and Love with darkling hands
  commixt
Poured, and no power to part them came
  betwixt,
But either's will, howbeit they seem at strife,
Was toward us one, as death itself and life
Are one sole doom toward all men, nor may
  one
Behold not darkness, who beholds the sun.'
  ' Ah, then,' she said, ' what word is this
  men hear
Of Merlin, how some doom too strange to
  fear

Was cast but late about him oversea,
Sweet recreant, in thy bridal Brittany ?
Is not his life sealed fast on him with sleep,
By witchcraft of his own and love's, to keep
Till earth be fire and ashes ?'
                              ' Surely,' said
Her lover, ' not as one alive or dead
The great good wizard, well beloved and well
Predestinate of heaven that casts out hell
For guerdon gentler far than all men's fate,
Exempt alone of all predestinate,
Takes his strange rest at heart of slumberland,
More deep asleep in green Broceliande
Than shipwrecked sleepers in the soft green
  sea
Beneath the weight of wandering waves : but
  he
Hath for those roofing waters overhead
Above him always all the summer spread
Or all the winter wailing : or the sweet
Late leaves marked red with autumn's burn-
  ing feet,
Or withered with his weeping, round the seer
Rain, and he sees not, nor may heed or hear
The witness of the winter : but in spring
He hears above him all the winds on wing
Through the blue dawn between the brighten-
  ing boughs,
And on shut eyes and slumber-smitten brows
Feels ambient change in the air and strength-
  ening sun,
And knows the soul that was his soul at one
With the ardent world's, and in the spirit of
  earth
His spirit of life reborn to mightier birth
And mixed with things of elder life than ours ;
With cries of birds, and kindling lamps of
  flowers,
And sweep and song of winds, and fruitful
  light
Of sunbeams, and the far faint breath of night,
And waves and woods at morning : and in all,
Soft as at noon the slow sea's rise and fall,
He hears in spirit a song that none but he
Hears from the mystic mouth of Nimue
Shed like a consecration ; and his heart,
Hearing, is made for love's sake as a part
Of that far singing, and the life thereof
Part of that life that feeds the world with
  love :
Yea, heart in heart is molten, hers and his,
Into the world's heart and the soul that is
Beyond or sense or vision ; and their breath
Stirs the soft springs of deathless life and
  death,

Death that bears life, and change that brings
forth seed
Of life to death and death to life indeed,
As blood recircling through the unsounded
veins
Of earth and heaven with all their joys and
pains.
Ah, that when love shall laugh no more nor
weep
We too, we too might hear that song and
sleep !'
   ' Yea,' said Iseult, ' some joy it were to be
Lost in the sun's light and the all-girdling sea,
Mixed with the winds and woodlands, and to
bear
Part in the large life of the quickening air,
And the sweet earth's, our mother : yet to pass
More fleet than mirrored faces from the glass
Out of all pain and all delight, so far
That love should seem but as the furthest star
Sunk deep in trembling heaven, scarce seen
or known,
As a dead moon forgotten, once that shone
Where now the sun shines—nay, not all
things yet,
Not all things always, dying, would I forget.'
   And Tristram answered amorously, and
said :
' O heart that here art mine, O heavenliest
head
That ever took men's worship here, which art
Mine, how shall death put out the fire at
heart,
Quench in men's eyes the head's remembered
light
That time shall set but higher in more men's
sight ?
Think thou not much to die one earthly day,
Being made not in their mould who pass away
Nor who shall pass for ever.'
                              ' Ah,' she said,
' What shall it profit me, being praised and
dead ?
What profit have the flowers of all men's
praise ?
What pleasure of our pleasure have the days
That pour on us delight of life and mirth ?
What fruit of all our joy on earth has earth ?
Nor am I—nay, my lover, am I one
To take such part in heaven's enkindling sun
And in the inviolate air and sacred sea
As clothes with grace that wondrous Nimue ?
For all her works are bounties, all her deeds
Blessings ; her days are scrolls wherein love
reads

The record of his mercies ; heaven above
Hath not more heavenly holiness of love
Than earth beneath, wherever pass or pause
Her feet that move not save by love's own
laws,
In gentleness of godlike wayfaring
To heal men's hearts as earth is healed by
spring
Of all such woes as winter : what am I,
Love, that have strength but to desire and
die,
That have but grace to love and do thee
wrong,
What am I that my name should live so long,
Save as the star that crossed thy star-struck
lot,
With hers whose light was life to Launcelot ?
Life gave she him, and strength, and fame
to be
For ever : I, what gift can I give thee ?
Peril and sleepless watches, fearful breath
Of dread more bitter for my sake than death
When death came nigh to call me by my name,
Exile, rebuke, remorse, and—O, not shame.
Shame only, this I gave thee not, whom none
May give that worst thing ever—no, not one.
Of all that hate, all hateful hearts that see
Darkness for light and hate where love should
be,
None for my shame's sake may speak shame
of thee.'
   And Tristram answering ere he kissed her,
smiled :
' O very woman, god at once and child,
What ails thee to desire of me once more
The assurance that thou hadst in heart before ?
For all this wild sweet waste of sweet vain
breath,
Thou knowest I know thou hast given me
life, not death.
The shadow of death, informed with shows
of strife,
Was ere I won thee all I had of life.
Light war, light love, light living, dreams in
sleep,
Joy slight and light, not glad enough to weep,
Filled up my foolish days with sound and
shine.
Vision and gleam from strange men's cast on
mine,
Reverberate light from eyes presaging thine
That shed but shadowy moonlight where thy
face
Now sheds forth sunshine in the deep same
place,

The deep live heart half dead and shallower
        then
Than summer fords which thwart not wan-
        dering men.
For how should I, signed sorrow's from my
        birth,
Kiss dumb the loud red laughing lips of
        mirth ?
Or how, sealed thine to be, love less than
        heaven on earth ?
My heart in me was held at restless rest,
Presageful of some prize beyond its quest,
Prophetic still with promise, fain to find the
        best.
For one was fond and one was blithe and one
Fairer than all save twain whose peers are
        none ;
For third on earth is none that heaven hath
        seen
To stand with Guenevere beside my queen.
Not Nimue, girt with blessing as a guard :
Not the soft lures and laughters of Ettarde :
Not she, that splendour girdled round with
        gloom,
Crowned as with iron darkness of the tomb,
And clothed with clouding conscience of a
        monstrous doom,
Whose blind incestuous love brought forth a
        fire
To burn her ere it burn its darkling sire,
Her mother's son, King Arthur : yet but
        late
We saw pass by that fair live shadow of
        fate,
The queen Morgause of Orkney, like a
        dream
That scares the night when moon and starry
        beam
Sicken and swoon before some sorcerer's eyes
Whose wordless charms defile the saintly
        skies,

Bright still with fire and pulse of blood and
        breath,
Whom her own sons have doomed for shame
        to death.'
 ' Death—yea,' quoth she, ' there is not said
        or heard
So oft aloud on earth so sure a word.
Death, and again death, and for each that
        saith
Ten tongues chime answer to the sound of
        death.
Good end God send us ever—so men pray.
But I—this end God send me, would I say,
To die not of division and a heart
Rent or with sword of severance cloven apart,
But only when thou diest and only where
        thou art,
O thou my soul and spirit and breath to me,
O light, life, love ! yea, let this only be,
That dying I may praise God who gave me
        thee,
Let hap what will thereafter.'
                        So that day
They communed, even till even was worn
        away,
Nor aught they said seemed strange or sad
        to say,
But sweet as night's dim dawn to weariness.
Nor loved they life or love for death's sake
        less,
Nor feared they death for love's or life's sake
        more.
And on the sounding soft funereal shore
They, watching till the day should wholly die,
Saw the far sea sweep to the far grey sky,
Saw the long sands sweep to the long grey
        sea.
And night made one sweet mist of moor and
        lea,
And only far off shore the foam gave light.
And life in them sank silent as the night.

VII.

THE WIFE'S VIGIL.

But all that year in Brittany forlorn,
More sick at heart with wrath than fear of
        scorn

And less in love with love than grief, an
        less
With grief than pride of spirit and bitterness

Till all the sweet life of her blood was
   changed
And all her soul from all her past estranged
And all her will with all itself at strife
And all her mind at war with all her life,
Dwelt the white-handed Iseult, maid and wife,
A mourner that for mourning robes had on
Anger and doubt and hate of things foregone.
For that sweet spirit of old which made her
   sweet
Was parched with blasts of thought as flowers
   with heat
And withered as with wind of evil will ;
Though slower than frosts or fires consume
   or kill
That bleak black wind vexed all her spirit
   still.
As ripples reddening in the roughening
   breath
Of the eager east when dawn does night to
   death,
So rose and stirred and kindled in her thought
Fierce barren fluctuant fires that lit not aught,
But scorched her soul with yearning keen as
   hate
And dreams that left her wrath disconsolate.
When change came first on that first heaven
   where all
Life's hours were flowers that dawn's light
   hand let fall,
The sun that smote her dewy cloud of days
Wrought from its showery folds his rainbow's
   rays,
For love the red, for hope the gentle green,
But yellow jealousy glared pale between.
Ere yet the sky grew heavier, and her head
Bent flowerwise, chill with change and fancies
   fled,
She saw but love arch all her heaven across
   with red,
A burning bloom that seemed to breathe and
   beat
And waver only as flame with rapturous heat
Wavers ; and all the world therewith smelt
   sweet,
As incense kindling from the rose-red flame :
And when that full flush waned, and love
   became
Scarce fainter, though his fading horoscope
From certitude of sight receded, hope
Held yet her April-coloured light aloft
As though to lure back love, a lamp sublime
   and soft.
But soon that light paled as a leaf grows pale
And fluttered leaf-like in the gathering gale

And melted even as dew-flakes, whose brief
   sheen
The sun that gave despoils of glittering
   green ;
Till harder shone 'twixt hope and love grown
   cold
A sallow light like withering autumn's gold,
The pale strong flame of jealous thought,
   that glows
More deep than hope's green bloom or love's
   enkindled rose :
As though the sunflower's faint fierce disk
   absorbed
The spirit and heart of starrier flowers dis-
   orbed.
   That same full hour of twilight's doors un-
   barred
To let bright night behold in Joyous Gard
The glad grave eyes of lovers far away
Watch with sweet thoughts of death the death
   of day
Saw lonelier by the narrower opening sea
Sit fixed at watch Iseult of Brittany.
As darkness from deep valleys void and bleak
Climbs till it clothe with night the sunniest
   peak
Where only of all a mystic mountain-land
Day seems to cling yet with a trembling hand
And yielding heart reluctant to recede,
So, till her soul was clothed with night in-
   deed,
Rose the slow cloud of envious will within
And hardening hate that held itself no sin,
Veiled heads of vision, eyes of evil gleam,
Dim thought on thought, and darkling dream
   on dream.
Far off she saw in spirit, and seeing abhorred,
The likeness wrought on darkness of her
   lord
Shine, and the imperial semblance at his
   side
Whose shadow from her seat cast down the
   bride,
Whose power and ghostly presence thrust her
   forth :
Beside that unknown other sea far north
She saw them, clearer than in present sight
Rose on her eyes the starry shadow of night ;
And on her heart that heaved with gathering
   fate
Rose red with storm the starless shadow of
   hate ;
And eyes and heart made one saw surge and
   swell
The fires of sunset like the fires of hell.

As though God's wrath would burn up sin
    with shame,
The incensed red gold of deepening heaven
    grew flame :
The sweet green spaces of the soft low sky
Faded, as fields that withering wind leaves
    dry :
The sea's was like a doomsman's blasting
    breath
From lips afoam with ravenous lust of death.
A night like desolation, sombre-starred,
Above the great walled girth of Joyous Gard
Spread forth its wide sad strength of shadow
    and gloom
Wherein those twain were compassed round
    with doom :
Hell from beneath called on them, and she
    heard
Reverberate judgment in the wild wind's word
Cry, till the sole sound of their names that
    rang
Clove all the sea-mist with a clarion's clang,
And clouds to clouds and flames to clustering
    flames
Beat back the dark noise of the direful names.
Fear and strong exultation caught her breath,
And triumph like the bitterness of death,
And rapture like the rage of hate allayed
With ruin and ravin that its might hath
    made ;
And her heart swelled and strained itself to
    hear
What may be heard of no man's hungering
    ear,
And as a soil that cleaves in twain for drouth
Thirsted for judgment given of God's own
    mouth
Against them, till the strength of dark desire
Was in her as a flame of hell's own fire.
Nor seemed the wrath which held her spirit
    in stress
Aught else or worse than passionate holiness,
Nor the ardent hate which called on judg-
    ment's rod
More hateful than the righteousness of God.
' How long, till thou do justice, and my wrong
Stand expiate ?   O long-suffering judge, how
    long ?
Shalt thou not put him in mine hand one day
Whom I so loved, to spare not but to slay ?
Shalt thou not cast her down for me to tread,
Me, on the pale pride of her humbled head ?
Do I not well, being angry ? doth not hell
Require them ? yea, thou knowest that I do
    well.

Is not thy seal there set of bloodred light
For witness on the brows of day and night ?
Who shall unseal it ? what shall melt away
Thy signet from the doors of night and day
No man, nor strength of any spirit above,
No prayer, nor ardours of adulterous love.
Thou art God, the strong lord over body and
    soul :
Hast thou not in the terrors of thy scroll
All names of all men written as with fire ?
Thine only breath bids time and space re-
    spire :
And are not all things evil in them done
More clear in thine eyes than in ours the sun
Hast thou not sight stretched wide enough to
    see
These that offend it, these at once and me ?
Is thine arm shortened or thine hand struck
    down
As palsied ? have thy brows not strength to
    frown ?
Are thine eyes blind with film of withering
    age ?
Burns not thine heart with righteousness or
    rage
Yet, and the royal rancour toward thy foes
Retributive of ruin ?   Time should close,
Thou said'st, and earth fade as a leaf grown
    grey,
Ere one word said of thine should pass away
Was this then not thy word, thou God most
    high,
That sin shall surely bring forth death and
    die,
Seeing how these twain live and have joy of
    life,
His harlot and the man that made me wife
For is it I, perchance, I that have sinned ?
Me, peradventure, should thy wasting wind
Smite, and thy sun blast, and thy storms de-
    vour
Me with keen fangs of lightning ? should thy
    power
Put forth on me the weight of its awakening
    hour ?
Shall I that bear this burden bear that weight
Of judgment ? is my sin against thee great,
If all my heart against them burn with all its
    hate ?
Thine, and not mine, should hate be ? nay,
    but me
They have spoiled and scoffed at, who can
    touch thee.
Me, me, the fullness of their joy drains dry,
Their fruitfulness makes barren : thou, not I.

ord, is it, whom their wrongdoing clothes
  with shame,
hat all who speak shoot tongues out at thy
  name
s all who hear mock mine ? Make me thy
  sword
t least, if even thou too be wronged, O Lord,
t all of these that wrong me : make mine
  hand
s lightning, or my tongue a fiery brand,
o burn or smite them with thy wrath : behold,
have nought on earth save thee for hope or
  hold,
ail me not thou : I have nought but this to
  crave,
Iake me thy mean to give them to the
  grave,
hy sign that all men seeing may speak thee
  just,
hy word which turns the strengths of sin to
  dust,
hy blast which burns up towers and thrones
  with fire.
ord, is this gift, this grace that I require,
o great a gift, Lord, for thy grace to give
And bid me bear thy part retributive ?
That I whom scorn makes mouths at, I
  might be
Thy witness if loud sin may mock at thee ?
For lo, my life is as a barren ear
Plucked from the sheaf : dark days drive past
  me here
Downtrodden, while joy's reapers pile their
  sheaves,
A thing more vile than autumn's weariest
  leaves,
For these the sun filled once with sap of
  life.
O thou my lord that hadst me to thy wife,
Dost thou not fear at all, remembering me,
The love that bowed my whole soul down to
  thee ?
Is this so wholly nought for man to dread,
Man, whose life walks between the quick and
  dead,
Naked, and warred about with wind and
  sea,
That one should love and hate as I do
  thee ?
That one should live in all the world his foe
So mortal as the hate that loves him so ?
Nought, is it nought, O husband, O my
  knight,
O strong man, and indomitable in fight,

That one more weak than foam-bells on the
  sea
Should have in heart such thoughts as I of
  thee ?
Thou art bound about with stately strengths
  for bands :
What strength shall keep thee from my
  strengthless hands ?
Thou art girt about with goodly guards and
  great :
What fosse may fence thee round as deep as
  hate ?
Thou art wise : will wisdom teach thee fear
  of me ?
Thou art great of heart : shall this deliver
  thee ?
What wall so massive, or what tower so
  high,
Shall be thy surety that thou shouldst not
  die,
If that which comes against thee be but I ?
Who shall rise up of power to take thy part,
What skill find strength to save, what strength
  find art,
If that which wars against thee be my
  heart ?
Not iron, nor the might of force afield,
Nor edge of sword, nor sheltering weight of
  shield,
Nor all thy fame since all thy praise began,
Nor all the love and laud thou hast of man,
Nor, though his noiseless hours with wool be
  shod,
Shall God's love keep thee from the wrath of
  God.
O son of sorrows, hast thou said at heart,
Haply, God loves thee, God shall take thy
  part,
Who hath all these years endured thee, since
  thy birth
From sorrow's womb bade sin be born on
  earth ?
So long he hath cast his buckler over thee,
Shall he not surely guard thee even from me ?
Yea, but if yet he give thee while I live
Into mine hands as he shall surely give,
Ere death at last bring darkness on thy
  face,
Call then on him, call not on me for grace,
Cast not away one prayer, one suppliant
  breath,
On me that commune all this while with
  death.
For I that was not and that was thy wife
Desire not but one hour of all thy life

Wherein to triumph till that hour be past ;
But this mine hour I look for is thy last.'
So mused she till the fire in sea and sky
Sank, and the northwest wind spake harsh on
    high,

And like the sea's heart waxed her heart that
    heard,   [word
Strong, dark, and bitter, till the keen wind's
Seemed of her own soul spoken, and the breath
All round her not of darkness, but of death.

VIII.

THE LAST PILGRIMAGE.

ENOUGH of ease, O Love, enough of light,
Enough of rest before the shadow of night.
Strong Love, whom death finds feebler ;
    kingly Love,
Whom time discrowns in season, seeing thy
    dove
Spell-stricken by the serpent ; for thy sake
These that saw light see night's dawn only
    break,
Night's cup filled up with slumber, whence
    men think   [to drink.
The draught more dread than thine was dire
O Love, thy day sets darkling : hope and fear
Fall from thee standing stern as death stands
    here.
    For what have these to do with fear or hope
On whom the gates of outer darkness ope,
On whom the door of life's desire is barred ?
Past like a cloud their days in Joyous Gard
Gleam like a cloud the westering sun stains
    red
Till all the blood of day's blithe heart be bled
And all night's heart requickened ; in their
    eyes
So flame and fade those far memorial skies,
So shines the moorland, so revives the sea,
Whereon they gazing mused of things to be
And wist not more of them than waters know
What wind with next day's change of tide
    shall blow.
Dark roll the deepening days whose waves
    divide
Unseasonably, with storm-struck change of
    tide.
Tristram from Iseult : nor may sorrow say
If better wind shall blow than yesterday
With next day risen or any day to come.
For ere the songs of summer's death fell
    dumb,

And autumn bade the imperial moorlands
    change
Their purples, and the bracken's bloom grow
    strange
As hope's green blossom touched with time's
    harsh rust,
Was all their joy of life shaken to dust,
And all its fires made ashes : by the strand
Where late they strayed and communed hand
    from hand
For the last time fell separate, eyes of eyes
Took for the last time leave, and saw the skies
Dark with their deep division. The last
    time—
The last that ever love's rekindling rhyme
Should keep for them life's days and nights in
    tune
With refluence of the morning and the moon
Alternative in music, and make one
The secrets of the stardawn and the sun
For these twain souls ere darkness held them
    fast ;
The last before the labour marked for last
And toil of utmost knighthood, till the wage
Of rest might crown his crowning pilgrimage
Whereon forth faring must he take farewell,
With spear for staff and sword for scallop
    shell
And scrip wherein close memory hoarded yet
Things holier held than death might well for-
    get ;
The last time ere the travel were begun
Whose goal is unbeholden of the sun,
The last wherewith love's eyes might yet be lit,
Came, and they could but dream they knew
    not it.
    For Tristram parting from her wist at heart
How well she wist they might not choose but
    part,

And he pass forth a pilgrim, when there came
A sound of summons in the high king's name
For succour toward his vassal Triamour,
King in wild Wales, now spoiled of all his
power,
As Tristram's father ere his fair son's birth,
By one the strongest of the sons of earth,
Urgan, an iron bulk of giant mould :
And Iseult in Tintagel as of old
Sat crowned with state and sorrow : for her
lord
At Arthur's hand required her back restored,
And willingly compelled against her will
She yielded, saying within her own soul still
Some season yet of soft or stormier breath
Should haply give her life again or death :
For now nor quick nor dead nor bright nor
dark
Were all her nights and days wherein King
Mark
Held haggard watch upon her, and his eyes
Were cloudier than the gradual wintering
skies
That closed about the wan wild land and sea.
And bitter toward him waxed her heart : but
he
Was rent in twain betwixt harsh love and hate
With pain and passion half compassionate
That yearned and laboured to be quit of
shame,
And could not : and his life grew smoulder-
ing flame,
And hers a cloud full-charged with storm and
shower,
Though touched with trembling gleams of
fire's bright flower
That flashed and faded on its fitful verge,
As hope would strive with darkness and
emerge
And sink, a swimmer strangled by the swal-
lowing surge.
But Tristram by dense hills and deepening
vales
Rode through the wild glad wastes of glorious
Wales,
High-hearted with desire of happy fight
And strong in soul with merrier sense of
might
Than since the fair first years that hailed him
knight :
For all his will was toward the war, so long
Had love repressed and wrought his glory
wrong,
So far the triumph and so fair the praise
Seemed now that kindled all his April days.

And here in bright blown autumn, while his
life
Was summer's yet for strength toward love or
strife,
Blithe waxed his hope toward battle, and high
desire
To pluck once more as out of circling fire
Fame, the broad flower whose breath makes
death more sweet
Than roses crushed by love's receding feet.
But all the lovely land wherein he went
The blast of ruin and ravenous war had rent ;
And black with fire the fields where home-
steads were,
And foul with festering dead the high soft air,
And loud with wail of women many a stream
Whose own live song was like love's deepen-
ing dream,
Spake all against the spoiler : wherefore still
Wrath waxed with pity, quickening all his
will,
In Tristram's heart for every league he rode
Through the aching land so broad a curse be-
strode
With so supreme a shadow : till one dawn,
Above the green bloom of a gleaming lawn,
High on the strait steep windy bridge that
spanned
A glen's deep mouth, he saw that shadow
stand
Visible, sword on thigh and mace in hand
Vast as the mid bulk of a roof-tree's beam.
So, sheer above the wild wolf-haunted stream,
Dire as the face disfeatured of a dream,
Rose Urgan : and his eyes were night and
flame ;
But like the fiery dawn were his that came
Against him, lit with more sublime desire
Than lifts toward heaven the leaping heart of
fire :
And strong in vantage of his perilous place
The huge high presence, red as earth's first
race,
Reared like a reed the might up of his mace,
And smote : but lightly Tristram swerved,
and drove
Right in on him, whose void stroke only clove
Air, and fell wide, thundering athwart : and he
Sent forth a stormier cry than wind or sea
When midnight takes the tempest for her
lord ;
And all the glen's throat seemed as hell's that
roared ;
But high like heaven's light over hell shone
Tristram's sword,

Falling, and bright as storm shows God's bare
   brand
Flashed as it shore sheer off the huge right
   hand
Whose strength was as the shadow of death
   on all that land.
And like the trunk of some green tree sawn
   through
Reeled Urgan, as his left hand grasped and
   drew
A steel by sorcerers tempered : and anew
Raged the red wind of fluctuant fight, till
   all
The cliffs were thrilled as by the clangorous
   call
Of storm's blown trumpets from the core of
   night,
Charging : and even as with the storm-wind's
   might
On Tristram's helm that sword crashed : and
   the knight
Fell, and his arms clashed, and a wild cry
   brake
From those far off that heard it, for his sake
Soul-stricken : and that bulk of monstrous
   birth
Sent forth again a cry more dire for mirth :
But ere the sunbright arms were soiled of
   earth
They flashed again, re-risen : and swift and
   loud
Rang the strokes out as from a circling cloud,
So dense the dust wrought over them its
   drifted shroud.
Strong strokes, within the mist their battle
   made,
Each hailed on other through the shifting
   shade
That clung about them hurtling as the swift
   fight swayed :
And each between the jointed corslet saw
Break forth his foe's bright blood at each grim
   flaw
Steel made in hammered iron : till again
The fiend put forth his might more strong for
   pain
And cleft the great knight's glittering shield
   in twain,
Laughing for very wrath and thirst to kill,
A beast's broad laugh of blind and wolfish
   will,
And smote again ere Tristram's lips drew
   breath
Panting, and swept as by the sense of
   death,

That surely should have touched and sealed
   them fast
Save that the sheer stroke shrilled aside, and
   passed
Frustrate : but answering Tristram smote
   anew,
And thrust the brute breast as with lightning
   through
Clean with one cleaving stroke of perfect
   might :
And violently the vast bulk leapt upright,
And plunged over the bridge, and fell : and
   all
The cliffs reverberate from his monstrous fall
Rang : and the land by Tristram's grace was
   free.
So with high laud and honour thence went he,
And southward set his sail again, and passed
The lone land's ending, first beheld and last
Of eyes that look on England from the sea :
And his heart mourned within him, knowing
   how she
Whose heart with his was fatefully made fast
Sat now fast bound, as though some charm
   were cast
About her, such a brief space eastward
   thence,
And yet might soul not break the bonds of
   sense
And bring her to him in very life and breath
More than had this been even the sea of death
That washed between them, and its wide
   sweet light
The dim strait's darkness of the narrowing
   night
That shuts about men dying whose souls put
   forth
To pierce its passage through ; but south and
   north
Alike for him were other than they were :
For all the northward coast shone smooth and
   fair,
And off its iron cliffs the keen-edged air
Blew summer, kindling from her mute bright
   mouth ;
But winter breathed out of the murmuring
   south,
Where, pale with wrathful watch on passing
   ships,
The lone wife lay in wait with wan dumb lips
Yet, sailing where the shoreward ripple
   curled
Of the most wild sweet waves in all the world
His soul took comfort even for joy to see
The strong deep joy of living sun and sea,

The large deep love of living sea and land,
As past the lonely lion-guarded strand
Where that huge warder lifts his couchant
    sides,
Asleep, above the sleepless lapse of tides,
The light sail swept, and past the unsounded
    caves
Unsearchable, wherein the pulse of waves
Throbs through perpetual darkness to and
    fro,
And the blind night swims heavily below
While heavily the strong noon broods above,
Even to the very bay whence very Love,
Strong daughter of the giant gods who
    wrought
Sun, earth, and sea out of their procreant
    thought,
Most meetly might have risen, and most
    divine
Beheld and heard things round her sound
    and shine
From floors of foam and gold to walls of
    serpentine.
For splendid as the limbs of that supreme
Incarnate beauty through men's visions gleam,
Whereof all fairest things are even but
    shadow or dream,
And lovely like as Love's own heavenliest
    face,
Gleams there and glows the presence and the
    grace
Even of the mother of all, in perfect pride of
    place.
For otherwhere beneath our world-wide sky
There may not be beheld of men that die
Aught else like this that dies not, nor may
    stress
Of ages that bow down men's works make less
The exultant awe that clothes with power its
    loveliness.
For who sets eye thereon soever knows
How since these rocks and waves first rolled
    and rose
The marvel of their many-coloured might
Hath borne this record sensible to sight,
The witness and the symbol of their own
    delight,
The gospel graven of life's most heavenly law.
Joy, brooding on its own still soul with awe,
A sense of godlike rest in godlike strife,
The sovereign conscience of the spirit of life.
Nor otherwhere on strand or mountain tower
Hath such fair beauty shining forth in flower
Put on the imperial robe of such imperious
    power.

For all the radiant rocks from depth to height
Burn with vast bloom of glories blossom-
    bright
As though the sun's own hand had thrilled
    them through with light
And stained them through with splendour ;
    yet from thence
Such awe strikes rapture through the spirit of
    sense
From all the inaccessible sea-wall's girth,
That exultation, bright at heart as mirth,
Bows deeper down before the beauty of earth
Than fear may bow down ever : nor shall one
Who meets at Alpine dawn the mounting sun
On heights too high for many a wing to climb
Be touched with sense of aught seen more
    sublime
Than here smiles high and sweet in face of
    heaven and time.
For here the flower of fire, the soft hoar bloom
Of springtide olive-woods, the warm green
    gloom
Of clouded seas that swell and sound with
    dawn of doom,
The keen thwart lightning and the wan grey
    light
Of stormy sunrise crossed and vexed with
    night,
Flash, loom, and laugh with divers hues in
    one
From all the curved cliff's face, till day be done,
Against the sea's face and the gazing sun.
And whensoever a strong wave, high in hope,
Sweeps up some smooth slant breadth of
    stone aslope,
That glowed with duskier fire of hues less
    bright,
Swift as it sweeps back springs to sudden sight
The splendour of the moist rock's fervent
    light,
Fresh as from dew of birth when time was
    born
Out of the world-conceiving womb of morn.
All its quenched flames and darkling hues
    divine
Leap into lustrous life and laugh and shine
And darken into swift and dim decline
For one brief breath's space till the next wave
    run
Right up, and ripple down again, undone,
And leave it to be kissed and kindled of the
    sun,
And all these things, bright as they shone
    before
Man first set foot on earth or sail from shore,

Rose not less radiant than the sun sees now
When the autumn sea was cloven of Tris-
tram's prow,
And strong in sorrow and hope and woful will
That hope might move not nor might sorrow
kill
He held his way back toward the wild sad
shore
Whence he should come to look on these no
more,
Nor ever, save with sunless eyes shut fast,
Sail home to sleep in home-born earth at last.
    And all these things fled fleet as light or
breath
Past, and his heart waxed cold and dull as
death,
Or swelled but as the tides of sorrow swell,
To sink with sullen sense of slow farewell.
So surely seemed the silence even to sigh
Assurance of inveterate prophecy,
' Thou shalt not come again home hither ere
thou die.'
And the wind mourned and triumphed, and
the sea
Wailed and took heart and trembled, nor
might he
Hear more of comfort in their speech, or see
More certitude in all the waste world's range
Than the only certitude of death and change.
And as the sense and semblance fluctuated
Of all things heard and seen alive or dead
That smote far off upon his ears or eyes
Or memory mixed with forecasts fain to rise
And fancies faint as ghostliest prophecies,
So seemed his own soul, changefully forlorn,
To shrink and triumph and mount up and
mourn.
Yet all its fitful waters, clothed with night,
Lost heart not wholly, lacked not wholly light,
Seeing over life and death one star in sight
Where evening's gates as fair as morning's ope,
Whose name was memory, but whose flame
was hope.
For all the tides of thought that rose and sank
Felt its fair strength wherefrom strong sorrow
shrank
A mightier trust than time could change or
cloy,
More strong than sorrow, more secure than
joy.
So came he, nor content nor all unblest,
Back to the grey old land of Merlin's rest.
    But ere six paces forth on shore he trod
Before him stood a knight with feet unshod,
And kneeling called upon him, as on God

Might sick men call for pity, praying aloud
With hands held up and head made bare and
bowed ;
' Tristram, for God's love and thine own dear
fame,
I Tristram that am one with thee in name
And one in heart with all that praise thee—I,
Most woful man of all that may not die
For heartbreak and the heavier scourge of
shame,
By all thy glory done our woful name
Beseech thee, called of all men gentlest
knight,
Be now not slow to do my sorrows right.
I charge thee for thy fame's sake through this
land,
I pray thee by thine own wife's fair white
hand,
Have pity of me whose love is borne away
By one that makes of poor men's lives his
prey,
A felon masked with knighthood : at his side
Seven brethren hath he night or day to ride
With seven knights more that wait on all his
will :
And here at hand ere yet one day fulfil
Its flight through light and darkness, shall
they fare
Forth, and my bride among them, whom they
bear
Through these wild lands his prisoner; and if
now
I lose her, and my prayer be vain, and thou
Less fain to serve love's servants than of yore,
Then surely shall I see her face no more.
But if thou wilt, for love's sake of the bride
Who lay most loved of women at thy side,
Strike with me, straight then hence behoves
us ride
And rest between the moorside and the sea
Where we may smite them passing : but for
me
Poor stranger, me not worthy scarce to touch
Thy kind strong hand, how shouldst thou do
so much ?
For now lone left this long time waits thy
wife
And lacks her lord and light of wedded life
Whilst thou far off art famous : yet thy fame,
If thou take pity on me that bear thy name
Unworthily, but by that name implore
Thy grace, how shall not even thy fame grow
more ?
But be thy will as God's among us done,
Who art far in fame above us as the sun :

Yet only of him have all men help and grace.'
And all the lordly light of Tristram's face
Was softened as the sun's in kindly spring.
'Nay, then may God send me as evil a thing
When I give ear not to such prayers,' he said,
'And make my place among the nameless dead
When I put back one hour the time to smite
And do the unrighteous griefs of good men right.
Behold, I will not enter in nor rest
Here in mine own halls till this piteous quest
Find end ere noon to-morrow : but do thou,
Whose sister's face I may not look on now,
Go, Ganhardine, with tiding of the vow
That bids me turn aside for one day's strife
Or live dishonoured all my days of life,
And greet for me in brother's wise my wife,
And crave her pardon that for knighthood's sake
And womanhood's, whose bands may no man break
And keep the bands of bounden honour fast,
I seek not her till two nights yet be past
And this my quest accomplished, so God please
By me to give this young man's anguish ease
And on his wrongdoer's head his wrong re-quite.'
And Tristram with that woful thankful knight
Rode by the seaside moorland wastes away
Between the quickening night and darkening day
Ere half the gathering stars had heart to shine.
And lightly toward his sister Ganhardine
Sped, where she sat and gazed alone afar
Above the grey sea for the sunset star,
And lightly kissed her hand and lightly spake
His tiding of that quest for knighthood's sake.
And the white-handed Iseult, bowing her head,
Gleamed on him with a glance athwart, and said :
'As God's on earth and far above the sun,
So toward his handmaid be my lord's will done.'
And doubts too dim to question or divine
Touched as with shade the spirit of Ganhar-dine,
Hearing ; and scarce for half a doubtful breath
His bright light heart held half a thought of death

And knew not whence this darkling thought might be,
But surely not his sister's work : for she
Was ever sweet and good as summer air,
And soft as dew when all the night is fair,
And gracious as the golden maiden moon
When darkness craves her blessing : so full soon
His mind was light again as leaping waves,
Nor dreamed that hers was like a field of graves
Where no man's foot dare swerve to left or right,
Nor ear dares hearken, nor dares eye take sight
Of aught that moves and murmurs there at night.
But by the sea-banks where at morn their foes
Might find them, lay those knightly name-fellows,
One sick with grief of heart and sleepless, one
With heart of hope triumphant as the sun
Dreaming asleep of love and fame and fight :
But sleep at last wrapped warm the wan young knight ;
And Tristram with the first pale windy light
Woke ere the sun spake summons, and his ear
Caught the sea's call that fired his heart to hear,
A noise of waking waters : for till dawn
The sea was silent as a mountain lawn
When the wind speaks not, and the pines are dumb,
And summer takes her fill ere autumn come
Of life more soft than slumber : but ere day
Rose, and the first beam smote the bounding bay,
Up sprang the strength of the dark East, and took
With its wide wings the waters as they shook,
And hurled them huddling on aheap, and cast
The full sea shoreward with a great glad blast,
Blown from the heart of morning : and with joy
Full-souled and perfect passion, as a boy
That leaps up light to wrestle with the sea
For pure heart's gladness and large ecstasy,
Up sprang the might of Tristram ; and his soul
Yearned for delight within him, and waxed whole
As a young child's with rapture of the hour
That brought his spirit and all the world to flower,

And all the bright blood in his veins beat time
To the wind's clarion and the water's chime
That called him and he followed it and stood
On the sand's verge before the grey great
flood
Where the white hurtling heads of waves that
met
Rose unsaluted of the sunrise yet.
And from his heart's root outward shot the
sweet
Strong joy that thrilled him to the hands and
feet,
Filling his limbs with pleasure and glad
might,
And his soul drank the immeasurable delight
That earth drinks in with morning, and the
free
Limitless love that lifts the stirring sea
When on her bare bright bosom as a bride
She takes the young sun, perfect in his pride,
Home to his place with passion : and the
heart
Trembled for joy within the man whose part
Was here not least in living : and his mind
Was rapt abroad beyond man's meaner kind
And pierced with love of all things and with
mirth
Moved to make one with heaven and heaven-
like earth
And with the light live water.   So awhile
He watched the dim sea with a deepening
smile,
And felt the sound and savour and swift flight
Of waves that fled beneath the fading night
And died before the darkness, like a song
With harps between and trumpets blown
along
Through the loud air of some triumphant day,
Sink through his spirit and purge all sense
away
Save of the glorious gladness of his hour
And all the world about to break in flower
Before the sovereign laughter of the sun ;
And he, ere night's wide work lay all undone,
As earth from her bright body casts off night,
Cast off his raiment for a rapturous fight
And stood between the sea's edge and the sea
Naked, and godlike of his mould as he
Whose swift foot's sound shook all the towers
of Troy ;
So clothed with might, so girt upon with joy,
As, ere the knife had shorn to feed the fire
His glorious hair before the unkindled pyre
Whereon the half of his great heart was laid,
Stood, in the light of his live limbs arrayed,

Child of heroic earth and heavenly sea,
The flower of all men : scarce less bright
than he,
If any of all men latter-born might stand,
Stood Tristram, silent, on the glimmering
strand.
Not long : but with a cry of love that rang
As from a trumpet golden-mouthed, he sprang
As toward a mother's where his head might
rest
Her child rejoicing, toward the strong sea's
breast
That none may gird nor measure : and his
heart
Sent forth a shout that bade his lips not part,
But triumphed in him silent : no man's voice,
No song, no sound of clarions that rejoice,
Can set that glory forth which fills with fire
The body and soul that have their whole
desire
Silent, and freer than birds or dreams are free
Take all their will of all the encountering sea.
And toward the foam he bent and forward
smote,
Laughing, and launched his body like a boat
Full to the sea-breach, and against the tide
Struck strongly forth with amorous arms made
wide
To take the bright breast of the wave to his
And on his lips the sharp sweet minute's kiss
Given of the wave's lip for a breath's space
curled
And pure as at the daydawn of the world.
And round him all the bright rough shudder-
ing sea
Kindled, as though the world were even as
he,
Heart-stung with exultation of desire ;
And all the life that moved him seemed to
aspire,
As all the sea's life toward the sun : and still
Delight within him waxed with quickening
will
More smooth and strong and perfect as a
flame
That springs and spreads, till each glad limb
became
A note of rapture in the tune of life,
Live music mild and keen as sleep and strife :
Till the sweet change that bids the sense grow
sure
Of deeper depth and purity more pure
Wrapped him and lapped him round with
clearer cold,
And all the rippling green grew royal gold

Between him and the far sun's rising rim.
And like the sun his heart rejoiced in him,
And brightened with a broadening flame of
mirth :
And hardly seemed its life a part of earth,
But the life kindled of a fiery birth
And passion of a new-begotten son
Between the live sea and the living sun.
And mightier grew the joy to meet full-faced
Each wave, and mount with upward plunge,
and taste
The rapture of its rolling strength, and cross
Its flickering crown of snows that flash and
toss
Like plumes in battle's blithest charge, and
thence
To match the next with yet more strenuous
sense ;
Till on his eyes the light beat hard and bade
His face turn west and shoreward through
the glad
Swift revel of the waters golden-clad,
And back with light reluctant heart he bore
Across the broad-backed rollers in to shore ;
Strong-spirited for the chance and cheer of
fight,
And donned his arms again, and felt the
might
In all his limbs rejoice for strength, and
praised
God for such life as that whereon he gazed,
And wist not surely its joy was even as fleet
As that which laughed and lapsed against his
feet,
The bright thin grey foam-blossom, glad and
hoar,
That flings its flower along the flowerless
shore
On sand or shingle, and still with sweet
strange snows,
As where one great white storm-dishevelled
rose
May rain her wild leaves on a windy land,
Strews for long leagues the sounding slope of
strand,
And flower on flower falls flashing, and anew
A fresh light leaps up whence the last flash
flew,
And cast its brief glad gleam of life away
To fade not flowerwise but as drops the day
Storm-smitten, when at once the dark devours
Heaven and the sea and earth with all their
flowers ;
No star in heaven, on earth no rose to see,
But the white blown brief blossoms of the sea.

That make her green gloom starrier than the
sky,
Dance yet before the tempest's tune, and die.
And all these things he glanced upon, and
knew
How fair they shone, from earth's least flake
of dew
To stretch of seas and imminence of skies,
Unwittingly, with unpresageful eyes,
For the last time. The world's half heavenly
face,
The music of the silence of the place,
The confluence and the refluence of the sea,
The wind's note ringing over wold and lea,
Smote once more through him keen as fire
that smote,
Rang once more through him one reverberate
note,
That faded as he turned again and went,
Fulfilled by strenuous joy with strong content,
To take his last delight of labour done
That yet should be beholden of the sun
Or ever give man comfort of his hand.
Beside a wood's edge in the broken land
An hour at wait the twain together stood,
Till swift between the moorside and the
wood
Flashed the spears forward of the coming
train ;
And seeing beside the strong chief spoiler's
rein
His wan love riding prisoner in the crew,
Forth with a cry the young man leapt, and
flew
Right on that felon sudden as a flame ;
And hard at hand the mightier Tristram
came,
Bright as the sun and terrible as fire :
And there had sword and spear their soul's
desire,
And blood that quenched the spear's thirst as
it poured
Slaked royally the hunger of the sword,
Till the fierce heart of steel could scarce
fulfil
Its greed and ravin of insatiate will.
For three the fiery spear of Tristram drove
Down ere a point of theirs his harness clove
Or its own sheer mid shaft splintered in twain ;
And his heart bounded in him, and was fain
As fire or wind that takes its fill by night
Of tempest and of triumph : so the knight
Rejoiced and ranged among them, great of
hand,
Till seven lay slain upon the heathery sand

Or in the dense breadth of the woodside fern.
Nor did his heart not mightier in him burn
Seeing at his hand that young knight fallen,
    and high
The red sword reared again that bade him die.
'But on the slayer exulting like the flame
Whose foot foreshines the thunder Tristram
    came
Raging, for piteous wrath had made him fire ;
And as a lion's look his face was dire
That flashed against his foeman ere the sword
Lightened, and wrought the heart's will of its
    lord,
And clove through casque and crown the
    wrongdoer's head.
And right and left about their dark chief dead
Hurtled and hurled those felons to and fro,
Till as a storm-wind scatters leaves and snow
His right hand ravening scattered them ; but
    one
That fled with sidelong glance athwart the sun
Shot, and the shaft flew sure, and smote
    aright,
Full in the wound's print of his great first fight
When at his young strength's peril he made
    free
Cornwall, and slew beside its bordering sea
The fair land's foe, who yielding up his
    breath
Yet left him wounded nigh to dark slow death.
And hardly with long toil thence he won home
Between the grey moor and the glimmering
    foam,
And halting fared through his own gate, and
    fell,
Thirsting : for as the sleepless fire of hell
The fire within him of his wound again
Burned, and his face was dark as death for
    pain,

And blind the blithe light of his eyes : but
    they
Within that watched and wist not of the fray
Came forth and cried aloud on him for woe.
And scarce aloud his thanks fell faint and slow
As men reared up the strong man fallen and
    bore
Down the deep hall that looked along the
    shore,
And laid him soft abed, and sought in vain
If herb or hand of leech might heal his pain.
And the white-handed Iseult hearkening heard
All, and drew nigh, and spake no wifely word
But gazed upon him doubtfully, with eyes
Clouded ; and he in kindly knightly wise
Spake with scant breath, and smiling : ' Surely
    this
Is penance for discourteous lips to kiss
And feel the brand burn through them, here
    to lie
And lack the strength here to do more than
    sigh
And hope not hence for pardon.' Then she
    bowed
Her head, still silent as a stooping cloud,
And laid her lips against his face ; and he
Felt sink a shadow across him as the sea
Might feel a cloud stoop toward it : and his
    heart
Darkened as one that wastes by sorcerous art
And knows not whence it withers : and he
    turned
Back from her emerald eyes his own, and
    yearned
All night for eyes all golden : and the dark
Hung sleepless round him till the loud first
    lark
Rang record forth once more of darkness done,
And all things born took comfort from the sun

IX.

THE SAILING OF THE SWAN.

FATE, that was born ere spirit and flesh were
    made,
The fire that fills man's life with light and
    shade ;
The power beyond all godhead which puts on
All forms of multitudinous unison,

A raiment of eternal change inwrought
With shapes and hues more subtly spun than
    thought,
Where all things old bear fruit of all things new
And one deep chord throbs all the music
    through,

The chord of change unchanging, shadow and
    light
Inseparable as reverberate day from night ;
Fate, that of all things save the soul of man
Is lord and God   since body and soul
    began ,
Fate, that keeps all the tune of things in
    chime ;
Fate, that breathes power upon the lips of
    time ;
That smites and soothes with heavy and heal-
    ing hand
All joys and sorrows born in life's dim land,
Till joy be found a shadow and sorrow a
    breath
And life no discord in the tune with death,
But all things fain alike to die and live
In pulse and lapse of tides alternative,
Through silence and through sound of peace
    and strife,
Till birth and death be one in sight of life ;
Fate, heard and seen of no man's eyes or ears,
To no man shown through light of smiles or
    tears,
And moved of no man's prayer to fold its
    wings ;
Fate, that is night and light on worldly things;
Fate, that is fire to burn and sea to drown,
Strength to build up and thunder to cast
    down ;
Fate, shield and screen for each man's life-
    long head,
And sword at last or dart that strikes it dead ;
Fate, higher than heaven and deeper than the
    grave,
That saves and spares not, spares and doth
    not save :
Fate, that in gods' wise is not bought and
    sold
For prayer or price of penitence or gold ;
Whose law shall live when life bids earth fare-
    well,
Whose justice hath for shadows heaven and
    hell ;
Whose judgment into no god's hand is given,
Nor is its doom not more than hell or heaven :
Fate, that is pure of love and clean of hate,
Being equal-eyed as nought may be but fate :
Through many and weary days of foiled desire
Leads life to rest where tears no more take
    fire ;
Through many and weary dreams of quenched
    delight
Leads life through death past sense of day
    and night.

25

Nor shall they feel or fear, whose date is
    done,
Aught that made once more dark the living
    sun
And bitterer in their breathing lips the breath
Than the dark dawn and bitter dust of death.
For all the light, with fragrance as of flowers,
That clothes the lithe live limbs of separate
    hours,
More sweet to savour and more clear to sight
Dawns on the soul death's undivided night.
No vigils has that perfect night to keep,
No fever-fits of vision shake that sleep.
Nor if they wake, and any place there be
Wherein the soul may feel her wings beat free
Through air too clear and still for sound or
    strife ;
If life were haply death, and death be life ;
If love with yet some lovelier laugh revive,
And song relume the light it bore alive,
And friendship, found of all earth's gifts most
    good,
Stand perfect in perpetual brotherhood ;
If aught indeed at all of all this be,
Though none might say nor any man might
    see,
Might he that sees the shade thereof not say
This dream were trustier than the truth of
    day.
Nor haply may not hope, with heart more
    clear,
Burn deathward, and the doubtful soul take
    cheer,
Seeing through the channelled darkness yearn
    a star
Whose eyebeams are not as the morning's are,
Transient, and subjugate of lordlier light,
But all unconquerable by noon or night,
Being kindled only of life's own inmost fire,
Truth, 'stablished and made sure by strong
    desire,
Fountain of all things living, source and
    seed,
Force that perforce transfigures dream to
    deed,
God that begets on time, the body of death,
Eternity : nor may man's darkening breath,
Albeit it stain, disfigure or destroy
The glass wherein the soul sees life and joy
Only, with strength renewed and spirit of
    youth,
And brighter than the sun's the body of Truth
Eternal, unimaginable of man,
Whose very face not Thought's own eyes may
    scan,

But see far off his radiant feet at least,
Trampling the head of Fear, the false high
    priest,
Whose broken chalice foams with blood no
    more,
And prostrate on that high priest's chancel
    floor,
Bruised, overthrown, blind, maimed, with
    bloodless rod,
The miscreation of his miscreant God.
That sovereign shadow cast of souls that dwell
In darkness and the prison-house of hell
Whose walls are built of deadly dread, and
    bound
The gates thereof with dreams as iron round,
And all the bars therein and stanchions
    wrought
Of shadow forged like steel and tempered
    thought
And words like swords and thunder-clouded
    creeds
And faiths more dire than sin's most direful
    deeds :
That shade accursed and worshipped, which
    hath made
The soul of man that brought it forth a shade
Black as the womb of darkness, void and vain,
A throne for fear, a pasturage for pain,
Impotent, abject, clothed upon with lies,
A foul blind fume of words and prayers that
    rise,
Aghast and harsh, abhorrent and abhorred,
Fierce as its God, blood-saturate as its Lord ;
With loves and mercies on its lips that hiss
Comfort, and kill compassion with a kiss
And strike the world black with their blasting
    breath ;
That ghost whose core of life is very death
And all its light of heaven a shadow of hell,
Fades, falls, wanes, withers by none other
    spell
But theirs whose eyes and ears have seen and
    heard
Not the face naked, not the perfect word
But the bright sound and feature felt from far
Of life which feeds the spirit and the star,
Thrills the live light of all the suns that roll,
And stirs the still sealed springs of every soul.
    Three dim days through, three slumberless
    nights long,
Perplexed at dawn, oppressed at evensong,
The strong man's soul now sealed indeed with
    pain,
And all its springs half dried with drought,
    had lain

Prisoner within the fleshy dungeon-dress
Sore chafed and wasted with its weariness.
And fain it would have found the star, and
    fain
Made this funereal prison-house of pain
A watch-tower whence its eyes might sweep,
    and see
If any place for any hope might be
Beyond the hells and heavens of sleep and
    strife,
Or any light at all of any life
Beyond the dense false darkness woven above,
And could not, lacking grace to look on love.
And in the third night's dying hour he spake,
Seeing scarce the seals that bound the day-
    spring break
And scarce the daystar burn above the sea :
' O Ganhardine, my brother true to me,
I charge thee by those nights and days we
    knew
No great while since in England, by the dew
That bathed those nights with blessing, and
    the fire
That thrilled those days as music thrills a lyre,
Do now for me perchance the last good deed
That ever love may crave or life may need
Ere love lay life in ashes : take to thee
My ship that shows aloft against the sea
Carved on her stem the semblance of a swan,
And ere the waves at even again wax wan
Pass, if it may be, to my lady's land,
And give this ring into her secret hand,
And bid her think how hard on death I lie,
And fain would look upon her face and die.
But as a merchant's laden be the bark
With royal ware for fraughtage, that King
    Mark
May take for toll thereof some costly thing ;
And when this gift finds grace before the king,
Choose forth a cup, and put therein my ring
Where sureliest only of one it may be seen,
And bid her handmaid bear it to the queen
For earnest of thine homage : then shall she
Fear, and take counsel privily with thee,
To know what errand there is thine from me
And what my need in secret of her sight.
But make thee two sails, one like sea-foam
    white
To spread for signal if thou bring her back,
And if she come not see the sail be black,
That I may know or ever thou take land
If these my lips may die upon her hand
Or hers may never more be mixed with mine.'
    And his heart quailed for grief in Ganhar-
    dine.

Hearing ; and all his brother bade he swore
Surely to do, and straight fare forth from
    shore.
But the white-handed Iseult hearkening heard
All, and her heart waxed hot, and every word
Thereon seemed graven and printed in her
    thought
As lines with fire and molten iron wrought.
And hard within her heavy heart she cursed
Both, and her life was turned to fiery thirst,
And all her soul was hunger, and its breath
Of hope and life a blast of raging death.
For only in hope of evil was her life.
So bitter burned within the unchilded wife
A virgin lust for vengeance, and such hate
Wrought in her now the fervent work of fate.
    Then with a south-west wind the Swan set
        forth,
And over wintering waters bore to north,
And round the wild land's windy westward
    end
Up the blown channel bade her bright way
    bend
East on toward high Tintagel : where at dark
Landing, fair welcome found they of King
    Mark,
And Ganhardine with Brangwain as of old
Spake, and she took the cup of chiselled gold
Wherein lay secret Tristram's trothplight ring,
And bare it unbeholden of the king
Even to her lady's hand, which hardly took
A gift whereon a queen's eyes well might look,
With grace forlorn of weary gentleness.
But, seeing, her life leapt in her, keen to
    guess
The secret of the symbol : and her face
Flashed bright with blood whence all its grief-
    worn grace
Took fire and kindled to the quivering hair.
And in the dark soft hour of starriest air
Thrilled through with sense of midnight, when
    the world
Feels the wide wings of sleep about it furled,
Down stole the queen, deep-muffled to her
    wan
Mute restless lips, and came where yet the
    Swan
Swung fast at anchor : whence by starlight she
Hoised snowbright sails and took the glim-
    mering sea.
    But all the long night long more keen and sore
His wound's grief waxed in Tristram ever-
    more,
And heavier always hung his heart asway
Between dim fear and clouded hope of day.

And still with face and heart at silent strife
Beside him watched the maiden called his
    wife,
Patient, and spake not save when scarce he
    spake,
Murmuring with sense distraught and spirit
    awake
Speech bitterer than the words thereof were
    sweet :
And hatred thrilled her to the hands and feet
Listening : for alway back reiterate came
The passionate faint burden of her name.
Nor ever through the labouring lips astir
Came any word of any thought of her,
But the soul wandering struggled and clung
    hard
Only to dreams of joy in Joyous Gard
Or wildwood nights beside the Cornish strand,
Or Merlin's holier sleep here hard at hand
Wrapped round with deep soft spells in dim
    Broceliande.
And with such thirst as joy's drained wine-cup
    leaves
When fear to hope as hope to memory cleaves
His soul desired the dewy sense of leaves,
The soft green smell of thickets drenched with
    dawn,
The faint slot kindling on the fiery lawn
As day's first hour made keen the spirit again
That lured and spurred on quest his hound
    Hodain,
The breeze, the bloom, the splendour and the
    sound,
That stung like fire the hunter and the hound,
The pulse of wind, the passion of the sea,
The rapture of the woodland : then would he
Sigh, and as one that fain would all be dead
Heavily turn his heavy-laden head
Back, and close eyes for comfort, finding none.
And fain he would have died or seen the sun,
Being sick at heart of darkness : yet afresh
Began the long strong strife of spirit and flesh
And branching pangs of thought whose
    branches bear
The bloodred fruit whose core is black, de-
    spair.
And the wind slackened and again grew great,
Palpitant as men's pulses palpitate
Between the flowing and ebbing tides of fa_
That wash their lifelong waifs of weal and w_
Through night and light and twilight to and
    fro.
Now as a pulse of hope its heartbeat throbbed,
Now like one stricken shrank and sank and
    sobbed,

Then, yearning as with child of death, put
    forth
A wail that filled the night up south and north
With woful sound of waters : and he said,
' So might the wind wail if the world were
    dead
And its wings wandered over nought but sea.
I would I knew she would not come to me,
For surely she will come not : then should I,
Once knowing I shall not look upon her, die.
I knew not life could so long breathe such
    breath
As I do. Nay, what grief were this, if death,
The sole sure friend of whom the whole world
    saith
He lies not, nor hath ever this been said,
That death would heal not grief—if death
    were dead
And all ways closed whence grief might pass
    with life ! '
Then softly spake his watching virgin wife
Out of her heart, deep down below her breath :
' Fear not but death shall come—and after
    death
Judgment.' And he that heard not answered
    her,
Saying—' Ah, but one there was, if truth not
    err,
For true men's trustful tongues have said it—
    one
Whom these mine eyes knew living while the
    sun
Looked yet upon him, and mine own ears
    heard
The deep sweet sound once of his godlike
    word—
Who sleeps and dies not, but with soft live
    breath
Takes always all the deep delight of death,
Through love's gift of a woman : but for me
Love's hand is not the hand of Nimue,
Love's word no still smooth murmur of the
    dove,
No kiss of peace for me the kiss of love.
Nor, whatsoe'er thy life's love ever give,
Dear, shall it ever bid me sleep or live ;
Nor from thy brows and lips and living breast
As his from Nimue's shall my soul take rest ;
Not rest but unrest hath our long love given—
Unrest on earth that wins not rest in heaven.
What rest may we take ever? what have we
Had ever more of peace than has the sea ?
Has not our life been as a wind that blows
Through lonelier lands than rear the wild
    white rose

That each year sees requickened, but for us
Time once and twice hath here or there done
    thus
And left the next year following empty and
    bare?
What rose hath our last year's rose left for heir,
What wine our last year's vintage ? and to me
More were one fleet forbidden sense of thee,
One perfume of thy present grace, one thought
Made truth one hour, ere all mine hours be
    nought,
One very word, breath, look, sign, touch of
    hand,
Than all the green leaves in Broceliande
Full of sweet sound, full of sweet wind and
    sun ;
O God, thou knowest I would no more but
    one,
I would no more but once more ere I die
Find thus much mercy. Nay, but then were I
Happier than he whom there thy grace hath
    found,
For thine it must be, this that wraps him
    round,
Thine only, albeit a fiend's force gave him
    birth,
Thine that has given him heritage on earth
Of slumber-sweet eternity to keep
Fast in soft hold of everliving sleep.
Happier were I, more sinful man than he,
Whom one love-worthier then than Nimue
Should with a breath make blest among the
    dead.'
    And the wan wedded maiden answering
    said,
Soft as hate speaks within itself apart :
' Surely ye shall not, ye that rent mine heart,
Being one in sin, in punishment be twain.'
    And the great knight that heard not spake
    again
And sighed, but sweet thought of sweet things
    gone by
Kindled with fire of joy the very sigh
And touched it through with rapture : ' Ay,
    this were
How much more than the sun and sunbright air,
How much more than the springtide, how
    much more
Than sweet strong sea-wind quickening wave
    and shore
With one divine pulse of continuous breath,
If she might kiss me with the kiss of death,
And make the light of life by death's look
    dim !'
    And the white wedded virgin answered him,

Inwardly, wan with hurt no herb makes
whole :
'Yea, surely, ye whose sin hath slain my soul,
Surely your own souls shall have peace in
death
And pass with benediction in their breath
And blessing given of mine their sin hath
slain.'
  And Tristram with sore yearning spake
again,
Saying : 'Yea, might this thing once be, how
should I,
With all my soul made one thanksgiving, die,
And pass before what judgment-seat may be,
And cry, "Lord, now do all thou wilt with
me,
Take all thy fill of justice, work thy will ;
Though all thy heart of wrath have all its fill,
My heart of suffering shall endure, and say,
For that thou gavest me living yesterday
I bless thee though thou curse me." Ay, and
well
Might one cast down into the gulf of hell,
Remembering this, take heart and thank his
fate—
That God, whose doom now scourges him
with hate,
Once, in the wild and whirling world above,
Bade mercy kiss his dying lips with love.
But if this come not, then he doth me wrong.
For what hath love done, all this long life
long,
That death should trample down his poor
last prayer
Who prays not for forgiveness ? Though
love were
Sin dark as hate, have we not here that
sinned
Suffered ? has that been less than wintry
wind
Wherewith our love lies blasted ? O my
own,
O mine and no man's yet save mine alone,
Iseult ! what ails thee that I lack so long
All of thee, all things thine for which I long ?
For more than watersprings to shadeless
sands,
More to me were the comfort of her hands
Touched once, and more than rays that set
and rise
The glittering arrows of her glorious eyes,
More to my sense than fire to dead cold air
The wind and light and odour of her hair,
More to my soul than summer's to the south
The mute clear music of her amorous mouth,

And to my heart's heart more than heaven's
great rest
The fullness of the fragrance of her breast,
Iseult, Iseult, what grace hath life to give
More than we twain have had of life, and
live ?
Iseult, Iseult, what grace may death not keep
As sweet for us to win of death, and sleep ?
Come therefore, let us twain pass hence and
try
If it be better not to live but die,
With love for lamp to light us out of life.'
  And on that word his wedded maiden wife
Pale as the moon in star-forsaken skies
Ere the sun fill them, rose with set strange
eyes
And gazed on him that saw not : and her
heart
Heaved as a man's death-smitten with a dart
That smites him sleeping, warm and full of
life :
So toward her lord that was not looked his
wife,
His wife that was not : and her heart within
Burnt bitter like an aftertaste of sin
To one whose memory drinks and loathes the
lee
Of shame or sorrow deeper than the sea ;
And no fear touched him of her eyes above
And ears that hoarded each poor word whence
love
Made sweet the broken music of his breath.
'Iseult, my life that wast and art my death,
My life in life that hast been, and that art
Death in my death, sole wound that cleaves
mine heart,
Mine heart that else, how spent soe'er, were
whole,
Breath of my spirit and anguish of my soul,
How can this be that hence thou canst not
hear,
Being but by space divided ? One is here,
But one of twain I looked at once to see ;
Shall death keep time and thou not keep with
me ?'
  And the white married maiden laughed at
heart,
Hearing, and scarce with lips at all apart
Spake, and as fire between them was her
breath ;
'Yea, now thou liest not : yea, for I am
death.'
  By this might eyes that watched without
behold
Deep in the gulfs of aching air acold

The roses of the dawning heaven that strew
The low soft sun's way ere his power shine
  through
And burn them up with fire : but far to west
Had sunk the dead moon on the live sea's
  breast,
Slain as with bitter fear to see the sun :
And eastward was a strong bright wind begun
Between the clouds and waters : and he said,
Seeing hardly through dark dawn her doubt-
  ful head,
'Iseult ?' and like a death-bell faint and clear
The virgin voice rang answer—'I am here.'
And his heart sprang, and sank again : and
  she
Spake, saying, 'What would my knightly
  lord with me ?'
And Tristram : ' Hath my lady watched all
  night
Beside me, and I knew not? God requite
Her love for comfort shown a man nigh dead.'
  'Yea, God shall surely guerdon it,' she
  said,
'Who hath kept me all my days through to
  this hour.'
  And Tristram : ' God alone hath grace and
  power
To pay such grace toward one unworthier
  shown
Than ever durst, save only of God alone,
Crave pardon yet and comfort, as I would
Crave now for charity if my heart were good,
But as a coward's it fails me, even for shame.'
  Then seemed her face a pale funereal
  flame
That burns down slow by midnight, as she
  said :
'Speak, and albeit thy bidding spake me
  dead,
God's love renounce me if it were not done.'
  And Tristram : ' When the sea-line takes
  the sun
That now should be not far off sight from
  far,
Look if there come not with the morning
  star
My ship bound hither from the northward
  back,
And if the sail be white thereof or black.'
  And knowing the soothfast sense of his
  desire
So sore the heart within her raged like fire
She could not wring forth of her lips a word,
But bowing made sign how humbly had she
  heard.

And the sign given made light his heart ; and
  she
Set her face hard against the yearning sea
Now all athirst with trembling trust of hope
To see the sudden gates of sunrise ope ;
But thirstier yearned the heart whose fiery
  gate
Lay wide that vengeance might come in to
  hate.
  And Tristram lay at thankful rest, and
  thought
Now surely life nor death could grieve him
  aught,
Since past was now life's anguish as a breath,
And surely past the bitterness of death.
For seeing he had found at these her hands
  this grace,
It could not be but yet some breathing-space
Might leave him life to look again on love's
  own face.
'Since if for death's sake,' in his heart he
  said,
' Even she take pity upon me quick or dead,
How shall not even from God's hand be com-
  passion shed ?
For night bears dawn, how weak soe'er and
  wan,
And sweet ere death, men fable, sings the
  swan.
So seems the Swan my signal from the sea
To sound a song that sweetens death to me
Clasped round about with radiance from above
Of dawn, and closer clasped on earth by love.
Shall all things brighten, and this my sign be
  dark ?'
  And high from heaven suddenly rang the
  lark,
Triumphant ; and the far first refluent ray
Filled all the hollow darkness full with day.
And on the deep sky's verge a fluctuant light
Gleamed, grew, shone, strengthened into per-
  fect sight,
As bowed and dipped and rose again the sail's
  clear white.
And swift and steadfast as a sea-mew's wing
It neared before the wind, as fain to bring
Comfort, and shorten yet its narrowing track.
And she that saw looked hardly toward him
  back,
Saying, ' Ay, the ship comes surely ; but her
  sail is black.'
And fain he would have sprung upright, and
  seen,
And spoken : but strong death struck sheer
  between,

And darkness closed as iron round his head :
And smitten through the heart lay Tristram
dead.

And scarce the word had flown abroad, and
wail
Risen, ere to shoreward came the snowbright
sail,
And lightly forth leapt Ganhardine on land,
And led from ship with swift and reverent
hand
Iseult : and round them up from all the
crowd
Broke the great wail for Tristram out aloud.
And ere her ear might hear her heart had
heard,
Nor sought she sign for witness of the word ;
But came and stood above him newly dead,
And felt his death upon her : and her head
Bowed, as to reach the spring that slakes all
drouth ;
And their four lips became one silent mouth.
So came their hour on them that were in life
Tristram and Iseult : so from love and strife
The stroke of love's own hand felt last and
best
Gave them deliverance to perpetual rest.
So, crownless of the wreaths that life had
wound,
They slept, with flower of tenderer comfort
crowned :
From bondage and the fear of time set free,
And all the yoke of space on earth and sea
Cast as a curb for ever : nor might now
Fear and desire bid soar their souls or bow,
Lift up their hearts or break them : doubt nor
grief
More now might move them, dread nor dis-
belief
Touch them with shadowy cold or fiery sting,
Nor sleepless languor with its weary wing,
Nor harsh estrangement, born of time's vain
breath,
Nor change, a darkness deeper far than death.
And round the sleep that fell around them
then
Earth lies not wrapped, nor records wrought
of men
Rise up for timeless token : but their sleep
Hath round it like a raiment all the deep ;
No change or gleam or gloom of sun and rain,
But all time long the might of all the main
Spread round them as round earth soft heaven
is spread,
And peace more strong than death round all
the dead.

For death is of an hour, and after death
Peace : nor for aught that fear or fancy saith,
Nor even for very love's own sake shall strife
Perplex again that perfect peace with life.
And if, as men that mourn may deem or
dream,
Rest haply here than there might sweeter
seem,
And sleep, that lays one hand on all, more
good
By some sweet grave's grace given of wold or
wood
Or clear high glen or sunbright wind-worn
down
Than where life thunders through the tram-
pling town
With daylong feet and nightlong overhead,
What grave may cast such grace round any
dead,
What so sublime sweet sepulchre may be
For all that life leaves mortal, as the sea ?
And these, rapt forth perforce from earthly
ground,
These twain the deep sea guards, and girdles
round
Their sleep more deep than any sea's gulf lies,
Though changeless with the change in shifting
skies,
Nor mutable with seasons : for the grave
That held them once, being weaker than a
wave,
The waves long since have buried : though
their tomb
Was royal that by ruth's relenting doom
Men gave them in Tintagel : for the word
Took wing which thrilled all piteous hearts
that heard
The word wherethrough their lifelong lot stood
shown,
And when the long sealed springs of fate were
known,
The blind bright innocence of lips that quaffed
Love, and the marvel of the mastering draught,
And all the fraughtage of the fateful bark,
Loud like a child upon them wept King Mark,
Seeing round the sword's hilt which long since
had fought
For Cornwall's love a scroll of writing
wrought,
A scripture writ of Tristram's hand, wherein
Lay bare the sinless source of all their sin,
No choice of will, but chance and sorcerous
art,
With prayer of him for pardon : and his
heart

Was molten in him, wailing as he kissed
Each with that kiss of kinship—' Had I wist,
Ye had never sinned nor died thus, nor had I
Borne in this doom that bade you sin and die
So sore a part of sorrow.'   And the king
Built for their tomb a chapel bright like spring
With flower-soft wealth of branching tracery
  made
Fair as the frondage each fleet year sees fade,
That should not fall till many a year were
  done.
There slept they wedded under moon and sun
And change of stars : and through the case-
  ments came
Midnight and noon girt round with shadow
  and flame
To illume their grave or veil it : till at last
On these things too was doom as darkness
  cast :

For the strong sea hath swallowed wall and
  tower,
And where their limbs were laid in woful hour
For many a fathom gleams and moves and
  moans
The tide that sweeps above their coffined bones
In the wrecked chancel by the shivered shrine :
Nor where they sleep shall moon or sunlight
  shine
Nor man look down for ever : none shall
  say,
Here once, or here, Tristram and Iseult lay :
But peace they have that none may gain who
  live,
And rest about them that no love can give,
And over them, while death and life shall
  be,
The light and sound and darkness of the
  sea.

ATALANTA IN CALYDON.

A TRAGEDY.

Τοὺς ζῶντας εὖ δρᾶν. κατθανὼν δ. πᾶς ἀνὴρ
Γῆ καὶ σκιά· τὸ μηδὲν εἰς οὐδὲν ῥίπει.

EUR. FR. Mel. 20. (537.)

TO THE MEMORY

OF

WALTER SAVAGE LANDOR

I NOW DEDICATE, WITH EQUAL AFFECTION, REVERENCE, AND REGRET,
A POEM INSCRIBED TO HIM WHILE YET ALIVE IN WORDS WHICH
ARE NOW RETAINED BECAUSE THEY WERE LAID BEFORE HIM ;
AND TO WHICH, RATHER THAN CANCEL THEM, I HAVE
ADDED SUCH OTHERS AS WERE EVOKED BY THE
NEWS OF HIS DEATH : THAT THOUGH LOSING
THE PLEASURE I MAY NOT LOSE THE HONOR
OF INSCRIBING IN FRONT OF MY WORK
THE HIGHEST OF CONTEMPORARY
NAMES.

ῳχεο δὴ Βορέηθεν ἀπότρομος· ἀλλά σε Νύμφαι
  ἤγαγον ἀσπασίαν ἡδύπνοοι καθ' ἅλα,
πληροῦσαι μέλιτος θεόθεν στόμα, μή τι Ποσειδῶν
  Βλάψῃ, ἐν ὠσὶν ἔχων σὴν μελίγηρυν ὄπα,
τοῖος ἀοιδὸς ἔφυς· ἡμεῖς δ' ἔτι κλαίομεν, οἵ σου
  δευόμεθ' οἰχομένου, καί σε ποθοῦμεν ἀεί.
εἶπε δὲ Πιερίδων τις ἀναστρεφθεῖσα πρὸς ἄλλην·
  ἦλθεν, ἰδού, πάντων φίλτατος ἦλθε βροτῶν,
στέμματα δρεψάμενος νεοθηλέα χερσὶ γεραιαῖς,
  καὶ πολιὸν δάφναις ἀμφεκάλυψε κάρα   10
ἡδύ τι Σικελικαῖς ἐπὶ πηκτίσιν, ἡδύ τι χόρδαις,
  ἀσόμενος· πολλὴν γὰρ μετέβαλλε λύραν,
πολλάκι δ' ἐν βήσσαισι καθήμενον εὖρεν Ἀπόλλων
  ἄνθεσι δ' ἔστεψεν, τερπνὰ δ' ἔδωκε λέγειν,
Πᾶνά τ' ἀείμνηστόν τε Πίτυν Κόρυθόν τε δύσεδρον,
  ἥν τ' ἐφίλησε θεὰν θνητὸς Ἀμαδρύαδα·
πόντου δ' ἐν μεγάροισιν ἐκοίμισε Κυμοδάμειαν,
  τήν τ' Ἀγαμεμνονίαν παῖδ' ἀπέδωκε πατρί,
πρὸς δ' ἱεροὺς Δελφοὺς θεόπληκτον ἔπεμψεν Ὀρέστην
  τειρόμενον στυγεραῖς ἔνθα καὶ ἔνθα θεαῖς   20

ῳχεο δὴ καὶ ἄνευθε φίλων καὶ ἄνευθεν ἀοιδῆς,
  δρεψόμενος μαλακῆς ἄνθεα Περσεφόνης.
ῳχεο· κοὐκ ἔτ' ἔσει, κοὐκ αὖ ποτέ σοι παρεδοῦμαι
  ἀζόμενος, χειρῶν χερσὶ θιγὼν ὁσίαις·
νῦν δ' αὖ μνησάμενον γλυκύπικρος ὑπήλυθεν οἰδὼς,
  οἷα τυχὼν οἵου πρὸς σέθεν οἷος ἔχω·
οὔποτε σοῖς γέρον, ὄμμα φίλοις φίλον ὄμμασι τέρψω,
  σῆς, γέρον, ἁψάμενος, φίλτατε, δεξιτερᾶς·
ἦ ψαφαρὰ κόνις, ἦ ψαφαρὸς βίος ἐστί· τὶ τουτων
  μεῖον ἐφημερίων ; οὐ κόνις ἀλλὰ βίος·   10
ἀλλά μοι ἡδύτερός γε πέλεις πολὺ τῶν ἔτ' ἐόντων,
  ἔπλεο γάρ· σοὶ μὴν ταῦτα θανόντι φέρω,
παῦρα μὲν· ἀλλ' ἀπὸ κῆρος ἐτήτυμα· μηδ' ἀποτρεφθῇς
  πρὸς δὲ βαλὼν ἔτι νῦν ἥσυχον ὄμμά δέχου·
οὐ γὰρ ἔχω, μέγα δὴ τι θέλων, σέθεν ἄξια δοῦναι
  θαπτομένου περ ἀπών· οὐ γὰρ ἔνεστιν ἔμοι·
οὐδὲ μελικρήτου παρέχειν γάνος· εἰ γὰρ ἐνείη
  καί σε χεροῖν ψαῦσαι καὶ σέ ποτ' αὖθις ἰδεῖν,
δάκρυσί τε σπονδαῖς τε κάρα φίλον ἀμφιπολεύειν
  ὀφθαλμούς θ' ἱεροὺς σοὺς ἱερόν τε δέμας.   20

εἴθ' ὄφελον. μάλα γὰρ τάδ' ἂν ἀμπαύσειε μερίμνης·
  νῦν δὲ πρόσωθεν ἄνευ σήματος οἶκτον ἔγω·
οὐδ' ἐπιτυμβίδιον θρηνῶ μέλος, ἀλλ' ἀπαμυνθεὶς,
  ἀλλ' ἀπάνευθεν ἔχων ἀμφιδακρυτὰ πάθη.
ἀλλὰ σὺ χαῖρε θανών, καὶ ἔχων γέρας ἴσθι πρὸς ἀνδρῶν
  πρός τε θεῶν, ἰνέροις εἴ τις ἔπεστι θεός.
χαῖρε γέρον, φίλε χαῖρε πατὲρ, πολὺ φέρτατ' ἀοιδῶν
  ὧν ἴδομεν, πολὺ δὴ φέρτατ' ἀεισομένων·
χαῖρε, καὶ ὄλβον ἔχοις, οἷόν γε θανόντες ἔχουσιν,
  ἡσυχίαν ἔχθρας καὶ φιλότητος ἄτερ.   30
σήματος οἰχομένου σοι μνήματ' ἐς ὕστερον ἔσται,
  σοί τε φίλη μνήμη μνήματος οἰχομένου·
ὃν Χάριτες κλαίουσι θεαὶ, κλαίει δ' Ἀφροδίτη
  καλλιχόροις Μουκῶν τερψαμένη στεφάνοις·
οὐ γὰρ ἅπαξ ἱερούς ποτε γῆρας ἔτριψεν ἀοιδούς·
  τήνδε τὸ σὸν φαίνει μνῆμα τόδ' ἀγλαΐαν.
ἢ φίλος ἦς μακάρεσσι βροτὸς σοὶ δ' εἴ τινι Νύμφαι
  δῶρα ποθεινὰ νέμειν, ὕστατα δῶρ', ἔδοσαν.
τὰς νῦν χάλκεος ὕπνος ἔβη καὶ ἀνήνεμος αἰών,
  καὶ συνθαπτόμεναι μοῖραν ἔχουσι μίαν.   40
εὕδεις καὶ σὺ, καλὸν καὶ ἀγάκλυτον ἐν χθονὶ κοίλῃ
  ὕπνον ἐφικόμενος, σῆς ἀπόνοσφι πάτρας,
τῆλε παρὰ ξανθοῦ Τυρσηνικὸν οἶδμα καθεύδεις
  νάματος, ἡ δ' ἔτι σὴ μαῖά σε γαῖα ποθεῖ,
ἀλλ' ἀπέχεις, καὶ πρόσθε φιλόπτολις ὢν περ ἀπεῖπας·
  εὕδε· μάκαρ δ' ἡμῖν οὐδ' ἀμέγαρτος ἔσει.
βαιὸς ἐπιχθονίων γε χρόνος καὶ μοῖρα κρατήσει,
  τοὺς δέ ποτ' εὐφροσύνη τοὺς δέ ποτ' ἄλγος ἔχει·
πολλάκι δ' ἢ βλάπτει φάος ἢ σκότος ἀμφικαλύπτει
  μυρομένους, δάκνει δ' ὕπνος ἐγρηγορότας·   50
οὐδ' ἔθ' ὅτ' ἐν τύμβοισι κάτεδραθεν ὄμμα θανόντων
  ἢ σκότος ἢ τι φέος δήξεται ἠελίου·
οὐδ' ὄναρ ἐννύχιον καὶ ἐνύπνιον οὐδ' ὕπαρ ἔσται
  ἤ ποτε τερπομένοις ἤ ποτ' ὀδυρομένοις·
ἀλλ' ἕνα πάντες ἀεὶ θᾶκον συνέχουσι καὶ ἕδραν
  ἀντὶ βροτῆς ἄβροτον, κάλλιμον ἄντι κακῆς.

THE ARGUMENT.

ALTHÆA, daughter of Thestius and Eurythemis, queen of Calydon, being with child of Meleager her first-born son, dreamed that she brought forth a brand burning; and upon his birth came the three Fates and prophesied of him three things, namely these; that he should have great strength of his hands, and good fortune in this life, and that he should live no longer when the brand then in the fire were consumed: wherefore his mother plucked it forth and kept it by her. And the child being a man grown sailed with Jason after the fleece of gold, and won himself great praise of all men living; and when the tribes of the north and west made war upon Ætolia, he fought against their army and scattered it. But Artemis, having at the first stirred up these tribes to war against Œneus, king of Calydon, because he had offered sacrifice to all the gods saving her alone, but her he had forgotten to honor, was yet more wroth because of the destruction of this army, and sent upon the land of Calydon a wild boar, which slew many and wasted all their increase; but him could none slay, and many went against him and perished. Then were all the chief men of Greece gathered together, and among them Atalanta, daughter of Iasius the Arcadian, a virgin; for whose sake Artemis let slay the boar, seeing she favored the maiden greatly; and Meleager having despatched it gave the spoil thereof to Atalanta, as one beyond measure enamored of her; but the brethren of Athæa his mother, Toxeus and Plexippus, with such others as misliked that she only should bear off the praise whereas many had borne the labor, laid wait for her to take away her spoil; but Meleager fought against them and slew them: whom when Althæa their sister beheld and knew to be slain of her son, she waxed for wrath and sorrow like as one mad, and taking the brand whereby the measure of her son's life was meted to him, she cast it upon a fire; and with the wasting thereof his life likewise wasted away, that being brought back to his father's house he died in a brief space; and his mother also endured not long after for very sorrow; and this was his end, and the end of that hunting.

ἴστω δ' ὅστις οὐχ ὑπόπτερος
φροντίσιν δαεὶς
τὰν ἁ παιδολύμας τάλαινα Θεστίας μήσατο
πυρδαῆ τινα πρόνοιαν,
καταίθουσα παιδὸς δαφοινὸν
δαλὸν ἥλικ᾿ ἐπεὶ μολὼν
ματρόθεν κελάδησε
σύμμετρόν τε διαὶ βίου
μοιρόκραντον ἐς ἆμαρ.

ÆSCH. Cho. 602–612.

THE PERSONS.

CHIEF HUNTSMAN.	TOXEUS.
CHORUS,	PLEXIPPUS.
ALTHÆA.	HERALD.
MELEAGER.	MESSENGER.
ŒNEUS.	SECOND MESSENGER.
ATALANTA.	

ATALANTA IN CALYDON.

MAIDEN, and mistress of the months
and stars
Now folded in the flowerless fields of
heaven,
Goddess whom all gods love with threefold
heart,
Being treble in thy divided deity,
A light for dead men and dark hours, a
foot
Swift on the hills as morning, and a hand
To all things fierce and fleet that roar and
range
Mortal, with gentler shafts than snow or
sleep;
Hear now and help and lift no violent
hand,
But favorable and fair as thine eye's beam
Hidden and shown in heaven; for I all
night
Amid the king's hounds and the hunting
men
Have wrought and worshipped toward
thee: nor shall man
See goodlier hounds or deadlier edge of
spears;
But for the end, that lies unreached at yet
Between the hands and on the knees of
gods.
O fair-faced sun killing the stars and dews
And dreams and desolation of the night !
Rise up, shine, stretch thine hand out,
with thy bow
Touch the most dimmest height of trembling
heaven,
And burn and break the dark about thy
ways,
Shot through and through with arrows; let
thine hair
Lighten as flame above that flameless
shell

Which was the moon, and thine eyes fill
the world,
And thy lips kindle with swift beams; let
earth
Laugh, and the long sea fiery from thy
feet
Through all the roar and ripple of stream-
ing springs
And foam in reddening flakes and flying
flowers
Shaken from hands and blown from lips of
nymphs
Whose hair or breast divides the wander-
ing wave
With salt close tresses cleaving lock to
lock,
All gold, or shuddering and unfurrowed
snow;
And all the winds about thee with their
wings,
And fountain-heads of all the watered
world;
Each horn of Achelous, and the green
Euenus, wedded with the straitening sea.
For in fair time thou comest; come also
thou,
Twin-born with him, and virgin, Artemis,
And give our spears their spoil, the wild
boar's hide.
Sent in thine anger against us for sin
done
And bloodless alters without wine or fire.
Him now consume thou; for thy sacrifice
With sanguine-shining steam divides the
dawn,
And one, the maiden rose of all thy maids,
Arcadian Atalanta, snowy-souled,
Fair as the snow and footed as the wind
From Ladon and well-wooded Mænalus
Over the firm hills and the fleeting sea
Hast thou drawn, hither, and many an
armèd king,

Heroes, the crown of men, like gods in
  fight.
Moreover out of all the Ætolian land,
From the full-flowered, Lelantian pasturage
To what of fruitful field the son of Zeus
Won from the roaring river and laboring
  sea
When the wild god shrank in his horn and
  fled
And foamed and lessened through his
  wrathful fords,
Leaving clear lands that steamed with
  sudden sun,
These virgins with the lightening of the
  day
Bring thee fresh wreaths and their own
  sweeter hair,
Luxurious locks and flower-like mixed
  with flowers,
Clean offering, and chaste hymns; but me
  the time
Divides from these things; whom do thou
  not less
Help and give honor, and to mine hounds
  good speed.
And edge to spears, and luck to each man's
  hand.

CHORUS.

When the hounds of spring are on winter's
    traces,
    The mother of months in meadow or
      plain
Fills the shadows and windy places
    With lisp of leaves and ripple of rain;
And the brown bright nightingale amorous
Is half assuaged for Itylus,
For the Thracian ships and the foreign
    faces,
    The tongueless vigil, and all the pain.

Come with bows bent and with emptying of
    quivers,
    Maiden most perfect, lady of light,
With a noise of winds and many rivers,
    With a clamor 'of waters, and with
      might;
Bind on thy sandals, O thou most fleet,
Over the splendor and speed of thy feet;
For the faint east quickens, the wan west
    shivers,
    Round the feet of the day and the feet
      of the night.

Where shall we find her, how shall we sing
  to her,

Fold our hands round her knees, and
    cling ?
O that man's heart were as fire and could
    spring to her,
    Fire, or the strength of the streams
      that spring !
For the stars and the winds are unto her
As raiment, as songs of the harp-player;
For the risen stars and the fallen cling to
    her,
    And the southwest-wind and the west-
      wind sing.

For winter's rains and ruins are over,
    And all the season of snows and sins;
The days dividing lover and lover,
    The light that loses, the night that
      wins;
And time remembered is grief forgotten,
And frosts are slain and flowers begotten,
And in green underwood and cover
    Blossom by blossom the spring begins.

The full streams feed on flower of rushes,
    Ripe grasses trammel a travelling foot,
The faint fresh flame of the young year
      flushes
From leaf to flower and flower to fruit;
And fruit and leaf are as gold and fire,
And the oat is heard above the lyre,
And the hoofèd heel of a satyr crushes
    The chestnut-husk at the chestnut-
      root.

And Pan by noon and Bacchus by night,
    Fleeter of foot than the fleet-foot kid,
Follows with dancing and fills with de-
      light
The Mænad and the Bassarid ;
And soft as lips that laugh and hide
The laughing leaves of the trees divide,
And screen from seeing and leave in sight
    The god pursuing, the maiden hid.

The ivy falls with the Bacchanal's hair
    Over her eyesbrows hiding her eyes ;
The wild vine slipping down leaves bare
    Her bright breast shortening into
      sighs ;
The wild vine slips with the weight of its
    leaves,
But the berried ivy catches and cleaves
To the limbs that glitter, the feet that
    scare
    The wolf that follows, the fawn that
      flies.

ALTHÆA.

What do ye singing? what is this ye sing?

CHORUS.

Flowers bring we, and pure lips that please
   the gods,
And raiment meet for service ; lest the day
Turn sharp with all its honey in our lips.

ALTHÆA.

Night, a black hound, follows the white
   fawn day,
Swifter than dreams the white flown feet
   of sleep ;
Will ye pray back the night with any
   prayers ?
And though the spring put back a little
   while
Winter, and snows that plague all men for
   sin,
And the iron time of cursing, yet I know
Spring shall be ruined with the rain, and
   storm
Eat up like fire the ashen autumn days.
I marvel what men do with prayers awake
Who dream and die with dreaming ; any
   god,
Yea the least god of all things called di-
   vine,
Is more than sleep and waking ; yet we
   say,
Perchance by praying a man shall match
   his god.
For if sleep have no mercy, and man's
   dreams
Bite t the blood and burn into the bone,
What shall this man do waking ?   By the
   gods,
He shall not pray to dream sweet things
   to-night,
Having dreamt once more bitter things
   than death.

CHORUS.

Queen, but what is it that hath burnt thine
   heart ?
For thy speech flickers like a blown-out
   flame.

ALTHÆA.

Look, ye say well, and know not what ye
   say ;

For all my sleep is turned into a fire,
And all my dreams to stuffs that kindles it.

CHORUS.

Yet one doth well being patient of the
   gods.

ALTHÆA.

Yea, lest they smite us with some four-foot
   plague.

CHORUS.

But when time spreads find out some herb
   for it.

ALTHÆA.

And with their healing herbs infect our
   blood.

CHORUS.

What ails thee to be jealous of their ways ?

ALTHÆA.

What if they give us poisonous drinks for
   wine ?

CHORUS.

They have their will ; much talking mends
   it not.

ALTHÆA.

And gall for milk, and cursing for a prayer ?

CHORUS.

Have they not given life, and the end of
   life ?

ALTHÆA.

Lo, where they heal, they help not ; thus
   they do,
They mock us with a little piteousness,
And we say prayers and weep ; but at the
   last,
Sparing awhile, they smite and spare no
   whit.

CHORUS.

Small praise man gets dispraising the high
   gods ;
What have they done that thou dishonorest
   them ?

ALTHÆA.

First Artemis for all this harried land
I praise not, and for wasting of the boar
That mars with tooth and tusk and fiery
   feet
Green pasturage and the grace of standing
   corn,
And meadow and marsh with springs and
   unblown leaves,
Flocks and swift herds and all that bite
   sweet grass,

I praise her not ; what things are these to praise ?

CHORUS.

But when the king did sacrifice, and gave
Each god fair dues of wheat and blood and
wine,
Her not with bloodshed nor burnt-offering
Revered he, nor with salt or cloven cake ;
Wherefore being wroth she plagued the
land ; but now
Takes off from us fate and her heavy
things.
Which deed of these twain were not good
to praise ?
For a just deed looks always either way
With blameless eyes, and mercy is no
fault.

ALTHÆA.

Yea, but a curse she hath sent above all
these
To hurt us where she healed us, and hath
lit
Fire where the old fire went out, and where
the wind
Slackened, hath blown on us with deadlier
air.

CHORUS.

What storm is this that tightens all our
sail ?

ALTHÆA.

Love, a thwart sea-wind full of rain and
foam.

CHORUS.

Whence blown, and born under what
stormier star ?

ALTHÆA.

Southward across Euenus from the sea.

CHORUS.

Thy speech turns toward Arcadia like
blown wind.

ALTHÆA.

Sharp as the north sets when the snows are
out.

CHORUS.

Nay, for this maiden hath no touch of
love.

ALTHÆA.

I would she had sought in some cold gulf
of sea
Love, or in dens where strange beasts
lurk, or fire,
Or snows on the extreme hills or iron
land

Where no spring is; I would she had
sought therein
And found, or ever love had found her
here.

CHORUS.

She is holier than all holy days or things,
The sprinkled water or fume of perfect
fire;
Chaste, dedicated to pure prayers, and
filled
With higher thoughts than heaven; a
maiden clean,
Pure iron, fashioned for a sword; and
man
She loves not; what should one such do
with love ?

ALTHÆA.

Look you, I speak not as one light of
wit,
But as a queen speaks, being heart-vexed;
for oft
I hear my brothers wrangling in mid hall,
And am not moved; and my son chiding
them,
And these things nowise move me, but I
know
Foolish and wise men must be to the end,
And feed myself with patience; but this
most,
This moves me, that for wise men as for
fools
Love is one thing, an evil thing, and turns
Choice words and wisdom into fire and
air.
And in the end shall no joy come, but
grief,
Sharp words and soul's division and fresh
tears
Flower wise upon the old root of tears
brought forth,
Fruit-wise upon the old flower of tears
sprung up,
Pitiful sighs, and much regrafted pain.
These things are in my presage, and
myself
Am part of them and know not; but in
dreams
The gods are heavy on me, and all the
fates
Shed fire across my eyelids mixed with
night,
And burn me blind, and disilluminate
My sense of seeing, and my perspicuous
soul
Darken with vision; seeing I see not, hear

And hearing am not holpen, but mine eyes
Stain many tender broideries in the bed
Drawn up about my face that I may weep
And the king wake not; and my brows and
  lips
Tremble and sob in sleeping, like swift
  flames
That tremble, or water when it sobs with
  heat
Kindled from under; and my tears fill my
  breast
And speek the fair-dyed pillows round the
  king
With barren showers and salter than the
  sea,
Such dreams divide me dreaming; for
  long since
I dreamed that out of this my womb had
  sprung
Fire and a firebrand; this was ere my son,
Meleager, a goodly flower in fields of fight,
Felt the light touch him coming forth, and
  wailed
Childlike; but yet he was not; and in time
I bare him, and my heart was great; for
  yet
So royally was never strong man born,
Nor queen so nobly bore as noble a thing
As this my son was: such a birth God sent
And such a grace to bear it. Then came
  in
Three weaving women, and span each a
  thread,
Saying This for strength and That for luck,
  and one
Saying Till the brand upon the hearth burn
  down,
So long shall this man see good days and
  live.
And I with gathered raiment from the bed
Sprang, and drew forth the brand, snd cast
  on it
Water, and trod the flame barefoot, and
  crushed
With naked hand spark beaten out of
  spark
And blew against and quenched it; for I
  said,
These are the most high Fates that dwell
  with us,
And we find favor a little in their sight,
A little, and more we miss of, and much
  time
Foils us; howbeit they have pitied me, O
  son,

26

And thee most piteous, thee a tenderer thing
Than any flower of fleshly seed alive.
Wherefore I kissed and hid him with my
  hands,
And covered under arms and hair, and
  wept,
And feared to touch him with my tears,
  and laughed;
So light a thing was this man, grown so
  great
Men cast their heads back, seeing against
  the sun
Blaze the armed man carven on his shield,
  and hear
The laughter of little bells along the brace
Ring, as birds singing or flutes blown, and
  watch,
High up the cloven shadow of either plume
Divide the bright light of the brass, and
  make
His helmet as a windy and wintering
  moon
Seen through blown cloud and plume-like
  drift, when ships
Drive, and men strive with all the sea, and
  oars
Break, and the beaks dip under, drinking
  death;
Yet was he then but a span long, and
  moaned
With inarticulate mouth inseparate words,
And with blind lips and fingers wrung my
  breast
Hard, and thrust out with foolish hands
  and feet,
Murmuring; but those gray women with
  bound hair
Who fright the gods frighted not him; he
  laughed
Seeing them, and pushed out hands to feel
  and haul
Distaff and thread, intangible; but they
Passed, and I hid the brand, and in my
  heart
Laughed likewise, having all my will of
  heaven.
But now I know not if to left or right
The gods have drawn us hither; for
  again
I dreamt, and saw the black brand burst
  on fire
As a branch bursts in flower, and saw the
  flame
Fade flower-wise, and Death came and
  with dry lips

Blew the charred ash into my breast; and
    Love
Trampled the ember and crushed it with
    swift feet.
This I have also at heart; that not for me,
Not for me only or son of mine, O girls,
The gods have wrought life, and desire of
    life,
Heart's love and heart's division; but for
    all
There shines one sun and one wind blows
    till night.
And when night comes the wind sinks and
    the sun,
And there is no light after, and no storm,
But sleep and much forgetfulness of
    things.
In such wise I gat knowledge of the gods
Years hence, and heard high sayings of one
    most wise,
Eurythemis my mother, who beheld
With eyes alive and spake with lips of
    these
As one on earth disfleshed and disallied
From breath or blood corruptible; such
    gifts
Time gave her, and an equal soul to these
And equal face to all things; thus she said.
But whatsoever intolerable or glad
The swift hours weave and unweave, I go
    hence
Full of mine own soul, perfect of myself,
Toward mine and me sufficient; and what
    chance
The gods cast lots for and shake out on us,
That shall we take, and that much bear
    withal
And now, before these gather to the hunt,
I will go arm my son and bring him forth,
Lest love or some man's anger work him
    harm.

CHORUS.

Before the beginning of years,
    There came to the making of man
Time, with a gift of tears;
    Grief, with a glass that ran;
Pleasure, with pain for leaven;
    Summer, with flowers that fell;
Remembrance fallen from heaven,
    And madness risen from hell;
Strength without hands to smite;
    Love that endures for a breath;
Night, the shadow of light,
    And life, the shadow of death.

And the high gods took in hand
    Fire, and the failing of tears,
And a measure of sliding sand
    From under the feet of the years;
And froth and drift of the sea;
    And dust of the laboring earth;
And bodies of things to be
    In the houses of death and of birth;
And wrought with weeping and laughter,
    And fashioned with loathing and love,
With life before and after
    And death beneath and above,
For a day and a night and a morrow,
    That his strength might endure for a span
With travail and heavy sorrow,
    The holy spirit of man.

From the winds of the north and the south
    They gathered as unto strife;
They breathed upon his mouth,
    They filled his body with life;
Eyesight and speech they wrought
    For the veils of the soul therein,
A time for labor and thought,
    A time to serve and to sin;
They gave him light in his ways,
    And love, and a space for delight,
And beauty and length of days,
    And night, and sleep in the night.
His speech is a burning fire;
    With his lips he travaileth;
In his heart is a blind desire,
    In his eyes foreknowledge of death;
He weaves, and is clothed with derision;
    Sows, and he shall not reap;
His life is a watch or a vision
    Between a sleep and a sleep.

MELEAGER.

O sweet new heaven and air without a star,
Fair day, be fair and welcome, as to men
With deeds to do and praise to pluck from
    thee.
Come forth a child, born with clear sound
    and light,
With laughter and swift limbs and pros-
    perous looks;
That this great hunt with heroes for the
    hounds
May leave thee memorable and us well
    sped.

ALTHÆA.

Son, first I praise thy prayer, then bid thee
    speed;

But the gods hear men's hands before their lips,
And heed beyond all crying and sacrifice
Light of things done and noise of laboring men.
But thou being armed and perfect for the deed,
Abide ; for like rain-flakes in a wind they grow,
The men thy fellows, and the choice of the world,
Bound to root out the tuskèd plague, and leave
Thanks and safe days and peace in Calydon.

MELEAGER.

For the whole city and all the low-lying land
Flames, and the soft air sounds with them that come ;
The gods give all these fruit of all their works.

ALTHÆA.

Set thine eye thither and fix thy spirit and say
Whom there thou knowest ; for sharp mixed shadow and wind
Blown up between the morning and the mist,
With steam of steeds and flash of bridle or wheel,
And fire, and parcels of the broken dawn,
And dust divided by hard light, and spears
That shine and shift as the edge of wild beasts' eyes,
Smite upon mine ; so fiery their blind edge
Burns, and bright points break up and baffle day.

MELEAGER.

The first, for many I know not, being far off,
Peleus the Larissæan, couched with whom
Sleeps the white sea-bred wife and silver-shod,
Fair as fled foam, a goddess; and their son
Most swift and splendid of men's children born,
Most like a god, full of the future fame.

ALTHÆA.

Who are these shining like one sundered star ?

MELEAGER.

Thy sister's sons, a double flower of men.

ALTHÆA.

O sweetest kin to me in all the world,
O twin-born blood of Leda, gracious heads
Like kindled lights in untempestuos heaven,
Fair flower-like stars on the iron foam of fight,
With what glad heart and kindliness of soul,
Even to the staining of both eyes with tears
And kindling of warm eyelids with desire,
A great way off I greet you, and rejoice
Seeing you so fair, and moulded like as gods.
Far off ye come, and least in years of these,
But lordliest, but worth love to look upon.

MELEAGER.

Even such (for sailing hither I saw far hence,
And where Eurotas hollows his moist rock
Nigh Sparta with a strenuous-hearted stream)
Even such I saw their sisters ; one swan-white,
The little Helen, and less fair than she
Fair Clytæmnestra, grave as pasturing fawns
Who feed and fear some arrow ; but at whiles,
As one smitten with love or wrung with joy,
She laughs and lightens with her eyes, and then
Weeps ; whereat Helen, having laughed, weeps too,
And the other chides her, and she being chid speaks naught,
But cheeks and lips and eyelids kisses her,
Laughing ; so fare they, as in their bloom-less bud
And full of unblown life, the blood of gods.

ALTHÆA.

Sweet days befall them and good loves and lords,
And tender and temperate honors of the hearth,
Peace, and a perfect life and blameless bed.
But who shows next an eagle wrought in gold,

That flames and beats broad wings against
the sun,
And with void mouth gapes after emptier
prey ?

MELEAGER.

Know by that sign the reign of Telamon
Between the fierce mouths of the encoun-
tering brine
On the strait reefs of twice-washed Salamis.

ALTHÆA.

For like one great of hand he bears himself,
Vine-chapleted, with savors of the sea,
Glittering as wine and moving as a wave.
But who girt round there roughly follows
him ?

MELEAGER.

Ancæus, great of hand, an iron bulk,
Lwo-edged for fight as the axe against his
arm,
Who drives against the surge of stormy
spears
Full-sailed ; him Cepheus follows, his twin-
born,
Chief name next his of all Arcadian men.

ALTHÆA.

Praise be with men abroad ; chaste lives
with us,
Home-keeping days and household rever-
ences.

MELEAGER.

Next by the left unsandalled foot know
thou
The sail and oar of this Ætolian land,
Thy brethren, Toxeus and the violent-
souled
Plexippus, over-swift with hand and tongue;
For hands are fruitful, but the ignorant
mouth
Blows and corrupts their work with barren
breath.

ALTHÆA.

Speech too bears fruit, being worthy ; and
air blows down
Things poisonous, and high-seated violen-
ces,
And with charmed words and songs have
men put out
Wild evil, and the fire of tyrannies.

MELEAGER.

Yea, all things have they, save the gods
and love.

ALTHÆA.

Love thou the law and cleave to things
ordained.

MELEAGER.

Law lives upon their lips whom these
applaud.

ALTHÆA.

How sayest thou these ? what god applauds
new things ?

MELEAGER.

Zeus, who hath fear and custom under foot.

ALTHÆA.

But loves not laws thrown down and lives
awry.

MELEAGER.

Yet is not less himself than his own law.

ALTHÆA.

Nor shifts and shuffles old things up and
down.

MELEAGER.

But what he will remoulds and discreates.

ALTHÆA.

Much, but not this, that each thing live its
life.

MELEAGER.

Nor only live, but lighten and lift up
higher.

ALTHÆA.

Pride breaks itself, and too much gained
is gone?

MELEAGER.

Things gained are gone, but great things
done endure.

ALTHÆA.

Child, if a man serve law through all his
life

And with his whole heart worship, him all
    gods
Praise ; but who loves it only with his lips,
And not in heart and deed desiring it
Hides a perverse will with obsequious
    words,
Him heaven infatuates and his twin-born
    fate
Tracks, and gains on him, scenting sins
    far off.
And the swift hounds of violent death
    devour.
Be man at one with equal-minded gods,
So shall he prosper ; not through laws torn
    up,
Violated rule and a new face of things.
A woman armed makes war upon herself,
Unwomanlike, and treads down use and
    wont
And the sweet common honor that she
    hath,
Love, and the cry of children, and the
    hand
Trothplight and mutual mouth of mar-
    riages.
This doth she, being unloved ; whom if
    one love,
Not fire nor iron and the wide-mouthed
    wars
Are deadlier than her lips or braider hair.
For of the one comes poison, and a curse
Falls from the other and burns the lives of
    men.
But thou, son, be not filled with evil
    dreams,
Nor with desire of these things ; for with
    time
Blind love burns out ; but if one feed it
    full
Till some discoloring stain dyes all his life,
He shall keep nothing praiseworthy, nor
    die
The sweet wise death of old men honor-
    able,
Who have lived out all the length of all
    their years
Blameless, and seen well-pleased the face
    of gods,
And without shame and without fear have
    wrought
Things memorable, and while their days
    held out
In sight of all men and the sun's great
    light

Have gat them glory and given of their
    own praise
To the earth that bare them and the day
    that bred,
Home friends and far-off hospitalities,
And filled with gracious and memorial
    fame
Lands loved of summer or washed by
    violent seas.
Towns populous and many unfooted ways,
And alien lips and native with their own.
But when white age and venerable death
Mow down the strength and life within
    their limbs,
Drain out the blood and darken their clear
    eyes,
Immortal honor is on them, having past
Through splendid life and death desirable
To the clear seat and remote throne of
    souls,
Lands indiscoverable in the unheard-of
    west,
Round which the strong stream of a sacred
    sea
Rolls without wind forever, and the snow
There shows not her white wings and windy
    feet,
Nor thunder nor swift rain saith anything,
Nor the sun burns, but all things rest and
    thrive;
And these, filled full of days, divine and
    dead,
Sages and singers fiery from the god,
And such as loved their land and all things
    good
And, best beloved of best men, liberty,
Free lives and lips, free hands of men free-
    born,
And whatsoever on earth was honorable
And whatsoever of all the ephemeral seed,
Live there a life no liker to the gods
But nearer than their life of terrene days.
Love thou such life and look for such a
    death.
But from the light and fiery dreams of love
Spring heavy sorrows and a sleepless life,
Visions not dreams, whose lids no charm
    shall close
Nor song assuage them walking; and swift
    death
Crushes with sterile feet the unripening
    ear,
Treads out the timeless vintage; whom do
    thou

Eschewing embrace the luck of this thy
life,
Not without honor; and it shall bear to
thee
Such fruit as men reap from spent hours
and wear.
Few men, but happy; of whom be thou, O
son,
Happiest, if thou submit thy soul to fate,
And set thine eyes and heart on hopes
high-born
And divine deeds and abstinence divine.
So shalt thou be toward all men all thy
days
As light and might communicable, and
burn
From heaven among the stars above the
hours,
And break not as a man breaks nor burn
down:
For to whom other of all heroic names
Have the gods given his life in hand as
thine ?
And gloriously hast thou lived, and made
thy life
To me that bare thee and to all men born
Thankworthy, a praise forever; and hast
won fame
When wild wars broke all round thy
father's house,
And the mad people of windy mountain
ways
Laid spears against us like a sea, and all
Ætolia thundered with Thessalian hoofs;
Yet these, as wind baffles the foam, and
beats
Straight back the relaxed ripple, didst thou
break
And loosen all their lances, till undone
And man from man they fell; for ye twain
stood
God against god, Ares and Artemis,
And thou the mightier; wherefore she un-
leashed
A sharp-toothed curse thou too shalt over-
come;
For in the greener blossom of thy life
Ere the full blade caught flower, and when
time gave
Respite, thou didst not slacken soul nor
sleep,
But with great hand and heart seek praise
of men
Out of sharp straits and many a grievous
thing,

Seeing the strange foam of undivided seas
On channels never sailed in, and by shores
Where the old winds cease not blowing,
and all the night
Thunders, and day is no delight to men.

CHORUS.

Meleager, a noble wisdom and fair words
The gods have given this woman; hear
thou these.

MELEAGER.

O mother, I am not fain to strive in speech
Nor set my mouth against thee, who art
wise
Even as they say and full of sacred words.
But one thing I know surely, and cleave to
this;
That though I be not subtle of wit as thou
Nor womanlike to weave sweet words, and
melt
Mutable minds of wise men as with fire,
I too, doing justly and reverencing the
gods,
Shall not want wit to see what things be
right.
For whom they love and whom reject,
being gods,
There is no man but seeth, and in good
time
Submits himself, refraining all his heart.
And I too as thou sayest have seen great
things;
Seen otherwhere, but chiefly when the sail
First caught between stretched ropes the
roaring west,
And all our oars smote eastward, and the
wind
First flung round faces of seafaring men
White splendid snow-flakes of the sunder-
ing foam,
And the first furrow in virginal green sea
Followed the plunging ploughshare of
hewn pine,
And closed, as when deep sleep subdues
man's breath
Lips close and heart subsides; and closing,
shone
Sunlike with many a Nereid's hair, and
moved
Round many a trembling mouth of doubtful
gods,
Risen out of sunless and sonorous gulfs
Through waning water and into shallow
light.

That watched us; and when flying the dove was snared
As with men's hands, but we shot after and sped
Clear through the irremeable Symplegades;
And chiefliest when hoar beach and herb-less cliff
Stood out ahead from Colchis, and we heard
Clefts hoarse with wind, and saw through narrowing reefs
The lightning of the intolerable wave
Flash, and the white wet flame of breakers burn
Far under a kindling south-wind, as a lamp
Burns and bends all its blowing flame one way;
Wild heights untravelled of the wind, and vales
Cloven seaward by their violent streams, and white
With bitter flowers and bright salt scurf of brine;
Heard sweep their sharp swift gales, and bowing birdwise
Shriek with birds' voices, and with furious feet
Tread loose the long skirts of a storm; and saw
The whole white Euxine clash together and fall
Full-mouthed, and thunderous from a thousand throats:
Yet we drew thither and won the fleece and won
Medea, deadlier than the sea; but there
Seeing many a wonder and fearful things to men
I saw not one thing like this one seen here,
Most fair and fearful, feminine, a god,
Faultless; whom I that love not, being unlike,
Fear, and give honor, and choose from all the gods.

OENEUS.

Lady, the daughter of Thestius, and thou, son,
Not ignorant of your strife nor light of wit,
Scared with vain dreams and fluttering like spent fire,
I come to judge between you, but a king
Full of past days and wise from years en-dured.
Nor thee I praise who art fain to undo things done;
Nor thee, who art swift to esteem them overmuch.
For what the hours have given is given, and this
Changeless; howbeit these change, and in good time
Devise new things and good, not one thing still.
Us have they sent now at our need for help
Among men armed a woman, foreign born,
Virgin, not like the natural flower of things
That grows and bears and brings forth fruit and dies;
Unlovable, no light for a husband's house,
Espoused; a glory among unwedded girls,
And chosen of gods who reverence maiden-hood.
These too we honor in honoring her; but thou,
Abstain thy feet from following, and thine eyes
From amorous touch; nor set toward hers thine heart.
Son, lest hate bear no deadlier fruit than love.

ALTHÆA.

O king, thou art wise, but wisdom halts; and just,
But the gods love not justice more than fate,
And smite the righteous and the violent mouth,
And mix with insolent blood the reverent man's,
And bruise the holier as the lying lips.
Enough; for wise words fail me, and my heart
Takes fire and trembles flamewise, O my son,
O child, for thine head's sake; mine eyes wax thick,
Turning toward thee, so goodly a weaponed man,
So glorious; and for love of thine own eyes
They are darkened, and tears burn them, fierce as fire,

And my lips pause and my soul sinks with love.

But by thine hand, by thy sweet life and eyes,

By thy great heart and these clasped knees, O son,

I pray thee that thou slay me not with thee.

For there was never a mother woman-born

Loved her sons better; and never a queen of men

More perfect in her heart toward whom she loved.

For what lies light on many and they forget,

Small things and transitory as a wind o' the sea,

I forget never; I have seen thee all thine years

A man in arms, strong and a joy to men

Seeing thine head glitter and thine hand burn its way

Through a heavy and iron furrow of sundering spears;

But always also a flower of three suns old,

The small one thing that lying drew down my life

To lie with thee and feed thee; a child and weak,

Mine, a delight to no man, sweet to me.

Who then sought to thee? who gat help? who knew

If thou wert goodly? nay, no man at all.

Or what sea saw thee, or sounded with thine oar,

Child? or what strange land shone with war through thee?

But fair for me thou wert, O little life,

Fruitless, the fruit of mine own flesh, and blind,

More than much gold, ungrown, a foolish flower.

For silver nor bright snow nor feather of foam

Was whiter, and no gold yellower than thine hair,

O child, my child; and now thou art lordlier grown,

Not lovelier, nor a new thing in mine eyes,

I charge thee by thy soul and this my breast,

Fear thou the gods and me and thine own heart,

Lest all these turn against thee; for who knows

What wind upon what wave of altering time

Shall speak a storm and blow calamity?

And there is nothing stabile in the world

But the gods break it; yet not less, fair son,

If but one thing be stronger, if one endure,

Surely the bitter and the rooted love

That burns between us, going from me to thee,

Shall more endure than all things. What dost thou,

Following strange loves? why wilt thou kill mine heart?

Lo, I talk wild and windy words, and fall

From my clear wits, and seem of mine own self

Dethroned, dispraised, disseated; and my mind,

That was my crown, breaks, and mine heart is gone,

And I am naked of my soul, and stand

Ashamed, as a mean woman; take thou thought:

Live if thou wilt, and if thou wilt not, look,

The gods have given thee life to lose or keep,

Thou shalt not die as men die, but thine end

Fallen upon thee shall break me unaware.

MELEAGER.

Queen, my whole heart is molten with thy tears,

And my limbs yearn with pity of thee, and love

Compels with grief mine eyes and laboring breath:

For what thou art I know thee, and this thy breast

And thy fair eyes I worship, and am bound

Toward thee in spirit and love thee in all my soul.

For there is nothing terribler to men

Than the sweet face of mothers, and the might.

But what shall be let be; for us the day

Once only lives a little, and is not found.

Time and the fruitful hour are more than we,

And these lay hold upon us; but thou, God,

Zeus, the sole steersman of the helm of things,

Father, be swift to see us, and as thou
  wilt
Help: or if adverse, as thou wilt, refrain.

CHORUS.

We have seen thee, O Love, thou art fair;
  thou art goodly, O Love;
Thy wings make light in the air as the
  wings of a dove.
Thy feet are as winds that divide the
  stream of the sea;
Earth is thy covering to hide thee, the garment of thee.
Thou art swift and subtle and blind as a
  flame of fire;
Before thee the laughter, behind thee the
  tears of desire;
And twain go forth beside thee, a man with
  a maid;
Her eyes are the eyes of a bride whom delight makes afraid;
As the breath in the buds that stir is her
  bridal breath:
But Fate is the name of her; and his name
  is Death.

For an evil blossom was born
  Of sea-foam and the frothing of blood,
  Blood-red and bitter of fruit,
    And the seed of it laughter and
    tears,
And the leaves of it madness and scorn;
  A bitter flower from the bud,
  Sprung of the sea without root,
    Sprung without graft from the years.

The weft of the world was untorn
  That is woven of the day on the night,
The hair of the hours was not white
  Nor the raiment of time over-worn,
  When a wonder, a world's delight,
A perilous goddess was born;
  And the waves of the sea as she came
Clove, and the foam at her feet,
  Fawning, rejoiced to bring forth
  A fleshly blossom, a flame
Filling the heavens with heat
  To the cold white ends of the north.
And in air the clamorous birds,
  And men upon earth that hear
Sweet articulate words
  Sweetly divided apart,
  And in shallow channel and mere
The rapid and footless herds,
  Rejoiced, being foolish of heart.

For all they said upon earth,
  She is fair, she is white like a dove,
  And the life of the world in her breath
Breathes, and is born at her birth;
  For they knew thee for mother of love,
  And knew thee not mother of death.

What hadst thou to do being born,
  Mother, when winds were at ease,
  As a flower of the springtime of corn,
  A flower of the foam of the seas?
For bitter thou wast from thy birth.
  Aphrodite, a mother of strife;
For before thee some rest was on earth,
  A little respite from tears,
  A little pleasure of life;
For life was not then as thou art,
  But as one that waxeth in years
Sweet-spoken, a fruitful wife;
  Earth had no thorn, and desire
No sting, neither death any dart;
  What hadst thou to do among these,
  Thou, clothed with a burning fire,
Thou, girt with sorrow of heart,
  Thou, sprung of the seed of the seas
As an ear from a seed of corn,
  As a brand plucked forth of a pyre,
  As a ray shed forth of the morn,
  For division of soul and disease,
For a dart and a sting and a thorn?
What ailed thee then to be born?
Was there not evil enough,
  Mother, and anguish on earth
Born with a man at his birth,
Wastes underfoot, and above
  Storm out of heaven, and dearth
Shaken down from the shining thereof
  Wrecks from afar overseas
  And peril of shallow and firth,
  And tears that spring and increase
In the barren places of mirth,
That thou, having wings as a dove,
  Being girt with desire for a girth,
  That thou must come after these.
That thou must lay on him love?

Thou shouldst not so have been born:
  But death should have risen with thee,
  Mother, and visible fear,
  Grief, and the wringing of hands,
And noise of many that mourn;
  The smitten bosom, the knee
  Bowed, and in each man's ear
  A cry as of perishing lands,
A moan as of people in prison,

A tumult of infinite griefs;
    And thunder of storm on the sands,
    And wailing of wives on the shore;
And under thee newly arisen,
    Loud shoals and shipwrecking reefs,
    Fierce air and violent light:
Sail rent and sundering oar,
    Darkness and noises of night;
Clashing of streams in the sea,
    Wave against wave as a sword,
    Clamor of currents, and foam;
        Rains making ruin on earth,
        Winds that wax ravenous and roam
As wolves in a wolfish horde;
Fruits growing faint in the tree,
    And blind things dead in their birth;
    Famine, and blighting of corn,
    When thy time was come to be born.

All these we know of ; but thee
    Who shall discern or declare ?
In the uttermost ends of the sea
    The light of thine eyelids and hair,
    The light of thy bosom as fire
        Between the wheel of the sun
And the flying flames of the air ?
    Wilt thou turn thee not yet nor have pity,
But abide with despair and desire
    And the crying of armies undone,
        Lamentation of one with another,
    And breaking of city by city;
The dividing of friend against friend,
    The severing of brother and brother;
Wilt thou utterly bring to an end ?
    Have mercy, mother !

For against all men from of old
    Thou hast set thine hand as a curse,
    And cast out gods from their places.
        These things are spoken of thee.
Strong kings and goodly with gold
    Thou hast found out arrows to pierce,
    And made their kingdoms and races
        As dust and surf of the sea.
All these, overburdened with woes
    And with length of their days waxen
        weak,
        Thou slewest; and sentest moreover
        Upon Tyro an evil thing.
Rent hair and a fetter and blows
    Making bloody the flower of the cheek,
        Though she lay by a god as a lover,
        Though fair, and the seed of a king.
For of old, being full of thy fire,

She endured not longer to wear
    On her bosom a saffron vest,
        On her shoulder an ashwood quiver;
Being mixed and made one through desire.
    With Enipeus and all her hair
        Made moist with his mouth, and her
            breast
        Filled full of the foam of the river.

ATALANTA.

Sun, and clear light among green hills, and
    day
Late risen and long sought after, and you
    just gods
Whose hands divide anguish and recom-
    pense,
But first the sun's white sister, a maid in
    heaven,
On earth of all maids worshipped,—hail,
    and hear,
And witness with me if not without sign
    sent,
Not without rule and reverence, I a maid
Hallowed, and huntress holy as whom I
    serve,
Here in your sight and eyeshot of these
    men
Stand, girt as they toward hunting, and my
    shafts
Drawn; wherefore all ye stand up on my
    side,
If I be pure and all ye righteous gods,
Lest one revile me, a woman, yet no wife,
That bear a spear for spindle, and this
    bow strung
For a web woven ; and with pure lips
    salute
Heaven, and the face of all the gods, and
    dawn
Filling with maiden flames and maiden
    flowers
The starless fold o' the stars, and making
    sweet
The warm wan heights of the air, moon-
    trodden ways
And breathless gates and extreme hills of
    heaven,
Whom, having offered water and bloodless
    gifts,
Flowers, and a golden circlet of pure hair,
Next Artemis I bid be favorable
And make this day all golden, hers and
    ours,
Gracious and good and white to the un-
    blamed end.

But thou, O well-beloved, of all my days
Bid it be fruitful, and a crown for all,
To bring forth leaves and bind round all
  my hair
With perfect chaplets woven for thine of
  thee.
For not without the word of thy chaste
  mouth,
For not without law given and clean com-
  mand,
Across the white straits of the running sea
From Elis even to the Acheloïan horn
I with clear winds came hither and gentle
  gods,
Far off my father's house, and left un-
  cheered
Iasius, and uncheered the Arcadian hills
And all their green-haired waters, and all
  woods
Disconsolate to hear no horn of mine
Blown, and behold no flash of swift white
  feet.

MELEAGER.

For thy name's sake and awe toward thy
  chaste head,
O holiest Atalanta, no man dares
Praise thee, though fairer than whom all
  men praise,
And godlike for thy grace of hallowed
  hair
And holy habit of thine eyes and feet
That make the blown foam neither swift
  nor white
Though the wind winnow and whirl it; yet
  we praise
Gods, found because of thee adorable
And for thy sake praiseworthiest from all
  men:
Thee therefore we praise also, thee as
  these,
Pure, and light lit at the hands of gods.

TOXEUS.

How long will ye whet spears with elo-
  quence,
Fight and kill beasts dry-handed with
  sweet words?
Cease, or talk still and slay thy boars at
  home.

PLEXIPPUS.

Why, if she ride among us for a man,
Sit thou for her and spin; a man grown
  girl

Is worth a woman weaponed; sit thou
  here

MELEAGER.

Peace, and be wise; no gods love idle
  speech

PLEXIPPUS.

Nor any man a man's mouth woman-
  tongued.

MELEAGER.

For my lips bite not sharper than mine
  hands.

PLEXIPPUS.

Nay, both bite soft, but no whit softly
  mine.

MELEAGER.

Keep thine hands clean; they have time
  enough to stain.

PLEXIPPUS.

For thine shall rest and wax not red to-
  day.

MELEAGER.

Have all thy will of words; talk out thine
  heart.

ALTHÆA.

Refrain your lips, O brethren, and my
  son,
Lest words turn snakes and bite you uttering them.

TOXEUS.

Except she give her blood before the gods,
What profit shall a maid be among men?

PLEXIPPUS.

Let her come crowned and stretch ner
  throat for a knife,
Bleat out her spirit and die, and so shall
  men
Through her too prosper and through
  prosperous gods;
But nowise through her living; shall she
  live
A flower-bud of the flower bed, or sweet
  fruit
For kisses and the honey-making mouth,
And play the shield for strong men and the
  spear?
Then shall the heifer and her mate lock
  horns,

And the bride overbear the groom, and
    men
Gods; for no less division sunders these;
Since all things made are seasonable in
    time,
But if one alter unseasonable are all.
But thou, O Zeus, hear me that I may
    slay
This beast before thee and no man halve
    with me
Nor woman, lest these mock thee, though
    a god,
Who hast made men strong, and thou be-
    ing wise be held
Foolish ; for wise is that thing which en-
    dures.

ATALANTA.

Men, and the chosen of all this people, and
    thou,
King, I beseech you a little bear with
    me.
For if my life be shameful that I live,
Let the gods witness and their wrath; but
    these
Cast no such word against me. Thou, O
    mine,
O holy, O happy goddess, if I sin
Changing the words of women and the
    works
For spears and strange men's faces, hast
    not thou
One shaft of all thy sudden seven that
    pierced
Seven through the bosom or shining throat
    or side,
All couched about one mothers' loosening
    knees,
All holy born, engraffed of Tantalus?
But if toward any of you I am overbold
That take thus much upon me, let him
    think
How I, for all my forest holiness,
Fame, and this armed and iron maiden-
    hood,
Pay thus much also; I shall have no man's
    love
Forever, and no face of children born
Or feeding lips upon me or fastening eyes
Forever, nor being dead shall kings my
    sons
Mourn me and bury, and tears on daughter's
    cheeks
Burn ; but a cold and sacred life, but
    strange,

But far from dances and the back-blowing
    torch,
Far off from flowers or any bed of man
Shall my life be forever: me the snows
That face the first o' the morning, and cold
    hills
Full of the land-wind and sea-travelling
    storms
And many a wandering wing of noisy
    nights
That know the thunder and hear the thick-
    ening wolves—
Me the utmost pine and footless frost of
    woods
That talk with many winds and gods, the
    hours
Re-risen, and white divisions of the dawn,
Springs thousand-tongued with the inter-
    mitting reed
And streams that murmur of the mother
    snow—
Me these allure, and know me ; but no
    man
Knows, and my goddess only. Lo now,
    see,
If one of all you these things vex at all.
Would God that any of you had all the
    praise
And I no manner of memory when I die,
So might I show before her perfect eyes
Pure, whom I follow, a maiden to my
    death.
But for the rest let all have all they will;
For is it a grief to you that I have part,
Being woman merely, in your male might
    and deeds
Done by main strength ? yet in my body is
    throned
As great a heart, and in my spirit, O
    men,
I have not less of godlike. Evil it were
That one a coward should mix with you,
    one hand
Fearful, one eye abase itself ; and these
Well might ye hate and well revile, not
    me.
For not the difference of the several flesh
Being vile or noble or beautiful or base
Makes praiseworthy, but purer spirit and
    heart
Higher than these meaner mouths and
    limbs, that feed,
Rise, rest, and are and are not; and for me,
What should I say ? but by the gods of the
    world

And this my maiden body, by all oaths
That bind the tongue of men and the evil
will,
I am not mighty-minded, nor desire
Crowns, nor the spoil of slain things nor
the fame;
Feed ye on these, eat and wax fat ; cry
out,
Laugh, having eaten, and leap without a
lyre
Sing, mix the wind with clamor, smite and
shake
Sonorus timbrels and tumultuous hair,
And fill the dance up with tempestuous
feet,
For I will none; but having prayed my
prayers
And made thank-offering for prosperities,
I shall go hence and no man see me more.
What thing is this for you to shout me
down,
What, for a man to grudge me this my
life
As it were envious of all yours, and I
A thief of reputations ? nay, for now,
If there be any highest in heaven, a god
Above all thrones and thunders of the
gods
Throned, and the wheel of the world roll
under him,
Judge he between me and all of you, and
see
If I transgress at all: but ye, refrain
Transgressing hands and reinless mouths,
and keep
Silence, less by much foam of violent words
And proper poison of your lips ye die.

ŒNEUS.

O flower of Tega, maiden, fleetest foot
And holiest head of women, have good
cheer
Of thy good words : but ye, depart with
her
In peace and reverence, each with blameless eye
Following his fate; exalt your hands and
hearts,
Strike, cease not, arrow on arrow and
wound on wound,
And go with gods and with the gods
return.

CHORUS.

Who hath given man speech ? or who hath
set therein

A thorn for peril and a snare for sin ?
For in the word his life is and his breath,
And in the word his death,
That madness and the infatuate heart may
breed
From the word's womb the deed
And life bring one thing forth ere all pass
by,
Even one thing which is ours yet cannot
die—
Death. Hast thou seen him ever any-
where,
Time's twin-born brother, imperishable as
he
Is perishable and plaintive, clothed with
care
And mutable as sand,
But death is strong and full of blood and
fair
And perdurable and like a lord of land ?
Nay, time thou seest not, death thou wilt
not see
Till life's right hand be loosened from
thine hand
And thy life-days from thee.
For the gods very subtly fashion
Madness with sadness upon earth :
Not knowing in anywise compassion,
Nor holding pity of any worth;
And many things they have given and
taken,
And wrought and ruined many things;
The firm land have they loosed and
shaken,
And sealed the sea with all her springs ;
They have wearied time with heavy burdens
And vexed the lips of life with breath :
Set men to labor and given them guerdons,
Death and great darkness after death :
Put moans into the bridal measure
And on the bridal wools a stain :
And circled pain about with pleasure,
And girdled pleasure about with pain ;
And strewed one marriage-bed with tears
and fire
For extreme loathing and supreme desire.

What shall be done with all these tears of
ours ?
Shall they make watersprings in the
fair heaven
To bathe the brows of morning ? or like
flowers
Be shed and shine before the starriest
hours,

Or made the raiment of the weeping
Seven?
Or rather, O our masters, shall they be
Food for the famine of the grievous sea,
A great well-head of lamentation
Satiating the sad gods? or fall and flow
Among the years and seasons to and fro,
And wash their feet with tribulation
And fill them full with grieving ere they
go?
Alas, our lords, and yet alas again,
Seeing all your iron heaven is gilt as gold
But all we smite thereat in vain;
Smite the gates barred with groanings
manifold,
But all the floors are paved with our
pain.
Yea, and with the weariness of lips and
eyes,
With breaking of the bosom, and with
sighs,
We labor, and are clad and fed with
grief
And filled with days we would not fain
behold
And nights we would not hear of; we wax
old,
All we wax old and wither like a leaf.
We are outcast, strayed between bright sun
and moon;
Our light and darkness are as leaves of
flowers,
Black flowers and white, that perish; and
the noon
As midnight, and the night as daylight
hours.
A little fruit a little while is ours
And the worm finds it soon.

But up in heaven the high gods one by one
Lay hands upon the draught that quick-
eneth,
Fulfilled with all tears shed and all things
done,
And stir with soft imperishable breath
The bubbling bitterness of life and
death,
And hold it to our lips and laugh; but
they
Preserve their lips from tasting night or
day,
Lest they too change and sleep, the fates
that spun,
The lips that made us and the hands that
slay:

Lest all these change, and heaven bow
down to none,
Change and be subject to the secular sway
And terrene revolution of the sun.
Therefore they thrust it from them, putting
time away.
I would the wine of time, made sharp and
sweet
With multitudinous days and nights and
tears
And many mixing savors of strange
years,
Were no more trodden of them under feet,
Cast out and spilt about their holy
places:
That life were given them as a fruit to
eat
And death to drink as water; that the
light
Might ebb, drawn backward from their
eyes, and night
Hide for one hour the imperishable
faces.
That they might rise up sad in heaven,
and know
Sorrow and sleep, one paler than young
snow,
One cold as blight of dew and ruinous
rain;
Rise up and rest and suffer a little, and
be
Awhile as all things born with us, and
we,
And grieve as men, and like slain men
be slain.

For now we know not of them; but one
saith
The gods are gracious, praising God;
and one,
When hast thou seen? or hast thou felt
his breath
Touch nor consume thy eyelids as the
sun,
Nor fill thee to the lips with fiery death?
None hath beheld him, none
Seen above other gods and shapes of
things,
Swift without feet and flying without
wings,
Intolerable, not clad with death or life,
Insatiable, not known of night or day,
The lord of love and loathing and of
strife
Who gives a star and takes a sun away;

Who shapes the soul, and makes her a bar-
ren wife
    To the earthy body and grievous growth
      of clay ;
Who turns the large limbs to a little flame
And binds the great sea with a little
    sand ;
Who makes desire, and slays desire with
    shame ;
    Who shakes the heaven as ashes in his
      hand ;
Who, seeing the light and shadow for the
    same,
    Bids day waste night as fire devours a
      brand,
Smites without sword, and scourges with-
    out rod ;
      The supreme evil, God.

Yea, with thine hate, O God, thou hast
    covered us,
    One saith, and hidden our eyes away
      from sight,
And made us transitory and hazardous,
    Light things and slight;
Yet have men praised thee, saying, He
    hath made man thus,
    And he doeth right.
Thou hast kissed us, and hath smitten ;
    thou hast laid
Upon us with thy left hand life, and said,
    Live: and again thou hast said, Yield up
      your breath,
And with thy right hand laid upon us
    death.
Thou hast sent us sleep, and stricken sleep
    with dreams,
    Saying, Joy is not, but love of joy shall
      be ;
Thou hast made sweet springs for all the
    pleasant streams,
    In the end thou hast made them bitter
      with the sea.
Thou hast fed one rose with dust of many
    men ;
    Thou hast marred one face with fire of
      many tears ;
    Thou hast taken love, and given us sor-
      row again ;
With pain thou hast filled us full to the
    eyes and ears.
Therefore because thou art strong, our
    father, and we
    Feeble ; and thou art against us, and
      thine hand

Constrains us in the shallows of the sea
    And breaks us at the limits of the land ;
Because thou hast bent thy lightnings as a
    bow,
    And loosed the hours like arrows ; and
      let fall
Sins and wild words and many a wingèd
    woe
    And wars among us, and one end of all;
Because thou hast made the thunder, and
    thy feet
Are as rushing water when the skies
Break, but thy face as an exceeding heat
    And flames of fire the eyelids of thine
      eyes ;
Because thou art over all who are over us;
    Because thy name is life and our name
      death ;
Because thou art cruel and men are piteous,
    And our hands labor and thine hand
      scattereth ;
Lo, with hearts rent and knees made
    tremulous,
    Lo, with ephemeral lips and casual
      breath,
    At least we witness of thee ere we die
That these things are not otherwise, but
    thus ;
    That each man in his heart sigheth. and
      saith,
    That all men even as I,
All we are against thee, against thee, O
    God most high.

But ye, keep ye on earth
    Your lips from over-speech,
Loud words and longing are so little
    worth ;
    And the end is hard to reach.
For silence after grievous things is good,
    And reverence, and the fear that makes
      men whole,
And shame, and righteous governance of
    blood,
    And lordship of the soul.
But from sharp words and wits men pluck
    no fruit,
And gathering thorns they shake the tree
    at root ;
For words divide and rend ;
But silence is most noble to the end.

ALTHÆA.

I heard within the house a cry of news
And came forth eastward hither, where the
    dawn

Cheers first these warder gods that face the
　　sun
And next our eyes unrisen ; for unaware
Came clashes of swift hoofs and trampling
　　feet
And through the windy pillared corridor
Light sharper than the frequent flames of
　　day
That daily fill it from the fiery dawn;
Gleams, and a thunder of people that cried
　　out,
And dust and hurrying horsemen; lo their
　　chief,
That rode with Œneus rein by rein, re-
　　turned.
What cheer, O herald of my lord the king ?

HERALD.

Lady, good cheer and great; the boar is
　　slain.

CHORUS.

Praised be all gods that look toward
　　Calydon.

ALTHÆA.

Good news and brief ; but by whose hap-
　　pier hand ?

HERALD.

A maiden's and a prophet's and thy son's.

ALTHÆA.

Well fare the spear that severed him and
　　life.

HERALD.

Thine own, and not an alien, hast thou
　　blest.

ALTHÆA.

Twice be thou too for my sake blest and
　　his.

HERALD.

At the king's word I rode afoam for thine.

ALTHÆA,

Thou sayest he tarrieth till they bring the
　　spoil ?

HERALD.

Hard by the quarry, where they breathe,
　　O queen.

ALTHÆA.

Speak thou their chance; but some bring
　　flowers and crown

These gods and all the lintel, and shed
　　wine,
Fetch sacrifice and slay; for heaven is
　　good.

HERALD.

Some furlongs northward where the brakes
　　begin
West of that narrowing range of warrior
　　hills
Whose brooks have bled with battle when
　　thy son
Smote Acarnania, there all they made
　　halt,
And with keen eye took note of spear and
　　hound,
Royally ranked; Laertes island-born,
The young Gerenian Nestor, Panopeus,
And Cepheus and Ancæus, mightiest
　　thewed,
Arcadians; next, and evil-eyed of these,
Arcadian Atalanta, with twain hounds
Lengthening the leash, and under nose and
　　brow
Glittering with lipless tooth and fire-swift
　　eye ;
But from her white-braced shoulder the
　　plumed shafts
Rang, and the bow shone from her side ;
　　next her
Meleager; like a sun in spring that strikes
Branch into leaf and bloom into the world,
A glory among men meaner; Iphicles,
And following him that slew the biform
　　bull
Pirithous, and divine Eurytion,
And, bride-bound to the gods, Æacides.
Then Telamon his brother, and Argive-
　　born
The seer and sayer of visions and of truth,
Amphiaraus; and a fourfold strength,
Thine, even thy mother's and thy sister's
　　sons.
And recent from the roar of foreign foam
Jason; and Dryas twin-begot with war,
A blossom of bright battle, sword and
　　man
Shining; and Idas, and the keenest eye
Of Lynceus, and Admetus twice-espoused,
And Hippasus and Hyleus, great in heart.
These having halted bade blow horns, and
　　rode
Through woods and waste lands cleft by
　　stormy streams,
Past yew-trees and the heavy hair of pines,

And where the dew is thickest under oaks,
This way and that; but questing up and
    down
They saw no trail nor scented; and one
    said,
Plexippus, Help, or help not, Artemis,
And we will flay thy boarskin with male
    hands;
But saying, he ceased and said not that he
    would,
Seeing where the green ooze of a sun-struck
    marsh
Shook with a thousand reeds untunable,
And in their moist and multitudinous
    flower
Slept no soft sleep, with violent visions
    fed,
The blind bulk of the immeasurable beast.
And seeing, he shuddered with sharp lust
    of praise
Through all his limbs, and launched a
    double dart,
And missed; for much desire divided him,
Too hot of spirit and feebler than his will,
That his hand failed, though fervent; and
    the shaft,
Sundering the rushes, in a tamarisk stem
Shook, and stuck fast; then all abode save
    one,
The Arcadian Atalanta; from her side
Sprang her hounds, laboring at the leash,
    and slipped,
And plashed ear-deep with plunging feet;
    but she
Saying, Speed it as I send it for thy sake,
Goddess, drew bow and loosed; the sudden
    string
Rang, and sprang inward, and the waterish
    air
Hissed, and the moist plumes of the song-
    less reeds
Moved as a wave which the wind moves
    no more.
But the boar heaved half out of ooze and
    slime
His tense flank trembling round the barbéd
    wound,
Hateful; and fiery with invasive eyes
    And bristling with intolerable hair
Plunged, and the hounds clung, and green
    flowers and white
Reddened and broke all round them where
    they came.
And charging with sheer tusk he drove,
    and smote

27

Hyleus; and sharp death caught his sudden
    soul,
And violent sleep shed night upon his
    eyes.
Then Peleus, with strong strain of hand
    and heart,
Shot; but the sidelong arrow slid, and
    slew
His comrade born and loving country-
    man,
Under the left arm smitten, as he no less
Poised a like arrow; and bright blood
    break afoam,
And falling, and weighed back by clamor-
    ous arms,
Sharp rang the dead limbs of Eurytion.
Then one shot happier, the Cadmean seer,
Amphiaraus; for his sacred shaft
Pierced the red circlet of one ravening
    eye
Beneath the brute brows of the sanguine
    boar,
Now bloodier from one slain; but he so
    galled
Sprang straight, and rearing cried no lesser
    cry
Than thunder and the roar of wintering
    streams
That mix their own foam with the yellower
    sea;
And as a tower that falls by fire in fight
With ruin of walls and all its archery,
And breaks the iron flower of war be-
    neath,
Crushing charred limbs and molten arms
    of men;
So through crushed branches and the
    reddening brake
Clamored and crashed the fervor of his
    feet,
And trampled, springing sideways from
    the tusk,
Too tardy a moving mould of heavy
    strength,
Ancæus; and as flakes of weak-winged
    snow
Break, all the hard thews of his heaving
    limbs
Broke, and rent flesh fell every way, and
    blood
Flew, and fierce fragments of no more a
    man.
Then all the heroes drew sharp breath, and
    gazed,
And smote not; but Meleager, but thy son,

Right in the wild way of the coming curse
Rock-rooted, fair with fierce and fastened
  lips,
Clear eyes, and springing muscle and
  shortening limb—
With chin aslant indrawn to a tightening
  throat,
Grave, and with gathered sinews, like a
  god,—
Aimed on the left side his well-handled
  spear
Grasped where the ash was knottiest hewn,
  and smote,
And with no missile wound, the monstrous
  boar
Right in the hairiest hollow of his hide
Under the last rib, sheer through bulk and
  bone,
Deep in; and deeply smitten, and to death,
The heavy horror with his hanging shafts
Leapt, and fell furiously, and from raging
  lips
Foamed out the latest wrath of all his life.
And all they praised the gods with mightier
  heart,
Zeus and all gods, but chiefliest Artemis,
Seeing; but Meleager bade whet knives and
  flay,
Strip and stretch out the splendor of the
  spoil;
And hot and horrid from the work all
  these
Sat, and drew breath and drank and made
  great cheer
And washed the hard sweat off their calmer
  brows.
For much sweet grass grew higher than
  grew the reed,
And good for slumber, and every holier
  herb,
Narcissus, and the low-lying melilote,
And all of goodliest blade and bloom that
  springs
Where, hid by heavier hyacinth, violet
  buds
Blossom and burn; and fire of yellower
  flowers
And light of crescent lilies, and such leaves
As fear the Faun's and know the Dryad's
  foot;
Olive and ivy and poplar dedicate,
And many a wellspring overwatched of
  these.
There now they rest; but me the king bade
  bear

Good tidings to rejoice this town and thee.
Wherefore be glad, and all ye give much
  thanks
For fallen is all the trouble of Calydon.

ALTHÆA.

Laud ye the gods; for this they have given
  is good
And what shall be they hide until their
  time.
Much good and somewhat grievous* hast
  thou said,
And either well; but let all sad things be,
Till all have made before the prosperous
  gods
Burnt-offering, and poured out the floral
  wine.
Look fair, O gods, and favorable; for we
Praise you with no false heart or flattering
  mouth
Being merciful, but with pure souls and
  prayer.

HERALD.

Thou hast prayed well; for whoso fears
  not these,
But once being prosperous waxes huge of
  heart,
Him shall some new thing unaware destroy.

CHORUS.

O that I now, I too were
By deep wells and water-floods,
Streams of ancient hills, and where
All the wan green places bear
Blossoms cleaving to the sod,
Fruitless fruit, and grasses fair
Or such darkest ivy-buds
As divide thy yellow hair,
Bacchus, and their leaves that nod
Round thy fawnskin brush the bare
Snow-soft shoulders of a god;
There the year is sweet, and there
Earth is full of secret springs,
And the fervent rose-cheeked hours,
Those that marry dawn and noon,
There are sunless, there look pale
In dim leaves and hidden air,
Pale as grass or latter flowers
Or the wild vine's wan wet rings
Full of dew beneath the moon,
And all day the nightingale
Sleeps, and all night sings;
There in cold remote recesses

That nor alien eye assail,
Feet, nor imminence of wings.
Nor a wind nor any tune,
Thou, O queen and holiest,
Flower the whitest of all things,
With reluctant lengthening tresses
And with sudden splendid breast
Save of maidens unbeholden,
There are wont to enter, there
Thy divine sweet limbs and golden
Maiden growth of unbound hair,
Bathed in waters white,
Shine, and many a maid's by thee
In moist woodland or the hilly
Flowerless brakes where wells abound
Out of all men's sight;
Or in lower pools that see
All their marges clothed all round
With the innumerable lily,
Whence the golden-girdled bee
Flits through flowering rush to fret
White or duskier violet,
Fair as those that in far years
With their buds left luminous
And their little leaves made wet
From the warmer dew of tears,
Mother's tears in extreme need,
Hid the limbs of Iamus,
Of thy brother's seed;
For his heart was piteous
Toward him, even as thine heart now
Pitiful toward us;
Thine, O goddess, turning hither
A benignant blameless brow;
Seeing enough of evil done
And lives withered as leaves wither
In the blasting of the sun;
Seeing enough of hunters dead,
Ruin enough of all our year,
Herds and harvests slain and shed
Herdsmen stricken many an one,
Fruits and flocks consumed together,
And great length of deadly days.
Yet with reverent lips and fear
Turn we toward thee, turn and praise
For this lightening of clear weather
And prosperities begun.
For not seldom, when all air
As bright water without breath
Shines, and when men fear not, fate
Without thunder unaware
Breaks, and brings down death.
Joy with grief ye great gods give,
Good with bad, and overbear
All the pride of us that live,

All the high estate,
As ye long since overbore,
As in old time long before,
Many a strong man and a great,
All that were.
But do thou, sweet, otherwise,
Having heed of all our prayer,
Taking note of all our sighs;
We beseech thee by thy light,
By thy bow, and thy sweet eyes,
And the kingdom of the night,
Be thou favorable and fair;
By thine arrows and thy might
And Orion overthrown;
By the maiden thy delight,
By the indissoluble zone
And the sacred hair.

MESSENGER.

Maidens, if ye will sing now, shift your
song,
Bow down, cry, wail for pity; is this a
time
For singing ? nay, for strewing of dust and
ash,
Rent raiment, and for bruising of the
breast.

CHORUS.

What new thing wolf-like lurks behind thy
words ?
What snake's tongue in thy lips ? what fire
in the eyes ?

MESSENGER.

Bring me before the queen and I will
speak.

CHORUS.

Lo, she comes forth as from thank-offering
made.

MESSENGER.

A barren offering for a bitter gift

ALTHÆA.

What are these borne on branches, and the
face
Covered ? no mean men living, but now
slain
Such honor have they, if any dwell with
death.

MESSENGER.

Queen, thy twain brethren and thy mother's
sons,

ALTHÆA.

Lay down your dead till I behold their
    blood
If it be mine indeed, and I will weep.

MESSENGER.

Weep if thou wilt, for these men shall no
    more.

ALTHÆA.

O brethren, O my father's sons, of me
Well loved and well reputed, I should
    weep
Tears dearer than the dear blood drawn
    from you
But that I know you not uncomforted,
Sleeping no shameful sleep, however slain,
For my son surely hath avenged you dead.

MESSENGER.

Nay, should thine own seed slay himself,
    O queen ?

ALTHÆA.

Thy double word brings forth a double
    death.

MESSENGER.

Know this then singly, by one hand they
    fell.

ALTHÆA.

What mutterest thou with thine ambiguous
    mouth ?

MESSENGER.

Slain by thy son's hand; is that saying so
    hard ?

ALTHÆA.

Our time is come upon us: it is here.

CHORUS.

O miserable, and spoiled at thine own
    hand.

ALTHÆA.

Wert thou not called Meleager from this
    womb ?

CHORUS.

A grievous huntsman hath it bred to thee.

ALTHÆA.

Wert thou born fire, and shalt thou not
    devour ?

CHORUS.

The fire thou madest, will it consume even
    thee ?

ALTHÆA.

My dreams are fallen upon me; burn thou
    too.

CHORUS.

Not without God are visions born and die.

ALTHÆA.

The gods are many about me; I am one.

CHORUS.

She groans as men wrestling with heavier
    gods.

ALTHÆA.

They rend me, they divide me, they de-
    stroy.

CHORUS.

Or one laboring in travail of strange births.

ALTHÆA.

They are strong, they are strong; I am
    broken, and these prevail.

CHORUS.

The god is great against her; she will die.

ALTHÆA.

Yea, but not now; for my heart too is
    great.
I would I were not here in sight of the sun.
But thou, speak all thou sawest, and I will
    die.

MESSENGER.

O queen, for queenlike hast thou borne
    thyself,
A little word may hold so great mischance.
For in division of the sanguine spoil
These men thy brethren wrangling bade
    yield up
The boar's head and the horror of the hide,
That this might stand a wonder in Caly-
    don,
Hallowed; and some drew toward them ;
    but thy son,
With great hands grasping all that weight
    of hair,
Cast down the dead heap clanging and
    collapsed
At female feet, saying, This thy spoil, not
    mine,
Maiden, thine own hand for thyself hath
    reaped,

And all this praise God gives thee: she
  thereat
Laughed, as when dawn touches the sacred
  night
The sky sees laugh and redden and divide
Dim lips and eyelids virgin of the sun,
Hers, and the warm slow breasts of morn-
  ing heave,
Fruitful, and flushed with flame from lamp-
  lit hours,
And maiden undulation of clear hair
Color the clouds; so laughed she from pure
  heart
Lit with a low blush to the braided hair,
And rose-colored and cold like very dawn,
Golden and godlike, chastely with chaste
  lips
A faint, grave laugh; and all they held
  their peace,
And she passed by them. Then one cried,
  Lo now,
Shall not the Arcadian shoot out lips
  at us,
Saying all we were despoiled by this one
  girl ?
And all they rode against her violently
And cast the fresh crown from her hair,
  and now
They had rent her spoil away, dishonoring
  her,
Save that Meleager, as a tame lion chafed,
Bore on them, broke them, as fire cleaves
  wood
So clove and drove them, smitten in twain;
  but she
Smote not nor heaved up hand; and this
  man first,
Plexippus, crying out, this for Love's sake,
  sweet,
Drove at Meleager, who with spear
  straightening
Pierced his cheek through; then Toxeus
  made for him,
Dumb, but his spear spake; vain and vio-
  lent words,
Fruitless; for him too, stricken through
  both sides,
The earth felt falling, and his horse's
  foam
Blanched thy son's face, his slayer; and
  these being slain,
None moved nor spake; but Œneus bade
  bear hence
These made of heaven infatuate in their
  deaths,

Foolish ; for these would baffle fate, and
  fell,
And they passed on, and all men honored
  her,
Being honorable, as one revered of heaven.

ALTHÆA.

What say ye, Women ? is all this not well
  done ?

CHORUS.

No man doth well but God hath part in
  him.

ALTHÆA.

But no part here; for these my brethren
  born
Ye have no part in, these ye know not of
As I that was their sister, a sacrifice
Slain in their slaying. I would I had died
  for these;
For this man dead walked with me, child
  by child,
And made a weak staff for my feebler feet
With his own tender wrist and hand, and
  held
And led me softly, and showed me gold
  and steel
And shining shapes of mirror and bright
  crown
And all things fair; and threw light spears,
  and brought
Young hounds to huddle at my feet and
  thrust
Tame heads against my little maiden
  breasts,
And please me with great eyes; and those
  days went,
And these are bitter, and I a barren
  queen
And sister miserable, a grievous thing
And mother of many curses ; and she
  too,
My sister Leda, sitting overseas
With fair fruits round her, and her faultless
  lord,
Shall curse me, saying, A sorrow and not
  a son,
Sister, thou barest, even a burning fire
A brand consuming thine own soul and
  me.
But ye now, sons of Thestius, make good
  cheer,
For ye shall have such wood to funeral
  fire

As no king hath; and flame that once burnt down
Oil shall not quicken or breath relume or wine
Refresh again; much costlier than fine gold,
And more than many lives of wandering men.

CHORUS.

O queen, thou hast yet with thee love-worthy things,
Thine husband, and the great strength of thy son.

ALTHÆA,

Who shall get brothers for me while I live ?
Who bear them ? who bring forth in lieu of these ?
Are not our fathers and our brethren one,
And no man like them ? are not mine here slain ?
Have we not hung together, he and I,
Flowerwise feeding as the feeding bees,
With mother-milk for honey ? and this man too,
Dead, with my son's spear thrust between his sides,
Hath he not seen us, later born than he,
Laugh with lips filled, and laughed again for love ?
There were no sons then in the world, nor spears,
Nor deadly births of women ; but the gods
Allowed us, and our days were clear of these.
I would I had died unwedded, and brought forth
No swords to vex the world; for these that spake
Sweet words long since and loved me will not speak
Nor love nor look upon men ; and all my life
I shall not hear nor see them living men.
But I too living, how shall I now live ?
What life shall this be with my son, to know
What hath been and desire what will not be,
Look for dead eyes and listen for dead lips,
And kill mine own heart with remembering them,

And with those eyes that see the slayer alive
Weep, and wring hands that clasp him by the hand ?
How shall I bear my dreams of them, to hear
False voices, feel the kisses of false mouths
And footless sound of perished feet, and then
Wake and hear only it may be their own hounds
Whine masterless in miserable sleep,
And see their boar spears and their beds and seats
And all the gear and housings of their lives
And not the men ? shall hounds and horses mourn,
Pine with strange eyes, and prick up hungry ears,
Famish and fail at heart for their dear lords,
And I not heed at all ? and those blind things
Fall off from life for love's sake, and I live ?
Surely some death is better than some life,
Better one death for him and these and me.
For if the gods had slain them it may be
I had endured it ; if they had fallen by war
Or by the nets and knives of privy death
And by hired hands while sleeping, this thing too
I had set my soul to suffer; or this hunt,
Had this despatched them, under tusk or tooth,
Torn, sanguine, trodden, broken ; for all deaths
Or honorable or with facile feet avenged
And hands of swift gods following, all save this,
Are bearable; but not for their sweet land
Fighting, but not a sacrifice, lo these
Dead ; for I had not then shed all mine heart
Out at mine eyes: then either with good speed,
Being just, I had slain their slayer atoningly,
Or strewn with flowers their fire and on their tombs

Hung crowns, and over them a song, and
  seen
Their praise outflame their ashes ; for all
  men,
All maidens, had come thither, and from
  pure lips
Shed songs upon them, from heroic eyes
Tears; and their death had been a death-
  less life;
But now, by no man hired nor alien
  sword,
By their own kindred are they fallen, in
  peace,
After much peril, friendless among friends,
By hateful hands they loved; and how shall
  mine
Touch these returning red and not from
  war,
These fatal from the vintage of men's
  veins,
Dead men my brethren ? how shall these
  wash off
No festal stains of undelightful wine
How mix the blood, my blood on them,
  with me,
Holding mine hand ? or how shall I say,
  son,
That am no sister ? but by night and day
Shall we not sit and hate each other, and
  think
Things hate-worthy ? not live with shame-
  fast eyes,
Brow-beaten, treading soft with fearful
  feet,
Each unupbraided, each without rebuke
Convicted, and without a word reviled
Each of another ? and I shall let thee live
And see thee strong and hear men for thy
  sake
Praise me, but these thou wouldest not let
  live
No man shall praise for ever ? these shall lie
Dead, unbeloved, unholpen, all through
  thee ?
Sweet were they toward me living, and
  mine heart
Desired them, but was then well satisfied,
That now is as men hungered ; and these
  dead
I shall want always to the day I die
For all things else and all men may re-
  new ;
Yea, son for son the gods may give and
  take,
But never a brother or sister any more.

CHORUS.

Nay, for the son lies close about thine
  heart,
Full of thy milk, warm from thy womb,
  and drains
Life and blood of life and all thy fruit,
Eats thee and drinks thee as who breaks
  bread and eats,
Treads wine and drinks, thyself a sect of
  thee;
And if he feed not, shall not thy flesh
  faint ?
Or drink not, are not thy lips dead for
  thirst ?
This thing moves more than all things,
  even thy son,
That thou cleave to him; and he shall
  honor thee,
Thy womb that bare him and the breasts
  he knew,
Reverencing most for thy sake all his gods.

ALTHÆA.

But these the gods too gave me, and these
  my son,
Not reverencing his gods nor mine own
  heart
Nor the old sweet years nor all venerable
  things,
But cruel, and in his ravin like a beast,
Hath taken away to slay them : yea, and
  she,
She the strange woman, she the flower,
  the sword,
Red from spilt blood, a mortal flower to
  men,
Adorable, detestable—even she
Saw with strange eyes and with strange
  lips rejoiced,
Seeing these mine own slain of mine own,
  and me
Made miserable above all miseries made,
A grief among all women in the world,
A name to be washed out with all men's
  tears.

CHORUS.

Strengthen thy spirit; is this not also a
  god,
Chance, and the wheel of all necessities ?
Hard things have fallen upon us from harsh
  gods,
Whom lest worse hap rebuke we not for
  these.

ALTHÆA.

My spirit is strong against itself, and I
For these things sake cry out on mine own
    soul
That it endures outrage, and dolorous
    days,
And life, and this inexpiable impotence.
Weak am I, weak and shameful; my breath
    drawn
Shames me, and monstrous things and
    violent gods.
What shall atone? what heal me? what
    bring back
Strength to the foot, light to the face?
    what herb
Assauge me? what restore me? what re-
    lease?
What strange things eaten or drunken, O
    great gods,
Make me as you or as the beasts that feed,
Slay and divide and cherish their own
    hearts?
For these ye show us; and we less than
    these
Have not wherewith to live as all these
    things
Which all their lives fare after their own
    kind
As who doth well rejoicing; but we ill,
Weeping or laughing, we whom eyesight
    fails,
Knowledge and light of face and perfect
    heart,
And hands we lack, and wit; and all our
    days
Sin, and have hunger, and die infatuated.
For madness have ye given us and not
    health,
And sins whereof we know not; and for
    these
Death, and sudden destruction unaware.
What shall we say now? what thing comes
    of us?

CHORUS.

Alas, for all this all men undergo.

ALTHÆA.

Wherefore I will not that these twain, O
    gods,
Die as a dog dies, eaten of creeping things,
Abominable, a loathing; but though dead
Shall they have honor and such funereal
    flame
As strews men's ashes in their enemies'
    face

And blinds their eyes who hate them: lest
    men say,
" Lo how they lie, and living had great
    kin,
And none of these hath pity of them, and
    and none
Regards them lying, and none is wrung at
    heart,
None moved in spirit for them, naked and
    slain,
Abhorred, abased, and no tears comfort
    them ";
And in the dark this grieve Eurythemis,
Hearing how these her sons come down to
    her
Unburied, unavenged, as kinless men,
And had a queen their sister.   That were
    shame
Worse than this grief.   Yet how to atone
    at all
I know not ; seeing the love of my born
    son,
A new-made mother's new born-love, that
    grows
From the soft child to the strong man,
    now soft,
Now strong as either, and still one sole
    same love,
Strives with me, no light thing to strive
    withal:
This love is deep, and natural to man's
    blood,
And ineffaceable with many tears.
Yet shall not these rebuke me though I
    die.
Nor she in that waste world with all her
    dead,
My mother, among the pale flocks fallen
    as leaves,
Folds of dead people, and alien from the
    sun ;
Nor lack some bitter comfort, some poor
    praise,
Being queen, to have borne her daughter
    like a queen,
Righteous; and though mine own fire burn
    me too,
She shall have honor and these her sons,
    though dead.
But all the gods will, all they do, and we
Not all we would, yet somewhat; and one
    choice
We have, to live and do just deeds and
    die.

CHORUS.

Terrible words she communes with, and
    turns
Swift fiery eyes in doubt against herself,
And murmurs as who talks in dreams with
    death.

ALTHÆA.

For the unjust also dieth, and him all men
Hate, and himself abhors the unrighteous-
    ness,
And seeth his own dishonor intolerable.
But I being just, doing right upon myself,
Slay mine own soul, and no man born
    shames me,
For none constrains nor shall rebuke, being
    done,
What none compelled me doing; thus these
    things fare
Ah, ah, that such things should so fare; ah
    me,
That I am found to do them and endure,
Chosen and constrained to chose, and bear
    myself
Mine own wound through mine cwn flesh
    to the heart
Violently stricken, a spoiler and a spoil,
A ruin ruinous, fallen on mine own son.
Ah, ah, for me too as for these; alas,
For that is done that shall be, and mine
    hand
Full of the deed, and full of blood mine
    eyes,
That shall see never nor touch anything
Save blood unstanched and fire unquench-
    able.

CHORUS.

What wilt thou do? what ails thee? for
    the house
Shakes ruinously; wilt thou bring fire for
    it?

ALTHÆA.

Fire in the roofs, and on the lintels fire.
Lo ye, who stand and weave, between the
    doors,
There; and blood drips from hand and
    thread, and stains
Threshold and raiment and me passing in
Flecked with the sudden sanguine drops of
    death.

CHORUS.

Alas that time is stronger than strong men,
Fate than all gods: and these are all fallen
    on us.

ALTHÆA.

A little since and I was glad; and now
I never shall be glad or sad again.

CHORUS.

Between two joys a grief grows unaware

ALTHÆA.

A little while and I shall laugh; and then
I shall weep never and laugh not any
    more.

CHORUS.

What shall be said? for words are thorns
    to grief.
Withhold thyself a little and fear the gods.

ALTHÆA.

Fear died when these were slain; and I am
    as dead.
And fear is of the living; these fear none.

CHORUS.

Have pity upon all people for their sake.

ALTHÆA.

It is done now; shall I put back my day?

CHORUS.

And end is come, an end; this is of God.

ALTHÆA.

I am fire, and burn myself; keep clear
    of fire.

CHORUS.

The house is broken, is broken; it shall
    not stand.

ALTHÆA.

Woe, woe for him that breaketh; and a
    rod
Smote it of old, and now the axe is here.

CHORUS.

Not as with sundering of the earth
    Nor as with cleaving of the sea
Nor fierce foreshadowings of a birth
    Nor flying dreams of death to be
Nor loosening of the large world's girth,
And quickening of the body of night,
    And sound of thunder in men's ears
And fire of lightning in men's sight,
    Fate, mother of desires and fears,

Bore unto men the law of tears;
But sudden, an unfathered flame,
    And broken out of night, she shone,
She, without body, without name,
    In days forgotten and foregone;
And heaven rang round her as she came
Like smitten cymbals, and lay bare;
    Clouds and great stars, thunders and
        snows,
The blue sad fields and folds of air,
    The life that breathes, the life that
        grows,
    All wind, all fire, that burns or blows,
Even all these knew her: for she is great;
    The daughter of doom, the mother of
        death
The sister of sorrow ; a lifelong weight
    That no man's finger lighteneth,
Nor any god can lighten fate;
A landmark seen across the way
    Where one race treads as the other trod;
An evil sceptre, an evil stay,
    Wrought for a staff, wrought for a rod,
    The bitter jealousy of God.
For death is deep as the sea,
    And fate as the waves thereof.
Shall the waves take pity on thee
    Or the south-wind offer thee love ?
Wilt thou take the night for thy day
Or the darkness for light on thy way
    Till thou say in thine heart, Enough ?
Behold, thou art over fair, thou art over
    wise;
The sweetness of spring in thine hair, and
    the light in thine eyes.
The light of the spring in thine eyes, and
    the sound in thine ears;
Yet thine heart shall wax heavy with sighs
    and thine eyelids with tears.
Wilt thou cover thine hair with gold; and
    with silver thy feet ?
Hast thou taken the purple to fold thee,
    and made thy mouth sweet ?
Behold, when thy face is made bare, he
    that loved thee shall hate;
Thy face shall be no more fair at the fall of
    thy fate.
For thy life shall fall as a leaf and be shed
    as the rain;
And the veil of thine head shall be grief;
    and the crown shall be pain.

AITHÆA.

o ye that wail, and ye that sing, make
    way

Till I be come among you. Hide your
    tears,
Ye little weepers, and your laughing lips,
Ye laughers for a little; lo mine eyes
That outweep heaven at rainiest, and my
    mouth
That laughs as gods laugh at us. Fate's
    are we,
Yet fate is ours a breathing-space; yea,
    mine,
Fate is made mine forever; he is my son,
My bedfellow, my brother. You strong
    gods,
Give place unto me; I am as any of you,
To give life and to take life. Thou old
    earth,
That hast made man and unmade; thou
    whose mouth
Looks red from the eaten fruits of thine
    own womb;
Behold me with what lips upon what food
I feed and fill my body, even with flesh
Made of my body. Lo, the fire I lit
I burn with fire to quench it; yea, with
    flame
I burn up even the dust and ash thereof.

CHORUS.

Woman, what fire is this thou burnest
    with ?

ALTHÆA.

Yea to the bone, yea to the blood and all.

CHORUS.

For this thy face and hair are as one fire.

ALTHÆA.

A tongue that licks and beats upon the
    dust.

CHORUS.

And in thine eyes are hollow light and
    heat.

ALTHÆA.

Of flame not fed with hand or frankin-
    cense.

CHORUS.

I fear thee for the trembling of thine eyes.

ALTHÆA.

Neither with love they tremble nor for

CHORUS.

And thy mouth shuddering like a shot bird.

ALTHÆA.

Not as the bride's mouth when the man kisses it.

CHORUS.

Nay, but what thing is this thing thou hast done?

ALTHÆA.

Look, I am silent, speak your eyes for me.

CHORUS.

I see a faint fire lightening from the hall.

ALTHÆA.

Gaze, stretch your eyes, strain till the lids drop off.

CHORUS.

Flushed pillars down the flickering vestibule.

ALTHÆA.

Stretch with your necks like birds: cry, chirp as they.

CHORUS.

And a long brand that blackens: and white dust.

ALTHÆA.

O children, what is this ye see? your eyes
Are blinder than night's face at fall of moon,
That is my son, my flesh, my fruit of life,
My travail, and the year's weight of my womb.
Meleager, a fire enkindled of mine hands,
And of mine hands extinguished; this is he.

CHORUS.

O gods, what word has flown out at thy mouth?

ALTHÆA.

I did this and I say this and I die.

CHORUS.

Death stands upon the doorway of thy lips,
And in thy mouth has death set up his house.

ALTHÆA.

O death, a little, a little while, sweet death,
Until I see the brand burnt down and die.

CHORUS.

She reels as any reed under the wind,
And cleaves unto the ground with staggering feet.

ALTHÆA.

Girls, one thing will I say and hold my peace.
I that did this will weep not nor cry out,
Cry ye and weep: I will not call on gods,
Call ye on them; I will not pity man,
Shew ye your pity. I know not if I live;
Save that I feel the fire upon my face
And on my cheek the burning of a brand.
Yea the smoke bites me, yea I drink the steam
With nostril and with eyelid and with lip
Insatiate and intolerant; and mine hands
Burn, and fire feeds upon mine eyes; I reel
As one made drunk with living, whence he draws
Drunken delight; yet I though mad for joy,
Loathe my long living and am waxen red
As with the shadow of shed blood; behold,
I am kindled with the flames that fade in him,
I am swollen with subsiding of his veins,
I am flooded with his ebbing; my lit eyes
Flame with the falling fire that leaves his lids
Bloodless; my cheek is luminous with blood
Because his face is ashen. Yet, O child,
Son, first-born, fairest—O sweet mouth, sweet eyes,
That drew my life out through my suckling breast,
That shone and clove my heart through,— O soft knees
Clinging, O tender treadings of soft feet,
Cheeks warm with little kissings,—O child, child,
What have we made each other? Lo, I felt
Thy weight cleave to me, a burden of beauty, O son,

Thy cradled brows and loveliest loving lips,
The floral hair, the little lightening eyes,
And all thy goodly glory : with mine hands
Delicately I fed thee, with my tongue
Tenderly spake, saying, Verily in God's time,
For all the little likeness of thy limbs,
Son, I shall make thee a kingly man to fight,
A lordly leader; and hear before I die,
" She bore the goodliest sword of all the world,"
Oh ! oh ! For all my life turns round on me ;
I am severed from myself, my name is gone,
My name that was a healing, it is changed,
My name is a consuming. From this time,
Though mine eyes reach to the end of all these things,
My lips shall not unfasten till I die.

SEMICHORUS.

She has filled with sighing the city,
    And the ways thereof with tears;
She arose, she girdled her sides,
She set her face as a bride's :
She wept, and she had no pity;
Trembled and felt no fears.

SEMICHORUS.

Her eyes were clear as the sun,
    Her brows were fresh as the day;
She girdled herself with gold,
    Her robes were manifold :
But the days of her worship are done,
    Her praise is taken away.

SEMICHORUS.

For she set her hand to the fire;
    With her mouth she kindled the same;
As the mouth of a flute-player,
So was the mouth of her;
With the might of her strong desire
    She blew the breath of the flame.

SEMICHORUS.

She set her hand to the wood,
    She took the fire in her hand;
As one who is nigh to death,
She panted with strange breath;
She opened her lips unto blood,
    She breathed and kindled the brand

SEMICHORUS.

As wood-dove newly shot,
    She sobbed and lifted her breast;
She sighed and covered her eyes,
Filling her lips with sighs;
She sighed, she withdrew herself not,
    She refrained not, taking not rest;

SEMICHORUS.

But as the wind which is drouth,
    And as the air which is death,
As storm that severeth ships,
Her breath severing her lips,
The breath came forth of her mouth
    And the fire came forth of her breath.

SECOND MESSENGER.

Queen, and you maidens, there is come on us
A thing more deadly than the face of death;
Meleager the good lord is as one slain.

SEMICHORUS.

Without sword, without sword is he stricken ;
    Slain, and slain without hand.

SECOND MESSENGER.

For as keen ice divided of the sun
His limbs divide, and as thawed snow the flesh
Thaws from off all his body to the hair.

SEMICHORUS.

He wastes as the embers quicken ;
    With the brand he fades as a brand.

SECOND MESSENGER.

Even while they sang and all drew hither and he
Lifted both hands to crown the Arcadian's hair
And fix the looser leaves, both hands fell down.

SEMICHORUS.

With rending of cheek and of hair
    Lament ye, mourn for him, weep.

SECOND MESSENGER.

Straightway the crown slid off and smote on earth.
First fallen; and he, grasping his own hair, groaned

And cast his raiment round his face and fell.

SEMICHORUS.

Alas for visions that were,
   And soothsayings spoken in sleep.

SECOND MESSENGER.

But the king twitched his reins in and leapt down
And caught him, crying out twice, "O child," and thrice
So that men's eyelids thickened with their tears.

SEMICHORUS.

Lament with a long lamentation,
   Cry, for an end is at hand.

SECOND MESSENGER.

O son, he said, son, lift thine eyes, draw breath,
Pity me; but Meleager with sharp lips
Gasped, and his face waxed like as sunburnt grass.

SEMICHORUS.

Cry aloud, O thou kingdom, O nation,
   O stricken, a ruinous land.

SECOND MESSENGER.

Whereat king Œnus, straightening feeble knees,
With feeble hands heaved up a lessening weight,
And laid him sadly in strange hands, and wept.

SEMICHORUS.

Thou art smitten, her lord, her desire,
   Thy dear blood wasted as rain.

SECOND MESSENGER.

And they with tears and rendings of the beard
Bear hither a breathing body, wept upon.
And lightening at each footfall, sick to death.

SEMICHORUS.

Thou madest thy sword as a fire,
   With fire for a sword thou art slain.

SECOND MESSENGER.

And lo the feast turned funeral and the crowns

Fallen; and the huntress and the hunter trapped;
And weeping and changed faces and veiled hair.

MELEAGER.

Let your hands meet
   Round the weight of my head
Lift ye my feet
   As the feet of the dead;
For the flesh of my body is molten, the limbs of it molten as lead.

CHORUS.

O thy luminous face,
   Thine imperious eyes !
O the grief, O the grace,
   As of the day when it dies !
Who is this bending over thee, lord, with tears and suppression of sighs !

MELEAGER,

Is a bride so fair ?
   Is a maid so meek ?
With unchapleted hair
   With unfilleted cheek,
Atalanta, the pure among women, whose name is as blessing to speak.

ATALANTA,

I would that with feet,
   Unsandled, unshod.
Overbold, overfleet,
   I had swum not nor trod
From Arcadia to Calydon, northward, a blast of the envy of God.

MELEAGER.

Unto each man his fate;
   Unto each as he saith
In whose fingers the weight
   Of the world is as breath;
Yet I would that in clamor of battle mine hands had laid hold upon death.

CHORUS.

Not with cleaving of shields
   And their clash in thine ear,
When the lord of fought fields
   Breaketh spearshaft from spear,
Thou art broken, our lord, thou art broken, with travail and labor and fear.

MELEAGER.

Would God he had found me
   Beneath fresh boughs !

Would God he had bound me
　　Unawares in mine house,
With light in mine eyes, and songs in my
　lips, and a crown on my brows !

CHORUS.

Whence art thou sent from us ?
　　Whither thy goal ?
How art thou rent from us,
　　Thou that wert whole,
As with severing of eyelids and eyes, as
　with sundering of body and soul !

MELEAGER.

My heart is within me
　　As an ash in the fire;
Whosoever hath seen me,
　　Without lute, without lyre,
Shall sing of me grievous things, even
　things that were ill to desire.

CHORUS.

Who shall raise thee
　　From the house of the dead ?
Or what man praise thee
　　That thy praise may be said ?
Alas thy beauty ! alas thy body ! alas
　thine head !

MELEAGER.

But thou, O mother,
　　That dreamer of dreams,
Wilt thou bring forth another
　　To feel the sun's beams
When I move among shadows a shadow,
　and wail by impassable streams ?

ŒNEUS.

What thing wilt thou leave me
　　Now this thing is done ?
A man wilt thou give me,
　　A son for my son,
For the light of mine eyes, the desire of
　my life, the desirable one ?

CHORUS.

Thou wert glad above others,
　　Yea, fair beyond word;
Thou wert glad among mothers;
　　For each man that heard
Of thee, praise there was added unto thee,
　as wings to the feet of a bird.

ŒNEUS.

Who shall give back
　　Thy face of old years,

With travail made black,
　　Grown gray among fears,
Mother of sorrow, mother of cursing,
　mother of tears ?

MELEAGER.

Though thou art as fire
　　Fed with fuel in vain,
My delight, desire,
　　Is more chaste than the rain,
More pure than the dewfall, more holy
　than stars are that live without stain.

ATALANTA.

I would that as water
　　My life's blood had thawn,
Or as winter's wan daughter
　　Leaves lowland and lawn
Spring-stricken, or ever mine eyes had be-
　held thee made dark in thy dawn.

CHORUS.

When thou dravest the men
　　Of the chosen of Thrace,
None turned him again
　　Nor endured he thy face
Clothed round with the blush of the battle,
　with light from a terrible place,

ŒNEUS.

Thou shouldst die as he dies
　　For whom none sheddeth tears ;
Filling thine eyes
　　And fulfilling thine ears.
With the brilliance of battle, the bloom
　and the beauty, the splendor of spears.

CHORUS.

In the ears of the world
　　It is sung, it is told,
And the light thereof hurled
　　And the noise thereof rolled
From the Acroceraunian snow to the ford
　of the fleece of gold.

MELEAGER.

Would God ye could carry me
　　Forth of all these;
Heap sand and bury me
　　By the Chersonese
Where the thundering Bosphorus answers
　the thunder of Pontic seas.

ŒNEUS.

Dost thou mock at our praise
　　And the singing begun

And the men of strange days
Praising my son
In the folds of the hills of home, high
places of Calydon?

MELEAGER.

For the dead man no home is;
Ah, better to be
What the flower of the foam is
In fields of the sea,
That the sea-waves might be as my rai-
ment, the gulf-stream a garment for me.

CHORUS.

Who shall seek thee and bring
And restore thee thy day,
When the dove dipt her wing
And the oars won their way,
Where the narrowing Symplegades whitened
the straits of Propontis with spray?

MELEAGER.

Will ye crown me my tomb
Or exalt me my name,
Now my spirits consume
Now my flesh is a flame?
Let the sea slake it once, and men speak
of me sleeping to praise me or shame.

CHORUS.

Turn back now, turn thee,
As who turns him to wake;
Though the life in thee burn thee,
Couldst thou bathe it and slake
Where the sea-ridge of Helle hangs heavier,
and east upon west waters break?

MELEAGER.

Would the winds blow me back
Or the waves hurl me home?
Ah, to touch in the track
Where the pine learnt to roam
Cold girdles and crowns of the sea-gods,
cool blossoms of water and foam!

CHORUS.

The gods may release
That they made fast;
Thy soul shall have ease
In thy limbs at the last;
But what shall they give thee for life, sweet
life that is overpast?

MELEAGER.

Not the life of men's veins,
Not of flesh that conceives;
But the grace that remains,
The fair beauty that cleaves
To the life of the rains in the grasses, the
life of the dews on the leaves.

CHORUS.

Thou wert helmsman and chief;
Wilt thou turn in an hour,
Thy limbs to the leaf,
Thy face to the flower,
Thy blood to the water, thy soul to the
gods who divide and devour?

MELEAGER.

The years are hungry,
They wail all their days;
The gods wax angry
And weary of praise;
And who shall bridle their lips? and who
shall straiten their ways?

CHORUS.

The gods guard over us
With sword and with rod;
Weaving shadow to cover us,
Heaping the sod,
That law may fulfil herself wholly, to
darken man's face before God.

MEL   G R.

O holy head f   n   lo thy
Guiltless, yet red from alien guilt, yet foul
With kinship of contam   ated lives,
Lo for their blood I die; and mine own
blood
For bloodshedding of mine is mixed there-
with,
That death may not discern me from m
kin.
Yet with clean heart I die and faultless
hand,
Not shamefully; thou therefore of thy
love
Salute me, and bid fare among the dead
Well, as the dead fare; for the best man
dead
Fares sadly; nathless I now faring well
Pass without fear where nothing is to fear,
Having thy love about me and thy good-
will,
O father, among dark places and men
dead.

ŒNEUS.

Child, I salute thee with sad heart and tears,
And bid thee comfort, being a perfect man
In fight, and honorable in the house of peace.
The gods give thee fair wage and dues of death,
And me brief days and ways to come at thee.

MELEAGER.

Pray thou thy days be long before thy death,
And full of ease and kingdom; seeing in death
There is no comfort and none aftergrowth,
Nor shall one thence look up and see day's dawn
Nor light upon the land whither I go.
Live thou and take thy fill of days and die
When thy day comes; and make not much of death
Lest ere thy day thou reap an evil thing.
Thou, too, the bitter mother and mother-plague
Of this my weary body,—thou too, queen,
The source and end, the sower and the scythe,
The rain that ripens and the drought that slays,
The sand that swallows and the spring that feeds,
To make me and unmake me,—thou, I say,
Althæa, since my father's ploughshare, drawn
Through fatal seedland of a female field,
Furrowed thy body, whence a wheaten ear
Strong from the sun and fragrant from the rains
I sprang and cleft the closure of thy womb,
Mother, I dying with unforgetful tongue
Hail thee as holy and worship thee as just
Who art unjust and unholy; and with my knees
Would worship, but thy fire and subtlety,
Dissundering them, devour me; for these limbs

Are as light dust and crumblings from mine urn
Before the fire has touched them; and my face
As a dead leaf or dead foot's mark on snow,
And all this body a broken barren tree
That was so strong, and all this flower of life
Disbranched and desecrated miserably,
And minished all that god-like muscle and might
And lesser than a man's: for all my veins
Fail me, and all mine ashen life burns down.
I would thou hadst let me live; but gods averse,
But fortune, and the fiery feet of change,
And time, these would not, these tread out my life,
These, and not thou; me, too, thou hast loved, and I
Thee; but this death was mixed with all my life,
Mine end with my beginning; and this law,
This only, slays me, and not my mother at all.
And let no brother or sister grieve too sore,
Nor melt their hearts out on me with their tears,
Since extreme love and sorrowing over-much
Vex the great gods, and overloving men
Slay and are slain for love's sake; and this house
Shall bear much better children; why should these
Weep ? but in patience let them live their lives
And mine pass by forgotten: thou alone,
Mother, thou sole and only, thou not these,
Keep me in mind a little when I die
Because I was thy first-born; let thy soul
Pity me, pity even me gone hence and dead,
Though thou wert wroth, and though thou bear again
Much happier sons, and all men later born
Exceedingly excel me; yet do thou
Forget not, nor think shame; I was thy son.

Time was I did not shame thee; and time
was
I thought to live and make thee honorable
With deeds as great as these men's; but
they live,
These, and I die; and what thing should
have been
Surely I know not; yet I charge thee, see-
ing
I am dead already, love me not the less,
Me, O my mother; I charge thee by these
gods,
My father's, and that holier breast of
thine,
By these that see me dying, and that which
nursed,
Love me not less, thy first-born: though
grief come,
Grief only, of me, and of all these great
joy,
And shall come always to thee; for thou
knowest
O mother, O breasts that bare me, for ye
know
O sweet head of my mother, sacred eyes,
Ye know my soul albeit I sinned, ye
know
Albeit I kneel not neither touch thy
knees,
But with my lips I kneel, and with my
heart
I fall about thy feet and worship thee.
And ye, farewell now, all my friends; and
ye,
Kinsmen, much younger and glorious
more than I
Sons of my mother's sister; and all fare-
well
That were in Colchis with me, and bare
down
The waves and wars that met us and though
times
Change, and though now I be not any-
thing,
Forget not me among you, what I did
In my good time; for even by all those
days,
Those days and this, and your own living
souls,
And by the light and luck of you that live,
And by this miserable spoil, and me
Dying, I beseech you, let my name not
die.

But thou, dear, touch me with thy rose-like
hands,
And fasten up mine eyelids with thy
mouth,
A bitter kiss; and grasp me with thine
arms
Printing with heavy lips my light waste
flesh,
Made light and thin by heavy-handed
fate,
And with thine holy maiden eyes drop
dew,
Drop tears for dew upon me who am
dead,
Me who have loved thee; seeing without
sin done
I am gone down to the empty weary
house
Where no flesh is nor beauty nor swift
eyes
Nor sound of mouth nor might of hands
and feet,
But thou, dear, hide my body with thy
veil,
And with thy raiment cover foot and head,
And stretch thyself upon me and touch
hands
With hands and lips with lips: be pitiful
As thou art maiden perfect; let no man
Defile me to despise me, saying, This
man
Die woman-wise, a woman's offering, slain
Through female fingers in his woof of life,
Dishonorable; for thou hast honored me,
And now for God's sake kiss me once and
twice
And let me go; for the night gathers me
And in the night shall no man gather
fruit.

ATALANTA.

Hail thou: but I with heavy face and
feet
Turn homeward and am gone out of thine
eyes.

CHORUS.

Who shall contend with his lords
　Or cross them or do them wrong?
Who shall bind them as with cords?
　Who shall tame them as with song?
Who shall smite them as with swords?
　For the hands of their kingdom are
strong.

28

ERECHTHEUS:

A TRAGEDY.

ὦ ταὶ λιπαραὶ καὶ ἰοστέφι νοι καὶ ἀοίδιμοι,
Ἑλλάδος ἔρεισμα, κλειναὶ Ἀθᾶναι, δαιμόνιον πτολίεθρον.

PIND. *Fr.* 47.

ΑΤ. τίς δὲ ποιμάνωρ ἔπεστι κἀπιδεσπόζει στρατοῦ;
ΧΟ. οὔτινος δοῦλοι κέκλη, ται φωτὸς οὐδ᾽ ὑπήκοοι.

ÆSCH. *Pers.* 241-2.

PERSONS.

ERECHTHEUS.
CHORUS OF ATHENIAN ELDERS.
PRAXITHEA.
CHTHONIA.

HERALD OF EUMOLPUS.
MESSENGER.
ATHENIAN HERALD.
ATHENA.

ERECHTHEUS.

MOTHER of life and death and all men's days,
Earth, whom I chief of all men born would
  bless,
And call thee with more loving lips than theirs
Mother, for of this very body of thine
And living blood I have my breath and live,
Behold me, even thy son, me crowned of men,
Me made thy child by that strong cunning
  God
Who fashions fire and iron, who begat

Me for a sword and beacon-fire on thee,
Me fostering of Pallas, in her shade
Reared, that I first might pay the nursing
  debt,
Hallowing her fame with flower of third-year
  feasts,   [steeds
And first bow down the bridled strength of
To lose the wild wont of their birth, and bear
Clasp of man's knees and steerage of his hand,
Or fourfold service of his fire-swift wheels

434

That whirl the four-yoked chariot ; me the
king
Who stand before thee naked now, and cry,
O holy and general mother of all men born,
But mother most and motherliest of mine,
Earth, for I ask thee rather of all the Gods,
What have we done ? what word mistimed or
work
Hath winged the wild feet of this timeless
curse
To fall as fire upon us ? Lo, I stand
Here on this brow's crown of the city's head
That crowns its lovely body, till death's hour
Waste it ; but now the dew of dawn and birth
Is fresh upon it from thy womb, and we
Behold it born how beauteous ; one day more
I see the world's wheel of the circling sun
Roll up rejoicing to regard on earth
This one thing goodliest, fair as heaven or he,
Worth a God's gaze or strife of Gods ; but
now
Would this day's ebb of their spent wave of
strife
Sweep it to sea, wash it on wreck, and leave
A costless thing contemned ; and in our stead,
Where these walls were and sounding streets
of men,
Make wide a waste for tongueless water-herds
And spoil of ravening fishes ; that no more
Should men say, Here was Athens. This shalt
thou
Sustain not, nor thy son endure to see,
Nor thou to live and look on ; for the womb
Bare me not base that bare me miserable,
To hear this loud brood of the Thracian foam
Break its broad strength of billowy-beating
war
Here, and upon it as a blast of death
Blowing, the keen wrath of a fire-souled king,
A strange growth grafted on our natural soil,
A root of Thrace in Eleusinian earth
Set for no comfort to the kindly land,
Son of the sea's lord and our first-born foe,
Eumolpus ; nothing sweet in ears of thine
The music of his making, nor a song
Toward hopes of ours auspicious ; for the note
Rings as for death oracular to thy sons
That goes before him on the sea-wind blown
Full of this charge laid on me, to put out
The brief light kindled of mine own child's
life,
Or with this helmsman hand that steers the
state
Run right on the under shoal and ridge of
death

The populous ship with all its fraughtage gone
And sails that were to take the wind of time
Rent, and the tackling that should hold out fast
In confluent surge of loud calamities
Broken, with spars of rudders and lost oars
That were to row toward harbor and find rest
In some most glorious haven of all the world
And else may never near it : such a song
The Gods have set his lips on fire withal
Who threatens now in all their names to bring
Ruin ; but none of these, thou knowest, have I
Chid with my tongue or cursed at heart for
grief,
Knowing how the soul runs reinless on sheer
death
Whose grief or joy takes part against the Gods.
And what they will is more than our desire,
And their desire is more than what we will.
For no man's will and no desire of man's
Shall stand as doth a God's will. Yet, O fair
Mother, that seest me how I cast no word
Against them, plead no reason, crave no cause,
Boast me not blameless, nor beweep me
wronged,
By this fair wreath of towers we have decked
thee with,
This chaplet that we give thee woven of walls,
This girdle of gate and temple and citadel
Drawn round beneath thy bosom, and fast
linked
As to thine heart's root—this dear crown of
thine,
This present light, this city—be not thou
Slow to take heed nor slack to strengthen her,
Fare we so short-lived howsoe'er, and pay
What price we may to ransom thee thy town,
Not me my life ; but thou that diest not, thou,
Though all our house die for this people's sake
Keep thou for ours thy crown our city, guard
And give it life the lovelier that we died.

CHORUS.

Sun, that hast lightened and loosed by thy
might
Ocean and Earth from the lordship of night,
Quickening with vision his eye that was veiled,
Freshening the force in her heart that had
failed,
That sister fettered and blinded brother
Should have sight by thy grace and delight o
each other,
Behold now and see
What profit is given them of thee ;
What wrath has enkindled with madness of mind

Her limbs that were bounden, his face that
　　was blind,
To be locked as in wrestle together, and light-
　　en
With fire that shall darken thy fire in the sky,
Body to body and eye against eye
　　In a war against kind,
Till the bloom of her fields and her high hills
　　whiten
　　With the foam of his waves more high.
For the sea-marks set to divide of old
The kingdoms to Ocean and Earth assigned,
The hoar sea-fields from the cornfields' gold,
His wine-bright waves from her vineyards' fold,
　　Frail forces we find
To bridle the spirit of Gods or bind
　　Till the heat of their hearts wax cold.
But the peace that was stablished between
　　them to stand
Is rent now in twain by the strength of his hand
Who stirs up the storm of his sons overbold
To pluck from fight what he lost of right,
By council and judgment of Gods that spake
And gave great Pallas the strife's fair stake,
The lordship and love of the lovely land,
The grace of the town that hath on it for crown
　　But a headband to wear
　　Of violets one-hued with her hair :
For the vales and the green high places of
　　earth
　　Holds nothing so fair,
And the depths of the sea bear no such birth
　　Of the manifold births they bear.
Too well, too well was the great stake worth
A strife divine for the Gods to judge,
A crowned God's triumph, a foiled God's
　　grudge,
Though the loser be strong and the victress
　　wise
Who played so long since for so large a prize,
The fruitful immortal anointed adored
Dear city of men without master or lord,
Fair fortress and fostress of sons born free,
Who stand in her sight and in thine, O sun,
Slaves of no man, subjects of none ;
A wonder enthroned on the hills and sea,
A maiden crowned with a fourfold glory
That none from the pride of her head may
　　rend,
Violet and olive-leaf purple and hoary,
Song-wreath and story the fairest of fame,
Flowers that the winter can blast not or bend ;
A light upon earth as the sun's own flame,
　　A name as his name,
　　Athens, a praise without end.

A noise is arisen against us of waters,
　　A sound as of battle come up from the sea.
Strange hunters are hard on us, hearts without
　　pity ;
They have staked their nets round the fair
　　young city,
That the sons of her strength and her virgin
　　daughters
　　Should find not whither alive to flee.
And we know not yet of the word unwritten,
　　The doom of the Pythian we have not heard
From the navel of earth and the veiled mid
　　altar
We wait for a token with hopes that falter,
With fears that hang on our hearts thought
　　smitten
　　Lest her tongue be kindled with no good
　　word.
O thou not born of the womb, nor bred
In the bride-night's warmth of a changed God's
　　bed,
But thy life as a lightning was flashed from the
　　light of thy father's head,
O chief God's child by a motherless birth,
If aught in thy sight we indeed be worth,
Keep death from us thou, that art none of the
　　Gods of the dead under earth.
　　Thou that hast power on us, save, if thou
　　wilt ;
　　Let the blind wave breach not thy wall
　　scarce built ;
But bless us not so as by bloodshed, impute
　　not for grace to us guilt,
　　Nor by price of pollution of blood set us
　　free ;
　　Let the hands be taintless that clasp thy
　　knee,
Nor a maiden be slain to redeem for a maiden
　　her shrine from the sea.
　　O earth, O sun, turn back
　　Full on his deadly track
Death, that would smite you black and mar
　　your creatures,
　　And with one hand disroot
　　All tender flower and fruit,
With one strike blind and mute the heaven's
　　fair features,
　　Pluck out the eyes of morn, and make
Silence in the east and blackness whence the
　　bright songs break.
　　Help, earth, help, heaven, that hear
　　The song-notes of our fear,
Shrewd notes and shrill, not clear or joyful
　　sounding ;
　　Hear, highest of Gods, and stay

Death on his hunter's way,
Full on his forceless prey his beagles hounding ;
Break thou his bow, make short his hand,
Maim his fleet foot whose passage kills the liv-
  ing land.
Let a third wave smite not us, father,
  Long since sore smitten of twain,
    Lest the house of thy son's son perish
    And his name be barren on earth.
Whose race wilt thou comfort rather
  If none to thy son remain ?
    Whose seed wilt thou choose to cherish
    If his be cut off in the birth ?
For the first fair graft of his graffing
  Was rent from its maiden root
    By the strong swift hand of a lover
    Who fills the night with his breath ;
On the lip of the stream low-laughing
  Her green soft virginal shoot
    Was plucked from the stream-side cover
    By the grasp of a love like death.
For a God's was the mouth that kissed her
  Who speaks, and the leaves lie dead,
    When winter awakes as at warning
    To the sound of his foot from Thrace.
Nor happier the bed of her sister
  Though Love's self laid her abed
    By a bridegroom beloved of the morning
    And fair as the dawn's own face.
For Procris, ensnared and ensnaring
  By the fraud of a twofold wile,
    With the point of her own spear stricken
    By the gift of her own hand fell.
Oversubtle in doubts, overdaring
  In deeds and devices of guile,
    And strong to quench as to quicken,
    O Love, have we named thee well ?
By thee was the spear's edge whetted
  That laid her dead in the dew,
    In the moist green glens of the midland
    By her dear lord slain and thee.
And him at the cliff's end fretted
  By the grey keen waves, him too,
    Thine hand from the white-browed
      headland
    Flung down for a spoil to the sea.
But enough now of griefs grey-growing
  Have darkened the house divine,
    Have flowered on its boughs and faded,
    And green is the brave stock yet.
O father all-seeing and all-knowing,
  Let the last fruit fall not of thine
    From the tree with whose boughs we are
      shaded,
    From the stock that thy son's hand set.

ERECHTHEUS.

O daughter of Cephisus, from all time
Wise have I found thee, wife and queen, of
  heart
Perfect ; nor in the days that knew not wind
Nor days when storm blew death upon our
  peace
Was thine heart swoln with seed of pride, or
  bowed
With blasts of bitter fear that break men's
  souls
Who lift too high their minds toward heaven,
  in thought
Too godlike grown for worship ; but of mood
Equal, in good time reverent of time bad,
And glad in ill days of the good that were.
Nor now too would I fear thee, now misdoubt
Lest fate should find thee lesser than thy doom,
Chosen if thou be to bear and to be great
Haply beyond all women ; and the word
Speaks thee divine, dear queen, that speaks
  thee dead,
Dead being alive, or quick and dead in one
Shall not men call thee living ? yet I fear
To slay thee timeless with my proper tongue,
With lips, thou knowest, that love thee ; and
  such work
Was never laid of Gods on men, such word
No mouth of man learnt ever, as from mine
Most loth to speak thine ear most loth shall
  take
And hold it hateful as the grave to hear.

PRAXITHEA.

That word there is not in all speech of man,
King, that being spoken of the Gods and thee
I have not heart to honor, or dare hold
More than I hold thee or the Gods in hate
Hearing ; but if my heart abhor it heard
Being insubmissive, hold me not thy wife
But use me like a stranger, whom thine hand
Hath fed by chance and finding thence no
  thanks
Flung off for shame's sake to forgetfulness.

ERECHTHEUS.

O, of what breath shall such a word be made,
Or from what heart find utterance ? Would my
  tongue
Were rent forth rather from the quivering root
Than made as fire or poison thus for thee.

PRAXITHEA.

But if thou speak of blood, and I that hear
Be chosen of all for this land's love to die
And save to thee thy city, know this well,
Happiest I hold me of her seed alive.

ERECHTHEUS.

O sun that seest, what saying was this of thine,
God, that thy power 'has breathed into my
    lips ?
For from no sunlit shrine darkling it came.

PRAXITHEA.

What portent from the mid oracular place
Hath smitten thee so like a curse that flies
Wingless, to waste men with its plagues? yet
    speak.

ERECHTHEUS.

Thy blood the Gods require not ; take this
    first.

PRAXITHEA.

To me than thee more grievous this should
    sound.

ERECHTHEUS.

That word rang truer and bitterer than it knew.

PRAXITHEA.

This is not then thy grief, to see me die ?

ERECHTHEUS.

Die shalt thou not, yet give thy blood to death.

PRAXITHEA.

If this ring worse I know not ; strange it rang.

ERECHTHEUS.

Alas, thou knowest not ; woe is me that know.

PRAXITHEA.

And woe shall mine be, knowing ; yet halt not
here.

ERECHTHEUS.

Guiltless of blood this state may stand n
    more.

PRAXITHEA.

Firm let it stand whatever bleed or fall.

ERECHTHEUS.

O Gods, that I should say it shall and weep.

PRAXITHEA.

Weep, and say this ? no tears should bath
    such words.

ERECHTHEUS.

Woe's me that I must weep upon them, woe

PRAXITHEA.

What stain is on them for thy tears to cleanse

ERECHTHEUS.

A stain of blood unpurgeable with tears.

PRAXITHEA.

Whence ? for thou sayest it is and is not min

ERECHTHEUS.

Hear then and know why only of all men I
That bring such news as mine is, I alone
Must wash good words with weeping ; I an
    thou,
Woman, must wail to hear men sing, must groa
To see their joy who love us ; all our friends
Save only we, and all save we that love
This holiness of Athens, in our sight
Shall lift their hearts up, in our hearing prais
Gods whom we may not ; for to these the
    give
Life of their children, flower of all their seed,
For all their travail fruit, for all their hopes
Harvest ; but we for all our good things, we
Have at their hands which fill all these folk ful
Death, barrenness, child-slaughter, curses, care
Sea-leaguer and land-shipwreck ; which c
    these,
Which wilt thou first give thanks for ? all ar
    thine.

PRAXITHEA.

That first they give who give this city good,
Or that first given to save it I give thanks
First, and thanks heartier from a happier tongue,
More than for any my peculier grace
Now me and not my country ; next for this,
That none of all these but for all these I
Just bear my burden, and no eye but mine
Weep of all women's in this broad land born
Who see their land's deliverance ; but much
    more,
But most for this I thank them most of all,
That this their edge of doom is chosen to pierce
My heart and not my country's ; for the sword
Drawn to smite there and sharpened for such
    stroke
Should wound more deep than any turned on
    me.

CHORUS.

Well fares the land that bears such fruit, and well
The spirit that breeds such thought and speech
    in man.

ERECHTHEUS.

O woman, thou hast shamed my heart with
    thine,
To show so strong a patience ; take then all ;
For all shall break not nor bring down thy
    soul.
The word that journeying to the bright God's
    shrine
Who speaks askance and darkling, but his
    name
Hath in it slaying and ruin broad writ out,
I heard, hear thou : thus saith he ; There shall
    die
One soul for all this people ; from thy womb
Came forth the seed that here on dry bare
    ground
Death's hand must sow untimely, to bring
    forth
Nor blade nor shoot in season, being by name
To the under Gods made holy, who require
For this land's life her death and maiden blood
To save a maiden city.   Thus I heard,
And thus with all said leave thee ; for save
    this
No word is left us, and no hope alive.

CHORUS.

He hath uttered too surely his wrath not ob-
    scurely, nor wrapt as in mists of his breath,
The master that lightens not hearts he enlight-
    ens, but gives them foreknowledge of death.
As a bolt from the cloud hath he sent it aloud
    and proclaimed it afar,
From the darkness and height of the horror
    of night hath he shown us a star.
Star may I name it and err not, or flame
    shall I say,
Born of the womb that was born for the
    tomb of the day?
O Night, whom other but thee for mother, and
    Death for the father, Night,
Shall we dream to discover, save thee and thy
    lover, to bring such a sorrow to sight ?
From the slumberless bed for thy bedfellow
    spread and his bride under earth
Hast thou brought forth a wild and insatiable
    child, an unbearable birth.
Fierce are the fangs of his wrath, and the
    pangs that they give ;
None is there, none that may bear them,
    not one that would live.

CHTHONIA.

Forth of the fine-spun folds of veils that hide
My virgin chamber toward the full-faced sun
I set my foot not moved of mine own will,
Unmaidenlike, nor with unprompted speed
Turn eyes too broad or doglike unabashed
On reverend heads of men and thence on thine,
Mother, now covered from the light and bow-
    ed
As hers who mourns her brethren ; but what
    grief
Bends thy blind head thus earthward, holds
    thus mute,
I know not till thy will be to lift up
Toward mine thy sorrow-muffled eyes and
    speak ;
And till thy will be would I know this not.

PRAXITHEA.

Old men and childless, or if sons ye have seen
And daughters, elder-born were these than
    mine,
Look on this child, how young of years, how
    sweet,
How scant of time and green of age her life
Puts forth its flower of girlhood ; and her gait
How virginal, how soft her speech, her eyes
How seemly smiling ; wise should all ye be,

All honorable and kindly men of age ;
Now give me counsel and one word to say
That I may bear to speak, and hold my peace
Henceforth for all time even as all ye now.
Dumb are ye all, bowed eyes and tongueless
    mouths.
Unprofitable ; if this were wind that speaks,
As much its breath might move you. Thou
    then, child,
Set thy sweet eyes on mine ; look through
    them well ;
Take note of all the writing of my face
As of a tablet or a tomb inscribed
That bears me record ; lifeless now, my life
Thereon that was think written ; brief to read,
Yet shall the scripture sear thine eyes as fire
And leave them dark as dead men's. Nay,
    dear child,
Thou hast no skill, my maiden, and no sense
To take such knowledge ; sweet is all thy lore,
And all this bitter ; yet I charge thee learn
And love and lay this up within thine heart,
Even this my word ; less ill it were to die
Than live and look upon thy mother dead,
Thy mother-land that bare thee ; no man slain
But him who hath seen it shall men count un-
    blest,
None blest as him who hath died and seen it
    not.

CHTHONIA.

That sight some God keep from me though I
    die.

PRAXITHEA.

A God from thee shall keep it ; fear not this.

CHTHONIA.

Thanks all my life long shall he gain of mine.

PRAXITHEA.

Short gain of all yet shall he get of thee.

CHTHONIA.

Brief be my life, yet so long live my thanks.

PRAXITHEA.

So long? so little ; how long shall they live ?

CHTHONIA.

Even while I see the sunlight and thine eyes.

PRAXITHEA.

Would mine might shut ere thine upon the sun.

CHTHONIA.

For me thou prayest unkindly ; change that
    prayer.

PRAXITHEA.

Not well for me thou sayest, and ill for thee.

CHTHONIA.

Nay, for me well, if thou shalt live, not I.

PRAXITHEA,

How live, and lose these loving looks of thine ?

CHTHONIA.

It seems I too, thus praying, then, love thee
    not.

PRAXITHEA.

Lov'st thou not life ? what wouldst thou do to
    die ?

CHTHONIA.

Well, but not more than all things, love I life.

PRAXITHEA.

And fain wouldst keep it as thine age allows ?

CHTHONIA.

Fain would I live, and fain not fear to die.

PRAXITHEA

That I might bid thee die not ! Peace ; no
    more.

CHORUS.

A Godlike race of grief the Gods have set
For these to run matched equal, heart with
    heart.

PRAXITHEA.

ild of the chief of Gods, and maiden
crowned,
ueen of these towers and fostress of their
king,
llas, and thou my father's holiest head,
living well of life nor stanched nor stained,
God Cephisus, thee too charge I next,
e to me judge and witness ; nor thine ear
all now my tongue invoke not, thou to me
ost hateful of things holy, mournfullest
f all old sacred streams that wash the world,
issus, on whose marge at flowery play
whirlwind-footed bridegroom found my
child
nd rapt her northward where mine elder-born
eeps now the Thracian bride-bed of a God
tolerable to seamen, but this land
inds him in hope for her sake favorable,
gracious son by wedlock ; hear me then
hou likewise, if with no faint heart or false
he word I say be said, the gift be given,
hich might I choose I had rather die than
give
r speak and die not.   Ere thy limbs were
made
r thine eyes lightened, strife, thou knowest,
my child,
wixt God and God had risen, which heavenlier name
ould here stand hallowed, whose more
liberal grace
ould win this city's worship, and our land
o which of these do reverence ; first the lord
hose wheels make lightnings of the foam-
flowered sea
ere on this rock, whose height brow-bound
with dawn
head and heart of Athens, one sheer blow
truck, and beneath the triple wound that
shook
he stony sinews and stark roots of the earth
prang toward the sun a sharp salt fount, and
sank
There lying it lights the heart up of the hill,
well of bright strange brine ; but she that
reared
hy father with her same chaste fostering hand
et for a sign against it in our guard
he holy bloom of the olive, whose hoar leaf
igh in the shadowy shrine of Pandrosus
ath honor of us all ; and of this strife
he twelve most high Gods judging with one
mouth

Acclaimed her victress; wroth whereat, as
wronged
That she should hold from him such prize and
place,
The strong king of the tempest-rifted sea
Loosed reinless on the low Thriasian plain
The thunders of his chariots, swallowing
stunned
Earth, beasts, and men, the whole blind found-
ering world
That was the sun's at morning, and ere noon
Death's ; nor this only prey fulfilled his mind ₁
For with strange crook-toothed prows of Carian
folk
Who snatch a sanguine life out of the sea,
Thieves keen to pluck their bloody fruit of
spoil
From the grey fruitless waters, has their God
Furrowed our shores to waste them, as the
fields
Were landward harried from the north with
swords
Aonian, sickles of man-slaughtering edge
Ground for no hopeful harvest of live grain
Against us in Bœotia ; these being spent,
Now this third time his wind of wrath has
blown
Right on this people a mightier wave of war,
Three times more huge a ruin ; such its ridge
Foam-rimmed and hollow like the womb of
heaven,
But black for shining, and with death for life
Big now to birth and ripe with child, full-blown
With fear and fruit of havoc, takes the sun
Out of our eyes, darkening the day, and blinds
The fair sky's face unseasonably with change,
A cloud in one and billow of battle, a surge
High reared as heaven with monstrous surf of
spears
That shake on us their shadow, till men's heads
Bend, and their hearts even with its forward
wind
Wither, so blasts all seed in them of hope
Its breath and blight of presage ; yea, even
now
The winter of this wind out of the deeps
Makes cold our trust in comfort of the Gods
And blind our eye toward outlook ; yet not
here,
Here never shall the Thracian plant on high
For ours his father's symbol, nor with wreaths
A strange folk wreathe it upright set and
crowned
Here where our natural people born behold
The golden Gorgon of the shield's defence

That screeens their flowering olive, nor strange
    Gods
Be graced, and Pallas here have praise no
    more.
And if this be not I must give my child,
Thee, mine own very blood and spirit of mine,
Thee to be slain. Turn from me, turn thine
    eyes
A little from me ; I can bear not yet
To see if still they smile on mine or no,
If fear make faint the light in them, or faith
Fix them as stars of safety. Need have we,
Sore need of stars that set not in mid storm,
Lights that outlast the lightnings ; yet my heart
Endures not to make proof of thine or these,
Not yet to know thee whom I made, and bare
What manner of woman ; had I borne thee
    man,
I had made no question of thine eyes or heart,
Nor spared to read the scriptures in them writ,
Wert thou my son ; yet couldst thou then but
    die
Fallen in sheer fight by chance and charge of
    spears
And have no more of memory, fill no tomb
More famous than thy fellows in fair field,
Where many share the grave, many the praise ;
But one crown shall one only girl my child
Wear, dead for this dear city, and give back life
To him that gave her and to me that bare,
And save two sisters living ; and all this,
Is this not all good ? I shall give thee, child,
Thee but by fleshly nature mine, to bleed
For dear land's love ; but if the city fall
What part is left me in my children then ?
But if it stand and thou for it lie dead,
Then hast thou in it a better part than we,
A holier portion than we all ; for each
Hath but the length of his own life to live,
And this most glorious mother-land on earth
To worship till that life have end ; but thine
Hath end no more than hers ; thou, dead,
    shalt live
Till Athens live not ; for the days and nights
Given of thy bare brief dark dividual life,
Shall she give thee half all her agelong own
And all its glory ; for thou givest her these ;
But with one hand she takes and gives again
More than I gave or she requires of thee.
Come therefore, I will make thee fit for death,
I that could give thee, dear, no gift at birth
Save of light life that breathes and bleeds,
    even I
Will help thee to this better gift than mine
And lead thee by this little living hand

That death shall make so strong, to that grea
    end
Whence it shall lighten like a God's, and strik
Dead the strong heart of battle that wou
    break
Athens ; but ye, pray for this land, old men,
That it may bring forth never child on earth
To love it less, for none may more, than we.

CHORUS.

Out of the north wind grief came forth,
    And the shining of a sword out of the se
Yea, of old the first-blown blast blew th
    prelude of this last,
    The blast of his trumpet upon Rhodope
Out of the north skies full of his cloud,
    With the clamour of his storms as of
    crowd
At the wheels of a great king crying aloud
At the axle of a strong king's car
That has girded on the girdle of war—
With hands that lightened the skies in sund
And feet whose fall was followed of thunde
    A God, a great God strange of name,
    With horse-yoke fleeter-hoofed than flam
To the mountain bed of a maiden came,
    Oreithyia, the bride mismated,
    Wofully wed in a snow-strewn bed
With a bridegroom that kisses the bride
    mouth dead ;
Without garland, without glory, withou
    song,
As a fawn by night on the hills belated,
Given over for a spoil unto the strong.
    From lips how pale so keen a wail
    At the grasp of a God's hand on her sl
    gave,
When his breath that darkens air made
    havoc of her hair,
    It rang from the mountain even to th
    wave ;
Rang with a cry, *Woe's me, woe is me !*
From the darkness upon Hæmus to the se
And with hands that clung to her new lor
    knee,
As a virgin overborne with shame,
She besought him by her spouseless fame,
By the blameless breasts of a maid unmar
    ed
And locks unmaidenly rent and harried,
    And all her flower of body, born
    To match the maidenhood of morn,
With the might of the wind's wrath wrench
    and torn.

Vain, all vain as a dead man's vision
Falling by night in his old friends' sight,
To be scattered with slumber and slain ere
light ;
Such a breath of such a bridegroom in that
hour
Of her prayers made mock, of her fears
derision,
And a ravage of her youth as of a flower.
With a leap of his limbs as a lion's, a cry from
his lips as of thunder,
In a storm of amorous godhead filled with
fire,
From the height of the heaven that was rent
with the roar of his coming in sunder,
Sprang the strong God on the spoil of his
desire.
And the pines of the hills were as green
reeds shattered,
And their branches as buds of the soft spring
scattered,
And the west wind and east, and the sound
of the south,
Fell dumb at the blast of the north wind's
mouth,
At the cry of his coming out of heaven.
And the wild beasts quailed in the rifts and
hollows
Where hound nor clarion of huntsman fol-
lows,
And the depths of the sea were aghast, and
whitened,
And the crowns of their waves were as flame
that lightened,
And the heart of the floods thereof was
riven.
But she knew not him coming for terror, she
felt not her wrong that he wrought her,
When her locks as leaves were shed before
his breath,
And she heard not for terror his prayer,
though the cry was a God's that besought
her,
Blown from lips that strew the world-wide
seas with death.
For the heart was molten within her to hear,
And her knees beneath her were loosened
for fear,
And her blood fast bound as a frost-bound
water,
And the soft new bloom of the green earth's
daughter
Wind-wasted as blossom of a tree ;
As the wild God rapt her from earth's breast
lifted,

On the strength of the stream of his dark
breath drifted,
From the bosom of earth as a bride from the
mother,
With storm for bridesman and wreck for
brother,
As a cloud that he sheds upon the sea.
Of this hoary-headed woe
Song made memory long ago ;
Now a younger grief to mourn
Needs a new song younger born.
Who shall teach our tongues to reach
What strange height of saddest speech,
For the new bride's sake that is given to be
A stay to fetter the foot of the sea,
Lest it quite spurn down and trample the town,
Ere the violets be dead that were plucked for
its crown,
Or its olive-leaf whiten and wither ?
Who shall say of the wind's way
That he journed yesterday,
Or the track of the storm that shall sound to-
morrow,
If the new be more than the grey-grown
sorrow ?
For the wind of the green first season
was keen,
And the blast shall be sharper that blew
between
That the breath of the sea blows hither.

HERALD OF EUMOLPUS.

Old men, grey borderers on the march of death,
Tongue-fighters, tough of talk and sinewy
speech,
Else nerveless, from no crew of such faint folk
Whose tongues are stouter than their hands
come I
To bid not you to battle ; let them strike
Whose swords are sharper than your keen-
tongued wail,
And ye, sit fast and sorrow ; but what man
Of all this land-folk and earth laboring herd
For heart or hand seems foremost, him I call
If heart be his to hearken, him bid forth
To try if one be in the sun's sight born
Of all that grope and grovel on dry ground
That may join hands in battle-grip for death
With them whose seed and strength is of the
sea.

CHORUS.

Know thou this much for all thy loud blast
blown,

We lack not hands to speak with, swords to
    plead,
For proof of peril, not of boisterous breath,
Sea-wind and storm of barren mouths that
    foam
And rough rock's edge of menace ; and short
    space
May lessen thy large ignorance and inform
This insolence with knowledge if there live
Men earth-begotten of no tenderer thews
Than knit the great joints of the grim sea's
    brood
With hasps of steel together ; heaven to help,
One man shall break, even on their own flood's
    verge,
That iron bulk of battle ; but thine eye
That sees it now swell higher than sand or
    shore
Haply shall see not when thine host shall
    shrink.

HERALD OF EUMOLPUS.

Not haply, nay, but surely, shall not thine.

CHORUS.

That lot shall no God give who fights for thee.

HERALD OF EUMOLPUS.

Shall Gods bear bit and bridle, fool, of men ?

CHORUS.

Nor them forbid we nor shalt thou constrain.

HERALD OF EUMOLPUS.

Yet say'st thou none shall make the good lot
    mine ?

CHORUS.

Of thy side none, nor moved for fear of thee.

HERALD OF EUMOLPUS.

Gods hast thou then to baffle Gods of ours ?

CHORUS.

Nor thine nor mine, but equal-souled are they.

HERALD OF EUMOLPUS.

Toward good and ill, then, equal-eyed of soul ?

CHORUS.

Nay, but swift-eyed to note where ill thoughts
    breed.

HERALD OF EUMOLPUS.

Thy shaft word-feathered flies yet far of me.

CHORUS.

Pride knows not, wounded, till the heart be
    cleft.

HERALD OF EUMOLPUS.

No shaft wounds deep whose wing is plumed
    with words.

CHORUS.

Lay that to heart, and bid thy tongue learn grace.

HERALD OF EUMOLPUS.

Grace shall thine own crave soon too late of
    mine.

CHORUS

Boast thou till then, but I wage words no more.

ERECHTHEUS.

Man, what shrill wind of speech and wrangling
    air
Blows in our ears a summons from thy lips
Winged with what message, or what gift or
    grace
Requiring ? none but what his hand may take
Here may the foe think hence to reap, nor this
Except some doom from Godward yield it him.

HERALD OF EUMOLPUS.

King of this land-folk, by my mouth to thee
Thus saith the son of him that shakes thine earth
Eumolpus ; now the stakes of war are set,
For land or sea to win by throw and wear ;
Choose therefore or to quit thy side and give
The palm unfought for to his bloodless hand,

Or by that father's sceptre, and the foot
Whose tramp far off makes tremble for pure
   fear
Thy soul-struck mother, piercing like a sword
The immortal womb that bare thee ; by the
   waves
That no man bridles and that bound thy world,
And by the winds and storms of all the sea,
He swears to raze from eyeshot of the sun
This city named not of his father's name,
And wash to deathward down one flood of doom
This whole fresh brood of earth yearned natural-
   ly,
Green yet and faint in its first blade, unblown
With yellow hope of harvest ; so do thou,
Seeing whom thy time is come to meet, for fear
Yield, or gird up thy force to fight and die.

ERECHTHEUS.

To fight then be it ; for if to die or live,
No man but only a God knows this much yet
Seeing us fare forth, who bear but in our hands
The weapons not the fortunes of our fight ;
For these now rest as lots that yet undrawn
Lie in the lap of the unknown hour ; but this
I know, not thou, whose hollow mouth of
   storm
Is but a warlike wind, a sharp salt breath
That bites and wounds not ; death nor life of
   mine
Shall give to death or lordship of strange kings
The soul of this live city, nor their heel
Bruise her dear brow discrowned, nor snaffle
   or goad
Wound her free mouth or stain her sanguine
   side
Yet masterless of man ; so bid thy lord
Learn ere he weep to learn it, and too late
Gnash teeth that could not fasten on her flesh,
And foam his life out in dark froth of blood
Vain as a wind's waif of the loud-mouthed sea
Torn from the wave's edge whitening. Tell
   him this ;
Though thrice his might were mustered for
   our scathe
And thicker set with fence of thorn-edged
   spears
Than sands are whirled about the wintering
   beach
When storms have swoln the rivers, and their
   blasts
Have breached the broad sea-banks with stress
   of sea,
That waves of inland and the main make war

As men that mix and grapple ; though his
   ranks
Were more to number than all wildwood
   leaves
The wind waves on the hills of all the world,
Yet should the heart not faint, the head not
   fall,
The breath not fail of Athens. Say, the Gods
From lips that have no more on earth to say
Have told thee this the last good news or ill
That I shall speak in sight of earth and sun
Or he shall hear and see them : for the next
That ear of his from tongue of mine may take
Must be the first word spoken underground
From dead to dead in darkness. Hence ; make
   haste,
Lest war's fleet foot be swifter than thy tongue
And I that part not to return again
On him that comes not to depart away
Be fallen before thee ; for the time is full,
And with such mortal hope as knows not fear
I go this high last way to the end of all.

CHORUS.

Who shall put a bridle in the mourner's lips to
   chasten them,
  Or seal up the fountains of his tears for
    shame ?
Song nor prayer nor prophecy shall slacken
   tears nor hasten them,
  Till grief be within him as a burnt-out flame ;
    Till the passion be broken in his breast
    And the might thereof molten into rest,
   'And the rain of eyes that weep be dry,
    And the breath be stilled of lips that sigh.
Death at last for all men is a harbor ; yet they
   flee from it,
  Set sails to the storm-wind and again to sea ;
Yet for all their labor no whit further shall they
   be from it,
  Nor longer but wearier shall their life's work
    be.
     And with anguish of travail until night
    Shall they steer into shipwreck out of
     sight,
    And with oars that break and shrouds that
     strain
    Shall they drive whence no ship steers
     again.
Bitter and strange is the word of the God most
   high,
    And steep the strait of his way.
Through a pass rock-rimmed and narrow the
   light that gleams

On the faces of men falls faint as the dawn of
dreams,
The dayspring of death as a star in an under sky
Where night is the dead men's day.
As darkness and storm is his will that on earth
is done,
As a cloud is the face of his strength.
King of kings, holiest of holies, and mightiest
of might,
Lord of the lords of thine heaven that are
humble in thy sight,
Hast thou set not an end for the path of the
fires of the sun,
To appoint him a rest at length?
Hast thou told not by measure the waves of
the waste wide sea,
And the ways of the wind their master and
thrall to thee?
Hast thou filled not the furrows with fruit
for the world's increase?
Has thine ear not heard from of old or thine
eye not read
The thought and the deed of us living, the
doom of us dead?
Hast thou made not war upon earth,
and again made peace?
Therefore, O father, that seest us whose lives
are a breath,
Take off us thy burden, and give us not wholly
to death.
For lovely is life, and the law wherein
all things live,
And gracious the season of each, and the hour
of its kind,
And precious the seed of his life in a wise
man's mind;
But all save life for his life will a base
man give.
But a life that is given for the life of the whole
live land,
From a heart unspotted a gift of a spotless
hand,
Of pure will perfect and free, for the land's
life's sake,
What man shall fear not to put forth his hand
and take?
For the fruit of a sweet life plucked in its pure
green prime
On his hand who plucks is as blood, on his
soul as crime.
With cursing ye buy not blessing, nor peace
with strife,
And the hand is hateful that chaffers with
death for life.
Hast thou heard, O my heart, and endurest

The word that is said,
What a garland by sentence found surest
Is wrought for what head?
With what blossomless flowerage of sea-foam
and blood-colored foliage inwound
It shall crown as a heifer's for slaughter the fore-
head for marriage uncrowned?
How the veils and the wreaths that should
cover
The brows of the bride
Shall be shed by the breath of what lover
And scattered aside?
With a blast of the mouth of what bridegroom
the crowns shall be cast from her hair,
And her head by what altar made humble be
left of them naked and bare?
At a shrine unbeloved of a God unbeholden a
gift shall be given for the land,
That its ramparts though shaken with clamor
and horror of manifold waters may stand:
That the crests of its citadels crowned and its
turrets that thrust up their heads to the sun
May behold him unblinded with darkness of
waves overmastering their bulwarks begun.
As a bride shall they bring her, a prey for the
bridegroom, a flower for the couch of her
lord;
They shall muffle her mouth that she cry not or
curse them, and cover her eyes from the
sword.
They shall fasten her lips as with bit and with
bridle, and darken the light of her face,
That the soul of the slayer may not falter, his
heart be not molten, his hand give not
grace.
If she weep then, yet may none that hear
take pity;
If she cry not, none should hearken though
she cried.
Shall a virgin shield thine head for love, O
city,
With a virgin's blood anointed as for pride?
Yet we held thee dear and hallowed of her
favor,
Dear of all men held thy people to her
heart;
Nought she loves the breath of blood, the
sanguine savour,
Who hath built with us her throne and
chosen her part.
Bloodless are her works, and sweet
All the ways that feel her feet;
From the empire of her eyes
Light takes life and darkness flies;
From the harvest of her hands

Wealth strikes root in prosperous lands ;
Wisdom of her word is made ;
At her strength is strength afraid ;
From the beam of her bright spear
War's fleet foot goes back for fear ;
In her shrine she reared the birth
Fire-begotten on live earth ;
Glory from her helm was shed
On his olive-shadowed head ;
By no hand but his shall she
Scourge the storms back of the sea,
To no fame but his shall give
Grace, being dead, with hers to live,
And in double name divine
Half the godhead of their shrine.
But now with what word, with what woe may
   we meet
The timeless passage of piteous feet,
Hither that bend to the last way's end
   They shall walk upon earth ?
What song be rolled for a bride black-stoled
And the mother whose hand of her hand hath
   hold ?
For anguish of heart is my soul's strength
   broken
And the tongue sealed fast that would fain have
   spoken,
To behold thee, O child of so bitter a birth
   That we counted so sweet,   ·
What way thy steps to what bride-feast tend,
What gift he must give that shall wed thee for
   token
 · If the bridegroom be goodly to greet.

CHTHONIA.

People, old men of my city, lordly wise and
   hoar of head,
I a spouseless bride and crownless but with
   garlands of the dead
From the fruitful light turn silent to my dark
   unchilded bed.

CHORUS.

Wise of word was he too surely, but with
   deadlier wisdom wise,
First who gave thee name from under earth,
   no breath from upper skies,
When foredoomed to this day's darkness, their
   first daylight filled thine eyes.

PRAXITHEA.

Child, my child that wast and art but death's
   and now no more of mine,

Half my heart is cloven with anguish by the
   sword made sharp for thine,
Half exalts its wing for triumph, that ¦I bare
   thee thus divine.

CHTHONIA.

Though for me the sword's edge thirst that sets
   no point against thy breast,
Mother, O my mother, where I drank of life
   and fell on rest,
Thine, not mine, is all the grief that marks
   this hour accurst and blest.

CHORUS.

Sweet thy sleep and sweet the bosom was that
   gave thee sleep and birth ;
Harder now the breast, and girded with no
   marriage-band for girth,
Where thine head shall sleep, the namechild
   of the lords of under earth.

PRAXITHEA.

Dark the name and dark the gifts they gave
   thee, child, in childbirth were,
Sprung from him that rent the womb of earth,
   a bitter seed to bear,
Born with groanings of the ground that gave
   him way toward heaven's dear air.

CHTHONIA.

Day to day makes answer, first to last, and life
   to death ; but I,
Born for death's sake, die for life's sake, if indeed this be to die,
This my doom that seals me deathless till the
   springs of time run dry.

CHORUS.

Children shalt thou bear to memory, that to
   man shalt bring forth none ;
Yea, the lordliest that lift eyes and hearts and
   songs to meet the sun,
Names to fire men's ears like music till the
   round world's race be run.

PRAXITHEA.

I thy mother, named of Gods that wreak revenge and brand with blame,

Now for thy love shall be loved as thou, and
　　famous with thy fame,
While this city's name on earth shall be for
　　earth her mightiest name.

CHTHONIA.

That I may give this poor girl's blood of mine
Scarce yet sun-warmed with summer, this thin
　　life
Still green with flowerless growth of seedling
　　days,
To build again my city ; that no drop
Fallen of these innocent veins on the cold
　　ground
But shall help to knit the joints of her firm walls
To knead the stones together, and make sure
The band about her maiden girdlestead
Once fastened, and of all men's violent hands
Inviolable for ever ; these to me
Were no such gifts as crave no thanksgiving,
If with one blow dividing the sheer life
I might make end, and one pang wind up all
And seal mine eyes from sorrow ; for such end
The Gods give none they love not ; but my heart,
That leaps up lightened of all sloth or fear
To take the sword's point, yet with one
　　thought's load
Flags, and falls back, broken of wing, that
　　halts
Maimed in mid flight for thy sake and borne
　　down,
Mother, that in the places where I played
An arm's length from thy bosom and no more
Shalt find me never, nor thine eye wax glad
To mix with mine its eyesight and for love
Laugh without word, filled with sweet light,
　　and speak
Divine dumb things of the inward spirit and
　　heart,
Moved silently ; nor hand or lip again
Touch hand or lid of either, but for mine
Shall thine meet only shadows of swift night,
Dreams and dead thoughts of dead things ; and
　　the bed
Thou strewedst, a sterile place for all time,
　　strewn
For my sleep only, with its void sad sheets
Shall vex thee, and the unfruitful coverlid
For empty days reproach me dead, that leave
No profit of my body, but am gone
As one not worth being born to bear no seed,
A sapless stock and branchless : yet thy womb
Shall want not honor of me, that brought forth
For all this people freedom, and for earth

From the unborn city born out of my blood
To light the face of all men evermore
Glory ; but lay thou this to thy great heart
Whereunder in the dark of birth conceived
Mine unlit life lay girdled with the zone
That bound thy bridal bosom ; set this thought
Against all edge of evil as a sword
To beat back sorrow, that for all the world
Thou brought'st me forth a saviour, who shall
　　save
Athens ; for none but I from none but thee
Shall take this death for garland ; and the men
Mine unknown children of unsounded years,
My sons unrisen shall rise up at thine hand,
Sown of thy seed to bring forth seed to thee,
And call thee most of all most fruitful found
Blessed ; but me too for my barren womb
More than my sisters for their children born
Shall these give honor, yea in scorn's own
　　place
Shall men set love and bring for mockery
　　praise
And thanks for curses ; for the dry wild vine
Scoffed at and cursed of all men that was I
Shall shed them wine to make the world's heart
　　warm,
That all eyes seeing may lighten, and all ears
Hear and be kindled ; such a draught to drink
Shall be the blood that bids this dust bring
　　forth,
The chaliced life here spilt on this mine earth,
Mine, my great father's mother ; whom I pray
Take me now gently, tenderly take home,
And softly lay in his my cold chaste hand
Who is called of men by my name, being of
　　Gods
Charged only and chosen to bring men under
　　earth,
And now must lead and stay me with his staff
A silent soul led of a silent God,
Toward sightless things led sightless ; and on
　　earth
I see now but the shadow of mine end,
And this last light of all for me in heaven.

PRAXITHEA.

Farewell I bid thee ; so bid thou not me,
Lest the Gods hear and mock us ; yet on these
I lay the weight not of this grief, nor cast
Ill words for ill deeds back ; for if one say
They have done men wrong, what hurt have
　　they to hear,
Or he what help to have said it ? surely, child,
If one among men born might say it and live

Blameless, none more than I may, who being
   vexed
Hold yet my peace; for now through tears
   enough
Mine eyes have seen the sun that from this day
Thine shall see never more; and in the night
Enough has blown of evil, and mine ears
With wail enough the winds have filled, and
   brought
Too much of cloud from over the sharp sea
To mar for me the morning; such a blast
Rent from these wide void arms and helpless
   breast
Long since one graft of me disbranched, and
   bore
Beyond the wild ways of the unwandered
   world
And loud wastes of the thunder-throated sea,
Springs of the night and openings of the
   heaven,
The old garden of the Sun; whence never
   more
From west or east shall winds bring back that
   blow
From folds of opening heaven or founts of
   night
The flower of mine once ravished, born my
   child
To bear strange children; nor on wings of
   theirs
Shall comfort come back to me, nor their sire
Breathe help upon my peril, nor his strength
Raise up my weakness; but of Gods and men
I drift unsteered on ruin, and the wave
Darkens my head with imminent height, and
   hangs
Dumb, filled too full with thunder that shall
   leave
These ears death-deafened when the tide finds
   tongue
And all its wrath bears on them; thee, O child,
I help not, nor am holpen; fain, ah fain,
More than was ever mother born of man,
Were I to help thee: fain beyond all prayer,
Beyond all thought fain to redeem thee, torn
More timeless from me sorrowing than the
   dream
That was thy sister; so shalt thou be too,
Thou but a vision, shadow-shaped of sleep,
By grief made out of nothing; now but once
I touch, but once more hold thee, one more
   kiss
This last time and none other ever more
Leave on thy lips and leave them. Go; thou
   wast

My heart, my heart's blood, life-blood of my
   life,
My child, my nursling; now this breast once
   thine
Shall rear again no children; never now
Shall any mortal blossom born like thee
Lie there, nor ever with small silent mouth
Draw the sweet springs dry for an hour that
   feed
The blind blithe life that knows not; never
   head
Rest here to make these cold veins warm, nor eye
Laugh itself open with the lips that reach
Lovingly toward a fount more loving; these
Death makes as all good lesser things now
   dead,
And all the latter hopes that flowered from
   these
And fall as these fell fruitless; no joy more
Shall man take of thy maidenhood, no tongue
Praise it; no good shall eyes get more of thee
That lightened for thy love's sake. Now, take
   note,
Give ear, O all ye people, that my word
May pierce your hearts through, and the stroke
   that cleaves
Be fruitful to them; so shall all that hear
Grow great at heart with child of thought most
   high
And bring forth seed in season; this my child,
This flower of this my body, this sweet life,
This fair live youth I give you, to be slain,
Spent, shed, poured out, and perish; take my
   gift
And give it death and the under Gods who
   crave
So much for that they give; for this is more,
Much more is this than all we; for they give
Freedom, and for a blast, an air of breath,
A little soul that is not, they give back
Light for all eyes, cheer for all hearts, and life
That fills the world's width full of fame and
   praise
And mightier love than children's. This they
   give,
The grace to make thy country great, and
   wrest
From time and death power to take hold on
   her
And strength to scathe for ever; and this gift,
Is this no more than man's love is or mine,
Mine and all mothers? nay, where that seems
   more,
Where one loves life of child, wife, father,
   friend,

29

Son, husband, mother, more than this, even
  there
Are all these lives worth nothing, all loves else
With this love slain and buried, and their tomb
A thing for shame to spit on ; for what love
Hath a slave left to love with ? or the heart
Base-born and bound in bondage fast to fear,
What should it do to love thee ? what hath he,
The man that hath no country ? Gods nor men
Have such to friend, yoked beast-like to base
  life,
Vile, fruitless, grovelling at the foot of death,
Landless and kinless thralls of no man's blood,
Unchilded and unmothered, abject limbs
That breed things abject ; but who loves on
  earth
Not friend, wife, husband, father, mother, child,
Nor loves his own life for his own land's sake,
But only this thing most, more this than all,
He loves all well and well of all is loved,
And this love lives for ever. See now, friends,
My countrymen, my brothers, with what heart
I give you this that of your hands again
The Gods require for Athens ; as I give
So give ye to them what their hearts would have
Who shall give back things better; yea, and these
I take for me to witness, all these Gods,
Were their great will more grievous than it is,
Not one but three, for this one thin-spun thread
A threefold band of children would I give
For this land's love's sake ; for whose love to-
  day
I bid thee, child, fare deathward and farewell.

CHORUS.

O wofullest of women, yet of all
Happiest, thy word be hallowed ; in all time
Thy name shall blossom, and from strange new
  tongues
High things be spoken of thee ; for such grace
The Gods have dealt to no man, that on none
Have laid so heavy sorrow. From this day
Live thou assured of godhead in thy blood,
And in thy fate no lowlier than a God
In all good things and evil ; such a name
Shall be thy child this city's and thine own,
Next hers that called it Athens. Go now
  forth
Blest, and grace with thee to the doors of
  death.

CHTHONIA.

O city, O glory of Athens, O crown of my
  father's land, farewell

CHORUS.

For welfare is given her of thee.

CHTHONIA.

O Goddess, be good to thy people, that in
  them dominion and freedom may dwell.

CHORUS.

Turn from us the strengths of the sea.

CHTHONIA.

Let glory's and theirs be one name in the
  mouths of all nations made glad with the
  sun.

CHORUS.

For the cloud is blown back with thy breath.

CHTHONIA.

With the long last love of mine eyes I salute thee, O land where my days now
  are done.

CHORUS.

But her life shall be born of thy death.

CHTHONIA.

I put on me the darkness thy shadow, my
  mother, and symbol, O Earth, of my
  name.

CHORUS.

For thine was her witness from birth.

CHTHONIA.

In thy likeness I come to thee darkling, a
  daughter whose dawn and her even are
  the same.

CHORUS.

Be thine heart to her gracious, O Earth.

CHTHONIA.

To thine own kind be kindly, for thy son's
  name's sake

CHORUS.

That sons unborn may praise thee and thy first-born son.

CHTHONIA.

Give me thy sleep, who give thee all my life awake.

CHORUS.

Too swift a sleep, ere half the web of day be spun.

CHTHONIA.

Death brings the shears or ever life wind up the weft.

CHORUS.

Their edge is ground and sharpened ; who shall stay his hand ?

CHTHONIA.

The woof is thin, a small short life, with no thread left.

CHORUS.

Yet hath it strength, stretched out, to shelter all the land.

CHTHONIA.

Too frail a tent for covering, and a screen too strait.

CHORUS.

Yet broad enough for buckler shall thy sweet life be.

CHTHONIA.

A little bolt to bar off battle from the gate.

CHORUS.

A wide sea-wall, that shatters the besieging sea.

CHTHONIA.

I lift up mine eyes from the skirts of the shadow,
　From the border of death to the limits of light ;
O streams and rivers of mountain and meadow
　That hallow the last of my sight,
　O father that wast of my mother
　Cephisus, O thou too his brother
　From the bloom of whose banks as a prey
　Winds harried my sister away,
　O crown on the world's head lying
　　Too high for its waters to drown,
　Take yet this one word of me dying,
　　O city, O crown.
Though land-wind and sea-wind with mouths that blow slaughter
　Should gird them to battle against thee again,
New-born of the blood of a maiden thy daughter,
　　The rage of their breath shall be vain.
　For their strength shall be quenched and made idle,
　And the foam of their mouths find a bridle,
　And the height of their heads bow down
　At the foot of the towers of the town.
　Be blest and beloved as I love thee
　　Of all that shall draw from thee breath ;
　Be thy life as the sun's is above thee ;
　　I go to my death.

CHORUS.

　Many loves of many a mood and many a kind
　Fill the life of man, and mould the secret mind ;
　Many days bring many dooms, to loose and bind ;
　Sweet in each in season, good the gift it brings,
　Sweet as change of night and day with altering wings,
Night that lulls world-weary day, day that comforts night,
Night that fills our eyes with sleep, day that fills with light.
　None of all is lovelier, loftier love is none,
　Less is bride's for bridegroom, mother's less for son,
　Child, than this that crowns and binds up all in one ;

Love of thy sweet light, thy fostering breast
    and hand,
Mother Earth, and city chosen, and natural land ;
Hills that bring the strong streams forth,
    heights of heavenlier air,
Fields aflower with winds and suns, woods
    with shadowing hair.
But none of the nations of men shall they liken
    to thee,
Whose children true-born and the fruit of thy
    body are we.
The rests are thy sons but in figure, in word
    are thy seed ;
We only the flower of thy travail, thy children
    indeed.
Of thy soil hast thou fashioned our limbs, of
    thy waters their blood,
And the life of thy springs everlasting is
    fount of our flood.
No wind oversea blew us hither adrift on thy
    shore,
None sowed us by land in thy womb that con-
    ceived us and bore.
But the stroke of the shaft of the sunlight that
    brought us to birth
Pierced only and quickened thy furrows to bear
    us, O Earth.
With the beams of his love wast thou cloven
    as with iron or fire,
And the life in thee yearned for his life, and
    grew great with desire.
And the hunger and thirst to be wounded and
    healed with his dart
Made fruitful the love in thy veins and the
    depth of thine heart.
And the showers out of heaven overflowing
    and liquid with love
Fulfilled thee with child of his godhead as rain
    from above.
Such desire had ye twain of each other, till
    molten in one
Ye might bear and beget of your bodies the
    fruits of the sun.
And the trees in their season brought forth and
    were kindled anew
By the warmth of the moisture of marriage,
    the child-bearing dew.
And the firstlings were fair of the wedlock of
    heaven and of earth ;
All countries were bounteous with blossom and
    burgeon of birth,
Green pastures of grass for all cattle, and life-
    giving corn ;
But here of thy bosom, here only, the man-
    child was born.

All races but one are as aliens engrafted or
    sown,
Strange children and changelings ; but we, O
    our mother, thine own.
Thy nurslings are others, and seedlings they
    know not of whom ;
For these hast thou fostered, but us thou hast
    borne in thy womb.
Who is he of us all, O beloved, that owe thee
    for birth,
Who would give not his blood for his birth's
    sake, O mother, O Earth ?
What landsman is he that was fostered and
    reared of thine hand
Who may vaunt him as we may in death
    though he die for the land ?
Well doth she therefore who gives thee in
    guerdon
    The bloom of the life of thy giving ;
And thy body was bowed by no fruitless burden,
    That bore such fruit of thee living.
    For her face was not darkened for fear,
    For her eyelids conceived not a tear,
        Nor a cry from her lips craved pity ;
    But her mouth was a fountain of song,
    And her heart as a citadel strong
        That guards the heart of the city.

MESSENGER.

High things of strong-souled men that loved
    their land
On brass and stone are written, and their deeds
On high days chanted ; but none graven or
    sung
That ever set men's eyes or spirits on fire,
Athenians, has the sun's height seen, or earth
Heard in her depth reverberate as from heaven,
More worth men's praise and good report of
    Gods
Than here I bring for record in your ears.
For now being come to the altar, where as
    priest
Death ministering should meet her, and his
    hand
Seal her sweet eyes asleep, the maiden stood,
With light in all her face as of a bride
Smiling, or shine of festal flame by night
Far flung from towers of triumph ; and her
    lips
Trembled with pride in pleasure, that no fear
Blanched them nor death before his time drank
    dry
The blood whose bloom fulfilled them ; for her
    cheeks

Lightened, and brighter than a bridal veil
Her hair enrobed her bosom and enrolled
From face to feet the body's whole soft length
As with a cloud sun-saturate ; then she spake
With maiden tongue words manlike, but her
   eyes
Lit mildly like a maiden's : *Countrymen,*
With more goodwill and height of happier
   heart
I give me to you than my mother bare,
And go more gladly this great way to death
Than young men bound to battle.   Then with
   face
Turned to the the shadowiest part of all the
   shrine
And eyes fast set upon the further shade,
Take me, dear Gods ; and as some form had
   shone
From the deep hollow shadow, some God's
   tongue
Answered, *I bless you that your guardian grace*
Gives me to guard this country, takes my blood,
Your child's by name, to heal it.   Then the
   priest
Set to the flower-sweet snow of her soft throat
The sheer knife's edge that severed it, and
   loosed
From the fair bondage of so spotless flesh
So strong a spirit ; and all that girt them
   round
Gazing, with souls that hung on that sad
   stroke,
Groaned, and kept silence after while a man
Might count how far the fresh blood crept, and
   bathed
How deep the dark robe and the bright shrine's
   base
Red-rounded with a running ring that grew
More large and duskier as the wells that fed
Were drained of that pure effluence : but the
   queen
Groaned not nor spake nor wept, but as a dream
Floats out of eyes awakening so past forth
Ghost-like, a shadow of sorrow, from all sight
To the inner court and chamber where she sits
Dumb, till word reach her of this whole day's
   end.

CHORUS.

More hapless born by far
   Beneath some wintrier star,
One sits in stone among high Lydian snows,
   The tomb of her own woes :
Yet happiest was once of the daughters of

Gods, and divine by her sire and her lord,
Ere her tongue was a shaft for the hearts of her
   sons, for the heart of her husband a sword.
   For she, too great of mind,
   Grown through her good things blind,
With goodless lips and fire of her own breath
   Spake all her house to death ;
But thou, no mother unmothered, nor kindled
   in spirit with pride of thy seed,
Thou hast hallowed thy child for a blameless
   blood-offering, and ransomed thy race by
   thy deed.

MESSENGER.

As flower is graffed on flower, so grief on grief
Engraffed brings forth new blossoms of strange
   tears,
Fresh buds and green fruits of an alien pain ;
For now flies rumor on a dark wide wing,
Murmuring of woes more than ye knew, most
   like
Hers whom ye hailed most wretched ; for the
   twain
Last left of all this house that wore last night
A threefold crown of maidens, and to-day
Should let but one fall dead out of the wreath,
If mad with grief we know not and sore love
For this their sister, or with shame soul-stung
To outlive her dead or doubt lest their lives too
The Gods require to seal their country safe
And bring the oracular doom to perfect end,
Have slain themselves, and fallen at the altar-
   foot
Lie by their own hands done to death ; and
   fear
Shakes all the city as winds a wintering tree,
And as dead leaves are men's hearts blown
   about
And shrunken with ill thoughts, and flowerless
   hopes
Parched up with presage, lest the piteous blood
Shed of these maidens guiltless fall and fix
On this land's forehead like a curse that cleaves
To the unclean soul's inexpiate hunted head
Whom his own crime tracks hotlier than a
   hound
To life's veiled end unsleeping ; and this hour
Now blackens toward the battle that must close
All gates of hope and fear on all their hearts
Who tremble toward its issue, knowing not yet
If blood may buy them surety, cleanse or soil
The helpless hands men raise and reach no stay.

CHORUS.

Ill thoughts breed fear, and fear ill words ; but
these
The Gods turn from us that have kept their
law.
　Let us lift up the strength of our hearts in
　　song,
　　And our souls to the height of the darkling
　　　day.
　If the wind in our eyes blow blood for
　　spray,
　Be the spirit that breathes in us life more
　　strong,
Though the prow reel round and the helm
　point wrong,
　And sharp reefs whiten the shoreward way.
For the steersman time sits hidden astern,
　With dark hand plying the rudder of doom,
　And the surf-smoke under it flies like fume
As the blast shears off and the oar-blades
　churn
The foam of our lives that to death return,
　Blown back as they break to the gulfing
　　gloom.
What cloud upon heaven is arisen, what
　shadow, what sound,
　From the world beyond earth, from the
　　night underground,
That scatters from wings unbeholden the weight
　of its darkness around ?
For the sense of my spirit is broken, and
　blinded its eye,
　As the soul of a sick man ready to die,
With fear of the hour that is on me, with dread
　if an end be not nigh.
O Eearth, O Gods of the land, have ye
　heart now to see and to hear
　What slays with terror mine eyesight and
　　seals mine ear ?
O fountains of streams everlasting, are all ye
　not shrunk up and withered for fear ?
Lo, night is arisen on the noon, and her
　hounds are in quest by day,
　And the world is fulfilled of the noise of
　　them crying for their prey,
And the sun's self stricken in heaven, and cast
　out of his course as a blind man astray.
　From east to west of the south sea-line
　Glitters the lightning of spears that shine ;
As a storm-cloud swoln that comes up from the
　skirts of the sea
　By the wind for helmsman to shoreward
　　ferried,

So black behind them the live storm serried
Shakes earth with the tramp of its foot, and
　the terror to be.
Shall the sea give death whom the land gave
　birth ?
O Earth, fair mother, O sweet live Earth,
Hide us again in thy womb from the waves of
　it, help us or hide.
　As a sword is the heart of the God thy brother,
　But thine as the heart of a new-made mother
To deliver thy sons from his ravin, and rage of
　his tide.
　O strong north wind, the pilot of cloud and
　　rain,
　For the gift we gave thee what gift hast thou
　　given us again ?
O God dark-winged, deep-throated, a terror to
　forth-faring ships by night,
　What bride-song is this that is blown on the
　　blast of thy breath ?
　A gift but of grief to thy kinsmen, a song but
　　of death,
For the bride's folk weeping, and woe for her
　father, who finds thee against him in fight.
　Turn back from us, turn thy battle, take heed
　　of our cry ;
　Let thy dread breath sound, and the waters
　　of war be dry ;
Let thy strong wrath shatter the strength of foe-
　men, the sword of their strength and the
　　shield ;
　　As vapors in heaven, or as waves or the
　　　wrecks of ships,
　　So break thou the ranks of their spears
　　　with the breath of thy lips,
Till their corpses have covered and clothed as
　with raiment the face of the sword-plough-
　　ed field.
　O son of the rose-red morning, O God twin-
　　born with the day,
　O wind with the young sun waking, and
　　winged for the same wide way,
Give up not the house of thy kin to the host
　thou hast marshalled from northward for prey.
　From the cold of thy cradle in Thrace, from
　　the mists of the fountains of night,
　From the bride-bed of dawn whence day
　　leaps laughing, on fire for his flight,
Come down with their doom in thine hand on
　the ships thou hast brought up against us
　　to fight.
For now not in word but in deed is the harvest
　of spears begun,
And its clamour outbellows the thunder, its
　lightning outlightens the sun

From the springs of the morning it thunders
and lightens across and afar
To the wave where the moonset ends and the
fall of the last low star.
With a trampling of drenched red hoofs and
an earthquake of men that meet,
Strong war sets hand to the scythe, and the
furrows take fire from his feet.
Earth groans from her great rent heart, and
the hollows of rocks are afraid,
And the mountains are moved, and the valleys
as waves in a storm-wind swayed.
From the roots of the hills to the plain's dim
verge and the dark loud shore,
Air shudders with shrill spears crossing, and
hurtling of wheels that roar.
As the grinding of teeth in the jaws of a lion
that foam as they gnash
Is the shriek of the axles that loosen, the shock
of the poles that crash.
The dense manes darken and glitter, the
mouths of the mad steeds champ,
Their heads flash blind through the battle,
and death's foot rings in their tramp.
For a fourfold host upon earth and in heaven
is arrayed for the fight,
Clouds ruining in thunder and armies encount-
ering as clouds in the night.
Mine ears are amazed with the terror of trumpets, with darkness mine eyes,
At the sound of the sea's host charging that
deafens the roar of the sky's.
White frontlet is dashed upon frontlet, and
horse against horse reels hurled,
And the gorge of the gulfs of the battle is wide
for the spoil of the world.
And the meadows are cumbered with shipwreck
of chariots that founder on land,
And the horsemen are broken with breach as
of breakers, and scattered as sand.
Through the roar and recoil of the charges
that mingle their cries and confound,
Like fire are the notes of the trumpets that
flash through the darkness of sound.
As the swing of the sea churned yellow that
sways with the wind as it swells
Is the lift and relapse of the wave of the char-
gers that clash with their bells ;
And the clang of the sharp shrill brass through
the burst of the wave as it shocks
Rings clean as the clear wind's cry through
the roar of the surge on the rocks :
And the heads of the steeds in their headgear
of war, and their corsleted breasts,

Gleam broad as the brows of the billows that
brighten the storm with their crests ;
Gleam dread as their bosoms that heave to the
shipwrecking wind as they rise,
Filled full of the terror and thunder of water,
that slays as it dies.
So dire is the glare of their foreheads, so fearful the fire of their breath,
And the light of their eyeballs enkindled so
bright with the lightnings of death ;
And the foam of their mouths as the sea's when
the jaws of its gulf are as graves,
And the ridge of their necks as the wind-shaken
mane on the ridges of waves :
And their fetlocks afire as they rear drip thick
with a dewfall of blood
As the lips of the rearing breaker with froth of
the manslaying flood :
And the whole plain reels and resounds as the
fields of the sea by night
When the stroke of the wind falls darkling,
and death is the seafarer's light.
But thou, fair beauty of heaven, dear face of
the day nigh dead,
What horror hath hidden thy glory, what hand
hath muffled thine head ?
O sun, with what song shall we call thee, or
ward off thy wrath by what name,
With what prayer shall we seek to thee,
soothe with what incense, assuage with
what gift,   .
If thy light be such only as lightens to deathward the seamen adrift
With the fire of his house for a beacon, that
foemen have wasted with flame ?
Arise now, lift up thy light ; give ear to us,
put forth thine hand,
Reach toward us thy torch of deliverance, a
lamp for the night of the land. ;
Thine eye is the light of the living, no lamp
for the dead ;
O, lift up the light of thine eye on the dark
of our dread.
Who hath blinded thee ? who hath prevailed
on thee ? who hath ensnared ?
Who hath broken thy bow, and the shafts
for thy battle prepared ?
Have they found out a fetter to bind thee, a
chain for thine arm that was bared ?
Be the name of thy conqueror set forth, and
the might of thy master declared ?
O God, fair God of the morning, O glory of
day,
What ails thee to cast from thy forehead its
garland away ?

To pluck from thy temples their chaplet enwreathed of the light,
And bind on the brows of thy godhead a
frontlet of night?
Thou hast loosened the necks of thine horses,
and goaded their flanks with affright,
To the race of a course that we know not on
ways that are hid from our sight.
As a wind through the darkness the wheels
of their chariot are whirled,
And the light of its passage is night on the
face of the world.
And there falls from the wings of thy glory
no help from on high,
But a shadow that smites us with fear and
desire of thine eye.
For our hearts are as reeds that a wind on the
water bows down and goes by,
To behold not thy comfort in heaven that hath
left us untimely to die.
But what light is it now leaps forth on the
land
Enkindling the waters and ways of the air
From thy forehead made bare,
From the gleam of thy bow-bearing hand?
Hast thou set not thy right hand again to the
string,
With the back-bowed horns bent sharp for
a spring
And the barbed shaft drawn,
Till the shrill steel sing and the tense nerve
ring
That pierces the heart of the dark with
dawn,
O huntsman, O king,
When the flame of thy face hath twilight in
chase
As a hound hath a blood-mottled fawn?
He has glanced into golden the grey sea-
strands,
And the clouds are shot through with the
fires of his hands,
And the height of the hollow of heaven that
he fills
As the heart of a strong man is quickened and
thrills;
High over the folds of the low-lying lands,
On the shadowless hills
As a guard on his watchtower he stands.
All earth and all ocean, all depth and all
height,
At the flash of an eyebeam are filled with his
might:
The sea roars backward, the storm drops
dumb,

And silence as dew on the fire of the fight
Falls kind in our ears as his face in our sight
With presage of peace to come.
Fresh hope in my heart from the ashes of
dread
Leaps clear as a flame from the pyres of the
dead,
　　That joy out of woe
May arise as the spring out of the tempest
and snow,
With the flower-feasted month in her hands
rose-red
Borne soft as a babe from the bearing-bed.
Yet it knows not indeed if a God be friend,
If rescue may be from the rage of the sea,
　　Or the wrath of its lord have end.
For the season is full now of death or of
birth,
To bring forth life, or an end of all ;
And we know not if anything stand or fall
That is girdled about with the round sea's
girth
　　As a town with its wall ;
But thou that art highest of the Gods most
high,
That art lord if we live, that art lord though
we die,
Have heed of the tongues of our terror that
cry
For a grace to the children of Earth.

ATHENIAN HERALD.

Sons of Athens, heavy-laden with the holy
weight of years,
Be your hearts as young men's lightened of
their loathlier load of fears ;
For the wave is sunk whose thunder shoreward
shook the shuddering lands
And unbreached of warring waters Athens like
a sea-rock stands.

CHORUS.

Well thy word has cheered us, well thy face
and glittering eyes, that spake
Ere thy tongue spake words of comfort ; yet
no pause behoves it make
Till the whole good hap find utterance that the
Gods have given at length.

ATHENIAN HERALD.

All is this, that yet the city stand unforced by
stranger strength.

CHORUS.

Sweeter sound might no mouth utter in man's
ear than this thy word.

ATHENIAN HERALD.

Feed thy soul then full of sweetness till some
bitter note be heard.

CHORUS.

None, if this ring sure, can mar the music fallen
from heaven as rain.

ATHENIAN HERALD.

If no fire of sun or star untimely sear the tender
grain.

CHORUS.

Fresh the dewfall of thy tidings on our hopes
reflowering lies.

ATHENIAN HERALD.

Till a joyless shower and fruitless blight them,
raining from thine eyes.

CHORUS.

Bitter springs have barren issues ; these bedew
grief's arid sands.

ATHENIAN HERALD.

Such thank-offerings ask such altars as expect
thy suppliant hands.

CHORUS.

Tears for triumph, wail for welfare, what strange
godhead's shrine requires ?

ATHENIAN HERALD.

Death or victory's be it, a funeral torch feeds
all its festal fires.

CHORUS.

Like a star should burn the beacon flaming
from our city's head.

ATHENIAN HERALD.

Like a balefire should the flame go up that says
the king is dead.

CHORUS.

Out of heaven, a wild-haired meteor, shoots
this new sign, scattering fear.

ATHENIAN HERALD.

Yea, the word has wings of fire that hovered,
loth to burn thine ear.

CHORUS.

From thy lips it leapt forth loosened on a shrill
and shadowy wing.

ATHENIAN HERALD.

Long they faltered, fain to hide it deep as death
that hides the king.

CHORUS.

Dead with him blind hope lies blasted by the
lightning of one sword.

ATHENIAN HERALD.

On thy tongue truth wars with error ; no man's
edge hath touched thy lord.

CHORUS.

False was thine then, jangling menace like a
warsteed's brow-bound bell ?

ATHENIAN HERALD.

False it rang not joy nor sorrow ; but by no
man's hand he fell.

CHORUS.

Vainly then good news and evil through so faint
a trumpet spake.

ATHENIAN HERALD.

All too long thy soul yet labors, as who sleeping fain would wake,

Waking, fain would fall on sleep again ; the
woe thou knowest not yet,
When thou knowest, shall make thy memory
thirst and hunger to forget.

CHORUS.

Long my heart has hearkened, hanging on thy
clamorous ominous cry,
Fain yet fearful of the knowledge whence it
looks to live or die ;
Now to take the perfect presage of thy dark
and side-long flight
Comes a surer soothsayer sorrowing, sable-
stoled as birds of night.

PRAXITHEA.

Man, what thy mother bare thee born to say
Speak ; for no word yet wavering on thy lip
Can wound me worse than thought forestalls or
fear.

ATHENIAN HERALD.

I have no will to weave too fine or far,
O queen, the weft of sweet with bitter speech,
Bright words with darkling ; but the brief
truth shown
Shall plead my pardon for a lingering tongue,
Loth yet to strike hope through the heart and
slay.
The sun's light still was lordly housed in heaven
When the twain fronts of war encountering
smote
First fire out of the battle ; but not long
Had the fresh wave of windy fight begun
Heaving, and all the surge of swords to sway,
When timeless night laid hold of heaven, and
took
With its great gorge the noon as in a gulf,
Strangled ; and thicker than the shrill-winged
shafts
Flew the fleet lightnings, held in chase through
heaven
By headlong heat of thunders on their trail
Loosed as on quest of quarry ; that our host
Smit with sick presage of some wrathful God
Quailed, but the foe as from one iron throat
With one great sheer sole thousand-throated
cry
Shook earth, heart-staggered from their shout,
and clove
The eyeless hollow of heaven ; and breached
therewith

As with an onset of strength-shattering sound
The rent vault of the roaring noon of night
From her throned seat of usurpation rang
Reverberate answer ; such response there
pealed
As though the tide's charge of a storming sea
Had burst the sky's wall, and made broad a
breach
In the ambient girth and bastion flanked with
stars
Guarding the fortress of the Gods, and all
Crashed now together on ruin ; and through
that cry
And higher above it ceasing one man's note
Tore its way like a trumpet : *Charge, make end,*
Charge, halt not, strike, rend up their strength
by the roots,
Strike, break them, make your birthright's
promise sure,
Show your hearts hardier than the fenced land
breeds
And souls breathed in you from no spirit of
earth,
Sons of the sea's waves ; and all ears that heard
Rang with that fiery cry, that the fine air
Thereat was fired, and kindling filled the plain
Full of that fierce and trumpet-quenching breath
That spake the clarions silent ; no glad song
For folk to hear that wist how dire a God
Begat this peril to them, what strong race
Fathered the sea-born tongue that sang them
death,
Threatening ; so raged through the red foam of
fight
Poseidon's son Eumolpus ; and the war
Quailed round him coming, and our side bore
back,
As a stream thwarted by the wind and sea
That meet it midway mouth to mouth, and beat
The flood back of its issue ; but the king
Shouted against them, crying, *O Father-God,*
Source of the God my father, from thine hand
Send me what end seems good now in thy sight,
But death from mine to this man ; and the
word
Quick on his lips yet like a blast of fire
Blew them together ; and round its lord that met
Paused all the reeling battle ; two main waves
Meeting, one hurled sheer from the sea-wall
back
That shocks it sideways, one right in from sea
Charging, that full in face takes at one blow
That whole recoil and ruin, with less fear
Startle men's eyes late shipwrecked ; for a
breath

Crest fronting crest hung, wave to wave rose
   poised,
Then clashed, breaker to breaker ; cloud with
   cloud
In heaven, chariot with chariot closed on earth,
One fourfold flash and thunder ; yet a breath,
And with the king's spear through his red
   heart's root
Driven, like a rock split from its hill-side, fell
Hurled under his own horsehoofs dead on earth
The sea-beast that made war on earth from sea,
Dumb, with no shrill note left of storming song,
Eumolpus ; and his whole host with one stroke
Spear-stricken through its dense deep iron
   heart
Fell hurtling from us, and in fierce recoil
Drew seaward as with one wide wail of waves,
Resorbed with reluctation ; such a groan
Rose from the fluctuant refluence of its ranks,
Sucked sullen back and strengthless ; but
   scarce yet
The steeds had sprung and wheels had bruised
   their lord
Fallen, when from highest height of the sund-
   ering heaven
The Father for his brother's son's sake slain
Sent a sheer shaft of lightning writhen and
   smote
Right on his son's son's forehead, that unhelmed
Shone like the star that shines down storm,
   and gave
Light to men's eyes that saw thy lord their king
Stand and take breath from battle ; then too
   soon
Saw sink down as a sunset in sea-mist
The high bright head that here in van of the
   earth
Rose like a headland, and through storm and
   night
Took all the sea's wrath on it ; and now dead
They bring thee back by war-forsaken ways
The strength called once thy husband, the great
   guard
That was of all men, stay of all men's lives,
They bear him slain of no man but a God,
Godlike ; and toward him dead the city's gates
Fling their arms open mother-like, through
   him
Saved ; and the whole clear land is purged of
   war.
What wilt thou say now of this weal and woe ?

PRAXITHEA.

I praise the Gods for Athens. O sweet Earth,

Mother, what joy thy soul has of thy son,
Thy life of my dead lord, mine own soul knows
That knows thee godlike ; and what grief
   should mine,
What sorrow should my heart have, who behold
Thee made so heavenlike happy ? This alone
I only of all these blessed, all thy kind,
Crave this for blessing to me, that in theirs
Have but a part thus bitter ; give me too
Death, and the sight of eyes that meet not
   mine.
And thee too from no godless heart or tongue
Reproachful, thee too by thy living name,
Father divine, merciful God, I call,
Spring of my life-springs, fountain of my stream,
Pure and poured forth to one great end with
   thine,
Sweet head sublime of triumph and these tears,
Cephisus, if thou seest as gladly shed
Thy blood in mine as thine own waves are
   given
To do this great land good, to give for love
The same lips drink and comfort the same
   hearts,
Do thou then, O my father, white-souled God,
To thy most pure earth-hallowing heart eterne
Take what thou gavest to be given for these,
Take thy child to thee ; for her time is full,
For all she hath borne she hath given, seen all
   she had
Flow from her, from her eyes and breasts and
   hands
Flow forth to feed this people ; but be thou,
Dear God and gracious to all souls alive,
Good to thine own seed also ; let me sleep,
Father'; my sleepless darkling day is done,
My day of life like night, but slumberless :
For all my fresh fair springs, and his that ran
In one stream's bed with mine, are all run out
Into the deep of death. The Gods have saved
Athens ; my blood has bought her at their
   hand,
And ye sit safe ; be glorious and be glad
As now for all time always, countrymen,
And love my dead for ever ; but me, me,
What shall man give for these so good as death ?

CHORUS.

From the cup of my heart I pour through my
   lips along
The mingled wine of a joyful and sorrowful
   song ;
Wine sweeter than honey and bitterer than
   blood that is poured

From the chalice of gold, from the point of the
　　two-edged sword.
For the city redeemed should joy flow forth as
　　a flood,
And a dirge make moan for the city polluted
　　with blood.
Great praise should the Gods have surely, my
　　country, of thee,
Were thy brow but as white as of old for thy
　　sons to see,
Were thy hands as bloodless, as blameless thy
　　cheek divine ;
But a stain on it stands of the life-blood offered
　　for thine.
What thanks shall we give that are mixed not
　　and marred with dread
For the price that has ransomed thine own
　　with thine own child's head ?
　　For a taint there cleaves to the people re-
　　　deemed with blood,
　　And a plague to the blood-red hand.
The rain shall not cleanse it, the dew nor the
　　sacred flood
　　That blesses the glad live land.
In the darkness of earth beneath, in the world
　　without sun,
　　The shadows of past things reign ;
And a cry goes up from the ghost of an ill deed
　　done,
And a curse for a virgin slain.

ATHENA.

Hear, men that mourn, and woman without
　　mate,
Hearken ; ye sick of soul with fear, and thou
Dumb-stricken for thy children ; hear ye too,
Earth, and the glory of heaven, and winds of
　　the air,
And the most holy heart of the deep sea,
Late worth, now full of quiet ; hear thou, sun,
Rolled round with the upper fire of rolling
　　heaven
And all the stars returning ; hill and streams,
Springs and fresh fountains, day that seest these
　　deeds,
Night that shalt hide not ; and thou child of
　　mine,
Child of a maiden, by a maid redeemed,
Blood-guiltless, though bought back with inno-
　　cent blood,
City mine own ; I Pallas bring thee word,
I virgin daughter of the most high God
Give all you charge and lay command on all
The word I bring be wasted not ; for this

The Gods have stablished and his soul hath
　　sworn,
That time nor earth nor changing sons of ma .
Nor waves of generations, nor the winds
Of ages risen and fallen that steer their tides
Through light and dark of birth and lovelier
　　death
From storm toward haven inviolable, shall see
So great a light alive beneath the sun
As the awless eye of Athens ; all fame else
Shall be to her fame as a shadow in sleep
To this wide noon at waking ; men most praised
In lands most happy for their children found
Shall hold as highest of honors given of God
To be but likened to the least of thine,
Thy least of all, my city ; thine shall be
The crown of all songs sung, of all deeds done
Thine the full flower of all time ; in thine hand
Shall time be like a sceptre, and thine head
Wear worship for a garland ; nor one leaf
Shall change or winter cast out of thy crown
Till all flowers wither in the world ; thine eyes
Shall first in man's flash lightning liberty,
Thy tongue shall first say freedom ; thy first hand
Shall loose the thunder terror as a hound
To hunt from sunset to the springs of the sun
Kings that rose up out of the populous east
To make their quarry of thee, and shall strew
With multitudinous limbs of myriad herds
The foodless pastures of the sea, and make
With wrecks immeasurable and unsummed
　　defeat
One ruin of all their many-folded flocks
Ill shepherded from Asia ; by thy side
Shall fight thy son the north wind, and the sea
That was thine enemy shall be sworn thy friend
And hand be struck in hand of his and thine
To hold faith fast for aye ; with thee, though
　　each
Make war on other, wind and sea shall keep
Peace, and take truce as brethren for thy sake
Leagued with one spirit and single-hearted
　　strength
To break thy foes in pieces, who shall meet
The wind's whole soul and might of the main
　　sea
Full in their face of battle, and become
A laughter to thee ; like a shower of leaves
Shall their long galleys rank by staggering rank
Be dashed adrift on ruin, and in thy sight
The sea deride them, and that lord of the air
Who took by violent hand thy child to wife
With his loud lips bemock them, by his
　　breath
Swept out of sight of being ; so great a grace

Shall this day give thee, that makes one in heart
With mine the deep sea's godhead, and his son
With him that was thine helmsman, king with
    king,
Dead man with dead ; such only names as these
Shalt thou call royal, take none else or less
To hold of men in honor ; but with me
Shall these be worshiped as one God, and mix
With mine the might of their mysterious names
In one same shrine served singly, thence to keep
Perpetual guard on Athens ; time and change,
Masters and lords of all men, shall be made
To thee that knowest no master and no lord
Servants ; the days that lighten heaven and
    nights
That darken shall be ministers of thine
To attend upon thy glory, the great years
As light-engraven letters of thy name
Writ by the sun's hand on the front of the
    earth
For world-beholden witness ; such a gift
For one fair chaplet of three lives enwreathed
To hang for ever from thy storied shrine,
And this thy steersman fallen with tiller in hand
To stand for ever at thy ship's helm seen,
Shall he that bade their threefold flower be
    shorn
And laid him low that planted, give thee back
In sign of sweet land reconciled with sea
And heavenlike earth with heaven ; such
    promise-pledge
I daughter without mother born of God
To the most woful mother born of man
Plight for continual comfort. Hail, and live
Beyond all human hap of mortal doom
Happy ; for so my sire hath sworn and I.

PRAXITHEA.

O queen Athena, from a heart made whole

Take as thou givest us blessing ; never tear
Shall stain for shame nor groan untune the
    song
That as a bird shall spread and fold its wings
Here in thy praise for ever, and fulfil
The whole world's crowning city crowned with
    thee
As the sun's eye fulfils and crowns with sight
The circling crown of heaven. There is no
    grief
Great as the joy to be made one in will
With him that is the heart and rule of life
And thee, God born of God ; thy name is ours,
And thy large grace more great than our de-
    sire.

CHORUS.

From the depth of the springs of my spirit a
    fountain is poured of thanksgiving,
  My country, my mother, for thee,
That thy dead for their death shall have life in
    thy sight and a name everliving
  At heart of thy people to be.
In the darkness of change on the waters of
    time they shall turn from afar
To the beam of this dawn for a beacon, the
    light of these pyres for a star.
They shall see thee who love and take comfort,
    who hate thee shall see and take warn-
    ing,
  Our mother that makest us free ;
And the sons of thine earth shall have help of
    the waves that made war on their morn-
    ing,
    And friendship and fame of the sea.

STUDIES IN SONG.

SONG FOR THE CENTENARY

WALTER SAVAGE LANDOR.

BORN JANUARY 30TH, 1775.

DIED SEPTEMBER 17TH, 1864.

There is delight in singing, though none hear
Beside the singer : and there is delight
In praising, though the praiser sit alone
And see the praised far off him, far above.

LANDOR.

DEDICATION.

TO MRS. LYNN LINTON.

Daughter in spirit elect and consecrate
By love and reverence of the Olympian sire
Whom I too loved and worshipped, seeing so great,
And found so gracious toward my long desire
To bid that love in song before his gate
Sound, and my lute be loyal to his lyre,
To none save one it now may dedicate
Song's new burnt-offering on a century's pyre.
And though the gift be light
As ashes in men's sight,
Left by the flame of no ethereal fire,
Yet, for his worthier sake
Than words are worthless, take
This wreath of words ere yet their hour expire:
So, haply, from some heaven above,
He, seeing, may set next yours my sacrifice of love.

May 24, 1880.

1.

FIVE years beyond an hundred years have seen
  Their winters, white as faith's and age's hue,
Melt, smiling through brief tears that broke
    between,
  And hope's young conquering colors reared
    anew,
Since, on the day whose edge for kings made
    keen
  Smote sharper once than ever storm-wind
    blew,
A head predestined for the girdling green
  That laughs at lightning all the seasons
    through,
    Nor frost or change can sunder
    Its crown untouched of thunder
Leaf from least leaf of all its leaves that grew
    Alone for brows too bold
    For storm to sear of old,
  Elect to shine in time s eternal view,
    Rose on the verge of radiant life
Between the winds and sunbeams mingling
    love with strife.

2.

The darkling day that gave its bloodred
    birth
  To Milton's white republic undefiled
That might endure so few fleet years on
    earth
  Bore in him likewise as divine a child ;
But born not less for crowns of love and mirth,
  Of palm and myrtle passionate and mild,
The leaf that girds about with gentler girth
  The brow steel-bound in battle, and the
    wild
    Soft spray that flowers above
    The flower-soft hair of love ;
  And the white lips of wayworn winter smil-
    ed
    And grew serene as spring's
    When with stretched clouds like wings
  Or wings like drift of snow-clouds massed
    and piled
    The godlike giant, softening, spread
  A shadow of stormy shelter round the new-
    born head.

3.

And o'er it brightening bowed the wild-haired
    hour,
And touched his tongue with honey and with
    fire,
And breathed between his lips the note of
    power
That makes of all the winds of heaven a
    lyre
Whose strings are stretched from topmost
    peaks that tower
To softest springs of waters that suspire,
With sounds too dim to shake the lowliest
    flower
Breathless with hope and dauntless with de-
    sire :
      And bright before his face
      That Hour became a Grace,
As in the light of their Athenian quire
      When the Hours before the sun
      And Graces were made one,
Called by sweet Love down from the aerial
    gyre
    By one dear name of natural joy,
To bear on her bright breast from heaven a
    heaven-born boy.

4.

Ere light could kiss the little lids in sunder
    Or love could lift them for the sun to
    smite,
His fiery birth-star as a sign of wonder
    Had risen, perplexing the presageful night
With shadow and glory around her sphere and
    under
    And portents prophesying by sound and
    sight ;
And half the sound was song and half was
    thunder,
    And half his life of lightning, half of
    light :
      And in the soft clenched hand
      Shone like a burning brand
A shadowy sword for swordless fields of
    fight ;
      Wrought only for such lord
      As so may wield the sword
That all things ill be put to fear and
    flight
    Even at the flash and sweep and gleam
Of one swift stroke beheld but in a shuddering
    dream.

5.

Like the sun's rays that blind the night's wild
    beasts
The sword of song shines as the swordsman
    sings ;
From the west wind's verge even to the ardu-
    ous east's
The splendor of the shadow that it flings
Makes fire and storm in heaven above the
    feasts
Of men fulfilled with food of evil things ;
Strikes dumb the lying and hungering lips of
    priests,
    Smites dead the slaying and ravening hands
    of kings ;
      Turns dark the lamp's hot light,
      And turns the darkness bright
As with the shadow of dawn's reverberate
    wings ;
      And far before its way
      Heaven, yearning toward the day,
Shines with its thunder and round its light-
    ning rings ;
    And never hand yet earlier played
With that keen sword whose hilt is cloud, and
    fire its blade.

6.

As dropping flakes of honey-heavy dew
    More soft than slumber's, fell the first note's
    sound
From strings the swift young hand strayed
    lightlier through
    Than leaves through calm air wheeling
    toward the ground
Stray down the drifting wind when skies are
    blue
    Nor yet the wings of latter winds un-
    bound,
Ere winter loosen all the Æolian crew
    With storm unleashed behind them like a
    hound.
      As lightly rose and sank
      Beside a green-flowered bank
The clear first notes his burning boyhood
    found
      To sing her sacred praise
      Who rode her city's ways
Clothed with bright hair and with high pur-
    pose crowned ;
    A song of soft presageful breath,
Prefiguring all his love and faith in life and
    death ;

7.

Who should love two things only and only
 praise
 More than all else for ever : even the glory
Of goodly beauty in women, whence all days
 Take light whereby death's self seems
  transitory ;
And loftier love than loveliest eyes can raise,
 Love that wipes off the miry stains and gory
From Time's worn feet, besmirched on blood-
  red ways,
 And lightens with his light the night of story ;
  Love that lifts up from dust
  Life, and makes darkness just,
 And purges as with fire of purgatory
  The dense disastrous air,
  To burn old falsehood bare
 And give the wind its ashes heaped and
  hoary ;
  Love, that with eyes of ageless youth
Sees on the breast of Freedom borne her nurs-
 ling Truth.

8.

For at his birth the sistering stars were one
 That flamed upon it as one fiery star ;
Freedom, whose light makes pale the mount-
  ing sun,
 And Song, whose fires are quenched when
  Freedom's are.
Of all that love not liberty let none
 Love her that fills our lips with fire from far
To mix with winds and seas in unison
 And sound athwart life's tideless harbor-bar
  Out where our songs fly free
  Across time's bounded sea,
A boundless flight beyond the dim's sun car,
  Till all the spheres of night
  Chime concord round their flight
 Too loud for blasts of warring change to
  mar,
  From stars that sang for Homer's birth
To these that gave our Landor welcome back
  from earth.

9.

Shine, as above his cradle, on his grave,
 Stars of our worship, lights of our desire !
For never man that heard the world's wind
  rave
 To you was truer in trust of heart and lyre :

30

Nor Greece nor England on a brow more
  brave
 Behold your flame against the wind burn
  higher:
Nor all the gusts that blanch life's worldly
  wave
 With surf and surge could quench its flaw-
  less fire :
  No blast of all that blow
  Might bid the torch burn low
 That lightens on us yet as o'er his pyre,
  Indomitable of storm,
  That now no flaws deform
 Nor thwart winds baffle ere it all aspire,
  One light of godlike breath and flame,
 To write on heaven with man's most glorious
  names his name.

10.

The very dawn was dashed with stormy dew
 And freaked with fire as when God's hand
  would mar
Palaces reared of tyrants, and the blue
 Deep heaven was kindled round her thunder-
  ous car,
That saw how swift a gathering glory grew
 About him risen, ere clouds could blind or
  bar
A splendor strong to burn and burst them
  through
 And mix in one sheer light things near and
  far.
  First flew before his path
  Light shafts of love and wrath,
 But winged and edged as elder warriors'
  are ;
  Then rose a light that showed
  Across the midsea road
 From radiant Calpe to revealed Masar
  The way of war and love and fate
 Between the goals of fear and fortune, hope
  and hate.

11.

Mine own twice banished fathers' harbor-land,
 Their nursing-mother France, the well-be-
  loved,
By the arduous blast of sanguine sunrise fanned,
 Flamed on him, and his burning lips were
  moved
As that live statue's throned on Lybian sand
 When morning moves it, ere her light faith
  roved

From promise, and her tyrant's poisonous
    hand
    Fed hope with Corsic honey till she proved
        More deadly than despair
        And falser even than fair,
    Though fairer than all elder hopes removed
        As landmarks by the crime
        Of inundating time ;
    Light faith by grief too loud too long re-
        proved :
        For even as in some darkling dance
Wronged love changed hands with hate, and
    turned his heart from France.

12.

But past the snows and summits Pyrenean
    Love stronger-winged held more prevailing
        flight,
That o'er Tyrrhene, Iberian, and Ægean
    Shores lightened with one storm of sound
        and light.
From earliest even to hoariest years one pæan
    Rang rapture through the fluctuant roar of
        fight,
From Nestor's tongue in accents Achillean
    On death's blind verge dominant over night.
        For voice as hand and hand
        As voice for one fair land
    Rose radiant, smote sonorous, past the height
        Where darkling pines enrobe
        The steel-cold Lake of Gaube,
    Deep as dark death and keen as death to
        smite,
    To where on peak or moor or plain
His heart and song and sword were one to
    strike for Spain.

13.

Resurgent at his lifted voice and hand
    Pale in the light of war or treacherous fate
Song bade before him all their shadows stand
    For whom his will unbarred their funeral
        grate.
The father by whose wrong revenged his land
    Was given for sword and fire to desolate
Rose fire-encircled as a burning brand,
    Great as the woes he wrought and bore were
        great.
        Fair as she smiled and died,
        Death's crowned and breathless bride
    Smiled as one living even on craft and hate :
        And pity, a star unrisen,
        Scarce lit Ferrante's prison

Ere night unnatural closed the natural gate
    That gave their life and love and light
To those fair eyes despoiled by fratricide of
    sight.

14.

Tears bright and sweet as fire and incense fell
    In perfect notes of music-measured pain
On veiled sweet heads that heard not love's
    farewell
    Sob through the song that bade them rise
        again ;
Rise in the light of living song, to dwell
    With memories crowned of memory : so the
        strain
Made soft as heaven the stream that girdles
    hell
    And sweet the darkness of the breathless
        plain,
        And with Elysian flowers
        Recrowned the wreathless hours
    That mused and mourned upon their works
        in vain ;
        For all their works of death
        Song filled with light and breath,
    And listening grief relaxed her lightening
        chain ;
        For sweet as all the wide sweet south
    She found the song like honey from the lion's
        mouth.

15.

High from his throne in heavens Simonides,
    Crowned with mild aureole of memorial
        tears
That the everlasting sun of all time sees .
    All golden, molten from the forge of years,
Smiled, as the gift was laid upon his knees
    Of song that hang like pearls in mourners'
        ears,
Mild as the murmuring of Hymettian bees
    And honied as their harvest, that endears
        The toil of flowery days ;
        And smiling perfect praise
    Hailed his one brother mateless else of
        peers :
        Whom we that hear not him
        For length of date grown dim
    Hear, and the heart grows glad of grief that
        hears ;
        And harshest heights of sorrowing hours,
    Like snows of Alpine April, melt from tears to
        flowers.

16.

Therefore to him the shadow of death was
none,
    The darkness was not, nor the temporal
        tomb :
And multitudinous time for him was one,
    Who bade before his equal seat of doom
Rise and stand up for judgment in the sun
    The weavers of the world's large-historied
        loom,
By their own works of light or darkness done
    Clothed round with light or girt about with
        gloom.
        In speech of purer gold
        Than even they spake of old
He bade the breath of Sidney's lips relume
        The fire of thought and love
        That made his bright life move
Through fair brief seasons of benignant
        bloom
    To blameles music ever, strong
As death and sweet as death-annihilating song.

17.

Thought gave his wings the width of time to
        roam,
    Love gave his thought strength equal to re-
        lease
From bonds of old forgetful years like foam
    Vanished, the fame of memories that de-
        crease ;
So strongly faith had fledged for flight from
        home
    The soul's large pinions till her strife should
        cease :
And through the trumpet of a child of Rome
    Rang the pure music of the flutes of Greece.
        As though some northern hand
        Reft from the Latin land
    A spoil more costly than the Colchian fleece
        To clothe with golden sound
        Of old joy newly found
And rapture as of penetrating peace
    The naked north-wind's cloudiest clime,
And give its darkness light of the old Sicilian
        time.

18.

He saw the brand that fired the towers of Troy
Fade, and the darkness at Œnone's prayer
Close upon her that closed upon her boy,
    For all the curse of godhead that she bare ;

And the Apollonian serpent gleam and toy
    With scathless maiden limbs and shudder-
        ing hair ;
And his love smitten in their dawn of joy
    Leave Pan the pine-leaf of her charge to
        wear ;
        And one in flowery coils
        Caught as in fiery toils
Smite Calydon with mourning unaware ;
        And where her low turf shrine
        Showed Modesty divine
The fairest mother's daughter far more fair
    Hide on her breast the heavenly shame
That kindled once with love should kindle
        Troy with flame.

19.

Nor less the light of story than of song
    With graver glories girt his godlike head,
Reverted alway from the temporal throng
    Of lives that live not toward the living dead.
The shadows and the splendors of their throng
    Made bright and dark about his board and
        bed
The lines of life and vision, sweet or strong
    With sound of lutes or trumpets blown,
        that led
        Forth of the ghostly gate
        Opening in spite of fate
Shapes of majestic or tumultuous tread,
        Divine and direful things,
        These foul as priests or kings,
    Those fair as heaven or love of freedom, red
        With blood and green with palms and
        white
With raiment woven of deeds divine and words
        of light.

20.

The thunder-fire of Cromwell, and the ray
    That keeps the place of Phocion's name
        serene
And clears the cloud from Kosciusko's day,
    Alternate as dark hours with bright between,
Met in the heaven of his high thought, which
        lay
    For all stars open that all eyes had seen
Rise on the night or twilight of the way
    Where feet of human hopes and fears had
        been.
        Again the sovereign word
        On Milton's lips was heard
    Living · again the tender three days' queen

Drew bright and gentle breath
  On the sharp edge of death :
And, staged again to show of mortal scene,
  Tiberius, ere his name grew dire,
Wept, stainless yet of empire, tears of blood
  and fire.

21.

Most ardent and most awful and most fond,
  The fervor of his Apollonian eye
Yearned upon Hellas, yet enthralled in bond
  Of time whose years beheld her and passed
    by
Silent and shameful, till she rose and donned
  The casque again of Pallas ; for her cry
Forth of the past and future, depths beyond
  This where the present and its tyrants lie,
    As one great voice of twain
    For him had pealed again,
  Heard but of hearts high as her own was
    high,
      High as her own and his
      And pure as love's heart is,
  That lives through hope at once and mem-
    ory die :
  And with her breath his clarion's blast
Was filled as cloud with fire or future souls
    with past.

22.

As a wave only obsequious to the wind
  Leaps to the lifting breeze that bids it leap,
Large-hearted, and its thickening mane be
    thinned
  By the strong god's breath moving on the
    deep
From utmost Atlas even the extremest Ind
  That shakes the plain where no men sow nor
    reap,
So, moved with wrath toward men that ruled
    and sinned
  And pity toward all tears he saw men
    weep,
      Arose to take man's part
      His loving lion heart,
  Kind as the sun's that has in charge to
    keep
      Earth and the seed thereof
      Safe in his lordly love,
  Strong as sheer truth and soft as very sleep ;
    The mightiest heart since Milton's leapt,
  The gentlest since the gentlest heart of Shake-
    speare slept.

23.

Like the wind's own on her divided sea
  His song arose on Corinth, and aloud
Recalled her Isthmian song and strife when
    she
    Was thronged with glories as with gods in
      crowd
And as the wind's own spirit her breath was
    free
  And as the heaven's own heart her soul was
    proud,
But freer and prouder stood no son than he
  Of all she bare before her heart was bowed;
    None higher than he who heard
    Medea's keen last word
  Transpierce her traitor, and like a rushing
    cloud
      That sundering shows a star
      Saw pass her thunderous car
  And a face whiter and deadlier than a shroud
    That lightened from it, and the brand
Of tender blood that falling seared his suppli-
    ant hand.

24.

More fair than all things born and slain of fate,
  More glorious than all births of days and
    nights,
He bade the spirit of man regenerate,
  Rekindling, rise and reassume the rights
That in high seasons of his old estate
  Clothed him and armed with majesties and
    mights
Heroic, when the times and hearts were great
  And in the depths of ages rose the heights
      Radiant of high deeds done
      And souls that matched the sun
  For splendor with the lightnings of their
    lights
      Whence even their uttered names
      Burn like the strong twin flames
  Of song that shakes a throne and steel that
    smites ;
    As on Thermopylæ when shone
Leonidas, on Syracuse Timoleon.

25.

Or, sweeter than the breathless buds when
    spring
  With smiles and tears and kisses bids them
    breathe,
Fell with its music from his quiring string

Fragrance of pine-leaves and odorous heath
Twined round the lute whereto he sighed to
    sing
Of the oak that screened and showed its
    maid beneath,
Who seeing her bee crawl back with broken
    wing
Faded, a fairer flower than all her wreath,
    And paler, though her oak
    Stood scathless of the stroke
More sharp than edge of axe or wolfish teeth,
    That mixed with mortals dead
    Her own half heavenly head
And life incorporate with a sylvan sheath,
    And left the wild rose and the dove
A secret place and sacred from all guests but
    Love.

26.

But in the sweet clear fields beyond the river
    Dividing pain from peace and man from
    shade
He saw the wings that there no longer quiver
    Sink of the hours whose parting footfalls
    fade
On ears which hear the rustling amaranth
    shiver
With sweeter sound of wind than ever made
Music on earth : departing, they deliver
    The soul that shame or wrath or sorrow
    swayed ;
    And round the king of men
    Clash the clear arms again,
Clear of all soil and bright as laurel braid,
    That rang less high for joy
    Through the gates fallen of Troy
Than here to hail the sacrificial maid,
Iphigeneia, when the ford
Fast-flowing of sorrows brought her father and
    their lord.

27.

And in the clear gulf of the hollow sea
    He saw light glimmering through the grave
    green gloom
That hardly gave the sun's eye leave to see
Cymodameia ; but nor tower nor tomb,
No tower on earth, no tomb of waves may be,
    That may not sometime by diviner doom
Be plain and previous to the poet ; he
    Bids time stand back from him and fate
    make room
    For passage of his feet,

    Strong as their own are fleet,
And yield the prey no years may reassume
    Through all their clamorous track,
    Nor night nor day win back
Nor give to darkness what his eyes illume
    And his lips bless for ever : he
Knows what earth knows not, sings truth sung
    not of the sea.

28.

Before the sentence of a curule chair
    More sacred than the Roman, rose and stood
To take their several doom the imperial pair
    Diversely borne of Venus, and in mood
Diverse as their one mother, and as fair,
    Though like two stars contrasted, and as good,
    Though different as dark eyes from golden hair;
    One as that iron planet red like blood
    That bears among the stars
    Fierce witness of her Mars
In bitter fire by her sweet light subdued ;
    One in the gentler skies
    Sweet as her amorous eyes :
One proud of worlds and seas and darkness
    rude
    Composed and conquered ; one content
With lightnings from loved eyes of lovers
    lightly sent.

29.

And where Alpheus and where Ladon ran
    Radiant, by many a rushy and rippling cove
More known to glance of god than wandering
    man,
    He sang the strife of strengths divine that
    strove,
Unequal, one with other, for a span,
    Who should be friends forever in heaven
    above
And here on pastoral earth : Arcadian Pan,
    And the awless lord of kings and shepherds,
    Love :
    All the sweet strife and strange
    With fervid counterchange
Till one fierce wail through many a glade
    and grove
    Rang, and its breath made shiver
    The reeds of many a river,
And the warm airs waxed wintry that it
    clove,
    Keen-edged as ice-retempered brand ;
Nor might god's hurt find healing save of god-
    like hand.

30.

As when the jarring gates of thunder ope
  Like earthquake felt in heaven, so dire a cry,
So fearful and so fierce—'Give the sword
      scope !'—
  Rang from a daughter's lips, darkening the
      sky
To the extreme azure of all its cloudless cope
  With starless horror ; nor the god's own eye
'Whose doom bade smite, whose ordinance
    bade hope,
  Might well endure to see the adulteress die,
    The husband-slayer fordone
    By swordstroke of her son,
Unutterable, unimaginable on high,
    On earth abhorrent, fell
    Beyond all scourge of hell,
Yet righteous as redemption : Love stood
    nigh,
  Mute, sister-like, and closer clung
Than all fierce forms of threatening coil and
    maddening tongue.

31.

All these things heard and seen and sung of old,
  He heard and saw and sang them. Once
    again
Might foot of man tread, eye of man behold
Things unbeholden save of ancient men,
Ways save by gods untrodden. In his hold
  The staff that stayed through some Ætnean
    glen
The steps of the most highest, most awful-
    souled
And mightiest-mouthed of singers, even as
    then
    Became a prophet's rod,
    A lyre on fire of God,
Being still the staff of exile : yea, as when
    The voice poured forth on us
    Was even of Æschylus,
And his one word great as the crying of ten,
  Crying in men's ears of wrath toward
    wrong,
Of love toward right immortal, sanctified with
    song.

32.

Him too whom none save one before him ever
  Beheld, nor since hath man again beholden,
Whom Dante seeing him saw not, nor the
    giver

Of all gifts back to man by time witholden,
Shakespeare—him too, whom sea-like ages
    sever,
  As waves divide men's eyes from lights up-
    holden
To landward, from our songs that find him
    never,
  Seeking, though memory fire and hope em-
    bolden—
    Him too this one song found,
    And raised at its sole sound
Up from the dust of darkling dreams and
    olden
    Legends forlorn of breath.
    Up from the deeps of death
Ulysses : him whose name turns all songs
    golden,
  The wise divine strong soul, whom fate
Could make no less than change and chance
    beheld him great.

33.

Nor stands the seer who raised him less august
  Before us, nor in judgment frail and rathe,
Less constant or less loving or less just,
  But fruitful-ripe and full of tender faith,
Holding all high and gentle names in trust
  Of time for honor ; so his quickening breath
Called from the darkness of their martyred
    dust
  Our sweet Saints Alice and Elizabeth,
    Revived and reinspired
    With speech from heavenward fired
By love to say what Love the Archangel
    saith
    Only, nor may such word
    Save by such ears be heard
As hear the tongues of angels after death
    Descending on them like a dove
Has taken all earthly sense of thought away
    but love.

34.

All sweet, all sacred, all heroic things,
  All generous names and loyal, and all wise,
With all his heart in all its wayfarings
  He sought, and worshipped, seeing them
    with his eyes
In very present glory, clothed with wings
  Of words and deeds and dreams immortal
    rise
Visible more than living slaves and kings.
  Audible more than actual vows and lies ;

These, with scorn's fieriest rod,
These and the Lord their God,
The Lord their likeness, tyrant of the skies
As they Lord Gods of earth,
These with a rage of mirth
He mocked and scourged and spat on, in
such wise
That none might stand before his rod,
And these being slain the Spirit alone be lord
or God.

35.

For of all souls for all time glorious none
Loved Freedom better, of all who have lov-
ed her best,
Than he who wrote that scripture of the sun
Writ as with fire and light on heaven's own
crest,
Of all words heard on earth the noblest one
That ever spake for souls and left them blest :
GLADLY WE SHOULD REST EVER, HAD WE
WON
FREEDOM : WE HAVE LOST, AND VERY
GLADLY REST.
O poet hero, lord
And father, we record
Deep in the burning tablets of the breast
Thankfully those divine
And living words of thine
For faith and comfort in our hearts imprest
With strokes engraven past hurt of years
And lines inured with fire of immemorial tears.

36.

But who being less than thou shall sing of thee
Words worthy of more than pity or less than
scorn ?
Who sing the golden garland woven of three,
Thy daughters, Graces mightier than the
morn,
More godlike than the graven gods men see
Made all but immortal, human born
And heavenly natured ? With the first came
He,
Led by the living hand, who left forlorn
Life by his death, and time
More by his life sublime
Than by the lives of all whom all men
mourn,
And even for mourning praise
Heaven, as for all those days
These dead men's lives clothed round with
glories worn

By memory till all time lie dead,
And higher than all behold the bay round
Shakespeare's head.

37.

Then, fairer than the fairest Grace of ours,
Came girt with Grecian gold the second
Grace,
And verier daughter of his most perfect hours
Than any of latter time or alien place
Named, or with hair inwoven of English
flowers
Only, nor wearing on her statelier face
The lordlier light of Athens. All the Powers
That graced and guarded round that holiest
race,
That heavenliest and most high
Time hath seen live and die,
Poured all their power upon him to retrace
The erased immortal roll
Of Love's most sovereign scroll
And Wisdom's warm from Freedom's wide
embrace,
The scroll that on Aspasia's knees
Laid once made manifest the Olympian Peri.
cles.

38.

Clothed on with tenderest weft of Tuscan
air,
Came laughing like Etrurian spring the
third,
With green Valdelsa's hill-flowers in her hair
Deep-drenched with May-dews, in her voice
the bird
Whose voice hath night and morning in it ;
fair
As the ambient gold of wall-flowers that
engird
The walls engirdling with a circling stair
My sweet San Gimignano : nor a word
Fell from her flowerlike mouth
Not sweet with all the south ;
As though the dust shrined in Certaldo
stirred
And spake, as o'er it shone
That bright Pentameron,
And his own vines again and chestnuts
heard
Boccaccio : nor swift Elsa's chime
Mixed not her golden babble with Petrarca's
rhyme.

39.

No lovelier laughed the garden which receives
  Yet, and yet hides not from our following
    eyes
With soft rose-laurels and strawberry-leaves,
  Ternissa, sweet as April-colored skies,
Bowed like a flowering reed when May's wind
    heaves
The reed-bed that the stream kisses and
    sighs,
In love that shrinks and murmurs and believes
  What yet the wisest of the starriest wise
    Whom Greeee might ever hear
    Speaks in the gentlest ear
  That ever heard love's lips philosophize
    With such deep reasoning words
    As blossoms use and birds,
  Nor heeds Leontion lingering till they rise
  Far off, in no wise over far,
Beneath a heaven all amorous of its first-born
    star.

40.

What sound, what storm and splendour of
    what fire,
  Darkening the light of heaven, lightening
    the night,
Rings, rages, flashes round what ravening
    pyre
  That makes time's face pale with its reflex
    light
And leaves on earth, who seeing might scarce
    respire,
  A shadow of red remembrance ? Right nor
    might
Alternating wore ever shapes more dire
  Nor manifest in all men's awful sight
    In form and face that wore
    Heaven's light and likeness more
  Than these, or held suspense men's hearts
    at height
    More fearful, since man first
    Slaked with man's blood his thirst,
  Than when Rome clashed with Hannibal in
    fight,
  Till tower on ruining tower was hurled
Where Scipio stood, and Carthage was not in
    the world.

41.

Nor lacked there power of purpose in his hand

Who carved their several praise in words o.
    gold
To bare the brows of conquerors and to brand,
  Made shelterless of laurels bought and sold
For price of blood or incense, dust or sand,
  Triumph or terror. He that sought of old
His father Ammon in a stranger's land,
  And shrank before the serpentining fold,
    Stood in our seer's wide eye
    No higher than man most high,
  And lowest in heart when highest in hope
    hold
    Fast as a scripture furled
    The scroll of all the world
  Sealed with his signet : nor the blind and
    bold
    First thief of empire, round whose head
Swarmed carrion flies for bees, on flesh for
    violets fed.*

42.

As fire that kisses, killing with a kiss,
  He saw the light of death, riotous and red,
Flame round the bent brows of Semiramis
  Re-risen, and mightier, from the Assyrian
    dead,
Kindling, as dawn a frost-bound precipice,
  The steady snows of Russia, for the tread
Of feet that felt before them crawl and hiss
  The snaky lines of blood violently shed
    Like living creeping things
    That writhe but have no stings
  To scare adulterers from the imperial bed
    Bowed with its load of lust,
    Or chill the ravenous gust
  That made her body a fire from heel to head ;
  Or change her high bright spirit and clear,
For all its mortal stains, from taint of fraud or
    fear.

43.

As light that blesses, hallowing with a look,
  He saw the godhead in Vittoria's face
Shine soft on Buonarroti's, till he took,
  Albeit himself God, a more godlike grace,
A strength more heavenly to confront and
    brook
All ill things coiled about his worldy race,
From the bright scripture of that present book

* Thy lifelong works, Napoleon, who shall write ?
  Time, in his children's blood who takes delight.

From the Greek of Landor

Wherein his tired grand eyes got power to
    trace
    Comfort more sweet than youth,
    And hope whose child was truth,
And love that brought forth sorrow for a
    space,
    Only that she might bear
    Joy : these things, written there,
Made even his soul's high heaven a heaven-
    lier place,
    Perused with eyes whose glory and glow
Had in their fires the spirit of Michael Angelo.

44.

With balms and dews of blessing he consoled
    The fair fame wounded by the black priest's
    fang,
Giovanna's, and washed off her blithe and
    bold
Boy-bridegroom's blood, that seemed so
    long to hang
On her fair hand, even till the stain of old
Was cleansed with healing song, that after
    sang
Sharp truth by sweetest singers' lips untold
    Of pale Beatrice, though her death-note rang
    From other strings divine
    Ere his rekindling line
With yet more piteous and intolerant pang
    Pierced all men's hearts anew
    That heard her passion through
Till fierce from throes of fiery pity sprang
    Wrath, armed for chase of monstrous
    beasts,
Strong to lay waste the kingdom of the seed of
    priests.

45.

He knew the high-souled humbleness, the
    mirth
And majesty of meanest men born free,
That made with Luther's or with Hofer's birth
    The whole world worthier of the sun to see :
The wealth of spirit among the snows, the
    dearth
Wherein souls festered by the servile sea
That saw the lowest of even crowned heads on
    earth
    Thronged round with worship in Parthenope.
    His hand bade Justice guide
    Her child Tyrannicide,
Light winged by fire that brings the dawn to
    be ;

And pierced with Tyrrel's dart
    Again the riotous heart
That mocked at mercy's tongue and man-
    hood's knee :
And oped the cell where kinglike death
Hung o'er her brows discrowned who bare
    Elizabeth.

46.

Toward Spenser or toward Bacon proud or
    kind
    He bared the heart of Essex, twain and one,
For the base heart that soiled the starry mind
    Stern, for the father in his child undone
Soft as his own toward children, stamped and
    signed
    With their sweet image visibly set on
As by God's hand, clear as his own designed
    The likeness radiant out of ages gone
    That none may now destroy
    Of that high Roman boy
Whom Julius and Cleopatra saw their son
    True-born of sovereign seed,
    Foredoomed even thence to bleed,
The stately grace of bright Cæsarion,
    The head unbent, the heart unbowed,
That not the shadow of death could make less
    clear and proud.

47.

With gracious gods he communed, honoring
    thus
    At once by service and similitude,
Service devout and worship emulous
    Of the same golden Muses once they wooed,
The names and shades adored of all of us,
    The nurslings of the brave world's earlier
    brood,
Grown gods for us themselves : Theocritus
    First, and more dear Catullus, names be-
    dewed
    With blessings bright like tears
    From the old memorial years,
And loves and lovely laughters, every mood
    Sweet as the drops that fell
    Of their own œnomel
From living lips to cheer the multitude
    That feeds on words divine, and grows
More worthy, seeing their world reblossom like
    a rose.

48.

Peace, the soft seal of long life's closing story,
  The silent music that no strange note jars,
Crowned not with gentler hand the years that
    glory
  Crowned, but could hide not all the spirit-
    ual scars
Time writes on the inward strengths of war-
    riors hoary
  With much long warfare, and with gradual
    bars
Blindly pent in : but these, being transitory,
  Broke, and the power came back that pass-
    ion mars :
    And at the lovely last
    Above all anguish past
Before his own the sightless eyes like stars
    Arose that watched arise
    Like stars in other skies
Above the strife of ships and hurtling cars
  The Dioscurian songs divine
That lighten all the world with lightning of
    their line.

49.

He sang the last of Homer, having sung
  The last of his Ulysses. Bright and wide
For him time's dark strait ways, like clouds
    that clung
  About the day-star, doubtful to divide,
Waxed in his spiritual eyeshot, and his tongue
  Spake as his soul bore witness, that descried,
Like those twin towering lights in darkness
    hung,

Homer, and grey Laertes at his side
    Kingly as kings are none
    Beneath a later sun,
And the sweet maiden ministering in pride
    To sovereign and to sage
    In their more sweet old age :
These things he sang, himself as old, and
    died.
  And if death be not, if life be,
As Homer and as Milton are in heaven is he.

50.

Poet whose large-eyed loyalty of love
  Was pure toward all high poets, all their
    kind
And all bright words and all sweet works
    thereof;
  Strong like the sun, and like the sunlight
    kind ;
Heart that no fear but every grief might move
  Wherewith men's hearts were bound of
    powers that bind ;
The purest soul that ever proof could prove
  From taint of tortuous or of envious mind ;
    Whose eyes elate and clear
    Nor shame nor ever fear
But only pity or glorious wrath could
    blind ;
    Name set for love apart,
    Held lifelong in my heart,
  Face like a father's toward my face inclined ;
No gift like thine are mine to give,
Who by thine own words only bid thee hail,
    and live.

OFF SHORE.

WHEN the might of the summer
    Is most on the sea ;
When the days overcome her
    With joy but to be,
With rapture of royal enchantment, and sor-
    cery that sets her not free,

  But for hours upon hours
    As a thrall she remains
    Spell-bound as with flowers

And content in their chains,
And her loud steeds fret not, and lift not
    lock of their deep white manes ;

    Then only, far under
      In the depths of her hold,
    Some gleam of its wonder
      Man's eye may behold,
Its wild weed forests of crimson and russet
    and olive and gold.

Still deeper and dimmer
And goodlier they glow
For the eyes of the swimmer
Who scans them below
As he crosses the zone of their flowerage that
knows not of sunshine and snow.

Soft blossomless frondage
And foliage that gleams
As to prisoners in bondage
The light of their dreams,
The desire of a dawn unbeholden, with hope
on the wings of its beams.

Not as prisoners entombed
Waxen haggard and wizen,
But consoled and illumed
In the depths of their prison
With delight of the light everlasting and vision
of dawn on them risen,

From the banks and the beds
Of the waters divine
They lift up their heads
And the flowers of them shine
Through the splendor of darkness that clothes
them of water that glimmers like wine.

Bright bank over bank
Making glorious the gloom,
Soft rank upon rank,
Strange bloom after bloom,
They kindle the liquid low twilight, and dusk
of the dim sea's womb.

Through the subtle and tangible
Gloom without form,
Their branches, infrangible
Ever of storm
Spread softer their sprays than the shoots of the
woodland when April is warm.

As the flight of the thunder, full
Charged with its word,
Dividing the wonderful
Depths like a bird,
Speaks wrath and delight to the heart of the
night that exults to have heard,

So swiftly, though soundless
In silence's ear,
Light, winged from the boundless
Blue depths full of cheer,
Speaks joy to the heart of the waters that part
not before him, but hear.

Light, perfect and visible
Godhead of God,
God indivisible,
Lifts but his rod,
And the shadows are scattered in sunder, and
darkness is light at his nod.

At the touch of his wand,
At the nod of his head
From the spaces beyond
Where the dawn hath her bed,
Earth, water, and air are transfigured, and
rise as one risen from the dead.

He puts forth his hand,
And the mountains are thrilled
To the heart as they stand
In his presence, fulfilled
With his glory that utters his grace upon
earth, and her sorrows are stilled.

The moan of her travail
That groans for the light
Till day spring unravel
The weft of the night,
At the sound of the strings of the music of
morning, falls dumb with delight.

He gives forth his word,
And the word that he saith,
Ere well it be heard,
Strikes darkness to death ;
For the thought of his heart is the sunrise, and
dawn as the sound of his breath.

And the strength of its pulses
That passion makes proud
Confounds and convulses
The depths of the cloud
Of the darkness that heaven was engirt with,
divided and rent as a shroud,

As the veil of the shrine
Of the temple of old
When darkness divine
Over noonday was rolled ;
So the heart of the night by the pulse of the
light is convulsed and controlled.

And the sea's heart, groaning
For glories withdrawn,
And the waves' mouths, moaning
All night for the dawn,
Are uplift as the hearts and the mouths of the
singers on leaside and lawn.

And the sound of the quiring
   Of all these as one,
Desired and desiring
   Till dawn's will be done,
Fills full with delight of them heaven till it
   burns as the heart of the sun.

Till the waves too inherit
   And waters take part
In the sense of the spirit
   That breathes from his heart,
And are kindled with music as fire when the
   lips of the morning part,

With music unheard
   In the light of her lips,
In the life-giving word
   Of the dewfall that drips
On the grasses of earth, and the wind that en-
   kindles the wings of the ships.

White glories of wings
   As of seafaring birds
That flock from the springs
   Of the sunrise in herds
With the wind for a herdsman, and hasten or
   halt at the change of his words.

As the watchword's change
   When the wind's note shifts,
And the skies grow strange,
   And the white squall drifts
Up sharp from the sea-line, vexing the sea
   till the low cloud lifts.

At the charge of his word
   Bidding pause, bidding haste,
When the ranks are stirred
   And the lines displaced,
They scatter as wild swans parting adrift on
   the wan green waste.

At the hush of his word
   In a pause of his breath
When the waters have heard
   His will that he saith,
They stand as a flock penned close in its fold
   for division of death.

As a flock by division
   Of death to be thinned,
As the shades in a vision
   Of spirits that sinned ;
So glimmer their shrouds and their sheetings
   as clouds on the stream of the wind.

But the sun stands fast,
   And the sea burns bright,
And the flight of them past
   Is no more than the flight
Of the snow-soft swarm of serene wings poised
   and afloat in the light.

Like flowers upon flowers
   In a festival way
When hours after hours
   Shed grace on the day,
White blossom-like butterflies hover and gleam
   through the snows of the spray.

Like snow-colored petals
   Of blossoms that flee
From storm that unsettles
   The flower as the tree
They flutter, a legion of flowers on the wing,
   through the field of the sea.

Through the furrowless field
   Where the foam-blossoms blow
And the secrets are sealed
   Of their harvest below
They float in the path of the sunbeams, as
   flakes or as blossoms of snow.

Till the sea's ways darken,
   And the God, withdrawn,
Give ear not or hearken
   If prayer on him fawn,
And the sun's self seem but a shadow, the
   noon as a ghost of the dawn.

No shadow, but rather
   God, father of song,
Shew grace to me, Father
   God, loved of me long,
That I lose not the light of thy face, that my
   trust in thee work me not wrong.

While yet I make forward
   With face toward thee
Not turned yet in shoreward,
   Be thine upon me ;
Be thy light on my forehead or ever I turn
   it again from the sea.

As a kiss on my brow
   Be the light of thy grace,
Be thy glance on me now
   From the pride of thy place:
As the sign of a sire to a son be the light on
   my face of thy face.

Thou wast father of olden
   Times hailed and adored,
And the sense of thy golden
   Great harp's monochord
Was the joy in the soul of the singers that
  hailed thee for master and lord.

Fair father of all
   In thy ways that have trod,
That have risen at thy call,
   That have thrilled at thy nod,
Arise, shine, lighten upon me, O sun that we
  see to be God.

As my soul has been dutiful
   Only to thee,
O God most beautiful,
   Lighten thou me,
As I swim through the dim long rollers, with
  eyelids uplift from the sea.

Be praised and adored of us
   All in accord,
Father and lord of us
   Alway adored,
The slayer and the stayer and the harper, the
  light of us all and our lord.

At the sound of thy lyre,
   At the touch of thy rod,
Air quickens to fire
   By the foot of thee trod,
The saviour and healer and singer, the living
  and visible God.

The years are before thee
   As shadows of thee,
As men that adore thee,
   As cloudlets that flee :
But thou art the God, and thy kingdom is
  heaven, and thy shrine is the sea.

AFTER NINE YEARS.

TO JOSEPH MAZZINI.

Prima dicte mihi, Summâ dicende Camenâ.

I.

THE shadows fallen of years are nine
Since heaven grew seven times more divine
With thy soul entering, and the dearth
Of soul on earth
Grew sevenfold sadder, wanting One
Whose light of life, quenched here and done,
Burns there eternal as the sun.

2.

Beyond all word, beyond all deed,
Beyond all thought beloved, what need
Hast death or love that speech should be,
Hast thou of me ?
I had no word, no prayer, no cry,
To praise or hail or mourn thee by,
As when thou too wast man as I.

3.

Nay, never, nor as any born
Save one whose name priests turn to scorn,
Who haply, though we know not now,
Was man as thou,
A wanderer branded with men's blame,
Loved past man's utterance : yea, the same,
Perchance, and as his name thy name.

4.

Thou was as very Christ—not he
Degraded into Deity,
And priest-polluted by such prayer
As poisons air,
Tongue-worship of the tongue that slays,
False faith and parricidal praise :
But the man crowned with suffering days.

5.

God only, being of all mankind
Most manlike, of most equal mind
And heart most perfect, more than can
Be heart of man
Once in ten ages, born to be
As haply Christ was, and as we
Knew surely, seeing, and worshipped thee.

6.

To know thee—this at least was ours,
God, clothed upon with human hours,
O face beloved, O spirit adored,

Saviour and lord !
That was not only for thine own
Redeemer—not of these alone
But all to whom thy word was known.

7.

Ten years have wrought their will with me
Since last my words took wing for thee
Who then was' even as now above
Me, and my love.
As then thou knewest not scorn, so now
With that beloved benignant brow
Take these of him whose light was thou.

FOR A PORTRAIT OF FELICE ORSINI.

STEADFAST as sorrow, fiery sad, and sweet
  With underthoughts of love and faith, more strong
  Than doubt and hate and all ill thoughts which throng,
Haply, round hope's or fear's world-wandering feet
That find no rest from wandering till they meet
  Death, bearing palms in hand and crowns of song ;
His face, who thought to vanquish wrong with wrong,
Erring, and make rage and redemption meet,
Havoc and freedom ; weaving in one weft
Good with his right hand, evil with his left ;
  But all a hero lived and erred and died ;
Looked thus upon the living world he left
  So bravely that with pity less than pride
  Men hail him Patriot and Tyrannicide.

EVENING ON THE BROADS.

OVER two shadowless waters, adrift as a pinnace in peril,
Hangs as in heavy suspense, charged with irresolute light,
Softly the soul of the sunset upholden awhile on the sterile
Waves and wastes of the land, half repossessed by the night.
Inland glimmer the shallows asleep and afar in the breathless
Twilight : yonder the depths darken afar and asleep.
Slowly the semblance of death out of heaven descends on the deathless
Waters : hardly the light lives on the face of the deep—
Hardly, but here for awhile.   All over the grey soft shallow
  Hover the colors and clouds of twilight, "oid of a star.

As a bird unfledged is the broad-winged night,
    whose winglets are callow
  Yet, but soon with their plumes will she
    cover her brood from afar,
Cover the brood of her worlds that cumber
    the skies with their blossom
  Thick as the darkness of leaf-shadowed
    spring is encumbered with flowers.
World upon world is enwound in the bountiful
    girth of her bosom,
Warm and lustrous with life lovely to look on
    as ours.
Still is the sunset adrift as a spirit in doubt
    that dissembles
  Still with itself, being sick of division and
    dimmed by dismay—
Nay, not so ; but with love and delight beyond
    passion it trembles,
  Fearful and fain of the night, lovely with
    love of the day :
Fain and fearful of rest that is like unto death,
    and begotten
  Out of the womb of the tomb, born of the
    seed of the grave :
Lovely with shadows of loves that are only
    not wholly forgotten,
  Only not wholly suppressed by the dark as a
    wreck by the wave.
Still there linger the loves of the morning and
    noon, in a vision
  Blindly beheld, but in vain : ghosts that are
    tired, and would rest.
But the glories beloved of the night rise all too
    dense for division,
  Deep in the depth of her breast sheltered as
    doves in a nest.
Fainter the beams of the loves of the daylight
    season enkindled
  Wane, and the memories of hours that were
    fair with the love of them fade :
Loftier, aloft of the lights of the sunset stricken
    and dwindled,
Gather the signs of the love at the heart of the
    night new-made.
New-made night, new-born of the sunset, im-
    measurable, endless,
  Opens the secret of love hid from of old in
    her heart,
In the deep sweet heart full-charged with fault-
    less love of the friendless
  Spirits of men that are eased when the wheels
    of the sun depart.
Still is the sunset afloat as a ship on the waters
    upholden,
  Full-sailed, wide-winged, poised softly forever
    asway—

Nay, not so, but at least for a little, awhile at
    the golden
  Limit of arching air fain for an hour to delay.
Here on the bar of the sand-bank, steep yet
    aslope to the gleaming
  Waste of the water without, waste of the
    water within,
Lights overhead and lights underneath seem
    doubtfully dreaming
  Whether the day be done, whether the night
    may begin.
Far and afar and farther again they falter and
    hover,
  Warm on the water and deep in the sky and
    pale on the cloud :
Colder again and slowly remoter, afraid to re-
    cover
  Breath, yet fain to revive, as it seems, from
    the skirt of the shroud.
Faintly the heartbeats shorten and pause of the
    light in in the westward
  Heaven, as eastward quicken the paces of
    star upon star
Hurried and eager of life as a child that strains
    to the breast-ward
  Eagerly, yearning forth of the deeps where
    the ways of them are,
Glad of the glory of the gift of their life and
    the wealth of its wonder,
  Fain of the night and the sea and the sweet
    wan face of the earth.
Over them air grows deeper, intense with de-
    light in them : under
  Things are thrilled in their sleep as with
    sense of a sure new birth.
But here by the sand-bank watching, with eyes
    on the sea-line, stranger
  Grows to me also the weight of the sea-
    ridge gazed on of me,
Heavily heaped up, changefully changeless,
    void though of danger
  Void not of menace, but full of the might of
    the dense dull sea.
Like as the wave is before me, behind is the
    bank deep-drifted ;
  Yellow and thick as the bank is behind me
    in front is the wave.
As the wall of a prison imprisoning the mere
    is the girth of it lifted :
  But the rampire of water in front is erect as
    the wall of a grave.
And the crests of it crumble and topple and
    change, but the wall is not broken :
  Standing still dry-shod, I see it as higher
    than my head,

Moving inland alway again, reared up as in
    token
  Still of impending wrath still in the foam of
    it shed.
And even in the pauses between them, divid-
    ing the rollers in sunder,
  High overhead seems ever the sea-line fixed
    as a mark,
And the shore where I stand as a valley behol-
    den of hills whence thunder
  Cloud and torrent and storm, darkening the
    depths of the dark.
Up to the sea, not upon it or over it, upward
    from under
  Seems he to gaze, whose eyes yearn after it
    here from the shore :
A wall of turbid water, aslope to the wide
    sky's wonder
  Of color and cloud, it climbs, or spreads as
    a slanted floor.
And the large lights change on the face of the
    mere like things that were living,
  Winged and wonderful, beams like as birds
    are that pass and are free :
But the light is dense as darkness, a gift with-
    held in the giving,
  That lies as dead on the fierce dull face of the
    landward sea.
Stained and stifled and soiled, made earthier
    than earth is and duller,
  Grimly she puts back light as rejected, a
    thing put away :
No transparent rapture, a molten music of
    color ;
  No translucent love taken and given of the
    day.
Fettered and marred and begrimed is the light's
    live self on her falling,
  As the light of a man's life lighted the fume
    of a dungeon mars :
Only she knows of the wind, when her wrath
    gives ear to him calling ;
  The delight of the light she knows not, nor
    answers the sun or the stars.
Love she hath none to return for the luminous
    love of their giving :
  None to reflect from the bitter and shallow
    response of her heart.
Yearly she feeds on her dead, yet herself seems
    dead and not living,
  Or confused as a soul heavy-laden with
    trouble that will not depart.
In the sound of her speech to the darkness the
    moan of her evil remorse is,
  Haply, for strong ships gnawed by the dog-
    toothed sea-bank's fang

And trampled to death by the rage of the feet
    of her foam-lipped horses
  Whose manes are yellow as plague, and as
    ensigns of pestilence hang,
That wave in the foul faint air of the breath of
    a death-stricken city ;
  So menacing heaves she the manes of her
    rollers knotted with sand,
Discolored, opaque, suspended in sign as of
    strength without pity,
  That shake with flameless thunder the low
    long length of the strand.
Here, far off in the farther extreme of the shore
    as it lengthens
  Northward, lonely for miles, ere ever a
    village begin,
On the lapsing land that recedes as the growth
    of the strong sea strengthens
  Shoreward, thrusting further and further its
    outworks in,
Here in Shakespeare's vision, a flower of her
    kin forsaken,
  Lay in her golden raiment alone on the wild
    wave's edge,
Surely by no shore else, but here on the bank
    storm-shaken,
  Perdita, bright as a dew-drop engilt of the sun
    on the sedge.
Here on a shore unbeheld of his eyes in a
    dream he beheld her
  Outcast, fair as a fairy, the child of a far-off
    king :
And over the babe-flower gently the head of a
    pastoral elder
  Bowed, compassionate, hoar as the hawthorn-
    blossom in spring,
And kind as harvest in autumn : a shelter of
    shade on the lonely
  Shelterless unknown shore scourged of im-
    placable waves :
Here, where the wind walks royal, alone in his
    kingdom, and only
  Sounds to the sedges a wail as of triumph
    that conquers and craves.
All these waters and wastes are his empire of
    old, and awaken
  From barren and stagnant slumber at only
    the sound of his breath :
Yet the hunger is eased not that aches in his
    heart, nor the goal overtaken
  That his wide wings yearn for and labor as
    hearts that yearn after death.
All the solitude sighs and expects with a blind
    expectation
  Somewhat unknown of its own sad heart,
    grown heart-sick of strife :

Till sometime its wild heart maddens, and
    moans, and the vast ululation
Takes wing with the clouds on the waters,
    and wails to be quit of its life.
For the spirit and soul of the waste is the wind,
    and his wings with their waving
Darken and lighten the darkness and light
    of it thickened or thinned,
But the heart that impels them is even as a
    conqueror's insatiably craving
That victory can fill not, as power cannot
    satiate the want of the wind.
All these moorlands and marshes are full of
    his might, and oppose not
Aught of defence nor of barrier, of forest or
    precipice piled :
But the will of the wind works ever as his that
    desires what he knows not,

And the wail of his want unfulfilled is as one
    making moan for her child.
And the cry of his triumph is even as the cry·
    ing of hunger that maddens
The heart of a strong man aching in vain as
    the wind's heart aches :
And the sadness itself of the land for its in-
    finite solitude saddens
More for the sound than the silence athirst
    for the sound that slakes.
And the sunset at last and the twilight are
    dead : and the darkness is breathless
With fear of the wind's breath rising that
    seems and seems not to sleep :
But a sense of the sound of it alway, a spirit
    unsleeping and deathless,
Ghost or God, evermore moves on the face
    of the deep.

THE EMPEROR'S PROGRESS.

A STUDY IN THREE STAGES.

(On the Busts of Nero in the Uffizj.)

I.

A CHILD of brighter than the morning's birth
    And lovelier than all smiles that may be
      smiled
Save only of little children undefiled,
Sweet, perfect, witless of their own dear worth,
Live rose of love, mute melody of mirth,
    Glad as a bird is when the woods are mild,
    Adorable as is nothing save a child,
Hails with wide eyes and lips his life on earth,
    His lovely life with all its heaven to be.
    And whoso reads the name inscribed or hears
Feels his own heart a frozen well of tears,
Child, for deep dread and fearful pity of thee
Whom God would not let rather die than see
    The incumbent horror of impending years.

II.

Man, that wast godlike being a child, and
    now,
    No less than kinglike, art no more in sooth
    For all thy grace and lordliness of youth,

The crown that bids men's branded foreheads
    bow
Much more has branded and bowed down thy
    brow
    And gnawn upon it as with fire or tooth
    Of steel or snake so sorely, that the truth
Seems here to bear false witness. Is it thou,
Child ? and is all the summer of all thy spring
    This ? are the smiles that drew men's kisses
    down
    All faded and transfigured to the frown
That grieves thy face ? Art thou this weary
    thing ?
    Then is no slave's load heavier than a crown
And such a thrall no bondman as a king.

III.

Misery, beyond all men's most miserable,
    Absolute, whole, defiant of defence,
    Inevitable, inexplacable, intense,
More vast than heaven is high, more deep than
    hell,
Past cure or charm of solace or of spell,

Possesses and pervades the spirit and sense
Whereto the expanse of the earth pays tribute ; whence
Breeds evil only, and broods on fumes that swell
Rank from the blood of brother and mother and wife.

"Misery of miseries, all is misery," saith
The heavy fair-faced hateful head, at strife
With its own lusts that burn with feverous breath
Lips which the loathsome bitterness of life
Leaves fearful of the bitterness of death.

THE RESURRECTION OF ALCILIA.

(Gratefully inscribed to Dr. A. B. Grosart.)

SWEET song-flower of the Mayspring of our song,
Be welcome to us, with loving thanks and praise
To his good hand who travelling on strange ways
Found thee forlorn and fragrant, lain along
Beneath dead leaves that many a winter's wrong
Had rained and heaped through nigh three centuries' maze

Above thy Maybloom, hiding from our gaze
The life that in thy leaves lay sweet and strong.
For thine have life, while many above thine head
Piled by the wind lie blossomless and dead.
So now disburdened of such load above
That lay as death's own dust upon thee shed
By days too deaf to hear thee like a dove
Murmuring, we hear thee, bird and flower of love.

THE FOURTEENTH OF JULY.

(On the refusal by the French Senate of the plenary amnesty demanded by Victor Hugo, in his speech of July 3rd, for the surviving exiles of the Commune.)

THOU shouldst have risen as never dawn yet rose,
Day of the sunrise of the soul of France,
Dawn of the whole world's morning, when the trance
Of all the world had end, and all its woes
Respite, prophetic of their perfect close.
Light of all tribes of men, all names and clans,
Dawn of the whole world's morning and of man's,

Flower of the heart of morning's mystic rose,
Dawn of the very dawn of very day,
When the sun brighter breaks night's ruinous prison,
Thou shouldst have risen as yet no dawn has risen,
Evoked of him whose word puts night away,
Our father, at the music of whose word
Exile had ended, and the world had heard.

July 5, 1880.

THE LAUNCH OF THE LIVADIA.

I.

GOLD, and fair marbles, and again more gold,
    And space of halls afloat that glance and
        gleam
    Like the green heights of sunset heaven, or
        seem
The golden steeps of sunrise red and cold
On deserts where dark exile keeps the fold
    Fast of the flocks of torment, where no beam
    Falls of kind light or comfort save in dream,
These we far off behold not, who behold
The cordage woven of curses, and the decks
    With mortal hate and mortal peril paven ;
    From stem to stern the lines of doom en-
        graven
That mark for sure inevitable wrecks
Those sails predestinate, though no storm vex,
    To miss on earth and find in hell their haven.

II.

All curses be about her, and all ill
    Go with her ; heaven be dark above her way,
    The gulf beneath her glad and sure of prey,
And, wheresoe'er her prow be pointed, still
The winds of heaven have all one evil will
    Conspirant even as hearts of kings to slay
    With mouths of kings to lie and smile and
        pray,
And chiefliest his whose wintrier breath makes
    chill

With more than winter's and more **poisonous**
    cold
The horror of his kingdom toward the
    north,
The deserts of his kingdom toward the east.
And though death hide not in her direful hold
    Be all stars adverse toward her that come
        forth
Nightly, by day all hours till all have ceased :

III.

Till all have ceased for ever, and the sum
    Be summed of all the sumless curses told
    Out on his head by all dark seasons rolled
Over its cursed and crowned existence, dumb
And blind and stark as though the snows made
    numb
    All sense within it, and all conscience cold,
    That hangs round hearts of less imperial
        mold
Like a snake feeding till their doomday come.
O heart fast bound of frozen poison, be
    All nature's as all true men's hearts to thee,
    A two-edged sword of judgment ; hope be
        far
And fear at hand for pilot oversea
    With death for compass and despair for star,
    And the white foam a shroud for the White
        Czar.

September 30, 1880.

SIX YEARS OLD.

TO H. W. M.

BETWEEN the springs of six and seven,
    Two fresh years' fountains, clear
Of all but golden sand for leaven,
    Child, midway passing here,
As earth for love's sake dares bless heaven,
    So dare I bless you, dear.

Between two bright well-heads, that brighten
    With every breath that blows
Too loud to lull, too low to frighten,
    But fain to rock, the rose,
Your feet stand fast, your lit smiles lighten,
    That might rear flowers from snows.

You came when winds unleashed were snarling
  Behind the frost-bound hours,
A snow-bird sturdier than the starling,
  A storm-bird fledged for showers,
That spring might smile to find you, dar-
    ling,
  First born of all the flowers.

Could love make worthy things of worthless,
  My song were worth an ear :
Its note should make the days most mirthless
  The merriest of the year,
And wake to birth all buds yet birthless
  To keep your birthday, dear.

But where your birthday brightens heaven
  No need has earth, God knows,
Of light or warmth to melt or leaven
  The frost or fog that glows
With sevenfold heavenly lights of seven
  Sweet springs that cleave the snows.

Could love make worthy music of you,
  And match my Master's powers,
Had even my love less heart to love you,
  A better song were ours ;
With all the rhymes like stars above you,
  And all the words like flowers.

      September 30, 1880.

A PARTING SONG.

(To a friend leaving England for a year's residence in Australia.)

THESE winds and suns of spring
    That warm with breath and wing
The trembling sleep of earth, till half awake
She laughs and blushes ere her slumber break,
    For all good gifts they bring
    Require one better thing,
For all the loans of joy they lend us, borrow
One sharper dole of sorrow,
To sunder soon by half a world of sea
Her son from England and my friend from me.

    Nor hope nor love nor fear
    May speed or stay one year,
Nor song nor prayer may bid, as mine would
    fain,
The seasons perish and be born again,
    Restoring all we lend,
    Reluctant, of a friend,
The voice, the hand, the presence and the
    sight
That lend their life and light
To present gladness and heart-strengthening
    cheer,
Now lent again for one reluctant year.

    So much we lend indeed,
    Perforce, by force of need,
So much we must ; even these things and no
    more
The far sea sundering and the sundered shore

    A world apart from ours,
    So much the imperious hours,
Exact and spare not ; but no more than these
All earth and all her seas
From thought and faith of trust and truth can
    borrow,
Not memory from desire, nor hope from sor-
    row.

    Through bright and dark and bright
    Returns of day and night
I bid the swift year speed and change and give
His breath of life to make the next year live
    With sunnier suns for us
    A life more prosperous,
And laugh with flowers more fragrant, that
    shall see
A merrier March for me,
A rosier-girdled race of night with day,
A goodlier April and a tenderer May.
    For him the inverted year
    Shall mark our seasons here
With alien alternation, and revive
This withered winter, slaying the spring alive
    With darts more sharply drawn
    As nearer draws the dawn
In heaven transfigured over earth transformed
And with our winters warmed
And wasted with our summers, till the beams
Rise on his face that rose on Dante's dreams.

Till fourfold morning rise
Of starshine on his eyes,
Dawn of the spheres that brand steep heaven
    across
At height of night with semblance of a cross
    Whose grace and ghostly glory
    Poured heaven on purgatory
Seeing with their flamelets risen all heaven
    grow glad
For love thereof it had
And lovely joy of loving ; so may these
Make bright with welcome now their southern
    seas.

O happy stars, whose mirth
    The saddest soul on earth   [bless,
That ever soared and sang found strong to
Lightening his life's harsh load of heaviness
    With comfort sown like seed
    In dream though not in deed   [vine,
On sprinkled wastes of darkling thought di-
Let all your lights now shine
With all as glorious gladness on his eyes
For whom in deed and not in dream they rise.

As those great twins of air
    Hailed once with oldworld prayer
Of all folk alway faring forth by sea,
So now may these for grace and guidance be,
    To guard his sail and bring
    Again to brighten spring

The face we look for and the hand we lack
Still, till they light him back,
As welcome as to first discovering eyes
Their light rose ever, soon on his to rise.

As parting now he goes
    From snow-time back to snows,
So back to spring from summer may next year
Restore him, and our hearts receive him here,
    The best good gift that spring
    Had ever grace to bring
At fortune's happiest hour of star-blest birth,
Back to love's homebright earth,
To eyes with eyes that commune, hand with
    hand,
And the old warm bosom of all our mother-
    land.

Earth and sea-wind and sea
    And stars and sunlight be
Alike all prosperous for him, and all hours
Have all one heart, and all that heart as ours.
    All things as good as strange
    Crown all the season's change
With changing flower and compensating fruit
From one year's ripening root ;
Till next year brings us, roused at spring's
    recall,
A heartier flower and goodlier fruit than all.

March 26, 1880.

BY THE NORTH SEA.

"We are what suns and winds and waters make us."—LANDOR.

SEA, *wind and sun, with light and sound and breath*
    The spirit of man fulfilling—these create
    That joy wherewith man's life grown passionate
Gains heart to hear and sense to read and faith
To know the secret word our Mother saith
    In silence, and to see, though doubt wax great
    Death as the shadow cast by life on fate,
Passing, whose shade we call the shadow of death.

Brother, to whom our Mother as to me
    Is dearer than all dreams of days undone,
This song I give you of the sovereign three
    That are as life and sleep and death are, one :
    A song the sea-wind gave me from the sea
    Where naught of man's endures before the sun.

BY THE NORTH SEA.

I

1.

A LAND that is lonelier than ruin ;
　A sea that is stranger than death :
Far fields that a rose never blew in,
　Wan waste where the winds lack breath ;
Waste endless and boundless and flowerless
　But of marsh-blossoms fruitless as free :
Where earth lies exhausted, as powerless
　　To strive with the sea.

2.

Far flickers the flight of the swallows,
　Far flutters the weft of the grass
Spun dense over desolate hollows
　More pale than the clouds as they pass :
Thick woven as the weft of a witch is
　Round the heart of a thrall that hath sinned,
Whose youth and the wrecks of its riches
　　Are waifs on the wind.

3.

The pastures are herdless and sheepless
　No pasture or shelter for herds :
The wind is relentless and sleepless
　And restless and songless the birds ;
Their cries from afar fall breathless,
　Their wings are as lightnings that flee ;
For the land has two lords that are deathless :
　　Death's self, and the sea.

4.

These twain, as a king with his fellow,
　Hold converse of desolate speech :
And her waters are haggard and yellow
　And crass with the scurf of the beach :
And his garments are grey as the hoary
　Wan sky where the day lies dim :
And his power is to her, and his glory,
　　As hers unto him.

5.

In the pride of his power she rejoices,
　In her glory he glows and is glad :
In her darkness the sound of his voice is,
　With his breath she dilates and is mad :
' If thou slay me, O death, and outlive me,
　Yet thy love hath fulfilled me of thee.'
' Shall I give thee not back if thou give me,
　　O sister, O sea ?'

6.

And year upon year dawns living,
　And age upon age drops dead :
And his hand is not weary of giving,
　And the thirst of her heart is not fed :
And the hunger that moans in her passion,
　And the rage in her hunger that roars,
A a wolf's that the winter lays lash on,
　　Still calls and implores.

7.

Her walls have no granite for girder,
　No fortalice fronting her stands :
But reefs the bloodguiltiest of murder
　Are less than the banks of her sands :
These number their slain by the thousand;
　For the ship hath no surety to be,
When the bank is abreast of her bows and
　　Aflush with the sea.

8.

No surety to stand, and no shelter
　To dawn out of darkness but one,
Out of waters that hurtle and welter
　No succor to dawn with the sun
But a rest from the wind as it passes,
　Where, hardly redeemed from the waves,
Lie thick as the blades of the grasses
　　The dead in their graves.

9.

A multitude noteless of numbers,
  As wild weeds cast on an heap :
And sounder than sleep are their slumbers,
  And softer than song is their sleep ;
And sweeter than all things and stranger
  The sense, if perchance it may be,
That the wind is divested of danger
    And scatheless the sea.

10.

That the roar of the banks they breasted
  Is hurtless as bellowing of herds,
And the strength of his wings that invested
  The wind, as the strength of a bird's ;
As the sea-mew's might or the swallow's
  That cry to him back if he cries,
As over the graves and their hollows
    Days darken and rise.

11.

As the souls of the dead men disburdened
  And clean of the sins that they sinned,
With a lovelier than man's life guerdoned
  And delight as a wave's in the wind,
And delight as the wind's in the billow,
  Birds pass, and deride with their glee
The flesh that has dust for its pillow
    As wrecks have the sea.

12.

When the days of the sun wax dimmer,
  Wings flash through the dusk like beams ;
As the clouds in the lit sky glimmer,
  The bird in the graveyard gleams ;

As the cloud at its wing's edge whitens
  When the clarions of sunrise are heard,
The graves that the bird's note brightens
    Grow bright for the bird.

13.

As the waves of the numberless waters
  That the wind cannot number who guides
Are ths sons of the shore and the daughters
  Here lulled by the chime of the tides :
And here in the press of them standing
  We know not if these or if we
Live truliest, or anchored to landing
    Or drifted to sea.

14.

In the valley he named of decision
  No denser were multitudes met
When the soul of the seer in her vision
  Saw nations for doom of them set ;
Saw darkness in dawn, and the splendor
  Of judgment, the sword and the rod ;
But the doom here of death is more tender
    And gentler the god.

15.

And gentler the wind from the dreary
  Sea-banks by the waves overlapped,
Being weary, speaks peace to the weary
  From slopes that the tide-stream hath
    sapped ;
And sweeter than all that we call so
  The seal of their slumber shall be
Till the graves that embosom them also
    Be sapped of the sea.

II.

1.

For the heart of the waters is cruel,
  And the kisses are dire of their lips,
And their waves are as fire is to fuel
  To the strength of the sea-faring ships,
Though the sea's eye gleam as a jewel
  To the sun's eye back as he dips.

2.

Though the sun's eye flash to the sea's
  Live light of delight and of laughter,
And her lips breathe back to the breeze
  The kiss that the wind's lips waft her
From the sun that subsides, and sees
  No gleam of the storm's dawn after.

3.

And the wastes of the wild sea-marches
    Where the borderers are matched in their
      might—
Bleak fens that the sun's weight parches,
    Dense waves that reject his light—
Change under the change-colored arches
    Of changeless morning and night.

4.

The waves are as ranks enrolled
    Too close for the storm to sever :
The fens lie naked and cold,
    But their heart fails utterly never :
The lists are set from of old,
    And the warfare endureth for ever.

III.

1.

Miles, and miles, and miles of desolation !
    Leagues on leagues on leagues without a
      change !
Sign or token of some eldest nation
    Here would make the strange land not so
      strange.
Time-forgotten, yea since time's creation,
    Seem these borders where the sea-birds
    range.

2.

Slowly, gladly, full of peace and wonder
    Grows his heart who journeys here alone.
Earth and all its thoughts of earth sink under
    Deep as deep in water sinks a stone.
Hardly knows it if the rollers thunder,
    Hardly whence the lonely wind is blown.

3.

Tall the plumage of the rush-flower tosses,
    Sharp and soft in many a curve and line
Gleam and glow the sea-colored marsh-mosses,
    Salt and splendid from the circling brine.
Streak on streak of glimmering seashine
    crosses
    All the land sea-saturate as with wine.

4.

Far, and far between, in divers orders,
    Clear grey steeples cleave the low grey sky ;
Fast and firm as time-unshaken warders,
    Hearts made sure by faith, by hope made
    high.
These alone in all the wild sea-borders
    Fear no blast of days and nights that die.

5.

All the land is like as one man's face is,
    Pale and troubled still with change of cares.
Doubt and death pervade her clouded spaces :
    Strength and length of life and peace are
    theirs ;
Theirs alone amid these weary places,
    Seeing not how the wild world frets and fares.

6.

Firm and fast where all is cloud that changes
    Cloud-clogged sunlight, cloud by sunlight
    thinned,
Stern and sweeet, above the sand-hill ranges
    Watch the towers and tombs of men that
    sinned
Once, now calm as earth whose only change is
    Wind, and light, and wind and cloud, and
    wind.

7.

Out and in and out the sharp straits wander,
    In and out and in the wild way strives,
Starred and paved and lined with flowers that
    squander
    Gold as golden as the gold of hives,
Salt and moist and multiform : but yonder,
    See, what sign of life or death survives ?

8.

Seen then only when the songs of olden
    Harps where young whose echoes yet endure,
Hymned of Homer when his years were golden,
    Known of only when the world was pure,
Here is Hades, manifest, beholden,
    Surely, surely here, if aught be sure !

9.

Where the border-line was crossed, that, sund-
ering
Death from life, keeps weariness from rest,
None can tell, who fares hereforward wondering;
None may doubt but here might end his quest.
Here life's lightning joys and woes once thun-
dering
Sea-like round him cease like storm sup-
pressed.

Here the wise wave-wandering steadfast-heart-
ed
Guest of many a lord of many a land
Saw the shape or shade of years departed,
Saw the semblance risen and hard at hand,
Saw the mother long from love's reach parted,
Anticleia, like a statue stand.

11.

Statue ? nay, nor tissued image woven
Fair on hangings in his father's hall ;
Nay, too fast her faith of heart was proven,
Far too firm her loveliest love of all;
Love wherethrough the loving heart was cloven,
Love that hears not when the loud Fates call.

12.

Love that lives and stands up re-created
Then when life has ebbed and anguish fled ;
Love more strong than death or all things
fated,

Child's and mother's, lit by love and led ;
Love that found what life so long awaited
Here, when life came down among the
dead.

13.

Here, where never came alive another,
Came her sod across the sundering tide
Crossed before by many a warrior brother
Once that warred on Ilion at his side ;
Here spread forth vain hands to clasp the
mother
Dead, that sorrowing for his love's sake
died.

14.

Parted, though by narrowest of divisions,
Clasp he might not, only might implore,
Sundered yet by bitterest of derisions,
Son, and mother from the son she bore—
Here ? But all dispeopled here of visions
Lies, forlorn of shadows even, the shore.

15.

All too sweet such men's Hellenic speech is
All too fain they lived of light to see,
Once to see the darkness of these beaches,
Once to sing this Hades found of me
Ghostless, all its gulfs and creeks and reaches,
Sky, and shore, and cloud, and waste, and
sea.

IV.

1.

But aloft and afront of me faring
Far forward as folk in a dream
That strive, between doubting and daring,
Right on till the goal for them gleam,
Full forth till their goal on them lighten,
The harbor where fain they would be,
What headlands there darken and brighten ?
What change in the sea ?

2.

What houses and woodlands that nestle
Save inland to lee of the hill

As it slopes from the headlands that wrestle
And succumb to the strong sea's will ?
Truce is not, nor respite, nor pity,
For the battle is waged not of hands
Where over the grave of a city
The ghost of it stands.

3.

Where the wings of the sea-wind slacken,
Green lawns to the landward thrive,
Fields brighten and pine-woods blacken,
And the heat in their heart is alive ;
They blossom and warble and murmur,
For the sense of their spirit is free :
But harder to shoreward and firmer
The grasp of the sea.

4.

Like ashes the low cliffs crumble,
　The banks drop down into dust,
The heights of the hills are made humble,
　As a reed's is the strength of their trust :
As a city's that armies environ,
　The strength of their stay is of sand :
But the grasp of the sea is as iron,
　　Laid hard on the land.

5.

A land that is thirstier than ruin :
　A sea that is hungrier than death ;
Heaped hills that a tree never grew in ;
　Wide sands where the wave draws breath ;
All solace is here for the spirit
　That ever for ever may be
For the soul of thy son to inherit
　　My mother, my sea.

6.

O delight of the headlands and beaches !
　O desire of the wind on the wold,
More glad than a man's when it reaches
　That end which it sought from of old
And the palm of possession is dreary
　To the sense that in search of it sinned ;
But nor satisfied ever nor weary
　　Is ever the wind.

7.

The delight that he takes but in living
　Is more than of all things that live :
For the world that has all things for giving
　Has nothing so goodly to give :
But more than delight his desire is,
　For the goal where his pinions would be
Is immortal as air or as fire is,
　　Immense as the sea.

8.

Though hence come the moan that he borrows
　From darkness and depth of the night,
Though hence be the spring of his sorrows,
　Hence too is the joy of his might ;
The delight that his doom is for ever
　To seek and desire and rejoice,
And the sense that eternity never
　　Shall silence his voice.

9.

That satiety never may stifle
　Nor weariness ever estrange
Nor time be so strong as to rifle
　Nor change be so great as to change
His gift that renews in the giving,
　The joy that exalts him to be
Alone of all elements living
　　The lord of the sea.

10.

What is fire, that its flame should consume
　　her?
　More fierce than all fires are her waves :
What is earth, that its gulfs should entomb
　　her?
　More deep are her own than their graves.
Life shrinks from his pinions that cover
　The darkness by thunders bedinned :
But she knows him, her lord and her lover,
　　The godhead of wind.

11.

For a season his wings are about her,
　His breath on her lips for a space ;
Such rapture he wins not without her
　In the width of his worldwide race.
Though the forests bow down, and the moun-
　　tains
　Wax dark, and the tribes of them flee,
His delight is more deep in the fountains
　　And springs of the sea.

12.

There are those too of mortals that love him
　There are souls that desire and require,
Be the glories of midnight above him
　Or beneath him the daysprings of fire :
And their hearts are as harps that approve him
　And praise him as chords of a lyre
That were fain with their music to move him
　　To meet their desire.

13.

To descend through the darkness to grace
　　them,
　Till darkness were lovelier than light :
To encompass and grasp and embrace them,
　Till their weakness were one with his might
With the strength of his wings to caress them

With the blast of his breath to set free ;
With the mouths of his thunders to bless them
   For sons of the sea.

14.

For these have the toil and the guerdon
   That the wind has eternally : these
Have part in the boon and the burden
   Of the sleepless unsatisfied breeze,
That finds not, but seeking rejoices
   That possession can work him no wrong :

And the voice at the heart of their voice is
   The sense of his song.

15.

For the wind's is their doom and their blessing ;
   To desire, and have always above
A possession beyond their possessing,
   A love beyond reach of their love.
Green earth has her sons and her daughters,
   And these have their guerdons ; but we
Are the wind's and the sun's and the water's,
   Elect of the sea.

V.

1.

For the sea too seeks and rejoices,
   Gains and loses and gains,
And the joy of her heart's own choice is
   As ours, and as ours are her pains :
As the thoughts of our hearts are her voices,
   And as hers is the pulse of our veins.

2.

Her fields that know not of dearth
   Nor lie for their fruit's sake fallow
Laugh large in the depth of their mirth :
   But inshore here in the shallow,
Embroiled with encumbrance of earth,
   Their skirts are turbid and yellow.

3.

The grime of her greed is upon her
   The sign of her deed is her soil ;
As the earth's is her own dishonor,
   And corruption the crown of her toil :
She hath spoiled and devoured, and her honor
   Is this, to be shamed by her spoil.

4.

But afar where pollution is none,
   Nor ensign of strife nor endeavor,
Where her heart and the sun's are one,
   And the soil of her sin comes never,
She is pure as the wind and the sun,
   And her sweetness endureth for ever.

VI.

1.

Death, and change, and darkness everlasting,
   Deaf, that hears not what the daystar saith,
Blind, past all remembrance and forecasting,
   Dead, past memory that it once drew breath;
These, above the washing tides and wasting,
   Reign, and rule this land of utter death.

2.

Change of change, darkness of darkness, hidden,
   Very death of very death, begun
When none knows,—the knowledge is for-
   bidden--

Self-begotten, self-proceeding, one,
Born, not made—abhorred, unchained, unchid
   den,
   Night stands here defiant of the sun.

3.

Change of change, and death of death begotten,
   Darkness born of darknes, one and three,
Ghostly godhead of a world forgotten,
   Crowned with heaven, enthroned on land and
   sea,
Here, where earth with dead men's bones is
   rotten,
   God of Time, thy likeness worships thee.

4.

Lo. thy likeness of thy desolation,
  Shape and figure of thy might, O Lord,
Formless form, incarnate miscreation
  Served of all things living and abhorred ;
Earth herself is here thine incarnation,
  Time of all things born on earth abored.

5.

All that worship thee are fearful of thee ;
  No man may not worship thee for fear :
Prayers nor curses prove not nor disprove thee,
  Move nor change thee with our change of
    cheer :
All at last, though all abhorred thee, love thee,
  God, the sceptre of whose throne is here.

6.

Here thy throne and sceptre of thy station,
  Here the palace paven for thy feet ;
Here thy sign from nation unto nation
  Passed as watchword for thy guards to greet,
Guards that go before thine exaltation,
  Ages, clothed with bitter years and sweet.

7.

Here, where sharp the sea-bird shrills his ditty,
  Flickering flame-wise through the clear live
    calm,
Rose triumphal, crowning all a city,
  Roofs exalted once with prayer and psalm,
Built of holy hands for holy pity,
  Frank and fruitful as a sheltering palm.

8.

Church and hospice wrought in faultless fash-
    ion,
  Hall and chancel bounteous and sublime,
Wide and sweet and glorious as compassion,
  Filled and thrilled with force of choral chime,
Filled with spirit of prayer and thrilled with
    passion,
  Hailed a God more merciful than Time.

9.

Ah, less mighty, less than Time prevailing,
  Shrunk, expelled, made nothing at his nod,
Less than clouds across the sea-line sailing,
  Lies he, stricken by his master's rod.

' Where is man ? ' the cloister murmurs wail-
    ing ;
  Back the mute shrine thunders—' Where is
    God ? '

10.

Here is all the end of all his glory—
  Dust, and grass, and barren silent stones.
Dead, like him, one hollow tower and hoary
  Naked in the sea-wind stands and moans,
Filled and thrilled with its perpetual story :
  Here, where earth is dense with dead men's
    bones.

11.

Low and loud and long, a voice for ever,
  Sounds the wind's clear story like a song.
Tomb from tomb the waves devouring sever,
  Dust from dust as years relapse along ;
Graves where men made sure to rest, and never
  Lie dismantled by the seasons' wrong.

12.

Now displaced, devoured and desecrated,
  Now by Time's hands darkly disinterred,
These poor dead that sleeping here awaited
  Long the archangel's re-creating word,
Closed about with roofs and walls high-gated
  Till the blast of judgment should be heard,

13.

Naked, shamed, cast out of consecration,
  Corpse and coffin, yea the very graves,
Scoffed at, scattered, shaken from their station,
  Spurned and scourged of wind and sea
    like slaves,
Desolate beyond man's desolation,
  Shrink and sink into the waste of waves.

14.

Tombs, with bare white piteous bones pro-
    truded,
  Shroudless, down the loose collapsing banks,
Crumble, from their constant place detruded,
  That the sea devours and gives not thanks.
Graves where hope and prayer and sorrow
    brooded
  Gape and slide and perish, ranks on ranks.

15.

Rows on rows and line by line they crumble,
  They that thought for all time through to be.
Scarce a stone whereon a child might stumble

Breaks the grim field paced alone of me.
Earth, and man, and all their gods wax
  humble,
Here, where Time brings pasture to the sea.

VII.

1.

But afar on the headland exalted,
  But beyond in the curl of the bay,
From the depth of his dome deep-vaulted
  Our father is lord of the day.
Our father and lord that we follow,
  For deathless and ageless is he ;
And his robe is the whole sky's hollow,
  His sandal the sea.

2.

Where the horn of the headland is sharper,
  And her green floor glitters with fire,
The sea has the sun for a harper,
  The sun has the sea for a lyre.
The waves are a pavement of amber,
  By the feet of the sea-winds trod
To receive in a god's presence-chamber
  Our father, the God.

3.

Time, haggard and changeful and hoary,
  Is master and God of the land :
But the air is fulfilled of the glory
  That is shed from our lord's right hand.
C father of all of us ever,
  All glory be only to thee
From heaven, that is void of thee never
  And earth, and the sea.

4.

O Sun, whereof all is beholden,
  Behold now the shadow of this death,
This place of the sepulchres, olden

And emptied and vain as a breath.
The bloom of the bountiful heather
  Laughs broadly beyond in thy light,
As dawn, with her glories to gather,
  At darkness and night.

5.

Though the Gods of the night lie rotten
  And their honor be taken away
And the noise of their names forgotten,
  Thou, Lord, art God of the day.
Thou art father and saviour and spirit,
  O Sun, of the soul that is free
And hath grace of thy grace to inherit
  Thine earth and thy sea.

6.

The hills and the sands and the beaches,
  The waters adrift and afar,
The banks and the creeks and the reaches,
  How glad of thee all these are !
The flowers, overflowing, overcrowded,
  Are drunk with the mad wind's mirth :
The delight of thy coming unclouded
  Makes music of earth.

7

I, last least voice of her voices,
  Give thanks that were mute in me long
To the soul in my soul that rejoices
  For the song that is over my song.
Time gives what he gains for the giving
  Or takes for his tribute of me ;
My dreams to the wind everliving,
  My song to the sea.

GRAND CHORUS OF BIRDS FROM ARISTOPHANES ATTEMPTED IN ENGLISH AFTER THE ORIGINAL METRE.

[I was allured into the audacity of this experiment by consideration of a fact which hitherto does not seem to have been taken into consideration by any translator of the half divine humourist in whose incomparable genius the highest qualities of Rabelais were fused and harmonized with the supremest gifts of Shelley : namely that his marvellous metrical invention of the anapæstic heptameter was almost exactly reproducible in a language to which all variations and combinations of anapæstic, iambic, or trochaic metre are as natural and pliable as all dactylic and spondaic forms of verse are unnatural and abhorrent. As it happens, this highest central interlude of . most adorable masterpiece is as easy to detach from its dramatic setting, and even from its lyrical context, as it was easy to give line for line of it in English. In two metrical points only does my version vary from the verbal pattern of the original. I have of course added rhymes, and double rhymes, as necessary makeweights for the imperfection of an otherwise inadequate lauguage ; and equally of course I have not attempted the impossible and undesirable task of reproducing the rare exceptional effect of a line overcharged on purpose with a preponderance of heavy-footed spondees : and this for the obvious reason that even if such a line—which I doubt— could be exactly represented, foot by foot and pause for pause, in English, this English line would no more be a verse in any proper sense of the word than is the line I am writing at this moment. And my main intention, or at least my main desire, in the undertaking of this brief adventure was to renew as far as possible for English ears the music of this resonant and thriumphant metre, which goes ringing at full gallop as of horses who

'dance as 'twere to the music

Their own hoofs make.'

I would not seem over curious in search of an apt or an inapt quotation ; but nothing can be fitter than a verse of Shakspere's to praise at once and to describe the most typical verse of Aristophanes.]

(The Birds, 685-723.)

COME on then, ye dwellers by nature in dark-
　ness, and like to the leaves' generations,
That are little of might, that are moulded of
　mire, unenduring and shadowlike nations,
Poor plumeless ephemerals, comfortless mor-
　tals, as visions of shadows fast fleeing,
Lift up your mind unto us that are deathless, and
　dateless the date of our being :
Us, children of heaven, us, ageless for aye, us,
　all of whose thoughts are eternal ;
That ye may from henceforth, having heard of
　us all things aright as to matters supernal,
Of the being of birds and beginning of gods,
　and of streams, and the dark beyond
　reaching,
Truthfully knowing aright, in my name bid
　Prodicus pack with his preaching.
It was Chaos and Night at the first, and the
　blackness of darkness, and Hell's broad
　border,
Earth was not, nor air, neither heaven ; when
　in depths of the womb of the dark with-
　out order
First thing first-born of the black-plumed

Night was a wind-egg hatched in her
　bosom,
Whence timely with seasons revolving again
　sweet Love burst out as a blossom,
Gold wings glittering forth of his back, like
　whirlwinds gustily turning,
He, after his wedlock with Chaos, whose wings
　are of darkness, in Hell broad-burning,
For his nestlings begat him the race of us first,
　and upraised us to light new-lighted.
And before this was not the race of the gods,
　until all things by Love were united ·
And of kind united with kind in communion
　of nature the sky and the sea are
Brought forth, and the earth, and the race of
　the gods everlasting and blest. So that
　we are
Far away the most ancient of all things blest.
　And that we are of Love's generation
There are manifest manifold signs. We have
　wings, and with us have the Love's hab-
　tation ;
And manifold fair young folk that forswore
　love once, ere the bloom of them ended,

Have the men that pursued and desired them
  subdued, by the help of us only befriended,
With such baits as a quail, a flamingo, a goose,
  or a cock's comb staring and splendid.
All best good things that befall men come from
  us birds, as is plain to all reason :
For first we proclaim and make known to
  them spring, and the winter and autumn
  in season ;
Bid sow, when the crane starts clanging for
  Afric, in shrill-voiced emigrant number,
And calls to the pilot to hang up his rudder
  again for the season, and slumber ;
And then weave a cloak for Orestes the thief,
  lest he strip men of theirs if it freezes.
And again thereafter the kite reappearing
  announces a change in the breezes,
And that here is the season for shearing your
  sheep of their spring wool.   Then does
  the swallow

Give you   notice to sell your greatcoat, and
  provide something light for the heat that's
  to follow.
Thus are we as Ammon or Delphi unto you,
  Dodona, nay, Phœbus Apollo.
For, as first ye come all to get auguries of birds,
  even such is in all things your carriage,
Be the matter a matter of trade, or of earning
  your bread, or of any one's marriage.
And all things ye lay to the charge of a bird that
  belong to discerning prediction :
Winged fame is a bird, as you reckon : you
  sneeze, and the sign's as a bird for con-
  viction :
All tokens are "birds" with you—sounds
  too, and lackeys, and donkeys.   Then
  must it not follow
That we ARE to you all as the manifest godhead that speaks in prophetic Apollo?

ATHENS:

AN ODE.

ERE from under earth again like fire the violet kindle, [*Str.* 1.
Ere the holy buds and hoar on olive-branches bloom,
Ere the crescent of the last pale month of winter dwindle,
Shrink, and fall as falls a dead leaf on the dead month's tomb,
Round the hills whose heights the first-born olive-blossom brightened,
Round the city brow-bound once with violets like a bride,
Up from under earth again a light that long since lightened
Breaks, whence all the world took comfort as all time takes pride.
Pride have all men in their fathers that were free before them,
In the warriors that begat us free-born pride have we :
But the fathers of their spirits, how may men adore them,
With what rapture may we praise, who bade our souls be free ?
Sons of Athens born in spirit and truth are all born free men;
Most of all, we, nurtured where the north wind holds his reign :
Children all we sea-folk of the Salaminian seamen,
Sons of them that beat back Persia they that beat back Spain.
Since the songs of Greece fell silent, none like ours have risen;
Since the sails of Greece fell slack, no ships have sailed like ours;
How should we lament not, if her spirit sit in prison ?
How should we rejoice not, if her wreaths renew their flowers ?
All the world is sweeter, if the Athenian violet quicken:
All the world is brighter, if the Athenian sun return:
All things foul on earth wax fainter, by that sun's light stricken:
All ill growths are withered, where those fragrant flower-lights burn.
All the wandering waves of seas with all their warring waters

Roll the record on forever of the sea-fight there,
When the capes were battle's lists, and all the straits were slaughter's,
And the myriad Medes as foam-flakes on the scattering air.
Ours the lightning was that cleared the north and lit the nations,
But the light that gave the whole world light of old was she :
Ours an age or twain, but hers are endless generations :
All the world is hers at heart, and most of all are we.

Ye that bear the name about you of her glory, [*Ant.* 1.
Men that wear the sign of Greeks upon you sealed,
Yours is yet the choice to write yourselves in story
Sons of them that fought the Marathonian field.
Slaves of no man were ye, said your warrior poet,
Neither subject unto man as underlings :
Yours is now the season here wherein to show it,
If the seed ye be of them that knew not kings.
If ye be not, swords nor words alike found brittle
From the dust of death to raise you shall prevail:
Subject swords and dead men's words may stead you little,
If their old king-hating heart within you fail.
If your spirit of old, and not your bonds, be broken,
If the kingless heart be molten in your breasts,
By what signs and wonders, by what word or token,
Shall ye drive the voltures from your eagles' nests ?
All the gains of tyrants Freedom counts for losses;
Nought of all the work done holds she worth the work,
When the slaves whose faith is set on crowns and crosses

Drive the Cossack bear against the tiger
   Turk.
Neither cross nor crown nor crescent shall ye
   bow to,
Nought of Araby nor Jewry, priest nor king:
As your watchword was of old, so be it now
   too:
   As from lips long stilled, from yours let
      healing spring.
Through the fights of old, your battle-cry was
   healing,
   And the Saviour that ye called on was the
      Sun:
Dawn by dawn behold in heaven your God,
   revealing
   Light from darkness as when Marathon was
      won.
Gods were yours yet strange to Turk or Gali-
   lean,
   Light and Wisdom only then as gods adored:
Pallas was your shield, your comforter was
   Pæan,
   From your bright world's navel spake the
      Sun your Lord.

Though the names be lost, and changed the
   signs of Light and Wisdom be,   [*Ep.* 1.
By these only shall men conquer, by these
   only be set free:
When the whole world's eye was Athens,
   these were yours, and theirs were ye.
Light was given you of your wisdom, light ye
   gave the world again:
As the sun whose godhead lightened on her
   soul was Hellas then:
Yea, the least of all her children as the chosen
   of other men.
Change your hearts not with your garments,
   nor your faith with creeds that change:
Truth was yours, the truth which time and
   chance transform not nor estrange:
Purer truth nor higher abides not in the reach
   of time's whole range.
Gods are they in all men's memories and for
   all time's periods,
They that hurled the host back seaward which
   had scourged the sea with rods:
Gods for us are all your fathers, even the
   least of these as gods.
In the dark of days the thought of them is
   with us, strong to save,
They that had no lord, and made the Great
   King lesser than a slave;
They that rolled all Asia back on Asia, broken
   like a wave.
No man's men were they, no master's and no
   God's but these their own:

32

Gods not loved in vain nor served amiss, nor
   all yet overthrown:
Love of country, Freedom, Wisdom, Light,
   and none save these alone.
King by king came up against them, sire and
   son, and turned to flee:
Host on host roared westward, mightier each
   than each, if more might be:
Field to field made answer, clamorous like as
   wave to wave at sea.
Strife to strife responded, loud as rocks to
   clangorous rocks respond
Where the deep rings wreck to seamen held
   in tempest's thrall and bond,
Till when war's bright work was perfect peace
   as radiant rose beyond:
Peace made bright with fruit of battle, stronger
   made for storm gone down,
With the flower of song held heavenward for
   the violet of her crown
Woven about the fragrant forehead of the fostress maiden's town.
Gods arose alive on earth from under stroke
   of human hands:
As the hands that wrought them, these are
   dead, and mixed with time's dead sands:
But the godhead of supernal song, though
   these now stand not, stands.
Pallas is not, Phœbus breathes no more in
   breathing brass or gold:
Clytæmnestra towers, Cassandra wails, forever: Time is bold,
But nor heart nor hand hath he to unwrite
   the scriptures writ of old.
Dead the great chryselephantine God, as dew
   last evening shed:
Dust of earth or foam of ocean is the symbol
   of his head:
Earth and ocean shall be shadows when Pro-
   metheus shall be dead.

Fame around her warriors living rang through
   Greece and lightened,   [*Str.* 2.
   Moving equal with their stature, stately
      with their strength:
Thebes and Lacedæmon at their breathing
   presence brightened,
   Sense or sound of them filled all the live
      land's breadth and length.
All the lesser tribes put on the pure Athenian
   fashion,
   One Hellenic heart was from the mountains
      to the sea:
Sparta's bitter self grew sweet with high half-
   human passion,
   And her dry thorns flushed aflower in strait
      Thermopylæ,

Fruitless yet the flowers had fallen, and all
the deeds died fruitless,
Save that tongues of after men, the children
of her peace,
Took the tale up of her glories, transient else
and rootless,
And in ears and hearts of all men left the
praise of Greece.
Fair the war-time was when still, as beacon
answering beacon,
Sea to land flashed fight, and thundered
note of wrath or cheer;
But the strength of noonday night hath power
to waste and weaken,
Nor may light be passed from hand to
hand of year to year
If the dying deed be saved not, ere it die for
ever,
By the hands and lips of men more wise
than years are strong;
If the soul of man take heed not that the
deed die never,
Clothed about with purple and gold of
story, crowned with song.
Still the burning heart of boy and man alike
rejoices,
Hearing words which made it seem of old
for all who sang
That their heaven of heavens waxed happier
when from free men's voices
Well-beloved Harmodius and Aristogeiton
rang.
Never fell such fragrance from the flower-
month's rose-red kirtle
As from chaplets on the bright friends'
brows who slew their lord:
Greener grew the leaf and balmier blew the
flower of myrtle
When its blossom sheathed the sheer tyran-
nicidal sword.
None so glorious garland crowned the feast
Panathenæan
As this wreath too frail to fetter fast the
Cyprian dove :
None so fiery song sprang sunwards annual
as the pæan
Praising perfect love of friends and perfect
country's love.

Higher than highest of all those heavens
wherefrom the starry   [*Ant. 2.*
Song of Homer shone above the rolling
fight,
Gleams like spring's green bloom on boughs
all gaunt and gnarry
Soft live splendor as of flowers of foam in
flight,

Glows a glory of mild-winged maidens upward mounting
Sheer through air made shrill with strokes
of smooth swift wings
Round the rocks beyond foot's reach, past
eyesight's counting,
Up the cleft where iron wind of winter
rings
Round a God fast clenched in iron jaws of
fetters,
Him who culled for man the fruitful flower
of fire,
Bared the darkling scriptures writ in dazzling
letters,
Taught the truth of dreams deceiving
men's desire,
Gave their water-wandering chariot-seats of
ocean
Wings, and bade the rage of war-steeds
champ the rein,
Showed the symbols of the wild birds' wheel-
ing motion,
Waged for man's sake war with God and all
his train.
Earth, whose name was also Righteousness, a
mother
Many-named and single-natured, gave
him breath
Whence God's wrath could wring but this
word and none other—
He may smite me, yet he shall not do to death.
Him the tongue that sang triumphant while
tormented
Sang as loud the sevenfold storm that
roared erewhile
Round the towers of Thebes till wrath might
rest contented :
Sang the flight from smooth soft-sanded
banks of Nile,
When like mateless doves that fly from snare
or tether
Came the suppliants landwards trembling
as they trod,
And the prayer took wing from all their
tongues together—
King of kings, most holy of holies, blessed
God.
But what mouth may chant again, what heart
may know it,
All the rapture that all hearts of men put on
When of Salamis the time-transcending poet
Sang, whose hand had chased the Mede at
Marathon?
Darker dawned the song with stormier wings
above the watch-fire spread   [*Ep. 2.*
Whence from Ida toward the hill of Hermes
leapt the light that said

Troy was fallen, a torch funereal for the king's triumphal head.
Dire indeed the birth of Leda's womb that had God's self to sire
Bloomed, a flower of love that stung the soul with fangs that gnaw like fire :
But the twin-born human-fathered sister-flower bore fruit more dire.
Scarce the cry that called on airy heaven and all swift winds on wing,
Wells of river-heads, and countless laugh of waves past reckoning,
Earth which brought forth all, and the orbèd sun that looks on everything,
Scarce that cry fills yet men's hearts more full of heart-devouring dread
Than the murderous word said mocking, how the child whose blood he shed
Might clasp fast and kiss her father where the dead salute the dead.
But the latter note of anguish from the lips that mocked her lord,
When her son's hand bared against the breast that suckled him his sword,
How might man endure, O Æschylus, to hear it and record?
How might man endure, being mortal yet, O thou most highest, to hear?
How record, being born of woman? Surely not thy Furies near,
Surely this beheld, this only, blasted hearts to death with fear.
Not the hissing hair, nor flakes of blood that oozed from eyes of fire,
Nor the snort of savage sleep that snuffed the hungering heart's desire
Where the hunted prey found hardly space and harbor to respire ;
She whose likeness called them—'Sleep ye, ho? what need of you that sleep?'
(Ah, what need indeed, where she was, of all shapes that night may keep
Hidden dark as death and deeper than men's dreams of hell are deep?)
She the murderess of her husband, she the huntress of her son,
More than ye was she, the shadow that no God withstands but one,
Wisdom equal-eyed and stronger and more splendid than the sun.
Yea, no God may stand betwixt us and the shadows of our deeds,
Nor the light of dreams that lighten darkness, nor the prayer that pleads,
But the wisdom equal-souled with heaven, the light alone that leads.
Light whose law bids home those childless children of eternal night,

Soothed and reconciled and mastered and transmuted in men's sight
Who behold their own souls, clothed with darkness once, now clothed with light.
King of kings and father crowned of all our fathers crowned of yore,
Lord of all the lords of song, whose head all heads bow down before,
Glory be to thee from all thy sons in all tongues evermore.

Rose and vine and olive and deep ivy-bloom entwining   [*Str.* 3.
Close the goodliest grave that e'er they closeliest might entwine
Keep the wind from wasting and the sun from too strong shining
    Where the sound and light of sweetest songs still float and shine.
Here the music seems to illume the shade, the light to whisper
Song, the flowers to put not odors only forth, but words
Sweeter far than fragrance : here the wandering wreaths twine crisper
    Far, and louder far exults the note of all wild birds.
Thoughts that change us, joys that crown and sorrows that enthrone us,
Passions that enrobe us with a clearer air than ours,
Move and breathe as living things beheld round white Colonus,
    Audibler than melodies and visibler than flowers.
Love, in fight unconquered, Love, with spoils of great men laden,
Never sang so sweet from throat of woman or of dove :
Love, whose bed by night is in the soft cheeks of a maiden,
    And his march is over seas, and low roofs lack not Love ;
Nor may one of all that live, ephemeral or eternal,
Fly nor hide from Love ; but whoso clasps him fast goes mad.
Never since the first-born year with flowers first-born grew vernal
    Such a song made listening hearts of lovers glad or sad.
Never sounded note so radiant at the rayless portal
Opening wide on the all-concealing lowland of the dead
As the music mingling, when her doomsday marked her mortal,

From her own and old men's voices round
the bride's way shed,
Round the grave her bride-house, hewn for
endless habitation,
Where, shut out from sunshine, with no
bridegroom by, she slept ;
But beloved of all her dark and fateful
generation,
But with all time's tears and praise be-
sprinkled and bewept :
Well-beloved of outcast father and self-
slaughtered mother,
Born, yet unpolluted, of their blind incestuous bed ;
Best-beloved of him for whose dead sake she
died, her brother,
Hallowing by her own life's gift her own
born brother's head :

Not with wine or oil nor any less libation
         [*Ant.* 3.
Hallowed, nor made sweet with humbler
perfume's breath ;
Not with only these redeemed from desecra-
tion,
But with blood and spirit of life poured
forth to death ;
Blood unspotted, spirit unsullied, life devoted,
Sister too supreme to make the bride's
hope good,
Daughter too divine as woman to be noted,
Spouse of only death in mateless maiden-
hood.
Yea, in her was all the prayer fulfilled, the
saying
All accomplished—*Would that fate would
let me wear*
*Hallowed innocence of words and all deeds,
weighing*
Well the laws thereof, begot on holier air,
Far on high sublimely stablished, whereof only
*Heaven is father ; nor did birth of mortal
mould*
*Bring them forth, nor shall oblivion lull to
lonely*
*Slumber. Great in these is God, and grows
not old.*
Therefore even that inner darkness where she
perished
Surely seems as holy and lovely, seen aright,
As desirable and as dearly to be cherished,
As the haunt closed in with laurels from
the light,
Deep inwound with olive and wild vine in-
woven,
Where a godhead known and unknown
makes men pale,
But the darkness of the twilight noon is cloven

Still with shrill sweet moan of many a
nightingale.
Closer clustering there they make sweet noise
together,
Where the fearful gods look gentler than
our fear,
And the grove thronged through with birds of
holiest feather
Grows nor pale nor dumb with sense of
dark things near.
There her father, called upon with signs of
wonder,
Passed with tenderest words away by ways
unknown,
Not by sea-storm stricken down, nor touched
of thunder,
To the dark benign deep underworld, alone.

Third of three that ruled in Athens, kings
with sceptral song for staff,   [*Ep.* 3.
Gladdest heart that God gave ever milk and
wine of thought to quaff,
Clearest eye that lightened ever to the broad
lip's lordliest laugh,
Praise be thine as theirs whose tragic brows
the loftier leaf engirds
For the live and lyric lightning of thy honey-
hearted words,
Soft like sunny dewy wings of clouds and
bright as crying of birds ;
Full of all sweet rays and notes that make of
earth and air and sea
One great light and sound of laughter from
one great God's heart, to be
Sign and semblance of the gladness of man's
life where men breathe free.
With no Loxian sound obscure God uttered
once, and all time heard,
All the soul of Athens, all the soul of England,
in that word :
Rome arose the second child of freedom :
northward rose the third.
Ere her Boreal dawn came kindling seas afoam
and fields of snow,
Yet again, while Europe groaned and grovel-
led, shone like suns aglow
Doria splendid over Genoa, Venice bright
with Dandolo.
Dead was Hellas, but Ausonia by the light
of dead men's deeds
Rose and walked awhile alive, though mocked
as whom the fen-fire leads
By the creed-wrought faith of faithless souls
that mock their doubts with creeds.
Dead are these, and man is risen again : and
haply now the Three
Yet coequal and triune may stand in story,
marked as free

By the token of the washing of the waters of
  the sea.
Athens first of all earth's kindred many-
  tongued and many-kinned
Had the sea to friend and comfort, and for
  kinsman had the wind:
She that bare Columbus next: then she that
  made her spoil of Ind.
She that hears not what man's rage but only
  what the sea-wind saith :
She that turned Spain's ships to cloud-wrack
  at the blasting of her breath,
By her strengths of strong-souled children and
  of strong winds done to death.
North and south the Great King's galleons
  went in Persian wise : and here

She, with Æschylean music on her lips that
  laughed back fear,
In the face of Time's grey godhead shook the
  splendor of her spear.
Fair as Athens then with foot upon her foeman's front, and strong
Even as Athens for redemption of the world
  from sovereign wrong,
Like as Athens crowned she stood before the
  sun with crowning song.
All the world is theirs with whom is freedom:
  first of all the free,
Blest are they whom song has crowned and
  clothed with blessing : these as we,
These alone have part in spirit with the sun
  that crowns the sea.

THE STATUE OF VICTOR HUGO.

I.

SINCE in Athens God stood plain for adora-
  tion,
Since the sun beheld his likeness reared in
  stone,
Since the bronze or gold of human consecra-
  tion
Gave to Greece her guardian's form and
  feature shown,
Never hand of sculptor, never heart of nation,
  Found so glorious a'm in all these ages
  flown
As 's theirs who rear for all time's acclamation
  Here the likeness of our mightiest and
  their own.

2.

Theirs and ours and all men's living who behold him
Crowned with garlands multiform and
  manifold ;
Praise and thanksgiving of all mankind enfold
  him
Who for all men casts abroad his gifts of
  gold.
With the gods of song have all men's tongues
  enrolled him,
With the helpful gods have all men's hearts
  enrolled :
Ours he is who love him, ours whose hearts'
  hearts hold him
Fast as his the trust that hearts like his
  may hold.

3.

He, the heart most high, the spirit on earth
  most blameless,
Takes in charge all spirits, holds all hearts
  in trust :
As the sea-wind's on the sea his ways are
  tameless,
As the laws that steer the world his works
  are just.
All most noble feel him nobler, all most shameless
Feel his wrath and scorn make pale their
  pride and lust :
All most poor and lowliest, all whose wrongs
  were nameless,
Feel his word of comfort raise them from
  the dust.

4.

Pride of place and lust of empire bloody-
  fruited
Knew the blasting of his breath on leaf and
  fruit :
Now the hand that smote the death-tree now
  disrooted
Plants the refuge-tree that has man's hope
  for root.
Ah, but we by whom his darkness was saluted,
  How shall now all we that see his day
  salute ?
How should love not seem by love's own
  speech confuted, [mute ?
Song before the sovereign singer not be

5.

With what worship, by what blessing, in what measure,
    May we sing of him, salute him, or adore,
With what hymn for praise, what thanksgiving for pleasure,
Who had given us more than heaven, and gives us more?
Heaven's whole treasury, filled up full with night's whole treasure,
Holds not so divine or deep a starry store
As the soul supreme that deals forth worlds at leisure
    Clothed with light and darkness, dense with flower and ore.

6.

Song had touched the bourn: fresh verses overflow it,
    Loud and radiant, waves on waves on waves that throng ;
Still the tide grows, and the sea-mark still below it
    Sinks and shifts and rises, changed and swept along.
Rose it like a rock? the waters overthrow it,
    And another stands beyond them sheer and strong :
Goal by goal pays down its prize, and yields its poet
    Tribute claimed of triumph, palm achieved of song

7.

Since his hand that holds the keys of fear and wonder
    Opened on the high priest's dreaming eyes a door
Whence the lights of heaven and hell above and under
    Shone, and smote the face that men bow down before,
Thrice again one singer's note had cloven in sunder
    Night, who blows again not one blast now but four,
And the fourfold heaven is kindled with his thunder,
    And the stars about his forehead are fourscore.

8.

From the deep soul's depths where alway love abounded
    First had risen a song with healing on its wings
Whence the dews of mercy raining balms unbounded

Shed their last compassion even on sceptre things.[1]
Even on heads that like a curse the crown surrounded
    Fell his crowning pity, soft as cleansing springs ;
And the sweet last note his wrath relenting sounded
    Bade men's heart's be melted not for slaves but kings.

9.

Next, that faith might strengthen fear and love embolden,
    On the creeds of priests a scourge of sunbeams fell :
And its flash made bare the deeps of heaven, beholden
    Not of men that cry, Lord, Lord, from church or cell.[2]
Hope as young as dawn from night obscure and olden
    Rose again, such power abides in truth's one spell:
Night, if dawn it be that touches her, grows golden,
    Tears, if such as angels weep, extinguish hell.

10.

Through the blind loud mills of barren blear-eyed learning
    Where in dust and darkness children's foreheads bow,
While men's labor, vain as wind or water turning
    Wheels and sails of dreams, makes life a leafless bough,
Fell the light of scorn and pity touched with yearning,
    Next, from words that shone as heaven's own kindling brow.[3]
Stars were these as watch-fires on the world's waste burning,
    Stars that fade not in the fourfold sunrise now.[4]

11.

Now the voice that faints not till all wrongs be wroken
    Sounds as might the sun's song from the morning's breast,

[1] *La Pitié Suprême.* 1879.
[2] *Religions et Religion.* 1880.
[3] *L'Âne.* 1880.
[4] *Les Quatre Vents de l'Esprit.* I. *Le Livre satirique.* II. *Le Livre dramatique.* III. *Le Livre lyrique.* IV. *Le Livre épique.* 1881.

All the seals of silence sealed of night are
broken,
All the winds that bear the fourfold word
are blest.
All the keen fierce east flames forth one fiery
token;
All the north is loud with life that knows
not rest,
All the south with song as though the stars
had spoken;
All the judgment-fire of sunset scathes the
west.

12.

Sound of pæan, roll of chanted panegyric,
Though by Pindar's mouth song's trumpet
spake forth praise,
March of warrior songs in Pythian mood or
Pyrrhic,
Though the blast were blown by lips of
ancient days,
Ring not clearer than the clarion of satiric
Song whose breath sweeps bare the plague-
infected ways
Till the world be pure as heaven is for the
lyric
Sun to rise up clothed with radiant sounds
as rays.

13.

Clear across the cloud-rack fluctuant and
erratic
As the strong star smiles that lets no
mourner mourn,
Hymned alike from lips of Lesbian choirs or
Attic
Once at evensong and morning newly born,
Clear and sure above the changes of dramatic
Tide and current, soft with love and keen
with scorn,
Smiles the strong sweet soul of maidenhood,
ecstatic
And inviolate as the red glad mouth of
morn.

14.

Pure and passionate as dawn, whose appari-
tion
Thrills with fire from heaven the wheels of
hours that whirl,
Rose and passed her radiance in serene tran-
sition
From his eyes who sought a grain and
found a pearl.
But the food by cunning hope for vain frui-
tion
Lightly stolen away from keeping of a
churl
Left the bitterness of death and hope's perdi-
tion

On the lip that scorn was wont for shame
to curl.[1]

15.

Over waves that darken round the wave-worn
rover
Rang his clarion higher than winds cried
round the ship,
Rose a pageant of set suns and storms blown
over,
Hands that held life's guerdons fast or let
them slip.
But no tongue may tell, no thanksgiving discover,
Half the heaven of blessing, soft with clouds
that drip,
Keen with beams that kindle, dear as love to
lover,
Opening by the spell's strength on his lyric
lip.

16.

By that spell the soul transfigured and dilated
Puts forth wings that widen, breathes a
brightening air,
Feeds on light and drinks of music, whence
elated
All her sense grows godlike, seeing all
depths made bare,
All the mists wherein before she sat belated
Shrink, till now the sunlight knows not if
they were;
All this earth transformed is Eden recreated,
With the breath of heaven remurmuring in
her hair.

17.

Sweeter far than aught of sweet that April
nurses
Deep in dew-dropt woodland folded fast
and furled
Breathes the fragrant song whose burning
dawn disperses
Darkness, like the surge of armies backward hurled,
Even as though the touch of spring's own
hand, that pierces
Earth with life's delight, had hidden in the
impearled
Golden bells and buds and petals of his verses
All the breath of all the flowers in all the
world.

18.

But the soul therein, the light that our souls
follow,
Fires and fills the song with more of prophet's pride,

[1] *Les Deux Trouvailles de Gallus.* I. *Mar-
garita, comédie.* II . *Esca, drame.*

More of life than all the gulfs of death may
swallow,
More of flame than all the might of night
may hide.
Though the whole dark age were loud and
void and hollow,
Strength of trust were here, and help for
all souls tried,
And a token from the flight of that strange
swallow [1]
Whose migration still is toward the wintry
side.

19.

Never came such token for divine solution
From the oraculous live darkness whence
of yore
Ancient faith sought word of help and retribu-
tion,
Truth to lighten doubt, a sign to go before.
Never so baptismal waters of ablution
Bathed the brows of exile on so stern a
shore,
Where the lightnings of the sea of revolution
Flashed across them ere its thunders yet
might roar.

20.

By the lightning's light of present revelation
Shown, with epic thunder as from skies that
frown,
Clothed in darkness as of darkling expiation,
Rose a vision of dead stars and suns gone
down,
Whence of old fierce fire devoured the star-
struck nation,
Till its wrath and woe lit red the raging
town,
Now made glorious with his statue's crowning
station,
Where may never gleam again a viler
crown.

21.

King, with time for throne and all the years
for pages,
He shall reign though all thrones else be
overhurled,
Served of souls that have his living words for
wages,
Crowned of heaven each dawn that leaves
his brows impearled ;
Girt about with robes unrent of storm that
rages,
Robes not wrought with hands, from no
loom's weft unfurled ;

Je suis une hirondelle étrange, car j'émigre
1 Du côté de l'hiver.
Le Livre Lyrique, liii.

All the praise of all earth's tongues in all
earth's ages,
All the love of all men's hearts in all the
world.

22.

Yet what hand shall carve the soul or cast the
spirit,
Mould the face of fame, bid glory's feature
glow ?
Who bequeath for eyes of ages hence to
inherit
Him, the Master, whom love knows not if
it know ?
Scarcely perfect praise of men man's work
might merit,
Scarcely bid such aim to perfect stature
grow,
Were his hand the hand of Phidias who shall
rear it,
And his soul the very soul of Angelo.

23.

Michael, awful angel of the world's last ses-
sion,
Once on earth, like him, with fire of suffering tried,
Thine it were, if man's it were, without transgression,
Thine alone, to take this toil upon thy
pride.
Thine, whose heart was great against the
world's oppression,
Even as his whose word is lamp and staff
and guide :
Advocate for man, untired of intercession,
Pleads his voice for slaves whose lords his
voice defied.

24.

Earth, with all the kings and thralls on earth,
below it,
Heaven alone, with all the worlds in heaven,
above,
Let his likeness rise for suns and stars to
know it,   [love :
High for men to worship, plain for men to
Brow that braved the tides which fain would
overflow it,
Lip that gave the challenge, hand that flung
the glove ;
Comforter and prophet, Paraclete and poet,
Soul whose emblems are an eagle and a
dove.

25.

Sun, that hast not seen a loftier head wax
hoary,
Earth, which hast not shown the sun a
nobler birth,

Time, that hast not on thy scroll defiled and
 gory
 One man's name writ brighter in its whole
  wide girth,
Witness, till the final years fulfil their story,
 Till the stars break off the music of their
  mirth,   [glory,
What among the sons of men was this man's
 What the vesture of his soul revealed on
  earth.

SONNETS.

HOPE AND FEAR.

BENEATH the shadow of dawn's aerial cope,
 With eyes enkindled as the sun's own
  sphere,
 Hope from the front of youtn in godlike
  cheer
Looks Godward, past the shades where blind
 men grope
Round the dark door that prayers nor dreams
 can ope,
 And makes for joy the very darkness dear
 That gives her wide wings play; nor dreams
  that fear
At noon may rise and pierce the heart of
 hope.
Then, when the soul leaves off to dream and
 yearn,
May truth first purge her eyesight to discern
 What once being known leaves time no
  power to appal;
Till youth at last, ere yet youth be not, learn
 The kind wise word that falls from years
  that fall—
 'Hope thou not much, and fear thou not
  at all.'

AFTER SUNSET.

' Si quis piorum Manibus locus.'

I.

STRAIGHT from the sun's grave in the deep
 clear west
 A sweet strong wind blows, glad of life:
  and I,
 Under the soft keen stardawn whence the
  sky
Takes life renewed, and all night's godlike
 breast
Palpitates, gradually revealed at rest
 By growth and change of ardors felt on
  high,

Make onward, till the last flame fall and die
And all the world by night's broad hand lie
 blest.
Haply, meseems, as from that edge of death,
 Whereon the day lies dark, a brightening
  breath
 Blows more of benediction than the morn,
So from the graves whereon grief gazing
 saith
 That half our heart of life there lies forlorn
 May light or breath at least of hope be
  born.

II.

The wind was soft before the sunset fled:
 Now, while the cloud-enshrouded corpse of
  day
 Is lowered along a red funereal way
Down to the dark that knows not white from
 red,
A clear sheer breeze against the night makes
 head,
 Serene, but sure of life as ere a ray
 Springs, or the dusk of dawn knows red
  from gray,
Being as a soul that knows not quick from
 dead.
From far beyond the sunset, far above,
 Full toward the starry soundless east it
  blows
 Bright as a child's breath breathing on a
  rose,
Smooth to the sense as plume of any dove;
 Till more and more as darkness grows and
  glows
Silence and night seem likest life and love.

III.

If light of life outlive the set of sun
 That men call death and end of all things,
  then
 How should not that which life held best
  for men
And proved most precious, though it seem
 undone
By force of death and woful victory won,
 Be first and surest of revival, when
 Death shall bow down to life arisen again ?
So shall the soul seen be the self-same one
That looked and spake with even such lips
 and eyes
As love shall doubt not then to recognize,
 And all bright thoughts and smiles of all
  time past
Revive, transfigured, but in spirit and sense
None other than we knew, for evidence
 That love's last mortal word was not his
  last.

A STUDY FROM MEMORY.

IF that be yet a living soul which here
    Seemed brighter for the growth of num-
        bered springs
    And clothed by Time and Pain with good-
        lier things
Each year it saw fulfilled a fresh fleet year,
Death can have changed not aught that made
        it dear;
    Half humorous goodness, grave-eyed mirth
        on wings
    Bright-balanced, blither-voiced than quiring
        strings;
Most radiant patience, crowned with conquer-
        ing cheer;
A spirit inviolable that smiled and sang
    By might of nature and heroic need
More sweet and strong than loftiest dream
        or deed;
A song that shone, a light whence music rang
    High as the sunniest heights of kindliest
        thought;
    All these must be, or all she was be nought.

TO DR. JOHN BROWN.

BEYOND the north wind lay the land of old
    Where men dwelt blithe and blameless,
        clothed and fed
    With joy's bright raiment and with love's
        sweet bread,
The whitest flock of earth's maternal fold.
None there might wear about his brows en-
        rolled
    A light of lovelier fame than rings your
        head,
    Whose lovesome love of children and the
        dead
All men give thanks for: I far off behold
A dear dead hand that links us, and a light
The blithest and benignest of the night,
    The night of death's sweet sleep, wherein
        may be
A star to show your spirit in present sight
    Some happier island in the Elysian sea
    Where Rab may lick the hand of Mar-
        jorie.

TO WILLIAM BELL SCOTT.

THE larks are loud above our leagues of whin
    Now the sun's perfume fills their glorious
        gold

With odor like the color: all the wold
Is only light and song and wind wherein
These twain are blent in one with shining din.
    And now your gift, a giver's kingly-souled,
    Dear old fast friend whose honors grow not
        old,
Bids memory's note as loud and sweet begin.
Though all but we from life be now gone
        forth
Of that bright household in our joyous north
Where I, scarce clear of boyhood just at end,
    First met your hand; yet under life's clear
        dome,
Now seventy strenuous years have crowned
        my friend,
    Shines no less bright his full-sheaved har
        vest-home.

A DEATH ON EASTER DAY.

THE strong spring sun rejoicingly may rise,
    Rise and make revel, as of old men said,
    Like dancing hearts of lovers newly wed:
A light more bright than ever bathed the
        skies
Departs for all time out of all men's eyes.
    The crowns that girt last night a living
        head
    Shine only now, though deathless, on the
        dead:
Art that mocks death, and Song that never
        dies.
Albeit the bright sweet mothlike wings be
        furled,
    Hope sees, past all division and defection,
    And higher than swims the mist of human
        breath,
The soul most radiant once in all the world
Requickened to regenerate resurrection
    Out of the likeness of the shadow of
        death.

ON THE DEATHS OF THOMAS CAR-
LYLE AND GEORGE ELIOT.

Two souls diverse out of our human sight
    Pass, followed one with love and each with
        wonder :
    The stormy sophist with his mouth of
        thunder,
Clothed with loud words and mantled in the
        might
Of darkness and magnificence of night ;

And one whose eye could smite the night in
sunder,
Searching if light or no light were there-
under,
And found in love of loving-kindness light.
Duty divine and Thought with eyes of fire
Still following Righteousness with deep desire
Shone sole and stern before her and above,
Sure stars and sole to steer by ; but more
sweet
Shone lower the loveliest lamp for earthly
feet,
The light of little children, and their love.

AFTER LOOKING INTO CARLYLE'S REMINISCENCES.

I.

THREE men lived yet when this dead man
was young
Whose names and words endure forever :
one
Whose eyes grew dim with straining toward
the sun,
And his wings weakened, and his angel's
tongue
Lost half the sweetest song was ever sung,
But like the strain half uttered earth hears
none,
Nor shall man hear till all men's songs are
done :
One whose clear spirit like an eagle hung
Between the mountains hallowed by his love
And the sky stainless as his soul above :
And one the sweetest heart that ever spake
The brightest words wherein sweet wisdom
smiled.
These deathless names by this dead snake
defiled
Bid memory spit upon him for their sake.

II.

Sweet heart, forgive me for thine own sweet
sake,
Whose kind blithe soul such seas of sorrow
swam,
And for my love's sake, powerless as I am
For love to praise thee, or like thee to make
Music of mirth where hearts less pure would
break,
Less pure than thine, our life-unspotted
Lamb.
Things hatefullest thou hadst not heart to
damn,
Nor wouldst have set thine heel on this dead
snake.

Let worms consume its memory with its
tongue,
The fang that stabbed fair Truth, the lip that
stung
Men's memories uncorroded with its breath.
Forgive me, that with bitter words like his
I mix the gentlest English name that is,
The tenderest held of all that know not
death.

A LAST LOOK.

SICK of self-love, Malvolio, like an owl
That hoots the sun rerisen where starlight
sank,
With German garters crossed athwart thy
frank
Stout Scottish legs, men watched thee snarl
and scowl,
And boys responsive with reverberate howl
Shrilled, hearing how to thee the springtime
stank
And as thine own soul all the world smelt
rank
And as thine own thoughts Liberty seemed
foul.
Now, for all ill thoughts nursed and ill words
given
Not all condemned, not utterly forgiven,
Son of the storm and darkness, pass in
peace.
Peace upon earth thou knewest not : now,
being dead,
Rest, with nor curse nor blessing on thine
head,
Where high-strung hate and strenuous envy
cease.

DICKENS.

CHIEF in thy generation born of men
Whom English praise acclaimed as Eng-
lish-born,
With eyes that matched the worldwide eyes
of morn
For gleam of tears or laughter, tenderest
then
When thoughts of children warmed their
light, or when
Reverence of age with love and labor worn,
Or godlike pity fired with godlike scorn,
Shot through them flame that winged thy
swift live pen:
Where stars and suns that we behold not
burn,

Higher even than here, though highest was
    here thy place,
    Love sees thy spirit laugh and speak and
      shine
With Shakespeare and the soft bright soul of
    Sterne
    And Fielding's kindliest might and Gold-
      smith's grace ;
    Scarce one more loved or worthier love
    than thine.

ON LAMB'S SPECIMENS OF DRAMA-
TIC POETS.

I.

IF all the flowers of all the fields on earth
    By wonder-working summer were made
    one,
    Its fragrance were not sweeter in the sun,
Its treasure-house of leaves were not more
    worth
Than those wherefrom thy light of musing
    mirth
    Shone, till each leaf whereon thy pen would
    run
    Breathed life, and all its breath was beni-
    son.
Beloved beyond all names of English birth,
More dear than mightier memories; gentlest
    name
That ever clothed itself with flower-sweet
    fame,
Or linked itself with loftiest names of old
    By right and might of loving; I, that am
Less than the least of those within thy fold,
    Give only thanks for them to thee, Charles
    Lamb.

II.

So many a year had borne its own bright bees
    And slain them since thy honey-bees were
    hived,
    John Day, in cells of flower-sweet verse
    contrived
So well with craft of moulding melodies,
Thy soul perchance in amaranth fields at ease
    Thought not to hear the sound on earth
    revived
    Of summer music from the spring derived
When thy song sucked the flower of flower-
    ing trees.
But thine was not the chance of every day:
Time, after many a darkling hour, grew sunny,
    And light between the clouds ere sunset
    swam,

Laughing, and kissed their darkness all
    away,
    When, touched and tasted and approved,
    thy honey
    Took subtler sweetness from the lips of
    Lamb.

TO JOHN NICHOL.

I.

FRIEND of the dead, and friend of all my
    days
    Even since they cast off boyhood, I salute
    The song saluting friends whose songs are
    mute
With full burnt-offerings of clear-spirited
    praise.
That since our old young years our several
    ways
    Have led through fields diverse of flower
    and fruit
    Yet no cross wind has once relaxed the
    root
We set long since beneath the sundawn's rays,
The root of trust whence towered the trusty
    tree,
    Friendship—this only and duly might impel
    My song to salutation of your own;
More even than praise of one unseen of me
    And loved—the starry spirit of Dobell,
    To mine by light and music only known.

II.

But more than this what moves me most of
    all
    To leave not all unworded and unsped
    The whole heart's greeting of my thanks
    unsaid
Scarce needs this sign, that from my tongue
    should fall
His name whom sorrow and reverent love
    recall,
    The sign to friends on earth of that dear
    head
    Alive, which now long since untimely dead
The wan gray waters covered for a pall.
Their trustless reaches dense with tangling
    stems
    Took never life more taintless of rebuke,
    More pure and perfect, more serene and
    kind,
Than when those clear eyes closed beneath
    the Thames,
    And made the now more hallowed name of
    Luke
    Memorial to us of morning left behind.

DYSTHANATOS.

Ad generem Cereris sine cæde et vulnere pauci
Descendunt reges, aut siccâ morte tyranni.

By no dry death another king goes down
    The way of kings. Yet may no free man's
      voice,
    For stern compassion and deep awe, re-
      joice
That one sign more is given against the
    crown,
That one more head those dark red waters
    drown
    Which rise round thrones whose trembling
      equipoise
    Is propped on sand and bloodshed and such
      toys
As human hearts that shrink at human frown.
The name writ red on Polish earth, the star
That was to outshine our England's in the
    far
    East heaven of empire—where is one that
      saith
Proud words now, prophesying of this White
    Czar?
    'In bloodless pangs few kings yield up
      their breath,
    Few tyrants perish by no violent death.'

EUONYMOS.

εὖ μὴν ἦ τιμήν ἐδίδου νικηφόρος ἀλκὴ
ἐκ νίκης ὄνομ' ἔσχε φόβου κἑαρ αἰὲν ἄθικτος.

A year ago red wrath and keen despair
    Spake, and the sole word from their dark-
      ness sent
    Laid low the lord not all omnipotent
Who stood most like a god of all that were
As gods for pride of power, till fire and air
    Made earth of all his godhead. Lightning
      rent
    The heart of empire's lurid firmament,
And laid the mortal core of manhood bare.
But when the calm crowned head that all
    revere
For valor higher than that which casts out
    fear,
    Since fear came near it never, comes near
      death,
Blind murder cowers before it, knowing that
    here
    No braver soul drew bright and queenly
      breath
    Since England wept upon Elizabeth.

ON THE RUSSIAN PERSECUTION OF THE JEWS.

O son of man, by lying tongues adored,
    By slaughterous hands of slaves with feet
      red-shod
In carnage deep as ever Christian trod
Profaned with prayer and sacrifice abhorred
And incense from the trembling tyrant's horde,
    Brute worshippers or wielders of the rod,
    Most murderous even of all that call thee
      God,
Most treacherous even that ever called thee
    Lord ;
Face loved of little children long ago,
    Head hated of the priests and rulers then,
    If thou see this, or hear these hounds of
      thine
    Run ravening as the Gadarean swine,
Say, was not this thy Passion, to foreknow
    In death's worst hour the works of Christian
      men?

BISMARCK AT CANOSSA.

Not all disgraced, in that Italian town,
    The imperial German cowered beneath
      thine hand,
    Alone indeed imperial Hildebrand,
And felt thy foot and Rome's, and felt her
    frown
And thine, more strong and sovereign than
    his crown,
    Though iron forged its blood-encrusted
      band.
But now the princely wielder of his land,
    For hatred's sake toward freedom, so bows
      down,
No strength is in the foot to spurn : its tread
Can bruise not now the proud submitted
    head :
    But how much more abased, much lower
      brought low,
And more intolerably humiliated,
    The neck submissive of the prosperous foe,
    Than his whom scorn saw shuddering in the
      snow !

QUIA NOMINOR LEO.

I.

What part is left thee, lion? Ravenous
    beast,
    Which hadst the world for pasture, and for
      scope

And compass of thine homicidal hope
The kingdom of the spirit of man, the feast
Of souls subdued from west to sunless east,
  From blackening north to bloodred south
    aslope,
All servile ; earth for footcloth of the pope,
And heaven for chancel-ceiling of the priest ;
Thou that hadst earth by right of rack and rod,
Thou that hadst Rome because thy name was
    God,
  And by thy creed's gift heaven wherein to
    dwell ;
Heaven laughs with all his light and might
    above
That earth has cast thee out of faith and
    love ;
  Thy part is but the hollow dream of hell.

II.

The light of life has faded from thy cause,
  High priest of heaven and hell and pur-
    gatory :
  Thy lips are loud with strains of oldworld
    story,
But the red prey was rent out of thy paws
Long since : and they that dying brake down
    thy laws
  Have with the fires of death-enkindled glory
  Put out the flame that faltered on thy hoary
High altars, waning with the world's applause.
This Italy was Dante's : Bruno died
Here : Campanella, too sublime for pride,
  Endured thy God's worst here, and hence
    went home.
And what art thou, that time's full tide should
    shrink
For thy sake downward ? What art thou, to
    think
  Thy God shall give thee back for birthright
    Rome ?

———

THE CHANNEL TUNNEL.

Not for less love, all glorious France, to thee,
  'Sweet enemy' called in days long since at
    end,
  Now found and hailed of England sweeter
    friend,
Bright sister of our freedom now, being free ;
Not for less love or faith in friendship we
  Whose love burnt ever toward thee re-
    prehend
  The vile vain greed whose pursy dreams
    portend
Between our shores suppression of the sea.

Not by dull toil of blind mechanic art
Shall these be linked for no man's force to
    part
  Nor length of years and changes to divide,
But union only of trust and loving heart
  And perfect faith in freedom strong to abide
  And spirit at one with spirit on either side.

———

SIR WILLIAM GOMM.

I.

At threescore years and five aroused anew
  To rule in India, forth a soldier went
  On whose bright-fronted youth fierce war
    had spent
Its iron stress of storm, till glory grew
Full as the red sun waned on Waterloo.
  Landing, he met the word from England
    sent
  Which bade him yield up rule : and he, con-
    tent,
Resigned it, as a mightier warrior's due ;
And wrote as one rejoicing to record
  That 'from the first' his royal heart was
    lord
  Of its own pride or pain ; that thought was
    none
Therein save this, that in her perilous strait
England, whose womb brings forth her sons
    so great,
  Should choose to serve her first her migh-
    tiest son.

II.

Glory beyond all flight of warlike fame
  Go with the warrior's memory who pre-
    ferred
  To praise of men whereby men's hearts
    are stirred,
And acclamation of his own proud name
With blare of trumpet-blasts and sound and
    flame
  Of pageant honor, and the titular word
That only wins men worship of the herd,
His country's sovereign good ; who overcame
Pride, wrath, and hope of all high chance on
    earth,
For this land's love that gave his great heart
    birth.
  O nursling of the sea-winds and the sea,
Immortal England, goddess ocean-born,
What shall thy children fear, what strengths
    not scorn,
  While children of such mould are born to
    thee ?

EUTHANATOS.

In memory of Mrs. Thellusson.

Forth of our ways and woes,
Forth of the winds and snows,
A white soul soaring goes,
  Winged like a dove:
So sweet, so pure, so clear,
So heavenly tempered here,
Love need not hope or fear her changed
  above:

Ere dawned her day to die,
So heavenly, that on high
Change could not glorify
  Nor death refine her:
Pure gold of perfect love,
On earth like heaven's own dove,
She cannot wear, above, a smile diviner.

Her voice in heaven's own quire
Can sound no heavenlier lyre
Than here: no purer fire
  Her soul can soar:
No sweeter stars her eyes
In unimagined skies
Beyond our sight can rise than here before.

Hardly long years had shed
Their shadows on her head:
Hardly we think her dead,
  Who hardly thought her
Old: hardly can believe
The grief our hearts receive
And wonder while they grieve, as wrong were
  wrought her.

But though strong grief be strong
No word or thought of wrong
May stain the trembling song,
  Wring the bruised heart,
That sounds or sighs its faint
Low note of love, nor taint
Grief for so sweet a saint, when such depart.

A saint whose perfect soul,
With perfect love for goal,
Faith hardly might control,
  Creeds might not harden:
A flower more splendid far
Than the most radiant star
Seen here of all that are in God's own garden.

Surely the stars we see
Rise and relapse as we,
And change and set, may be

But shadows too.
But spirits that man's lot
Could neither mar nor spot
Like these false lights are not, being heavenly
  true.

Not like these dying lights
Of worlds whose glory smites
The passage of the nights
  Through heaven's blind prison:
Not like their souls who see,
If thought fly far and free,
No heavenlier heaven to be for souls rerisen,

A soul wherein love shone
Even like the sun, alone,
With fervor of its own
  And splendor fed,
Made by no creeds less kind
Toward souls by none confined,
Could Death's self quench or blind, Love's
  self were dead.

———

FIRST AND LAST.

Upon the borderlands of being,
  Where life draws hardly breath
Between the lights and shadows fleeing
  Fast as a word one saith,
Two flowers rejoice our eyesight, seeing
  The dawns of birth and death.

Behind the babe his dawn is lying
  Half risen with notes of mirth
From all the winds about it flying
  Through new-born heaven and earth:
Before bright age his day for dying
  Dawns equal-eyed with birth.

Equal the dews of even and dawn,
  Equal the sun's eye seen
A hand's breadth risen and half withdrawn
  But no bright hour between
Brings aught so bright by stream or lawn
  To noonday growths of green.

Which flower of life may smell the sweeter
  To love's insensual sense,
Which fragrance move with offering meeter
  His soothed omnipotence,
Being chosen as fairer or as fleeter,
  Borne hither or borne hence,

Love's foiled omniscience knows not: this
  Where more than all he knows

With all his lore of bale and bliss,
  The choice of rose and rose,
One red as lips that touch with his,
  One white as moonlit snows.

No hope is half so sweet and good,
  No dream of saint or sage
So fair as these are: no dark mood
  But these might best assuage;
The sweet red rose of babyhood,
  The white sweet rose of age.

LINES ON THE DEATH OF EDWARD JOHN TRELAWNY.

LAST high star of the years whose thunder
  Still men's listening remembrance hears,
  Last light left of our fathers' years,
Watched with honor and hailed with wonder
Thee too then have the years borne under,
  Thou too then hast regained thy peers.

Wings that warred with the winds of morn-
    ing,
  Storm-winds rocking the red great dawn,
  Close at last, and a film is drawn
Over the eyes of the storm-bird, scorning
Now no longer the loud wind's warning,
  Waves that threaten or waves that fawn.

Peers were none of thee left us living,
  Peers of theirs we shall see no more.
  Eight years over the full fourscore
Knew thee: now shalt thou sleep, forgiving
All griefs past of the wild world's giving,
  Moored at last on the stormless shore.

Worldwide liberty's lifelong lover,
  Lover no less of the strength of song,
  Sea-king, swordsman, hater of wrong,
Over thy dust that the dust shall cover
Comes my song as a bird to hover,
  Borne of its will as of wings along.

Cherished of thee were this brief song's
    brothers
  Now that follows them, cherishing thee.
  Over the tides and the tideless sea
Soft as a smile of the earth our mother's
Flies it faster than all those others,
  First of the troop at thy tomb to be.

Memories of Greece and the mountain's
    hollow
  Guarded alone of thy loyal sword

Hold thy name for our hearts in ward:
Yet more fain are our hearts to follow
One way now with the southward swallow
  Back to the grave of the man their lord.

Heart of hearts, art thou moved not, hearing
  Surely, if hearts of the dead may hear,
  Whose true heart it is now draws near?
Surely the sense of it thrills thee, cheering
Darkness and death with the news now near-
    ing—
  Shelley, Trelawny rejoins thee here

ADIEUX À MARIE STUART.

I.

QUEEN, for whose house my fathers fought,
  With hopes that rose and fell,
Red star of boyhood's fiery thought,
  Farewell.

They gave their lives, and I, my queen,
  Have given you of my life,
Seeing your brave star burn high between
  Men's strife.

The strife that lightened round their spears
  Long since fell still: so long
Hardly may hope to last in years
  My song.

But still through strife of time and thought
  Your light on me too fell:
Queen, in whose name we sang or fought,
  Farewell.

II.

There beats no heart on either border
  Wherethrough the north blasts blow
But keeps your memory as a warder
  His beacon-fire aglow.

Long since it fired with love and wonder
  Mine, for whose April age
Blithe midsummer made banquet under
  The shade of Hermitage.

Soft sang the burn's blithe notes, that gather
  Strength to ring true:
And air and trees and sun and heather
  Remembered you.

Old border ghosts of fight or fairy
  Or love or teen,

These they forgot, remembering Mary
    The Queen.

III.

Queen once of Scots and ever of ours
    Whose sires brought forth for you
Their lives to strew your way like flowers,
    Adieu.

Dead is full many a dead man's name
    Who died for you this long
Time past: shall this too fare the same,
    My song?

But surely, though it die or live,
    Your face was worth
All that a man may think to give
    On earth.

No darkness cast of years between
    Can darken you:
Man's love will never bid my queen
    Adieu.

IV.

Love hangs like light about your name
    As music round the shell:
No heart can take of you a tame
    Farewell.

Yet, when your very face was seen,
    Ill gifts were yours for giving:
Love gat strange guerdons of my queen
    When living.

O diamond heart unflawed and clear,
    The whole world's crowning jewel!
Was ever heart so deadly dear
    So cruel?

Yet none for you of all that bled
    Grudged once one drop that fell:
Not one to life reluctant said
    Farewell.

V.

Strange love they have given you, love dis-
        loyal,
    Who mock with praise your name,
To leave a head so rare and royal
    Too low for praise or blame.

You could not love nor hate, they tell us
    You had nor sense nor sting:
In God's name, then, what plague befell us
    To fight for such a thing?

'Some faults the gods will give,' to fetter
    Man's highest intent:

33

But surely you were something better
    Than innocent!

No maid that strays with steps unwary
    Through snares unseen,
But one to live and die for; Mary,
    The Queen.

VI.

Forgive them all their praise, who blot
    Your fame with praise of you:
Then love may say, and falter not,
    Adieu.

Yet some you hardly would forgive
    Who did you much less wrong
Once; but resentment should not live
    Too long.

They never saw your lip's bright bow,
    Your swordbright eyes,
The bluest of heavenly things below
    The skies.

Clear eyes that love's self finds most like
    A swordblade's blue,
A swordblade's ever keen to strike,
    Adieu.

VII.

Though all things breathe or sound of fight
    That yet make up your spell,
To bid you were to bid the light
    Farewell.

Farewell the song says only, being
    A star whose race is run:
Farewell the soul says never, seeing
    The sun.

Yet, wellnigh as with flash of tears,
    The song must say but so
That took your praise up twenty years
    Ago.

More bright than stars or moons that vary,
    Sun kindling heaven and hell,
Here, after all these years, Queen Mary,
    Farewell.

HERSE.

When grace is given us ever to behold
    A child some sweet months old,
Love, laying across our lips his finger, saith,
    Smiling, with bated breath,

Hush ! for the holiest thing that lives is here,
  And heaven's own heart how near !
How dare we, that may gaze not on the sun,
  Gaze on this verier one ?
Heart, hold thy peace; eyes, be cast down
    for shame;
  Lips, breathe not yet its name.
In heaven they know what name to call it; we,
  How should we know ?   For, see !
The adorable sweet living marvellous
  Strange light that lightens us
Who gaze, desertless of such glorious grace,
  Full in a babe's warm face !
All roses that the morning rears are nought,
  All stars not worth a thought,
Set this one star against them, or suppose
  As rival this one rose.
What price could pay with earth's whole
    weight of gold
  One least flushed roseleaf's fold
Of all this dimpling store of smiles that shine
  From each warm curve and line,
Each charm of flower-sweet flesh, to reillume
  The dappled rose-red bloom
Of all its dainty body, honey-sweet
  Clenched hands and curled-up feet,
That on the roses of the dawn have trod
  As they came down from God,
And keep the flush and color that the sky
  Takes when the sun comes nigh,
And keep the likeness of the smile their grace
  Evoked on God's own face
When, seeing this work of his most heavenly
    mood,
  He saw that it was good ?
For all its warm sweet body seems one smile,
  And mere men's love too vile
To meet it, or with eyes that worship dims
  Read o'er the little limbs,
Read all the book of all their beauties o'er,
  Rejoice, revere, adore,
Bow down and worship each delight in turn,
  Laugh, wonder, yield, and yearn.
But when our trembling kisses dare, yet dread,
  Even to draw nigh its head,
And touch, and scarce with touch or breath
    surprise
  Its mild miraculous eyes
Out of their viewless vision—O, what then,
  What may be said of men ?
What speech may name a new-born child?
    what word
  Earth ever spake or heard ?
The best men's tongue that ever glory knew
  Called that a drop of dew
Which from the breathing creature's kindly
    womb

Came forth in blameless bloom.
We have no word, as had those men most
    high,
  To call a baby by.
Rose, ruby, lily, pearl of stormless seas—
  A better word than these,
A better sign it was than flower or gem
  That love revealed to them:
They knew that whence comes light of quick-
    ening flame,
  Thence only this thing came,
And only might be likened of our love
  To somewhat born above,
Not even to sweetest things dropped else on
    earth,
  Only to dew's own birth.
Nor doubt we but their sense was heavenly
    true,
  Babe, when we gaze on you,
A dew-drop out of heaven whose colors are
  More bright than sun or star,
As now, ere watching love dare fear or hope,
  Lips, hands, and eyelids ope,
And all your life is mixed with earthly leaven.
  O child, what news from heaven?

TWINS.

Affectionately inscribed to W. M. R.
                    and L. R.

April, on whose wings
Ride all gracious things,
Like the star that brings
  All things good to man,
Ere his light, that yet
Makes the month shine, set,
And fair May forget
  Whence her birth began,

Brings, as heart would choose,
Sound of golden news,
Bright as kindling dews
  When the dawn begins;
Tidings clear as mirth,
Sweet as air and earth
Now that hail the birth,
  Twice thus blest, of twins.

In the lovely land
Where with hand in hand
Lovers wedded stand
  Other joys before
Made your mixed life sweet :
Now, as Time sees meet,

Three glad blossoms greet
  Two glad blossoms more.

Fed with sun and dew,
While your joys were new,
First arose and grew
  One bright olive-shoot :
Then a fair and fine
Slip of warm-haired pine
Felt the sweet sun shine
  On its leaf and fruit.

And it wore for mark
Graven on the dark
Beauty of its bark
  That the noblest name
Worn in song of old
By the king whose bold
Hand had fast in hold
  All the flower of fame.

Then, with southern skies
Flattered in her eyes,
Which, in lovelier wise
  Yet, reflect their blue
Brightened more, being bright
Here with life's delight,
And with love's live light
  Glorified anew,

Came, as fair as came
One who bore her name
(She that broke as flame
  From the swan-shell white),
Crowned with tender hair
Only, but more fair
Than all queens that were
  Themes of oldworld fight,

Of your flowers the third
Bud, or new-fledged bird
In your hearts' nest heard
  Murmuring like a dove
Bright as those that drew
Over waves where blew
No loud wind the blue
  Heaven-hued car of love.

Not the glorious grace
Even of that one face
Potent to displace
  All the towers of Troy
Surely shone more clear
Once with childlike cheer
Than this child's face here
  Now with living joy.

After these again
Here in April's train
Breaks the bloom of twain
  Blossoms in one birth
For a crown of May
On the front of day
When he takes his way
  Over heaven and earth.

Half a heavenly thing
Given from heaven to Spring
By the sun her king,
  Half a tender toy,
Seems a child of curl
Yet too soft to twirl ;
Seems the flower-sweet girl
  By the flower-bright boy.

All the kind gods' grace,
All their love, embrace
Ever either face,
  Ever brood above them :
All soft wings of hours
Screen them as with flowers
From all beams and showers :
  All life's seasons love them.

When the dews of sleep
  Falling lightliest keep
Eyes too close to peep
Forth and laugh off rest,
Joy from face to feet
Fill them, as is meet :
Life to them be sweet
  As their mother's breast.

When those dews are dry,
And in day's bright eye
Looking full they lie
  Bright as rose and pearl,
All returns of joy
Pure of time's alloy
Bless the rose-red boy,
  Guard the rose-white girl.

POSTCRIPT.

Friends, if I could take
Half a note from Blake
Or but one verse make
  Of the Conqueror's mine,
Better than my best
Song above your nest
I would sing : the quest
  Now seems too divine.

THE SALT OF THE EARTH.

IF childhood were not in the world,
 But only men and women grown ;
No baby-locks in tendrils curled,
 No baby-blossoms blown ;

Though men were stronger, women fairer,
 And nearer all delights in reach,
And verse and music uttered rarer
 Tones of more godlike speech ;

Though the utmost life of life's best hours
 Found, as it cannot now find, words ;
Though desert sands were sweet as flowers
 And flowers could sing like birds,

But children never heard them, never
 They felt a child's foot leap and run :
This were a drearier star than ever
 Yet looked upon the sun.

SEVEN YEARS OLD.

I.

SEVEN white roses on one tree,
 Seven white loaves of blameless leaven,
Seven white sails on one soft sea,
Seven white swans on one lake's lee,
Seven white flowerlike stars in heaven,
All are types unmeet to be
 For a birthday's crown of seven.

II.

Not the radiance of the roses,
 Not the blessing of the bread,
Not the breeze that ere day grows is
ᵛresh for sails and swans, and closes
 Wings above the sun's grave spread,
When the starshine on the snows is
 Sweet as sleep on sorrow shed.

III.

Nothing sweetest, nothing best,
 Holds so good and sweet a treasure
As the love wherewith once blest
Joy grows holy, grief takes rest,
 Life, half tired with hours to measure,
Fills his eyes and lips and breast
 With most light and breath of pleasure ;

IV.

As the rapture unpolluted,
 As the passion undefiled,
By whose force all pains heart-rooted

Are transfigured and transmuted,
 Recompensed and reconciled,
Through the imperial, undisputed,
 Present godhead of a child.

V.

Brown bright eyes and fair bright head,
 Worth a worthier crown than this is,
Worth a worthier song instead,
 Sweet grave wise round mouth, full fed
With the joy of love, whose bliss is
More than mortal wine and bread,
 Lips whose words are sweet as kisses,

VI.

Little hands so glad of giving,
 Little heart so glad of love,
Little soul so glad of living,
 While the strong swift hours are weaving
Light with darkness woven above,
Time for mirth and time for grieving,
 Plume of raven and plume of dove,

VII.

I can give you but a word
 Warm with love therein for leaven,
But a song that falls unheard
 Yet on ears of sense unstirred
Yet by song so far from heaven,
Whence you came the brightest bird,
 Seven years since, of seven times seven.

EIGHT YEARS OLD.

I.

Sun, whom the faltering snow-cloud fears,
 Rise, let the time of year be May,
Speak now the word that April hears,
 Let March have all his royal way;
Bid all spring raise in winter's ears
 All tunes her children hear or play,
Because the crown of eight glad years
 On one bright head is set to-day.

II.

What matters cloud or sun to-day
 To him who wears the wreath of years
So many, and all like flowers at play
 With wind and sunshine, while his ears
Hear only song on every way ?
 More sweet than spring triumphant hears
Ring through the revel-rout of May
 Are these, the notes that winter fears.

III.

Strong-hearted winter knows and fears
    The music made of love at play,
Or haply loves the tune he hears
    From hearts fulfilled with flowering May,
Whose molten music thaws his ears
    Late frozen, deaf but yesterday
To sounds of dying and dawning years,
    Now quickened on his deathward way.

IV.

For deathward now lies winter's way
    Down the green vestibule of years
That each year brightens day by day
    With flower and shower till hope scarce
        fears
And fear grows wholly hope of May.
    But we—the music in our ears
Made of love's pulses as they play
    The heart alone that makes it hears.

V.

The heart it is that plays and hears
    High salutation of to-day.
Tongue falters, hand shrinks back, song fears
    Its own unworthiness to play
Fit music for those eight sweet years,
    Or sing their blithe accomplished way.
No song quite worth a young child's ears
    Broke ever even from birds in May.

VI.

There beats not in the heart of May,
    When summer hopes and springtide fears,
There falls not from the height of day,
    When sunlight speaks and silence hears,
So sweet a psalm as children play
    And sing, each hour of all their years,
Each moment of their lovely way,
    And know not how it thrills our ears.

VII.

Ah child, what are we, that our ears
    Should hear you singing on your way,
Should have this happiness ? The years
    Whose hurrying wings about us play
Are not like yours, whose flower-time fears
    Nought worse than sunlit showers in May,
Being sinless as the spring, that hears
    Her own heart praise her every day.

VIII.

Yet we too triumph in the day
    That bare, to entrance our eyes and ears,
To lighten daylight, and to play
    Such notes as darkness knows and fears,
The child whose face illumes our way,

Whose voice lifts up the heart that hears
Whose hand is as the hand of May
    To bring us flowers from eight full years.

———

COMPARISONS.

CHILD, when they say that others
    Have been or are like you,
Babes fit to be your brothers,
    Sweet human drops of dew,
Bright fruit of mortal mothers,
    What should one say or do ?

We know the thought is treason,
    We feel the dream absurd;
A claim rebuked of reason,
    That withers at a word:
For never shone the season
    That bore so blithe a bird.

Some smiles may seem as merry,
    Some glances gleam as wise,
From lips as like a cherry
    And scarce less gracious eyes;
Eyes browner than a berry,
    Lips red as morning's rise.

But never yet rang laughter
    So sweet in gladdened ears
Through wall and floor and rafter
    As all this household hears
And rings response thereafter
    Till cloudiest weather clears.

When those your chosen of all men,
    Whose honey never cloys,
Two lights whose smiles enthrall men
    Were called at your age boys,
Those mighty men, while small men,
    Could make no merrier noise.

Our Shakespeare, surely, daffed not
    More lightly pain aside
From radiant lips that quaffed not
    Of forethought's tragic tide:
Our Dickens, doubtless, laughed not
    More loud with life's first pride.

The dawn were not more cheerless
    With neither light nor dew
Than we without the fearless
    Clear laugh that thrills us through
If ever child stood peerless,
    Love knows that child is you.

WHAT IS DEATH?

LOOKING on a page where stood
Graven of old on old-world wood
Death, and by the grave's edge grim,
Pale, the young man facing him,
Asked my well-beloved of me
Once what strange thing this might be,
　　Gaunt and great of limb.

Death, I told him: and, surprise
Deepening more his wildwood eyes
(Like some sweet fleet thing's whose breath
Speaks all spring though nought it saith),
Up he turned his rosebright face
Glorious with its seven years' grace,
　　Asking—What is death?

————

A CHILD'S PITY.

No sweeter thing than children's ways and
　　wiles,
　　Surely, we say, can gladden eyes and ears:
Yet sometime sweeter than their words or
　　smiles
　　Are even their tears.

To one for once a piteous tale was read,
　　How, when the murderous mother croco-
　　dile
Was slain, her fierce brood famished, and lay
　　dead,
　　Starved, by the Nile.

In vast green reed-beds on the vast gray slime
　　Those monsters motherless and helpless
　　lay,
Perishing only for the parent's crime
　　Whose seed were they.

Hours after, toward the dusk, our blithe
　　small bird
　　Of Paradise, who has our hearts in keeping,
Was heard or seen, but hardly seen or heard,
　　For pity weeping.

He was so sorry, sitting still apart,
　　For the poor little crocodiles, he said.
Six years had given him, for an angel's heart,
　　A child's instead.

Feigned tears the false beast shed for murder-
　　ous ends,
　　We know from travellers' tales of croco-
　　diles:

But these tears wept upon them of my friend's
　　Outshine his smiles.

What heavenliest angels of what heavenly city
　　Could match the heavenly heart in children
　　here ?
The heart that hallowing all things with its
　　pity
Casts out all fear ?

So lovely, so divine, so dear their laughter
　　Seems to us, we know not what could be
　　more dear :
But lovelier yet we see the sign thereafter
　　Of such a tear.

With sense of love half laughing and half
　　weeping
　　We met your tears, our small sweet-spirited
　　friend :
Let your love have us in its heavenly keeping
　　To life's last end.

————

A CHILD'S LAUGHTER.

ALL the bells of heaven may ring,
All the birds of heaven may sing,
All the wells on earth may spring,
All the winds on earth may bring
　　All sweet sounds together ;
Sweeter far than all things heard,
Hand of harper, tone of bird,
Sound of woods at sundawn stirred,
Welling water's winsome word,
　　Wind in warm wan weather,

One thing yet there is, that none
Hearing ere its chime be done
Knows not well the sweetest one
Heard of man beneath the sun,
　　Hoped in heaven hereafter ;
Soft and strong and loud and light,
Very sound of very light
Heard from morning's rosiest height,
When the soul of all delight
　　Fills a child's clear laughter.

Golden bells of welcome rolled
Never forth such notes, nor told
Hours so blithe in tones so bold,
As the radiant mouth of gold
　　Here that rings forth heaven.
If the golden-crested wren
Were a nightingale—why, then,

Something seen and heard of men
Might be half as sweet as when
    Laughs a child of seven.

A CHILD'S THANKS.

How low soe'er men rank us,
    How high soe'er we win,
The children far above us
Dwell, and they deign to love us,
With lovelier love than ours,
And smiles more sweet than flowers ;
As though the sun should thank us
    For letting light come in.

With too divine complaisance,
    Whose grace misleads them thus,
Being gods, in heavenly blindness
They call our worship kindness,
Our pebble-gift a gem :
They think us good to them,
Whose glance, whose breath, whose presence,
    Are gifts too good for us.

The poet high and hoary
    Of meres that mountains bind
Felt his great heart more often
Yearn, and its proud strength soften
From stern to tenderer mood,
At thought of gratitude
Shown than of song or story
    He heard of hearts unkind.

But with what words for token
    And what adoring tears
Of reverence risen to passion,
In what glad prostrate fashion
Of spirit and soul subdued,
May man show gratitude
For thanks of children spoken
    That hover in his ears?

The angels laugh, your brothers,
    Child, hearing you thank me,
With eyes whence night grows sunny,
And touch of lips like honey,
And words like honey-dew:
But how shall I thank you?
For gifts above all others
    What guerdon-gift may be?

What wealth of words caressing,
    What choice of songs found best,
Would seem not as derision,
Found vain beside the vision

And glory from above
Shown in a child's heart's love?
His part in life is blessing;
    Ours, only to be blest.

A CHILD'S BATTLES.

πύξ ἀρετὰν εὑρών.—PINDAR.

PRAISE of the knights of old
May sleep: their tale is told,
    And no man cares:
The praise which fires our lips is
A knight's whose fame eclipses
    All of theirs.

The ruddiest light in heaven
Blazed as his birth-star seven
    Long years ago:
All glory crown that old year
Which brought our stout small soldier
    With the snow !

Each baby born has one
Star, for his friends a sun,
    The first of stars:
And we, the more we scan it,
The more grow sure your planet,
    Child, was Mars.

For each one flower, perchance,
Blooms as his cognizance :
    The snowdrop chill,
The violet unbeholden,
For some: for you the golden
    Daffodil.

Erect, a fighting flower,
It breasts the breeziest hour
    That ever blew,
And bent or broke things brittle
Or frail, unlike a little
    Knight like you.

Its flower is firm and fresh
And stout like sturdiest flesh
    Of children: all
The strenuous blast that parches
Spring hurts it not till March is
    Near his fall.

If winds that prate and fret
Remark, rebuke, regret,
    Lament, or blame
The brave plant's martial passion,
It keeps its own free fashion
    All the same.

We that would fain seem wise
Assume grave mouths and eyes
    Whose looks reprove
Too much delight in battle:
But your great heart our prattle
    Cannot move.

We say, small children should
Be placid, mildly good
    And blandly meek:
Whereat the broad smile rushes
Full on your lips, and flushes
    All your cheek.

If all the stars that are
Laughed out, and every star
    Could here be heard,
Such peals of golden laughter
We should not hear, as after
    Such a word.

For all the storm saith, still,
Stout stands the daffodil:
    For all we say,
Howe'er he look demurely,
Our martialist will surely
    Have his way.

We may not bind with bands
Those large and liberal hands,
    Nor stay from fight,
Nor hold them back from giving:
No lean mean laws of living
    Bind a knight.

And always here of old
Such gentle hearts and bold
    Our land has bred:
How durst her eye rest else on
The glory shed from Nelson
    Quick and dead?

Shame were it, if but one
Such once were born her son,
    That one to have borne,
And brought him ne'er a brother:
His praise should bring his mother
    Shame and scorn.

A child high-souled as he
Whose manhood shook the sea
    Smiles haply here:
His face, where love lies basking,
With bright shut mouth seems asking,
    What is fear?

The sunshine-colored fists
Beyond his dimpling wrists
    Were never closed
For saving or for sparing—
For only deeds of daring
    Predisposed.

Unclenched, the gracious hands
Let slip their gifts like sands
    Made rich with ore
That tongues of beggars ravish
From small stout hands so lavish
    Of their store.

Sweet hardy kindly hands
Like these were his that stands
    With heel on gorge
Seen trampling down the dragon
On sign or flask or flagon,
    Sweet Saint George.

Some tournament, perchance,
Of hands that couch no lance,
    Might mark this spot
Your lists, if here some pleasant
Small Guenevere were present,
    Launcelot.

My brave bright flower, you need
No foolish song, nor heed
    It more than spring
The sighs of winter stricken
Dead when your haunts requicken
    Here, my king.

Yet O, how hardly may
The wheels of singing stay
    That whirl along
Bright paths whence echo raises
The phantom of your praises,
    Child, my song!

Beyond all other things
That give my words fleet wings,
    Fleet wings and strong,
You set their jesses ringing
Till hardly can I, singing,
    Stint my song.

But all things better, friend,
And worse must find an end:
    And, right or wrong,
'Tis time, lest rhyme should baffle,
I doubt to put a snaffle
    On my song.

And never may your ear
Aught harsher hear or fear,
   Nor wolfish night
Nor dog-toothed winter snarling
Behind your steps, my darling,
   My delight!

For all the gifts you give
Me, dear, each day you live,
   Of thanks above
All thanks that could be spoken
Take not my song in token,
   Take my love.

A CHILD'S FUTURE.

WHAT will it please you, my darling, hereafter to be?
Fame upon land will you look for, or glory
   by sea?
Gallant your life will be always, and all of it
   free.
Free as the wind when the heart of the twilight is stirred
Eastward, and sounds from the springs of the
   sunrise are heard:
Free—and we know not another as infinite
   word.

Darkness or twilight or sunlight may compass
   us round,
Hate may arise up against us, or hope may
   confound;
Love may forsake us; yet may not the spirit
   be bound.

Free in oppression of grief as in ardor of joy
Still may the soul be, and each to her strength
   as a toy:
Free in the glance of the man as the smile of
   the boy.
Freedom alone is the salt and the spirit that
   gives
Life, and without her is nothing that verily
   lives:
Death cannot slay her: she laughs upon
   death and forgives.

Brightest and hardiest of roses anear and afar
Glitters the blithe little face of you, round as
   a star:
Liberty bless you and keep you to be as you
   are.

England and liberty bless you and keep you
   to be
Worthy the name of their child and the sight
   of their sea:
Fear not at all; for a slave, if he fears not, is
   free.

SONNETS

ON ENGLISH DRAMATIC POETS.—(1590–1650.)

I.

CHRISTOPHER MARLOWE.

CROWNED, girdled, garbed and shod with
   light and fire,
Son first-born of the morning, sovereign
   star!
Soul nearest ours of all, that wert most far,
Most far off in the abysm of time, thy lyre
Hung highest above the dawn-enkindled
   quire
Where all ye sang together, all that are,
And all the starry songs behind thy car
Rang sequence, all our souls acclaim thee sire.

'If all the pens that ever poets held
   Had fed the feeling of their masters'
     thoughts,'
   And as with rush of hurtling chariots
The flight of all their spirits were impelled
   Toward one great end, thy glory—nay, not
     then,   [men.
   Not yet might'st thou be praised enough of

II.

WILLIAM SHAKESPEARE.

NOT if men's tongues and angels' all in one
   Spake, might the word be said that might
     speak Thee.

Streams, winds, woods, flowers, fields,
mountains, yea, the sea,
What power is in them all to praise the sun?
His praise is this,—he can be praised of none.
Man, woman, child, praise God for him ;
but he
Exults not to be worshipped, but to be.
He is ; and, being, beholds his work well
done.
All joy, all glory, all sorrow, all strength, all
mirth,
Are his : without him, day were night on
earth.
Time knows not his from time's own period.
All lutes, all harps, all viols, all flutes, all
lyres,
Fall dumb before him ere one string suspires.
All stars are angels ; but the sun is God.

III.

BEN JONSON.

BROAD-BASED, broad-fronted, bounteous,
multiform,
With many a valley impleached with ivy
and vine,
Wherein the springs of all the streams run
wine,
And many a crag full-faced against the storm,
The mountain where thy Muse's feet made
warm
Those lawns that revelled with her dance
divine
Shines yet with fire as it was wont to shine
From tossing torches round the dance
aswarm.

Nor less, high-stationed on the gray grave
heights,
High-thoughted seers with heaven's heart-
kindling lights
Hold converse : and the herd of meaner
things
Knows or by fiery scourge or fiery shaft
When wrath on thy broad brows has risen,
and laughed,
Darkening thy soul with shadow of thunderous wings.

IV.

BEAUMONT AND FLETCHER.

AN hour ere sudden sunset fired the west,
Arose two stars upon the pale deep east.

The hall of heaven was clear for night's
high feast,
Yet was not yet day's fiery heart at rest.
Love leapt up from his mother's burning
breast
To see those warm twin lights, as day de-
creased,
Wax wider, till when all the sun had ceased
As suns they shone from evening's kindled
crest.
Across them and between, a quickening fire,
Flamed Venus, laughing with appeased desire.
Their dawn, scarce lovelier for the gleam
of tears,
Filled half the hollow shell 'twixt heaven and
earth
With sound like moonlight, mingling moan
and mirth,
Which rings and glitters down the darkling
years.

V.

PHILIP MASSINGER.

CLOUDS here and there arisen an hour past
noon
Checkered our English heaven with length-
ening bars
And shadow and sound of wheel-winged
thunder-cars
Assembling strength to put forth tempest
soon,
When the clear still warm concord of thy tune
Rose under skies unscared by reddening
Mars
Yet, like a sound of silver speech of stars,
With full mild flame as of the mellowing moon.
Grave and great-hearted Massinger, thy face
High melancholy lights with loftier grace
Than gilds the brows of revel : sad and wise,
The spirit of thought that moved thy deeper
song,
Sorrow serene in soft calm scorn of wrong,
Speaks patience yet from thy majestic eyes.

VI.

JOHN FORD

HEW hard the marble from the mountain's
heart
Where hardest night holds fast in iron
gloom

Gems brighter than an April dawn in bloom,
That his Memnonian likeness thence may
  start
Revealed, whose hand with high funereal art
  Carved night, and chiselled shadow : be
  the tomb
That speaks him famous graven with signs
  of doom
Intrenched inevitably in lines athwart,
As on some thunder-blasted Titan's brow
  His record of rebellion. Not the day
  Shall strike forth music from so stern a
  chord,
Touching this marble : darkness, none knows
  how,
  And stars impenetrable of midnight, may.
So looms the likeness of thy soul, John Ford.

VII.

JOHN WEBSTER.

Thunder: the flesh quails, and the soul
  bows down.
  Night : east, west, south, and northward,
  very night.
Star upon struggling star strives into sight,
Star after shuddering star the deep storms
  drown.
The very throne of night, her very crown,
  A man lays hand on, and usurps her right.
  Song from the highest of heaven's imperious
  height
Shoots, as a fire to smite some towering town.
Rage, anguish, harrowing fear, heart-crazing
  crime,
Make monstrous all the murderous face of
  Time
  Shown in the spheral orbit of a glass
Revolving. Earth cries out from all her
  graves.
Frail, on frail rafts, across wide-wallowing
  waves,
  Shapes here and there of child and mother
  pass.

VIII.

THOMAS DECKER.

Out of the depths of darkling life where sin
  Laughs piteously that sorrow should not
  know

Her own ill name, nor woe be counted woe ·
Where hate and craft and lust make drearier
  din
Than sounds through dreams that grief holds
  revel in ;
  What charm of joy-bells ringing, streams
  that flow,
  Winds that blow healing in each note they
  blow,
Is this that the outer darkness hears begin?

O sweetest heart of all thy time save one,
Star seen for love's sake nearest to the sun,
  Hung lamplike o'er a dense and doleful
  city,
Not Shakespeare's very spirit, howe'er more
  great,
Than thine toward man was more compassion-
  ate,
  Nor gave Christ praise from lips more sweet
  with pity.

IX.

THOMAS MIDDLETON.

A wild moon riding high from cloud to cloud,
  That sees and sees not, glimmering far
  beneath,
  Hell's children revel along the shuddering
  heath
With dirge-like mirth and raiment like a
  shroud :
A worse fair face than witchcraft's, passion-
  proud,
  With brows blood-flecked behind their
  bridal wreath
  And lips that bade the assassin's sword find
  sheath
Deep in the heart whereto love's heart was
  vowed :
A game of close contentious crafts and creeds
  Played till white England bring black Spain
  to shame :
A son's bright sword and brighter soul, whose
  deeds
  High conscience lights for mother's love
  and fame :
Pure gypsy flowers, and poisonous courtly
  weeds:
  Such tokens and such trophies crown thy
  name.

x.

THOMAS HEYWOOD.

Tom, if they loved thee best who called thee
        Tom,
    What else may all men call thee, seeing thus
        bright
    Even yet the laughing and the weeping
        light
That still thy kind old eyes are kindled from?
Small care was thine to assail and overcome
    Time and his child Oblivion : yet of right
    Thy name has part with names of lordlier
        might
For English love and homely sense of home,
Whose fragrance keeps thy small sweet bay-
        leaf young
    And gives it place aloft among thy peers
Whence many a wreath once higher strong
        Time has hurled :
And this thy praise is sweet on Shakespeare's
        tongue—
    ' O good old man, how well in thee appears
    The constant service of the antique world ! '

xi.

GEORGE CHAPMAN.

High priest of Homer, not elect in vain,
    Deep trumpets blow before thee, shawms
        behind
    Mix music with the rolling wheels that
        wind
Slow through the laboring triumph of thy
        train :
Fierce history, molten in thy forging brain,
    Takes form and fire and fashion from thy
        mind,
    Tormented and transmuted out of kind :
But howsoe'er thou shift thy strenuous strain,
Like Tailor * smooth, like Fisher † swollen,
        and now
    Grim Yarrington ‡ scarce bloodier marked
        than thou,
    Then bluff as Mayne's § or broad-mouthed
        Barry's ‖ glee,
Proud still with hoar predominance of brow

* Author of *The Hog hath lost his Pearl.*
† Author of *Fuimus Troes, or the True Trojans.*
‡ Author of *Two Tragedies in One.*
§ Author of *The City Match.*
‖ Author of *Ram-Alley, or Merry Tricks.*

And beard like foam swept off the broad
        blown sea,
Where'er thou go, men's reverence goes
        with thee.

xii.

JOHN MARSTON.

The bitterness of death and bitterer scorn
    Breathes from the broad-leafed aloe-plant
        whence thou
    Wast fain to gather for thy bended brow
A chaplet by no gentler forehead worn.
Grief deep as hell, wrath hardly to be borne,
    Ploughed up thy soul till round the furrow-
        ing plough
    The strange black soil foamed, as a black
        beaked prow
Bids night-black waves foam where its track
        has torn.
Too faint the phrase for thee that only saith
Scorn bitterer than the bitterness of death
    Pervades the sullen splendor of thy soul,
Where hate and pain make war on force and
        fraud
And all the strengths of tyrants ; whence un-
        flawed
    It keeps this noble heart of hatred whole.

xiii.

JOHN DAY.

Day was a full-blown flower in heaven, alive
    With murmuring joy of bees and birds
        aswarm,
    When in the skies of song yet flushed and
        warm
With music where all passion seems to strive
For utterance, all things bright and fierce to
        drive
    Struggling along the splendor of the storm,
    Day for an hour put off his fiery form,
And golden murmurs from a golden hive
Across the strong bright summer wind were
        heard,
    And laughter soft as smiles from girls at
        play
    And loud from lips of boys brow-bound
        with May.
Our mightiest age let fall its gentlest word,

When Song, in semblance of a sweet small
    bird,
Lit fluttering on the light swift hand of Day.

XIV.

JAMES SHIRLEY.

THE dusk of day's decline was hard on dark
    When evening trembled round thy glow-
       worm lamp
    That shone across her shades and dewy
       damp
A small clear beacon whose benignant spark
Was gracious yet for loiterers' eyes to mark,
    Though changed the watchword of our
       English camp
    Since the outposts rang round Marlowe's
       lion ramp,
    When thy steed's pace went ambling round
       Hyde Park.

And in the thickening twilight under thee
Walks Davenant, pensive in the paths where
    he,
The blithest throat that ever carolled love
    In music made of morning's merriest heart,
Glad Suckling, stumbled from his seat above
And reeled on slippery roads of alien art.

XV.

THE TRIBE OF BENJAMIN.

SONS born of many a loyal Muse to Ben,
    All true-begotten, warm with wine or ale,
    Bright from the broad light of his presence,
       Hail!
Prince Randolph, nighest his throne of all
    his men,
Being highest in spirit and heart who hailed
    him then
    King, nor might other spread so blithe a
       sail :
    Cartwright, a soul pent in with narrower
       pale,
Praised of thy sire for manful might of pen:
Marmion, whose verse keeps alway keen and
    fine
The perfume of their Apollonian wine
    Who shared with that stout sire of all and
       thee
The exuberant chalice of his echoing shrine:
    Is not your praise writ broad in gold which
       he
Inscribed, that all who praise his name
    should see?

XVI.

ANONYMOUS PLAYS:

'ARDEN OF FEVERSHAM.'

MOTHER whose womb brought forth our man
    of men,
    Mother of Shakespeare, whom all time ac-
       claims
    Queen therefore, sovereign queen of Eng-
       lish dames,
Throned higher than sat thy sonless empress
    then,
Was it thy son's young passion-guided pen
    Which drew, reflected from encircling
       flames,
A figure marked by the earlier of thy names
Wife, and from all her wedded kinswomen
Marked by the sign of murderess? Pale and
    great,
    Great in her grief and sin, but in her death
    And anguish of her penitential breath
Greater than all her sin or sin-born fate,
    She stands, the holocaust of dark desire,
    Clothed round with song forever as with
       fire.

XVII.

ANONYMOUS PLAYS.

YE too, dim watchfires of some darkling hour,
    Whose fame forlorn time saves not nor pro-
       claims
    Forever, but forgetfulness defames
And darkness and the shadow of death de-
    vour,
Lift up ye too your light, put forth your
    power,
    Let the far twilight feel your soft small
       flames
    And smile, albeit night name not even their
       names,
Ghost by ghost passing, flower blown down
    on flower :
That sweet-tongued shadow, like a star's that
    passed
Singing, and light was from its darkness cast
    To paint the face of Painting fair with
       praise : *
And that wherein forefigured smiles the pure
Fraternal face of Wordsworth's Elidure
    Between two child-faced masks of merrier
       days.†

    Doctor Dodypol.   † *Nobody and Somebody.*

XVIII.

ANONYMOUS PLAYS.

MORE yet and more, and yet we mark not all:
The Warning fain to bid fair women heed
Its hard brief note of deadly doom and
deed; *
The verse that strewed too thick with flowers
the hall
Whence Nero watched his fiery festival; †
That iron page wherein men's eyes who
read
See bruised and marred between two babes
that bleed,
A mad red-handed husband's martyr fall ; ‡
The scene which crossed and streaked with
mirth the strife
Of Henry with his sons and witchlike wife; §
And that sweet pageant of the kindly fiend,
Who, seeing three friends in spirit and heart
made one,
Crowned with good hap the true-love wiles
he screened
In the pleached lanes of pleasant Edmon-
ton. ‖

XIX.

THE MANY.

I.

GREENE, garlanded with February's few
flowers,
Ere March came in with Marlowe's rapt-
urous rage:
Peele, from whose hand the sweet white
locks of age
Took the mild chaplet woven of honored
hours:
Nash, laughing hard: Lodge, flushed from
lyric bowers:
And Lilly, a goldfinch in a twisted cage
Fed by some gay great lady's pettish page
Till short sweet songs gush clear like short
spring showers:
Kid, whose grim sport still gambolled over
graves:
And Chettle, in whose fresh funereal verse

---

* *A Warning for fair Women.*
† *The Tragedy of Nero.*
‡ *A Yorkshire Tragedy.*
§ *Look about you.*
‖ *The Merry Devil of Edmonton.*

Weeps Marian yet on Robin's wildwood
hearse:
Cooke, whose light boat of song one soft
breath saves,
Sighed from a maiden's amorous mouth
averse :
Live likewise ye : Time takes not you for
slaves.

XX.

THE MANY.

II.

HAUGHTON, whose mirth gave woman all her
will:
Field, bright and loud with laughing flower
and bird
And keen alternate notes of laud and gird:
Barnes, darkening once with Borgia's deeds
the quill
Which tuned the passion of Parthenophil:
Blithe burly Porter, broad and bold of word:
Wilkins, a voice with strenuous pity stirred:
Turk Mason: Brewer, whose tongue drops
honey still:
Rough Rowley, handling song with Esau's
hand:
Light Nabbes: lean Sharpham, rank and
raw by turns,
But fragrant with a forethought once of
Burns:
Soft Davenport, sad-robed, but blithe and
bland:
Brome, gypsy-led across the woodland
ferns:
Praise be with all, and place among our band.

XXI.

EPILOGUE.

OUR mother, which wast twice, as history
saith,
Found first among the nations: once, when
she
Who bore thine ensign saw the God in thee
Smite Spain, and bring forth Shakespeare :
once, when death
Shrank, and Rome's bloodhounds cowered,
at Milton's breath:
More than thy place, then first among the
free,

More than that sovereign lordship of the
  sea
Bequeathed to Cromwell from Elizabeth,
More than thy fiery guiding-star, which Drake
Hailed, and the deep saw lit again for Blake,
More than all deeds wrought of thy strong
  right hand,

This praise keeps most thy fame's memorial
  strong,
That thou wast head of all these streams of
  song,
And time bows down to thee as Shakespeare's land.

A DARK MONTH.

'La maison sans enfants !'—VICTOR HUGO.

I.

A MONTH without sight of the sun
  Rising or reigning or setting
Through days without use of the day,
Who calls it the month of May?
  The sense of the name is undone
  And the sound of it fit for forgetting.

We shall not feel if the sun rise,
  We shall not care when it sets :
If a nightingale make night's air
As noontide, why should we care ?
Till a light of delight that is done rise,
  Extinguishing gray regrets ;

Till a child's face lighten again
  On the twilight of older faces ;
Till a child's voice fall as the dew
On furrows with heat parched through
And all but hopeless of grain,
  Refreshing the desolate places—

Fall clear on the ears of us hearkening
  And hungering for food of the sound
And thirsting for joy of his voice :
Till the hearts in us hear and rejoice,
And the thoughts of them doubting and
    darkening
  Rejoice with a glad thing found.

When the heart of our gladness is gone,
  What comfort is left with us after ?
When the light of our eyes is away,
What glory remains upon May,
What blessing of song is thereon
  If we drink not the light of his laughter ?

No small sweet face with the daytime
  To welcome, warmer than noon !

No sweet small voice as a bird's
  To bring us the day's first words !
Mid May for us here is not Maytime
  No summer begins with June.

A whole dead month in the dark,
  A dawn in the mists that o'ercome he.
Stifled and smothered and sad—
Swift speed to it barren and bad !
And return to us, voice of the lark,
  And remain with us, sunlight of summer.

II.

ALAS, what right has the dawn to glimmer,
  What right has the wind to do aught but
    moan ?
All the day should be dimmer
  Because we are left alone.

Yestermorn like a sunbeam present
  Hither and thither a light step smiled,
And made each place for us pleasant
  With the sense or the sight of a child.

But the leaves persist as before, and after
  Our parting the dull day still bears flowers;
And songs less bright than his laughter
  Deride us from birds in the bowers.

Birds, and blossoms, and sunlight only,
  As though such folly sufficed for spring !
As though the house were not lonely
  For want of the child its king !

III.

ASLEEP and afar to-night my darling
  Lies, and heeds not the night,
If winds be stirring or storms be snarling ;
  For his sleep is its own sweet light.

I sit where he sat beside me quaffing
   The wine of story and song
Poured forth of immortal cups, and laughing
   When mirth in the draught grew strong.

I broke the gold of the words, to melt it
   For hands but seven years old,
And they caught the tale as a bird, and felt it
   More bright than visible gold.

And he drank down deep, with his eyes broad
    beaming,
   Here in this room where I am,
The golden vintage of Shakespeare, gleaming
   In the silver vessels of Lamb.

Here by my hearth where he was I listen
   For the shade of the sound of a word,
Athirst for the birdlike eyes to glisten,
   For the tongue to chirp like a bird.

At the blast of battle, how broad they bright-
    ened,
   Like fire in the spheres of stars,
And clung to the pictured page, and lightened
   As keen as the heart of Mars!

At the touch of laughter, how swift it twit-
    tered
   The shrillest music on earth ;
How the lithe limbs laughed and the whole
    child glittered
   With radiant riot of mirth!

Our Shakespeare now, as a man dumb-
    stricken,
   Stands silent there on the shelf:
And my thoughts, that had song in the heart
    of them, sicken,
   And relish not Shakespeare's self.

And my mood grows moodier than Hamlet's
    even,
   And man delights not me,
But only the face that morn and even
   My heart leapt only to see.

That my heart made merry within me seeing,
   And sang as his laugh kept time :
But song finds now no pleasure in being,
   And love no reason in rhyme.

IV.

MILD May-blossom and proud sweet bay-
    flower,
   What, for shame, would you have with us
   here ?

It is not the month of the May-flower
   This, but the fall of the year.

Flowers open only their lips in derision,
   Leaves are as fingers that point in scorn :
The shows we see are a vision :
   Spring is not verily born.

Yet boughs turn supple and buds grow sappy
   As though the sun were indeed the sun :
And all our words are happy
   With all their birds save one.

But spring is over, but summer is over,
   But autumn is over, and winter stands
With his feet sunk deep in the clover
   And cowslips cold in his hands.

His hoar grim head has a hawthorn bonnet,
   His gnarled gaunt hand has a gay green
    staff
With new-blown rose-blossom on it :
   But his laugh is a dead man's laugh.

The laugh of spring that the heart seeks after,
   The hand that the whole world yearns to
    kiss,
It rings not here in his laughter,
   The sign of it is not this.

There is not strength in it left to splinter
   Tall oaks, nor frost in his breath to sting :
Yet it is but a breath as of winter,
   And it is not the hand of spring.

V.

THIRTY-ONE pale maidens, clad
   All in mourning dresses,
Pass, with lips and eyes more sad
That it seems they should be glad,
Heads discrowned of crowns they had,
   Gray for golden tresses.

Gray their girdles too for green,
   And their veils dishevelled:
None would say, to see their mien,
That the least of these had been
Born no baser than a queen,
   Reared where flower-fays revelled.

Dreams that strive to seem awake,
   Ghosts that walk by daytime,
Weary winds the way they take,
Since, for one child's absent sake,
May knows well, whate'er things make
   Sport, it is not Maytime.

VI.

A HAND at the door taps light
As the hand of my heart's delight:
It is but a full-grown hand,
Yet the stroke of it seems to start
Hope like a bird in my heart,
  Too feeble to soar or to stand.

To start light hope from her cover
Is to raise but a kite for a plover
If her wings be not fledged to soar.
Desire, but in dreams, cannot ope
The door that was shut upon hope
  When love went out at the door.

Well were it if vision could keep
The lids of desire as in sleep
  Fast locked, and over his eyes
A dream with the dark soft key
In her hand might hover, and he
  Their keeper till morning rise;

The morning that brings after many
Days fled with no light upon any
  The small face back which is gone;
When the loved little hands once more
Shall struggle and strain at the door
  They beat their summons upon.

VII.

IF a soul for but seven days were cast out of
  heaven and its mirth,
They would seem to her fears like as seventy
  years upon earth.

Even and morrow should seem to her sorrow
  as long
As the passage of numberless ages in slumberless song.

Dawn, roused by the lark, would be surely as
  dark in her sight
As her measureless measure of shadowless
  pleasure was bright.

Noon, gilt but with glory of gold, would be
  hoary and gray
In her eyes that had gazed on the depths, un-
  amazed with the day.

Night hardly would seem to make darker her
  dream never done,
When it could but withhold what a man may
  behold of the sun.

For dreams would perplex, were the days that
  should vex her but seven,

34

The sight of her vision, made dark with
  division from heaven.

Till the light on my lonely way lighten that
  only now gleams,
I too am divided from heaven and derided of
  dreams.

VIII.

A TWILIGHT fire-fly may suggest
  How flames the fire that feeds the sun;
' A crooked figure may attest
  In little space a million.'

But this faint-figured verse, that dresses
  With flowers the bones of one bare month,
Of all it would say scarce expresses
  In crooked ways a millionth.

A fire-fly tenders to the father
  Of fires a tribute something worth:
My verse, a shard-borne beetle rather,
  Drones over scarce-illumined earth.

Some inches round me though it brighten
  With light of music-making thought,
The dark indeed it may not lighten,
  The silence moves not, hearing nought.

Only my heart is eased with hearing,
  Only mine eyes are soothed with seeing,
A face brought nigh, a footfall nearing,
  Till hopes take form and dreams have
    being.

IX.

As a poor man hungering stands with insatiate
  eyes and hands
    Void of bread
Right in sight of men that feast while his
  famine with no least
    Crumb is fed,

Here across the garden-wall can I hear strange
  children call,
    Watch them play,
From the windowed seat above, whence the
  goodlier child I love
    Is away.

Here the sights we saw together moved his
  fancy like a feather
    To and fro,

Now to wonder, and thereafter to the sunny
    storm of laughter
        Loud and low—

Sights engraven on storied pages where man's
    tale of seven swift ages
        All was told—
Seen of eyes yet bright from heaven—for the
    lips that laughed were seven
        Sweet years old.

X.

WHY should May remember
    March, if March forget
The days that began with December,
    The nights that a frost could fret?

All their griefs are done with
    Now the bright months bless
Fit souls to rejoice in the sun with,
    Fit heads for the wind's caress;

Souls of children quickening
    With the whole world's mirth,
Heads closelier than field-flowers thickening
    That crowd and illuminate earth,

Now that May's call musters
    Files of baby bands
To marshal in joyfuller clusters
    Than the flowers that encumber their hands.

Yet morose November
    Found them no less gay,
With nought to forget or remember
    Less bright than a branch of may.

All the seasons moving
    Move their minds alike
Applauding, acclaiming, approving
    All hours of the year that strike.

So my heart may fret not,
    Wondering if my friend
Remember me not or forget not
    Or ever the month find end.

Not that love sows lighter
    Seed in children sown,
But that life being lit in them brighter
    Moves fleeter than even our own.

May nor yet September
    Binds their hearts, that yet

Remember, forget, and remember,
    Forget, and recall, and forget.

XI.

As light on a lake's face moving
    Between a cloud and a cloud
Till night reclaim it, reproving
    The heart that exults too loud,

The heart that watching rejoices
    When soft it swims into sight
Applauded of all the voices
    And stars of the windy night,

So brief and unsure, but sweeter
    Than ever a moondawn smiled,
Moves, measured of no tune's metre,
    The song in the soul of a child;

The song that the sweet soul singing
    Half listens, and hardly hears,
Though sweeter than joy-bells ringing
    And brighter than joy's own tears;

The song that remembrance of pleasure
    Begins, and forgetfulness ends
With a soft swift change in the measure
    That rings in remembrance of friends

As the moon on the lake's face flashes,
    So haply may gleam at whiles
A dream through the dear deep lashes
    Whereunder a child's eye smiles,

And the least of us all that love him
    May take for a moment part
With angels around and above him,
    And I find place in his heart.

XII.

CHILD, were you kinless and lonely—
    Dear, were you kin to me—
My love were compassionate only
    Or such as it needs would be.

But eyes of father and mother
    Like sunlight shed on you shine:
What need you have heed of another
    Such new strange love as is mine?

It is not meet if unruly
    Hands take of the children's bread
And cast it to dogs; but truly
    The dogs after all would be fed.

On crumbs from the children's table
  That crumble, dropped from above
My heart feeds, fed with unstable
  Loose waifs of a child's light love.

Though love in your heart were brittle
  As glass that breaks with a touch,
You haply would lend him a little
  Who surely would give you much.

XIII.

HERE is a rough
  Rude sketch of my friend,
Faint-colored enough
  And unworthily penned.

Fearlessly fair
  And triumphant he stands,
And holds unaware
  Friends' hearts in his hands;

Stalwart and straight
  As an oak that should bring
Forth gallant and great
  Fresh roses in spring.

On the paths of his pleasure
  All graces that wait
What metre shall measure,
  What rhyme shall relate?

Each action, each motion,
  Each feature, each limb,
Demands a devotion
  In honor of him:

Head that the hand
  Of a god might have blest,
Laid lustrous and bland
  On the curve of its crest:

Mouth sweeter than cherries
  Keen eyes as of Mars,
Browner than berries
  And brighter than stars.

Nor color nor wordy
  Weak song can declare
The stature how sturdy,
  How stalwart his air.

As a king in his bright
  Presence-chamber may be,
So seems he in height—
  Twice higher than your knee.

As a warrior sedate
  With reserve of his power,
So seems he in state—
  As tall as a flower:

As a rose overtowering
  The ranks of the rest
That beneath it lie cowering,
  Less bright than their best

And his hands are as sunny
  As ruddy ripe corn
Or the browner-hued honey
  From heather-bells borne.

When summer sits proudest,
  Fulfilled with its mirth,
And rapture is loudest
  In air and on earth,

The suns of all hours
  That have ripened the roots
Bring forth not such flowers
  And beget not such fruits.

And well though I know it,
  As fain would I write,
Child, never a poet
  Could praise you aright.

I bless you? the blessing
  Were less than a jest
Too poor for expressing;
  I come to be blest,

With humble and dutiful
  Heart, from above:
Bless me, O my beautiful
  Innocent love!

This rhyme in your praise
  With a smile was begun;
But the goal of his ways
  Is uncovered to none,

Nor pervious till after
  The limit impend;
It is not in laughter
  These rhymes of you end.

XIV.

SPRING, and fall, and summer, and winter,
  Which may Earth love least of them all,
Whose arms embrace as their signs imprint
      her,
  Summer, or winter, or spring, or fall?

The clear-eyed spring with the wood-birds
    mating,
The rose-red summer with eyes aglow,
The yellow fall with serene eyes waiting,
    The wild-eyed winter with hair all snow?

Spring's eyes are soft, but if frosts benumb
    her
As winter's own will her shrewd breath
    sting :
Storms may rend the raiment of summer,
    And fall grow bitter as harsh-lipped spring.

One sign for summer and winter guides me,
    One for spring, and the like for fall :
Whichever from sight of my friend divides me,
    That is the worst ill season of all.

XV.

WORSE than winter is spring
If I come not to sight of my king :
But then what a spring will it be
When my king takes homage of me !

I send his grace from afar
Homage, as though to a star;
As a shepherd whose flock takes flight
May worship a star by night.

As a flock that a wolf is upon
My songs take flight and are gone:
No heart is in any to sing
Aught but the praise of my king.

Fain would I once and again
Sing deeds and passions of men :
But ever a child's head gleams
Between my work and my dreams.

Between my hand and my eyes
The lines of a small face rise,
And the lines I trace and retrace
Are none but those of the face.

XVI.

TILL the tale of all this flock of days alike
    All be done,
Weary days of waiting till the month's hand
    strike
    Thirty-one,
Till the clock's hand of the month break off,
    and end
    With the clock,
Till the last and whitest sheep at last be
    penned
    Of the flock,

I their shepherd keep the count of night and
    day
    With my song,
Though my song be, like this month which
    once was May
    All too long.

XVII.

THE incarnate sun, a tall strong youth,
    On old Greek eyes in sculpture smiled:
But trulier had it given the truth
    To shape him like a child.

No face full-grown of all our dearest
    So lightens all our darkness, none
Most loved of all our hearts hold nearest
    So far outshines the sun,

As when with sly shy smiles that feign
    Doubt if the hour be clear, the time
Fit to break off my work again
    Or sport of prose or rhyme,

My friend peers in on me with merry
    Wise face, and though the sky stay dim
The very light of day, the very
    Sun's self comes in with him.

XVIII.

OUT of sight,
    Out of mind !
Could the light
    Prove unkind?

Can the sun
    Quite forget
What was done
    Ere he set ?

Does the moon
    When she wanes
Leave no tune
    That remains

In the void
    Shell of night
Overcloyed
    With her light?

Must the shore
    At low tide
Feel no more
    Hope or pride,

No intense
 Joy to be,
In the sense
 Of the sea—

In the pulses
 Of her shocks
It repulses,
 When its rocks

Thrill and ring
 As with glee ?
Has my king
 Cast off me,

Whom no bird
 Flying south
Brings one word
 From his mouth ?

Not the ghost
 Of a word
Riding post
 Have I heard,

Since the day
 When my king
Took away
 With him spring,

And the cup
 Of each flower
Shrivelled up
 That same hour,

With no light
 Left behind.
Out of sight,
 Out of mind !

XIX.

BECAUSE I adore you
 And fall
On the knees of my spirit before you—
 After all,

You need not insult,
 My king,
With neglect, though your spirit exult
 In the spring,

Even me, though not worth,
 God knows,
One word of you sent me in mirth,
 Or one rose

Out of all in your garden
 That grow
Where the frost and the wind never harden
 Flakes of snow,

Nor ever is rain
 At all,
But the roses rejoice to remain
 Fair and tall—

The roses of love,
 More sweet
Than blossoms that rain from above
 Round our feet,

When under high bowers
 We pass,
Where the west wind freckles with flowers
 All the grass.

But a child's thoughts bear
 More bright
Sweet visions by day, and more fair
 Dreams by night,

Than summer's whole treasure
 Can be :
What am I that his thought should take
  pleasure,
 Then, in me ?

I am only my love's
 True lover,
With a nestful of songs, like doves
 Under cover,

That I bring in my cap
 Fresh caught,
To be laid on my small king's lap—
 Worth just nought.

Yet it haply may hap
 That he,
When the mirth in his veins is as sap
 In a tree,

Will remember me too
 Some day
Ere the transit be thoroughly through
 Of this May—

Or perchance, if such grace
 May be,
Some night when I dream of his face,
 Dream of me.

Or if this be too high
　　A hope
For me to prefigure in my
　　Horoscope,

He may dream of the place
　　Where we
Basked once in the light of his face
　　Who now see

Nought brighter, not one
　　Thing bright,
Than the stars and the moon and the sun,
　　Day nor night.

XX.

Day by darkling day,
　　Overpassing, bears away
Somewhat of the burden of this weary May.

Night by numbered night,
　　Waning, brings more near in sight
Hope that grows to vision of my heart's de-
　　light.

Nearer seems to burn
　　In the dawn's rekindling urn
Flame of fragrant incense, hailing his return.

Louder seems each bird
　　In the brightening branches heard
Still to speak some ever more delightful word.

All the mists that swim
　　Round the dawns that grow less dim
Still wax brighter and more bright with hope
　　of him.

All the suns that rise
　　Bring that day more near our eyes
When the sight of him shall clear our clouded
　　skies.

All the winds that roam
　　Fruitful fields of fruitless foam
Blow the bright hour near that brings his
　　bright face home.

XXI.

I hear of two far hence
　　In a garden met,
And the fragrance blown from thence
　　Fades not yet.

The one is seven years old,
　　And my friend is he:

But the years of the other have told
　　Eighty-three.

To hear these twain converse
　　Or to see them greet
Were sweeter than softest verse
　　May be sweet.

The hoar old gardener there
　　With an eye more mild
Perchance than his mild white hair
　　Meets the child.

I had rather hear the words
　　That the twain exchange
Than the songs of all the birds
　　There that range,

Call, chirp, and twitter there
　　Through the garden-beds
Where the sun alike sees fair
　　Those two heads,

And which may holier be
　　Held in heaven of those
Or more worth heart's thanks to see
　　No man knows.

XXII.

Of such is the kingdom of heaven.
　　No glory that ever was shed
From the crowning star of the seven
　　That crown the north world's head,

No word that ever was spoken
　　Of human or godlike tongue,
Gave ever such godlike token
　　Since human harps were strung.

No sign that ever was given
　　To faithful or faithless eyes
Showed ever beyond clouds riven
　　So clear a Paradise.

Earth's creeds may be seventy times seven
　　And blood have defiled each creed:
If of such be the kingdom of heaven,
　　It must be heaven indeed.

XXIII.

The wind on the downs is bright
　　As though from the sea:
And morning and night
　　Take comfort again with me.

He is nearer to-day,
　　Each night to each morning saith,

Whose return shall revive dead May
With the balm of his breath.

The sunset says to the moon,
　He is nearer to-night
Whose coming in June
　Is looked for more than the light.

Bird answers to bird,
　Hour passes the sign on to hour,
And for joy of the bright news heard
　Flower murmurs to flower.

The ways that were glad of his feet
　In the woods that he knew
Grow softer to meet
　The sense of his footfall anew.

He is near now as day,
　Says hope to the new-born light:
He is near now as June is to May,
　Says love to the night.

XXIV.

GOOD things I keep to console me
　For lack of the best of all,
A child to command and control me,
　Bid come and remain at his call.

Sun, wind, and woodland and highland,
　Give all that ever they gave:
But my world is a cultureless island,
　My spirit a masterless slave.

And friends are about me, and better
　At summons of no man stand:
But I pine for the touch of a fetter,
　The curb of a strong king's hand.

Each hour of the day in her season
　Is mine to be served as I will:
And for no more exquisite reason
　Are all served idly and ill.

By slavery my sense is corrupted,
　My soul not fit to be free :
I would fain be controlled, interrupted,
　Compelled as a thrall may be.

For fault of spur and of bridle
　I tire of my stall to death:
My sail flaps joyless and idle
　For want of a small child's breath.

XXV.

WHITER and whiter
　The dark lines grow,

And broader opens and brighter
　The sense of the text below.

Nightfall and morrow
　Bring nigher the boy
Whom wanting we want not sorrow,
　Whom having we want no joy.

Clearer and clearer
　The sweet sense grows
Of the word which hath summer for hearer,
　The word on the lips of the rose.

Duskily dwindles
　Each deathlike day,
Till June rearising rekindles
　The depth of the darkness of May.

XXVI.

'In his bright radiance and collateral light
Must I be comforted, not in his sphere.'

STARS in heaven are many,
　Suns in heaven but one:
Nor for man may any
　Star supplant the sun.

Many a child as joyous
　As our far-off king
Meets as though to annoy us
　In the paths of spring.

Sure as spring gives warning,
　All things dance in tune:
Sun on Easter morning,
　Cloud and windy moon,

Stars between the tossing
　Boughs of tuneful trees,
Sails of ships recrossing
　Leagues of dancing seas;

Best, in all this playtime,
　Best of all in tune,
Girls more glad than Maytime,
　Boys more bright than June;

Mixed with all those dances,
　Far through field and street
Sing their silent glances,
　Ring their radiant feet.

Flowers wherewith May crowned us
　Fall ere June be crowned:
Children blossom round us
　All the whole year round.

Is the garland worthless
   For one rose the less,
And the feast made mirthless?
   Love, at least, says yes.

Strange it were, with many
   Stars enkindling air,
Should but one find any
   Welcome: strange it were,

Had one star alone won
   Praise for light from far:
Nay, love needs his own one
   Bright particular star.

Hope and recollection
   Only lead him right
In its bright reflection
   And collateral light.

Find as yet we may not
   Comfort in its sphere:
Yet these days will weigh not
   When it warms us here;

When full-orbed it rises,
   Now divine afar:
None in all the skies is
   Half so good a star;

None that seers importune
   Till a sign be won:
Star of our good fortune,
   Rise and reign, our sun!

XXVII.

I PASS by the small room now forlorn
   Where once each night as I passed I knew
A child's bright sleep from even to morn
   Made sweet the whole night through.

As a soundless shell, as a songless nest,
   Seems now the room that was radiant then
And fragrant with his happier rest
   Than that of slumbering men.

The day therein is less than the day,
   The night is indeed night now therein:
Heavier the dark seems there to weigh,
   And slower the dawns begin,

As a nest fulfilled with birds, as a shell
   Fulfilled with breath of a god's own hymn,
Again shall be this bare blank cell,
   Made sweet again with him.

XXVIII.

SPRING darkens before us,
   A flame going down,
With chant from the chorus
   Of days without crown—
Cloud, rain, and sonorous
   Soft wind on the down.

She is wearier not of us
   Than we of the dream
That spring was to love us
   And joy was to gleam
Through the shadows above us
   That shift as they stream.

Half dark and half hoary,
   Float far on the loud
Mild wind, as a glory
   Half pale and half proud
From the twilight of story,
   Her tresses of cloud;

Like phantoms that glimmer
   Of glories of old
With ever yet dimmer
   Pale circlets of gold
As darkness grows grimmer
   And memory more cold.

Like hope growing clearer
   With wane of the moon,
Shines toward us the nearer
   Gold frontlet of June,
And a face with it dearer
   Than midsummer noon.

XXIX.

YOU send me your love in a letter,
   I send you my love in a song:
Ah child, your gift is the better,
   Mine does you but wrong.

No fame, were the best less brittle,
   No praise, were it wide as earth,
Is worth so much as a little
   Child's love may be worth.

We see the children above us
   As they might angels above:
Come back to us, child, if you love us,
   And bring us your love.

XXX.

No time for books or for letters:
   What time should there be?
No room for tasks and their fetters:
   Full room to be free.

The wind and the sun and the Maytime
 Had never a guest
More worthy the most that his playtime
 Could give of its best.

If rain should come on, peradventure,
 (But sunshine forbid!)
Vain hope in us haply might venture
 To dream as it did.

But never may come, of all comers
 Least welcome, the rain,
To mix with his servant the summer's
 Rose-garlanded train!

He would write, but his hours are as busy
 As bees in the sun,
And the jubilant whirl of their dizzy
 Dance never is done.

The message is more than a letter,
 Let love understand,
And the thought of his joys even better
 Than sight of his hand.

XXXI.

WIND, high-souled, full-hearted
 South-west wind of the spring!
Ere April and earth had parted,
 Skies, bright with thy forward wing,
Grew dark in an hour with the shadow behind
 it, that bade not a bird dare sing.

Wind whose feet are sunny,
 Wind whose wings are cloud,
With lips more sweet than honey
 Still, speak they low or loud,
Rejoice now again in the strength of thine
 heart: let the depth of thy soul wax
 proud.

We hear thee singing or sighing,
 Just not given to sight,
All but visibly flying
 Between the clouds and the light,

And the light in our hearts is enkindled, the
 shadow therein of the clouds put to
 flight.

From the gift of thine hands we gather
 The core of the flowers therein,
Keen glad heart of heather,
 Hot sweet heart of whin,
Twin breaths in thy godlike breath close
 blended of wild spring's wildest or
 kin.

All but visibly beating
 We feel thy wings in the far
Clear waste, and the plumes of them fleet-
 ing,
 Soft as swan's plumes are,
And strong as a wild swan's pinions, and
 swift as the flash of the flight of a star.

As the flight of a planet enkindled
 Seems thy far soft flight
Now May's reign has dwindled
 And the crescent of June takes light
And the presence of summer is here, and the
 hope of a welcomer presence in sight.

Wind, sweet-souled, great-hearted
 Southwest wind on the wold!
From us is a glory departed
 That now shall return as of old,
Borne back on thy wings as on eagle's ex-
 panding, and crowned with the sun-
 dawn's gold.

There is not a flower but rejoices,
 There is not a leaf but has heard:
All the fields find voices,
 All the woods are stirred:
There is not a nest but is brighter because of
 the coming of one bright bird.

Out of dawn and morning,
 Noon and afternoon,
The sun to the world gives warning
 Of news that brightens the moon;
And the stars all night exult with us, hearing
 of joy that shall come with June.

SUNRISE.

IF the wind and the sunlight of April and
August had mingled the past and hereafter

In a single adorable season whose life were a
rapture of love and of laughter,

And the blithest of singers were back with a
song; if again from his tomb as from
prison,

If again from the night or the twilight of ages
Aristophanes had arisen,

With the gold-feathered wings of a bird that
were also a god upon earth at his
shoulders,

And the gold-flowing laugh of the manhood
of old at his lips, for a joy to beholders,

He alone unrebuked of presumption were
able to set to some adequate measure

The delight of our eyes in the dawn that re-
stores them the sun of their sense and
the pleasure.

For the days of the darkness of spirit are
over for all of us here, and the season

When desire was a longing, and absence a
thorn, and rejoicing a word without
reason.

For the roof overhead of the pines is astir
with delight as of jubilant voices,

And the floor underfoot of the bracken and
heather alive as a heart that rejoices.

For the house that was childless awhile, and
the light of it darkened, the pulse of it
dwindled,

Rings radiant again with a child's bright feet,
with the light of his face is rekindled.

And the ways of the meadows that knew him,
the sweep of the down that the sky's
belt closes,

Grow gladder at heart than the soft wind
made them whose feet were but fragrant with roses,

Though the fall of the year be upon us, who
trusted in June and by June were de-
frauded,

And the summer that brought us not back
the desire of our eyes be gone hence
unapplauded.

For July came joyless among us, and August
went out from us arid and sterile,

And the hope of our hearts, as it seemed,
was no more than a flower that the
seasons imperil,

And the joy of our hearts, as it seemed, than
a thought which regret had not heart
remember,

Till four dark months overpast were atoned
for, and summer began in September.

Hark, April again as a bird in the house with
a child's voice hither and thither:

See, May in the garden again with a child's
face cheering the woods ere they
wither.

June laughs in the light of his eyes, and July
on the sunbright cheeks of him slumbers,

And August glows in a smile more sweet
than the cadence of gold-mouthed
numbers.

In the morning the sight of him brightens the
sun, and the noon with delight in him
flushes,

And the silence of nightfall is music about
him as soft as the sleep that it hushes.

We awake with a sense of a sunrise that is
not a gift of the sundawn's giving,

And a voice that salutes us is sweeter than
all sounds else in the world of the living.

And a presence that warms us is brighter
than all in the world of our visions beholden,

Though the dreams of our sleep were as
those that the light of a world without
grief makes golden.

For the best that the best of us ever devised
as a likeness of heaven and its glory,

What was it of old, or what is it and will be
forever, in song or in story,

Or in shape or in color of carven or painted
resemblance, adored of all ages,

But a vision recorded of children alive in the
pictures of old or the pages?

Where children are not, heaven is not, and
heaven if they come not again shall be
never:

But the face and the voice of a child are assurance of heaven and its promise forever.

A MIDSUMMER HOLIDAY.

THE SEABOARD.

THE sea is at ebb, and the sound of her utmost word
Is soft as the least wave's lapse in a still small reach.
From bay into bay, on quest of a goal deferred,
From headland ever to headland and breach to breach
Where earth gives ear to the message that all days preach
With changes of gladness and sadness that cheer and chide,
The lone way lures me along by a chance untried
That haply, if hope dissolve not and faith be whole,
Not all for nought shall I seek, with a dream for guide,
The goal that is not, and ever again the goal.

The trackless ways are untravelled of sail or bird ;
The hoar wave hardly recedes from the soundless beach.
The silence of instant noon goes nigh to be heard,
The viewless void to be visible : all and each,
A closure of calm no clamor of storm can breach
Concludes and confines and absorbs them on either side,
All forces of light and of life and the live world's pride,
Sands hardly ruffled of ripples that hardly roll
Seem ever to show as in reach of a swift brief stride
The goal that is not, and ever again the goal.

The waves are a joy to the seamew, the meads to the herd,
And a joy to the heart is a goal that it may not reach.
No sense that for ever the limits of sense engird,
No hearing or sight that is vassal to form or speech,
Learns ever the secret that shadow and silence teach,
Hears ever the notes that or ever they swell subside,
Sees ever the light that lights not the loud world's tide,
Clasps ever the cause of the lifelong scheme's control
Wherethrough we pursue, till the waters of life be dried,
The goal that is not, and ever again the goal.

Friend, what have we sought or seek we, whate'er betide,
Though the seaboard shift its mark from afar descried,
But aims whence ever anew shall arise the soul ?
Love, thought, song, life, but show for a glimpse and hide
The goal that is not, and ever again the goal.

A HAVEN.

EAST and north a waste of waters, south and west
Lonelier lands than dreams in sleep would feign to be,
When the soul goes forth on travel, and is prest
Round and compassed in with clouds that flash and flee.
Dells without a streamlet, downs without a tree,
Cirques of hollow cliff that crumble, give their guest
Little hope, till hard at hand he pause, to see
Where the small town smiles, a warm still sea-side nest.

Many a lone long mile, by many a headland's crest,
Down by many a garden dear to bird and bee,
Up by many a sea-down's bare and breezy breast,
Winds the sandy strait of road where flowers run free.
Here along the deep steep lanes by field and lea
Knights have carolled, pilgrims chanted, on their quest,
Haply, ere a roof rose toward the bleak strand's lee,
Where the small town smiles, a warm still sea-side nest.

Are the wild lands cursed perchance of time,
    or blest,
Sad with fear or glad with comfort of the sea?
Are the ruinous towers of churches fallen on
    rest
Watched of wanderers woful now, glad once
    as we,
When the night has all men's eyes and hearts
    in fee,
When the soul bows down dethroned and
    dispossest?
Yet must peace keep guard, by day's and
    night's decree,
Where the small town smiles, a warm still
    sea-side nest.

Friend, the lonely land is bright for you and
    me
All its wild ways through : but this methinks
    is best,
Here to watch how kindly time and change
    agree
Where the small town smiles, a warm still
    sea-side nest.

ON A COUNTRY ROAD.

ALONG these low pleached lanes, on such a
    day,
So soft a day as this, through shade and sun,
With glad grave eyes that scanned the glad
    wild way,
And hearts still hovering o'er a song begun,
And smile that warmed the world with beni-
    son,
Our father, lord long since of lordly rhyme,
Long since hath haply ridden, when the lime
Bloomed broad above him, flowering where
    he came.
Because thy passage once made warm this
    clime,
Our father Chaucer, here we praise thy name.

Each year that England clothes herself with
    May,
She takes thy likeness on her. Time hath
    spun
Fresh raiment all in vain and strange array
For earth and man's new spirit, fain to shun
Things past for dreams of better to be won,
Through many a century since thy funeral
    chime
Rang, and men deemed it death's most dire-
    ful crime

To have spared not thee for very love or
    shame:
And yet, while mists round last year's me-
    mories climb,
Our father Chaucer, here we praise thy name.

Each turn of the old wild road whereon we
    stray,
Meseems, might bring us face to face with
    one
Whom seeing we could not but give thanks,
    and pray
For England's love our father and her son
To speak with us as once in days long done
With all men, sage and churl and monk and
    mime,
Who knew not as we know the soul sublime
That sang for song's love more than lust of
    fame,
Yet, though this be not, yet, in happy time,
Our father Chaucer, here we praise thy name.

Friend, even as bees about the flowering
    thyme,
Years crowd on years, till hoar decay begrime
Names once beloved; but, seeing the sun the
    same,
As birds of autumn fain to praise the prime,
Our father Chaucer, here we praise thy name.

THE MILL GARDEN.

STATELY stand the sunflowers, glowing down
    the garden-side,
Ranged in royal rank arow along the warm
    gray wall,
Whence their deep disks burn at rich midnoon
    afire with pride,
Even as though their beams indeed were sun-
    beams, and the tall
Sceptral stems bore stars whose reign endures,
    not flowers that fall.
Lowlier laughs and basks the kindlier flower
    of homelier fame,
Held by love the sweeter that it blooms in
    Shakespeare's name,
Fragrant yet as though his hand had touched
    and made it thrill,
Like the whole world's heart, with warm new
    life and gladdening flame.
Fair befall the fair green close that lies below
    the mill!

Softlier here the flower-soft feet of refluent
    seasons glide,

Lightlier breathes the long low note of change's
    gentler call.
Wind and storm and landslip feed the lone
    sea's gulf outside,
Half a seamew's first flight hence; but scarce
    may these appal
Peace, whose perfect seal is set for signet here
    on all.

Steep and deep and sterile, under fields no
    plough can tame,
Did the cliffs full-fledged with poppies red as
    love or shame,
Wide wan daisies bleak and bold, or herbage
    harsh and chill;
Here the full clove pinks and wallflowers
    crown the love they claim.
Fair befall the fair green close that lies below
    the mill!

All the place breathes low, but not for fear
    lest ill betide,
Soft as roses answering roses, or a dove's re-
    call.
Little heeds it how the seaward banks may
    stoop and slide,
How the winds and years may hold all outer
    things in thrall,
How their wrath may work on hoar church
    tower and boundary wall.
Far and wide the waste and ravin of their rule
    proclaim
Change alone the changeless lord of things,
    alone the same:
Here a flower is stronger than the winds that
    work their will,
Or the years that wing their way through dark-
    ness toward their aim.
Fair befall the fair green close that lies below
    the mill!

Friend, the home that smiled us welcome
    hither when we came,
When we pass again with summer, surely
    should reclaim
Somewhat given of heart's thanksgiving more
    than words fulfil—
More than song, were song more sweet than
    all but love, might frame.
Fair befall the fair green close that lies
    below the mill!

A SEA-MARK.

RAINS have left the sea-blanks ill to climb:
Waveward sinks the loosening seaboard's
    floor:

Half the sliding cliffs are mire and slime.
Earth, a fruit rain-rotted to the core,
Drops dissolving down in flakes, that pour
Dense as gouts from eaves grown foul with
    grime.
One sole rock which years that scathe not
    score
Stands a sea-mark in the tides of time.

Time were even as even the rainiest clime,
Life were even as even this lapsing shore,
Might not aught outlive their trustless prime:
Vainly fear would wail or hope implore,
Vainly grief revile or love adore
Seasons clothed in sunshine, rain, or rime.
Now for me one comfort held in store
Stands a sea-mark in the tides of time.

Once, by fate's default or chance's crime,
Each apart, our burdens each we bore;
Heard, in monotones like bells that chime,
Chime the sounds of sorrows, float and soar
Joy's full carols, near or far before;
Heard not yet across the alternate rhyme
Time's tongue tell what sign set fast of yore
Stands a sea-mark in the tides of time.

Friend, the sign we knew not heretofore
Towers in sight here present and sublime.
Faith in faith established evermore
Stands a sea-mark in the tides of time.

THE CLIFFSIDE PATH.

SEAWARD goes the sun, and homeward by the
    down
We, before the night upon his grave be sealed.
Low behind us lies the bright steep murmur-
    ing town,
High before us heaves the steep rough silent
    field.

Breach by ghastlier breach, the cliffs collaps-
    ing yield:
Half the path is broken, half the banks divide;
Flawed and crumbled, riven and rent, they
    cleave and slide
Toward the ridged and wrinkled waste of
    girdling sand
Deep beneath, whose furrows tell how far and
    wide
Wind is lord and change is sovereign of the
    strand.

Star by star on the unsunned waters twiring
    down,
Golden spear-points glance against a silver
    shield.

Over banks and bents, across the headland's
   crown,
As by pulse of gradual plumes through
   twilight wheeled,
Soft as sleep, the waking wind awakes the
   weald.
Moor and copse and fallow, near or far
   descried,
Feel the mild wings move, and gladden where
   they glide:
Silence, uttering love that all things understand,
Bids the quiet fields forget that hard beside
Wind is lord and change is sovereign of the
   strand.

Yet may sight, ere all the hoar soft shade
   grow brown,
Hardly reckon half the rifts and rents unhealed
Where the scarred cliffs downward sundering
   drive and drown,
Hewn as if with stroke of swords in tempest
   steeled,
Wielded as the night's will and the wind's
   may wield.
Crowned and zoned in vain with flowers of
   autumn-tide,
Soon the blasts shall break them, soon the
   waters hide ;
Soon, where late we stood, shall no man
   ever stand.
Life and love seek harborage on the landward side :
Wind is lord and change is sovereign of the
   strand.

Friend, though man be less than these, for
   all his pride,
Yet, for all his weakness, shall not hope
   abide ?
Wind and change can wreck but life and
   waste but land :
Truth and trust are sure, though here till all
   subside
Wind is lord and change is sovereign of the
   strand.

IN THE WATER.

THE sea is awake, and the sound of the song
   of the joy of her waking is rolled
From afar to the star that recedes, from anear
   to the wastes of the wild wide shore.
Her call is a trumpet compelling us homeward : if dawn in her east be acold,

From the sea shall we crave not her grace to
   rekindle the life that it kindled before,
Her breath to requicken. her bosom to rock
   us, her kisses to bless as of yore ?
For the wind, with his wings half open, at
   pause in the sky, neither fettered nor
   free,
Leans waveward and flutters the ripple to
   laughter : and fain would the twain of
   us be
Where lightly the wave yearns forward from
   under the curve of the deep dawn's
   dome,
And, full of the morning and fired with the
   pride of the glory thereof and the glee,
Strike out from the shore as the heart in us
   bids and beseeches, athirst for the foam.

Life holds not an hour that is better to live
   in : the past is a tale that is told,
The future a sun-flecked shadow, alive and
   asleep, with a blessing in store.
As we give us again to the waters, the rapture
   of limbs that the waters enfold
Is less than the rapture of spirit whereby,
   though the burden it quits were sore,
Our souls and the bodies they wield at their
   will are absorbed in the life they
   adore—
In the life that endures no burden, and bows
   not the forehead, and bends not the
   knee—
In the life everlasting of earth and of heaven,
   in the laws that atone and agree,
In the measureless music of things, in the
   fervor of forces that rest or that roam,
That cross and return and reissue, as I after
   you and as you after me
Strike out from the shore as the heart in us
   bids and beseeches, athirst for the
   foam.

For, albeit he were less than the least of
   them, haply the heart of a man may be
   bold
To rejoice in the word of the sea as a mother's
   that saith to the son she bore,
Child, was not the life in thee mine, and my
   spirit the breath in thy lips from of
   old ?
Have I let not thy weakness exult in my
   strength, and thy foolishness learn of
   my lore ?
Have I helped not or healed not thine anguish, or made not the might of thy
   gladness more ?

And surely his heart should answer, The light
of the love of my life is in thee.
She is fairer than earth, and the sun is not
fairer, the wind is not blither than she :
From my youth hath she shown me the joy of
her bays that I crossed, of her cliffs
that I clomb.
Till now that the twain of us here, in desire
of the dawn and in trust of the sea,
Strike out from the shore as the heart in us
bids and beseeches, athirst for the
foam.

Friend, earth is a harbor of refuge for winter,
a covert whereunder to flee
When day is the vassal of night, and the
strength of the hosts of her mightier
than he ;
But here is the presence adored of me, here
my desire is at rest and at home.
There are cliffs to be climbed upon land, there
are ways to be trodden and ridden :
but we
Strike out from the shore as the heart in us
bids and beseeches, athirst for the
foam.

THE SUNBOWS.

SPRAY of song that springs in April, light of
love that laughs through May,
Live and die and live forever: nought of all
things far less fair
Keeps a surer life than these that seem to
pass like fire away.
In the souls they live which are but all the
brighter that they were ;
In the hearts that kindle, thinking what delight of old was there.
Wind that shapes and lifts and shifts them
bids perpetual memory play
Over dreams and in and out of deeds and
thoughts which seem to wear
Light that leaps and runs and revels through
the springing flames of spray.

Dawn is wild upon the waters where we drink
of dawn to-day:
Wide, from wave to wave rekindling in re-
bound through radiant air,
Flash the fires unwoven and woven again of
wind that works in play,
Working wonders more than heart may note
or sight may wellnigh dare,
Wefts of rarer light than colors rain from
heaven, though this be rare.

Arch on arch unbuilt in building, reared and
ruined ray by ray,
Breaks and brightens, laughs and lessens,
even till eyes may hardly bear
Light that leaps and revels through
the springing flames of spray.

Year on year sheds light and music rolled
and flashed from bay to bay
Round the summer capes of time and winter
headlands keen and bare
Whence the soul keeps watch, and bids her
vassal memory watch and pray,
If perchance the dawn may quicken, or perchance the midnight spare.
Silence quells not music, darkness takes not
sunlight in her snare ;
Shall not joys endure that perish ? Yea,
saith dawn, though night say nay:
Life on life goes out, but very life enkindles
everywhere
Light that leaps and runs and revels through
the springing flames of spray.

Friend, were life no more than this is, well
would yet the living fare.
All aflower and all afire and all flung heavenward, who shall say
Such a flash of life were worthless ? This is
worth a world of care—
Light that leaps and runs and revels through
the springing flames of spray.

ON THE VERGE.

HERE begins the sea that ends not till the
world's end. Where we stand,
Could we know the next high sea-mark set
beyond these waves that gleam,
We should know what never man hath
known, nor eye of man hath scanned.
Nought beyond these coiling clouds that melt
like fume of shrines that steam
Breaks or stays the strength of waters till
they pass our bounds of dream.
Where the waste Land's End leans westward,
all the seas it watches roll
Find their border fixed beyond them, and a
worldwide shore's control:
These whereby we stand no shore beyond us
limits: these are free.
Gazing hence, we see the water that grows
iron round the Pole,
From the shore that hath no shore beyond it
set in all the sea.

Sail on sail along the sea-line fades and
flashes; here on land
Flash and fade the wheeling wings on wings
of mews that plunge and scream.
Hour on hour along the line of life and time's
evasive strand
Shines and darkens, wanes and waxes, slays
and dies: and scarce they seem
More than motes that thronged and trembled
in the brief noon's breath and beam.
Some with crying and wailing, some with
notes like sound of bells that toll,
Some with sighing and laughing, some with
words that blessed and made us whole,
Passed, and left us, and we know not what
they were, nor what were we.
Would we know, being mortal? Never breath
of answering whisper stole
From the shore that hath no shore beyond it
set in all the sea.

Shadows, would we question darkness? Ere
our eyes and brows be fanned
Round with airs of twilight, washed with dews
from sleep's eternal stream,
Would we know sleep's guarded secret? Ere
the fire consume the brand,

Would it know if yet its ashes may requicken?
yet we deem
Surely man may know, or ever night unyoke
her starry team,
What the dawn shall be, or if the dawn shall
be not: yea, the scroll
Would we read of sleep's dark scripture,
pledge of peace or doom of dole.
Ah, but here man's heart leaps, yearning toward the gloom with venturous glee,
Though his pilot eye behold nor bay nor harbor, rock nor shoal,
From the shore that hath no shore beyond it
set in all the sea.

Friend, who knows if death indeed have life
or life have death for goal?
Day nor night can tell us, nor may seas declare nor skies unroll
What has been from everlasting, or if aught
shall always be.
Silence answering only strikes response reverberate on the soul
From the shore that hath no shore beyond it
set in all the sea.

A NEW-YEAR ODE.

TO VICTOR HUGO.

I.

TWICE twelve times have the springs of years
refilled
  Their fountains from the river-head of
  time
Since by the green sea's marge, ere autumn
chilled
  Waters and woods with sense of changing
  clime,
A great light rose upon my soul, and thrilled
  My spirit of sense with sense of spheres in
  chime,
Sound as of song wherewith a God would
build
  Towers that no force of conquering war
  might climb.
      Wind shook the glimmering sea
      Even as my soul in me
  Was stirred with breath of mastery more
  sublime,
      Uplift and borne along
      More thunderous tides of song,

Where wave rang back to wave more rapturous rhyme
      And world on world flashed lordlier
      light
Than ever lit the wandering ways of ships by
night.

II.

The spirit of God, whose breath of life is
song,
  Moved, though his word was human, on
  the face
Of those deep waters of the soul, too long
  Dumb, dark, and cold, that waited for the
  grace
Wherewith day kindles heaven: and as some
throng
  Of quiring wings fills full some lone chill
  place
With sudden rush of life and joy, more strong
  Than death or sorrow or all night's dark-
  ling race,

So was my heart, that heard
All heaven in each deep word,
Filled full with light of thought, and waxed
apace
Itself more wide and deep,
To take that gift and keep
And cherish while my days fulfilled their
space;
A record wide as earth and sea,
The Legend writ of Ages past and yet to be.

III.

As high the chant of paradise and Hell
Rose, when the soul of Milton gave it wings;
As wide the sweep of Shakespeare's empire
fell,
When life had bared for him her secret
springs ;
But not his various soul might range and dwell
Amid the mysteries of the founts of things ;
Nor Milton's range of rule so far might swell
Across the kingdoms of forgotten kings
Men, centuries, nations, time,
Life, death, love, trust, and crime,
Rang record through the change of smitten
strings
That felt an exile's hand
Sound hope for every land
More loud than storm's cloud-sundering
trumpet rings,
And bid strong death for judgment rise,
And life bow down for judgment of his awless
eyes.

IV.

And death, soul-stricken in his strength re-
signed
The keeping of the sepulchres to song ;
And life was humbled, and his height of mind
Brought lower than lies a grave-stone fallen
along;
And like a ghost and like a God mankind
Rose clad with light and darkness ; weak
and strong,
Clean and unclean, with eyes afire and blind,
Wounded and whole, fast bound with cord
and thong,
Free; fair and foul, sin-stained,
And sinless ; crowned and chained;
Fleet-limbed, and halting all his lifetime long;
Glad of deep shame, and sad
For shame's sake; wise, and mad ;
Girt round with love and hate of right and
wrong;
Armed and disarmed for sleep and
strife;

35

Proud, and sore fear made havoc of his pride of
life.

V.

Shadows and shapes of fable and storied sooth
Rose glorious as with gleam of gold unpriced;
Eve, clothed with heavenly nakedness and
youth
That matched the morning's ; Cain, self-
sacrificed
On crime's first altar: legends wise as truth,
And truth in legends deep embalmed and
spiced ;
The stars that saw the starlike eyes of Ruth,
The grave that heard the clarion call of
Christ.
And higher than sorrow and mirth
The heavenly song of earth
Sprang, in such notes as might have well
sufficed
To still the storms of time
And sin's contentious clime
With peace renewed of life reparadised:
Earth, scarred not yet with temporal
scars;
Goddess of gods, our mother, chosen among
the stars.

VI.

Earth fair as heaven, ere change and time set
odds
Between them, light and darkness know not
when.
And fear, grown strong through panic periods,
Crouched, a crowned worm, in faith's Ler-
nean fen,
And love lay bound, and hope was scourged
with rods,
And death cried out from desert and from
den,
Seeing all the heaven above him dark with
gods
And all the world about him marred of men.
Cities that nought might purge
Save the sea's whelming surge
From all the pent pollutions in their pen
Deep death drank down, and wrought
With wreck of all things, nought
That none might live of all their names
again,
Nor aught of all whose life is breath
Serve any God whose likeness was not like
to death,

VII.

Till by the lips and eyes of one live nation
  The blind mute world found grace to see
    and speak,
And light watched rise a more divine creation
  At that more godlike utterance of the Greek,
Let there be freedom.   Kings whose orient
    station
  Made pale the morn, and all her presage
    bleak,
Girt each with strengths of all his generation,
  Dim tribes of shamefaced soul and sun-swart
    cheek,
      Twice, urged with one desire,
      Son following hard on sire,
  With all the wrath of all a world to wreak,
      And all the rage of night
      Afire against the light
  Whose weakness makes her strong-winged
    empire weak,
      Stood up to unsay that saying, and fell
Too far for song, though song were thousand-
    tongued, to tell.

VIII.

From those deep echoes of the loud Ægean
  That rolled response whereat false fear was
    chid
By songs of joy sublime and Sophoclean,
  Fresh notes reverberate westward rose to bid
All wearier times take comfort from the pæan
  That tells the night what deeds the sunrise
    did,
Even till the lawns and torrents Pyrenean
  Ring answer from the records of the Cid.
      But never force of fountains
      From sunniest hearts of mountains
Wherein the soul of hidden June was hid
      Poured forth so pure and strong
      Springs of reiterate song,
  Loud as the streams his fame was reared
    amid,
      More sweet than flowers they feed,
      and fair
With grace of lordlier sunshine and more
    lambent air.

IX.

A star more prosperous than the storm-clothed
    east's
  Clothed all the warm south-west with light
    like spring's
When hands of strong men spread the wolves
    their feasts

And from snake-spirited princes plucked
    the stings;
Ere earth, grown all one den of hurtling beasts,
  Had for her sunshine and her watersprings
The fire of hell that warmed the hearts of
    priests,
  The wells of blood that slaked the lips of
    kings.
      The shadow of night made stone
      Stood populous and alone,
  Dense with its dead and loathed of living
    things
      That draw not life from death,
      And as with hell's own breath
  And clangor of immitigable wing
      Vexed the fair face of Paris, made
Foul in its murderous imminence of sound and
    shade.

X.

And all these things were parcels of the vision
  That moved a cloud before his eyes, or
    stood
A tower half shattered by the strong collision
  Of spirit and spirit, of evil gods with good ;
A ruinous wall rent through with grim division,
  Where time had marked his every mon-
    strous mood
Of scorn and strength and pride and self-
    derision :
  The Tower of Things, that felt upon it
    brood
      Night, and about it cast
      The storm of all the past
  Now mute and forceless as a fire subdued :
      Yet through the rifted years
      And centuries veiled with tears
  And ages as with very death imbrued
      Freedom, whence hope and faith
      grow strong,
Smiles, and firm love sustains the indissoluble
    song.

XI.

Above the cloudy coil of days deceased,
  Its might of flight, with mists and storms
    beset,
Burns heavenward, as with heart and hope
    increased,
  For all the change of tempests, all the fret
Of frost or fire, keen fraud or force released
  Wherewith the world once wasted knows
    not yet
If evil or good lit all the darkling east
  From the ardent moon of sovereign **Maho-**
    met

Sublime in work and will
The song sublimer still
Salutes him, ere the splendor shrink and
set ;
Then with imperious eye
And wing that sounds the sky
Soars and sees risen as ghosts in concourse
met
The old world's seven elder wonders,
firm
As dust and fixed as shadows, weaker than
the worm.

XII.

High witness borne of knights high-souled
and hoary
Before death's face and empire's rings and
glows
Even from the dust their life poured forth left
gory,
As the eagle's cry rings after from the snows
Supreme rebuke of shame clothed round with
glory
And hosts whose track the false crowned
eagle shows ;
More loud than sounds through stormiest
song and story
The laugh of slayers whose names the sea-
wind knows ;
More loud than peals on land
In many a red wet hand
The clash of gold and cymbals as they close ;
Loud as the blast that meets
The might of marshalled fleets
And sheds it into shipwreck, like a rose
Blown from a child's light grasp in sign
That earth's high lords are lords not over
breeze and brine.

XIII.

Above the dust and mire of man's dejection
The wide-winged spirit of song resurgent
sees
His wingless and long-laboring resurrection
Up the arduous heaven, by sore and strange
degrees,
Mount, and with splendor of the soul's re-
flection
Strike heaven's dark sovereign down upon
his knees,
Pale in the light of orient insurrection,
And dumb before the almightier lord's
decrees
Who bade him be of yore,
Who bids him be no more:

And all earth's heart is quickened as the
sea's
Even as when sunrise burns
The very sea's heart yearns
That heard not on the midnight-walking
breeze
The wail that woke with evensong
From hearts of poor folk watching all the
darkness long.

XIV.

Dawn and the beams of sunbright song illume
Love, with strange children at her piteous
breast,
By grace of weakness from the grave-mouthed
gloom
Plucked, and by mercy lulled to living rest,
Soft as the nursling's nigh the grandsire's
tomb
That fell on sleep, a bird of rifled nest ;
Soft as the lips whose smile unsaid the doom
That gave their sire to violent death's arrest.
Even for such love's sake strong,
Wrath fires the inveterate song
That bids hell gape for one whose bland
mouth blest
All slayers and liars that sighed
Prayer as they slew and lied
Till blood had clothed his priesthood as a
vest,
And hears, though darkness yet be
dumb
The silence of the trumpet of the wrath to
come.

XV.

Nor lacked these lights of constellated age
A star among them fed with life more dire,
Lit with his bloodred fame whose withering
rage
Made earth for heaven's sake one funereal
pyre
And life in faith's name one appointed stage
For death to purge the souls of men with
fire.
Heaven, earth, and hell on one thrice tragic
page
Mixed all their light and darkness: one
man's lyre
Gave all their echoes voice;
Bade rose-cheeked love rejoice,
And cold-lipped craft with ravenous fear
conspire,
And fire-eyed faith smite hope
Dead, seeing enthroned as Pope

And crowned of heaven on earth at hell's
　　　desire
　　　　　Sin, called by death's incestuous name
Borgia: the world that heard it flushed and
　　　quailed with shame.

XVI.

Another year, and hope triumphant heard
　　　The consummating sound of song that spake
Conclusion to the multitudinous word
　　　Whose expectation held her spirit awake
Till full delight for twice twelve years deferred
　　　Bade all souls entering eat and drink, and
　　　take
A third time comfort given them, that the
　　　third
　　Might heap the measure up of twain, and
　　　make
　　　　　The sinking year sublime
　　　　　Among all sons of time
And fair in all men's memories for his sake.
　　　　　Each thought of ours became
　　　　　Fire, kindling from his fame,
And music winding in his wide song's wake.
　　　　　Yea, and the world bore witness here
How great a light was risen upon this dark-
　　　ening year.

XVII.

It was the dawn of winter: sword in sheath,
　　　Change, veiled and mild, came down the
　　　gradual air
With cold slow smiles that hid the doom
　　　beneath.
Five days to die in yet were autumn's, ere
The last leaf withered from his flowerless
　　　wreath.
South, east and north, our skies were all
　　　blown bare,
But westward over glimmering holt and
　　　heath
　　　Cloud, wind, and light had made a heaven
　　　more fair
　　　　　Than ever dream or truth
　　　　　Showed earth in time's keen youth
When men with angels communed unaware.
　　　　　Above the sun's head, now
　　　　　Veiled even to the ardent brow,
Rose two sheer wings of sundering cloud,
　　　that were
　　　　　As a bird's poised for vehement flight,
Full-fledged with plumes of tawny fire and
　　　hoar gray light.

XVIII.

As midnight black, as twilight brown, they
　　　spread,
　　　But feathered thick with flame that streak-
　　　ed and lined
Their living darkness, ominous else of dread,
　　　From south to northmost verge of heaven
　　　inclined
Most like some giant angel's, whose bent head
　　　Bowed earthward, as with message for
　　　mankind
Of doom or benediction to be shed
　　　From passage of his presence.　Far be-
　　　hind,
　　　　　Even while they seemed to close,
　　　　　Stoop, and take flight, arose
Above them, higher than heavenliest thought
　　　may find
　　　　　In light or night supreme
　　　　　Of vision or of dream,
　　　Immeasurable of men's eyes or mounting
　　　mind,
　　　　　Heaven, manifest in manifold
Light of pure pallid amber, cheered with fire
　　　of gold.

XIX.

And where the fine gold faded all the sky
　　　Shone green as the outer sea when April
　　　glows,
Inlaid with flakes and feathers fledged to
　　　fly
Of cloud suspense in rapture and repose,
With large live petals, broad as love bids lie
Full open when the sun salutes the rose,
And small rent sprays where with the heavens
　　　most high
　　　Were strewn as autumn strews the garden-
　　　close
　　　　　With ruinous roseleaves whirled
　　　　　About their wan chill world,
　　　Through wind-worn bowers that now no
　　　music knows,
　　　　　Spoil of the dim dusk year
　　　　　Whose utter night is near,
And near the flower of dawn beyond it
　　　blows;
　　　　　Till east and west were fire and light,
As though the dawn to come had flushed the
　　　coming night.

XX.

The highways paced of men that toil or play,
　　　The byways known of none but lonely feet,
Were paven of purple woven of night and
　　　day

With hands that met as hands of friends
    might meet—
As though night's were not lifted up to slay
And day's had waxed not weaker. Peace
    more sweet
Than music, light more soft than shadow, lay
    On downs and moorlands wan with day's
    defeat,
        That watched afar above
        Life's very rose of love
Let all its lustrous leaves fall, fade, and
    fleet,
        And fill all heaven and earth
        Full as with fires of birth
Whence time should feed his years with
    light and heat:
        Nay, not life's, but a flower more strong
Than life or time or death, love's very rose
    of song.

XXI.

Song visible, whence all men's eyes were lit
    With love and loving wonder: song that
    glowed
Through cloud and change on souls that knew
    not it
    And hearts that wist not whence their com-
    fort flowed,
Whence fear was lightened of her fever-fit,
    Whence anguish of her life-compelling load.
Yea, no man's head whereon the fire alit,
    Of all that passed along that sunset road
        Westward, no brow so drear,
        No eye so dull of cheer,
    No face so mean whereon that light abode,
        But as with alien pride
        Strange godhead glorified
    Each feature flushed from heaven with fire
    that showed
        The likeness of its own life wrought
By strong transfiguration as of living thought.

XXII.

Nor only clouds of the everlasting sky,
    Nor only men that paced that sunward way
To the utter bourne of evening, passed not by
    Unblest or unillumined: none might say,
Of all things visible in the wide world's eye,
    That all too low for all that grace it lay:
The lowliest lakelets of the moorland nigh,
    The narrowest pools where shallowest wave-
    lets play,
        Were filled from heaven above
        With light like fire of love,
    With flames and colors like a dawn in May,

As hearts that lowlier live
    With light of thoughts that give
Light from the depth of souls more deep
    than they
        Through song's or story's kindling
        scroll,
The splendor of the shadow that reveals the
    soul.

XXIII.

For, when such light is in the world, we share,
    All of us, all the rays thereof that shine:
Its presence is alive in the unseen air,
    Its fire within our veins as quickening wine;
A spirit is shed on all men everywhere,
    Known or not known of all men for divine.
Yea, as the sun makes heaven, that light
    makes fair
    All souls of ours, all lesser souls than thine,
        Priest, prophet, seer and sage,
        Lord of a subject age
That bears thy seal upon it for a sign;
        Whose name shall be thy name,
        Whose light thy light of fame,
The light of love that makes thy soul a
    shrine;
        Whose record through all years to be
Shall bear this witness written—that its womb
    bare thee.

XXIV.

O mystery, whence to one man's hand was
    given
    Power upon all things of the spirit, and
    might
Whereby the veil of all the years was riven
    And naked stood the secret soul of night !
O marvel, hailed of eyes whence cloud is
    driven,
    That shows at last wrong reconciled with
    right
By death divine of evil and sin forgiven!
    O light of song, whose fire is perfect light!
        No speech, no voice, no thought,
        No love, avails us aught
For service of thanksgiving in his sight
        Who hath given us all for ever
        Such gifts that man gave never
So many and great since first Time's wings
    took flight.
        Man may not praise a spirit above
Man's: life and death shall praise him: we
    can only love.

XXV.

Life, everlasting while the worlds endure,
    Death, self-abased before a power more
    high,

Shall bear one witness, and their word stand
sure,
That not till time be dead shall this man die.
Love, like a bird, comes loyal to his lure;
Fame flies before him, wingless else to fly.
A child's heart toward his kind is not more
pure,
An eagle's toward the sun no lordlier eye.
Awe sweet as love and proud
As fame, though hushed and bowed
Yearns toward him silent as his face goes
by: .
All crowns before his crown
Triumphantly bow down,
For pride that one more great than all
draws nigh:
All souls applaud, all hearts acclaim,
One heart benign, one soul supreme, one con-
quering name.

———

NOTES.

ST. V.
V. 3. La Légende des Siècles: Le Sacre
de la Femme.
4. La Conscience.
7. Booz endormi.
8. Première rencontre du Christ avec
le tombeau.
9. La Terre: Hymme.

ST. V.
VI. 3. Les Temps Paniques.
9. La Ville Disparue.
VII.   Les Trois Cents.
VIII. 1. Le Détroit de l'Euripe: La Chan
son de Sophocle à Salamine.
7. Le Romancero del Cid.
IX. 3. Le Petit Roi de Galice.
5. Le Jour des Rois.
9. Montfaucon.
X.   La vision d'ou est sorti ce livre.
XI. 9. L'an neuf de l'Hégire.
12. Les sept merveilles du monde.
XII. 1. Les quatre jours d'Elciis.
4. Le Régiment du baron Madruce.
7. La Chanson des Aventuriers de
la Mer.
9. Les Reîtres.
12. La Rose de l'Infante.
XIII. 1. Le Satyre.
12. Les paysans au bord de la mer.
XIV. 1. Les pauvres gens.
5. Petit Paul.
7. Guerre Civile.
9. La Vision de Dante.
15. La Trompette du Jugement.
XV.   Torquemada (1882).
XVI.   La Légende des Siècles: tome
cinquiéme et dernier (1883).
XVII.   November 25, 1883.

———

LINES ON THE MONUMENT OF GIUSEPPE MAZZINI.

ITALIA, mother of the souls of men,
Mother divine,
Of all that served thee best with sword or
pen,
All sons of thine,

Thou knowest that here the likeness of the
best.
Before thee stands;
The head most high, the heart found faith-
fulest,
The purest hands.

Above the fume and foam of time that flits,
The soul, we know,
Now sits on high where Alighieri sits
With Angelo.

Not his own heavenly tongue hath heavenly
speech
Enough to say
What this man was, whose praise no thought
may reach,
No words can weigh.

Since man's first mother brought to mortal
birth
Her first-born son,
Such grace befell not ever man on earth
As crowns this one.

Of God nor man was ever this thing said,
That he could give
Life back to her who gave him, whence his
dead mother might live.

But this man found his mother dead and
slain,
　　With fast sealed eyes,
And bade the dead rise up and live again,
　　And she did rise.

And all the world was bright with her through
him:
　　But dark with strife,
Like heaven's own sun that storming clouds
bedim,
　　Was all his life.

Life and the clouds are vanished: hate and
fear
　　Have had their span
Of time to hurt, and are not: he is here,
　　The sunlike man.

City superb that hadst Columbus first
　　For sovereign son,
Be prouder that thy breast hath later nurst
　　This mightier one.

Glory be his forever, while his land
　　Lives and is free,
As with controlling breath and sovereign
hand
　　He bade her be.

Earth shows to heaven the names by thou-
sands told
　　That crown her fame,
But highest of all that heaven and earth be-
hold
　　Mazzini's name.

────

LES CASQUETS.

FROM the depth of the waters that lighten
and darken
　　With change everlasting of life and of
death,
Where hardly by noon if the lulled ear
hearken
　　It hears the sea's as a tired child's breath,
Where hardly by night if an eye dare scan it
　　The storm lets shipwreck be seen or heard,
As the reefs to the waves and the foam to the
granite

　　Respond one merciless word,
Sheer seen and far, in the sea's live heaven,
　　A seamew's flight from the wild sweet land,
White-plumed with foam if the wind wake,
seven

Black helms as of warriors that stir not
stand.
From the depths that abide and the waves
that environ
　　Seven rocks rear heads that the midnight
masks;
And the strokes of the swords of the storm
are as iron
　　On the steel of the wave-worn casques.

Be night's dark word as the word of a wizard,
　　Be the word of dawn as a god's glad word.
Like heads of the spirits of darkness visore
　　That see not forever, nor ever have heard,
These basnets, plumed as for fight or plume-
less,
　　Crowned of the storm and by storm dis-
crowned,
Keep ward of the lists where the dead lie
tombless
　　And the tale of them is not found.

Nor eye may number nor hand may reckon
　　The tithes that are taken of life by the dark,
Or the ways of the path, if doom's hand
beckon,
　　For the soul to fare as a helmless bark—
Fare forth on a way that no sign showeth,
　　Nor aught of its goal or of aught between ;
A path for her flight which no fowl knoweth,
　　Which the vulture's eye hath not seen.

Here still, though the wave and the wind
seem lovers
　　Lulled half asleep by their own soft words,
A dream as of death in the sun's light hovers,
　　And a sign in the motions and cries of the
birds.
Dark auguries and keen from the sweet sea-
swallows
　　Strike noon with a sense as of midnight's
breath,
And the wing that flees and the wing that
follows
　　Are as types of the wings of death.

For here, when the night roars round, and
under
　　The white sea lightens and leaps like fire,
Acclaimed of storm and applauded in thunder,
　　Sits death on the throne of his crowned
desire.
Yea, hardly the hand of the god might fashion
　　A seat more strong for his strength to take
For the might of his heart and the pride of
his passion
　　To rejoice in the wars they make.

When the heart in him brightens with blithe-
ness of battle
And the depth of its thirst is fulfilled with
strife,
And his ear with the ravage of bolts that
rattle,
And the soul of death with the pride of life,
Till the darkness is loud with his dark thanks-
giving
And wind and cloud are as chords of his
hymn,
There is nought save death in the deep night
living
And the whole night worships him.

Heaven's height bows down to him, signed
with his token,
And the sea's depth, moved as a heart that
yearns,
Heaves up to him, strong as a heart half
broken,
A heart that breaks in a prayer that burns.
Of cloud is the shrine of his worship moulded,
But the altar therein is of sea-shaped stone,
Whereon, with the strength of his wide wings
folded,
Sits death in the dark, alone.

He hears the word of his servant spoken,
The word that the wind his servant saith ;
Storm writes on the front of the night his
token,
That the skies may seem to bow down to
death.
But the clouds that stoop and the storms that
minister
Serve but as thralls that fulfil their tasks ;
And his seal is not set save here on the
sinister
Crests reared of the crownless casques.

Nor flame nor plume of the storm that crowned
them
Gilds or quickens their stark black strength.
Life lightens and murmurs and laughs right
round them,
At peace with the noon's whole breadth and
length,
At one with the heart of the soft-souled
heaven,
At one with the life of the kind wild land:
But its touch may unbrace not the strengths
of the seven
Casques hewn of the storm-wind's hand.

No touch may loosen the black braced helm-
lets
For the wild elves' heads of the wild waves
wrought.
As flowers on the sea are her small green
realmlets,
Like heavens made out of a child's heart's
thought ;
But these as thorns of her desolate places,
Strong fangs that fasten and hold lives fast :
And the vizors are framed as for formless
faces
That a dark dream sees go past.

Of fear and of fate are the frontlets fashioned,
And the heads behind them are dire and
dumb.
When the heart of the darkness is scarce im-
passioned,
Thrilled scarce with sense of the wrath to
come,
They bear the sign from of old engraven,
Though peace be round them and strife
seem far,
That here is none but the night-wind's haven,
With death for the harbor bar.

Of the iron of doom are the casquets carven,
That never the rivets thereof should burst.
When the heart of the darkness is hunger-
starven,
And the throats of the gulfs are agape for
thirst,
And stars are as flowers that the wind bids
wither,
And dawn is as hope struck dead by fear,
The rage of the ravenous night sets hither,
And the crown of her work is here.

All shores about and afar lie lonely,
But lonelier are these than the heart of
grief,
These loose-linked rivets of rock, whence only
Strange life scarce gleams from the sheer
main reef,
With a blind wan face in the wild wan morn-
ing,
With a live lit flame on its brows by night,
That the lost may lose not its word's mute
warning
And the blind by its grace have sight.

Here, walled in with the wide waste water,
Grew the grace of a girl's lone life,
The sea's and the sea-wind's foster-daughter,
And peace was hers in the main mid strife.
For her were the rocks clothed round with
thunder,

And the crests of them carved by the storm-
        smith's craft:
For her was the mid storm rent in sunder
        As with passion that wailed and laughed.

For her the sunrise kindled and scattered
        The red rose-leaflets of countless cloud:
For her the blasts of the springtide shattered
        The strengths reluctant of waves back-
        bowed.
For her would winds in the mid sky levy
        Bright wars that hardly the night bade
        cease:
At noon, when sleep on the sea lies heavy,
        For her would the sun make peace.

Peace rose crowned with the dawn on golden
        Lit leagues of triumph that flamed and
        smiled:
Peace lay lulled in the moon-beholden
        Warm darkness making the world's heart
        mild.
For all the wide waves' troubles and treasons,
        One word only her soul's ear heard
Speak from stormless and storm-rent seasons,
        And ought save peace was the word.

All her life waxed large with the light of it,
        All her heart fed full on the sound:
Spirit and sense were exalted in sight of it,
        Compassed and girdled and clothed with
        it round.
Sense was none but a strong still rapture,
        Spirit was none but a joy sublime,
Of strength to curb and of craft to capture
        The craft and the strength of Time.

Time lay bound as in painless prison
        There, close in with a strait small space.
Never thereon as a strange light risen
        Change had unveiled for her grief's far
        face.
Three white walls flung out from the base-
        ment
Girt the width of the world whereon
Gazing at night from her flame-lit casement
        She saw where the dark sea shone.

Hardly the breadth of a few brief paces,
        Hardly the length of a strong man's stride,
The small court flower-lit with children's
        faces
        Scarce held scope for a bird to hide.
Yet here was a man's brood reared and hidden
        Between the rocks and the towers and the
        foam
Where peril and pity and peace were bidden
        As guests to the same sure home.

Here would pity keep watch for peril,
        And surety comfort his heart with peace.
No flower save one, where the reefs lie sterile,
        Gave of the seed of its heart's increase.
Pity and surety and peace most lowly
        Were the root and the stem and the bloom
        of the flower:
And the light and the breath of the buds
        kept holy
        That maid's else blossomless bower.

With never a leaf but the seaweed's tangle,
        Never a bird's but the seamew's note,
It heard all round it the strong storms wran-
        gle,
        Watched far past it the waste wrecks float.
But her soul was stilled by the sky's endur-
        ance,
        And her heart made glad with the sea's
        content;
And her faith waxed more in the sun's assur-
        ance
        For the winds that came and went.

Sweetness was brought for her forth of the
        bitter
        Sea's strength, and light of the deep sea's
        dark,
From where green lawns on Alderney glitter
        To the bastioned crags of the steeps of
        Sark.
These she knew from afar beholden,
        And marvelled haply what life would be
On moors that sunset and dawn leave golden,
        In dells that smile on the sea.

And forth she fared as a stout-souled rover,
        For a brief blithe raid on the bounding
        brine:
And light winds ferried her light bark over
        To the lone soft island of fair-limbed kine.
But the league-long length of its wild green
        border,
        And the small bright streets of serene St.
        Anne,
Perplexed her sense with a strange disorder
        At sight of the works of man.

The world was here, and the world's confu-
        sion,
        And the dust of the wheels of revolving
        life,
Pain, labor, change, and the fierce illusion
        Of strife more vain than the sea's old strife.
And her heart within her was vexed, and
        dizzy
        The sense of her soul as a wheel that
        whirled:

She might not endure for a space that busy
  Loud coil of the troublous world.

Too full, she said, was the world of trouble,
  Too dense with noise of contentious things,
And shews less bright than the blithe foam's
    bubble
  As home she fared on the smooth wind's
    wings.
For joy grows loftier in air more lonely,
  Where only the sea's brood fain would be;
Where only the heart may receive in it only
  The love of the heart of the sea.

A BALLAD OF SARK.

High beyond the granite portal arched across
  Like the gateway of some godlike giant's
    hold
Sweep and swell the billowy breasts of moor
    and moss
  East and westward, and the dell their slopes
    enfold
Basks in purple, glows in green, exults in
    gold.
Glens that know the dove and fells that hear
    the lark
Fill with joy the rapturous island, as an ark
  Full of spicery wrought from herb and
    flower and tree.
None would dream that grief even here may
    disembark
  On the wrathful woful marge of earth and
    sea.

Rocks emblazoned like the mid shield's royal
    boss
  Take the sun with all their blossom broad
    and bold.
None would dream that all this moorland's
    glow and gloss
  Could be dark as tombs that strike the
    spirit acold
  Even in eyes that opened here, and here
    behold
Now no sun relume from hope's belated
    spark
Any comfort, nor may ears of mourners hark
  Though the ripe woods ring with golden-
    throated glee,
While the soul lies shattered, like a stranded
    bark
  On the wrathful woful marge of earth and
    sea.

Death and doom are they whose crested tri
    umphs toss
  On the proud plumed waves whence mourn-
    ing notes are tolled.
Wail of perfect woe and moan for utter loss
Raise the bride-song through the graveyard
    on the wold
Where the bride-bed keeps the bridegroom
    fast in mould.
Where the bride, with death for priest and
    doom for clerk,
Hears for choir the throats of waves like
    wolves that bark,
  Sore anhungered, off the drear Eperquerie,
Fain to spoil the strongholds of the strength
    of Sark
  On the wrathful woful marge of earth and
    sea.

Prince of storm and tempest, lord whose
    ways are dark,
Wind whose wings are spread for flight that
    none may mark,
  Lightly dies the joy that lives by grace of
    thee.
Love through thee lies bleeding, hope lies
    cold and stark,
  On the wrathful woful marge of earth and
    sea.

NINE YEARS OLD.

February 4, 1883.

I.

Lord of light, whose shrine no hands destroy,
  God of song, whose hymn no tongue
    refuses,
Now, though spring far hence be cold and coy
  Bid the golden mouths of all the Muses
Ring forth gold of strains without alloy,
  Till the ninefold rapture that suffuses
Heaven with song bid earth exult for joy,
  Since the child whose head this dawn
    bedews is
Sweet as once thy violet-cradled boy.

II.

Even as he lay lapped about with flowers,
  Lies the life now nine years old before us
Lapped about with love in all its hours;
  Hailed of many loves that chant in chorus
Loud or low from lush or leafless bowers,
  Some from hearts exultant born sonorous,
Some scarce louder-voiced than soft-tongued
    showers

Two months hence, when spring's light
    wings poised o'er us
High shall hover, and her heart be ours.

III.

Even as he, though man-forsaken, smiled
    On the soft kind snakes divinely bidden
There to feed him in the green mid-wild
    Full with hurtless honey, till the hidden
Birth should prosper, finding fate more mild,
    So full-fed with pleasures unforbidden,
So by love's lures blamelessly beguiled,
    Laughs the nursling of our hearts un-
        chidden
Yet by change that mars not yet the child.

IV.

Ah, not yet! Thou, lord of night and day,
    Time, sweet father of such blameless
        pleasure,
Time, false friend who tak'st thy gifts away,
    Spare us yet some scantlings of the treasure,
Leave us yet some rapture of delay,
    Yet some bliss of blind and fearless leisure
Unprophetic of delight's decay,
    Yet some nights and days wherein to meas-
        ure
All the joys that bless us while they may.

V.

Not the waste Arcadian woodland, wet
    Still with dawn and vocal with Alpheus,
Reared a nursling worthier love's regret,
    Lord, than this, whose eyes beholden free
        us
Straight from bonds the soul would fain forget,
    Fain cast off, that night and day might see
        us
Clear once more of life's vain fume and fret:
    Leave us, then, whate'er thy doom decree
        us,
Yet some days wherein to love him yet.

VI.

Yet some days, wherein the child is ours,
    Ours, not thine, O lord whose hand is o'er
        us
Always, as the sky with suns and showers
    Dense and radiant, soundless or sonorous;
Yet some days for love's sake, ere the bowers
    Fade wherein his fair first years kept chorus
Night and day with Graces robed like hours,
    Ere this worshipped childhood wane be-
        fore us,
Change, and bring forth fruit—but no more
    flowers.

VII.

Love we may the thing that is to be,
    Love we must: but how forego this olden
Joy, this flower of childish love, that we
    Held more dear than aught of Time is
        holden—
Time, whose laugh is like as Death's to see—
    Time, who heeds not aught of all beholden,
Heard, or touched in passing—flower or tree,
    Tares or grain of leaden days or golden—
More than wind has heed of ships at sea?

VIII.

First the babe, a very rose of joy,
    Sweet as hope's first note of jubilation,
Passes: then must growth and change
        destroy
Next the child, and mar the consecration
Hallowing yet, ere thought or sense annoy,
    Childhood's yet half heavenlike habitation,
Bright as truth and frailer than a toy;
    Whence its guest with eager gratulation
Springs, and life grows larger round the boy.

IX.

Yet, ere sunrise wholly cease to shine,
    Ere change come to chide our hearts, and
        scatter
Memories marked for love's sake with a sign,
    Let the light of dawn beholden flatter
Yet some while our eyes that feed on thine,
    Child, with love that change not time can
        shatter,
Love, whose silent song says more than mine
    Now, though charged with elder loves and
        latter
Here it hails a lord whose years are nine.

AFTER A READING.

For the seven times seventh time love would
    renew the delight without end or alloy
That it takes in the praise as it takes in the
    presence of eyes that fulfil it with joy;
But how shall it praise them and rest unre-
    buked by the presence and pride of the
    boy?

Praise meet for a child is unmeet for an elder
    whose winters and springs are nine:
What song may have strength in its wings to
    expand them, or light in its eyes to shine,
That shall seem not as weakness and darkness
    if matched with the theme I would fain
    make mine?

The round little flower of a face that exults in
    the sunshine of shadowless days
Defies the delight it enkindles to sing of it
    aught not unfit for the praise
Of the sweetest of all things that eyes may re-
    joice in and tremble with love as they gaze.

Such tricks and such meanings abound on the
    lips and the brows that are brighter than
    light,
The demure little chin, the sedate little nose,
    and the forehead of sun-stained white,
That love overflows into laughter and laughter
    subsides into love at the sight.

Each limb and each feature has action in tune
    with the meaning that smiles as its speaks
From the fervor of eyes and the fluttering
    of hands in a foretaste of fancies and
    freaks,
When the thought of them deepens the dimples
    that laugh in the corners and curves of his
    cheeks.

As a bird when the music within her is yet too
    intense to be spoken in song,
That pauses a little for pleasure to feel how
    the notes from withinwards throng,
So pauses the laugh at his lips for a little, and
    waxes within more strong.

As the music elate and triumphal that bids
    all things of the dawn bear part
With the tune that prevails when her passion
    has risen into rapture of passionate art.
So lightens the laughter made perfect that
    leaps from its nest in the heaven of his
    heart.

Deep, grave and sedate is the gaze of expect-
    ant intensity bent for a while.
And absorbed on its aim as the tale that en-
    thralls him uncovers the weft of its wile,
Till the goal of attention is touched, and
    expectancy kisses delight in a smile.

And it seems to us here that in Paradise hardly
    the spirit of Lamb or of Blake
May hear or behold aught sweeter than
    lightens and rings when his bright thoughts
    break
In laughter that well might lure them to look,
    and to smile as of old for his sake.

O singers that best loved children, and best
    for their sakes are beloved of us here,

In the world of your life everlasting, where
    love has no thorn and desire has no fear,
All else may be sweeter than aught is on
    earth, nought dearer than these are dear.

———

MAYTIME IN MIDWINTER.

A NEW year gleams on us, tearful
    And troubled and smiling dim
As the smile on a lip still fearful,
    As glances of eyes that swim:
But the bird of my heart makes cheerful
    The days that are bright for him.

Child, how may a man's love merit
    The grace you shed as you stand,
The gift that is yours to inherit?
    Through you are the bleak days bland;
Your voice is a light to my spirit;
    You bring the sun in your hand.

The year's wing shows not a feather
    As yet of the plumes to be;
Yet here in the shrill gray weather
    The spring's self stands at my knee,
And laughs as we commune together,
    And lightens the world we see.

The rains are as dews for the christening
    Of dawns that the nights benumb:
The spring's voice answers me listening
    For speech of a child to come,
While promise of music is glistening
    On lips that delight keeps dumb.

The mists and the storms receding
    At sight of you smile and die:
Your eyes held wide on me reading
    Shed summer across the sky:
Your heart shines clear for me, heeding
    No more of the world than I.

The world, what is it to you, dear,
    And me, if its face be gray,
And the new-born year be a shrewd year
    For flowers that the fierce winds fray?
You smile, and the sky seems blue, dear,
    You laugh, and the month turns May.

Love cares not for care, he has daffed her
    Aside as a mate for guile:
The sight that my soul yearns after
    Feeds full my sense for awhile;
Your sweet little sun-faced laughter,
    Your good little glad grave smile.

Your hands through the bookshelves flutter;
  Scott, Shakespeare, Dickens, are caught;
Blake's visions, that lighten and mutter;
  Molière—and his smile has nought
Left on it of sorrow, to utter
  The secret things of his thought.

No grim thing written or graven
  But grows, if you gaze on it, bright;
A lark's note rings from the raven,
  And tragedy's robe turns white;
And shipwrecks drift into haven;
  And darkness laughs, and is light.

Grief seems but a vision of madness;
  Life's key-note peals from above
With nought in it more of sadness
  Than broods on the heart of a dove:
At sight of you, thought grows gladness,
  And life, through love of you, love.

A DOUBLE BALLAD OF AUGUST.

(1884.)

ALL Afric, winged with death and fire,
Pants in our pleasant English air.
Each blade of grass is tense as wire,
And all the wood's loose trembling hair
Stark in the broad and breathless glare
Of hours whose touch wastes herb and tree.
This bright sharp death shines everywhere ;
Life yearns for solace toward the sea.

Earth seems a corpse upon the pyre ;
The sun, a scourge for slaves to bear.
All power to fear, all keen desire,
Lies dead as dreams of days that were
Before the new-born world lay bare
In heaven's wide eye, whereunder we
Lie breathless till the season spare :
Life yearns for solace toward the sea.

Fierce hours, with ravening fangs that tire
On spirit and sense, divide and share
The throbs of thoughts that scarce respire,
The throes of dreams that scarce forbear
One mute immitigable prayer
For cold perpetual sleep to be
Shed snowlike on the sense of care.
Life yearns for solace toward the sea.

The dust of ways where men suspire
Seems even the dust of death's dim lair.
But though the feverish days be dire
The sea-wind rears and cheers its fair

Blithe broods of babes that here and there
Make the sands laugh and glow for glee
With gladder flowers than gardens wear.
Life yearns for solace toward the sea.

The music dies not off the lyre
That lets no soul alive despair.
Sleep strikes not dumb the breathless choir
Of waves whose note bids sorrow spare.
As glad they sound, as fast they fare,
As when fate's word first set them free
And gave them light and night to wear.
Life yearns for solace toward the sea.

For there, though night and day conspire
To compass round with toil and snare
And changeless whirl of change, whose gyre
Draws all things deathwards unaware,
The spirit of life they scourge and scare,
Wild waves that follow on waves that flee
Laugh, knowing that yet, though earth despair
Life yearns for solace toward the sea.

HEARTSEASE COUNTRY.

TO ISABEL SWINBURNE.

THE far green westward heavens are bland,
  The far green Wiltshire downs are clear
As these deep meadows hard at hand :
  The sight knows hardly far from near,
  Nor morning joy from evening cheer.
In cottage garden-plots their bees
  Find many a fervent flower to seize
  And strain and drain the heart away
From ripe sweet-williams and sweet-peas
  At every turn on every way.

But gladliest seems one flower to expand
  Its whole sweet heart all round us here ;
'Tis Heartsease Country, Pansy Land.
  Nor sounds nor savors harsh and drear
  Where engines yell and halt and veer
Can vex the sense of him who sees
  One flower-plot midway, that for trees
  Has poles, and sheds all grimed or gray
For bowers like those that take the breeze
  At every turn on every way.

Content even there they smile and stand,
  Sweet thought's heart-easing flowers, nor
  fear.
With reek and roaring steam though fanned,
  Nor shrink nor perish as they peer.
  The heart's eye holds not those more dear

That glow between the lanes and leas
Where'er the homeliest hand may please
    To bid them blossom as they may
Where light approves and wind agrees
    At every turn on every way.

Sister, the word of winds and seas
Endures not as the word of these
    Your wayside flowers whose breath would
        say
How hearts that love may find heart's ease
    At every turn on every way.

A BALLAD OF APPEAL.

TO CHRISTINA G. ROSSETTI.

SONG wakes with every wakening year
    From hearts of birds that only feel
Brief spring's deciduous flower-time near:
    And song more strong to help or heal
    Shall silence worse than winter seal?
From love-lit thought's remurmuring cave
The notes that rippled, wave on wave,
    Were clear as love, as faith were strong;
And all souls blessed the soul that gave
    Sweet water from the well of song.

All hearts bore fruit of joy to hear,
    All eyes felt mist upon them steal
For joy's sake, trembling toward a tear,
    When, loud as marriage-bells that peal,
    Or flutelike soft, or keen like steel,
Sprang the sheer music; sharp or grave,
We heard the drift of winds that drave,
    And saw, swept round by ghosts in throng,
Dark rocks, that yielded, where they clave,
    Sweet water from the well of song.

Blithe verse made all the dim sense clear
    That smiles of babbling babes conceal:
Prayer's perfect heart spake here: and here
    Rose notes of blameless woe and weal,
    More soft than this poor song's appeal.
Where orchards bask, where cornfields wave,
They dropped like rains that cleanse and lave,
    And scattered all the year along,
Like dewfall on an April grave,
    Sweet water from the well of song.

Ballad, go bear our prayer, and crave
Pardon, because thy lowlier stave
    Can do this plea no right, but wrong.
Ask nought beside thy pardon, save
    Sweet water from the well of song.

CRADLE SONGS.

(TO A TUNE OF BLAKE'S.)

I.

BABY, baby bright,
Sleep can steal from sight
Little of your light:

Soft as fire in dew,
Still the life in you
Lights your slumber through.

Four white eyelids keep
Fast the seal of sleep
Deep as love is deep:

Yet, though closed it lies,
Love behind them spies
Heaven in two blue eyes.

II.

Baby, baby dear,
Earth and heaven are near
Now, for heaven is here.

Heaven is every place
Where your flower-sweet face
Fills our eyes with grace.

Till your own eyes deign
Earth a glance again,
Earth and heaven are twain.

Now your sleep is done,
Shine, and show the sun
Earth and heaven are one.

III.

Baby, baby sweet,
Love's own lips are meet
Scarce to kiss your feet.

Hardly love's own ear,
When your laugh crows clear,
Quite deserves to hear.

Hardly love's own wile,
Though it please awhile,
Quite deserves your smile.

Baby full of grace,
Bless us yet a space:
Sleep will come apace.

IV.

Baby, baby true,
Man, whate'er he do,
May deceive not you.

Smiles whose love is guile,
Worn a flattering while,
Win from you no smile.

One, the smile alone
Out of love's heart grown,
Ever wins your own.

Man, a dunce uncouth,
Errs in age and youth:
Babies know the truth.

V.

Baby, baby fair,
Love is fain to dare
Bless your haughtiest air.

Baby blithe and bland,
Reach but forth a hand
None may dare withstand;

Love, though wellnigh cowed,
Yet would praise aloud
Pride so sweetly proud.

No! the fitting word
Even from breeze or bird
Never yet was heard.

VI.

Baby, baby kind,
Though no word we find
Bear us yet in mind.

Half a little hour,
Baby bright in bower,
Keep this thought aflower—

Love it is, I see,
Here with heart and knee
Bows and worships me.

What can baby do,
Then, for love so true ?—
Let it worship you.

VII.

Baby, baby wise,
Love's divine surmise
Lights your constant eyes.

Day and night and day
One mute word would they,
As the soul saith, say.

Trouble comes and goes;
Wonder ebbs and flows;
Love remains and glows.

As the fledgeling dove
Feels the breast above.
So your heart feels love.

PELAGIUS.

I.

THE sea shall praise him and the shores
      bear part
    That reared him when the bright south
      world was black
    With fume of creeds more foul than hell's
      own rack,
Still darkening more love's face with loveless
      art
Since Paul, faith's fervent Antichrist, of
      heart
    Heroic, haled the world vehemently back
    From Christ's pure path on dire Jehovah's
      track,
And said to dark Elisha's Lord, ' Thou art.'
But one whose soul had put the raiment on
Of love that Jesus left with James and John
    Withstood that Lord whose seals of love
      were lies,
Seeing what we see—how, touched by Truth's
      bright rod,
The fiend whom Jews and Africans called
      God
    Feels his own hell take hold on him and
      dies.

II.

The world has no such flower in any land,
    And no such pearl in any gulf the sea,
    As any babe on any mother's knee.
But all things blessed of men by saints are
      banned:
God gives them grace to read and understand
    The palimpsest of evil, writ where we,
    Poor fools and lovers but of love, can see
Nought save a blessing signed by Love's own
      hand.
The smile that opens heaven on us for them
    Hath sin's transmitted birthmark hid there-
      in:

The kiss it craves calls down from heaven
    a rod.
If innocence be sin that Gods condemn,
    Praise we the men who so being born in sin
      First dared the doom and broke the
      bonds of God.

III.

Man's heel is on the Almighty's neck who
    said,
    Let there be hell, and there was hell—on
      earth.
    But not for that may men forget their
      worth—
Nay, but much more remember them—who
    led
The living first from dwellings of the dead,
    And rent the cerecloths that were wont to
      engirth
    Souls wrapped and swathed and swaddled
      from their birth
With lies that bound them fast from heel to
    head.
Among the tombs when wise men all their
    lives
Dwelt, and cried out, and cut themselves
    with knives,
These men, being foolish, and of saints ab-
    horred,
    Beheld in heaven the sun by saints reviled,
Love, and on earth one everlasting Lord
    In every likeness of a little child.

LOUIS BLANC.

THREE SONNETS TO HIS MEMORY.

I.

THE stainless soul that smiled through glori-
    ous eyes;
    The bright grave brow whereon dark for-
      tune's blast
    Might blow, but might not bend it, nor
      o'ercast,
Save for one fierce fleet hour of shame, the
    skies
Thrilled with warm dreams of worthier days
    to rise
And end the whole world's winter; here at
    last,
If death be death, have passed into the
    past;
If death be life, live, though their semblance
    dies.

Hope and high faith inviolate of distrust
    Shone strong as life inviolate of the grave
      Through each bright word and lineament
      serene.
Most loving righteousness and love most just
    Crowned, as day crowns the dawn-en-
      kindled wave,
    With visible aureole thine unfaltering
      mien.

II.

Strong time and fire-swift change, with light-
    nings clad
    And shod with thunders of reverberate
      years,
    Have filled with light and sound of hopes
      and fears
The space of many a season, since I had
Grace of good hap to make my spirit glad,
    Once communing with thine: and memory
    hears
    The bright voice yet that then rejoiced
    mine ears,
Sees yet the light of eyes that spake, and
    bade
Fear not, but hope, though then time's heart
    were weak
    And heaven by hell shade-stricken, and the
    range
    Of high-born hope made questionable and
    strange
As twilight trembling till the sunlight speak.
    Thou sawest the sunrise and the storm in
    one
    Break: seest thou now the storm-compell-
    ing sun?

III.

Surely thou seest, O spirit of light and fire,
    Surely thou canst not choose, O soul, but
    see
    The days whose dayspring was beheld of
    thee
Ere eyes less pure might have their hope's de-
    sire,
Beholding life in heaven again respire
    Where men saw nought that was or was to
    be,
    Save only death imperial. Thou and he
Who has the heart of all men's hearts for
    lyre,
Ye twain, being great of spirit as time is
    great,
    And sure of sight as truth's own heaven-
    ward eye,

Beheld the forms of forces passing by
And certitude of equal-balanced fate,
Whose breath forefelt makes darkness pal-
  pitate,
And knew that light should live and darkness
  die.

VOS DEOS LAUDAMUS:

THE CONSERVATIVE JOURNALIST'S ANTHEM.

' As a matter of fact, no man living, or who ever lived
—not CÆSAR or PERICLES, not SHAKESPEARE or
MICHAEL ANGELO—could confer honor more than he
took on entering the House of Lords.'—*Saturday Review*, December 15, 1883.

' Clumsy and shallow snobbery—can do no hurt.'—
Ibid.

I.

O LORDS our Gods, beneficent, sublime,
  In the evening, and before the morning
    flames,
  We praise, we bless, we magnify your
    names.
The slave is he that serves not, his the crime
And shame, who hails not as the crown of
    Time
  That House wherein the all-envious world
    acclaims
  Such glory that the reflex of it shames
All crowns bestowed of men for prose or
    rhyme.
The serf, the cur, the sycophant is he
Who feels no cringing motion twitch his knee
  When from a height too high for Shake-
    speare nods
The wearer of a higher than Milton's crown.
Stoop, Chaucer, stoop: Keats, Shelley, Burns,
    bow down:
  These have no part with you, O Lords our
    Gods.

II.

O Lords our Gods, it is not that ye sit
  Serene above the thunder, and exempt
  From strife of tongues and casualties that
    tempt
Men merely found by proof of manhood fit
For service of their fellows: this is it
  Which sets you past the reach of Time's
    attempt,
  Which gives us right of justified contempt
For commonwealths built up by mere men's
    wit:

That gold unlocks not, nor may flatteries ope,
The portals of your heaven; that none may
    hope
  With you to watch how life beneath you
    plods,
Save for high service given, high duty done;
That never was your rank ignobly won:
  For this we give you praise, O Lords our
    Gods.

III.

O Lords our Gods, the times are evil: you
  Redeem the time, because of evil days.
  While abject souls in servitude of praise
Bow down to heads untitled, and the crew
Whose honor dwells but in the deeds they
    do,
  From loftier hearts your nobler servants
    raise
More manful salutation: yours are bays
That not the dawn's plebeian pearls bedew;
Yours, laurels plucked not of such hands as
    wove
Old age its chaplet in Colonos' grove.
  Our time, with heaven and with itself at
    odds,
Makes all lands else as seas that seethe and
    boil;
But yours are yet the corn and wine and oil,
  And yours our worship yet, O Lords our
    Gods.

ON THE BICENTENARY OF COR-
NEILLE,

CELEBRATED UNDER THE PRESIDENCY OF
VICTOR HUGO.

SCARCE two hundred years are gone, and the
    world is past away
  As a noise of brawling wind, as a flash of
    breaking foam,
  That beheld the singer born who raised up
    the dead of Rome;
And a mightier now than he bids him too
    rise up to-day.
All the dim great age is dust, and its king is
    tombless clay,
  But its loftier laurel green as in living eyes
    it clomb,
  And his memory whom it crowned hath
    his people's hearts for home,
And the shade across it falls of a lordlier-
    flowering bay.

Stately shapes about the tomb of their mighty
    maker pace,
Heads of high-plumed Spaniards shine, souls
    revive of Roman race,
Sound of arms and words of wail through the
    glowing darkness rise,
    Speech of hearts heroic rings forth of lips
      that know not breath,
And the light of thoughts august fills the pride
    of kindling eyes
    Whence of yore the spell of song drove the
      shadow of darkling death.

IN SEPULCRETIS.

'Vidistis ipso rapere de rogo cœnam.'—CATULLUS,
LIX. 3.
'To publish even one line of an author which he
himself has not intended for the public at large—es-
pecially letters which are addressed to private persons
—is to commit a despicable act of felony.'—HEINE.

I.

IT is not then enough that men who give
    The best gift given of man to man should
    feel,
    Alive, a snake's head ever at their heel:
Small hurt the worms may do them while
    they live—
Such hurt as scorn for scorn's sake may for-
    give.
    But now, when death and fame have set
    one seal
    On tombs whereat Love, Grief, and Glory
    kneel,
Men sift all secrets, in their critic sieve,
Of graves wherein the dust of death might
    shrink
    To know what tongues defile the dead
    man's name
    With loathsome love, and praise that stings
    like shame.
Rest once was theirs, who had crossed the
    mortal brink:
    No rest, no reverence now: dull fools un-
    dress
    Death's holiest shrine, life's veriest naked-
    ness.

II.

A man was born, sang, suffered, loved, and
    died.
    Men scorned him living: let us praise him
    dead.

His life was brief and bitter, gently led
And proudly, but with pure and blameless
    pride.
He wrought no wrong toward any; satisfied
    With love and labor, whence our souls are
    fed
    With largesse yet of living wine and bread.
Come, let us praise him: here is nought to
    hide.
Make bare the poor dead secrets of his heart,
    Strip the stark-naked soul, that all may
    peer,
    Spy, smirk, sniff, snap, snort, snivel, snar
    and sneer:
Let none so sad, let none so sacred part
    Lie still for pity, rest unstirred for shame,
    But all be scanned of all men. This is
    fame.

III.

'Now, what a thing it is to be an ass!'*
    If one, that strutted up the brawling streets
    As foreman of the flock whose concourse
    greets
Men's ears with bray more dissonant than
    brass,
Would change from blame to praise as coarse
    and crass
    His natural note, and learn the fawning
    feats
    Of lapdogs, who but knows what luck he
    meets?
But all in vain old fable holds her glass.

Mocked and reviled by men of poisonous
    breath,
    A great man dies: but one thing worst was
    spared;
    Not all his heart by their base hands lay
    bared.
One comes to crown with praise the dust of
    death;
    And lo, through him this worst is brought
    to pass.
Now, what a thing it is to be an ass!

IV.

Shame, such as never yet dealt heavier stroke
    On heads more shameful, fall on theirs
    through whom
    Dead men may keep inviolate not their
    tomb,
But all its depths these ravenous grave-worms
    choke.
And yet what waste of wrath were this, to
    invoke

* *Titus Andronicus*, Act iv., Scene 2.

Shame on the shameless? Even their twin-
born doom,
Their native air of life, a carrion fume,
Their natural breath of love, a noisome smoke,
The bread they break, the cup whereof they
drink,
The record whose remembrance damns
their name,
Smells, tastes, and sounds of nothing but
of shame.
If thankfulness nor pity bids them think
What work is this of theirs, and pause be-
times,
Not Shakespeare's grave would scare them
off with rhymes.

LOVE AND SCORN.

I.

LOVE, loyallest and lordliest born of things,
Immortal that shouldst be, though all else
end,
In plighted hearts of fearless friend with
friend,
Whose hand may curb or clip thy plume-
plucked wings?
Not grief's nor time's: though these be lords
and kings
Crowned, and their yoke bid vassal pas-
sions bend,
They may not pierce the spirit of sense, or
blend
Quick poison with the soul's live watersprings.
The true clear heart whose core is manful
trust
Fears not that very death may turn to dust
Love lit therein as toward a brother born,
If one touch make not all its fine gold rust,
If one breath blight not all its glad ripe
corn,
And all its fire be turned to fire of scorn.

II.

Scorn only, scorn begot of bitter proof
By keen experience of a trustless heart,
Bears burning in her new-born hand the
dart
Wherewith love dies heart-stricken, and the
roof
Falls of his palace, and the storied woof
Long woven of many a year with life's
whole art
Is rent like any rotten weed apart,
And hardly with reluctant eyes aloof

Cold memory guards one relic scarce exempt
Yet from the fierce corrosion of contempt,
And hardly saved by pity. Woe are we
That once we loved, and love not; but we
know
The ghost of love, surviving yet in show,
Where scorn has passed, is vain as grief
must be.

III.

O sacred, just, inevitable scorn,
Strong child of righteous judgment, whom
with grief
The rent heart bears, and wins not yet
relief,
Seeing of its pain so dire a portent born,
Must thou not spare one sheaf of all the corn,
One doit of all the treasure? not one sheaf,
Not one poor doit of all? not one dead leaf
Of all that fell and left behind a thorn?
Is man so strong that one should scorn
another?
Is any as God, not made of mortal mother,
That love should turn in him to gall and
flame?
Nay: but the true is not the false heart's
brother:
Love cannot love disloyalty: the name
That else it wears is love no more, but
shame.

ON THE DEATH OF RICHARD
DOYLE.

A LIGHT of blameless laughter, fancy-bred,
Soft-souled and glad and kind as love or
sleep,
Fades, and sweet mirth's own eyes are fain
to weep
Because her blithe and gentlest bird is dead.
Weep, elves and fairies all, that never shed
Tear yet for mortal mourning: you that keep
The doors of dreams whence naught of ill
may creep,
Mourn once for one whose lips your honey
fed.
Let waters of the Golden River steep
The rose-roots whence his grave blooms
rosy-red
And murmuring of Hyblæan hives be deep
About the summer silence of its bed,
And nought less gracious than a violet peep
Between the grass grown greener round his
head.

IN MEMORY OF HENRY A. BRIGHT.

YET again another, ere his crowning year,
  Gone from friends that here may look for
    him no more.
Never now for him shall hope set wide the
    door,
Hope that hailed him hither, fain to greet
    him here.
All the gracious garden-flowers he held so
    dear,
  Oldworld English blossoms, all his home-
    stead store.
  Oldworld grief had strewn them round his
    ' bier of yore,
Bidding each drop leaf by leaf as tear by tear;
Rarer lutes than mine had borne more tune-
    ful token,
  Touched by subtler hands than echoing
    time can wrong,
  Sweet as flowers had strewn his graveward
    path along.
Now may no such old sweet dirges more be
    spoken,
Now the flowers whose breath was very song
    are broken,
  Nor may sorrow find again so sweet a song.

A SOLITUDE.

SEA beyond sea, sand after sweep of sand,
  Here ivory smooth, here cloven and ridged
    with flow
  Of channelled waters soft as rain or snow,
Stretch their lone length at ease beneath the
    bland
Gray gleam of skies whose smile on wave and
    strand
  Shines weary like a man's who smiles to
    know·
  That now no dream can mock his faith with
    show,
Nor cloud for him seem living sea or land.

Is there an end at all of all this waste,
These crumbling cliffs defeatured and defaced,
These ruinous heights of sea-sapped walls
    that slide
  Seaward with all their banks of bleak blown
    flowers
Glad yet of life, ere yet their hope subside
  Beneath the coil of dull dense waves and
    hours ?

VICTOR HUGO: L'ARCHIPEL DE LA MANCHE.

SEA and land are fairer now, nor aught is all
    the same,
  Since a mightier hand than Time's hath
    woven their votive wreath.
Rocks as swords half drawn from out the
    smooth wave's jewelled sheath,
Fields whose flowers a tongue divine hath
    numbered name by name,
Shores whereby the midnight or the noon
    clothed round with flame
  Hears the clamor jar and grind whic'
    utters from beneath
  Cries of hungering waves like beasts fast
    bound that gnash their teeth,
All of these the sun that lights them lights
    not like his fame;
None of these is but the thing it was before
    he came.
  Where the darkling overfalls like dens of
    torment seethe,
High on tameless moorlands, down in
    meadows bland and tame,
Where the garden hides, and where the
    wind uproots the heath,
Glory now henceforth forever, while the
    world shall be,
Shines, a star that keeps not time with change
    on earth and sea.

THE TWILIGHT OF THE LORDS.

I.

Is the sound a trumpet blown, or a bell for
    burial tolled,
  Whence the whole air vibrates now to the
    clash of words like swords—
  'Let us break their bonds in sunder, and
    cast away their cords;
Long enough the world has mocked us, and
    marvelled to behold
How the grown man bears the curb whence
    his boyhood was controlled?'
Nay, but hearken: surer counsel more sober
    speech affords:
  'Is the past not all inscribed with the
    praises of our Lords?
Is the memory dead of deeds done of yore,
    the love grown cold
That should bind our hearts to trust in their
    counsels wise and bold?
  These that stand against you now, sense-
    less crowds and heartless hordes,

Are not these the sons of men that withstood
  your kings of old?
  Theirs it is to bind and loose; theirs the
  key that knows the wards,
Theirs the staff to lead or smite; yours, the
  spades and ploughs and hods:
Theirs to hear and yours to cry, Power is
  Yours, O Lords our Gods.'

II.

Hear, O England: these are they that would
  counsel thee aright.
  Wouldst thou fain have all thy sons sons of
  thine indeed, and free?
  Nay, but then no more at all as thou hast
  been shalt thou be:
Needs must many dwell in darkness, that
  some may look on light;
Needs must poor men brook the wrong that
  ensures the rich man's right.
  How shall kings and lords be worshipped,
  if no man bow the knee?
  How, if no man worship these, may thy
  praise endure with thee?
How, except thou trust in these, shall thy
  name not lose its might?
These have had their will of thee since the
  Norman came to smite:
Sires on grandsires, even as wave after
  wave along the sea,
Sons on sires have followed, steadfast as
  clouds or hours in flight.
  Time alone hath power to say, time alone
  hath eyes to see,
If your walls of rule be built but of clay-com-
  pacted sods,
If your place of old shall know you no more,
  O Lords our Gods.

III.

Through the stalls wherein ye sit sounds a
  sentence while we wait,
  Set your house in order: is it not builded
  on the sand?
  Set your house in order, seeing the night is
  hard at hand.
As the twilight of the Gods in the northern
  dream of fate
Is this hour that comes against you, albeit
  this hour come late.
  Ye whom Time and Truth bade heed, and
  ye would not understand,
  Now an axe draws nigh the tree overshad-
  owing all the land,
And its edge of doom is set to the root of all
  your state.

Light is more than darkness now, faith than
  fear and hope than hate;
  And what morning wills, behold, all the
  night shall not withstand.
Rods of office, helms of rule, staffs of wise
  men, crowns of great.
  While the people willed, ye bare; now
  their hopes and hearts expand,
Time with silent foot makes dust of your
  broken crowns and rods,
And the lordship of your godhead is gone, O
  Lords our Gods.

CLEAR THE WAY!

CLEAR the way, my lords and lackeys! you
  have had your day.
Here you have your answer—England's yea
  against your nay:
Long enough your house has held you : up,
  and clear the way!

Lust and falsehood, craft and traffic, precedent and gold,
Tongue of courtier, kiss of harlot, promise
  bought and sold,
Gave you heritage of empire over thralls of
  old.

Now that all these things are rotten, all their
  gold is rust,
Quenched the pride they lived by, dead the
  faith and cold the lust,
Shall their heritage not also turn again to
  dust?

By the grace of these they reigned, who left
  their sons their sway:
By the grace of these, what England says her
  lords unsay:
Till at last her cry go forth against them—
  Clear the way!

By the grace of trust in treason knaves have
  lived and lied:
By the force of fear and folly fools have fed
  their pride:
By the strength of sloth and custom reason
  stands defied.

Lest perchance your reckoning on some latter
  day be worse,
Halt and hearken, lords of lands and princes
  of the purse,
Ere the tide be full that comes with blessing
  and with curse.

Where we stand, as where you sit, scarce
    falls a sprinkling spray;
But the wind that swells, the wave that fol-
    lows, none shall stay:
Spread no more of sail for shipwreck: out,
    and clear the way!

A WORD FOR THE COUNTRY.

MEN, born of the land that for ages
    Has been honored where freedom was
        dear,
Till your labor wax fat on its wages
    You shall never be peers of a peer.
        Where might is, the right is:
            Long purses make strong swords.
        Let weakness learn meekness;
            God save the House of Lords!

You are free to consume in stagnation:
    You are equal in right to obey:
You are brothers in bonds, and the nation
    Is your mother—whose sons are her prey.
        Those others your brothers,
            Who toil not, weave, nor till,
        Refuse you and use you
            As waiters on their will.

But your fathers bowed down to their masters
    And obeyed them and served and adored.
Shall the sheep not give thanks to their
        pastors?
Shall the serf not give praise to his lord?
        Time, waning and gaining,
            Grown other now than then,
        Needs pastors and masters
            For sheep, and not for men.

If his grandsire did service in battle,
    If his grandam was kissed by a king,
Must men to my lord be as cattle
    Or as apes that he leads in a string?
        To deem so, to dream so,
            Would bid the world proclaim
        The dastards for bastards,
            Not heirs of England's fame.

Not in spite but in right of dishonor,
    There are actors who trample your boards
Till the earth that endures you upon her
    Grows weary to bear you, my lords.
        Your token is broken,
            It will not pass for gold:
        Your glory looks hoary,
            Your sun in heaven turns cold.

They are worthy to reign on their brothers,
    So contemn them as clods and as carles,
Who are Graces by grace of such mothers
    As brightened the bed of King Charles.
        What manner of banner,
            What fame is this they flaunt,
        That Britain, soul-smitten,
            Should shrink before their vaunt?

Bright sons of sublime prostitution,
    You are made of the mire of the street
Where your grandmothers walked in pollution
    Till a coronet shone at their feet.
        Your Graces, whose faces
            Bear high the bastard's brand,
        Seem stronger no longer
            Than all this honest land.

But the sons of her soldiers and seamen,
    They are worthy forsooth of their hire,
If the father won praise from all free men,
    Shall the sons not exult in their sire?
        Let money make sunny
            And power make proud their lives,
        And feed them and breed them
            Like drones in drowsiest hives.

But if haply the name be a burden
    And the souls be no kindred of theirs,
Should wise men rejoice in such guerdon
    Or brave men exult in such heirs?
        Or rather the father
            Frown, shamefaced on the son.
        And no men but foemen,
            Deriding, cry ' Well done'?

Let the gold and the land they inherit
    Pass ever from hand into hand:
In right of the forefather's merit
    Let the gold be the son's, and the land.
        Soft raiment, rich payment,
            High place, the state affords;
        Full measure of pleasure:
            But now no more, my lords,

Is the future beleaguered with dangers
    If the poor be far other than slaves?
Shall the sons of the land be as strangers
    In the land of their forefathers' graves?
        Shame were it to bear it,
            And shame it were to see:
        If free men you be, men,
            Let proof proclaim you free.

' But democracy means dissolution:
    See, laden with clamor and crime,
How the darkness of dim revolution

Comes deepening the twilight of time !'
　Ah, better the fetter
　　That holds the poor man's hand
　Than peril of sterile
　　Blind change that wastes the land.

' Gaze forward through clouds that environ ;
　It shall be as it was in the past :
Not with dreams, but with blood and with
　iron,
　Shall a nation be moulded to last.'
　　So teach they, so preach they,
　　　Who dream themselves the dream
　　　That hallows the gallows
　　　And bids the scaffold stream.

' With a hero at head, and a nation
　Well gagged and well drilled and well
　　cowed,
And a gospel of war and damnation,
　Has not empire a right to be proud ?'
　　Fools prattle and tattle
　　　Of freedom, reason, right,
　　　The beauty of duty,
　　　The loveliness of light.

' But we know, we believe it, we see it,
　Force only has power upon earth.'
So be it ! and ever so be it
　For souls that are bestial by birth !
　　Let Prussian with Russian
　　　Exchange the kiss of slaves :
　　　But sea-folk are free folk
　　　By grace of winds and waves.

Has the past from the sepulchres beckoned ?
　Let answer from Englishmen be——
No man shall be lord of us reckoned
　Who is baser, not better, than we.
　　No coward, empowered
　　　To soil a brave man's name :
　　　For shame's sake and fame's sake,
　　　Enough of fame and shame.

Fame needs not the golden addition;
　Shame bears it abroad as a brand.
Let the deed, and no more the tradition,
　Speak out and be heard through the land.
　　Pride, rootless and fruitless,
　　　No longer takes and gives:
　　　But surer and purer
　　　The soul of England lives.

He is master and lord of his brothers
　Who is worthier and wiser than they.
Him only, him surely, shall others,
　Else equal, observe and obey.
　　Truth, flawless and awless,
　　　Do falsehood what it can,

Makes royal the loyal
　And simple heart of man.

Who are these, then, that England should
　hearken,
　Who rage and wax wroth and grow pale
If she turn from the sunsets that darken
　And her ship for the morning set sail ?
　　Let strangers fear dangers :
　　　All know, that hold her dear,
　　　Dishonor upon her
　　　Can only fall through fear.

Men, born of the landsmen and seamen
　Who served her with souls and with swords.
She bids you be brothers, and free men,
　And lordless, and fearless of lords.
　　She cares not, she dares not
　　　Care now for gold or steel :
　　　Light lead her, truth speed her,
　　　God save the Commonweal !

A WORD FOR THE NATION.

I.

A word across the water
　Against our ears is borne,
Of threatenings and of slaughter,
　Of rage and spite and scorn :
We have not, alack, an ally to befriend us,
And the season is ripe to extirpate and end
　us :
Let the German touch hands with the Gaul,
And the fortress of England must fall ;
And the sea shall be swept of her seamen,
　And the waters they ruled be their graves,
And Dutchmen and Frenchmen be free men,
　　And Englishmen slaves.

II.

Our time once more is over,
　Once more our end is near ;
A bull without a drover,
　The Briton reels to rear,
And the van of the nations is held by his
　betters,
And the seas of the world shall be loosed
　from his fetters,
And his glory shall pass as a breath,
And the life that is in him be death :
And the sepulchre sealed on his glory
　For a sign to the nations shall be
As of Tyre and of Carthage in story,
　　Once lords of the sea.

III.

The lips are wise and loyal,
　The hearts are brave and true,
Imperial thoughts and royal
　Make strong the clamorous crew,
Whence louder and prouder the noise of defiance
Rings rage from the grave of a trustless alliance,
And bids us beware and be warned,
As abhorred of all nations and scorned,
As a swordless and spiritless nation,
　A wreck on the waste of the waves.
So foams the released indignation
　Of masterless slaves.

IV.

Brute throats that miss the collar,
　Bowed backs that ask the whip,
Stretched hands that lack the dollar,
　And many a lie-seared lip,
Forefeel and foreshow for us signs as funereal
As the signs that were regal of yore and imperial ;
We shall pass as the princes they served,
We shall reap what our fathers deserved,
And the place that was England's be taken
　By one that is worthier than she,
And the yoke of her empire be shaken
　Like spray from the sea.

V.

French hounds, whose necks are aching
　Still from the chain they crave,
In dog-day madness breaking
　The dog-leash, thus may rave :
But the seas that for ages have fostered and fenced her
Laugh, echoing the yell of their kennel against her
And their moan if destruction draw near them
And the roar of her laughter to hear them ;
For she knows that if Englishmen be men
　Their England has all that she craves;
All love and all honor from free men,
　All hatred from slaves.

VI.

All love that rests upon her
　Like sunshine and sweet air,
All light of perfect honor
　And praise than ends in prayer,
She wins not more surely, she wears not more proudly,

Than the token of tribute that clatters thu.
　loudly,
The tribute of foes when they meet
That rattles and rings at her feet,
The tribute of rage and of rancor,
　The tribute of slaves to the free,
To the people whose hope hath its anchor
　Made fast in the sea.

VII.

No fool that bows the back he
　Feels fit for scourge or brand,
No scurril scribes that lackey
　The lords of Lackeyland,
No penman that yearns, as he turns on his pallet,
For the place or the pence of a peer or a valet,
No whelp of as currish a pack
As the litter whose yelp it gives back,
Though he answer the cry of his brother
　As echoes might answer from caves,
Shall be witness as though for a mother
　Whose children were slaves.

VIII.

But those found fit to love her,
　Whose love has root in faith,
Who hear, though darkness cover
　Time's face, what memory saith,
Who seek not the service of great men or small men
But the weal that is common for comfort of all men,
Those yet that in trust have beholden
Truth's dawn over England grow golden
And quicken the darkness that stagnates
　And scatter the shadows that flee,
Shall reply for her meanest as magnates
　And masters by sea.

IX.

And all shall mark her station,
　Her message all shall hear,
When, equal-eyed, the nation
　Bids all her sons draw near,
And freedom be more than tradition or faction,
And thought be no swifter to serve her than action,
And justice alone be above her,
That love may be prouder to love her,
And time on the crest of her story
　Inscribe, as remembrance engraves,
The sign that subdues with its glory
　Kings, princes, and slaves.

A WORD FROM THE PSALMIST.

Ps. xciv. 8.

I.

TAKE heed, ye unwise among the people:
  O ye fools, when will ye understand?'
From pulpit or choir beneath the steeple,
  Though the words be fierce, the tones
    are bland.
But a louder than the Church's echo thunders
  In the ears of men who may not choose but
    hear;
And the heart in him that hears it leaps and
  wonders,
  With triumphant hope astonished, or with
    fear.
  For the names whose sound was power
    awaken
    Neither love nor reverence now nor
      dread;
    Their strongholds and shrines are stormed
      and taken,
      Their kingdom and all its works are
      dead.

II.

Take heed: for the tide of time is risen:
  It is full not yet, though now so high
That spirits and hopes long pent in prison
    Feel round them a sense of freedom
    nigh,
And a savor keen and sweet of brine and
  billow,
And a murmur deep and strong of deepen-
  ing strength.
Though the watchman dream, with sloth or
  pride for pillow,
  And the night be long, not endless is its
    length.
    From the springs of dawn, from clouds
    that sever,
    From the equal heavens and the east-
      ward sea,
    The witness comes that endures forever,
    Till men be brethren and thralls be
    free.

III.

But the wind of the wings of dawn ex-
  panding
  Strikes chill on your hearts as change
    and death.
Ye are old, but ye have not understand-
  ing;

And proud, but your pride is a dead
  man's breath.
And your wise men, toward whose words and
  signs ye hearken
And your strong men, in whose hands ye
  put your trust,
Strain eyes to behold but clouds and dreams
  that darken,
Stretch hands that can find but weapons
  red with rust.
  Their watchword rings, and the night rejoices,
    But the lark's note laughs at the night-
    bird's notes—
    ' Is virtue verily found in voices?
    Or is wisdom won when all win votes?

IV.

  ' Take heed, ye unwise indeed, who listen
    When the wind's wings beat and shift
    and change;
  Whose hearts are uplift, whose eyeballs
    glisten,
With desire of new things great and strange.
Let not dreams misguide nor any visions wrong
  you:
  That which has been, it is now as it was
    then.
Is not Compromise of old a god among you?
  Is not Precedent indeed a king of men?
  But the windy hopes that lead mislead
    you,
    And the sounds ye hear are void and
    vain.
  Is a vote a coat? will franchise feed you,
    Or words be a roof against the rain?

V.

  ' Eight ages are gone since kingship enter-
    ed,
    With knights and peers at its harness-
    ed back,
  And the land, no more in its own strength
    centred,
    Was cast for a prey to the princely pack.
But we pared the fangs and clipped the raven-
  ing claws of it,
  And good was in time brought forth of an
    evil thing,
  And the land's high name waxed lordlier in
    war because of it.
  When chartered Right had bridled and
    curbed the king.
    And what so fair has the world behold-
    en,

And what so firm has withstood the
years,
As Monarchy bound in chains all golden,
And Freedom guarded about with peers?

VI.

'How think ye? know not your lords and
masters
What collars are meet for brawling
throats?
Is change not mother of strange disasters?
Shall plague or peril be stayed by votes?
Out of precedent and privilege and order
Have we plucked the flower of compromise,
whose root
Bears blossoms that shine from border again
to border,
And the mouths of many are fed with its
temperate fruit.
Your masters are wiser than ye, their
henchmen:
Your lords know surely whereof ye
have need.
Equality? Fools, would you fain be
Frenchmen?
Is equity more than a word indeed?

VII.

'Your voices, forsooth, your most sweet
voices,
Your worthy voices, your love, your hate,
Your chioce, who know not whereof your
choice is,
What stays are these for a stable state?
Inconstancy, blind and deaf with its own
fierce babble,
Swells ever your throats with storm of un-
certain cheers:
He leans on straws who leans on a light-
souled rabble;
His trust is frail who puts not his trust in
peers.'
So shrills the message whose word con-
vinces
Of righteousness knaves, of wisdom
fools;
That serfs may boast them because of
princes,
And the weak rejoice that the strong
man rules.

VIII.

True friends, ye people, are these, the
faction
Full-mouthed that flatters and snarls and
bays,

That fawns and foams with alternate action
And mocks the names that it soils with
praise.
As from fraud and force their power had first
beginning,
So by righteousness and peace it may not
stand,
But by craft of state and nets of secret spin-
ning,
Words that weave and unweave wiles like
ropes of sand,
Form, custom, and gold, and laws grown
hoary,
And strong tradition that guards the
gate:
To these, O people, to these give glory,
That your name among nations may be
great.

IX.

How long—for haply not now much longer—
Shall fear put faith in a faithless creed,
And shapes and shadows of truths be
stronger
In strong men's eyes than the truth in-
deed?
If freedom be not a word that dies when
spoken,
If justice be not a dream whence men must
wake,
How shall not the bonds of the thraldom of
old be broken,
And right put might in the hands of them
that break?
For clear as a tocsin from the steeple
Is the cry gone forth along the land,
Take heed, ye unwise among the people:
O ye fools, when will ye understand?

A BALLAD AT PARTING.

SEA to sea that clasps and fosters England,
uttering evermore
Song eterne and praise immortal of the indomitable shore,
Lifts aloud her constant heart up, south to
north and east to west,
Here in speech that shames all music, there
in thunder-throated roar,
Chiming concord out of discord, waking rapture out of rest.
All her ways are lovely, all her works and
symbols are divine,
Yet shall man love best what first bade leap
his heart and bend his knee;

Yet where first his whole soul worshipped
shall his soul set up her shrine:
Nor may love not know the lovelier, fair as
both beheld may be,
Here the limitless north-eastern, there the
strait south-western sea.

Though their chant bear all one burden, as
ere man was born it bore;
Though the burden be diviner than the songs
all souls adore;
Yet may love not choose but choose between them which to love the best.
Me the sea my nursing-mother, me the Channel green and hoar,
Holds at heart more fast than all things,
bares for me the goodlier breast.
Lifts for me the lordlier love-song, bids for
me more sunlight shine,
Sounds for me the stormier trumpet of the
sweeter strain to me.
So the broad pale Thames is loved not like
the tawny springs of Tyne:
Choice is clear between them for the soul
whose vision holds in fee
Here the limitless north-eastern, there the
strait south-western sea.

Choice is clear, but dear is either; nor has
either not in store

Many a likeness, many a written sign of spirit-
searching lore,
Whence the soul takes fire of sweet remembrance, magnified and blest.
Thought of songs whose flame-winged feet
have trod the unfooted water-floor.
When the lord of all the living lords of
souls bade speed their quest;
Soft live sound like children's babble down
the rippling sand's incline,
Or the lovely song that loves them, hailed
with thankful prayer and plea;
These are parcels of the harvest here whose
gathered sheaves are mine,
Garnered now, but sown and reaped where
winds make wild with wrath or glee
Here the limitless north-eastern, there the
strait south-western sea.

Song, thy name is freedom, seeing thy
strength was born of breeze and brine.
Fare now forth and fear no fortune: such a
seal is set on thee.
Joy begat and memory bare thee, seeing in
spirit a twofold sign,
Even the sign of those thy fosters, each as
thou from all time free,
Here the limitless north-eastern, there the
strait south-western sea.

A CENTURY OF ROUNDELS.

DEDICATION.

TO

CHRISTINA G. ROSSETTI.

*Songs light as these may sound, though deep
and strong
The heart spake through them, scarce should
hope to please
Ears tuned to strains of loftier thoughts than
throng
        Songs light as these.*

*Yet grace may set their sometime doubt at ease,
Nor need their too rash reverence fear to wrong
The shrine it serves at and the hope it sees.*

*For childlike loves and laughters thence prolong
Notes that bid enter, fearless as the breeze,
Even to the shrine of holiest-hearted song,
        Songs light as these.*

IN HARBOR.

I.

GOODNIGHT and goodbye to the life whose
signs denote us
As mourners clothed with regret for the life
gone by;
To the waters of gloom whence winds of the
dayspring float us
        Goodnight and goodbye.

A time is for mourning, a season for grief to
 sigh;
But were we not fools and blind, by day to
 devote us
As thralls to the darkness, unseen of the sundawn's eye?

We have drunken of Lethe at length, we have
 eaten of lotus;
What hurts it us here that sorrows are born
 and die?
We have said to the dream that caressed and
 the dread that smote us
  Goodnight and goodbye.

II.

Outside of the port ye are moored in, lying
Close from the wind and at ease from the
 tide,
What sounds come swelling, what notes fall
 dying
  Outside?

They will not cease, they will not abide:
Voices of presage in darkness crying
Pass and return and relapse aside.

Ye see not, but hear ye not wild wings flying
To the future that wakes from the past that
 died?
Is grief still sleeping, is joy not sighing
  Outside?

THE WAY OF THE WIND.

THE wind's way in the deep sky's hollow
None may measure, as none can say
How the heart in her shows the swallow
  The wind's way.

Hope nor fear can avail to stay
Waves that whiten on wrecks that wallow,
Times and seasons that wane and slay.

Life and love, till the strong night swallow
Thought and hope and the red last ray,
Swim the waters of years that follow
  The wind's way.

'HAD I WIST.'

HAD I wist, when life was like a warm wind
 playing
Light and loud through sundawn and the
 dew's bright mist,

How the time should come for hearts to sight
 in saying
  ' Had I wist '—
Surely not the roses, laughing as they kissed,
Not the lovelier laugh of seas in sunshine
 swaying,
Should have lured my soul to look thereon
 and list.

Now the wind is like a soul cast out and
 praying
Vainly, prayers that pierce not ears when
 hearts resist:
Now mine own soul sighs, adrift as wind and
 straying,
  ' Had I wist.'

RECOLLECTIONS.

I.

YEARS upon years, as a course of clouds that
 thicken
Thronging the ways of the wind that shifts
 and veers,
Pass, and the flames of remembered fires requicken
  Years upon years.

Surely the thought in a man's heart hopes or
 fears
Now that forgetfulness needs must here have
 stricken
Anguish, and sweetened the sealed-up springs
 of tears.

Ah, but the strength of regret that strain and
 sicken,
Yearning for love that the veil of death en-
 dears,
Slackens not wing for the wings of years that
 quicken—
  Years upon years.

II.

Years upon years, and the flame of love's high
 altar
Trembles and sinks, and the sense of listening
 ears
Heeds not the sound that it heard of love's
 blithe psalter.
  Years upon years.

Only the sense of heart that hearkens hears,
Louder than dreams that assail and doubts
 that palter,

Sorrow that slept and that wakes ere sundawn
    peers.

Wakes, that the heart may behold, and yet
    not falter,
Faces of children as stars unknown of, spheres
Seen but of love, that endures though all
    things alter,
        Years upon years.

III.

Years upon years, as a watch by night that
    passes,
Pass, and the light of their eyes is fire that
    sears
Slowly the hopes of the fruit that life amasses
        Years upon years.

Pale as the glimmer of stars on moorland
    meres
Lighten the shadows reverberate from the
    glasses
Held in their hands as they pass among their
    peers.

Lights that are shadows, as ghosts on grave-
    yard grasses,
Moving on paths that the moon of memory
    cheers,
Show but as mists over cloudy mountain
    passes
        Years upon years.

TIME AND LIFE.

I.

Time, thy name is sorrow, says the stricken
Heart of life, laid waste with wasting flame,
Ere the change of things and thoughts re-
    quicken,
        Time, thy name.

Girt about with shadow, blind and lame,
Ghosts of things that smite and thoughts that
    sicken
Hunt and hound thee down to death and
    shame.

Eyes of hours whose paces halt or quicken
Read in bloodred lines of loss and blame,
Writ where cloud and darkness round it
    thicken,
        Time, thy name.

II.

Nay, but rest is born of me for healing,
—So might haply time, with voice represt,
Speak : is grief the last gift of my dealing?
        Nay, but rest.

All the world is wearied, east and west,
Tired with toil to watch the slow sun wheeling,
Twelve loud hours of life's laborious quest.

Eyes forspent with vigil, faint and reeling,
Find at last my comfort, and are blest,
Not with rapturous light of life's revealing—
        Nay, but rest.

A DIALOGUE.

I.

Death, if thou wilt, fain would I plead with
    thee :
Canst thou not spare, of all our hopes have
    built,
One shelter where our spirits fain would be,
        Death, if thou wilt?

No dome with suns and dews impearled and
    gilt,
Imperial : but some roof of wildwood tree,
Too mean for sceptre's heft or swordblade's
    hilt.

Some low sweet roof where love might live,
    set free
From change and fear and dreams of grief or
    guilt ;
Canst thou not leave life even thus much to
    see,
        Death, if thou wilt?

II.

Man, what art thou to speak and plead with
    me ?
What knowest thou of my workings, where
    and how
What things I fashion? Nay, behold and
    see,
        Man, what art thou ?

Thy fruits of life, and blossoms of thy bough,
What are they but my seedlings? Earth and
    sea
Bear nought but when I breathe on it must
    bow.

Bow thou too down before me : though thou
     be
Great, all the pride shall fade from off thy
     brow,
When Time and strong Oblivion ask of thee,
     Man, what art thou?

III.

Death, if thou be or be not, as was said,
Immortal ; if thou make us nought, or we
Survive : thy power is made but of our dread,
     Death, if thou be.

Thy might is made out of our fear of thee :
Who fears thee not, hath plucked from off
     thine head
The crown of cloud that darkens earth and
     sea.

Earth, sea, and sky, as rain or vapor shed,
Shall vanish ; all the shows of them shall
     flee :
Then shall we know full surely, quick or
     dead,
     Death, if thou be.

PLUS ULTRA.

FAR beyond the sunrise and the sunset rises
Heaven, with worlds on worlds that lighten
     and respond :
Thought can see not thence the goal of hope's
     surmises
     Far beyond.

Night and day have made an everlasting
     bond
Each with each to hide in yet more deep dis-
     guises
Truth, till souls of men that thirst for truth
     despond.

All that man in pride of spirit slights or
     prizes,
All the dreams that make him fearful, fain,
     or fond,
Fade at forethought's touch of life's unknown
     surprises
     Far beyond.

A DEAD FRIEND.
I.

GONE, O gentle heart and true,
     Friend of hopes foregone,

Hopes and hopeful days with you
Gone ?

Days of old that shone
Saw what none shall see anew,
     When we gazed thereon.

Soul as clear as sunlit dew,
     Why so soon pass on,
Forth from all we loved and knew
Gone ?

II.

Friend of many a season fled,
     What may sorrow send
Toward thee now from lips that said
     ' Friend ? '

Sighs and songs to blend
Praise with pain uncomforted
     Though the praise ascend ?

Darkness hides no dearer head :
     Why should darkness end
Day so soon, O dear and dead
     Friend ?

III.

Dear in death, thou hast thy part
     Yet in life, to cheer
Hearts that held thy gentle heart
     Dear.

Time and chance may sear
Hope with grief, and death may part
     Hand from hand's clasp here :

Memory, blind with tears that start,
     Sees through every tear
All that made thee, as thou art,
     Dear.

IV.

True and tender, single-souled,
     What should memory do
Weeping o'er the trust we hold
     True ?

Known and loved of few,
But of these, though small their fold,
     Loved how well were you !

Change, that makes of new things old,
     Leaves one old thing new ;
Love which promised truth, and told
     True.

V.

Kind as heaven, while earth's control
     Still had leave to bind

Thee, thy heart was toward man's whole
    Kind.

Thee no shadows blind
Now: the change of hours that roll
    Leaves thy sleep behind

Love, that hears thy death-bell toll
    Yet, may call to mind
Scarce a soul as thy sweet soul
    Kind

VI.

How should life, O friend, forget
    Death, whose guest art thou?
Faith responds to love's regret,
    How?

Still, for us that bow
Sorrowing, still, though life be set,
    Shines thy bright mild brow.

Yea, though death and thou be met,
    Love may find thee now
Still, albeit we know not yet
    How.

VII.

Past as music fades, that shone
    While its life might last;
As a song-bird's shadow flown
    Past!

Death's reverberate blast
Now for music's lord has blown
    Whom thy love held fast.

Dead thy king, and void his throne:
    Yet for grief at last
Love makes music of his own
    Past.

———

PAST DAYS.

I.

DEAD and gone, the days we had together,
Shadow-stricken all the lights that shone
Round them, flown as flies the blown-foam's
    feather,
    Dead and gone.

Where we went, we twain, in time foregone,
Forth by land and sea, and cared not whether,
If I go again, I go alone.

Bound am I with time as with a tether;
Thee perchance death leads enfranchised on.
Far from deathlike life and changeful wea-
    ther,
    Dead and gone.

II.

Above the sea and sea-washed town we dwelt
We twain together, two brief summers, free
From heed of hours as light as clouds that
    melt
    Above the sea.

Free from all heed of aught at all were we,
Save chance of change that clouds or sun-
    beams dealt
And gleam of heaven to windward or to lee.

The Norman downs with bright gray waves
    for belt
Were more for us than inland ways might be;
A clearer sense of nearer heaven was felt
    Above the sea.

III.

Cliffs and downs and headlands which the
    forward-hasting
Flight of dawn and eve empurples and em-
    browns,
Wings of wild sea-winds and stormy seasons
    wasting
    Cliffs and downs,
These, or ever man was, were: the same sky
    frowns,
Laughs, and lightens, as before his soul, fore-
    casting
Times to be, conceived such hopes as time
    discrowns.
These we loved of old: but now for me the
    blasting
Breath of death makes dull the bright small
    seaward towns,
Clothes with human change these all but
    everlasting
    Cliffs and downs.

———

AUTUMN AND WINTER.

I.

THREE months bade wane and wax the win-
    tering moon
Between two dates of death, while men were
    fain
Yet of the living light that all too soon
    Three months bade wane.

Cold autumn, wan with wrath of wind and
　　rain,
Saw pass a soul sweet as the sovereign tune
That death smote silent when he smote again.

First went my friend, in life's mid light of
　　noon,
Who loved the lord of music: then the strain
Whence earth was kindled like as heaven in
　　June
　　Three months bade wane.

II.

A herald soul before its master's flying
Touched by some few moons first the dark-
　　ling goal
Where shades rose up to greet the shade,
　　espying
　　A herald soul;

Shades of dead lords of music, who control
Men living by the might of men undying,
With strength of strains that make delight of
　　dole.

The deep dense dust on death's dim thresh-
　　old lying
Trembled with sense of kindling sound that
　　stole
Through darkness, and the night gave ear,
　　descrying
　　A herald soul.

III.

One went before, one after, but so fast
They seem gone hence together, from the
　　shore
Whence we now gaze: yet ere the mightier
　　passed
　　One went before;

One whose whole heart of love, being set of
　　yore
On that high joy which music lends us, cast
Light round him forth of music's radiant
　　store.

Then went, while earth on winter glared
　　aghast,
The mortal god he worshipped, through the
　　door
Wherethrough so late, his lover to the last,
　　One went before.

IV.

A star had set an hour before the sun
Sank from the skies wherethrough his heart's
　　pulse yet
Thrills audibly: but few took heed, or none,
　　A star had set.

All heaven rings back, sonorous with regret,
The deep dirge of the sunset: how should one
Soft star be missed in all the concourse met?

But, O sweet single heart whose work is done,
Whose songs are silent, how should I forget
That ere the sunset's fiery goal was won
　　A star had set?

THE DEATH OF RICHARD WAGNER.

I.

MOURNING on earth, as when dark hours
　　descend,
Wide-winged with plagues, from heaven;
　　when hope and mirth
Wane, and no lips rebuke or reprehend
　　Mourning on earth.

The soul wherein her songs of death and
　　birth,
Darkness and light, were wont to sound and
　　blend,
Now silent, leaves the whole world less in
　　worth.

Winds that make moan and triumph, skies
　　that bend,
Thunders, and sound of tides in gulf and firth,
Spake through his spirit of speech, whose
　　death should send
　　Mourning on earth.

II.

The world's great heart, whence all things
　　strange and rare
Take form and sound, that each inseparate
　　part
May bear its burden in all tuned thoughts
　　that share
　　The world's great heart—

The fountain forces, whence like steeds that
　　start
Leap forth the powers of earth and fire and
　　air,
Seas that revolve and rivers that depart—

Spake, and were turned to song: yea, all they
were,
With all their works, found in his mastering
art
Speech as of powers whose uttered word laid
bare
    The world's great heart.

III.

From the depths of the sea, from the well-
springs of earth, from the wastes of the
midmost night,
From the fountains of darkness and tempest
and thunder, from heights where the soul
would be,
The spell of the mage of music evoked their
sense, as an unknown light
    From the depths of the sea.

As a vision of heaven from the hollows of
ocean, that none but a god might see,
Rose out of the silence of things unknown of
a presence, a form, a might,
And we heard as a prophet that hears God's
message against him, and may not flee.

Eye might not endure it, but ear and heart
with a rapture of dark delight,
With a terror and wonder whose care was
joy, and a passion of thought set free,
Felt inly the rising of doom divine as a sundawn risen to sight
    From the depths of the sea

TWO PRELUDES.

I.

LOHENGRIN.

LOVE, out of the depth of things,
As a dewfall felt from above,
From the heaven whence only springs
    Love—

Love, heard from the heights thereof,
The clouds and the watersprings,
Draws close as the clouds remove.

And the soul in it speaks and sings,
A swan sweet-souled as a dove,
An echo that only rings
    Love.
37

II.

TRISTAN UND ISOLDE.

Fate out of the deep sea's gloom,
When a man's heart's pride grows great,
And nought seems now to foredoom
    Fate,

Fate, laden with fears in wait,
Draws close through the clouds that loom,
Till the soul see, all too late,

More dark than a dead world's tomb,
More high than the sheer dawn's gate,
More deep than the wide sea's womb,
    Fate.

THE LUTE AND THE LYRE.

DEEP desire, that pierces heart and spirit to
the root,
Finds reluctant voice in verse that yearns like
soaring fire,
Takes exultant voice when music holds in
high pursuit
    Deep desire.

Keen as burns the passion of the rose whose
buds respire,
Strong as grows the yearning of the blossom
towards the fruit,
Sounds the secret half unspoken ere the deep
tones tire.

Slow subsides the rapture that possessed
love's flower soft lute,
Slow the palpitation of the triumph of the
lyre:
Still the soul feels burn a flame unslaked
though these be mute,
    Deep desire.

PLUS INTRA.

SOUL within sense, immeasurable obscure,
Insepulchred and deathless, through the dense
Deep elements may scarce be felt as pure
    Soul within sense.

From depth and height by measurers left im
mense,
Thro' sound and shape and color, comes the
unsure
Vague utterance, fitful with supreme suspense.

All that may pass, and all that must endure,
Song speaks not, painting shows not : more
intense
And keen than these, art wakes with music's
lure
　　Soul within sense.

———

CHANGE.

BUT now life's face beholden
　　Seemed bright as heaven's bare brow
With hope of gifts withholden
　　But now.

From time's full-flowering bough
Each bud spake bloom to embolden
Love's heart, and seal his vow.

Joy's eyes grew deep with olden
　　Dreams, born he wist not how ;
Thought's meanest garb was golden ;
　　But now !

———

A BABY'S DEATH.

I.

A LITTLE SOUL scarce fledged for earth
Takes wing with heaven again for goal
Even while we hailed as fresh from birth
　　A little soul.

Our thoughts ring sad as bells that toll,
Not knowing beyond this blind world's girth
What things are writ in heaven's full scroll.

Our fruitfulness is there but dearth,
And all things held in time's control
Seem there, perchance, ill dreams, not worth
　　A little soul.

II.

The little feet that never trod
Earth, never strayed in field or street,
What hand leads upward back to God
　　The little feet ?

A rose in June's most honied heat.
When life makes keen the kindling sod,
Was not so soft and warm and sweet.

Their pilgrimage's period
A few swift moons have seen complete
Since mother's hand first clasped and shod
　　The little feet.

III.

The little hands that never sought
Earth's prizes, worthless all as sands,
What gift has death, God's servant, brought
　　The little hands ?

We ask : but love's self silent stands,
Love, that lends eyes and wings to thought
To search where death's dim heaven expands

Ere this, perchance, though love know nought,
Flowers fill them, grown in lovelier lands,
Where hands of guiding angels caught
　　The little hands.

IV.

The little eyes that never knew
Light other than of dawning skies,
What new life now lights up anew
　　The little eyes ?

Who knows but on their sleep may rise
Such light as never heaven let through
To lighten earth from Paradise ?

No storm, we know, may change the blue
Soft heaven that haply death descries:
No tears, like these in ours, bedew
　　The little eyes.

V.

Was life so strange, so sad the sky,
　　So strait the wide world's range,
He would not stay to wonder why
　　Was life so strange ?

Was earth's fair house a joyless grange
　　Beside that house on high
Whence　Time that bore him failed to es-
　　trange ?

That here at once his soul put by
　　All gifts of time and change,
And left us heavier hearts to sigh
　　' Was life so strange ? '

VI.

Angel by name love called him, seeing so fair
　　The sweet small frame !
Meet to be called, if ever man's child were,
　　Angel by name.

Rose-bright and warm from heaven's own
　　heart he came,
　　And might not bear
The cloud that covers earth's wan face with
　　shame.

His little light of life was all too rare
    And soft a flame:
Heaven yearned for him till angels hailed
    him there
        Angel by name.

VII.

The song that smiled upon his birthday here
Weeps on the grave that holds him undefiled
Whose loss makes bitterer than a soundless
    tear
        The song that smiled.

His name crowned once the mightiest ever
    styled
Sovereign of arts, and angel: fate and fear
Knew then their master, and were reconciled

But we saw born beneath some tenderer
    sphere
Michael, an angel and a little child,
Whose loss bows down to weep upon his bier
        The song that smiled.

ONE OF TWAIN.

I.

ONE of twain, twin-born with flowers that
    waken,
Now hath passed from sense of sun and rain :
Wind from off the flower-crowned branch
    hath shaken
        One of twain.

One twin flower must pass, and one remain :
One, the word said soothly, shall be taken,
And another left : can death refrain?

Two years since was love's light song mis-
    taken,
Blessing then both blossoms, half in vain?
Night outspeeding light hath overtaken
        One of twain.

Night and light? O thou of heart unwary,
Love, what knowest thou here at all aright,
Lured, abused, misled as men by fairy
        Night and light?

Haply, where thine eyes behold but night,
Soft as o'er her babe the smile of Mary
Light breaks flowerwise into new-born sight.

What though night of light to thee be chary?
What though stars of hope like flowers take
    flight?
Seest thou all things here, where all see vary
        Night and light?

DEATH AND BIRTH.

DEATH and birth should dwell not near to-
    gether :
Wealth keeps house not, even for shame, with
    dearth:
Fate doth ill to link in one brief tether
        Death and birth.

Harsh the yoke that binds them, strange the
    girth
Seems that girds them each with each: yet
    whether
Death be best, who knows, or life on earth?

Ill the rose-red and the sable feather
Blend in one crown's plume, as grief with
    mirth:
Ill met still are warm and wintry weather,
        Death and birth.

BIRTH AND DEATH.

BIRTH and death, twin-sister and twin-brother,
Night and day, on all things that draw breath,
Reign, while time keeps friends with one
    another
        Birth and death.

Each brow-bound with flowers diverse of
    wreath,
Heaven they hail as father, earth as mother,
Faithful found above them and beneath.

Smiles may lighten tears, and tears may
    smother
Smiles, for all that joy or sorrow saith :
Joy nor sorrow knows not from each other
        Birth and death.

BENEDICTION.

BLEST in death and life beyond man's guessing
Little children live and die, possest
Still of grace that keeps them past expressing
    Blest.

Each least chirp that rings from every nest,
Each least touch of flower-soft fingers pressing
Aught that yearns and trembles to be prest,

Each least glance, gives gifts of grace, re-
  dressing
Grief's worst wrongs : each mother's nurturing
  breast
Feeds a flower of bliss, beyond all blessing
  Blest.

ETUDE RÉALISTE.

I.

A BABY's feet, like sea-shells pink,
  Might tempt, should heaven see meet,
An angel's lips to kiss, we think,
  A baby's feet.

Like rose-hued sea-flowers toward the heat
  They stretch and spread and wink
Their ten soft buds that part and meet.

No flower-bells that expand and shrink
  Gleam half so heavenly sweet
As shine on life's untrodden brink
  A baby's feet

II.

A baby's hands, like rosebuds furled,
  Whence yet no leaf expands,
Ope if you touch, though close upcurled,
  A baby's hands.

Then, even as warriors grip their brands
  When battle's bolt is hurled,
They close, clenched hard like tightening
  bands.

No rosebuds yet by dawn impearled
  Match, even in loveliest lands,
The sweetest flowers in all the world–
  A baby's hands.

III.

A baby's eyes, ere speech begin
  Ere lips learn words or sighs,
Bless all things bright enough to win
  A baby's eyes.

Love, while the sweet thing laughs and lies,
  And sleep flows out and in,
Lies perfect in them Paradise.

Their glance might cast out pain and sin,
  Their speech make dumb the wise,
By mute glad godhead felt within
  A baby's eyes.

BABYHOOD.

I.

A BABY shines as bright
  If winter or if May be
On eyes that keep in sight
  A baby.

Though dark the skies or gray be,
  It fills our eyes with light,
If midnight or midday be.

Love hails it, day and night,
  The sweetest thing that may be,
Yet cannot praise aright
  A baby.

II.

All heaven, in every baby born,
All absolute of earthly leaven,
Reveals itself, tho' man may scorn
  All heaven.

Yet man might feel all sin forgiven,
All grief appeased, all pain outworn,
By this one revelation given.

Soul, now forgot thy burdens borne:
Heart, be thy joys now seven times seven:
Love shows in light more bright than morn
  All heaven.

III.

What likeness may define, and stay not
  From truth's exactest way,
A baby's beauty ? Love can say not
  What likeness may.

The Mayflower loveliest held in May
  Of all that shine and stay not
Laughs not in rosier disarray.

Sleek satin, swansdown, buds that play not
  As yet with winds that play,
Would fain be matched with this, and may
  not:
  What likeness may ?

IV.

Rose, round whose bed
Dawn's cloudlets close
Earth's brightest-bred
   Rose !

No song, love knows,
May praise the head
Your curtain shows.

Ere sleep has fled,
The whole child glows
One sweet live red
   Rose

FIRST FOOTSTEPS

A LITTLE way, more soft and sweet
Than fields aflower with May,
A babe's feet, venturing, scarce complete
   A little way.

Eyes full of dawning day
Look up for mother's eyes to meet,
   Too blithe for song to say.

Glad as the golden spring to greet
Its first live leaflet's play,
Love, laughing, leads the little feet
   A little way.

A NINTH BIRTHDAY.

FEBRUARY 4, 1883.

I.

THREE times thrice hath winter's rough white
   wing
Crossed and curdled wells and streams with
   ice
Since his birth whose praises love would sing
   Three times thrice.

Earth nor sea bears flower nor pearl of price
Fit to crown the forehead of my king.
Honey meet to please him, balm, nor spice.

Love can think of nought but love to bring
Fit to serve or do him sacrifice
Ere his eyes have looked upon the spring
   Three times thrice.

II.

Three times thrice the world has fallen on
   slumber,
Shone and waned and withered in a trice,
Frost has fettered Thames and Tyne and
   Humber
   Three times thrice,

Fogs have swoln too thick for steel to slice,
Cloud and mud have soiled with grime and
   umber
Earth and heaven, defaced as souls with vice.

Winds have risen to wreck, snows fallen to
   cumber.
Ships and chariots, trapped like rats or mice,
Since my king first smiled, whose years now
   number
   Three times thrice.

III.

Three times thrice, in wine of song full-flow-
   ing,
Pledge, my heart, the child whose eyes
   suffice,
Once beheld, to set thy joy-bells going
   Three times thrice.

Not the lands of palm and date and rice
Glow more bright when summer leaves them
   glowing,
Laugh more light when suns and winds entice.

Noon and eve and midnight and cock-crowing,
Child whose love makes life as paradise,
Love should sound your praise with clarions
   blowing
   Three times thrice.

NOT A CHILD.

I.

' NOT a child : I call myself a boy,'
Says my king, with accent stern yet mild,
Now nine years have brought him change of
   joy ;
      ' Not a child.'

How could reason be so far beguiled,
Err so far from sense's safe employ,
Stray so wide of truth, or run so wild ?

Seeing his face bent over book or toy,
Child I called him, smiling : but he smiled
Back, as one too high for vain annoy—
　　　Not a child.

II.

Not a child? alack the year !
What should ail an undefiled
Heart, that he would fain appear
　　　Not a child?

Men, with years and memories piled
Each on other, far and near,
Fain again would so be styled:

Fain would cast off hope and fear,
Rest, forget, be reconciled:
Why would you so fain be, dear,
　　　Not a child?

III.

Child or boy, my darling, which you will,
Still your praise finds heart and song employ,
Heart and song both yearning toward you still,
　　　Child or boy.

All joys else might sooner pall or cloy
Love than this which inly takes its fill,
Dear, of sight of your more perfect joy.

Nay, be aught you please, let all fulfil
All your pleasure; be your world your toy:
Mild or wild we love you, loud or still,
　　　Child or boy.

――――

TO DORA DORIAN.

CHILD of two strong nations, heir
Born of high-souled hope that smiled
Seeing for each brought forth a fair
　　　Child,

By thy gracious brows, and wild
Golden-clouded heaven of hair,
By thine eyes elate and mild,

Hope would fain take heart to swear
Men should yet be reconciled,
Seeing the sign she bids thee bear,
　　　Child.

THE ROUNDEL.

A ROUNDEL is wrought as a ring or a star-
　　　bright sphere,
With craft of delight and with cunning of
　　　sound unsought,
That the heart of the hearer may smile if to
　　　pleasure his ear
　　　　　A roundel is wrought.

Its jewel of music is carven of all or of
　　　aught—
Love, laughter or mourning—remembrance of
　　　rapture or fear—
That fancy may fashion to hang in the ear of
　　　thought.

As a bird's quick song runs round, and the
　　　hearts in us hear
Pause answer to pause, and again the same
　　　strain caught,
So moves the device whence, round as a pearl
　　　or tear,
　　　　　A roundel is wrought.

――――

AT SEA.

' FAREWELL and adieu ' was the burden pre-
　　　vailing
Long since in the chant of a home-faring
　　　crew;
And the heart in us echoes, with laughing or
　　　wailing,
　　　　　Farewell and adieu.

Each year that we live shall we sing it anew,
With a water untravelled before us for sailing
And a water behind us that wrecks may be-
　　　strew.

The stars of the past and the beacons are
　　　paling,
The heavens and the waters are hoarier of hue;
But the heart in us chants not an all unavail-
　　　ing
　　　　　Farewell and adieu.

――――

WASTED LOVE.

WHAT shall be done for sorrow
　　With love whose race is run ?
Where help is none to borrow,
　　What shall be done ?

In vain his hands have spun
The web, or drawn the furrow:
No rest their toil hath won.

His task is all gone thorough,
And fruit thereof is none:
And who dare say to-morrow
What shall be done?

BEFORE SUNSET.

LOVE'S twilight wanes in heaven above,
On earth ere twilight reigns:
Ere fear may feel the chill thereof,
Love's twilight wanes.

Ere yet the insatiate heart complains
'Too much, and scarce enough,'
The lip so late athirst refrains.

Soft on the neck of either dove
Love's hands let slip the reins:
And while we look for light of love
Love's twilight wanes.

A SINGING LESSON.

FAR-FETCHED and dear-bought, as the prov-
erb rehearses,
Is good, or was held so, for ladies: but
nought
In a song can be good if the turn of the verse
is
Far-fetched and dear-bought.

As the turn of a wave should it sound, and
the thought
Ring smooth, and as light as the spray that
disperses
Be the gleam of the words for the garb thereof wrought.

Let the soul in it shine through the sound as
it pierces
Men's hearts with possession of music unsought.
For the bounties of song are no jealous god's
mercies,
Far-fetched and dear-bought.

FLOWER-PIECES.

I.

LOVE LIES BLEEDING.

LOVE lies bleeding in the bed whereover
Roses lean with smiling mouths or pleading :
Earth lies laughing where the sun's dart clove
her:
Love lies bleeding.

Stately shine his purple plumes, exceeding
Pride of princess: nor shall maid or lover
Find on earth a fairer sign worth heeding.

Yet may love, sore wounded, scarce recover
Strength and spirit again, with life receding:
Hope and joy, wind-winged, about him
hover:
Love lies bleeding.

II.

LOVE IN A MIST.

Light love in a mist, by the midsummer moon
misguided,
Scarce seen in the twilight garden if gloom
insist,
Seems vainly to seek for a star whose gleam
has derided
Light love in a mist.

All day in the sun, when the breezes do all
they list,
His soft blue raiment of cloudlike blossom
abided
Unrent and unwithered of winds and of rays
that kissed.

Blithe-hearted or sad, as the cloud or the sun
subsided,
Love smiled in the flower with a meaning
whereof none wist
Save two that beheld, as a gleam that before
them glided,
Light love in a mist.

THREE FACES.

I.

VENTIMIGLIA.

THE sky and sea glared hard and bright and
blank:
Down the one steep street, with slow steps
firm and free

A tall girl paced, with eyes too proud to thank
    The sky and sea.

One dead flat sapphire, void of wrath or glee,
Through bay on bay shone blind from bank to
    bank
The weary Mediterranean, drear to see.

More deep, more living, shone her eyes that
    drank
The breathless light and shed again on me,
Till pale before their splendor waned and
    shrank
    The sky and sea.

II.

GENOA.

Again the same strange might of eyes, that
    saw
In heaven and earth nought fairer, overcame
My sight with rapture of reiterate awe,
    Again the same.

The self-same pulse of wonder shook like
    flame
The spirit of sense within me: what strange
    law
Had bid this be, for blessing or for blame?

To what veiled end that fate or chance foresaw
Came forth this second sister face, that came
Absolute, perfect, fair, without a flaw,
    Again the same?

III.

VENICE.

OUT of the dark pure twilight, where the
    stream
Flows glimmering, streaked by many a birdlike
    bark
That skims the gloom whence towers and
    bridges gleam
    Out of the dark,

Once more a face no glance might choose
    but mark
Shone pale and bright, with eyes whose deep
    slow beam
Made quick the twilight, lifeless else and
    stark.

The same it seemed, or mystery made it
    seem,

As those before beholden; but St. Mark
Ruled here the ways that showed it like a
    dream
    Out of the dark.

EROS.

I.

EROS, from rest in isles far-famed,
With rising Anthesterion rose,
And all Hellenic heights acclaimed
    Eros.

The sea one pearl, the shore one rose,
All round him all the flower-month flamed
And lightened, laughing off repose.

Earth's heart, sublime and unashamed,
Knew, even perchance as man's heart knows,
The thirst of all men's nature named
    Eros.

II.

Eros, a fire of heart untamed,
A light of spirit in sense that glows,
Flamed heavenward still ere earth defamed
    Eros.

Nor fear nor shame durst curb or close
His golden godhead, marred and maimed,
Fast round with bends that burnt and froze.

Ere evil faith struck blind and lamed
Love, pure as fire or flowers or snows,
Earth hailed as blameless and unblamed
    Eros.

III.

Eros, with shafts by thousands aimed
At laughing lovers round in rows,
Fades from their sight whose tongues pro-
    claimed
    Eros.

But higher than transient shapes or shows
The light of love in life inflamed
Spring toward no goal that these disclose.

Above those heavens which passion claimed
Shines, veiled by change that ebbs and flows,
The soul in all things born or framed.
    Eros.

SORROW.

SORROW, on wing through the world forever,
Here and there for awhile would borrow
Rest, if rest might haply deliver
    Sorrow.

One thought lies close in her heart gnawn
    through
With pain, a weed in a dried up-river,
A rust-red share in an empty furrow.

Hearts that strain at her chain would sever
The link where yesterday frets to-morrow !
All things pass in the world, but never
    Sorrow.

SLEEP.

SLEEP, when a soul that her own clouds cover
Wails that sorrow should always keep
Watch, nor see in the gloom above her
    Sleep.

Down, through darkness naked and steep,
Sinks, and the wings of his comforts cover
Close the soul, though her wouud be deep.

God beloved of us, all men's lover,
All most weary that smile or weep
Feel thee afar or anear them hover,
    Sleep.

ON AN OLD ROUNDEL.

Translated by D. G. Rossetti from the French of Villon.

I.

DEATH, from thy rigor a voice appealed,
And men still hear what the sweet cry saith,
Crying aloud in thine ears fast sealed,
    Death.

As a voice in a vision that vanisheth,
Through the grave's gate barred and the
    portal steeled
The sound of the wail of it travelleth.

Wailing aloud from a heart unhealed,
It woke response of melodious breath
From lips now too by thy kiss congealed,
    Death.

II.

Ages ago, from the lips of a sad glad poet
Whose soul was a wild dove lost in the whirl-
    ing snow,
The soft keen plaint of his pain took voice to
    show it
    Ages ago.

So clear, so deep, the divine drear accents
    flow,
No soul that listens may choose but thrill to
    know it,
Pierced and wrung by the passionate music's
    throe.

For us there murmurs a nearer voice below it,
Known once of ears that never again shall
    know
Nor mute as the mouth which felt death's
    wave o'erflow it
    Ages ago.

A LANDSCAPE BY COURBET.

Low lies the mere beneath the moorside, still
And glad of silence : down the wood sweeps
    clear
To the soft verge where fed with many a rill
    Low lies the mere.

The wind speaks only summer : eye nor ear
Sees aught at all of dark, hears aught of shrill,
From sound or shadow felt or fancied here.

Strange, as we praise the dead man's might
    and skill,
Strange that harsh thoughts should make such
    heavy cheer,
While, clothed with peace by heaven's most
    gentle will,
    Low lies the mere.

A FLOWER-PIECE BY FANTIN.

HEART'S EASE or pansy, pleasure or thought,
Which would the picture give us of those ?
Surely the heart that conceived it sought
    Heart's ease.

Surely by glad and divine degrees
The heart impelling the hand that wrought
Wrought comfort here for a soul's disease.

Deep flowers, with lustre and darkness fraught,
From glass that gleams as the chill still seas
Lean and lend for a heart distraught
    Heart's ease.

A NIGHT-PIECE BY MILLET.

WIND and sea and cloud and cloud-forsaking
Mirth of moonlight where the storm leaves
    free
Heaven awhile, for all the wrath of waking
    Wind and sea.

Bright with glad mad rapture, fierce with glee,
Laughs the moon, born on past cloud's o'er-
    taking
Fast, it seems, as wind or sail can flee.

One blown sail beneath her, hardly making
Forth, wild-winged for harborage yet to be
Strives and leaps and pants beneath the break-
    ing
    Wind and sea.

'MARZO PAZZO.'

MAD March, with the wind in his wings wide-
    spread,
Leaps from heaven, and the deep dawn's arch
Hails re-risen again from the dead
    Mad March.

Soft small flames on rowan and larch
Break forth as laughter on lips that said
Naught till the pulse in them beat love's
    march.

But the heartbeat now in the lips rose-red
Speaks life to the world, and the winds that
    parch
Bring April forth as a bride to wed
    Mad March.

DEAD LOVE.

DEAD love, by treason slain, lies stark,
White as a dead stark-stricken dove :
None that pass by him pause to mark
    Dead love.

His heart, that strained and yearned and
    strove
As toward the sundawn strives the lark,
Is cold as all the old joy thereof.

Dead men, re-risen from dust, may hark
When rings the trumpet blown above :
It will not raise from out the dark
    Dead love.

DISCORD.

UNRECONCILED by life's fleet years, that fled
With changeful clang of pinions wide and wild,
Though two great spirits had lived, and hence
    had sped
    Unreconciled ;

Though time and change, harsh time's impe-
    rious child,
That wed strange hands together, might not
    wed
High hearts by hope's misprision once be-
    guiled;

Faith, by the ligh from either's memory shed,
Sees, radiant as their ends were undefiled,
One goal for each—not twain among the dead
    Unreconciled.

CONCORD.

RECONCILED by death's mild hand, that giving
Peace gives wisdom, not more strong than
    mild,
Love beholds them, each without misgiving
    Reconciled.

Each on earth alike of earth reviled,
Hated, feared, derided, and forgiving,
Each alike had heaven at heart, and smiled.

Both bright names, clothed round with man's
    thanksgiving ;
Shine, twin stars above the storm-drifts piled,
Dead and deathless, whom we saw not living
    Reconciled.

MOURNING.

ALAS my brother ! the cry of the mourners of
    old
    That cried on each other

All crying aloud on the dead as the death-
note rolled,
 Alas my brother!

As flashes of dawn that mists from an east
 wind smother
  With fold upon fold,
The past years gleam that linked us one with
 another.

Time sunders hearts as of brethren whose
 eyes behold
  No more their mother :
But a cry sounds yet from the shrine whose
 fires wax cold,
  Alas my brother!

APEROTOS EROS.

STRONG as death, and cruel as the grave,
Clothed with cloud and tempest's blackening
 breath,
Known of death's dread self, whom none
 outbrave,
  Strong as death,

Love, brow-bound with anguish for a wreath,
Fierce with pain, a tyrant-hearted slave,
Burns above a world that groans beneath.

Hath not pity power on thee to save,
Love? hath power no pity? Nought he saith,
Answering : blind he walks as wind or wave,
  Strong as death.

TO CATULLUS.

MY brother, my Valerius, dearest head
Of all whose crowning bay-leaves crown their
 mother,
Rome, in the notes first heard of thine I read
 My brother.

No dust that death or time can strew may
 smother
Love and the sense of kinship inly bred
From loves and hates at one with one another.

To thee was Cæsar's self nor dear nor dread,
Song and the sea were sweeter each than
 other :
How should I living fear to call thee dead
 My brother?

'INSULARUM OCELLE.'

SARK, fairer than aught in the world than the
 lit skies cover,
Laughs inly behind her cliffs, and the seafarers mark
As a shrine where the sunlight serves, though
 the blown clouds hover,
  Sark.

We mourn, for love of a song that outsang
 the lark,
That nought so lovely beholden of Sirmio's
 lover
Made glad in Propontis the flight of his
 Pontic bark.

Here earth lies lordly, triumphal as heaven is
 above her,
And splendid and strange as the sea that
 upbears as an ark,
As a sign for the rapture of storm-spent eyes
 to discover,
  Sark.

IN SARK.

ABREAST and ahead of the sea is a crag's front
 cloven asunder
With strong sea-breach and with wasting of
 winds whence terror is shed
As a shadow of death from the wings of the
 darkness on waters that thunder
  Abreast and ahead.

At its edge is a sepulchre hollowed and hewn
 for a lone man's bed,
Propped open with rock and agape on the
 sky and the sea thereunder,
But roofed and walled in well from the wrath
 of them slept its dead.

Here might not a man drink rapture of rest,
 or delight above wonder,
Beholding, a soul disembodied, the days
 and the nights that fled,
With splendor and sound of the tempest
 around and above him and under,
  Abreast and ahead?

IN GUERNSEY.

I.

THE heavenly bay, ringed round with cliffs
 and moors,
Storm-stained ravines, and crags that lawns
 inlay,

Soothes as with love the rocks whose guard
        secures
    The heavenly bay.

O friend, shall time take ever this away,
This blessing given of beauty that endures,
This glory shown us, not to pass but stay?

Though sight be changed for memory, love
        ensures
What memory, changed by love to sight,
        would say—
The word that seals forever mine and yours
    The heavenly bay.

II.

My mother sea, my fostress, what new strand,
What new delight of waters, may this be,
The fairest found since time's first breezes
        fanned
    My mother sea?

Once more I give me body and soul to thee,
Who hast my soul forever : cliff and sand
Recede, and heart to heart once more are we.

My heart springs first and plunges, ere my
        hand
Strike out from shore : more close it brings
        to me,
More near and dear than seems my father-
        land,
    My mother sea.

III.

Across and along, as the bay's breadth
        opens, and o'er us
Wild autumn exults in the wind, swift rapt-
        ure and strong
Impels us, and broader the wide waves
        brighten before us
    Across and along.

The whole world's heart is uplifted, and knows
        not wrong ;
The whole world's life is a chant to the sea-
        tide's chorus ;
Are we not as waves of the water, as notes
        of the song?

Like children unworn of the passions and
        toils that wore us,
We breast for a season the breadth of the
        seas that throng,
Rejoicing as they, to be borne as of old they
        bore us
    Across and along.

IV.

On Dante's track by some funereal spell
Drawn down through desperate ways that
        lead not back
We seem to move, bound forth past flood and
        fell
    On Dante's track.

The gray path ends : the gaunt rocks gape:
        the black
Deep hollow tortuous night, a soundless shell,
Glares darkness: are the fires of old grown
        slack ?

Nay, then, what flames are these that leap
        and swell
As 'twere to show, where earth's foundations
        crack,
The secrets of the sepulchres of hell
    On Dante's track ?

V.

By mere men's hands the flame was lit, we
        know,
From heaps of dry waste whin and casual
        brands:
Yet, knowing, we scarce believe it kindled
        so
    By mere men's hands.

Above, around, high-vaulted hell expands,
Steep, dense, a labyrinth walled and roofed
        with woe
Whose mysteries even itself not understands.

The scorn in Farinata's eyes aglow
Seems visible in this flame : there Geryon
        stands:
No stage of earth's is here, set forth to show
    By mere men's hands.

VI.

Night, in utmost noon forlorn and strong, with
        heart athirst and fasting,
Hungers here, barred up forever, whence as
        one whom dreams affright
Day recoils before the low-browed lintel threat-
        ening doom and casting
    Night.

All the reefs and islands, all the lawns and
        highlands, clothed with light,
Laugh for love's sake in their sleep outside:
        but here the night speaks, blasting
Day with silent speech and scorn of all things
        known from depth to height

Lower than dive the thoughts of spirit-
stricken fear in souls forecasting
Hell, the deep void seems to yawn fear's
reach, and higher than sight
Rise the walls and roofs that compass it
about with everlasting
Night.

VII.

The house accurst, with cursing sealed and
signed,
Heeds not what storms about it burn and
burst:
Not fear more fearful than its own may find
The house accurst.

Barren as crime, anhungered and athirst,
Blank miles of moor sweep inland, sere and
blind,
Where summer's best rebukes not winter's
worst.

The low bleak tower with nought save wastes
behind
Stares down the abyss whereon chance reared
and nursed

This type and likeness of the accurst man's
mind,
The house accurst.

VIII.

Beloved and blest, lit warm with love and
fame,
The house that had the light of the earth for
guest
Hears for his name's sake all men hail its
name
Beloved and blest.

This eyrie was the homeless eagle's nest
When storm laid waste his eyrie: hence he
came
Again when storm smote sore his mother's
breast.

Bow down men bade us, or be clothed with
blame
And mocked for madness: worst, they sware,
was best
But grief shone here, while joy was one with
shame,
Beloved and blest.

C.

ENVOI.

FLY, white butterflies, out to sea,
Frail pale wings for the winds to try,
Small white wings that we scarce can see,
Fly.

Here and there may a chance-caught
eye

Note in a score of you twain or three
Brighter or darker of mould or dye.

Some fly light as a laugh of glee,
Some fly soft as a low long sigh:
All to the haven where each would be,
Fly.

ASTROPHEL.

AFTER READING SIR PHILIP SIDNEY'S ARCADIA IN THE GARDEN OF AN OLD ENGLISH MANOR
HOUSE.

I.

A STAR in the silence that follows
The song of the death of the sun
Speaks music in heaven, and the hollows
And heights of the world are as one;
One lyre that outsings and outlightens
The rapture of sunset, and thrills
Mute night till the sense of it brightens
The soul that it fills.

The flowers of the sun that is sunken
Hang heavy of heart as of head;
The bees that have eaten and drunken
The soul of their sweetness are fled;
But a sunflower of song, on whose
honey
My spirit has fed as a bee,
Makes sunnier than morning was sunny
The twilight for me.

The letters and lines on the pages
　　That sundered mine eyes and the flowers
Wax faint as the shadows of ages
　　That sunder their season and ours;
As the ghosts of the centuries that sever
　　A season of colourless time
From the days whose remembrance is ever,
　　　As they were, sublime.

The season that bred and that cherished
　　The soul that I commune with yet,
Had it utterly withered and perished
　　To rise not again as it set,
Shame were it that Englishmen living
　　Should read as their forefathers read
The books of the praise and thanksgiving
　　　Of Englishmen dead.

O light of the land that adored thee
　　And kindled thy soul with her breath,
Whose life, such as fate would afford thee,
　　Was lovelier than aught but thy death,
By what name, could thy lovers but know it,
　　Might love of thee hail thee afar,
Philisides, Astrophel, poet
　　　Whose love was thy star?

A star in the moondawn of Maytime,
　　A star in the cloudland of change;
Too splendid and sad for the daytime
　　To cheer or eclipse or estrange;
Too sweet for tradition or vision
　　To see but through shadows of tears
Rise deathless across the division
　　　Of measureless years.

The twilight may deepen and harden
　　As nightward the stream of it runs
Till starshine transfigure a garden
　　Whose radiance responds to the sun's:
The light of the love of thee darkens
　　The lights that arise and that set:
The love that forgets thee not hearkens
　　　If England forget.

II.

Bright and brief in the sight of grief and love
　　the light of thy lifetime shone,
Seen and felt by the gifts it dealt, the grace it
　　gave, and again was gone:
Ay, but now it is death, not thou, whom time
　　has conquered as years pass on.

Ay, not yet may the land forget that bore and
　　loved thee and praised and wept,
Sidney, lord of the stainless sword, the name
　　of names that her heart's love kept
Fast as thine did her own, a sign to light thy
　　life till it sank and slept.

Bright as then for the souls of men thy brave
　　Arcadia resounds and shines,
Lit with love that beholds above all joys and
　　sorrows the steadfast signs,
Faith, a splendour that hope makes tender,
　　and truth, whose presage the soul divines.

All the glory that girds the story of all thy life
　　as with sunlight round,
All the spell that on all souls fell who saw
　　thy spirit, and held them bound,
Lives for all that have heard the call and
　　cadence yet of its music sound.

Music bright as the soul of light, for wings an
　　eagle, for notes a dove,
Leaps and shines from the lustrous lines
　　wherethrough thy soul from afar above
Shone and sang till the darkness rang with
　　light whose fire is the fount of love.

Love that led thee alive, and fed thy soul with
　　sorrows and joys and fears,
Love that sped thee, alive and dead, to fame's
　　fair goal with thy peerless peers,
Feeds the flame of thy quenchless name with
　　light that lightens the rayless years.

Dark as sorrow though night and morrow
　　may lower with presage of clouded
　　fame,
How may she that of old bare thee, may Sid-
　　ney's England, be brought to shame?
How should this be, while England is? What
　　need of answer beyond thy name?

III.

From the love that transfigures thy glory,
　　From the light of the dawn of thy death,
The life of thy song and thy story
　　Took subtler and fierier breath.
And we, though the day and the morrow
　　Set fear and thanksgiving at strife,
Hail yet in the star of thy sorrow
　　　The sun of thy life.

Shame and fear may beset men here, and bid
    thanksgiving and pride be dumb:
Faith, discrowned of her praise, and wound
    about with toils till her life wax
    numb,
Scarce may see if the sundawn be, if darkness
    die not and dayrise come.

But England, enmeshed and benetted
    With spiritless villainies round,
With counsels of cowardice fretted,
    With trammels of treason enwound,
Is yet, though the season be other
Than wept and rejoiced over thee,
Thine England, thy lover, thy mother,
    Sublime as the sea.

Hers wast thou: if her face be now less bright,
    or seem for an hour less brave,
Let but thine on her darkness shine, thy
    saviour spirit revive and save,
Time shall see, as the shadows flee, her shame
    entombed in a shameful grave.

If death and not life were the portal
    That opens on life at the last,
If the spirit of Sidney were mortal
    And the past of it utterly past,
Fear stronger than honour was ever,
    Forgetfulness mightier than fame,
Faith knows not if England should never
    Subside into shame.

Yea, but yet is thy sun not set, thy sunbright
    spirit of trust withdrawn:
England's love of thee burns above all hopes
    that darken or fears that fawn:
Hers thou art: and the faithful heart that
    hopes begets upon darkness dawn.

The sunset that sunrise will follow
    Is less than the dream of a dream:
The starshine on height and on hollow
    Sheds promise that dawn shall redeem:
The night, if the daytime would hide it,
    Shows lovelier, aflame and afar,
Thy soul and thy Stella's beside it,
    A star by a star.

A NYMPHOLEPT.

SUMMER, and noon, and a splendour of silence,
    felt,
    Seen, and heard of the spirit within the
    sense.
Soft through the frondage the shades of the
    sunbeams melt,
    Sharp through the foliage the shafts of
    them, keen and dense,
    Cleave, as discharged from the string of
    the God's bow, tense
As a war-steed's girth, and bright as a war-
    rior's belt.
Ah, why should an hour that is heaven
    for an hour pass hence?

I dare not sleep for delight of the perfect hour,
    Lest God be wroth that his gift should be
    scorned of man.
The face of the warm bright world is the face
    of a flower,
    The word of the wind and the leaves that
    the light winds fan
    As the word that quickened at first into
    flame, and ran,

Creative and subtle and fierce with invasive
    power,
    Through darkness and cloud, from the
    breath of the one God, Pan.

The perfume of earth possessed by the sun
    pervades
    The chaster air that he soothes but with
    sense of sleep.
Soft, imminent, strong as desire that prevails
    and fades,
    The passing noon that beholds not a
    cloudlet weep
    Imbues and impregnates life with delight
    more deep
Than dawn or sunset or moonrise on lawns
    or glades
    Can shed from the skies that receive it and
    may not keep.

The skies may hold not the splendour of sun-
    down fast;
    It wanes into twilight as dawn dies down
    into day.

And the moon, triumphant when twilight is
    overpast,
  Takes pride but awhile in the hours of her
    stately sway.
But the might of the noon, though the
    light of it pass away,
Leaves earth fulfilled of desires and of dreams
    that last;
  But if any there be that hath sense of
    them none can say

For if any there be that hath sight of them,
    sense, or trust
  Made strong by the might of a vision, the
    strength of a dream,
His lips shall straiten and close as a dead
    man's must,
  His heart shall be sealed as the voice of a
    frost-bound stream.
For the deep mid mystery of light and of
    heat that seem
To clasp and pierce dark earth, and enkindle
    dust,
  Shall a man's faith say what it is? or a
    man's guess deem?

Sleep lies not heavier on eyes that have
    watched all night
  Than hangs the heat of the noon on the
    hills and trees.
Why now should the haze not open, and yield
    to sight
  A fairer secret than hope or than slumber
    sees?
I seek not heaven with submission of lips
    and knees,
With worship and prayer for a sign till it leap
    to light:
  I gaze on the gods about me, and call on
    these.

I call on the gods hard by, the divine dim
    powers
  Whose likeness is here at hand, in the
    breathless air,
In the pulseless peace of the fervid and silent
    flowers,
  In the faint sweet speech of the waters
    that whisper there.
Ah, what should darkness do in a world
    so fair?
The bent-grass heaves not, the couch-grass
    quails not or cowers;
  The wind's kiss frets not the rowan's or
    aspen's hair.

But the silence trembles with passion of sound
    suppressed,
  And the twilight quivers and yearns to the
    sunward, wrung
With love as with pain; and the wide wood's
    motionless breast
  Is thrilled with a dumb desire that would
    fain find tongue
And palpitates, tongueless as she whom
    a man-snake stung,
Whose heart now heaves in the nightingale,
    never at rest
  Nor satiated ever with song till her last be
    sung.

Is it rapture or terror that circles me round,
    and invades
  Each vein of my life with hope—if it be
    not fear?
Each pulse that awakens my blood into rap-
    ture fades,
  Each pulse that subsides into dread of a
    strange thing near
  Requickens with sense of a terror less
    dread than dear.
Is peace not one with light in the deep green
    glades
  Where summer at noonday slumbers?
    Is peace not here?

The tall thin stems of the firs, and the roof
    sublime
  That screens from the sun the floor of the
    steep still wood,
Deep, silent, splendid, and perfect and calm
    as time,
  Stand fast as ever in sight of the night
    they stood,
  When night gave all that moonlight and
    dewfall could.
The dense ferns deepen, the moss glows warm
    as the thyme:
  The wild heath quivers about me: the
    world is good.

Is it Pan's breath, fierce in the tremulous
    maidenhair,
  That bids fear creep as a snake through
    the woodlands, felt
In the leaves that it stirs not yet, in the mute
    bright air,
  In the stress of the uns? For here has
    the great God dwelt:

For hence were the shafts of his love or
his anger dealt.
For here has his wrath been fierce as his love
was fair,
When each was as fire to the darkness its
breath bade melt.

Is it love, is it dread, that enkindles the trem-
bling noon,
That yearns, reluctant in rapture that
fear has fed,
As man for woman, as woman for man?
Full soon,
If I live, and the life that may look on him
drop not dead,
Shall the ear that hears not a leaf quake
hear his tread,
The sense that knows not the sound of the
deep day's tune
Receive the God, be it love that he brings
or dread.

The naked noon is upon me: the fierce dumb
spell,
The fearful charm of the strong sun's
imminent might,
Unmerciful, steadfast, deeper than seas that
swell,
Pervades, invades, appals me with loveless light,
With harsher awe than breathes in the
breath of night.
Have mercy, God who art all! For I know
thee well,
How sharp is thine eye to lighten, thine
hand to smite.

The whole wood feels thee, the whole air fears
thee: but fear
So deep, so dim, so sacred, is wellnigh
sweet.
For the light that hangs and broods on the
woodlands here,
Intense, invasive, intolerant, imperious,
and meet
To lighten the works of thine hands and
the ways of thy feet,
Is hot with the fire of the breath of thy life,
and dear
As hope that shrivels or shrinks not for
frost or heat.

Thee, thee the supreme dim godhead, approved afar,

Perceived of the soul and conceived of the
sense of man,
We scarce dare love, and we dare not fear:
the star
We call the sun, that lit us when life
began
To brood on the world that is thine by
his grace for a span,
Conceals and reveals in the semblance of
things that are
Thine imminent presence, the pulse of thy
heart's life, Pan.

The fierce mid noon that awakens and warms
the snake
Conceals thy mercy, reveals thy wrath:
and again
The dew-bright hour that assuages the twilight brake
Conceals thy wrath and reveals thy mercy:
then
Thou art fearful only for evil souls of
men
That feel with nightfall the serpent within
them wake,
And hate the holy darkness on glade and
glen.

Yea, then we know not and dream not if ill
things be,
Or if aught of the work of the wrong of
the world be thine.
We hear not the footfall of terror that treads
the sea,
We hear not the moan of winds that assail
the pine:
We see not if shipwreck reign in the
storm's dim shrine;
If death do service and doom bear witness
to thee
We see not,—know not if blood for thy
lips be wine.

But in all things evil and fearful that fear
may scan,
As in all things good, as in all things
fair that fall,
We know thee present and latent, the lord
of man;
In the murmuring of doves, in the clam-
ouring of winds that call
And wolves that howl for their prey; in
the midnight's pall,

38

In the naked and nymph-like feet of the
  dawn, O Pan,
  And in each life living, O thou the God who
  art all.

Smiling and singing, wailing and wringing
  of hands,
  Laughing and weeping, watching and sleeping, still
Proclaim but and prove but thee, as the
  shifted sands
  Speak forth and show but the strength
  of the sea's wild will
  That sifts and grinds them as grain in the
  storm-wind's mill.
In thee is the doom that falls and the doom
  that stands:
  The tempests utter thy word, and the
  stars fulfil.

Where Etna shudders with passion and pain
  volcanic
  That rend her heart as with anguish that
  rends a man's,
Where Typho labours, and finds not his thews
  Titanic,
  In breathless torment that ever the flame's
  breath fans,
  Men felt and feared thee of old, whose
  pastoral clans
Were given to the charge of thy keeping; and
  soundless panic
  Held fast the woodland whose depths and
  whose heights were Pan's.

And here, though fear be less than delight,
  and awe
  Be one with desire and with worship of
  earth and thee,
So mild seems now thy secret and speechless
  law,
  So fair and fearless and faithful and godlike she,
  So soft the spell of thy whisper on stream
  and sea,
Yet man should fear lest he see what of old
  men saw
  And withered: yet shall I quail if thy
  breath smite me.

Lord God of life and of light and of all things
  fair,
  Lord God of ravin and ruin and all things
  dim,

Death seals up life, and darkens the sunbright
  air,
  And the stars that watch blind earth in
  the deep night swim
  Laugh, saying, 'What God is your God,
  that ye call on him?
What is man, that the God who is guide of
  our way should care
  If day for a man be golden, or night be
  grim?'

But thou, dost thou hear? Stars too but
  abide for a span,
  Gods too but endure for a season; but
  thou, if thou be
God, more than shadows conceived and
  adored of man,
  Kind Gods and fierce, that bound him or
  made him free,
  The skies that scorn us are less in thy sight
  than we,
Whose souls have strength to conceive and
  perceive thee, Pan,
  With sense more subtle than senses that
  hear and see.

Yet may not it say, though it seek thee and
  think to find
  One soul of sense in the fire and the frost-
  bound clod,
What heart is this, what spirit alive or blind,
  That moves thee: only we know that the
  ways we trod
  We tread, with hands unguided, with feet
  unshod,
With eyes unlightened; and yet, if with steadfast mind,
  Perchance may we find thee and know
  thee at last for God.

Yet then should God be dark as the dawn
  is bright,
  And bright as the night is dark on the
  world—no more.
Light slays not darkness, and darkness absorbs not light;
  And the labour of evil and good from
  the years of yore
  Is even as the labour of waves on a sunless shore.
And he who is first and last, who is depth and
  height,
  Keeps silence now, as the sun when the
  woods wax hoar.

The dark dumb godhead innate in the fair
world's life
    Imbues the rapture of dawn and of noon
with dread,
Infects the peace of the star-shod night with
strife,
    Informs with terror the sorrow that guards
the dead.
    No service of bended knee or of humbled
head
May soothe or subdue the God who has
change to wife:
    And life with death is as morning with
evening wed.

And yet, if the light and the life in the light
that here
    Seem soft and splendid and fervid as sleep
may seem
Be more than the shine of a smile or the flash
of a tear,
    Sleep, change, and death are less than a
spell-struck dream,
    And fear than the fall of a leaf on a starlit
stream.
And yet, if the hope that hath said it absorb
not fear,
    What helps it man that the stars and the
waters gleam?

What helps it man, that the noon be indeed
intense,
    The night be indeed worth worship? Fear
and pain
Were lords and masters yet of the secret sense,
    Which now dares deem not that light is as
darkness, fain
    Though dark dreams be to declare it, cry-
ing in vain.
For whence, thou God of the light and the
darkness, whence
    Dawns now this vision that bids not the
sunbeams wane?

What light, what shadow, diviner than dawn
or night,
    Draws near, makes pause, and again—
or I dream—draws near?
More soft than shadow, more strong than
the strong sun's light,
    More pure than moonbeams—yea, but the
rays run sheer
    As fire from the sun through the dusk
of the pinewood, clear

And constant; yea, but the shadow itself is
bright
    That the light clothes round with love that
is one with fear.

Above and behind it the noon and the woodland lie,
    Terrible, radiant with mystery, superb and
subdued,
Triumphant in silence; and hardly the sacred
sky
    Seems free from the tyrannous weight of
the dumb fierce mood
    Which rules as with fire and invasion of
beams that brood
The breathless rapture of earth till its hour
pass by
    And leave her spirit released and her peace
renewed.

I sleep not: never in sleep has a man beholden
    This. From the shadow that trembles
and yearns with light
Suppressed and elate and reluctant—obscure
and golden
    As water kindled with presage of dawn or
night—
    A form, a face, a wonder to sense and
sight,
Grows great as the moon through the month;
and her eyes embolden
    Fear, till it change to desire, and desire to
delight.

I sleep not: sleep would die of a dream so
strange;
    A dream so sweet would die as a rainbow
dies,
As a sunbow laughs and is lost on the waves
that range
    And reck not of light that flickers or spray
that flies.
    But the sun withdraws not, the woodland
shrinks not or sighs,
No sweet thing sickens with sense or with
fear of change;
    Light wounds not, darkness blinds not,
my steadfast eyes.

Only the soul in my sense that receives the
soul
    Whence now my spirit is kindled with
breathless bliss

Knows well if the light that wounds it with
　　love makes whole,
　　If hopes that carol be louder than fears
　　　　that hiss,
　　If truth be spoken of flowers and of waves
　　　　that kiss,
Of clouds and stars that contend for a sun-
　　bright goal.
　　And yet may I dream that I dream not
　　　　indeed of this?

An earth-born dreamer, constrained by the
　　bonds of birth,
　　Held fast by the flesh, compelled by his
　　　　veins that beat
And kindle to rapture or wrath, to desire or
　　to mirth,
　　May hear not surely the fall of immortal
　　　　feet,
　　May feel not surely if heaven upon earth
　　　　be sweet;
And here is my sense fulfilled of the joys of
　　earth,
　　Light, silence, bloom, shade, murmur of
　　　　leaves that meet.

Bloom, fervour, and perfume of grasses and
　　flowers aglow,
　　Breathe and brighten about me: the dark-
　　　　ness gleams,
The sweet light shivers and laughs on the
　　slopes below,
　　Made soft by leaves that lighten and
　　　　change like dreams;
　　The silence thrills with the whisper of
　　　　secret streams
That well from the heart of the woodland:
　　these I know:
　　Earth bore them, heaven sustained them
　　　　with showers and beams.

I lean my face to the heather, and drink the
　　sun
　　Whose flame-lit odour satiates the flowers:
　　　　mine eyes
Close, and the goal of delight and of life is
　　one:
　　No more I crave of earth or her kindred
　　　　skies.

No more? But the joy that springs from
　　them smiles and flies:
The sweet work wrought of them surely, the
　　good work done,
　　If the mind and the face of the season be
　　　　loveless, dies.

Thee, therefore, thee would I come to, cleave
　　to, cling,
　　If haply thy heart be kind and thy gifts
　　　　be good,
Unknown sweet spirit, whose vesture is soft
　　in spring,
　　In summer splendid, in autumn pale as
　　　　the wood
　　That shudders and wanes and shrinks as
　　　　a shamed thing should,
In winter bright as the mail of a war-worn
　　king
　　Who stands where foes fled far from the
　　　　face of him stood.

My spirit or thine is it, breath of thy life or
　　of mine,
　　Which fills my sense with a rapture that
　　　　casts out fear?
Pan's dim frown wanes, and his wild eyes
　　brighten as thine,
　　Transformed as night or as day by the
　　　　kindling year.
　　Earth-born, or mine eye were withered
　　　　that sees, mine ear
That hears were stricken to death by the
　　sense divine,
　　Earth-born I know thee: but heaven is
　　　　about me here.

The terror that whispers in darkness and
　　flames in light,
　　The doubt that speaks in the silence of
　　　　earth and sea,
The sense, more fearful at noon than in mid-
　　most night,
　　Of wrath scarce hushed and of imminent
　　　　ill to be,
　　Where are they? Heaven is as earth,
　　　　and as heaven to me
Earth: for the shadows that sundered them
　　here take flight;
　　And nought is all, as am I, but a dream
　　　　of thee.

ON THE SOUTH COAST.

To Theodore Watts.

Hills and valleys where April rallies his
    radiant squadron of flowers and birds,
Steep strange beaches and lustrous reaches
    of fluctuant sea that the land engirds,
Fields and downs that the sunrise crowns
    with life diviner than lives in words,

Day by day of resurgent May salute the sun
    with sublime acclaim,
Change and brighten with hours that lighten
    and darken, girdled with cloud or flame;
Earth's fair face in alternate grace beams,
    blooms, and lowers, and is yet the same.

Twice each day the divine sea's play makes
    glad with glory that comes and goes
Field and street that her waves keep sweet,
    when past the bounds of their old repose,
Fast and fierce in renewed reverse, the foam-
    flecked estuary ebbs and flows.

Broad and bold through the stays of old staked
    fast with trunks of the wildwood tree,
Up from shoreward, impelled far forward, by
    marsh and meadow, by lawn and lea,
Inland still at her own wild will swells, rolls,
    and revels the surging sea.

Strong as time, and as faith sublime,—clothed
    round with shadows of hopes and fears,
Nights and morrows, and joys and sorrows,
    alive with passion of prayers and tears,—
Stands the shrine that has seen decline eight
    hundred waxing and waning years.

Tower set square to the storms of air and
    change of season that glooms and glows,
Wall and roof of it tempest-proof, and equal
    ever to suns and snows,
Bright with riches of radiant niches and pil-
    lars smooth as a straight stem grows.

Aisle and nave that the whelming wave of
    time has whelmed not or touched or
    neared,
Arch and vault without stain or fault, by
    hands of craftsmen we know not reared,
Time beheld them, and time was quelled;
    and change passed by them as one that
    feared.

Time that flies as a dream, and dies as dreams
    that die with the sleep they feed,
Here alone in a garb of stone incarnate stands
    as a god indeed,
Stern and fair, and of strength to bear all
    burdens mortal to man's frail seed.

Men and years are as leaves or tears that
    storm or sorrow is fain to shed:
These go by as the winds that sigh, and none
    takes note of them quick or dead:
Time, whose breath is their birth and death,
    folds here his pinions, and bows his head.

Still the sun that beheld begun the work
    wrought here of unwearied hands
Sees, as then, though the Red King's men
    held ruthless rule over lawless lands,
Stand their massive design, impassive, pure
    and proud as a virgin stands.

Statelier still as the years fulfil their count,
    subserving her sacred state,
Grows the hoary grey church whose story
    silence utters and age makes great:
Statelier seems it than shines in dreams the
    face unveiled of unvanquished fate.

Fate, more high than the star-shown sky,
    more deep than waters unsounded, shines
Keen and far as the final star on souls that
    seek not for charms or signs;
Yet more bright is the love-shown light of
    men's hands lighted in songs or shrines.

Love and trust that the grave's deep dust can
    soil not, neither may fear put out,
Witness yet that their record set stands fast,
    though years be as hosts in rout,
Spent and slain; but the signs remain that
    beat back darkness and cast forth doubt.

Men that wrought by the grace of thought
    and toil things goodlier than praise dare
    trace,
Fair as all that the world may call most fair,
    save only the sea's own face,
Shrines or songs that the world's change
    wrongs not, live by grace of their own
    gift's grace.

Dead, their names that the night reclaims—
    alive, their works that the day relumes—
Sink and stand, as in stone and sand engraven:
    none may behold their tombs:
Nights and days shall record their praise
    while here this flower of their grafting
    blooms.

Flower more fair than the sun-thrilled air
    bids laugh and lighten and wax and rise,
Fruit more bright than the fervent light sus-
    tains with strength from the kindled skies,
Flower and fruit that the deathless root of
    man's love rears though the man's name
    dies.

Stately stands it, the work of hands unknown
    of: statelier, afar and near,
Rise around it the heights that bound our
    landward gaze from the seaboard here;
Downs that swerve and aspire, in curve and
    change of heights that the dawn holds
    dear.

Dawn falls fair on the grey walls there con-
    fronting dawn, on the low green lea,
Lone and sweet as for fairies' feet held sacred,
    silent and strange and free,
Wild and wet with its rills; but yet more fair
    falls dawn on the fairer sea.

Eastward, round by the high green bound of
    hills that fold the remote fields in,
Strive and shine on the low sea-line fleet
    waves and beams when the days begin;
Westward glow, when the days burn low, the
    sun that yields and the stars that win.

Rose-red eve on the seas that heave sinks
    fair as dawn when the first ray peers;
Winds are glancing from sunbright Lancing
    to Shoreham, crowned with the grace of
    years;
Shoreham, clad with the sunset, glad and
    grave with glory that death reveres.

Death, more proud than the kings' heads
    bowed before him, stronger than all
    things, bows
Here his head: as if death were dead, and
    kingship plucked from his crownless
    brows,
Life hath here such a face of cheer as change
    appals not and time avows.

Skies fulfilled with the sundown, stilled and
    splendid, spread as a flower that spreads,
Pave with rarer device and fairer than
    heaven's the luminous oyster-beds,
Grass-embanked, and in square plots ranked,
    inlaid with gems that the sundown sheds.

Squares more bright and with lovelier light
    than heaven that kindled it shines with
    shine
Warm and soft as the dome aloft, but heaven-
    lier yet than the sun's own shrine:
Heaven is high, but the water-sky lit here
    seems deeper and more divine.

Flowers on flowers, that the whole world's
    bowers may show not, here may the sun-
    set show,
Lightly graven in the waters paven with
    ghostly gold by the clouds aglow:
Bright as love is the vault above, but love-
    lier lightens the wave below.

Rosy grey, or as fiery spray full-plumed, or
    greener than emerald, gleams
Plot by plot as the skies allot for each its
    glory, divine as dreams
Lit with fire of appeased desire which sounds
    the secret of all that seems;

Dreams that show what we fain would know,
    and know not save by the grace of
    sleep,
Sleep whose hands have removed the bands
    that eyes long waking and fain to weep
Feel fast bound on them—light around them
    strange, and darkness above them steep.

Yet no vision that heals division of love from
    love, and renews awhile
Life and breath in the lips where death has
    quenched the spirit of speech and smile,
Shews on earth, or in heaven's mid mirth,
    where no fears enter or doubts defile,

Aught more fair than the radiant air and
    water here by the twilight wed,
Here made one by the waning sun whose last
    love quickens to rosebright red
Half the crown of the soft high down that
    rears to northward its wood-girt head.

There, when day is at height of sway, men's
    eyes who stand, as we oft have stood,

High where towers with its world of flowers
the golden spinny that flanks the
wood,
See before and around them shore and seaboard glad as their gifts are good.

Higher and higher to the north aspire the
green smooth-swelling unending downs;
East and west on the brave earth's breast
glow girdle-jewels of gleaming towns;
Southward shining, the lands declining subside in peace that the sea's light
crowns.

Westward wide in its fruitful pride the plain
lies lordly with plenteous grace;
Fair as dawn's when the fields and lawns
desire her glitters the glad land's face:
Eastward yet is the sole sign set of elder days
and a lordlier race.

Down beneath us afar, where seethe in wilder
weather the tides aflow,
Hurled up hither and drawn down thither in
quest of rest that they may not know,
Still as dew on a flower the blue broad stream
now sleeps in the fields below.

Mild and bland in the fair green land it smiles,
and takes to its heart the sky;
Scarce the meads and the fens, the reeds and
grasses, still as they stand or lie,
Wear the palm of a statelier calm than rests
on waters that pass them by.

Yet shall these, when the winds and seas of
equal days and coequal nights
Rage, rejoice, and uplift a voice whose sound
is even as a sword that smites,
Felt and heard as a doomsman's word from
seaward reaches to landward heights,

Lift their heart up, and take their part of
triumph, swollen and strong with rage,
Rage elate with desire and great with pride
that tempest and storm assuage;
So their chime in the ear of time has rung
from age to rekindled age.

Fair and dear is the land's face here, and fair
man's work as a man's may be:
Dear and fair as the sunbright air is here the
record that speaks him free;
Free by birth of a sacred earth, and regent
ever of all the sea.

AN AUTUMN VISION.

OCTOBER 31, 1889.

Ζεφύρου γίγαντος αὔρᾳ.

I.

Is it Midsummer here in the heavens that
illumine October on earth?
Can the year, when his heart is fulfilled with
desire of the days of his mirth,
Redeem them, recall, or remember?
For a memory recalling the rapture of earth,
and redeeming the sky,
Shines down from the heights to the depths:
will the watchword of dawn be July
When to-morrow acclaims November?
The stern salutation of sorrow to death or
repentance to shame
Was all that the season was wont to accord
her of grace or acclaim;
No lightnings of love and of laughter.
But here, in the laugh of the loud west wind
from around and above,
In the flash of the waters beneath him, what
sound or what light but of love
Rings round him or leaps forth after?

II.

Wind beloved of earth and sky and sea beyond all winds that blow,
Wind whose might in fight was England's
on her mightiest warrior day,
South-west wind, whose breath for her was
life, and fire to scourge her foe,
Steel to smite and death to drive him down
an unreturning way,
Well-beloved and welcome, sounding all the
clarions of the sky,
Rolling all the marshalled waters toward
the charge that storms the shore,
We receive, acclaim, salute thee, we who live
and dream and die,
As the mightiest mouth of song that ever
spake acclaimed of yore.
We that live as they that perish praise thee,
lord of cloud and wave,
Wind of winds, clothed on with darkness
whence as lightning light comes forth.

We that know thee strong to guard and smite,
　　to scatter and to save,
We to whom the south-west wind is dear
　　as Athens held the north.
He for her waged war as thou for us against
　　all powers defiant,
Fleets full-fraught with storm from Per-
　　sia, laden deep with death from Spain:
Thee the giant god of song and battle hailed
　　as god and giant,
Yet not his but ours the land is whence thy
　　praise should ring and rain;
Rain as rapture shed from song, and ring as
　　trumpets blown for battle,
Sound and sing before thee, loud and
　　glad as leaps and sinks the sea:
Yea, the sea's white steeds are curbed and
　　spurred of thee, and pent as cattle,
Yet they laugh with love and pride to
　　live, subdued not save of thee.
Ears that hear thee hear in heaven the sound
　　of widening wings gigantic,
Eyes that see the cloud-lift westward see
　　thy darkening brows divine;
Wings whose measure is the limit of the limit-
　　less Atlantic,
Brows that bend, and bid the sovereign
　　sea submit her soul to thine.

III.

Twelve days since is it—twelve days gone,
Lord of storm, that a storm-bow shone
Higher than sweeps thy sublime dark wing,
Fair as dawn is and sweet like spring?

Never dawn in the deep wide east
Spread so splendid and strange a feast,
Whence the soul as it drank and fed
Felt such rapture of wonder shed.

Never spring in the wild wood's heart
Felt such flowers at her footfall start,
Born of earth, as arose on sight
Born of heaven and of storm and light.

Stern and sullen, the grey grim sea
Swelled and strove as in toils, though free,
Free as heaven, and as heaven sublime,
Clear as heaven of the toils of time.

IV.

Suddenly, sheer from the heights to the depths
　　of the sky and the sea,
Sprang from the darkness alive as a vision of
　　life to be

Glory triune and transcendent of colour afar
　　and afire,
Arching and darkening the darkness with
　　light as of dream or desire.
Heaven, in the depth of its height, shone wist-
　　ful and wan from above:
Earth from beneath, and the sea, shone
　　stricken and breathless with love.
As a shadow may shine, so shone they; as
　　ghosts of the viewless blest,
That sleep hath sight of alive in a rapture of
　　sunbright rest,
The green earth glowed and the grey sky
　　gleamed for a wondrous while;
And the storm's full frown was crossed by the
　　light of its own deep smile.
As the darkness of thought and of passion is
　　touched by the light that gives
Life deathless as love from the depth of a
　　spirit that sees and lives,
From the soul of a seer and a singer, wherein
　　as a scroll unfurled
Lies open the scripture of light and of dark-
　　ness, the word of the world,
So, shapeless and measureless, lurid as an-
　　guish and haggard as crime,
Pale as the front of oblivion and dark as the
　　heart of time,
The wild wan heaven at its height was assailed
　　and subdued and made
More fair than the skies that know not of
　　storm and endure not shade.
The grim sea-swell, grey, sleepless, and sad
　　as a soul estranged,
Shone, smiled, took heart, and was glad of its
　　wrath: and the world's face changed.

V.

Up from moorlands northward gleaming
　　Even to heaven's transcendent height,
Clothed with massive cloud, and seeming
　　All one fortress reared of night,
Down to where the deep sea, dreaming
　　Angry dreams, lay dark and white,
White as death and dark as fate,
Heaving with the strong wind's weight,
Sad with stormy pride of state,
One full rainbow shone elate.

Up from inmost memory's dwelling
　　Where the light of life abides,
Where the past finds tongue, foretelling
　　Time that comes and grace that guides,

Power that saves and sways, compelling
  Souls that ebb and flow like tides,
Shone or seemed to shine and swim
Through the cloud-surf great and grim,
Thought's live surge, the soul of him
  By whose light the sun looks dim.

In what synod were they sitting,
  All the gods and lords of time,
Whence they watched as fen-fires flitting
  Years and names of men sublime,
When their counsels found it fitting
  One should stand where none might
      climb—
None of man begotten, none
Born of men beneath the sun
Till the race of time be run,
Save this heaven-enfranchised one?

With what rapture of creation
  Was the soul supernal thrilled,
With what pride of adoration
  Was the world's heart fired and filled,
Heaved in heavenward exultation
  Higher than hopes or dreams might build,
Grave with awe not known while he
Was not, mad with glorious glee
As the sun-saluted sea,
When his hour bade Shakespeare be?

VI.

There, clear as night beholds her crowning
  seven,
The sea beheld his likeness set in heaven.
The shadow of his spirit full in sight
Shone: for the shadow of that soul is
  light.
Nor heaven alone bore witness: earth avowed
Him present, and acclaimed of storm aloud.
From the arching sky to the ageless hills and
  sea
The whole world, visible, audible, was he:
Each part of all that wove that wondrous
  whole
The raiment of the presence of his soul.
The sun that smote and kissed the dark to
  death
Spake, smiled, and strove, like song's trium-
  phant breath;
The soundless cloud whose thunderous heart
  was dumb
Swelled, lowered, and shrank to feel its con-
  queror come.

Yet high from heaven its empire vast and
  vain
Frowned, and renounced not night's reluctant
  reign.
The serpentine swift sounds and shapes
  wherein
The stainless sea mocks earth and death and
  sin,
Crawls dark as craft, or flashes keen as hate,
Subdued and insubmissive, strong like fate
And weak like man, bore wrathful witness yet
That storms and sins are more than suns that
  set;
That evil everlasting, girt for strife
Eternal, wars with hope as death with life.
The dark sharp shifting wind that bade the
  waves
Falter, lose heart, bow down like foes made
  slaves,
And waxed within more bitter as they bowed,
Baffling the sea, swallowing the sun with
  cloud,
Devouring fast as fire on earth devours
And hungering hard as frost that feeds on
  flowers,
Clothed round with fog that reeked as fume
  from hell,
And darkening with its miscreative spell
Light, glad and keen and splendid as the
  sword
Whose heft had known Othello's hand its
  lord,
Spake all the soul that hell drew back to greet
And felt its fire shrink shuddering from his
  feet.
Far off the darkness darkened, and recoiled,
And neared again, and triumphed: and the
  coiled
Colourless cloud and sea discoloured grew
Conscious of horror huge as heaven, and knew
Where Goneril's soul made chill and foul the
  mist,
And all the leprous life in Regan hissed.
Fierce homeless ghosts, rejected of the pit,
From hell to hell of storm fear watched them
  flit.
About them and before, the dull grey gloom
Shuddered, and heaven seemed hateful as
  the tomb
That shrinks from resurrection; and from out
That sullen hell which girt their shades about
The nether soul that lurks and lowers within
Man, made of dust and fire and shame and
  sin,

Breathed: all the cloud that felt it breathe and blight
Was blue as plague or black as thunderous night.
Elect of hell, the children of his hate
Thronged, as to storm sweet heaven's triumphal gate.
The terror of his giving rose and shone
Imminent: life had put its likeness on.
But higher than all its horrent height of shade
Shone sovereign, seen by light itself had made,
Above the woes of all the world, above
Life, sin, and death, his myriad-minded love.
From landward heights whereon the radiance leant
Full-fraught from heaven, intense and imminent,
To depths wherein the seething strengths of cloud
Scarce matched the wrath of waves whereon they bowed,
From homeborn pride and kindling love of home
To the outer skies and seas of fire and foam,
From splendour soft as dew that sundawn thrills
To gloom that shudders round the world it fills,
From midnights murmuring round Titania's ear
To midnights maddening round the rage of Lear,
The wonder woven of storm and sun became
One with the light that lightens from his name.
The music moving on the sea that felt
The storm-wind even as snows of springtide melt
Was blithe as Ariel's hand or voice might make
And bid all grief die gladly for its sake.
And there the soul alive in ear and eye
That watched the wonders of an hour pass by
Saw brighter than all stars that heaven inspheres
The silent splendour of Cordelia's tears,
Felt in the whispers of the quickening wind
The radiance of the laugh of Rosalind,
And heard, in sounds that melt the souls of men
With love of love, the tune of Imogen.

VII.

For the strong north-east is not strong to subdue and to slay the divine south-west,
And the darkness is less than the light that it darkens, and dies in reluctant rest.
It hovers and hangs on the labouring and trembling ascent of the dawn from the deep,
Till the sun's eye quicken the world and the waters, and smite it again into sleep.
Night, holy and starry, the fostress of souls, with the fragrance of heaven in her breath,
Subdues with the sense of her godhead the forces and mysteries of sorrow and death.
Eternal as dawn's is the comfort she gives: but the mist that beleaguers and slays
Comes, passes, and is not: the strength of it withers, appalled or assuaged by the day's.
Faith, haggard as Fear that had borne her, and dark as the sire that begat her, Despair,
Held rule on the soul of the world and the song of it saddening through ages that were;
Dim centuries that darkened and brightened and darkened again, and the soul of their song
Was great as their grief, and sublime as their suffering, and strong as their sorrows were strong.
It knew not, it saw not, but shadows triune, and evoked by the strength of their spell
Dark hell, and the mountain of anguish, and heaven that was hollower and harder than hell.
These are not: the womb of the darkness that bare them rejects them, and knows them no more:
Thought, fettered in misery and iron, revives in the light that it lived in of yore.
For the soul that is wisdom and freedom, the spirit of England redeemed from her past,
Speaks life through the lips of the master and lord of her children, the first and the last.
Thought, touched by his hand and redeemed by his breath, sees, hears, and accepts from above
The limitless lightnings of vision and passion, the measureless music of love.

A SWIMMER'S DREAM.

NOVEMBER 4, 1889.

Somno mollior unda.

I.

DAWN is dim on the dark soft water,
  Soft and passionate, dark and sweet.
Love's own self was the deep sea's daughter,
  Fair and flawless from face to feet,
Hailed of all when the world was golden,
Loved of lovers whose names beholden
Thrill men's eyes as with light of olden
  Days more glad than their flight was fleet.

So they sang: but for men that love her,
  Souls that hear not her word in vain,
Earth beside her and heaven above her
  Seem but shadows that wax and wane.
Softer than sleep's are the sea's caresses,
Kinder than love's that betrays and blesses,
Blither than spring's when her flowerful tresses
  Shake forth sunlight and shine with rain.

All the strength of the waves that perish
  Swells beneath me and laughs and sighs,
Sighs for love of the life they cherish,
  Laughs to know that it lives and dies,
Dies for joy of its life, and lives
Thrilled with joy that its brief death gives—
Death whose laugh or whose breath forgives
  Change that bids it subside and rise.

II.

Hard and heavy, remote but nearing,
  Sunless hangs the severe sky's weight,
Cloud on cloud, though the wind be veering
  Heaped on high to the sundawn's gate.
Dawn and even and noon are one,
Veiled with vapour and void of sun;
Nought in sight or in fancied hearing
  Now less mighty than time or fate.

The grey sky gleams and the grey seas glimmer,
  Pale and sweet as a dream's delight,
As a dream's where darkness and light seem dimmer,
  Touched by dawn or subdued by night.
The dark wind, stern and sublime and sad,
Swings the rollers to westward, clad
With lustrous shadow that lures the swimmer,
  Lures and lulls him with dreams of light.

Light, and sleep, and delight, and wonder,
  Change, and rest, and a charm of cloud,
Fill the world of the skies whereunder
  Heaves and quivers and pants aloud
All the world of the waters, hoary
Now, but clothed with its own live glory,
That mates the lightning and mocks the thunder
  With light more living and word more proud.

III.

Far off westward, whither sets the sounding strife,
  Strife more sweet than peace, of shoreless waves whose glee
Scorns the shore and loves the wind that leaves them free,
Strange as sleep and pale as death and fair as life,
  Shifts the moonlight-coloured sunshine on the sea.

Toward the sunset's goal the sunless waters crowd,
  Fast as autumn days toward winter: yet it seems
Here that autumn wanes not, here that woods and streams
Lose not heart and change not likeness, chilled and bowed
  Warped and wrinkled: here the days are fair as dreams.

IV.

O russet-robed November,
  What ails thee so to smile?
Chill August, pale September,
  Endured a woful while,
And fell as falls an ember
  From forth a flameless pile:
But golden-girt November
  Bids all she looks on smile.

The lustrous foliage, waning
  As wanes the morning moon,
Here falling, here refraining,
  Outbraves the pride of June

With statelier semblance, feigning
    No fear lest death be soon:
As though the woods thus waning
    Should wax to meet the moon.

As though, when fields lie stricken
    By grey December's breath,
These lordlier growths that sicken
    And die for fear of death
Should feel the sense requicken
    That hears what springtide saith
And thrills for love, spring-stricken
    And pierced with April's breath.

The keen white-winged north-easter
    That stings and spurs thy sea
Doth yet but feed and feast her
    With glowing sense of glee:
Calm chained her, storm released her,
    And storm's glad voice was he:
South-wester or north-easter,
    Thy winds rejoice the sea.

V.

A dream, a dream is it all—the season,
    The sky, the water, the wind, the shore?
A day-born dream of divine unreason,
    A marvel moulded of sleep—no more?
For the cloudlike wave that my limbs while
      cleaving
Feel as in slumber beneath them heaving
Soothes the sense as to slumber, leaving
    Sense of nought that was known of yore.

A purer passion, a lordlier leisure,
    A peace more happy than lives on land,
Fulfils with pulse of diviner pleasure
    The dreaming head and the steering hand.
I lean my cheek to the cold grey pillow,
The deep soft swell of the full broad billow,
And close mine eyes for delight past measure,
    And wish the wheel of the world would
      stand.

The wild-winged hour that we fain would
      capture
Falls as from heaven that its light feet
      clomb,
So brief, so soft, and so full the rapture
    Was felt that soothed me with sense of
      home.
To sleep, to swim, and to dream, for ever—
Such joy the vision of man saw never;
For here too soon will a dark day sever
    The sea-bird's wing from the sea-wave's
      foam.

A dream, and more than a dream, and dim-
      mer
    At once and brighter than dreams that
      flee,
The moment's joy of the seaward swimmer
    Abides, remembered as truth may be.
Not all the joy and not all the glory
Must fade as leaves when the woods wax
      hoary;
For there the downs and the sea-banks glim-
      mer,
And here to south of them swells the sea.

GRACE DARLING.

TAKE, O star of all our seas, from not an
    alien hand,
    Homage paid of song bowed down before
    thy glory's face,
Thou the living light of all our lovely stormy
    strand,
    Thou the brave north-country's very glory
    of glories, Grace.

Loud and dark about the lighthouse rings and
    glares the night;
    Glares with foam-lit gloom and darkling
    fire of storm and spray,

Rings with roar of winds in chase and rage
    of waves in flight,
    Howls and hisses as with mouths of snakes
    and wolves at bay.
Scarce the cliffs of the islets, scarce the walls
    of Joyous Gard,
    Flash to sight between the deadlier light-
    nings of the sea:
Storm is lord and master of a midnight evil-
    starred,
    Nor may sight or fear discern what evil
    stars may be.

Dark as death and white as snow the sea-
swell scowls and shines,
Heaves and yearns and pants for prey,
from ravening lip to lip,
Strong in rage of rapturous anguish, lines
on hurtling lines,
Ranks on charging ranks, that break and
rend the battling ship.
All the night is mad and murderous: who
shall front the night?
Not the prow that labours, helpless as a
storm-blown leaf,
Where the rocks and waters, darkling depth
and beetling height,
Rage with wave on shattering wave and
thundering reef on reef.
Death is fallen upon the prisoners there of
darkness, bound
Like as thralls with links of iron fast in
bonds of doom;
How shall any way to break the bands of
death be found,
Any hand avail to pluck them from that
raging tomb?
All the night is great with child of death: no
stars above
Show them hope in heaven, no lights from
shoreward help on earth.
Is there help or hope to seaward, is there help
in love,
Hope in pity, where the ravening hounds
of storm make mirth?
Where the light that shows the naked eyeless
face of Death
Nearer, laughing dumb and grim across
the loud live storm?
Not in human heart or hand or speech of
human breath,
Surely, nor in saviours found of mortal
face or form.
Yet below the light, between the reefs, a skiff
shot out
Seems a sea-bird fain to breast and brave
the strait fierce pass
Whence the channelled roar of waters driven
in raging rout,
Pent and pressed and maddened, speaks
their monstrous might and mass.
Thunder heaves and howls about them,
lightning leaps and flashes,
Hard at hand, not high in heaven, but
close between the walls
Heaped and hollowed of the storms of old,
whence reels and crashes

All the rage of all the unbaffled wave that
breaks and falls
Who shall thwart the madness and the gladness of it, laden
Full with heavy fate, and joyous as the
birds that whirl?
Nought in heaven or earth, if not one mortal-
moulded maiden,
Nought if not the soul that glorifies a northland girl.
Not the rocks that break may baffle, not the
reefs that thwart
Stay the ravenous rapture of the waves that
crowd and leap
Scarce their flashing laughter shows the hunger of their heart,
Scarce their lion-throated roar the wrath at
heart they keep.
Child and man and woman in the grasp of
death clenched fast
Tremble, clothed with darkness round
about, and scarce draw breath,
Scarce lift eyes up toward the light that saves
not, scarc may cast
Thought or prayer up, caught and tram-
melled in the snare of death.
Not as sea-mews cling and laugh or sun their
plumes and sleep
Cling and cower the wild night's waifs of
shipwreck, blind with fear,
Where the fierce reef scarce yields foothold
that a bird might keep,
And the clamorous darkness deadens eye
and deafens ear.
Yet beyond their helpless hearing, out of
hopeless sight,
Saviours, armed and girt upon with
strength of heart, fare forth,
Sire and daughter, hand on oar and face
against the night,
Maid and man whose names are beacons
ever to the North.
Nearer now; but all the madness of the storming surf
Hounds and roars them back; but roars
and hounds them back in vain:
As a pleasure-skiff may graze the lake-em-
banking turf,
So the boat that bears them grates the
rock where-toward they strain.
Dawn as fierce and haggard as the face of
night scarce guides
Toward the cries that rent and clove the
darkness, crying for aid,

Hours on hours, across the engorged reluctance of the tides,
Sire and daughter, high-souled man and
mightier-hearted maid.
Not the bravest land that ever breasted war's
grim sea,
Hurled her foes back harried on the lowlands whence they came,
Held her own and smote her smiters down,
while such durst be,
Shining northward, shining southward, as
the aurorean flame,
Not our mother, not Northumberland, brought
ever forth,
Though no southern shore may match the
sons that kiss her mouth,
Children worthier all the birthright given of
the ardent north
Where the fire of hearts outburns the suns
that fire the south.
Even such fire was this that lit them, not from
lowering skies
Where the darkling dawn flagged, stricken
in the sun's own shrine,
Down the gulf of storm subsiding, till their
earnest eyes
Find the relics of the ravening night that
spared but nine.
Life by life the man redeems them, head by
storm-worn head,
While the girl's hand stays the boat whereof
the waves are fain:
Ah, but woe for one, the mother clasping fast
her dead!
Happier, had the surges slain her with
her children slain.
Back they bear, and bring between them safe
the woful nine,
Where above the ravenous Hawkers fixed
at watch for prey
Storm and calm behold the Longstone's
towering signal shine

Now as when that labouring night brought
forth a shuddering day.
Now as then, though like the hounds of
storm against her snarling
All the clamorous years between us storm
down many a fame
As our sires beheld before us we behold Grace
Darling
Crowned and throned our queen, and as
they hailed we hail her name.
Nay, not ours alone, her kinsfolk bcrn, though
chiefliest ours,
East and west and south acclaim her queen
of England's maids,
Star more sweet than all their stars and flower
than all their flowers,
Higher in heaven and earth than star that
sets or flower that fades.
How should land or sea that nurtured her
forget, or love
Hold not fast her fame for us while aught
is borne in mind?
Land and sea beneath us, sun and moon and
stars above,
Bear the bright soul witness, seen of all
but souls born blind.
Stars and moon and sun may wax and wane,
subside and rise,
Age on age as flake on flake of showering
snows be shed:
Not till earth be sunless, not till death strike
blind the skies,
May the deathless love that waits on deathless deeds be dead.

Years on years have withered since beside
the hearth once thine
I, too young to have seen thee, touched
thy father's hallowed hand:
Thee and him shall all men see for ever, stars
that shine
While the sea that spared thee girds and
glorifies the land.

LOCH TORRIDON.

To E. H.

THE dawn of night more fair than morning
rose,
Stars hurrying forth on stars, as snows on
snows

Haste when the wind and winter bid them
speed.
Vague miles of moorland road behind us lay
Scarce traversed ere the day

Sank, and the sun forsook us at our need,
Belated. Where we thought to have rested,
    rest
Was none; for soft Maree's dim quivering
    breast,
Bound round with gracious inland girth of
    green
And fearless of the wild wave-wandering
    West,
Shone shelterless for strangers; and unseen
The goal before us lay
Of all our blithe and strange and strenuous
    day.
For when the northering road faced westward
    —when
The dark sharp sudden gorge dropped sea-
    ward—then,
Beneath the stars, between the steeps, the
    track
We followed, lighted not of moon or sun,
And plunging whither none
Might guess, while heaven and earth were
    hoar and black,
Seemed even the dim still pass whence none
    turns back:
And through the twilight leftward of the way,
And down the dark, with many a laugh and
    leap,
The light blithe hill-streams shone from scaur
    to steep
In glittering pride of play;
And ever while the night grew great and deep
We felt but saw not what the hills would
    keep
Sacred awhile from sense of moon or star;
And full and far
Beneath us, sweet and strange as heaven may
    be,
The sea.

The very sea: no mountain-moulded lake
Whose fluctuant shapeliness is fain to take
Shape from the steadfast shore that rules it
    round,
And only from the storms a casual sound:
The sea, that harbours in her heart sublime
The supreme heart of music deep as time,
And in her spirit strong
The spirit of all imaginable song.

Not a whisper or lisp from the waters: the
    skies were not silenter. Peace
Was between them; a passionless rapture of
    respite as soft as release.

Not a sound, but a sense that possessed and
    pervaded with patient delight
The soul and the body, clothed round with
    the comfort of limitless night.
Night infinite, living, adorable, loved of the
    land and the sea:
Night, mother of mercies, who saith to the
    spirits in prison, Be free.
And softer than dewfall, and kindlier than
    starlight, and keener than wine,
Came round us the fragrance of waters, the
    life of the breath of the brine.
We saw not, we heard not, the face or the
    voice of the waters: we knew
By the darkling delight of the wind as the
    sense of the sea in it grew.
By the pulse of the darkness about us en-
    kindled and quickened, that here,
Unseen and unheard of us, surely the goal
    we had faith in was near.
A silence diviner than music, a darkness
    diviner than light,
Fulfilled as from heaven with a measureless
    comfort the measure of night.

But never a roof for shelter
  And never a sign for guide
    Rose doubtful or visible: only
      And hardly and gladly we heard
The soft waves whisper and welter,
  Subdued, and allured to subside,
    By the mild night's magic: the lonely
      Sweet silence was soothed, not stirred,
By the noiseless noise of the gleaming
  Glad ripples, that played and sighed,
    Kissed, laughed, recoiled, and relented,
      Whispered, flickered, and fled.
No season was this for dreaming
  How oft, with a stormier tide,
    Had the wrath of the winds been
      vented
      On sons of the tribes long dead:
The tribes whom time, and the changes
  Of things, and the stress of doom,
    Have erased and effaced; forgotten
      As wrecks or weeds of the shore
In sight of the stern hill-ranges
  That hardly may change their gloom
    When the fruits of the years wax rotten
      And the seed of them springs no more.
For the dim strait footway dividing
  The waters that breathed below
    Led safe to the kindliest of shelters
      That ever awoke into light:

And still in remembrance abiding
  Broods over the stars that glow
    And the water that eddies and welters
    The passionate peace of the night.

All night long, in the world of sleep,
Skies and waters were soft and deep:
Shadow clothed them, and silence made
Soundless music of dream and shade:
All above us, the livelong night,
Shadow, kindled with sense of light;
All around us, the brief night long,
Silence, laden with sense of song.
Stars and mountains without, we knew,
Watched and waited, the soft night through:
All unseen, but divined and dear,
Thrilled the touch of the sea's breath near:
All unheard, but alive like sound,
Throbbed the sense of the sea's life round:
Round us, near us, in depth and height,
Soft as darkness and keen as light.

And the dawn leapt in at my casement: and
    there, as I rose, at my feet
No waves of the landlocked waters, no lake
    submissive and sweet,
Soft slave of the lordly seasons, whose breath
    may loose it or freeze;
But to left and to right and ahead was the
    ripple whose pulse is the sea's.
From the gorge we had travelled by star-
    light the sunrise, winged and aflame,
Shone large on the live wide wavelets that
    shuddered with joy as it came;
As it came and caressed and possessed them,
    till panting and laughing with light
From mountain to mountain the water was
    kindled and stung to delight.
And the grey gaunt heights that embraced
    and constrained and compelled it were
    glad,
And the rampart of rock, stark naked, that
    thwarted and barred it, was clad
With a stern grey splendour of sunrise: and
    scarce had I sprung to the sea
When the dawn and the water were wedded,
    the hills and the sky set free.

The chain of the night was broken: the waves
    that embraced me and smiled
And flickered and fawned in the sunlight,
    alive, unafraid, undefiled,
Were sweeter to swim in than air, though ful-
    filled with the mounting morn,
Could be for the birds whose triumph rejoiced
    that a day was born.
And a day was arisen indeed for us. Years
    and the changes of years
Clothed round with their joys and their sor-
    rows, and dead as their hopes and their
    fears,
Lie noteless and nameless, unlit by remem-
    brance or record of days
Worth wonder or memory, or cursing or
    blessing, or passion or praise,
Between us who live and forget not, but
    yearn with delight in it yet,
And the day we forget not, and never may live
    and may think to forget.
And the years that were kindlier and
    fairer, and kindled with pleasures as
    keen,
Have eclipsed not with lights or with shadows
    the light on the face of it seen.
For softly and surely, as nearer the boat that
    we gazed from drew,
The face of the precipice opened and bade us
    as birds pass through,
And the bark shot sheer to the sea
    through the strait of the sharp steep
    cleft,
The portal that opens with imminent ram-
    pires to right and to left,
Sublime as the sky they darken and strange
    as a spell-struck dream,
On the world unconfined of the mountains,
    the reign of the sea supreme,
The kingdom of westward waters, wherein
    when we swam we knew
The waves that we clove were boundless, the
    wind on our brows that blew
Had swept no land and no lake, and had
    warred not on tower or on tree,
But came on us hard out of heaven, and alive
    with the soul of the sea.

THE PALACE OF PAN.

INSCRIBED TO MY MOTHER.

SEPTEMBER, all glorious with gold, as a king
  In the radiance of triumph attired,
Outlightening the summer, outsweetening the
    spring,
Broods wide on the woodlands with limitless
    wing,
  A presence of all men desired.

Far eastward and westward the sun-coloured
    lands
  Smile warm as the light on them smiles;
And statelier than temples upbuilded with
    hands,
Tall column by column, the sanctuary stands
  Of the pine-forest's infinite aisles.

Mute worship, too fervent for praise or for
    prayer,
  Possesses the spirit with peace,
Fulfilled with the breath of the luminous air,
The fragrance, the silence, the shadows as fair
  As the rays that recede or increase.

Ridged pillars that redden aloft and aloof,
  With never a branch for a nest,
Sustain the sublime indivisible roof,
To the storm and the sun in his majesty proof,
  And awful as waters at rest.

Man's hand hath not measured the height
    of them thought
  May measure not, awe may not know;
In its shadow the woofs of the woodland are
    wrought;
As a bird is the sun in the toils of them caught,
  And the flakes of it scattered as snow.

As the shreds of a plumage of gold on the
    ground
  The sun-flakes by multitudes lie,
Shed loose as the petals of roses discrowned
On the floors of the forest engilt and em-
    browned
  And reddened afar and anigh.

Dim centuries with darkling inscrutable hands
  Have reared and secluded the shrine
For gods that we know not, and kindled as
    brands
On the altar the years that are dust, and their
    sands
  Time's glass has forgotten for sign.

A temple whose transepts are measured by
    miles,
  Whose chancel has morning for priest,
Whose floor-work the foot of no spoiler
    defiles,
Whose musical silence no music beguiles,
  No festivals limit its feast.

The noon's ministration, the night's and the
    dawn's,
  Conceals not, reveals not for man,
On the slopes of the herbless and blossomless
    lawns,
Some track of a nymph's or some trail of a
    faun's
  To the place of the slumber of Pan.

Thought, kindled and quickened by worship
    and wonder
  To rapture too sacred for fear
On the ways that unite or divide them in
    sunder,
Alone may discern if about them or under
  Be token or trace of him here.

With passionate awe that is deeper than panic
  The spirit subdued and unshaken
Takes heed of the godhead terrene and
    Titanic
Whose footfall is felt on the breach of volcanic
  Sharp steeps that their fire has forsaken.

By a spell more serene than the dim necro-
    mantic
  Dead charms of the past and the night,
Or the terror that lurked in the noon to make
    frantic
Where Etna takes shape from the limbs of
    gigantic
  Dead gods disanointed of might,

The spirit made one with the spirit whose
    breath
  Makes noon in the woodland sublime
Abides as entranced in a presence that saith
Things loftier than life and serener than
    death,
  Triumphant and silent as time.

PINE RIDGE: September, 1893.

39

A YEAR'S CAROLS.

JANUARY.

HAIL, January, that bearest here
On snowbright breasts the babe-faced year
That weeps and trembles to be born.
Hail, maid and mother, strong and bright,
Hooded and cloaked and shod with white,
  Whose eyes are stars that match the morn
Thy forehead braves the storm's bent bow,
Thy feet enkindle stars of snow.

FEBRUARY.

Wan February with weeping cheer,
Whose cold hand guides the youngling year
  Down misty roads of mire and rime,
Before thy pale and fitful face
The shrill wind shifts the clouds apace
  Through skies the morning scarce may
    climb.
Thine eyes are thick with heavy tears,
But lit with hopes that light the year's.

MARCH.

Hail, happy March, whose foot on earth
Rings as the blast of martial mirth
  When trumpets fire men's hearts for fray.
No race of wild things winged or finned
May match the might that wings thy wind
  Through air and sea, through scud and
    spray
Strong joy and thou were powers twin-born
Of tempest and the towering morn.

APRIL.

Crowned April, king whose kiss bade earth
Bring forth to time her lordliest birth
  When Shakespeare from thy lips drew
    breath
And laughed to hold in one soft hand
A spell that bade the world's wheel stand,
  And power on life, and power on death,
With quiring suns and sunbright showers
Praise him, the flower of all thy flowers.

MAY.

Hail, May, whose bark puts forth full-sailed
For summer; May, whom Chaucer hailed
  With all his happy might of heart,
And gave thy rosebright daisy-tips
Strange fragrance from his amorous lips
  That still thine own breath seems to part
And sweeten till each word they say
Is even a flower of flowering May.

JUNE.

Strong June, superb, serene, elate
With conscience of thy sovereign state
  Untouched of thunder, though the storm
Scathe here and there thy shuddering skies
And bid its lightning cross thine eyes
  With fire, thy golden hours inform
Earth and the souls of men with life
That brings forth peace from shining strife.

JULY.

Hail, proud July, whose fervent mouth
Bids even be morn and north be south
  By grace and gospel of thy word,
Whence all the splendour of the sea
Lies breathless with delight in thee
  And marvel at the music heard
From the ardent silent lips of noon
And midnight's rapturous plenilune.

AUGUST.

Great August, lord of golden lands,
Whose lordly joy through seas and strands
  And all the red-ripe heart of earth
Strikes passion deep as life, and stills
The folded vales and folding hills
  With gladness too divine for mirth,
The gracious glories of thine eyes
Make night a noon where darkness dies.

SEPTEMBER.

Hail, kind September, friend whose grace
Renews the bland year's bounteous face
  With largess given of corn and wine
Through many a land that laughs with
    love
Of thee and all the heaven above,
  More fruitful found than all save thine
Whose skies fulfil with strenuous cheer
The fervent fields that knew thee near.

OCTOBER.

October of the tawny crown,
Whose heavy-laden hands drop down
  Blessing, the bounties of thy breath
And mildness of thy mellowing might
Fill earth and heaven with love and light
  Too sweet for fear to dream of death
Or memory, while thy joy lives yet,
To know what joy would fain forget.

NOVEMBER.

Hail, soft November, though thy pale
Sad smile rebuke the words that hail
  Thy sorrow with no sorrowing words
Or gratulate thy grief with song
Less bitter than the winds that wrong
  Thy withering woodlands, where the birds
Keep hardly heart to sing or see
How fair thy faint wan face may be.

DECEMBER.

December, thou whose hallowing hands
On shuddering seas and hardening lands
  Set as a sacramental sign
The seal of Christmas felt on earth
As witness toward a new year's birth
  Whose promise makes thy death divine,
The crowning joy that comes of thee
Makes glad all grief on land or sea.

ENGLAND: AN ODE.

I.

SEA and strand, and a lordlier land than sea-
    tides rolling and rising sun
Clasp and lighten in climes that brighten with
    day when day that was here is done,
Call aloud on their children, proud with
    trust that future and past are one.

Far and near from the swan's nest here the
    storm-birds bred of her fair white breast,
Sons whose home was the sea-wave's foam,
    have borne the fame of her east and west;
North and south has the storm-wind's mouth
    rung praise of England and England's
    quest.

Fame, wherever her flag flew, never forbore
    to fly with an equal wing:
France and Spain with their warrior train
    bowed down before her as thrall to king;
India knelt at her feet, and felt her sway more
    fruitful of life than spring.

Darkness round them as iron bound fell off
    from races of elder name,
Slain at sight of her eyes, whose light bids
    freedom lighten and burn as flame;
Night endures not the touch that cures of
    kingship tyrants, and slaves of shame.

All the terror of time, where error and fear
    were lords of a world of slaves,
Age on age in resurgent rage and anguish
    darkening as waves on waves,
Fell or fled from a face that shed such grace
    as quickens the dust of graves.

Things of night at her glance took flight: the
    strengths of darkness recoiled and
    sank:
Sank the fires of the murderous pyres where-
    on wild agony writhed and shrank:
Rose the light of the reign of right from gulfs
    of years that the darkness drank.

Yet the might of her wings in flight, whence
    glory lightens and music rings,
Loud and bright as the dawn's, shall smite
    and still the discord of evil things,
Yet not slain by her radiant reign, but dark-
    ened now by her sail-stretched wings.

II.

Music made of change and conquest, glory
    born of evil slain,
Stilled the discord, slew the darkness, bade
    the lights of tempest wane,
Where the deathless dawn of England rose in
    sign that right should reign.

Mercy, where the tiger wallowed mad and
    blind with blood and lust,
Justice, where the jackal yelped and fed,
    and slaves allowed it just,
Rose as England's light on Asia rose, and
    smote them down to dust.

Justice bright as mercy, mercy girt by justice
    with her sword,
Smote and saved and raised and ruined, till
    the tyrant-ridden horde
Saw the lightning fade from heaven and knew
    the sun for God and lord.

Where the footfall sounds of England, where
the smile of England shines,
Rings the tread and laughs the face of freedom, fair as hope divines
Days to be, more brave than ours and lit by
lordlier stars for signs.

All our past acclaims our future: Shakes-
peare's voice and Nelson's hand,
Milton's faith and Wordsworth's trust in this
our chosen and chainless land,
Bear us witness: come the world against her,
England yet shall stand.

Earth and sea bear England witness if he lied
who said it; he
Whom the winds that ward her, waves
that clasp, and herb and flower and
tree
Fed with English dews and sunbeams, hail
as more than man may be.

No man ever spake as he that bade our England be but true,
Keep but faith with England fast and firm,
and none should bid her rue;
None may speak as he: but all may know the
sign that Shakespeare knew.

III.

From the springs of the dawn, from the depths
of the noon, from the heights of the night
that shine,
Hope, faith, and remembrance of glory that
found but in England her throne and her
shrine,
Speak louder than song may proclaim them,
that here is the seal of them set for a
sign.

And loud as the sea's voice thunders applause
of the land that is one with the sea

Speaks Time in the ear of the people that
never at heart was not inly free
The word of command that assures us of life,
if we will but that life shall be;

If the race that is first of the races of men who
behold unashamed the sun
Stand fast and forget not the sign that is given
of the years and the wars that are done,
The token that all who are born of its blood
should in heart as in blood be one.

The word of remembrance that lightens as
fire from the steeps of the storm-lit past
Bids only the faith of our fathers endure in
us, firm as they held it fast:
That the glory which was from the first upon
England alone may endure to the last.

That the love and the hate may change not,
the faith may not fade, nor the wrath
nor scorn,
That shines for her sons and that burns for
her foemen as fire of the night or the
morn:
That the births of her womb may forget not
the sign of the glory wherein they were
born.

A light that is more than the sunlight, an air
that is brighter than morning's breath,
Clothes England about as the strong sea
clasps her, and answers the word that it
saith;
The word that assures her of life if she change
not, and choose not the ways of death.

Change darkens and lightens around her,
alternate in hope and in fear to be:
Hope knows not if fear speak truth, nor
fear whether hope be not blind as she:
But the sun is in heaven that beholds her immortal, and girdled with life by the sea.

ETON: AN ODE.

FOR THE FOUR HUNDRED AND FIFTIETH ANNIVERSARY OF THE FOUNDATION OF THE COLLEGE.

I.

Four hundred summers and fifty have shone
on the meadows of Thames and died
Since Eton arose in an age that was darkness,
and shone by his radiant side
As a star that the spell of a wise man's word
bade live and ascend and abide.

And ever as time's flow brightened, a river
more dark than the storm-clothed
sea,
And age upon age rose fairer and larger in
promise of hope set free,
With England Eton her child kept pace as a
fostress of men to be.

And ever as earth waxed wiser, and softer
the beating of time's wide wings,
Since fate fell dark on her father, most hapless
and gentlest of star-crossed kings,
Her praise has increased as the chant of the
dawn that the choir of the noon outsings.

II.

Storm and cloud in the skies were loud, and
lightning mocked at the blind sun's
light;
War and woe on the land below shed heavier
shadow than falls from night;
Dark was earth at her dawn of birth as here
her record of praise is bright.

Clear and fair through her morning air the
light first laugh of the sunlit stage
Rose and rang as a fount that sprang from
depths yet dark with a spent storm's
rage,
Loud and glad as a boy's, and bade the sunrise
open on Shakespeare's age.

Lords of state and of war, whom fate found
strong in battle, in counsel strong,

Here, ere fate had approved them great,
abode their season, and thought not long:
Here too first was the lark's note nursed that
filled and flooded the skies with song.

III.

Shelley, lyric lord of England's lordliest
singers, here first heard
Ring from lips of poets crowned and dead
the Promethean word
Whence his soul took fire, and power to out-
soar the sunward-soaring bird.

Still the reaches of the river, still the light on
field and hill,
Still the memories held aloft as lamps for
hope's young fire to fill,
Shine, and while the light of England lives
shall shine for England still.

When four hundred more and fifty years have
risen and shone and set,
Bright with names that men remember, loud
with names that men forget,
Haply here shall Eton's record be what
England finds it yet.

THE UNION.

I.

THREE in one, but one in three,
God, who girt her with the sea,
Bade our Commonweal to be:
   Nought, if now not one.
Though fraud and fear would sever
The bond assured for ever,
Their shameful strength shall never
   Undo what heaven has done.

II.

South and North and West and East
Watch the ravens flock to feast,
Dense as round some death-struck beast,
   Black as night is black.
Stand fast as faith together
In stress of treacherous weather
When hounds and wolves break tether
   And Treason guides the pack.

III.

Lovelier than thy seas are strong,
Glorious Ireland, sword and song
Gird and crown thee: none may wrong,
   Save thy sons alone.
The sea that laughs around us
Hath sundered not but bound us:
The sun's first rising found us
   Throned on its equal throne.

IV.

North and South and East and West,
All true hearts that wish thee best
Beat one tune and own one quest,
   Staunch and sure as steel.
God guard from dark disunion
Our threefold State's communion,
God save the loyal Union,
   The royal Commonweal!

EAST TO WEST.

SUNSET smiles on sunrise: east and west
    are one,
Face to face in heaven before the sovereign
    sun.
From the springs of the dawn everlasting
    a glory renews and transfigures the
    west,
From the depths of the sunset a light as of
    morning enkindles the broad sea's
    breast,
And the lands and the skies and the waters
    are glad of the day's and the night's
    work done.

Child of dawn, and regent on the world-
    wide sea,
England smiles on Europe, fair as dawn
    and free.

Not the waters that gird her are purer, nor
    mightier the winds that her waters
    know.
But America, daughter and sister of England,
    is praised of them, far as they flow:
Atlantic responds to Pacific the praise of her
    days that have been and shall be.

So from England westward let the watch-
    word fly,
So for England eastward let the seas reply;
Praise, honour, and love everlasting be sent
    on the wind's wings, westward and
    east,
That the pride of the past and the pride of the
    future may mingle as friends at feast,
And the sons of the lords of the world-wide
    seas be one till the world's life die.

MUSIC: AN ODE.

I.

WAS it light that spake from the dark-
    ness, or music that shone from the
    word,
When the night was enkindled with sound
    of the sun or the first-born bird?
Souls enthralled and entrammelled in bond-
    age of seasons that fall and rise,
Bound fast round with the fetters of flesh, and
    blinded with light that dies,
Lived not surely till music spake, and the
    spirit of life was heard.

II.

Music, sister of sunrise, and herald of life
    to be,
Smiled as dawn on the spirit of man, and
    the thrall was free.

Slave of nature and serf of time, the bondman
    of life and death,
Dumb with passionless patience that breathed
    but forlorn and reluctant breath,
Heard, beheld, and his soul made answer,
    and communed aloud with the sea.

III.

Morning spake, and he heard: and the
    passionate silent noon
Kept for him not silence: and soft from
    the mounting moon
Fell the sound of her splendour, heard as
    dawn's in the breathless night,
Not of men but of birds whose note bade
    man's soul quicken and leap to light:
And the song of it spake, and the light and
    the darkness of earth were as chords
    in tune.

INSCRIPTIONS FOR THE FOUR SIDES OF A PEDESTAL.

I.

MARLOWE, the father of the sons of song
  Whose praise is England's crowning praise,
    above
All glories else that crown her, sweet and
    strong
  As England, clothed with light and fire
    of love,
And girt with might of passion, thought, and
    trust,
Stands here in spirit, sleeps not here in dust.

II.

Marlowe, a star too sovereign, too superb,
  To fade when heaven took fire from
    Shakespeare's light,
A soul that knew but song's triumphal curb
  And love's triumphant bondage, holds
    of right
His pride of place, who first in place and time
Made England's voice as England's heart
    sublime.

III.

Marlowe bade England live in living song:
  The light he lifted up lit Shakespeare's
    way:
He spake, and life sprang forth in music,
    strong
  As fire or lightning, sweet as dawn of
    day.
Song was a dream where day took night to
    wife:
'Let there be life,' he said: and there was life.

IV.

Marlowe of all our fathers first beheld
  Beyond the tidal ebb and flow of things
The tideless depth and height of souls, im-
    pelled
  By thought or passion, borne on waves or
    wings,
Beyond all flight or sight but song's: and he
First gave our song a sound that matched our
    sea.

ON THE DEATH OF RICHARD BURTON.

NIGHT or light is it now, wherein
Sleeps, shut out from the wild world's din,
  Wakes, alive with a life more clear,
One who found not on earth his kin?

Sleep were sweet for awhile, were dear
Surely to souls that were heartless here,
  Souls that faltered and flagged and fell,
Soft of spirit and faint of cheer.

A living soul that had strength to quell
Hope the spectre and fear the spell,
  Clear-eyed, content with a scorn sublime
And a faith superb, can it fare not well?

Life, the shadow of wide-winged time,
Cast from the wings that change as they
    climb,
  Life may vanish in death, and seem
Less than the promise of last year's prime.

But not for us is the past a dream
Wherefrom, as light from a clouded stream,
  Faith fades and shivers and ebbs away,
Faint as the moon if the sundawn gleam.

Faith, whose eyes in the low last ray
Watch the fire that renews the day,
  Faith which lives in the living past,
Rock-rooted, swerves not as weeds that
    sway.

As trees that stand in the storm-wind fast
She stands, unsmitten of death's keen blast,
  With strong remembrance of sunbright
    spring
Alive at heart to the lifeless last.

Night, she knows, may in no wise cling
To a soul that sinks not and droops not
    wing,
  A sun that sets not in death's false
    night
Whose kingdom finds him not thrall but
    king.

Souls there are that for soul's affright
Bow down and cower in the sun's glad
    sight,
  Clothed round with faith that is one
    with fear,
And dark with doubt of the live world's
    light.

But him we hailed from afar or near
As boldest born of the bravest here
  And loved as brightest of souls that
   eyed
Life, time, and death with unchangeful
 cheer,

A wider soul than the world was wide,
Whose praise made love of him one with
 pride,
  What part has death or has time in him,
Who rode life's lists as a god might ride?

While England sees not her old praise
 dim,

While still her stars through the world's
 night swim,
  A fame outshining her Raleigh's fame,
A light that lightens her loud sea's rim,

Shall shine and sound as her sons proclaim
The pride that kindles at Burton's name.
  And joy shall exalt their pride to be
The same in birth if in soul the same.

But we that yearn for a friend's face—we
Who lack the light that on earth was he—
  Mourn, though the light be a quench-
   less flame
That shines as dawn on a tideless sea.

ELEGY.

1869–1891.

AUVERGNE, Auvergne, O wild and woful land,
 O glorious land and gracious, white as
  gleam
The stairs of heaven, black as a flameless
 brand,
  Strange even as life, and stranger than a
   dream,

Could earth remember man, whose eyes
 made bright
The splendour of her beauty, lit by day
Or soothed and softened and redeemed by
 night,
  Wouldst thou not know what light has
   passed away?

Wouldst thou not know whom England,
 whom the world,
  Mourns? For the world whose wildest
  ways he trod,
And smiled their dangers down that coiled
 and curled
  Against him, knows him now less man
   than god.

Our demigod of daring, keenest-eyed
  To read and deepest read in earth's dim
  things,
A spirit now whose body of death has died
And left it mightier yet in eyes and wings,

The sovereign seeker of the world, who
 now
  Hath sought what world the light of
  death may show,
Hailed once with me the crowns that load
 thy brow,
  Crags dark as midnight, columns bright
   as snow.

Thy steep small Siena, splendid and content
  As shines the mightier city's Tuscan
  pride
Which here its face reflects in radiance,
 pent
  By narrower bounds from towering side
   to side,

Set fast between the ridged and foamless
 waves
  Of earth more fierce and fluctuant than
  the sea,
The fearless town of towers that hails and
 braves
  The heights that gird, the sun that brands
   Le Puy;

The huddled churches clinging on the
 cliffs
  As birds alighting might for storm's sake
  cling,

Moored to the rocks as tempest-narried
  skiffs
  To perilous refuge from the loud wind's
    wing;

The stairs on stairs that wind and change
    and climb
  Even up to the utmost crag's edge curved
    and curled,
More bright than vision, more than faith
    sublime,
  Strange as the light and darkness of the
    world;

Strange as are night and morning, stars and
    sun,
  And washed from west and east by day's
    deep tide,
Shine yet less fair, when all their heights are
    won,
  Than sundawn shows thy pillared moun-
    tain-side.

Even so the dawn of death, whose light
    makes dim
  The starry fires that life sees rise and set,
Shows higher than here he shone before us
    him
  Whom faith forgets not, nor shall fame
    forget.

Even so those else unfooted heights we
    clomb
  Through scudding mist and eddying
    whirls of cloud,
Blind as a pilot beaten blind with foam,
  And shrouded as a corpse with storm's
    grey shroud,

Foot following foot along the sheer straight
    ledge
  Where space was none to bear the wild
    goat's feet
Till blind we sat on the outer footless edge
  Where darkling death seemed fain to share
    the seat,

The abyss before us, viewless even as time's,
  The abyss to left of us, the abyss to
    right,
Bid thought now dream how high the freed
    soul climbs
  That death sets free from change of day
    and night.

The might of raging mist and wind whose
    wrath

Shut from our eyes the narrowing rock we
    trod,
The wondrous world it darkened, made our
    path
  Like theirs who take the shadow of death
    for God.

Yet eastward, veiled in vapour white as snow,
  The grim black herbless heights that scorn
    the sun
And mock the face of morning rose to show
  The work of earth-born fire and earthquake
    done.

And half the world was haggard night,
    wherein
  We strove our blind way through: but far
    above
Was light that watched the wild mists whirl
    and spin,
  And far beneath a land worth light and
    love.

Deep down the Valley of the Curse, un-
    daunted
  By shadow and whisper of winds with
    sins for wings
And ghosts of crime wherethrough the
    heights live haunted
  By present sense of past and monstrous
    things,

The glimmering water holds its gracious way
  Full forth, and keeps one happier hand's-
    breadth green
Of all that storm-scathed world whereon the
    sway
  Sits dark as death of deadlier things un-
    seen.

But on the soundless and the viewless river
  That bears through night perchance again
    to day
The dead whom death and twin-born fame
    deliver
  From life that dies, and time's inveterate
    sway,

No shadow save of falsehood and of fear
  That brands the future with the past, and
    bids
The spirit wither and the soul grow sere,
  Hovers or hangs to cloud life's opening
    lids,

If life have eyes to lift again and see,
  Beyond the bounds of sensual sight or
    breath,
What life incognisable of ours may be
  That turns our light to darkness deep as
    death.

Priests and the soulless serfs of priests may
    swarm
  With vulturous acclamation, loud in lies,
About his dust while yet his dust is warm
  Who mocked as sunlight mocks their base
    blind eyes,

Their godless ghost of godhead, false and
    foul
  As fear his dam or hell his throne: but we,
Scarce hearing, heed no carrion church-wolf's
    howl:
  The corpse be theirs to mock; the soul is
    free.

Free as ere yet its earthly day was done
  It lived above the coil about us curled:
A soul whose eyes were keener than the sun,
  A soul whose wings were wider than the
    world.

We, sons of east and west, ringed round with
    dreams,
  Bound fast with visions, girt about with
    fears,
Live, trust, and think by chance, while
    shadow seems
  Light, and the wind that wrecks a hand
    that steers.

He, whose full soul held east and west in
    poise,
  Weighed man with man, and creed of
    man's with creed,
And age with age, their triumphs and their
    toys,
  And found what faith may read not and
    may read.

Scorn deep and strong as death and life, that
    lit
  With fire the smile at lies and dreams out-
    worn
Wherewith he smote them, showed sublime
    in it
  The splendour and the steadfastness of
    scorn.

What loftier heaven, what lordlier air, what
    space
  Illimitable, insuperable, infinite,
Now to that strong-winged soul yields ampler
    place
  Than passing darkness yields to passing
    light,

No dream, no faith can tell us: hope and
    fear,
  Whose tongues were loud of old as chil-
    dren's, now
From babbling fall to silence: change is
    here,
  And death; dark furrows drawn by time's
    dark plough.

Still sunward here on earth its flight was bent,
  Even since the man within the child began
To yearn and kindle with superb intent
  And trust in time to magnify the man.

Still toward the old garden of the Sun, whose
    fruit
  The honey-heavy lips of Sophocles
Desired and sang, wherein the unwithering
    root
  Sprang of all growths that thought brings
    forth and sees

Incarnate, bright with bloom or dense with
    leaf
  Far-shadowing, deep as depth of dawn or
    night:
And all were parcel of the garnered sheaf
  His strenuous spirit bound and stored
    aright.

And eastward now, and ever toward the
    dawn,
  If death's deep veil by life's bright hand be
    rent,
We see, as through the shadow of death with-
    drawn,
  The imperious soul's indomitable ascent.

But not the soul whose labour knew not
    end—
  But not the swordman's hand, the crested
    head—
The royal heart we mourn, the faultless
    friend,
  Burton—a name that lives till fame be
    dead.

A SEQUENCE OF SONNETS ON THE DEATH OF ROBERT BROWNING.

I.

THE clearest eyes in all the world they read
  With sense more keen and spirit of sight
    more true
Than burns and thrills in sunrise, when
  the dew
Flames, and absorbs the glory round it shed,
As they the light of ages quick and dead,
  Closed now, forsake us: yet the shaft
    that slew
  Can slay not one of all the works we knew,
Nor death discrown that many-laurelled head.

The works of words whose life seems light-
  ning wrought,
And moulded of unconquerable thought,
And quickened with imperishable flame,
Stand fast and shine and smile, assured
  that nought
  May fade of all their myriad-moulded fame,
  Nor England's memory clasp not Brown-
    ing's name.

December 13, 1889.

II.

Death, what hast thou to do with one for
  whom
  Time is not lord, but servant? What least
    part
Of all the fire that fed his living heart,
Of all the light more keen than sundawn's
  bloom
That lit and led his spirit, strong as doom
  And bright as hope, can aught thy breath
    may dart
  Quench? Nay, thou knowest he knew
    thee what thou art,
A shadow born of terror's barren womb,
That brings not forth save shadows. What
  art thou,
To dream, albeit thou breathe upon his
  brow,
  That power on him is given thee,—that
    thy breath
Can make him less than love acclaims him
  now,
  And hears all time sound back the word it
    saith?
What part hast thou then in his glory,
  Death?

III.

A graceless doom it seems that bids us
  grieve:
  Venice and winter, hand in deadly hand,
  Have slain the lover of her sunbright
    strand
And singer of a stormbright Christmas Eve.
A graceless guerdon we that loved receive
  For all our love, from that the dearest
    land
  Love worshipped ever. Blithe and soft
    and bland,
Too fair for storm to scathe or fire to cleave,
Shone on our dreams and memories ever-
  more
The domes, the towers, the mountains and
  the shore
  That gird or guard thee, Venice: cold and
    black
Seems now the face we loved as he of yore.
  We have given thee love—no stint, no
    stay, no lack:
  What gift, what gift is this thou hast given
    us back?

IV.

But he—to him, who knows what gift is
  thine,
  Death? Hardly may we think or hope,
    when we
Pass likewise thither where to-night is he,
Beyond the irremeable outer seas that shine
And darken round such dreams as half
  divine
  Some sunlit harbour in that starless sea
  Where gleams no ship to windward or to
    lee,
To read with him the secret of thy shrine.

There too, as here, may song, delight, and
  love,
The nightingale, the sea-bird, and the dove,
Fulfil with joy the splendour of the sky
Till all beneath wax bright as all above:
  But none of all that search the heavens,
    and try
  The sun, may match the sovereign eagle's
    eye.

December 14.

v.

Among the wondrous ways of men and time
He went as one that ever found and
sought
And bore in hand the lamplike spirit of
thought
To illume with instance of its fire sub-
lime
The dusk of many a cloudlike age and clime.
No spirit in shape of light and darkness
wrought,
No faith, no fear, no dream, no rapture,
nought
That blooms in wisdom, nought that burns in
crime,
No virtue girt and armed and helmed with
light,
No love more lovely than the snows are white,
No serpent sleeping in some dead soul's
tomb,
No song-bird singing from some live soul's
height,
But he might hear, interpret, or illume
With sense invasive as the dawn of doom.

VI.

What secret thing of splendour or of shade
Surmised in all those wandering ways
wherein
Man, led of love and life and death and
sin,
Strays, climbs, or cowers, allured, absorbed,
afraid,
Might not the strong and sunlike sense invade
Of that full soul that had for aim to win
Light, silent over time's dark toil and din,

Life, at whose touch death fades as dead
things fade?
O spirit of man, what mystery moves in thee
That he might know not of in spirit, and
see
The heart within the heart that seems to
strive,
The life within the life that seems to be,
And hear, through all thy storms that
whirl and drive,
The living sound of all men's souls alive?

VII.

He held no dream worth waking: so he said,
He who stands now on death's triumphal
steep,
Awakened out of life wherein we sleep
And dream of what he knows and sees,
being dead.
But never death for him was dark or dread:
'Look forth' he bade the soul, and fear
not. Weep,
All ye that trust not in his truth, and keep
Vain memory's vision of a vanished head
As all that lives of all that once was he
Save that which lightens from his word: but
we,
Who, seeing the sunset-coloured waters
roll,
Yet know the sun subdued not of the sea,
Nor weep nor doubt that still the spirit is
whole,
And life and death but shadows of the
soul.

December 15.

SUNSET AND MOONRISE.

NEW YEAR'S EVE, 1889.

ALL the west, whereon the sunset sealed
the dead year's glorious grave
Fast with seals of light and fire and cloud
that light and fire illume,
Glows at heart and kindles earth and
heaven with joyous blush and bloom,
Warm and wide as life, and glad of death that
only slays to save.
As a tide-reconquered sea-rock lies aflush
with the influent wave

Lies the light aflush with darkness, lapped
about by lustrous gloom,
Even as life with death, and fame with
time, and memory with the tomb,
Where a dead man hath for vassals Fame the
serf and Time the slave.

Far from earth as heaven, the steadfast light
withdrawn, superb, suspense,
Burns in dumb divine expansion of illimitable flower:

Moonrise whets the shadow's edges keen as
noontide: hence and thence
Glows the presence from us passing,
shines and passes not the power.

Souls arise whose word remembered is as
spirit within the sense:
All the hours are theirs of all the seasons:
death has but his hour.

BIRTHDAY ODE.

AUGUST 6, 1891.

I.

LOVE and praise, and a length of days whose
shadow cast upon time is light,
Days whose sound was a spell shed round
from wheeling wings as of doves in flight,
Meet in one, that the mounting sun to-day
may triumph, and cast out night.

Two years more than the full fourscore lay
hallowing hands on a sacred head—
Scarce one score of the perfect four uncrowned
of fame as they smiled and fled:
Still and soft and alive aloft their sunlight
stays though the suns be dead.

Ere we were or were thought on, ere the love
that gave us to life began,
Fame grew strong with his crescent song, to
greet the goal of the race they ran,
Song with fame, and the lustrous name with
years whose changes acclaimed the man.

II.

Soon, ere time in the rounding rhyme of
choral seasons had hailed us men,
We too heard and acclaimed the word whose
breath was life upon England then—
Life more bright than the breathless light of
soundless noon in a songless glen.

Ah, the joy of the heartstruck boy whose ear
was opened of love to hear!
Ah, the bliss of the burning kiss of song and
spirit, the mounting cheer

Lit with fire of divine desire and love that
knew not if love were fear!

Fear and love as of heaven above and earth
enkindled of heaven were one;
One white flame, that around his name
grew keen and strong as the worldwied
sun;
Awe made bright with implied delight, as
weft with weft of the rainbow spun.

III.

He that fears not the voice he hears and loves
shall never have heart to sing:
All the grace of the sun-god's face that bids
the soul as a fountain spring
Bids the brow that receives it bow, and hail
his likeness on earth as king.

We that knew when the sun's shaft flew
beheld and worshipped, adored and
heard:
Light rang round it of shining sound, whence
all men's hearts were subdued and
stirred:
Joy, love, sorrow, the day, the morrow, took
life upon them in one man's word.

Not for him can the years wax dim, nor
downward swerve on a darkening way:
Upward wind they, and leave behind such
light as lightens the front of May:
Fair as youth and sublime as truth we find
the fame that we hail to-day.

THRENODY.

OCTOBER 6, 1892.

I.

LIFE, sublime and serene when time had
　　power upon it and ruled its breath,
Changed it, bade it be glad or sad, and hear
　　what change in the world's ear saith,
Shines more fair in the starrier air whose
　　glory lightens the dusk of death.

Suns that sink on the wan sea's brink, and
　　moons that kindle and flame and fade,
Leave more clear for the darkness here the
　　stars that set not and see not shade
Rise and rise on the lowlier skies by rule of
　　sunlight and moonlight swayed.

So, when night for his eyes grew bright, his
　　proud head pillowed on Shakespeare's
　　breast,
Hand in hand with him, soon to stand where
　　shine the glories that death loves best,
Passed the light of his face from sight, and
　　sank sublimely to radiant rest.

II.

Far above us and all our love, beyond all reach
　　of its voiceless praise,
Shines for ever the name that nevertshall feel
　　the shade of the changeful days
Fall and chill the delight that still sees winter's
　　light on it shine like May's.

Strong as death is the dark day's breath whose
　　blast has withered the life we see

Here where light is the child of night, and
　　less than visions or dreams are we:
Strong as death; but a word, a breath, a
　　dream is stronger than death can be.

Strong as truth and superb in youth eternal,
　　fair as the sundawn's flame
Seen when May on her first-born day bids
　　earth exult in her radiant name,
Lives, clothed round with its praise and
　　crowned with love that dies not, his love-
　　lit fame.

III.

Fairer far than the morning star, and sweet
　　for us as the songs that rang
Loud through heaven from the choral Seven
　　when all the stars of the morning sang,
Shines the song that we loved so long—since
　　first such love in us flamed and sprang.

England glows as a sunlit rose from mead to
　　mountain, from sea to sea,
Bright with love and with pride above all
　　taint of sorrow that needs must be,
Needs must live for an hour, and give its
　　rainbow's glory to lawn and lea.

Not through tears shall the new-born years be-
　　hold him, crowned with applause of men,
Pass at last from a lustrous past to life that
　　lightens beyond their ken,
Glad and dead, and from earthward led to
　　sunward, guided of Imogen.

THE BALLAD OF MELICERTES.

IN MEMORY OF THEODORE DE BANVILLE.

DEATH, a light outshining life, bids heaven
　　resume
　　Star by star the souls whose light made
　　earth divine.
Death, a night outshining day, sees burn and
　　bloom
　　Flower by flower, and sun by sun, the fames
　　that shine
Deathless, higher than life beheld their
　　sovereign sign.

Dead Simonides of Ceos, late restored,
Given again of God, again by man de-
　　plored,
　　Shone but yestereve, a glory frail as
　　breath.
Frail? But Fame's breath quickens, kindles,
　　keeps in ward,
　　Life so sweet as this that dies and casts off
　　death.

Mother's love, and rapture of the sea, whose
womb
  Breeds eternal life of joy that stings like
  brine,
Pride of song, and joy to dare the singer's
doom,
  Sorrow soft as sleep and laughter bright as
  wine,
Flushed and filled with fragrant fire his lyric
line.
As the sea-shell utters, like a stricken
chord,
Music uttering all the sea's within it stored,
  Poet well-beloved, whose praise our sor-
  row saith,
So thy songs retain thy soul, and so record
  Life so sweet as this that dies and casts off
  death.

Side by side we mourned at Gautier's golden
tomb:
  Here in spirit now I stand and mourn at
  thine.
Yet no breath of death strikes thence, no
shadow of gloom,

Only light more bright than gold of the in-
most mine,
Only steam of incense warm from love's
own shrine.
Not the darkling stream, the sundering
Stygian ford,
Not the hour that smites and severs as a
sword,
  Not the night subduing light that per-
  isheth,
Smite, subdue, divide from us by doom ab-
horred,
  Life so sweet as this that dies and casts off
  death.

Prince of song more sweet than honey, lyric
lord,
Not thy France here only mourns a light
adored,
  One whose love-lit fame the world in-
  heriteth.
Strangers too, now brethren, hail with heart's
accord
  Life so sweet as this that dies and casts off
  death.

AU TOMBEAU DE BANVILLE.

LA plus douce des voix qui vibraient sous
le ciel
Se tait: les rossignols ailés pleurent le frère
Qui s'envole au-dessus de l'âpre et sombre
terre,
Ne lui laissant plus voir que l'être essentiel,

Esprit qui chante et rit, fleur d'une âme sans
fiel.
L'ombre élyséenne, où la nuit n'est que
lumière,

Revoit, tout revêtu de splendeur douce et
fière,
Mélicerte, poète à la bouche de miel.

Dieux exilés, passants célestes de ce monde,
Dont on entend parfois dans notre nuit pro-
fonde
Vibrer la voix, frémir les ailes, vous savez
S'il vous aima, s'il vous pleura, lui dont la vie
Et le chant rappelaient les vôtres. Recevez
L'âme de Mélicerte affranchie et ravie.

LIGHT: AN EPICEDE.

TO PHILIP BOURKE MARSTON.

LOVE will not weep because the seal is broken
  That sealed upon a life beloved and brief
Darkness, and let but song break through for
token

How deep, too far for even thy song's
relief,
Slept in thy soul the secret springs of
grief.

Thy song may soothe full many a soul hereafter,
  As tears, if tears will come, dissolve despair;
As here but late, with smile more bright than
laughter,
  Thy sweet strange yearning eyes would
  seem to bear
Witness that joy might cleave the clouds of
care.

Two days agone, and love was one with pity
  When love gave thought wings toward the
  glimmering goal
Where, as a shrine lit in some darkling city,
  Shone soft the shrouded image of thy soul:
And now thou art healed of life; thou art
healed, and whole.

Yea, two days since, all we that loved thee
pitied:
  And now with wondering love, with shame
  of face,
We think how foolish now, how far unfitted,
  Should be from us, toward thee who hast
  run thy race,
  Pity—toward thee, who hast won the painless place;

The painless world of death, yet unbeholden
  Of eyes that dream what light now lightens thine
And will not weep. Thought, yearning
toward those olden

Dear hours that sorrow sees and sees not
shine,
  Bows tearless down before a flameless
  shrine:

A flameless altar here of life and sorrow
  Quenched and consumed together. These
  were one,
One thing for thee, as night was one with
morrow
  And utter darkness with the sovereign sun:
And now thou seest life, sorrow, and dark-
ness done.

And yet love yearns again to win thee
hither;
  Blind love, and loveless, and unworthy
  thee:
Here where I watch the hours of darkness
wither
  Here where mine eyes were glad and sad
  to see
  Thine that could see not mine, though
  turned on me.

But now, if aught beyond sweet sleep lie
hidden,
  And sleep be sealed not fast on dead men's
  sight
For ever, thine hath grace for ours forbidden,
  And sees us compassed round with change
  and night:
Yet light like thine is ours, if love be
light.

THRENODY.

WATCHING here alone by the fire whereat
last year
Sat with me the friend that a week since yet
was near,
  That a week has borne so far and hid so
  deep,
  Woe am I that I may not weep,
  May not yearn to behold him here.

Shame were mine, and little the love I bore
him were,
Now to mourn that better he fares than love
may fare
  Which desires, and would not have indeed,
  its will,
  Would not love him so worse than ill,
  Would not clothe him again with care.

Yet can love not choose but remember,
hearts but ache,
Eyes but darken, only for one vain thought's
poor sake,
  For the thought that by this hearth's now
  lonely side
  Two fast friends, on the day he died,
  Looked once more for his hand to take.

Let thy soul forgive them, and pardon heal
the sin,
Though their hearts be heavy to think what
then had been,
  The delight that never while they live may
  be—
  Love's communion of speech with thee,
  Soul and speech with the soul therein.

O my friend, O brother, a glory veiled and
    marred!
Never love made moan for a life more evil-
    starred.
    Was it envy, chance, or chance-compelling
      fate,
    Whence thy spirit was bruised so late,
    Bowed so heavily, bound so hard?

Now released, it may be,—if only love might
    know—
Filled and fired with sight, it beholds us
    blind and low

With a pity keener yet, if that may be,
Even than ever was this that we
Felt, when love of thee wrought us
    woe.

None may tell the depths and the heights of
    life and death.
What we may we give thee: a word that sor-
    row saith,
    And that none will heed save sorrow:
      scarce a song.
    All we may, who have loved thee long,
    Take: the best we can give is breath.

A DIRGE.

A BELL tolls on in my heart
    As though in my ears a knell
    Had ceased for awhile to swell,
But the sense of it would not part
From the spirit that bears its part
    In the chime of the soundless bell.

Ah dear dead singer of sorrow,
    The burden is now not thine
    That grief bade sound for a sign
Through the songs of the night whose morrow
Has risen, and I may not borrow
    A beam from its radiant shrine.

The burden has dropped from thee
    That grief on thy life bound fast;
    The winter is over and past
Whose end thou wast fain to see.
Shall sorrow not comfort me
    That is thine no longer—at last?

Good day, good night, and good morrow,
    Men living and mourning say.
    For thee we could only pray
That night of the day might borrow
Such comfort as dreams lend sorrow:
    Death gives thee at last good day.

A REMINISCENCE.

THE rose to the wind has yielded: all its
    leaves
    Lie strewn on the graveyard grass, and
      all their light
And colour and fragrance leave our sense
    and sight
Bereft as a man whom bitter time be-
    reaves
Of blossom at once and hope of garnered
    sheaves,
    Of April at once and August. Day to
      night
Calls wailing, and life to death, and depth
    to height,

And soul upon soul of man that hears and
    grieves.

Who knows, though he see the snow-cold
    blossom shed,
If haply the heart that burned within the
    rose,
The spirit in sense, the life of life be dead?
    If haply the wind that slays with storming
      snows
Be one with the wind that quickens? Bow
    thine head,
    O Sorrow, and commune with thine heart:
      who knows?

VIA DOLOROSA.

THE days of a man are threescore years and
ten.
The days of his life were half a man's,
whom we
Lament, and would yet not bid him back,
to be
Partaker of all the woes and ways of men.
Life sent him enough of sorrow: not again
Would anguish of love, beholding him set
free,
Bring back the beloved to suffer life and see
No light but the fire of grief that scathed him
then.
We know not at all: we hope, and do not
fear.
We shall not again behold him, late so near,
Who now from afar above, with eyes alight
And spirit enkindled, haply toward us here
Looks down unforgetful yet of days like
night
And love that has yet his sightless face in
sight.

February 15, 1887.

I.

TRANSFIGURATION.

BUT half a man's days—and his days were
nights.
What hearts were ours who loved him,
should we pray
That night would yield him back to dark-
ling day,
Sweet death that soothes, to life that spoils
and smites?
For now, perchance, life lovelier than the
light's
That shed no comfort on his weary way
Shows him what none may dream to see or
say
Ere yet the soul may scale those topless
heights
Where death lies dead, and triumph. Haply
there
Already may his kindling eyesight find
Faces of friends—no face than his more
fair—
And first among them found of all his
kind
Milton, with crowns from Eden on his hair,
And eyes that meet a brother's now not
blind.

II.

DELIVERANCE.

O DEATH, fair Death, sole comforter and
sweet,
Nor Love nor Hope can give such gifts
as thine.
Sleep hardly shows us round thy shadowy
shrine
What roses hang, what music floats, what
feet
Pass and what wings of angels. We repeat
Wild words or mild, disastrous or divine,
Blind prayer, blind imprecation, seeing no
sign
Nor hearing aught of thee not faint and
fleet
As words of men or snowflakes on the wind.
But if we chide thee, saying 'Thou hast
sinned, thou hast sinned,
Dark Death, to take so sweet a light away
As shone but late, though shadowed, in
our skies,'
We hear thine answer—'Night has given
what day
Denied him: darkness hath unsealed his
eyes.'

III.

THANKSGIVING.

COULD love give strength to thank thee!
Love can give
Strong sorrow heart to suffer: what we
bear
We would not put away, albeit this
were
A burden love might cast aside and live.
Love chooses rather pain than palliative,
Sharp thought than soft oblivion. May
we dare
So trample down our passion and our
prayer
That fain would cling round feet now fugi-
tive
And stay them—so remember, so forget,
What joy we had who had his presence yet,
What griefs were his while joy in him was
ours
And grief made weary music of his breath,
As even to hail his best and last of hours
With love grown strong enough to thank
thee, Death?

IV.

LIBITINA VERTICORDIA.

SISTER of sleep, healer of life, divine
As rest and strong as very love may be,
To set the soul that love could set not
    free,
To bid the skies that day could bid not
    shine,
To give the gift that life withheld was thine.
    With all my heart I loved one borne from
        me:
    And all my heart bows down and praises
        thee,
Death, that hast now made grief not his but
    mine.

O Changer of men's hearts, we would not
    bid thee
    Turn back our hearts from sorrow: this
        alone
    We bid, we pray thee, from thy sovereign
        throne
And sanctuary sublime where heaven has hid
    thee,
    Give: grace to know of those for whom we
        weep
That if they wake their life is sweet as sleep.

V.

THE ORDER OF RELEASE.

THOU canst not give it. Grace enough is
    ours
    To know that pain for him has fallen on
        rest.
    The worst we know was his on earth: the
        best,
We fain would think,—a thought no fear
    deflowers—
Is his, released from bonds of rayless hours.
    Ah, turn our hearts from longing; bid our
        quest
    Cease, as content with failure. This thy
        guest
Sleeps, vexed no more of time's imperious
    powers,
The spirit of hope, the spirit of change and
    loss,
The spirit of love bowed down beneath his
    cross,
    Nor now needs comfort from the strength
        of song.

Love, should he wake, bears now no cross
    for him:
Dead hope, whose living eyes like his were
    dim,
    Has brought forth better comfort, strength
        more strong.

VI.

PSYCHAGOGOS.

As Greece of old acclaimed thee God and
    man,
    So, Death, our tongue acclaims thee: yet
        wast thou
    Hailed of old Rome as Romans hail thee
        now,
Goddess and woman. Since the sands first
    ran
That told when first man's life and death
    began,
    The shadows round thy blind ambiguous
        brow
    Have mocked the votive plea, the pleading
        vow
That sought thee sorrowing, fain to bless
    or ban.

But stronger than a father's love is thine,
    And gentler than a mother's. Lord and
        God,
Thy staff is surer than the wizard rod
That Hermes bare as priest before thy shrine
    And herald of thy mercies. We could
        give
Nought, when we would have given: thou
    bidst him live.

VII.

THE LAST WORD.

So many a dream and hope that went and
    came,
So many and sweet, that love thought like
    to be,
Of hours as bright and soft as those for
    me
That made our hearts for song's sweet love
    the same,
Lie now struck dead, that hope seems one
    with shame.
    O Death, thy name is Love: we know it,
        and see
    The witness: yet for very love's sake we
Can hardly bear to mix with thine his name.

Philip, how hard it is to bid thee part
Thou knowest, if aught thou knowest where
    now thou art
    Of us that loved and love thee. None
    may tell

What none but knows—how hard it is to
    say
The word that seals up sorrow, darkens day,
    And bids fare forth the soul it bids fare·
    well.

IN MEMORY OF AURELIO SAFFI.

THE wider world of men that is not ours
    Receives a soul whose life on earth was
    light.
Though darkness close the date of human
    hours,
    Love holds the spirit and sense of life in
    sight,
    That may not, even though death bid fly,
    take flight.
Faith, love, and hope fulfilled with memory,
    see
As clear and dear as life could bid it be
The present soul that is and is not he.

He, who held up the shield and sword of
    Rome
    Against the ravening brood of recreant
    France,
Beside the man of men whom heaven took
    home
    When earth beheld the spring's first eye-
    beams glance
    And life and winter seemed alike a trance
Eighteen years since, in sight of heaven and
    spring
That saw the soul above all souls take
    wing,
He too now hears the heaven we hear not
    sing.

He too now dwells where death is dead, and
    stands
    Where souls like stars exult in life to be:
Whence all who linked heroic hearts and
    hands
    Shine on our sight, and give it strength to
    see
    What hope makes fair for all whom faith
    makes free:
Free with such freedom as we find in sleep,
The light sweet shadow of death, when dreams
    are deep
And high as heaven whence light and light-
    ning leap.

And scarce a month yet gone, his living
    hand
    Writ loving words that sealed me friend of
    his.
Are heaven and earth as near as sea to
    strand?
    May life and death as bride and bridegroom
    kiss?
    His last month's written word abides, and
    is;
Clear as the sun that lit through storm and
    strife
And darkling days when hope took fear to
    wife
The faith whose fire was light of all his
    life.

A life so fair, so pure of earthlier leaven,
    That none hath won through higher and
    harder ways
The deathless life of death which earth calls
    heaven;
    Heaven, and the light of love on earth,
    and praise
    Of silent memory through subsiding days
Wherein the light subsides not whence the
    past
Feeds full with life the future. Time holds
    fast
Their names whom faith forgets not, first
    and last.

Forget? The dark forgets not dawn, nor we
    The suns that sink to rise again, and shine
Lords of live years and ages. Earth and sea
    Forget not heaven that makes them seem
    divine,
    Though night put out their fires and bid
    their shrine
Be dark and pale as storm and twilight. Day,
Not night, is everlasting: life's full sway
Bids death bow down as dead, and pass
    away.

What part has death in souls that past all
  fear
  Win heavenward their supernal way, and
  smite
With scorn sublime as heaven such dreams
  as here
  Plague and perplex with cloud and fire the
  light
  That leads men's waking souls from glimmering night
To the awless heights of day, whereon man's
  awe,
Transfigured, dies in rapture, seeing the
  law
Sealed of the sun that earth arising saw?

Faith, justice, mercy, love, and heaven-born
  hate
  That sets them all on fire and bids them be
More than soft words and dreams that wake
  too late,
  Shone living through the lordly life that
  we
  Beheld, revered, and loved on earth, while
  he
Dwelt here, and bade our eyes take light
  thereof;
Light as from heaven that flamed or smiled
  above
In light or fire whose very hate was love.

No hate of man, but hate of hate whose foam
  Sheds poison forth from tongues of snakes
  and priests,
And stains the sickening air with steams
  whence Rome
  Now feeds not full the God that slays and
  feasts;
  For now the fangs of all the ravenous
  beasts
That ramped about him, fain of prayer and
  prey,
Fulfil their lust no more: the tide of day
Swells, and compels him down the deathward
  way.

Night sucks the Church its creature down,
  and hell
  Yawns, heaves, and yearns to clasp its
  loathliest child
Close to the breasts that bore it. All the
  spell
  Whence darkness saw the dawn in heaven
  defiled
  Is dumb as death: the lips that lied and
  smiled
Wax white for fear as ashes. She that bore
The banner up of darkness now no more
Sheds night and fear and shame from shore
  to shore.

When they that cast her kingdom down
  were born,
  North cried on south and east made moan
  to west
For hopes that love had hardly heart to
  mourn,
  For Italy that was not. Kings on quest,
  By priests whose blessings burn as curses
  blest,
Made spoil of souls and bodies bowed and
  bound,
Hunted and harried, leashed as horse or
  hound,
And hopeless of the hope that died unfound.

And now that faith has brought forth fruit
  to time,
  How should not memory praise their
  names, and hold
Their record even as Dante's life sublime,
  Who bade his dream, found fair and false
  of old,
  Live? Not till earth and heaven be dead
  and cold
May man forget whose work and will made
  one
Italy, fair as heaven or freedom won,
And left their fame to shine beside her sun.

April 1890.

THE FESTIVAL OF BEATRICE.

DANTE, sole standing on the heavenward
  height,
  Beheld and heard one saying, 'Behold
  me well:
I am, I am Beatrice.' Heaven and hell
Kept silence, and the illimitable light

Of all the stars was darkness in his sight
  Whose eyes beheld her eyes again, and fell
Shame-stricken. Since her soul took flight
  to dwell
In heaven, six hundred years have taken
  flight.

And now that heavenliest part of earth
whereon
Shines yet their shadow as once their presence shone
   To her bears witness for his sake,
as he

For hers bare witness when her face was
gone:
   No slave, no hospice now for grief—but
free
From shore to mountain and from Alp to
sea.

THE MONUMENT OF GIORDANO BRUNO.

I.

Not from without us, only from within,
   Comes or can ever come upon us light
   Whereby the soul keeps ever truth in
sight.
No truth, no strength, no comfort man may
win,
No grace for guidance, no release from
sin,
   Save of his own soul's giving. Deep and
bright
   As fire enkindled in the core of night
Burns in the soul where once its fire has
been
The light that leads and quickens thought,
inspired
   To doubt and trust and conquer. So he
said
   Whom Sidney, flower of England, lordliest
head
Of all we love, loved: but the fates re-
quired
A sacrifice to hate and hell, ere fame
Should set with his in heaven Giordano's
name.

II.

Cover thine eyes and weep, O child of hell,
   Grey spouse of Satan, Church of name
abhorred.
   Weep, withered harlot, with thy weeping
lord,
Now none will buy the heaven thou hast to
sell
At price of prostituted souls, and swell
   Thy loveless list of lovers. Fire and sword
   No more are thine: the steel, the wheel, the
cord,
The flames that rose round living limbs,
and fell
In lifeless ash and ember, now no more
   Approve thee godlike. Rome, redeemed
at last
   From all the red pollution of thy past,
Acclaims the grave bright face that smiled of
yore
Even on the fire that caught it round and
clomb
To cast its ashes on the face of Rome.

June 9,1889.

LIFE IN DEATH.

He should have followed who goes forth
before us,
   Last born of us in life, in death first-born:
   The last to lift up eyes against the morn,
The first to see the sunset. Life, that bore us
Perchance for death to comfort and restore
us,
   Of him hath left us here awhile forlorn,
   For him is as a garment overworn,
And time and change, with suns and stars in
chorus,

Silent. But if, beyond all change or time,
A law more just, more equal, more sublime
   Than sways the surge of life's loud sterile
sea
Sways that still world whose peace environs
him,
Where death lies dead as night when stars
wax dim,
   Above all thought or hope of ours is he.

August 2, 1891.

EPICEDE.

As a vesture shalt thou change them, said
    the prophet,
    And the raiment that was flesh is turned to
      dust;
Dust and flesh and dust again the likeness
    of it,
    And the fine gold woven and worn of youth
      is rust.
Hours that wax and wane salute the shade
    and scoff it,
    That it knows not aught it doth nor aught
      it must:
Day by day the speeding soul makes haste to
    doff it,
    Night by night the pride of life resigns its
      trust.

Sleep, whose silent notes of song loud life's
    derange not,
    Takes the trust in hand awhile as angels
      may:
Joy with wings that rest not, grief with wings
    that range not,
    Guard the gates of sleep and waking, gold
      or grey.
Joys that joys estrange, and griefs that griefs
    estrange not,
    Day that yearns for night, and night that
      yearns for day,
As a vesture shalt thou change them, and
    they change not,
    Seeing that change may never change or
      pass away.

Life of death makes question, 'What art thou
    that changest?
    What am I, that fear should trust or faith
      should doubt?
I that lighten, thou that darkenest and es-
    trangest,
    Is it night or day that girds us round about?
Light and darkness on the ways wherein thou
    rangest
    . Seen as one, and beams as clouds they put
      to rout.
Strange is hope, but fear of all things born
    were strangest,
    Seeing that none may strive with change to
      cast it out.

·Change alone stands fast, thou sayest, O
    death: I know not:

What art thou, my brother death, that thou
    shouldst know?
Men may reap no fruits of fields wherein they
    sow not;
    Hope or fear is all the seed we have to sow.
Winter seals the sacred springs up that they
    flow not:
    Wind and sun and change unbind them,
      and they flow.
Am I thou or art thou I? The years that
    show not
    Pass, and leave no sign when time shall be
      to show.'

Hope makes suit to faith lest fear give ear to
    sorrow:
    Doubt strews dust upon his head, and goes
      his way.
All the golden hope that life of death would
    borrow,
    How, if death require again, may life re-
      pay?
Earth endures no darkness whence no light
    yearns thorough;
    God in man as light in darkness lives, they
      say:
Yet, would midnight take assurance of the
    morrow,
    Who shall pledge the faith or seal the bond
      of day?

Darkness, mute or loud with music or with
    mourning,
    Starry darkness, winged with wind or
      clothed with calm,
Dreams no dream of grief or fear or wrath or
    warning,
    Bears no sign of race or goal or strife or
      palm.
Word of blessing, word of mocking or of
    scorning,
    Knows it none, nor whence its breath sheds
      blight or balm.
Yet a little while, and hark, the psalm of
    morning:
    Yet a little while, and silence takes the
      psalm.

All the comfort, all the worship, all the won-
    der,
    All the light of love that darkness holds in
      fee,

All the song that silence keeps or keeps not
under,
Night, the soul that knows gives thanks
for all to thee.
Far beyond the gates that morning strikes in
sunder,

Hopes that grief makes holy, dreams that
fear sets free,
Far above the throne of thought, the lair of
thunder,
Silent shines the word whose utterance fills
the sea.

MEMORIAL VERSES ON THE DEATH OF WILLIAM BELL SCOTT.

A LIFE more bright than the sun's face, bowed
Through stress of season and coil of cloud,
Sets: and the sorrow that casts out fear
Scarce deems him dead in his chill shroud,

Dead on the breast of the dying year,
Poet and painter and friend, thrice dear
For love of the suns long set, for love
Of song that sets not with sunset here,

For love of the fervent heart, above
Their sense who saw not the swift light move
That filled with sense of the loud sun's lyre
The thoughts that passion was fain to prove

In fervent labour of high desire
And faith that leapt from its own quenched
pyre
Alive and strong as the sun, and caught
From darkness light, and from twilight fire.

Passion, deep as the depths unsought
Whence faith's own hope may redeem us
nought,
Filled full with ardour of pain sublime
His mourning song and his mounting thought.

Elate with sense of a sterner time,
His hand's flight clomb as a bird's might
climb
Calvary: dark in the darkling air
That shrank for fear of the crowning crime,

Three crosses rose on the hillside bare,
Shown scarce by grace of the lightning's glare
That clove the veil of the temple through
And smote the priests on the threshold there.

The soul that saw it, the hand that drew,
Whence light as thought's or as faith's glance
flew,

And stung to life the sepulchral past,
And bade the stars of it burn anew,

Held no less than the dead world fast
The light live shadows about them cast,
The likeness living of dawn and night,
The days that pass and the dreams that
last.

Thought, clothed round with sorrow as light,
Dark as a cloud that the moon turns bright,
Moved, as a wind on the striving sea,
That yearns and quickens and flags in flight,

Through forms of colour and song that he
Who fain would have set its wide wings free
Cast round it, clothing or chaining hope
With lights that last not and shades that
flee.

Scarce in song could his soul find scope,
Scarce the strength of his hand might ope
Art's inmost gate of her sovereign shrine,
To cope with heaven as a man may cope.

But high as the hope of a man may shine
The faith, the fervour, the life divine
That thrills our life and transfigures, rose
And shone resurgent, a sunbright sign,

Through shapes whereunder the strong soul
glows
And fills them full as a sunlit rose
With sense and fervour of life, whose light
The fool's eye knows not, the man's eye
knows.

None that can read or divine aright
The scriptures writ of the soul may slight
The strife of a strenuous soul to show
More than the craft of the hand may write.

None may slight it, and none may know
How high the flames that aspire and glow
  From heart and spirit and soul may climb
And triumph; higher than the souls lie low

Whose hearing hears not the livelong rhyme,
Whose eyesight sees not the light sublime,
  That shines, that sounds, that ascends and
    lives
Unquenched of change, unobscured of time.

A long life's length, as a man's life gives
Space for the spirit that soars and strives
  To strive and soar, has the soul shone
    through
That heeds not whither the world's wind
    drives

Now that the days and the ways it knew
Are strange, are dead as the dawn's grey dew
  At high midnoon of the mounting day
That mocks the might of the dawn it slew.

Yet haply may not—and haply may—
No sense abide of the dead sun's ray
  Wherein the soul that outsoars us now
Rejoiced with ours in its radiant sway.

Hope may hover, and doubt may bow,
Dreaming. Haply—they dream not how—
  Not life but death may indeed be dead
When silence darkens the dead man's
    brow.

Hope, whose name is remembrance, fed
With love that lightens from seasons fled,
  Dreams, and craves not indeed to know,
That death and life are as souls that
    wed.

But change that falls on the heart like
    snow
Can chill not memory nor hope, that show
  The soul, the spirit, the heart and head,
Alive above us who strive below.

AN OLD SAYING.

MANY waters cannot quench love,
  Neither can the floods drown it.
Who shall snare or slay the white dove
  Faith, whose very dreams crown it,
Gird it round with grace and peace, deep,
Warm, and pure, and soft as sweet sleep?
Many waters cannot quench love,
  Neither can the floods drown it.

Set me as a seal upon thine heart,
  As a seal upon thine arm.
How should we behold the days depart
  And the nights resign their charm?
Love is as the soul: though hate and fear
Waste and overthrow, they strike not here.
Set me as a seal upon thine heart,
  As a seal upon thine arm.

A MOSS-ROSE.

IF the rose of all flowers be the rarest
  That heaven may adore from above,
And the fervent moss-rose be the fairest
  That sweetens the summer with love,

Can it be that a fairer than any
  Should blossom afar from the tree?
Yet one, and a symbol of many,
  Shone sudden for eyes that could see.

In the grime and the gloom of November
  The bliss and the bloom of July
Bade autumn rejoice and remember
  The balm of the blossoms gone by.

Would you know what moss-rose now it may be
  That puts all the rest to the blush,
The flower was the face of a baby,
  The moss was a bonnet of plush.

TO A CAT.

I.

STATELY, kindly, lordly friend,
        Condescend
Here to sit by me, and turn
Glorious eyes that smile and burn,
Golden eyes, love's lustrous meed,
On the golden page I read.

All your wondrous wealth of hair,
        Dark and fair,
Silken-shaggy, soft and bright
As the clouds and beams of night,
Pays my reverent hand's caress
Back with friendlier gentleness.

Dogs may fawn on all and some
        As they come;
You, a friend of loftier mind,
Answer friends alone in kind.
Just your foot upon my hand
Softly bids it understand.

Morning round this silent sweet
        Garden-seat
Sheds its wealth of gathering light,
Thrills the gradual clouds with might,
Changes woodland, orchard, heath,
Lawn, and garden there beneath.

Fair and dim they gleamed below:
        Now they glow
Deep as even your sunbright eyes,
Fair as even the wakening skies.
Can it not or can it be
Now that you give thanks to see?

May not you rejoice as I,
        Seeing the sky
Change to heaven revealed, and bid

Earth reveal the heaven it hid
All night long from stars and moon,
Now the sun sets all in tune?

What within you wakes with day
        Who can say?
All too little may we tell,
Friends who like each other well,
What might haply, if we might,
Bid us read our lives aright.

II.

Wild on woodland ways your sires
        Flashed like fires;
Fair as flame and fierce and fleet
As with wings on wingless feet
Shone and sprang your mother, free,
Bright and brave as wind or sea.

Free and proud and glad as they,
        Here to-day
Rests or roams their radiant child,
Vanquished not, but reconciled,
Free from curb of aught above
Save the lovely curb of love.

Love through dreams of souls divine
        Fain would shine
Round a dawn whose light and song
Then should right our mutual wrong—
Speak, and seal the love-lit law
Sweet Assisi's seer foresaw.

Dreams were theirs; yet haply may
        Dawn a day
When such friends and fellows born,
Seeing our earth as fair at morn,
May for wiser love's sake see
More of heaven's deep heart than we.

HAWTHORN DYKE.

ALL the golden air is full of balm and bloom
    Where the hawthorns line the shelving
        dyke with flowers.
Joyous children born of April's happiest
        hours,
High and low they laugh and lighten, know-
        ing their doom

Bright as brief—to bless and cheer they know
        not whom,
    Heed not how, but washed and warmed
        with suns and showers
    Smile, and bid the sweet soft gradual banks
        and bowers
Thrill with love of sunlit fire or starry gloom.

All our moors and lawns all round rejoice;
    but here
All the rapturous resurrection of the
    year
Finds the radiant utterance perfect, sees
    the word

Spoken, hears the light that speaks it. Far
    and near,
All the world is heaven: and man and
    flower and bird
Here are one at heart with all things seen
    and heard.

THE BROTHERS.

THERE were twa brethren fell on strife;
  Sweet fruits are sair to gather:
The tane has reft his brother of life;
  And the wind wears owre the heather.

There were twa brethren fell to fray;
  Sweet fruits are sair to gather:
The tane is clad in a cloak of clay;
  And the wind wears owre the heather.

O loud and loud was the live man's cry,
  (Sweet fruits are sair to gather)
'Would God the dead and the slain were I!'
  And the wind wears owre the heather.

O sair was the wrang and sair the fray,'
  (Sweet fruits are sair to gather)
But liefer had love be slain than slay.'
  And the wind wears owre the heather.

'O sweet is the life that sleeps at hame,'
  (Sweet fruits are sair to gather)
'But I maun wake on a far sea's faem.'
  And the wind wears owre the heather.

'And women are fairest of a' things fair,'
  (Sweet fruits are sair to gather)
But never shall I kiss woman mair.'
  And the wind wears owre the heather.

Between the birk and the aik and the thorn
  (Sweet fruits are sair to gather)
He's laid his brother to lie forlorn:
  And the wind wears owre the heather.

Between the bent and the burn and the broom
  (Sweet fruits are sair to gather)
He's laid him to sleep till dawn of doom:
  And the wind wears owre the heather.

He's tane him owre the waters wide,
  (Sweet fruits are sair to gather)

Afar to fleet and afar to bide:
  And the wind wears owre the heather.

His hair was yellow, his cheek was red,
  (Sweet fruits are sair to gather)
When he set his face to the wind and fled:
  And the wind wears owre the heather.

His banes were stark and his een were
    bright
  (Sweet fruits are sair to gather)
When he set his face to the sea by night.
  And the wind wears owre the heather.

His cheek was wan and his hair was grey
  (Sweets fruits are sair to gather)
When he came back hame frae the wide
    world's way:
  And the wind wears owre the heather.

His banes were weary, his een were dim,
  (Sweet fruits are sair to gather)
And nae man lived and had mind of him:
  And the wind wears owre the heather.

'O whatten a wreck wad they seek on land'
  (Sweet fruits are sair to gather)
'That they houk the turf to the seaward
    hand?'
  And the wind wears owre the heather.

'O whatten a prey wad they think to take'
  (Sweet fruits are sair to gather)
'That they delve the dykes for a dead man's
    sake?'
  And the wind wears owre the heather.

A bane of the dead in his hand he's tane;
  Sweet fruits are sair to gather:
And the red blood brak frae the dead white
    bane.
  And the wind wears owre the heather.

He's cast it forth of his auld faint hand;
　Sweet fruits are sair to gather:
And the red blood ran on the wan wet sand.
　And the wind wears owre the heather.

'O whatten a slayer is this,' they said,
　(Sweet fruits are sair to gather)
　That the straik of his hand should raise his
　　dead?'
And the wind wears owre the heather.

'O weel is me for the sign I take'
　(Sweet fruits are sair to gather)
'That now I may die for my auld sin's sake.'
　And the wind wears owre the heather.

'For the dead was in wait now fifty year,'
　(Sweet fruits are sair to gather)
'And now shall I die for his blood's sake
　here.'
　And the wind wears owre the heather.

JACOBITE SONG.

Now who will speak, and lie not,
　And pledge not life, but give?
Slaves herd with herded cattle:
The dawn grows bright for battle,
And if we die, we die not;
　And if we live, we live.

The faith our fathers fought for,
　The kings our fathers knew,
We fight but as they fought for:
We seek the goal they sought for,
　The chance they hailed and knew,
The praise they strove and wrought for,
　To leave their blood as dew
　On fields that flower anew.

Men live that serve the stranger;
　Hounds live that huntsmen tame:
These life-days of our living
Are days of God's good giving
Where death smiles soft on danger
　And life scowls dark on shame.

And what would you do other,
　Sweet wife, if you were I?
And how should you be other,
My sister, than your brother,
　If you were man as I,
Born of our sire and mother,
　With choice to cower and fly,
　And chance to strike and die?

No churl's our oldworld name is,
　The lands we leave are fair:
But fairer far than these are,

But wide as all the seas are,
But high as heaven the fame is
　That if we die we share.

Our name the night may swallow,
　Our lands the churl may take:
But night nor death may swallow,
Nor hell's nor heaven's dim hollow,
　The star whose height we take,
The star whose light we follow
　For faith's unfaltering sake
　Till hope that sleeps awake.

Soft hope's light lure we serve not,
　Nor follow, fain to find:
Dark time's last word may smite her
Dead, ere man's falsehood blight her:
But though she die, we swerve not,
　Who cast not eye behind.

Faith speaks when hope dissembles:
　Faith lives when hope lies dead:
If death as life dissembles,
And all that night assembles
　Of stars at dawn lie dead,
Faint hope that smiles and trembles
　May tell not well for dread:
　But faith has heard it said.

Now who will fight, and fly not,
　And grudge not life to give?
And who will strike beside us,
　If life's or death's light guide us?
For if we live, we die not,
　And if we die, we live.

THE BALLAD OF DEAD MEN'S BAY.

THE sea swings owre the slants of sand,
All white with winds that drive
The sea swirls up to the still dim strand,
Where nae man comes alive.

At the grey soft edge of the fruitless surf
A light flame sinks and springs;
At the grey soft rim of the flowerless turf
A low flame leaps and clings.

What light is this on a sunless shore,
  What gleam on a starless sea?
Was it earth's or hell's waste womb that
        bore
  Such births as should not be?

As lithe snakes turning, as bright stars burn-
        ing,
  They bicker and beckon and call;
As wild waves churning, as wild winds yearn-
        ing,
  They flicker and climb and fall.

A soft strange cry from the landward rings—
  'What ails the sea to shine?'
A keen sweet note from the spray's rim
        springs—
  'What fires are these of thine?'

A soul am I that was born on earth
  For ae day's waesome span:
Death bound me fast on the bourn of
        birth
  Ere I were christened man.

'A light by night, I fleet and fare
  Till the day of wrath and woe;
On the hems of earth and the skirts of air
  Winds hurl me to and fro.'

'O well is thee, though the weird be strange
  That bids thee flit and flee;
For hope is child of the womb of change,
  And hope keeps watch with thee.

'When the years are gone, and the time is
        come
  God's grace may give thee grace;
And thy soul may sing, though thy soul were
        dumb
  And shine before God's face.

'But I, that lighten and revel and roll
  With the foam of the plunging sea,
No sign is mine of a breathing soul
  That God should pity me.

'Nor death, nor heaven, nor hell, nor birth
  Hath part in me nor mine:
Strong lords are these of the living earth
  And loveless lords of thine.

'But I that know nor lord nor life
  More sure than storm or spray,
Whose breath is made of sport and strife,
  Whereon shall I find stay?'

'And wouldst thou change thy doom with
        me,
  Full fain with thee would I:
For the life that lightens and lifts the sea
  Is more than earth or sky.

'And what if the day of doubt and doom
  Shall save nor smite not me?
I would not rise from the slain world's tomb
  If there be no more sea.

'Take he my soul that gave my soul,
  And give it thee to keep;
And me, while seas and stars shall roll
  Thy life that falls on sleep.'

That word went up through the mirk mid
        sky,
  And even to God's own ear:
And the Lord was ware of the keen twin cry,
  And wroth was he to hear.

He's tane the soul of the unsained child
  That fled to death from birth;
He's tane the light of the wan sea wild,
  And bid it burn on earth.

He's given the ghaist of the babe new-born
  The gift of the water-sprite,
To ride on revel from morn to morn
  And roll from night to night.

He's given the sprite of the wild wan sea
  The gift of the new-born man,
A soul for ever to bide and be
  When the years have filled their span.

When a year was gone and a year was come,
  O loud and loud cried they—
'For the lee-lang year thou hast held us dumb
  Take now thy gifts away!'

O loud and lang they cried on him,
  And sair and sair they prayed:
'Is the face of thy grace as the night's face
    grim
  For those thy wrath has made?'

A cry more bitter than tears of men
  From the rim of the dim grey sea;—
'Give me my living soul again,
  The soul thou gavest me,
The doom and the dole of kindly men,
  To bide my weird and be!'

A cry more keen from the wild low land
  Than the wail of waves that roll;—
'Take back the gift of a loveless hand,
  Thy gift of doom and dole,
The weird of men that bide on land;
  Take from me, take my soul!'

The hands that smite are the hands tha
    spare;
  They build and break the tomb;
They turn to darkness and dust and air
  The fruits of the waste earth's womb;
But never the gift of a granted prayer,
  The dole of a spoken doom.

Winds may change at a word unheard,
  But none may change the tides:
The prayer once heard is as God's own word;
  The doom once dealt abides.

And ever a cry goes up by day,
  And ever a wail by night;
And nae ship comes by the weary bay
But her shipmen hear them wail and pray,
  And see with earthly sight
The twofold flames of the twin lights play
Where the sea-banks green and the sea-floods
    grey
Are proud of peril and fain of prey,
  And the sand quakes ever; and ill fare they
  That look upon that light.

DEDICATION.

1893.

THE sea of the years that endure not
  Whose tide shall endure till we die
And know what the seasons assure not,
  If death be or life be a lie,
Sways hither the spirit and thither,
  A waif in the swing of the sea
Whose wrecks are of memories that wither
  As leaves of a tree.

We hear not and hail not with greeting
  The sound of the wings of the years,
The storm of the sound of them beating,
  That none till it pass from him hears:
But tempest nor calm can imperil
  The treasures that fade not or fly;
Change bids them not change and be sterile,
  Death bids them not die.

Hearts plighted in youth to the royal
  High service of hope and of song,
Sealed fast for endurance as loyal,
  And proved of the years as they throng,

Conceive not, believe not, and fear not
  That age may be other than youth;
That faith and that friendship may hear not
  And utter not truth.

Not yesterday's light nor to-morrow's
  Gleams nearer or clearer than gleams,
Though joys be forgotten and sorrows
  Forgotten as changes of dreams,
The dawn of the days unforgotten
  That noon could eclipse not or slay,
Whose fruits were as children begotten
  Of dawn upon day.

The years that were flowerful and fruitless,
  The years that were fruitful and dark,
The hopes that were radiant and rootless,
  The hopes that were winged for their mark,
Lie soft in the sepulchres fashioned
  Of hours that arise and subside,
Absorbed and subdued and impassioned,
  In pain or in pride.

But far in the night that entombs them
  The starshine as sunshine is strong,
And clear through the cloud that resumes
    them
  Remembrance, a light and a song,
Rings lustrous as music and hovers
  As birds that impend on the sea,
And thoughts that their prison-house covers
  Arise and are free.

Forgetfulness deep as a prison
  Holds days that are dead for us fast
Till the sepulchre sees rearisen
  The spirit whose reign is the past,
Disentrammelled of darkness, and kindled
  With life that is mightier than death,
When the life that obscured it has dwindled
  And passed as a breath.

But time nor oblivion may darken
  Remembrance whose name will be joy
While memory forgets not to hearken,
  While manhood forgets not the boy
Who heard and exulted in hearing
  The songs of the sunrise of youth
Ring radiant above him, unfearing
  And joyous as truth.

Truth, winged and enkindled with rapture
  And sense of the radiance of yore,
Fulfilled you with power to recapture
  What never might singer before—
The life, the delight, and the sorrow
  Of troublous and chivalrous years
That knew not of night or of morrow,
  Of hopes or of fears.

But wider the wing and the vision
  That quicken the spirit have spread
Since memory beheld with derision
  Man's hope to be more than his dead.
From the mists and the snows and the thun-
    ders
  Your spirit has brought for us forth
Light, music, and joy in the wonders
  And charms of the north.

The wars and the woes and the glories
  That quicken and lighten and rain
From the clouds of its chronicled stories,
  The passion, the pride, and the pain,
Whose echoes were mute and the token
  Was lost of the spells that they spake,
Rise bright at your bidding, unbroken
  Of ages that break.

For you, and for none of us other,
  Time is not: the dead that must live
Hold commune with you as a brother
  By grace of the life that you give.
The heart that was in them is in you,
  Their soul in your spirit endures:
The strength of their song is the sinew
  Of this that is yours.

Hence is it that life, everlasting
  As light and as music, abides
In the sound of the surge of it, casting
  Sound back to the surge of the tides,
Till sons of the sons of the Norsemen
  Watch, hurtling to windward and lee,
Round England, unbacked of her horsemen,
  The steeds of the sea.

SPECIMENS OF MODERN POETS

THE HEPTALOGIA

OR

THE SEVEN AGAINST SENSE

A CAP WITH SEVEN BELLS

PREFACE

To the collector of First Editions The Heptalogia has long been known as one of the less accessible volumes issued anonymously by Mr. Swinburne. In Mr. Thomas J. Wise's bibliography of the poet the facts are stated with sufficient clearness: it is also made evident that the work is destined by its author to remain *introuvable*.

That a series of such inimitable parodies should be forever restricted to a few undaunted bibliophiles would seem a woeful injustice to every outstanding lover of Letters. The sum total of first rate parody has never run to excess in English literature. *John Jones* is without doubt the choicest example of literary banter in the language.

We have added *Disgust: A Dramatic Monologue*. This is now reprinted from *The Fortnightly Review*, December 1, 1881. It parodies Lord Tennyson's *Despair: A Dramatic Monologue*, which had appeared in *The Nineteenth Century* for November, 1881.

The following is a list of the seven parodies, with the names of the poets to whom they severally apply:

THE HIGHER PANTHEISM IN A NUTSHELL.

ONE, who is not, we see: but one, whom we
  see not, is:
Surely this is not that: but that is assuredly
  this.

What, and wherefore, and whence? for under is over and under:
If thunder could be without lightning, lightning could be without thunder.

Doubt is faith in the main: but faith, on the
  whole, is doubt:
We cannot believe by proof: but could we
  believe without?

Why, and whither, and how? for barley and
  rye are not clover:
Neither are straight lines curves: yet over is
  under and over.

Two and two may be four: but four and four
  are not eight:
Fate and God may be twain: but God is the
  same thing as fate.

Ask a man what he thinks, and get from a man
  what he feels:
God, once caught in the fact, shews you a fair
  pair of heels.

Body and spirit are twins: God only knows
  which is which:
The soul squats down in the flesh, like a
  tinker drunk in a ditch.

One and two are not one: but one and nothing is two:
Truth can hardly be false, if falsehood cannot
  be true.

Once the mastodon was: pterodactyls were
  common as cocks:
Then the mammoth was God: now is He a
  prize ox.

Parallels all things are: yet many of these are
  askew:
You are certainly I: but certainly I am not
  you.

Springs the rock from the plain, shoots the
  stream from the rock:
Cocks exist for the hen: but hens exist for the
  cock.

God, whom we see not, is: and God, who is
  not, we see:
Fiddle, we know, is diddle: and diddle, we
  take it, is dee.

JOHN JONES.

I.

AT THE PIANO.

I.

LOVE me and leave me; what love bids re-
  trieve me? can June's fist grasp May?
Leave me and love me; hopes eyed once
  above me like spring's sprouts, decay;
Fall as the snow falls, when summer leaves
  grow false—cards packed for storm's
  play!

II.

Nay, say Decay's self be but last May's elf,
  wing shifted, eye sheathed—
Changeling in April's crib rocked, who lets
  'scape rills locked fast since frost
  breathed—

Skin cast (think!) adder-like, now bloom
  bursts bladder-like,—bloom frost bequeathed?

III.

Ah, how can fear sit and hear as love hears it
  grief's heart's cracked grate's screech?
Chance lets the gate sway that opens on hate's
  way and shews on shame's beach
Crouched like an imp sly change watch sweet
  love's shrimps lie, a toothful in each.

IV.

Time feels his tooth slip on husks wet from
  Truth's lip, which drops them and
  grins—
Shells where no throb stirs of life left in lob-
  sters since joy thrilled their fins—

41

Hues of the prawn's tail or comb that makes
    dawn stale,[1] so red for our sins!

V.

Years blind and deaf use the soul's joys as
    refuse, heart's peace as manure,
Reared whence, next June's rose shall bloom
    where our moons rose last year, just as
    pure:
Moons' ends match roses' ends: men by
    beasts' noses' ends mete sin's stink's cure.

VI.

Leaves love last year smelt now feel dead
    love's tears melt—flies caught in time's
    mesh!
Salt are the dews in which new time breeds
    new sin, brews blood and stews flesh;
Next year may see dead more germs than this
    weeded and reared them afresh.

VII.

Old times left perish, there's new time to
    cherish; life just shifts its tune;
As, when the day dies, earth, half afraid, eyes
    the growth of the moon;
Love me and save me, take me or waive me;
    death takes one so soon!

II.

BY THE CLIFF.

I.

Is it daytime (guess),
    You that feed my soul
      To excess
With that light in those eyes
And those curls drawn like a scroll
In that round grave guise?
      No or yes?

II.

Oh, the end, I'd say!
    Such a foolish thing
      (Pure girls' play!)
As a mere mute heart,
    Was it worth a kiss, a ring,
This? for two must part—
      Not to-day.

III.

Look, the whole sand crawls,
    Hums, a heaving hive,
      Scrapes and scrawls—
Such a buzz and burst!
    Here just one thing's not alive,
One that was at first—
      But life palls.

IV.

Yes, my heart, I know,
    Just my heart's stone dead—
      Yes, just so.
Sick with heat, those worms
    Drop down scorched and overfed—
No more need of germs!
      Let them go.

V.

Yes, but you now, look,
    You, the rouged stage female
      With a crook,
Chalked Arcadian sham,
    You that made my soul's sleep's dream ail—
Your soul fit to damn?
      Shut the book.

III.

ON THE SANDS.

I.

THERE was nothing at all in the case (con-
    ceive)
    But love; being love, it was not (under-
    stand)
Such a thing as the years let fall (believe)
    Like the rope's coil dropt from a fisher-
    man's hand
When the boat's hauled up—"by your leave!"

II.

So—well! How that crab writhes—leg after
    leg
    Drawn, as a worm draws ring upon
    ring
Gradually, not gladly! Nay, but, Meg,
    Is it more than the ransom (say) of a
    king
(Take my meaning at least) that I beg?

---

[1] ' Whose youth and freshness
Wrinkles Apollo's, and makes stale the morning.'—SHAKESPEARE.

III.

Not so! You were ready to learn, I think,
 What the world said! 'He loves you too
 well (suppose)
For such leanings! These poets, their love's
 mere ink—
 Like a flower, their flame flashes—a rose-
 bud, blows—
Then it all drops down at a wink!

IV.

'Ah, the instance! A curl of a blossomless
 vine
 The vinedresser passing it sickens to see
And mutters "Much hope (under God) of
 His wine
 From the branch and the bark of a barren
 tree
Spring reared not, and winter lets pine—

V.

' "His wine that should glorify (saith He)
 the cup
 That a man beholding (not tasting) might
 say
'Pour out life at a draught, drain it dry,
 drink it up,
 Give this one thing, and huddle the rest
 away—
Save the bitch, and who cares for the pup?'

VI.

' "Let it rot then!" which saying, he leaves it
 —we'll guess,
 Feels (if the sap move at all) thus much—
Yearns, and would blossom, would quicken
 no less,
 Bud at an eye's glance, flower at a touch—
"Die, perhaps, would you not, for her?—
 "Yes

VII.

'Note the hitch there! That's piteous—so
 much being done,
 (He'll think some day, your lover) so little
 to do!
Such infinite days to wear out, once begun!
 Since the hand its glove holds, and the foot-
 sole its shoe—
Overhead too there's always the sun!'

VIII.

Oh, no doubt they had said so, your friends—
 been profuse
 Of good counsel, wise hints—'where the
 trap lurks, walk warily—
Squeeze the fruit to the core ere you count on
 the juice!
 For the graft may fail, shift, wax, change
 colour, wane, vary, lie—'
You were cautious, God knows—to what use?

IX.

This crab's wiser, it strikes me—no twist but
 implies life—
 Not a curl but's so fit you could find none
 fitter—
For the brute from its brutehood looks up
 thus and eyes life—
 Stoop your soul down and listen, you'll
 hear it twitter,
Laughing lightly,—my crab's life's the wise
 life!

X.

Ah, now, look you—tail foremost, the beast
 sets seaward—
 The sea draws it, sand sucks it—he's wise,
 my crab!
From the napkin out jumps his one talent—
 good steward,
 Just judge! So a man shirks the smile or
 the stab,
And sets his sail duly to leeward!

XI.

Trust me? Hardly! I bid you not lean (remark)
 On my spirit, your spirit—my flesh, your
 flesh—
Hold my hand, and tread safe through the
 horrible dark—
 Quench my soul as with sprinklings of
 snow, then refresh
With some blast of new bellows the spark!

XII.

By no means! This were easy (men tell me)
 to say—
 'Give her all, throw your chance up, fall
 back on her heart!'

(Say my friends) 'she must change! after
    night follows day—'
No such fool! I am safe set in hell, for my
    part—
So let heaven do the worst now he may!

XIII.

What they bid me? Well, this, nothing more
    —'Tell her this—
"You are mine, I yours, though the whole
    world fail—
Though things are not, I know there is one
    thing which is—
    Though the oars break, there's hope for us
      yet—hoist the sail!
Oh, your heart! what's the heart? but your
    kiss!"

XIV.

'Then she breaks, she drops down, she lies
    flat at your feet—
    Take her then!' Well, I knew it—what
      fools are men!
Take the bee by her horns, will your honey
    prove sweet?
    Sweet is grass—will you pasture your cows
      in a fen?
Oh, if contraries could but once meet!

XV.

Love you call it? Some twitch in the moon's
    face (observe)
    Wet blink of her eyelid, tear dropt about
      dewfall,
Cheek flushed or obscured—does it make the
    sky swerve?
    Fetch the test, work the question to rags,
      bring to proof all—
Find what souls want and bodies deserve!

XVI.

Ah, we know you! Your soul works to infinite
    ends,
    Frets, uses life up for death's sake, takes
      pains,
Flings down love's self—'but you, bear me
    witness, my friends!
    Have I lost spring? count up (see) the
      winter's fresh gains!
is the shrub spoilt? the pine's hair impends!'

XVII.

What, you'd say—'Mark how God works!
    Years crowd, time wears thin,
    Earth keeps good yet, the sun goes on,
      stars hold their own,
And you'll change, climb past sight of the
    world, shift your skin,
    Never heeding how life moans—more flesh
      now, less bone!"
For that cheek's worn waste outline (death's
    grin)

XVIII.

Pleads with time still—"what good if I lose
    this? but see—" '
    (There's the crab gone!) ' "I said, 'Though
      earth sinks,' " ' (you perceive?
Ah, true, back there!) your soul now—' " 'yet
    some vein might be
    (Could one find it alive in the heart's core's
      pulse, cleave
Through the life-springs where 'you' melts in
    'me')—

XIX.

' " 'Some true vein of the absolute soul, which
    survives
    All that flesh runs to waste through'—and
      lo, this fails!
Here's death close on us! One life? a million
    of lives!
    Why choose one sail to watch of these in-
      finite sails?
Time's a tennis-play! thank you, no, fives!

XX.

' "Stop life's ball then!" Such folly! melt
    earth down for that,
    Till the pure ore eludes you and leaves you
      raw scoriæ!
Pish, the vein's wrong!' But you, friends—
    come, what were you at
    When God spat you out suddenly? what
      was the story He
Cut short thus, the growth He laid flat?

XXI.

Wait! the crab's twice alive, mark! Oh,
    worthy, your soul,
    Of strange ends, great results, novel la-
      bours! Take note,

I reject this for one! (ay, now, straight to the
hole!
  Safe in sand there—your skirts smooth out
  all as they float!)
I, shirk drinking through flaws in the bowl?

XXII.

Or suppose now that rock's cleft—grim,
scored to the quick,
  As a man's face kept fighting all life through
  gets scored,
Mossed and marked with grey purulent
leprosies, sick,
  Flat and foul as man's life here (be swift
  with your sword—
Cut the soul out, stuck fast where thorns
prick!)

XXIII.

—Say it let the rock's heart out, its meaning,
the thing
  All was made for, devised, ruled out gradually, planned—
Ah, that sea-shell, perhaps—since it lies, such
a ring
  Of pure colour, a cup full of sunbeams, to
  stand
(Say, in Lent) at the priest's hand—(no
king!)

XXIV.

Blame the cleft then? Praise rather! So—
just a chance gone!
  Had you said—'Save the seed and secure
  souls in flower'—
Ah, how time laughs, years palpitate, pro
grapples con,
  Till one day you shrug shoulders—'Well,
  gone, the good hour!
Till one night—'Is God off now? or on?

IV.

UP THE SPOUT.

I.

Hi! Just you drop that! Stop, I say!
  Shirk work, think slink off, twist friend's
  wrist?
Where that spined sand's lined band's the
  bay—
  Lined blind with true sea's blue, as due—
Promising—not to pay?

II.

For the sea's debt leaves wet the sand;
  Burst worst fate's weights in one burst gun?
A man's own yacht, blown—What? off land?
  Tack back, or veer round here, then—
  queer!
Reef points, though—understand?

III.

I'm blest if I do. Sigh? be blowed!
  Love's doves make break life's ropes, eh?
  Tropes!
Faith's brig, baulked, sides caulked, rides at
road;
  Hope's gropes befogged, storm-dogged and
  bogged—
Clogged, water-logged, her load!

IV.

Stowed, by Jove, right and tight, away!
  No show now how best plough sea's brow,
Wrinkling—breeze quick, tease thick, ere day,
  Clear sheer wave's sheen of green, I mean,
With twinkling wrinkles—eh?

V.

Sea sprinkles winkles, tinkles light
  Shells' bells—boy's joys that hap to snap!
It's just sea's fun, breeze done, to spite
  God's rods that scourge her surge, I'd
  urge—
Not proper, is it—quite?

VI.

See, fore and aft, life's craft undone!
  Crank plank, split spritsail—mark, sea's
  lark!
That grey cold sea's old sprees, begun
  When men lay dark i' the ark, no spark,
All water—just God's fun!

VII.

Not bright, at best, his jest to these
  Seemed—screamed, shrieked, wreaked on
  kin for sin!
When for mirth's yell earth's knell seemed
  please
  Some dumb new grim great whim in him
Made Jews take chalk for cheese.

VIII.

Could God's rods bruise God's Jews?   Their
    jowls
  Bobbed, sobbed, gaped, aped the plaice in
    face:
None heard, 'tis odds, his—God's—folk's
    howls.
  Now, how must I apply, to try
This hookiest-beaked of owls?

IX.

Well, I suppose God knows—I don't.
  Time's crimes mark dark men's types, in
    stripes
Broad as fen's lands men's hands were wont
  Leave grieve unploughed, though proud
    and loud
With birds' words—No! he won't!

X.

One never should think good impossible.
  Eh? say I'd hide this Jew's oil's cruse—
His shop might hold bright gold, engrossible
  By spy—spring's air takes there no care
To wave the heath-flower's glossy bell!

XI.

But gold bells chime in time there, coined—
  Gold! Old Sphinx winks there—'Read
    my screed!'
Doctrine Jews learn, use, burn for, joined
  (Through new craft's stealth) with health
    and wealth—
At once all three purloined!

XII.

I rose with dawn, to pawn, no doubt,
  (Miss this chance, glance untried aside?)
John's shirt, my—no! Ay, so—the lout!
  Let yet the door gape, store on floor
And not a soul about?

XIII.

Such men lay traps, perhaps—and I'm
  Weak—meek—mild—child of woe, you
    know!
But theft, I doubt, my lout calls crime.
  Shrink? Think! Love's dawn in pawn—
    you spawn
Of Jewry! Just in time!

V.

OFF THE PIER.

I.

ONE last glance at these sands and stones!
  Time goes past men, and lives to his liking,
Steals, and ruins, and sometimes atones.
  Why should he be king, though, and why
    not I king?
There now, that wind, like a swarm of sick
    drones!

II.

Is it heaven or mere earth (come!) that moves
    so and moans?
  Oh, I knew, when you loved me, my soul
    was in flowerage—
Now the frost comes; from prime, though, I
    watched through to nones,
  Read love's litanies over—his age was not
    our age!
No more flutes in this world for me now, dear!
    trombones.

III.

All that youth once denied and made mouths
    at, age owns.
  Facts put fangs out and bite us; life stings
    and grows viperous;
And times fugues are a hubbub of meaning-
    less tones.
  Once we followed the piper; now why not
    the piper us?
Love, grown grey, plays mere solos; we want
    antiphones.

IV.

And we sharpen our wits up with passions for
    hones,
  Melt down loadstars for magnets, use
    women for whetstones,
Learn to bear with dead calms by remember-
    ing cyclones,
  Snap strings short with sharp thumbnails,
    till silence begets tones,
Burn our souls out, shift spirits, turn skins
    and change zones;

V.

Then the heart, when all's done with, wakes,
    whimpers, intones
  Some lost fragment of tune it thought sweet
    ere it grew sick;

(Is it life that disclaims this, or death that
    disowns?)
  Mere dead metal, scrawled bars—ah, one
    touch, you make music!
Love's worth saving, youth doubts, but ex-
    perience depones.

VI.

Think, what use, when youth's saddle galls
    bay's back or roan's,
  To seek chords on love's keys to strike,
    other than his chords?
There's an error joy winks at and grief half
    condones,
  Or life's counterpoint grates the C major
    of discords—
'Tis man's choice 'twixt sluts rose-crowned
    and queens age dethrones.

¹ First edition :—

And my face bear his brand—mine, that once bore Love's badge elate!

VII.

I for instance might groan as a bag-pipe
    groans,
  Give the flesh of my heart for sharp sorrows
    to flagellate,
Grief might grind my cheeks down, age make
    sticks of my bones,
  (Though a queen drowned in tears must be
    worth more than Madge elate)¹
Rose might turn burdock, and pine-apples
    cones;

VIII.

My skin might change to a pitiful crone's,
  My lips to a lizard's, my hair to weed,
My features, in fact, to a series of loans;
  Thus much is conceded; now, you, concede
You would hardly salute me by choice, John
    Jones?

THE POET AND THE WOODLOUSE.

SAID a poet to a woodlouse—'Thou art cer-
    tainly my brother;
  I discern in thee the markings of the fingers
    of the Whole;
And I recognize, in spite of all the terrene
    smut and smother,
  In the colours shaded off thee, the sugges-
    tions of a soul.

'Yea,' the poet said, 'I smell thee by some
    passive divination,
  I am satisfied with insight of the measure
    of thine house;
What had happened I conjecture, in a blank
    and rhythmic passion,
  Had the æons thought of making thee a
    man, and me a louse.

The broad lives of upper planets, their ab-
    sorption and digestion,
  Food and famine, health and sickness, I
    can scrutinize and test;
Through a shiver of the senses comes a reso-
    nance of question,
  And by proof of balanced answer I decide
    that I am best.

'Man the fleshly marvel, always feels a cer-
    tain kind of awe stick
  To the skirts of contemplation, cramped
    with nympholeptic weight:
Feels his faint sense charred and branded by
    the touch of solar caustic,
  On the forehead of his spirit feels the foot-
    print of a Fate.'

'Notwithstanding which, O poet,' spake the
    woodlouse, very blandly,
  'I am likewise the created,—I the equi-
    poise of thee;
I the particle, the atom, I behold on either
    hand lie
  The inane of measured ages that were
    embryos of me.

'I am fed with intimations, I am clothed with
    consequences,
  And the air I breathe is coloured with apoc-
    alyptic blush:
Ripest-budded odours blossom out of dim
    chaotic stenches,
  And the Soul plants spirit-lilies in sick
    leagues of human slush.

'I am thrilled half cosmically through by
　　cryptophantic surgings,
　　Till the rhythmic hills roar silent through
　　　a spongious kind of blee:
And earth's soul yawns disembowelled of
　　her pancreatic organs,
　　Like a madrepore if mesmerized, in rapt
　　　catalepsy.

'And I sacrifice, a Levite—and I palpitate, a
　　poet;—
　　Can I close dead ears against the rush and
　　　resonance of things?
Symbols in me breathe and flicker up the
　　heights of the heroic;
　　Earth's worst spawn, you said, and cursed
　　　me? look! approve me! I have wings.

'Ah, men's poets! men's conventions crust
　　you round and swathe you mist-like,
　　And the world's wheels grind your spirits
　　　down the dust ye overtrod:
We stand sinlessly stark-naked in effulgence
　　of the Christlight,
　　And our polecat chokes not cherubs; and
　　　our skunk smells sweet to God.

'For He grasps the pale Created by some
　　thousand vital handles,
　　Till a Godshine, bluely winnowed through
　　　the sieve of thunder-storms,

Shimmers up the non-existent round the
　　churning feet of angels;
　　And the atoms of that glory may be seraphs,
　　　being worms.

'Friends, your nature underlies us and your
　　pulses overplay us;
　　Ye, with social sores unbandaged, can ye
　　　sing right and steer wrong?
For the transient cosmic, rooted in imperish-
　　able chaos,
　　Must be kneaded into drastics as material
　　　for a song.

'Eyes once purged from homebred vapours
　　through humanitarian passion
　　See that monochrome a despot through a
　　　democratic prism;
Hands that rip the soul up, reeking from
　　divine evisceration,
　　Not with priestlike oil anoint him, but a
　　　stronger-smelling chrism.

'Pass, O poet, retransfigured! God, the
　　psychometric rhapsode,
　　Fills with fiery rhythms the silence, stings
　　　the dark with stars that blink;
All eternities hang round him like an old
　　man's clothes collapsèd,
　　While he makes his mundane music—AND
　　HE WILL NOT STOP, I THINK.'

THE PERSON OF THE HOUSE.

IDYL CCCLXVI.

THE ACCOMPANIMENTS.

1. THE MONTHLY NURSE.
2. THE CAUDLE.
3. THE SENTENCES.

THE KID.

1. THE MONTHLY NURSE.

THE sickly airs had died of damp;
　　Through huddling leaves the holy chime
Flagged; I, expecting Mrs. Gamp,
　　Thought—'Will the woman come in time?'

Upstairs I knew the matron bed
　　Held her whose name confirms all joy
To me; and tremblingly I said
　　'Ah! will it be a girl or boy?'
And, soothed, my fluttering doubts began
　　To sift the pleasantness of things;
Developing the unshapen man,
　　An eagle baffled of his wings;
Considering, next, how fair the state
　　And large the license that sublimes
A nineteenth-century female fate—
　　Sweet cause that thralls my liberal rhymes!
And Chastities and colder Shames,
　　Decorums mute and marvellous,
And fair Behaviour that reclaims
　　All fancies grown erroneous,

Moved round me musing, till my choice
  Faltered.   A female in a wig
Stood by me, and a drouthy voice
  Announced her—Mrs. Betsy Prig.

2. THE CAUDLE.

SWEET Love that sways the reeling years,
  The crown and chief of certitudes,
For whose calm eyes and modest ears
  Time writes the rule and text of prudes—
That, surpliced, stoops a nuptial head
  Nor chooses to live blindly free,
But, with all pulses quieted,
  Plays tunes of domesticity—
That Love I sing of and have sung
  And mean to sing till Death yawn sheer,
He rules the music of my tongue,
  Stills it or quickens there or here.
I say but this: as we went up
  I heard the Monthly give a sniff
And '*if* the big dog makes the pup—'
  She murmured—then repeated 'if!'
The caudle on a slab was placed;
  She snuffed it, snorting loud and long;
I fled—I would not stop to taste—
  And dreamed all night of things gone wrong.

3. THE SENTENCES.

I.

ABORTIVE Love is half a sin;
  But Love's abortions dearer far
Than wheels without an axle-pin
  Or life without a married star.

II.

My rules are hard to understand
  For him whom sensual rules depress;
A bandbox in a midwife's hand
  May hold a costlier bridal dress.

III.

I like her not; in fact I loathe;
  Bugs hath she brought from London beds.'
Friend! wouldst thou rather bear their growth
  Or have a baby with two heads?

IDYL CCCLXVI.

THE KID.

My spirit, in the doorway's pause,
  Fluttered with fancies in my breast;
Obsequious to all decent laws,
  I felt exceedingly distressed.

I knew it rude to enter there
  With Mrs. V. in such a state;
And, 'neath a magisterial air,
  Felt actually indelicate.
I knew the nurse began to grin;
  I turned to greet my Love.   Said she—
'Confound your modesty, come in!
  —What shall we call the darling, V.?'
(There are so many charming names!
  Girls'—Peg, Moll, Doll, Fan, Kate,
    Blanche, Bab:
  Boys'—Mahershahal-hashbaz, James,
    Kit, Nick, Dick, Mark, Aminadab.)
Lo, as the acorn to the oak,
  As well-heads to the river's height,
As to the chicken the moist yolk,
  As to high noon the day's first white—
Such is the baby to the man.
  There, straddling one red arm and leg,
Lay my last work, in length a span,
  Half hatched, and conscious of the egg.
A creditable child, I hoped;
  And half a score of joys to be
Through sunny lengths of prospects oped
  Smooth to the bland futurity.
O, fate surpassing other dooms,
  O, hope above all wrecks of time!
O, light that fills all vanquished glooms,
  O, silent song o'ermastering rhyme!
I covered either little foot,
  I drew the strings about its waist;
Pink as the unshell'd inner fruit,
  But barely decent, hardly chaste,
Its nudity had startled me;
  But when the petticoats were on,
'I know,' I said; 'its name shall be
  Paul Cyril Athanasius John.'
'Why,' said my wife, 'the child's a girl.'
  My brain swooned, sick with failing sense;
With all perception in a whirl,
  How could I tell the difference?
'Nay,' smiled the nurse, 'the child's a
  boy.'
And all my soul was soothed to hear
  That so it was: then startled Joy
Mocked Sorrow with a doubtful tear.
And I was glad as one who sees
  For sensual optics things unmeet:
As purity makes passion freeze,
  So faith warns science off her beat.
Blessed are they that have not seen,
  And yet, not seeing, have believed:
To walk by faith, as preached the Dean,
  And not by sight, have I achieved.

Let love, that does not look, believe;
  Let knowledge, that believes not, look:
Truth pins her trust on falsehood's sleeve,
  While reason blunders by the book.

Then Mrs. Prig addressed me thus;
  'Sir, if you'll be advised by me,
You'll leave the blessed babe to us;
  It's my belief he wants his tea.'

LAST WORDS OF A SEVENTH-RATE POET.

BILL, I feel far from quite right—if not
    further: already the pill
Seems, if I may say so, to bubble inside me.
    A poet's heart, Bill,
Is a sort of a thing that is made of the tender-
    est young bloom on a fruit.
You may pass me the mixture at once, if you
    please—and I'll thank you to boot
For that poem—and then for the julep. This
    really is damnable stuff!
(Not the poem, of course.) Do you snivel,
    old friend? well, it's nasty enough,
But I think I can stand it—I think so—ay,
    Bill, and I could were it worse.
But I'll tell you a thing that I can't and I
    won't. 'Tis the old, old curse—
The gall of the gold-fruited Eden, the lure
    of the angels that fell.
'Tis the core of the fruit snake-spotted in the
    hush of the shadows of hell,
Where a lost man sits with his head drawn
    down, and a weight on his eyes.
You know what I mean, Bill—the tender and
    delicate mother of lies,
Woman, the devil's first cousin—no doubt by
    the female side.
The breath of her mouth still moves in my
    hair, and I know that she lied,
And I feel her, Bill, sir, inside me—she oper-
    ates there like a drug.
Were it better to live like a beetle, to wear the
    cast clothes of a slug,
Be the louse in the locks of the hangman, the
    mote in the eye of the bat,
Than to live and believe in a woman, who
    must one day grow aged and fat?
You must see it's preposterous, Bill, sir.
    And yet, how the thought of it clings!
I have lived out my time—I have prigged lots
    of verse—I have kissed (ah, that stings!)
Lips that swore I had cribbed every line that
    I wrote on them—cribbed—honour
    bright!
Then I loathed her; but now I forgive her;
    perhaps after all she was right.

Yet I swear it was shameful—unwoman*l*y,
    Bill, sir—to say that I fibbed.
Why, the poems were mine, for I bought them
    in print. Cribbed? of course they were
    cribbed.
Yet I wouldn't say, cribbed from the French
    —Lady Bathsheba thought it was
    vulgar—
But picked up on the banks of the Don, from
    the lips of a highly intelligent Bulgar.
I'm aware, Bill, that's out of all metre—I
    can't help it—I'm none of your sort
Who set metres, by Jove, above morals—not
    exactly. They don't go to Court—
As I mentioned one night to that cowslip-
    faced pet, Lady Rahab Redrabbit
(Whom the Marquis calls Drabby for short).
    Well, I say, if you want a thing, grab it—
That's what I did, at least, when I took that
    danseuse to a swell *cabaret*,
Where expense was no consideration. A
    poet, you see, now and then must be
    gay.
(I declined to give more, I remember, than
    fifty centeems to the waiter;
For I asked him if that was enough; and the
    jackanapes answered—*Peut-être*.
Ah, it isn't in you to draw up a *menu* such as
    ours was, though humble:
When I told Lady Shoreditch, she thought it
    a regular *grand tout ensemble*.)
She danced the heart out of my body—I can
    see in the glare of the lights,
I can see her again as I saw her that evening,
    in spangles and tights.
When I spoke to her first, her eye flashed so,
    I heard—as I fancied—the spark whiz
From her eyelid—I said so next day to that
    jealous old fool of a Marquis.
She reminded me, Bill, of a lovely volcano,
    whose entrails are lava—
Or (you know my *penchant* for original
    types) of the upas in Java.
In the curve of her sensitive nose was a
    singular species of dimple,

Where the flush was the mark of an angel's
    creased kiss—if it wasn't a pimple.
Now I'm none of your bashful John Bulls
    who don't know a pilau from a pug-
    garee
Nor a chili, by George, from a chopstick. So,
    sir, I marched into her snuggery,
And proposed a light supper by way of a
    finish. I treated her, Bill,
To six *entrées* of ortolans, sprats, maraschino,
    and oysters. It made her quite ill.
Of which moment of sickness I took some
    advantage. I held her like this,
And availed myself, sir, of her sneezing, to
    shut up her lips with a kiss.
The waiters, I saw, were quite struck; and
    I felt, I may say, *entre nous*
Like Don Juan, Lauzun, Almaviva, Lord
    Byron, and old Richelieu.
(You'll observe, Bill, that rhyme's quite
    Parisian; a Londoner, sir, would have
    cited old Q.)
These are moments that thrill the whole spirit
    with spasms that excite and exalt.
I stood more than the peer of the great Casa-
    nova—you know—de Seingalt.
She was worth, sir, I say it without hesitation,
    two brace of her sisters.
Ah, why should all honey turn rhubarb—all
    cherries grow onions—all kisses leave
    blisters?
Oh, and why should I ask myself questions?
    I've heard such before—once or twice.
Ah, I can't understand it—but, O, I imagine
    it strikes me as nice.
There's a deity shapes us our ends, sir, rough-
    hew them, my boy, how we will—
As I stated myself in a poem I published last
    year, you know, Bill—
Where I stated myself that that was the ques-
    tion—to be, or, by Jove, not to be.
Ah, it's something—you'll think so hereafter
    —to wait on a poet like me.
Had I written no more than those verses on
    that Countess I used to call Pussy—
Yes, Minette or Manon—and—you'll hardly
    believe it—she said they were all out of
    Musset.
Now I don't say they weren't—but what then?
    and I don't say they were—I'll bet
    pounds against pennies on
The subject—I wish I may never die Lau-
    reate, if some of them weren't out of
    Tennyson.

And I think—I don't like to be certain, with
    Death, so to speak, by me, frowning—
But I think there were some—say a dozen,
    perhaps, or a score—out of Browning.
As for poets who go on a contrary tack to
    what I go and you go—
You remember my lyrics *translated*—like
    'sweet bully Bottom'—from Hugo?
Though I will say it's curious that simply on
    just that account there should be
Men so bold as to say that not one of my
    poems was written by me.
It would stir the political bile or the physical
    spleen of a drab or a Tory
To hear critics assign to his hand the Con-
    fessional, Bill, and the Laboratory.
Yes, it's singular—nay, I can't think of a
    parallel (ain't it a high lark?
As that Countess would say)—there are few
    men believe it was I wrote the Ode to a
    Skylark.
And it often has given myself and Lord Al-
    bert no end of diversion
To hear fellows maintain to my face it was
    Wordsworth who wrote the Excursion.
When they know that whole reams of the
    verses recur in my authorized works
Here and there, up and down! Why such
    readers are infidels—heretics—Turks.
And the pitiful critics who think in their paltry
    presumption to pay me a
Pretty compliment, pairing me off, sir, with
    Keats—as if *he* could write Lamia!
While I never produced a more characteristic
    and exquisite book,
One that gave me more real satisfaction, than
    did, on the whole, Lalla Rookh.
Was it there that I called on all debtors,
    being pestered myself by a creditor, (he
Isn't paid yet) to rise, by the proud appella-
    tion of bondsmen—hereditary?
Yes—I think so. And yet, on my word, I
    can't think why I think it was so.
It more probably was in the poem I made a
    few seasons ago
On that Duchess—her name now? ah, thus
    one outlives a whole cycle of joys!
Fair supplants black as brown succeeds
    golden. The poem made rather a noise.
And indeed I have seen worse verses; but
    as for the woman, my friend—
Though his neck had been never so stiff, she'd
    have made a philosopher bend.

As the broken heart of a sunset that bleeds
    pure purple and gold
In the shudder and swoon of the sickness of
    colour, the agonies old
That engirdle the brows of the day when he
    sinks with a spasm into rest
And the splash of his kingly blood is dashed
    on the skirts of the west,
Even such was my own, when I felt how
    much sharper than any snake's tooth
Was the passion that made me mistake Lady
    Eve for her niece Lady Ruth.
The whole world, colourless, lapsed. Earth
    fled from my feet like a dream,
And the whirl of the walls of Space was about
    me, and moved as a stream
Flowing and ebbing and flowing all night to
    a weary tune
('Such as that of my verses'? Get out!) in
    the face of a sick-souled moon.
The keen stars kindled and faded and fled,
    and the wind in my ears
Was the wail of a poet for failure—you
    needn't come snivelling tears
And spoiling the mixture, confound you, with
    dropping your tears into that!
I know I'm pathetic—I must be—and you
    soft-hearted and fat,
And I'm grateful of course for your kind-
    ness—there, don't come hugging me,
    now—
But because a fellow's pathetic, you needn't
    low like a cow.

I should like—on my soul, I should like—
    to remember—but somehow I can't—
If the lady whose love has reduced me to this
    was the niece or the aunt.
But whichever it was, I feel sure, when I
    published my lays of last year
(You remember their title—The Tramp—
    only seven-and-sixpence—not dear),
I sent her a copy (perhaps her tears fell on
    the title-page—yes—
I should like to imagine she wept)—and the
    Bride of Bulgaria (MS.)
I forwarded with it. The lyrics, no doubt,
    she found bitter—and sweet;
But the Bride she rejected, you know, with
    expressions I will not repeat.
Well—she did no more than all publishers
    did. Though my prospects were marred,
I can pity and pardon them. Blindness, mere
    blindness! And yet it was hard.

For a poet, Bill, is a blossom—a bird—a
    billow—a breeze—
A kind of creature that moves among men as
    a wind among trees.
I with the heat of my heart still burning
    against all bars
As the fire of the dawn, so to speak, in the
    blanched blank brows of the stars—
I with my tremulous lips made pale by musi-
    cal breath—
I with the shade in my eyes that was left by
    the kisses of death—
(For Death came near me in youth, and
    touched my face with his face,
And put in my lips the songs that belong to
    a desolate place—
Desolate truly, my heart and my life, till her
    kiss filled them up!)
I with my soul like wine poured out with my
    flesh for the cup—
It was hard for me—it was hard—Bill, Bill,
    you great owl, was it not?
For the day creeps in like a Fate: and I
    think my grand passion is rot:
And I dreamily seem to perceive, by the light
    of a life's dream done,
The lotion at six, and the mixture at ten, and
    the draught before one.

Yes—I feel rather better. Man's life is a
    mull, at the best;
And the patent perturbator pills are like
    bullets of lead in my chest.
When a man's whole spirit is like the lost
    Pleiad, a blown-out star,
Is there comfort in Holloway, Bill? is there
    hope of salvation in Parr?
True, most things work to their end—and an
    end that the shroud overlaps.
Under lace, under silk, under gold, sir, the
    skirt of a winding-sheet flaps—
Which explains, if you think of it, Bill,
    why I can't, though my soul thereon
    broodeth,
Quite make out if I loved Lady Tamar as
    much as I loved Lady Judith.
Yet her dress was of violet velvet, her hair was
    hyacinth-hued,
And her ankles—no matter. A face where
    the music of every mood
Was touched by the tremulous fingers of pas
    sionate feeling, and made
Strange melodies, scornful, but sweeter than
    strings whereon sorrow has played

To enrapture the hearing of mirth when his
  garland of blossom and green
Turns to lead on the anguished forehead—
  'you don't understand what I mean'?
Well, of course I knew you were stupid—
  you always were stupid at school—
Now don't say you weren't—but I'm hanged
  if I thought you were quite such a
  fool!
You don't see the point of all this? I was
  talking of sickness and death—
In that poem I made years ago, I said this—
  'Love, the flower-time whose breath
Smells sweet through a summer of kisses and
  perfumes an autumn of tears
Is sadder at root than a winter—its hopes
  heavy-hearted like fears.
Though I love your Grace more than I love
  little Letty, the maid of the mill,
Yet the heat of your lips when I kiss them'
  (you see we were intimate, Bill)
'And the beat of the delicate blood in your
  eyelids of azure and white
Leave the taste of the grave in my mouth
  and the shadow of death on my sight.
Fill the cup—twine the chaplet—come into
  the garden—get out of the house—
Drink to *me* with your eyes—there's a banquet behind, where worms only carouse!
As I said to sweet Katie, who lived by the
  brook on the land Philip farmed—
Worms shall graze where my kisses found
  pasture!' The Duchess, I may say, was
  charmed.
It was read to the Duke, and he cried like a
  child. If you'll give me a pill,
I'll go on till past midnight. That poem was
  said to be—Somebody's, Bill.
But you see you can always be sure of my
  hand as the mother that bore me
By the fact that I never write verse which
  has never been written before me.
Other poets—I blush for them, Bill—may
  adore and repudiate in turn a
Libitina, perhaps, or Pandemos; my Venus,
  you know, is Laverna.
Nay, that epic of mine which begins from
  foundations the Bible is built on—
'Of man's *first* disobedience'—I've heard it
  attributed, dammy, to Milton.
Well, it's lucky for them that it's not worth
  my while, as I may say, to break spears
With the hirelings, forsooth, of the press who
  assert that Othello was Shakespeare's.

When he that can run, sir, may read—if he
  borrows the book, or goes on tick—
In my poems the bit that described how
  the Hellespont joins the Propontic.
There are men, I believe, who will tell you
  that Gray wrote the whole of The
  Bard—
Or that I didn't write half the Elegy, Bill, in
  a Country Churchyard.
When you know that my poem, The Poet,
  begins—'Ruin seize thee!' and ends
With recapitulations of horrors the poet in-
  vokes on his friends.
And I'll swear, if you look at the dirge on my
  relatives under the turf, you
Will perceive it winds up with some lines on
  myself—and begins with the curfew.
Now you'll grant it's more probable, Bill—as
  a man of the world, if you please—
That all these should have prigged from
  myself than that I should have prigged
  from all these.
I could cry when I think of it, friend, if such
  tears would comport with my dignity,
That the author of Christabel ever should
  smart from such vulgar malignity.
(You remember perhaps that was one of the
  first little things that I carrolled
After finishing Marmion, the Princess, the
  Song of the Shirt, and Childe Harold.)
Oh, doubtless it always has been so—Ah,
  doubtless it always will be—
There are men who would say that myself is
  a different person from me.
Better the porridge of patience a poor man
  snuffs in his plate
Than the water of poisonous laurels distilled
  by the fingers of hate.

'Tis a dark-purple sort of a moonlighted
  kind of a midnight, I know;
You remember those verses I wrote on Irene,
  from Edgar A. Poe?
It was Lady Aholibah Levison, daughter of
  old Lord St. Giles,
Who inspired those delectable strains, and
  rewarded her bard with her smiles.
I recited her charms, in conjunction with
  those of a girl at the *café*,
In a poem I published in collaboration with
  Templeton (Taffy).
There are prudes in a world full of envy—
  and some of them thought it too
  strong

To compare an earl's daughter by name with a girl at a French *restaurant*.

I regarded her, though, with the chivalrous eyes of a knight-errant on quest;

I may say I don't know that I ever felt prouder, old friend, of a conquest.

And when *I*'ve been made happy, I never have cared a brass farthing who knew it; I

Thank my stars I'm as free from mock-modesty, friend, as from vulgar fatuity.

You may see by my shortness of speech that my time's almost up: I perceive

That my new-fangled brevity strikes you: but don't—though the public will—grieve.

As it's sometimes my whim to be vulgar, it's sometimes my whim to be brief;

As when once I observed, after Heine, that 'she was a harlot, and I' (which is true) 'was a thief.'

(Though you hardly should cite this particular line, by the way, as an instance of absolute brevity:

I'm aware, man, of that; so you needn't disgrace yourself, sir, by such grossly mistimed and impertinent levity.)

I don't like to break off, any more than you wish me to stop: but my fate is

Not to write half a million such rhymes without blockheads exclaiming—

JAM SATIS.

SONNET FOR A PICTURE.

THAT nose is out of drawing. With a gasp,
She pants upon the passionate lips that ache
With the red drain of her own mouth, and make
A monochord of colour. Like an asp,
One lithe lock wriggles in his rutilant grasp.
Her bosom is an oven of myrrh, to bake
Love's white warm shewbread to a browner cake.

The lock his fingers clench has burst its hasp.
The legs are absolutely abominable.
Ah! what keen overgust of wild-eyed woes
Flags in that bosom, flushes in that nose?
Nay! Death sets riddles for desire to spell,
Responsive. What red hem earth's passion sews,
But may be ravenously unripped in hell?

NEPHELIDIA.

FROM the depth of the dreamy decline of the dawn through a notable nimbus of nebulous noonshine,

Pallid and pink as the palm of the flag-flower that flickers with fear of the flies as they float,

Are they looks of our lovers that lustrously lean from a marvel of mystic miraculous moonshine,

These that we feel in the blood of our blushes that thicken and threaten with throbs through the throat?

Thicken and thrill as a theatre thronged at appeal of an actor's appalled agitation,

Fainter with fear of the fires of the future than pale with the promise of pride in the past;

Flushed with the famishing fullness of fever that reddens with radiance of rathe recreation,

Gaunt as the ghastliest of glimpses that gleam through the gloom of the gloaming when ghosts go aghast?

Nay, for the nick of the tick of the time is a tremulous touch on the temples of terror,

Strained as the sinews yet strenuous with strife of the dead who is dumb as the dust-heaps of death:

Surely no soul is it, sweet as the spasm of erotic emotional exquisite error,

Bathed in the balms of beatified bliss, beatific itself by beatitude's breath.

Surely no spirit or sense of a soul that was soft to the spirit and soul of our senses

Sweetens the stress of suspiring suspicion that sobs in the semblance and sound of a sigh;

Only this oracle opens Olympian, in mystical moods and triangular tenses—

'Life is the lust of a lamp for the light that is
  dark till the dawn of the day when we die.'
Mild is the mirk and monotonous music of
  memory, melodiously mute as it may be,
While the hope in the heart of a hero is
  bruised by the breach of men's rapiers,
  resigned to the rod;
Made meek as a mother whose bosom-beats
  bound with the bliss-bringing bulk of a
  balm-breathing baby,
As they grope through the grave-yard of
  creeds, under skies growing green at a
  groan for the grimness of God.

Blank is the book of his bounty beholden
  of old, and its binding is blacker than
  bluer:
Out of blue into black is the scheme of the
  skies, and their dews are the wine of the
  bloodshed of things;
Till the darkling desire of delight shall be
  free as a fawn that is freed from the fangs
  that pursue her,
Till the heart-beats of hell shall be hushed
  by a hymn from the hunt that has harried the kennel of kings.

DISGUST.

A DRAMATIC MONOLOGUE.

A woman and her husband, having been con-
verted from free thought to Calvinism, and being
utterly miserable in consequence, resolve to end themselves by poison. The man dies, but the woman is
rescued by application of the stomach-pump.

I.

PILLS? talk to me of your pills? Well, that, I
  must say, is cool.
Can't bring my old man round? he was always a stubborn old fool.
If I hadn't taken precautions—a warning to
  all that wive—
He might not have been dead, and I might
  not have been alive.

II.

You would like to know, if I please, how it
  was that our troubles began?
You see, we were brought up Agnostics, I
  and my poor old man.
And we got some idea of selection and evolu-
  tion, you know—
Professor Huxley's doing—where does he expect to go!

III.

Well, then came trouble on trouble on trouble
  —I may say, a peck—
And his cousin was wanted one day on the
  charge of forging a cheque—
And his puppy died of the mange—my parrot
  choked on its perch.
This was the consequence, was it, of not going
  weekly to church?

IV.

So we felt that the best if not only thing that
  remained to be done
On an earth everlastingly moving about a
  perpetual sun,
Where worms breed worms to be eaten of
  worms that have eaten their betters--
And reviewers are barely civil—and people
  get spiteful letters—
And a famous man is forgot ere the minute
  hand can tick nine—
Was to send in our P. P. C., and purchase a
  package of strychnine.

V.

Nay—but first we thought it was rational—
  only fair—
To give both parties a hearing—and went to
  the meeting-house there,
At the curve of the street that runs from the
  Stag to the old Blue Lion.
"Little Zion" they call it—a deal more
  "little" than "Zion."

VI.

And the preacher preached from the text,
  "Come out of her." Hadn't we
  come?
And we thought of the Shepherd in Pickwick
  —and fancied a flavour of rum
Balmily borne on the wind of his words—and
  my man said, "Well,
Let's get out of this, my dear—for his text has
  a brimstone smell."

VII.

So we went, O God, out of chapel—and gazed,
ah God, at the sea.
And I said nothing to him. And he said
nothing to me.

VIII.

And there, you see, was an end of it all. It
was obvious, in fact,
That, whether or not you believe in the doctrine taught in a tract,
Life was not in the least worth living. Because, don't you see?
Nothing that can't be, can, and what must be,
must. Q. E. D.
And the infinitesimal sources of Infinite Un-
ideality
Curve in to the central abyss of a sort of a
queer Personality
Whose refraction is felt in the nebulæ strewn
in the pathway of Mars
Like the parings of nails Æonian—clippings
and snippings of stars—
Shavings of suns that revolve and evolve and
involve—and at times
Give a sweet astronomical twang to remark-
ably hobbling rhymes.

IX.

And the sea curved in with a moan—and we
thought how once—before
We fell out with those atheist lecturers—once,
ah, once and no more,
We read together, while midnight blazed like
the Yankee flag,
A reverend gentleman's work—the Conver-
sion of Colonel Quagg.
And out of its pages we gathered this lesson
of doctrine pure—
Zephaniah Stockdolloger's gospel—a word
that deserves to endure
Infinite millions on millions of infinite Æons
to come—
"Vocation," says he, "is vocation, and duty
duty. Some."

X.

And duty, said I, distinctly points out—and
vocation, said he,
Demands as distinctly—that I should kill you,
and that you should kill me.
The reason is obvious—we cannot exist without creeds—who can?
So we went to the chemist's—a highly re-
spectable church-going man—
And bought two packets of poison. You
wouldn't have done so Wait.
It's evident, Providence is not with you,
ma'am, the same thing as Fate.
Unconscious cerebration educes God from a
fog,
But spell God backwards, what then? Give it
up? the answer is, dog.
(I don't exactly see how this last verse is to
scan,
But that's a consideration I leave to the secular man.)

XI.

I meant of course to go with him—as far as
I pleased—but first
To see how my old man liked it—I thought
perhaps he might burst.
I didn't wish it—but still it's a blessed release
for a wife—
And he saw that I thought so—and grinned
in derision—and threatened my life
If I made wry faces—and so I took just a sip
—and he—
Well—you know how it ended—he didn't
get over me.

XII.

Terrible, isn't it? Still, on reflection, it might
have been worse.
He might have been the unhappy survivor,
and followed my hearse.
"Never do it again"? Why, certainly not.
You don't
Suppose I should think of it, surely? But
anyhow—there—I won't.

INDEX.

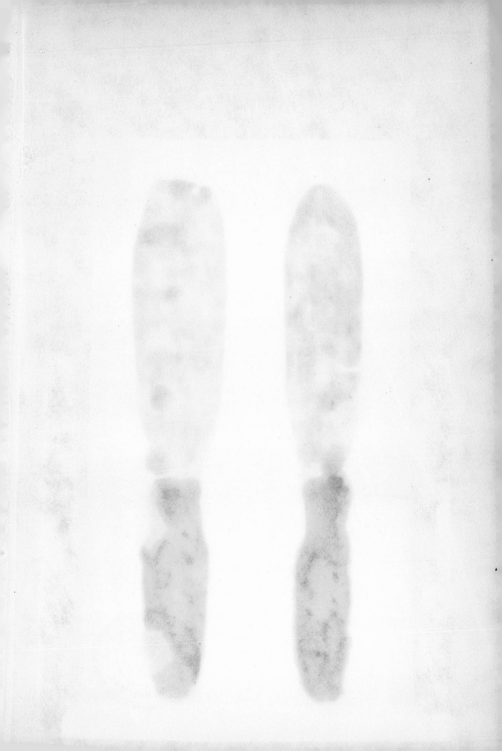

DATE DUE

JAN 0 2 1996	
MAY 0 6 1998	